The 1998 World Book

YEAR BOOK

The Annual Supplement to The World Book Encyclopedia

■ ■ ■ A REVIEW OF THE EVENTS OF 1997 ■ ■ ■

World Book, Inc.

a Scott Fetzer company

Chicago ▪ London ▪ Sydney ▪ Toronto

World Book, Inc.
525 W. Monroe
Chicago, IL 60661

ISBN: 0-7166-0498-1
ISSN 0084-1439
Library of Congress Catalog Card Number: 62-4818

Printed in the United States of America.

Staff

EDITORIAL

Executive Editor
Darlene R. Stille

Managing Editor
Scott Thomas

Senior Editor
Kristina Vaicikonis

Staff Editors
Tim Frystak
Jay Lenn
Al Smuskiewicz
Peter Uremovic

Contributing Editors
David L. Dreier
Mark Dunbar
Jennifer Parello

Editorial Assistant
Ethel Matthews

Cartographic Services
H. George Stoll, Head
Wayne K. Pichler, Senior
Cartographer
Susan E. Ryan, Staff
Cartographer

Index Services
David Pofelski, Head
Pam Hori

Statistical Services
Jay Powers, Head

Permissions Editor
Janet Peterson

ART

Executive Director
Roberta Dimmer

Senior Designer, Year Book
Brenda B. Tropinski

Senior Designers
Cari L. Biamonte
Melanie J. Lawson

Senior Photographs Editor
Sandra M. Dyrlund

Art Production Assistant
Jon Whitney

RESEARCH SERVICES

Researchers
Karen A. McCormack
Mitchell C. Bassler
Nicholas V. Kilzer

Library Services
Jon Fjortoft, Head

PRODUCTION

Vice President
Daniel N. Bach

Manufacturing/Pre-Press
Sandra Van den Broucke,
Director
Barbara Podczerwinski,
Manufacturing Manager
Joann Seastrom,
Production Manager

Proofreaders
Anne Dillon
Carol Seymour

Text Processing
Curley Hunter
Gwendolyn Johnson

PUBLISHER
Michael Ross

EDITOR IN CHIEF
Robert J. Janus

Contributors

Contributors not listed on these pages are members of *The World Book Year Book* editorial staff.

■ **ALEXIOU, ARTHUR G.,** B.S., M.S., E.E.; Senior assistant secretary, UNESCO/IOC. **[Ocean]**

■ **ANDREWS, PETER J.,** B.A., M.S.; Free-lance writer. **[Chemistry]**

■ **APSELOFF, MARILYN FAIN,** B.A., M.A.; Professor of English, Kent State University, Ohio. **[Literature for children]**

■ **ASKER, JAMES R.,** B.A.; Washington Bureau Chief, *Aviation Week & Space Technology* magazine. **[Space exploration]**

■ **BARBER, PEGGY,** B.A., M.L.S.; Associate executive director for public policy and programs, American Library Association. **[Library]**

■ **BARNHART, BILL,** B.A., M.S.T., M.B.A.; Financial markets columnist, *Chicago Tribune.* **[Stocks and bonds]**

■ **BAYNHAM, SIMON,** B.A., M.A., Ph.D.; Consultant, Research Institute for the Study of Conflict and Terrorism, London. **[Africa Special Report: The Hutu and Tutsi: A Conflict Beyond Borders]**

■ **BOULDREY, BRIAN,** B.A., M.F.A.; Free-lance editor and instructor. **[Radio; San Francisco]**

■ **BOYD, JOHN D.,** B.S.; Economics reporter, *Bridge News.* **[Economics; International trade; Manufacturing]**

■ **BRADSHER, HENRY S.,** A.B., B.J.; Foreign affairs analyst. **[Asia and Asian country articles]**

■ **BRETT, CARLTON E.,** B.A., M.S., Ph.D.; Professor of geology and biology, University of Rochester. **[Paleontology]**

■ **BRODY, HERB,** B.S.; Senior editor, *Technology Review* magazine. **[Internet]**

■ **BUERKLE, TOM,** B.A.; Correspondent, *International Herald Tribune.* **[Europe and Western European nation articles]**

■ **CAMPBELL, GEOFFREY A.,** B.J.; Free-lance writer. **[Civil rights; Courts; Supreme Court of the United States]**

■ **CAMPBELL, LINDA P.,** B.A., M.S.L.; Senior reporter, *Fort Worth Star-Telegram.* **[Civil rights; Courts; Supreme Court of the United States]**

■ **CARDINALE, DIANE P.,** B.A.; Assistant communications director, Toy Manufacturers of America. **[Toys and games]**

■ **CASEY, MIKE,** B.S., M.A.; Assistant editor, *Kansas City Star.* **[Automobile]**

■ **CATES, WARD MITCHELL,** Ed.D.; Associate professor, Lehigh University **[World Book supplement: Computerized instruction]**

■ **CHISWICK, BARRY R.,** B.A., M.A., Ph.D.; Research professor, University of Illinois at Chicago. **[Immigration Special Report: Immigration: The Latest Wave]**

■ **CLAMPITT, CYNTHIA A.,** B.A.; Free-lance writer, editor, and photographer. **[Literature, Children's Special Report: The Creator of Thomas, the Tank Engine]**

■ **CLARK, KAREN LIN,** B.S.; Solutions editor, *San Diego Union-Tribune.* **[World Book supplement: San Diego]**

■ **COHEN, STUART E.** M.Arch.; Associate professor of architecture, University of Illlinois at Chicago. **[World Book supplement: House]**

■ **CORNELL, VINCENT J.,** B.A., M.A., Ph.D.; Andrew W. Mellon assistant professor of religion, Duke University. **[Islam]**

■ **DeFRANK, THOMAS M.,** B.A., M.A.; Washington bureau chief, *New York Daily News.* **[Armed forces]**

■ **DeLANCEY, MARK W.,** B.A., M.A., Ph.D.; Professor of government and international studies, University of South Carolina. **[Africa and African country articles]**

■ **DELPAR, HELEN,** Ph.D., Professor of history, University of Alabama. **[World Book supplement: Exploration]**

■ **DILLON, DAVID,** B.A., M.A., Ph.D.; Architecture critic, *The Dallas Morning News.* **[Architecture]**

■ **DIRDA, MICHAEL,** B.A., M.A., Ph.D.; Writer and editor, *The Washington Post Book World.* **[Poetry]**

■ **DUCKETT, LUCINDA,** B.A.; Assistant chief of staff, (Sydney) *Daily Telegraph.* **[Australia]**

■ **EATON, WILLIAM J.,** B.S., M.S.; Curator, Hubert H.Humphrey Fellowship Program, University of Maryland. **[U.S. government articles]**

■ **ELLIS, GAVIN,** Assistant editor, *New Zealand Herald.* **[New Zealand]**

■ **FARR, DAVID M. L.,** D.Phil.; Professor emeritus of history, Carleton University. **[Canada; Canadian provinces; Canadian territories; Canadian prime minister]**

■ **FISHER, ROBERT W.,** B.A., M.A.; Free-lance writer. **[Labor and employment]**

■ **FITZGERALD, MARK,** B.A.; Midwest editor, *Editor & Publisher* magazine. **[Newspaper]**

■ **FOX, THOMAS C.,** B.A., M.A.; Publisher and editor, *National Catholic Reporter.* **[Roman Catholic Church]**

■ **FRICKER, KAREN,** B.A., M.A.; Free-lance theater writer. **[Theater]**

■ **FRIEDMAN, EMILY,** B.A.; Health-policy columnist, *Journal of the American Medical Association.* **[Health-care issues]**

■ **GADOMSKI, FRED,** B.S., M.S.; Meteorologist, Pennsylvania State University. **[Weather]**

■ **GARVIE, MAUREEN,** B.A., B.Ed., M.A.; Teacher and writer, Queen's University. **[Canadian literature]**

■ **GATTY, BOB,** Editor, *Grocery Headquarters.* **[Food]**

■ **GIBSON, ERIC,** B.A.; Executive editor, *ARTnews.* **[Art]**

■ **GOLDNER, NANCY,** B.A.; Free-lance dance critic. **[Dance]**

■ **HARAKAS, STANLEY SAMUEL,** B.A., B.D., Th.D.; Professor emeritus, Holy Cross Greek Orthodox School of Theology. **[Eastern Orthodox Churches]**

■ **HAVERSTOCK, NATHAN A.,** A.B.; Affiliate scholar, Oberlin College. **[Latin America and Latin American country articles]**

■ **HELMS, CHRISTINE,** B.A., Ph.D.; Director, Research and Analysis, Future Management Services. **[Middle East and Middle Eastern country articles; North African country articles]**

■ **HENDERSON, HAROLD,** B.A.; Staff writer, Chicago *Reader.* **[Chicago]**

■ **HOFFMAN, ANDREW J.,** B.S., M.S., Ph.D.; Assistant professor of Organizational Behavior, Boston University. **[Environmental pollution]**

■ **HOWELL, LEON,** A.B., M.Div.; Free-lance journalist. **[Religion]**

■ **JOHANSON, DONALD C.,** B.S., M.A., Ph.D.; Director and professor, Institute of Human Origins. **[Anthropology]**

■ **JONES, TIM,** B.S.; Media writer, *Chicago Tribune.* **[Telecommunications]**

KILGORE, MARGARET, B.A., M.B.A.; Editor, Phillips-Van Buren, Incorporated. **[Los Angeles]**

KING, MIKE, Reporter, *The Montreal Gazette*. **[Montreal]**

KLINTBERG, PATRICIA P., B.A.; Washington editor, *Farm Journal*. **[Agriculture]**

KLOBUCHAR, LISA, B.A.; Free-lance editor and writer. **[Disabled; Nobel prizes; People in the news; Pulitzer prizes]**

LAL, ANIL, M.A.; Instructor of English, Truman College. **[World Book supplement, India]**

LAL, VINAY, Ph. D.; Assistant professor of history, University of California at Los Angeles. **[World Book supplement, India]**

LAWRENCE, ALBERT, B.A., M.A., M.Ed.; President, OutExcel! **[Chess]**

LEWIS, DAVID C., M.D.; Professor of medicine and community health, Brown University. **[Drug abuse]**

MARCH, ROBERT H., A.B., M.A., Ph.D.; Professor of physics, University of Wisconsin at Madison. **[Physics]**

MARSCHALL, LAURENCE A., B.S., Ph.D.; Professor of physics, Gettysburg College. **[Astronomy]**

MARTY, MARTIN E., Ph.D.; Fairfax M. Cone distinguished service professor, University of Chicago. **[Protestantism]**

MATHER, IAN J., B.A., M.A.; Diplomatic editor, *The European*, London. **[Ireland; Northern Ireland; United Kingdom]**

MATHESON, KATY, M.A.; Free-lance writer **[World Book supplement: Ballet]**

MAUGH, THOMAS H., II, Ph.D.; Science writer, *Los Angeles Times*. **[Biology]**

McLEESE, DON, B.A., M.A.; Columnist/critic-at-large, *Austin American-Statesman*. **[Popular music]**

MESSENGER, ROBERT, B.A.; Free-lance writer/editor. **[City; Crime; Literature, American; Washington, D.C.]**

MINER, TODD, B.S., M.S.; Meteorologist, Pennsylvania State University. **[Weather]**

MORITZ, OWEN, B.A.; Urban-affairs editor, *New York Daily News*. **[New York City]**

MORRIS, BERNADINE, B.A., M.A.; Free-lance fashion writer. **[Fashion]**

MULLINS, HENRY T., B.S., M.S., Ph.D.; Professor of Earth science, Syracuse University. **[Geology]**

NGUYEN, J. TUYET, M.A.; United Nations correspondent, Deutsche Presse-Agentur. **[Population; United Nations]**

OGAN, EUGENE, B.A., M.A., Ph.D.; Professor emeritus of anthropology, University of Minnesota. **[Pacific Islands]**

PEREZ, LOUIS A., JR., Ph.D.; professor of history, University of North Carolina. **[World Book supplement, Cuba]**

RAPHAEL, MARC LEE, B.A., M.A., Ph.D.; Professor of religion, College of William and Mary. **[Judaism]**

REICH, BERNARD, Ph.D.; professor of political science and international affairs, George Washington University. **[World Book supplement, Jerusalem]**

REID, RON, B.A.; Sportswriter, *The Philadelphia Inquirer*. **[Sports articles]**

ROSE, MARK I., B.A., M.A., Ph.D.; Managing editor, *Archaeology* magazine. **[Archaeology]**

RUBENSTEIN, RICHARD E., B.A., M.A., J.D.; Professor of conflict resolution and public affairs, George Mason University. **[Terrorism]**

SAVAGE, IAN, B.A., M.A., Ph.D.; Assistant professor of economics and transportation, Northwestern University. **[Aviation; Transportation]**

SEGAL, TROY, B.A.; Free-lance writer. **[Television]**

SHAPIRO, HOWARD, B.S.; Travel editor, *The Philadelphia Inquirer*. **[Philadelphia]**

SHERWONIT, BILL, B.A., M.S.; Free-lance writer. **[Sports Special Report: Iditarod: Celebrating the Dog Days of Winter]**

SOLNICK, STEVEN L., B.A., M.A., Ph.D.; Assistant professor of political science, Columbia University. **[Baltic states and other former Soviet republic articles]**

STEIN, DAVID LEWIS, B.A., M.S.; Urban affairs columnist, *The Toronto Star*. **[Toronto]**

STEINBERG, LAURENCE, Ph.D.; Professor of psychology, Temple University. **[World Book supplement, Adolescent]**

STOKER, CAROL, B.A.; Reporter, *Boston Globe*. **[Gardening]**

STUART, ELAINE, B.A.; Managing editor, Council of State Governments. **[State government]**

TANNER, JAMES C., B.S.J.; Former news editor—energy, *The Wall Street Journal*. **[Energy supply]**

TATUM, HENRY K., B.A.; Associate editorial page editor, *The Dallas Morning News*. **[Dallas]**

TAYLOR, DAVID, B.A., M.A., Ph.D.; Senior lecturer in South Asian Politics at the School of Oriental and African Studies, University of London. **[India Special Report: India: 50 Years of Independence]**

THIEME, JOHN A., B.A., M.Phil., Ph.D.; Professor of new literature in English, University of Hull. **[Literature, World]**

THOMAS, GRAHAM, M.A., M.A., M.Ed.; Head of the Briefing Office of the School of Oriental and African Studies, University of London. **[Hong Kong Special Report: Hong Kong 1997: Capitalism Comes to China]**

THOMAS, PAULETTE, B.A.; Reporter, *The Wall Street Journal*. **[Bank]**

TOCH, THOMAS W., B.A., M.A.; Senior editor, *U.S. News & World Report*. **[Education]**

TOMB, GEOFFREY, B.A.; Reporter, *The Miami Herald* **[Miami]**

TONRY, MICHAEL, A.B., LL.B.; Professor of law and public policy, University of Minnesota Law School. **[Prison]**

von RHEIN, JOHN, B.A., B.A.; Classical music critic, *Chicago Tribune*. **[Classical music]**

WALTER, EUGENE J., Jr., B.A.; Free-lance writer. **[Conservation; Zoos]**

WOLCHIK, SHARON L., M.A., Ph.D.; Professor of Political Sciences and International Relations, George Washington University. **[Eastern European country articles]**

WOODS, MICHAEL, B.S.; Science editor, *The Toledo* (Ohio) *Blade* and *Pittsburgh Post-Gazette*. **[Biology Special Report: Is It Wrong to Clone People?; AIDS; Computer; Drugs; Electronics; Magazine; Medicine; Mental health; Public health; Safety]**

WRIGHT, ANDREW G., B.A., Associate editor, *Engineering News-Record*. **[Building and construction]**

WUNTCH, PHILIP, B.A.; Film critic, *The Dallas Morning News*. **[Motion pictures]**

Contents

Cross-Reference Tabs

A tear-out page of Cross-Reference Tabs for insertion in *The World Book Encyclopedia* appears before page 1.

The Year in Brief **10**

A month-by-month review of the major news stories of 1997.

Update **36 to 432**

The major world events of 1997 are reported in more than 250 alphabetically arranged Update articles—from "Afghanistan" and "Africa" to "Yugoslavia" and "Zoos." Included are Special Reports that provide an in-depth focus on especially noteworthy developments.

The Year's

Major News Stories

From China's change of leadership and take-over of Hong Kong to the tragic death of Britain's Princess Diana, 1997 was a year of memorable news events. On these two pages are stories that the editors picked as some of the most important of the year, along with details on where to find information about them in this volume.   *The Editors*

▲ **Stock market boom—and bust**
Traders at the New York Stock Exchange on October 23 watch as the Dow Jones Industrial Average, which had surged to above the 8000 mark, drops 187 points in response to faltering Asian markets. Still, the U.S. market remained strong at year-end. See **Asia,** page 82; **Economics,** page 191; **Stocks and bonds,** page 389.

Tobacco settlement
In an effort to avoid further litigation resulting from smoking-related diseases, the five major U.S. tobacco companies in June agree to a settlement with the states under which they will pay $368.5 billion to the states and the U.S. government over 25 years. The measure awaited approval at year-end. See **Courts,** page 164.

▲ **China regains Hong Kong**
Fireworks explode over Hong Kong at midnight between June 30th and July 1 to celebrate its return to China after more than a century of British rule. China pledged not to stifle Hong Kong's freewheeling economy, a promise many observers considered dubious. See **Hong Kong** Special Report: **Hong Kong 1997: Capitalism Comes to China,** page 224.

Zaire falls to rebels, becomes Congo
In May, after a seven-month civil war, rebel forces under the leadership of Laurent Kabila end the 31-year reign of Zaire's President Mobutu Sese Seko, who dies soon afterward of cancer. Zaire's new president renames the country the Democratic Republic of Congo. See **Africa,** page 42; **Congo (Kinshasa)** page 155.

Farewell to Mother Teresa ▶
Mother Teresa, the Roman Catholic nun who spent much of her life caring for the poor in the slums of Calcutta, India, dies of heart disease on September 5 at the age of 87. See **Roman Catholic Church,** page 357; **Roman Catholic Church** Special Report: **Mother Teresa: Saint of the Gutters,** page 358.

A big Labour victory in the U.K.
Britain's Labour Party, led by Tony Blair, rolls to a resounding election victory on May 1, winning 179 seats in Parliament. Blair, 43, becomes the youngest British prime minister in more than a century. See **United Kingdom,** page 411. **People in the news,** page 333.

▲ **Deadly smog in Asia**
Smog generated by smoke from out-of-control forest fires on four Indonesian Islands shrouds Kuala Lumpur, Malaysia, in late September. See **Asia,** page 86; **Indonesia,** page 263; **Malaysia,** page 299.

▲ **Honoring Diana**
Mourners in London on September 6 toss bouquets of flowers onto the hearse carrying the body of Britain's Princess Diana, killed in an August 31 car crash in Paris. See **Diana** Special Report: **Diana, Princess of Wales (1961-1997),** page 180; **United Kingdom,** page 412.

Jiang takes the reins in China
The ailing Deng Xiaoping, 92, leader of China since 1978, dies in February. President Jiang Zemin, Deng's designated successor, assumes the top post and says he will continue the Communist nation's program of economic reforms. See **China,** page 144; **People in the news,** page 337.

Cloning in the spotlight
Researchers in Scotland announce in February that they have developed a way to clone mammals using cells from adults, opening the possibility of creating human clones. A debate on the moral issues involved in human cloning had begun by year-end. See **Biology** Special Report: **Is It Wrong to Clone People?** page 108.

▲ **A new Guggenheim art museum in Spain**
The new Guggenheim Museum in Bilbao, Spain, opened in October. The titanium-clad structure—an outpost of New York City's Solomon R. Guggenheim Museum—was the work of American architect Frank O. Gehry. The building was hailed by critics as one of the great art museum designs of the 1900's. See **Architecture,** page 61; **Art,** page 80.

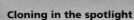

1997

The Year in Brief

A month-by-month listing of the most significant world events that occurred during 1997.

1 **An off-duty Israeli soldier** empties the clip of his M-16 automatic rifle into the open-air market in Hebron on the West Bank and wounds seven Arabs before being overpowered by other Israeli soldiers. The incident, according to the gunman, is to keep Hebron from being handed over to Palestinian control.

3 **The Serbian government**, dominated by Slobodan Milošević, rejects a call endorsed by 54 nations to install in office those candidates who were victorious in the Nov. 17, 1996, local elections, but who were disqualified by their opposition to Milošević.

4 **Winter storms,** which have battered at the West Coast for two weeks, result in massive flooding in Washington, Oregon, and northern California and cause the death of more than 30 people, the evacuation of 125,000 people, and damage to property in excess of $1 billion.

7 **Newt Gingrich,** a Republican from Georgia, is reelected speaker of the U.S. House of Representatives. Nine Republicans, disturbed by Gingrich's admission that he had violated various ethical standards of the House, defected from the party by voting for other candidates or by abstaining.

9 **All 26 passengers and 3 crew members** aboard a twin-engine, turboprop plane are killed when the commuter plane crashes on approach to the Detroit Metropolitan Airport during a heavy snowstorm.

11 **Bulgarians by the tens of thousands** take to the streets of Sofia, the capital, demanding early elections in order to oust the highly unstable, Socialist-controlled government. Police, swinging clubs and firing guns, work their way through the crowds to free lawmakers trapped in the parliament building.

15 **Israeli Prime Minister Benjamin Netanyahu** and Palestinian leader Yasir Arafat agree on the details and timing of an Israeli pullout of Hebron, the largely Palestinian city on the West Bank of the Jordan River. Hebron is sacred to both Jews and Muslims as the traditional burial place of the Biblical prophet Abraham. By January 17, Israel removes its troops from 80 percent of the city of Hebron.

17 **Ireland's High Court grants a divorce,** the first in the country's modern history. Irish voters in 1995 narrowly approved a constitutional amendment allowing divorce.

18 **Paul E. Tsongas,** the 1992 Democratic presidential candidate credited with forcing fellow candidates to deal with the nation's economic problems, dies at the age of 55.

19 **Two bombs explode** in a Tulsa, Oklahoma, abortion clinic, which was hit by firebombs on January 1. Similar bombings took place at an Atlanta, Georgia, abortion clinic during the week of January 12.

20 **William Jefferson Clinton,** the 42nd president of the United States, is inaugurated for a second term in Washington, D.C.

21 **Members of the U.S. House** of Representatives vote to reprimand Speaker Newt Gingrich for using tax-exempt money to promote a Republican Party agenda and for giving false information to the ethics committee investigating his behavior. It is the most severe rebuke ever delivered to a presiding officer of the House.

22 **A federal jury** in Greensboro, North Carolina, awards Food Lion, a supermarket chain, more than $5.5 million in punitive damages for a 1992 segment of the American Broadcasting Company (ABC) television show "Prime Time Live" that accused the chain of selling spoiled meat.

23 **Madeleine K. Albright**, the former U.S. Ambassador to the United Nations, is sworn in as the first female secretary of state of the United States. She was unanimously confirmed in her position by the Senate on January 22.

26 **The Green Bay Packers** win Super Bowl XXXI, 35 to 21, over the New England Patriots. The Green Bay Packers had not won a National Football League title for 29 years.

28 **South Africa's** Truth and Reconciliation Commission, a committee investigating abuses under apartheid, announces that former policemen had confessed to a number of notorious murders, including the 1977 killing of Black Consciousness Movement leader Steve Biko.

January
1997

S	M	T	W	TH	F	S
				1	2	3	4
5	6	7	8	9	10	11
12	13	14	15	16	17	18
19	20	21	22	23	24	25
26	27	28	29	30	31	

29 **America Online Inc. (AOL)**, the internet subscription service, agrees to offer credits and million of dollars in refunds to compensate customers for network traffic jams.

30 **The Internal Revenue Service (IRS)**, after admitting to a congressional panel that it had spent $4 billion on computer systems that do not work, proposes hiring independent contractors to process paper tax returns.

President Bill Clinton is sworn in for a second term on January 20 on the west steps of the the U.S. Capitol as his wife, Hillary, holds the Bible, and his daughter, Chelsea, and Vice President Al Gore look on.

February
1997

2 **Algerian rebels** kill more than 30 people in a town south of Algiers, the capital. The victims were associated with a dissident member of a fundamentalist Muslim rebel faction, one of a number of groups battling the government and each other in Algeria's five-year-old civil war.

3 **Sergeant Major of the Army** Gene McKinney, the U.S. Army's top-ranking enlisted man and a member of the committee that reviews army sexual-harassment policies, is accused of sexually assaulting a female colleague.

5 **Former Prime Minister** Benazir Bhutto's Pakistan People's Party concedes that the Pakistan Muslim League, headed by Nawaz Sharif, has taken 134 of the National Assembly's 217 seats in the February 3 elections. The People's Party wins only 19 seats.

6 **The German government** announces that the number of Germans without jobs rose in January to 4.66 million, 12.2 percent of the work force and the nation's highest unemployment rate since 1933, the year Adolf Hitler became chancellor.

7 **Ron Robertson,** head of the District of Columbia police union, describes the streets of the nation's capital as a war zone and calls on the federal government to take control of the police force. Forty-five people have been murdered since January 1 on the streets of Washington, D.C.

10 **A civil court jury** in Santa Monica, California, orders O. J. Simpson to pay $25 million in punitive damages to the families of Simpson's exwife, Nicole Brown Simpson, and her friend Ronald L. Goldman, who were murdered in 1994. On February 4, the same jury, ruling against Simpson in the wrongful-death suit brought by the Brown and Goldman families, ordered Simpson to pay $8.5 million in compensatory damages.

Chinese leaders (from left) President Jiang Zemin, Prime Minister Li Peng, and Chairman of National Congress Qiao Shi pay their respects on February 24 to "paramount leader" Deng Xiaoping.

13 **The Dow Jones Industrial Average**, a composite of the stock prices of 30 major companies listed on the New York Stock Exchange, climbs 60.81 points to close at 7,022.44. The push beyond 7,000, coming only 82 trading days after the Dow cleared the 6,000-point level, is the fastest 1000-point jump in Wall Street history.

14 **Forty-nine dolphins and three whales** are found dead in the Gulf of California near Culiacán, Mexico. Biologists suspect that the cause is a chemical used by drug traffickers to mark sites where drugs are dropped in the ocean.

15 **More than 60 countries**, meeting in Geneva, Switzerland, agree to open their telecommunications markets to foreign competition, a move that could push down the cost of international telephone calls, which average $1 a minute, by 80 percent.

17 **The Department of Health** and Human Services announces that the U.S. government will pay teaching hospitals not to train physicians. University of Pennsylvania professor Alan Hillman called the program, which is designed to reduce the surplus of doctors, "an amazing treatment of health care as a commodity."

19 **Deng Xiaoping**, leader of one fifth of all human beings on Earth, dies at the age of 92. "Paramount leader" of China for 18 years, Deng was the last of the generation of Communist revolutionaries who transformed China from a chaotic, feudal state to a world power.

21 **Kenneth Starr** announces he has changed his mind and will not resign as the Justice Department's independent counsel until the investigation into the failed Arkansas real estate venture known as Whitewater is completed. Starr had announced his resignation on February 17, sparking widespread speculation that he had failed to collect sufficient evidence to prosecute President Clinton or First Lady Hillary Rodham Clinton for their possible roles in the Whitewater project.

22 **Embryologist Ian Wilmut** announces that he and his research group at the Roslin Institute near Edinburgh, Scotland, have cloned an adult animal. Using a mammary cell from an adult ewe, Wilmut and his team prepared the DNA to be accepted by an egg from another ewe. After removing the DNA from the egg, they replaced it with the DNA from the donor ewe. The egg was then implanted in a third ewe, which gave birth in July 1996 to a healthy lamb with DNA that perfectly matches that of the donor ewe.

23 **Wielding a semiautomatic weapon**, a 69-year-old Palestinian immigrant opens fire on a crowd of 90 to 100 people on the 86th-floor open-air observation deck atop New York City's Empire State Building. One person is fatally shot and seven are wounded before the gunman turns the gun on himself.

26 **Chairman of the Federal Reserve System** Alan Greenspan publicly warns that stock prices may be "unsustainably high."

27 **Officials of the Centers for Disease** Control and Prevention announce that deaths from AIDS throughout the United States have dropped "substantially." The AIDS death rate was 13 percent lower in the first six months of 1996 compared with the same period in 1995. The decline is attributed to the benefits of drug therapies introduced in the late 1990's to fight HIV, the virus that causes AIDS.

March
1997

S	M	T	W	TH	F	S
						1
2	3	4	5	6	7	8
9	10	11	12	13	14	15
16	17	18	19	20	21	22
23	24	25	26	27	28	29
30	31					

Workers from the medical examiner's office remove the bodies of some of the 39 members of the Heaven's Gate cult who committed mass suicide on March 26 in a mansion near San Diego, California.

1 Thunderstorms and tornadoes, sweeping across Arkansas, Mississippi, Kentucky, West Virginia, and Ohio, leave 48 people dead.

5 Clinton Administration officials admit that Margaret A. Williams, Hillary Rodham Clinton's chief of staff, accepted—in the White House in 1995—a $50,000 campaign donation to the Democratic Party from Johnny Chung, a California businessman. Federal law prohibits solicitation or receipt of political contributions in government offices.

6 China's legislature revises the nation's criminal code for the first time since 1979, introducing laws regulating insider trading and money laundering and eliminating laws covering a variety of "counterrevolutionary" crimes.

7 The most severe flooding along the Ohio River since 1964 crests at Louisville, Kentucky, 15.7 feet (4.8 meters) above flood stage. It leaves 29 people dead and tens of thousands homeless in West Virginia, Ohio, Indiana, Tennessee, and Kentucky.

8 **Hostage crisis** negotiations between Peruvian officials and the Túpac Amaru collapse when the Marxist rebels discover that government security police are digging a tunnel beneath the Japanese ambassador's residence in Lima, the capital, where the Túpac Amaru have held 72 people hostage since Dec. 17, 1996.

10 **The Federal Bureau** of Investigation (FBI) issues a statement flatly refuting President Bill Clinton's claim, made during a news conference earlier in the day, that he and senior staff members had not been told that the FBI had warned White House officials in 1996 that China might be attempting to illegally funnel money into U.S. political campaigns.

11 **The U.S. Senate** approves a measure to investigate "illegal and improper" campaign fund-raising activities in the executive and legislative branches of the government.

12 **Japanese Prime Minister** Ryutaro Hashimoto publicly apologizes for his government's "inadequate" response to a March 11 fire that triggered an explosion at the Tokaimura nuclear-waste reprocessing plant, exposing 21 workers to low-level radiation. A similar accident in December 1995 at Monju, Japan's only fast-breeder reactor, triggered widespread criticism of Japan's nuclear industry.

13 **A 23-year-old Jordanian soldier** opens fire on a group of Israeli junior-high school girls visiting Naharayim. Seven girls die and six are wounded before the attacker is subdued.

In Tiranë, the capital of Albania, looters carry off the remains of the city's dwindling food supply, while the police arm civilians in the hope that they will defend the government of authoritarian ruler Sali Berisha, who refuses to resign the presidency. The U.S. State Department warns that all Americans in Albania should leave immediately.

14 **The giant food corporation H. J. Heinz** announces that it will lay off 2,500 employees—5.8 percent of its work force—shut down at least 25 domestic and international plants, and sell its frozen-foods subsidiary, Ore-Ida Foods Incorporated.

15 **Zairian rebels** take the important, eastern city of Kisangani, a Congo River port of more than 300,000 residents, from the Zairian army, which puts up token resistance. Kisangani's fall signals the downfall of President Mobutu Sese Seko, who has ruled Zaire for 31 years.

17 **Anthony Lake,** President Bill Clinton's nominee for Central Intelligence Agency (CIA) director, withdraws his name from consideration after his confirmation, delayed for three months, is threatened with additional delays by the U.S. Senate Intelligence Committee.

18 **The Presidential Advisory Committee** on Gulf War Veterans' Illnesses, a panel charged with investigating illnesses associated with the Persian Gulf War, presents evidence that the March 1991 demolition of an enemy ammunition depot in Iraq released clouds of nerve gas. The gas may have spread as far as 165 miles (265 kilometers) in a southerly direction, exposing hundreds of thousands of American troops to low doses of toxic chemicals.

20 **The Liggett Group, Inc.,** which manufactures the Chesterfield, L & M, and Lark brands of cigarettes, acknowledges that tobacco is addictive and causes cancer. The Liggett spokesperson also concedes that tobacco companies historically have marketed their products to minors in an attempt to lure children as young as 14 years old into a lifetime smoking habit.

24 **Director of the Kenya Wildlife Service** David Western announces his support for lifting the 20-year ban on big-game hunting on private land in order to cull overpopulations of such nonendangered species as zebra, antelope, and wart hogs, which overrun farmers' fields.

25 **The Federal Reserve** banking system, under the leadership of Chairman Alan Greenspan, votes to raise interest rates for the first time in more than two years.

26 **The bodies of 39 mass suicide victims** are discovered in a mansion in the San Diego suburb of Rancho Santa Fe. The dead—21 women and 18 men—belonged to a cult named Heaven's Gate. They apparently had believed that a space ship traveling behind Comet Hale-Bopp, visible in the night sky, would pick up and transport them to a better world.

29 **A dozen tornadoes** rampage through Tennessee, leaving more than 40 people homeless. In Chattanooga, tornadoes snap trees and utility poles designed to withstand winds of up to 160 miles per hour (270 kilometers per hour). Two people were killed when the same series of storms cut through Indiana and Kentucky late on March 28.

April
1997

S	M	T	W	TH	F	S
		1	2	3	4	5
6	7	8	9	10	11	12
13	14	15	16	17	18	19
20	21	22	23	24	25	26
27	28	29	30			

1 **A spring storm**, which the National Weather Service brands the third worst in Boston history, blankets the Northeast with more than 2.5 feet (76 centimeters) of snow.

2 **A U.S. Department of Agriculture** (USDA) spokesperson announces that 153 Michigan schoolchildren have been diagnosed with the viral infection hepatitis A, transmitted through contaminated strawberries served as part of the school lunch program conducted by the USDA.

3 **Helmut Kohl,** architect of the 1990 unification of Germany, announces that he will run in 1998 for a fifth term as chancellor.

6 **Algerian eyewitnesses** report that more than 90 civilians have been killed since April 3 by Islamic militants, groups that have battled the government in a civil war for five years.

8 **The U.S. Court of Appeals** for the Ninth Circuit declares constitutional California's Proposition 209—a measure that banned the use of racial and sex-based preferences in affirmative-action programs. Implementation of the proposition was blocked by an injunction issued by a federal district court judge soon after it was passed by voters in November 1996.

9 **A National Aeronautics and Space** Administration spokesperson reveals highly detailed photographs of Europa, a large moon orbiting Jupiter, that suggest a thin crust of ice covering a global ocean of water.

13 **A 21-year-old Professional Golf Association** rookie, Tiger Woods, wins the Masters Tournament in Augusta, Georgia.

15 **A fire rages** through 70,000 tents housing thousands of people who had journeyed to Mecca in Saudi Arabia for an annual pilgrimage that is one of Islam's holiest rituals. At least 340 people die and more than 1,300 people are injured.

19 **India's coalition government** names Inder Kumar Gujral prime minister, ending the political chaos that brought down the previous prime minister, H. D. Deve Gowda, on March 11.

21 **At Grand Forks, North Dakota,** the Red River of the North, swollen by record levels of melting snow, crests at 54 feet (16.5 meters). Ninety percent of the city, now empty of its 50,000 inhabitants, is under water—in some areas to levels of 15 feet (4.5 meters). A fire broke out in the downtown area on the afternoon of April 19. Hampered by floodwater, fire fighters were unable to battle the blaze, which engulfed whole blocks of historic structures.

Fire fighters survey the ruins of an entire block of downtown Grand Forks, North Dakota, which burned in April 1997 when catastrophic flooding blocked efforts to battle the fire.

22 **Peruvian soldiers** storm the Japanese ambassador's residence in Lima and rescue 72 hostages taken prisoner by the Túpac Amaru Revolutionary Army on Dec. 17, 1996. Two soldiers and all 14 of the revolutionaries are killed. One hostage later dies of a heart attack.

24 **At Philadelphia's Academy** of Natural Sciences, an international team of paleontologists announce the recent discovery in China of an extraordinary trove of dinosaur fossils. The team has unearthed the fossilized internal organs of dinosaurs and the fossil of a dinosaur containing the remains of a mammal it had just eaten.

27 **A Texas couple is held hostage** in a travel trailer in the Davis Mountains of West Texas by members of a militant group that calls itself the Republic of Texas. The group claims that Texas remains an independent nation because its 1845 annexation by the United States was illegal.

29 **Lori Fortier, a key witness** for the trial of Timothy J. McVeigh—the man accused of the April 19, 1995, bombing of the Alfred P. Murrah Federal Building in Oklahoma City, Oklahoma—testifies in federal court in Denver that McVeigh called the Oklahoma City building "an easy target" and told her, in October 1994, that he planned to blow it up.

May
1997

S	M	T	W	TH	F	S
				1	2	3
4	5	6	7	8	9	10
11	12	13	14	15	16	17
18	19	20	21	22	23	24
25	26	27	28	29	30	31

1 **British voters,** after 18 years of a Conservative Party government, sweep the Labour Party into power in the House of Commons and party leader Tony Blair into 10 Downing Street—the prime minister's residence. It is the worst defeat for Conservatives since 1832.

2 **President Bill Clinton** and Republican leaders in Congress agree on a plan that will balance the federal budget in five years.

3 **Five members** of the militant Republic of Texas, including leader Richard L. McLaren, surrender after seven days of stand-off with Texas law-enforcement officials. The stand-off began after the group abducted a local couple.

11 **World chess champion** Garry Kasparov loses the final game of a six-game match to Deep Blue, an International Business Machines RS/6000 ST computer. The defeat marks the first time a machine has bested a world-class chess champion.

12 **The deputy chief of a Mount Everest** search-and-rescue service announces that six climbers from three expeditions attempting to scale the mountain's north face were lost in a blizzard on May 11 and are probably dead. The year before, eight climbers died while attempting to climb the mountain.

14 **Russia and the North Atlantic Treaty** Organization (NATO), a military alliance consisting of the United States, Canada, and 14 Western European countries, agree to terms under which NATO will expand its membership to include European countries that were former satellites of the Soviet Union. NATO, formed in 1949 to discourage a Soviet attack on non-Communist countries, agrees to establish a NATO-Russian security council.

17 **Rebel leader Laurent Kabila** pronounces himself president of Zaire and changes the country's name to the Democratic Republic of Congo. Mobutu Sese Seko, who controlled the country for nearly 32 years, fled the capital on May 16.

21 **British officials meet** with leaders of Sinn Fein, the political arm of the Irish Republican Army (IRA) for the first time since the IRA broke a cease-fire in February 1996.

22 **America's first female B-52 pilot,** First Lieutenant Kelly Flinn, agrees to a general discharge from the U.S. Air Force rather than face charges of adultery, lying, fraternization, and disobedience of direct orders.

23 **Mohammed Khatami,** a moderate who campaigned on a platform of social reform, is overwhelmingly elected president of Iran.

24 **Soldiers of the Taliban,** the Islamic fundamentalist group that controls much of Afghanistan, capture Mazar-e-Sharif, a northern city that was the last obstacle to uniting the country for the first time since the Soviet invaders left in 1989.

25 **Senator Strom Thurmond,** the oldest person ever to serve in the U.S. Congress, breaks the record of Senator Carl Hayden of Arizona to become the longest-serving senator in history. The 94-year-old Republican to date has served in the Senate for 41 years and 10 months.

27 **The U.S. Supreme Court** rules 9 to 0 that a sitting president of the United States can be sued while in office for actions unrelated to official duties. The decision allows Paula Corbin Jones, a former employee of the state of Arkansas, to sue President Bill Clinton for sexual harassment.

Violent tornadoes cut through central Texas. In Jarrell, 27 people are killed when a tornado, with winds up to 260 miles (418 kilometers) per hour, rips through the town of 1,000 residents.

Rebel soldiers prepare on May 21 to advance into Kinshasa, the capital of Zaire, which was renamed the Democratic Republic of Congo by rebel leader and new president, Laurent Kabila.

7 **The United Nations war crimes tribunal,** meeting in the Netherlands, finds Dušan Tadić, a Bosnian Serb, guilty on multiple counts of war crimes and crimes against humanity. Tadić's conviction is the first made by the tribunal, which is investigating atrocities committed in the former Yugoslavia during the Bosnian War.

10 **An earthquake of 7.1 magnitude** shakes a mountainous region in northeastern Iran. Some 200 villages are leveled, leaving at least 4,000 people dead, 6,000 injured, and 50,000 homeless. Three major earthquakes and dozens of aftershocks have rocked northeastern Iran since early February.

June
1997

S	M	T	W	TH	F	S
1	2	3	4	5	6	7
8	9	10	11	12	13	14
15	16	17	18	19	20	21
22	23	24	25	26	27	28
29	30					

1 **French voters reject** the conservative policies of President Jacques Chirac and give the Socialist Party and its allies a resounding mandate to form a government that will give jobs and social programs priority over France's participation in the European Union's new currency. Chirac, who called elections one year ahead of schedule in the hope of gaining public support for his austere economic policies, must now name Socialist Party leader Lionel Jospin prime minister.

2 **Timothy J. McVeigh is found guilty** by a federal jury of 11 counts of conspiracy and murder for the bombing of the Alfred P. Murrah Federal Building in Oklahoma City, Oklahoma, on April 19, 1995. The explosion resulted in the death of 168 people. On June 13, the jury sentences McVeigh to death.

3 **Canadian Prime Minister** Jean Chrétien's Liberal Party wins sufficient seats in the national election to retain control of Parliament, but the election, which the prime minister called early, cost the Liberals 19 seats.

5 **Algerians vote** for a multiparty parliament for the first time since the outbreak of civil war in 1992 between the government and Islamic fundamentalists.

6 **The Department of Labor** reports that the U.S. unemployment rate, which has fallen for the fourth consecutive month, stands at 4.8 percent, its lowest level since 1973.

7 **A member of Sinn Fein**, the political wing of the Irish Republican Army (IRA), wins a seat in the Parliament of the Republic of Ireland in Dublin. Caoimhghin O'Caolain will be the first IRA member to enter parliament since Ireland won independence from Great Britain in 1922.

14 **A report issued** by the General Accounting Office, the investigative arm of Congress, finds "substantial evidence" linking health problems experienced by more than 80,000 veterans of the Persian Gulf War to nerve gas and other chemical weapons, including aflatoxin, a liver carcinogen.

Members of the Chinese armed forces raise the Chinese Flag at the stroke of midnight between June 30 and July 1, marking the moment Hong Kong reverts to Chinese rule, ending more than 150 years of British sovereignty.

15 **Rebel forces in Colombia** release 70 state soldiers and marines, some of whom were held hostage since August 1996, after the government in Bogotá agrees to withdraw all military forces from an area in southern Colombia around the city of Cartagena del Chairá.

16 **Hours after two Royal Ulster Constabulary** officers in Northern Ireland were shot in the head, the Irish Republican Army (IRA) claims responsibility for the murders. British officials call off further contact with Sinn Fein, the political arm of the IRA. The new British Labour government first met with Sinn Fein leaders in May, breaking a silence that began when the IRA shattered a cease-fire in February 1996.

17 **Bodyguard units** loyal to Cambodia's first prime minister, Prince Norodom Ranariddh, exchange rocket and gun fire with similar units loyal to the second prime minister, Hun Sen, in the streets of Phnom Penh. A rocket explodes in the garden of the U.S. embassy, throwing people from their beds and shattering windows.

18 **Necmettin Erbakan,** Turkey's first pro-Islamic prime minister, resigns under intense pressure from senior army officials, who claim that the prime minister has undermined the nonreligious basis on which the Turkish republic had been governed since its founding in 1923.

19 **The Convention on International Trade** in Endangered Species votes to allow limited international trade in elephant ivory from three southern African countries.

20 **Tobacco companies,** state attorneys general, and lawyers representing individuals and health groups come to an historic $368.5-billion agreement, which, if ratified by the U.S. Congress and signed by the president, would allow the U.S. Food and Drug Administration to regulate nicotine as an addictive drug.

22 **The U.S. Justice Department's** Bureau of Justice Statistics announces that the prison population in the United States now stands at nearly 1.2 million. In 1996, 55,900 new inmates, an increase of 5 percent from 1995, were incarcerated in the nation's overcrowded prisons.

23 **The U.S. Supreme Court,** in a 5-to-4 decision, rules that sexual offenders judged dangerous but not mentally ill can be confined to state mental institutions for indefinite periods after completing prison sentences. The decision upholds a 1994 Kansas law intended to protect citizens from sexual offenders deemed likely to repeat the crimes for which they were imprisoned.

24 **The U.S. Air Force** issues "The Roswell Report—Case Closed"—a 231-page statement claiming that the mysterious bodies supposedly discovered in Roswell, New Mexico, in 1947 were not aliens from unidentified flying objects, as many people have asserted, but rather dummies used in high-altitude parachute tests.

25 **An unmanned cargo vessel** collides with the Mir space station, sending Mir reeling. The impact, which punctured the outer skin of the station, shuts down much of the ship's power.

26 **The U.S. Supreme Court** unanimously rules that states can ban doctor-assisted suicide.

30 **More than 150 years** of British colonial rule in Hong Kong ends on the stroke of midnight between June 30 and July 1 as the People's Republic of China takes control of Hong Kong. The transfer of power is marked by martial music, dancing dragons, extravagant fireworks, and speeches by President Jiang Zemin of China and Prince Charles of Great Britain.

1 **Chinese President Jiang Zemin,** appearing before a huge crowd in Beijing, the capital, exhorts Taiwan to follow the leads of Hong Kong and Macao and reunite with China. The Portuguese colony of Macao is scheduled to be reintegrated into China in December 1999.

2 **The *Diamond Grace,*** a Japanese-owned tanker, spills 400,000 gallons (1.5 million liters) of oil into Tokyo Bay after running aground.

4 **The American spacecraft Pathfinder** lands on Mars after a 7-month, 309-million-mile (495-million-kilometer) journey from Earth. Designed to transmit data and pictures of the Martian landscape, the craft opens its three exterior panels to announce to Earth its textbook-perfect arrival on Mars. Attached to the craft is a six-wheeled rover—named Sojourner—that will begin exploring the surface of Mars.

5 **Sixteen-year-old Martina Hingis** beats Jana Novotna to win the women's singles tennis championship at Wimbledon.

6 **Hun Sen,** second prime minister of Cambodia, seizes absolute control of the government in Phnom Penh, the capital, after two days of street fighting between forces loyal to him and a royalist faction loyal to Prince Norodom Ranariddh, the first prime minister.

7 **Results of Mexico's July 5 election** reveal that the party that has held power since 1929, the Institutional Revolutionary Party, has lost control of the Chamber of Deputies. Cuauhtémoc Cárdenas Solórzano, founder of the emerging leftist Party of the Democratic Revolution, is overwhelmingly elected to the powerful post of mayor of Mexico City, regarded by some as a stepping stone to the presidency.

Montgomery Ward, the Chicago-based company that invented mail-order retailing, declares bankruptcy after 125 years in business.

8 **The North Atlantic Treaty Organization** (NATO) invites three former Soviet bloc countries—Poland, the Czech Republic, and Hungary—to join the military alliance that consists of the United States, Canada, and 14 other Western countries. NATO was formed in 1949 to discourage a Soviet attack on the non-Communist countries of Europe.

10 **Scientists at the University of Munich** in Germany announce that they have analyzed DNA extracted from the skull of a Neanderthal specimen. Results suggest that Neanderthals did not interbreed with anatomically modern humans, as has long been speculated, and that Neanderthals appear to have separated from the hominid line leading to modern humans four times as long ago as anthropologists had thought.

15 **Fashion designer Gianni Versace** is shot and killed on the front steps of his mansion in Miami Beach's art deco South Beach area. Police suspect Andrew Cunanan, believed to have previously killed four men in a three-state murder spree in April and May.

July
1997

S	M	T	W	TH	F	S
		1	2	3	4	5
6	7	8	9	10	11	12
13	14	15	16	17	18	19
20	21	22	23	24	25	26
27	28	29	30	31		

17 **The Woolworth Corporation** announces that all remaining F. W. Woolworth stores—approximately 400—are to be closed.

19 **The Irish Republican Army (IRA)** announces a cease-fire of terrorist activities. The organization's last cease-fire ended in February 1996.

20 **Rivers across central Europe** continue to rise after 10 days of torrential rain. Nearly 100 people are killed by the flooding, described as the worst of the century.

21 **Canadian fishermen**, angry because of a U.S.-Canadian dispute over who gets to fish for salmon in the international waters of the Pacific Northwest, ignore a court order to break up a 200-boat blockade of the *Malaspina,* an Alaskan ferry, held in the port of Prince Rupert, British Columbia, since July 19.

23 **A three-month, nationwide manhunt** ends when Andrew Cunanan, accused of killing five men in a four-state murder spree, shoots himself aboard a Miami Beach houseboat.

24 **Scientists responsible** for producing the sheep Dolly through cloning announce they have created another sheep through cloning containing a human gene coded for the production of a pharmaceutically useful protein.

25 **K. R. Narayanan takes the oath of office** as president of India. He is the first untouchable, or member of the lowest rung in the Hindu caste system, to attain high office in India.

27 **A journalist reveals** that he saw Pol Pot, notorious leader of Cambodia's Khmer Rouge guerrillas, on July 22. It is the first time the founder of the fanatical Maoist movement has been sighted by an outsider in nearly two decades.

The Sojourner, *left,* **a six-wheeled rover transported to Mars by the American spacecraft Pathfinder that landed on July 4, examines a rock on the surface of the red planet. Pathfinder, designed to transmit data about the Martian landscape, successfully completed its mission and provided people on Earth with pictures of Mars, which were posted by NASA for public view on the World Wide Web.**

August
1997

1 **The National Cancer Institute** announces that fallout from nuclear blasts in 1952, 1953, 1955, and 1957 at the Nevada Test Site near Las Vegas may have been the cause of thousands of cases of thyroid cancer.

3 **Ash, superheated gas, and molten rock** from Montserrat's Soufriere Hills Volcano flow into Plymouth, destroying houses in the historic center of the capital of the Caribbean island.

6 **A Korean Air Lines jumbo jet** en route to Guam from Seoul, South Korea, crashes into the jungle on the U.S.-held Pacific island, killing 226 of the 254 people aboard.

6 **Apple Computer Inc.** announces the formation of an alliance between Apple and its archrival, Microsoft Corporation. Microsoft agrees to buy $150 million of nonvoting Apple stock.

8 **The United Nations Children's Fund** warns that some 80,000 North Korean children are in imminent danger of dying from hunger. An additional 800,000 North Korean children are suffering from malnutrition.

12 **As many as 600 people are killed** and thousands more are forced from their homes in Burundi during renewed clashes between Hutu rebels and the Tutsi-dominated Burundian army. Since 1993, when the latest round of fighting between Hutu guerrillas and army soldiers began, more than 150,000 Burundians have died.

13 **The Canadian province of Ontario** shuts down seven nuclear reactors operated by Ontario Hydro in response to a report that the safety of the utility's entire nuclear power system has been compromised by poor management.

14 **Paleoanthropologist** Lee Berger announces that he and colleagues at the University of Witwatersrand in Johannesburg, South Africa, have found the earliest-known fossilized footprints of an anatomically modern human being. Discovered on the edge of Langebaan Lagoon north of Cape Town, the prints are believed to have been made approximately 117,000 years ago.

15 **The U.S. Department of Agriculture** issues a public-health alert, warning that as much as 1.2 million pounds (544,300 kilograms) of frozen hamburger patties tainted with *E. coli* 0157:H7 bacteria has been sold nationwide by the Hudson Foods Company of Rogers, Arkansas.

18 **Officials of the Teamsters Union** announce a tentative agreement with United Parcel Service (UPS), ending a 15-day strike against the world's largest package-delivery company.

22 **Government officials** reveal that the thermoplastic skin of the B-2 stealth bomber loses its ability to evade radar in heat, moderate humidity, and rain. The bomber regularly fails 26 percent of flight tests as a result of damage to its sensitive skin.

24 **India asks Pakistan for a cease-fire** after both nations' troops exchange two days of near-continuous gunfire across their borders adjacent to the disputed state of Kashmir.

25 **More than 40 Algerian civilians,** mostly women and children, are murdered in attacks attributed to Islamic militant groups waging a civil war against the government.

26 **Former President of South Africa** F. W. de Klerk resigns as head of the National Party, the country's leading opposition party, and retires from politics.

28 **The Department of Commerce** announces that the U.S. economy grew at a robust rate of 3.6 percent during the second quarter of 1997.

29 **The British government** invites Sinn Fein, the political wing of the Irish Republican Army (IRA), to participate in peace talks in Belfast on September 15.

31 **Diana, Princess of Wales,** and former wife of Prince Charles, heir to the throne of Great Britain, dies in a car crash in Paris. Authorities believe the Mercedes bearing the princess entered a tunnel at a speed exceeding 100 miles (160 kilometers) per hour in an attempt to escape from photographers pursuing on motorcycles. The Princess's companion in the car, Emad al-Fayed—Egyptian-born heir to a fortune that includes Harrod's Department Store in London and the Ritz Hotel in Paris—dies, as does the driver. A bodyguard survives. Police reports indicate that the driver may have been drunk.

A United Parcel Service employee walks the picket line outside a UPS distribution center in New Haven, Connecticut, in August during a nationwide strike. The strike was settled on August 18.

September
1997

S	M	T	W	TH	F	S
		1	2	3	4	5	6
7	8	9	10	11	12	13
14	15	16	17	18	19	20
21	22	23	24	25	26	27
28	29	30				

3 **Southeastern Asia currencies**, led by the Thai baht and the Malaysian ringgit, again plunge to record lows against the dollar. The value of the ringgit has slipped 15 percent since July 2.

4 **Three suicide bombers,** dressed as women, detonate bombs in a Jerusalem shopping area packed with Israelis and tourists, killing eight people including themselves. Nearly 200 people are wounded.

5 **Mother Teresa,** the Roman Catholic nun whose work on behalf of the poor of the world earned her the 1979 Nobel Peace Prize, dies in Calcutta, India. She was 87 years old.

Queen Elizabeth II of Great Britain expresses her sorrow over the death of her former daughter-in-law, Diana, Princess of Wales, who was killed in a car crash on August 31. In a televised statement, the Queen refers to Diana, who was divorced from Prince Charles in 1996, as "an exceptional and gifted human being."

6 **Diana, Princess of Wales,** is buried on an ornamental island at Althorp, the ancestral house of her family, the Spencers, in Northamptonshire, following a funeral in London's Westminster Abbey. Millions of people, standing in silence, lined the streets, 20 deep, along which the cortege passed on its way to the Abbey. An estimated 1 billion people around the world watched the service on television.

9 **Panic among passengers** aboard an overcrowded ferry in waters along the coast of Haiti capsizes the 60-foot (18-meter) vessel, causing the death by drowning of at least 245 people.

11 **The citizens of Scotland** vote to establish a legislature, their first since 1707. The referendum grants wide-ranging power to a Scottish legislature that will function under the leadership of the British monarch and prime minister.

12 **Chinese President Jiang Zemin,** who also heads China's Communist Party, announces at the opening of the 15th party congress in Beijing that the Chinese government will sell more than 300,000 state-owned enterprises.

13 **Mother Teresa**, who was called a living saint for her work in the slums of Calcutta, is entombed after a funeral service that was closed to most of the poor to whom she had devoted her life. To ensure the safety of visiting dignitaries, the Indian army barred crowds from the funeral.

Tens of thousands of people line London's streets on September 6 to watch the coffin of Diana, Princess of Wales, transported by horse-drawn gun carriage to Westminster Abbey for her funeral service. Diana died on August 31 at age 36.

15 **American Home Products Corporation** of Madison, New Jersey, announces the immediate withdrawal of two prescription diet pills, including fenfluramine. The U.S. Food and Drug Administration asked that the drugs be withdrawn after uncovering evidence suggesting that they may cause heart valve damage to as many as 30 percent of the people taking them. In 1996, physicians prescribed a diet drug combination containing fenfluramine and phenfermine to more than 18 million Americans.

18 **A tourist bus** outside Cairo's Egyptian Museum is attacked by men wielding automatic weapons. Ten people die in the assault.

26 **An Indonesian Airbus**, en route from Jakarta to Sumatra, crashes on approach to the airport, killing all 234 people aboard.

28 **Italian Prime Minister** Romano Prodi announces a $500-million fund to aid victims of the two earthquakes that shook central Italy on September 26.

29

3 Attorney General Janet Reno announces that she has found no evidence that President Bill Clinton misused his office to raise money, improperly allowed contributors to stay overnight at the White House, or sought contributions in exchange for political favors.

4 Chicago's Field Museum of Natural History pays $8.36 million at Sotheby's auction house in New York City for Sue, the most complete *Tyrannosaurus rex* fossil yet discovered.

5 The Clinton Administration releases a videotape showing President Bill Clinton greeting potential campaign donors at a series of coffees in the West Wing of the White House before the 1996 presidential election. The tape is released two days after Attorney General Janet Reno cleared Clinton of allegations of campaign finance abuse.

6 Sheik Ahmed Yassin, founder of the Islamic movement Hamas, returns to his home in Gaza after being released on October 1 by Israel in exchange for two Israeli intelligence agents who had been held in Jordan for attempting to assassinate Khaled Meshal, a political leader of Hamas. Yassin had been imprisoned in Israel for eight years for his role in terrorist activities. The two Israeli agents allegedly attempted to kill Meshal by injecting a poison into his ear. After capturing the agents, Jordan demanded and received from Israel an antidote to the poison.

7 Astronomers announce the discovery of a star —in the direction of the constellation Sagittarius, 25,000 light-years from Earth—that is the brightest star yet observed in the Milky Way.

8 The Mars Global Surveyor yields the strongest evidence to date that Mars, like Earth, has a crust, a mantle, and an iron core. The finding lends support to the theory that the planet might once have been hospitable to life.

9 A hurricane unleashes flash floods and landslides along the Pacific coast of Mexico, killing 150 people. The storm dumps 16 inches (40.6 centimeters) of rain on the Mexican resort city of Acapulco.

10 The Nobel Peace Prize is awarded to the International Campaign to Ban Landmines and to its American coordinator, Jody Williams. Hours after the award is announced, Russian President Boris Yeltsin declares that Russia has decided to sign an international treaty banning land mines.

The major tobacco companies settle the first class-action lawsuit over the effects of smoking on nonsmokers by agreeing to spend $300 million for the study of tobacco-related diseases.

12 Singer/songwriter John Denver, 53, dies when his plane crashes into California's Monterey Bay.

14 The U.S. Supreme Court removes the last legal obstacle to the Oregon law that allows physician-assisted suicide. Oregon voters adopted the measure in a statewide referendum in 1994.

October
1997

S	M	T	W	TH	F	S
			1	2	3	4
5	6	7	8	9	10	11
12	13	14	15	16	17	18
19	20	21	22	23	24	25
26	27	28	29	30	31	

18 McNeil Consumer Products Company, the makers of Tylenol, the most popular pain reliever in the United States, announce that future advertising and bottle labels will inform consumers that too much of the drug can harm children. Overdoses of acetaminophen—Tylenol's active ingredient—have been blamed for liver damage and the deaths of several U.S. children.

20 The U.S. Justice Department charges the Microsoft Corp. with violating a 1995 antitrust pact and files a petition in court to fine Microsoft $1 million per day until the Redmond, Washington-based software giant stops demanding that U.S. personal computer makers package only Microsoft software for browsing the Internet.

Stock prices and currency values fall sharply in Asia markets amid fears that East Asia's economic crisis is spreading to other regions. Stocks plunged in Hong Kong, Malaysia, South Korea, Taiwan, and Thailand. The currencies of South Korea, Taiwan, and Thailand hit record lows against the dollar.

26 President Jiang Zemin of China lands in Honolulu, Hawaii, to begin a state visit to the United States, the first by a Chinese leader in 12 years.

The Florida Marlins win baseball's World Series, defeating the Cleveland Indians 3-2 in the 11th inning of the seventh and final game. The Marlins were the first baseball team ever to win the series without finishing the regular season first in its league.

27 A worldwide plunge in stock prices forces the New York Stock Exchange to halt trading for the first time since President John F. Kennedy was assassinated in 1963. The Dow Jones Industrial Average ends the day down 7.2 percent, the worst since October 1987 and the 12th-worst day in the history of the exchange.

Traders on the floor of the New York Stock Exchange on October 23 react to a worldwide stock slide triggered by a market panic in Hong Kong. The Dow Jones Industrial Average falls 186.88 points in response to deteriorating economic conditions throughout Southeast Asia.

November

1997

S	M	T	W	TH	F	S
						1
2	3	4	5	6	7	8
9	10	11	12	13	14	15
16	17	18	19	20	21	22
23	24	25	26	27	28	29
30						

2 **Iraq blocks two Americans** on the United Nations (UN) weapons inspection team from entering the country, its second such action in less than a week. Officials of the Clinton Administration respond that the United States will ask the UN Security Council to force Iraqi President Saddam Hussein to allow Americans into Iraq as team members.

3 **Prime Minister Chavalit Yongchaiyudh** of Thailand resigns after weeks of public protest sparked by the country's financial crisis.

President Saddam Hussein of Iraq threatens to shoot down American U-2 spy planes used by an international team monitoring disarmament. The United States announces that it has no plans to ground the planes.

5 **An independent panel of experts** concludes that the practice of acupuncture is an effective therapy for certain medical conditions, especially those involving nausea and pain, and should be integrated into standard medical practice.

7 **The U.S. government** reports that unemployment fell in October to 4.7 percent, the lowest rate in the United States since 1973.

8 **Chinese engineers** close a 130-foot (40-meter) wide gap in a dam as they complete the diversion of the Yangtze River and forge ahead with a hydroelectric power project that is forcing more than 1 million people to relocate.

10 **Louise Woodward,** a British *au pair* (live-in baby sitter) who had faced a long prison sentence following her murder conviction for the death of a child in her care, is released by a Massachusetts judge who reduces her charge to involuntary manslaughter and sentences her to the 279 days she had already served in jail.

12 **Four American** businessmen and their Pakistani driver are shot and killed in Pakistan as they drive through Karachi. Police suspect the assailants were avenging the U.S. conviction of a Pakistani citizen for killing two CIA employees.

17 **Gunmen open fire** near a temple built during the time of the pharaohs in Egypt. Fifty-eight foreign tourists and four Egyptians are killed in the worst attack yet on tourists in Egypt.

19 **Bobbi McCaughey**, a 29-year-old woman in Carlisle, Iowa, gives birth to seven babies, the first time in the United States that so many infants have been born alive.

An Egyptian police officer guards Queen Hatshepsut's temple in Luxor after gun-wielding terrorists stormed the popular tourist site on November 17 and killed 58 foreign tourists and 4 Egyptians.

21 **Iraqi President Saddam Hussein** allows UN inspectors—including Americans—to resume their search for weapons in Iraq.

South Korea, which has the world's 11th-biggest economy, announces that it will seek emergency assistance from the International Monetary Fund to avert a financial crisis.

27 **Sudden bursts of high winds** disrupt Macy's Thanksgiving Day Parade in New York City. Two spectators are hospitalized with serious head injuries when a six-story-tall Cat in the Hat balloon strikes a lamppost and plunges on top of the crowd.

28 **India's fourth prime minister** in 18 months resigns, deepening the political chaos that has overtaken the country since a 1996 election produced a fractured Parliament. Prime Minister I. K. Gujral resigns his government after three weeks of heated political fighting in Parliament. The speaker of Parliament, fearing violence, adjourns Parliament indefinitely.

30 **Czech Prime Minister Václav Klaus** resigns following President Václav Havel's call for a new government. Klaus, a noted reform economist, lost standing as the result of a campaign finance scandal in his party.

December
1997

S	M	T	W	TH	F	S
		1	2	3	4	5	6
7	8	9	10	11	12	13
14	15	16	17	18	19	20
21	22	23	24	25	26	27
28	29	30	31			

President Bill Clinton greets people on the streets of Sarajevo on December 22 after pledging continued U.S. military support of peace-keeping efforts in Bosnia-Herzegovina. On December 19, Clinton had announced that U.S. troops would remain in Bosnia as part of an international peacekeeping force past the June 1998 departure deadline.

1 **A 14-year-old boy shoots eight students** at a high school in West Paducah, Kentucky, killing two girls and critically injuring a third. The boy, a juvenile, is charged with murder, attempted murder, and burglary.

2 **The U.S. Food and Drug Administration** (FDA) approves the irradiation of red meat, a measure that could nearly eliminate bacteria that cause food poisoning from the meat supply. According to the FDA, irradiation is safe, does not alter the nutritional content of food, and does not change the flavor or aroma of meat.

President Farooq Leghari of Pakistan resigns from office after a month-long political battle with Prime Minister Nawaz Sharif.

Attorney General Janet Reno refuses to appoint an independent prosecutor to investigate fund-raising activities by President Bill Clinton and Vice President Albert Gore during the 1996 presidential campaign.

3 **South Korea agrees** to the largest international economic bailout in history—a $57-billion loan package that will overhaul the world's 11th largest economy. South Korea must severely cut public spending, which may result in rising unemployment and bankruptcies.

4 **The National Basketball Association** suspends Latrell Sprewell, a guard with the Golden State Warriors, for one year without pay for choking and threatening to kill his coach, P. J. Carlesimo. The Warriors terminated Sprewell's $32-million contract on December 3.

6 **A Russian military transport plane** smashes into an apartment complex in Irkutsk, a city in southern Siberia, killing more than 60 people and injuring dozens more. The plane crashed seconds after taking off fully loaded with fuel. Rescuers battle not only fire and smoke from the crash, but subzero temperatures as well.

10 **Gerry Adams,** the Northern Irish nationalist, meets with British Prime Minister Tony Blair at 10 Downing Street, the official residence of British prime ministers, in London. At the meeting, Adams, leader of Sinn Fein, the political wing of the Irish Republican Army (IRA), makes a commitment to nonviolence. It has been 76 years since the last IRA leader, Michael Collins, crossed the threshold at 10 Downing Street.

11 **Negotiators** for more than 150 countries meeting in Kyoto, Japan, agree tentatively to a package of measures that would legally obligate industrialized countries to cut emissions of heat-trapping greenhouse gases. The nations have one year to ratify the treaty.

16 **More than 700 television viewers** in Tokyo, Japan, suffer epilepsylike seizures while watching the hit cartoon "Pokemon." According to doctors, the seizures could have been triggered by a cartoon character with flashing eyes.

17 **The value of the yen** soars after Japanese Prime Minister Ryutaro Hashimoto announces a sweeping economic stimulus package that includes income-tax cuts of 2 trillion yen, or more than $15 billion.

A lioness, named Nala after a character in the Disney film *The Lion King,* is recaptured after being at large in central Florida for more than 24 hours. Nala escaped from her cage at a zoo in Kissimmee, Florida, as keepers were erecting a platform to protect her from heavy rains.

18 **South Koreans,** angered by the ruling party's mismanagement of the economy, elect an opposition candidate president for the first time in the country's history. Kim Dae Jung, head of the National Congress for New Politics, is elected to lead the nation, succeeding Kim Yong-sam.

President Bill Clinton announces that U.S. troops will stay in Bosnia as part of an international peacekeeping force past their mission's departure deadline of June 1998. There are approximately 8,000 Americans serving in Bosnia as part of a NATO-led force.

19 **A Singaporean passenger jet** crashes in a marsh in Indonesia, killing all 104 people on board. It is the third major plane crash in a week. A Tajik airliner crashed in the United Arab Emirates on December 15, killing 85 people, and a Ukrainian plane crashed in Greece on December 17 killing 70 people.

22 **President Bill Clinton** makes his first visit to Sarajevo, the capital of Bosnia-Herzegovina, pledging continued U.S. military support of peacekeeping efforts in Bosnia.

23 **Terry L. Nichols is convicted** of conspiring to bomb the Oklahoma City Federal Building and of involuntary manslaughter. The federal jury also acquits Nichols of murder charges. The jury finds that Nichols conspired with Timothy McVeigh in planning the 1995 blast that killed 168 people. Earlier in 1997, McVeigh was convicted on 11 counts and sentenced to death.

Gunmen spraying rifle fire and swinging machetes charge into a mountain village in Chiapas, Mexico, killing 45 Indians, including 15 children, and wounding at least 13 people. Some 300 people have been killed in the southern Mexican state since clashes began in 1994 between armed militia and Indian guerrillas fighting for greater rights.

28 **The Hong Kong government** announces that every chicken in the territory—more than 1.2 million—will be killed to combat a potentially deadly strain of flu, which scientists believe people can contract directly from chicken!

31 Michael Kennedy, son of the late Senator Robert F. Kennedy and nephew of President John F. Kennedy, dies at age 39 in a skiing accident in Aspen, Colorado.

1997

Update

The major events of 1997 are summarized in more than 250 alphabetically arranged articles, from "Afghanistan" to "Zoos." Included are Special Reports that offer in-depth looks at subjects, ranging from life work of Mother Teresa to how governments worldwide respond to the pressures of immigration. The Special Reports can be found on the following pages under their respective Update article titles.

ICE SKATIN

IRELAND

KENYA

LATIN A

LITERATUR

MENTAL HEA

NEWS

RIZES NO

PAKISTAN

POLAND

PSYCHOLO

MALIA SO

SPORTS SRI LANK

SWIMMIING SWITZERLAND SYRIA TAIWAN TELECOMMUNICATIONS

UKRAINE UNITED KINGDOM UNITED NATIONS UNITED STATES

HURRICANE PAULINE HITS ACAPULCO, MEXICO, SEE PAGE 427

Afghanistan. The Taliban, a fundamentalist Muslim militia group, battled several smaller regional groups in 1997 for total control of Afghanistan. In 1996, the Taliban captured Afghanistan's capital, Kabul, and formed a new national government. By early 1997, the Taliban controlled the southern two-thirds of the country. The United Nations was unsuccessful in negotiating a peace agreement between the warring factions.

The Taliban was composed primarily of Pashtuns, Afghanistan's largest ethnic group. The faction also included soldiers from the country's former Communist regime and its guerrilla opponents. Pakistan reportedly aided and armed the Taliban. The Taliban's main opponents for control of the country consisted of a coalition that included ethnic Tajiks in northeastern Afghanistan, led by Ahmad Shah Massoud; Uzbeks and Turkmen in the northwest, led by Abdul Rashid Dostam; and a Hazara ethnic group of Shiite Muslims in the north-central region, led by Abdul Karim Khalili.

Fighting in early 1997 took place between Kabul and the Salang tunnel through the mountains of the Hindu Kush chain. The Taliban launched an offensive in the northwest after Massoud forces blocked the Salang tunnel. On May 24, the Taliban captured Dostam's capital at Mazar-i-Sharif, and Dostam fled to Turkey. After the fall of Mazar-i-Sharif, Pakistan broke ranks with most other countries by extending diplomatic recognition to the Taliban government. Massoud charged on August 13 that Pakistan backed the Taliban so the faction would permit pipelines to carry oil and gas across Afghanistan to Pakistan.

Islamic law. The Taliban attempted to impose the same rigid interpretation of Islamic law on Mazar-i-Sharif as it had on other cities under its control. Severe restrictions were imposed on women working in public or appearing unveiled outside the house. The strict rules made it difficult for foreign aid workers to supply Afghanistan with desperately needed food and medical help. On May 27, Mazar-i-Sharif citizens revolted against the restrictions. Hundreds of Taliban members were killed in the worst uprising against the faction since 1995. In early September 1997, Dostam returned to Mazar-i-Sharif and regained power.

Prime minister killed. Coalition leaders backed Burhanuddin Rabbani, the leader who had governed Kabul before it was captured by the Taliban, as figurehead leader of the coalition. On Aug. 13, 1997, Rabbani named a Pashtun diplomat, Abdul Rahim Ghafurzai, prime minister. Ghafurzai was killed on August 21 in a plane crash.

Opium production. The United Nations reported on September 10 that opium production in Afghanistan had increased 26 percent, despite Taliban pledges to curtail production of the drug.

☐ Henry S. Bradsher

See also **Asia** (Facts in brief table); **Pakistan**.

Africa

The trend toward more democratic governments continued in Africa in 1997, though its momentum slowed. Despite democratic successes, war and violence remained a fact of African life. A particularly disturbing trend was the intervention of African governments in the domestic conflicts of their neighbors, an outgrowth of ethnic hostilities and the floods of refugees crossing borders to escape violence. As a result, internal wars threatened to become regional wars, particularly in West Africa and—most dramatically—around the Great Lakes of Central Africa.

Contrasts in democracy. Nigeria, Africa's most populous state, and South Africa represented opposite ends of the democratic spectrum. Nigeria's dictator, General Sani Abacha, remained firmly in power in 1997. The "popular" clamor for Abacha to run for president in national elections scheduled for 1998 was well-orchestrated by the government and indicative of the realities of the "democratic transition" supposedly underway.

Moshood Abiola, whose 1993 election as Nigeria's president was overthrown by the military, remained in prison. In an effort to squelch opposition to its rule, the regime in March 1997 charged a number of dissidents, including Wole Soyinka, exiled winner of the 1986 Nobel Prize for literature, with treason.

South Africa presented a brighter picture. The Truth and Reconciliation Commission heard confessions and exposed information in several of the most notorious assassinations of activists opposed to the former government's policy of *apartheid* (racial separation). The Truth and Reconciliation Commission, established to reconcile the divisions caused by apartheid, also held public hearings on violence within the antiapartheid movement.

The country's various political parties, however, continued struggling to overcome the public's view that the parties represented races rather than a platform or ideology. A lack of economic growth and a resulting higher unemployment rate also threatened South Africa's political stability.

Successes. In 1997, Liberians rejoiced at the end of an eight-year civil war that had caused more than 100,000 deaths. Armies demobilized and disarmed. Elections took place on July 19. And a new government took charge on August 2.

In Madagascar, a government crisis that included the impeachment of the country's president was resolved by a peaceful and fair election. Former Marxist dictator Didier Ratsiraka regained the presidency on February 9 after winning a fair runoff election in December 1996 against former President Albert Zafy. Zafy, charged with wrongdong by Madagas-

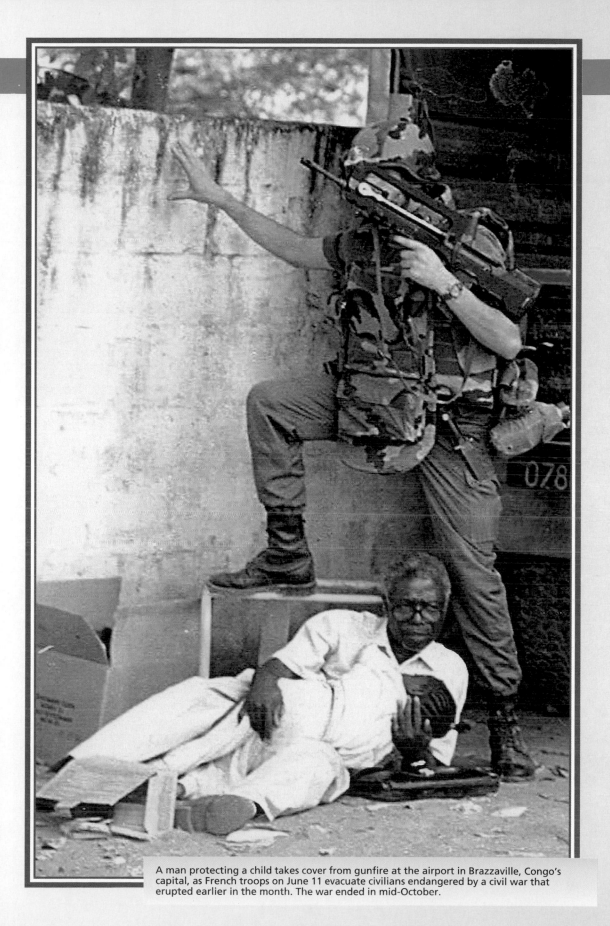

A man protecting a child takes cover from gunfire at the airport in Brazzaville, Congo's capital, as French troops on June 11 evacuate civilians endangered by a civil war that erupted earlier in the month. The war ended in mid-October.

Facts in brief on African political units

Country	Population	Government	Monetary unit*	Foreign trade (million U.S.$) Exports†	Imports†
Algeria	29,806,000	President Liamine Zeroual; Prime Minister Ahmed Ouyahia	dinar (58.18 = $1)	10,240	10,250
Angola	12,212,000	President José Eduardo dos Santos	readj. kwanza (257,128.00 = $1)	2,989	1,140
Benin	5,900,000	President Mathieu Kerekou	CFA franc (596.99 = $1)	189	694
Botswana	1,620,000	President Sir Ketumile Masire	pula (3.72 = $1)	1,800	1,800
Burkina Faso	11,119,000	Popular Front Chairman, Head of State, & Head of Government Blaise Compaoré	CFA franc (596.99 = $1)	305	535
Burundi	6,937,000	President Pierre Buyoya; Prime Minister Pascal-Firmin Ndimira	franc (349.40 = $1)	40	130
Cameroon	14,389,000	President Paul Biya	CFA franc (596.99 = $1)	2,047	1,245
Cape Verde	424,000	President Antonio Mascarenhas Monteiro; Prime Minister Carlos Wahnon Veiga	escudo (95.11 = $1)	9	252
Central African Republic	3,555,000	President Ange Patasse	CFA franc (596.99 = $1)	171	175
Chad	6,904,000	President Idriss Deby	CFA franc (596.99 = $1)	251	220
Comoros	724,000	President Mohamed Taki Abdoulkarim	franc (447.74 = $1)	22	69
Congo (Brazzaville)	2,809,000	President Pascal Lissouba; Prime Minister David Charles Ganao	CFA franc (596.99 = $1)	1,173	670
Congo (Kinshasa)	48,042,000	President Laurent Kabila	new zaire (117,500.00 = $1)	438	397
Djibouti	616,000	President Hassan Gouled Aptidon; Prime Minister Barkat Gourad Hamadou	franc (177.72 = $1)	16	219
Egypt	66,547,000	President Hosni Mubarak; Prime Minister Kamal Ahmed al-Ganzouri	pound (3.40 = $1)	3,540	13,041
Equatorial Guinea	430,000	President Teodoro Obiang Nguema Mbasogo; Prime Minister Serafin Seriche Dougan	CFA franc (596.99 = $1)	86	50
Eritrea	3,816,000	President Isaias Afworki	Ethiopian birr	33	420
Ethiopia	60,053,000	President Negasso Gidada	birr (6.69 = $1)	372	1,033
Gabon	1,161,000	President El Hadj Omar Bongo; Prime Minister Paulin Obame	CFA franc (596.99 = $1)	2,712	881
Gambia	1,217,000	Head of State Yahya Jammeh	dalasi (10.43 = $1)	16	140
Ghana	19,016,000	President Jerry John Rawlings	cedi (2,230.00 = $1)	1,252	2,175
Guinea	7,308,000	President Lansana Conté	franc (1,132.00 = $1)	562	688
Guinea-Bissau	1,142,000	President João Bernardo Vieira	CFA franc (596.99 = $1)	24	71
Ivory Coast	15,684,000	President Henri Konan Bédié	CFA franc (596.99 = $1)	4,177	3,157
Kenya	30,738,000	President Daniel T. arap Moi	shilling (62.85 = $1)	2,067	2,852
Lesotho	2,216,000	King Letsie III; Prime Minister Ntsu Mokhehle	maloti (4.72 = $1)	142	1,000
Liberia	3,339,000	President Charles Taylor	dollar (1 = $1)	396	272
Libya	5,965,000	Leader of the Revolution Muammar Muhammad al-Qadhafi; General People's Committee Secretary (Prime Minister) Abd al Majid al-Qaud	dinar (0.39 = $1)	11,213	5,356

Country	Population	Government	Monetary unit*	Foreign trade (million U.S.$) Exports†	Imports†
Madagascar	14,125,000	President Didier Ratsiraka	franc (4,975.00 = $1)	366	529
Malawi	11,724,000	President Bakili Muluzi	kwacha (17.73 = $1)	405	475
Mali	11,806,000	President Alpha Oumar Konare; Prime Minister Ibrahima Boubacar Keita	CFA franc (596.99 = $1)	452	755
Mauritania	2,450,000	President Maaouya Ould Sid Ahmed Taya	ouguiya (165.55 = $1)	437	222
Mauritius	1,154,000	President Sir Cassam Uteem; Prime Minister Navinchandra Ramgoolam	rupee (21.67 = $1)	1,537	1,959
Morocco	28,548,000	King Hassan II; Prime Minister Abdellatif Filali	dirham (9.59 = $1)	6,736	9,718
Mozambique	17,703,000	President Joaquím Alberto Chissano; Prime Minister Pascoal Manuel Mocumbi	metical (11,495.00 = $1)	169	784
Namibia	1,663,000	President Sam Nujoma; Prime Minister Hage Geingob	rand (4.72 = $1)	1,300	1,200
Niger	10,093,000	President, Niger National Council, Ibrahim Bare Mainassara; Prime Minister Amadou Boubacar Cisse	CFA franc (596.99 = $1)	259	373
Nigeria	121,513,000	Head of State, Chairman, Federal Executive Council Sani Abacha	naira (21.89 = $1)	9,376	6,517
Rwanda	7,261,000	President Pasteur Bizimungu	franc (299.55 = $1)	51	248
São Tomé and Príncipe	141,000	President Miguel Trovoada	dobra (2,390.00 = $1)	7	24
Senegal	8,993,000	President Abdou Diouf; Prime Minister Habib Thiam	CFA franc (596.99 = $1)	871	1,383
Seychelles	75,000	President France Albert René	rupee (5.07 = $1)	53	233
Sierra Leone	4,833,000	President Ahmad Tejan Kabbah	leone (780.00 = $1)	47	212
Somalia	11,811,000	No functioning government	shilling (2,620.00 = $1)	81	81
South Africa	44,223,000	State President Nelson Mandela	rand (4.72 = $1)	28,145	29,105
Sudan	30,392,000	President Umar Hasan Ahmad al-Bashir	pound (1,428.60 = $1)	556	1,185
Swaziland	928,000	King Mswati III; Prime Minister Barnabas Sibusiso Dlamini	lilangeni (4.72 = $1)	798	827
Tanzania	32,211,000	President Benjamin William Mkapa; Prime Minister Frederick Sumaye	shilling (616.48 = $1)	758	1,386
Togo	4,527,000	President Gnassingbé Eyadéma	CFA franc (596.99 = $1)	209	385
Tunisia	9,363,000	President Zine El Abidine Ben Ali; Prime Minister Hamed Karoui	dinar (1.13 = $1)	5,518	7,746
Uganda	23,204,000	President Yoweri Kaguta Museveni; Prime Minister Kintu Musoke	shilling (1,145.50 = $1)	461	1,055
Zambia	10,204,000	President Frederick Chiluba	kwacha (1,336.00 = $1)	1,216	1,523
Zimbabwe	11,989,000	President Robert Mugabe	dollar (12.42 = $1)	2,115	2,661

*Exchange rates as of Oct. 24, 1997, or latest available data.   †Latest available data.

car's parliament, had resigned in September 1996.

In Chad, the party of President Idriss Deby, who won the presidency in a multiparty vote in July 1996, collected 63 of 125 seats in parliamentary elections in January and February 1997. These elections completed a transition to a multiparty system begun in 1993, three years after Deby, a former guerrilla leader, seized power. Opposition leaders voiced some complaints about voting irregularities, but those disputes were handled peaceably by the courts.

Setback in Mali. Mali's reputation as a model of African democracy was tarnished in 1997. In April, Malian courts nullified the results of parliamentary elections held earlier that month, because of widespread disorganization and confusion about voter eligibility and the location of polling places. Opposition parties then decided to boycott the rescheduled parliamentary elections held on July 20 and August 3.

Many outside observers defended President Alpha Oumar Konare's commitment to democratic principles, arguing that opposition forces boycotted the elections because they knew they would lose. In August, Konare jailed 10 opposition leaders on charges of involvement in the murder of a police officer at a political meeting.

Allegations of election fraud. In Gambia, a planned transition from military to civilian rule was completed with a new civilian president, Yahya Jammeh, in 1996 and parliamentary elections on Jan. 3, 1997. Observers claimed that the results, however, were less than democratic. President Yahya Jammeh, an army captain who overthrew an elected government in 1994, retired from the military and won the presidency in a disputed election in September 1996. In the 1997 parliamentary elections, opposition politicians were allowed to run for office, but they were forbidden to campaign until two weeks before the polling.

In Cameroon, President Paul Biya, under intense domestic pressure to move faster toward democracy, called for elections on October 12. The opposition, responding to a history of fraudulent elections, demanded that the government establish an independent electoral commission to oversee the vote. Biya refused. The three major opposition parties then boycotted the elections, and the stability of the country grew more precarious.

Deterioration in Kenya. Kenya presented another difficult political situation. Kenya had once enjoyed one of Africa's more successful economies and a political process that was stable if not democratic. In 1997, however, Kenya faced a worsening economic decline and growing political instability. Responding violently to a series of prodemocracy demonstrations staged across the country, government forces killed or injured tens of thousands of demonstrators.

In August, gangs linked to the party of President

Daniel arap Moi attacked civilians along the coast of the Indian Ocean in an effort to frighten opposition forces there.

Moi easily won a fifth term in office in general elections held on December 29, only two days before a constitutionally mandated deadline. Moi had stalled on announcing a date for elections for most of 1997 and had legalized Safina, the main opposition group, only a month before the vote. Safina, which had sought government approval for two years, failed to unite prodemocracy groups behind a single challenger to Moi.

The Angolan civil war seemed close to resolution in 1997, but progress in disarming the forces of rebel leader Jonas Savimbi and integrating his supporters and the territory he controlled into a united government came to a standstill. On April 11, a new government of Unity and National Reconciliation was established, with representatives of Savimbi's forces taking part. Savimbi, however, consistently delayed following agreements on disarmament and reconciliation negotiated by the United Nations (UN).

By late June, tensions were high, and there had been several clashes between the national army and the rebels. On August 28, the UN Security Council voted to impose air and travel sanctions against Angola, but in September the UN delayed their implementation in the hope that Savimbi would cooperate.

Fall of a dictator. After 32 years of dictatorship, Zaire's President Mobutu Sese Seko was driven from power in May by rebel forces led by Laurent Kabila. The rebels took only a few months to overwhelm the demoralized Zairian Army. Kabila immediately renamed the country the Democratic Republic of the Congo, which was similar to the country's original name. (The country is also known as Congo [Kinshasa] to distinguish it from its smaller neighbor, the People's Republic of the Congo, also called Congo [Brazzaville].)

Mobutu, ill with cancer, fled to Morocco, where he died on September 7. Kabila faced the daunting challenge of reuniting the country, establishing democratic rule, and stimulating a long-stagnant economy.

War in the other Congo. Civil war erupted on June 5 in Congo (Brazzaville) when President Pascal Lissouba sent troops to disarm opposition militias led by former dictator Denis Sassou-Nguesso. The two long-time enemies were scheduled to compete in a presidential election on July 27. The armed struggle seemed deadlocked until mid-October, when Angolan forces invaded to support Sassou-Nguesso. The strengthened rebels then seized the country's two major cities and Sassou-Nguesso declared victory.

Foreign intervention. More disturbing than the level of violence within the Congos and other countries in Central Africa was the degree of foreign involvement in the conflicts. Neighboring states increasingly intervened, either with arms or military forces, in domestic conflicts. Angolan aid, which proved decisive in Sassou-Nguesso's victory in Congo (Brazzaville), was given in retaliation for the support Congo's President Lissouba had provided to Savimbi's forces in Angola. Rwanda and Congo (Kinshasa) also supported Sassou-Nguesso.

The civil war in Congo (Kinshasa) itself drew in neighboring countries. Angola's President José Eduardo dos Santos aided Laurent Kabila in his war against Mobutu because Mobutu had supported Savimbi. Rwanda played an even more decisive role in Kabila's victory, though Kabila had steadfastly denied receiving outside assistance.

However, Rwanda's vice president admitted in July that Mobutu's overthrow was part of a plan to destroy the Hutu guerrilla movement, based in Hutu refugee camps across the border from Rwanda in eastern Congo (Kinshasa). Mobutu provided a haven for Hutu refugees from Rwanda, including many members of the military forces that slaughtered hundreds of thousands of Rwanda's Tutsi in 1994.

Western interference. Involvement in the affairs of African nations was not limited to their African neighbors. Western powers, particularly the United States and France, were actively involved in African politics and wars. Many observers interpreted events around the Great Lakes of central Africa in the context of a Franco-American trade competition.

The United States provided military assistance to Rwanda and was involved in the conflict in Congo (Kinshasa), both former French colonies. In the civil war in Congo (Brazzaville), the French, who have very significant petroleum interests in their former colony, provided crucial support for Sassou-Nguesso.

France's influence in Central Africa seemed to be in decline, however. In July 1997, France's newly elected Socialist government announced it would withdraw about one-third of its 7,900 troops in Africa over the next five years and reevaluate its subsidies to its African allies.

Other conflicts. Fighting was ongoing in several other parts of Africa. In Uganda, the war between the government of Yoweri Museveni and the rebel Lord's Resistance Army (LRA) continued with no end in sight in 1997. Variously described as Christian fundamentalists, revolutionaries, terrorists, and criminals, the LRA received support from Sudan, which accused Museveni of supporting the rebels in the Sudan civil war. Ethnic and regional jealousies inflamed the situation. Previous rulers of Uganda came from the north, the LRA's area. Museveni was from the south.

Hope for peace in Sierra Leone, so high in 1996, was dashed on May 25, 1997, by a *coup d'état* (overthrow) against elected President Ahmed Tejan Kab-

bah. Major Johnny Paul Koromah took power in the face of worldwide condemnation. The Organization of African Unity, the UN, the United States, and many other countries condemned the coup and demanded Kabbah's restoration. Nigerian military forces in the country to oversee the transition to democracy attacked Koromah's forces. The Nigerians were defeated in their first attempt. In October the Nigerian Air Force began bombing raids on Koromah's troops. On October 8, the UN voted sanctions against Koromah. On October 23, Koromah agreed to give up power—but not before 2001.

Economic news. Although the political news from Africa had a gloomy tone, the economic news was brighter. Africa in 1997 experienced its second consecutive year of economic growth. African economies grew by 3.9 percent in 1996, the last year for which data were available, and were expected to expand by 4.2 percent in 1997. Eleven countries experienced economic growth rates of 6 percent or higher, much greater than in recent years.

Domestic reforms that boosted international trade and reduced government ownership of industry provided some economic stimulation. Other factors included good weather for Africa's many farmers and improving world economic conditions, especially important for a continent where the overwhelming majority of countries depend heavily on exports of raw materials. Higher oil exports accounted for much of the good news. The growth rates of African oil exporters outpaced those of exporters of agricultural products and minerals. Nonoil exports declined during 1997. However, there was no assurance that the improvement would continue.

Population rates in Africa continued to exceed economic growth rates. Africa's population was expected to increase by 300 million people in the next 15 years, reaching 1.25 billion by 2025. If a country's population grows faster than its economy, the quality of life inevitably declines. And many Africans in the 1990's experienced a decline in their standard of living, in spite of overall economic growth.

According to the UN's Human Poverty Index, 9 of the world's 10 poorest countries are in Africa: Burundi, Madagascar, Guinea, Mozambique, Mali, Ethiopia, Burkina Faso, Sierra Leone, and Niger. The UN index measures deprivation rather than income—for example, low life expectancy, lack of education, and lack of access to clean water.

Health problems remained an urgent priority in Africa. AIDS was perhaps the most widely known of these problems, but numerous other diseases, including tuberculosis and malaria, continued to afflict the continent. For many Africans, nutrition and health care remained inadequate in 1997.

☐ Mark DeLancey

See also the various African country articles; **Africa** Special Report: **The Hutu and the Tutsi—A Conflict Beyond Borders; France.**

THE HUTU AND TUTSI: A CONFLICT BEYOND BORDERS

The centuries-old conflict between Hutu and Tutsi was significant far beyond the borders of Rwanda and Burundi. It also played a critical role in the revolution in Zaire.

By Simon Baynham

O n May 17, 1997, Laurent Kabila proclaimed himself president of Zaire and immediately renamed Africa's third largest country the Democratic Republic of Congo. The day before, Mobutu Sese Seko, president of Zaire for nearly 32 years, surrendered power and fled into exile. Mobutu's flight left the weary people of Zaire's capital, Kinshasa, waiting for the arrival of Kabila's rebel guerrillas. On May 20, Kabila entered the capital in a heavily guarded motorcade. By that time, the commander of Mobutu's elite presidential guard—the only force capable of putting up a defense—had boarded a speedboat for Brazzaville, capital of the Republic of the Congo across the Congo River.

The forcible overthrow of the Mobutu regime in Zaire was highly significant to far more people than the country's 45 million citizens. The revolt was also a critical development in the Hutu–Tutsi ethnic conflict that has plagued Africa's Great Lakes region—Burundi, Rwanda, Tanzania, Uganda, and the Democratic Republic of Congo (Zaire)—and nearby Angola for decades.

The ethnic rivalry between Hutu and Tutsi originated when Tutsi entered the lands of the Hutu before 1400 and subjugated the Hutu. The rivalry festered from the 1890's to the mid-1900's as the reigning European colonial powers perpetuated Tutsi rule over the Hutu, who constituted a majority in the region. The rivalry became inflamed when Rwanda and Burundi gained independence from Belgium in the early 1960's. The turmoil resulting from the rivalry spread to neighboring states, such as Zaire, when hundreds of thousands of refugees criss-crossed the region in a desperate search for peace and safety. By the mid-1990's, the Hutu-Tutsi conflict in Rwanda and Burundi had poisoned the political atmosphere of the entire Great Lakes region.

The seeds of conflict

Most historians of east and central Africa believe that the Hutu descended from a number of *Bantu* clans (a large group of African peoples made up of many individual but related tribes) that settled in the area that is now Burundi and Rwanda between A.D. 400 and 700. The *agrarian* (crop-raising) clans, who came to be referred to as Hutu, cleared much of the forest that had been home for several thousand years to the Twa, hunter-gatherer relatives of the pygmies. By approximately 1400, a group of different tribal and racial stock arrived—the *pastoralist* (cattle-herding) Tutsi. Successive waves of nomadic Tutsi herdsmen dominated the Hutu and subjected them to the authority of an expanding Tutsi kingdom.

Some historians disagree with this assessment and insist that Hutu and Tutsi are not, in fact, different ethnic groups, but rather different social classes of the same group. These historians argue that Tutsi can be identified solely by their possession of cattle, which allowed them to establish a patron relationship over the agrarian Hutu. These scholars also point out that Tutsi and Hutu share a common Bantu language.

During Burundi's and Rwanda's colonial period, Europeans calculated that 85 percent of the people of Rwanda and Burundi were Hutu, 14 percent were Tutsi, and 1 percent were Twa. The census takers used cattle ownership as a major criterion of ethnic origin. These percentages continued to be commonly accepted by demographers as accurate for the tribal composition of Rwanda and Burundi in the mid-1990's.

The creation of Ruanda-Urundi

Rwanda and Burundi are small for African states—only 10,169 square miles (26,338 square kilometers) and 10,747 square miles (27,834 square kilometers), respectively, and they were not artificially created by European conquerors. Both countries had existed as established feudal monarchies for several centuries before being discovered by European explorers, and both countries survived Western conquest and occupation.

Rwanda and Burundi—two remote, land-locked, mountainous kingdoms—were first explored by a European, the German Count von Gützen, in 1894, and both countries became part of the colonial territory known as German East Africa. Following Germany's defeat in World War I (1914-1918), the area—then known as the Territory of Ruanda-Urundi—was *mandated* (given over for administration) to Belgium by the League of Nations, a now-defunct international peace association that was headquartered in Geneva, Switzerland.

After World War II (1939-1945), Ruanda-Urundi became a United Nations trust territory, which Belgium continued to administer through Tutsi chiefs. The Belgians relied on the martial Tutsi to strengthen their authority—much to the resentment of the Hutu, who made up the majority of residents.

Roman Catholic and Protestant missionaries established churches and schools in Ruanda-Urundi in the late 1890's. In part, ideas about education and equality learned from the missionaries fueled *nationalism* (patriotic feelings for one's own nation) that, in turn, launched the movement for independence that spread through the territories after World War II. Tutsi traditionalists in both Ruanda and Urundi, however, were determined that independence would not mean rule under a Hutu majority. Similarly, Hutu extremists, resentful of Tutsi domination during the colonial period, decided that they would need to destroy the Tutsi hold on power before Tutsi domination could be finalized with the onset of independence. The views of Hutu moderates, who believed that Hutu and Tutsi could share power in a national government, were ignored.

Violence erupts

In 1959, Hutu farmers in the Ruandan, or northern, region of Ruanda-Urundi, organized by the Party of the Hutu Emancipation Movement, revolted against their Tutsi overlords. The Hutu greatly outnumbered the Tutsi in the fierce and brutal revolt. By the time Belgian security forces suppressed the violence, approximately

Africa

Rwanda Uganda
Dem. Rep. of Congo Tanzania
Burundi
Angola

The author

Simon Baynham, Director of Research from 1989 to 1996 at Pretoria's Africa Institute of South Africa, is currently Consultant at the Research Institute for the Study of Conflict and Terrorism, in London.

150,000 people—most of whom were Tutsi—had been killed. The Tutsi king, Kigeri V, along with thousands of his subjects, was forced into exile. A referendum in September 1961 abolished the monarchy.

Both Ruanda and Urundi gained independence in 1962. Ruanda was named Rwanda and was established as a republic, led by President Grégoire Kayibanda, a Hutu. Urundi, which changed its name to Burundi, was established as a constitutional monarchy. Burundi's elected legislature was dominated by Tutsi, and the country's ruler was Tutsi King Mwambutsa IV. Independence did not, however, settle the animosities between the two tribal groups in either country.

Hutu and Tutsi in Rwanda

Tutsi exiles, primarily from Burundi, invaded Rwanda in late 1963 in an attempt to restore a Tutsi monarchy. Their invasion unleashed mass reprisals, resulting in the death of 15,000 Tutsi at the hands of Hutu and the flight of an estimated 150,000 to 200,000 people, most of whom were Tutsi.

Civilian rule in Rwanda ended in July 1973 when a Hutu—Defense Minister Juvénal Habyarimana—staged a *coup d'etat* (an overthrow of the government) and established a one-party state. Habyarimana remained in office for the next 21 years.

In 1990, some 10,000 guerrillas belonging to the Tutsi-dominated Rwandan Patriotic Front, an Uganda-based group of Tutsi refugees and moderate Hutu, invaded Rwanda. Troops from Zaire assisted the small Rwandan army in halting the rebel advance on Rwanda's capital, Kigali, but intermittent fighting continued until 1993.

Renewed violence followed the February 1994 assassination of government minister Félicien Gatabazi—a Hutu moderate who had advocated a peaceful settlement with the Tutsi rebels. The murder was eclipsed in April 1994 by the death of President Habyarimana, who was killed in a plane crash with Burundi President Cyprien Ntaryamira (also a Hutu). Authorities were unable to determine who or what was responsible for the crash, but the event ushered in an orgy of violence. Hutu militants in the Rwandan armed forces slaughtered some 500,000 people, mainly Tutsi, in three-months. Then-UN Secretary-General Boutros Boutros-Ghali labeled the Hutu violence against Tutsi as genocide. The Tutsi-controlled Rwandan Patriotic Front responded with another invasion and captured Kigali in July 1994.

After seizing the capital, Rwandan Patriotic Front soldiers forced the Rwandan army and huge numbers of Hutu civilians into Zaire. Before the month was out, more than 2 million Rwandans had fled, most into enormous refugee settlements around the Zairian city of Goma. In mid-July 1994, a new Rwandan government was established with Hutus—Pasteur Bizimungu and Faustin Twagiramungu— as president and prime minister. While the Rwandan Patriotic Front leaders emphasized national reconciliation, real power was held by the Front's militia, under the control of General Paul Kagame, a Tutsi.

Foreign relations

The Hutu–Tutsi conflict influenced foreign relations between several central-African countries. The governments of Rwanda, Burundi, and Uganda all aided in the overthrow of President Mobutu in Zaire.

President Pasteur Bizimungu of Rwanda

President Pierre Buyoya of Burundi

President Yoweri Museveni of Uganda

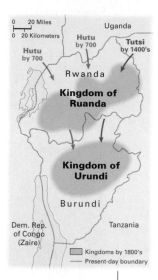

Kingdoms by 1800's
Present-day boundary

Ancient kingdoms

The Hutu came to the area that is now Rwanda and Burundi from the north and northwest sometime by A.D. 700. The Tutsi had arrived from the northeast and had subjugated the Hutu by 1400. By 1800, the kingdoms of Ruanda and Urundi occupied the regions occupied by contemporary Rwanda and Burundi.

Tribal tensions in Burundi

Political life in Burundi after independence was also dominated by Hutu–Tutsi tensions and recurrent ethnic violence. UN-sponsored elections in 1961 swept the National Unity and Progress Party, supported by the Hutu majority, into power. Between independence in 1962 and the end of the monarchy in 1966, King Mwambutsa's attempts to extend his constitutional authority and restrict the powers of the government forced the fall of seven consecutive governments.

In October 1965, Hutu police and military officers attacked the palace. King Mwambutsa, fearing for his life, fled the country. However, loyal troops under Michel Micombero, a Tutsi, repulsed the attack, providing a pretext for Tutsi retaliation.

The army and police were purged of Hutu, and every Hutu political leader of standing was killed. In November 1966, Micombero deposed King Ntare V, who had gained the throne by deposing his father, Mwambutsa. Micombero proclaimed a republic, with himself as head of state.

The abolition of the monarchy removed the last potentially unifying force in Burundi, opening the way for Tutsi domination. With Micombero in power, the Tutsi eliminated almost the entire educated Hutu population. As many as 200,000 people may have been killed. An additional 150,000 Hutu fled the country. In 1976, Micombero was overthrown by his cousin, Jean-Baptiste Bagaza, who was overthrown in 1987 by another Tutsi, Pierre Buyoya. A 1988 Hutu uprising led to the death of another 20,000 Hutu and the emigration of 60,000 more people to Rwanda.

Nevertheless, President Buyoya indicated some sympathy for the grievances of Burundi's majority Hutu by appointing a Hutu prime minister and moving cautiously toward a democratic constitution. Following the country's first multiparty elections in 1993, Melchior Ndadaye became Burundi's first Hutu head of state. He honored a campaign promise by appointing Sylvie Kinigi, a Tutsi woman, as prime minister. Kinigi was one of Africa's first women premiers.

Four months later, President Ndadaye was killed during an attempted coup staged by elements of the army. His assassination provoked a new wave of bloodletting during which more than 100,000 people died. The military embarked upon a "pacification campaign." This campaign included forcing another 700,000 Hutu to flee Burundi for Rwanda, Tanzania, and Zaire.

In 1994, Cyprien Ntaryamire, who had replaced Ndadaye as president, was killed with Rwanda's President Habyarimana when their airplane crashed. Sylvestre Ntibantunganya, another Hutu, became president of Burundi. The violence continued during Ntibantunganya's presidency until July 1996 when Burundi's military leadership reinstalled Pierre Buyoya, a Tutsi, as head of state. Between 1993 and 1996, at least 150,000 people had died.

Refugee crisis

The migration into Zaire in 1994 of at least one million Rwandan Hutu—who left their homes in fear of reprisals for the massacre of some 500,000 Tutsi—was unprecedented in its size and long-term effects. Although governments in the Great Lakes region had grown accustomed to disorderly mass migrations since independence in the 1960's, none had been forced to deal with a migration the size of the Rwandan immigration into Zaire. In addition to the familiar housing, food, and medical problems of refugees, the Zairian government also had to contend with the presence of Hutu extremists—the Interahamwe—in the Zairian refugee camps. The Interahamwe were intent on undermining Rwanda's Tutsi-led government and used the crowded conditions of the refugee camps to hide their activities and identities. The group intimidated large numbers of Hutu moderates to work with them.

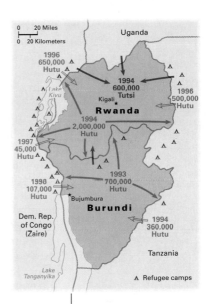

In addition to the danger the Hutu Interahamwe posed to the Rwandan government, their presence in the refugee camps of eastern Zaire helped spark the Zairian revolution. The Interahamwe came to the aid of Mobutu's Zairian security forces in their attacks on a group of Zairian ethnic Tutsi known as the Banyamulenge. While the Banyamulenge had lived in Zaire's diamond-rich eastern Kivu province for at least 200 years, Mobutu had repeatedly called the ethnic Tutsi "foreigners" and urged that they be treated as rebels and expelled. The Banyamulenge were joined by Laurent Kabila's forces—the Alliance of Democratic Forces for the Liberation of Congo-Zaire.

Neighboring countries aid the revolution

The revolution gained momentum when Rwanda and Burundi—both led by Tutsi governments that sympathized with the Banyamulenge—came to the aid of the Banyamulenge and their allies, Laurent Kabila's rebels. The governments of Rwanda and Burundi provided armed assistance in the fight against Mobutu's forces and the Interahamwe.

Uganda also lent support to the rebellion against Mobutu. Uganda was the closest ally of Rwanda's Tutsi government and, therefore, supported Rwanda's efforts to clean out the troublesome Interaham-we camps in Zaire. Observers also believe that President Museveni of Uganda aided Laurent Kabila to induce Kabila to clamp down on Uganda's own Islamic-militant rebels, who used eastern Zaire to launch attacks on Uganda. Observers credited Museveni with supporting Tutsi regimes in Rwanda and Burundi as an expedient way to impose stability in central Africa.

Angola supported Kabila's push to drive Mobutu from Zaire because Mobutu had allowed Angolan rebels—the National Union for

Refugees on the move

In the mid-1990's, massacres and reprisals kept millions of Hutu and Tutsi refugees moving between Rwanda, Burundi, Uganda, Tanzania, and the Democratic Republic of Congo (Zaire).

the Total Independence of Angola—to export diamonds and import weapons through Zaire. Angolan military support of Kabila's forces west and southeast of Kinshasa helped pave the way for Kabila's assumption of power.

In a series of lightning strikes, the disciplined corps of some 15,000 predominantly Tutsi fighters under Kabila seized the provincial capitals Bukavu and Goma in eastern Zaire by early November 1996. What had begun as a Tutsi-led uprising quickly developed into a popularly supported revolution. Within seven months, the rebel forces had over-run all of Zaire, scoring victory after victory against the unpaid, ill-equipped, and demoralized army of President Mobutu, who had alienated his own people and Zaire's neighbors by threatening to deport the "alien" Banyamulenge Tutsi.

Later in November 1996, approximately 650,000 Hutu refugees left their camps in Zaire and returned to Rwanda. Their return followed a series of conciliatory statements made by the Tutsi government. This left approximately 350,000 refugees in Zaire. As many as 100,000 of the remaining refugees—believed to include many perpetrators of the 1994 massacre—were driven out of camps around Bukavu and Goma by forces under the control of Laurent Kabila. Instead of re-turning to Rwanda, the refugees trekked west, into Zaire's interior, walking through miles of mountainous jungle and surviving on insects and wild plants.

Between April and June 1997, another 45,000 refugees were *repatriated* (sent back) to Rwanda in what was one of the UN's biggest and most expensive airlifts. At the end of 1997, at least 200,000 refugees from the 1994 migration remained unaccounted for.

History of the Hutu-Tutsi conflict

by 1400's • Cattle-herding Tutsi invade the land of the Hutu, an agricultural group, and establish a monarchy.

1894 • Germany colonizes the area, then called Ruanda-Urundi, as part of the German East Africa territory and maintains the Tutsi royalty in positions of power.

1923 • Belgian forces occupy German East Africa and, after Germany's defeat in World War I (1914-1918), administer the area. The Belgians maintain Tutsi royalty in administrative government positions.

1959 • Ruandan Hutu revolt and overthrow the Tutsi. About 150,000 Tutsi are killed and 150,000 more flee to Urundi and neighboring countries.

1962 • After Belgium grants independence to Ruanda, a Hutu, Grégoire Kayibanda, becomes president of the newly established Republic of Rwanda.

• After Belgium grants independence to Urundi, the Kingdom of Burundi is established as a constitutional monarchy with a Tutsi king.

1963 • Refugee Tutsi invade Rwanda but are defeated. As many as 15,000 Tutsi are killed in Hutu reprisals. Some 200,000 Tutsi flee to Burundi, Uganda, Congo, and Tanzania.

1966 • Tutsi military leader Michel Micombero overthrows the king of Burundi. Micombero establishes a republic and declares himself president.

Fears of new genocide

Laurent Kabila, prior to his May 1997 entry into Kinshasa, had threatened to overrun refugee camps in eastern Zaire because of their use as havens by Hutu extremists. During late 1996 and the first few months of 1997, reports circulated that Kabila's rebels and the Banyamulenge had slaughtered Rwandan Hutu refugees, mainly in the vicinity of Kisangani, in northeastern Zaire. Some news stories reported that earth-moving equipment had been used to bury the bodies in mass graves. In other areas, refugees had simply vanished.

Throughout 1997, President Kabila repeatedly thwarted UN attempts to mount on-the-spot inquiries into the atrocities. In October, two human rights organizations, Human Rights Watch/Africa in New York City and the International Federation of Human Rights Leagues in Paris, reported that Kabila's troops continued to kill large numbers of civilian refugees. Kabila finally allowed a UN team into the Republic of Congo in mid-November to begin an investigation.

Prospects for the Republic of Congo's future

When President Kabila took office, he was surrounded by the Banyamulenge Tutsi on whose military muscle he had ridden to power. Kabila faced the daunting task of forming a truly national administration in a country with more than 250 tribes. Western powers appeared to have accepted Kabila's plan to put off elections until 1999. However, representatives of the United States, the European Union (an organization of 15 Western European countries), the World Bank, and the International Monetary Fund, after a meeting in September 1997, set conditions for Kabila. Unless Kabila provided a plan to

1972 • Some 3,000 Tutsi are killed during an attempted Hutu uprising in Burundi. Tutsi retaliate by killing at least 100,000 Hutu. About 150,000 more Hutu flee to neighboring countries.

1973 • Rwandan Hutu military leader Juvenal Habyarimana overthrows President Kayibanda.

1993 • A Hutu, Melchior Ndadaye, wins Burundi's first multiparty presidential election but is slain in a Tutsi coup. More than 100,000 Hutu and Tutsi die in the subsequent fighting, and about 700,000 Hutu flee to Rwanda, Tanzania, and Zaire.

1994 • A Hutu, Cyprien Ntaryamire, is elected president of Burundi.

• Ntaryamire and Rwandan military leader Habyarimana die in a suspicious airplane crash over Rwanda.

• Hutu militants kill up to 500,000 Tutsi in Rwanda, and a new Hutu-dominated government is formed, with Pasteur Bizimungu as president.

• The Tutsi-dominated Rwandan Patriotic Front defeats government forces and drives 2 million Hutu into Zaire, Tanzania, and Burundi.

• Tutsi in Zaire are attacked by Hutu militia among the refugees.

1996 • The Tutsi-dominated military suspends the Burundi constitution, disbands the legislature, and installs Pierre Buyoya as president.

1997 • Some 1.5 million Hutu refugees return to Rwanda from Zaire and Tanzania.

Rwandan Hutu abandon their refugee camp in eastern Zaire and begin the long trek home in November 1996. By early 1997, some 1.5 million Hutu refugees had returned to Rwanda from Zaire and Tanzania.

reconstruct the economy, granted permission for the UN team to investigate charges of atrocities, and made progress on democracy and human rights issues, no financial assistance would be provided.

Prospects for peace

Prospects for peace and democracy in Burundi remained grim in 1997, as ethnic rivals continued to see extermination as a solution to tribal conflict. President Buyoya's government had done little since resuming power in 1996 to reach meaningful political compromises with the Hutu majority. By mid-1997, many Hutu had begun to support the Hutu militias that mounted widespread attacks against an essentially Tutsi military government. Buyoya's cabinet responded by forcing 250,000 Hutu into "regroupment" camps, making it easier for the army to find and kill Hutu extremist guerrillas.

In Rwanda, Hutu rebels began filtering back into the country from Congo in May 1997 and continued their attempts to overthrow Rwanda's Tutsi-controlled government. By October, some 4,000 people had died in the fighting.

In addition, the return of Hutu refugees to Rwanda created a housing crisis, since many Hutu houses had been taken over by Tutsi who had been similarly displaced during an earlier refugee cycle. As many as 2,000 of the returning Hutu refugees were accused of planning the 1994 annihilation of Tutsi, and some 85,000 other Hutu were accused of lesser crimes. Trials under the jurisdiction of both Rwandan courts and the UN International Criminal Tribunal for Rwanda began in January 1997.

Although violence in Rwanda increased after the refugees' return, the Tutsi who controlled the country claimed that Rwanda's cycle of bloodletting could be broken. The government's commitment to national reconciliation was generally acknowledged by the international community. However, old tensions over tribal animosities could be quickly rekindled in a country with one of the most densely packed populations in Africa.

Planning a stable future

Many political analysts believe that there are basically three ways by which the Hutu and Tutsi could move toward a stable future. One possible solution would be the formation of a government that acknowledges the right of both the majority Hutu and the minority Tutsi to share governing power. Such a system was adopted in South Africa, where Nelson Mandela's Government of National Unity shared power beyond the membership of Mandela's own party, the African National Congress.

Another solution would be the election of government leaders with no regard for tribal affiliation. Ugandan President Museveni espoused such a model. Museveni refused to allow political parties to campaign in Uganda because tribal rivalries were so fierce in that country that Museveni believed multiparty politics would continue to divide people along tribal and religious lines.

Finally, some analysts have suggested that the only hope for peace between the Hutu and Tutsi would be to establish separate countries—a Hutuland and a Tutsiland—for the two tribes. Because of the current lack of consensus on these matters, it may be that an outside peace-brokering mission, such as one sponsored by the Organization of African Unity, could provide a solution. However, political analysts agree that unless the leaders and the people accept the politics of a shared humanity and mutual respect, Hutu and Tutsi—and the countries of which they are a part—will be doomed to an even bleaker future well into the 21st century. ■ ■ ■

For further reading:

Dostert, Pierre Etienne. *Africa 1997.* Stryker-Post, 1997.
Edwards, Mike. "Central Africa's Cycle of Violence." *National Geographic,* June 1997, pp. 124-133.

Additional resoures

United Nations High Commissioner for Refugees Home Page (http://www.unhcr.ch) Includes up-to-date information on refugee movements throughout the world, including those in the Great Lakes region of Africa. Also includes background information on countries of the world, including Rwanda, Burundi, and other countries of central Africa.

Agriculture. In 1997, American farmers planted more soybeans than wheat, a reflection of the Agriculture Improvement and Reform Act of 1996, which ended government restrictions on planting. Harvests were good, prices were above average, and exports reached near-record levels. However, economic turmoil in Southeast Asia—the fastest growing U.S. export market—raised the spectre of recession in that region and reduced demand for U.S. products in 1997.

World farm production. According to a U.S. Department of Agriculture (USDA) report in December, world wheat production in 1997 reached record levels at 604 million metric tons. Increased production in Russia, Australia, and Ethiopia offset poor crops in Kazakstan, South Africa, and Eastern Europe. Nonetheless, world consumption of wheat depleted stocks to some of the lowest levels on record.

Production of small grains—including corn, grain sorghum, barley, oats, rye, millet, and mixed grains—declined from the 1996 harvest by 3.0 percent to 886 million metric tons. Drought reduced China's coarse grain crop by 20 percent. Larger corn crops in Eastern Europe and the European Union (EU), an organization of 15 Western European countries, and greater barley production in Australia and Russia did not offset small-grain losses in other countries.

Rice production in 1997 increased 1 percent due to larger crops in Brazil, China, India, and South Korea. Global consumption of rice continued to increase, however, and was expected to reduce reserve stocks in coming years. Better cotton crops in China, the United States, and Syria increased production to 90 million bales, 1 percent above the 1996 crop. However, world trade in cotton declined in 1997 by 2 percent due to economic problems in Brazil and Indonesia. Oilseed production was up 8 percent from 1996, raising stocks to near normal levels.

U.S. farm production. The 1997 corn crop—9.35 billion bushels, the third largest on record—was up slightly from the 9.2 billion-bushel crop harvested in 1996. Nearly 7.3 billion bushels were consumed at home in 1997, primarily by livestock. Increased soybean planting nudged production 9 percent above 1996 levels to a record 2.7 billion bushels. The wheat crop rebounded in 1997 at 2.5 billion bushels, 10 percent higher than in 1996. Rice production in 1997 increased 6 percent, while cotton production at 18.8 million bales nearly equaled 1996's 18.94 million bale crop.

U.S. agricultural exports in 1997 totaled $57.4 billion, down slightly from the $60 billion record in 1996. Export sales of red meats, poultry, and vegetables exceeded sales of bulk grains for the 12th straight year. Meat exports to Japan in 1997 fell below the 1996 record, due to an economic downturn and food safety concerns.

Reduced competition in 1997 increased U.S. corn exports by 4 percent over 1996 levels to 1.875 billion bushels and soybeans by 11 percent to a record 980 million bushels. Cotton exports in 1997 were steady due to increased sales to Mexico of fabric, thread, and yarn. Imports of Mexican apparel made from U.S. cotton increased from 4 percent of the U.S. clothing market in 1990 to 15 percent in 1997. Rice exports in 1997 were up 9 percent from 1996 primarily because of increased sales to Hong Kong, Indonesia, and the EU.

Crop revenue protection. American farmers bought protection in 1997 against low yields and low prices with a new type of crop insurance called Crop Revenue Coverage (CRC). CRC was tested in a 1996 pilot program for corn and soybean growers in Iowa and Nebraska and in selected areas for winter wheat. In 1997, CRC was available for corn and soybeans in 13 states and for cotton, sorghum, and spring wheat in other selected areas. The USDA also announced that this federally subsidized program would be available to farmers in most states for 1998 crops of corn, soybeans, grain sorghum, and cotton. Interest in the program grew, partly because government farm-program payments, which totaled $5.8 billion in 1997, were scheduled to end in 2002.

Tax relief. On August 5, President Bill Clinton signed into law the Tax Payer Relief Act of 1997. Provisions in the law lowered the maximum tax rate on the sale of assets from 28 percent to 20 percent and raised the tax-exempt value on an inherited estate from $600,000 to $1.3 million. An income-averaging measure in the law stipulated that farmers could determine their taxable income in 1998, 1999, and 2000, based on the average income from the three previous years. The new law was expected to save farmers $1.6 billion in taxes in 1998.

Conservation program. In May 1997, the USDA reported that more than 16 million acres (6.5 million hectares) of environmentally fragile farmland were accepted into the new 10-year Conservation Reserve Program. In this program, the government rents land—at an average rate of $50 an acre—to keep it out of production to prevent soil erosion, improve air quality, and preserve wildlife habitats.

The World Food Prize, awarded by the World Food Prize Foundation of Iowa City, Iowa, was given in October to professors Ray F. Smith of the University of California at Berkeley and Perry L. Adkisson of Texas A&M University in College Station. Smith and Adkisson were honored for developing Integrated Pest Management (IPM), a pest-control system that uses a variety of approaches that are safer for consumers and the environment. The methods include using genetically altered plants that are resistant to pests and tracking pest infestation problems to determine the appropriate level and timing of pesticide use. The World Food Prize was created to recognize outstanding individual achievement in improving the quality, quantity, or availability of food in the world.

Food safety problems in 1997, in the United States and abroad, stirred debate about the ever-increasing global trade in agricultural products. The focus remained the suspected link between bovine spongiform encephalopathy (BSE) or "mad cow disease," and Creutzfeldt-Jakob disease (CJD) in humans. Both BSE and CJD destroy brain cells. According to some scientists, beef from cattle infected with BSE may cause CJD in humans. In Europe, a 10-percent drop in beef consumption in 1997 was linked to consumer worries about the risk of CJD infection.

U.S. pork sales to Japan declined due to consumer reaction to swine disease in Taiwan, which lost 20 percent of its hog industry to foot-and-mouth disease in 1996. An outbreak of hog cholera in the Netherlands in 1997 also lowered pork sales.

Reaction to food safety problems. Illnesses associated with imported fruit and meat helped scuttle the Clinton Administration's effort in 1997 to get congressional permission for "fast-track" negotiating—presidential authority to negotiate trade agreements that Congress could not amend. U.S. competitors in agricultural trade were expected to benefit from the Congressional rejection of "fast-track" negotiating. For example, the Free Trade Agreement between Canada and Chile, scheduled to go into effect in 1998, was expected to hurt U.S. exports since a similar agreement would not be negotiated and approved by Congress quickly enough.

In addition, the World Trade Organization (WTO) in Geneva, Switzerland—the arbiter of trade disputes among member countries—agreed in May 1997 that the EU should lift its import ban against U.S. beef produced with hormones. The WTO said trade could not be limited because of allegations of health risks that were not supported by scientific proof. An EU appeal of the decision was expected to have a chance of prevailing in 1998, when the rules for arbitration were scheduled to be renegotiated. The EU planned to argue for giving more weight in the negotiating process to consumer opinion rather than focusing only on scientific evidence.

The EU in July 1997 decided to label food products made from corn and soybeans that may contain genetically modified organisms (GMO's). GMO's are plants containing added genes that make them less susceptible to insect damage, thus reducing the need for chemical pesticides. Labeling was seen as less damaging to U.S. exports than a proposal to segregate shipments of GMO grain and non-GMO grain. Nonetheless, Brazil stood ready to fill Europe's needs for non-GMO grain as soon as labeling began.

The U.S. Food and Drug Administration approved on December 2 the irradiation of red meat, a process that bombards meat with radiation to kill harmful bacteria. The FDA determined that irradiation is safe for consumers, does not alter the nutritional content of meat, and does not affect the flavor of meat.

□ Patricia Peak Klintberg

AIDS. In February 1997, the U.S. Centers for Disease Control and Prevention (CDC) in Atlanta, Georgia, reported that deaths in the United States from acquired immune deficiency syndrome (AIDS) had decreased for the first time since 1981, when the CDC began tracking the disease. AIDS-related deaths declined from about 24,900 in the first six months of 1995 to about 22,000 during the same period of 1996. The CDC attributed the decline in deaths partly to new drugs and to therapies that use drug combinations to attack the human immunodeficiency virus (HIV), the virus that causes AIDS.

In April 1997, the CDC reported that 581,429 people in the United States as of December 1996 had been diagnosed with AIDS and 362,004 people had died of AIDS-related illnesses. The CDC also estimated that in 1997 about 1 million people in the United States were infected with HIV.

Worldwide cases. The World Health Organization (WHO), an agency of the United Nations based in Geneva, Switzerland, reported in November 1997 that an estimated 30.6 million people worldwide were infected with HIV. The estimate was significantly higher than the 1996 figure of 22.6 million people. Although WHO attributed some of the increase to more accurate methods of collecting data, the 1997 statistics indicated a rapid spread of HIV infection. WHO also estimated that the death toll from AIDS in 1997 was about 2.3 million people.

Treatment guidelines. In June, the first guidelines for the treatment of AIDS patients were issued by a panel of experts convened by the U.S. Department of Health and Human Services (HHS) and the Henry J. Kaiser Family Foundation, a health care philanthropy based in Menlo Park, California. HHS officials said the guidelines were necessary because new drugs and new ways of monitoring the condition of patients made treatment decisions more difficult.

The panel recommended that physicians monitor the progression of HIV by testing both the *viral load* (level of HIV in the patient's blood) and the number of CD4 T-cells, immune system cells that are destroyed by HIV. The guidelines recommended a treatment that combined three drugs, including one protease inhibitor, which blocks the production of an enzyme called *protease,* a substance in the human body that HIV uses to reproduce itself.

The experts also concluded that the treatment should begin in the early stages of AIDS to reduce the damage HIV does to the immune system. The treatment was also recommended for patients who had no AIDS symptoms but had a particularly high viral load or low CD4 T-cell count. Since the combination therapy is a powerful drug treatment, the panelists also provided information about the benefits and risks for patients. □ Michael Woods

Air pollution. See Environmental pollution.

Alabama. See State government.

Alaska. See State government.

Albanians in the port of Durres attempt to flee the country illegally by jumping aboard a foreign ship in March after violence erupted throughout the country. The violence was triggered by financial fraud that robbed about half of Albania's citizens of their life savings.

Albania. The collapse of several private investment schemes involving an estimated half of all Albanian citizens led to widespread rioting and unrest in 1997. Protests, which began in late 1996, were particularly numerous in the south. Rioters burned government buildings and clashed with police. Although the government banned questionable investment schemes in January 1997 and vowed to compensate investors, many of whom had lost their life's savings, public unrest continued to escalate.

The crisis caused the government to declare a state of emergency in March. In an effort to reduce the unrest, President Sali Berisha named a member of the opposition Socialist Party, Bashkim Fino, as prime minister on March 11. In April, Italy organized an international mission, Operation *Alba* (Dawn), and sent more than 6,000 troops to restore order, permit humanitarian aid to be delivered, and provide security during national elections. The mission ended in August, but a small contingent of advisers remained in Albania to help revive the military and to retrain the police.

President Berisha had been reelected by the parliament, which his Democratic Party controlled, in March, but in elections held June 29 and August 6, Berisha's party retained only 27 seats. The Socialist Party formed a coalition that controlled 117 out of the parliament's 155 seats. International observers called the elections valid despite such irregularities as election-related shootings. Voters also rejected a referendum to restore the Albanian monarchy.

Berisha resigned as president after his party's defeat. Rexhep Mejdani, an official of the Socialist Party, succeeded him. Medjani appointed Fatos Nano, the Socialist Party leader who had been imprisoned in 1993 by Berisha's government, as prime minister. The new government promised to restore public order, further reform the economy, and compensate victims of the investment schemes.

Aftermath. The financial collapse and the breakdown of public order that followed ended the rapid growth of Albania's economy. Unemployment, which stood at 12 percent in January 1997, rose sharply in the first half of the year, as rioting shut down much of the nation's industry. Inflation reached 31.9 percent in April. In August, the government of Greece agreed to grant work permits to illegal Albanian immigrants. Italy, however, announced plans to gradually send back some 10,000 Albanians who had entered Italy illegally since March.

Albanian authorities issued an arrest warrant in August for Leka Zogu, the pretender to the Albanian throne, after his participation in a demonstration at which a gunfight broke out. During the financial crisis, about 1 million military weapons had been removed from storage or openly distributed to rioters by police. In September, about 800,000 weapons remained in private hands. □ Sharon L. Wolchik

See also **Europe** (Facts in brief table); **Italy**.

Algeria. On Aug. 29, 1997, as many as 300 civilians were massacred in Reis, a village south of the capital Algiers, in the most brutal attack on civilians since the country's civil war began in 1992. On Sept. 5, 1997, as many as 150 civilians were killed in Beni Massous, a village west of Algiers, and on September 23, up to 200 villagers were massacred in Baraki, east of Algiers. The massacres were the worst of dozens of such incidents that took the lives of hundreds of Algerian civilians in 1997. Women and children were killed and left beheaded in most of the attacks. One of the most shocking incidents in Algeria during 1997 occurred on September 29, when 12 teachers, 11 of them women, had their throats slashed in front of their students.

The military-backed government of President Liamine Zeroual blamed the killings on Islamic rebels. However, diplomats in Algiers believed that military hard-liners in the government initiated some of the massacres in an attempt to discredit officials who wanted to negotiate with the rebels.

The military had usurped power in 1992 by canceling parliamentary elections that seemed certain to empower the Islamic Salvation Front (FIS). Between 1992 and 1997, fighting between Islamic extremists and the military claimed approximately 80,000 lives, including many civilians.

The Islamic Salvation Army (the military wing of FIS) called for a truce to begin on Oct. 1, 1997. The truce, however, had little effect on the sporadic violence, which escalated through the rest of the year. Other militant groups continued fighting.

Elections. Parliamentary elections on June 5 left President Zeroual in control of 57 percent of the National Assembly's 380 seats. His party, the National Democratic Rally, won 156 seats, and an allied party, the National Liberation Front, took 62 seats.

Some Algerians hoped the elections would spur a national dialogue, but the polling was marred by charges of fraud and vote-rigging. In addition, critics noted that a 1996 constitutional referendum had banned parties formed on religious or ethnic platforms, thereby disenfranchising many Algerians. FIS was among the groups banned from the elections.

Rebels freed. After the 1997 elections, Zeroual made a bid for reconciliation by freeing FIS spiritual leader Abassi Madani, who had been sentenced to a 12-year jail term in 1992. Another FIS leader, Abdelkader Hachani, was also released after the elections. However, the continued imprisonment of Ali Belhadj, a militant FIS leader jailed with Madani in 1992, angered many Muslims. After the Aug. 29, 1997, massacre in Reis, Madani was arrested again and placed under house arrest.

Europe. In 1997, many European states took action against suspected FIS supporters living outside Algeria. On February 7, France jailed six Algerians for up to five years each for dealing in forged passports. On March 3, Switzerland announced that Al-

An Algerian woman screams in anger and frustration after her husband is killed in a January raid on their village near Algiers. The Algerian government blamed Islamic rebels for the hundreds of civilian deaths that occurred during such attacks in 1997.

gerians were banned from buying or carrying weapons in public—rights granted to Swiss nationals and legal aliens. On June 23, a German court jailed four Algerians, including two sons of Madani, for up to three years each for smuggling weapons and forging passports.

Economy. In late February, the government announced that Algeria had a trade surplus of $4.3 billion in 1996, a marked upswing from 1995's $521-million deficit. The improvement in the trade balance was partly due to import cuts of some $1.7 billion. In addition, Algeria earned $12.5 billion in 1996 from oil and gas exports—nearly a 30-percent increase over 1995. However, the government also revealed in 1997 that major manufacturing industries suffered a drop in production of nearly 13 percent between 1995 and 1996, due partly to lack of material and other effects of the civil war. State-owned companies, many of which the government was trying to privatize in 1997, remained overstaffed and inefficient. Unemployment, which stood at about 30 percent in 1997, also remained a problem. Unemployment was cited as a major cause for the appeal of militant Islam to people under age 30, who make up more than two-thirds of Algeria's population. □ Christine Helms

See also **Africa** (Facts in brief table).
Angola. See Africa.
Animal. See Biology; Conservation; Zoos.

Anthropology. The first successful isolation of DNA from the bones of a Neanderthal was reported in July 1997 by genetics expert Svante Pääbo of the University of Munich, Germany. DNA—deoxyribonucleic acid—is the molecule genes are made of. Neanderthals were primitive human beings who lived in parts of Europe and Asia from about 80,000 to 30,000 years ago. Anthropologists have long debated whether Neanderthals were ancestors of modern humans or an evolutionary dead end.

Pääbo and his team extracted mitochondrial DNA (mtDNA)—a form of DNA found in cellular structures called mitochondria—from the upper arm bone of the original Neanderthal skeleton discovered in Germany in 1856, thought to be less than 100,000 years old. It was possible to isolate mtDNA because that form of DNA is hundreds to thousands of times more common in cells than nuclear DNA. The researchers compared a sequence of the Neanderthal mtDNA with similar sequences in mtDNA taken from more than 2,000 living people from around the world and found that the Neanderthal mtDNA differed significantly from all the modern mtDNA.

Pääbo's team concluded from this finding that Neanderthals did not interbreed with anatomically modern human populations and therefore were not ancestors of human beings. For paleoanthropologists favoring the "Out of Africa" theory—that modern humans arose in Africa and replaced Neanderthals throughout the world—this conclusion was welcome news. It was not welcomed by the "multiregionalists," who argue that modern humans arose semi-independently in different parts of the world. In the multiregional scenario, Neanderthals bequeathed their genes to modern humans. But Pääbo's work was based on only the mtDNA of a single specimen, so the issue was far from settled. His provocative findings were certain to stimulate further efforts to retrieve and study DNA from the fossils of early human beings.

Important fossil find in Spain. Anthropologists in Spain reported in May 1997 that they had discovered the remains of a previously unknown species that is one of the oldest known human ancestors. The fossils, discovered from 1994 to 1996, were found in caves in the Gran Dolina area of northern Spain and were determined through the geological dating of surrounding rock samples to be at least 780,000 years old. The discoverers, led by anthropologist José Maria Bermúdez de Castro, named the species *Homo antecessor,* from the Latin word meaning *man who explores* or *who goes first.*

The specimens included the partial face of a boy as well as the remains of five other individuals. In all, there were some 80 fossils, mostly skulls, teeth, and jaws. The fossils were from male and female teenagers and young adults.

The researchers noted an unusual combination of modern and primitive anatomical traits in the specimens. In some respects, the boy's face, with sunken cheekbones and a projecting nose, is strikingly modern. But the forehead, with strong brow ridges and a heavily constructed lower jaw lacking a chin, are much more primitive. The overall anatomy of the Gran Dolina fossils led the Spanish anthropologists to conclude that the remains represent a new species ancestral to both modern humans and extinct Neanderthals. They also suggested that the ancestor of *H. antecessor* was an African species, *Homo ergaster,* dated to 1.6 million years ago.

The scientists concluded that in northerly regions, *H. antecessor* evolved into a previously discovered species called *Homo heidelbergensis*—remains of which have been found in Africa and Europe—which in turn gave rise to the Neanderthals. In Africa, they theorized, *H. antecessor* evolved directly into modern humans. This view signaled a major revision in the human family tree, because most anthropologists accept *H. heidelbergensis* as the common ancestor of both the Neanderthals and modern humans. The Spanish researchers' theory removes *H. heidelbergensis* as a direct ancestor to modern humans.

Many anthropologists expressed caution about accepting these conclusions because the fossils came from young individuals whose features might have been due to change later in life. Nonetheless, the remains constitute the oldest accurately dated human fossils in Europe.

Ancient human footprints. The discovery of fossilized human footprints 117,000 years old was reported in August 1997 by paleoanthropologist Lee Berger of the University of the Witwatersrand in Johannesburg, South Africa. A single individual, probably a small woman, made the two impressions while walking in wet sand, which later hardened into rock. The footprints, the oldest ever found of anatomically modern human beings, were hailed as a remarkable discovery. Although anthropologists have unearthed many fossilized remains of early humans' teeth and bones, only rarely do they find traces of their soft anatomy, such as feet.

The footprints were discovered in 1995 by South African geologist David Roberts and authenticated in 1997. A detailed investigation of the prints, found in limestone on the edge of a lagoon some 60 miles (100 kilometers) north of Cape Town, revealed that they had a distinctly modern aspect.

Fossils of anatomically modern humans, dated at 60,000 to 120,000 years ago, have been found at the tip of South Africa at the mouth of the Klasies River. Berger and his team speculated that the footprints by the lagoon might have been made by a member of that same group of people. The discovery of the footprints adds weight to the idea that anatomically modern humans evolved in Africa and later migrated to Europe and Asia. □ Donald C. Johanson

See also **Archaeology.**

Archaeology.

In March 1997, divers working under a permit from the state of North Carolina announced that they had discovered remains that they believed to be from *Queen Anne's Revenge,* the flagship of the British pirate Blackbeard. The remains were found off the coast of North Carolina. Among the items recovered by the salvagers were a bronze bell inscribed with the year 1709, a 24-pound (11-kilogram) cannonball, and the brass barrel of a *blunderbuss* (a short musket). Blackbeard had apparently removed any treasure from the ship before it sank in 1718, after running aground on a sandbar in the Pamlico River near Beaufort, North Carolina.

Queen Anne's Revenge, which accommodated a crew of approximately 125, was one of at least four ships under the command of Blackbeard, who died in 1718. The ship was 103 feet (31 meters) long and 24½ feet (7½ meters) wide and had 40 cannons, 15 of which were found by the divers.

Roman ships. The discovery of the largest group of ancient shipwrecks ever found in deep water was announced in July 1997. The find, located approximately 2,500 feet (760 meters) beneath the surface of the Mediterranean Sea and 100 miles (160 kilometers) north of Tunis, a city on the coast of North Africa, consisted of five ancient Roman sailing ships dating from between approximately 100 B.C. and A.D. 400. Three other ships, dating from the late 1700's to the early 1900's, were also discovered.

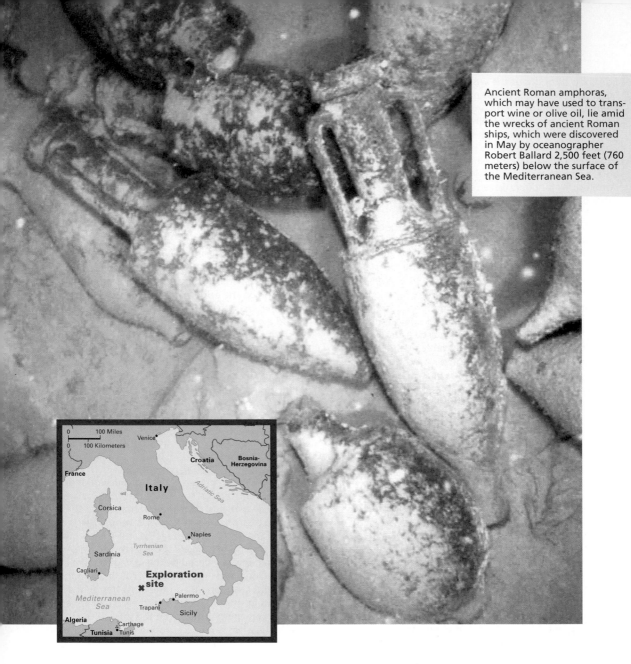

Ancient Roman amphoras, which may have used to transport wine or olive oil, lie amid the wrecks of ancient Roman ships, which were discovered in May by oceanographer Robert Ballard 2,500 feet (760 meters) below the surface of the Mediterranean Sea.

0   100 Miles
0   100 Kilometers
Venice
Croatia
Bosnia-Herzegovina
France
Italy
Adriatic Sea
Corsica
Rome
Naples
Tyrrhenian Sea
Sardinia
Cagliari
Exploration site
Mediterranean Sea
Palermo
Trapani
Sicily
Algeria
Carthage
Tunisia   Tunis

In the hold of one of the Roman ships, researchers discovered cut building stones, which were apparently part of a prefabricated temple. The ships were discovered by a research team led by oceanographer Robert Ballard, who had previously found the wrecks of the British passenger ship *Titanic,* which sank in 1912, and the German battleship *Bismarck,* which sank in 1941. Ballard, using a U.S. Navy submarine equipped with special sonar and photographic arrays, was attempting to trace ancient trade routes in the Mediterranean and Black seas.

Ice Age hunting. U.S. and Czech researchers concluded in an August 1997 report that people who lived between 29,000 and 22,000 years ago used nets for hunting small game such as hare and

fox. The conclusions were based on impressions of textiles woven from nettles or hemp that had been preserved in clay found in the 1920's in caves in what is now the Czech Republic. The findings suggested that hunters of the time relied on small game to a greater extent than archaeologists had previously thought. The report noted that hunting small game with nets would have been more efficient and safer than hunting large game with spears.

English temple. In November 1997, archaeologists with English Heritage, a government agency that takes care of historic sites, announced that they had found remains of the largest-known prehistoric temple in Great Britain. The 5,000-year-old temple, in Somerset, consisted of nine concentric circles of wooden posts surrounded by a circular ditch more than 400 feet (122 meters) in diameter. Archaeologists said that the temple was twice as large as any previous "timber temples" found in England.

Cypriot sculptures. In January 1997, four limestone sculptures of lions and two *sphinxes* (statue of lions with a human heads) were discovered during restoration work on a royal tomb, dating from the 500's B.C. and located south of Nicosia, Cyprus. The lions, which are life-sized or larger, were carved in a crouching position with teeth bared and tongues protruding. The sphinxes were executed in a style similar to Egyptian sphinxes of the same era, reflecting Egyptian control of Cyprus from 565 to 545 B.C. The tomb was located in the ancient city of Tamassos, capital of one of the 11 kingdoms on ancient Cyprus.

Anasazi cannibalism. Evidence that Anasazi Indians, ancestors of the modern-day Pueblo Indians, engaged in cannibalism was reported in April 1997 by researchers from Soil Systems Incorporated of Phoenix, an archaeological contractor. The evidence, consisting of seven sets of human remains that had apparently been dismembered and defleshed, was found at a site dating from the 1100's in southwestern Colorado. The bones had marks from cutting, battering, and burning, suggesting that the bodies were butchered, cooked, and eaten.

The researchers proposed that the cannibalism was associated with violent conflict between Anasazi communities in the mid 1100's that was contemporary with a period of drought and cultural collapse. Some scholars were not convinced that the evidence indicated cannibalism and suggested that warfare, ritual execution, and mortuary practices offered alternative explanations.

Louisiana mounds. In September 1997, researchers led by archaeologist Joseph Saunders of Northeast Louisiana University, in Monroe, reported that they had discovered that earthen mounds in northeastern Louisiana were the oldest known structures made by humans in North America—1,900 years older than the oldest of previously known mounds. Scientific dating methods indicated that the mounds were built between 5,000 and 5,400 years ago. The researchers studied 11 mounds laid out in an oval enclosing almost 22 acres (9 hectares). The largest mound is 25 feet (7.5 meters) tall. The other mounds range from 3 feet (90 centimeters) to 14 feet (4.25 meters) in height.

There are hundreds of earthen mounds made by American Indians in the valleys of the Mississippi and Ohio rivers. Archaeologists believe that some mounds were used as burial places, ceremonial sites, or platforms for houses. The purpose of the Louisiana mounds remains unknown, although they do not appear to have been used as burial places.

☐ Mark Rose

See also **Anthropology; Geology.**

Architecture. Two extraordinary art museums, one in Spain and the other in the United States, topped the 1997 architectural news. The Guggenheim Museum in Bilbao, Spain, which opened in October, was designed by American architect Frank O. Gehry. The museum, partially clad in silvery titanium, is a stunning sculpture of tilting walls and undulating roofs that resembles a gigantic flower opening to the sun. Within its 18 galleries are works by prominent modern artists from the collection of the Guggenheim in New York City. Both critics and artists agreed that the new Guggenheim is the most poetic—and possibly prophetic—structure of the late 20th century.

American architect Richard Meier's Getty Center opened in December 1997. Spread over a hillside overlooking Los Angeles, the art center's six buildings are reached by a Disneyesque tramway. Meier's pristine geometry, dazzling light, and refined detailing are all on display, though his signature white porcelain panels have been muted to reduce glare. Five two-story pavilions, surrounding an open courtyard, contain the Getty's permanent collection, which focuses on European painting and sculpture as well as the history of photography. At $1 billion, the Getty was the most expensive art museum ever built and Los Angeles's strongest challenge to date to the cultural dominance of New York City.

The Georgia O'Keeffe Museum opened July 17 in Santa Fe, New Mexico. Designed by New York architect Richard Gluckman, it was the first museum devoted exclusively to a female artist. While its bland adobe exterior reflects strict city ordinances controlling building design in Santa Fe's historic district, the museum's nine galleries, created from the shell of a Spanish Baptist church, are as varied and brilliantly illuminated as O'Keeffe's paintings.

Frank Lloyd Wright's Monona Terrace Community and Convention Center in Madison, Wisconsin—perhaps the most exotic architectural project of 1997—opened in July. Designed in the 1930's, then shelved for political and financial reasons, the center was revived in the early 1990's by Wright's successors, Taliesin Associates. Monona Terrace contains three levels of meeting rooms and a dramatic rooftop garden overlooking Lake Monona. Wright conceived the project as a way to connect the community, the cityscape, and the state capitol. Madison residents in 1997 were as divided—pro and con—about Wright's project as they had been about the works he created during his lifetime (1867–1959).

Memorials. The Franklin Delano Roosevelt Memorial opened in May 1997 on the Tidal Basin in Washington, D.C.'s West Potomac Park. Landscape architect Lawrence Halprin arranged massive granite blocks into four outdoor "rooms," one for each of Roosevelt's terms as U.S. president from 1933 to 1945. Halprin integrated waterfalls, sculptures, and

quotations to commemorate the man and his era. The memorial is the largest in Washington, covering 7.5 acres (3.0 hectares). Architecturally, it is a transitional work that falls between the heroic classicism of the Lincoln and Jefferson memorials and the spare abstraction of Maya Ying Lin's Vietnam Veterans Memorial.

Three architects from Locus Bold Design in Berlin, Germany, won the international competition to create a memorial to the victims of the 1995 bombing of the Alfred P. Murrah Federal Building in Oklahoma City, Oklahoma. The centerpiece of the proposed memorial is a lawn, tracing the foundation of the destroyed building and filled with 168 empty chairs—one for each victim.

Restorations. New York City's 42nd Street, a historic theater district that in the 1970's had become an area of adult entertainment, made a comeback in 1997 as a family entertainment center, anchored by the New Amsterdam Theater. Purchased by the Walt Disney Company as a home for its musicals, the landmark theater reopened in May. Brilliantly restored by Hardy Holzman Pfeiffer Architects, the 1903 theater is an art nouveau masterpiece, emblazoned with cherubs, murals of fanciful creatures, and swirling plaster trees and vines that culminate in the most dazzling theater ceiling in the United States.

In Chicago, Daniel Burnham's famed Orchestra Hall was renovated as part of the $110-million Symphony Center. Architects Skidmore, Owings & Merrill modernized the hall's acoustics with a special floating canopy and designed a dramatic glass rotunda that connects the hall to a library, rehearsal rooms, a restaurant, and classrooms in adjacent buildings.

Washington, D.C.'s National Airport got a new passenger terminal in July 1997 designed by architect Cesar Pelli. Reminiscent of the great train stations of the mid- to late-1800's, the terminal features a dramatic vaulted concourse of painted steel and arched windows, from which pavilions with shops and restaurants reach toward the runways. More than a piece of urban infrastructure, the terminal rekindles the romance of arrival and departure.

Architecture prizes. Richard Meier was awarded the 1997 Gold Medal from the American Institute of Architects in February. The jury praised his "single-minded pursuit of the essence of modern architecture," which Meier defined as the "precise manipulation of geometry in light."

The 1997 Pritzker Prize—a $100,000 award given annually for lifetime contribution to architectural design—was awarded in May to Norwegian architect Sverre Fehn. His use of gray stone and native woods follows the tradition of romantic Scandinavian modernism established by Alvar Aalto and Eliel Saarinen.

☐ David Dillon

See also **Art; Washington, D.C.; Washington, D.C. Special Report: A Look at the FDR Memorial.**

The Monona Terrace Community and Convention Center, *left,* overlooking a lake in Madison, Wisconsin, opened in July. The opening came more than 60 years after the structure was originally designed by Frank Lloyd Wright, who died in 1959. The Guggenheim Museum in Bilbao, Spain, *below,* designed by Frank O. Gehry, opened to critical acclaim in October 1997. The building's irregularly shaped exterior is sheathed in titanium.

Argentina. A political coalition comprised of the center-right Radical Civic Union and the left-wing Front for a Country in Solidarity (Frepaso) captured control of the House of Deputies in midterm elections on Oct. 25, 1997. The coalition victory was a stunning defeat for President Carlos Saúl Menem's Peronist Party, which lost majority control.

Political observers gave much of the credit for the election victory to an extraordinarily popular candidate, Graciela Fernández Meijide, 66, who gave up her place in the Senate to run for deputy of the Buenos Aires province, historically a Peronist stronghold. Fernández Meijide had been a high-profile human rights activist since 1976, when her 17-year-old son, Pablo, disappeared during political conflicts.

"Good governance." The main issues of the campaign surfaced earlier in 1997, when the International Monetary Fund (IMF), a United Nations agency, made Argentina a test case for granting credit to a country based on "good governance." To be eligible for a three-year line of credit, Argentina was required to take steps to create new jobs, increase spending on health and education, overhaul the tax system, increase the independence of the courts, safeguard private property rights, and open government ledgers to public inspection.

Protests broke out in several provinces in 1997 over salary cuts, limited government assistance for the poor, high unemployment rates, and large job layoffs. In April in the province of Neuquén, demonstrators set up roadblocks to protest the privatization of a state-owned oil company. The privatization eliminated the jobs of approximately half of the workers in the cities of Cutral-Có and Plaza Huincúl. A teachers' strike, also in Neuquén, ended in violence that left one teacher dead. Similar protests occurred in at least nine other provinces.

President Menem described the protests in Neuquén as evidence of a new "subversive threat." But *La Nacion*, a conservative newspaper in Buenos Aires, was more sympathetic to the protesters, coining the word *la pueblada* (the people's uprising) to describe the demonstrations.

Violent retribution. On January 25, police found the body of José Luis Cabezas, a photographer who had exposed corruption in the Buenos Aires provincial police force in 1996. The murder was one of an estimated 800 violent attacks on journalists since Menem became president in 1989.

On Sept. 11, 1997, four men carrying police identification attacked Adolfo Francisco Scilingo, a former Navy captain. In 1995, he had revealed the Argentine Navy's role in killing political dissidents between 1976 and 1983, the years of the military dictatorship's so-called "dirty war" against political opponents. Scilingo's assailants carved the initials of three journalists to whom he had allegedly leaked information in 1995 on the retired officer's face.

University students and antiriot police clash in Buenos Aires on May 28, 1997. The riot, one of many violent antigovernment protests in 1997, broke out during a march staged to increase funding of education.

The Argentine government announced plans in August 1997 to issue $3 billion in bonds to compensate the relatives of the thousands of people who "disappeared" during the dirty war in an attempt to heal old wounds,

Judicial corruption. Between January and August, the Argentine Congress removed 10 federal judges on grounds of corruption. In one highly publicized incident, Judge Hernán Bernasconi was accused of planting evidence in a drug trafficking case in an alleged effort to frame Guillermo Cóppola, a popular sports agent. Former finance minister Domingo Cavallo added to public resentment over corruption by charging that during his tenure as minister, President Menem's "cabinet members regularly called judges and prosecutors to give them instructions on how to handle important cases."

Return of ancestral lands. About 100 Colla Indians, dressed in traditional broad-brimmed hats and red ponchos, attended a March 19 ceremony in Buenos Aires at which they were given title to their ancestral lands in northwest Argentina. From 1994 to 1997, the government restored nearly 4 million acres (1.6 million hectares) of land to the nation's 600,000 *indigenous* (native) peoples.

☐ Nathan A. Haverstock

See also **Latin America** (Facts in brief table).

Arizona. See State government.

Arkansas. See State government.

Armed forces. The U.S. armed forces were buffeted in 1997 by allegations of sexual misconduct among the ranks, reaching from enlisted men to the vice chairman of the Joint Chiefs of Staff.

Nominee derailed. Air Force General Joseph W. Ralston withdrew his name from consideration as chairman of the Joint Chiefs of Staff in June, after a political furor erupted over an extramarital relationship he had engaged in during the 1980's. Ralston, vice chairman of the joint chiefs of staff, withdrew after it became clear that some members of the Senate Armed Services Committee and the Congressional Women's Caucus were opposed to his nomination. Ralston had been Secretary of Defense William S. Cohen's first choice for the chairmanship.

Cohen's second candidate, Army General Henry H. Shelton, commander of the U.S. Special Operations Command, was sworn in as chairman of the Joint Chiefs of Staff in October 1997, succeeding retiring Army General John Shalikashvili. Shelton became the first Green Beret officer to head the U.S. military.

The first female B-52 bomber pilot was dismissed from the Air Force in May in the wake of allegations that she had lied to superior officers about a relationship with a married civilian. First Lieutenant Kelly Flinn, a pilot at Minot Air Force Base, North Dakota, agreed to accept a general discharge in exchange for avoiding a court-martial. Flinn was

charged in February with adultery, fraternization, making false statements, conduct unbecoming an officer, and disobeying an order to end a relationship with a Minot soccer coach who was married to a woman enlisted in the Air Force.

Flinn's supporters claimed she was the victim of a sexist double standard and was treated more harshly than male officers who had also been charged with sexual misconduct. Senior Air Force officers contended that Flinn's behavior was a threat to military order and discipline and could not be tolerated. Flinn had sought an honorable discharge, which would have allowed her to continue flying in the Air Force Reserves or the National Guard.

Sergeant major charged. The Army announced in October that it would court-martial its highest-ranking enlisted soldier, Sergeant Major of the Army Gene C. McKinney, on 20 counts of alleged criminal behavior, including sexual assault, adultery, and obstruction of justice. Most of the charges involved alleged sexual misconduct with five female soldiers and a Navy enlisted woman. The Army later removed McKinney as the Army's top enlisted soldier and promoted Command Sergeant Major Robert Hall to the position.

The case was triggered in February when McKinney's former public relations assistant, retired Sergeant Major Brenda Hoster, alleged that McKinney had made unwanted sexual advances during an April 1996 military conference in Hawaii. McKinney denied all the charges against him and claimed that they were racially motivated. McKinney was the first African American to hold the rank of sergeant major of the army.

Sexual misconduct. An investigation of sexual misconduct that began in November 1996 at the Army's training center at the Aberdeen Proving Ground in Maryland continued in 1997, as the Army charged 12 Aberdeen base staff members with crimes ranging from inappropriate sexual comments to rape. By September, nine soldiers had been discharged from the service. In the most serious case, Staff Sergeant Delmar Simpson was convicted in April of rape and sentenced to 25 years in a military prison. Four other soldiers were convicted of other charges of sexual misconduct.

Army personnel conducting a 10-month internal investigation of sexual misconduct concluded in September that "sexual harassment exists throughout the Army, crossing gender, rank, and racial lines." The study found that 72 percent of Army women and 63 percent of the men had witnessed "sexist behavior," 47 percent of the women reported unwelcome sexual attention, 15 percent of the women were the victims of sexual coercion, and 7 percent of the women were victims of sexual assault.

The Army instituted a series of policy changes designed to remedy the problem, including tighter screening of drill sergeants who train female recruits and extended training in ethics and values. The former Aberdeen commander and several subordinates were issued letters of reprimand.

Air Force top general resigns. Air Force Chief of Staff General Ronald R. Fogleman resigned in July, in part to protest Defense Secretary Cohen's decision to punish several officers for security lapses at an Air Force facility in Saudi Arabia that had been bombed by terrorists in 1996. Cohen agreed with the conclusions of outside experts that the attack, which killed 19 U.S. airmen, could have been prevented by stricter security arrangements. However, Fogleman supported two Air Force reviews that concluded that security was adequate at the Khobar Towers apartment complex.

Fogleman retired one year before the scheduled end of his four-year term as the Air Force's top officer. In a statement, he said that he felt "out of step" with his civilian bosses and feared he would be considered "a divisive force" if he did not step down.

A-10 crashes. An Air Force A-10 jet pilot abruptly broke off from formation during a routine training mission in Arizona and vanished on April 2, 1997. The wreckage of the plane was discovered three weeks later and 800 miles (1,280 kilometers) away on a Colorado mountainside. DNA tests confirmed that remains found at the crash site were those of the pilot, Captain Craig Button. In October, Air Force investigators ruled that Button had committed suicide in a spontaneous action.

An A-10 crash on May 27 killed one of the few women flying combat jets for the Air Force. Captain Amy Lynn Svoboda died when her jet crashed during a training flight near Gila Bend, Arizona, about 100 miles (160 kilometers) northwest of Tucson. Both she and Button had been stationed at Davis-Monthan Air Force Base, Arizona. Svoboda was the first female Air Force pilot to die on duty.

Flights grounded. In September, Defense Secretary Cohen ordered a 24-hour worldwide grounding of all U.S. military training flights, following five jet crashes in four days. In the most serious of the incidents, an Air Force C-141 cargo jet collided with a German military transport plane off the South African coast on September 13, killing more than 30 crew members and passengers.

An Air Force F-117 Stealth fighter crashed near a Baltimore, Maryland, residential area during an air show on September 14. No one was killed or seriously injured. A pilot was killed on September 14 when a Navy F/A-18 jet fighter crashed during a training exercise in Oman. On September 15, a Marine Corps F/A-18 crashed near Cape Hatteras, North Carolina, killing two crew members. Two Air National Guard F-16 fighter jets collided over the Atlantic Ocean off the New Jersey coast during exercises on September 16. The pilot of one plane flew his damaged aircraft back to a base while two crew members in the second jet ejected before that jet crashed.

The temporary halt, or stand-down, was designed to allow for a full review of training flight frequency, safety procedures, and maintenance. The halt did not apply to operational missions, such as protecting the "no-fly zone" over Iraq and supporting peacekeeping operations in Bosnia.

Following the stand-down order, an Air Force B-1 bomber on a training mission crashed in southeastern Montana near the Wyoming state line on September 19, killing all four crew members. On October 2, one crew member died when a Navy F-14 fighter jet on a routine training mission crashed in the Atlantic Ocean off the North Carolina coast. Two crew members of a T-38 jet were killed on October 22 following a mid-air collision with an F-16 at Edwards Air Force Base, California. On November 6, a third F-16 crashed near the desert town of Brownwood, Texas.

Base closings. The U.S. Senate in July rejected President Bill Clinton's plans to close several military bases. The action blocked the Department of Defense from proceeding with two previously approved rounds of base closings scheduled for 1999 and 2001. Defense officials sought to close bases in order to divert funds for improving weapons systems. However, members of Congress in 1997 became increasingly reluctant to agree with the president's plan.

Defense budget. The Department of Defense submitted its $259.4 billion budget for fiscal 1998 to Congress in February 1997. The budget allocated more money for operational readiness and peacekeeping operations than for new weapons.

On November 18, President Clinton signed a $268-billion defense bill. The bill provided money to expand the military B-2 bomber fleet, but included an option to use the money to repair and modernize the existing fleet instead. President Clinton opposed purchasing additional B-2 bombers, a radar-evading plane. Other key provisions of the defense bill included $720 million for a Navy destroyer, $2.2 billion for the Air Force F-22 fighter jet program, and $529 million for nine transport planes.

Peacekeeping operations. Approximately 8,500 American soldiers remained on duty in Bosnia-Herzegovina in 1997 as part of a multinational peacekeeping force. The troops were scheduled to be withdrawn by June 30, 1998, but on Dec. 18, 1997, President Clinton announced plans to extend the operation indefinitely. The 1998 defense appropriations bill, passed by Congress in September 1997, allowed the president to request that Congress continue to fund the American military contingent.

Former POW named ambassador. In May, Douglas Peterson, a retired Air Force pilot and Congressman, became the first U.S. ambassador to Vietnam since the fall of South Vietnam in 1973. Peterson was a prisoner of war in North Vietnam for more than six years during the Vietnam War (1957-1975).

Command changes. Sheila Widnall, the first woman to serve as secretary of the Air Force, stepped down in October 1997 to return to teaching. Daryl L. Jones, a Florida state legislator and an Air Force Academy graduate, was nominated to succeed her. General Michael Ryan was nominated as Air Force chief of staff in August to replace General Fogleman, after Fogleman's July resignation. In September, Congress confirmed Army General Wesley K. Clark as commander of the North American Treaty Organization and all American military forces in Europe. In May, the Senate confirmed Claudia Kennedy as the Army's first female three-star general. She was also confirmed as the Army's deputy chief of staff for intelligence.

VMI admits women. Virginia Military Institute (VMI), a state-supported military college in Lexington, opened its doors to female cadets for the first time in the school's 158-year history on August 18. Thirty-one women were admitted in the freshman class of more than 400. VMI had been ordered by the U.S. Supreme Court in 1996 to admit women.

Anthrax vaccinations. An Army spokesperson announced on Dec. 15, 1997, that all members of the armed services will be vaccinated against anthrax, a deadly biological agent, beginning in 1998. The Army feared that at least 10 countries, including Iraq, were capable of developing biological weapons from anthrax bacteria. □ Thomas M. DeFrank

See also **Armed forces** Special Report.

First Lieutenant Kelly Flinn, *left,* was dismissed from the U.S. Air Force in May after disobeying an order to end a relationship with a civilian man married to an enlisted person. In June, Air Force General Joseph Ralston, *below,* withdrew his name from consideration as chairman of the Joint Chiefs of Staff after news of an earlier extramarital relationship touched off a political furor.

Armed Forces of the World

By Peter Uremovic

In 1997, the world's military situation was much different than it had been a decade before. In 1987, the military strength of much of the world was controlled by the globe's two superpowers—the Soviet Union and the United States, as it had been for more than four decades following World War II (1939-1945). These nations were engaged in an intense rivalry that became known as the Cold War. Military experts of the era expected that if the Cold War were to heat up, the conflict would ignite in Europe. In response to that fear, both sides developed and stockpiled tremendous arsenals of nuclear weapons.

To check Soviet military power in Europe, the United States helped found the North Atlantic Treaty Organization (NATO) in 1949, joined by Belgium, Canada, Denmark, France, Greece, Iceland, Luxembourg, the Netherlands, Norway, Portugal, Spain, Turkey, and West Germany. Each member pledged to respond to an attack on an ally as an attack on itself. To counter NATO, the Soviet Union engineered its own alliance, the Warsaw Pact, in 1955. This alliance comprised the Communist, Eastern European nations that separated Western Europe and the Soviet Union.

The collapse of the Soviet Union in 1991 triggered a great shift in the balance of military power. NATO, with the loss of its principal enemy, began to greatly reduce its military posture. Soviet and U.S. allies in other parts of the world were also affected and could no longer rely on Cold-War competition to encourage the superpowers to supply them with weapons or training.

The changes that occurred since the collapse of the Soviet Union were often dramatic, sometimes fascinating. The following pages present an overview showing how the world's military forces stood in 1997 in relation to the Cold War era.

The author

Peter Uremovic is a
Staff Editor on the
World Book Year Book.

The military forces of the world's largest powers generally became smaller during the 1990's. The exceptions were in areas where regional conflicts occurred, such as in the Middle East or the Balkans, where nations increased their military posture.

ARMED FORCES

NATIONS WITH THE WORLD'S LARGEST STANDING ARMED FORCES

1997 Personnel		1987 Personnel	
CHINA	2.8 million	USSR	5.2 million
UNITED STATES	1.4 million	CHINA	3.2 million
RUSSIA	1.2 million	UNITED STATES	2 million
INDIA	1.1 million	INDIA	1.3 million
NORTH KOREA	1.1 million	VIETNAM	1.3 million
SOUTH KOREA	672,000	NORTH KOREA	838,000
TURKEY	639,000	TURKEY	654,000
PAKISTAN	587,000	IRAN*	654,000
IRAN	518,000	SOUTH KOREA	629,000
VIETNAM	492,000	PAKISTAN	480,000

*Figure includes other associated military personnel.
Sources: *The Military Balance 1997/98* and *The Military Balance 1987/88*.

NATIONS WITH THE WORLD'S LARGEST RESERVE FORCES*

	1997	1987
RUSSIA/USSR	20 million	6.2 million
NORTH KOREA	4.7 million	540,000
SOUTH KOREA	4.5 million	4.8 million
UNITED STATES	3.6 million	1.7 million
VIETNAM	3 to 4 million	500,000
TAIWAN	1.7 million	1.5 million
BRAZIL	1.3 million	1.1 million
INDIA	1.3 million	200,000
CHINA	1.2 million	4.4 million
UKRAINE†	1 million	

*Reserve forces are defined as nonoperational forces that can be activated in an emergency.
†Ukraine was part of the USSR in 1987.
Sources: *The Military Balance 1997/98* and *The Military Balance 1987/88*.

NATIONS REPORTING THE LARGEST NUMBERS OF WOMEN IN THE ARMED FORCES

	1997	1987
UNITED STATES	198,500	203,000
RUSSIA/USSR	153,000	*
CHINA	136,000	*
FRANCE	17,350	14,700
UNITED KINGDOM	14,950	16,100
JAPAN	9,900	*
SOUTH AFRICA	8,000	3,200
AUSTRALIA	7,500	*
CANADA	6,500	7,740
GREECE	5,100	1,800
BELARUS	3,400	*
BELGIUM	2,760	3,460
NETHERLANDS	2,600	1,600
NEW ZEALAND	1,340	*
DENMARK	960	800
BRUNEI	600	150
CYPRUS (ROC)	445	*
FINLAND	300	*
INDIA	200	*
SPAIN	200	*
IRELAND	100	*
BAHAMAS	70	*

*Not reported
Sources: *The Military Balance 1997/98* and *The Military Balance 1987/88*.

NATIONS WITH MOST SOLDIERS PER POPULATION IN 1997

	Population (in millions)	Soldiers per 1,000 people
NORTH KOREA	23.5	44.3
ISRAEL	5.3	34.9
JORDAN	4.1	27.3
SÃO TOMÉ & PRÍNCIPE*	0.1	22 to 26
SYRIA	15.1	21.2
UNITED ARAB EMIRATES	2.9	20.5
GREECE	10.5	20.3
TAIWAN	21.3	20
DJIBOUTI	0.4	19
IRAQ	20.6	18.9

*Rough estimate
Source: *World Military Expenditures and Arms Transfers 1996*.

MILITARY FORCES IN EUROPE, 1997, 1994, AND 1987

	Troops	Tanks/ Armored Vehicles	Artillery	Combat aircraft*
1997				
NATO	2.2 million	35,565	14,010	5,439
(BUDAPEST/TASHKENT GROUP)†	2.1 million	46,156	18,868	7,063
1994				
NATO	2.3 million	41,179	16,274	5,985
(BUDAPEST/TASHKENT GROUP)†	2.5 million	54,091	20,629	8,066
1987				
NATO	2.4 million	22,200	11,100	3,292
WARSAW PACT	2.3 million	52,200	37,000	7,524

*Includes ground-based fixed-wing combat aircraft and attack helicopters.
†The Budapest/Tashkent Group consists of the former Eastern Bloc countries Armenia, Azerbaijan, Belarus, Bulgaria, Czech Republic, Georgia, Hungary, Moldova, Poland, Romania, Russia, Slovakia, and Ukraine.
Sources: *The Military Balance 1986/87*, *The Military Balance 1995/96*, and *The Military Balance 1997/98*.

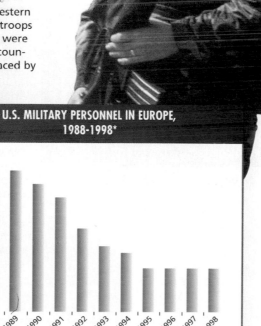

Post-Cold War Europe

Military forces in Europe—including those of non-European NATO members—were significantly realigned after 1990. For example, Canada completed a total withdrawal of its personnel and equipment from Europe by January 1997. The United States by 1995 had withdrawn more than 400,000 soldiers. These troops were replaced by Western European forces. Similarly, troops of the former Soviet Union were pulled out of Eastern Bloc countries in the 1990's and replaced by individual national forces.

U.S. MILITARY PERSONNEL IN EUROPE, 1988-1998*

*Figure includes only personnel assigned to bases on land.
Source: U.S. Department of Defense.

The armies of the world's developed nations became more reliant on technology than on manpower during the 1990's. Expenditures for personnel decreased while expenditures for equipment increased.

ARMIES

NATIONS WITH THE LARGEST ARMIES

	1997 Personnel	1987 Personnel
CHINA	2.1 million	2.3 million
INDIA	980,000	1.1 million
NORTH KOREA	923,000	750,000
SOUTH KOREA	560,000	542,000
TURKEY	525,000	542,000
PAKISTAN	520,000	450,000
UNITED STATES	495,000	774,100
RUSSIA/USSR	420,000	2 million
VIETNAM	420,000	1.1 million
BURMA*	400,000	170,000
IRAN	350,000	305,000
IRAQ	350,000	955,000
EGYPT	320,000	320,000
TAIWAN	240,000	270,000
GERMANY	239,950	(East) 120,000
		(West) 332,000
INDONESIA	220,000	216,000
FRANCE	219,900	279,900
SYRIA	215,000	300,000
BRAZIL	200,000	197,000
ITALY	188,300	265,000

*Rough estimate
Sources: *The Military Balance 1997/98* and *The Military Balance 1987/88*.

NATIONS REPORTING THE GREATEST NUMBER OF WOMEN IN THE ARMY

	1997	1987
UNITED STATES	72,000	76,000
FRANCE	9,000	6,250
UNITED KINGDOM	6,800	6,500
SOUTH AFRICA	4,000	2,500
GREECE	2,700	1,400
AUSTRALIA	2,600	*
BELGIUM	1,600	*
CANADA	1,600	*
SRI LANKA	1,000	*
NEW ZEALAND	500	*
DENMARK	460	*
BRUNEI	250	*

*Not reported
Sources: *The Military Balance 1997/98* and *The Military Balance 1987/88*.

NATIONS WITH THE GREATEST TANK AND ARMORED VEHICLE STRENGTH

	1997	1987
RUSSIA/USSR	53,700	118,000
UNITED STATES	33,000	40,100
CHINA	15,200	14,250
ISRAEL	10,600	13,800
UKRAINE*	10,400	
GERMANY	9,500	(East) 7,100
		(West) 8,400
SYRIA	9,100	7,900
EGYPT	8,700	5,300
INDIA	8,300	3,700
TURKEY	7,850	7,450
FRANCE	6,900	5,550
NORTH KOREA	6,000	2,600
IRAQ	5,600	8,600
UNITED KINGDOM	5,540	5,020
BULGARIA	4,860	3,160
BELARUS*	4,760	
SOUTH KOREA	4,600	2,350
POLAND	4,370	11,170
GREECE	4,260	4,040

*Ukraine and Belarus were part of the USSR in 1987.
Sources: *The Military Balance 1997/98* and *The Military Balance 1987/88*.

ARMIES WITH THE GREATEST NUMBER OF ATTACK HELICOPTERS*

	1997	1987
UNITED STATES	1,460	1,400
RUSSIA	1,060	1,080
CHINA	380	0
FRANCE	340	550
UNITED KINGDOM	270	270
UKRAINE†	270	
GERMANY	200	(East) 0
		(West) 210
ITALY	130	120
IRAQ	120	180
IRAN	100	1

*Some nations allocated attack helicopters to other branches besides the army.
†Ukraine was part of the USSR in 1987.
Sources: *The Military Balance 1997/98* and *The Military Balance 1987/88*.

Air force size and equipment strength generally remained stable between 1987 and 1997 because of the tactical advantage offered by air power.

AIR FORCES

NATIONS WITH THE WORLD'S LARGEST AIR FORCES

	1997 Personnel	1987 Personnel
CHINA	470,000	470,000
UNITED STATES	382,200	606,000
RUSSIA/USSR	130,000	454,000
UKRAINE*	124,400	
INDIA	110,000	115,000
NORTH KOREA	85,000	53,000
FRANCE	83,400	96,000
GERMANY	76,900	(East) 40,000
		(West) 108,700
TAIWAN	68,000	77,000
ITALY	63,600	73,000
TURKEY	63,000	57,400
UNITED KINGDOM	56,700	93,500
POLAND	56,100	80,000
SOUTH KOREA	52,000	33,000
BRAZIL	50,000	50,700
ROMANIA	47,600	32,000
PAKISTAN	45,000	17,600
JAPAN	44,100	45,000
THAILAND	43,000	48,000
SYRIA	40,000	45,000

*Ukraine was part of the USSR in 1987.
Sources: The Military Balance 1997/98 and The Military Balance 1987/88.

NATIONS REPORTING THE GREATEST NUMBER OF WOMEN IN THE AIR FORCE

	1997	1987
UNITED STATES	65,000	69,000
FRANCE	5,950	5,850
UNITED KINGDOM	4,950	6,300
AUSTRALIA	2,700	*
GREECE	1,100	200
BELGIUM	900	*
CANADA	830	*
SOUTH AFRICA	800	300
NETHERLANDS	720	*
NEW ZEALAND	500	*
DENMARK	300	*
GERMANY	230	*

*Not reported
Sources: The Military Balance 1997/98 and The Military Balance 1987/88.

AIR FORCES WITH LONG-RANGE STRATEGIC BOMBERS

	Range (km)*	Max. speed (Mach)†	Weapon load (1,000's kg)**
UNITED STATES			
B-52G	4,600	0.95	29.5
B-52H	6,140	0.95	29.5
B-1B	4,580	1.25	61
B-2A	5,840	‡	18
RUSSIA and UKRAINE			
Tu-95	5,690	0.9	11.3
Tu-160	7,300	2.3	16.3
CHINA			
H-6	2,180	0.91	145

*Maximum distance an aircraft can fly to complete its mission
†Mach 1 is the speed of sound.
**Maximum weight of weapons an aircraft is able to carry
‡The B-2A's top speed is classified.
Source: The Military Balance 1995/96.

AIR FORCES WITH THE GREATEST COMBAT AIRCRAFT STRENGTH, 1997 AND 1987

	1997	1987
CHINA	3,740	5,380
UNITED STATES	3,740	4,880
RUSSIA/USSR	1,850	4,920
UKRAINE*	1,170	
INDIA	780	701
FRANCE	600	520
NORTH KOREA	600	840
SYRIA	590	480
EGYPT	570	440
SOUTH KOREA	460	480
GERMANY	450	(East) 330
		(West) 30
ISRAEL	450	680
PAKISTAN	430	380
ITALY	400	460
TAIWAN	400	560
JAPAN	370	390
POLAND	360	660
ROMANIA	310	370
BRAZIL	270	190
THAILAND	210	160

*Ukraine was part of the USSR in 1987.
Sources: The Military Balance 1997/98 and The Military Balance 1987/88.

In 1997, the United States remained the world's most formidable sea power. Its fleet of aircraft carriers extended America's military presence to virtually anywhere in the world.

NAVIES

NATIONS WITH THE WORLD'S LARGEST NAVIES

	1997 Personnel	1987 Personnel
UNITED STATES	441,8000	583,800
CHINA	275,000	340,000
RUSSIA/USSR	201,000	477,000
FRANCE	60,400	68,900
INDIA	54,000	47,000
THAILAND	51,000	42,000
BRAZIL	50,100	33,000
TURKEY	47,900	51,000
NORTH KOREA	47,000	35,000
ITALY	43,000	50,300
JAPAN	42,500	45,000
UNITED KINGDOM	38,200	58,800
TAIWAN	38,000	38,000
SOUTH KOREA	35,000	29,000
SPAIN	31,800	51,000
GERMANY	27,760	(East) 16,000
		(West) 36,400
INDONESIA	31,000	30,000
MEXICO	28,400	19,200
CHILE	26,600	20,300
PERU	22,000	20,500

Sources: *The Military Balance 1997/98* and *The Military Balance 1987/88.*

NATIONS REPORTING THE GREATEST NUMBER OF WOMEN IN THE NAVY

	1997	1987
UNITED STATES	53,000	48,600
UNITED KINGDOM	3,200	3,300
FRANCE	2,400	1,500
AUSTRALIA	2,200	*
JAPAN	1,800	*
GREECE	1,300	200
NETHERLANDS	1,200	*
CANADA	650	*
SOUTH AFRICA	500	300
GERMANY	420	*
NEW ZEALAND	340	*
BELGIUM	260	*
DENMARK	200	*

*Not reported
Sources: *The Military Balance 1997/98* and *The Military Balance 1987/88.*

NATIONS WITH AIRCRAFT CARRIERS IN 1997

Vessel	Year of commission
ARGENTINA	
Veinticinco de Mayo	1945
BRAZIL	
Minas Gerais	1945
CHINA	
n/a	[under construction]
FRANCE	
Charles de Gaulle	1999*
Foch	1963
Clemenceau	1961
INDIA	
Viraat	1959
ITALY	
Giuseppe Garibaldi	1985
RUSSIA	
Admiral Kuznetsov	1991
Admiral Gorshkov	1987
SPAIN	
Principe de Asturias	1988
UNITED KINGDOM	
Ark Royal	1985
Illustrious	1982
Invincible	1980
UNITED STATES	
Ronald Reagan	2002*
Harry S Truman	1998
John C. Stennis	1996
George Washington	1992
Abraham Lincoln	1989
Theodore Roosevelt	1986
Carl Vinson	1982
Dwight D. Eisenhower	1977
Nimitz	1975
John F. Kennedy	1968
Enterprise	1961
Constellation	1961
Kitty Hawk	1961
Independence	1959

*Projected year of commissioning
Source: *Jane's Fighting Ships 1997-98.*

NATIONS WITH THE LARGEST FLEETS OF SURFACE WARSHIPS IN 1997

	Cruisers*	Destroyers†	Corvettes**	Frigates††
UNITED STATES	30	56	none	33
CHINA	none	18	none	35
RUSSIA	8	22	76	104
TAIWAN	none	13	6	14
THAILAND	none	none	5	14
SOUTH KOREA	none	7	28	9
TURKEY	none	5	none	16
INDIA	none	5	23	13
UNITED KINGDOM	none	13	none	22
BRAZIL	none	none	4	14
NORTH KOREA	none	none	5	3
INDONESIA	none	none	16	17
ITALY	1	4	8	18
JAPAN	none	41	none	17
VIETNAM	none	none	3	7
MEXICO	none	3	none	4
CHILE	none	4	none	4
PHILIPPINES	none	none	10	1
PAKISTAN	none	3	none	8

*CRUISER is a large warship used to escort aircraft carriers and for independent operations with destroyers.

†DESTROYER is a major warship used to defend larger warships and amphibious and merchant ships from enemy attack.

**CORVETTE is a fast, highly maneuverable warship of the destroyer class.

††FRIGATE is a warship used chiefly to escort amphibious and merchant ships.

Source: Jane's Fighting Ships 1997-98.

NATIONS WITH ATTACK SUBMARINES*

	1997	1987
RUSSIA	138	200
UNITED STATES	82	96
CHINA	50	50
UNITED KINGDOM	12	28

*Attack submarines search out and destroy enemy submarines and surface ships. They may also attack land targets and gather information about enemy vessels.

Sources: *The Military Balance 1997/98* and *The Military Balance 1987/88*.

NATIONS WITH THE LARGEST MARINE CORPS, 1997 AND 1987

	1997 Personnel	1987 Personnel
UNITED STATES	174,900	199,600
TAIWAN	30,000	39,000
VIETNAM	30,000	27,000
SOUTH KOREA	25,000	25,000
THAILAND	22,000	20,000
RUSSIA/USSR	19,000	18,000
BRAZIL	14,600	15,000
INDONESIA	12,000	12,000
COLOMBIA	9,000	5,000
MEXICO	8,600	8,600

Sources: *The Military Balance 1997/98* and *The Military Balance 1987/88*.

NATIONS WITH BALLISTIC MISSILE SUBMARINES* IN 1997

Class name	Number in service	Year first commisioned
CHINA		
Xia	1	1987
Golf	1	1966
FRANCE		
Triomphant	4	1996
L'Inflexible M4	3	1976
RUSSIA		
Bory	1	2002†
Antyey	12	1986
Delfin	7	1985
Skat	1	1980**
Akula	6	1981
Kalmar	12	1976
Murena	5	1972
UNITED KINGDOM		
Vanguard	4	1993
UNITED STATES		
Ohio	18	1981

*Ballistic missile submarines are designed to attack enemy cities and military bases ashore. They carry long-range missiles that can strike targets from about 1,500 to 4,000 miles (2,400 to 6,400 kilometers) away.

†Projected year of commissioning

**Specific year unknown

Source: *Jane's Fighting Ships 1997-98*.

The Strategic Arms Reduction Treaty (START), signed in 1991 by the United States and the Soviet Union, and START II, signed in 1993 by the United States and Russia, mandated substantial cuts in the number of nuclear warheads and their delivery systems maintained by the two nations. After the breakup of the Soviet Union in 1991, the former Soviet republics of Belarus, Kazakstan, and Ukraine, which had inherited strategic nuclear weapons from the Soviet Union, ratified START, pledging to eliminate their nuclear stockpiles by December 2001. Besides the five declared nuclear powers, four other nations—Israel, India, North Korea, and Pakistan—were assumed by intelligence experts to possess nuclear weapons in 1997, but have never officially declared this capability.

——— NUCLEAR WEAPONS ———

NATIONS WITH STRATEGIC NUCLEAR WEAPONS IN 1997*

Declared powers

EST. NUMBER OF WARHEADS

RUSSIA	12,000
UNITED STATES	10,000
FRANCE	480
CHINA	450
UNITED KINGDOM	200

*Strategic nuclear weapons are designed to attack targets from great distances, generally 6,500 miles (10,500 kilometers) from the launch site.
Source: *The Financial Times*

STRATEGIC NUCLEAR WEAPONS IN OTHER NATIONS*

Undeclared capability	Nations Relinquishing weapons
ISRAEL	ARGENTINA
INDIA	BELARUS
NORTH KOREA	BRAZIL
PAKISTAN	KAZAKSTAN
	SOUTH AFRICA
	UKRAINE

*Strategic nuclear weapons are designed to attack targets from great distances, generally 6,500 miles (10,500 kilometers) from the launch site.
Source: *The Financial Times*

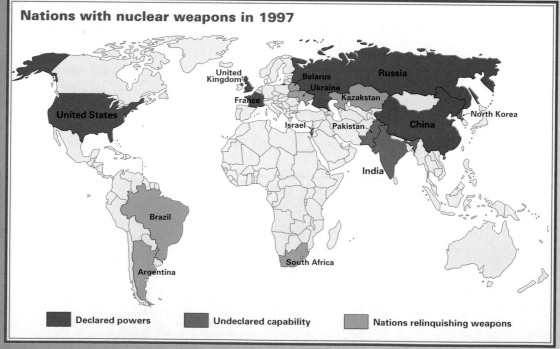

Nations with nuclear weapons in 1997

Declared powers   Undeclared capability   Nations relinquishing weapons

Source: *The Financial Times*

NUCLEAR TESTS 1945-1994

	Atmospheric	Underground	Total
UNITED STATES	215	815	1,030
USSR/RUSSIA	219	496	715
FRANCE*	50	160	210
UNITED KINGDOM	21	24	45
CHINA*	23	20	43
INDIA		1	1
		GRAND TOTAL	2,044

*France and China carried out additional tests in 1995 and 1996.
Source: Bulletin of the Atomic Scientists

NUCLEAR MISSILE SITES IN THE UNITED STATES*

NEW MEXICO	2,850
GEORGIA	2,000
WASHINGTON	1,600
NEVADA	1,450
NORTH DAKOTA	965
WYOMING	592
MISSOURI	550
TEXAS	520
LOUISIANA	455
MONTANA	455
NEBRASKA	255
CALIFORNIA	175
VIRGINIA	175
SOUTH DAKOTA	138
COLORADO	138

*Exact locations of U.S. nuclear weapons remain an official secret.
Source: Bulletin of the Atomic Scientists

United States and USSR/ Russia: Total Strategic Nuclear Warheads, 1945-1996

Source: Natural Resources Defense Council

On a global scale, military spending between 1987 and 1997 dropped sharply, except in the Middle East and other areas of regional antagonism, where military spending remained a priority.

MILITARY SPENDING

NATIONS WITH LARGEST MILITARY BUDGETS, 1994 AND 1986*

1994†		1986	
UNITED STATES	238,194**	UNITED STATES	335,048**
FRANCE	39,426	UNITED KINGDOM	42,867
UNITED KINGDOM	32,677	FRANCE	41,081
GERMANY	31,448	GERMANY	39,889
JAPAN	30,766	JAPAN	24,811
ITALY	21,380	ITALY	20,186
SAUDI ARABIA	15,633	SAUDI ARABIA	17,077
SOUTH KOREA	11,763	IRAN	15,556††
TAIWAN	10,885	CANADA	11,233
CANADA	9,430	SPAIN	8,827

*Reliable figures for some nations, including Russia, are unavailable.
†Latest available data.
**Figures in US$ million, constant 1990 dollars.
††Estimate
Source: *SIPRI Yearbook 1996*

NATIONS WITH THE LARGEST MILITARY BUDGETS AS PERCENT OF GROSS NATIONAL PRODUCT, 1994 AND 1986

1994*	Percentage	1986	Percentage
SAUDI ARABIA	10.9†	OMAN	23.8†
ISRAEL	9.5	SAUDI ARABIA	23.0
JORDAN	8.2	ISRAEL	16.9
CROATIA	7.7	SYRIA	14.4
ANGOLA	6.4**	LIBYA	12.7
MOZAMBIQUE	5.8**	JORDAN	11.5
PAKISTAN	5.7**	MOZAMBIQUE	10.2
CYPRUS	5.6	UNITED ARAB EMIRATES	8.7
ITALY	5.6	MONGOLIA	8.5
BAHRAIN	5.3**	EGYPT	7.8

*Latest available data.
†Figures in US$ million, constant 1990 dollars.
**Estimate
Source: *SIPRI Yearbook 1996*

THE WORLD'S BIGGEST ARMS EXPORTERS, 1995 AND 1991

1995*		1991	
UNITED STATES	9,894†	UNITED STATES	12,568†
USSR/RUSSIA	3,905	USSR/RUSSIA	4,657
GERMANY	1,964	GERMANY	2,520
UNITED KINGDOM	1,663	UNITED KINGDOM	1,143
CHINA	868	CHINA	1,104
FRANCE	815	FRANCE	1,071
UZBEKISTAN	464	YUGOSLAVIA	543
NETHERLANDS	448	SWITZERLAND	386
CZECH REPUBLIC	326	ITALY	346
ITALY	324	NETHERLANDS	306

*Latest available data.
†Figures in US$ million, constant 1990 dollars.
Source: *SIPRI Yearbook 1996*

THE WORLD'S BIGGEST ARMS IMPORTERS, 1995 AND 1991

1995*	
CHINA	1,696†
SOUTH KOREA	1,677
EGYPT	1,555
TURKEY	1,125
MALAYSIA	1,120
KUWAIT	1,117
TAIWAN	980
SAUDI ARABIA	961
THAILAND	888
JAPAN	799

1991	
JAPAN	2,386
INDIA	1,799
ISRAEL	1,309
EGYPT	1,234
AFGHANISTAN	1,212
SAUDI ARABIA	1,208
PORTUGAL	1,062
FRANCE	981
TURKEY	954
GERMANY	929

*Latest available data.
†Figures in US$ million, constant 1990 dollars.
Source: *SIPRI Yearbook 1996*

WORLDWIDE DEFENSE SPENDING TRENDS, 1986 AND 1994*

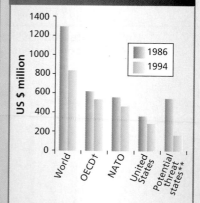

Legend: 1986, 1994
Y-axis: US $ million
X-axis: World, OECD†, NATO, United States, Potential threat states**

*Latest available data
†Organization for Economic Cooperation and Development
**Potential threat states for 1986 includes nations of the Warsaw Pact, China, Cuba, Iran, Iraq, Libya, North Korea, Syria, and Vietnam; 1994 states include Russia, Belarus, China, Cuba, Iran, Iraq, Libya, North Korea, Syria, and Vietnam.
Source: *SIPRI Yearbook 1996*

The prestige of United Nations peacekeeping missions waxed and waned with the success or failure of its many operations, but the UN in 1997 remained the world's principal instrument of maintaining peace.

UN PEACEKEEPING OPERATIONS*

Africa

Region: Western Sahara
Implemented: September 1991
Participating

Nations	Police[†]	Troops**	Observers[‡]
28	9	26	248

Nation: Liberia
Implemented: September 1993
Participating

Nations	Police	Troops	Observers
10	0	7	84

Region: Angola
Implemented: July 1997
Participating

Nations	Police	Troops	Observers
32	n/a	n/a	n/a

Asia

Nation: India (state of Jammu and Kashmir
Implemented: January 1949
Participating

Nations	Police	Troops	Observers
8	0	0	42

The Balkans

Nation: Macedonia
Implemented: March 1995
Participating

Nations	Police	Troops	Observers
27	26	1,039	35

Nation: Bosnia and Herzegovina
Implemented: December 1995
Participating

Nations	Police	Troops	Observers
34	1,579	5	0

Nation: Croatia (eastern Slavonia)
Implemented: January 1996
Participating

Nations	Police	Troops	Observers
31	408	4,749	100

Nation: Croatia (Prevlaka Peninsula)
Implemented: January 1996
Participating

Nations	Police	Troops	Observers
25	0	0	28

Caribbean

Nation: Haiti
Implemented: August 1997
Participating

Nations	Police	Troops	Observers
9	n/a	n/a	n/a

Former Soviet Union

Region: Georgia and province of Abkhazia
Implemented: August 1993
Participating

Nations	Police	Troops	Observers
23	0	0	120

Nation: Tajikistan
Implemented: December 1994
Participating

Nations	Police	Troops	Observers
8	0	0	24

Mediterranean

Nation: Cyprus
Implemented: March 1964
Participating

Nations	Police	Troops	Observers
8	35	1,162	0

Middle East

Region: Middle East
Implemented: June 1948
Participating

Nations	Police	Troops	Observers
20	0	0	169

Region: Golan Heights
Implemented: June 1974
Participating

Nations	Police	Troops	Observers
4	0	1,032	0

Region: Lebanon
Implemented: March 1978
Participating

Nations	Police	Troops	Observers
10	0	4,473	0

Persian Gulf

Region: Iraq-Kuwait border
Implemented: April 1991
Participating

Nations	Police	Troops	Observers
33	0	891	197

*As of September 1997
[†]Police are civilian peacekeeping authorities.
**Troops are military peacekeepers.
[‡]Observers are military or civilian monitors.
Source: United Nations Department of Peace-keeping Operations

Armenia. Robert Kocharyan became prime minister of Armenia in March 1997, after Armen Sarkisyan resigned due to ill health. In November 1996, Kocharyan had been elected president of the self-proclaimed Republic of Nagorno-Karabakh, an Armenian enclave claimed by neighboring Azerbaijan. Kocharyan was not a member of President Levon Ter-Petrosyan's ruling Pan-National Movement, and his appointment triggered rumors of a split within the party. In late August 1997, Kocharyan fired 24 high-ranking officials, but denied that a rift existed between him and the Movement.

Armenia signed a treaty with Russia in August that arranged closer economic and military ties. This move was denounced by Azerbaijan. In September, Ter-Petrosyan said he would consider a plan created by European mediators to end the ongoing war with Azerbaijan. Armenia had occupied a large part of Azerbaijan, including Nagorno-Karabakh, since 1993. The plan called for Armenia's withdrawal from these areas, allowing their status to be decided later.

On Sept. 25, 1997, opposition leader Vazgen Manukyan announced a new "mass resistance movement" to coordinate opposition to Ter-Petrosyan's rule. Manukyan had been defeated by Ter-Petrosyan in a disputed election in September 1996. He denounced Ter-Petrosyan's new flexibility on Nagorno-Karabakh as "treason." □ Steven L. Solnick

See also **Azerbaijan; Asia** (Facts in brief table).

Art. In 1997, devastating earthquakes in central Italy damaged the treasured artworks of the Basilica of St. Francis of Assisi. The quakes destroyed *frescoes* (wall and ceiling paintings) attributed to Giovanni Cimabue and Giotto, artists from the late 1200's and early 1300's, who are considered the principal founders of Italian Renaissance painting.

Four people investigating damage from the first quake on Sept. 26, 1997, were killed when a second quake nine hours later brought down sections of the church's vaulted ceiling covered with a fresco depicting St. Jerome and portraits of saints attributed to Giotto. A fresco of St. Matthew by Cimabue and a decorative section of starry sky were also damaged.

The earthquakes, including a third quake on October 7, also damaged the *tympanum* (a triangular architectural crown) on the north facade of the church. Before a fourth earthquake struck on October 14, authorities had placed a metal cage around the tympanum to prevent it from collapsing.

The unusual architecture of the church may have saved its most precious possession—a cycle of frescoes depicting the life of St. Francis, attributed by many art historians to Giotto. The paintings, located in the lower basilica, a separate church beneath the main church, survived the quakes. While authorities were confident that the church itself could be repaired, they were less optimistic about the frescoes, which had been reduced to a pile of rubble.

The new Guggenheim Museum in Bilbao, Spain, a city in the northern Basque region, opened in October. Designed by American architect Frank O. Gehry, the $100-million Bilbao Guggenheim is a highly abstract structure clad in titanium. The 112,000-square-foot (10,400-square-meter) exhibition space includes a boat-shaped gallery measuring more than 430 feet (130 meters) long. Hailed as the greatest museum design of the decade—the century, according to some critics—the Guggenheim opened with more than 240 works on view, including 50 new acquisitions.

The Bilbao facility was one of the latest overseas outposts of New York City's Solomon R. Guggenheim Museum. Under the directorship of Thomas Krens since 1988, the Guggenheim expanded its operations worldwide by forming partnerships with local governments to build and operate museums that display parts of the Guggenheim collection. Another branch, Deutsche Guggenheim Berlin, opened in November 1997 with "Visions of Paris: Robert Delaunay's Series," three series of paintings from the early 1900's. Deutsche Guggenheim—much smaller than the New York or Bilbao Guggenheims—is housed in Berlin's newly renovated Deutsche Bank.

The Getty Center. In December 1997, the Getty Center, designed by architect Richard Meier, opened in Los Angeles. The $1-billion complex consists of six buildings on a hilltop overlooking the city. The Center affords the J. Paul Getty Trust a high-profile headquarters for its varied operations, including a museum and a conservation institute, which were previously dispersed around Los Angeles.

In July, the Getty announced that Barry Munitz, the 56-year-old chancellor of the California State University system, was to replace Harold M. Williams as president and chief executive officer of the J. Paul Getty Trust in January 1998. The retiring Williams was responsible for shaping the trust from a single museum awash in cash in the early 1980's into a cultural powerhouse—a combination think tank, museum, and financial godfather to a number of projects.

Chinese art collection. The Metropolitan Museum of Art in New York City opened its renovated Chinese galleries in May 1997. The pride of the new galleries were 11 paintings given by the C. C. Wang Family Collection, including *The Riverbank*, a rare silk scroll from the 900's by Dong Yuan, whose landscape forms greatly influenced later Chinese artists. The expanded permanent collection, which was arranged to reflect the historical context of the work, firmly established the new galleries as one of the finest collections of Chinese art outside of China.

Ganz collection. Fifty-seven works of art from the collection of the late Victor and Sally Ganz—perhaps the most important post-World War II (after 1945) American collectors of modern and contemporary art—sold for $206.5 million at New York City's Christie's, an auction house. The sale, which brought

in a record price for a private collection, included masterpieces by Pablo Picasso as well as works by German-born sculptor Eva Hesse and American artists Jasper Johns, Frank Stella, and Robert Rauschenberg.

Major exhibitions of 1997. "Picasso: The Early Years, 1892-1906," an exhibition at the National Gallery of Art in Washington, D.C., and the Museum of Fine Arts in Boston, traced the artist's formative years from ages 11 to 25—the brink of his breakthrough into cubism, a style that depicts three-dimensional objects in terms of a structure of intersecting planes. "Exiles and Émigrés: The Flight of European Artists from Hitler" featured artists, such as Piet Mondrian from the Netherlands and Max Beckmann from Germany, who fled the Nazis in the 1930's and 1940's. The exhibit, which opened at the Los Angeles County Museum of Art and traveled to museums in Montreal and Berlin, looked at how American culture changed the work of the artists and how they influenced American art.

"Bill Viola," a traveling exhibit that opened at the Los Angeles County Museum of Art, presented a survey of the pioneering video artist. In New York City, "Robert Rauschenberg: A Retrospective" at the Solomon R. Guggenheim, the SoHo Guggenheim, and the Ace Gallery spanned the entire career of this pivotal American pop-art figure. The Phillips Collection in Washington, D.C., presented "Arthur Dove: A Retrospective Exhibition," work by the artist credited as the first American to break into abstract art. "Richard Diebenkorn," which began a four-city tour at the Whitney Museum of American Art in New York City, presented a retrospective of the San Francisco painter known for his fusion of abstract expressionist brushwork and

Giotto's frescoes, *above,* of St. Francis and St. Clair in Italy's Basilica of St. Francis of Assisi, show signs of damage from an earthquake on Sept. 26, 1997. A second quake on the same day triggered the collapse of sections of the church's ceiling, *left,* destroying works by artists Giotto and Cimabue.

the saturated color of French artist Henri Matisse.

"The Private Collection of Edgar Degas" at the Metropolitan Museum of Art brought together more than 200 paintings, drawings, and prints once owned by the French impressionist painter and sculptor. Degas had collected more than 5,000 works by artists whom he admired and whose art influenced his own work. "Stanley Spencer: An English Vision" at the Hirshhorn Museum in Washington, D.C., was the first extended view of the eccentric English realist painter who died in the early 1950's.

Trouble for Sotheby's. In February 1997, Sotheby's, an auction house based in London, began an in-house investigation after the firm was accused of smuggling foreign artwork. The investigation followed a broadcast on British television of a secretly shot film of Roeland Kollewijn, a Sotheby's painting specialist in Milan, Italy, allegedly agreeing to smuggle a painting to London. The film followed the painting as it was allegedly delivered to George Gordon, Old Masters specialist at Sotheby's in London, where the painting sold for about $12,000 in 1996.

The secret taping was arranged by Peter Watson, whose book *Sotheby's: The Inside Story* was published in 1997. Watson accused the auction house of smuggling not just Italian works, but also Asian art and antiquities. In response to the allegations, Sotheby's appointed a committee to look into "international trade issues and auction practices."

In July, Sotheby's announced that sales of Greek and Roman antiquities and Indian and Himalayan artwork were being transferred from London to New York City, and two experts in those areas had resigned from their positions in London. Sotheby's claimed that the changes were not related to the allegations of smuggling made earlier in the year.

The U.S. Department of Justice began in 1997 to investigate possible unfair trade practices and antitrust violations among U.S. art dealers. Sotheby's, Christie's, and several galleries—including PaceWildenstein, Acquavella, and Hirschl & Adler—were served subpoenas for financial documents, travel records, and other materials. At issue was the possible existence of bidding "rings." In such an arrangement, a group of dealers refrain from bidding against each other for the same object at auction in order to keep the price as low as possible. After the artwork has been resold by one of the group, the profits are then divided among the other dealers.

Deaths. Willem de Kooning, the last of the first-generation abstract expressionist painters and a pivotal figure in post-World War II American art, died at age 92 on March 19. Roy Lichtenstein, an early and highly influential pop artist known for his paintings of comic strips, died at age 73 on September 29. Roger Brown, a leading painter in the Chicago Imagist school, died at the age of 55 on November 22.

☐ Eric Gibson

See also **Architecture; Deaths.**

Asia

Many Asian countries experienced escalating financial troubles in 1997, which threatened economic growth and contributed to regional poverty. Southeast Asia was hit hard by plunging stock and currency values. In late 1997, sections of Southeast Asia were clouded in smoke from jungle fires that degraded air quality and raised health concerns in the region.

Economic decline. In the 1970's and 1980's, many Asian countries led the world in economic growth. The economies in long impoverished countries such as Taiwan and South Korea became so strong that these nations evolved into industrial leaders. This so-called "Asian miracle" of prosperity spread in the 1980's to Southeast Asia. China's economy boomed when it relaxed its Communist system, and India began to prosper as the state loosened its control of the economy.

In the early 1990's, Japan, the leading economic power in Asia, entered an economic slowdown that left many banks with unpaid loans on overvalued property. Economic stagnation continued in 1997, and a drop in industrial production and in household spending brought Japan to the brink of recession. Experts blamed the weak economy on an increase in sales taxes—from 3 to 5 percent—in April and on a decline in public investment. While these actions reduced Japan's budget deficit, the largest deficit of any major industrial nation, they also stalled growth.

China's growth. In 1997, some international economists predicted that China would have the world's largest economy by 2020, and Chinese economists estimated that it would surpass the U.S. economy by 2030. However, the benefits of China's emerging prosperity were not evenly distributed. Although new industry boosted the country's economy, many workers were paid very low salaries and lived in poverty. In 1997, China attempted to strengthen its economy by reducing high subsidies to inefficient state-owned industries. Easy access to foreign investment money helped China greatly expand its industrial capacity, resulting in a capacity far greater than the country was capable of utilizing.

Poverty in India. According to an August 1997 report released by the World Bank, an affiliate of the United Nations (UN), 35 percent of India's 975 million people subsisted on less than $1 a day. The report concluded that India's antipoverty programs were underfunded, and the administration of the programs was too expensive.

The economies of Southeast Asia teetered in 1997, stalling growth in Thailand, Indonesia, Malaysia, and the Philippines. These countries had previously lured foreign companies to the region by providing a work force willing to produce export goods

Tourists stroll along the Great Wall at Badaling, China, shopping for souvenirs in kiosks. In 1997, the massive wall, which had held the line for centuries against invaders, was overrun by the commercialism sweeping through China.

for low pay. As industry grew in these nations, basic infrastructure, such as municipal services, roads, and electricity, failed to keep up with the increasing needs of the business community. Production rates of workers in much of Southeast Asia lagged behind wage increases. As a result, production costs in these countries increased. Foreign investors began looking elsewhere for cheap workers and moved factories to such places as Vietnam and China. In Southeast Asia, only Singapore continued to attract industry in 1997 by providing advanced methods of production.

Most Southeast Asian countries continued to attract foreign investment but used it to finance non-productive assets, such as luxury housing—much of which sat empty. This resulted in a decline in foreign-trade earnings, which in turn resulted in the inability to repay foreign loans. As investors began to lose confidence in the economies of many Southeast Asian countries, values of regional currencies plunged.

Monetary values for Thailand's currency dropped more than 33 percent in the first nine months of 1997, while its stock market fell 53 percent. Malaysia's currency fell almost by 33 percent, and its stock market plunged 52 percent. Indonesia's currency fell 32 percent, and its stock market fell 41.6 percent. Singapore's currency also dipped in value, and South

Facts in brief on Asian countries

Country	Population	Government	Monetary unit*	Foreign trade (million U.S.$)	
				Exports†	Imports†
Afghanistan	23,731,000	No functioning government	afghani (4,750.00 = $1)	188	616
Armenia	3,726,000	President Levon Ter-Petrossian	dram (486.34 = $1)	248	661
Australia	18,758,000	Governor General William Deane; Prime Minister John Howard	dollar (1.41 = $1)	60,536	65,428
Azerbaijan	7,801,000	President Heydar A. Aliyev	manat (3,950.00 = $1)	631	961
Bangladesh	128,558,000	President Shahabuddin Ahmed; Prime Minister Sheikh Hasina Wajed	taka (44.55 = $1)	3,297	6,615
Bhutan	1,756,000	King Jigme Singye Wangchuck	ngultrum (36.23 = $1)	71	114
Brunei	300,000	Sultan Sir Hassanal Bolkiah	dollar (1.58 = $1)	2,296	1,695
Burma (Myanmar)	49,447,000	Prime Minister, State Peace and Development Council Chairman Than Shwe	kyat (6.25 = $1)	691	1,361
Cambodia (Kampuchea)	11,052,000	King Norodom Sihanouk; Prime Minister Ung Huot; Prime Minister Hun Sen	riel (3,000.00 = $1)	241	631
China	1,264,774,000	Communist Party General Secretary and President Jiang Zemin; Premier Li Peng	yuan (8.28 = $1)	151,197	138,944
Georgia	5,500,000	President Eduard Shevardnadze	lari (not available)	140	250
India	986,026,000	President Kircheril Raman Narayanan; Prime Minister Inder Kumar Gujral**	rupee (36.23 = $1)	33,057	37,378
Indonesia	206,491,000	President Suharto; Vice President Try Sutrisno	rupiah (3,605.00 = $1)	49,814	42,929
Iran	71,569,000	Leader of the Islamic Revolution Ali Hoseini-Khamenei; President Mohammad Khatami-Ardakani	rial (3,000.00 = $1)	16,000	13,000
Japan	125,922,000	Emperor Akihito; Prime Minister Ryutaro Hashimoto	yen (121.62 = $1)	410,924	349,173
Kazakstan	17,457,000	President Nursultan Nazarbayev	tenge (76.66 = $1)	6,230	4,261
Korea, North	25,121,000	Korean Workers' Party General Secretary Kim Chong-il	won (2.20 = $1)	840	1,270
Korea, South	46,262,000	President Kim Yong-sam; Prime Minister Ko Kon	won (929.85 = $1)	130,346	150,676
Kyrgyzstan	4,960,000	President Askar Akayev	som (12.10 = $1)	380	439

Korea and Hong Kong experienced irregularities in the values of their currencies.

Regional economies. In 1997, Malaysian Prime Minister Mahathir bin Mohamad accused international currency speculators of wanting "to destroy weak countries" by driving down the value of their currencies. His efforts to insulate the Malaysian economy backfired, however, amid policy disputes within his government and criticism from international bankers and economists. Bankers worried that Mahathir helped destabilize the region's financial markets. The World Bank called for higher standards of banking supervision and clearer accounting methods.

Thailand in 1997 stopped its practice of boosting

the value of its currency at the expense of depleting its foreign-exchange reserves. Thailand sought help from the International Monetary Fund (IMF), a UN agency that promotes economic growth by providing short-term credit to member nations. IMF terms typically require countries to reduce government economic controls, cut deficits and subsidies, and open markets to world trade, thus allowing for a more competitive marketplace.

The IMF also agreed to help the Philippines and Indonesia. All three countries reduced large infrastructure investments on projects such as dams and power plants, which would have increased debts without producing income quickly. The countries

Country	Population	Government	Monetary unit*	Foreign trade (million U.S.$)	
				Exports†	Imports†
Laos	5,296,000	President Nouhak Phoumsavan; Prime Minister Khamtai Siphandon	kip (1,310.00 = $1)	348	587
Malaysia	21,398,000	Paramount Ruler Tuanku Ja'afar Ibni Al-Marhum Tuanku Abdul Rahman; Prime Minister Mahathir bin Mohamad	ringgit (3.39 = $1)	78,258	78,429
Maldives	269,000	President Maumoon Abdul Gayoom	rufiyaa (11.77 = $1)	59	302
Mongolia	2,556,000	President Natsagiun Bagabandi; Prime Minister Mendsaikhan Enkhsaikhan	tugrik (800.32 = $1)	423	438
Nepal	23,603,000	King Birendra Bir Bikram Shah Dev; Prime Minister Lokendra Bahadur Chand	rupee (56.95 = $1)	349	1,378
New Zealand	3,683,000	Governor General Sir Michael Hardie-Boys; Prime Minister Jennifer Shipley	dollar (1.60 = $1)	14,442	14,725
Pakistan	152,766,000	President Farooq Leghari;†† Prime Minister Nanaz Sharif	rupee (44.01 = $1)	9,321	12,131
Papua New Guinea	4,596,000	Governor General Wiwa Korowi; Prime Minister William Skate	kina (1.47 = $1)	2,650	1,452
Philippines	71,654,000	President Fidel Ramos	peso (35.25 = $1)	20,417	34,122
Russia	146,120,000	President Boris Yeltsin	ruble (5,888.50 = $1)	88,703	61,147
Singapore	2,919,000	President Ong Teng Cheong; Prime Minister Goh Chok Tong	dollar (1.58 = $1)	125,059	131,340
Sri Lanka	19,034,000	President Chandrika Kumaratunga; Prime Minister Sirimavo Bandaranaike	rupee (59.88 = $1)	4,095	5,412
Taiwan	22,106,000	President Li Teng-hui; Vice President Lien Chan	dollar (30.37 = $1)	93,000	85,100
Tajikistan	6,603,000	President Emomali Rahmonov; National Assembly Chairman Safarali Rajabov	ruble (400.00 = $1)	769	656
Thailand	60,626,000	King Phumiphon Adunyadet; Prime Minister Chuan Leekpai	baht (38.55= $1)	56,191	73,426
Turkmenistan	4,361,000	President Saparmurat Niyazov	manat (not available)	1,939	777
Uzbekistan	24,320,000	President Islam Karimov	sum (57.90 = $1)	4,590	4,721
Vietnam	79,247,000	Communist Party General Secretary Do Muoi; President Le Duc Anh; Prime Minister Vo Van Kiet	dong (12,297.00 = $1)	5,200	7,500

*Exchange rates as of Oct. 24, 1997, or latest available data.   †Latest available data.   **Resigned November 28.   ††Resigned December 2.

also postponed investments in other vital projects, such as creating public transport systems.

Interest rates rose in Southeast Asia in 1997 as foreign businesses pulled investment capital from the region. Higher interest rates made it harder for domestic businesses to operate. Rising rates also resulted in slowed economic growth, increased unemployment, and greater social tensions.

Forest fires in July burned out of control in jungles of four major Indonesian islands—Sumatra, Kalimantan, Sulawesi, and Irian Jaya. By September, when an estimated 3,000 square miles (7,770 square kilometers) of jungle were on fire, smoke stretched some 2,000 miles (3,200 kilometers) across parts of six nations—Brunei, Indonesia, Malaysia, the Philippines, Singapore, and Thailand. It was the fifth and worst outbreak of Indonesian fires in 15 years.

Corporations deliberately set jungle fires to clear land for farms used to grow trees for palm oil, rubber, or pulp wood. Indonesia outlawed commercial burning in 1995, after the region suffered smog problems. The law, however, was rarely enforced. In 1997, fires were made even worse by a weather phenomenon known as El Niño, which caused drought in the region.

Smoke from the fires, combined with industrial emissions and car exhausts, created severe smog over large metropolitan areas, such as Singapore and Kuala Lumpur, Malaysia. An Indonesian official estimated that 20 million Indonesians suffered respiratory problems as a result of the smog. Medical experts predicted that the breathing of these pollutants inflicted long-term health damage on thousands of people.

On September 26, the crash of an Indonesian airliner on Sumatra, which killed all 234 people aboard, was blamed on the smoke. Authorities later suggested that the crash may have resulted from miscommunication between the pilot and air traffic control.

Malaysia sent 2,000 firefighters to the Indonesian jungles to aid in dousing the fires. Many other nations also sent firefighters. By early October, the fires were reduced through the efforts of firefighters and the onset of the rainy season.

Several nations criticized Indonesia for initially calling the haze a natural disaster. Officials in Southeast Asia charged that the companies participating in setting the fires had pressured Indonesia into not enforcing its law against burning.

Massive cities. In April, the Asian Development Bank, a UN affiliate, predicted that by 2025 Asia would have 20 cities with populations exceeding 10 million people. In 1997, only nine Asian cities—Beijing, Bombay, Calcutta, Jakarta, Osaka, Seoul, Shanghai, Tianjin, and Tokyo—had populations exceeding 10 million. The bank expected the populations of Bangkok, Dhaka, Karachi, Manila, Bangalore, Hyderabad, Lahore, Madras, New Delhi, and Shenyang to skyrocket by the year 2025. The bank reported that

environmental conditions were worsening in the cities, and an annual investment of between $20 and $40 billion would be needed by 2007 to sustain productivity and improve the quality of urban life.

Territorial disputes flared in 1997 between Japan, China, and Taiwan. On May 6, a right-wing member of Japan's largest opposition political party planted a Japanese flag on an island claimed by all three countries. The island, situated in a chain of uninhabited rocks 125 miles (200 kilometers) northeast of Taiwan, was called the Diaoyu Island by China and the Senkakus by Japan. On May 26, the Japanese coast guard blocked all Taiwanese and Chinese attempts to reach the island.

On March 7, Vietnamese officials criticized China for positioning an oil exploration rig 75 miles (120 kilometers) off Vietnam's central coast, an area they claimed was inside their exclusive economic zone.

The Association of Southeast Asian Nations (ASEAN) in 1997 neared its goal of including all 10 regional countries in its membership. Created in 1967 as a bulwark against Communism, ASEAN emphasized cooperation between member nations. On July 23, 1997, ASEAN admitted Burma and Laos to its membership, which included Brunei, Indonesia, Malaysia, the Philippines, Singapore, Thailand, and Vietnam. A 1997 *coup* (government overthrow) in Cambodia delayed its membership in ASEAN.

Singapore held parliamentary elections on Jan. 2, 1997. The People's Action Party, which had ruled the island state since its creation in 1965, won 65 percent of the vote and took 81 out of 83 seats in the Singapore Parliament.

Mongolia. Nachagyn Bagabandy was elected president on May 18, 1997, winning 61 percent of the vote. President Punsalmaagiyn Ochirbat received only 30 percent of the vote. Bagabandy represented the Mongolian People's Revolutionary Party, the former Communist party that had ruled Mongolia until 1996. Ochirbat's Democratic Union coalition continued to hold control of the parliament and government after the May 1997 elections.

Nepal failed in 1997 to establish a stable government as minority parties maneuvered for power. Prime Minister Sher Bahadur Deuba lost a confidence vote in parliament on March 6 and resigned. He was succeeded by Lokendra Bahadur Chand, whose small, right-wing parliamentary faction had been part of Deuba's coalition. Chand's faction then teamed up with the Communist party, the largest in parliament, to oust Deuba. The foreign minister in Chand's cabinet, Prakash Chandra Lohani, resigned on June 10, charging the Communists with "widespread rigging and intimidation" in local elections. Chand resigned October 4 after losing a confidence motion introduced by the main opposition party, and Surya Bahadur Thapa became prime minister on October 6. ☐ Henry S. Bradsher

See also the various Asian country articles.

Astronomy.

In 1997, an unusually bright comet lit the spring sky. Astronomers received a flood of data from spacecraft exploring Jupiter and Mars and discovered a new galaxy. Telescopes in space revealed a huge fountain of antimatter and showed, for the first time, the sources of mysterious bursts of gamma rays observed in past decades.

Water on a Jovian moon? In February 1997, the Galileo spacecraft, which has orbited Jupiter and its satellites since 1995, photographed what appeared to be a layer of ice covering Europa, one of Jupiter's four largest moons. The images, made during Galileo's closest approach to Europa—a distance of 360 miles (580 kilometers)—strongly reinforced astronomers' suspicion that an ocean of liquid water or slush may lie beneath the icy layer. The pictures showed broken pieces of what appeared to be ice, resembling the icebergs in Earth's polar seas, and what looked like frozen outflows of water that may have erupted, like geysers, from a source of liquid water underneath. Scientists conjectured that Europa's interior may be warmed by gravitational stresses caused by Jupiter and Jupiter's other satellites, making the interior warm enough for liquid water to exist—a condition necessary for life. To explore this possibility, Galileo's mission, originally scheduled to end Dec. 7, 1997, was extended to the end of 1999 to allow for more Europa fly-bys.

A mysterious gamma-ray burst was observed for a long enough period in February 1997 for astronomers to catch a glimpse of its source. Such bursts of intense radiation were first spotted by U.S. spy satellites. But the bursts had occurred so randomly and disappeared so quickly—in some cases in $\frac{1}{100}$ of a second—that astronomers had been unable to measure the direction of incoming bursts or to photograph one. Using the Italian-Dutch BeppoSAX satellite, astronomers spotted the burst and, hours later, a fading X-ray source that may have been the burst as it cooled. Astronomers on the Canary Islands took the first images, and cameras on the Hubble Space Telescope photographed the burst for a month thereafter. However, the source remained unclear. Some astronomers detected movement in the source of the February burst—a sign that the source may lie in the Milky Way. But observations of another gamma-ray burst, caught in May, indicated that the burst was located billions of *light-years* (the distance light travels in a year, about 5.9 trillion miles [9.5 trillion kilometers]) beyond the Milky Way.

Hale-Bopp, the brightest comet observed in almost 30 years, made its closest approach to both the sun and the Earth on April 1, 1997. Discovered by amateur astronomers Alan Hale and Thomas Bopp in 1995, the comet was visible in many areas of the United States, even to the naked eye. Hale-Bopp was not only brighter than most comets, it was also larger. Astronomers estimated that its nucleus was approximately 25 miles (40 kilometers) wide, while most comets' nuclei typically measured 6 miles (10 kilometers) wide. Hale-Bopp was also unique for its three tails. While most comets have a dust tail and a tail made of *ions* (electrically charged atoms or molecules), Hale-Bopp had a third tail of sodium atoms as well.

A fountain of antimatter near the center of the Milky Way Galaxy was discovered by astrophysicists in April 1997. Antimatter, which is identical to ordinary matter but opposite in electrical charge, becomes visible when it collides with regular matter, producing energy that can be detected as gamma rays. Scientists used the National Atmospheric and Space Agency's Compton Gamma Ray Observatory satellite to map the high-energy radiation from the Milky Way. The cloud of antimatter stretched as far as 3,000 light-years above the center of the galaxy. Some researchers speculated that the antimatter may have been released by exploding stars called supernovae, while others proposed that the source may have been a black hole.

The Mars Pathfinder spacecraft landed on Mars on July 4, 1997, after a seven-month journey from Earth. Pathfinder released Mars Sojourner Rover, a small robotic vehicle, which photographed the Martian surface and analyzed rocks and soil under the direction of scientists on Earth. Data from Sojourner showed that the landing site may have lain in the path of floodwaters that, hundreds of millions of years ago, scoured the area and littered it with debris. The high quartz content of one of the Martian rocks indicated that Mars may have been more molten shortly after it formed than most astronomers had thought.

In September, the Global Surveyor went into orbit around Mars, beginning a long-term, highly detailed mapping project of the planet's surface. Measurements by Surveyor revealed a patchy Martian magnetic field. The field appeared to emanate from scattered magnetic hot spots.

The most distant galaxy ever seen was reported by astronomers in August 1997. Using the Hubble Space Telescope and the Keck Telescope in Hawaii, astronomers found a galaxy that they estimated to be some 13 billion light-years from Earth. Many astronomers believe that the universe is about 14 billion years old. Therefore, since light from the galaxy took 13 billion years to reach Earth, astronomers were able to view the galaxy as it appeared shortly after the big bang, the theoretical cosmic explosion in which the universe may have originated.

The brightest star ever seen in the Milky Way was photographed in September 1997 by astronomers using the Hubble Space Telescope. Dubbed Pistol Star for the shape of its *nebula* (surrounding cloud of gas and dust), the star was estimated to be about 25,000 light-years from Earth and to be 10 million times as bright as the sun.   □ Laurence A. Marschall

See also **Space exploration.**

Bright, compact regions of star formation stand out in an image of the most distant galaxy yet discovered. Astronomers reported in August that they had found the galaxy, which lies about 13 billion *light-years* (the distance light travels in a year) from Earth, from photographs taken from the Hubble Space Telescope.

Astronomers in 1997 observed the most distant galaxy, the brightest star, one of the brightest comets in 30 years, and the surfaces of Mars and the satellites of Jupiter. They also saw the birth of new stars in a galactic collision.

Astronomy 1997

The Pathfinder spacecraft rests on the surface of Mars after a perfect landing on July 4, 1997. Pathfinder released Mars Sojourner Rover, a small roving robot that analyzed the soil and rocks found on Mars, and then relayed the findings back to scientists on Earth.

Hale-Bopp, the brightest comet observed in almost 30 years, illuminates the sky above Stonehenge, an ancient monument in southwestern England, on March 28, 1997. Hale-Bopp made its closest approach to both the sun and Earth on April 1.

Astronomers believe the ice-like ridges, hills, and domes crisscrossing the crust of Jupiter's moon Europa, photographed on Feb. 20, 1997, by Galileo spacecraft, may suggest the existence of water.

Astronomy
continued

A Hubble Space Telescope image of the colliding Antennae galaxies, released in October 1997, allows astronomers to view the orange and yellow galactic centers and to observe new stars forming in the areas of blue light. An older, black-and-white photo taken with a ground-based telescope, *above left,* offers no such detail.

The brightest star yet discovered in the Milky Way shines at the center of a Hubble Space Telescope image taken in September 1997. Astronomers estimate that the star, dubbed the Pistol Star because of the shape of the *nebula* (gas cloud) surrounding it, may be 100 times more massive than the sun.

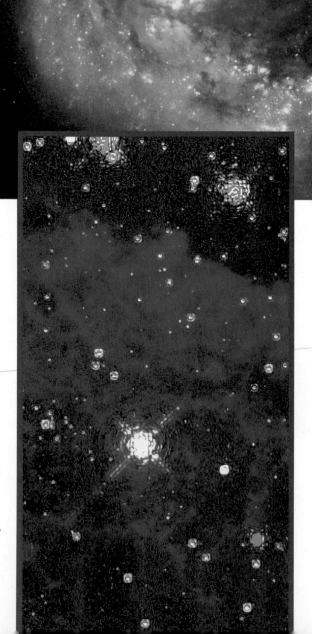

Australia. The economy of Australia grew in 1997 for the sixth year in a row, enjoying a growth rate of 3.2 percent coupled with the lowest inflation rate in the industrialized world—1.7 percent in the quarter ending in June. The unemployment rate, however, remained stubbornly high, at approximately 8.5 percent throughout 1997. Repeated cuts in interest rates since mid-1996 had failed to create jobs. In February 1997, Prime Minister John Howard announced a jobs program for people 18 to 24 years old, after being criticized for an unemployment rate that ran as high as 28 percent among youth.

Travel expenses scandal. Three federal ministers and two members of Howard's staff resigned in September following allegations that they had falsely claimed thousands of dollars worth of travel expenses. Observers called the scandal—known as the "Travel Rorts Affair" (*rort* is Australian slang for a dishonest scheme)—one of the most serious ever faced by an Australian prime minister. The scandal also spread to the Senate, where the deputy president and a member of the opposition were forced to resign.

A poll taken in September indicated that the travel expenses scandal had adversely affected Howard's popularity. Only 36 percent of the Australians polled expressed satisfaction with his performance as prime minister.

Constitutional convention. In August, the Senate approved convening a constitutional convention in February 1998 to debate whether Australia should remain a commonwealth of Great Britain or become an independent republic. In November 1997, the Australian citizens chose half of the 152 convention delegates. The other delegates were appointed by the government. A 1997 poll indicated that 54 percent of Australians favored the establishment of a republic, while 30 percent favored retaining the British monarch as Australia's head of state.

Industrial relations. The Workplace Relations Act went into effect in January 1997, causing considerable discontent among many Australian workers. The act reduced the power of unions, making it easier for employers to dismiss employees and enabling employers to reach nonunion agreements containing no-strike clauses directly with individual workers. The government claimed that the act was vital to update rigid and cumbersome industrial laws. Unions, which staged a number of strikes across Australia to protest the act, maintained that it would adversely affect working conditions.

Gold price crisis. The Reserve Bank, Australia's central bank, triggered a worldwide slump in gold prices when it revealed in July that it had secretly sold two-thirds of Australia's gold stocks during the previous six months. The bank announced that it could no longer justify maintaining 20 percent of its official reserve assets in gold when Australia had huge reserves of unmined gold.

Offensive comments leaked. In July, Australia's relations with its South Pacific neighbors were damaged when Australian government papers were accidentally leaked to the press at a summit of South Pacific economic ministers. The papers described a number of South Pacific political leaders and government officials as incompetent, drunk, vain, or corrupt and described certain South Pacific neighboring states as teetering on bankruptcy. Observers said the incident entrenched perceptions of Australia as a patronizing "big brother" to its smaller neighbors, including Fiji, Tonga, Papua New Guinea, and Samoa.

In August, Australian Foreign Minister Alexander Downer visited several South Pacific nations and attempted to heal relations with the message that the leaked papers did not reflect official policies of the Australian government.

New political party. Pauline Hanson, a controversial independent member of parliament, founded a new political party—the One Nation Party—in April. Hanson had been elected in 1996 after a campaign in which she called for a halt to immigration, declaring that Australia was "in danger of being swamped by Asians." Meetings to establish One Nation branches around the country in 1997 encountered demonstrations, many of which became violent. Polls indicated that between 5 and 9 percent of Australian voters supported One Nation in 1997. Critics blamed Hanson for the reduction in the number of Asian students enrolling in Australian universities in 1997.

Aborigines. A government report issued in May disclosed that from 1910 to 1970, 10 to 33 percent of the children of *Aborigines* (native Australians) had been forcibly removed from their parents. According to the report, most of the children had been placed with white adoptive parents or in children's homes under a policy that aimed to assimilate Aborigines into white society. The report recommended that the Australian government offer financial compensation to Aborigines affected by the policy.

Prime Minister Howard, however, ruled out government compensation and blocked parliamentary attempts at issuing a formal apology. He said that Australians should not have to "accept guilt and blame for past actions over which they had no control." Howard did express his "deep personal sorrow" to Aborigines.

By June 1997, more than 1,500 Aboriginal people had begun to sue state governments over the distress caused by the past removal of children from their families. However, the Australian High Court in late July ruled that the law that had allowed Aborigines to be separated from their families in the Northern Territory had been valid and had not, as the May report claimed, authorized *genocide* (the extermination of a culture or racial group). The court decided that Aborigines had no direct entitlement to compensation, even if their constitutional rights had been violated.

Land claims. In May 1997, Prime Minister Howard proposed a plan that would allow Australian farmers to continue agricultural activities on land claimed by Aborigines. The plan would also require Aborigines to face strict tests for registering land claims. Howard's plan responded to the concerns of farmers who feared that a 1996 High Court ruling would allow Aborigines to lay claim to land that farmers had leased from the government.

On Dec. 23, 1996, the High Court had ruled that pastoral land leases held by white farmers did not necessarily prevent Aborigines from making claims on the land. The court ruled that white and Aboriginal claims could coexist where they did not directly conflict. The case heard by the court involved land in northern Queensland claimed by the Wik and Thayorre Aborigines. Howard's plan was designed to give Australian farmers security while stopping short of extinguishing native claims.

Euthanasia. The Northern Territory's Rights of the Terminally Ill Act, the first act legalizing *euthanasia* (mercy killing), was overturned by legislation passed by the Australian Senate in March 1997. The law had gone into effect in July 1996. Following the Senate action, Northern Territory officials announced that they would fight for the right to retain the law by taking the case to the High Court. Polls indicated that 70 percent of Australians favored legal euthanasia.

Guns banned. The possession of automatic weapons in Australia became illegal on Sept. 30, 1997, and punishable by fines of up to $5,500 or jail terms of as long as 10 years. (All monetary figures are in Australian dollars.) Gun owners had surrendered more than 600,000 weapons to the government in a "buy back" scheme instituted after 35 people were killed by a gunman with an automatic rifle in Tasmania in 1996.

Cyclone Justin killed two people and caused as much as $200 million in damage when it hit the coast of northern Queensland in March 1997. The banana industry reported that 50 to 60 percent of its crop had been damaged, at a loss of $130 million. The sugar industry lost $50 million due to the cyclone, representing a 10 percent drop in yield.

2000 Olympics. In May, the Sydney Organising Committee for the Olympic Games (SOCOG) estimated that the cost of staging the Summer Olympics in Sydney in the year 2000 would be $5.5 billion—far greater than the committee had previously predicted. However, SOCOG announced in September that plans for the games were ahead of schedule. The main stadium was expected to be completed in July 1999, and all venues were to be finished by the end of 1999.   □ Lucinda Duckett

See also **Asia** (Facts in brief table).

Austria. Chancellor Franz Vranitzky, Austria's long-serving leader, announced his immediate resignation on Jan. 18, 1997. Vranitzky's announcement followed growing dissent within his Social Democratic Party over the Social Democrats' poor showing in an October 1996 election for the European Parliament. The October election had marked the first time that the party had received less than 30 percent of the vote in a nationwide election.

Vranitzky had been chancellor since 1986 and had helped steer Austria into the European Union (EU), an organization of 15 Western European countries, in 1995. During his tenure, however, support for the country's two major political parties—the Social Democratic Party and the People's Party—eroded, and the right-wing, anti-immigrant Freedom Party rose in popularity.

The new chancellor, Social Democrat Viktor Klima, whom Vranitzky named as his successor on Jan. 19, 1997, had served as finance minister under Vranitzky. As chancellor, Klima maintained the governing coalition backed by the Social Democrats and the People's Party and continued to pursue a package of budget reductions begun in 1996. The package was designed to reduce the deficit by $9.7 billion to qualify Austria for participation in a single European currency due to be launched by the EU in 1999. The government froze spending levels in April 1997 for the remainder of the year to ensure that the deficit target was achieved.

The budget cutbacks restrained the country's economy. The European Commission, the administrative arm of the EU, forecast in October 1997 that Austrian gross domestic product would grow by 1.9 percent in 1997, up from 1.6 percent in 1996 but below the average rate for European countries. The commission projected that the deficit would decline to 2.8 percent, meeting the requirement for joining the single currency.

Privatizations. The ruling coalition agreed on Jan. 12, 1997, to sell the government's 70-percent stake in Creditanstalt Bankverein AG, the country's second-largest bank, to Bank Austria AG, the largest bank, for $1.55 billion. Attempts to sell the bank, which had been founded by the Rothschild family in the 1850's, had stirred political controversy since 1990 because of the close ties between Austria's political parties and its major companies. Creditanstalt was closely allied with the People's Party, as Bank Austria was with the Social Democrats. As part of the sale, the Social-Democrat-controlled city of Vienna agreed to reduce its ownership of Bank Austria from 45 percent to less than 25 percent within five years. The government also sold its 44-percent stake in the tobacco company Austria Tabakwerke AG for $402 million on Oct. 30, 1997. The sale was one of a series of privatizations of state-owned companies.   □ Tom Buerkle

See also **Europe** (Facts in brief table).

Automobile sales in 1997 remained nearly constant with sales in 1996. According to *Ward's Automotive Reports,* domestic and foreign cars and light-trucks sales in the United States totaled 11,505,568 units by Sept. 30, 1997, a slight decrease compared with 11,582,394 total sales in the first nine months of 1996. Throughout 1997, motorists opted for light trucks over cars, triggering competition among automakers. The increased competition forced automakers to delay price increases.

Foreign automakers gain ground. One sign of the stiffer competition in 1997 was a shift in the U.S. market share of sales of automobiles. Foreign automakers gained U.S. market share at the expense of General Motors Corporation (GM) and Chrysler Corporation, while Ford Motor Company held its own. The Big Three took 71.4 percent of the car market through the first nine months of 1997, a drop from 72.8 percent during the first nine months of 1996.

Asian automakers had captured 24.8 percent of the American market by the end of September 1997, compared with 23.7 percent for the same period in 1996, and Toyota and Honda car models experienced exceptionally strong sales in 1997. Analysts believed Honda and Toyota succeeded because they produced vehicles that the American market found appealing and because a weaker yen in relation to a stronger dollar lowered prices on imports.

European automakers also increased sales in the United States, gaining 3.8 percent of the U.S. market by Sept. 30, 1997, compared with 3.4 percent for the same nine-month period in 1996.

Top sellers. The Toyota Camry was the best-selling automobile in the United States in 1997. By September 30, Camry sales had reached a total of 301,346 units. The Honda Accord ranked second, with sales of 268,049 units. Sales of both cars outdistanced the Ford Taurus, which sold 261,863 units in the first nine months of 1997. Mercedes-Benz U.S. sales increased to 79,943 vehicles by Sept. 30, 1997, a 21 percent increase over the same period in 1996.

Big Three. Labor difficulties hit GM and Chrysler in 1997, with strikes costing the two automakers nearly $1 billion in profits. Although the Big Three had settled national contracts with the United Auto Workers union in 1996, the companies bargained plant-by-plant agreements with the local unions in 1997. The strikes generally centered on company proposals to shift work from union plants to outside companies and union requests for added workers.

A 29-day strike at a Chrysler engine plant in Detroit, which ended May 8, caused the shut-down of seven assembly plants and cut vehicle shipments. The strike cost Chrysler more than $438 million. Through the first nine months of 1997, Chrysler had a market share of 15.2 percent, a drop from the 16.3-percent share it had held during the first nine months of 1996. By Sept. 30, 1997, Chrysler's net income was

$1.9 billion, compared with $2.7 billion for the same period during 1996.

At GM, disputes with union workers led to several local strikes that cost the number-one automaker more than $490 million. General Motors reported that the walkouts hurt production and kept the company from improving its market share. Through September, the GM market share was 31.1 percent, slightly lower than its 31.6-percent share in 1996. Analysts predicted that in 1998 GM would benefit from new models introduced in 1997 as well as from additional models planned for 1998. In September 1997, the automaker reported a nine-month net earnings of $5 billion, compared with $4.2 billion for the same period in 1996.

Ford settled local contracts without strikes and reaped profits from new vehicles introduced in 1996 and 1997. Sales of the Ford Expedition, a large sport utility vehicle, reached 156,052 units by the end of September. Ford's F-series pickup truck remained the nation's most popular vehicle, with sales of 536,968 units through September. These successes helped Ford capture a market share of 25.1 percent, a minor increase over the 25-percent market share Ford held in the first nine months of 1996. Successful sales also helped propel Ford's net income to $5.1 billion by September 1997, compared with $3.2 billion for the same period in 1996.

On March 17, 1997, Ford announced it would cease production of the Thunderbird after 43 years because of slow sales. Ford officials hinted that the automaker might introduce a redesigned Thunderbird after the turn of the century.

Light-truck sales increase. Americans continued their fondness for light trucks, particularly sport-utility vehicles, in 1997. Sales for such models as the Ford Explorer, Chevrolet Suburban, and Jeep Cherokee rose to 1,761,198 units by the end of September. Sales increased by 14 percent over the same nine-month period in 1996. Throughout 1997, both domestic and foreign automakers strived to design light trucks and sport-utility vehicles that would meet the needs of a variety of motorists.

New vehicles. Automakers unveiled several new 1998 models in the fall of 1997. Chrysler introduced the new Dodge Durango, aimed at buyers wanting something larger than the standard medium-sized sport-utility vehicle. The Durango featured a standard 6-cylinder, 175-horsepower engine, though a larger V8 engine was an option.

Mercedes-Benz introduced the new Mercedes M-Class sport utility vehicle. In May 1997, the German automaker rolled its first sport-utility vehicle off an assembly line at a new plant in Alabama.

Ford introduced the 4-wheel-drive Lincoln Navigator to attract motorists wanting a luxury sport-utility vehicle. The design of the Navigator was closely based on the Ford Expedition.

GM pursued luxury sales with a redesigned Cadil-

The 1998 Corvette, *left*, the first new Corvette from Chevrolet in 13 years, features a redesigned engine and chassis. Some industry critics hailed the new Corvette as an almost perfect car.

F O C U S

A renewed interest in sports cars resulted in the redesign and upgrading of old favorites as well as new models in 1997.

Automobiles 1997

O N

The Mercedes-Benz SLK, *above,* a popular new model with both industry critics and motorists, includes a 4-cylinder, 185-horsepower engine. The roof—metal but convertible—folds into the trunk, emulating a similar feature of Ford products of the late 1950's. The 1997 Boxster, *left,* the first new Porsche in 19 years, offers a 6-cylinder, 201-horsepower engine.

lac Seville. The Seville's engine came in both 275-horsepower and 300-horsepower versions. In 1997, GM attempted to increase sales of the luxury car in Europe and Asia to compensate for the dwindling market for luxury cars in the United States.

In 1997, Honda showcased its new 1998 Accord, which featured a redesigned body. The Accord, which had sold well through the 1990's, was offered with either a 2.3-liter, 4-cylinder engine or a more powerful 3.0-liter, V6 engine.

Airbags. A major car safety controversy centered in 1997 on the use of airbags. Although air-bags had saved approximately 2,600 lives in the United States between 1990 and 1997, they were blamed for the deaths of approximately 85 adults and children be-

tween 1991 and 1997. Most victims were killed in low-speed accidents by the force of the airbag inflation.

In response to the concern, federal safety regulators on Nov. 18, 1997, announced that some consumers, beginning in January 1998, would be able to purchase on-off switches to temporarily deactivate airbags. Motorists eligible for the switches would include people with medical conditions that place them at high risk from an airbag deployment and people who could not avoid placing rear-facing infant car seats in the front passenger seat. Consumers had to obtain permission from the National Highway Traffic Safety Administration to have switches installed in a vehicle. ☐ Mike Casey

See also **Transportation.**

Automobile racing. Controversy continued to plague Indy-car racing in 1997, with the Indy Racing League (IRL) and Championship Auto Racing Teams (CART) still competing as rival entities. In 1997, Jeff Gordon and Jacques Villeneuve both achieved repeated successes. In March, John Nemecheck, the 27-year-old brother of Winston Cup driver Joe Nemecheck, became the first fatality of the three-year Craftsman Truck Series. Nemechek hit the wall on the 144th lap of the Florida Dodge Dealers 400 in Miami. He died a few days later.

The IRL dropped a controversial rule that had guaranteed 25 of the 33 starting positions in the Indianapolis 500 to regular drivers on the IRL circuit. To avoid the embarrassing situation of having to bump Lyn St. James and Johnny Unser—who had managed higher qualifying speeds than seven of the designated starters—officials expanded the field to 35 cars. This change was to become permanent beginning in 1998.

But CART and IRL remained divided by an IRL provision requiring all teams to use chassis and engines built by league suppliers, an expensive option that effectively prevented CART teams from returning to the Indy 500. CART also opposed the IRL ban against turbocharged engines, a rule that produced much slower qualifying times at the 1997 Indianapolis 500. Only two drivers exceeded 213 miles (343 kilometers) per hour in qualifying rounds.

The 81st Indianapolis 500 was rained out on Sunday, May 25, and again the next day, although the drivers managed 15 laps before the second rainout call. A crash reduced the starting field to 29 cars on May 27, when the race finally was won by Arie Luyendyk, a Dutchman from Scottsdale, Arizona. In his second Indy victory since 1990, Luyendyk took home a record $1,553,650 in prize money. Canadian Scott Goodyear, Luyendyk's hard-luck teammate, came in second by 0.57 of a second, because a race official inadvertently had left the caution light on through half of the final lap.

CART. The 17-event CART season ran from March through September and included races in Australia, Brazil, and Vancouver, British Columbia. Paul Tracy won three consecutive races early in the year, at Nazareth, Pennsylvania; Rio de Janeiro; and Madison, Illinois. Alex Zanardi also got off to a quick start in the series and went on to win the series title.

NASCAR. Jeff Gordon was the 1997 star of the popular 33-race Winston Cup stock-car series. In February, Gordon, at age 25, became the youngest driver ever to win the Daytona 500, arguably the premier event on the National Association for Stock Car Auto Racing (NASCAR) circuit. At the end of the season, Gordon had finished first 10 times, and his winnings totaled more than $4 million. Gordon clinched the championship in the final race of the year on November 23 at the NAPA 500 in Atlanta.

Formula One. The Grand Prix season consisted of 15 races—11 in Europe and one each in Australia, Brazil, Argentina, and Canada. The final race of the season, the European Grand Prix in Jerez, Spain, was held on Oct. 26, 1997. Jacques Villeneuve trailed Michael Schumacher by one point in the season standings. The two collided in the 48th lap of the race. Schumacher was out of the race, but Villeneuve was able to finish and clinch the title. Schumacher denied deliberately ramming Villeneuve.

Endurance. A Dyson Ford Mark III driven by a team of six drivers won the 24 Hours of Daytona in February. The finish was one of the most gripping in series history. The Ford's engine began to overheat in the 23rd hour. Driver Butch Leitzinger was clinging to a one-lap lead and could ill-afford to make a pit stop. In an intense final hour, Leitzinger managed to nurse the smoking car through the final laps. The Ford crossed the finish line in a cloud of smoke to win the race by one lap and 14.891 seconds. In June, Michele Alboreto, Stefan Johanson, and Tom Kristensen drove a Joest Porsche to victory in the Lemans 24 Hours, held June 15 and 16 in France.

Dragsters. The National Hot Rod Association (NHRA) sponsored a 22-race schedule in 1997. Season champions included Gary Scelzi in the top fuel division, John Force in funny cars for the seventh time in eight years, and Jim Yates in the pro stock division for the second year in a row. ☐ Ron Reid

Aviation. Boeing Aircraft Company of Seattle, Washington, and McDonnell Douglas Corporation of St. Louis, Missouri, completed a $14-billion merger in August 1997 to form the world's largest aerospace manufacturer. European Commission, the executive arm of the European Union, and the U.S. Federal Trade Commission approved the merger.

The Star Alliance, an international partnership of five airlines, was announced in May 1997. The partners—United Airlines, a subsidiary of U.S.-based UAL Corp., Air Canada, Germany's Lufthansa, Thai International Airways, and SAS of Scandinavia—planned to coordinate frequent-flyer programs, marketing, reservations, and schedules. They also agreed to share facilities, purchasing, and technology. Brazil's Varig Airlines joined the alliance in October.

European airlines. British Airways purchased the insolvent French airline Air Liberte in February 1997, giving the British carrier a major presence in France. British Airways had acquired Paris-based TAT European Airlines in 1996. Lufthansa became fully privatized in October 1997, when the German government sold its remaining shares in the airline. The EC approved an Italian government aid package for Alitalia after the airline announced a loss of $790 million for 1996, its ninth year in the red.

American Airlines pilots went on strike on Feb. 15, 1997. U.S. President Bill Clinton responded by imposing a 60-day mediation period. The Allied

The Lockheed Martin-Boeing F-22 Raptor fighter jet is unveiled in April 1997. The Raptor, flown for the first time in September, was designed to replace the U.S. Air Force's aging fleet of F-15's.

Pilots Association approved a new contract agreement on May 5. The airline was allowed to purchase the 50- and 70-seat regional jets that it wanted to use on short-haul routes. The pilots received a stock options program, a 9 percent wage increase over five years, and assurances that, in the event of job reductions, pilots who fly larger planes would have priority over lower-paid, commuter-airline pilots.

Deadly crashes. A Korean Air 747 crashed into a hill as it approached Guam International Airport on August 6, killing 226 passengers and crew. A preliminary investigation attributed the accident—which 28 people survived—to rainy weather and a flaw in a ground-based altitude warning program.

In Indonesia's worst air disaster, all 234 passengers and crew died when an Airbus A-300 crashed on Sumatra on September 26. Investigators stated that poor visibility caused by forest fires that blanketed much of southern Southeast Asia with thick smog may have contributed to the crash.

Accident investigations. In November 1997, the Federal Bureau of Investigation ended its search for clues that a terrorist bomb or missile caused the crash of Trans World Airlines Flight 800 off Long Island, New York, in July 1996. All 230 passengers and crew died in the crash. Although the investigators were not certain what caused the crash, they believed that mechanical or electrical problems may have been to blame, particularly vapors that may

have ignited in the almost-empty center fuel tank. The National Transportation Safety Board (NTSB), a U.S. government agency that makes safety recommendations to the Federal Aviation Administration (FAA), recommended that aircraft manufacturers and airlines fill empty fuel tanks with *inert* (inactive) gases or insulate the tanks to keep them cool.

In August 1997, the NTSB issued its final report on the fire aboard a ValuJet Airlines flight over the Florida Everglades in May 1996. The fire caused a crash that killed all 110 passengers and crew. The NTSB blamed maintenance contractor Sabre-Tech of Phoenix, Arizona, for improperly preparing and identifying oxygen generators that ignited on the plane; ValuJet for failing to properly oversee the contractor; and the FAA for failing to require smoke detectors and fire-suppression systems in the cargo holds of aircraft, a requirement the NTSB had been recommending since 1988. In July 1997, ValuJet announced a merger with Orlando, Florida-based Air-Ways Corp. and changed its name to AirTran.

Investigators of the 1996 collision of a Saudi Arabian Airlines jet and a Kazakstan Airlines flight over India concluded in May 1997 that the crash was caused by the Kazakstan aircraft's descent below the altitude to which air traffic controllers had assigned it. The crash, one of the deadliest midair collisions in aviation history, resulted in the deaths of all 349 passengers and crew aboard the two planes.

FAA rulings. In March 1997, the FAA ordered U.S. airlines to replace the rudder-control systems on Boeing 737 jets with new ones that reduce the risk of a loss of control. The NTSB had reported that loss of rudder control probably caused the 1994 crash of a USAir flight near Pittsburgh, Pennsylvania, and may have caused the 1991 crash of a United Airlines flight near Colorado Springs, Colorado.

In July 1997, the FAA required changes in the flight data recorders on U.S. transport planes. Recorders in new aircraft must monitor at least 88 *parameters* (categories of information, such as air speed), while recorders in older aircraft must monitor 17 or 18 parameters. Previously, recorders were required to monitor only 11 parameters. The NTSB stated that additional parameters would significantly aid in investigating the causes of crashes.

Industry profits. Airlines worldwide earned a total net profit of $4 billion in 1996, 23 percent less than 1995 earnings. The International Air Transport Association attributed the drop to higher fuel costs.

Around-the-world flight. San Antonio, Texas, businesswoman Linda Finch completed a historic 73-day solo flight around the world in May 1997. Her flight marked the 60th anniversary of the ill-fated flight of Amelia Earhart, who disappeared over the Pacific Ocean in 1937. Finch piloted a restored aircraft similar to that used by Earhart. ☐ Ian Savage

See also **People in the news.**

Azerbaijan. Relations between Azerbaijan and Armenia deteriorated when a three-year cease-fire came close to collapsing early in 1997. In March, Azerbaijani officials accused Armenia of concentrating troops near the contested border between the two countries. In April, fighting erupted around the disputed Armenian enclave of Nagorno-Karabakh, part of the territory that Armenian troops had occupied since 1993.

However, in the spring of 1997 both nations began to signal greater flexibility over the issue of Nagorno-Karabakh. In May, Azerbaijani President Heydar A. Aliyev indicated that he was prepared to build a lucrative oil pipeline across Armenia in exchange for the return of Nagorno-Karabakh. Armenia rejected the offer, but the exchange did lead both sides to repeat their willingness to consider proposals to end the conflict. In June, a peace plan was presented by European mediators that called for troops in the disputed areas to be replaced by international peacekeepers while negotiations were held.

In July, Azerbaijan, Russia, and the breakaway Russian region of Chechnya signed an agreement to develop a pipeline system to transport Azerbaijani oil to Russian ports for export. However, Turkmenistan disputed Azerbaijan's claims to oil deposits in some areas of the Caspian Sea. ☐ Steven L. Solnick

See also **Armenia; Asia** (Facts in brief table).

Bahamas. See West Indies.

Bahrain. On March 26, 1997, a state court sentenced 15 Bahrainis to jail terms ranging from 3 to 15 years for their involvement in an alleged Iranian-backed plot to overthrow the ruling Al Khalifa family and install a fundamentalist Islamic government. The convicted Bahrainis were Shiite Muslims said to be militants belonging to the pro-Iranian Bahraini Hezbollah (Party of God). Most Bahrainis and Iranians are Shiite Muslims, while the Al Khalifas are Sunni Muslims. Shiites and Sunnis form the two major sects of Islam. The human rights group Amnesty International criticized the trials because they were closed to the public and the evidence against the accused was not made available to the press.

Bahrain had been wracked since December 1994 with arson, bombings, and demonstrations—mainly by Shiites protesting political and economic discrimination by Sunnis. As of late 1997, more than 30 people had been killed in the violence, and hundreds of citizens had been arrested. Although U.S. officials stated that Iran was involved in some of the disorder, they believed that much of the unrest was homegrown. One demand of Bahraini dissidents in 1997 was the restoration of the parliament, dissolved in 1975 by the Al Khalifas.

U.S. presence. Responding to reports that Americans were being targeted for terrorist attacks, the United States in April imposed a 7 p.m. curfew on 1,000 U.S. land-based Navy personnel stationed in Bahrain and warned all U.S. citizens in Bahrain to avoid public places. The United States also began diverting shore leaves of naval personnel stationed in the Persian Gulf from Bahrain to the United Arab Emirates. Bahrain had been named the headquarters of the U.S. Fifth Fleet in 1995.

Gulf relations. Bahrain and Qatar agreed in March 1997 to exchange ambassadors for the first time since they gained independence from Great Britain in 1971. It was hoped that the move would improve relations between the two countries. In 1996, Qatar had accused Bahrain of helping to plot a *coup* (overthrow) attempt against its government, and Bahrain had convicted two Qataris for spying. The Qataris were later pardoned and freed.

Improved relations between the two countries were encouraged by the Gulf Cooperation Council (GCC), a regional Arab group promoting cooperation in military and economic matters. The GCC had feared that conflicting claims by the two countries over the Hawar Islands, a cluster of small Persian Gulf islands, could negatively affect the unity of the GCC itself. The islands are potentially rich in oil and gas reserves. While Qatar has vast supplies of natural gas reserves, Bahrain's oil reserves have dwindled substantially. Bahrain was the smallest Arab oil producer in 1997, with a daily production of 40,000 barrels of crude oil. ☐ Christine Helms

See also **Middle East** (Facts in brief table).

Ballet. See Dance.

A fire in a gas field operated by a U.S.-owned company in Maulvi-Bazar, a city in northeast Bangladesh, forces the evacuation of thousands of people in April 1997.

Bangladesh. A struggle between Bangladesh's two main political parties continued in 1997 to threaten government and economic stability. The Bangladesh National Party (BNP), led by former Prime Minister Khaleda Ziaur Rahman (known as Zia), organized strikes against Prime Minister Hasina Wajed, and in July, four national strikes brought the country to a standstill.

In 1996, Hasina organized similar strikes—costing 54 working days—that forced Zia to resign as prime minister and pressured the government to turn over power to a caretaker government, which conducted parliamentary elections in June 1996. The Awami League, headed by Hasina, won more parliamentary seats than the BNP and the Jatiya Party and, in a coalition with Jatiya, formed a new government headed by Hasina.

Ershad freed. The Jatiya Party was led by former Bangladesh president Hussain Mohammad Ershad, who had lost power in a 1990 uprising led by Hasina and Zia. Hussain was later sentenced to 23 years in prison for illegal arms possession and corruption and ran the Jatiya Party from prison. On Jan. 9, 1997, Hussain was released on bail. The BNP charged that Hasina had made a deal to free Hussain.

The economy. Domestic output grew at 5.7 percent—up from 5.3 percent in 1996—and agricultural production rose, but industrial growth slowed in fiscal 1997. Exports rose 13.5 percent, and inflation stood at 4 percent. While economic prospects in Bangladesh improved somewhat, experts warned that political turmoil threatened to stall financial gains. The Metropolitan Chamber of Commerce in the capital, Dhaka, warned that the federal government was engaged in poor financial practices, and the American Chamber of Commerce in Dhaka expressed concern about "the sustainability of political stability."

In 1997, labor unions criticized efforts by the Bangladesh government to sell inefficient state-owned companies. Although such companies lost an estimated $500 million in 1996—an enormous sum for one of the world's poorest countries—labor unions expressed concern that opening the companies to competition in the private sector might cause many companies to go bankrupt.

Hurricane damage. On May 19, 1997, a hurricane with winds of 125 miles (200 kilometers) per hour killed approximately 600 people and destroyed more than 400,000 houses in Bangladesh. Early evacuation of more than 1 million people saved thousands of lives.

Bangladesh has a tragic history of devastation by hurricanes (known locally as cyclones). A 1970 hurricane killed an estimated 300,000 people in coastal villages, and a 1991 hurricane killed 138,000 people. In the mid-1990's, the government developed an early warning system to speed evacuation to new concrete shelters.　　　　　□ Henry S. Bradsher

See also **Asia** (Facts in brief table).

Bank. In September 1997, the Federal Deposit Insurance Corporation (FDIC), a government agency that insures deposits at U.S. banks and savings and loans (S&L's), reported that profits at U.S. banks rose to $29.1 billion in the first half of 1997, up from $25.5 billion during the first half of 1996. Profits continued to rise in the third quarter, and analysts predicted that 1997 would be the sixth straight year of record profits for the banking industry. The FDIC also reported that no banks or S&L's became insolvent between mid-1996 and mid-1997—the first 12 consecutive months without a bank failure in 35 years. The strength of the banking industry in 1997 was partly due to the strong American economy. The growing use of automated services and increased fees for the use of ATM's (automatic teller machines) also contributed to high bank profits.

Consumer debt was the only weak link for the industry in 1997, as it had been in 1996. The rate at which banks wrote off bad credit-card loans in the second reporting quarter of 1997 rose to its highest level in more than 14 years. Credit card losses in the quarter amounted to 5.22 percent (or $5.22 of every $100 charged), up from 4.48 percent in the second quarter of 1996.

S&L earnings. The FDIC reported in 1997 that earnings for S&L's fell to $3.42 billion for the first half of 1997, compared to $3.75 billion for the first half of 1996. The declining profits were partly attributed to higher taxes paid by S&L's, according to the FDIC.

Bank mergers. The pace of bank mergers slowed in 1997, compared to 1995 and 1996. However, the November 1997 acquisition of CoreStates Financial Corporation of Philadelphia by First Union Corporation of Charlotte, North Carolina, involved the highest price ever paid for a U.S. bank—$16.3 billion. Another large transaction between banks had occurred in March, when First Bank System Inc. of Minneapolis purchased U.S. Bancorp of Portland, Oregon, for $9.1 billion.

Commercial banks became involved in a number of mergers with investment banks, securities firms, and insurance companies in 1997. These mergers were triggered by regulation changes that overrode a 1933 law that had blocked banks from merging with other financial service companies. In addition, the surging stock market of 1997 lifted the value of banks, making transactions more affordable.

In January, Banc One Corp. of Columbus, Ohio, bought credit-card issuer First USA Inc. of Dallas for $7.3 billion. In June, NationsBank Corp. of Charlotte agreed to buy the investment firm Montgomery Securities Inc. of San Francisco for $1.2 billion. In July, Washington Mutual Inc., a Seattle financial services company, acquired Great Western Financial Corp., a Chatsworth, California S&L, for $7 billion.

S&L's. The Office of Thrift Supervision, the government agency that regulates S&L's, expected to receive 32 charter applications in 1997—twice the number it received in 1993. Many of the 1997 applications were from brokerage companies, banks, and insurance companies, including investment giant Merrill Lynch and Co. Inc. of New York City; Travelers Insurance Group Inc. of Hartford, Connecticut; State Farm Mutual Automobile Insurance Co. of Bloomington, Illinois; and insurance underwriter Transamerica Corp. of San Francisco. S&L charters were attractive in 1997 because of the distinctions between S&L's and banks. S&L's could underwrite insurance, while banks could not. S&L's had greater latitude than did banks to open branches outside home states.

S&L insurance premiums. In December 1996, the FDIC announced that the S&L deposit insurance fund was fully capitalized. As a result, in 1997, for the first time since 1989, most S&L's were not required to pay any insurance premiums on deposits. Some S&L's were required to pay small premiums. Previously, S&L's had been required to pay much larger deposit insurance premiums than banks to help fund the government bailout of S&L's mandated by the Financial Reform and Recovery Act of 1989. From the mid-1980's to the early 1990's, many S&L's became insolvent because they had been paying higher interest rates to depositors than they were taking in on loan charges. Under terms of the 1989 act, the government spent $50 billion to buy and sell off the assets of failed S&L's.

Second largest bank. In December, Union Bank of Switzerland and Swiss Bank Corp. announced that they would merge, creating the world's second largest bank. The only bank larger than the new bank, called United Bank of Switzerland, was Japan's Bank of Tokyo-Mitsubishi. The new bank controlled nearly $600 billion in assets. Analysts said that the merger would result in the loss of 13,000 jobs worldwide.

Interest rates. The Federal Reserve Board, the top banking regulator in the United States, raised interest rates once during 1997. In March, the board raised its *federal funds target rate* (the interest rate that banks charge each other for short-term loans) by a quarter-point, to 5.5 percent. The board adjusts interest rates to balance economic growth with inflation. If the economy is growing quickly and prices are rising, the board typically raises bank interest rates to slow down the economy. If the economy is sluggish, it lowers interest rates to entice businesses to expand and spur economic growth. In the first half of 1997, the U.S. economy grew at a healthy pace of 4.1 percent, but inflation remained low.

Mortgages. The Federal Reserve Board reported in 1997 that U.S. lending institutions turned down 48.8 percent of mortgage applications from black Americans in 1996, compared to just 24.1 percent of mortgage applications from white Americans. The report was part of the board's effort to monitor how mortgage money is distributed racially. In contrast to this report, the Joint Center for Housing Studies at

Harvard University in Cambridge, Massachusetts, reported in 1997 that the number of minority homeowners in the United States rose 38 percent between 1985 and 1995, compared to a rise of just 9 percent for white homeowners.

Credit unions. In October 1997, the U.S. Supreme Court heard arguments in a case that was expected to establish whether workers from different occupations and communities could join the same credit union. Credit unions are associations that make loans to members at low rates of interest. The low rates are possible because credit unions, unlike banks, are exempt from taxes. The case heard by the court was *AT&T Family Federal Credit Union v. First National Bank and Trust Co.* The bank, located in Asheboro, North Carolina, filed a lawsuit against the credit union, located in Winston-Salem, North Carolina, contending that it was violating the law by having members from a large number of diverse occupations. In 1982, the National Credit Union Administration, the government agency that regulates all federally chartered credit unions, abandoned guidelines that had required members of credit unions to have similar occupations or live in the same communities. Credit unions, since the 1982 changes, became increasingly competitive with banks, which claimed that credit unions were expanding beyond their original mandate.

□ Paulette Thomas

Baseball. In its fifth season without a full-time commissioner, Major League Baseball in 1997 had yet to regain the audience it lost in 1994, when a player strike forced the cancellation of the World Series. In an attempt to boost sagging attendance figures, major league owners scheduled interleague games during the regular season for the first time since the major leagues were formed. The 1997 season also commemorated the 50th anniversary of Jackie Robinson's debut as the first African American athlete in the major leagues. Other highlights included a home-run record quest by Mark McGwire and Ken Griffey, Jr., and the first World Series championship ever won by a wild-card play-off team.

Interleague play. Regular-season games between National League (NL) and American League (AL) clubs were played for the first time in 1997. As expected, the most anticipated interleague games were played between teams from the same city, such as the White Sox and Cubs in Chicago and the Mets and Yankees in New York. The crossover scheduling proved an unqualified hit at the box office, drawing an average of 33,400 fans per game—a 20 percent increase over other regular-season games. The National League dominated the first season of interleague play, compiling a 117-to-97 record against the American League.

Salaries. Baseball's selective salary boom was most evident in 1997 in the case of Chicago White

Final standings in major league baseball

American League

Eastern Division	W.	L.	Pct.	G.B.
Baltimore Orioles	98	64	.605	—
New York Yankees*	96	66	.593	2
Detroit Tigers	79	83	.488	19
Boston Red Sox	78	84	.481	20
Toronto Blue Jays	76	86	.469	22

Central Division	W.	L.	Pct.	G.B.
Cleveland Indians	86	75	.534	—
Chicago White Sox	80	81	.497	6
Milwaukee Brewers	78	83	.484	8
Minnesota Twins	68	94	.420	18½
Kansas City Royals	67	94	.416	19

Western Division	W.	L.	Pct.	G.B.
Seattle Mariners	90	72	.556	—
Anaheim Angels	84	78	.519	6
Texas Rangers	77	85	.475	13
Oakland Athletics	65	97	.401	25

American League champions—Cleveland Indians (defeated New York, 3 games to 2)

National League

Eastern Division	W.	L.	Pct.	G.B.
Atlanta Braves	101	61	.623	—
Florida Marlins*	92	70	.568	9
New York Mets	88	74	.543	13
Montreal Expos	78	84	.481	23
Philadelphia Phillies	68	94	.420	33

Central Division	W.	L.	Pct.	G.B.
Houston Astros	84	78	.519	—
Pittsburgh Pirates	79	83	.488	5
Cincinnati Reds	76	86	.469	8
St. Louis Cardinals	73	89	.451	11
Chicago Cubs	68	94	.420	16

Western Division	W.	L.	Pct.	G.B.
San Francisco Giants	90	72	.556	—
Los Angeles Dodgers	88	74	.543	2
Colorado Rockies	83	79	.512	7
San Diego Padres	76	86	.469	14

National League champions—Florida Marlins (defeated Atlanta, 4 games to 2)

World Series champions—Florida Marlins (defeated Cleveland, 4 games to 3)

Offensive leaders

Batting average—Frank Thomas, Chicago — .347
Runs scored—Ken Griffey, Jr., Seattle — 125
Home runs—Ken Griffey, Jr., Seattle[†] — 56
Runs batted in—Ken Griffey, Jr., Seattle — 147
Hits—Nomar Garciaparra, Boston — 209
Stolen bases—Brian L. Hunter, Detroit — 74
Slugging percentage—Ken Griffey, Jr., Seattle — .646

Leading pitchers

Games won—Roger Clemens, Toronto — 21
Earned run average (162 or more innings)—
Roger Clemens, Toronto — 2.05
Strikeouts—Roger Clemens, Toronto — 292
Saves—Randy Myers, Baltimore — 45
Shut-outs—Roger Clemens, Toronto;
Pat Hentgen, Toronto (tie) — 3
Complete games—Roger Clemens, Toronto;
Pat Hentgen, Toronto (tie) — 9

Awards**

Most Valuable Player—Ken Griffey, Jr., Seattle
Cy Young—Roger Clemens, Toronto
Rookie of the Year—Nomar Garciaparra, Boston
Manager of the Year—Davey Johnson, Baltimore

Offensive leaders

Batting average—Tony Gwynn, San Diego — .372
Runs—Craig Biggio, Houston — 146
Home runs—Larry Walker, Colorado[†] — 49
Runs batted in—Andres Galarraga, Colorado — 140
Hits—Tony Gwynn, San Diego — 220
Stolen bases—Tony Womack, Pittsburgh — 60
Slugging percentage—Larry Walker, Colorado — .720

Leading pitchers

Games won—Danny Neagle, Atlanta — 20
Earned run average (162 or more innings)—
Pedro Martinez, Montreal — 1.90
Strikeouts—Curt Schilling, Philadelphia — 319
Saves—Jeff Shaw, Cincinnati — 42
Shut-outs—Carlos Perez, Montreal — 5
Complete games—Pedro Martinez, Montreal — 13

Awards**

Most Valuable Player—Larry Walker, Colorado
Cy Young—Pedro Martinez, Montreal
Rookie of the Year—Scott Rolen, Philadelphia
Manager of the Year—Dusty Baker, San Francisco

*Qualified for wild-card play-off spot.
[†]Mark McGwire, St. Louis, hit a total of 58 major league home runs—34 in the American League and 24 in the National League.
**Selected by the Baseball Writers Association of America.

Sox outfielder Albert Belle, whose $10-million salary exceeded the entire $9-million annual payroll of the Pittsburgh Pirates. The New York Yankees led both leagues with a $58.5 million payroll. The 1997 median salary for major league baseball players was $450,000. More than a third of the players had salaries of at least $1 million, and 280 earned more than $1 million. A total of 48 players received the league minimum salary of $150,000.

Regular season. The Atlanta Braves had the best record (101-61) in the major leagues for 1997 and won the NL Eastern Division title by 9 games. The Houston Astros (84-78) won the Central Division by 5 games, and the San Francisco Giants (90-72) won the Western Division by 2 games. The Florida Marlins made the play-offs as a "wild-card" team because their 92-70 record was best among NL teams that did not win a division title.

The 1997 AL winners were Baltimore (98-64) by 2 games for the Eastern Division title, Seattle (90-72) by 6 games in the Western Division, and Cleveland (86-75) by 6 games for the Central Division title. The Yankees (96-66) were the AL's wild-card entry.

Play-offs. The first round of the National League play-offs was marked by a pair of sweeps, as Atlanta took 3 straight games from Houston and Florida beat San Francisco, 3 games to 0. The NL championship series saw Florida eliminate Atlanta—a team that had played in four of the previous five World Series—4 games to 2. The Marlins, a five-year-old

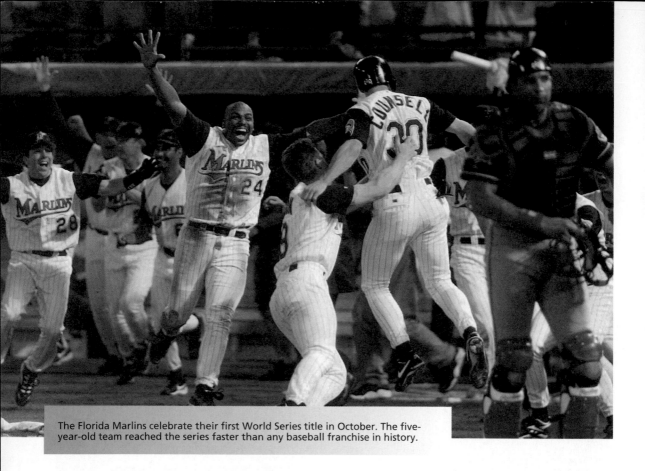

The Florida Marlins celebrate their first World Series title in October. The five-year-old team reached the series faster than any baseball franchise in history.

franchise, reached the World Series faster than any expansion team in history. They also became the first wild-card team to reach the series.

In the American League, the Baltimore Orioles defeated Seattle, 3 games to 1, and Cleveland came back to beat the Yankees after New York was 4 outs away from eliminating the Indians in the fourth game. Cleveland won the AL crown, 4 games to 2 over the Orioles, winning each game by 1 run.

The 1997 World Series, disparaged by a network television executive who said he hoped it would end as quickly as possible, was played in oppressive humidity in Miami and freezing cold in Cleveland. The latter contributed to a deluge of errors and perhaps the worst pitching performances ever seen in the championship round. But the 1997 series also gave fans a deciding seventh game for the first time in a decade.

The series opened on October 18 in Miami, where the Marlins won, 7-4. The Marlins scored all of their runs off Orel Hershiser, starting pitcher for the Indians. Cleveland came back the next night to win, 6-1. The television ratings of the first two games set an all-time World Series low.

Snow fell during batting practice before Game 3 in Cleveland. The two teams combined for 6 errors and 16 walks in the cold. In the 9th inning, the Marlins scored 7 runs on 4 hits, 3 walks, a wild pitch, and a record 3 errors. At 4 hours, 12 minutes, it was the second-longest World Series game in history. The game ended in a 14-11 victory for Florida. The Indians tied the series with a 10-3 victory in Game 4.

Florida won Game 5, 8-7, despite eight walks by starting pitcher Livan Hernandez. Through the first five games, Marlins pitchers had a collective earned run average (ERA) of 8.20, compared to 6.91 for Cleveland. In the previous 92 World Series, only one team had ever reached an ERA of 5.00.

Cleveland tied the series again in Game 6 in Miami, 4-1, when Chad Ogea, the Indians' starting pitcher, drove in runs with a single and a double. But the Marlins won it all with a 3-2 victory in the 11th inning of Game 7, which began on October 26 and ended after midnight. Edgar Renteria drove in the winning run with a single off Indians pitcher Charles Nagy. Livan Hernandez, a Cuban defector whose pitching contributed to two Marlins victories, was named the most valuable player of the series.

Stars. Mark McGwire, traded by the AL's Oakland A's to the NL's St. Louis Cardinals in July, became the first player to hit home runs against 20 different teams. Both McGwire and Seattle's Ken Griffey, Jr., challenged the single-season record of 61 home runs, set by Roger Maris in 1961. McGwire hit 58 homers, 34 with Oakland and 24 with St. Louis. Griffey led the AL with 56 home runs, and Larry Walker of the Colorado Rockies was declared the NL home run champion, with 49.

Tony Gwynn of the San Diego Padres won the NL batting title for the fourth year in a row and the eighth time in 14 seasons, with a .372 average. Gwynn, at age 37, also led the major leagues with 220 hits. He set personal bests with 17 home runs, 119 RBI, 68 extra-base hits, and 324 total bases.

The Toronto Blue Jay's Roger Clemens also had a noteworthy 1997 season. He led the AL in wins, ERA, and strikeouts, becoming the first pitcher to lead all three categories since Detroit's Hal Newhouser in 1945. In November 1997, Clemens became the first AL pitcher to win a fourth Cy Young Award. Pedro Martinez of Montreal won the NL Cy Young Award.

Expansion. On November 6, Major League Baseball approved a division realignment plan in preparation for the debut of two teams in 1998. The plan put the Tampa Bay Devil Rays in the AL East and the Arizona Diamondbacks in the NL West. In addition, the Milwaukee Brewers moved from the AL Central to the NL Central, and the Detroit Tigers switched from the AL East to the AL Central in 1998.

Hall of Fame. Four men were inducted into the Baseball Hall of Fame on August 3, 1997: pitcher Phil Niekro, who won 318 games in his 24-year career; infielder Nelson (Nellie) Fox, a 12-time all-star of the 1950's and 1960's; Tommy Lasorda, who spent 20 years as manager of the Los Angeles Dodgers; and shortstop Willie Wells, a Negro League star of the 1920's to the 1940's.   □ Ron Reid

Basketball. There was a decidedly familiar look to two of the three major basketball championships decided during the 1996-1997 season. The Chicago Bulls took the National Basketball Association (NBA) title for the fifth time in seven seasons under coach Phil Jackson, and the University of Tennessee won the National Collegiate Athletic Association (NCAA) women's championship for the second straight year under coach Pat Summitt. However, the NCAA men's championship went to the University of Arizona for the first time.

Professional. The Bulls were virtually unstoppable through most of the season, winning 49 of their first 56 games, but injuries late in the season cut their winning percentage over the final 26 games. The Bulls still managed to lead the league in scoring, with an average of 103.1 points per game, and compiled a 69-13 record, the second best in NBA history. These statistics effectively silenced critics who suggested the Chicago dynasty was crumbling.

The primary forces behind Chicago's success once again were Michael Jordan and Scottie Pippen. With a string of dominating performances and a remarkable will to win, Jordan averaged 29.6 points per game, enhancing his reputation as the greatest player of all time. Pippen averaged 20.2 points per game and led his team in three-point field goals (156).

The division winners were the Bulls, the Miami Heat (61-21) the Utah Jazz (64-18) and the Seattle

The 1996-1997 college basketball season

College tournament champions

NCAA	(Men)	Division I:	Arizona
		Division II:	California State-Bakersfield
		Division III:	Illinois Wesleyan
NCAA	(Women)	Division I:	Tennessee
		Division II:	North Dakota
		Division III:	New York University
NAIA	(Men)	Division I:	Life University (Ga.)
		Division II:	Bethel College (Ind.)
	(Women)	Division I:	Southern Nazarene (Okla.)
		Division II:	Northwest Nazarene (Ida.)
NIT (Men)			Michigan
Junior College	(Men)	Division I:	Indian Hills (Ia.)
		Division II:	Beaver County (Penn.)
		Division III:	Eastfield (Tex.)
	(Women)	Division I:	Trinity Valley (Tex.)
		Division II:	Kirkwood (Ia.)
		Division III:	Anoka-Ramsey (Minn.)

Men's college champions

Conference	School
America East	Boston University*
Atlantic Coast	Duke (reg. season)
	North Carolina (tournament)
Atlantic Ten	
Eastern Division	St Joseph's (Penn.)*
Western Division	Xavier (Ohio)
Big East	
Big East 7	Georgetown—Providence (tie; reg. season)
Big East 6	Villanova—Boston College*
	(tie; reg. season)
Big Sky	Northern Arizona (reg. season)
	Montana (tournament)
Big South	Liberty—N.C. Asheville (tie; reg. season)
	Charleston Southern (tournament)
Big Ten	Minnesota†
Big Twelve	Kansas*
Big West	
Eastern Division	Utah State—Nevada—New Mexico State
	(tie; reg. season)
Western Division	Pacific*
Colonial	Old Dominion*—N.C.-Wilmington
	(tie; reg. season)
Conference USA	Marquette (tournament)
Red Division	Tulane (reg. season)
White Division	N.C. Charlotte—Memphis (tie; reg. season)
Blue Division	Cincinnati (reg. season)
Ivy League	Princeton†
Metro Atlantic	Iona (reg. season)
	Fairfield (tournament)
Mid-American	Bowling Green—Miami (Ohio)*
	(tie; reg. season)
Mid-Continent	Valparaiso*
Mid-Eastern	Coppin State*
Midwestern	Butler*
Missouri Valley	Illinois State*
Northeast	Long Island*
Ohio Valley	Murray State*—Austin Peay
Pacific Ten	UCLA†
Patriot League	Navy*
Southeastern	Kentucky (tournament)
Eastern Division	South Carolina (reg. season)
Western Division	Mississippi (reg. season)
Southern	
North Division	Marshall—Davidson (tie; reg. season)
South Division	Chattanooga*
Southland	Southwest Texas State*—McNeese State—Northeast Louisiana (tie; reg. season)
Southwestern	Mississippi Valley State (reg. season)
	Jackson State (tournament)
Sun Belt	New Orleans—South Alabama*
	(tie; reg. season)
Trans America	
Eastern Division	College of Charleston (S.C.)*
Western Division	Samford (reg. season)
West Coast	St Mary's (Calif.)*—Santa Clara
	(tie; reg. season)
Western	
Mountain Division	Utah*
Pacific Division	Hawaii—Fresno State (tie; reg. season)

*Regular season and conference tournament champion.
†No tournament played.

Basketball

SuperSonics (57-25). The Bulls stormed through the NBA play-offs, beating the Washington Bullets (3 games to 0) the Atlanta Hawks (4 to 1) and Miami (4 to 1) to win the Eastern Conference title. Utah took the Western Conference by defeating the Los Angeles Clippers (3 games to 0), the Los Angeles Lakers (4 to 1), and the Houston Rockets (4 to 2).

The Bulls took the first two games of the final, best-of-seven series in Chicago before the Jazz drew even with a pair of victories in Salt Lake City. Chicago came back to win the pivotal fifth game in Utah. Jordan turned in a legendary performance, shrugging off flu symptoms to score 38 points in a 90-88 victory. The Bulls claimed the NBA championship, 4 games to 2, with a 90-86 victory that fittingly concluded the hard-fought series. Jordan scored 39 points. Steve Kerr clinched the game with a 17-foot (5-meter) jump shot.

People. Dennis Rodman, the Bulls's rainbow-haired defensive forward, led the NBA in rebounds for the sixth straight year, but he received far more attention for his "bad-boy" image. In January, he received an 11-game suspension for kicking a courtside cameraman. During the finals, Rodman drew a $50,000 fine—the highest in NBA history—for making a derogatory remark about Mormons.

On Dec. 3, 1997, the Golden State Warriors announced they had terminated the $32-million con-

tract of their all-star guard Latrell Sprewell. During a practice session two days earlier, Sprewell had choked Warriors head coach P. J. Carlesimo and reportedly threatened to kill him. On December 4, the NBA suspended Sprewell for a year without pay—the longest suspension the league's 51-year history.

Jordan won the NBA's scoring title for the ninth time. Pat Riley of Miami was the NBA's coach of the year. Atlanta's 7-foot-2-inch (218-centimeter) center Dikembe Mutombo was the NBA's top defensive player for the second time in three years.

Professional women. The eight-team American Basketball League (ABL) played its first season in 1997, to critical acclaim and consistent, if small attendance. The Columbus Quest became the first ABL champion by defeating the Richmond Rage in the final series, 3 games to 2.

The Women's National Basketball Association (WNBA) debuted during the summer of 1997. The WNBA enjoyed marketing help from the NBA, but had trouble establishing significant attendance and television ratings. The Houston Comets won the WNBA's first title, defeating the New York Liberty, 65-51, in a single-game elimination.

College men. The University of Kansas went into the 64-team NCAA championship tournament in March with a regular-season record of 33 wins and 1 loss. However, Kansas was eliminated in the second round by the University of Arizona (19 and 9).

Arizona joined the three surviving top-ranked teams in the Final Four in Indianapolis and scored another major upset by beating the University of North Carolina, 66-58, to reach the NCAA final. The University of Kentucky reached the final for the second straight year by beating the University of Minnesota, 78-69. The final game was a hard-fought contest that Arizona won in overtime, 84-79. Arizona guard Miles Simon scored 30 points and was voted the outstanding player of the tournament.

Voters named Tim Duncan of Wake Forest University player of the year and Arizona's Lute Olsen coach of the year. The consensus All-American team included Duncan, Danny Fortson of the University of Cincinnati, Ron Mercer of Kentucky, Raef LaFrentz of Kansas, and Keith Van Horn of the University of Utah. After the season ended, Rick Pitino opted to leave Kentucky, accepting a reported 10-year, $70-million contract to become head coach of the NBA's Boston Celtics. He was replaced by Tubby Smith, who became Kentucky's first African American coach. In October, Dean Smith, who won more games (879) than any other coach in college basketball history, retired after 36 seasons at North Carolina.

College women. The University of Tennessee overcame inexperience to become the first women's team in 13 years to win back-to-back NCAA titles. Tennessee went into the 1997 NCAA tournament with a 26-and-10 record, a third-ranked team that had finished fifth in the Southeastern Conference. But Tennessee took a

Houston Comets forward Tina Thompson drives to the net over New York's Rebecca Lobo in the WNBA championship game in August. Women's basketball became an increasingly popular spectator sport in 1997.

The Chicago Bulls add another NBA championship trophy to their collection in June. The 1996-1997 title was the team's fifth in seven years.

National Basketball Association standings

Eastern Conference

Atlantic Division

	W.	L.	Pct.	G.B.
Miami Heat*	61	21	.744	—
New York Knicks*	57	25	.695	4
Orlando Magic*	45	37	.549	16
Washington Bullets*	44	38	.537	17
New Jersey Nets	26	56	.317	35
Philadelphia 76ers	22	60	.268	39
Boston Celtics	15	67	.183	46

Central Division

	W.	L.	Pct.	G.B.
Chicago Bulls*	69	13	.841	—
Atlanta Hawks*	56	26	.683	13
Charlotte Hornets*	54	28	.659	15
Detroit Pistons*	54	28	.659	15
Cleveland Cavaliers	42	40	.512	27
Indiana Pacers	39	43	.476	30
Milwaukee Bucks	33	49	.402	36
Toronto Raptors	30	52	.366	39

Western Conference

Midwest Division

	W.	L.	Pct.	G.B.
Utah Jazz*	64	18	.780	—
Houston Rockets*	57	25	.695	7
Minnesota Timberwolves*	40	42	.488	24
Dallas Mavericks	24	25	.293	40
Denver Nuggets	21	61	.256	43
San Antonio Spurs	20	62	.244	44
Vancouver Grizzlies	14	68	.171	50

Pacific Division

	W.	L.	Pct.	G.B.
Seattle SuperSonics*	57	25	.695	—
Los Angeles Lakers*	56	26	.683	1
Portland Trail Blazers*	49	33	.598	8
Phoenix Suns*	40	42	.488	17
Los Angeles Clippers*	36	46	.439	21
Sacramento Kings	34	48	.415	23
Golden State Warriors	30	52	.366	27

*Made play-offs

NBA champions—Chicago Bulls (defeated Utah Jazz, 4 games to 2)

Individual leaders

Scoring

	G.	F.G.	F.T.	Pts.	Avg.
Michael Jordan, Chicago	82	920	480	2,431	29.6
Karl Malone, Utah	82	864	521	2,249	27.4
Glen Rice, Charlotte	79	722	464	2,115	26.8
Mitch Richmond, Sacramento	81	717	457	2,095	25.9
Latrell Sprewell, Golden State	80	649	493	1,938	24.2
Allen Iverson, Philadelphia	76	625	382	1,787	23.5
Hakeem Olajuwon, Houston	78	727	351	1,010	23.2
Patrick Ewing, New York	78	655	439	1,751	22.4
Kendall Gill, New Jersey	82	644	427	1,789	21.8
Gary Payton, Seattle	82	706	254	1,785	21.8

Rebounding

	G.	Off.	Def.	Tot.	Avg.
Dennis Rodman, Chicago	55	320	563	883	16.1
Dikembe Mutombo, Atlanta	80	268	661	929	11.6
Anthony Mason, Charlotte	73	186	643	829	11.4
Ervin Johnson, Denver	82	231	682	913	11.1
Patrick Ewing, New York	78	175	659	834	10.7
Chris Webber, Washington	72	238	505	743	10.3
Vin Baker, Milwaukee	78	267	537	804	10.3
Loy Vaught, L.A. Clippers	82	222	595	817	10.0
Shawn Kemp, Seattle	81	275	532	807	10.0

huge step toward retaining its title with a second-round victory over the University of Connecticut (91-81), a top-ranked team with a 33-and-0 regular season record.

The University of North Carolina was the other top-ranked team that failed to make the Final Four. Stanford and Old Dominion completed the Final Four line-up by beating the University of Georgia (82-47) and the University of Florida (53-51), respectively. In the Final Four at Cincinnati, Old Dominion rallied from a 15-point deficit to nip Stanford in overtime, 83-82 and set up a rematch with Tennessee, a 80-66 winner over Notre Dame.

Tennessee avenged its loss to Old Dominion earlier in the season with a 68-59 victory in the NCAA final. Tennessee sophomore guard Chamique Holdsclaw, who scored 24 points in the final game, was voted the tournament's outstanding player.

Kara Wolters, center from Connecticut, was voted player of the year, and her coach, Geno Auriemma, won coach of the year honors. Most selectors picked Wolters, Holdsclaw, Kate Starbird of Stanford, and Clarisse Machanguana and Ticha Penicheiro of Old Dominion to the All-American team.

International. In July, Yugoslavia defeated Italy, 61-49, to win the European Basketball Championship in Barcelona, Spain. This was Yugoslavia's second straight European basketball title. □ Ron Reid

Belarus. President Alexander Lukashenko continued to exercise strict control over Belarus in 1997, despite increasing criticism from domestic and international observers. Lukashenko had installed a new, handpicked parliament in November 1996, but the former parliament continued to meet in 1997, claiming that it was the legitimate national legislature. Lukashenko responded by closing down offices of rival political parties and arresting opposition leaders. He also held tight control over the media, barring any direct criticism of his regime.

International organizations were united in their opposition to Lukashenko's escalating political repression. In June, the Organization for Security and Cooperation in Europe, the continent's leading international security organization, warned that Belarus's government was clearly building a totalitarian regime. The World Bank, a United Nations agency that provides loans to countries for development, criticized the state's continuing control over the Belarusian economy and refused to resume aid programs to Belarus, which it had suspended in 1994.

In September 1997, the Soros Foundation shut down its operations in Belarus, claiming political harassment. The Soros Foundation, a private charitable organization, had spent millions of dollars since the fall of the Soviet Union in 1991 to promote democracy and free speech in Belarus and the other former Soviet states. Belarusian tax authorities seized the foundation's bank accounts in May 1997, demanding that the foundation pay taxes.

Relations with Russia. On May 23, Lukashenko and Russian President Boris Yeltsin signed a charter of political and economic union. While both presidents had suggested the charter would reintegrate the two countries, the final document did not do so. Russia opposed assuming responsibility for Belarus's unreformed economic system. Belarus opposed surrendering the formal trappings of statehood that were prized by many Belarusian nationalists.

The limitations of the new relationship with Russia became clearer in July and August when Belarusian police arrested two teams of Russian journalists working for a Russian state television network. Yeltsin and other Russian diplomats protested the arrests, which occurred while the journalists were filming reports on Belarusian border guards. The diplomatic crisis forced Lukashenko to postpone a planned trip to Russia. All of the journalists were ultimately released from prison, but a few of them faced trial under Belarus's restrictive media laws.

Relations with Russia were also tested when Gazprom, the Russian natural gas monopoly, sharply reduced fuel shipments to Belarus in July. Gazprom officials claimed that Belarus owed them more than $150 million in unpaid debts. Regular shipments of fuel were resumed after a new payment schedule was negotiated. □ Steven L. Solnick

See also **Europe** (Facts in brief table); **Russia**.

Belgium struggled in 1997 with the fear and discord that had erupted in the country in August 1996, when police had discovered a network believed to be responsible for the abduction, sexual abuse, and murder of four girls. Public concern rose again in March 1997 when police found the body of a 9-year-old girl missing since 1992 in a Brussels garage. A convicted child molester, who was apparently not involved in the other murders, was charged with her abduction and rape. In October 1997, the public was again outraged when police arrested a Hungarian-born Protestant pastor, Andras Pandy, after finding human remains in his house. The police had been investigating the disappearance of two of Pandy's former wives and four of his children.

Child abduction ring. A parliamentary inquiry into the investigation of the girls' murders resulted in intense criticism of Belgium's police and judicial system for failing to find the girls in time to prevent their deaths despite numerous leads to the chief suspects. The committee report, issued in April 1997, blamed the failures on rivalries between Belgium's police forces and blunders by individual investigators. The committee failed to uncover evidence that the suspects had been protected by senior politicians or justice officials, but it refused to rule out the possibility of such protection. In October, the government of Prime Minister Jean-Luc Dehaene introduced legislation to merge two of the country's three police forces in response to the report.

Cools case. During 1997, judges released four of six men arrested in 1996 for possible involvement in the 1991 slaying of Andre Cools, the former deputy prime minister. Lack of progress in the murder investigation raised fresh doubts that the crime—which many Belgians believed to have been politically motivated—would ever be solved.

Renault dispute. French automaker Renault announced in February 1997 that it would shut its assembly plant in the Brussels suburb of Vilvoorde and lay off 3,100 workers. The Belgian government charged Renault with violating laws requiring companies to consult with workers before closing facilities and lobbied the French government to reverse the decision. France allowed Renault to proceed with the closure. The factory's last car was completed on September 5.

Economic growth accelerated during 1997, raising Belgium's hopes of qualifying for the single European currency due to be launched in 1999. But the country's unemployment rate remained high at 9.7 percent. The government predicted in October 1997 that the budget deficit would shrink below 3 percent of gross domestic product, the limit for countries joining the single currency. □ Tom Buerkle

See also **Europe** (Facts in brief table).

Belize. See Latin America.

Benin. See Africa.

Bhutan. See Asia.

Biology. Man's best friend—the dog—has been a companion to humans much longer than scientists had previously believed, according to new genetic findings reported in June 1997 by researchers at the University of California at Los Angeles (UCLA). Although scientists have long known that dogs were the first animals to be domesticated, most thought that event occurred only 10,000 to 20,000 years ago, based on studies of fossilized bones found at human habitation sites. The new evidence showed, however, that dogs became a separate species far earlier—perhaps more than 100,000 years ago. The evidence also revealed that dogs are descended entirely from wolves, with no genetic contribution from jackals or coyotes, as many researchers had supposed.

The UCLA investigators analyzed mitochondrial DNA from 162 wolves from around the world and from 140 dogs belonging to 67 breeds. DNA—deoxyribonucleic acid—is the molecule that genes are made of. Mitochondria are tiny cellular structures that are inherited only from the mother and, thus, make a useful tool for studying genetic lineages. The investigators used techniques that enabled them to compare the sequences of molecular subunits in the DNA samples. Because sequences change at a steady rate over time as *mutations* (genetic alterations) occur in them, such comparisons enable scientists to determine how long it has been since related species diverged from a common ancestor.

The UCLA team concluded that dogs evolved from wolves between 60,000 and 135,000 years ago. Most modern dog breeds, in contrast, are no more than a few hundred years old. They were created by the selective breeding of existing dogs.

Rebirth after a fire. The fires that blacken vegetation in Western deserts also provide the trigger for a dramatic regrowth of plant life, but not in the way that scientists had believed, botanists at Occidental College in Los Angeles reported in May. Biologists had thought that it was the exposure of seeds to heat from the fire itself that triggered their germination, but the Occidental researchers found that the real stimulus is the gas nitrogen dioxide, a component of smoke.

Botanists Jon E. Keeley and C. J. Fotheringham studied seeds of whispering bells, a flowering plant that is usually one of the first species to reappear after a fire. They found that seeds exposed only to heat remained dormant, but those exposed to either smoke or nitrogen dioxide alone underwent nearly 100 percent germination.

Why songbirds sing. An unusual experiment reported in March by neurobiologist Evan Balaban of the Neurosciences Institute in San Diego showed that the unique songs of birds are genetically programmed rather than learned from their parents, as most biologists had previously believed. Balaban cut a hole in the shells of three-day-old fertilized chicken eggs, exposing the neural stem, from which the brain grows. Using special stains to identify the parts of the brain that are thought to control bird song, he removed those tissues and replaced them with corresponding cells from the brains of quails. The embryos were then allowed to develop normally and hatch.

Balaban said the chicks sang like quail. Chickens normally emit a single squawk with little head movement. The altered chicks, in contrast, bobbed their heads up and down rapidly and emitted the three-note song characteristic of quail. Otherwise, Balaban reported, the chicks behaved completely like chickens.

Huddled masses. Male emperor penguins sit on a nest for 105 to 115 days, enduring the fierce Antarctic winter without food, to incubate the single egg laid by their mates. Most biologists believed that the birds could not put on enough body fat to survive the ordeal unaided. In fact, they are aided—by their fellow penguins. That finding was reported in January by biologist Yvon Le Maho and her colleagues at the National Center for Scientific Research in Strasbourg, France.

The research team studied 18 male emperor penguins living in a huddled group of 3,000 birds in Antarctica and 10 penguins kept isolated in outdoor pens. They found that the huddled penguins used 17 percent less energy to maintain their body temperature than those living separately. Without the warmth gained from huddling, the penguins would run out of energy three weeks early and would have to abandon their egg to search for food, the team concluded.

When life exploded. Biologists have long known that the number of species of plants and animals increased sharply some 500 million years ago in what is known as the Cambrian explosion, but scientists have never understood what factors led to this sudden rise in diversity. Geologists at the California Institute of Technology in Pasadena reported in July that the cause may have been a sudden movement of the Earth's mantle and crust, the planet's two outermost layers, that led to a realignment of the continents. The repositioning of the continents, the investigators theorized, created new biological niches for animals to evolve into.

The scientists, led by geologist Joseph L. Kirschvink, based their conclusion on a study of residual magnetism in rocks, which told them how the rocks have moved over the eons, transported on the drifting continents. The team concluded that shifting masses within the Earth unbalanced the planet, causing the mantle and crust to change position by as much as 90 degrees over a period of perhaps 15 million years. The accompanying disruptions in climate and ecosystems may have led to the rapid evolution of new species, the researchers said.

□ Thomas H. Maugh II

Is It Wrong to Clone People?

The cloning of sheep and other animals in 1997 ignited an ethical controversy over the possible cloning of human beings.

By Michael Woods

Scientists in Scotland shocked the world on Feb. 22, 1997, by announcing that they had *cloned* (produced an exact genetic copy of) an adult sheep. The resulting ewe, born in July 1996 and named Dolly, represented a major advance in genetics research. She was the first clone of an adult mammal. Later in 1997, scientists announced that they had used various cloning techniques to produce other sheep (capable of secreting proteins potentially useful in pharmaceuticals) as well as monkeys and calves. By the end of 1997, it seemed to many observers that cloning technology was on the verge of revolutionizing livestock breeding, drug production, and medical research.

Immediately after the announcement of Dolly's birth, however, church officials, theologians, ethicists, and politicians voiced the widespread concern that human beings might be cloned, and this ignited an international ethical and legal debate. While scientists claimed they had no intention of cloning humans, the creation of Dolly proved that it was technically possible to take a body cell from a human being and use it to clone that person. People recalled such science-fiction tales as the 1978 movie *The Boys from Brazil*, in which Nazis living in South America cloned Adolf Hitler from preserved tissue, and believed that a nightmare was about to come true. What if an individual with the means to do so decided to produce dozens of copies of himself or herself? What if parents desired a "designer child"—a clone, perhaps, of supermodel Cindy Crawford, basketball star Michael Jordan, or chess champion Garry Kasparov? What if parents stopped giving birth to babies and, instead, reproduced themselves from skin cells? Would human cloning lead to people produced solely to serve as donors for organ transplants? Would babies that were products of cloning grow up to be normal, or would they be defective in some way?

Reaction to Dolly

Polls taken in February 1997 revealed the public's concern. A Gallup Poll indicated that 88 percent of people in the United States thought that the cloning of a human being would be "morally wrong," and a TIME/CNN poll indicated that 74 percent of Americans thought that human cloning was "against God's will." Among the religious organizations that spoke out against human cloning was the Roman Catholic Church, which, four days after Dolly's announcement, called for a global ban on human cloning.

Politicians generally reacted negatively to the news of Dolly's birth. In March 1997, the British government announced that it planned to stop providing funds for cloning research at the Scottish institute where Dolly was produced. Also in March, U.S. President Bill Clinton warned scientists against the temptation "to play God," and he issued a 90-day moratorium on the use of U.S. government funds for research into the cloning of humans. Clinton also asked the National Bioethics Advisory Commission (NBAC)—a panel of 18 experts in science, law, and ethics—to develop recommendations for a national policy on human cloning. (The NBAC had been created by Clinton in 1995 to explore the ethical issues concerning the biotechnology industry.) The U.S. Congress introduced two bills that, if passed, would permanently ban federal funding for research into human cloning. A third bill would mandate a $5,000 fine on anyone conducting such research. Senator Christopher Bond of Missouri, the sponsor of one of the bills, said, "There are aspects of human life that should be off limits to science."

The Public Health and Safety Subcommittee of the Senate Labor and Human Resources Committee held a hearing in March 1997 during which several scientists and ethicists presented their opinions on cloning. Among those testifying before the subcommittee was Ian Wilmut, the scientist who led the team that produced Dolly. Wilmut surprised many when he announced that he too supported a ban on human cloning. He said that he had never heard of an ethically acceptable reason for cloning a human. When Senator Tom Harkin of Iowa predicted human cloning in his lifetime, Wilmut replied, "I hope you're wrong."

Opposite page:
Dolly, the first clone of an adult mammal, is presented to the world in February 1997.

The author

Michael Woods is the Science Editor of the *Pittsburgh Post-Gazette* and *Toledo Blade,* Washington Bureau.

As the controversy raged, it became apparent that public leaders were often confused as to what a clone is and is not. A clone is an exact genetic copy of a gene, a cell, or a whole organism (such as a plant or animal). The clone contains precisely the same genetic information as the original. The cells of a tumor, for example, originate from a single cancer cell and are, therefore, clones. Identical twins originate from division of a fertilized egg into two identical eggs. They are clones. Copies of genes or cells made through genetic engineering are also clones. When applied to whole plants or animals, cloning means producing an identical individual *asexually* (without fusion of an egg and sperm).

Plant breeders have long employed cloning techniques to produce desired varieties of plants without use of seeds. Most apple trees, for example, are grown from buds cut from trees that have previously produced a desired kind of fruit. The buds are *grafted* (attached by placing into slits cut in plants) to roots of other trees. The resulting apple trees are clones of the trees from which the buds were cut.

In the 1950's, scientists developed a technique called *nuclear transfer* to produce clones of certain kinds of animals. In nuclear transfer, scientists remove the *nucleus* (the part of a cell that contains an organism's genetic information and controls growth and development) from an unfertilized egg cell and replace it with the nucleus of a cell—called the donor cell—taken from another organism. The resulting cell develops into a small embryo, which is implanted into the womb of a surrogate mother. Following the pregnancy, the surrogate mother gives birth to an offspring genetically identical to the organism from which the donor cell was taken. This technique, originally used to clone frogs, was first applied to the cloning of mammals in the 1980's—using donor cells taken from mouse embryos.

Making of Dolly

Dolly was produced with a new variation of nuclear transfer developed by Wilmut, Keith H. S. Campbell, and their colleagues at the Roslin Institute and PPL Therapeutics PLC, both near Edinburgh, Scotland. The birth of Dolly shocked scientists because she was produced from a donor cell taken from an adult rather than from an embryo. Many researchers had previously tried to transfer nuclei from cells taken from adults, but the resulting embryos had died. These failures led scientists to conclude that only the genes of an embryo had the ability to direct the development of a complete individual. They also assumed that genes lose this ability as their cells become part of specialized tissue, such as skin, muscle, nerve, bone, and hair. Cloning an adult mammal appeared to be impossible.

The researchers in Scotland accomplished the seemingly impossible by removing cells from the udder of a 6-year-old ewe and depriving them of almost all nutrients for five days. Wilmut and Campbell believed that nutrient deprivation would help to reprogram genes in the cells, making them capable of directing the development of a complete animal. To produce Dolly, the scientists fused one of the

Do you think that cloning of human beings would be morally acceptable or morally wrong?

Morally wrong 88%
Morally acceptable 6%

Source: Gallup Poll,
Feb. 24-26, 1997

Is it against God's will to clone human beings?

Yes 74%
No 19%

Source: TIME/CNN poll,
Feb. 26-27, 1997

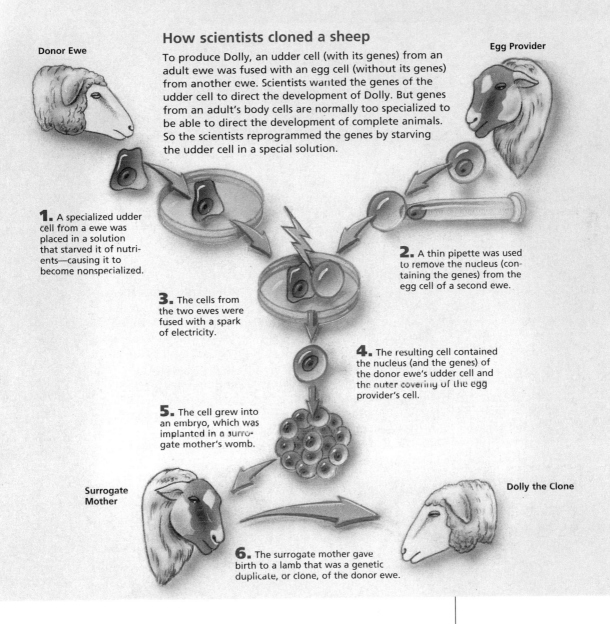

How scientists cloned a sheep

Donor Ewe

Egg Provider

To produce Dolly, an udder cell (with its genes) from an adult ewe was fused with an egg cell (without its genes) from another ewe. Scientists wanted the genes of the udder cell to direct the development of Dolly. But genes from an adult's body cells are normally too specialized to be able to direct the development of complete animals. So the scientists reprogrammed the genes by starving the udder cell in a special solution.

1. A specialized udder cell from a ewe was placed in a solution that starved it of nutrients—causing it to become nonspecialized.

2. A thin pipette was used to remove the nucleus (containing the genes) from the egg cell of a second ewe.

3. The cells from the two ewes were fused with a spark of electricity.

4. The resulting cell contained the nucleus (and the genes) of the donor ewe's udder cell and the outer covering of the egg provider's cell.

5. The cell grew into an embryo, which was implanted in a surrogate mother's womb.

Surrogate Mother

Dolly the Clone

6. The surrogate mother gave birth to a lamb that was a genetic duplicate, or clone, of the donor ewe.

reprogrammed udder cells with an *enucleated* (without a nucleus) egg cell from another ewe. The resulting embryo was placed in a surrogate mother ewe, which gave birth to Dolly 148 days later. The technique employed by Wilmut and his colleagues was inefficient in that it was repeated 277 times before yielding a surviving offspring. In August 1997, a U.S. company announced that it had developed a more efficient and advanced cloning technique that enabled them, within only 15 attempts, to produce a calf.

The reason scientists first cloned mammals from adult cells was to develop a better way of producing *transgenic animals* (animals with genes from species other than their own) for commercial and medical use. The biotechnology firm that helped fund research on Dolly, PPL Therapeutics, genetically alters female mammals to produce human proteins in their milk and investigates how such proteins could be used to treat human diseases. The first such transgenic animal produced through cloning, a sheep named Polly, was introduced to the press in July 1997 by the same scientists who created Dolly. Besides being used to produce pharmaceutically useful proteins, transgenic animals can be used to improve livestock and to produce modified organs capable of being transplanted into humans. The techniques currently employed to produce transgenic animals are expensive, slow, and inefficient. Experts hoped that cloning might streamline the production of such animals—enabling them to be mass produced.

Concerns about human cloning

While many scientists and medical ethicists applaud the cloning of research animals, a number of them nevertheless fear the consequences of any attempts to clone humans. In early June 1997, NBAC concluded that cloning was not yet safe enough for use with humans, because attempts at human cloning could result in the loss of many embryos and fetuses. Also, no one knows what the long-term health effects of cloning might be. Any attempt to create a child through cloning, therefore, would be "morally unacceptable." The panel noted that cloning research should be allowed to continue as long as the researchers do not try to use human embryos to create babies. NBAC recommended that President Clinton's moratorium on the use of federal funds for human cloning research be continued indefinitely and that Congress consider passing a law making it illegal to create a child through cloning. The panel recommended that such a law should expire in three to five years, allowing Congress to review advances in cloning technology and determine whether a continued ban was justified. President Clinton sent a bill to Congress that embodied the panel's recommendations.

In apparent justification of NBAC's cautionary recommendations, scientists said in late June that some of Dolly's *chromosomes* (structures that carry genes) had undergone subtle changes normally found only in cells from older animals. These changes, which probably resulted from the fact that the cell used to produce Dolly came from a 6-year-old ewe, raised the possibility that Dolly could age and die prematurely. Dolly also might face a high risk of genetic defects because her genes were inherited only from a female animal. An organism may need a complete set of maternal and paternal genes. Scientific evidence indicates that some genes work normally only when inherited from the father, and others work normally only when inherited from the mother.

The ethical debate over cloning also encompassed the possible psychological impact on the offspring. Would a human clone tend to have a diminished sense of individuality? Perhaps human clones would think that they were genetically destined to the same fate as

---

If you had the chance, would you clone yourself?

No 91%
Yes 7%

Source: TIME/CNN poll, Feb. 26-27, 1997

Should the federal government regulate the cloning of animals?

Yes 65%
No 29%

Source: TIME/CNN poll, Feb. 26-27, 1997

Arguments used against and in defense of human cloning

Against

Cloning might lead to the creation of genetically engineered groups of people for specific purposes, such as warfare or slavery.

Cloning might lead to an attempt to improve the human race according to an arbitrary standard.

Cloning could result in the introduction of additional defects in the human gene pool.

Cloning is unsafe. There are too many unknown factors that could adversely affect the offspring.

A clone might have a diminished sense of individuality.

A clone might have fewer rights than other people.

Doctors might use clones as sources of organs for organ transplants.

Cloning is at odds with the traditional concept of family.

Cloning is against God's will.

Some aspects of human life should be off limits to science.

In defense of

Cloning would enable infertile couples to have children of their own.

Cloning would give couples who are at risk of producing a child with a genetic defect the chance to produce a healthy child.

Cloning could shed light on how genes work and lead to the discovery of new treatments for genetic diseases.

A ban on cloning may be unconstitutional. It would deprive people of the right to reproduce and restrict the freedom of scientists.

A clone would not really be a duplicate, because environmental factors would mold him or her into a unique individual.

A clone would have as much of a sense of individuality as do twins.

A clone would have the same rights as do all other people.

Cloning is comparable in safety to a number of other medical procedures.

Objections to cloning are similar to objections raised against previous scientific achievements, for example, heart transplants and test-tube babies, that later came to be widely accepted.

113

Ian Wilmut, *left*, the scientist who created Dolly, and Harold Varmus, the director of the National Institutes of Health, testify before a U.S. Senate subcommittee in March 1997 on the ethical issues involved in the cloning of human beings.

the persons from whom their donor cells came.

Ethical questions have also been raised about cloning's effects on parenting and family life. Parents of clones might value their children according to how closely they met some overly detailed, preordained specifications. Cloning, therefore, could undermine basic elements of a loving, nurturing family, such as the acceptance of each child as a unique individual.

Cloning might have society-wide effects, as well. What would happen to a world that separated reproduction from love and other human relationships? Would society use cloning for *eugenics* (attempting to scientifically improve the human race according to arbitrary standards)? Ethicists have voiced concerns that cloning, combined with various techniques of genetic engineering, could lead to efforts to selectively breed children who are healthier, more intelligent, or even designed for warfare or slavery.

Misconceptions about cloning

Scientists and medical ethicists who argue in favor of human cloning claim that much of the public's concern is based on misconceptions. They note that, although many people believe that cloning would produce an instant carbon copy of an adult person, cloning would, in reality, produce what amounts to a delayed identical twin, several years or even decades younger than the person who donated the cell from which the clone was produced. Identical twins are genetic carbon copies, but they are separate individuals. They often look different because of different preferences in clothing and hairstyle. They may have different moral values, academic achievements, occupations, and tastes in music.

Another misconception that scientists suggest clouds the issue of human cloning is the question of how genes influence an individual's development. Human beings do not inherit a fixed, unchangeable genetic blueprint from their parents. Scientists believe that physical and mental traits result from complex interactions between genes and the environment in which an individual grows up and lives—including the chemical environment surrounding the fetus in the womb. Two people can inherit the same set of genes and turn out very differently, because environmental factors often determine how genes are expressed. A person might, for example, inherit genes for large body size, but those genes will not be fully expressed unless the person receives proper nutrition. Genes for musical ability may be expressed only if a person grows up in a family that loves music.

Some ethicists voice fears that human clones might be considered less than human and might be used for spare parts in organ transplants or for other unethical purposes. Legal experts, however, claim that clones would have all the legal rights and protections of other people. They note that society never questioned the legal rights of offspring resulting from other reproductive technologies, such as *in vitro fertilization* (the technology that produces "test-tube babies").

Perhaps the strongest argument put forth in favor of human cloning is that cloning could provide the only avenue available to some infertile couples for producing children. In cases of fertile couples in which one member carries a gene for a disease, cloning using a cell from the other member could assure that the couple has a healthy child of its own. Some U.S. legal experts claim that preventing a couple from choosing cloning as a method of reproduction could be unconstitutional. Scientists and ethicists who favor human cloning research also argue that cloning may provide a better understanding of the nature of genetic diseases and aid in the production of embryos from which cells could be obtained to grow various organs for organ transplants.

Will humans be cloned?

Although many laboratories around the world conducted animal cloning research in 1997, no laboratory acknowledged that it attempted to clone humans. However, noting that when a feat is technically possible, it is usually performed, a number of ethicists stated that it was simply a matter of time before a human being would be cloned. They argued that governments should establish strict regulations based on conditions under which human cloning might be acceptable, rather than spend time creating unenforceable laws that ban the procedure.

To much of the public, the sudden possibility of human cloning might have seemed like the latest in a series of radical and frightening scientific developments that society has had to confront throughout the last century—from the splitting of the atom to the proliferation of computers, from artificial life-support systems to test-tube babies. As society at the dawn of the next century weighs the benefits versus the harm of many scientific developments, human cloning may present the most thought-provoking challenge yet. ■ ■ ■

Boating. Yachtsmen the world over were appalled in March 1997 when a Maori activist walked into the Auckland, New Zealand, boating club where the America's Cup was on display and proceeded to beat the 150-year-old silver trophy with a sledgehammer. By August, the cup was back in New Zealand, after being repaired in London by Garrard, the royal silversmith and jeweler that had originally created it. New Zealand had won the America's Cup from the defending U.S. champion in 1995.

Sailing. *Adela,* a 170-foot (51-meter) schooner built in 1995, won the first Atlantic Challenge Cup on June 1, 1997. The 3,000-mile (4,800-kilometer) ocean race started with a 15-boat fleet that left Sandy Hook, New Jersey, on May 17 and finished at The Lizard, a point of land off the southwest coast of England. *Adela* took nearly 15 full days for the voyage because easterly headwinds impeded its progress. The 92-year-old record for the traditional course—12 days, 4 hours, 1 minute, and 19 seconds—set under ideal weather conditions by the legendary schooner *Atlantic,* was never threatened.

Pat Henry, a 56-year-old architect from Bloomington, Illinois, became the first American woman to sail solo around the world. She finished the final leg of her 27,000-mile (43,400-kilometer), 8-year passage on May 5, when she piloted her 31-foot (9.5-meter) sailboat, *Southern Cross,* into Acapulco, Mexico. Henry, a grandmother, was also the oldest woman of any nationality to complete the solo voyage. She said she financed most of her trip by painting and selling watercolors along the way.

The Worrell 1000, a catamaran race along 1,000 miles (1,600 kilometers) of coastline from Florida to Virginia, was reintroduced in May, eight years after being discontinued. The 13-day race subjected its 13-team fleet of double-hulled sailboats to two overnight stages along the way. Randy Smyth, the two-time Olympic silver medalist who had won Worrell twice before, gained his third victory in record-breaking fashion. Smyth and his teammate, Jason Sneed, took more than a day off Smyth's 1985 record (99 hours, 45 minutes) by completing their 1997 trek in 75 hours, 17 minutes.

The record for sailing around the world also was beaten in 1997, by the 90-foot (27-meter) French *trimaran* (3-hulled boat) *Sport-Elec.* Oliver Kersauson and his six-man crew returned to the southwest coast of England, their starting point, after circling the globe in 71 days, 14 hours, 22 minutes, and 8 seconds. Their voyage was almost three days faster than the former record of 74 days, set in 1994.

Powerboats. In June 1997 in Detroit, *Miss Budweiser* overcame wind and rough water to win the Gold Cup race, the most prestigious event on the American Power Boat Association circuit. The victory was *Miss Budweiser*'s 11th in 35 years. The boat's driver, Dave Villwock, had won the 1996 Gold Cup driving *PICO American Dream.* □ Ron Reid

Bolivia. On Aug. 6, 1997, Hugo Banzer Suárez, 71, was sworn in for a five-year term as president of Bolivia. Banzer and Vice President Jorge Quiroga, 36, were elected by Bolivia's Congress, which selects the leaders if no candidates receive more than 50 percent of the popular vote. Banzer and Quiroga, members of the right-wing Democratic National Action party, received 22.3 percent of votes in the June elections. A retired general, Banzer had seized power in Bolivia in a military *coup* (take-over) in 1971 and had run unsuccessfully for president five times since being ousted in another coup in 1978.

In January 1997, two Spanish banks, Argentaria and Banco Bilbao Vizcaya, won bids to administer privatized pension funds. In 1997, some 300,000 Bolivians, aged 65, began receiving payments amounting to $250 annually.

On July 12, Bolivia's government confirmed that the remains of the Argentine-born leftist guerrilla leader, Ernesto (Ché) Guevara, had been found in a mass grave near Vallegrande, Bolivia. Guevara, who figured prominently in the 1959 Communist revolution in Cuba, was executed by the Bolivian army in October 1967 for attempting to overthrow the Bolivian government. Guevara's remains were returned to his family in Cuba in July 1997.

□ Nathan A. Haverstock

Books. See **Canadian literature; Literature, American; Literature, Children's; Literature, World.**

Bosnia-Herzegovina. Vladimir Soljić, a Croat, became president of the Muslim-Croat Federation of Bosnia in March 1997. Bosnia consists of two substates—a Muslim-Croat federation and a Serb republic. The president of the Serb Republic, Biljana Plavšić, spent much of 1997 battling hard-line Serb leaders loyal to her predecessor, Radovan Karadzić, who had resigned under international pressure in 1996. Plavšić, who had been Karadzić's hand-picked successor, lost the support of fellow hard-liners as she moderated her political stance. Although Plavšić held the title of president, Karadzić and his allies were believed to exercise control behind the scenes.

On May 2, 1997, Dušan Tadić, a Bosnian Serb, became the first person since the end of World War II (1939–1945) to be convicted of war crimes by an international court. He was sentenced in July 1997 to 20 years in prison for his role in the ethnic persecution of Bosnian Muslims and Croats during the Bosnian War (1992–1995).

Hard-liners in the Serb republic clashed with North Atlantic Treaty Organization (NATO) forces in August 1997, when NATO troops seized local police stations in two Bosnian Serb towns that were being used to stockpile weapons. In October, NATO forces seized several television transmitters used by Bosnian Serb hard-liners to transmit hate messages and anti-NATO propaganda. NATO troops were sent to Bosnia in 1995 to police the agreement to end the

A mourner visits a Croat-Muslim cemetery on April 17, the Muslim holiday of Bajram, in the Bosnian capital, Sarajevo, a city struggling to rebuild itself from the devastation of a civil war that raged from 1992 to 1995.

civil war. Approximately 32,000 NATO soldiers were in Bosnia at the end of 1997. They were expected to remain there until at least June 1998.

Politics. On July 3, 1997, Plavšić dissolved the Bosnian Serb parliament, which was dominated by hard-liners. She founded a new, more moderate political party to contest the parliamentary elections in November. The official election results, announced in December, revealed that the hard-liners had lost control of parliament. However, no party, including Plavšić's, received a strong enough mandate to forge a stable government in the near future.

Economy. Leaders of the two Bosnian substates agreed in April to establish a joint central bank and a single currency. In June, officials of the World Bank, a UN affiliate, said that they expected Bosnia's economy to grow by 30 to 35 percent in 1997, after being almost totally destroyed by the Bosnian War. Foreign aid and reconstruction efforts fueled most of the recovery. However, the country received only 2 percent of the nearly $2 billion in reconstruction aid it was scheduled to receive in 1997, because its leaders refused to comply with the agreement that ended the war. As a result, citizens in the Serb republic continued to experience delays in receiving social assistance payments, and unemployment remained above 50 percent.   □ Sharon L. Wolchik

See also **Europe** (Facts in brief table).

Botswana. See Africa.

Bowling highlights in 1997 included the first $2-million career earnings winner on the men's Professional Bowlers Association (PBA) tour and a single-season earnings record on the Ladies Professional Bowlers Tour (LPBT). The year 1997 also marked the final telecast of the PBA tour on the ABC television network. ABC dropped the series, one of the longest running sports programs on TV, after years of declining ratings, saying that the audience had grown older and less desirable to advertisers. Announcer Chris Schenkel, 73, who had been with the series since its debut in 1962, received a standing ovation at the final telecast.

PBA. In 1997, Walter Ray Williams, Jr., of Stockton, California, became the first bowler to earn $2 million in career prize money. Williams reached the milestone on June 23, at a regional tournament in Fairview Heights, Illinois. The $4,000 first prize raised his career earnings to $2,002,373. Williams, whose exceptional hand-eye coordination helped him become a six-time world champion horseshoe pitcher, took 13 years to win his first $1 million in bowling. He needed only four years to win his second million.

The year's eight PBA tournaments offered a total of $4.6 million in purses. Williams led the 1997 tour, winning three tournaments and earning $322,044. He also led the PBA in scoring, with an average of 222 pins per game. Parker Bohn, III, of Jackson, New Jersey, was second in earnings with $273,185. Pete

Weber of St. Ann, Missouri, came in third with $252,184. Major tournament winners in 1997 included John Gant in the Brunswick Tournament of Champions, Rick Steelsmith in the PBA Championship, and rookie Jason Queen in the ABC Masters.

LPBT. On the 20-tournament women's tour, Wendy McPherson of Henderson, Nevada, enjoyed record success. She won four individual titles and boosted the single-season LPBT earnings record to $154,025. McPherson also led the LPBT tour in scoring, averaging 214.68 pins per game. Carol Gianotti-Block of Perth, Australia, also topped $100,000 in earnings in 1997. Sandra Jo Shiery-Odom won the Women's International Bowling Congress Queens tournament. Marianne DiRupo won the Hammer Players championship, and Kim Adler won the Sam's Town Invitational. On July 10 in Danville, Virginia, Michelle Feldman, 21, of Skaneateles, New York, became the first woman in bowling history to bowl a 300 game on national television.

Seniors. Gary Dickinson of Edmond, Oklahoma, was the top money winner on the seniors tour, with more than $143,000 in earnings. Dickinson won the American Bowling Congress Senior Masters on August 16 in Akron, Ohio. It was Dickinson's third title of 1997, and the $60,000 first prize was his biggest in 28 years as a pro. Larry Laub won the PBA Championship, and George Pappas took the Showboat Tournament of Champions.   □ Ron Reid

Boxing. The boxing scene took some bizarre twists in 1997. The year saw Riddick Bowe, the former World Boxing Association (WBA) heavyweight champion, end a short-lived venture in the United States Marine Corps; Oliver McCall, a heavyweight contender, suffer an apparent breakdown during a championship bout; and former heavyweight champ Mike Tyson bite off the top of Evander Holyfield's right ear during a WBA title fight.

Bowe and McCall. Bowe shocked the boxing world in January 1997 when he joined the U.S. Marine Corps. However, he dropped out after three days of basic training at the Marine Corp's facility at Parris Island, South Carolina. Bowe retired from boxing in April, ending a career that had earned $100 million in purses.

Oliver McCall met Lennox Lewis in Las Vegas, Nevada, on February 7, to compete for the vacant World Boxing Council (WBC) heavyweight title. The fight ended in Round 5, after McCall mysteriously stopped fighting in the fourth round. Before the fifth round, he stood in his corner, crying. Lewis was declared the winner by technical knockout.

A heavyweight chomp. Mike Tyson, the former WBA and WBC champion, fought current WBA champion Evander Holyfield on June 28 in Las Vegas. In the third round, Tyson was cut over the left eye by a head butt from Holyfield, which the referee ruled was accidental. Moments later, during a clinch,

World champion boxers

World Boxing Association

Division	Champion	Country	Date won
Heavyweight	Evander Holyfield	U.S.A.	11/96
Light heavyweight	Lou Del Valle	U.S.A.	9/97
	Darius Michalczewski	Germany	6/97
	Virgil Hill	U.S.A.	9/92
Middleweight	Julio Cesar Green	U.S.A.	8/97
	William Joppy	U.S.A.	6/96
Welterweight	Ike Quartey	Ghana	6/94
Lightweight	Orzubek Nazarov	Russia	10/93
Featherweight	Wilfredo Vazquez	Puerto Rico	5/96
Bantamweight	Nana Konadu	Ghana	6/97
	Daorung Chuwatana	Thailand	10/96
Flyweight	Jose Bonilla	Venezuela	11/96

World Boxing Council

Division	Champion	Country	Date won
Heavyweight	Lennox Lewis	United Kingdom	2/97
Light heavyweight	Roy Jones	U.S.A.	8/97
	Montell Griffin	U.S.A.	3/97
	Roy Jones	U.S.A.	11/96
Middleweight	Keith Holmes	U.S.A.	3/96
Welterweight	Oscar de la Hoya	U.S.A.	4/97
	Pernell Whitaker	U.S.A.	3/93
Lightweight	Steve Johnston	U.S.A.	3/97
	Jean-Baptiste Mendy	France	4/96
Featherweight	Luisito Espinosa	Philippines	12/95
Bantamweight	S. Singmanassak	Thailand	8/96
Flyweight	Chatchai Sasakul	Thailand	11/97
	Yuri Arbachakov	Russia	6/92

Tyson bit Holyfield's right ear, tearing away a piece of tissue. The bout continued a few moments more, after Holyfield received treatment for the bite. Tyson then bit Holyfield again, on the left ear, and was disqualified. Observers said that Tyson appeared frustrated by the cut, the doubtful impact of his punches, and the points he was losing. The sudden end to the fight set off a wave of brawling throughout the arena. The fight grossed more than $130 million and was the richest in history.

Many observers called Tyson's apology to Holyfield on June 29 insincere and self-serving. On July 9, Nevada boxing officials fined Tyson 10 percent of his earnings for the fight—a total of $3 million—and revoked his boxing license, effectively banning him from boxing in the United States for at least a year.

On Nov. 8, 1997, Evander Holyfield won the International Boxing Federation's heavyweight title from Michael Moorer in Las Vegas. The fight ended when Moorer failed to answer the ninth round bell.

Other divisions. Oscar De La Hoya took the WBC welterweight title from Pernell Whitaker in April. He defended it with impressive victories over David Kamau in June, Hector "Macho" Camacho in September, and Wilfredo Rivera in December.

Sugar Ray Leonard, age 40, attempted a comeback in March, after retiring from boxing in 1991. Leonard was easily beaten by Hector Camacho in the fifth round of the fight. ☐ Ron Reid

Mike Tyson bites the ear of heavyweight champion Evander Holyfield in a June 28 title fight. Moments later, Tyson was disqualified for biting Holyfield again.

Brazil. On June 4, 1997, President Fernando Henrique Cardoso obtained the right to run for a second term as president in 1998, when the Brazilian Senate passed a constitutional amendment that allows the president, state governors, and mayors to serve for two consecutive terms. Cardoso's reputation for integrity, however, was severely tarnished in the process.

On May 13, 1997, a São Paulo newspaper, *A Fôlha de São Paulo,* revealed that members of the Chamber of Deputies, the lower house of the legislature, had allegedly taken bribes for voting for the measure in January and February.

Ronivón Santiago and João Maia, deputies who revealed their role in the scandal on a secretly recorded audio tape, resigned on May 21, the day of the first vote in the Senate. The two men, who admitted receiving bribes of nearly $200,000 each, alleged that four other deputies had received equal sums. The money was reported to have come from Sérgio Motta, the minister of communications, and had been paid to the deputies by Amazonino Mendes, the governor of Amazonas state.

Austerity measures. On November 10, the Brazilian government announced tax increases of about 10 percent, budget cuts, and job layoffs in an effort to reduce the budget deficit. The announcement followed a 6-percent plunge in Brazil's stock market on November 7. The government expected the austerity measures to restore international confidence in the economy and to prevent the devaluation of Brazil's currency, the *real*.

Landless march on Brasília. On April 17, the first anniversary of a police massacre of 19 protesters in the northern state of Pará, 1,500 landless workers marched on the capital, Brasília, to demand land reform. They were welcomed by tens of thousands of supporters drawing attention to the inequality of land distribution in Brazil, where 20 percent of the people own 88 percent of the land.

State mining company privatized. The Brazilian government on May 6 sold 41.75 percent of the state-owned mining company, Companhia Vale do Rio Doce (CVRD). The sale was the largest privatization effort yet conducted in Latin America. A consortium, led by a Brazilian steelmaker, Companhia Siderúrgica Nacional, won the privatized shares of CVRD with a $3.13 billion bid. NationsBank Corporation of the United States provided a loan of $1.1 billion for the purchase.

More than 120 legal challenges were filed in court in a futile effort to block the sale of what many economists regarded as one of Brazil's most important assets. In 1997, CVRD was the world's largest exporter of iron ore, the third largest mining enterprise, and Latin America's leading gold producer. Some Brazilians viewed the sale as a "first step" toward turning over all of the assets of Brazil's Amazon basin, where CVRD operates, to foreigners.

Foreign buy-outs of Brazilian companies. In 1997, foreign companies continued to buy Brazilian enterprises at a feverish pace. Bayer AG, a German chemicals giant, paid $51.6 million for a majority stake in Central de Polímeros de Bahia, which makes plastics for computers and automobile shock absorbers. On March 27, the London-based HSBC Holdings PLC announced that it was buying Banco Bamerindus do Brasil, a bank with 1,300 branches in Brazil, for $1 billion.

Cellular phone licenses. On July 9, the Bell South Corporation of the United States and three Brazilian companies—the Safra Group, a banking and industrial conglomerate; O Estado de São Paulo, a media company; and Splice, a maker of telecommunications equipment—paid $2.5 billion for a 15-year license to sell cellular phones in metropolitan São Paulo, a market with some 18 million people. On August 8, Bell South and the Safra Group announced that they would pay $512 million for a license to provide cellular service in a six-state area of northeast Brazil. The Brazilian government also sold licenses for a mobile phone network within the state of São Paulo for $1.74 billion to a group of companies led by Telia AB of Sweden.

☐ Nathan A. Haverstock

See also **Latin America** (Facts in brief table).

British Columbia. See Canadian provinces.

Brunei. See Asia.

Building and construction. Construction on two long awaited art museums was completed in 1997. In October, the Guggenheim Museum, designed by American architect Frank O. Gehry, opened in Bilbao, a city in the Basque region of northern Spain. The $100-million art complex consists of several connected buildings with irregularly shaped exteriors of titanium and glass. The exhibition space covers more than 112,000 square feet (10,400 square meters)—larger than either of the Guggenheim museums in New York City. The striking structure, considered by many to be Gehry's most ambitious design to date, is the central element in Bilbao's goal to establish itself as an international cultural center.

The Getty Center, designed by American architect Richard Meier, was opened in Los Angeles in December. Under construction for more than eight years, the Getty Center, a campus of six buildings joined by plazas and terraces, cost about $1 billion. The complex is located on a 710-acre (287-hectare) hilltop that visitors reach by taking a tram from a parking lot at the base of the hill.

China's Three Gorges Dam. In November, work was completed on the first phase of the Three Gorges Dam, the largest flood-control and hydroelectric power project in the world. The $24.5-billion project was designed to generate 18,200 megawatts of electricity by taming China's Yangtze River, which

The Sky Tower, at 1,076 feet (328 meters) the highest structure in the Southern Hemisphere, opened in Auckland, New Zealand, in July 1997. The tower, featuring a revolving restaurant and four observation decks, was designed to resist earthquake damage and to withstand wind gusts of 125 miles (200 kilometers) per hour.

flows west to east for 3,915 miles (6,300 kilometers).

Construction workers, in the first phase, cut a diversion channel through the river's bank to redirect the flow of the river temporarily. On the opposite bank, workers began removing about 2.05 billion cubic feet (58 million cubic meters) of granite to build a five-step navigation lock for river traffic. A *cofferdam* (temporary dam) was also constructed to block the flow of the river before the next phase of the project begins, building the permanent dam. Scheduled for completion in 2009, the dam will require almost 530 million cubic feet (15 million cubic meters) of concrete to complete a structure 7,550 feet (2,300 meters) long and 590 feet (180 meters) high.

The project continued to draw worldwide criticism during 1997. Many scientists opposed the dam, which will flood a 135-mile (220-kilometer) stretch of riverbank that is rich in cultural and archeological artifacts. The project will also displace about 1.2 million people who live along the Yangtse River.

African water project. In May, construction of the Letsibogo Dam was completed across the Motlutse River in Botswana in southern Africa. Work also continued on the North-South Water Project pipeline, a 220-mile (350-kilometer) aqueduct made of steel and glass-reinforced plastic that will transport water to Gaborone, the capital city of Botswana. The $330-million dam and pipeline are part of a 30-year master water plan to help transform the country from an agrarian society to a developing, urban nation.

California reservoir. In 1997, the Metropolitan Water District of Southern California continued construction on the Eastside Reservoir, a lake 90 miles (145 kilometers) southeast of Los Angeles with a capacity of 800,000 acre-feet (987 million cubic meters). The lake will be large enough to provide a six-month reserve of water to the public agency's 16 million customers. Three dams will contain the lake in a 7.5-square-mile (19.4-square-kilometer) valley that is high enough for water to flow by gravity to most customers in the network.

The Eastside Reservoir project was the largest earthmoving job in the United States in 1997. With a fleet of specialized equipment that operated 20 hours a day, crews excavated and backfilled 250,000 cubic yards (190,000 cubic meters) of earth daily. The $1.9-billion project, scheduled to be completed in 1999 and filled by 2003, was expected to double the Metropolitan Water District's storage capacity in order to replace water from aqueducts that are damaged from earthquakes.

Earthquake resistant freeway. In July 1997, a nearly 3-mile (4.8-kilometer) stretch of the Cypress Freeway opened in the San Francisco Bay area. The new road replaced the double-decker expressway that collapsed in the 1989 Loma Prieta earthquake, killing 42 people. The new six-lane, single-level freeway is a structurally complicated network of earth-quake-resistant ramps, interchanges, and connectors. Engineers designed concrete and steel piles that were extended into the ground to a depth of 90 feet (27 meters) and large girders and columns that were made 30 times stronger than those supporting the old freeway. The new portion of the expressway swings around the city of Oakland to connect Interstate 880 in the south to Interstate 80 and the San Francisco-Oakland Bay Bridge. Other portions of the expressway were scheduled for completion in 1998.

Sports facilities. In 1997, contractors rushed to complete several sports venues around the United States in time for various sports seasons. The U.S. Open tennis tournament in August inaugurated the nearly 23,000-seat, $250-million Arthur Ashe Stadium at the U.S. Tennis Association's National Tennis Center in New York City. The MCI Center, with seating for about 20,000 people, opened in Washington, D.C., in December. The $175-million stadium, which sits above two levels of subterranean parking and two subway stations, was the new home to the National Basketball Association's Washington Wizards and the National Hockey League's Washington Capitals. In September, the Washington Redskins moved into the National Football League's largest open-air stadium, the Jack Kent Cooke Stadium in Raljon, Maryland. □ Andrew G. Wright

See also **Architecture.**

Bulgaria. More than 100 people were injured on Jan. 10, 1997, in clashes between opposition protesters and police in Bulgaria's parliament building. The violence erupted after the Socialist majority in parliament refused to allow a vote on a measure proposed by opposition parties that included a call for early elections. The violence came amid weeks of daily protests, strikes, and a blockade of important intersections in Sofia, the country's capital. The protests had forced the resignation of the Socialist prime minister, Zhan Videnov, and his government two weeks earlier, on Dec. 21, 1996.

Bulgaria's newly elected president, Petar Stoyanov, a member of the largest opposition group, the center-right Union of Democratic Forces (UDF), took office on Jan. 22, 1997. He moved quickly to forge a compromise between the ruling and opposition parties. Under the agreement, Stoyanov dissolved the legislature in February and appointed an interim government to rule until early elections in April.

In the April 19 elections, the UDF and its coalition partner, the People's Union, won 137 of the 240 seats in the legislature. The defeated Socialists retained just 58 seats. Ivan Kostov, leader of the UDF and a former finance minister, became prime minister. The Kostov government pledged to continue the economic measures and the war on crime begun by the interim government.

Economy. Foreign investment in Bulgaria declined sharply in early 1997 in reaction to the economic and political turmoil. Inflation, which stood at 43.8 percent in January, rocketed to 243 percent in February. By May, inflation had eased to 5.6 percent. Economists expected the unemployment rate, which had reached 13.4 percent in early 1997, to double in the next two years.

IMF Loan. On April 11, the International Monetary Fund (IMF) approved a $658-million loan to Bulgaria. In accordance with an agreement made between the IMF and the interim government in March, Bulgaria established a currency board in July to oversee a strict monetary policy and a program to reduce the nation's budget deficit. While the government aimed to privatize 40 percent of state-owned businesses in 1997, only 1 percent of these had been sold in the first three months of the year. Thirty of the largest of these enterprises were earmarked for sale to foreign buyers.

Foreign affairs. Turkey in February agreed not to expel some 200,000 ethnic Turks who had entered Turkey from Bulgaria illegally. Bulgaria's leaders in 1997 reaffirmed their interest in joining Western institutions. However, they refused to eliminate the country's arsenal of medium-range nuclear missiles.

☐ Sharon L. Wolchik

See also **Europe** (Facts in brief table).

Burkina Faso. See Africa.

Burma became a member of the Association of Southeast Asian Nations (ASEAN), an organization fostering cooperation primarily in economic development, on July 23, 1997. Burma was admitted to ASEAN despite human rights and narcotics trafficking charges against the governing *junta* (military group that holds power after a coup or revolution), which had seized power in 1988. The junta changed its name in November 1997 from the State Law and Order Restoration Council to the State Peace and Development Council.

Burma, which is officially known as Myanmar, gained admission into ASEAN only months after it attacked Thailand, another ASEAN member. In January and February 1997, Burmese troops had crossed into Thailand and burned refugee camps of the Karen National Union, an ethnic minority group that had long fought for independence from Burma.

U.S. boycott. On April 22, the United States government imposed a ban on new U.S. investments in Burma after the junta refused to meet with Daw Aung San Suu Kyi, leader of the National League for Democracy. The League had won parliamentary elections in 1990, but the junta imprisoned many League members and refused to allow parliament to convene.

When the U.S. ban took effect in May 1997, the junta arrested several League members. Most ASEAN member nations ignored the ban, and China contin-

Bulgarians raise extra cash by hauling an abandoned car to sell for scrap when inflation rose by nearly 200 percent in February 1997. The inflation rate in Bulgaria eased by May.

ued to increase its trade with and its military aid to Burma. In September, British Foreign Secretary Robin Cook said that Burma would not be invited to an April 1998 meeting in London that was planned for improving relations between Europe, China, Japan, South Korea, and most ASEAN member nations.

Suu Kyi, who had often been under house arrest since 1989, made a rare public appearance on April 14, 1997, to celebrate the Buddhist new year. In May, the junta blocked a party meeting at Suu Kyi's house by detaining at least 60 League members. In September, the League cancelled a meeting with the junta's top secretary, Lieutenant General Khin Nyunt, because Suu Kyi was not invited.

Burma's economy experienced severe inflation in 1997 as the currency, the kyat, lost more than half of its value. Imports were financed by money sent home by overseas workers and drug money. Few new enterprises were launched in Burma in 1997.

Riot. On March 16 and March 17, a riot erupted at a gathering of Buddhist monks in Mandalay. Fighting broke out between local Muslims and the monks, who were meeting to air grievances against the local government. According to some published reports, army troops provoked the riots to justify a crackdown on widespread *dissidence* (disagreements with government policy).   □ Henry S. Bradsher

See also **Asia** (Facts in brief table); **Thailand.**

Burundi. The Hutu-Tutsi ethnic conflict continued in Burundi in 1997, despite peacemaking efforts by neighboring African countries. Between 1993 and 1996, at least 150,000 people had died in the armed conflict between Burundi's minority Tutsi, who controlled the government and army, and the Hutu, who made up 85 percent of the population. During 1997, frequent attacks by Hutu rebels were followed by severe reprisals by the army.

Hutu camps. By mid-1997, an estimated 250,000 Hutu civilians had been forced into camps in about 12 "protection zones" by the military government of President Pierre Buyoya, the leader of a successful 1996 coup against Burundi's Hutu civilian president. Buyoya claimed the protection zones would ensure the safety of Hutu civilians, who had also suffered from attacks by Hutu rebels. Hutu leaders, however, charged that the camps were established to prevent Hutu farmers from aiding the rebels and to provide the government with victims for reprisals. Human rights groups reported that the camp residents were suffering from inadequate shelter, food, and water.

Peacemaking efforts. Under the leadership of Julius Nyerere, former president of Tanzania, the leaders of Burundi's neighboring states continued to pressure Buyoya's government to end the ethnic conflict. In 1996, the group had imposed an embargo on landlocked Burundi, demanding that Buyoya reopen parliament, reestablish political parties, and

negotiate a peaceful settlement with the rebels. In March 1997, Buyoya agreed to the first two of these conditions, though the absence of Hutus in the government limited their effect. Buyoya also proclaimed his willingness to open talks with the rebels.

On April 18, leaders of neighboring states eased their embargo after meeting with Buyoya in Tanzania. On September 4, however, they concluded that Burundi's government had made no progress toward resolving the conflict and that sanctions should continue. Although the embargo created hardships for Burundians, enough smuggling occurred to prevent the embargo from undermining the government.

Internal dissent. In mid-September, Charles Mukasi of the Tutsi Union of National Progress filed a court challenge to the government's policy against negotiation. He was immediately arrested but released the following day. Buyoya stated publicly that he wanted to talk with the leader of the Congo (Kinshasa)-based National Council for the Defense of Democracy—the main Hutu rebel group. However, some Tutsi civilian groups continued to oppose negotiations.   □ Mark DeLancey

See also **Africa** (Facts in brief table); **Africa** Special Report: **The Hutu and Tutsi—A Conflict Beyond Borders; Congo (Kinshasa); Rwanda.**

Bus. See Transportation

Business. See Bank; Economics; Labor; Manufacturing.

Cabinet, U.S. President Bill Clinton reshuffled his Cabinet in 1997 as he began his second term in office. He selected Madeleine K. Albright as the first woman to become secretary of state, promoting her from the post of U.S. ambassador to the United Nations. Albright became the highest-ranking woman ever to serve in the U.S. government. Former Senator William S. Cohen (R., Maine) was also swiftly confirmed as secretary of defense. Both Albright and Cohen were confirmed by the Senate on January 22 with votes of 99 to zero.

Alexis Herman's confirmation as secretary of labor faced a long delay following opposition by Senate Republicans. Critics argued that Herman may have engaged in improper political fund-raising while director of the White House Office of Public Liaison. The Senate confirmed Herman's appointment by a vote of 85 to 13 on April 30, but only after Clinton withdrew a plan urging federal agencies to award federal construction projects to companies that employ only unionized labor. In August, Herman played a key role in the settlement of a teamsters' union strike against United Parcel Service.

Federico F. Peña was confirmed as secretary of energy on March 12. He had served as secretary of transportation during President Clinton's first term (1993-1997). The Senate also confirmed in 1997 Rodney E. Slater, former chairman of the Arkansas Highway Commission, as secretary of transportation;

William M. Daley, the son of former Chicago Mayor Richard J. Daley, as secretary of commerce; and Andrew Cuomo, the son of former New York Governor Mario Cuomo, as secretary of housing and urban development.

In 1997, the president reappointed Attorney General Janet Reno, Secretary of the Treasury Robert Rubin, Secretary of Education Richard W. Riley, Secretary of Interior Bruce Babbitt, Secretary of Agriculture Dan Glickman, Secretary of Health and Human Services Donna Shalala, and Secretary of Veterans Affairs Jesse Brown. Brown resigned in July.

The president's nominee to head the Central Intelligence Agency (CIA), Anthony Lake, withdrew his name from consideration on March 17, after some senators questioned Lake's personal finances and leadership of the White House National Security Council. On March 19, Clinton named George Tenet, the deputy CIA director, to run the agency.

Former Housing Secretary Henry Cisneros was indicted on December 11 on charges of conspiracy, obstructing justice, and making false statements during a Senate confirmation hearing in 1993 about payments he had made to woman with whom he had an extramarital relationship. ☐ William J. Eaton

See also **Labor and employment; People in the news.**

California. See Los Angeles; San Francisco; State government.

Cambodia. Hun Sen, second prime minister and head of the Cambodian People's Party (CPP), staged a military *coup* (overthrow) on July 5, 1997, ousting the first prime minister and eliminating any effective governmental role for the National United Front for an Independent, Neutral, Peaceful, and Cooperative Cambodia (FUNCINPEC) Party. The CPP and FUNCINPEC had run the government in coalition since 1993.

The CPP had been a Communist party when put in power by the Vietnamese who invaded Cambodia in 1979. FUNCINPEC had taken the largest number of votes in the 1993 elections, which were supervised by the United Nations (UN). Following the elections, the UN had failed to carry out its mandate to disarm political factions and set up a neutral government. FUNCINPEC was forced to form a coalition government with the CPP when Hun Sen refused to give up his party's army or its control over the government. Prince Ranariddh, head of FUNCINPEC and son of King Norodom Sihanouk, became first prime minister, and Hun Sen was named second prime minister.

In 1997, both parties attempted to win the support of the Khmer Rouge, the Communist movement that had ruled Cambodia from 1975 to 1979. A faction of the Khmer Rouge eager to make peace with the government agreed to support FUNCINPEC. Ranariddh also formed an alliance with Sam Rainsy, a

Residents of Phnom Penh flee the city in July 1997 as armed conflict between supporters of Cambodia's two prime ministers erupts in the capital.

Cambodia

Cambodian politician whose criticisms of the CPP had angered Hun Sen. Rainsy narrowly escaped a grenade attack on March 30, 1997, that killed 16 people. Hun Sen was blamed for the attack.

Fearing that the alliances would give FUNCINPEC the strength it needed to win elections scheduled for May 1998, Hun Sen, on July 4, 1997, ordered CPP troops to attack FUNCINPEC's forces in the capital, Phnom Penh. On July 6—the day the Khmer Rouge was to enter into an alliance with FUNCINPEC—the CPP took control of the government, and Ranariddh fled the country.

FUNCINPEC's armed forces retreated to northwest Cambodia. In mid-August, CPP troops drove 30,000 FUNCINPEC soldiers and refugees into a small area in the north near Thailand. A UN investigation found that Hen Sen's forces subsequently tortured and executed at least 40 FUNCINPEC military officers and officials, including Interior Minister Ho Sok, who once tried to arrest a Hun Sen supporter for narcotics trading. Theng Bunma, a businessman widely accused of drug dealing, claimed to have financed the coup. Following the coup, the United States and many other countries suspended economic aid to Cambodia.

On August 6, the Cambodian parliament stripped Ranariddh of power and elected Foreign Minister Ung Huot as first prime minister. Hun Sen called for Ranariddh's arrest and asked that he be tried by a military court on charges of illegally importing weapons. Prince Ranariddh, in exile, claimed that Hun Sen had staged the coup to avoid investigations into drug trafficking. King Sihanouk returned to Cambodia from China for two months and attempted to arrange peace talks between Hun Sen and Ranariddh, but Hun Sen rejected the offer. King Sihanouk returned to China in October, after announcing that he would no longer fulfill his constitutional function and would prefer to abdicate.

Pol Pot captured. Pol Pot, the reclusive leader of the hard-line Communist faction of the Khmer Rouge, was sentenced to life imprisonment in July after Khmer Rouge guerrillas convicted him of ordering the murder of government officials. In mid-June, mutinous Khmer Rouge forces had captured Pol Pot after he orchestrated the executions of 10 government negotiators and his former defense minister, Son Sen.

Pol Pot oversaw the deaths of more than 1.5 million people—a quarter of Cambodia's population—when the Khmer Rouge ruled Cambodia in the late 1970's. He was last seen by journalists in 1979, when he gave a news conference after his government was toppled by a Vietnamese invasion. In 1996, the Khmer Rouge split into factions led by Pol Pot and by Ieng Sary, leader of the Khmer Rouge's guerrilla forces. The Pol Pot faction had provoked violent unrest in Cambodia. □ Henry S. Bradsher

See also **Asia** (Facts in brief table).

Canada

Canada emerged from a general election on June 2, 1997, with its Parliament composed for the first time of five officially recognized political parties. Each of the parties owed its success to the election's most significant component—regional voting. Even the victorious Liberal Party of Prime Minister Jean Chrétien lost its standing as a national party. The Liberals won only a scattering of seats in Western Canada Provinces (British Columbia, Alberta, Saskatchewan, and Manitoba) and lost nearly all their seats in the Atlantic or Maritime Provinces (New Foundland, New Brunswick, Prince Edward Island, and Nova Scotia). At the root of this regional split lay the issue of national unity—an issue that had dominated Canada's political agenda since the referendum for the secession of Quebec was narrowly defeated in 1995.

The campaign. Chrétien called for a general election on April 27, 1997, six months before the end of the usual four-year term for Canadian governments. He was unable to explain convincingly why he had called an early election. Many observers believed that Chrétien, who enjoyed high ratings in public opinion polls, was hoping to exploit the problems plaguing the separatist Bloc Québécois (BQ) and the right-wing Reform Party to strengthen the Liberals' position, particularly in Western Canada.

Before the election, the Liberals held 174 of 295 seats in the House of Commons. Two other parties each held 50 seats: the BQ, the official opposition party following its second-place showing in the 1993 election; and the Reform Party. In the 1993 election, neither the right-of-center Progressive Conservative Party nor the liberal New Democratic Party had won the 12 seats needed to qualify for participation in parliamentary debates.

During the campaign, the Liberals emphasized their steady management of the Canadian union. They also trumpeted their success in cutting the annual federal deficit from $45 billion in 1993 to $17 billion in fiscal 1997-1998. Under attack for cutting spending on social programs, the Liberals promised to restore $700 million in payments to the provinces for health care and education and to increase spending on crime prevention and job training for youth. (All monetary figures are in Canadian dollars.) Chrétien also promised to delay any new talks on Quebec's status until the government had the support of a majority of the provinces.

Election results. Chrétien's accommodating approach to Quebec's claims of special status earned him little respect in Western Canada, while voters in the economically weak Atlantic Provinces resented his cutbacks in unemployment insurance benefits. Nevertheless, the Liberals managed to win 155 of

Queen Elizabeth II of Great Britain participates in a June 24, 1997, ceremony in New-foundland, including a reenactment of John Cabot's 1497 landing, to mark the 500th anniversary of the arrival of the first English ships in North America.

The House of Commons of the first session of the 36th Parliament convened on Sept. 22, 1997. As of Nov. 1, 1997, the House of Commons consisted of the following members: 155 Liberal Party, 44 Bloc Québécois, 59 Reform Party, 21 New Democratic Party, 20 Progressive Conservative Party, and 1 Independent. This table shows each legislator and party affiliation. An asterisk (*) denotes those who served in the 35th Parliament.

Alberta
Diane Ablonczy, Ref.*
Rob Anders, Ref.*
Leon E. Benoit, Ref.*
Cliff Breitkreuz, Ref.*
Rick Casson, Ref.
David Chatters, Ref.*
Ken Epp, Ref.*
Peter Goldring, Ref.
Deborah Grey, Ref.*
Art Hanger, Ref.*
Grant Hill, Ref.*
Rahim Jaffer, Ref.
Dale Johnston, Ref.*
Jason Kenney, Ref.
David Kilgour, Lib.*
Eric Lowther, Ref.
Preston Manning, Ref.*
Ian McClelland, Ref.*
Anne McLellan, Lib.*
Bob Mills, Ref.*
Deepak Obhrai, Ref.
Charlie Penson, Ref.*
Jack Ramsay, Ref.*
Monte Solberg, Ref.*
Myron Thompson, Ref.*
John Williams, Ref.*

British Columbia
Jim Abbott, Ref.*
David Anderson, Lib.*
Chuck Cadman, Ref.
Raymond Chan, Lib.*
John Cummins, Ref.*
Elizabeth Davies, N.D.P.
Harbance Singh Dhaliwal, Lib.*
John Duncan, Ref.*
Reed Elley, Ref.
Paul Forseth, Ref.*
Hedy Fry, Lib.*
Bill Gilmour, Ref.*
Jim Gouk, Ref.*
Gurmant Grewal, Ref.
Richard M. Harris, Ref.*
Jim Hart, Ref.*
Jay Hill, Ref.*
M. Sophia Leung, Lib.
Gary Lunn, Ref.
Keith Martin, Ref.*
Philip Mayfield, Ref.*
Grant McNally, Ref.
Ted McWhinney, Lib.*
Val Meredith, Ref.*
John Reynolds, Ref.
Nelson Riis, N.D.P.*
Svend J. Robinson, N.D.P.*
Werner Schmidt, Ref.*
Mike Scott, Ref.*
Darrel Stinson, Ref.*
Chuck Strahl, Ref.*
Randy White, Ref.*
Ted White, Ref.*

Manitoba
Reg Alcock, Lib.*
Lloyd Axworthy, Lib.*

Bill Blaikie, N.D.P.*
Rick Borotsik, P.C.
Bev Desjarlais, N.D.P.
Ronald J. Duhamel, Lib.*
John Harvard, Lib.*
Howard Hilstrom, Ref.
Jake E. Hoeppner, Ref.*
David Iftody, Lib.*
Inky Mark, Ref.
Pat Martin, N.D.P.
Rey D. Pagtakhan, Lib.*
Judy Wasylycia-Leis, N.D.P.

New Brunswick
Gilles Bernier, P.C.
Claudette Bradshaw, Lib.
Jean Dubé, P.C.
Yvon Godin, N.D.P.
John Herron, P.C.
Charles Hubbard, Lib.*
Andy Scott, Lib.*
Greg Thompson, P.C.
Angela Vautour, N.D.P.
Elsie Wayne, P.C.*

Newfoundland
George S. Baker, Lib.*
Gerry Byrne, Lib.*
Norman Doyle, P.C.
Bill Matthews, P.C.
Fred J. Mifflin, P.C.*
Lawrence D. O'Brien, Lib.*
Charlie Power, P.C.

Northwest Territories
Ethel Blondin-Andrew, Lib.*
Nancy Karetak-Lindell, Lib.

Nova Scotia
Scott Brison, P.C.
Bill Casey, P.C.
Michelle Dockrill, N.D.P.
Gordon Earle, N.D.P.
Gerald Keddy, P.C.
Wendy Lill, N.D.P.
Peter Mackay, P.C.
Peter Mancini, N.D.P.
Alexa McDonough, N.D.P.
Mark Muise, P.C.
Peter Stoffer, N.D.P.

Ontario
Peter Adams, Lib.*
Sarkis Assadourian, Lib.*
Jean Augustine, Lib.*
Sue Barnes, Lib.*
Colleen Beaumier, Lib.*
Réginald Bélair, Lib.*
Mauril Bélanger, Lib.*
Eugène Bellemare, Lib.*
Carolyn Bennett, Lib.
Maurizio Bevilacqua, Lib.*
Raymond Bonin, Lib.*
Paul Bonwick, Lib.

Don Boudria, Lib.*
Bonnie Brown, Lib.*
John Bryden, Lib.*
Sarmite Bulte, Lib.
Charles Caccia, Lib.*
Murray Calder, Lib.*
John Cannis, Lib.*
Elinor Caplan, Lib.
Aileen Carroll, Lib.
Marlene Catterall, Lib.*
Brenda Chamberlain, Lib.*
Hec Clouthier, Lib.
Shaughnessy Cohen, Lib.*
David M. Collenette, Lib.*
Joe Comuzzi, Lib.*
Sheila Copps, Lib.*
Roy Cullen, Lib.*
Paul DeVillers, Lib.*
Stan Dromisky, Lib.*
Arthur C. Eggleton, Lib.*
John Finlay, Lib.*
Joe Fontana, Lib.*
Roger Gallaway, Lib.*
John Godfrey, Lib.*
Bill Graham, Lib.*
Herb Gray, Lib.*
Ivan Grose, Lib.*
Albina Guarnieri, Lib.*
Mac Harb, Lib.*
Tony Ianno, Lib.*
Ovid L. Jackson, Lib.*
Jim Jones, P.C.
Joe Jordan, Lib.
Jim Karygiannis, Lib.*
Stan Keyes, Lib.*
Bob Kilger, Lib.*
Gar Knutson, Lib.*
Karen Kraft Sloan, Lib.*
Walt Lastewka, Lib.*
Derek Lee, Lib.*
Judi Longfield, Lib.
Steve Mahoney, Lib.
Gurbax Singh Malhi, Lib.*
John Maloney, Lib.*
John Manley, Lib.*
Sergio Marchi, Lib.*
Diane Marleau, Lib.*
Larry McCormick, Lib.*
John McKay, Lib.
Dan McTeague, Lib.*
Peter Milliken, Lib.*
Dennis J. Mills, Lib.*
Maria Minna, Lib.*
Andy Mitchell, Lib.*
Ian Murray, Lib.*
Lynn Myers, Lib.
Robert D. Nault, Lib.*
John Nunziata, Ind.*
Pat O'Brien, Lib.*
John O'Reilly, Lib.*
Gilbert Parent, Lib.*
Carolyn Parrish, Lib.*
Janko Peric, Lib.*
Jim Peterson, Lib.*

Beth Phinney, Lib.*
Jerry Pickard, Lib.*
Gary Pillitteri, Lib.*
David Pratt, Lib.
Carmen Provenzano, Lib.
Karen Redman, Lib.
Julian Reed, Lib.*
John Richardson, Lib.*
Allan Rock, Lib.*
Brent St. Denis, Lib.*
Benoît Serré, Lib.*
Alex Shepherd, Lib.*
Bob Speller, Lib.*
Paul Steckle, Lib.*
Christine Stewart, Lib.*
Jane Stewart, Lib.*
Paul Szabo, Lib.*
Andrew Telegdi, Lib.*
Paddy Torsney, Lib.*
Rose-Marie Ur, Lib.*
Tony Valeri, Lib.*
Lyle Vanclief, Lib.*
Joseph Volpe, Lib.
Tom Wappel, Lib.*
Susan Whelan, Lib.*
Bryon Wilfert, Lib.
Bob Wood, Lib.*

Prince Edward Island
Wayne Easter, Lib.*
Lawrence MacAulay, Lib.*
Joe McGuire, Lib.*
George Proud, Lib.*

Quebec
Hélène Alarie, B.Q.
Mark Assad, B.Q.*
Gérard Asselin, B.Q.*
André Bachand, P.C.
Claude Bachand, B.Q.*
Eleni Bakopanos, Lib.*
Michel Bellehumeur, B.Q.*
Stéphane Bergeron, B.Q.*
Yvan Bernier, B.Q.*
Gilles Bernier, P.C.*
Robert Bertrand, B.Q.*
Bernard Bigras, B.Q.
Pierre Brien, B.Q.*
René Canuel, B.Q.*
Martin Cauchon, Lib.*
Yvon Charbonneau, Lib.
Jean J. Charest, P.C.*
Jean Chrétien, Lib.*
Jean-Guy Chrétien, B.Q.*
Denis Coderre, Lib.
Paul Crête, B.Q.*
Madeleine Dalphond-Guiral, B.Q.*
Pierre de Savoye, B.Q.*
Maud Debien, B.Q.*
Odina Desrochers, B.Q.
Stéphane Dion, Lib.*
Nunzio Discepola, Lib.*
Claude Drouin, Lib.
Antoine Dubé, B.Q.*
Gilles Duceppe, B.Q.*

The Senate of the first session of the 36th Parliament convened on Sept. 30, 1997. As of Nov. 1, 1997, the Senate consisted of 52 Liberals, 47 Progressive Conservatives, and 3 Independents. The first date in each listing shows when the senator was appointed. The second date in each listing shows when the senator's term expires. A senator's term expires when the senator reaches the age of 75. Senators appointed before 1965 need not retire at the age of 75. An * denotes the senator who was appointed before 1965. Though Orville H. Phillips was appointed in 1963, he has elected to retire at the age of 75. Thus, his end-of-term date of 1999 is indicated.

Maurice Dumas, B.Q.*
Sheila Finestone, Lib.*
Raymonde Folco, Lib.
Fournier Ghislain, B.Q.
Alfonso Gagliano, Lib.*
Christiane Gagnon, B.Q.*
Michel Gauthier, B.Q.*
Jocelyne Girard-Bujold, B.Q.
Maurice Godin, B.Q.*
Monique Guay, B.Q.*
Michel Gulmond, B.Q.*
André Harvey, P.C.
Marlene Jennings, Lib.
Francine Lalonde, B.Q.*
René Laurin, B.Q.*
Raymond Lavigne, Lib.*
Ghislain Lebel, B.Q.*
Réjean Lefebvre, B.Q.*
Clifford Lincoln, Lib.*
Yvan Loubier, B.Q.*
Richard Marceau, B.Q.
Jean-Paul Marchand, B.Q.*
Paul Martin, Lib.*
Marcel Massé, Lib.*
Réal Ménard, B.Q.*
Paul Mercier, B.Q.*
Gilbert Normand, Lib.
Denis Paradis, Lib.*
Bernard Patry, Lib.*
Gilles-A. Perron, B.Q.
Pierre S. Pettigrew, Lib.*
Pauline Picard, B.Q.*
Louis Plamondon, B.Q.*
David Price, P.C.
Lucienne Robillard, Lib.*
Yves Rocheleau, B.Q.*
Jacques Saada, Lib.
Benoît Sauvageau, B.Q.*
Caroline St-Hilaire, B.Q.
Diane St-Jacques, P.C.
Guy St-Julien, Lib.
Yolande Thibeault, Lib.
Stéphan Tremblay, B.Q.*
Suzanne Tremblay, B.Q.*
Daniel Turp, B.Q.
Pierrette Venne, B.Q.*

Saskatchewan
Chris Axworthy, N.D.P.*
Roy Bailey, Ref.
Garry Breitkreuz, Ref.*
Ralph E. Goodale, Lib.*
Allan Kerpan, Ref.*
Derrek Konrad, Ref.
Rick Laliberte, N.D.P.
Lee Morrison, Ref.*
Lorne Nystrom, N.D.P.
Jim Pankiw, Ref.
Dick Proctor, N.D.P.
Gerry Ritz, Ref.
John Solomon, N.D.P.*
Maurice Vellacott, Ref.

Yukon Territory
Louise Hardy, N.D.P.

Province	Term
Alberta	
Joyce Fairbairn, Lib.	1984-2014
Jean B. Forest, Lib.	1996-2001
Ronald D. Ghitter, P.C.	1993-2010
Daniel Hays, Lib.	1984-2014
Nicholas W. Taylor, Lib.	1996-2002
British Columbia	
Jack Austin, Lib.	1975-2007
Pat Carney, P.C.	1990-2010
Edward M. Lawson, Ind.	1970-2004
Len Marchand, Lib.	1984-2008
Raymond J. Perrault, Lib.	1973-2001
Gerry St. Germain, P.C.	1993-2012
Manitoba	
Sharon Carstairs, Lib.	1994-2017
Duncan J. Jessiman, P.C.	1993-1998
Janis G. Johnson, P.C.	1990-2021
Gildas L. Molgat, Lib.	1970-2002
Mira Spivak, P.C.	1986-2009
Terrance R. Stratton, P.C.	1993-2013
New Brunswick	
John G. Bryden, Lib.	1994-2012
Erminie J. Cohen, P.C.	1993-2001
Eymard G. Corbin, Lib.	1984-2009
Mabel M. DeWare, P.C.	1990-2001
Noel A. Kinsella, P.C.	1990-2014
Rose-Marie Losier-Cool, Lib.	1995-2012
Brenda Robertson, P.C.	1984-2004
Fernand Robichaud, Lib.	1997-2006
Louis J. Robichaud, Lib.	1973-2000
Jean-Maurice Simard, P.C.	1985-2006
Newfoundland	
Ethel M. Cochrane, P.C.	1986-2012
C. William Doody, P.C.	1979-2006
P. Derek Lewis, Lib.	1978-1999
Gerald R. Ottenheimer, P.C.	1987-2009
William J. Petten, Lib.	1968-1998
William Rompkey, Lib.	1995-2011
Northwest Territories	
Willie Adams, Lib.	1977-2009
Nova Scotia	
John M. Buchanan, P.C.	1990-2006
Peggy Butts, Lib.	1997-1999
Gérald J. Comeau, P.C.	1990-2021
J. Michael Forrestall, P.C.	1990-2007
Alasdair B. Graham, Lib.	1972-2004
Michael Kirby, Lib.	1984-2016
Finlay MacDonald, P.C.	1984-1998
Wilfred P. Moore, Lib.	1996-2017
Donald H. Oliver, P.C.	1990-2013
John B. Stewart, Lib.	1984-1999
Ontario	
Norman K. Atkins, P.C.	1986-2009
Peter Bosa, Lib.	1977-2002
Anne C. Cools, Lib.	1984-2018
Consiglio Di Nino, P.C.	1990-2013
Richard J. Doyle, P.C.	1985-1998

Province	Term
Ontario cont'd	
John T. Eyton, P.C.	1990-2009
Jean-Robert Gauthier, Lib.	1994-2004
Jerahmiel S. Grafstein, Lib.	1984-2010
Stanley Haidasz, Lib.	1978-1998
James F. Kelleher, P.C.	1990-2005
William M. Kelly, P.C.	1982-2000
Colin Kenny, Lib.	1984-2018
Wilbert Joseph Keon, P.C.	1990-2010
Marjory LeBreton, P.C.	1993-2015
Michael Arthur Meighen, P.C.	1990-2014
Lorna Milne, Lib.	1995-2009
Lowell Murray, P.C.	1979-2011
Landon Pearson, Lib.	1994-2005
P. Michael Pitfield, Ind.	1982-2012
Marie-P. Poulin, Lib.	1995-2020
Richard J. Stanbury, Lib.	1968-1998
Peter Stollery, Lib.	1981-2010
Andrew Thompson, Lib.	1967-1999
Eugene Whelan, Lib.	1996-1999
Prince Edward Island	
M. Lorne Bonnell, Lib.	1971-1998
Catherine Callbeck, Lib.	1997-2014
Orville H. Phillips, P.C.*	1963-1999
Eileen Rossiter, P.C.	1986-2004
Quebec	
W. David Angus, P.C.	1993-2012
Lise Bacon, Lib.	1994-2009
Marisa Ferretti Barth, Lib.	1997-2006
Gérald A. Beaudoin, P.C.	1988-2004
Roch Bolduc, P.C.	1988-2003
Michel Cogger, P.C.	1986-2014
Pierre De Bané, Lib.	1984-2013
Philippe D. Gigantès, Lib.	1984-1998
Jacques Hébert, Lib.	1983-1998
Céline Hervieux-Payette, Lib.	1995-2016
Leo Kolber, Lib.	1983-2004
John Lynch-Staunton, P.C.	1990-2005
Shirley Maheu, Lib.	1996-2006
Léonce Mercier, Lib.	1996-2001
Pierre Claude Nolin, P.C.	1993-2025
Lucia Pépin, Lib.	1997-2011
Marcel Prud'homme, Ind.	1993-2009
Jean-Claude Rivest, P.C.	1993-2018
Fernand Roberge, P.C.	1993-2015
Charlie Watt, Lib.	1984-2019
Dalia Wood, Lib.	1979-1999
Quebec divisional	
Normand Grimard, P.C.	1990-2000
Thérèse Lavoie-Roux, P.C.	1990-2003
Saskatchewan	
Raynell Andreychuk, P.C.	1993-2019
James Balfour, P.C.	1979-2003
Eric A. Berntson, P.C.	1990-2016
Leonard J. Gustafson, P.C.	1993-2008
Herbert O. Sparrow, P.C.	1968-2005
David Tkachuk, P.C.	1993-2020
Yukon Territory	
Paul Lucier, Lib.	1975-2005

Jean Chrétien—prime minister
Andy Scott—solicitor general of Canada
Don Boudria—leader of the government in the House of Commons
Lloyd Axworthy—minister of foreign affairs
Pierre Pettigrew—minister of human resources development
Arthur Eggleton—minister of national defence
Herb Dhaliwal—minister of national revenue
Lyle Vanclief—minister of agriculture and agri-food
Alfonso Gagliano—minister of public works and government services; deputy leader of the government in the House of Commons
Jane Stewart—minister of Indian affairs and Northern development
David Anderson—minister of fisheries and oceans
Alasdair Graham—leader of the government in the Senate
Herb Gray—deputy prime minister
Sheila Copps—minister of Canadian heritage
Lucienne Robillard—minister of citizenship and immigration
John Manley—minister of industry
Allan Rock—minister of health
Paul Martin—minister of finance
David Collenette—minister of transport
Marcel Massé—president of the Treasury Board; minister responsible for infrastructure
Stéphane Dion—president of the Queen's Privy Council for Canada; minister of intergovernmental affairs
Ralph Goodale—minister of natural resources and minister responsible for the Canadian Wheat Board
Anne McLellan—minister of justice; attorney general of Canada
Hedy Fry—secretary of state (multiculturalism/ status of women)
Gilbert Normand—secretary of state (agriculture and agri-food, fisheries and oceans)
Ethel Blondin-Andrew—secretary of state (children and youth)
Fred Mifflin—minister of veterans affairs; secretary of state (Atlantic Canada Opportunities Agency)
Christine Stewart—minister of the environment
David Kilgour—secretary of state (Latin America and Africa)
Raymond Chan—secretary of state (Asia-Pacific)
Ronald Duhamel—secretary of state (science, research, and development; Western economic diversification)
Jim Peterson—secretary of state (international financial institutions)
Lawrence MacAulay—minister of labor
Martin Cauchon—secretary of state (Federal Office of Regional Development—Quebec)
Andrew Mitchell—secretary of state (parks)
Sergio Marchi—minister for international trade
Diane Marleau—minister for international cooperation; minister responsible for la Francophonie

*As of Dec. 31, 1997.

Premiers of Canadian provinces

Province	Premier
Alberta	Ralph Klein
British Columbia	Glen Clark
Manitoba	Gary Filmon
New Brunswick	Frank McKenna
Newfoundland	Brian Tobin
Nova Scotia	Russell McLellan
Ontario	Mike Harris
Prince Edward Island	Pat Binns
Quebec	Lucien Bouchard
Saskatchewan	Roy Romanow

Government leaders of territories

Northwest Territories	Don Morin
Yukon Territory	Piers MacDonald

301 seats in an expanded Commons, 4 more than required for a majority. The Liberal Party's strongholds were Ontario, where they swept up 101 of 103 seats, and Quebec, where they gained 7 seats for a total of 26. Outside of Ontario, the Liberals won a majority of seats only in Newfoundland and Prince Edward Island. In the Atlantic Provinces as a whole, the party lost 20 seats, including all 11 of their seats in Nova Scotia. In 1993, by comparison, the Liberals won 31 of 32 available seats. Hopes of a Liberal resurgence in Western Canada were dashed by the loss of 2 seats, leaving the Liberals with only 15 of 88 seats.

Strong Western support enabled the right-wing Reform Party to gain its new position as the official opposition. Reform candidates, who criticized the Liberals' "tired" approach to Quebec separation, won 60 districts, including 24 of 26 seats in Alberta and 25 of 34 seats in British Columbia. Although Reform candidates attracted about half of the conservative vote in Ontario, the party's goal of expanding beyond the West failed. Reform not only failed to win any new seats, it failed to retain even the one district it had won in 1993.

The Progressive Conservatives (PC's), who had plummeted from a governing majority in 1984 to holding only two seats in Parliament in 1993, made gains in the 1997 elections. The PC's won 20 districts, including 13 in the Atlantic Provinces. Propelled by the popularity of Jean Charest, their 38-year-old bilingual leader, the PC's took five seats in Quebec, a gain of four seats.

The separatist BQ suffered a moral defeat in 1997. In the 1993 election, the party had taken 49 percent of Quebec's popular vote. In 1997, it attracted only 38 percent. As a result, BQ representation in the Commons fell from 50 to 44 seats. Many political observers considered Gilles Duceppe, the party's new leader, inept in Parliament as well as on the campaign trail.

The biggest surprise of the election may have been the success of the left-of-center New Democratic Party (NDP). The party more than doubled its representation in the Commons, rising from 9 to 21 seats. NDP candidates were particularly successful in Nova Scotia, where they picked up six new seats. The party outpaced the Liberals in Saskatchewan 5 seats to 1, and it picked up three new seats in Manitoba. The NDP's success was widely credited to a vigorous new leader from Nova Scotia, Alexa McDonough, who promised to fight for jobs and expanded social programs.

Regional voting ranked as the most significant consequence of the June election. Traditionally, Canada's sectional differences had been negotiated and reconciled within the structure of the national parties. Now they had been brought out in the open. Although parties representing such distinctly different political viewpoints were unlikely to combine against the Liberals, their number increased the prospect of a fractious and tempestuous Parliament.

Cabinet. Prime Minister Chrétien and a new Cabinet were sworn in on June 11. The expanded Cabinet consisted of 28 full ministers and 8 junior ministers. Eight members of the new cabinet were women. The most important change was the movement of Albertan Anne McLellan from minister of natural resources to the major post of minister of justice. Paul Martin, Chrétien's heir apparent, continued as finance minister, and Lloyd Axworthy remained as minister of foreign affairs.

Federal-provincial relations. On the intractable question of national unity, Chrétien moved ahead on two fronts. He deliberately avoided any discussion of constitutional change, realizing that after years of struggling with the question, Canadians preferred to consider other problems, such as unemployment. Chrétien also continued to meet provincial demands for greater power. The government gave more control over the selection of immigrants to three provinces that requested firmer control, as well as funds to support the provincial programs.

On April 21, the government satisfied one of Quebec's long-standing grievances by giving that province responsibility for managing job training. Four other provinces entered into similar agreements, which Chrétien praised as an example of "flexible federalism."

Hard line on secession. Chrétien followed a harder line on Quebec separation in 1997 than in previous years. On February 28, the government filed legal arguments against secession before the Supreme Court of Canada. The government contended that because Canada's constitution has no provision for secession, Quebec could not declare its independence unilaterally. The high court's review of the case was set tentatively for February 1998.

In August 1997, Stéphane Dion, Chrétien's minister for intergovernmental affairs, released two open letters on the dangerous consequences of secession. Dion, a former professor of constitutional law from Montreal, argued that Quebec would invite anarchy if it attempted to leave Canada in a manner outside the law. Such a momentous step, Dion wrote, could be taken only with the consent of all parties concerned.

Secession, Dion warned, is one of the most "consequence-laden choices" any society can make. Contrary to contentions by Quebec's government, Dion argued that international law provides no support for a declaration of independence by Quebec. Secession could be considered only if the decision were based on a "substantial consensus" of Quebec's population expressed in a referendum asking a clear question.

Dion's letters presented a more aggressive tone than the federal government had previously used

Federal spending in Canada
Estimated budget for fiscal 1997-1998*

Department or agency	Millions of dollars†
Agriculture and agri-food	1,505
Canadian heritage	2,524
Citizenship and immigration	652
Environment	517
Finance	66,038
Fisheries and oceans	1,077
Foreign affairs and international trade	3,224
Governor general	10
Health	1,776
Human resources development	24,906
Indian affairs and northern development	4,308
Industry	3,237
Justice	736
National defence	9,917
National revenue	2,269
Natural resources	697
Parliament	272
Privy Council	150
Public works and government services	3,586
Solicitor general	2,535
Transport	1,754
Treasury board	1,481
Veterans affairs	1,922
Total	**135,093**

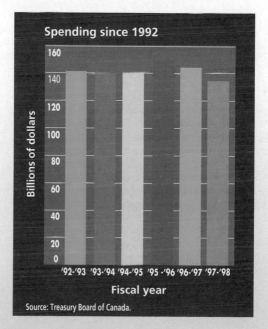

Spending since 1992

Source: Treasury Board of Canada.

* April 1, 1997, to March 31, 1998.
† Canadian dollars; $1 = U.S. $0.72 as of Oct. 24, 1997.

Canadian fishing boats blockade an Alaskan-bound U.S. ferry at Prince Rupert, British Columbia, in July 1997, to protest the alleged overfishing of salmon by Alaskan fishermen.

and were clearly intended to give pause to Quebecers holding moderate opinions on secession.

Provincial response. The premiers of Canada's nine provinces other than Quebec entered into the unity debate for the first time in five years with their own message to Quebec. At their annual conference in August, Premier Roy Romanow of Saskatchewan urged his fellow premiers to show more leadership on the issue. The nine met again in September in Calgary, Alberta. After an 11-hour discussion, they issued a seven-point constitutional statement on national unity that recognized Quebec's "unique character" within a federation in which all Canadians are equal and all provinces enjoy "equality of status." Each province agreed to hold public hearings on the

issue and then distill those results into resolutions that would be approved by each provincial legislature. These statements would constitute a good-will gesture that could be used by the federalists in the next referendum, expected in 1998.

Within Quebec, public support for separation seemed to decline in 1997. In a poll conducted in late September, 53 percent percent of Québécois respondents stated that they would prefer to see the province remain in a renewed Canadian federal state rather than secede.

Economy. The Canadian economy forged ahead in 1997, propelled by a consumer demand stronger than at any time since the country's recovery from the 1990-1992 recession. Retail sales and housing

construction rose, while interest rates remained low. Inflation, as measured by the consumer price index, stood at a marginal 1.5 to 2 percent for the year. The only disappointing factor in a period of buoyant growth was a stubborn unemployment rate that hovered around 9 percent, which was nearly double the rate in the United States.

Budget. Finance Minister Paul Martin, aided by an improving economy and rising government revenues, in 1997 continued his attack on Canada's federal deficit. In a budget released on February 18, he announced a deficit target of $17 billion for the 1997-1998 fiscal year, the lowest federal deficit since 1982.

For 1997-1998, Martin estimated revenues at

$137.8 billion and spending at $151.8 billion. The operating deficit of $14 billion was augmented by a $3-billion spending reserve. Martin's budget included no new taxes. The most important new social program was a tax benefit to help 2.5 million children in low-income families. The benefit addressed the problem of families that found themselves better off on welfare than in low-paying jobs.

Criticism of military command. A scathing condemnation of the leadership of Canada's armed forces was released on June 30, 1997, by a three-person commission of inquiry. The commission had been appointed in March 1995 to investigate the 1993 torture-killing of a Somali teen-ager and the shooting of two other Somali civilians by Canadian units in the United Nations (UN) peacekeeping mission in Somalia.

In January 1997, then-Defense Minister Douglas Young ordered the commission to conclude its hearings by March 31 and report its findings by June 30. Young said the inquiry had dragged on too long, had cost too much, and was damaging the morale of the military forces. Many observers criticized Young for halting the investigation before the commission could hear testimony on the teen-ager's death and on alleged attempts by senior government officials and high-ranking military officers to cover up the incident. The critics accused the Canadian government of trying to protect senior officials and prevent the findings from becoming an issue in the 1997 elections.

The commission's five-volume report, entitled *Dishonoured Legacy*, concluded that "systemic, organizational and leadership failures" were "pervasive" in Canada's armed forces. The findings contradicted the armed forces' claim that the misdeeds in Somalia had been the work of "a few rotten apples." Singled out for censure were 12 senior officers who, the commission said, "refused to acknowledge error and blamed subordinates."

In October, new Defense Minister Arthur Eggleton presented a package of reforms that included the establishment of an eight-member civilian watchdog committee and greater independence for military police from the military chain of command. Critics dismissed the changes as inadequate. In September, Eggleton appointed Lieutenant General Maurice Baril, commander of Canada's land forces, as the new chief of defense staff. The former commander of Canada's land forces, General Jean Boyle, had resigned in 1996 after having been accused of tampering with documents.

Ban on land mines. On Sept. 18, 1997, a total of 89 countries formally adopted a Canadian-initiated treaty banning the production, export, stockpiling, and use of antipersonnel land mines. Land mines kill approximately 9,600 civilians and maim another 14,000 people annually. An estimated 110 million land mines are buried in about 30 countries.

Canada

Canadian census results

Province and territory populations*

Alberta	2,696,826
British Columbia	3,724,500
Manitoba	1,113,898
New Brunswick	738,133
Newfoundland	551,792
Northwest Territories	64,402
Nova Scotia	909,282
Ontario	10,753,573
Prince Edward Island	134,557
Quebec	7,138,795
Saskatchewan	990,237
Yukon Territory	30,766
Canada	**28,846,761**

City and metropolitan area populations*

	Metropolitan area	City
Toronto, Ont.	4,263,757	653,734
Montreal, Que.	3,326,510	1,016,376
Vancouver, B.C.	1,831,665	514,008
Ottawa-Hull	1,010,498	
Ottawa, Ont.		323,340
Hull, Que.		62,339
Edmonton, Alta.	862,597	616,306
Calgary, Alta.	821,628	768,082
Quebec, Que.	671,889	167,264
Winnipeg, Man.	667,209	618,477
Hamilton, Ont.	624,360	322,352
London, Ont.	398,616	325,646
Kitchener, Ont.	382,940	178,420
St. Catharines-Niagara	372,406	
St. Catharines, Ont.		130,926
Niagara Falls, Ont.		76,917
Halifax, N.S.	332,518	113,910
Victoria, B.C.	304,287	73,504
Windsor, Ont.	278,685	197,694
Oshawa, Ont.	268,773	134,364
Saskatoon, Sask.	219,056	193,647
Regina, Sask.	193,652	180,400
St. John's, Nfld.	174,051	101,936
Sudbury, Ont.	160,488	92,059
Chicoutimi-Jonquière	160,454	
Chicoutimi, Que.		63,061
Jonquière, Que.		56,503
Sherbrooke, Que.	147,384	76,786
Trois-Rivières, Que.	139,956	48,419
Saint John, N.B.	125,705	72,494
Thunder Bay, Ont.	125,562	113,662

*Figures are based on the 1996 census.
Source: Statistics Canada.

The Canadian government, frustrated over the slow pace of the UN Conference on Disarmament in dealing with the land-mine problem, had launched the treaty initiative in October 1996. Led by Foreign Minister Axworthy, the so-called Ottawa Process called for disarmament negotiations to proceed at a faster-than-normal rate. The initiative quickly gained momentum with the endorsement of humanitarian organizations and widespread publicity provided by the late Diana, Princess of Wales.

During the talks, the United States unsuccessfully attempted to amend the treaty to allow the continued use of antipersonnel mines in South Korea. The United States insisted the mines were essential to protect outnumbered South Korean forces from the North Korean army. On Nov. 3, 1997, Prime Minister Chrétien and Jody Williams, the American coordinator of the International Campaign to Ban Landmines and winner of the 1997 Nobel Peace Prize, pushed a button that triggered the explosion of the last operational stocks of Canadian land mines. More than 100 countries signed the land-mine treaty in Ottawa, Canada's capital, on December 5.

Pacific salmon dispute. The most significant dispute between Canada and the United States in 1997 arose from both nations' mounting demands for larger shares of the migratory Pacific salmon catch. Since 1993, both countries had disregarded the 1985 Pacific Salmon Treaty, which laid down guidelines to ensure the conservation and equitable division of stocks of five types of salmon. The collapse in June 1997 of talks to restore the treaty and the decision by each country to set its own salmon quotas resulted in an anxious atmosphere in Pacific Northwest fishing grounds during the 1997 season.

Canada charged that in waters off the Alaskan Panhandle and at the southern end of Vancouver Island, U.S. fishermen had caught three to four times more Canada-bound sockeye and chinook salmon than was permitted under the treaty. American fishermen claimed that Canada was catching more than its share of U.S.-bound coho, an endangered species.

Several factors complicated the situation. In Canada, ocean fisheries fell under federal jurisdiction, while in the United States they were controlled by individual states. In addition, private fishing interests could block agreement, under U.S. law, on any U.S. negotiating position. Competition between ocean fishers and commercial fish farms had lowered prices for salmon and led to overfishing as ocean fishers sought to maintain their incomes. In an effort to cull Canada's salmon fleet, Chrétien's government had restricted the fishing grounds of British Columbia's fishermen, thus reducing their catch.

From July 19 to July 21, approximately 200 Canadian fishing boats blockaded an Alaska-bound U.S. ferry docked at Prince Rupert, British Columbia. During the summer, both Canada and the United States allowed their fishermen to intercept fish heading toward the other's spawning grounds. On July 24, Premier Glen Clark of British Columbia heated the atmosphere by threatening to cancel the renewal of an agreement allowing U.S. naval vessels to use a submarine-testing facility on Vancouver Island.

In August, the two countries each appointed a representative to discuss how the negotiation process might be reinvigorated. William Ruckelshaus, former head of the U.S. Environmental Protection Agency, and David Strangway, former president of the University of British Columbia, were directed to meet with private fishing stakeholders to work out a new formula for negotiations. ☐ David M. L. Farr

See also **Canadian prime minister; Canadian provinces; Canadian territories; Toronto.**

Canadian literature.

The lives of men at the turn of the *millennium* (period of 1,000 years) and society's changing expectations of men provoked the interest of three established Canadian writers whose works were published in 1997: Carol Shields, who won a 1995 Pulitzer Prize for *The Stone Diaries*, traces the life of a florist turned landscape architect in *Larry's Party*; Mordecai Richler broke an eight-year literary silence with *Barney's Version*, in which a difficult man reveals truths about his marriages and a suspected murder; in *The Underpainter*, Jane Urquhart depicts a 75-year-old American minimalist painter exploring the layers of his past.

Fiction. Two of the year's most popular books were genre fiction by newcomers. Manitoban Susie Maloney's thriller, *A Dry Spell*, about a charismatic rainmaker seemed likely to be made into a movie. Kathy Reichs's *De'já Dead* is a tautly plotted mystery pitting a serial killer against a protagonist who is, like the author, a forensic anthropologist.

Lynn Crosbie's controversial *Paul's Case* uses fictionalized letters as a literary device to explore the mind of serial murderer Paul Bernardo. Nino Ricci's *Where She Has Gone* completed the author's acclaimed trilogy by taking his protagonist back to the character's home village in Italy. In *Any Known Blood*, Lawrence Hill follows five generations of a black family from slavery in Virginia to suburban Ontario. Eric McCormack's *First Blast of the Trumpet Against the Monstrous Regiment of Women* consolidated his reputation as master of the "sexual gothic." *In the Wings* by Carole Corbeil takes as its premise two lovers cast as Hamlet and Gertrude in a production of Shakespeare's *Hamlet*. Travel writer Ronald Wright in *A Scientific Romance* moves to a future Great Britain affected by global warming, while Brian Moore sets *The Magician's Wife* in the French court of Napoleon III and in North Africa.

Margaret Gibson's *Opium Dreams* evokes the relationship between a daughter and her father, who is afflicted with Alzheimer's disease. Michael Helm's *The Projectionist* chronicles a high-school teacher's struggles for self-respect. First-rate story collections included Elizabeth Hay's semiautobiographical *Small Change* about difficult friendships and Sandra Birdsell's *The Two-Headed Calf*, a collection of unsettling tales set in or near Winnipeg, Manitoba. French works from Quebec newly available in English included *These Festive Nights* by Marie-Claire Blais, translated by Sheila Fischman, which celebrates a child's birth near the end of the 1990's. Monique Proulx's *Aurora Montrealis*, a politically charged story sequence set in Montreal, was translated by Matt Cohen.

Poetry. Poems that Pat Lowther had completed before she was murdered by her husband in 1975 provide the basis for *Time Capsule*. Esta Spalding's eloquent book-length poem, *Anchoress*, focuses on a young woman who commits suicide to protest the Persian Gulf War. Other notable collections of 1997 included Dionne Brand's *Land to Light On;* Don McKay's *Pausing for Breathing Apparatus*; Marilyn Bowering's *Autobiography*; and Patrick Friesen's apocalyptic litany of the century, *A Broken Bowl.*

Children's books. *The House of Wooden Santas*, an illustrated Christmas story set on Cape Breton Island, was a departure for young-adult novelist Kevin Major. *The Parrot* by Laszlo and Raffaella Gal retells an Italian folktale about a brave girl and a parrot prince, while Ludmilla Zeman's *The First Red Maple Leaf* explains the seasons in folktale form. Author-illustrator Robin Muller tells a tale of hope in a grim Victorian setting in *The Angel Tree*. In junior novels, Martha Brooks's *Bone Dance* focuses on two young people with *Métis* (mixed American Indian and European) ancestry struggling with death and loss. *Wish Me Luck* by James Heneghan is based on the sinking of a ship carrying children being evacuated from Great Britain to Canada during World War II (1939–1945).

Nonfiction. Ottawa writer Lawrence Martin created headlines with *The Antagonist: Lucien Bouchard and the Politics of Delusion*, which describes Bouchard, a leader of the Quebec separatist movement, as "the greatest threat to unity" in Canada. Alberta writer Frank Dabbs's *Preston Manning: The Roots of Reform* profiles the leader of the Reform Party while placing him in a historical context. John Crosbie's *No Holds Barred* reprises that outspoken politician's 30-year public life. "Neoconservative excess" comes under attack in *Beyond Greed* by Hugh Segal, once an aide to Prime Minister Brian Mulroney.

John Ralston Saul examines the ideologies dividing Canada in *Reflections of a Siamese Twin*. In *Somalia Cover-Up*, Peter Desbarats castigates Canada's government and defense establishment for its handling of the torture death of a Somali teen-ager. The unraveling story of the Bre-X gold stock scandal spawned a rush of books, including *The Bre-X Fraud* by business reporters Douglas Goold and Andrew Willis and *Bre-X: The Inside Story* by Diane Francis. Stand-outs in environmental writing were David Suzuki and Amanda McConnell's *The Sacred Balance: Rediscovering Our Place in Nature*, an exploration of our spiritual relationship with Earth, and Wayne Grady's *The Quiet Limit of the World: An Expedition to the North Pole to Investigate Global Warming*, a recounting of a scientific expedition.

Biography. James King's *The Life of Margaret Laurence* reveals that the novelist took her own life in 1987 rather than succumb to terminal illness. *Glenn Gould: The Ecstasy and Tragedy of Genius* by Peter Ostwald presents a psychological profile of the pianist. In *Thin Ice: Coming of Age in Canada*, humorist Bruce McCall remembers growing up in Canada in the 1950's. Sports stories included *Fury: Inside the Life of Theoren Fleury* by Andrew Malcolm, about the captain of the Calgary Flames, and *Zero Tollerance*, six-time national skating champion Toller Cranston's idiosyncratic version of his career.

Awards. Winners of the 1997 Governor-General's Awards for books in English were Jane Urquhart for *The Underpainter* (fiction); Rachel Manley for *Drumblair—Memories of a Jamaican Childhood* (nonfiction); Ian Ross for *fareWel* (drama); Dionne Brand for *Land to Light On* (poetry); Kit Pearson for *Awake and Dreaming* (children's literature—text); Barbara Reid for *The Party* (children's literature—illustration); and Howard Scott for *The Euguelion* (translation).

Winners of the Governor-General's Awards in French were Claudette Charbonneau-Tissot for *Cet imperceptible mouvement* (fiction); Roland Viau for *Enfants du néant et mangeurs d'ames* (nonfiction); Yvan Bienvenue for *Dits et Inédits* (drama); Pierre Nepveu for *Romans-fleuves* (poetry); Michel Noel for *Pien* (children's literature-text); Stephane Poulin for *Poil de serpent, dent d'araignée* (children's literature-illustration); and Marie José Thériault for *Arracher les montagnes* (translation).

Barney's Version by Mordecai Richler won the 1997 Giller Prize, while Anne Michaels took the Chapters/Books in Canada First Novel Award for *Fugitive Pieces*. □ Maureen McCallum Garvie

See also **Literature, American; Literature for children; Literature, World.**

Canadian prime minister

Canadian prime minister Jean Chrétien led his Liberal Party to victory in parliamentary elections on June 2, 1997, becoming the first Liberal prime minister to win a back-to-back majority in 44 years. The election was a mixed victory, however. The Liberals' strength in the House of Commons dropped from 174 seats to 155. While Chrétien won his own seat in the St. Maurice region of Quebec for the 10th time, his margin of victory slipped dramatically. In the 1993 election, he had taken the district by 6,000 votes. In 1997, he won by fewer than 400 votes.

In a nationwide poll conducted in May, Chrétien ranked first among Canadian party leaders on most national issues. However, on the question of who would best represent Canada in a future referendum on independence for Quebec, Chrétien trailed Jean Charest, the strongly federalist leader of the Progressive Conservative Party (PC). In the June Parliamentary election, the PC's made inroads in Quebec, where Chrétien's policies to reform Canada's federal structure failed to attract French-speaking voters.

Chrétien remained committed in 1997 to North American free trade and close economic integration with the United States. However, he fervently defended Canada's separate identity. On an official visit to Washington, D.C., in April, Chrétien characterized his relationship with President Bill Clinton as "good but not cozy." □ David M. L. Farr

See also **Canada.**

Canadian provinces. Although four provinces continued to struggle in 1997 to cut government spending, the other six provinces in the Canadian federation enjoyed success in their efforts to contain government spending and projected balanced budgets, or even surpluses, for fiscal year 1997-1998 (April 1, 1997, to March 31, 1998). In some provinces, government leaders cautiously turned their attention to increasing spending on health care and education, areas that had borne the brunt of budget-slashing efforts.

Alberta. Premier Ralph Klein led his right-of-center Progressive Conservative Party (PCP) to a decisive reelection victory on March 11, 1997. The PCP won 63 of 83 seats in the provincial legislature and captured 51 percent of the popular vote, up from 45 percent in the 1993 election. The centrist provincial Liberal Party lost 14 seats, which reduced its total to 18, of which 16 were in Edmonton, the capital.

The PCP rode to victory mainly on its success in vigorously paring provincial expenditures. The cuts, painful to those on social assistance and in need of medical services, had led to four consecutive balanced budgets and the lowest taxes in any Canadian province. Budgets presented by the government in February and April 1997 predicted a surplus of $144 million (all amounts are in Canadian dollars) for fiscal year 1997-1998. The surplus for fiscal 1996-1997 was estimated at $2.23 billion, much of it representing high revenues from a booming energy sector.

Klein invited more than 100 government leaders and representatives of public agencies and private organizations to a two-day summit on September 29 and 30 to recommend how to spend the surplus. The delegates proposed increased funding for education and health services and rejected new tax cuts. Between 1992 and 1997, Alberta fell from first to last among Canadian provinces in *per capita* (per person) spending on health care.

British Columbia. The New Democratic Party (NDP) government of Premier Glen Clark, which narrowly retained power in 1996, broke new ground with social welfare measures in 1997. In July, the provincial legislature unanimously passed legislation allowing the province to sue tobacco companies for medical costs relating to tobacco addiction. British Columbia's health-care system paid out an estimated $500 million annually to treat smoking-related illnesses. Also in July, British Columbia became the first province in Canada to extend family-support laws to same-sex couples. Under the law, gay and lesbian couples who separate would have the same legal rights and responsibilities for child support, visitation, and custody as do heterosexual couples.

The Clark government made peace with one of British Columbia's largest employers on August 5, when it announced an out-of-court settlement with

Alcan Aluminum Limited. Alcan had threatened to sue the province because of the government's 1995 cancellation of Alcan's planned powerhouse at the Kemano hydroelectric project in northwest British Columbia. The government had blocked the powerhouse, intended to supply energy for an expansion of Alcan's aluminum smelter in Kitimat, because of concerns that it would dry up the Nechako River and destroy a salmon run. Under the terms of the 1997 settlement, the government agreed to supply Alcan with taxpayer-subsidized electricity if the company built a $1.2-billion aluminum smelter, employing approximately 2,000 workers, in Kitimat.

Manitoba. The worst flood to hit Manitoba in the 1900's drove at least 27,000 people from their houses and caused an estimated $400 million in damage in late April and early May. At least 445,000 acres (180,000 hectares) of farmland were inundated when the meltoff from huge snowfalls in southern Manitoba and neighboring North Dakota swelled the Red River of the North, which flows north across the Canada-United States border and through southern Manitoba. The river also runs through Winnipeg, Manitoba's capital.

A floodway built to the east of Winnipeg in 1968 provided crucial protection against the raging water. To safeguard the southwestern side of the city, workers in 1997 constructed a dike 7 feet (2 meters) high and 25 miles (40 kilometers) long in only five days. Although the barriers saved Winnipeg, they created a 775-square-mile (2,000-square-kilometer) lake extending 55 miles (90 kilometers) to the U.S. border. Residents of towns south of Winnipeg complained that the barriers worsened the flooding in their areas.

New Brunswick. Premier Frank McKenna, who dominated New Brunswick's government for a decade, announced his resignation on Oct. 7, 1997. His successor, Ray Frenette, a former government minister, was chosen by the Liberal Party caucus and sworn in on October 13.

McKenna's resignation fell on the 10th anniversary of his dramatic 1987 victory in provincial elections, in which his Liberal Party had swept all 58 seats in the legislature. McKenna, an energetic and enthusiastic leader, had made it plain for some time that he considered 10 years in power long enough for any politician. From 1987 to 1997, McKenna had taken New Brunswick from a budget deficit of $360 million to a $180-million budget surplus. In addition to devising innovative approaches to social programs, he had attracted at least 40 customer service centers providing more than 5,000 new jobs to New Brunswick, one of Canada's poorest provinces.

Heated protests in three communities in northeastern New Brunswick led McKenna's government in July to reverse its decision to close three French-language elementary schools. Although enrollment in the schools had declined, the government agreed that the schools were too important to French-speaking residents of the region to be sacrificed for budgetary considerations.

Newfoundland. Voters in Newfoundland overwhelmingly supported a government proposal to establish a *nondenominational* (nonreligious) public school system in a referendum held on Sept. 2, 1997. In 1995, the province's voters had narrowly approved government plans to take control of publicly financed schools from the religious denominations that had been operating them for more than 100 years.

People in Newfoundland on May 19, 1997, cheered the partial reopening of the Newfoundland cod fishing industry, closed down in 1992 because of severely declining stocks. In 1997, fishers were allowed to catch limited amounts of cod off the southern coast of Newfoundland and in the northern Gulf of St. Lawrence. The reopening provided temporary work for at least 3,000 fishers and workers in area processing plants. When the fishing ban was imposed in 1992, Newfoundland's cod industry had employed at least 30,000 fishers and plant workers.

Some environmentalists, scientists, and fishers contended that lifting the fishing ban was a reckless attempt by Canada's Liberal government to curry favor with voters before national elections in June 1997. The government, however, pointed to scientific studies reporting an increase in cod stocks and reiterated a plan to prevent overfishing.

On November 17, oil began flowing from the Hibernia project, Canada's first off-shore oil field. The field, 195 miles (315 kilometers) southeast of St. John's, took 20 years to develop at a cost of $5.8 billion. Hibernia oil reserves were estimated at more than 750 million barrels.

Nova Scotia. Premier John Savage, who narrowly escaped being ousted as head of Nova Scotia's Liberal Party in 1995, announced his resignation on March 20, 1997. After leading his party to victory in legislative elections in 1993, Savage had watched his popularity steadily decline.

Savage had infuriated other Liberals by refusing to replace workers in government jobs with party members. He also endured severe public criticism for the tough measures—called "savage" cuts—his government took to reduce the province's $417-million budget deficit, the worst in Nova Scotia's history. These measures included cutting or freezing public service salaries, closing hospitals, and combining municipalities. By fiscal year 1996-1997, the Savage government had produced the province's first budget surplus—$4.7 million—in 25 years.

The continuing public outcry over service cuts, however, had hurt the Liberal administration and threatened its electoral prospects. With an increasingly discontented party caucus, Savage stepped down. His successor, Russell MacLellan, a member of

Canadian provinces

Canada's parliament since 1979, was selected after a bitter fight at a party convention on July 12, 1997.

Ontario. The massive restructuring of Ontario's provincial and municipal governments, scheduled to take effect on Jan. 1, 1998, dominated Canada's largest province in 1997. In part, the plan by the PCP government of Premier Mike Harris involved cutting government spending by consolidating municipalities, hospitals, and school boards. In April, the government prevailed against widespread opposition in its plan to merge the six municipalities of metropolitan Toronto into a single megacity.

The centerpiece of the government's restructuring plan was legislation authorizing "downloading"—shifting responsibility and funding for public services from the provincial government to municipal governments. Nearly all elements of the plan, which covered public housing, health programs, and mass transit, met with fierce resistance from legislators. Most contentious was a proposal to increase municipal funding for welfare from 20 percent to 50 percent. In return, the province would pay for public education.

Although the government retreated on its proposed funding formula, it passed on an additional $2.5 billion in welfare costs to Ontario's municipalities. However, a threatened revolt against the "downloading" bill by some PCP legislators forced the government to provide up to $800 million to municipalities to cushion the effects of the transfer.

In late September, the Harris government averted a province-wide strike by public service unions by retreating on legislation that would have restricted the unions' bargaining power. Among the bill's provisions was a two-year ban on strikes by public employees and the establishment of a government-appointed commission with the power to impose labor settlements. Public service unions angrily threatened walkouts that could have involved 450,000 employees. In response, the government amended the bill, protecting employees' right to strike and the use of arbitrators chosen by both sides in a dispute.

A two-week strike from October 27 to November 7 by five unions representing Ontario's 126,000 elementary and high school teachers failed to halt legislation that centralized authority over school funding, class size, teacher preparation time, and other educational issues. Such issues previously had been regulated by local school boards.

Charges of incompetence rocked Ontario Hydro, the province-owned utility whose 19 nuclear-powered generators supplied 60 percent of Ontario's electricity. In August, the utility released an internal report on its nuclear division that detailed severe management problems, inadequate maintenance, and "minimally acceptable" safety standards. A number of senior managers resigned, and Ontario Hydro temporarily shut down nine reactors for repairs and upgrading.

Prince Edward Island. The Confederation Bridge, the world's longest bridge over a waterway that freezes in winter, opened on May 31, 1997. The new bridge extends 8 miles (13 kilometers) across the Northumberland Strait to link Prince Edward Island to mainland New Brunswick. The bridge, which replaced a car-ferry service staffed by 680 workers, was built by a private consortium that was to collect tolls to recoup construction costs. The federal government agreed to buy the bridge by paying the consortium $41.9 million annually for 35 years. Built to last 100 years, the new span shortened travel time across the strait from 45 to 12 minutes, which was expected to increase tourism.

Quebec. A census report published in April revealed that Quebec's population had dropped below 25 percent of the total Canadian population for the first time since the province joined the confederation in 1867. Although Quebec's population grew by 3.5 percent from 1991 to 1996—to 7.1 million—it was outpaced by Canada's overall 5.7-percent growth rate. The population shift could affect Quebec's share of seats in the House of Commons and, thus, its importance in the federation.

The separatist Parti Québécois (PQ) government of Premier Lucien Bouchard continued its cost-cutting measures, determined to put the province's financial house in order before calling for another referendum on Quebec's independence from the

Thousands of pedestrians cross the new Confederation Bridge on its opening day, May 31. The Confederation is the first bridge to link Prince Edward Island with mainland Canada.

Canadian federation. A 1995 referendum on sovereignty narrowly failed. Concessions from Quebec's 430,000 public employees on March 21, 1997, allowed the provincial government to cut payroll costs by $1.5 billion.

The provincial budget for fiscal 1997-1998, presented on March 25, 1997, called for deeper cuts in spending for health, education, and other social services. The government also reduced its payments to municipalities by $400 million a year. Although the budget forecast a $2.2-billion deficit, the government reaffirmed its commitment to a balanced budget by fiscal 2000. Lower provincial income tax rates scheduled to begin in 1998 were offset by future increases in retail sales taxes and user fees.

An amendment allowing Quebec to replace school boards based on religion with boards based on language passed the House of Commons on Nov. 18, 1997. The amendment removed a section of Canada's constitution that guaranteed the existence of Protestant and Roman Catholic schools in Montreal and Quebec City. Some religious groups opposed the plan, contending that it would eliminate religious instruction in Quebec.

Saskatchewan enjoyed a healthy economy in 1997 due to 1996 grain harvests that were 25 percent higher than average and substantial revenues from oil fields. The fiscally conservative NDP government of Premier Roy Romanow balanced the prov-

ince's books for the fourth successive year

Finance Minister Janice MacKinnon, in a budget released on March 20, 1997, lopped 2 percent from the provincial sales tax. The cut represented a small break to residents who had endured higher taxes since 1991, when the Romanow government came to power determined to reduce public debt while maintaining key social programs. The budget projected a surplus of $24 million even though the province increased spending on highways, because of the gradual disappearance of railway lines and grain elevators in rural Saskatchewan.

A scandal involving members of the PCP, which had governed Saskatchewan before the NDP took office in 1991, threatened to destroy the provincial party. Twenty PC's, mostly former members of the provincial legislature, were accused of falsifying expense claims. In trials underway since 1995, 14 had been convicted of fraud.

While the PC's anguished over their future in Saskatchewan, four members still sitting in the provincial legislature joined with four disaffected members of the Liberal Party on Aug. 8, 1997, to form the new right-wing Saskatchewan Party. In November, the party held its first convention, approving a platform calling for a balanced budget, lower taxes, and more privatization of government services.   □ David M. L. Farr

See also **Canada; Montreal.**

139

Canadian territories. The Northwest Territories moved in 1997 toward division and the creation of the new territory of Nunavut in April 1999. Nunavut was to be formed from the eastern part of the Territories, which is largely populated by Inuit, a people native to the region.

The territorial budget, introduced by Finance Minister John Todd on Jan. 27, 1997, was designed to eliminate any legacy of debt for the new governments. Spending cuts of $200 million (Canadian dollars) in the last two budgets permitted the minister to project a surplus of almost $9 million for fiscal year 1997-1998 (April 1, 1997, to March 31, 1998). The government also cut 500 public service jobs.

Representatives from the future territory Nunavut and the parent Northwest Territories continued to meet throughout 1997 to devise a system for delivering government services to communities scattered across the North. A plan to require each electoral district to elect one male and one female member to the assembly of Nunavut was rejected by voters in a referendum held on May 26. The proposal, which would have been the first of its kind in Canada, was intended to open debate on social problems by bringing more women into the legislature.

The Yukon prepared to celebrate in 1998 the 100th anniversary of the spectacular gold rush of 1898, which brought thousands of people to the territory's mineral-laden creeks. The main concerns of the Yukon's 32,000 inhabitants in 1997, however, were less festive: diversifying an economy still heavily dependent on mining and transferring more decision-making powers to territorial agencies from the federal government. The Yukon government was scheduled to assume control over lands, forest, minerals, and water in 1999.

Mining news. The Yukon, with an unemployment rate exceeding 15 percent in 1997, cheered the announcement in August that the Anvil Range Mining Corporation, the territory's principal private employer, would reopen its silver-lead-zinc mine at Faro in November for at least four months. The mine was closed in late 1996 because of low zinc and lead prices on world markets.

In August 1997, road building and underground reconstruction began at the Sa Dena Hes mine in southeastern Yukon. Low zinc and lead prices also had contributed to the 1992 shutdown of the mine, owned by Cominco Limited. Cominco said the mine could be reopened as early as spring 1998 if world mineral prices rose.

Work continued on what would be the first diamond mine in North America, at Lac de Gras in the central Northwest Territories. The mine, expected to begin production by 1999, boosted employment in the Territories. Residents comprised nearly 60 percent of the mine's work force, with native people making up 18 percent of workers.   □ David M. L. Farr

Cape Verde. See Africa.

Census. A plan by the U.S. Census Bureau to use statistical sampling to supplement traditional counting methods for the 2000 census became snarled in a partisan political dispute in 1997. Sampling techniques would enable the bureau to estimate a region's total population based on a representative sample rather than a count of every person.

In April, the U.S. House of Representatives attached a measure banning the Census Bureau from developing sampling tools to an $8.6-million emergency spending bill providing relief for flood-stricken communities in the Midwest. President Bill Clinton vetoed the disaster relief bill in part because it prohibited sampling, but on June 12 signed a revised bill that had eliminated the ban on sampling. However, further conflict arose in September after the House attached a measure prohibiting sampling to a spending bill for the U.S. Commerce Department, which oversees the Census Bureau.

The Clinton Administration and Republican congressional leaders compromised in November and agreed to permit the Census Bureau to experiment with statistical sampling techniques in 1998. Statistical sampling methods as well as traditional methods—door-to-door and mail census measurements—were to be used in Sacramento, California. The results would be compared with the results of traditional methods collected from 11 counties in South Carolina and on the Menominee Indian Reservation in northern Wisconsin.

In exchange for allowing the experiment, Republicans were given the right to pursue an expedited hearing before the U.S. Supreme Court on the legality of sampling. Taxpayers will pay for the lawsuit. The compromise also established an eight-member, bipartisan census monitoring board to oversee the preparation and implementation of the 2000 census.

Republicans contended that sampling techniques violate the U.S. Constitution's requirement for an "actual enumeration," or counting, of the population. Republican members of Congress also claimed that the results could be used to create congressional districts dominated by minority voters, who tend to support the Democratic Party. Democrats maintained that sampling would prevent undercounting minorities in the census. According to the Census Bureau, statistical sampling provides an accurate count of the population and the best way to avoid undercounting people residing in remote rural areas and large urban areas.

The Census Bureau had announced in 1996 that it planned to count 10 percent of all households in the year 2000 using statistical sampling techniques. The bureau also planned to explore such techniques on 750,000 households nationwide to correct any undercount of minorities.   □ William J. Eaton

See also **Population**.

Central African Republic. See Africa.

Chad. See Africa.

Chemistry. In May 1997, biochemist James H. Tumlinson of the United States Department of Agriculture explained how a corn plant under attack by caterpillars sounds an alarm. When a hungry caterpillar bites down on a corn leaf, the plant releases compounds into the air that are a signal for help. Wasps answer the call and lay their eggs on the caterpillar, which becomes a meal for wasp larvae.

Tumlinson and his colleagues at the Agricultural Research Service station in Gainesville, Florida, identified and synthesized a chemical, volicitin, in caterpillar saliva that causes a corn plant to call for help. They found that the compound has the same wasp-summoning effect when applied to a potato leaf.

The scientists speculated that volicitin may be the key to a better understanding of the wars between plants and their insect predators and could lead to new ways of protecting crops. A goal of agricultural research is to develop pest-control methods that are kinder to the environment than artificial pesticides.

Vanishing fingerprints. A puzzle commonly encountered by police inspectors—why the fingerprints of children disappear from a crime scene—was solved in 1997 by chemist Michelle Buchanan of the Oak Ridge National Laboratory in Tennessee. Buchanan found that the fingerprints of youngsters differ chemically from the prints of adults.

Buchanan's chemical expertise was called on by Art Bohanan, a detective with the Knoxville, Tennessee, Police Department. Bohanan wanted to know why no fingerprints of a young kidnapping victim could be found in a car that witnesses said they had seen the child riding in. Bohanan's frustrations over missing finger prints had long been shared by investigators everywhere in crimes involving juveniles:

Buchanan took samples of fingertip secretions from both adults and children. She tested the samples using gas chromatography/mass spectroscopy, a sensitive method for analyzing chemicals, and found important differences. The main difference was in the output of the skin's oil glands, which after puberty produce compounds called alkyl esters. It is these large molecules, Buchanan said, that cause adults' fingerprints to persist at a crime scene. Buchanan found that children's oil glands produce a higher percentage of small molecules that can evaporate quickly, causing fingerprints to vanish.

Understanding the differences between adult and juvenile prints offers the possibility of developing a special kit for detecting children's fingerprints. Until then, Buchanan recommended, detectives should act quickly to recover fingerprints when they suspect that a youngster's prints are present at a crime scene.

Protecting nerve cells. In victims of spinal injury, stroke, and certain neurological disorders such as multiple sclerosis, nerve cells come under heavy attack from destructive molecules called free radicals. In August, scientists at Washington University in St. Louis, Missouri, described a promising new method of protecting nerve cells from free radicals.

The technique involves chemically modified versions of molecules called buckyballs, which are a form of carbon. A buckyball molecule consists of 60 carbon atoms arranged in a shape resembling a soccer ball. Buckyballs are like sponges to free radicals. By way of comparison, one molecule of vitamin C neutralizes a lone free radical, whereas a single buckyball molecule can sop up 30 free radicals. Washington University neurologist Laura L. Dugan and her colleagues decided to see if buckyballs could be used to protect nerve cells from free radicals.

The researchers first changed buckyballs into a form that would dissolve in water and thus could be used in the body. They then added the modified buckyballs to test tubes filled with nerve cells that had been deprived of nutrients, simulating the effects of a stroke. They found that the buckyballs cut the death rate of the nerve cells by 75 percent.

Taking the experiment a step further, the scientists administered the altered buckyballs to mice that had been engineered to carry the human gene for amyotrophic lateral sclerosis (Lou Gehrig's disease), a degenerative condition of the nervous system. The mice lived 8 to 10 days longer than untreated mice, suggesting that buckyballs may have potential for treating human disorders. ☐ Peter J. Andrews

Chess. In May 1997, Deep Blue, a supercomputer developed by International Business Machines Corporation (IBM) of Armonk, New York, defeated Professional Chess Association World Champion Garry Kasparov of Russia in a six-game match by the score of 3.5 to 2.5. The match, held in New York City, was the first competition in which a computer beat a reigning world chess champion under tournament conditions. In February 1996, Kasparov had defeated a less advanced version of Deep Blue.

Most chess experts agreed that Kasparov, whose chess skills were judged superior to those of Deep Blue, was intimidated by the supercomputer. Except in the single game that he won, Kasparov exhibited an uncharacteristic caution. Playing the final game with the score even, Kasparov became unnerved. He made a drastic mistake early in the game, suffering one of the shortest and few defeats of his career.

Kasparov accused the IBM team of breaking the match rules by allowing humans to intervene in the computer's play. IBM denied the charges and declined Kasparov's challenge to a rematch, announcing that Deep Blue was to be used only for research.

Tournaments. In September 1997, Joel Benjamin, IBM's grandmaster consultant for the Deep Blue-Kasparov match, won for the second time the U.S. Chess Championship, held in Chandler, Arizona. Esther Epstein of Newton, Massachusetts, won the 1997 U.S. Women's Chess Championship, also in

An audience of chess enthusiasts watches Garry Kasparov play against Deep Blue, an IBM supercomputer, in the May 1997 six-game match that pitted man against machine. The computer won, the first time a machine ever bested a world chess champion in tournament play.

Chandler in September. In August, Alex Yermolinsky of Euclid, Ohio, won the U.S. Open Chess Championship in Orlando, Florida. In April, Dmitry Gurevich of Chicago topped a field of international champions to win the National Open Chess Championship in Las Vegas. In March, Turkish player Suat Atalik won the U.S. All-Masters Chess Championship in Chicago over a record 130 participants.

Young U.S. Champions. Eighteen-year-old Tal Shaked of Tucson, Arizona, won the U.S. Junior Championship, held in Bloomington, Illinois, in June. In Zagan, Poland, Shaked became 1997 World Junior Champion, going undefeated at the annual World Chess Federation tournament. In May in New Brunswick, New Jersey, 12-year-old Matthew Traldi of Easton, Pennsylvania, posted a perfect 6-0 score to become the youngest player ever to win the title of U.S. Amateur East Champion.

The 1997 Super Nationals Scholastic Chess Championships, consisting of all three U.S. Chess Federation school championships held simultaneously in Knoxville, Tennessee, attracted more than 4,300 players in April, demonstrating the growing popularity of chess among young people. Shelby School of Payson, Arizona, became National Elementary Champion. J. R. Masterman School of Philadelphia won both the National Junior High School and National High School titles.   □ Al Lawrence

See also **Computer.**

Chicago. Francis E. George was installed as archbishop of the Archdiocese of Chicago on May 6, 1997, following a five-month search. The 60-year-old Chicago native was appointed by Pope John Paul II to succeed the late Joseph Cardinal Bernardin as spiritual leader of the area's more than 2 million Roman Catholics.

Education. Ninth- and eleventh-graders attending Chicago's public schools showed marked improvement in reading and mathematics on the Iowa Test of Basic Skills in scores reported April 30. Nevertheless, 115 schools were placed on the city's academic probation list, up from the 109 schools on probation during the 1995-1996 school year. On Sept. 18, 1997, the Illinois State Board of Education placed 93 city schools on its new Academic Early Warning List, down from the 148 schools on such a list in 1995-1996. Schools are placed on the Academic Early Warning List if more than 50 percent of their students' scores on state tests do not meet state standards for two years, or if student test scores decline for three years. The schools are then given two to four years to improve their students' performance before closure of the school is considered.

Redevelopment. In 1997, for the third year in a row, more than 2,000 housing units were completed in the city of Chicago, many in locations near downtown that had once been considered undesirable. In September, USX Realty Development, a division of

Pittsburgh, Pennsylvania-based USX Corporation, offered 570 acres (231 hectares) on the far southeast side for sale to developers for $85 million. The parcel, former site of U.S. Steel's South Works, borders Lake Michigan and was approved for residential use by the Illinois Environmental Protection Agency. The Chicago Park District announced in May that it would spend $30 million to refurbish harbors and beaches along the south lakefront.

The Sears Tower was purchased in December 1997 for $844 million by Toronto-based Trizec Hahn Corporation. The 110-story skyscraper was the tallest building in the world from 1973 to 1996.

The Field Museum of Natural History in Chicago, outbidding museums throughout the United States, purchased Sue, the most complete skeleton of a *Tyrannosaurus rex* yet discovered, in October 1997 for $8.4 million. The museum planned to complete a fossil-preparation lab by the year 2000 in which visitors will watch paleontologists prepare the 65-million-year-old dinosaur for permanent display.

Scandal. Mayor Richard Daley issued an executive order on Oct. 27, 1997, barring the mayor's staff and security detail from outside employment and barring the same employees and their spouses from conducting business with the city. The order also forbade city employees to accept loans from city contractors and required contractors to name their lawyers, lobbyists, and consultants. The order, issued in response to reports of questionable dealings by

Brian McRae of the Cubs beats a pickoff tag by Mario Valdez of the White Sox in June in the first of three interleague games in Chicago in 1997. Both teams wore vintage uniforms to commemorate their last match—the 1906 World Series.

members of the City Council and the mayor's administration, went into effect December 1.

Sports. The Chicago Bulls won their fifth National Basketball Association championship in seven years on June 13. The team beat the Utah Jazz by a score of 90 to 86 in the sixth game of the series.

Crime. Alleged mob hit man Harry Aleman was convicted September 30 of a 1972 murder for which he had originally been acquitted. He was retried because the judge who heard the case in 1977 was found to have taken a $10,000 bribe to fix the trial.

Deaths. Ardis Krainik, who built the Lyric Opera of Chicago into a financially solid artistic force, died Jan. 18, 1997. Sir Georg Solti, conductor of the Chicago Symphony Orchestra from 1969 to 1991, died on Sept. 5, 1997, at the age of 84. Architect Bertrand Goldberg died October 8 at age 84. Goldberg designed Chicago's distinctive Marina City towers. Roger Brown, a leading painter in the Chicago Imagist school, died November 22, at the age of 55.

Pulitzer Prize-winning columnist Mike Royko, one of the best-known journalists in the United States, died on April 29 at age 64. Royko's columns for the *Chicago Daily News,* the *Chicago Sun-Times,* and the *Chicago Tribune* were characterized by blunt language—especially when Royko wrote in the persona of the fictional Slats Grobnik. ☐ Harold Henderson

Children's books. See **Literature for children.**

Chile. General Augusto Pinochet Ugarte, at age 82, announced on Sept. 11, 1997, that he would step down as commander of Chile's armed forces on March 11, 1998. The announcement was made on the 24th anniversary of the *coup* (takeover) that ousted the elected socialist government of Salvador Allende. From 1973 to 1990, Pinochet had been dictator of Chile. He voluntarily yielded the presidency to a democratically elected civilian in 1990. Pinochet's 1997 announcement was viewed as a positive step toward achieving full-fledged democracy in Chile. The retiring general was credited with numerous achievements, particularly the creation of a free-market economy that had enjoyed record growth, low inflation, and low unemployment since 1985.

Hantavirus, a rodent-transmitted microorganism that causes respiratory problems and high fever, claimed the lives of at least 13 people in Chile and sent dozens of others to hospitals in 1997. The disease kills about 60 percent of those who contract it.

Douglas Tompkins, a wealthy American, was granted Chilean approval on July 7 to establish a 677,000-acre (274,000-hectare) nature preserve in Chile. Tompkins guaranteed public access to the park and agreed to transfer its ownership to a private trust run by seven board members—four chosen by Tompkins and three by private Chilean academic and religious institutions. ☐ Nathan A. Haverstock

See also **Latin America** (Facts in brief table).

China. Jiang Zemin became leader of the People's Republic of China in February 1997, following the death of Deng Xiaoping, the paramount leader of China since 1978. Jiang embraced Deng's legacy of economic reforms, which had introduced elements of capitalism into China's socialistic system in the 1980's and 1990's. At the 15th Communist Party Congress in September 1997, Jiang presented a program to reduce the number of the nation's ailing state-owned industries. In October, Jiang met with President Bill Clinton in Washington, D.C., where the two leaders concluded trade agreements but did not resolve differences on human-rights issues.

Deng's legacy. Deng, who had long suffered from Parkinson disease, died at age 92 on February 19 of complications from a lung infection. Deng was the last of China's leaders who helped Mao Zedong lead the Chinese Communist Party to power in 1949. Observers considered Deng more practical than the visionary Mao. As Mao's policies became more radical in the 1950's and 1960's, Deng often was at odds with the hard-line Marxist regime. When Mao launched the Cultural Revolution in 1966, trying to remake Chinese society according to his own vision, Deng was exiled from power. After Mao's death in 1976, Deng assumed leadership. Convinced that China had wasted 20 years on ideological disputes, Deng set ideology aside and concentrated on economic development. He transformed China into a global economic power by relaxing Marxist principles that called for a centrally controlled economy.

The economic reforms established by Deng raised the standard of living in China. In 1978, when Deng began policy changes, the average income of Chinese peasants amounted to the equivalent of $72 a year. (All amounts are in 1997 U.S. dollars.) Urban residents in 1978 had an average income of $158 a year. At the time of Deng's death in 1997, the World Bank, a United Nations agency that promotes economic growth by providing short-term credit to member nations, estimated that China's per capita income was approximately the equivalent of $1,500 per year. Many experts in 1997 predicted that China would be one of the world's largest economies by the early to mid-2000's.

Deng's successor. Deng chose Jiang, age 71, an electrical engineer and longtime Communist Party official, as his successor. Many dismissed Jiang as a political lightweight when he became head of the Communist Party after the 1989 massacre of prodemocracy demonstrators near Tiananmen Square in the capital, Beijing. However, in the 1990's, Jiang steadily accumulated power. In 1997, he held the titles of president, general secretary of the Communist Party, and chairman of the Central Military Commission. World leaders credited Jiang with the smooth handling of both Deng's death and the return of Hong Kong to Chinese rule at midnight on the morning of July 1. At the Communist

Police, determined to prevent a repeat of the 1989 demonstrations in Tiananmen Square that left more than 100 people dead, escort a protester from the square on Feb. 25, 1997, the day of Deng Xiaoping's memorial service.

Party Congress, held in September in Beijing, Jiang further strengthened his position.

The 15th Communist Party Congress, a gathering of more than 2,000 delegates representing the party's 58 million members, met in September to approve leaders, elect a new Central Committee, and draft policy through the year 2002. In a move that signaled his growing influence, Jiang succeeded in keeping his rival, Qiao Shi, the top official of China's parliament, the National People's Congress, off the 19-member Politburo and the 193-member Central Committee. Qiao, who was in charge of China's security and law enforcement agencies, had been a favored candidate for the position of general secretary of the Communist Party in 1989. However, Jiang had captured the post when in 1989 Qiao wavered on how to handle the student demonstrators in Beijing.

In 1997, observers expected that Prime Minister Li Peng would replace Qiao as head of the National People's Congress after Qiao relinquishes the post in 1998. At the September 1997 congress, Li retained his position in the Politburo but was constitutionally barred from seeking a third term as premier after his term expires in March 1998. The Communist Party leadership picked Deputy Prime Minister Zhu Rongji, who was widely expected to succeed Li, to replace Qiao as the third-highest ranking member in the party. Zhu, an economic planner, was credited with

lowering China's inflation rate from 24 percent in 1994 to 2 percent in 1997.

Fighting corruption. Wei Jianxing, head of the party's corruption-fighting discipline commission, was named in 1997 to the standing committee of the Politburo, the party's ultimate decision-making body. Wei's appointment to the committee came hours after Jiang vowed to battle political corruption. Jiang told the congress that the "fight against corruption is a grave political struggle vital to the very existence of the party and the state." Prior to the congress, the party had announced that it would prosecute Chen Xitong, a former Beijing party secretary and mayor, who was believed to have embezzled more than $20 million before being removed from office in 1995.

Military loses power. The Communist Party leadership for the first time in decades did not elect a military officer to the standing committee. General Liu Huaqing, senior deputy chairman of the Central Military Commission and a Jiang rival, was dropped from the committee at the September 1997 congress. Noting to the congress that China's armed forces should be subordinate to the needs of economic development, Jiang announced that army forces would be reduced by 500,000 persons by the year 2000, down from approximately 2.8-million troops in 1997.

145

China

Economic reform. Jiang endorsed a limited program of economic reform at the congress that could eventually reduce Communist Party control. He stated that the party would continue to maintain a monopoly on China's political structure but would loosen its control on the economy. According to Jiang, the state must retain "a dominant position in major industries and key areas that concern the life-blood of the national economy." He added that strong international competition in China's economy required restructuring state enterprises.

The government announced plans to combine 118,000 state-owned industries, half of which lost money, into 512 large enterprises in economically strategic fields. Observers judged many of the state companies, which employed approximately 100 million employees in 1997, to be inefficient and over-staffed. The government paid billions of dollars in subsidies annually to keep the companies afloat. Jiang's 1997 plan would convert many of the enter-prises to a shareholding system that would greatly increase the number of companies that sell stock publicly and would more clearly define the owner-ship of those that do not.

However, the sale of state-owned companies could throw an estimated 25 million people out of work. Jiang urged workers, many of whom had a strong sense of entitlement bred by a Communist system, to "change their ideas about employment and improve their own quality to meet the new re-quirements of reform and development."

Growing prosperity. In 1997, China continued to maintain one of the fastest-growing economies in the world. From 1992 through 1996, China's *gross domestic product* (the value of all goods and services produced within a country) rose an average of 12.1 percent a year. The incomes of residents in urban ar-eas grew an average 7.2 percent during the same period and incomes of rural residents grew an aver-age of 5.7 percent.

Deputy Prime Minister Zhu forecast in 1997 that the economy would continue to grow an average of 8 percent annually through the year 2000, but eco-nomic problems across Asia threatened this growth. Encouraged by the growing prosperity, many Chi-nese couples chose to have more than one child. In an effort to slow population growth, the govern-ment for many years had imposed fines on families that had more than one child.

Foreign investment. In the first half of the 1990's, foreigners invested more than $100 billion in factory construction in China. However, investor con-fidence in China grew shaky in 1997 because of con-stant changes in China's legal and tax systems, wide-spread corruption, and rising crime.

Hong Kong. Investors were concerned about China's takeover of Hong Kong. In 1996, more than 60 percent of all foreign investment in China had flowed through Hong Kong, and Hong Kong-based companies had employed 6 million people in China.

Hong Kong ceased to be a British dependency and became a special administrative region of China in 1997. China in 1842 ceded Hong Kong island to Great Britain, and in 1898, Britain negotiated a 99-year lease for an adjacent area. In the early 1980's, China had refused to renew Britain's lease and the countries had jointly declared that Britain would turn over Hong Kong to China in 1997. The declara-tion further stated that Hong Kong, under Chinese sovereignty, would retain for 50 years its capitalist system, British common law, and international guar-antees of human rights.

Ethnic conflicts raged throughout 1997 in the western region of Xinjiang, China's largest province. Ethnic Uighurs, Muslims who made up about 60 per-cent of the region's population, claimed that the government used excessive force and police intimi-dation to deny them access to mosques and religious teachings. The Uighurs feared that non-Muslim Chi-nese settlers would reduce them to a minority.

Monk convicted. Tibetan Buddhist monk Chad-rel Rinpoche, was sentenced to six years in prison in 1997 on charges that he had leaked state secrets to the Dalai Lama, Tibet's supreme religious leader who went into exile in 1959. (Tibet was absorbed by Chi-na in 1951.) The monk had led a government-ap-proved search for the 11th reincarnation of the Panchen Lama, Tibet's second most important reli-gious leader. In 1995, the Dalai Lama announced the name of the new Panchen Lama. China then selected another child as the new Panchen Lama.

The Taiwan National Assembly approved con-stitutional changes on July 18, 1997, that brought the island closer to full independence from China. The island of Taiwan separated from China in 1949, but in 1997 China still regarded Taiwan as its prov-ince. The amendment expanded presidential power and virtually eliminated the provincial government. China warned that the amendment would not lessen China's claim to Taiwan and threatened that the act could lead to war.

Jiang visits U.S. China and the United States reached an agreement on trade pacts during an Oc-tober 29 meeting in Washington, D.C., between Jiang and Clinton. China agreed to buy $3 billion worth of American civilian airplanes and to elimi-nate stiff tariffs on U.S. technology. Clinton agreed to lift a 12-year ban on the sale of U.S. nuclear tech-nology to China after Jiang agreed to abandon a nu-clear cooperation program with Iran. However, the two leaders clashed over American concerns about political and religious rights in China. Jiang offered no apologies for China's jailing of political dissidents and warned the United States not to interfere in China's internal affairs. □ Henry S. Bradsher

See also **Asia** (Facts in brief table); **Hong Kong** Special Report: **Hong Kong 1997: Capitalism Comes to China; Taiwan.**

City. United States President Bill Clinton began his second term in 1997 by focusing on the needs of American cities. Soon after his January inauguration, Clinton asked the Department of Housing and Urban Development (HUD) to devise a long-term plan for responding to the various social and economic problems faced by cities. The plan and a description of the problems addressed by the plan were issued in a June report entitled "The State of the Cities."

Problems. The report identified four major problems that city officials struggled with in 1997—unemployment, poverty concentrations, middle-class migration, and the need to move people off of welfare and into jobs. Despite low unemployment in the United States as a whole, the unemployment rate in large U.S. cities remained stubbornly high in 1997, generally 30 to 50 percent higher than in the surrounding suburbs. The report linked the high unemployment rates with rising poverty rates, which had created dense, isolated ghettos for the poor. According to the report, providing the necessary social services to these poor areas was creating a huge strain on city finances in 1997. Contributing to the increase in urban poverty concentrations was a migration of much of the middle class to the suburbs. As middle class people left the cities, they took a large number of small businesses with them and weakened the tax base. Welfare reform laws, signed by Clinton in 1996, forced many cities in 1997 to try to develop plans to create jobs for an estimated 1 million poor people scheduled to be dropped from welfare rolls by the year 2000.

HUD plan. The HUD report recommended an "urban empowerment agenda" designed to correct the problems faced by cities. The agenda consisted of six main areas requiring federal involvement: (1) bringing private-sector investment to the inner cities; (2) creating long-term, comprehensive plans for urban development; (3) working with city governments, private businesses, community organizations, and citizens to shape responses to problems; (4) creating performance measurements to ensure that cities achieve positive results with federal money; (5) promoting such traditional values as hard work, self-reliance, and dedication to family; and (6) helping cities work together to create solutions to wide, regional problems.

In a June 1997 speech to the National Conference of Mayors in San Francisco, President Clinton discussed the HUD plan, emphasizing that the role of the federal government was to help cities work on solutions to problems, not to tell cities what to do. Clinton referred to the mayors as "America's most effective and creative public officials."

Fiscal health. According to an annual survey by the National League of Cities (NLC), an organization based in Washington, D.C., which seeks to improve the quality of life in American cities, 1997 was the fourth straight year of improving fiscal health for

50 largest cities in the world

Rank	Urban center*	Population
1.	Tokyo-Yokohama, Japan	29,042,000
2.	Mexico City, Mexico	25,399,000
3.	São Paulo, Brazil	22,966,000
4.	Seoul, South Korea	20,163,000
5.	New York City, U.S.	14,641,000
6.	Bombay, India	14,225,000
7.	Osaka-Kobe-Kyoto, Japan	14,150,000
8.	Calcutta, India	13,350,000
9.	Rio de Janeiro, Brazil	13,316,000
10.	Teheran, Iran	12,629,000
11.	Buenos Aires, Argentina	12,498,000
12.	Manila, Philippines	11,914,000
13.	Jakarta, Indonesia	11,775,000
14.	Cairo, Egypt	11,674,000
15.	Moscow, Russia	10,907,000
16.	Lagos, Nigeria	10,785,000
17.	Delhi, India	10,758,000
18.	Los Angeles, U.S.	10,533,000
19.	Karachi, Pakistan	10,072,000
20.	Paris, France	8,780,000
21.	London, U.K.	8,766,000
22.	Lima, Peru	8,373,000
23.	Istanbul, Turkey	8,095,000
24.	Taipei, Taiwan	7,871,000
25.	Shanghai, China	7,330,000
26.	Essen, Germany	7,314,000
27.	Bogotá, Colombia	7,226,000
28.	Bangkok, Thailand	7,010,000
29.	Madras, India	6,868,000
30.	Chicago, U.S.	6,551,000
31.	Pusan, South Korea	6,106,000
32.	Bangalore, India	6,060,000
33.	Santiago, Chile	5,998,000
34.	Beijing, China	5,916,000
35.	Hong Kong	5,887,000
36.	Dhaka, Bangladesh	5,736,000
37.	Lahore, Pakistan	5,314,000
38.	Tianjin, China	5,141,000
39.	Nagoya, Japan	5,129,000
40.	Kinshasa, Congo	4,931,000
41.	Madrid, Spain	4,902,000
42.	Baghdad, Iraq	4,821,000
43.	Milan, Italy	4,812,000
44.	St. Petersburg, Russia	4,712,000
45.	Belo Horizonte, Brazil	4,655,000
46.	Barcelona, Spain	4,625,000
47.	Shenyang, China	4,546,000
48.	Ahmadabad, India	4,440,000
49.	Hyderabad, India	4,382,000
50.	Ho Chi Minh City, Vietnam	4,224,000

*An urban center is a continuous built-up area, similar to a metropolitan area, having a population density of at least 5,000 persons per square mile (1,900 per square kilometer).
Source: 1997 estimates based on data from the U.S. Bureau of the Census.

U.S. cities. More than two-thirds of the 338 cities surveyed by the NLC reported that they were better able to meet their financial needs in 1997 than in 1996. Thirty-six percent of the cities reported that in 1997 they would add government jobs, 29 percent said they would increase spending, and 24 percent said they would increase productivity levels.

Statistics from the survey showed that only 12 percent of cities cut capital spending in fiscal year 1997, compared to 61 percent in 1992 (during an economic recession). According to the survey, city *financial reserves* (financial resources saved for future uses), were expected to average 18.3 percent of spending in 1997, compared to 10 percent in 1992.

The "new pragmatism." In 1997, a number of U.S. mayors were applauded by political observers for having adopted a nonpolitical, business-style management philosophy for their cities. These mayors, sometimes referred to as "new pragmatists" or "new progressives," included Democrats Richard Daley of Chicago, Ed Rendell of Philadelphia, Michael White of Cleveland, and John Norquist of Milwaukee, as well as Republicans Rudolph Giuliani of New York City, Richard Riordan of Los Angeles, and Stephen Goldsmith of Indianapolis, Indiana. Each of these mayors often broke rank with his party in an attempt to address concerns of citizens regardless of party, race, or class.

The "new pragmatist" mayors tended to focus on such basic issues as crime, jobs, and education. In 1997, for the fifth consecutive year, cities reported large drops in violent crime. Much of this drop was credited to the fact that city governments had more police on the streets and adopted more aggressive policing tactics.

Mayor Goldsmith was generally credited with being the most ambitious mayor in applying business practices to government. In 1992, Goldsmith had required that Indianapolis's public employee union compete with private companies for city contracts. Auto mechanics of the public employee union won their contract after turning down salary increases to make their bid more competitive. The money saved by the new auto contract resulted in increased efficiency. In 1997, auto repair costs were down 29 percent, repair times were improved, and customer complaints had fallen by more than 90 percent, compared to 1992.

Education reform. In October 1997, the Illinois State Board of Education reported that in 1997 Chicago schools had their highest graduation and attendance rates in almost a decade. The board also reported that Chicago students made significant gains in standardized test scores, particularly in math and science. Many observers credited the improvements to Mayor Daley's takeover of the Chicago school board in 1995.

The five-person board appointed by Daley eliminated a $1.3-billion deficit and radically changed the

50 largest cities in the United States

Rank	City	Population*
1.	New York City, N.Y.	7,380,906
2.	Los Angeles, Calif.	3,553,638
3.	Chicago, Ill.	2,721,547
4.	Houston, Tex.	1,744,058
5.	Philadelphia, Pa.	1,478,002
6.	San Diego, Calif.	1,171,121
7.	Phoenix, Ariz.	1,159,014
8.	San Antonio, Tex.	1,067,816
9.	Dallas, Tex.	1,053,292
10.	Detroit, Mich.	1,000,272
11.	San Jose, Calif.	838,744
12.	Indianapolis, Ind.	746,737
13.	San Francisco, Calif.	735,315
14.	Jacksonville, Fla.	679,792
15.	Baltimore, Md.	675,401
16.	Columbus, Ohio	657,053
17.	El Paso, Tex.	599,865
18.	Memphis, Tenn.	596,725
19.	Milwaukee, Wis.	590,503
20.	Boston, Mass.	558,394
21.	Washington, D.C.	543,213
22.	Austin, Tex.	541,278
23.	Seattle, Wash.	524,704
24.	Nashville, Tenn.	511,263
25.	Cleveland, Ohio	498,246
26.	Denver, Colo.	497,840
27.	Portland, Ore.	480,824
28.	Fort Worth, Tex.	479,716
29.	New Orleans, La.	476,625
30.	Oklahoma City, Okla.	469,852
31.	Tucson, Ariz.	449,002
32.	Charlotte, N.C.	441,297
33.	Kansas City, Mo.	441,259
34.	Virginia Beach, Va.	430,385
35.	Honolulu, Hawaii	423,475
36.	Long Beach, Calif.	421,904
37.	Albuquerque, N. Mex.	419,681
38.	Atlanta, Ga.	401,907
39.	Fresno, Calif.	396,011
40.	Tulsa, Okla.	378,491
41.	Las Vegas, Nev.	376,906
42.	Sacramento, Calif.	376,243
43.	Oakland, Calif.	367,230
44.	Miami, Fla.	365,127
45.	Omaha, Nebr.	364,253
46.	Minneapolis, Minn.	358,785
47.	St. Louis, Mo.	351,565
48.	Pittsburgh, Pa.	350,363
49.	Cincinnati, Ohio	345,818
50.	Colorado Springs, Colo.	345,127

*1996 estimates.
Source: U.S. Bureau of the Census.

50 largest metropolitan areas in the United States

Rank	Metropolitan area	Population*
1.	Los Angeles-Long Beach, Calif.	9,138,789
2.	New York City, N.Y.	8,570,212
3.	Chicago, Ill.	7,724,770
4.	Boston-Worcester-Lawrence-Lowell-Brockton, Mass.	5,768,968
5.	Philadelphia, Pa.-N.J.	4,950,866
6.	Washington, D.C.-Md.-Va.-W.Va.	4,509,932
7.	Detroit, Mich.	4,320,203
8.	Houston, Tex.	3,710,844
9.	Atlanta, Ga.	3,431,983
10.	Dallas, Tex.	2,957,910
11.	Riverside-San Bernadino, Calif.	2,949,387
12.	Minneapolis-St. Paul, Minn.-Wis.	2,723,137
13.	Nassau-Suffolk, N.Y.	2,659,476
14.	San Diego, Calif.	2,644,132
15.	Phoenix-Mesa, Ariz.	2,563,582
16.	St. Louis, Mo.-Ill.	2,547,686
17.	Baltimore, Md.	2,469,985
18.	Pittsburgh, Pa.	2,394,702
19.	Cleveland-Lorain-Elyria, Ohio	2,224,974
20.	Seattle-Bellevue-Everett, Wash.	2,197,451
21.	Oakland, Calif.	2,195,411
22.	Tampa-St. Petersburg-Clearwater, Fla.	2,180,484
23.	Miami, Fla.	2,031,336
24.	Newark, N.J.	1,936,096
25.	Denver, Colo.	1,831,308
26.	Portland-Vancouver, Ore.-Wash.	1,710,260
27.	Kansas City, Mo.-Kan.	1,663,453
28.	San Francisco, Calif.	1,645,815
29.	New Haven-Bridgeport-Stamford-Waterbury-Danbury, Conn.	1,625,513
30.	Cincinnati, Ohio-Ky.-Ind.	1,591,837
31.	San Jose, Calif.	1,565,253
32.	Norfolk-Virginia Beach-Newport News, Va.	1,540,446
33.	Fort Worth-Arlington, Tex.	1,491,965
34.	Indianapolis, Ind.	1,476,865
35.	San Antonio, Tex.	1,460,809
36.	Milwaukee-Waukesha, Wis.	1,457,939
37.	Sacramento, Calif.	1,456,955
38.	Columbus, Ohio	1,437,512
39.	Fort Lauderdale, Fla.	1,412,165
40.	Orlando, Fla.	1,390,574
41.	New Orleans, La.	1,315,294
42.	Bergin-Passaic, N.J.	1,308,655
43.	Charlotte-Gastonia-Rock Hill, N.C.-S.C.	1,289,177
44.	Salt Lake City-Ogden, Ut.	1,199,323
45.	Buffalo-Niagra Falls, N.Y.	1,184,052
46.	Las Vegas, Nev.-Ariz.	1,138,750
47.	Greensboro-Winston-Salem-High Point, N.C.	1,123,840
48.	Hartford, Conn.	1,115,223
49.	Nashville, Tenn.	1,093,836
50.	Rochester, N.Y.	1,088,516

*1995 estimates.
Source: U.S. Bureau of the Census.

standards for achievement. The board mandated that students who lacked required skills would have to either attend summer school or repeat the same grade. In 1996, the first year that the requirements were in effect, 48 percent of the city's ninth-graders and 25 percent of eighth-graders were refused promotion to the next grade. In 1997, Chicago had nearly 90,000 students in summer school. Chicago schools that failed to improve substandard performances faced wholesale changes in administration and teachers.

In 1997, other U.S. cities were looking to Chicago as a model for saving their troubled public schools. However, some observers credited the gains in Chicago to local school reforms initiated in 1988—not to Mayor Daley's board.

Long-range planning. Many large U.S. cities were considering long-range plans for city development in 1997. New York City officials reacted in 1997 to a report issued in 1996 by the Regional Plan Association (RPA), an influential independent research and advocacy group. The report, called "A Region at Risk," emphasized the dangers of urban sprawl. According to the report, developed land around New York City increased by 65 percent between 1970 and 1990, even though the city's population increased by just 8 percent during the same period. The rapid growth in developed land was causing concerns about environmental issues and living conditions. The RPA report maintained that New York City needed massive investment not only in open spaces, but also in education, transportation, water and waste systems, and downtown neighborhoods to remain competitive with other cities.

New York City officials had mixed responses to the RPA report. Some officials supported policy changes based on the report, advocating new investment in rail transit, housing, jobs, and open spaces. Other officials, including Mayor Giuliani, were critical of the report, calling the multibillion-dollar cost of its proposals unrealistic. The problems discussed in the RPA report were similar to the problems faced by most large U.S. cities in 1997.

Fast growth in Sun Belt. In November, the U.S. Bureau of the Census released a list of the U.S. cities with the fastest growing populations since 1990. The 10 fastest-growing cities were in California, Florida, Texas, Arizona, and Nevada—states in the so-called "Sun Belt." Many of the cities on the list were suburbs of larger, more established cities. Others, near the Mexican border, were being populated by large numbers of Mexican immigrants.

The 10 fastest-growing cities in the United States were: (1) Henderson, Nevada, (2) Chandler, Arizona, (3) Pembroke Pines, Florida, (4) Palmdale, California, (5) Plano, Texas, (6) Las Vegas, Nevada, (7) Scottsdale, Arizona, (8) Laredo, Texas, (9) Coral Springs, Florida, and (10) Corona, California.

☐ Robert Messenger

Civil rights. On Aug. 28, 1997, a California law went into effect that banned state-run affirmative action programs. Affirmative action programs were created to increase representation of certain racial or ethnic groups and women in areas of employment and education. The law, approved by California voters in a November 1996 initiative, eliminated affirmative action considerations from state hiring and contracting decisions and from admission policies at state colleges. Such decisions and policies were to be based solely on the qualifications of applicants, according to the new law.

U.S. District Judge Thelton Henderson blocked enforcement of the antiaffirmative action initiative soon after it was passed. A three-judge panel of the Ninth U.S. Circuit Court of Appeals overruled Henderson's order in April 1997 but delayed the law from going into effect while a coalition of civil rights groups sought a rehearing. In August, the full appeals court declined the rehearing request, clearing the way for the law to take effect.

The passage of the California law led lawmakers in several other states and cities to put forward similar ballot initiatives. In November, voters in Houston rejected an initiative to ban affirmative action programs from city contracting and hiring policies.

Civil rights director. On December 15, President Bill Clinton appointed Bill Lann Lee acting director of the U.S. Justice Department's civil rights division. Lee had been a legal counsel for the National Association for the Advancement of Colored People. Clinton's action defied Republican members of the U.S. Senate who had blocked Senate consideration of Lee's nomination as director. The Republican senators had objected to Lee's strong support of affirmative action. Clinton promised to resubmit Lee's nomination to the Senate in 1998.

Church fires. In February 1997, Gary Cox and Timothy Welch, two former members of the Ku Klux Klan, were sentenced to nearly 20 years in prison for burning down two predominantly African American churches in South Carolina in 1995. In August 1997, two other former Klansmen—Arthur Haley and Hubert Rowell—were sentenced to lengthy prison terms for conspiring with Cox and Welch.

The two arsons were among 429 church fires that were investigated by the National Church Arson Task Force, a panel of U.S. Justice Department and Treasury Department officials, established by President Clinton in June 1996. The panel had been charged with determining if the church fires were isolated incidents or part of a national conspiracy. Nearly 4 out of 10 of the blazes involved churches that were predominantly African American.

In June 1997, the task force reported that the fires at "African American and other houses of worship were motivated by a wide array of factors, including not only blatant racism or religious hatred, but also financial profit, burglary and personal revenge." The task force, which found no evidence of a national conspiracy, noted that only a small number of the 110 people convicted in the attacks had links to the Ku Klux Klan or other hate groups.

Sex discrimination. In January 1997, two of four female cadets admitted in autumn 1996 to The Citadel, a state-supported military college in Charleston, South Carolina, left the school after complaining they had been harassed and hazed. Among other complaints, Kim Messer and Jeanie Mentavlos claimed that male cadets poured nail polish remover over the clothes they were wearing and set their clothes on fire. Following an internal investigation conducted by The Citadel, 14 male cadets were punished or resigned from the school.

In August 1997, David Schwacke, a South Carolina state prosecutor, decided that criminal charges would not be filed against the accused male cadets, because there were too many discrepancies in the evidence and in the accounts of witnesses. In September, Mentavlos sued the school, its governing board, the officer in charge of her barracks, and five male cadets—alleging federal civil rights violations.

The previously all-male Citadel first integrated women into its student body in 1995. The freshman class for the 1997-1998 school year at the Citadel included 20 women.

Another previously all-male, state-supported military college, Virginia Military Institute (VMI) in Lexington, Virginia, enrolled women for the first time in August 1997, when 31 female cadets began classes. The school became coeducational as a result of a 1996 U.S. Supreme Court decision that ruled that VMI's gender-based admissions policy violated the Constitution's equal protection guarantees.

Army scandal. A sexual harassment scandal involving the U.S. Army, which began in 1996, continued to unfold in 1997 as several supervisors at training bases were prosecuted and punished for misconduct. To combat what the Army admitted was widespread sexual harassment within the ranks, the Army announced in September that it was revamping its drill sergeant training system with a greater focus on ethics and values.

Many of the harassment incidents occurred at Aberdeen Proving Ground, an Army training base in Maryland. Following an investigation, the Army charged 12 Aberdeen supervisors, most of whom were drill sergeants, with various misdeeds. Staff Sergeant Delmar Simpson was sentenced to 25 years in prison and ordered dishonorably discharged after being convicted in April of raping six female trainees at Aberdeen during 1995 and 1996. Simpson maintained his innocence. Four other Aberdeen supervisors were convicted of sexual misconduct.

Top-ranking man accused. A military judge ruled in October 1997 that Sergeant Major of the Army Gene McKinney, the Army's top-ranking enlisted man, should be court-martialed on charges of sexual misconduct. McKinney had been suspended from duty in February, after former aide Brenda Hoster, a retired sergeant major, accused him of making improper sexual advances toward her. Five other women who served under his command later came forward with complaints against McKinney. The court-martial of McKinney, who pled innocent to the charges, was scheduled for 1998.

Race relations. President Clinton launched what he described as a much-needed national discussion of race relations in June 1997 by appointing a panel to advise him on the issue. The panel, headed by black historian John Hope Franklin, consisted of three whites, two blacks, one Hispanic, and one Korean American. Members said they would focus on education and economic opportunity.

Homosexual rights. In July, Hawaii became the first state in the United States to allow unmarried individuals to extend their medical insurance and certain other benefits to homosexual partners living in the same household. The law also applied to roommates and to siblings living together. In December, New Jersey authorities ruled that homosexual and unmarried heterosexual couples could jointly adopt children who are in state custody. Most states allow individual homosexuals, but not couples, to adopt.

☐ Geoffrey A. Campbell and Linda P. Campbell

See also **Armed forces; Supreme Court of the United States.**

Classical music. In 1997, a number of music critics expressed concern about the future of classical music. According to these critics, a decline in government funding for the arts, an abandonment of music education by public schools, and an aging and shrinking audience were contributing to the potential demise of classical music. According to *Who Killed Classical Music?*, a book by British critic Norman Lebrecht published in 1997, the transformation of classical music from a nonprofit art form into a branch of show business controlled by a small group of corporate promoters had contributed to the problem. Lebrecht blamed the huge sums of money siphoned out of the business by these promoters and their superstar clients—including "The Three Tenors" Luciano Pavarotti, Placido Domingo, and Jose Carreras—for the financial difficulties faced by many orchestras, opera companies, and organizations that present serious music.

More optimistic critics responded that classical music would likely adjust to and survive its current difficulties. According to these critics, the classical-music audience was declining only at those institutions whose management refused to change outdated marketing strategies.

More orchestras. In June, optimistic news was reported in Washington, D.C., at the annual meeting of the American Symphony Orchestra League, an association of orchestral groups that range from youth to professional orchestras. Statistics presented at the meeting revealed that the number of symphony orchestras in the United States increased from approximately 1,100 in 1972 to 1,800 in 1997. Although eight professional orchestras filed for bankruptcy tween 1986 and 1996, six of them were later reorganized. A seventh orchestra was in the midst of a reorganization effort in late 1997.

Concert halls renovated. Another sign that classical music was in much stronger shape in 1997 than many feared was the boom in concert hall renovations. Among the symphonic and opera facilities starting, continuing, or completing multimillion dollar overhauls in 1997 were Orchestra Hall in Chicago, the Academy of Music in Philadelphia, the Kennedy Center Concert Hall in Washington, D.C., and War Memorial Opera House in San Francisco. Most renovations were undertaken to update cramped and outdated facilities.

The Shine phenomenon. Many music critics interpreted the success of pianist David Helfgott as an example of how popular culture can distort classical music. The 49-year-old Australian pianist, who had spent much of his life in mental institutions, soared to fame in 1997 through the depiction of his life in the motion picture *Shine*, which won an Academy Award in March for Geoffrey Rush, the actor who portrayed Helfgott. The movie's success led to a recording contract and a 60-concert international tour for Helfgott. He made his U.S. debut at Boston's Symphony Hall on March 4. The so-called "Shine Tour" dismayed music critics, who noted that performances by the real Helfgott were erratic, technically and musically inept, and unworthy of the unprecedented publicity barrage.

Breakthrough for women. In February, the Vienna Philharmonic Orchestra, one of the world's oldest and most revered symphony orchestras, ended its ban on admitting women musicians as full members. Harpist Anna Lelkes, who had played with the 143-member ensemble for 26 years without the full salary and privileges that male musicians enjoyed, became the first woman admitted into the orchestra. In 1996, the Austrian government had threatened to cut funding for the 155-year-old institution if it remained exclusively male.

Mozart discoveries. As reported in June 1997, David Buch, a professor of music history at the University of Northern Iowa in Cedar Falls, discovered a copy of the little-known opera, *The Philosopher's Stone,* inscribed with notations proving that portions of it were composed by Wolfgang Amadeus Mozart. The notations showed that Mozart and other composers collaborated on the work in Vienna, Austria, in 1790. Buch discovered the copy in a library in Hamburg, Germany, in July 1996. He also discovered evidence in 1996 that a second Viennese opera, *The Beneficent Dervish,* contained passages written by Mozart in 1790. The discoveries, though

The king of Egypt reviews his victorious troops in a presentation of the spectacular "Triumphal March" scene from Giuseppe Verdi's tragic opera *Aida*, produced by Arena di Verona in Verona, Italy, in July 1997.

consisting of only small amounts of music, shed new light on one of Mozart's masterpieces, *The Magic Flute*, which was composed during the same period.

New operas. American opera composers and librettists continued in 1997 to find inspiration in historical figures. Myron Fink's *The Conquistador*, which had its first performance by the San Diego Opera on March 1, took as its title character the Spanish conquistador Don Luis de Carvahal. *Jackie O*, by composer Michael Daugherty and librettist Wayne Koestenbaum, was a Broadway-style pop-opera based on the life and times of former first lady Jacqueline Kennedy Onassis. The work was premiered by the Houston Opera Studio on March 14. On July 26, the Santa Fe (New Mexico) Opera premiered Peter Lieberson's *Ashoka's Dream*, the central figure of which was Emperor Ashoka, a ruler of ancient India.

New instrumental music. Esa-Pekka Salonen, the Finnish-born music director of the Los Angeles Philharmonic, conducted the first performance of his orchestral work, *L.A. Variations*, in Los Angeles on January 16. *Concerto for Violin and Guitar*, by American composer Aaron Jay Kernis, was debuted on February 6 by violinist Nadja Salerno-Sonnenberg and cellist Sharon Isbin with the St. Paul (Minnesota) Chamber Orchestra. *Cello Concerto No. 1*, written by English composer Bernard Rands in honor of the 70th birthday of Russian cellist Mstislav Rostropovich, was premiered on April 3. Rostropovich was the

soloist, playing with the Boston Symphony Orchestra. Russian-born Sofia Gubaidulina, one of Europe's leading composers, attended the world premiere of her *Concerto for Viola and Orchestra* on April 17 in Chicago. Violist Yuri Bashmet performed with the Chicago Symphony Orchestra. The American composer Elliott Carter had his newest orchestral work, *Allegro Scorrevole,* premiered by the Cleveland Orchestra on May 22. The work was inspired by a poem by Richard Crashaw, an English poet of the 1600's.

Notable deaths in 1997 included that of the Hungarian-born conductor and pianist Sir Georg Solti, 84, who died on September 5. Solti's tireless pursuit of musical perfection during his 22 years as music director of the Chicago Symphony Orchestra (ending with his retirement in 1991) helped to make that ensemble world famous.

Composers Hugo Weisgall and Conlon Nancarrow, both 84, died in 1997. Weisgall was one of the nation's most widely respected composers of opera and vocal music. Nancarrow, who wrote mostly for the player piano, was regarded as one of the century's few truly visionary composers. Sir Rudolf Bing, 95, head of New York City's Metropolitan Opera (the Met) from 1950 to 1972, died on Sept. 2, 1997. He helped establish the Met as one of the most prominent opera companies in the world. □ John von Rhein

See also **Motion pictures; People in the news; Popular music.**

Colombia. By August 1997, a full year before the end of President Ernesto Samper Pizano's four-year term, the Samper Administration had proved to be disastrous for Colombia by almost any standard. Economic growth, which had reached nearly 5 percent in 1994, was estimated to have fallen to 1.5 percent in 1997. Colombia's foreign debt soared from $17 billion in 1994 to $32 billion in 1997. During the same period, government spending swelled from 20 to 33 percent of Colombia's *gross domestic product* (the value of all goods and services produced in a country in a given year).

A lack of leadership from President Samper created a vacuum quickly filled by right-wing paramilitary groups and leftist guerrillas. By the end of 1997, the guerrillas controlled an estimated 50 percent of Colombia. Charges of drug payoffs and political corruption further crippled the administration and put Colombia at odds with former allies.

Rebel gains. On June 15, Samper brokered a deal with the Revolutionary Armed Forces of Colombia (FARC), the largest leftist group, to free 70 soldiers, some of whom had been held since August 1996. Although Samper reportedly regarded the deal as a successful political move, he was forced to withdraw troops from several large areas of the country in exchange for the captured soldiers.

Rebels belonging to the National Liberation Army (ELN), a smaller leftist force, had carried out

Grammy Award winners in 1997

Classical Album, *Corigliano: Symphony No. 1, Of Rage and Remembrance;* National Symphony Orchestra, Washington Oratorio Society Men's Chorus, Leonard Slatkin, conductor.

Orchestral Performance, *Prokofiev: Romeo and Juliet (Scenes From the Ballet);* San Francisco Symphony, Michael Tilson Thomas, conductor.

Opera Recording, *Britten: Peter Grimes;* City of London Sinfonia, London Symphony Chorus, Richard Hickox, conductor.

Choral Performance, *Walton: Belshazzar's Feast;* Bournemouth Symphony Chorus, Andrew Litton, conductor.

Classical Performance, Instrumental Solo with Orchestra, *Bartok: The Three Piano Concertos;* Yefim Bronfman, piano; Los Angeles Philharmonic, Esa-Pekka Salonen, conductor.

Classical Performance, Instrumental Solo without Orchestra, *The Romantic Master;* Earl Wild, piano.

Chamber Music Performance, *Corigliano: String Quartet;* Cleveland Quartet.

Small Ensemble Performance, *Boulez: . . . Explosante-Fixe . . . ;* Ensemble Intercontemporain, Pierre Boulez, conductor.

Classical Vocal Performance, *Opera Arias (works of Mozart, Wagner, Borodin, etc.);* Bryn Terfel, bass-baritone; Met Orchestra, James Levine, conductor.

Classical Contemporary Composition, *Corigliano: String Quartet;* Cleveland Quartet.

more than 41 attacks by August 1997 on the vital Cano-Limón pipeline, which transports about half of Colombia's exported oil. During an attack on July 6, the rebels shot down a military helicopter, killing all 24 people aboard. The attacks disrupted Colombia's economy and caused severe environmental damage.

Elections disrupted. The armed groups unleashed a series of attacks intended to disrupt municipal elections scheduled for October 26. In the months before the election, leftist rebels or right-wing paramilitary groups had reportedly killed at least 53 candidates and kidnapped more than 200 others. The violence forced Samper to withdraw federal troops from additional areas of Colombia and to cancel elections in at least 20 municipalities.

Several supporters of the president were murdered in 1997. The most prominent, Senator Jorge Cristo, a member of the ruling Liberal Party and close ally of the president, was killed, as was his bodyguard, on August 8 in Cucutá, a border town in northwestern Colombia.   □ Nathan A. Haverstock

See also **Latin America** (Facts in brief table).

Colorado. See State government.

Common Market. See Europe.

Commonwealth of Independent States. See Armenia; Azerbaijan; Belarus; Georgia; Kazakstan; Kyrgyzstan; Russia; Ukraine; Uzbekistan.

Comoros. See Africa.

Computer. Apple Computer Incorporated of Cupertino, California, shocked the personal computer (PC) industry in August by unexpectedly forming an alliance with its historic rival, Microsoft Corporation, of Redmond, Washington. As part of the agreement, Microsoft invested $150 million in Apple to help bolster Apple's troubled financial situation. Microsoft also paid Apple $100 million to settle a long-standing lawsuit charging Microsoft with copying Apple's Macintosh operating system (MacOS) in the design of Microsoft's Windows operating system.

Rescuing Apple. Steven P. Jobs had returned to Apple—the company he helped found—as an advisor in December 1996, when Apple purchased his company, NeXT Software. Jobs was forced out of Apple in 1985. In July 1997, Apple's board of directors ousted Gilbert F. Amelio after just 18 months as chief executive. Although Jobs maintained that he would not take Amelio's position, he became the company's temporary leader while a new chief executive was sought. In August, Jobs replaced all but two members of Apple's board. In September, Apple purchased Power Computing Corporation of Round Rock, Texas, for $100 million. Power Computing had been the largest maker of Macintosh *clones* (PC's based on the MacOS). Jobs also announced that Apple would not renew the licensing deals it had made with other clone builders, thereby eliminating competition in the Macintosh market.

Steven Jobs of Apple (at podium) and Microsoft chairman Bill Gates (on screen) shock the computer industry at an Apple software developers conference in August by announcing that they had formed an alliance.

Faster chips. Intel Corporation of Santa Clara, California, introduced Pentium MMX and Pentium II *microprocessor chips* (collections of circuits that execute software instructions) in 1997. The MMX was a version of Intel's Pentium chip, modified to enhance sound and video. The Pentium II was a new design whose premium version ran at 300 *megahertz* (cycles per second). Motorola Corporation of Schaumburg, Illinois, and International Business Machines Corporation (IBM) of Armonk, New York, makers of the PowerPC chip, also unveiled a new design in 1997—it ran at up to 350 megahertz. PowerPC chips were used only with Macintoshes, while Pentium chips were used only with Windows machines.

Cheaper PC's spur sales. More than 40 million American households owned a PC in 1996, an increase of about 4 percent over 1995, according to a March 1997 report by Computer Intelligence, an industry research firm in La Jolla, California. Analysts predicted even more growth in 1997, due largely to the debut of PC's priced below $1,000. Before 1997, PC's in this price range generally had been stripped-down versions of more expensive models that would run many popular software titles poorly, if at all. According to the research firm Audits & Surveys, Inc., of New York City, the availability of more affordable home PC's boosted sales by 16 percent by mid-1997 after no growth through April. □ Michael Woods

See also **Internet; People in the news.**

Congo (Brazzaville).

The democratically elected government of the People's Republic of the Congo fell in October 1997 to the country's former military dictator, who won a four-month civil war with foreign help. The People's Republic of the Congo, which has a population of 2.5 million, is often referred to as Congo (Brazzaville) to distinguish it from the Democratic Republic of the Congo—formerly named Zaire—its much larger neighbor across the Congo River.

By the end of the civil war, more than 10,000 people had been killed, and Brazzaville, Congo's capital, lay ruined and largely abandoned. The war also thwarted an economic boom promised by a surge in oil production.

Presidential election. The war broke out as Congo was preparing for a presidential election, scheduled for July 27. The leading contenders were President Pascal Lissouba and Denis Sassou-Nguesso, a former army colonel who had led the country's military government from 1979 to 1993. In 1992, Lissouba had defeated Sassou-Nguesso in the country's first multiparty elections since gaining independence from France in 1960. After his defeat, Sassou-Nguesso had retreated to the countryside, where he trained a 5,000-man private militia called the Cobras.

In May 1997, Sassou-Nguesso moved back to Brazzaville and announced his candidacy for president. On June 5, Lissouba sent government troops to Sassou-Nguesso's quarters to disarm the Cobras. Fierce fighting broke out, causing most of Brazzaville's 900,000 residents to abandon the city.

Stalemate and intervention. The conflict remained stalemated for months. In mid-October, however, 3,500 Angolan troops, supported by tanks and airplanes, attacked Brazzaville in support of Sassou-Nguesso. Additional Angolan forces crossed Congo's southwestern border with Angola and attacked government positions there. Angolan support for Sassou-Nguesso came in retaliation for Lissouba's aid to Angolan rebel forces in the Congo led by Jonas Savimbi. Sassou-Nguesso also reportedly received aid from France, which held extensive oil operations in Congo, a former French colony. French leaders were reported to have been angered by Lissouba's decision —later reversed under pressure—to grant contracts to a United States oil company.

On October 14, Lissouba fled Brazzaville. The next day, the Cobras took control of the capital, and Sassou-Nguesso declared victory.

Aftermath. Sassou-Nguesso, who was sworn in as president on October 22, pledged to form a national unity government and hold free elections. However, the record of his previous rule, marked by economic mismanagement, corruption, and political oppression, led observers to question his sincerity. □ Mark DeLancey

See also **Africa** (Facts in brief table).

Congo (Kinshasa).

The 31-year rule of President Mobutu Sese Seko of Zaire collapsed in May 1997 after a seven-month rebellion, which had been supported by at least three neighboring countries. Laurent Kabila, leader of the rebel Alliance of Democratic Forces for the Liberation of Congo Zaire (ADFL), became the new leader of the country, which Kabila renamed the Democratic Republic of the Congo in May. The country is also known as Congo (Kinshasa).

The civil war began in October 1996 with an uprising by members of the country's minority Tutsi people in eastern Zaire, along the country's eastern borders with Rwanda and Uganda. With Mobutu's support, Hutu refugee camps in eastern Zaire had become a base for exiled Hutu militants fighting Rwanda's Tutsi-backed government. Rebels fighting the Ugandan Army had also established guerrilla camps there.

The ADFL, which was backed by Rwandan troops and weapons and Ugandan money and weaponry, quickly swept through eastern Zaire. Mobutu's army launched a counteroffensive on Jan. 20, 1997, from Kisangani, the largest city in the eastern part of the country. However, the army, which included many *mercenary* (working for money only) soldiers generally offered little resistance. Mobutu, ill with cancer and living in Europe, was unable to invigorate his government or his troops. On March 15, ADFL forces,

South African President Nelson Mandela (center) leads peace talks in April with Zaire's President Mobutu (left) and rebel leader Laurent Kabila. The negotiations failed to settle the civil war, which led to Mobutu's downfall in May.

aided by Angola, captured Kisangani.

Talks between the government and the ADFL in April as well as continuing negotiations by other African states and Western nations failed to produce a peaceful settlement of the conflict. On May 17, the rebels captured Kinshasa, the capital. Mobutu went into exile and died on September 7.

Aftermath. At his inauguration as president on May 29, Kabila promised to hold a referendum on a new constitution by December 1998 and legislative elections by April 1999. However, Kabila had already banned public demonstrations and activities by political parties. On July 25, 1997, government soldiers shot at least three people during an antigovernment demonstration in Kinshasa.

Refugee investigation. Kabila agreed in September to allow United Nations (UN) investigators to probe allegations by officials of human-rights and foreign-aid organizations that his forces and Rwandan allies had murdered thousands of Rwandan Hutu refugees in eastern Congo during the civil war. The agreement came after Western governments had threatened to withhold aid to Congo. Kabila's government had refused entry to the UN's first team of investigators. Kabila then demanded the removal of the team's leader for issuing a report containing evidence of 134 alleged massacres of Hutu refugees by Kabila's forces.   □ Mark DeLancey

See also **Africa** (Facts in brief table).

Congress of the United States. The U.S. Congress and President Bill Clinton in 1997 agreed on landmark legislation to cut taxes, reduce spending, and achieve a balanced federal budget by the year 2002. Representatives of both parties claimed a major victory when the president, on Aug. 5, 1997, signed separate budget and tax bills. One provision of the compromise included a $400-per-child tax credit for children age 16 or younger beginning in 1998. The credit was available for families with annual incomes up to $110,000.

The balanced-budget bill was to lower spending by $263 billion over five years and result in a balanced budget for the first time since 1969. Reductions included cuts in Medicare, the federal health program for the elderly and disabled.

Gingrich sanctioned. The U.S. House of Representatives voted 395 to 28 on Jan. 21, 1997, to formally reprimand Speaker Newt Gingrich (R., Georgia) and fine him $300,000 for bringing discredit upon the House of Representatives. The House Ethics Committee found that Gingrich improperly used tax-exempt donations for political purposes and then submitted false information to the House Ethics Committee. It was the first sanction imposed on a speaker in the history of the House of Representatives. Gingrich admitted to the charges as part of a plea agreement with the committee. Representative Nancy Johnson (R., Connecticut), chair of the

Members of the United States Senate

The Senate of the second session of the 105th Congress consisted of 45 Democrats and 55 Republicans when it convened on Jan. 27, 1998. The first date in each listing shows when the senator's term began. The second date in each listing shows when the senator's term expires.

State	Term	State	Term	State	Term
Alabama		**Louisiana**		**Ohio**	
Richard C. Shelby, R.	1987-1999	John B. Breaux, D.	1987-1999	John H. Glenn, Jr., D.	1974-1999
Jeff Sessions, R.	1997-2003	Mary L. Landrieu, D.	1997-2003	Mike DeWine, R.	1995-2001
Alaska		**Maine**		**Oklahoma**	
Theodore F. Stevens, R.	1968-2003	Olympia Snowe, R.	1995-2001	Don Nickles, R.	1981-1999
Frank H. Murkowski, R.	1981-1999	Susan M. Collins, R.	1997-2003	James M. Inhofe, R.	1994-2003
Arizona		**Maryland**		**Oregon**	
John McCain III, R.	1987-1999	Paul S. Sarbanes, D.	1977-2001	Ron Wyden, D.	1996-1999
Jon Kyl, R.	1995-2001	Barbara A. Mikulski, D.	1987-1999	Gordon Smith, R.	1997-2003
Arkansas		**Massachusetts**		**Pennsylvania**	
Dale Bumpers, D.	1975-1999	Edward M. Kennedy, D.	1962-2001	Arlen Specter, R.	1981-1999
Tim Hutchinson, R.	1997-2003	John F. Kerry, D.	1985-2003	Rick Santorum, R.	1995-2001
California		**Michigan**		**Rhode Island**	
Dianne Feinstein, D.	1992-2001	Carl Levin, D.	1979-2003	John H. Chafee, R.	1976-2001
Barbara Boxer, D.	1993-1999	Spencer Abraham, R.	1995-2001	Jack Reed, D.	1997-2003
Colorado		**Minnesota**		**South Carolina**	
Ben N. Campbell, R.	1993-1999	Paul D. Wellstone, D.	1991-2003	Strom Thurmond, R.	1955-2003
Wayne Allard, R.	1997-2003	Rod Grams, R.	1995-2001	Ernest F. Hollings, D.	1966-1999
Connecticut		**Mississippi**		**South Dakota**	
Christopher J. Dodd, D.	1981-1999	Thad Cochran, R.	1978-2003	Thomas A. Daschle, D.	1987-1999
Joseph I. Lieberman, D.	1989-2001	Trent Lott, R.	1989-2001	Tim Johnson, D.	1997-2003
Delaware		**Missouri**		**Tennessee**	
William V. Roth, Jr., R.	1971-2001	Christopher S. (Kit) Bond, R.	1987-1999	Fred Thompson, R.	1994-2003
Joseph R. Biden, Jr., D.	1973-2003	John Ashcroft, R.	1995-2001	Bill Frist, R.	1995-2001
Florida		**Montana**		**Texas**	
Bob Graham, D.	1987-1999	Max Baucus, D.	1978-2003	Phil Gramm, R.	1985-2003
Connie Mack III, R.	1989-2001	Conrad Burns, R.	1989-2001	Kay Bailey Hutchison, R.	1993-2001
Georgia		**Nebraska**		**Utah**	
Paul Coverdell, R.	1993-1999	J. Robert Kerrey, D.	1989-2001	Orrin G. Hatch, R.	1977-2001
Max Cleland, D.	1997-2003	Chuck Hagel, R.	1997-2003	Robert F. Bennett, R.	1993-1999
Hawaii		**Nevada**		**Vermont**	
Daniel K. Inouye, D.	1963-1999	Harry M. Reid, D.	1987-1999	Patrick J. Leahy, D.	1975-1999
Daniel K. Akaka, D.	1990-2001	Richard H. Bryan, D.	1989-2001	James M. Jeffords, R.	1989-2001
Idaho		**New Hampshire**		**Virginia**	
Larry E. Craig, R.	1991-2003	Robert C. Smith, R.	1990-2003	John W. Warner, R.	1979-2003
Dirk Kempthorne, R.	1993-1999	Judd Gregg, R.	1993-1999	Charles S. Robb, D.	1989-2001
Illinois		**New Jersey**		**Washington**	
Carol Moseley-Braun, D.	1993-1999	Frank R. Lautenberg, D.	1982-2001	Slade Gorton, R.	1989-2001
Richard J. Durbin, D.	1997-2003	Robert G. Torricelli, D.	1997-2003	Patty Murray, D.	1993-1999
Indiana		**New Mexico**		**West Virginia**	
Richard G. Lugar, R.	1977-2001	Pete V. Domenici, R.	1973-2003	Robert C. Byrd, D.	1959-2001
Dan R. Coats, R.	1989-1999	Jeff Bingaman, D.	1983-2001	John D. Rockefeller IV, D.	1985-2003
Iowa		**New York**		**Wisconsin**	
Charles E. Grassley, R.	1981-1999	Daniel P. Moynihan, D.	1977-2001	Herbert Kohl, D.	1989-2001
Tom Harkin, D.	1985-2003	Alfonse M. D'Amato, R.	1981-1999	Russell D. Feingold, D.	1993-1999
Kansas		**North Carolina**		**Wyoming**	
Sam Brownback, R.	1996-1999	Jesse A. Helms, R.	1973-2003	Craig Thomas, R.	1995-2001
Pat Roberts, R.	1997-2003	Lauch Faircloth, R.	1993-1999	Mike Enzi, R.	1997-2003
Kentucky		**North Dakota**			
Wendell H. Ford, D.	1974-1999	Kent Conrad, D.	1987-2001		
Mitch McConnell, R.	1985-2003	Byron L. Dorgan, D.	1992-1999		

Members of the United States House of Representatives

The House of Representatives of the second session of the 105th Congress consisted of 203 Democrats, 227 Republicans, 1 independent and 4 vacancies (not including representatives from American Samoa, the District of Columbia, Guam, Puerto Rico, and the Virgin Islands), when it convened on Jan. 27, 1998. There were 207 Democrats, 227 Republicans, and 1 independent when the first session of the 105th Congress convened. This table shows congressional district, legislator, and party affiliation. Asterisk (*) denotes those who served in the 104th Congress; dagger (†) denotes "at large."

Alabama
1. Sonny Callahan, R.*
2. Terry Everett; R.*
3. Bob Riley, R.
4. Robert Aderholt, R.
5. Bud Cramer, D.*
6. Spencer Bachus, R.*
7. Earl Hilliard, D.*

Alaska
†Donald E. Young, R.*

Arizona
1. Matt Salmon, R.*
2. Ed Pastor, D.*
3. Bob Stump, R.*
4. John Shadegg, R.*
5. Jim Kolbe, R.*
6. J. D. Hayworth, R.*

Arkansas
1. Marion Berry, D.
2. Vic Snyder, D.
3. Asa Hutchinson, R.
4. Jay Dickey, R.*

California
1. Frank Riggs, R.*
2. Wally Herger, R.*
3. Vic Fazio, D.*
4. John Doolittle, R.*
5. Robert T. Matsui, D.*
6. Lynn Woolsey, D.*
7. George E. Miller, D.*
8. Nancy Pelosi, D.*
9. Ronald V. Dellums, D.*
10. Ellen Tauscher, D.
11. Richard Pombo, R.*
12. Tom Lantos, D.*
13. Fortney H. (Peter) Stark, D.*
14. Anna Eshoo, D.*
15. Tom Campbell, R.*
16. Zoe Lofgren, D.*
17. Sam Farr, D.*
18. Gary Condit, D.*
19. George Radanovich, R.*
20. Calvin Dooley, D.*
21. William M. Thomas, R.*
22. Walter H. Capps, D.**
23. Elton Gallegly, R.*
24. Brad Sherman, D.
25. Howard McKeon, R.*
26. Howard L. Berman, D.*
27. James E. Rogan, R.
28. David Dreier, R.*
29. Henry A. Waxman, D.*
30. Xavier Becerra, D.*
31. Matthew Martinez, D.*
32. Julian C. Dixon, D.*
33. Lucille Roybal-Allard, D.*
34. Esteban E. Torres, D.*
35. Maxine Waters, D.*
36. Jane Harman, D.*
37. Juanita Millender-McDonald, D.*
38. Steve Horn, R.*
39. Edward Royce, R.*
40. Jerry Lewis, R.*
41. Jay Kim, R.*

**Died Oct. 28, 1997

†† Died Jan. 5, 1998

42. George E. Brown, Jr., D.*
43. Kenneth Calvert, R.*
44. Sonny Bono, R.* ††
45. Dana Rohrabacher, R.*
46. Loretta Sanchez, D.
47. C. Christopher Cox, R.*
48. Ronald C. Packard, R.*
49. Brian Bilbray, R.*
50. Bob Filner, D.*
51. Randy (Duke) Cunningham, R.*
52. Duncan L. Hunter, R.*

Colorado
1. Diana DeGette, D.
2. David E. Skaggs, D.*
3. Scott McInnis, R.*
4. Bob Schaffer, R.
5. Joel Hefley, R.*
6. Daniel Schaefer, R.*

Connecticut
1. Barbara B. Kennelly, D.*
2. Sam Gejdenson, D.*
3. Rosa DeLauro, D.*
4. Christopher Shays, R.*
5. James H. Maloney, D.
6. Nancy L. Johnson, R.*

Delaware
†Michael Castle, R.*

Florida
1. Joe Scarborough, R.*
2. Allen Boyd, D.
3. Corrine Brown, D.*
4. Tillie Fowler, R.*
5. Karen Thurman, D.*
6. Clifford B. Stearns, R.*
7. John Mica, R.*
8. Bill McCollum, R.*
9. Michael Bilirakis, R.*
10. C. W. Bill Young, R.*
11. Jim Davis, D.
12. Charles Canady, R.*
13. Dan Miller, R.*
14. Porter J. Goss, R.*
15. Dave Weldon, R.*
16. Mark Foley, R.*
17. Carrie Meek, D.*
18. Ileana Ros-Lehtinen, R.*
19. Robert Wexler, D.
20. Peter Deutsch, D.*
21. Lincoln Diaz-Balart, R.*
22. E. Clay Shaw, Jr., R.*
23. Alcee Hastings, D.*

Georgia
1. Jack Kingston, R.*
2. Sanford Bishop, D.*
3. Mac Collins, R.*
4. Cynthia A. McKinney, D.*
5. John Lewis, D.*
6. Newt Gingrich, R.*
7. Bob Barr, R.*
8. Saxby Chambliss, R.*
9. Nathan Deal, R.*
10. Charlie Norwood, R.*
11. John Linder, R.*

Hawaii
1. Neil Abercrombie, D.*
2. Patsy T. Mink, D.*

Idaho
1. Helen Chenoweth, R.*
2. Michael Crapo, R.*

Illinois
1. Bobby Rush, D.*
2. Jesse L. Jackson, Jr., D.*
3. William O. Lipinski, D.*
4. Luis Gutierrez, D.*
5. Rod R. Blagojevich, D.
6. Henry J. Hyde, R.*
7. Danny Davis, D.
8. Philip M. Crane, R.*
9. Sidney R. Yates, D.*
10. John Edward Porter, R.*
11. Gerald Weller, R.*
12. Jerry F. Costello, D.*
13. Harris W. Fawell, R.*
14. J. Dennis Hastert, R.*
15. Thomas W. Ewing, R.*
16. Donald Manzullo, R.*
17. Lane A. Evans, D.*
18. Ray LaHood, R.*
19. Glenn Poshard, D.*
20. John Shimkus, R.

Indiana
1. Peter J. Visclosky, D.*
2. David McIntosh, R.*
3. Tim Roemer, D.*
4. Mark Souder, R.*
5. Steve Buyer, R.*
6. Danny L. Burton, R.*
7. Edward A. Pease, R.
8. John Hostettler, R.*
9. Lee H. Hamilton, D.*
10. Julia M. Carson, D.

Iowa
1. Jim Leach, R.*
2. Jim Nussle, R.*
3. Leonard Boswell, D.
4. Greg Ganske, R.*
5. Tom Latham, R.*

Kansas
1. Jerry Moran, R.
2. Jim Ryun, R.*
3. Vince Snowbarger, R.
4. Todd Tiahrt, R.*

Kentucky
1. Edward Whitfield, R.*
2. Ron Lewis, R.*
3. Anne Northup, R.
4. Jim Bunning, R.*
5. Harold (Hal) Rogers, R.*
6. Scotty Baesler, D.*

Louisiana
1. Robert L. Livingston, Jr., R.*
2. William J. Jefferson, D.*
3. W. J. (Billy) Tauzin, R.*
4. Jim McCrery, R.*
5. John Cooksey, R.
6. Richard Hugh Baker, R.*
7. Chris John, D.

Maine
1. Thomas Allen, D.
2. John Baldacci, D.*

Maryland
1. Wayne T. Gilchrest, R.*
2. Robert Ehrlich, Jr., R.*
3. Benjamin L. Cardin, D.*
4. Albert Wynn, D.*
5. Steny H. Hoyer, D.*
6. Roscoe Bartlett, R.*
7. Elijah Cummings. D.*
8. Constance A. Morella, R.*

Massachusetts
1. John W. Olver, R.*
2. Richard E. Neal, D.*
3. James McGovern, D.
4. Barney Frank, D.*
5. Martin Meehan, D.*
6. John Tierney, D.
7. Edward J. Markey, D.*
8. Joseph P. Kennedy II, D.*
9. John Joseph Moakley, D.*
10. William Delahunt, D.

Michigan
1. Bart Stupak, D.*
2. Peter Hoekstra, R.*
3. Vernon Ehlers, R.*
4. Dave Camp, R.*
5. James Barcia, D.*
6. Frederick S. Upton, R.*
7. Nick Smith, R.*
8. Debbie Stabenow, D.
9. Dale E. Kildee, D.*
10. David E. Bonior, D.*
11. Joseph Knollenberg, R.*
12. Sander M. Levin, D.*
13. Lynn Rivers, D.*
14. John Conyers, Jr., D.*
15. Carolyn Kilpatrick, D.
16. John D. Dingell, D.*

Minnesota
1. Gil Gutknecht, R.*
2. David Minge, D.*
3. Jim Ramstad, R.*
4. Bruce F. Vento, D.*
5. Martin O. Sabo, D.*
6. William P. Luther, D.*
7. Collin C. Peterson, D.*
8. James L. Oberstar, D.*

Mississippi
1. Roger Wicker, R.*
2. Bennie Thompson, D.*
3. Charles Pickering, R.
4. Mike Parker, R.*
5. Gene Taylor, D.*

Missouri
1. William L. (Bill) Clay, D.*
2. James Talent, R.*
3. Richard A. Gephardt, D.*
4. Ike Skelton, D.*
5. Karen McCarthy, D.*
6. Pat Danner, D.*
7. Roy Blunt, R.
8. Jo Ann Emerson, R.*
9. Kenny Hulshof, R.

Montana
†Rick Hill, R.

Nebraska
1. Doug Bereuter, R.*
2. Jon Christensen, R.*
3. Bill Barrett, R.*

Nevada
1. John Ensign, R.*
2. Jim Gibbons, R.

New Hampshire
1. John E. Sununu, R.
2. Charles Bass, R.*

New Jersey
1. Robert E. Andrews, D.*
2. Frank LoBiondo, R.*
3. H. James Saxton, R.*
4. Christopher H. Smith, R.*
5. Marge Roukema, R.*
6. Frank Pallone, Jr., D.*
7. Bob Franks, R.*
8. William Pascrell, D.
9. Steven Rothman, D
10. Donald M. Payne, D.*
11. Rodney Frelinghuysen, R.*
12. Mike Pappas, R.
13. Robert Menendez, D.*

New Mexico
1. Steven H. Schiff, R.*
2. Joe Skeen, R.*
3. Bill Redmond, R.

New York
1. Michael Forbes, R.*
2. Rick Lazio, R.*
3. Peter King, R.*
4. Carolyn McCarthy, D.
5. Gary L. Ackerman, D.*
6. Floyd Flake, D.*‡
7. Thomas J. Manton, D.*
8. Jerrold Nadler, D.*
9. Charles E. Schumer, D.*
10. Edolphus Towns, D.*
11. Major R. Owens, D.*
12. Nydia Velázquez, D.*
13. Vito J. Fossella, R.
14. Carolyn Maloney, D.*

15. Charles B. Rangel, D.*
16. José E. Serrano, D.*
17. Eliot L. Engel, D.*
18. Nita M. Lowey, D.*
19. Sue Kelly, R.*
20. Benjamin A. Gilman, R.*
21. Michael R. McNulty, D.*
22. Gerald B. H. Solomon, R.*
23. Sherwood L. Boehlert, R.*
24. John McHugh, R.*
25. James Walsh, R.*
26. Maurice Hinchey, D.*
27. William Paxon, R.*
28. Louise M. Slaughter, D.*
29. John J. LaFalce, D.*
30. Jack Quinn, R.*
31. Amo Houghton, R.*

North Carolina
1. Eva Clayton, D.*
2. Bob Etheridge, D.
3. Walter Jones, Jr., R.*
4. David Price, D.
5. Richard Burr, R.*
6. Howard Coble, R.*
7. Mike McIntyre, D.
8. W. G. (Bill) Hefner, D.*
9. Sue Myrick, R.*
10. Cass Ballenger, R.*
11. Charles H. Taylor, R.*
12. Melvin Watt, D.*

North Dakota
†Earl Pomeroy, D.*

Ohio
1. Steve Chabot, R.*
2. Rob Portman, R.*
3. Tony P. Hall, D.*
4. Michael G. Oxley, R.*
5. Paul E. Gillmor, R.*
6. Ted Strickland, D.
7. David L. Hobson, R.*
8. John A. Boehner, R.*
9. Marcy Kaptur, D.*
10. Dennis Kucinich, D.
11. Louis Stokes, D.*
12. John R. Kasich, R.*
13. Sherrod Brown, D.*
14. Thomas C. Sawyer, D.*
15. Deborah Pryce, R.*
16. Ralph Regula, R.*
17. James A. Traficant, Jr., D.*
18. Bob Ney, R.*
19. Steven LaTourette, R.*

Oklahoma
1. Steve Largent, R.*
2. Tom Coburn, R.*
3. Wes Watkins, R.
4. J. C. Watts, R.*
5. Ernest Jim Istook, R.*
6. Frank Lucas, R.*

Oregon
1. Elizabeth Furse, D.*
2. Robert Smith, R.
3. Earl Blumenauer, D.*
4. Peter A. DeFazio, D.*
5. Darlene Hooley, D.

Pennsylvania
1. Thomas M. Foglietta, D.*§
2. Chaka Fattah, D.*
3. Robert A. Borski, Jr., D.*
4. Ron Klink, D.*
5. John Peterson, R.
6. Tim Holden, D.*
7. W. Curtis Weldon, R.*
8. Jim Greenwood, R.*
9. E. G. (Bud) Shuster, R.*
10. Joseph M. McDade, R.*
11. Paul E. Kanjorski, D.*
12. John P. Murtha, D.*
13. Jon Fox, R.*
14. William J. Coyne, D.*
15. Paul McHale, D.*
16. Joseph Pitts, R.
17. George W. Gekas, R.*
18. Michael Doyle, D.*
19. William F. Goodling, R.*
20. Frank Mascara, D.*
21. Philip English, R.*

Rhode Island
1. Patrick Kennedy, D.*
2. Robert Weygand, D.

South Carolina
1. Mark Sanford, R.*
2. Floyd Spence, R.*
3. Lindsey Graham, R.*
4. Bob Inglis, R.*
5. John M. Spratt, Jr., D.*
6. James Clyburn, D.*

South Dakota
†John Thune, R.

Tennessee
1. William Jenkins, R.
2. John J. Duncan, Jr., R.*
3. Zach Wamp, R.*
4. Van Hilleary, R.*
5. Bob Clement, D.*
6. Bart Gordon, D.*
7. Ed Bryant, R.*
8. John S. Tanner, D.*
9. Harold E. Ford, Jr., D.

Texas
1. Max Sandlin, D.
2. Jim Turner, D.
3. Sam Johnson, R.*
4. Ralph M. Hall, D.*
5. Pete Sessions, R.
6. Joe Barton, R.*
7. Bill Archer, R.*
8. Kevin Brady, R.
9. Nick Lampson, D.
10. Lloyd Doggett, D.*
11. Chet Edwards, D.*
12. Kay Granger, R.
13. William Thornberry, R.*
14. Ron Paul, R.
15. Rubén Hinojosa, D.
16. Silvestre Reyes, D.
17. Charles W. Stenholm, D.*
18. Sheila Jackson Lee, D.*
19. Larry Combest, R.*

20. Henry B. Gonzalez, D.*
21. Lamar S. Smith, R.*
22. Tom DeLay, R.*
23. Henry Bonilla, R.*
24. Martin Frost, D.*
25. Ken Bentsen, D.
26. Richard K. Armey, R.*
27. Solomon P. Ortiz, D.*
28. Ciro Rodriguez, D.
29. Gene Green, D.*
30. Eddie Bernice Johnson, D.*

Utah
1. James V. Hansen, R.*
2. Merrill Cook, R.
3. Christopher Cannon, R.

Vermont
†Bernard Sanders, Ind.*

Virginia
1. Herbert H. Bateman, R.*
2. Owen B. Pickett, D.*
3. Robert Scott, D.*
4. Norman Sisisky, D.*
5. Virgil Goode, D.
6. Robert Goodlatte, R.*
7. Thomas J. (Tom) Bliley, Jr., R.*
8. James P. Moran, Jr., D.*
9. Rick C. Boucher, D.*
10. Frank R. Wolf, R.*
11. Thomas Davis III, R.*

Washington
1. Rick White, R.*
2. Jack Metcalf, R.*
3. Linda Smith, R.*
4. Doc Hastings, R.*
5. George Nethercutt, R.*
6. Norman D. Dicks, D.*
7. Jim McDermott, D.*
8. Jennifer Dunn, R.*
9. Adam Smith, D

West Virginia
1. Alan B. Mollohan, D.*
2. Robert E. Wise, Jr., D.*
3. Nick J. Rahall II, D.*

Wisconsin
1. Mark Neumann, R.*
2. Scott Klug, R.*
3. Ron Kind, D.
4. Gerald D. Kleczka, D.*
5. Thomas Barrett, D.*
6. Thomas E. Petri, R.*
7. David R. Obey, D.*
8. Jay Johnson, D.
9. F. James Sensenbrenner, Jr., R.*

Wyoming
†Barbara Cubin, R.*

Nonvoting representatives
American Samoa
Eni F. H. Faleomavaega, D.*

District of Columbia
Eleanor Holmes Norton, D.*

Guam
Robert Underwood, D.*

Puerto Rico
Carlos Romero-Barceló, D.*

Virgin Islands
Donna Christian-Green, D.

‡Resigned Nov. 16, 1997.　　　§Resigned Nov. 11, 1997.

committee, said the reprimand showed that "no one is above the rules of the House."

On April 17, Gingrich announced a plan to borrow $300,000 from retired Republican Senator Bob Dole (R., Kansas) in order to pay the fine.

Republican rebellion. In a bizarre internal rebellion in July, Speaker Gingrich fought off an attempted *coup* (overthrow) by junior Republican House members who tried to oust him from the speakership. Reports differed on who was involved, but on July 17, Representative Bill Paxon (R., New York), who some viewed as Gingrich's potential successor, resigned as head of the House Republican leadership team. However, Paxon denied having anything to do with the failed coup.

Some reports claimed that House Majority Leader Dick Armey (R., Texas), Majority Whip Tom DeLay (R., Texas), and Representative John Boehner (R., Ohio), chairman of the House Republican conference, were also involved in the attempted coup. All three Republican representatives, however, denied involvement.

Fund-raising allegations. Partisan warfare erupted sporadically between the Republican-controlled Congress and the Clinton Administration during 1997 over allegations of campaign fund-raising abuses. Both the U.S. Senate and the House of Representatives investigated fund-raising tactics used by President Clinton and Vice President Al Gore during the 1996 presidential campaign.

The Senate Governmental Affairs Committee hearings spotlighted ties between the Democratic National Committee (DNC) and contributions from Asian businesses. Senator Fred Thompson (R., Tennessee) had hoped to expose an Asian plot to influence the presidential election. Although the Democratic Party returned $3 million in contributions it deemed illegal or inappropriate—approximately three-quarters of which had been raised by three Asian American businessmen—the committee was unable to provide proof of any illegal activity.

The committee also criticized President Clinton for inviting political contributors to stay overnight in the White House and for videotapes that showed him hosting fund-raising coffees in the Executive Mansion. President Clinton responded that he did nothing improper.

On Sept. 9, 1997, former DNC leader Donald L. Fowler admitted to the Senate committee that he had arranged meetings between members of the Clinton Administration and major contributors to the Democratic Party. On September 18, Roger Tamraz, who contributed more than $300,000 to the DNC during the 1996 campaign, was invited to the White House despite a warrant for his arrest issued in Lebanon on embezzlement charges. Tamraz testified in 1997 that he had been seeking U.S. government backing for an overseas oil pipeline project and donated money to the Democratic Party to gain

access to high-ranking government officials.

Vice President Al Gore also came under attack from Republicans on the committee for his presence in April 1996 at the Buddhist Hsi Lai Temple in Hacienda Heights, California, when illegal donations of $65,000 were given to the Democratic National Committee. Three Buddhist nuns testified during the Senate committee hearing in September 1997 that the temple had illegally reimbursed its members for contributions. Vice President Gore denied that he knew it was a fund-raising event.

In October, the Senate Governmental Affairs Committee ended its probe into campaign financing without uncovering hard evidence of abuses. The House of Representatives Reform and Oversight Committee was still investigating election fund-raising when Congress adjourned in November.

Telephone inquiry. Both President Clinton and Vice President Gore also were attacked in 1997 by Republicans in Congress for allegedly breaking a law by making telephone calls from the White House to solicit donations to the Democratic Party. Attorney General Janet Reno began a preliminary investigation in September into whether an independent counsel should be named to conduct a formal inquiry into the president's and vice president's phone calls. Although the Justice Department continued its probe of fund-raising abuses through 1997, Reno announced on December 2 that she would not appoint an independent counsel to investigate the allegations about Clinton and Gore.

Republican fund-raising. The Republican National Committee (RNC) also was criticized for its role in a questionable Hong Kong loan to a nonprofit group allied with the GOP (Grand Old Party, or Republican Party). Former RNC Chairman Haley Barbour in July denied using the National Policy Forum (NPF), a conservative organization he founded in 1993, to funnel more than $2 million from a Hong Kong-based company to the RNC during the 1994 elections.

Democrats on the Senate Governmental Affairs Committee investigating campaign fund-raising abuses had alleged that Barbour asked Hong Kong businessman Ambrous Tung Young, head of Young Brothers Development Corporation, for funds that were sent to the RNC. Barbour insisted that it was legal for the NPF—a nonprofit organization until the Internal Revenue Service revoked its tax-exempt status for partisanship—to accept foreign donations. Barbour claimed that the NPF used $1.6 million it received from Young to repay a debt to the RNC.

Statistical sampling techniques slated for use in the year 2000 census triggered debate in Congress in 1997. In April, the House of Representatives attached to an $8.6-billion spending bill providing disaster aid to flood-stricken Midwestern states a measure that banned the U.S. Census Bureau from developing sampling tools for the 2000 census.

Republican members of the U.S. Congress celebrate the news in July 1997 of a balanced-budget agreement. The legislation was signed in August.

Sampling is used to estimate a region's total population based on a representative sample rather than a count of every person. The president vetoed the bill in June 1997, in part because it prohibited sampling. The president later signed a revised bill from which the ban on sampling had been removed.

The conflict was renewed in September after the House attached another measure prohibiting sampling to a spending bill for the U.S. Commerce Department, which oversees the Census Bureau. In November, Republican congressional leaders and the Clinton Administration finally compromised. The Census Bureau was allowed to experiment with statistical sampling techniques in various regions during 1998. However, the compromise also allowed Repub-

licans to pursue an expedited hearing before the U.S. Supreme Court on the constitutionality of statistical sampling measures.

Chemical weapons ban. The Senate on April 24, 1997, voted 74 to 26 to ratify the Chemical Weapons Convention, a treaty requiring the destruction of poison-gas weapons. The United States was the 88th nation to ratify the treaty.

The treaty originally received strong support from GOP members of Congress, but in 1997, Republicans opposing the treaty, led by Senator Jesse Helms (R., North Carolina), maintained that it was unenforceable and ineffective. Some analysts also argued that the treaty would provide all nations access to chemical weapons.

161

Congressional improprieties. Representative Jay C. Kim (R., California), and his wife, June Kim, pleaded guilty on August 11 to charges stemming from illegal contributions of $250,000 to his campaigns between 1992 and 1997. In 1995 and 1996, five South Korean companies or subsidiaries had pleaded guilty to laundering campaign donations through Kim. Kim had originally denied any wrongdoing and did not plan to resign from the House.

A U.S. District Court judge in July 1997 sentenced former Representative Mel Reynolds (D., Illinois) to six years in prison for bank fraud and campaign finance violations. Reynolds was already serving a five-year jail term for having had a sexual relationship with a minor.

A circuit court judge in March convicted former Representative Wes S. Cooley (R., Oregon) of lying about his military service in a 1994 voter's pamphlet and sentenced him to two years' probation and 100 hours of community service.

A U.S. district judge in February 1997, sentenced former House of Representatives postmaster Robert V. Rota to four months in prison for allowing former representatives Dan Rostenkowski (D., Illinois) and Joseph Kolter (D., Pennsylvania) to exchange stamps for money. Rota also received a $2,000 fine and paid $5,000 in restitution to Congress.

In special congressional elections in 1997, voters on April 12 elected Texas State Representative Ciro Rodriguez, a Democrat, to fill the seat of Representative Frank Tejeda (D., Texas), who died in January. In New Mexico, Republican Bill Redmond won a May 13 election to succeed Representative Bill Richardson (D., New Mexico), who left Congress in February after being named U.S. ambassador to the United Nations. On November 4, voters elected Republican Vito Fossella to succeed Representative Susan Molinari (R., New York), who had resigned in August to become a news anchorperson.

Election inquiry ends. The Senate's Rules Committee voted 16 to 0 on October 1 to drop an inquiry into the November 1996 election of Senator Mary Landrieu (D., Louisiana). Her Republican opponent, Woody Jenkins, had claimed voter fraud and corruption during the election. The Rules Committee reported that while it had uncovered "isolated incidents of fraud," there was no compelling evidence to overturn the election.

Congressional pay raise. Under legislation signed by President Clinton in October, members of Congress would receive a cost-of-living pay increase beginning in 1998. The 2.3-percent increase raised the basic salary from $133,600 to $136,672. The increase was part of a spending bill for the U.S. Treasury Department and other agencies.

Although the legislation did not specifically mention pay increases, a 1989 law permits Congress to receive a cost-of-living increase unless the House and Senate vote to prevent it. The House voted 231 to 192 on Sept. 17, 1997, to approve the Treasury Department spending bill without deleting the pay-increase provision. On September 24, the House again voted on the pay increase, this time approving the measure 229 to 199, after some representatives accused members of trying to "sneak" the pay raise through without a debate. The Senate on October 1 voted 55 to 45 in favor of the Treasury Department legislation, which also allowed the pay increase. Congress last received a pay raise in 1992.

Gold coin approved. Congress approved legislation in November 1997 for a gold-colored $1 coin and a redesigned quarter, which will honor the 50 states. The legislation requires the secretary of the treasury to approve the design of the gold-colored coin, which replaces the Susan B. Anthony $1 coin minted from 1979 to 1981. The Susan B. Anthony $1 coin proved to be widely unpopular because it looked and felt too much like a quarter.

Beginning in 1999, five new quarters commemorating 5 of the 50 states are to be issued annually for 10 years. The eagle on one side of the coin will be replaced with designs commemorating each state. The portrait of George Washington will remain on the face of the coin. □ William J. Eaton

See also **Census; Congress of the United States; Democratic Party; Elections; People in the News; Republican Party; Taxation; United States president.**

Connecticut. See State government.

Conservation. On May 31, 1997, the United States National Park Service dedicated nearly 11,000 acres (4,455 hectares) of tallgrass prairie in the Flint Hills of eastern Kansas as the Tallgrass Prairie National Preserve. The preserve is dominated by such native American grasses as big bluestem, Indian grass, switchgrass, and sideoats gramma. Wildflowers on the preserve include purple prairie coneflower, Indian paintbrush, and blue vervain. The preserve is also prime nesting territory for numerous grassland birds, such as sparrows and meadowlarks.

The National Park Service acquired only 180 acres (73 hectares) of the preserve. The balance of the land remained in the control of the National Park Trust, a private conservation organization based in Washington, D.C., that purchases ecologically valuable land. The National Park Service and National Park Trust planned to manage the preserve jointly.

Everglades purchase. Vice President Al Gore announced in June that the federal government had purchased 31,000 acres (12,555 hectares) of private land near Everglades National Park as part of President Bill Clinton's goal to restore the natural flow of water in the Everglades, an area of marshes, swamps, and forests in southern Florida. The land, which cost $50 million, was to be organized as a state park to preserve habitat for Florida panthers, black bears, and other wildlife. Much of the land had once been slated for real-estate development.

In 1947, the U.S. Army Corps of Engineers began to create a network of levees, canals, pumping stations, and reservoirs that altered the flow of water in the Everglades to reduce flooding, bring more drinking water to Miami, and provide land for real-estate developers and sugar cane growers. The project destroyed much of the natural ecosystem and drastically reduced wildlife populations.

Sugar conflict in the Everglades. On April 17, 1997, U.S. Representatives Dan Miller (R., Florida) and Charles Schumer (D., New York) reintroduced a bill in the House that would, if passed, eliminate federal price supports of the sugar industry in the Everglades area. The bill had been narrowly defeated in the House of Representatives in 1996.

Environmentalists argued that the elimination of price supports would cut the amount of land in the Everglades that is used for growing sugar cane, resulting in a decrease in pollution caused by the runoff of agricultural chemicals. The sugar industry claimed that the elimination of price supports would put many sugar growers out of business and eliminate thousands of jobs in southern Florida.

Weevils aid Everglades. In August 1997, the U.S. Department of Agriculture began to release Australian weevils, also called snout beetles, into the Everglades. The department hoped that the snout beetles would destroy melaleuca trees, which were introduced into the Everglades from Australia toward the end of the 1800's. Used for landscaping and erosion control, melaleuca trees spread more rapidly than was anticipated and took over areas previously dominated by native plants.

Five years of laboratory research indicated that snout beetles, which eat only melaleucas, would not end up becoming pests—as introduced species often become in nature. Scientists believed that the snout beetles, used along with aerial spraying of herbicides and other methods, would keep melaleucas under control.

Property rights. On March 19, 1997, the U.S. Supreme Court ruled that the Endangered Species Act permits any landowners who believe they are being harmed by efforts to save endangered species to file lawsuits against the federal government. Lower courts had previously ruled that the Endangered Species Act permitted only landowners who were attempting to protect endangered species to file lawsuits. However, Justice Antonin Scalia, who wrote the majority opinion, stated that the Endangered Species Act was intended not only for species protection but also "to avoid needless economic dislocation produced by agency officials zealously but unintelligently pursuing their environmental objectives."

Conservationists were angered by the court's ruling. They anticipated that it would result in an increase in the number of developers, agricultural organizations, limber companies, property rights

A Zimbabwe parks department employee displays elephant tusks from a nationally owned stockpile. In June, a United Nations agency ruled that Zimbabwe and two other African nations could sell stockpiled ivory to fund elephant conservation.

groups, and state agencies suing the federal government in hopes of reversing economically costly conservation measures.

Conservation innovation. In March, the San Diego City Council approved a nature conservation plan that won praise from both environmentalists and real-estate developers. According to the plan, certain undeveloped plots of private land were to be purchased by the city and permanently preserved as natural habitat, while other private sites were to be designated for unrestricted development. San Diego expected to spend more than $60 million to acquire the land. The plan was to benefit at least 85 endangered animal species plus many endangered plant species. Several other southern California communities had similar plans under consideration in 1997.

Ivory for sale. On June 19, 1997, delegates at the 10th United Nations Convention on International Trade in Endangered Species (CITES), meeting in Harare, Zimbabwe, voted to allow three southern African nations—Zimbabwe, Botswana, and Namibia—to resume the sale of ivory. CITES is an international agreement, signed by more than 120 nations, that regulates trade in wildlife and wildlife products. All commercial trade in ivory had been banned by CITES since 1989 in order to protect declining numbers of African elephants.

During the 1980's, the African elephant population plunged from an estimated 1.3 million animals to 500,000, primarily due to poachers killing the elephants for their ivory. After the 1989 ivory ban, the elephant population began to increase. By 1997, Zimbabwe, Botswana, and Namibia all had large numbers of elephants. They also had stockpiled ivory confiscated from poachers and obtained from the culling of herds and from natural deaths. The June CITES vote allowed these nations to sell a total of 60 tons (54 metric tons) of their ivory to Japan. The revenue obtained, estimated at $30 million, was to be used primarily to compensate farmers whose crops had been eaten by hungry elephants, to build elephant-proof fences, and to monitor elephants.

Animal protectionists feared that the ivory sales would be an incentive to poachers to resume the slaughter of elephants and sell illegally obtained ivory along with the legal product. The United States, Australia, Israel, and several European countries opposed the resumption of the ivory trade.

Decline of the apes. In April, the World Wildlife Fund (WWF), an international conservation organization with headquarters near Geneva, Switzerland, warned that habitat destruction and other pressures could lead to the extinction in the wild of the great apes (gorillas, chimpanzees, and orangutans). Unrestricted logging, expansion of agricultural land, oil and mineral exploration, and encroaching human population in Africa and Asia were among the factors responsible for the loss of ape habitat. Other pressures on ape populations in 1997 were caused by

poachers hunting apes for food and trophies and by land mines planted as part of human warfare.

WWF reported that the most endangered of the great apes was the mountain gorilla. Only about 620 of the primates survived in central Africa in 1997. Between 1900 and 1997, according to WWF, chimpanzee numbers decreased from several million to fewer than 200,000, and orangutan numbers decreased from 100,000 to fewer than 30,000.

Siberian conservation. In February, Yakutia (also called the Sakha Republic), a Russian republic in Siberia, announced that it was setting aside 270,000 square miles (700,000 square kilometers)—one-quarter of its land area—for nature reserves. The government's primary conservation goal was to save the endangered Siberian crane, a white and red bird that is sacred to the people of Yakutia. At 48 inches (122 centimeters) in height, the Siberian crane is one of the world's largest birds. Hundreds of the cranes nest in Yakutia each summer. Other animals in the reserves include polar bears, reindeer, and walruses.

Despite being protected in Yakutia, the cranes remained in peril in 1997 because the world's largest hydroelectric project was under construction in the region in China where the cranes winter. Conservation groups were trying to persuade China to take actions to protect the cranes.   □ Eugene J. Walter, Jr.

Costa Rica. See **Latin America** (Facts in brief table).

Courts. On June 2, 1997, a federal jury in Denver, Colorado, found Timothy J. McVeigh, 29, guilty on 11 counts of murder and conspiracy in connection with the April 19, 1995, bombing of the Alfred P. Murrah Federal Building in Oklahoma City, Oklahoma. On June 13, 1997, the seven-man, five-woman jury recommended that McVeigh, a decorated U.S. Army veteran who served in the Persian Gulf War (1991), be executed for his role in the attack. The Oklahoma City bombing, the most destructive terrorist attack ever committed on U.S. soil, killed 168 people and injured more than 500 others.

On Dec. 23, 1997, a federal jury convicted Terry L. Nichols, a second defendant charged in the attack, of conspiring to bomb the Oklahoma City federal building. The jury also found Nichols guilty of involuntary manslaughter in the deaths of eight federal law enforcement officers. The jury acquitted him of charges that he helped carry out the attack.

Tobacco litigation. The tobacco industry on June 20 agreed to a proposed national settlement that would end lawsuits by states seeking reimbursement for health-care costs resulting from smoking. Tobacco manufacturers—Philip Morris Companies; RJR Nabisco Holdings Corporation; B.A.T. Industries P.L.C., the British parent of the Brown & Williamson Tobacco Corporation; and the Loews Corporation, which owns the Lorillard Tobacco Company—agreed to pay $368.5 billion to the states and the federal government during a 25-year period. After 25 years, the annual fine would be reduced to $15 billion but continue indefinitely. The money would be used to pay for uninsured children's health care, to reimburse states for the cost of treating ill smokers, and to pay for antismoking advertising. The proposed settlement would allow future individual claims from smokers for medical bills or lost wages, but bans future class-action suits and suits brought by individuals.

The tobacco agreement had to be approved by President Bill Clinton and the U.S. Congress. In October 1997, Republican Congressional leaders predicted that the tobacco legislation might be approved in early 1998.

On July 3, 1997, Mississippi reached a $3.6-billion settlement with the tobacco companies. Mississippi was the first state to take tobacco companies to court and became the first state to receive a guaranteed share of the proposed national settlement. On August 25, the tobacco industry agreed to an $11.3-billion settlement with Florida.

Megan's law. A jury in a New Jersey court sentenced convicted child molester Jesse K. Timmendequas, 36, to death on June 20 for raping and strangling 7-year-old Megan Kanka in 1994. The child's slaying in Hamilton Township, New Jersey, led her parents to campaign for laws requiring that communities be notified when convicted sex offenders move into the neighborhood. Timmendequas moved into a house across from Kanka's family after he had served time in prison for sex crimes against young girls.

By 1997, more than 40 states and the federal government had adopted a law requiring that convicted sex offenders register with authorities when they move to a community. On August 20, the Third Circuit Court of Appeals upheld New Jersey's version of Megan's Law, and on August 22, the Second Circuit Court of Appeals upheld New York's version.

Implants. In the first class-action lawsuit over silicone breast implants, a Louisiana jury in August found the Dow Chemical Company of Midland, Michigan, negligent in the testing of silicone used in the implants and in hiding information about the potential health risks of the implants from con-

Fred Goldman (left) embraces his daughter Kim (center) and wife, Patti, following the Feb. 4, 1997, verdict finding O. J. Simpson liable for the wrongful death of Goldman's son, Ronald, and Simpson's ex-wife, Nicole.

sumers. Lawyers for the women who received breast implants claimed that Dow Chemical was involved in the production and safety testing of silicone used in the devices. The company argued that it did not make or test implants. However, Dow Corning, which is partially owned by Dow Chemical, was once the nation's largest implant producer.

On August 25, Dow Corning offered to pay $2.4 billion to settle the claims by more than 300,000 women who maintained that leaking implants had led to various health problems.

Au pair trial. In one of the most closely watched court cases of 1997, a 19-year-old *au pair* (live-in baby sitter) was convicted of second-degree murder, only to be set free after the charge against her was reduced to manslaughter. Louise Woodward, an English woman, was charged with the February shaking death of 8-month-old Matthew Eappen. A jury on October 30 convicted Woodward of second-degree murder after the prosecution and defense had agreed to prohibit them from considering a lesser charge of manslaughter. Woodward faced a mandatory sentence of life with no possibility of parole for 15 years. On November 10, Judge Hiller Zobel changed Woodward's conviction from second-degree murder to manslaughter and sentenced her to the 279 days she had already served since her arrest. Zobel ruled that while Woodward had killed the infant by violently shaking him, the action did not constitute murder because she had not acted with malice.

O. J. Simpson. On February 4, a civil jury in Santa Monica, California, found former football star and sports commentator O. J. Simpson liable for the June 12, 1994, deaths of his ex-wife, Nicole Brown Simpson, and her friend, Ronald L. Goldman. The jury unanimously awarded $8.5 million in compensatory damages to Goldman's parents, Fred Goldman and Sharon Rufo. On Feb. 10, 1997, the jurors ordered Simpson to pay $25 million in punitive damages to Fred Goldman and to Louis and Juditha Brown, the parents of Nicole Brown Simpson. On April 28, a judge denied a new trial request, saying there was no validity to defense claims of juror misconduct.

☐ Geoffrey A. Campbell and Linda P. Campbell

See also **Crime; Supreme Court of the United States.**

Crime in the United States declined in 1997 nationwide for the sixth consecutive year, according to the results of government studies. The Federal Bureau of Investigation (FBI) announced on November 23 that serious crime—a category that includes violent crime and property crime—decreased 4 percent between January and June 1997, compared with the first six months of 1996. According to Uniform Crime Reporting Program figures, which are collected from law enforcement agencies nationwide, violent crime decreased by 5 percent and property crime decreased by 4 percent during the first six months of 1997, compared with the same period in 1996.

According to the FBI, murder and robbery each declined 9 percent between January and July 1997, compared with the first six months of 1996. Aggravated assault in the first six months of 1997 fell 3 percent and forcible rape fell 2 percent. The FBI reported a 9 percent decrease in arson and a 5 percent decrease in both motor vehicle theft and burglary during the same period.

The FBI report revealed that all U.S. cities in the first six months of 1997 showed a decline in serious crime. Cities with a population of more than 250,000 people reported the greatest decrease, a drop of 6 percent. Crime also fell in most states: 6 percent in Northeastern states; 5 percent in Midwestern and Western states; and 3 percent in Southern states.

In a separate survey reflecting the downward

trend, the U.S. Department of Justice reported on Nov. 15, 1997, that violent crime in 1996 dropped 10 percent compared with 1995 statistics. According to the results of the National Crime Victimization Survey, conducted by the Bureau of Justice Statistics, violent crime reached its lowest recorded level since the survey began in 1973.

The most significant drop, according to the survey, was in the category of rapes and sexual assaults, which dropped 17.6 percent in 1996 from the 1995 level. Property crimes also decreased 8.3 percent overall, with the largest drop—20.1 percent—in motor vehicle theft. Personal thefts, such as stolen purses and wallets, decreased 21.1 percent.

Attorney General Janet Reno announced on Oct. 2, 1997, that juvenile arrests in the United States also declined in 1996 compared with 1995 arrest rates. The arrest rate for juveniles for violent crimes declined 9.2 percent in 1996. The FBI reported that 1996 marked the second consecutive year of decline following seven years of increases.

Crime analysts claimed that the reason behind the drop in the crime rate was the new aggressive approach taken by law enforcement, which included the constant presence of police in a community and the active enforcement of laws, even minor laws such as public drunkenness. Some criminologists pointed to demographic changes that reduced the number of potential criminals on the streets, such as the large increase in the number of people in jail and the decrease in the number of U.S. teen-agers.

Killing spree. A highly publicized series of murders, which began in April, ended on July 23, 1997, when Andrew Cunanan, 27, of San Diego, committed suicide in a Miami Beach, Florida, houseboat. Cunanan was the prime suspect in five murders, including the death of fashion designer Gianni Versace.

Cunanan allegedly killed two friends in the Minneapolis, Minnesota, area, a businessman in Chicago, and a cemetery caretaker in New Jersey. In each case a car belonging to the victim was stolen and left near the scene of the next crime. On July 15, Cunanan allegedly shot and killed Versace outside his Miami Beach mansion.

On July 23, a caretaker reported seeing a man resembling Cunanan inside the houseboat and hearing a gunshot. Police surrounded the boat for several hours before entering and finding Cunanan's body. The suicide left many unanswered questions, including what may have prompted the murders.

Murder mystery. Police in Boulder, Colorado, in 1997 continued their investigation into the Dec. 26, 1996, murder of 6-year-old JonBenet Ramsey. Ramsey had been a child beauty pageant-contestant and was named Little Miss Colorado of 1995.

On Dec. 26, 1996, Ramsey's parents called police to report the child as missing. Her body was found later that day in the basement of the family's house. A handwritten ransom note demanding $118,000 was discovered elsewhere in the house. An autopsy report released in August 1997 revealed that Ramsey had been strangled and that her skull had been fractured.

Ramsey's parents, John and Patsy Ramsey, soon became the focus of the police investigation. However, the couple's attorneys repeatedly delayed requests by the police for an interview. In May, after being interviewed by investigators, John and Patsy Ramsey called a press conference to deny any involvement in their daughter's death.

Allegations surfaced throughout 1997 about feuds between the Boulder Police Department and the Boulder district attorney, who had connections with the attorneys representing the Ramseys. In October, Boulder's police chief removed the lead detective from the case and criticized the media for irresponsible coverage of the murder.

Comedian's son murdered. Ennis Cosby, the only son of famed comedian Bill Cosby, was shot to death on January 16 after stopping on a Los Angeles freeway ramp to change a flat tire. Los Angeles police on March 13 charged an 18-year-old immigrant from Ukraine, Mikhail Markhasev, with the murder. Police investigators concluded that Markhasev had allegedly shot Cosby during a botched attempt to steal the victim's car. □ Robert Messenger

See also **Terrorism; United Kingdom; United States, Government of the.**

Croatia. On Dec. 12, 1997, President Franjo Tudjman's vow that Croatia would not participate in any sort of new Balkan alliance became federal law. The Croatian parliament passed a constitutional amendment banning Croatia's entry into a new Yugoslav federation or union of Balkan nations. However, Croatia began to take steps to improve its chances for membership in broader alliances, including the North Atlantic Treaty Organization (NATO), a military partnership of 16 Western European and North American nations, and in the European Union (EU), an organization of 15 Western European countries.

Relations with the West. Western countries and international organizations were hesitant to hold membership talks with Croatia in 1997. Despite agreeing to the provisions of the 1995 Dayton peace agreement that ended the Bosnian War (1992–1995), Tudjman had failed by mid-1997 to fulfill his promise to hand over many war-crimes suspects for trial or to improve Croatia's poor human-rights record.

In April 1997, however, Croatia began to comply with the Dayton agreement by surrendering indicted war criminal Zlatko Aleksovski to the international war crimes tribunal in The Hague, the Netherlands. In October, Croatia turned over 10 Bosnian Croats suspected of war crimes to the tribunal.

Elections. In April 1997 elections, Tudjman's Croatian Democratic Union party (HDZ) retained control of the Croatian parliament. However, oppo-

The body of Andrew Cunanan is removed from a Miami Beach houseboat after his July 23 suicide. Cunanan was the prime suspect in a killing spree that left five men dead.

Croatia

sition parties won council races in several major cities, and HDZ only narrowly won a majority in Zagreb, the nation's capital. In May, Tudjman appointed ethnic Serbs to fill two of the five seats in the parliament reserved for presidential appointees.

Tudjman was elected to a second five-year term as president in June, winning 61 percent of the vote. International observers called the election "free but unfair," alleging bias on the part of the media.

Croatia's economy continued to benefit from a stable exchange rate, single-digit inflation, and increased foreign investment in 1997. Croatia's *gross domestic product* (the total value of goods and services produced in a country in a given period) was expected to grow by 5 percent in 1997. Unemployment stood at 17.4 percent in October.

Eastern Slavonia, the last remaining Serb-held part of Croatia, remained under the administration of the UN in 1997. The UN was due to recall its troops and return administration of the region to Croatia on Jan. 15, 1998. In November 1997, Croatian Foreign Minister Mate Granić formally invited UN police to remain in Eastern Slavonia for nine months after the January 15 deadline. The Serbs, fearing for their safety under Croatian rule, had repeatedly asked for the UN to extend its presence in the region.   □ Sharon L. Wolchik

See also **Bosnia-Herzegovina; Europe** (Facts in brief table).

Cuba. Canadian Foreign Minister Lloyd Axworthy visited Cuba in January 1997—the first visit by a high-ranking Canadian official since 1976. Cuban Foreign Minister Roberto Robaina welcomed Axworthy, noting, "Your country does not share the policy of isolation." Observers interpreted the remark as a reference to U.S. policy prohibiting American companies from trading with Cuba. On Jan. 22, 1997, Axworthy and Fidel Castro pledged to cooperate to improve human rights in Cuba and protect investors from restrictions in the Helms-Burton Act of 1996, a U.S. law targeting foreign businesses in Cuba.

U.S. President Bill Clinton on Jan. 3, 1997, announced he would suspend indefinitely a provision of the Helms-Burton law that allows U.S. citizens whose Cuban property was confiscated after the 1959 Communist revolution to sue foreign companies that use that property.

On Jan. 28, 1997, the Clinton Administration pledged that the U.S. and the international community would provide substantial economic aid to Cuba to promote a peaceful transition to democracy when President Castro is no longer in power.

Sugar harvest. In June 1997, the Cuban government reduced its estimate of the size of the 1996-1997 sugar harvest to 4.2 million metric tons, nearly 2 million metric tons less than originally estimated. Officials blamed the poor harvest on a 1996 hurricane and the lack of foreign financing for crops.

Aleida Guevara speaks at a July 1997 ceremony in Havana, Cuba, honoring her father, leftist guerrilla Ernesto (Ché) Guevara, who fought with Fidel Castro (center) in the 1959 revolution. The ceremony was held upon the return to Cuba of Ché Guevara's remains by Bolivia, where he had been executed in 1967.

Hotel bombings. Cuban authorities characterized a rash of hotel bombings that began in April 1997 as a vast "terrorist plan" to disrupt foreign travel to Cuba. On September 4, three hotels and one restaurant were hit with bombs, one of which killed an Italian tourist. On September 11, Cuban authorities arrested Raúl Ernesto Cruz León, a former Salvadoran soldier described as a "mercenary agent" recruited by Cuban exiles in Miami. Cruz reportedly confessed to carrying out some of the bombings.

Charges of insect attack. At an August 25 meeting of 138 nations that had signed the 1972 Biological and Toxin Weapons Convention, Cuba charged that a U.S. State Department airplane on Oct. 21, 1996, had sprayed the island with *Thrips palmi*, insects that devour some plants. The United States denied the allegation, but the convention established a committee to investigate the charges.

Christmas holiday. On Dec. 14, 1997, President Castro granted Cubans a public Christmas holiday on Dec. 25, 1997, as a concession to Pope John Paul II, who was scheduled to visit Cuba in January 1998.

Cable News Network (CNN) broadcast live from Cuba on March 17, 1997. CNN, the first U.S. media company to maintain a permanent bureau in Cuba since 1969, was the only U.S. agency allowed by Cuba to set up a bureau.   □ Nathan A. Haverstock

See also **Latin America** (Facts in brief table).

Cyprus. See Middle East.

Czech Republic. Public support for the government of Prime Minister Václav Klaus declined sharply in 1997, because of a financial crisis. On November 30, a scandal involving his party's fund raising activities during the 1996 national elections forced Klaus out of office. On Dec. 17, 1997, President Václav Havel named Josef Tosovsky, head of the national bank, as prime minister. Tosovsky, who held no party affiliation, was expected to serve only until parliamentary elections could be held.

Crisis and scandal. The Czech economy began to weaken in late 1996, as the result of a *trade deficit* (more goods being imported than exported). By the spring of 1997, the deficit had grown out of control. In April, the government responded by adopting an austerity program that included budget cuts and new restrictions on imports. To boost public confidence in his government, Klaus replaced three cabinet members in early June. The government won a vote of confidence in parliament on June 10, but only by a 2-vote margin.

In November, Czech journalists discovered that Klaus's Civic Democratic Party had $5 million in a secret Swiss bank account. The reporters also revealed that party leaders had accepted $225,000 in 1996 from a businessman who was interested in purchasing a state-owned steel mill.

Economy. The failure of several large banks and a series of financial scandals caused the Czech currency to drop sharply in value in May 1997, triggering a recession. Consumer prices rose 9.9 percent in August, the steepest climb since June 1995. Unemployment declined to 3.8 percent in May 1997, but reached 4.9 percent at the end of October and was expected to continue to rise. The trade deficit, which reached $1.9 billion in the first quarter of 1997, fell to $290 million by October.

The economic situation was made worse by the devastating floods that covered much of the northern provinces of Moravia and eastern Bohemia in July. Forty-nine people died in the floods, which caused $1.8 billion in damage. The Czech government pledged $350 million in flood relief aid.

Foreign affairs. The Czech Republic was one of three countries invited in 1997 to join the North Atlantic Treaty Organization, a military alliance of 16 Western European and North American nations, in 1997. In July, officials of the European Union (EU), an organization of 15 Western European countries, recommended that the Czech Republic be invited to participate in talks about joining the EU in 1998.

A reconciliation pact was signed by Czech and German leaders in January 1997. Germany apologized for annexing Czech lands betwen 1938 and 1945. The Czechs expressed regret for expelling almost 3 million ethnic Germans after the end of World War II (1939–1945).   □ Sharon L. Wolchik

See also **Europe** (Facts in brief table).

Dallas public schools spent much of 1997 in turmoil. The appointment of Yvonne Gonzalez as the first Hispanic superintendent of schools in January was hailed by many, but her tenure was marked by a series of clashes between Hispanics and African Americans at school board meetings. In April, Gonzalez launched an investigation into employee payroll fraud, which resulted in 13 indictments. However, in September Gonzalez herself was forced to resign after pleading guilty to federal charges of misapplying district funds. Gonzalez was accused of using $16,279 in public funds to purchase furniture for her office and apartment. She also faced a sexual harassment lawsuit filed by the district's chief financial officer, Matthew Harden, Jr.

City council scandal. Former Dallas city council member Paul Fielding began serving a 41-month prison term in October after pleading guilty to fraud and extortion charges. Fielding was accused of using his public office to extort a lucrative cleaning contract for a client, of lying during bankruptcy proceedings, and of conspiring to defraud investors.

Downtown revitalization. Two real estate companies announced plans on May 15 to develop 700 apartment units in six historic downtown Dallas buildings. The announcement by Columbus Realty Trust and Southwest Properties brought to nearly 7,000 the number of residential units built or rehabilitated in the downtown area during the 1990's.

Unsnarling traffic. The Dallas City Council approved a Texas Department of Transportation plan on September 10 to unsnarl one of the 10 most congested freeway interchanges in the United States. The state pledged $1 billion to relieve traffic problems at the site of the merger of interstate highways 30 and 35, known as the "mixmaster," just south of downtown Dallas. The plan includes the building of a toll road along the Trinity River as a reliever parkway.

Baylor Hospital preserved. The Baylor University Board of Regents withdrew a proposal in March to sell the 12-hospital Baylor Health Care System to a for-profit hospital chain. The regents then relinquished control of the hospital chain to the system's board. The suggested sale of Baylor Medical Center and several suburban nonprofit hospitals to Santa Barbara, California-based Tenet Healthcare Corporation for $1.2 billion had caused an uproar among Dallas citizens and Baylor University alumni. The Baylor Health Care System spends more than $65 million a year on the care of indigent people and $9 million on research and development.

Pollution. In September, the Environmental Protection Agency downgraded air quality assessments in the Dallas-Fort Worth area from "moderate" to "serious." The agency cited the failure of state and local officials to address pollution problems.

Arts. Dallas real estate developer Raymond D. Nasher announced in April that he would build a park in the Downtown Arts District to house a rotating display from his world-renowned sculpture collection. Museums in Europe, New York, and Washington, D.C., had sought the Nasher collection, which contains works by such artists as Pablo Picasso, Alexander Calder, Henry Moore, and Auguste Rodin. Nasher's decision is expected to attract international tourists to Dallas.

Arena agreement. The Dallas City Council ratified an agreement with the owners of the Dallas Mavericks basketball team and Stars hockey team in October to build a $230-million downtown arena. If Dallas voters approve the agreement in 1998, the city will finance $125 million of the construction costs with a 5-percent tax increase on rental cars and a 2-percent tax increase on hotel and motel rooms. The majority owner of the Mavericks, Ross Perot, Jr., threatened to move his team to a suburban location if an arena proposal could not be worked out.

Cowboys accuser prosecuted. Former exotic dancer Nina Shahravan, 24, received a 90-day jail sentence in September 1997, after admitting that she falsely accused two Dallas Cowboys football players of sexual assault. Shahravan recanted a claim that Erik Williams assaulted her in December 1996 while Michael Irvin held a gun to her head. Shahravan could face deportation to her native Iran as a result of the conviction.   □ Henry K. Tatum

See also **City.**

Dance. Lavish full-length ballets were the box-office draw in dance in the United States in 1997, but few companies could afford to produce them independently. The American Ballet Theater (ABT) and the San Francisco Ballet split the $2-million cost of *Othello,* based on Shakespeare's tragedy, while the Houston Ballet and the Pittsburgh Ballet Theater joined economic forces to stage a $1-million *Dracula.*

Dracula, created by Houston Ballet artistic director Ben Stevenson, commemorated the 100th anniversary of Bram Stoker's novel. Stevenson, however, eliminated many of the novel's subplots to focus on Count Dracula himself and emphasize the erotic drive of Dracula's thirst for blood. Another unique concept was to give Dracula 18 wives—instead of the 3 wives in the novel—to provide the full *corps de ballet* (dancers who perform as a group) of traditional ballets. *Dracula* was first performed on March 13, 1997, at the Wortham Theater Center in Houston, Texas, and became a major artistic success for Stevenson. The production was reprised in Los Angeles from July 15 to July 20, and the Pittsburgh Ballet Theater opened its 1997-1998 season on Oct. 9, 1997, with the production.

Othello, created by modern-dance choreographer Lar Lubovitch, was premiered by ABT on May 23 during the troupe's annual spring run at New York City's Metropolitan Opera House. San Francisco Ballet was scheduled to dance the work in 1998 in the newly refurbished War Memorial Opera House.

Living up to its big-budget conception, *Othello* was more impressive for its spectacular decor than for its choreography and dramatic conception. Critics paid particular attention to George Tsypin's set, which featured huge chunks of cracked glass, symbolizing themes of power and fragility, and a sensational boat carrying Iago and Othello to Venice.

Other ABT projects. Far more satisfying artistically was ABT's new production of a comic masterpiece of the 1800's, *Coppelia,* which opened Feb. 11, 1997, at the Orange County Performing Arts Center in Costa Mesa, California. Choreographer Frederic Franklin brought to the ballet the same warmth and wit he remembered it having when he danced the ballet's hero in the 1940's. Despite the success of *Coppelia* and other acclaimed three-act story ballets, critics wondered if ABT's repertory was not being pointed too far in this direction. Under the leadership of Kevin McKenzie, ABT corrected the bias in a two-week season of short ballets beginning Nov. 4, 1997, at New York's City Center Theater. Two small-scale works premiered—*Carnation's Dream,* a ballet for three men by Nacho Duato; and a *pas de deux* (dance for two) by Jean-Christophe Maillot.

In 1997, ABT joined the Coca-Cola Company's National Scholarship Program, which gives financial aid to students to study at local ballet schools until they graduate from high school. ABT offered summer courses to students in the scholarship program.

Timothy O'Keefe dances the title role in the critically acclaimed Houston Ballet production of *Dracula* with Susan Cummins. *Dracula* was also performed in 1997 by the Pittsburgh Ballet Theater.

Tours. Some of the most prominent American troupes traveled throughout the world in addition to touring in the United States. The Alvin Ailey American Dance Theater visited South Africa for the first time from June 17 to June 29. The troupe gave 13 performances in Johannesburg and gave master classes, lecture demonstrations, and special performances for children in many townships and cities throughout the country.

The Paul Taylor Dance Company began 1997 in India, premiering Taylor's *Prime Numbers* on January 10 in New Delhi as part of India's 50th anniversary celebration of independence from Great Britain. In September, the troupe traveled to Moscow, the only American dance group invited to celebrate the city's 850th anniversary. From October 22 to November 5, the Taylor company, including the apprentice Taylor 2, toured several Alaskan towns and cities.

The New York City Ballet split for the first time in its 49-year history for overseas tours. In September and October, one half traveled to Brazil, while the other half danced in Korea, Taiwan, and Australia. On the company's home turf, the New York State Theater at the Lincoln Center, the major event of the year was the January 22 premiere of *Brandenburg*, a work by Jerome Robbins set to four of composer Johann Sebastian Bach's *Brandenburg Concertos*. Critics applauded *Brandenburg* for the fascinating patterns that Robbins devised for the ensemble and for the slightly mysterious edge of the duets for

171

Dance

the two leading couples. On November 25, opening night of the troupe's winter season, Merrill Ashley danced for the last time with the New York City Ballet after 31 years with the company.

The Sydney Dance Company, one of Australia's outstanding contemporary troupes, opened an 11-city U.S. tour at the University of Texas in Austin on October 21. The tour concluded as an engagement at New York City's Joyce Theater from November 18 through November 30. The tour featured artistic director Graeme Murphy's *Free Radicals,* a full-length piece set to a percussive score for metal salad bowls, ceramic pots, the dancer's bodies, and other unconventional "instruments." Other companies more familiar to Americans visited the United States, including Pina Bausch's Tanztheater Wuppertal, a German troupe that performed at the Brooklyn Academy of Music's Next Wave Festival in New York City, and Great Britain's Royal Ballet, which was a centerpiece of the second annual Lincoln Center Festival in July. The Royal's Darcey Bussell again proved to be one of the greatest ballerinas in the world.

Troubled companies. Most dance seasons produce a story of a company dramatically reviving after near collapse. On Jan. 22, 1997, the dancers of the Dance Theater of Harlem in New York City went on strike—the first time that unionized dancers had done so in the United States. The strike issue involved not only money but the dancers' belief that artistic director Arthur Mitchell, who founded the company in 1969, wielded unnecessary control. The strike was bitter, with Mitchell publicly denouncing the dancers. Several veteran dancers quit the company before the 19-day strike was resolved. Out of the turmoil came a newly energized company that dazzled critics when the Dance Theater of Harlem performed at the Kennedy Center in Washington, D.C., in April and at the Aaron Davis Hall in New York City's Harlem neighborhood in September.

The Martha Graham Dance Company, whose namesake was one of the great choreographers of the century, came close to extinction in 1997. Only the nonunion junior company performed on a steady basis. The main troupe canceled its major engagement of the year at the City Center in New York for lack of money. Long-time associates of Graham, who had taught at the Graham school and rehearsed the dancers, continued to leave the company, endangering the Graham legacy.

New leadership. Bruce Marks resigned as head of the Boston Ballet as of June 30, 1997. Marks, who had turned the Boston Ballet into one of the most successful regional troupes in the United States since becoming its head in 1985, was succeeded by Anna-Marie Holmes, a long-time associate of Marks. Pittsburgh Ballet Theater's director, Patricia Wilde, retired in July 1997 and was replaced by Terry Orr, formerly a ballet master at ABT. ☐ Nancy Goldner

Deaths in 1997 included those listed below, who were Americans unless otherwise indicated.

Anderson, Eugenie (1909–March 31), a founder of Americans for Democratic Action who was the first woman appointed a United States ambassador when posted to Denmark by President Harry Truman in 1949.

Arcaro, Eddie (1916–November 14), America's premier jockey for more than 30 years who won the Kentucky Derby five times and twice swept the Triple Crown.

Arensberg, Conrad (1910–February 10), anthropologist whose prescriptions for precise scientific observation and interpretation contributed to anthropology's refocus from primitive groups to complex modern societies.

Auerbach, Oscar (1905–January 15), pathologist who in 1964 discovered in lung tissue the first evidence that a link existed between smoking and cancer. The discovery is cited as the beginning of the antismoking movement.

Awdry, Wilbert (1911–March 21), Anglican minister and British children's writer who became internationally known for his 26 "Thomas the Tank Engine" books.

Baker, LaVern (1922–March 10), rhythm-and-blues singer of the 1950's and 1960's best known for "Tweedlee Dee," "Jim Dandy," and "I Cried a Tear."

Berlin, Isaiah (1909–November 5), philosopher and conversationalist who was revered for his intellect and wit.

Berry, Richard (1935–January 23), songwriter who wrote "Louie Louie," the legendary rock song whose allegedly lewd lyrics, slurred in the 1963 Kingsmen recording, came under a 30-month investigation by the FBI.

Bing, Rudolf (1902–September 2), manager from 1950 to 1972 of New York City's Metropolitan Opera. Bing integrated the company, hired artists to design productions, and transformed the Met into the world's largest and most prominent opera company.

Blackstone, Harry, Jr., (1934–May 14), classical magician who turned women into tigers, cut his wife in half with a buzz saw, and made elephants disappear on stage.

Chien-shiung Wu, physicist

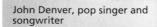

John Denver, pop singer and songwriter

Brennan, William (1906–July 24), U.S. Supreme Court justice whose liberal vision of the U.S. Constitution and commitment to equal rights contributed to reshaping the nation's law as well as its political and social life. Appointed by President Dwight Eisenhower in 1956, Brennan wrote 1,360 opinions during his 33 years on the court and has been called the most influential associate justice in history.

Burroughs, William S. (1914–August 2), Beat Generation writer who defined "hip" to cultist followers of *Naked Lunch* as well as *Junkie, Exterminator!* and *Cities of the Red Night.*

Calment, Jeanne (1875–August 5), 122-year-old French woman who, according to the *Guinness Book of World Records,* was the world's oldest human being.

Calvin, Melvin (1911–January 8), biochemist who received the Nobel Prize for chemistry in 1961 for detecting how plants process carbon dioxide and water into sugar.

Robert Mitchum, motion-picture actor

Red Skelton, comedian

Cheatham, Doc (Adolphus Anthony Cheatham) (1905–June 2), jazz trumpeter who accompanied Bessie Smith, played for Louis Armstrong and Cab Calloway at the Cotton Club, and performed with Benny Goodman's quintet.

Claster, Nancy (1915–April 26), housewife who was pressed into service by her producer husband as "Miss Nancy" on the children's program "Romper Room" and who with the aid of a Magic Mirror was able to "see" her pupils at home.

Cooke, Jack Kent (1912–April 6), Canadian-born owner of the Washington Redskins football team, Los Angeles Lakers basketball team, and Los Angeles Kings hockey team.

Cousteau, Jacques (1910–June 25), French oceanographer and author of *The Silent World* who coinvented SCUBA (self-contained underwater breathing apparatus), made a series of award-winning films and groundbreaking television documentaries championing underwater exploration and environmental causes, and is believed to have explored more of the Earth than any other person in history.

Cruso, Thalassa (1909–June 11), English-born plant expert who found celebrity in the 1960's as the eccentric hostess of "Making Things Grow" on public television.

Danilova, Alexandra (1903–July 13), ballet star whose career extended from dancing before the czar in St. Petersburg to appearing for Sergei Diaghilev with the Ballet Russes and performing the earliest abstract works of Fyodor Lopukhov and George Balanchine.

Danowski, Ed (1912–February 1), star football halfback who led the New York Giants to two National Football League titles in 1934 and 1938.

Davis, Gail (1924–March 15), actress who from 1955 to 1958 played the title character in the television series *Annie Oakley,* the first western to star a woman.

Davis, Kingsley (1908–February 27), demographics expert who coined the term "zero population growth" to describe his solution to overpopulation.

de Kooning, Willem (1904–March 19), Dutch-born artist associated with the American abstract expressionism movement of the 1950's.

Deng Xiaoping (1904–February 19), "paramount leader" of China for 18 years and the architect of the economic modernization that radically improved the standard of living of one-fifth of the world's population.

Denver, John (1944–October 12), singer and writer of songs that celebrated country pleasures, such as "Take Me Home, Country Roads," "Sunshine on My Shoulders," and "Rocky Mountain High."

Diana, Princess of Wales (1961–August 31), glamorous former wife of Prince Charles, heir to the British throne, known for her warmth and ease with people.

Dicke, Robert (1916–March 4), physicist who contributed to the development of radar and accurately predicted the existence of a microwave echo of the Big Bang.

Dickey, James (1923–January 19), poet and teacher who received the National Book Award in 1966 for his poetry but was best known for his 1970 novel *Deliverance.*

Dixon, Jeane (1918–January 25), astrologer and self proclaimed psychic who won fame for apparently predicting the 1963 death of President John F. Kennedy.

Dorris, Michael (1945–April 11), author of *A Yellow Raft in Blue Water* who spearheaded Native American studies programs and won the National Book Award in 1989 for *The Broken Cord,* an account of fetal alcohol syndrome.

Esau, Katherine (1898–June 4), biologist called the "grand dame of botany" who was recognized as a leading authority on plant anatomy and morphology.

Farley, Chris (1964–December 18), comedian and actor whose out-of-control, highly physical brand of comedy enlivened television's "Saturday Night Live" from 1990 to 1995 and such films as *Black Sheep* and *Tommy Boy.*

Faye, Joey (1909–April 26), burlesque comic and character actor who is credited with inventing classic comic routines, including "Slowly I Turn" and "Floogle Street."

Fenneman, George (1919–May 29), television personality best known as the "You Bet Your Life" announcer whom host Groucho Marx called "the perfect straight man."

Flood, Curt (1938–January 20), St. Louis Cardinals All–Star center fielder (1958–1969) who refused to be traded to another baseball team and sued for the right to decide his own fate, which led to the free-agent system.

Fujita, Nobuo (1912–September 30), Japanese pilot who flew bombing runs over Oregon in 1942, which were apparently the only time enemy aircraft ever bombed the U.S. mainland.

Geneen, Harold S. (1910–November 21), former International Telephone and Telegraph Corporation president who was considered the architect of the international conglomerate.

Deaths

Ginsberg, Allen (1926–April 5), poet whose early works, notably "Howl" and "Kaddish," helped define the Beat Generation and shape the social activism and sexual revolution of the 1960's and 1970's.

Goizuta, Roberto C. (1931–October 18), Cuban refugee who became chairman of the Coca-Cola Company.

Goldberg, Bertrand (1913–October 9), architect who reshaped the Chicago skyline in the 1960's with twin cylindrical apartment towers known as Marina City.

Graham, R. K. (Robert Klark Graham) (1906–February 13), businessman who transformed CR-39—the plastic used in World War II bomber windows—into lightweight eyeglass lenses and who was instrumental in developing contact lenses and establishing a sperm bank stocked with donations from Nobel Prize laureates.

Hanff, Helene (1916–April 9), writer who was acclaimed for *84, Charing Cross Road,* a 1970 memoir consisting of letters, cranky and charming, exchanged over a 20-year period between Hanff and the manager of an antiquarian book shop in London.

Harriman, Pamela Digby (1920–February 5), political hostess and U.S. Ambassador to France who began a public life as the daughter-in-law of British Prime Minister Winston Churchill.

Hassett, Buddy (1911–August 23), first baseman with the Brooklyn Dodgers, Boston Braves, and New York Yankees in the late 1930's and early 1940's who came to be called the "Bronx thrush" for his propensity for breaking into song on the field.

Hershey, Alfred D. (1908–May 22), scientist who shared the 1969 Nobel Prize in physiology and medicine for proving that DNA is the molecule that contains genetic information by demonstrating that a virus, consisting of DNA surrounded by a coat of protein, leaves its coat behind as it invades a cell.

Herzog, Chaim (1919–April 17), Israeli general and military intelligence director who was made first military governor of the occupied West Bank and elected to two successive terms as president.

Hogan, Ben (1912–July 25), professional golfer who was one of the greatest players in the history of the sport. Hogan was one of four players to win all four major professional championships.

Hornberger, H. Richard (1924–November 4), surgeon who wrote the novel *M*A*S*H,* the inspiration for the film and the long-running television series.

Hutchence, Michael (1960–November 22), lead singer of the Australian rock group INXS, whose performance style was compared to Mick Jagger's.

Hutson, Don (1913–June 26), football player with the Green Bay Packers in the 1930's and 1940's who was called one of the greatest wide receivers in the game's history.

Alexandra Danilova, ballet dancer

Doc Cheatham, jazz musician

Jacobs, Helen (1908–June 2), tennis champion of the 1930's who won the U.S. national title from 1932 to 1935 and Wimbledon in 1936.

Jagan, Cheddi (1918–March 6), dentist and political leader who led Guyana to independence and served as prime minister in the 1960's and president in the 1990's.

James, Dennis (1916–June 3), television personality who claimed more than 20 TV firsts, including making the first commercial, broadcasting the first sports commentary, and hosting the first audience participation show.

Jaeckel, Richard (1926–June 13), character actor known for his portrayal of tough World War II soldiers in such films as *Guadalcanal Diary, On a Wing and a Prayer,* and *The Dirty Dozen.*

Johnson, Lyman T. (1906–October 3), a grandson of slaves and the plaintiff in a lawsuit that led to the integration of the University of Kentucky in 1949.

Kempton, Murray (1917–May 5), Pulitzer Prize-winning columnist, called the journalistic conscience of his generation, who wrote for such publications as *The New York Post, New York Newsday,* and *The New Republic.*

Krainik, Ardis (1929–January 18), Lyric Opera of Chicago director who joined the company as a secretary, premiered as a singer on its stage in 1956, moved into management, and was credited with saving the company from financial ruin while reestablishing its artistic credentials.

Kuralt, Charles (1934–July 4), journalist, Vietnam War correspondent, and anchor of the weekly "CBS News Sunday Morning" television program who, after tiring of reporting war and civil conflict, earned recognition and affection for his idiosyncratic reports "On the Road."

Keith, Brian (1921–June 24), actor who appeared in more than 40 films, but was best known for his roles in eight television series, including "Family Affair" (1966–1971) and "Hardcastle & McCormick" (1983–1986).

Kendrew, John C. (1917–August 23), British molecular biochemist who won the 1962 Nobel Prize in chemistry for decoding the structure of myoglobin, a muscle protein similar to the oxygen-carrying hemoglobin in blood.

Lane, Burton (1912–January 5), composer of songs for the Broadway musicals *Finian's Rainbow* and *On a Clear Day You Can See Forever* and for more than 30 Hollywood productions, including *Royal Wedding* with Fred Astaire.

Leonard, Walter "Buck" (1907–November 27), baseball player and Hall of Famer regarded as the greatest first baseman in the history of the Negro leagues.

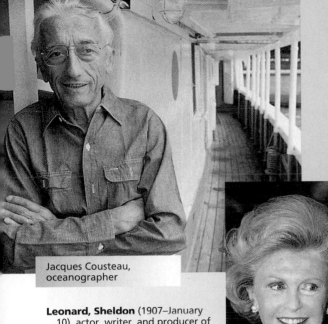

Jacques Cousteau, oceanographer

Mobutu Sese Seko (1930–September 7), president of Zaire who was driven from power in May 1997 after nearly 32 years in office. The word "kleptocracy" was coined to describe government under Mobutu, who is said to have accumulated $5 billion during his tenure in office.

Mother Teresa (1910–September 5) Roman Catholic nun whose work on behalf of the poor of the world earned her the 1979 Nobel Peace Prize and international acclaim as a "living saint."

Pamela Harriman, U.S. ambassador to France

Allen Ginsberg, poet

Leonard, Sheldon (1907–January 10), actor, writer, and producer of such television situation comedies as "The Dick Van Dyke Show" and "The Andy Griffith Show."

Lewis, Robert (1909–November 23), Broadway director and teacher of acting who helped found the Actors Studio in New York City.

Lichtenstein, Roy (1923–September 29), master of American Pop Art who was best known for his oversized, ironic paintings that appeared to reproduce the text and image of a comic-strip panel in original Ben Day dot colors.

Louis, Jean (1907–April 20), Academy Award-winning designer who created the strapless, flesh-colored dress into which Marilyn Monroe was sewn to sing "Happy Birthday" to President John F. Kennedy in 1962.

Lukas, J. Anthony (1933–June 5), nonfiction writer who received Pulitzer prizes for both newspaper articles and for *Common Ground*, a book detailing Boston's agony over school busing.

Maar, Dora (1907–July 16), photographer and painter who was best known for being Pablo Picasso's mistress and his model for the "weeping women" portraits of the late 1930's and early 1940's.

Maples, William R. (1937–February 27), forensic anthropologist who positively identified the remains of Czar Nicholas II of Russia, Spanish explorer Francisco Pizarro, and "Elephant Man" John Merrick.

Mas Canosa, Jorge (1939–November 23), Cuban refugee who built the Cuban-American National Foundation into one of the most powerful U.S. lobbying groups.

Meredith, Burgess (1907–September 9), actor who appeared in such films as *Of Mice and Men, The Day of the Locust,* and *Rocky.* Meredith created the Penguin on the 1960's "Batman" series.

Michener, James A. (1907–October 16), writer who won the Pulitzer Prize with his first book, *Tales of the South Pacific* (1948) and became one of the best-selling authors of all times with such epic novels as *Hawaii, The Source, Chesapeake,* and *Texas.*

Mitchum, Robert (1907–July 1), actor who appeared in more than 100 films who was known for playing both heroes, as in *The Story of a G.I.* and the television miniseries *The Winds of War,* and antiheros in such noir classic movies as *Cape Fear, Out of the Past,* and *Farewell, My Lovely.*

Namias, Jerome (1910–February 10), meteorological researcher who studied how the upper layers of oceans affect weather patterns and pioneered the development of extended weather forecasting.

Notorious B.I.G. (Christopher Wallace) 1975–March 9), hip-hop artist and rapper who was murdered, like his West Coast rival, Tupac Shakur, in a drive-by shooting.

Nyro, Laura (1947–April 8), songwriter of "And When I Die" (recorded by Blood, Sweat and Tears), "Eli's Coming' (Three Dog Night), and "Stoned Soul Picnic" (the Fifth Dimension) and singer whose 1968 "Eli and the Thirteenth Confession" album influenced the music of her time.

Payton, Lawrence (1948–June 20), singer with the Four Tops whose hits included "Baby, I Need Your Loving," "I Can't Help Myself (Sugar Pie, Honey Bunch)," and "Standing in the Shadows of Love."

Parker, Tom (1910–January 21), one-time carnival barker and show-business promoter, known by the honorary title Colonel, who orchestrated the career of Elvis Presley from 1955 until the singer's death in 1977.

Pasqualini, Jean (1926–October 9), translator whose book about the years he spent as a political prisoner in China's labor camps exposed the horrors of China's penal system.

Paulson, Pat (1927–April 25), comedian and deadpan parodist of political doubletalk who ran five tongue-in-cheek campaigns for president of the United States.

Porter, Don (1912–February 11), television actor who played Ann Sothern's boss on the situation comedy "Private Secretary" and Sally Field's father on "Gidget."

Pritchard, James (1910–January 1), archaeologist of Biblical sites who discovered the locations of the palace of King Herod in Jericho, Phoenician villages in Lebanon, and Gibeon.

Pritchett, V. S. (Sir Victor Sawdon Pritchett) (1900–March 20), English writer who was acclaimed for his meticulously wrought short stories about the lives of ordinary, middle-class people.

Deaths

Reynolds, Marjorie (1921–February 1), actress who began her career as a child in silent films, appeared opposite Bing Crosby and Fred Astaire in *Holiday Inn,* and played Peg Riley with William Bendix on the early television comedy "The Life of Riley."

Richter, Sviatosloav (1915–August 1), self-taught Russian pianist who was known for his technical brilliance, unique color and tonal quality, and imaginative interpretations of Chopin and Schumann.

Robbins, Harold (1916–October 14), a writer whose formula of sex, money, and power made him one of the best-selling authors of his day. His books included *The Dream Merchants* (1949), *The Carpetbaggers* (1961), and *The Betsy* (1971).

Rosario, Edwin (1963–December 1), boxer who was a three-time lightweight world champion.

Rossi, Aldo (1931–September 4), Italian architect who was considered "an architect's architect" for the monumental simplicity of his geometric designs. In 1990, Rossi was awarded the Pritzker Prize, architecture's highest honor.

Rosten, Leo (1908–February 19), author of *The Joys of Yiddish* and creator of one of American literature's most enduring comic characters, Hyman Kaplan, the Jewish "Mr. Malaprop" protagonist of three books and a Broadway musical.

Rowse, A. L. (1904–October 3), authority on Shakespeare and Elizabethan England, best known for his identification of the Dark Lady of Shakespeare's sonnets as Emilia Bassano Lanier, the daughter of an Italian court musician.

Royko, Mike (1932–April 29), colorful Chicago newspaper columnist who became nationally known for the wit with which he shot barbs at venal and hypocritical politicians and "fat cats."

Rudolph, Paul (1918–August 8), architect of abstract, modernist buildings whose concrete megastructures, such as the Yale University Art and Architecture Building, exerted a profound influence on architecture in the mid-1900's and laid the foundation for the "brutalist" school.

Saudek, Robert (1911–March 13), television executive who in 1952 created "Omnibus," the Sunday-afternoon series that gave TV audiences their first exposure to such talents as Leonard Bernstein, Mike Nichols and Elaine May, Igor Stravinski, and Dr. Seuss.

Schramm, David (1945–December 19), astrophysicist and authority on the Big Bang theory on the origin of the universe. Schramm combined astrophysics, nuclear physics, and particle physics in his research on the early universe and reckoning of the number of elementary-particle families in the universe.

Serber, Robert (1909–June 1), theoretical physicist who was J. Robert Oppenheimer's colleague on the Manhattan Project, the enterprise to develop an atomic weapon during World War II.

Shabazz, Betty (1936–June 23), widow of Black Muslim leader Malcolm X, civil rights activist, and public speaker who was admired as a dynamic symbol of African American perseverance.

Shoemaker, Eugene Merle (1928–July 18), planetary geologist and astronomer who, with his wife, Carolyn, is credited with discovering 32 comets, including Comet Shoemaker-Levy.

Jimmy Stewart,
motion-picture actor

LaVern Baker,
rhythm-and-blues singer

Shomo, Frank (1889–March 20), last known survivor of the Johnstown Flood—the May 31, 1889, disaster resulting from the collapse of an earthen dam, which unleashed a wall of water that slammed into Johnstown, Pennsylvania, killing 2,209 people.

Simjian, Luther G. (1905–October 23), inventor regarded as "the second Thomas Edison," who held more than 200 patents that included the automated teller machine and the self-focusing camera.

Skelton, Red (1913–September 17), actor and clown whose characters—Clem Kaddidlehopper, Freddie the Freeloader, the sea gulls Gertrude and Heathcliffe—delighted vaudeville, radio, film, and television audiences for more than 80 years.

Solti, Sir Georg (1912–September 5), Hungarian-born conductor who for 22 years led the Chicago Symphony Orchestra to international acclaim. Solti won more Grammy Awards than any other recording artist, classical or popular, in history.

Spitzer, Jr., Lyman (1914–March 31), astrophysicist who headed Princeton University's Plasma Physics Laboratory, inspired the Hubble Space Telescope, and pioneered research into the use of nuclear fusion as a clean, limitless source of energy.

Stewart, James (1908–July 2), lanky, drawling movie actor who, in more than 70 motion pictures, created an American archetype, the essentially decent but troubled man confronted by crisis. Stewart, who starred in such classics as *Mr. Smith Goes to Washington, The Philadelphia Story, Rear Window, Vertigo,* and *Anatomy of a Murder,* may be best remembered for his role as George Bailey in the beloved Christmas classic *It's a Wonderful Life.*

Stewart, T. Dale (1901–October 29), a physical anthropologist who was director of the

Smithsonian's National Museum of Natural History in Washington, D.C.

Stone, Jon (1931–March 27), "Captain Kangaroo" television producer who came out of retirement at the age of 36 to help write, produce, and direct "Sesame Street" as well as participate, with Muppet creator Jim Henson, in the conception of Big Bird, Oscar the Grouch, and the Cookie Monster.

Gianni Versace, fashion designer

Sir Georg Solti, conductor

Jeanne Calment, oldest living person

Sumii, Sue (1902–June 23), Japanese novelist whose multivolume *The River with No Bridge* drew world attention to the social status of the burakumin, Japanese "untouchables" discriminated against as descendants of people who performed such "unclean" work as the slaughtering of animals and tanning of hides.

Tanaka, Tomoyuki (1910–April 2), Japanese producer who made 220 movies, including films with director Akira Kurosawa, but who was best known for *Godzilla*. Tanaka made 21 sequels before the creature awakened from the ocean depths by hydrogen bomb tests was felled in the 1995 *Godzilla Versus Destroyer*.

Tartikoff, Brandon (1949–August 27), television executive who was named president of National Broadcasting Corporation (NBC) entertainment at the age of 31. In the 1980's Tartikoff transformed NBC, ranked third in viewership after ABC and CBS, into a ratings powerhouse by programming such hit shows as "Cheers" and "Cosby."

Thimann, Kenneth (1904–January 15), botanist whose discoveries of how hormones control plant development advanced human understanding of plant physiology.

Tombaugh, Clyde W. (1906–January 17), self-taught astronomer who in 1930 discovered Pluto, the solar system's ninth, smallest, and usually most distant planet.

Tsongas, Paul E. (1941–January 18), former congressman and senator from Massachusetts who as a Democratic candidate for president in 1992 was credited with forcing fellow candidates to deal with serious issues, including the nation's economic problems.

Tutuola, Amos (1920–June 8), Nigerian writer whose fanciful and grammatically playful interpretations of Nigerian folk tales, including *The Palmwine Drinkard*, celebrated and preserved the traditions of Yoruba storytelling.

Vander Meer, Johnny (1914–October 6), baseball player who, in 1938, pitched two consecutive no-hit games, the only pitcher in major league baseball history to do so.

Versace, Gianni (1946–July 15), Italian designer who dressed such celebrities as Princess Diana, Madonna, and Elton John and was credited with reviving the fashion industry by creating designs that combined the influence of art and film with the energy of popular culture.

Weaver, Robert C. (1907–July 17), author, educator, and civil-rights strategist who served in President Franklin Roosevelt's so-called "black cabinet" and in President Lyndon Johnson's cabinet as the first Secretary of Housing and Urban Development.

Willem De Kooning, painter

Weisgall, Hugo (1912–March 11), neoclassical composer best known for his opera based on Pirandello's *Six Characters in Search of an Author.*

Weston, Joanie (1935–May 10), athlete who once hit eight home runs in a single college softball game but became nationally known as the "blond bombshell" of Roller Derby in that event's golden era of the 1950's and 1960's.

Wethered, Joyce (1901–November 18), stylish English athlete described by *The Encyclopedia of Golf* as "the supreme woman golfer of her age, perhaps of all time.'

White, Augusta (1906–March 27), songwriter who, with husband John I. White, wrote "Get Along, Little Dogie" and other ballads of the American West.

White, Jesse (1919–January 9), character actor best known for his stage and film portrayal of a comedic male nurse in *Harvey* and as a lonely Maytag repairman on television commercials.

Widerberg, Bo (1930–May 1), Swedish director who made three films—*All Things Fair, Adalen 31,* and *Raven's End*—that were nominated for Academy Awards for best foreign film, but who was largely known for the lushly romantic *Elvira Madigan.*

Wu, Chien-Shiung (1912–February 16), physicist who performed an experiment on subatomic particles involving the so-called weak force that overthrew the principle of conservation of parity—that nature in effect does not differentiate between left and right—a law of symmetry that physicists had considered incontrovertible. Wu, who was the first woman to be elected president of the American Physical Society, helped develop a process that produced large quantities of uranium 235, the first atomic bomb fuel, while working on the Manhattan Project during World War II.

Yokoi, Shoichi (1915– September 22), Japanese soldier in World War II (1939-1945) who, rather than surrender to American troops, remained hidden in the jungles of Guam until discovered in 1972.

Young, Coleman A. (1918–November 29), politician who became the first black mayor of Detroit in 1973 and was elected to a record five terms, running the motor city for 20 years.

Zale, Tony (1913–March 20), boxer who in the 1940's was twice middleweight champion of the world and earned induction into the boxing Hall of Fame for his three title bouts with Rocky Graziano.

Zehnder, Bruno (1945–July 7), Swiss wildlife photographer who was known for his images of Antarctica, particularly its emperor penguins.

Zinnemann, Fred (1907–March 14), movie director known for his films—*From Here to Eternity, High Noon,* and *A Man for All Seasons*—which centered around moral crises.

Ben Hogan,
professional golfer

178

Democratic Party. The Democratic Party went on the defensive and deeply into debt during 1997 as officials from the U.S. Congress and the U.S. Justice Department investigated the possibility of illegal fund-raising practices during U.S. President Bill Clinton's 1996 reelection campaign.

The U.S. Senate Governmental Reform Committee began hearings in July 1997 to investigate fund-raising excesses during the campaign. At the start of the hearings, Senator Fred Thompson (R., Tennessee), chairman of the committee, alleged that China had tried to influence the 1996 election by making illegal campaign contributions to Democrats, including the president.

Before the start of the Senate committee hearings, the Democratic Party had conceded that some donations may have been illegal. In February 1997, the party announced that it would return more than $3 million in contributions that it had deemed illegal or inappropriate. About three-quarters of the contributions had been raised by three Asian American businessmen—John Huang, Johnny Chung, and Charles Yah Lin Trie. Many of the contributions that were returned to donors came from individuals or businesses located in Asia.

By October, when the hearings adjourned, the committee had failed to provide proof of campaign corruption. Analysts claimed that the hearings did reveal some allegedly improper fund-raising actions, which might prove potentially harmful to President Clinton or Vice President Al Gore.

Buying access. In September, former Democratic National Committee (DNC) Chairman Donald Fowler told the Senate committee that he had contacted high-level Clinton Administration officials to arrange meetings with big-money contributors seeking government favors. One donor, Roger Tamraz, testified on September 18 that he had contributed $300,000 to the Democratic Party to gain access to high-ranking government officials. Tamraz freely admitted attempting to gain government backing for an overseas oil pipeline project.

Throughout the hearings, Republicans criticized President Clinton for inviting political contributors to stay overnight in the White House. The president was also criticized for additional campaign financing abuses after videotapes revealed that he had hosted fund-raising coffees in the executive West Wing of the White House. The president maintained that he had done nothing improper.

Phone calls. Republicans also attacked President Clinton and Vice President Gore in 1997 for allegedly breaking a law by making telephone calls from their government offices to solicit donations for the Democratic Party.

Republican leaders pushed Attorney General Janet Reno to appoint an independent investigator to examine the allegations. In September, Reno launched a Justice Department investigation into whether the president or vice president broke the law. While the Justice Department continued its investigation of fund-raising improprieties through 1997, Reno announced on December 2 that she had not uncovered sufficient evidence of wrongdoing to appoint an independent counsel to further investigate the president or vice president.

Democratic debt. The multiple investigations of fund-raising practices were costly for the Democratic Party. On May 19, Steve Grossman, DNC national chairman, announced that the Democratic Party owed $16 million in debts. Legal bills for staff members connected to the controversial fund-raising issue accounted for most of the debt. Grossman said that the party would reduce spending in the hope of eliminating the debt by the end of 1998.

"Soft money" donations. Donald Fowler, national chairman of the DNC in early 1997, said on January 21 that the Democratic Party would no longer accept contributions from foreign citizens or from U.S. subsidiaries of foreign corporations. Fowler also said that the Democratic Party would limit controversial "soft money" contributions to $100,000. Soft money refers to individual contributions to political parties that are not subject to the same stringent restrictions placed on contributions to candidates.

The Federal Election Commission (FEC) reported on September 22 that both the Democratic and Republican parties raised record amounts of soft money in the first six months of 1997, despite the fund-raising furor. The FEC reported that the Democratic Party received $13.7 million. In comparison, the Republican Party received $21.7 million.

Gubernatorial elections. Democratic candidates suffered major losses in off-year elections in 1997. On Nov. 4, New Jersey Governor Christine Todd Whitman, a Republican, defeated Democrat Jim McGreevey, a state senator and mayor of Woodbridge, New Jersey, by one percentage point.

Lieutenant Governor Don Beyer of Virginia, a Democrat, lost the governor's race to former State Attorney General James S. Gilmore III, a Republican. Gilmore, whose victory led a Republican sweep of the top three state offices, succeeded Governor George Allen, a Republican.

Mayoral races. Democrats lost mayoral races in the nation's two largest cities in 1997. In New York City on Nov. 4, Mayor Rudolph W. Giuliani easily defeated Democrat Ruth Messinger, Manhattan borough president. Messinger was defeated even though New York City's registered Democrats outnumbered registered Republicans by a 5-to-1 margin. In Los Angeles on April 8, Democratic state Senator Tom Hayden lost the mayoral election to incumbent Richard J. Riordan, a Republican.

☐ William J. Eaton

See also **Congress of the United States; Elections; People in the news; Republican Party; U.S. President.**

Denmark enjoyed the benefits of one of Europe's strongest economies in 1997 as growth accelerated and unemployment fell to one of the lowest rates on the continent. Rising employment and higher wages generated strong demand from consumers, while low interest rates and buoyant exports encouraged companies to increase investment. The European Commission forecast in October that Denmark's economic output would grow by 3.5 percent in 1997, up from 2.7 percent in 1996 and nearly a full percentage point above the European average. The unemployment rate was projected to decline to 6.0 percent from 6.7 percent in 1996.

The government continued its restrictive spending policy in 1997 in an effort to prevent the strong economy from driving up inflation. The budget policy also was intended to guarantee the stability of Danish currency—the crown—despite the government's decision to keep Denmark out of the single European currency planned for 1999. Prime Minister Poul Nyrup Rasmussen announced a supplementary budget package in October 1997 for 1998 containing $1 billion in spending cuts and tax increases designed to slow the economy to a more sustainable growth rate. As a result of the budgetary restraint, Denmark was expected to post a budget surplus of 1.3 percent of gross domestic product in 1997. Only two other European countries, Luxembourg and Ireland, were expected to run budget surpluses.

European Union. Denmark's relations with its partners in the European Union (EU), a group of 15 Western European countries, improved in 1997, and Prime Minister Rasmussen gave Danish backing to the Treaty of Amsterdam, an EU agreement signed in October. The treaty limited the ability of national governments to veto EU policies but was less ambitious than the Treaty on European Union signed in Maastricht in 1992, which many Danes felt had infringed on their nation's sovereignty. The Danish government planned a referendum on the new treaty in 1998, after a High Court ruling on a constitutional challenge to the Maastricht treaty.

Local elections. A new right-wing party made a strong showing in local elections on Nov. 18, 1997, after campaigning for tough curbs on immigration. The People's Party, founded in 1995, received 6.8 percent of the votes cast, ranking it fifth among Denmark's numerous political parties. Support for the country's two leading parties eroded. The vote for the Social Democratic Party, which heads Denmark's coalition government, slipped to 33.1 percent from 34.3 percent in the previous local election in 1993. The opposition Liberal Party's share fell to 25 percent from 27.2 percent. The 1997 election was seen by many as a test run for national parliamentary elections due to be held in 1998. ☐ Tom Buerkle

See also **Europe** (Facts in brief table); **Immigration** Special Report: **Immigration: The Latest Wave; Ireland.**

Diana,
Princess of Wales
(1961-1997)

When Diana, Princess of Wales, was killed in a car crash at age 36 on Aug. 31, 1997, the sudden shock of her death touched off an extraordinary outpouring of grief around the world. On every continent, people stood for hours in lines at British embassies to sign books of condolence. Kensington Palace, Diana's residence in London, was awash in thousands of bouquets of flowers left by the people who admired her.

The length of the route her casket would travel was extended several times in the days before the funeral as the estimates of the expected crowd

grew ever larger. Millions of people lined the streets of London, and an estimated 2 billion people watched on television, as Diana's coffin—followed on foot by her sons, Prince William and Prince Henry; her former husband, Prince Charles; her brother, Charles, ninth Earl Spencer; and her former father-in-law, Prince Philip—was pulled on a horse-drawn caisson to Westminster Abbey, where British monarchs have been crowned since William the Conqueror became king in 1066. The scene was eerily reminiscent of Diana's wedding day 16 years earlier when she rode in a glass coach past crowds of well-wishers and television cameras toward what she would later call the "fairy story that everybody wanted to work."

In spite of her fame, fortune, and beauty, many people felt a kinship with Diana, whose willingness to expose her emotions and flaws broke traditional ideas of royal behavior. Diana's battle to overcome marital and emotional problems won the admiration of millions of people—particularly women—who shared similar struggles. Diana was a divorcee and a single mother, whose search for love and security often led to pain and humiliation. She publicly admitted living with a poor self-image, which manifested itself in eating disorders, self-mutilation, and suicide attempts. "The world . . . cherished her for her vulnerability, whilst admiring her for her honesty," said her brother Charles in his eulogy of Diana.

British Prime Minister Tony Blair called Diana "the people's princess," a glamorous woman who led a life of privilege yet had the ability to relate to people of all backgrounds. "Diana profoundly influenced [Great Britain] and the world," said the Very Reverend Dr. Wesley Carr, the dean of Westminster. "Although a princess, she was someone for whom, from afar, we dared to feel affection, and by whom we were all intrigued."

The facts of Diana's life were trumpeted in headlines and chronicled in photographs by the world press, which tracked her every move and her many transformations. Diana first appeared before the spotlight as a shy, young kindergarten teacher who won the heart of the most eligible bachelor in the world. Next, she became an elegant trendsetter, whose image on magazine covers guaranteed skyrocketing sales of the publications. Then, she was portrayed as a mother who strove to put her sons in touch with ordinary people, allowing them to experience life outside the royal enclave. After her marriage

The author

Jennifer Parello is a Managing Editor with World Book Annuals.

Diana arrives at Wetherby school in 1989 with her sons Henry, *left*, and William, *right,* on their first day of classes. She broke with royal tradition by sending her sons to school with other children, rather than having them tutored at home.

crumbled, she translated her own pain into the desire to comfort the suffering of others and used her international celebrity to champion charitable causes.

A legend is born

Lady Diana Spencer was born on July 1, 1961, the daughter of Viscount Althorp, on an estate neighboring Sandringham, the royal family's country house in Norfolk. When Diana was 6 years old, her parents divorced, an event that haunted her throughout her life. Everything in Diana's "tormented psyche turned on what happened to her at age 6 and left her to a loneliness that nothing could cure," wrote her friend Clive James, a British journalist.

A poor student, Diana ended her formal education at age 16. In 1979, she moved to London where she worked as a nanny, a house cleaner, and a kindergarten teacher. At age 19, Diana began dating Prince Charles, heir to the throne of Great Britain, who was 12 years her senior and a former boyfriend of Diana's sister Sarah. "She [Diana] taught him how to tap-dance on the terrace [at Sandringham]," a family friend said at the time of their engagement. "He thought she was adorable. Who wouldn't?"

Diana and Charles married on July 29, 1981, in a ceremony watched on television by an estimated 1 billion people around the world. The wedding was a diversion from Great Britain's worst economic recession in 50 years. Diana's effect on Britain was "like the sun coming up; coming up giggling," according to one journalist. The newlyweds were so popular that a poll conducted in 1981 showed that 73 percent of the British public approved of the immediate abdication of Queen Elizabeth II in favor of Charles.

The wedding made Diana an international celebrity and a popular target of the press and the *paparazzi* (photographers who are paid large sums of money for candid pictures of famous people). Early in her marriage, Diana developed a conflicted relationship with the press. At times she would share confidences with reporters and invite photographers to take her picture. At other times, she would fly into a rage at the sight of members of the press. Initially, Diana seemed to greet the ever-present photographers with grace and calm. However, she confided to a friend that she was "terrified of them. Everywhere I turn, they are there, poking their cameras at me, asking me questions, following me whenever I step outside. I don't know how I'm going to cope."

The royal couple's first son, William, was born in June 1982. Diana gave birth to their second child, Henry, in September 1984. Diana's devotion to her sons was unquestioned even by those who criticized other aspects of her behavior. Defying royal tradition, Diana was openly affectionate with her children. "I hug my children to death and get into bed with them at night," she said of her parenting style. "I always feed them love and affection; it's so important." Diana went to great lengths to expose her sons to everyday situations and ordinary people. For example, when they went to Disney World in Orlando, Florida, they stood in lines with other tourists. She also took her sons with her to visit homeless shelters and AIDS hospices.

Diana hugs a child during a 1991 visit to a hospital in Brazil, *left*. She was admired for her devotion to the sick and needy. Wearing a dress by Christina Stambolian, *below*, Diana attends a social event in 1994. She adopted a sleek, elegant style after she separated from Prince Charles.

By the mid-1980's, Diana was regarded as one of the most fashionable women in the world. The girl who once favored sweaters and frilly dresses had become the standard against which elegance was judged. In the years before her divorce, she often spent more than $1 million annually on clothes and accessories. Her sophisticated image made her a permanent feature on magazine covers and on best-dressed lists.

The royal marriage crumbles

The public image of Diana as a happy wife and mother masked private despair. In the 1980's, Diana was overwhelmed by the pressures of royal life. She later complained that she received no support or guidance in carrying out her duties from her husband or Queen Elizabeth II. In an interview broadcast in 1995 on BBC television, Diana said that during most of her marriage, she had "a feeling of being no good at everything and useless and hopeless and failed in every direction." In response to her unhappiness, she half-heartedly tried to kill herself several times, cut her arms with a lemon peeler, and developed *bulimia nervosa* (an eating disorder characterized by binge eating of high calorie foods, often followed by self-induced vomiting).

In 1986, the press began hinting that the marriage was in trouble. Stories reported that the couple had few common interests. Charles enjoyed hunting, polo, painting, and spending time in the country. Diana preferred the city, going to lunch with friends, and attending rock concerts. Diana also claimed that Charles was jealous of her popularity with the public, which was charmed by Diana's warmth and her ease in dealing with people. While the rest of the royal family avoided physical contact, Diana went out of her way to touch and hug people. Her most celebrated demonstration of physical contact came in 1987, when Diana shook hands with an AIDS patient at a time when people were terrified to touch people with the disease. "With that handshake, she educated the world about compassion, love, and understanding," said David Harvey, director of the National Policy Center for Children, Youth and Families in Washington, D.C.

In 1992, Charles and Diana announced that they had agreed to separate. The unraveling of the marriage proved to be just as public as their courtship and wedding. Both used the press to berate each other and to confess infidelities. Diana encouraged friends to cooperate with Andrew Morton, the author of *Diana: Her True Story,* a book published in 1992 that sympathetically detailed Diana's emotional problems and portrayed the royal family as cold, manipulative, and cruel to Diana. Diana also gave interviews and read and made revisions to the manuscript before its publication. In 1995, Diana admitted in a BBC interview that she had entered into an extramarital relationship only after learning that Charles was involved with another woman. "There were three of us in this marriage," she said, "so it was a bit crowded." The divorce, which stripped Diana of her title Her Royal Highness, became final in August 1996.

"Queen of people's hearts"

Since she would never become queen of Great Britain, Diana announced that she wanted to transform herself into the "queen of people's hearts" by carving out a global role for herself. She spent the last year of her life traveling the world, drawing public attention to her favorite causes—the banning of land mines, care for the homeless, and treatment for cancer, AIDS, leprosy, and childhood diseases. In June 1997, Diana raised millions of dollars for charity by selling 79

Paparazzi mob Diana as she leaves the British National Ballet on Aug. 28, 1996, the day her divorce was finalized. The press tracked her every move, making her one of the most photographed people in history.

of her most extravagant dresses at an auction.

In the summer of 1997, Diana began seeing Emad (Dodi) Fayed, the son of the owner of Harrods Department Store in London and the Ritz Hotel in Paris. The paparazzi, who could earn as much as $1 million for a picture of Diana and Fayed, hounded the couple as they vacationed in the south of France. On August 30, photographers followed the couple to Paris, where Diana planned to spend a final evening before returning to London to visit her sons. Following a late supper, Diana and Fayed attempted to flee a pack of paparazzi pursuing the couple's chauffeured car on motorcycles. Henri Paul, the driver of the car, who was later revealed to have been intoxicated, sped away from the photographers and—driving at more than 90 miles (145 kilometers) per hour—crashed the car into a cement pillar in a tunnel. Fayed and Paul were killed instantly. Photographers arrived at the scene moments after the crash and took pictures of Diana as she lay dying in the wreckage. Still alive when she was pulled from the car by rescue workers, Diana died later in a Paris hospital. French authorities detained several paparazzi to determine whether they violated a law that requires anyone at an accident scene to aid those in distress.

The day before Diana's funeral, her former mother-in-law, Queen Elizabeth II, made a rare televised statement. "No one who knew Diana will ever forget her," the Queen said in a broadcast from Buckingham Palace. As she spoke, she stood next to a window through which hundreds of mourners could be seen placing flowers near the palace gates. "Millions of others who never met her, but felt they knew her, will remember her." ▪ ▪ ▪

In the days preceding Diana's funeral on Sept. 6, 1997, tens of thousands of bouquets are deposited at Kensington Palace, *above*, her residence in London. A young mourner, *inset*, watches the funeral crowds from her perch on the Victoria Memorial outside of Buckingham Palace.

Disabled. The United States Justice Department indicted 20 members of a Mexico-based organized crime ring in August 1997 on charges that they had smuggled Mexicans who were deaf into the United States and had forced them to work as trinket peddlers on the streets of New York City. The operation was uncovered after about 60 Mexicans were found living in two New York City apartments in July. The immigrants claimed that they had been lured to the United States by promises of a better life and that they had been virtually enslaved. Their captors confiscated their identification papers, forced them to work up to 18 hours a day, took most of the money they earned, and beat them if they failed to meet daily quotas. The ring was run by a family of Mexican Americans, many of whom were also deaf.

A surgical implant—the Freehand System—that may restore limited use of hands to quadriplegics who are capable of some upper-body movement was approved by the Food and Drug Administration on August 18. The system is the first device capable of restoring movement to a paralyzed limb. Manufactured by Cleveland-based NeuroControl Corporation, the system uses a small implant to send electrical pulses down a wire to electrodes attached to arm and hand muscles. Users can learn to control these pulses to trigger the hand to open and close. The device will enable some quadriplegics to perform tasks such as eating and grooming.   □ Lisa Klobuchar

Disasters. Severe flooding occurred throughout the world in 1997. Floods in Asia, Central Europe, North America, and South America left thousands of people dead and homeless. Disasters that resulted in 25 or more deaths in 1997 include the following:

Aircraft crashes

January 9—Detroit, Michigan. A commuter plane en route to Detroit from Cincinnati, Ohio, during a heavy snowstorm crashes on approach to the Detroit Metropolitan Airport, killing all 26 passengers and 3 crew members.

February 4—Shaar Yishuv, Israel. In the worst air disaster in Israeli history, 73 men are killed when two army helicopters collide in midair between the Sea of Galilee and the Israel-Lebanon border.

July 12—Santiago de Cuba, Cuba. An aging, Russian-made Cuban airliner carrying 39 passengers and 5 crew members to Havana crashes into the Caribbean off the southeast coast of Cuba minutes after takeoff from Santiago de Cuba. There are no survivors.

August 5—Guam. A Korean Air Lines jumbo jet en route to Guam from Seoul, South Korea, crashes into the jungle, killing 226 of the 254 passengers and crew members aboard the plane.

September 3—Phnom Penh, Cambodia. At least 64 people die when a Vietnamese Airlines Tu-134 jet crashes on approach to the Phnom Penh airport. Two passengers, including a 4-year-old boy, survive.

September 13—South Atlantic off Namibia. A German military plane with a crew of 24 and a U.S. Air Force transport plane with 9 people aboard disappear off the coast of West Africa. A Namibian ship discovers a large oil slick and wreckage from both planes.

September 26—Medan, Indonesia. An Indonesian Airbus A–300 becomes lost, partially because of a thick blanket of smoke from hundreds of Indonesian forest fires and crashes, killing all 234 people aboard.

October 11—Nuevo Berlin, Uruguay. An Argentine airliner crashes in Uruguay, killing all 75 people aboard.

December 6—Irkutsk, Russia. A Russian military transport plane smashes into an apartment complex, killing more than 60 people and injuring dozens more.

December 19—Sungsang, Indonesia. A passenger jet crashes into a marsh, killing all 104 people on board.

Earthquakes

February 4—Northeastern Iran. Two earthquakes, one registering a magnitude of 6.1 and the other registering 5.4, level 20 villages and leave an estimated 80 people dead and 25,000 homeless.

February 28—Ardabil and Meshkinshahr, Iran. An earthquake with a magnitude of 6.1 devastates more than 80 towns and villages on the edge of the Talish Mountains in northwest Iran, resulting in the deaths of 965 people.

February 28—Baluchistan Province, Pakistan. An earthquake with a magnitude of 7.3 kills more than 100 people in western Pakistan.

May 10—Northeastern Iran. An earthquake with a magnitude of 7.1 shakes a remote mountainous region. Two hundred villages are leveled, leaving at least 4,000 people dead, 6,000 injured, and 50,000 homeless.

May 22—Kosamghat, India. People are buried in their beds in central India by an earthquake with a magnitude of 6.0. At least 38 people are killed and 1,000 are injured.

July 10—Cariaco, Venezuela. An earthquake with a magnitude of 6.9 flattens buildings, including two schools, along Venezuela's Caribbean coast, leaving at least 65 people dead, 460 injured, and 500 families homeless.

Explosions and fires

January 29—Changsha, China. A fire, believed to have been set by arsonists, in the restaurant of the Yanshan Hotel in Changsha, the capital of China's Hunan Province, results in the death of 30 people.

February 23—Baripada, India. More than 120 people die and 165 others are injured when a fire sweeps through a cluster of temporary buildings set up to shelter some 12,000 pilgrims who had gathered to seek the blessing of Swami Nigamananda, a Hindu guru.

March 7—Pingdingshan County, China. A series of gas explosions in three separate but interconnected coal mines kills 86 miners in central China.

March 19—Jalalabad, Afghanistan. The headquarters of the Islamic Taliban militia is flattened and at least 30 people are killed when approximately 220 tons (200 metric tons) of explosives detonate during an accidental blast at an ammunition dump.

April 15—Mecca, Saudi Arabia. A fire sweeps through some 70,000 tents housing tens of thousands of people who had journeyed to Mecca for the *hajj*, the annual pilgrimage involving as many as 2 million visitors that is one of Islam's holiest rituals. More than 340 people die, and more than 1,200 others are injured.

June 7—Thanjavur, India. A fire, started by firecrackers, sweeps through a 1,000-year-old Hindu temple, triggering a stampede among the worshippers that results in the deaths of at least 60 people.

June 13—New Delhi, India. Sixty people die and 200 others are injured when suburban movie patrons, at-

Investigators examine the wreckage of Korean Air Flight 801, which crashed into a jungle near Guam, killing 226 of the 254 passengers and crew members aboard.

tempting to escape a fire, find most exit doors in the crowded theater bolted shut.

July 11—Pattaya, Thailand. Ninety people die when a kitchen fire races through the 17-story Royal Jomtien Hotel in the Thai beach resort of Pattaya, 68 miles (110 kilometers) south of Bangkok, the capital. Most victims are trapped behind locked emergency exits.

September 14—Vishakhapatnam, India. A leak in a pipeline triggers an explosion and fire that kills at least 35 people at a Hindustan Petroleum Corporation refinery. More than 100,000 people in Vishakhapatnam, India, are forced to evacuate.

September 29—Santiago, Chile. A fire in the children's wing of a facility for mentally disabled people in a Santiago suburb causes the roof to collapse on residents trapped in their beds, killing 31 children and teen-agers.

Shipwrecks

February 14—Homa Bay, Kenya. An outboard motor-powered boat, overloaded with passengers, capsizes on Lake Victoria, drowning at least 35 people.

February 20—Sri Lanka. A boat headed for India capsizes 35 miles (56 kilometers) off Sri Lanka's coast, drowning 165 Tamils fleeing from Sri Lanka's civil war.

March 35—The Adriatic Sea. At least 79 passengers and crew members drown when an Italian navy frigate twice rams a boat with 117 Albanian refugees, mostly women and children, crowded into the hold. The boat, an Albanian naval vessel apparently hijacked by gangsters who used it to ferry refugees to Italy for a price, went down in 2,400 feet (731 meters) of water.

September 9—Haiti. Panic among passengers aboard an overcrowded ferry capsizes the 60-foot (18-meter) vessel, causing the death by drowning of at least 245 people. The ferry, cruising along Haiti's central coast, was licensed to carry 80 passengers.

Storms and floods

January 6—West Coast of the United States. Winter storms, which battered the West Coast for two weeks, result in massive flooding in Washington, Oregon, and Northern California, causing the deaths of 36 people, the evacuation of more than 125,000 people, and at least $1 billion in damages.

January 8—Western Europe. The death toll from days of record low temperatures in Western Europe reaches 250. Lows of -6 °F (-21 °C) are recorded in the county of Kent, south of London; 7 °F (-14 °C) in Brussels; and -4 °F (-20 °C) in Berlin.

January 27—Antananarivo, Madagascar. More than 50 people are killed and 500,000 left homeless when a tropical cyclone strikes southern Madagascar.

February 1—United States. Thunderstorms and tornadoes, sweeping across Arkansas, Mississippi, Kentucky, West Virginia, and Ohio, leave 48 people dead.

February 18—Ccocha and Tamburco, Peru. Rains trigger the collapse of a mountainside in the Andes, burying two villages and killing as many as 300 people.

March 7—Louisville, Kentucky. The most severe flooding along the Ohio River since 1964 crests at Louisville, Kentucky, 15.7 feet (4.78 meters) above flood stage, and leaves 29 people dead and thousands homeless in West Virginia, Ohio, Indiana, Tennessee, and Kentucky.

March 26—Northern Afghanistan. At least 100 people are buried alive when an avalanche of snow crashes over them as they are walking along a highway toward the Salang Tunnel, where they were to catch a bus.

May 19—Bangladesh. More than 600 people are killed when a cyclone with winds of 125 miles (200 kilometers) per hour sweeps over the islands of Maheshkhali, Kutubdia, and St. Martin's and crashes into the area around Cox's Bazar on the flat southeastern coast. The storm destroys approximately 400,000 houses, leaving as many as 1 million people homeless.

May 23—Manila, Philippines. Three days of torrential rains trigger widespread flooding, landslides, and downed power lines that cause the death of 29 people and bring the Philippine capital, Manila, to a standstill.

May 27—Jarrell, Texas. Twenty-seven people are killed and more than 300 houses are leveled when a tornado, with winds up to 260 miles (418 kilometers) per hour, rips through Jarrell, Texas, a town of 1,000 residents.

July 10—Guangdong Province, China. Beijing officials announce that more than 40 people have been killed and tens of thousands left homeless by record floods along the Pearl River in China's Guangdong Province, adjacent to Hong Kong.

July 14—Zheijiang and Jiangxi provinces, China. Officials in Beijing announce that more than 100 people have died in July and 10,000 mines and factories have been closed as a result of severe flooding in eastern and southern China.

July 20—Central Europe. Rivers across central Europe continue to rise after 10 days of torrential rain. In Poland and the Czech Republic, nearly 100 people are dead and property damage is estimated at more than $2 billion.

August 11—Himachal Pradesh, India. Heavy rains in northern India swell the Sutlej and Andhara rivers, triggering floods that leave more than 135 people dead when trees, bridges, and whole villages are washed away. Nearly 600 Indians died in floods during the June through August monsoon season of 1997.

August 27—Punjab Province, Pakistan. Flooding due to unusually heavy monsoon rains leads to the destruction of some 400 villages and the death of 37 people from the collapse of buildings.

September 27—Dhaka, Bangladesh. A cyclone, with 90-mile (144-kilometer) per-hour winds, hits the coast of Bangladesh along the Bay of Bengal, primarily in the district of Bhola, destroying tens of thousands of houses and killing at least 35 people.

October 9—Acapulco, Mexico. A hurricane pounds the Pacific Coast, causing flash floods and landslides. At least 150 people die, 40 of them in Acapulco.

October 31—Ribeira Quente, Portugal. A mud slide kills at least 26 people living in a village on Sao Miguel, the biggest of the nine islands in the Portuguese archipelago.

November 3—Ho Chi Minh City, Vietnam. A typhoon pummels Vietnam's southern coast with winds of more than 80 miles (128 kilometers) per hour, killing hundreds of people. At least 1,000 fishing boats and nearly 4,000 crew members are missing in the wake of the most devastating storm to hit the country in decades.

November 7—Badajoz, Spain. Rain storms cut a path of destruction across southern Spain and Portugal, killing 31 people.

November 11—Bardera, Somalia. At least 130 people die in flooding caused by rain storms that began in late October. They are the heaviest rains in 30 years in southern Somalia.

Other disasters

January 20—Hyderabad, Pakistan. A batch of homemade liquor kills at least 32 men, ranging in age from 12 to 70 years old.

March 3—Punjab Province, Pakistan. A runaway 17-car train carrying 1,500 passengers jumps its tracks, killing more than 125 people.

April 8—Dharmadi, India. Thirty-eight passengers die when a bus plunges 148 feet (45 meters) down a gorge northeast of Jammu, the winter capital of the state of Jammu and Kashmir.

April 27—Hunan Province, China. Ninety people die and 300 are injured when a train traveling cross-country on the Guangzhou-Beijing rail line crashes into the rear of a train waiting at a station, derailing 13 cars.

May 4—Kisangani, Congo (Kinshasa). Thousands of Rwandan refugees swarm onto a train leaving the Biaro refugee camp in Zaire. The severe overcrowding forces some to the bottom of the cars, suffocating and crushing to death more than 100 people.

September 4—Ankara, Turkey. Two buses collide on a highway between Ankara and Istanbul, killing 33 people and injuring 40 other passengers.

September 14—Madhya Pradesh, India. More than 100 people are killed and 400 others are injured when five cars of an overcrowded passenger train plunge off a bridge and into the Hansdev River near the city of Raigarth.

September 16—Maseer, Egypt. A truck transporting boys and girls ranging in age from 12 to 17 to work in cotton fields skids off the road into a canal, killing 29 of the children and injuring 50 more.

September 19—Vietnam. Thirty people die and 22 others are injured when a 60-passenger bus plunges off a highway and sinks in the South China Sea.

October 20—Freetown, Sierra Leone. At least 70 people die when a tractor-pulled flatbed trailer, on which they were traveling, overturns.

Drug abuse. Illicit drug use in the United States dropped from an estimated 18.0 percent of all 12- to 17-year-old children in 1995 to 16.7 percent in 1996, according to the U.S. Department of Health and Human Service's National Household Survey on Drug Abuse (NHSDA). The study, released in August 1997, surveyed 18,269 people, age 12 and older. (All estimates are based on the number of people reporting the use of a substance at least once during the year prior to the survey, unless otherwise noted.)

Among all people age 12 and over, the NHSDA estimated that 10.8 percent, or approximately 23 million people, used illegal drugs. Marijuana continued to be the most popular illegal drug, used by 77 percent of those who used illegal drugs, or 8.6 percent of the total population. An estimated 1.9 percent used cocaine, 1.7 percent used hallucinogens, and 0.2 percent used heroin.

According to Monitoring the Future, a survey released in December 1997 by the University of Michigan Institute for Social Research in Ann Arbor, the number of eighth-grade students reporting the use of illegal drugs dropped from 29.4 percent in 1995 to 28.5 percent in 1996. However, the percentage of high school seniors reporting daily use of marijuana increased from 4.9 percent in 1995 to 5.8 percent in 1996. The American Medical Association's National Longitudinal Study of Adolescent Health, released in September 1997, noted that students in grades 7 through 12 who had strong attachments to their parents and teachers were less likely to use drugs, smoke cigarettes, or drink alcohol.

Heroin use. Although the 1997 NHSDA indicated that a small percentage of the population used heroin (0.2 percent), there was an upward trend in the number of new users, 90 percent of whom were under the age of 26. The resurgence of the drug's popularity was attributed to the availability of cheaper and purer forms. Experts worried that the drug's low price and the fact that it could be easily used—by smoking, sniffing, or snorting—attracted people who otherwise would not have tried the drug.

Experts who study trends in drug use warned, however, that the purity of heroin sold on the street would eventually degrade. As the street supply becomes less pure and, therefore, less potent, users addicted to heroin through smoking, sniffing, or snorting would be more likely to inject the drug to maintain their addiction, thereby putting themselves at risk for contracting AIDS and other diseases that are transmitted by sharing needles.

Alcohol. According to the 1997 NHSDA, 32 percent of 18- to 25-year-olds reported "binge drinking" at least once during the month prior to the survey. Binge drinking was defined by the NHSDA as consuming five or more drinks within a couple of hours. Deaths from binge drinking on college campuses drew much publicity in 1997. □ David Lewis

Drugs. On Sept. 15, 1997, American Home Products Corporation of Madison, New Jersey, withdrew its drugs fenfluramine and dexfenfluramine from the market at the urging of the United States Food and Drug Administration (FDA). Concerns first arose about fenfluramine in July 1997, when a study by physicians at the Mayo Clinic in Rochester, Minnesota, and the MeritCare Medical Center in Fargo, North Dakota, linked its use (when combined with a drug called phentermine) with heart valve disorders in 24 women. Heart valves are leaflike flaps of tissue that regulate blood flow through the heart. Subsequent reports attributed other cases of heart valve disorders to dexfenfluramine. The fenfluramine-phentermine combination, called "fen-phen," had been a popular diet-drug combination in 1997.

Thalidomide. On September 22, the FDA informed Celgene Corporation, a chemical manufacturer in Warren, New Jersey, that the corporation would be allowed to market thalidomide as a treatment for leprosy. Thalidomide had previously been used as a sedative for pregnant women but was banned throughout the world in the early 1960's after it was linked to thousands of cases of severe birth defects. The FDA said the new use of the drug would be restricted to avoid birth defects.

Heart drug. In May 1997, the FDA approved a new drug designed to prevent congestive heart failure, the first since 1983. Congestive heart failure, which kills about 40,000 Americans annually, is a condition in which the heart cannot pump sufficient amounts of blood to adequately supply the body. Studies showed that the new drug—carvedilol, sold under the brand name Coreg—substantially reduces the need for hospitalization and lowers the risk of death among patients. Coreg can also be used to treat *hypertension* (high blood pressure).

Parkinson drug. In July 1997, the FDA approved the first new drug for Parkinson disease since 1989. Parkinson disease is a brain disorder in which patients produce low amounts of dopamine, a chemical needed for the normal function of nerve cells in the brain. The disease causes such symptoms as muscle rigidity and tremors. The new drug—pramipexole dihydrochloride, sold under the brand name Mirapex—stimulates nerve cells in the brain just as dopamine does.

Alzheimer's slowed. The first evidence that drug treatment can slow the progression of Alzheimer's disease, a brain disorder that causes increasing loss of memory and other mental abilities, was reported in April 1997. A two-year study financed by the National Institutes of Health (NIH), a government biomedical research agency based in Bethesda, Maryland, found that consequences of Alzheimer's disease, such as being admitted into a nursing home, were slowed by as much as seven months in Alzheimer's patients taking vitamin E or selegiline, a drug already used for Parkinson disease.

Home drug test. In January, the FDA approved the first home test kit for drug abuse. "Dr. Brown's Home Drug Testing System" can detect the presence of marijuana, PCP, amphetamines, cocaine, heroin, codeine, and morphine in urine. The FDA stated that the kit, developed by Personal Health and Hygiene, Incorporated of Silver Spring, Maryland, gives parents a new option to help assure that their children are not using drugs.

The user of the kit collects urine in vials, which are labeled with an identification number and sent to a laboratory for analysis. Results of the analyses are available one to three days after the laboratory receives the samples.

Flu vaccine. In July, the NIH announced that an experimental influenza vaccine administered as a nasal spray, rather than an injection, was highly effective in protecting children from the flu.

A study financed by the NIH and Aviron, a biotechnology company in Mountain View, California, found that only 1 percent of 1,070 children who were given the vaccine developed influenza. By comparison, 18 percent of 532 children who received a placebo developed the flu. Aviron announced that the vaccine would not be available until at least 1999 because additional tests were needed.

Faster drug approvals. In November, President Bill Clinton signed legislation establishing new FDA procedures designed to speed the approval of prescription drugs. The new procedures were expected to reduce by at least one year the average time it takes for a newly developed drug to become available to consumers. In 1997, new drugs typically took 12 to 15 years after initial development to arrive on the market.

Simpler drug labels. The FDA proposed rules in February to improve consumer information on nonprescription drug labels. Wording on new labels would be easier for consumers to understand, and the labels would carry more prominent warnings about side effects. The proposed change would apply to about 100,000 over-the-counter drugs.

The FDA proposed the new rules because consumers "self-treat" many more health problems than physicians actually treat. According to the FDA, 60 to 90 percent of all illnesses are initially self-treated. The new rules, which the FDA announced would go into effect in 1999 or 2000, were designed to make it easier for consumers to select proper drugs.

Drug dosages for kids. In August 1997, President Clinton proposed regulations requiring manufacturers to study the effects of prescription drugs on children and list proper dosages for children on labels. According to the FDA, approximately 80 percent of prescription drugs are not labeled for children's use, despite the fact that physicians often prescribe such drugs to children. □ Michael Woods

See also **AIDS; Drug abuse; Medicine.**

Eastern Orthodox Churches.
On Sept. 26, 1997, Russian President Boris Yeltsin signed into law a bill that gave a higher status to Russian Orthodoxy, Buddhism, Islam, and Judaism—religions that had been officially recognized by the former Soviet government—than to religions or sects either not recognized by the Soviet government or introduced in Russia since the 1991 fall of the Soviet Union. Patriarch Alexie II of Moscow supported the law, which limits the activities of dissident Orthodox congregations, Roman Catholics, evangelical Christians, and other foreign-based religions. According to the 1997 law, the newer religious organizations, many of which had enjoyed rapid growth since 1991, may not run schools, distribute religious literature, or control television and radio stations.

Ecumenical Patriarch Bartholomew, the head of the Orthodox Church in Constantinople (Istanbul, Turkey), received a Congressional Gold Medal on Oct. 21, 1997, from U.S. President Bill Clinton in recognition of the patriarch's "contribution to religious understanding and peace." After leaving Washington, D.C., Bartholomew, the spiritual leader of all Orthodox Christians, visited congregations in 11 other U.S. cities.

Orthodox Church in Cyprus. In August, more than 600 Orthodox Greek Cypriots were allowed to visit the Monastery of St. Andreas for the first time since 1974, when Turkish Army invaders took control

Nearly 1,000 Russian Orthodox pilgrims in June pass beneath an ancient tree, a site of pilgrimage since an image of St. Nicholas was found there in 1383.

of the island's northern region. Tension between the two groups, nonetheless, continued during 1997. In January, St. Anastasia Church in the Turkish Cypriot region was leased to private developers as a site for a hotel complex. Since 1974, more than 100 churches and monasteries under the control of Muslim Cypriots had been stripped of their sacred objects or converted into mosques, recreation areas, or stables.

New leadership. On March 9, 1997, Petros Papapetrou, the Metropolitan of Cameroon in Africa, was installed as the new Patriarch of Alexandria, Egypt. Papapetrou succeeded Patriarch Parthenios, who died in July 1996.

Exhibitions of religious art. The Metropolitan Museum of Art in New York City presented, in the spring of 1997, "The Glory of Byzantium," an exhibit of artwork from the middle era of the Byzantine Empire (800's to 1200's). The more than 350 articles in the exhibit included paintings, mosaics, manuscripts, chalices, and other religious objects of the Eastern Orthodox Church.

The exhibit "The Treasures of Mount Athos" opened on June 21, 1997, in Thessaloniki, Greece. Mount Athos is a secluded Orthodox Christian commonwealth of 20 monasteries, dating back to the mid-900's, in northern Greece. Hundreds of religious art objects from 16 of the monasteries were allowed to leave the sacred location for public display for the first time.   □ Stanley Samuel Harakas

Economics. Most regions of the world began 1997 showing substantial economic strength and low inflation. The combination fueled sharp gains in global stock markets. The second half of 1997, however, brought a wave of severe financial market declines that struck Asia, spread to Latin America, and threatened economic prosperity worldwide. The rapid spread of crisis underscored how interconnected the world economy had become in an era of expanding international trade.

Analysts remained uncertain at the end of 1997 of the global economic outlook for 1998. Strong growth with low inflation was expected to continue in the United States, which would help other regions recover from economic setbacks. The U.S. economy was projected to slow from its fast pace in 1997, partly because a shrinking pool of available U.S. labor would hamper further business expansion. Weakened Asian economies would also curb demand for exported U.S. products while increasing imports to the United States to compete against American goods.

A midyear forecast by the Organization for Economic Cooperation and Development in Europe, a Paris-based multinational association working to promote economic and social welfare, expected the overall 1997 economic growth of its members to average 3 percent. By the end of 1997, analysts believed that percentage was overly optimistic.

Economics

The strong U.S. economy fueled debate among analysts for most of 1997. Many economists wondered whether the growth was too fast to avoid future inflation and whether the Federal Reserve System (the Fed), the nation's central bank, should raise interest rates to slow the economic growth; or whether years of investment in high-technology equipment had created a new era that permitted stronger output of goods with lower inflation than in past years.

The U.S. gross domestic product (GDP)—the total output of goods and services produced in the United States—rose 4.9 percent in the January-March quarter of 1997 and 3.3 percent in both the second quarter and third quarter. A strong economy and reduced government spending cut the deficit for fiscal 1997, which ended September 30, to $22.6 billion. It was the lowest deficit since 1974 and within reach of a long-held policy goal of erasing the federal deficit.

Early in 1997, Fed Chairman Alan Greenspan cautioned that the fast GDP growth had threatened the ability of manufacturers to produce desired goods, which could fuel inflation in 1998. In response, the Fed on March 25, 1997, tightened slightly the pace at which new money was created, which increased the short-term interest rate banks charged to one another from 5.25 percent to 5.5 percent. The rate increase was meant to prolong the economic expansion by sustaining the low inflation.

As the economy slowed and inflation remained low, the Fed enacted no further policy changes through 1997. The U.S. economic scenario was also brightened by continued low unemployment rates. According to the U.S. Bureau of Labor Statistics, the nation's November unemployment rate—the percentage of workers unable to find a job—fell to 4.6 percent, the lowest level since October 1973.

Asian economies sustained major setbacks in 1997. Japan's fluctuating economy faltered in the April–June quarter after the government, on April 1, increased a consumption tax on goods from 3 percent to 5 percent in an attempt to decrease the budget deficit. Spending sharply decreased for the remainder of that quarter as Japanese consumers stockpiled goods prior to March 31.

Collapsing currencies of smaller nations in Southeast Asia also triggered concern on world markets. In mid-May, currency traders, who viewed the economy of Thailand as having become too overextended to support its growth, began to bid down Thailand's currency, the baht. The Thai government on July 2 announced that it would seek financial assistance from the International Monetary Fund (IMF), a United Nations affiliate that provides short-term credit to more than 175 nations. In response, the value of the baht dropped even lower.

The devaluation of currency in mid-1997 continued to spread across Asia, affecting the Philippines,

Selected key U.S. economic indicators

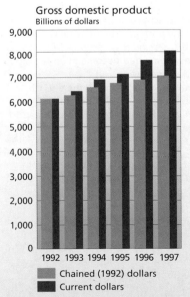

Gross domestic product
Billions of dollars

Chained (1992) dollars
Current dollars

Sources: U.S. Department of Commerce and U.S. Department of Labor, except 1997 figures, which are estimates from The Conference Board.

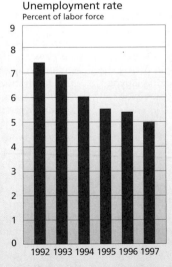

Unemployment rate
Percent of labor force

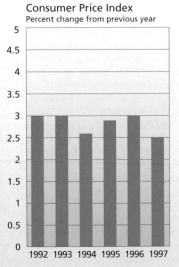

Consumer Price Index
Percent change from previous year

The gross domestic product (GDP) measures the value in current prices of all goods and services produced within a country in a year. Many economists believe the GDP is an accurate measure of the nation's total economic performance. Constant dollars show the amount adjusted for inflation. The unemployment rate is the percentage of the total labor force that is unemployed and actively seeking work. The Consumer Price Index measures inflation by showing the change in prices of selected goods and services consumed by urban families and individuals.

Malaysia, and Indonesia. Falling currency values forced some countries to seek assistance from the IMF or to increase interest rates in an effort to protect the value of their currency. These actions cut deeply into international business investment.

In December, South Korea, the world's 11th-largest economy, agreed to terms for the largest international economic rescue in history. The $57-billion loan package was arranged to assist South Korea pay its debts. The IMF was joined by the World Bank, the Asian Development Bank, the United States, and several other nations in financing the loan package.

In Japan, stock values continued to decline in late 1997 as investors became increasingly aware of the precarious condition of many Japanese banks and financial institutions. In November, Yamaichi Securities, Japan's fourth-largest brokerage firm, announced that it was insolvent. The corporate failure was the largest in Japan since the end of World War II (1939–1945).

Latin American nations kept a watchful eye on their economies in late 1997 following the Asian crisis. Economists paid special attention to Brazil, which had enjoyed a three-year economic boom. In November, the Brazilian government increased interest rates to 43 percent in an attempt to maintain the value of its currency, the real. Some economists cautioned that such tough policies could strangle future economic growth.

Stock markets crash. Currency crises in Asia led to a plunge in the Hang Seng Index, Hong Kong's stock market, in late October. On October 23, stocks lost 10.4 percent of their value in the Hong Kong stock market, causing a frantic sell-off of stocks in the rest of Asia and throughout Europe, Latin America, and the United States. The Dow Jones Industrial Average—statistics that show the trend of prices of selected stocks and bonds traded on the New York Stock Exchange—fell 554 points on October 27, a record point loss. However, many economists maintained that, after considerable growth, such a decline was inevitable. The Dow rebounded a record 337 points on October 28, prompting reassurances from U.S. President Bill Clinton that the U.S. economy remained strong. Toward the end of 1997, global stock markets resumed their gains.

Future predictions. While many analysts in late 1997 remained uncertain of the global economic outlook in 1998, some international observers maintained that the financial woes that marked 1997 in Asia and Latin America would probably not continue. In European and the North American nations, analysts also predicted continued solid economic expansions that could prevent the financial crises of 1997 from triggering a worldwide recession.

□ John D. Boyd

See also **International trade; Labor and employment; Manufacturing.**

Ecuador. Rapidly shifting leadership dominated the political situation in Ecuador in 1997. On February 6, Ecuador's Chamber of Representatives removed from office President Abdala Bucarám Ortíz on grounds of "mental incapacity" and incompetence. During the political turmoil following Bucarám's removal, Vice President Rosalia Arteaga served as interim president, becoming—if only for two days—Ecuador's first female head of state.

On Feb. 11, 1997, the Chamber selected Fabián Alarcón, the 49-year-old leader of the legislature, to serve as interim president until presidential elections in 1998. Nicknamed *El Bailarin* (the dancer) for his fancy political footwork while leading the 16-party legislature, Alarcón won endorsement as interim president in a public referendum on May 25, 1997.

President Alarcón attempted to trim a government deficit of $1.3 billion by reducing public spending and reforming the nation's customs service. However, he had little room to maneuver with 45 percent of the $4-billion annual budget earmarked for payments on foreign and domestic debts.

On April 9, Ecuador's Supreme Court issued a warrant for the arrest of former President Bucarám and four of his former aides on charges of misappropriating more than $80 million in government funds. Panama's government granted Bucarám political asylum on April 28. □ Nathan A. Haverstock

See also **Latin America** (Facts in brief table).

Education. The number of students enrolled in elementary and secondary schools in the United States in the fall of 1997 reached 52.2 million. Another 14.1 million students enrolled in colleges and universities. The nation's elementary and secondary schools spent $339.7 billion to educate students, while colleges and universities spent $224.5 billion.

President Bill Clinton sought to lead a national effort to strengthen the educational system in 1997. ``My number-one priority for the next four years is to ensure that Americans have the best education in the world,'' he declared in his State of the Union address in February. The president announced a 10-point plan to strengthen education. It included expanding federal funding for preschool education, connecting schools and libraries to the Internet, and enlisting a million volunteers to ensure that every student could read by the end of the third grade.

National tests. The president also called for new national tests in his address as a way to spur educators to raise academic standards. He proposed that the federal government pay for the development of a fourth-grade reading test and an eighth-grade math test that states and school systems could use voluntarily. The president's testing proposal ran into strong opposition in the U.S. Congress from conservative Republican advocates of local control of education and liberal Democrats who feared that minority students might do poorly on the new national exams. In a compromise measure approved in November, Congress postponed funding the new testing program for one year.

State tests. Some states did not wait for the standoff in the nation's capital to be resolved. In August, North Carolina issued monetary rewards and regulatory penalties to its 1,600 elementary and middle schools as part of its first-year effort to make educators more accountable for what their students learn. Under the plan, those teachers whose students achieved high scores on end-of-the-year tests were rewarded with $500 to $1,000. Schools whose students did not score well had to enact improvement plans specified by state officials.

Report cards issued on the nation's schools in 1997 were used by advocates of national examinations as evidence of the need for local educators to set higher standards. In February, the National Assessment of Education Progress (NAEP), an independent, federally funded program that measures the performance of national samples of students, reported that only 21 percent of 4th graders, 24 percent of 8th graders, and 16 percent of 12th graders were proficient in math. However, those percentages were slightly higher than the percentage of students that had scored in the proficient category in math four years earlier.

In October, the NAEP reported that only 26 percent of 4th and 8th graders and 18 percent of 12th graders were proficient in science. In addition, only 3 percent of students at each grade level had advanced knowledge of the subject. The performance of minority students was particularly alarming. Among 12th graders, as many as 77 percent of African Americans and 67 percent of Hispanics demonstrated a "below basic" mastery of science. They were unable to demonstrate such knowledge as identifying ice as the solid form of water.

The results of the Third International Mathematics and Science Study, announced in June, were more promising. U.S. fourth graders placed high among 26 countries in science and above average in math. U.S. 8th graders scored above average in science but below average in math.

Students themselves advocated higher standards in 1997. In February, Public Agenda, a New York-based research organization, issued the results of an extensive study of high school students called "Getting By: What American Teenagers Really Think About Their Schools." Half of the respondents to the survey said that standards in their schools were not sufficiently challenging.

The U.S. Supreme Court reversed itself in June when it ruled that public-school systems could send remedial teachers into parochial schools to work with needy children. A 1985 Supreme Court decision had forbidden such teachers from working with children on parochial school premises, citing the constitutional separation of church and state.

The charter school movement, in which private individuals or companies operate taxpayer-funded public schools, spread rapidly in 1997. By year's end, the number of such schools in the nation had more than doubled, with 780 charter schools in 23 states enrolling over 150,000 students. The popularity of charter schools reflected dissatisfaction with traditional public schools and a growing belief that the rules, regulations, and strong traditions in public education made the reform of existing public schools very difficult. President Clinton gave the charter school movement a boost in 1997 by budgeting $100 million to help open new charter schools.

The number of new companies to manage charter schools for profit also increased in 1997. At least 10 such companies ran more than 100 public schools in 12 states. The largest was the Edison Project, L.P., a New York City-based firm launched by Christopher Whittle, a former publishing executive. By September the Edison Project had revenues of $65 million and was operating 25 schools in 8 states.

Tuition vouchers. There was also vocal support in 1997, especially among the Republican leaders of the U.S. House of Representatives, for the idea of giving parents publicly funded vouchers to send their students to private schools. However, a Wisconsin court in January struck down a plan to expand a voucher program that had been created in the early 1990's in Milwaukee, and in May, an appeals court upheld the decision. The courts ruled that the planned expansion, to include Roman Catholic and other parochial schools, violated the state's constitutional ban on government aid to religion.

Also in May, an Ohio court struck down the nation's only other voucher plan, involving public, private, and religious schools in Cleveland, on the same grounds. The two-year-old program involving 2,000 students was allowed to remain in place until a further ruling by a higher Ohio court.

Increasing costs were cited by experts as significant barriers to college admissions in 1997. In September, the College Board, an organization of schools and colleges, reported that the average college tuition increased 5 percent for the 1997–1998 school year, more than double the rate of inflation for the same period.

A commission on college costs warned in a June 1997 report that additional years of higher-than-inflation tuition hikes would shut millions of students out of higher education. The 18-person commission was created by the Council for Aid to Education, a subsidiary of the Santa Monica, California-based Rand Corporation. Its report, "Breaking the Social Contract: The Fiscal Crisis in Higher Education," urged colleges and universities to take such cost-cutting steps as requiring faculty members to teach more courses and trimming course offerings.

Congress reacted to the problem of rising tuition costs by approving President Clinton's Hope Scholarship program in November. Under the program, students in the first two years of college would be eligible for a $1,500 tax credit each year.

Limitations on affirmative action programs in some states resulted in fewer admission applications from minority students in 1997. In Texas, where a federal court in 1996 had barred the use of race in college admissions decisions, the University of Texas at Austin reported in May 1997 that 21 percent fewer African Americans applied for admission for the 1997–1998 school year than had the previous year. Applications by Hispanics dropped by 17 percent. At the law school of the University of California at Los Angeles, where the board of regents had voted in 1995 to end race-based admissions, only 21 African American students were admitted for the 1997–1998 school year, down from 100 in 1996–1997.

Albert Shanker, the president of the American Federation of Teachers (AFT) and one of the nation's leading educators, died on Feb. 22, 1997. Shanker led the crusade to unionize public school teaching early in the 1960's. He won the nation's first teacher collective-bargaining contract as a militant leader of the United Federation of Teachers in New York City. In 1974, Shanker became president of the AFT, one of the nation's largest teachers' unions. Shankar was succeeded as president of the AFT in May 1997 by Sandra Feldman, president of the United Federation of Teachers. □ Thomas Toch

Egypt. Violent attacks in 1997 by Islamic militants against tourists and Coptic Christians stunned Egyptians. The most shocking incident occurred on November 17, when 58 foreign tourists and 4 Egyptians were murdered at the ancient temple of Queen Hatshepsut in Luxor. Militants killed the tourists in the hope that tourism, a vital part of Egypt's economy, would be weakened. Islamic militants had declared war on the Egyptian government in 1992.

On Feb. 12, 1997, militants stormed a church in the southern town of Abu Qurgas, killing 10 Coptic Christians. On March 13, Islamic gunmen slew 13 men, 9 of them Copts, in the southern village of Nag Dawoud. On September 18, 10 people, including 9 German tourists, were gunned down by militants who attacked a bus by Cairo's Egyptian Museum.

The Egyptian parliament extended a 1981 law in February 1997 that granted the government emergency powers to combat violence into the year 2000. The law permitted prolonged detention of suspected dissidents and their trial by military courts.

Tension with Israel. Relations between Egypt and Israel worsened in 1997. Tension began in February, when Israeli Prime Minister Benjamin Netanyahu approved the construction of a new Jewish settlement in East Jerusalem. Egyptian President Hosni Mubarak criticized the action because the status of East Jerusalem remained an issue to be negotiated in final discussions of the Arab-Israeli peace process.

Presidential security guards patrol prime tourist attractions in Egypt, such as the Sphinx and Great Pyramids in Giza, after 58 foreign tourists were massacred in November at an ancient temple in Luxor. The country depends heavily on tourism as a source of foreign currency.

El Salvador

Palestinians hoped that East Jerusalem would become their capital.

Another issue of contention between Israel and Egypt in 1997 concerned the case of Azam Azam, an Israeli convicted by an Egyptian court of spying for Israel. Netanyahu, who insisted that Azam was innocent, asked Mubarak to intercede in the case, but Mubarak refused. Azam was sentenced in August to life in prison with 15 years of hard labor.

Canal project. On January 9, President Mubarak inaugurated a government project to build a 192-mile- (309-kilometer-) long canal to transport water from the Nile River to Egypt's Western Desert. It was hoped that the canal, scheduled to be completed in the year 2017, would transform 1 million acres (405,000 hectares) of desert into farmland. Where Egypt would find the estimated $2 billion dollars needed to complete the project remained unresolved at the end of 1997.

Female circumcision. In December, Egypt's Supreme Administrative Court upheld a 1996 government decree that had banned *female circumcision* (the full or partial removal of genitalia on females). The court decision overturned a June ruling by a mid-level court that had struck down the government decree. Egyptian Islamic conservatives argued in favor of female circumcision on both religious and medical grounds. □ Christine Helms

See also **Israel; Middle East** (Facts in brief table).

El Salvador. The Farabundo Martí National Liberation Front, a leftist political party known as FMLN, made significant gains in elections in El Salvador on March 16, 1997. The FMLN was founded by former rebels who had signed a peace accord with the Salvadoran government in 1992.

The FMLN's Hector Silva won the 1997 race for mayor of San Salvador, the capital. The mayoralty is considered the country's second most important political office and a potential stepping stone to the presidency. The FMLN captured the mayoralties in 54 other municipalities and won 27 seats in the 84-seat national Legislative Assembly. The ruling conservative National Republican Alliance won 28 seats.

Pedro Antonio Andrade, a former leftist rebel who was an informant for the U.S. Central Intelligence Agency (CIA) in the 1980's, was deported from the United States to El Salvador on Nov. 3, 1997. The CIA had provided Andrade with a U.S. visa in 1990 despite allegations that he had masterminded a 1985 attack in San Salvador that left six Americans and seven Salvadorans dead.

In early July 1997, Salvadoran officials uncovered an investment fraud that cheated at least 1,400 investors out of an estimated $115 million. President Armando Calderón Sol fired the government's top banking regulator, Rafael Rodrígues Loucel, in the wake of investigations. □ Nathan A. Haverstock

See also **Latin America** (Facts in brief table).

Elections. Republicans in 1997 won major victories in off-year elections in New Jersey and Virginia and reelected mayors in New York City and Los Angeles, the nation's two largest cities. The Democratic Party, which was outspent by the Republicans in most key state races, also lost two of the three contests for open seats in the U.S. House of Representatives. Major ballot issues in several states failed to gain voter support in 1997.

Gubernatorial races. New Jersey Governor Christine Todd Whitman, a Republican, narrowly won reelection to a second term on November 4. Whitman defeated her Democratic challenger, state Senator Jim McGreevey, by only 1 percentage point. Whitman was once regarded as a rising star of the Republican Party, but lost the support of many conservative Republicans because of her moderate position on such social issues as abortion. During the campaign, McGreevey, who was also the mayor of Woodbridge, New Jersey, contended that Whitman had not done enough to reduce high automobile insurance premiums and local property taxes.

In Virginia, former State Attorney General James S. Gilmore III, a Republican, easily captured the governor's race against Democratic Lieutenant Governor Don Beyer. Gilmore, whose victory led a Republican sweep of the state's top three offices, focused his campaign on ending an unpopular personal property tax on cars and trucks. Republican John Hager defeated Democrat L. F. Payne in the race for lieutenant governor. Republican state Senator Mark Earley won the race for attorney general, defeating Democrat William Dolan. The triple victory for Republicans confirmed a conservative trend in Virginia, which once was a Democratic Party stronghold.

Incumbent mayoral victories. Republican Richard J. Riordan cruised to a second term as mayor of Los Angeles on April 8, 1997, by defeating his Democratic opponent, state Senator Tom Hayden, by a margin of nearly 2 to 1. New York City Mayor Rudolph Giuliani overwhelmed his Democratic opponent, longtime Manhattan Borough President Ruth Messinger, on November 4 to also win a second term. Giuliani received 57 percent of the vote, becoming the first Republican to be reelected mayor since Fiorello LaGuardia in 1937. The 1997 outcome was remarkable because registered Democrats outnumber Republicans by 5 to 1 in New York City. Giuliani, however, downplayed party ties and emphasized delivery of city services and a reduction in street crime.

Elsewhere in the November 4 elections, Detroit Mayor Dennis Archer defeated state Representative Ed Vaughn to win a second term. In Minneapolis, Minnesota, Mayor Sharon Sayles Belton, a Democrat, won a bitter battle for reelection against Republican Barbara Carlson, a former city council member. Across the river in St. Paul, Minnesota, Republican Mayor Norm Coleman easily defeated Democratic state Senator Sandy Pappas. Pittsburgh Mayor Tom Murphy, a Democrat, overwhelmed Republican challenger Harry Frost. Thomas Menino, a Democrat, became the first mayor in Boston's history to run unopposed in the general election. Menino won a second term in office. Cleveland Mayor Michael White, a Democrat, won a third term by defeating city council member Helen Smith.

In a hotly contested race in Miami, Florida, former mayor Xavier Suarez upset incumbent Joe Carollo in a November 13 runoff election. In another stronger-than-expected challenge, Mayor Bill Campbell of Atlanta, Georgia, won a second term by defeating City Council President Marvin Arrington in a November 25 runoff election. Candidates in neither city received a majority of the votes in the November 4 general election.

Special congressional elections. In a race for an open seat in the House of Representatives that drew national attention, Brooklyn and Staten Island, New York, voters on November 4 elected Republican Vito Fossella over his Democratic foe, State Assemblyman Eric Vitaliano. During the final weeks of the campaign, Vitaliano was bombarded by negative television ads paid for by the Republican National Committee. Fossella, who received financial backing from the national Republican Party, succeeded Republican Susan Molinari, who resigned on August 1 to become a television anchorwoman.

Texas State Representative Ciro Rodriguez, a Democrat, on April 12 won the seat left vacant by the death of Representative Frank Tejeda (D., Texas). In New Mexico, Republican Bill Redmond was elected on May 13 to replace former Democratic Representative Bill Richardson, who left Congress after being named U.S. Ambassador to the United Nations.

On a closely watched ballot issue, Oregon voters on November 4 turned back, by a 60 to 40 margin, an effort to repeal a state law granting the right to physician-assisted suicide. The Death With Dignity Act, approved by Oregon voters in 1994, had not taken effect because of a court challenge. In October 1997, the U.S. Supreme Court rejected an appeal to block the act. The Supreme Court's action and the decision by voters made Oregon the first state to make legalized doctor-assisted suicide available to terminally ill patients.

Washington state voters rejected the legalization of marijuana for medical use, a measure to prohibit job discrimination because of sexual orientation, and an initiative requiring trigger locks on all handguns sold or traded. New York state voters turned down a call for a constitutional convention and a request to borrow $2.4 billion to build and renovate schools.

☐ William J. Eaton

See also **Congress of the United States; Democratic Party; Republican Party; State government; United States, Government of the.**

Electric power. See Energy supply.

Electronics. The transition to high-definition television (HDTV) in the United States formally began in April 1997, when the federal government cleared the way for the first update of the nation's broadcast-television standard in more than 40 years.

Phasing in HDTV. In April, the U.S. Federal Communications Commission (FCC) began the transition to HDTV by licensing a second channel to approximately 1,600 television stations nationwide, over which they could broadcast digital signals. HDTV was also known as digital television because HDTV signals were to be broadcast *digitally* (as a series of 0's and 1's). Plans called for the stations to use this dual-channel approach until 2006, after which nondigital television broadcasts would end. At that time, the estimated 240 million conventional television sets in use in 1997 would become nonfunctional unless they were equipped with a *converter box* (a device that converts the digital signal to the older format).

The new broadcast standard promised several improvements over the old system. For example, HDTV produced sharper video and more lifelike audio than traditional television. Unlike traditional TV screens, which were nearly square, HDTV screens were wider than they were tall, like a movie screen. In addition, HDTV included six channels of audio instead of the conventional two-channel stereo, producing a surround-sound effect similar to a movie theater. Furthermore, because they were digital, HDTV sets could work together with home-computer systems, enabling television broadcasts to incorporate interactive content, somewhat like the World Wide Web.

In May, Mitsubishi Consumer Electronics America of Cypress, California, announced that it would begin selling high-end HDTV sets in the United States in 1998. Mitsubishi announced that their large-screen, projection-type sets would cost $8,000 to $11,000. In June 1997, American television maker Zenith Electronics Corporation, of Glenview, Illinois, said its first high-end digital sets would cost between $7,000 and $11,000.

Satellite TV boom. About 1 million households per year were switching from cable television to Direct-to-Home (DTH) satellite systems, according to a study reported in March 1997 by the Consumer Electronics Manufacturing Association (CEMA). DTH systems received broadcasts directly from satellites in orbit around the Earth.

In place of a cable connection, DTH subscribers needed to purchase a small satellite dish about 16 inches (40 centimeters) in diameter. DTH systems broadcast their programs digitally, which enabled them to offer excellent picture and sound quality. In addition, DTH offered a greater variety of programming than was available on most cable systems. CEMA projected that 4.4 million DTH systems would be sold in 1997, up from 3.5 million in 1996.

DVD audio. A group of consumer electronics manufacturers and record companies agreed in July on technical standards for a new generation of digital audio players. The first of these new players were expected to become available in 1999.

Instead of the traditional *CD* (compact disc), which first became popular in the 1980's, the new players used a high-capacity disc known as a *digital versatile disc* (DVD), which could store seven times more music than a traditional audio CD. Traditional CD players used a two-channel (left and right) stereo sound system that was developed in the 1960's. DVD players used a six-channel audio format that delivered much more realistic sound reproduction.

Sales of electronics equipment and components totaled about $409 billion in 1996, a 6-percent increase from 1995, the Electronics Industries Association (EIA) reported in March 1997. EIA is the main trade organization of American electronics manufacturers and is based in Arlington, Virginia. In July, EIA reported that sales during the first half of 1997 totaled $219 billion, a 9-percent increase from the same period in 1996. The biggest increase occurred in sales of cellular telephones, pagers, and other telecommunications equipment, which rose by 14 percent. Sales of computers and computer equipment rose by 6 percent. □ Michael Woods

See also **Television**.

Employment. See Economics; Labor.
Endangered species. See Conservation.

Energy Supply. Thriving economies in many nations, growing populations, and increasing numbers of vehicles caused the world's demand for energy to continue to increase in 1997. Despite the increased demand, energy prices were relatively stable and low in 1997 due to ample energy supplies. The petroleum, natural gas, and coal industries remained the chief beneficiaries of gains in energy use.

Petroleum. In 1997, the world used gasoline, heating oil, and other petroleum products at a rate of some 73.8 million barrels a day, according to the International Energy Agency (IEA), an energy-research group based in Paris. One barrel consists of 42 gallons (159 liters) of petroleum. The IEA estimated that in 1998 global petroleum use would rise to an average of 75.6 million barrels a day.

The American Petroleum Institute (API), a Washington, D.C.-based group of petroleum companies, reported that U.S. petroleum demand in 1997 averaged slightly more than 18.5 million barrels a day through November. This amount was 1.2 percent greater than the amount used during the first 11 months of 1996. Approximately half of the petroleum that the United States uses is imported.

Gasoline is the chief petroleum product in the United States because of the huge and ever-growing numbers of cars and trucks in the country. To meet the demand for gasoline and other fuels, U.S. refineries operated at record levels during much of

1997. In August, during the peak of the U.S. driving season, gasoline output averaged 8 million barrels a day according to the API—the greatest amount ever recorded for that month.

Petroleum costs. Prices of gasoline rose slightly in early 1997 and then declined. During most of 1997, gasoline prices remained under $1.20 a gallon at many pumps in the United States. Analysts said that gasoline was about as cheap as ever after adjustments were made for inflation and taxes. Petroleum products remained relatively inexpensive in 1997 because of the competitive nature of the oil industry and widespread perceptions that the market may soon face an oil glut. Costs of other energy was held down by cheap petroleum.

The cost of crude oil, from which gasoline is made, fell in early 1997 after a run-up in prices during 1996. Over most of 1997, crude oil prices ranged between approximately $19 and $20 a barrel. Analysts projected similar prices for 1998. In 1996, crude oil prices had averaged approximately $22 a barrel.

OPEC. In November 1997, the Organization of Petroleum Exporting Countries (OPEC), an association of 11 oil-producing nations, announced a 10 percent rise in its production quota to help supply the rising demand for petroleum. OPEC nations produce nearly all of world's exported oil. The quota increase, which suggested an additional 2.5 million barrels a day in the market, was the first major increase in official OPEC supply limits in four years. Some analysts expected the increase to lead to lower petroleum prices in 1998. However, other analysts pointed out that except for Iraq, whose oil sales were restricted by the United Nations because of its 1990 invasion of Kuwait, OPEC nations were already exceeding production quotas in 1996, and many of the nations were producing to capacity.

The Energy Information Administration (EIA), an agency of the U.S. Department of Energy, projected that the actual increase in OPEC's oil flow in 1998 would only be between 500,000 and 800,000 barrels a day, pushing total OPEC output to between 28.5 and 28.8 million barrels a day. The extra crude was expected to come mainly from Saudi Arabia, the only OPEC nation with significant excess capacity.

Natural gas. After a sharp increase in 1996, natural gas use held steady in the United States for most of 1997. The EIA reported that the United States burned slightly less than 16.2 trillion cubic feet (454 billion cubic meters) of natural gas in the first nine months of 1997, approximately the same amount as in the first nine months of 1996. The EIA also reported that U.S. natural gas prices averaged $2.34 per thousand cubic feet through June 1997, up from $2.05 in the first six months of 1996. Natural gas prices declined from October to December 1997, contrary to the rise in prices typically seen during colder months. Analysts said the main reason for the price decline was an expectation that the 1997–1998

A fire fueled by toxic chemicals erupts after an explosion of unknown origin at the Shell Oil Company chemical refinery near Houston, Texas, in June.

winter would be milder than normal over much of the United States due to the effects of El Niño, a periodic warming of Pacific Ocean currents.

Coal. U.S. coal production from January through September 1997 totaled 812 million short tons (736 million metric tons), according to the EIA. This amount was 2 percent greater than the amount produced during the first nine months of 1996.

Environmental concerns. A November 1997 report by the Washington, D.C.-based Independent Petroleum Association of America, an organization of independent oil and gas producers, projected that overall energy consumption in the United States would increase by 1.7 percent in 1998, compared to 1997. According to the study, natural gas, coal, and petroleum would have the largest gains. Accelerating use of these fossil fuels added to concerns that emissions from their burning may lead to a warming of global climate. The burning of fossil fuels releases carbon dioxide into the atmosphere. Carbon dioxide is a *greenhouse gas* (a gas that helps trap heat in the lower atmosphere). In December, representatives from 150 nations met in Kyoto, Japan, to draft an international agreement calling for reductions in emissions of greenhouse gases.　　　□ James Tanner

See also **Environmental pollution; Petroleum and gas.**

Engineering. See Building and construction.
England. See United Kingdom.

Environmental pollution. A special ses-
sion of the United Nation's (UN) General Assembly was held in New York City in June 1997 to determine how best to implement ambitious environmental goals made at the 1992 UN Earth Summit in Rio de Janeiro, Brazil. However, disagreement among delegates caused the 1997 meeting, dubbed "Earth Summit + 5," to fail to produce a strategy for implementing the goals in a way that both protects the environment and promotes economic well-being. Delegates could not agree on plans to protect global forests, help developing countries conserve their environmental resources, or reduce emissions of *greenhouse gases* (gases, such as those generated from the burning of fossil fuels, blamed for the gradual warming of the atmosphere). Most environmentalists were highly critical of the session.

Kyoto meeting. In December, delegates from more than 150 nations attended the UN's third Conference of the Parties (COP-3), held in Kyoto, Japan, to set binding protocols for reductions in emissions of greenhouse gases. Disagreement arose between United States delegates, who favored relatively modest cuts in emissions to offset any potential economic consequences, and European delegates, who favored deep cuts. Following a visit to the conference by U.S. Vice President Al Gore, delegates reached a compromise agreement that called for most developed nations to reduce emissions of car-

bon dioxide and five other greenhouse gases to more than 5 percent below 1990 levels by the year 2012. Several members of the U.S. Senate, which must ratify the agreement before it can take effect in the United States, criticized the plan for not requiring developing nations to reduce emissions.

Black market CFC's. In September 1997, delegates from more than 100 countries agreed at a conference in Montreal, Canada, to implement an import/export licensing system to curb the smuggling of chlorofluorocarbons (CFC's), chemicals blamed for thinning the atmosphere's ozone layer. The ozone layer helps protect living things from excessive exposure to the sun's ultraviolet rays, which can cause cancer and other health problems. In 1987, an international agreement called the Montreal Protocol mandated the gradual phase-out of CFC's and other chemicals that thin the ozone layer. CFC's, which were commonly used in air-conditioning systems, subsequently became increasingly difficult to obtain. In 1997, U.S. officials acknowledged that CFC smuggling ranked second, behind narcotics, as a source of black market profits.

Economic value of nature. In May, a group of 13 economists, ecologists, and geographers, led by ecological economist Robert Costanza of the University of Maryland in Catonsville, published a report that attempted to assess the economic value of nature. Based on an economic analysis of various activities performed as part of natural processes—including food production, pollination, soil formation, erosion control, climate regulation, water-supply maintenance, and the provision of raw materials—the group estimated that nature provides at least $33 trillion worth of services annually.

The report indicated that the value of services provided by nature far exceeds the value of services provided by the human economy. In 1997, the total gross national product of the world (the value of all the goods and services produced by people) was approximately $18 trillion.

Salmon "war." From July 19 to July 21, approximately 200 Canadian fishing boats, banding together to form a floating barricade, prevented the Alaskan ferry *Malaspina* from leaving port at Prince Rupert, British Columbia. The barricade was a demonstration of frustration at the lack of progress in a long-running dispute between U.S. and Canadian fishermen over how to divide the Pacific-coast salmon catch. The Canadians said that Alaskan fishermen took three to four times more sockeye salmon than was allowed under terms of the 1985 Pacific Salmon Treaty, signed by the two countries. The treaty was established to help regulate the salmon catch, which was declining due to a number of factors, including overfishing and pollution.

To ease tensions worsened by the incident, Canadian Foreign Minister Lloyd Axworthy and U.S. Deputy Secretary of State Strobe Talbott agreed on July

23, 1997, to restart negotiations concerning rights to the 1997 salmon catch. The negotiations had collapsed in June. Tensions remained, however. In September, British Columbia filed a lawsuit, seeking $300 million in damages from the United States, contending that U.S. fishermen violated the Pacific Salmon Treaty.

Japanese oil spills. The Japanese coast was hit by two major oil spills within seven months in 1997. On January 2, the aging Russian tanker *Nakhodka* broke up in rough waters in the Sea of Japan approximately 240 miles (390 kilometers) northwest of Tokyo. The bulk of the freighter sank at the scene, but the ship's bow drifted for five days before running aground on January 7. Creating the worst oil spill in Japan in 20 years, the wreck released more than 1.3 million gallons (4.9 million liters) of heavy crude oil into the sea. The oil slick, measuring 500 yards by 5.5 miles (460 meters by 9 kilometers), caused widespread environmental damage to Japan's waters and coastline. Thousands of sea birds perished after they encountered the heavy oil.

On July 2, the Japanese tanker *Diamond Grace* ran aground on a shallow reef in Tokyo Bay, rupturing 2 of the ship's 14 oil tanks and spilling 400,000 gallons (1.5 million liters) of light crude oil into the bay. Driven by strong winds, the oil slick stretched 9 miles by 11 miles (14 by 18 kilometers) at one point, spanning the bay's entire width. Much of the oil evaporated, due to its light weight. Most of the remaining oil was scooped up in a 10-day cleanup operation that involved a flotilla of more than 300 ships. Nevertheless, residents who lived near the spill complained of a nauseating odor. Environmentalists were concerned about the effects of the spill on the bay's fish catch, valued at $200 million annually.

New air pollution rules. In June, President Clinton announced much stricter limits on the amounts of soot and smog released into the atmosphere by U.S. industries. The new regulations had been advocated by Carol Browner, head of the Environmental Protection Agency (EPA), who claimed that 15,000 people die every year from exposure to soot and smog. Hundreds of thousands of asthma sufferers would benefit the most from the regulations, according to an EPA spokesperson. However, industrial groups claimed that the health benefits of the new regulations would be much smaller than the EPA announced. The private groups also said that the regulations would be harmful to the economy. The regulations were not scheduled to go into effect for several years, in order to give states and cities time to decide how best to implement them.

Forest protection. In November, President Clinton signed legislation to provide $250 million in federal funds for a $380-million land-purchase agreement that U.S. and California officials made in 1996. The agreement called for the government to pur-

chase and preserve 7,500 acres (3,038 hectares) of California redwood forest from Charles Hurwitz, the owner of a Houston logging and mining firm. Hurwitz had sought compensation from the government for the land after federal officials told him in 1996 that environmental regulations would prevent him from logging on the land. After Clinton signed the legislation, California Governor Pete Wilson proposed a ballot measure to provide $130 million of state funds toward the land purchase.

Hurwitz was one of several entrepreneurs in 1997 who sought cash or other compensation from the government after being prevented from exploiting the natural resources on their land. Some environmentalists complained that many of these entrepreneurs were cheating the government by inflating land values.

Water filtration. New York City announced a plan in January to purchase land around upstate reservoirs and preserve it as a natural water-filtration system. The land, in its natural state, helps to prohibit the flow of municipal and agricultural pollutants into the reservoirs, which are New York City's primary sources of drinking water. By preserving the land, city officials expected to avoid the need to build a new water filtration plant at an estimated cost of $4 billion. ☐ Andrew Hoffman

See also **Canada.**

Equatorial Guinea. See Africa.

Estonia. Mart Siimann replaced Tiit Vahi as prime minister of Estonia in March 1997, after Vahi nearly lost a no-confidence vote in the parliament. Vahi's popularity had suffered amid accusations of improper real estate dealings in the capital, Tallinn. Siimann vowed to continue Vahi's economic policies.

In July, Estonia became the only one of the three Baltic republics of the former Soviet Union to be invited to apply for membership in the European Union (EU), an alliance of 15 western European nations. EU leaders said that Estonia's steady progress in economic reform since gaining independence in 1991 had earned it the special distinction. Estonia was richer than Baltic neighbors Lithuania and Latvia, with low debt, steady economic growth, and a nearly balanced budget. In addition, Estonia had one of the strongest currencies of the post-Soviet states and one of the most liberal trade policies. EU membership offered Estonia greater opportunities to expand trade with other European states.

Negotiations continued during 1997 on a treaty with Russia to set the official border between the two countries. While a draft of the treaty was adopted in 1996, both parties continued to disagree over details. Russia also continued to complain that the roughly 400,000 Russians in Estonia were being denied full citizenship rights. ☐ Steven L. Solnick

See also **Europe** (Facts in brief table).

Ethiopia. See Africa.

The nations of Europe took historic steps in 1997 to heal the East-West divide that had split the continent since the end of World War II (1939-1945). The North Atlantic Treaty Organization (NATO), a military alliance of Western European and North American countries, established a forum in May for security cooperation with its Cold War adversary, Russia. The Cold War was the intense U.S.-Russian rivalry that began after World War II and ended when the Soviet Union fell in 1991. In December 1997, NATO also invited three Eastern European countries to join the organization. The moves toward military reconciliation between East and West were matched in the political arena by the European Union (EU), the political and economic bloc of 15 Western European nations. In July, the EU invited five Eastern European countries to begin membership negotiations. Europe's economic upturn in 1997 was expected to enable most EU countries to qualify for participation in a single European currency, due to be launched in 1999.

NATO reform. The most dramatic changes in Europe in 1997 involved the NATO alliance. NATO had struggled to redefine its role since the collapse of the Berlin Wall in 1989 and the fall of Communism in the former Soviet Union in 1991. In 1997, NATO sought to expand the alliance into Eastern Europe to ensure the region's permanent conversion to democracy and free-market economics and to deepen cooperation with Russia despite that country's opposition to NATO expansion.

U.S. President Bill Clinton and leaders of the NATO allies signed an agreement called the Founding Act with Russian President Boris Yeltsin at a summit meeting in Paris on May 27. The act created a Permanent Joint Council in Brussels, Belgium, between the alliance and Russia to consider joint actions, such as arms control and peacekeeping missions, and to facilitate consultations in times of crisis. The council gave Russia a voice—but not a veto—on NATO issues. As part of the act, NATO stated it had no intention of deploying nuclear weapons in any of the new Eastern European member countries.

NATO leaders, in another summit meeting on July 8 in Madrid, Spain, recommended offering membership to nations of the former Soviet-led Warsaw Pact alliance. NATO extended offers to Hungary, the Czech Republic, and Poland, the Eastern European countries that had made the most progress toward becoming free-market democracies. The alliance completed membership negotiations by December 1997 and aimed to obtain congressional and parliamentary ratifications of NATO expansion in time to allow the countries to enter in 1999, NATO's 50th anniversary.

EU enlargement. The European Union also took steps in 1997 to admit new members from Eastern Europe. EU leaders fulfilled a precondition for enlargement by agreeing to constitutional reforms at a summit meeting in Amsterdam, the Netherlands, in June. The reforms, called the Treaty of Amsterdam, sought to limit the ability of national governments to veto EU policies and to curb the growth of members in the European Parliament and the European Commission, the EU executive agency. The changes, which are likely to be ratified quickly by all EU members, were intended to ensure that the EU could continue to function with as many as a dozen future new members.

In July 1997, the European Commission identified five Eastern European countries—the Czech Republic, Estonia, Hungary, Poland, and Slovenia—as ready to enter negotiations for EU membership. The countries were judged on their commitment to democracy and the extent of their economic reforms. At a meeting in Luxembourg in December, EU leaders agreed to open negotiations in 1998 with those countries as well as with Cyprus, which the EU had previously ruled eligible for membership. EU leaders also agreed to deepen cooperation with Bulgaria, Latvia, Lithuania, Romania, and Slovakia, which had been deemed not yet ready for membership.

Monetary union. The EU made progress in 1997 toward achieving the planned 1999 launch of a single currency. At the Amsterdam summit in June, EU leaders endorsed a Pact for Stability and Growth that was designed to guarantee the strength of the future currency, the euro. The pact sought to reassure Germany that it would not suffer by giving up the highly valued German mark for the euro by setting permanent limits on national budget deficits and steep fines for countries that violated the limits.

Accelerated economic growth across Europe also improved the prospects that many countries would launch the single currency. Low interest rates and an increase in exports were expected to boost *gross domestic product* (GDP—the value of all goods and services produced in a country in a given year) by an average rate of 2.6 percent in EU nations, compared with 1.8 percent in 1996. The positive effect of faster growth on government tax revenues, combined with continued restraints on public spending, put most EU countries in good shape to meet the low-deficit requirement for joining the single currency. The European Commission predicted in October 1997 that all EU countries except Greece would meet the budget-deficit limit of no more than 3 percent of GDP in 1997. Great Britain, Denmark, and Sweden declared that they would not join the single currency initially,

A bitter cold snap in Europe in early 1997 drives temperatures in Paris to −14 °F (−26 °C) on January 3, freezing the city's famed fountains.

Country	Population	Government	Monetary unit*	Foreign trade (million U.S.$)	
				Exports†	Imports†
Albania	3,548,000	President Rexhep Mejdani; Prime Minister Fatos Nano	lek (148.18 = $1)	141	601
Andorra	75,000	Co-sovereigns bishop of Urgel, Spain, and the president of France; Prime Minister Marc Forne	French franc & Spanish peseta	46	920
Austria	8,076,000	President Thomas Klestil; Chancellor Viktor Klima	schilling (12.54 = $1)	57,540	66,272
Belarus	10,048,000	President Alexander Lukashenko	ruble (26,530.00 = $1)	4,156	4,644
Belgium	10,273,000	King Albert II; Prime Minister Jean-Luc Dehaene	franc (36.75 = $1)	165,807	152,791
				(includes Luxembourg)	
Bosnia-Herzegovina	3,947,000	Chairman of the collective presidency Alija Izetbegović	dinar (not available)	no statistics available	
Bulgaria	8,654,000	President Petar Stoyanov; Prime Minister Ivan Kostov	lev (1,772.60 = $1)	5,091	5,026
Croatia	4,457,000	President Franjo Tudjman	kuna (6.26 = $1)	4,512	7,788
Czech Republic	10,327,000	President Václav Havel; Prime Minister Václav Klaus**	koruna (33.25 = $1)	21,924	27,778
Denmark	5,197,000	Queen Margrethe II; Prime Minister Poul Nyrup Rasmussen	krone (6.78 = $1)	48,775	43,221
Estonia	1,509,000	President Lennart Meri; Prime Minister Mart Silman	kroon (14.25 = $1)	2,041	3,182
Finland	5,162,000	President Martti Ahtisaari; Prime Minister Paavo Lipponen	markka (5.33 = $1)	38,442	29,271
France	58,609,000	President Jacques Chirac; Prime Minister Lionel Jospin	franc (5.97 = $1)	289,350	274,071
Germany	81,664,000	President Roman Herzog; Chancellor Helmut Kohl	mark (1.78 = $1)	521,137	455,706
Greece	10,523,000	President Konstandinos Stephanopoulos; Prime Minister Costas Simitis	drachma (279.70 = $1)	9,392	21,489
Hungary	10,009,000	President Arpad Goncz; Prime Minister Gyula Horn	forint (198.74 = $1)	12,647	15,854
Iceland	277,000	President Olafur Grimsson; Prime Minister David Oddsson	krona (72.41 = $1)	1,637	2,175
Ireland	3,590,000	President Mary McAleese; Prime Minister Bertie Ahern	pound (punt) (0.68 = $1)	48,154	35,763
				(includes San Marino)	
Italy	57,221,000	President Oscar Scalfaro; Prime Minister Romano Prodi	lira (1,738.52 = $1)	250,992	206,912
Latvia	2,504,000	President Guntis Ulmanis; Prime Minister Guntars Krasts	lat (0.59 = $1)	1,443	2,219
Liechtenstein	31,000	Prince Hans Adam II; Prime Minister Mario Frick	Swiss franc	1,636	not available

but the 11 other EU countries were expected to launch the single currency on schedule in 1999. EU leaders planned to select the launch countries in May 1998, based on final economic figures for 1997.

Unemployment remained high in Europe in 1997, however, as growth was too slow to generate many new jobs. The unemployment rate remained at an average of almost 11 percent across the EU and above 12 percent in Finland, France, Germany, and Italy. The French and Italian governments promised late in 1997 to try reducing the standard work week to 35 hours around the year 2000 from about 40 hours in 1997 so that companies would be forced to hire more workers. However, other countries, includ-

ing Germany and Great Britain, considered the idea impractical. EU leaders held a jobs summit in Luxembourg in November at the demand of France, but did not agree on a plan for increasing employment.

Swing to the left. The election in 1997 of a Labour government led by Tony Blair in Great Britain and of a Socialist government led by Lionel Jospin in France put left-of-center parties in control of a majority of EU governments for the first time. Socialist or Social-Democratic parties headed 9 of the 15 EU governments. However, left-wing governments remained committed to the single-currency's required policies, including low budget deficits, deregulation, and the privatization of state-owned businesses.

Country	Population	Government	Monetary unit*	Foreign trade (million U.S.$) Exports†	Imports†
Lithuania	3,696,000	President Algirdas Brazauskas; Prime Minister Gediminas Vagnorius	litas (4.00 = $1)	3,280	4,405
Luxembourg	418,000	Grand Duke Jean; Prime Minister Jean-Claude Juncker	franc (36.75 = $1)	165,807 (includes Belgium)	152,791
Macedonia	2,213,000	President Kiro Gligorov	denar (55.02 = $1)	1,204	1,719
Malta	373,000	President Ugo Mifsud Bonnici; Prime Minister Alfred Sant	lira (0.39 = $1)	1,723	2,653
Moldova	4,479,000	President Petru Lucinschi; Prime Minister Ion Ciubuc	leu (4.61 = $1	802	1,079
Monaco	33,000	Prince Rainier III	French franc	no statistics available	
Netherlands	15,760,000	Queen Beatrix; Prime Minister Wim Kok	guilder (2.01 = $1)	197,245	180,642
Norway	4,391,000	King Harald V; Prime Minister Kjell Magne Bondevik	krone (7.18 = $1)	49,331	35,087
Poland	40,858,000	President Aleksander Kwasniewski; Prime Minister Jerzy Buzek	zloty (3.40 = $1)	24,410	36,966
Portugal	9,814,000	President Jorge Sampaio; Prime Minister Antonio Guterres	escudo (181.33 = $1)	23,754	33,933
Romania	22,698,000	President Emil Constantinescu; Prime Minister Victor Ciorbea	leu (7,729.00 = $1)	8,460	9,828
Russia	146,120,000	President Boris Yeltsin; Prime Minister Viktor Chernomyrdin	ruble (5,888.50 = $1)	88,703	61,147
San Marino	26,000	2 captains regent appointed by Grand Council every 6 months	Italian lira	250,992 (includes Italy)	206,912
Slovakia	5,422,000	President Michal Kovac; Prime Minister Vladimir Meciar	koruna (33.82 = $1)	8,841	10,911
Slovenia	1,945,000	President Milan Kucan; Prime Minister Janez Drnovsek	tolar (168.06 = $1)	8,123	9,399
Spain	39,752,000	King Juan Carlos I; Prime Minister José Maria Aznar	peseta (150.15 = $1)	102,000	121,793
Sweden	8,894,000	King Carl XVI Gustaf; Prime Minister Göran Persson	krona (7.62 = $1)	79,919	64,447
Switzerland	7,374,000	President Arnold Koller	franc (1.48 = $1)	76,204	74,469
Turkey	65,331,000	President Süleyman Demirel; Prime Minister Mesut Yilmaz	lira (183,136.00 = $1)	23,083	42,465
Ukraine	51,134,000	President Leonid Kuchma	hryvna (1.88 = $1)	11,567	11,379
United Kingdom	59,056,000	Queen Elizabeth II; Prime Minister Tony Blair	pound (0.61 = $1)	262,094	287,432
Yugoslavia	10,755,000	President Slobodan Milosević; Prime Minister Radoje Kontić	new dinar (5.90 = $1)	no statistics available	

*Exchange rates as of Oct. 24, 1997, or latest available data. †Latest available data. **Resigned Nov. 29, 1997.

The political pendulum swung in the opposite direction in Eastern Europe. Solidarity, the conservative, union-based group that led Poland's struggle to overturn Communism in the 1980's, established a coalition government after winning 201 of 460 seats in parliamentary elections on Sept. 21, 1997. Solidarity formed a coalition with the pro-business Freedom Union. Jerzy Buzek, a veteran Solidarity adviser, became prime minister. The coalition defeated the Democratic Left Alliance, the former Communists who had governed Poland since 1993.

In Bulgaria, a coalition of conservative parties defeated the former Communists in an April 1997 election. The coalition tried to prevent the country's bankruptcy by adopting an austerity program of budget cuts in return for aid from Western countries and the International Monetary Fund, an organization that provides short-term loans to its members.

The Balkans. NATO countries continued in 1997 to try bringing a lasting peace to the former Yugoslavia. The United Nations (UN) increased pressure on Bosnia, Croatia, and Serbia to hand over suspected war criminals for trial before the International Criminal Tribunal in The Hague, the Netherlands. In July, for the first time, troops from the NATO-led UN Stabilization Force actively pursued those charged by the tribunal with war crimes. The troops killed one Bosnian Serb officer and wounded another. A potential breakthrough occurred on October 6, when 10 Bosnian Croats charged with murdering Muslims during the war surrendered to the tribunal.

The political situation in the former Yugoslavia remained confused. Slobodan Milošević, the Serbian president widely blamed for having instigated the war in 1991 to create a greater Serbia, saw his power challenged in 1997. Milošević resigned the Serbian presidency on July 23 because of a two-term limit, but had himself elected president of the Yugoslav Federation, which includes Serbia and Montenegro. In October, Milošević's political opponent, Milo Djukanović, defeated a Milošević ally for the Montenegran presidency. Djukanović blocked constitutional changes that would have transferred broad powers to the Yugoslav presidency. Milošević's power increased in December, when Milan Milutinović, Milošević's ally and hand-picked successor, won the Serbian presidency amid allegations of fraud.

In the Serb-controlled half of Bosnia, UN forces supported President Biljana Plavšić in her attempt to seize real control from forces loyal to the former president and war-crimes suspect Radovan Karadzić. UN peacekeepers seized four television transmitters from Karadzić's forces on October 1 and turned them over to Plavšić's supporters. Plavšić had promised to implement the 1995 Dayton peace agreement that ended the war. In December 1997 elections, no party, including Plavšić's, received a strong enough mandate to forge a stable government in the near future. In mid-December, President Clinton stated that U.S. troops—part of the NATO force in Bosnia—would stay in that country indefinitely.

The UN also struggled with Croatia over the plight of some 350,000 ethnic Serbs who had been driven from the Croatian region of Eastern Slavonia during the war. U.S. Secretary of State Madeleine Albright told Croatian President Franjo Tudjman in May that the United States would block aid unless Croatia allowed the Serb refugees to return. In June, the UN extended the stay of 5,000 peacekeeping forces in Eastern Slavonia because the government refused to allow the refugees to return.

Albania. Law and order broke down in Albania in March after several fraudulent investment schemes collapsed, wiping out an estimated $2 billion in savings in Europe's poorest country. Some 16,000 Albanians crossed the Adriatic Sea to flee violence that erupted. Italy obtained a peacekeeping mandate from the UN and led a force of more than 6,000 soldiers from nine European countries into Albania in April. The force enabled Albania to restore order and hold elections on June 29, in which the opposition Socialist Party defeated the Democratic Party of President Sali Berisha. Berisha resigned on July 23. The Socialists then installed their leader, Fatos Nano, as prime minister and the party's secretary-general, Rexhep Mejdani, as president. The peacekeeping force withdrew in August.

EU–U.S. clashes. The European Commission, which rules on antitrust matters for the EU, threatened in early 1997 to block the $14-billion merger of U.S. civilian aircraft makers Boeing Company of Seattle, Washington, and McDonnell Douglas Corporation of St. Louis, Missouri. The commission claimed that the merger would increase Boeing's dominance of the aircraft-building industry at the expense of Airbus Industrie, the European consortium that was Boeing's only competitor. However, the commission approved the merger on July 30 after Boeing agreed to drop its exclusive-supplier agreements with three major U.S. airlines and promised not to pressure subcontractors into not working with Airbus.

The EU also fought against U.S. trade sanctions on foreign companies that do business with Cuba, Iran, and Libya. The EU called the sanctions an unjust effort by the United States to impose its laws on other countries. When the EU in April challenged the sanctions' legality at the World Trade Organization, a group that oversees international economic relations, the United States suspended sanctions against European companies. The suspension remained in effect at the end of 1997 despite failure to reach a settlement and a decision in September by French oil company Total SA to invest $2 billion in natural gas production in Iran. □ Tom Buerkle

See also the various European country articles.

Explosion. See **Disasters.**

Fashion. The international fashion industry was shocked and saddened in 1997 by the murder of Gianni Versace, the Italian designer. Versace was shot and killed on July 15 outside his mansion in Miami Beach, Florida, allegedly by Andrew Cunanan, a suspect in four other murders.

Versace, a flamboyant designer who merged the worlds of fashion and entertainment, had gained critical acclaim with his latest collections. His clients included Diana, Princess of Wales, Sylvester Stallone, Madonna, and such supermodels as Naomi Campbell and Claudia Schiffer. Versace's design house was expected to survive under the management of his sister, Donatella, who took over design, and his brother, Santo, who took control of finances.

Paris's design houses, eager to maintain influence, attempted to reinvent themselves in 1997 by hiring young, edgy designers. In June, Paris design house Jacques Fath, maker of couture (made-to-order) fashions and ready-to-wear clothing, hired Russian-born Elena Nazaroff to design the company's ready-to-wear line but later dismissed her because her designs were considered edgy. Three cutting-edge designers were also hired at established ready-to-wear houses: Martin Margiela at Hermes, Stella McCartney at Chloe, and Marc Jacobs at Vuitton.

Halston. The big name for revival in 1997 in the United States was Halston, which had dominated U.S. fashion in the 1970's and early-1980's. Roy Hal-

FOCUS ON

Fashion 1997

Popular fashions in 1997 included casual dress at the office and a return to the styles of the 1970's.

Almost everyone—men, women, boys, girls, even heads of state—took to wearing baseball caps in the United States in 1997. President Bill Clinton dons a cap to greet constituents in August.

Monochromatic shirt and tie combinations introduced subtlety to men's dress clothes in 1997. Styles of the 1970's—close-fitting knit tops, flared pant legs, and tall platform shoes—continued their appeal, particularly with the young. Lime green was the spring color of 1997.

ston Frowick, who died in 1990, was a couture designer and a producer of ready-to-wear clothing. Halston International was formed in 1996 by Marc Setton and Jack Setton, who had acquired the rights to most of the Halston products. The new company introduced more than 20 products in 1997 under the labels Halston Lifestyle, a moderately priced offering, and Signature, the designer collection.

The new Halston line, produced under the leadership of designer and creative director Randolph Duke, included women's clothing, menswear, home furnishings, shoes, jewelry, and other accessories. According to managing director Carmine Porcelli, the products expressed the Halston philosophy: a "clean, pure, simple, and comfortable American style."

Trends in 1997. The activity in design houses in 1997 was intended to spark interest in fashion, which had peaked in the 1980's. Designers discovered that people might like to look at outrageous fashion pictures but did not necessarily view them as an invitation to buy. Some marketing techniques for clothing even drew criticism. A style of photography that came to be called "heroin chic"—featuring disheveled young people staring vacantly into space—sparked controversy in the press after President Bill Clinton chastised the fashion industry and publishers for delivering inappropriate messages.

To restore an interest in fashion, designers offered styles that fit an increasingly relaxed era. Women in the professional workplace dressed more

207

casually and consequently needed fewer clothes. With pants accepted in most offices in the United States, the pants suit superseded the more traditional jacket and skirt for women. Retailers, therefore, stocked more pants than skirts in 1997. Sportswear for men and women—including casual jackets, T-shirts, sweaters, and sneakers—continued to be acceptable for many occasions.

Even for formal occasions, the elaborately draped dress of the past was not considered appropriate in the late 1990's. Figure-slimming dresses were the fashion, even in floor-length styles. At most black-tie events, black was the dominant color for women, though a certain amount of embroidery and lace added a decorative effect. Luxury was expressed subtly, in precious fibers, such as silk and cashmere, but the styles remained casual.

Fur sales, which had declined significantly in the early 1990's after years of criticism from antifur activists, showed signs of a comeback in 1997. Retailers reported in 1997 that 1996 fur sales were as much as 20 percent higher than the previous year. However, the elaborate floor-length mink was no longer the coat of choice. Designers used curly lamb, raccoon, beaver, and a host of other furs in styles as casual as pea jackets. Other designers added fur trim to suits, fashioned fur handbags, and wove fur into the fabric of evening gowns. ☐ Bernadine Morris

See also **Deaths.**

Finland

Finland enjoyed one of Europe's strongest economic recoveries in 1997. The Finnish economy finally regained the ground lost in the 1990–1993 recession, when its *gross domestic product* (the value of all goods and services produced in a country in a given year) fell by about 12 percent because of the economic collapse of the former Soviet Union, which had been Finland's chief export market.

The European Commission, the executive arm of the European Union (EU)—a group of 15 Western European nations, forecast that economic growth in Finland would accelerate to 4.6 percent in 1997 from 3.3 percent in 1996. The growth rate was almost double the average of other EU countries. Unemployment, which peaked at more than 17 percent in 1994, was forecast to drop to 13.8 percent in 1997.

The economy was driven by higher exports of paper products and electronic goods, while lower interest rates revived demand from Finnish consumers. Short-term interest rates fell, reflecting confidence in the government's intention to lead Finland into the single currency, expected to be launched by the EU in 1999. The Finnish currency, the markka, was stable after the government pegged its value to other EU currencies. The EU forecast a budget deficit of 1.4 percent for 1997, well below the 3 percent ceiling for countries wishing to join the single currency.

Finland's employers federation and its leading trade unions agreed in November 1997 to create a so-called buffer fund. The buffer fund was created to allay the fears of some unions that Finland would become vulnerable to severe recessions after entering the single currency, because the country would no longer be able to devalue its currency or set its own interest rates.

Minister resigns. The Social Democratic-led government of Prime Minister Paavo Lipponen was shaken in September 1997 when Budget Minister Arja Alho reduced the amount a Finnish court had fined former Social Democratic leader Ulf Sundquist from 11 million markka to just over 1 million markka. The court had imposed the fine for losses incurred by a bank Sundquist had managed. When leading opposition parties complained that Alho was showing favoritism, Alho resigned, and the Lipponen government faced a no-confidence vote in parliament, which it survived.

Energy companies merge. The government announced on December 16 that it would merge two state-owned companies, Neste Oy and Imatran Voyma Oy. The union would create Finland's largest energy company, with 16,000 employees and $10 billion in sales, and make the companies more competitive in international markets. ☐ Tom Buerkle

See also **Europe** (Facts in brief table).

Fire. See Disasters.

Flood. See Disasters.

Florida. See State government.

Food. The largest recall of meat in United States history occurred on Aug. 21, 1997, when Hudson Foods, Inc. of Rogers, Arkansas, recalled 25 million pounds (11 million kilograms) of ground beef processed at the company's Columbus, Nebraska, plant. The recall followed reports that at least 16 people in Colorado became ill after eating beef traced to the plant. The beef was contaminated with a rare, potentially deadly strain of *Escherichia coli* bacteria.

The contamination may have occurred at one of the plants that supplied beef to Hudson, according to the company. The recall cost Hudson its main customer when Burger King Corporation of Miami, Florida, announced on August 24 that it would no longer purchase ground beef from Hudson. In early September, Hudson was acquired by Tyson Foods, Incorporated of Springdale, Arkansas.

The incident prompted the U.S. Department of Agriculture (USDA) to request in August that legislation be proposed in the U.S. Congress giving the USDA authority to stop the distribution and order the recall of meat and poultry that pose a probable threat to public health. The incident also helped prompt the Food and Drug Administration (FDA) to announce in December that meat processing plants in the United States would be allowed to expose beef to *gamma radiation* (high-energy waves similar to those used in radiation therapy) in order to kill bacterial contaminants.

Other food-borne illnesses. In May, the government of Guatemala announced that, at the request of the FDA, it was suspending exports of fresh raspberries to the United States. The Centers for Disease Control and Prevention (CDC) in Atlanta, Georgia, had linked Guatemalan raspberries to outbreaks of *cyclosporiasis,* an infectious disease characterized by severe diarrhea.

In August, the CDC announced that alfalfa sprouts contaminated with *E. coli* had sickened at least 70 people in Michigan and Virginia in 1997. Also in 1997, hepatitis outbreaks in Michigan were linked to coleslaw and imported raspberries.

Food imports. In October, U.S. President Bill Clinton proposed that the FDA be granted authority to ban imports of fruits and vegetables from countries that did not have food-safety standards similar to those of the United States. Clinton's proposal came in response to increasing numbers of food-borne illnesses traced to imported foods.

New food safety rules. New federal regulations requiring meat, poultry, and seafood plants to adopt so-called Hazard Analysis Critical Control Points (HACCP) procedures began to be implemented in 1997. The regulations, which were not to be fully carried out until the year 2000, require companies to introduce measures to prevent or minimize contamination in their processing systems and to monitor the results.

Juice safety. In August 1997, the FDA announced that it planned to propose an HACCP program for the juice industry. The announcement followed several cases in 1996 and 1997 in which unpasteurized juices, which are not treated to destroy disease-causing microorganisms, had been linked to illnesses and at least one death.

Revised RDA's. In August 1997, the National Academy of Sciences, an organization that advises the government on scientific matters, issued revisions to the Recommended Dietary Allowances (RDA's), guidelines for proper vitamin and mineral intake. The guidelines, renamed Dietary Reference Intakes, concerned the five bone-building nutrients—calcium, vitamin D, phosphorus, magnesium, and fluoride. Revised guidelines for the other nutrients were scheduled to be issued in six separate announcements between 1998 and 2000.

Organic foods. In December 1997, the USDA announced that it would, for the first time, regulate *organic foods* (foods grown or raised without the use of pesticides, synthetic fertilizers, or added hormones). The USDA proposed regulations defining which products could be labeled organic and setting standards for the production and handling of organically grown crops and organically raised meat and poultry. Between 1990 and 1997, sales of organic foods in the United States increased by more than 20 percent annually, according to the USDA. In 1996, sales totaled $3.5 billion. ☐ Bob Gatty

Football. Problems continued to plague both college and professional football in 1997. On the collegiate level, the bowl alliance invented to determine the season's undisputed—if unofficial—national champion was inadvertently derailed for the second straight year. In the professional ranks, the continuing impact of free agency reduced the talent level and diminished the quality of play throughout the 30-team National Football League (NFL), a trend that was especially noticeable on plays that involved field goal attempts, punts, and kickoffs.

"Who's number one?" Although most coaches and athletic directors continued to endorse a national championship playoff system for major college teams, college presidents generally remained opposed to the idea. In 1997, the University of Michigan Wolverines eliminated most fans' doubts about which was the best team by storming through its 11-game regular season unbeaten and untied to rank No. 1 in both the Associated Press media poll and the USA Today/CNN coaches poll. A matchup with No. 2-ranked University of Nebraska (11-1) to decide the national championship through competition rather than the polls was once again denied, however, because the Big 10 and Pacific 10 conferences remained obligated in 1997 to match up their respective champions in the nonalliance Rose Bowl.

Michigan captured its first national championship in 50 years by beating Washington State, 21 to 16, on January 1, 1998, in the Rose Bowl at Pasadena, California. It was the first Rose Bowl appearance by Washington State since 1931. Washington State's last-minute comeback drive ran out of time with the Cougars on Michigan's 26-yard line. Nebraska beat Tennessee on January 2, in the Orange Bowl, 42 to 17.

College football in 1997 saw such perennial powers as Notre Dame (7-5), Alabama (4-7), Southern California (6-5), Texas (4-7), and Oklahoma (4-8) all finish out of the top 25 in the polls. Michigan's perfect record, in contrast, reflected great improvement after four straight four-loss seasons.

On Dec. 13, 1997, Charles Woodson, Michigan's versatile junior cornerback, became the first primarily defensive player ever to win the Heisman Trophy as college football's best player. In addition to 7 interceptions on defense, Woodson returned 33 punts, caught 11 passes, carried the ball from scrimmage, scored 4 touchdowns, and completed a pass as an offensive player.

Woodson amassed 1,815 points to beat out Peyton Manning, the University of Tennessee senior quarterback, in the voting for the Heisman Trophy. Manning, who had 1,542 points, set career records for passing yardage (10,669), touchdowns (84), and the most 300-yard passing games (17) in Southeastern Conference history. Washington State

University of Michigan cornerback Charles Woodson (left) gracefully deflects a pass. In 1997, Woodson became the first defensive player ever to win the Heisman Trophy, which honors college football's best player.

Professional. On the first weekend of January, in the NFL's National Football Conference (NFC) playoffs, defending NFL champion Dallas Cowboys beat the Minnesota Vikings, 40 to 15, and the San Francisco 49ers shut out the Philadelphia Eagles, 14 to 0. The Cowboys, however, were beaten the next week by Carolina, 26 to 17, and Green Bay eliminated San Francisco, 35 to 14, in Green Bay.

In the American Football Conference (AFC), the Jacksonville Jaguars, a second-year expansion team, pulled off the upset of the season when they eliminated the heavily favored Denver Broncos, 30 to 27, at Denver's Mile High Stadium. Denver had not lost a game at home during the regular season. The New England Patriots beat the defending AFC champion Pittsburgh Steelers, 28 to 3.

Both home teams prevailed in the AFC and NFC championship games. New England won the AFC title by beating Jacksonville, 20 to 6, and Green Bay captured the NFC crown for the first time in 29 years by defeating Carolina, 30 to 13.

On January 26 in New Orleans, Louisiana, Green Bay met New England in Super Bowl XXXI at the Superdome. Once again, the NFL championship—which no AFC team has won since 1984—went to the NFC team. The Packers beat the Patriots, 35 to 21. Desmond Howard, the smallest man on either roster, won Most Valuable Player honors after he returned a kickoff 99 yards for the game's final touchdown, establishing a new Super Bowl record for kickoff return yardage.

As the 1997-1998 season began, new coaches were calling the shots at 10 NFL franchises. Among them were Dick Vermeil at the St. Louis Rams, the former Philadelphia Eagles head coach, who returned to the NFL after 14 years, and Mike Ditka, who became head coach of the New Orleans Saints after a 10-year stint with the Chicago Bears that ended in 1992. San Francisco head coach Steve Mariucci set a record for first-year coaches by winning 11 of his first 12 games, while Jim Fassell, another first-time head coach, turned the 6-and-10 New York Giants into division champions. Bill Parcells moved from New England to the New York Jets and turned that team—which had won only one game in 1996—into a 9-7 division contender.

quarterback Ryan Leaf came in third in the voting, with 861 points.

Eddie Robinson retired in 1997, at age 78, after a 57-year career as head football coach at Grambling State University in Louisiana. Robinson led teams to 408 victories, more than any other coach in history. He was succeeded by Doug Williams, who played for Robinson from 1974 through 1976 before he moved on to a nine-year NFL career that included MVP honors in Super Bowl XXII, as quarterback for the Washington Redskins. In December 1997, Tom Osborne also decided to retire after 25 seasons at Nebraska, where he was hailed leading his teams to 25 consecutive bowl appearances and criticized for coddling players who frequently ran afoul of the law.

National Football League final standings

American Conference

Eastern Division	W.	L.	T.	Pct.
New England Patriots*	10	6	0	.625
Miami Dolphins*	9	7	0	.563
New York Jets	9	7	0	.563
Buffalo Bills	6	10	0	.375
Indianapolis Colts	3	13	0	.188

Central Division	W.	L.	T.	Pct.
Pittsburgh Steelers*	11	5	0	.688
Jacksonville Jaguars*	11	5	0	.688
Tennessee Oilers	8	8	0	.500
Cincinnati Bengals	7	9	0	.438
Baltimore Ravens	6	9	1	.188

Western Division	W.	L.	T.	Pct.
Kansas City Chiefs*	13	3	0	.813
Denver Broncos*	12	4	0	.750
Seattle Seahawks	8	8	0	.500
Oakland Raiders	4	12	0	.250
San Diego Chargers	4	12	0	.250

*Made play-offs

Individual statistics

Leading scorers, touchdowns

	TD's	Rush	Rec.	Ret.	Pts.
Karim Abdul-Jabbar, Miami	16	15	1	0	96
Terrell Davis, Denver	15	15	0	0	90
Joey Galloway, Seattle	12	0	12	0	72
James Jett, Oakland	12	0	12	0	72
Rod Smith, Denver	12	0	12	0	72

Leading scorers, kicking

	PAT att./made	FG att./made	Longest	Pts.
Mike Hollis, Jacksonville	41/41	31/36	52	134
Jason Elam, Denver	46/46	26/36	53	124
John Hall, N.Y. Jets	36/36	28/41	55	120
Cary Blanchard, Indianapolis	21/21	32/41	50	117
Olindo Mare, Miami	33/33	28/36	50	117

Leading quarterbacks

	Att.	Comp.	Yds.	TD's	Int.
Jim Harbaugh, Indianapolis	309	189	2,060	10	4
Mark Brunell, Jacksonville	435	264	3,281	18	7
Drew Bledsoe, New England	522	314	3,706	28	15
Warren Moon, Seattle	528	313	3,678	25	16
Dan Marino, Miami	548	319	3,780	16	11
Jeff Blake, Cincinnati	317	184	2,125	8	7
Vinny Testaverde, Baltimore	470	271	2,971	18	15
Elvis Grbac, Kansas City	314	179	1,943	11	6
Neil O'Donnell, N.Y. Jets	460	259	2,796	17	7
John Elway, Denver	502	280	3,635	27	11

Leading receivers

	Passes caught	Rec. yards	Avg. gain	TD's
Tim Brown, Oakland	104	1,408	13.5	5
Keenan McCardell, Jacksonville	85	1,164	13.7	5
Jimmy Smith, Jacksonville	82	1,324	16.1	4
Yancey Thigpen, Pittsburgh	79	1,398	17.7	7
O. J. McDuffie, Miami	76	943	12.4	1
Marvin Harrison, Indianapolis	73	866	11.9	6
Joey Galloway, Seattle	72	1,049	14.6	12
Andre Rison, Kansas City	72	1,092	15.2	7
Shannon Sharpe, Denver	72	1,107	15.4	3
Keyshawn Johnson, N.Y. Jets	70	963	13.8	5

Leading rushers

	Rushes	Yards	Avg.	TD's
Terrell Davis, Denver	369	1,750	4.8	15
Jerome Bettis, Pittsburgh	375	1,665	4.4	7
Eddie George, Tennessee	357	1,399	3.9	6
Napoleon Kaufman, Oakland	272	1,294	4.8	6
Curtis Martin, New England	274	1,160	4.2	4
Corey Dillon, Cincinnati	233	1,129	4.8	10
Adrian Murrell, N.Y. Jets	300	1,086	3.6	7
Marshall Faulk, Indianapolis	264	1,054	4.0	7
Gary Brown, San Diego	253	945	3.7	4
Karim Abdul-Jabbar, Miami	283	892	3.2	15

Leading punters

	Punts	Yards	Avg.	Longest
Tom Tupa, New England	78	3,569	45.8	73
Chris Gardocki, Indianapolis	67	3,034	45.3	72
Leo Araguz, Oakland	93	4,189	45.0	63
Bryan Barker, Jacksonville	66	2,964	44.9	64
Darren Bennett, San Diego	89	3,972	44.6	66

National Conference

Eastern Division	W.	L.	T.	Pct.
New York Giants*	10	5	1	.656
Washington Redskins	8	7	1	.531
Philadelphia Eagles	6	9	1	.406
Dallas Cowboys	6	10	0	.375
Arizona Cardinals	4	12	0	.250

Central Division	W.	L.	T.	Pct.
Green Bay Packers*	13	3	0	.813
Tampa Bay Buccaneers*	10	6	0	.625
Detroit Lions*	9	7	0	.563
Minnesota Vikings*	9	7	0	.563
Chicago Bears	4	12	0	.250

Western Division	W.	L.	T.	Pct.
San Francisco 49ers*	13	3	0	.813
Atlanta Falcons	7	9	0	.438
Carolina Panthers	7	9	0	.438
New Orleans Saints	6	10	0	.375
St. Louis Rams	5	11	0	.313

Individual statistics

Leading scorers, touchdowns

	TD's	Rush	Rec.	Ret.	Pts.
Barry Sanders, Detroit	14	11	3	0	84
Cris Carter, Minnesota	13	0	13	0	78
Antonio Freeman, Green Bay	12	0	12	0	72
Dorsey Levens, Green Bay	12	7	5	0	72
Mike Alstott, Tampa Bay	10	7	3	0	60
Jamal Anderson, Atlanta	10	7	3	0	60
Raymont Harris, Chicago	10	10	0	0	60

Leading scorers, kicking

	PAT att./made	FG att./made	Longest	Pts.
Richie Cunningham, Dallas	24/24	34/37	53	126
Gary Anderson, San Francisco	38/39	29/36	51	125
Ryan Longwell, Green Bay	48/48	24/30	50	120
Jason Hanson, Detroit	39/40	26/30	55	117
Jeff Wilkins, St. Louis	32/32	25/37	52	107

Leading quarterbacks

	Att.	Comp.	Yds.	TD's	Int.
Steve Young, San Francisco	356	241	3,029	19	6
Brad Johnson, Minnesota	452	275	3,036	20	12
Brett Favre, Green Bay	513	304	3,867	35	16
Chris Chandler, Atlanta	342	202	2,692	20	7
Erik Kramer, Chicago	477	275	3,011	14	14
Scott Mitchell, Detroit	509	293	3,484	19	14
Troy Aikman, Dallas	518	292	3,283	19	12
Trent Dilfer, Tampa Bay	386	217	2,555	21	11
Ty Detmer, Philadelphia	244	134	1,567	7	6
Danny Kanell, N.Y. Giants	294	156	1,740	11	9

Leading receivers

	Passes caught	Total yards	Avg. gain	TD's
Herman Moore, Detroit	104	1,293	12.4	8
Rob Moore, Arizona	97	1,584	16.3	8
Cris Carter, Minnesota	89	1,069	12.0	13
Irving Fryar, Philadelphia	86	1,316	15.3	6
Antonio Freeman, Green Bay	81	1,243	15.3	12
Johnnie Morton, Detroit	80	1,057	13.2	6
Michael Irvin, Dallas	75	1,180	15.7	9
Frank Sanders, Arizona	75	1,017	13.6	4
Jake Reed, Minnesota	68	1,138	16.7	6
Bert Emanuel, Atlanta	65	991	15.2	9

Leading rushers

	Rushes	Yards	Avg.	TD's
Barry Sanders, Detroit	335	2,053	6.1	11
Dorsey Levens, Green Bay	329	1,435	4.4	7
Robert Smith, Minnesota	232	1,266	5.5	6
Ricky Watters, Philadelphia	285	1,110	3.9	7
Emmitt Smith, Dallas	261	1,074	4.1	4
Raymont Harris, Chicago	275	1,033	3.8	10
Garrison Hearst, San Francisco	234	1,019	4.4	4
Jamal Anderson, Atlanta	290	1,002	3.5	7
Warrick Dunn, Tampa Bay	224	978	4.4	4
Fred Lane, Carolina	182	809	4.4	7

Leading punters

	Punts	Yards	Avg.	Longest
Mark Royals, New Orleans	88	4,038	45.9	66
Matt Turk, Washington	84	3,788	45.1	62
Craig Hentrich, Green Bay	75	3,378	45.0	65
Jeff Feagles, Arizona	91	4,028	44.3	62
Mitch Berger, Minnesota	73	3,133	42.9	65

Football

The 1997 college football season

College conference champions

Conference	School
Atlantic Coast	Florida State
Atlantic Ten	Middle Atlantic: Villanova
	New England: New Hampshire
Big East	Syracuse
Big Sky	Eastern Washington
Big Ten	Michigan
Big Twelve	Nebraska
Big West	Utah State—Nevada (tie)
Conference USA	Southern Mississippi
Gateway	Western Illinois
Ivy League	Harvard
Metro Atlantic	Georgetown
Mid-American	Marshall
Mid-Eastern	Hampton
Northeast	Robert Morris
Ohio Valley	Eastern Kentucky
Pacific 10	Washington State—UCLA (tie)
Patriot	Colgate
Pioneer	Dayton
Southeastern	Tennessee
Southern	Georgia Southern
Southland	McNeese State—Northwestern State (tie)
Southwestern	Southern
Western Athletic	Colorado State

Major bowl games

Bowl	Winner	Loser
Alamo	Purdue 33	Oklahoma State 20
Aloha	Washington 51	Michigan State 23
Amos Alonzo Stagg (Div. III)	Mount Union (Ohio) 61	Lycoming (Pa.) 12
Blue-Gray	Gray 31	Blue 24
Carquest	Georgia Tech 35	West Virginia 30
Citrus	Florida 21	Penn State 6
Cotton	UCLA 29	Texas A&M 23
Fiesta	Kansas State 35	Syracuse 18
Gator	North Carolina 42	Virginia Tech 3
Heritage	Southern 34	So. Carolina State 28
Holiday	Colorado State 35	Missouri 24
Humanitarian	Cincinnati 35	Utah State 19
Independence	Louisiana State 27	Notre Dame 9
Insight.com	Arizona 20	New Mexico 14
Las Vegas	Oregon 41	Air Force 13
Liberty	So. Mississippi 41	Pittsburgh 7
Motor City	Mississippi 34	Marshall 31
Orange	Nebraska 42	Tennessee 17
Outback	Georgia 33	Wisconsin 6
Peach	Auburn 21	Clemson 17
Rose	Michigan 21	Washington State 16
Sugar	Florida State 31	Ohio State 14
Sun	Arizona State 17	Iowa 7
NCAA Div. I-AA	Youngstown State 10	McNeese State 9
NCAA Div. II	Northern Colorado 51	New Haven 0
NAIA	Findlay 14	Willamette 7

All-America team (as picked by AP)

Offense
Quarterback—Peyton Manning, Tennessee
Running backs—Curtis Enis, Penn State; Ricky Williams, Texas
Wide receivers—Jacquez Green, Florida; Randy Moss, Marshall
Tight end—Alonzo Mayes, Oklahoma State
Center—Olin Kreutz, Washington
Other linemen—Alan Faneca, Louisiana State; Benji Olson, Washington; Chad Overhauser, UCLA; Aaron Taylor, Nebraska
All-purpose—Tim Dwight, Iowa
Place-kicker—Martin Gramatica, Kansas State

Defense
Linemen—Greg Ellis, North Carolina; Jason Peter, Nebraska; Andre Wadsworth, Florida State; Grant Wistrom, Nebraska
Linebackers—Sam Cowart, Florida State; Andy Katzenmoyer, Ohio State; Anthony Simmons, Clemson; Brian Simmons, North Carolina
Backs—Dré Bly, North Carolina; Donovin Darius, Syracuse; Brian Lee, Wyoming; Charles Woodson, Michigan
Punter—Chad Kessler, Louisiana State

Player awards
Heisman Trophy (best player)—Charles Woodson, Michigan
Lombardi Award (best lineman)—Grant Wistrom, Nebraska
Outland Trophy (best interior lineman)—Aaron Taylor, Nebraska

The 1997-1998 NFL season got underway on August 31, the earliest start in history. San Francisco, Green Bay, and the surprising New York Giants won the National Conference division titles. They qualified for the playoffs with the three remaining NFC teams with the best records—Tampa Bay, Detroit, and Minnesota. Division titles in the American Conference went to Pittsburgh, Kansas City, and New England. The wild-card play-off contenders were Jacksonville, Miami, and Denver.

People. The season's most exciting player was Barry Sanders, the Detroit Lions running back, who proved yet again in his ninth season that he had no peer at eluding defenders. Sanders rushed for 2,053 yards, becoming the third running back ever to compile 2,000 yards in a season. It was Sanders's ninth consecutive 1,000-yard season, an NFL record.

On July 26 in Canton, Ohio, Don Shula, Wellington Mara, Michael Haynes, and Mike Webster were inducted into the Pro Football Hall of Fame. Shula won a record 347 games during the 32 years he coached the Baltimore Colts and Miami Dolphins. His Miami team of 1972 compiled a 17-0 record that has never been equaled. Mara started out as a New York Giants training camp ball boy in 1926 and was president of the club in 1997. Haynes, a Raiders cornerback, and Webster, a Steelers center, helped their teams win the Super Bowl.

Jack Kent Cooke, owner of the Washington Redskins for 23 years, died in April at age 84. Cooke spent $300 million to build a new home for his club, Jack Kent Cooke Stadium, but died before it opened in September 1997. Falcons owner Rankin Smith died of heart failure in Atlanta on October 25. He was 72.

Other leagues. The Toronto Argonauts won the Canadian Football League (CFL) Grey Cup for the second straight year by beating the overmatched Saskatchewan Roughriders, 47 to 23, on Nov. 16, 1997. It was Toronto's 14th Grey Cup championship in 21 appearances, and the first time a team won consecutive Grey Cup games in 15 years. Toronto quarterback Doug Flutie, who led his team to a 15-3 regular-season record, completed 30 of 38 passes for 352 yards and three touchdowns. He was the game's Most Valuable Player for the third time since 1992.

The World League of American Football, sponsored by the NFL, contested a 10-game season from April to June in six European cities. The Barcelona Dragons beat the Rhein Fire, 38 to 24, to win the World Bowl on June 22, 1997. Barcelona quarterback John Kitna completed 23 of 31 passes for a record 401 yards and two touchdowns.

In April 1997, the NFL agreed to provide financial and marketing assistance to help promote the CFL. As part of the new agreement, the two leagues planned to discuss playing an annual "World Classic Bowl," possibly beginning in June 1998, with the previous season's World League champion facing the CFL champion. ☐ Ron Reid

France underwent great political change in 1997 as President Jacques Chirac's conservative allies lost control of the National Assembly (the lower house of parliament) to the Socialist Party. The Socialists had pledged to make jobs a top priority over budget austerity, but once in power they struggled to reconcile their promise with the demands of the single European currency, to be introduced in 1999.

Elections. Chirac dissolved the National Assembly on April 21, 1997, 10 months ahead of schedule. He claimed the conservatives needed a fresh, five-year mandate to carry out a series of reforms, including the budget reductions required for the single currency, tax cuts, and further privatization of industry. The voters, however, delivered a strong rebuke to the government and to Prime Minister Alain Juppé, whose tough economic policies and reputation for arrogance had made him extremely unpopular.

In two rounds of voting on May 25 and June 1, the Socialists won 241 seats in the 577-member National Assembly. With the support of the Communist Party, the Ecologists, and other left-wing allies, the Socialists controlled a majority of 319 seats and formed a government. Lionel Jospin, the Socialist Party leader, became prime minister of a government of "cohabitation," in which a conservative president—Jacques Chirac—shares power with a left-wing parliament.

Supporters in Paris celebrate the Socialist Party's victory at the polls on June 1, 1997. The Socialists gained control of the National Assembly and the premiership.

The center-right coalition, which had held 80 percent of the seats in the previous parliament, captured only 242 seats. The far-right, anti-immigrant National Front won 14.9 percent of the vote and its first parliamentary seat. In February, the town of Vitrolles elected the first National Front candidate to win a mayoral contest with an *absolute majority* (more than 50 percent of the vote).

European reaction. The election result shocked Europe because Jospin had promised to reject the austerity policies required for the single currency and instead try to stimulate employment. Such a shift threatened to delay the start of European economic and monetary union, planned for 1999, or produce a weak euro, as the single currency is to be named. However, Jospin pursued a more moderate course in 1997, in the face of pressure from Germany and the European Union (EU)—an organization of 15 Western European countries—as well as from financial markets, which briefly depressed the value of French stocks, bonds, and the franc. He signed a budget stability pact at the Amsterdam EU summit meeting in June 1997. The pact sought to guarantee a stable euro by requiring countries that joined the single currency to maintain low budget deficits permanently or face stiff fines. In return, EU countries held a special summit meeting on employment in Luxembourg in November. At that meeting, the EU agreed to set national targets for employment policies, including the offer of jobs or training opportunities to the young and long-term unemployed.

Economy. France drew strength from a general European economic upswing in 1997, but the recovery was not sufficient to reduce the country's unemployment rate. Unemployment reached a post-World War II (after 1945) high of 12.8 percent in February 1997. The economy was forecast to grow by 2.3 percent during 1997, up from 1.1 percent in 1996.

In July 1997, the government announced budget cuts totaling 32 billion francs ($5.2 billion) and corporate tax increases. The measures were designed to bring the 1997 budget deficit nearer to 3 percent of gross domestic product, the maximum allowed for countries joining the single currency. In September, the government introduced a new budget containing spending restraints and tax increases to meet the 3 percent deficit limit in 1998.

The government introduced legislation in August 1997 aimed at creating 350,000 jobs in government and related agencies over five years, a central campaign pledge of the Socialists. In December, it adopted legislation that called for reducing the work week from 39 hours to 35 by the year 2000. The Socialists hoped the reduction would spur companies to hire new workers. Business leaders said the move would reduce competitiveness and cost jobs.

Industrial policy. The Socialists also sought to steer a middle course toward business. They abandoned their opposition to the sale of state-owned companies but slowed the pace of privatization begun under the conservatives. In October 1997, the Socialists sold nearly 25 percent of France Telecom, the national telephone company, to the public and to employees. The sale was the country's largest privatization, raising 42 billion francs ($6.8 billion).

The automaker Renault, of which 46 percent is owned by the French government, stirred a Europe-wide debate over factory closings by announcing plans in February to close its plant near the Belgian capital of Brussels. The Belgian government protested that the sudden announcement violated Belgian laws requiring companies to consult workers before layoffs. The Socialists responded by pressing Renault to provide more compensation and job-hunting assistance to the Belgian workers.

Clashes with United States. In June, the Socialists halted a reconciliation between the French military and the North Atlantic Treaty Organization (NATO) begun by President Chirac. The government stated that France would not rejoin NATO's integrated command, because the United States would not agree to turn over command of NATO forces based in southern Europe to a European commander.

France challenged U.S. commercial policy in September, when the government defended a $2-billion contract signed by French oil company Total SA with Iran. A 1996 U.S. law imposed sanctions on foreign companies that invested more than $40 million annually in Iran. Supported by other European countries, France claimed that interacting with Iran was

more likely to moderate its behavior than isolating it. France threatened to counter sanctions with a trade war. The U.S. government agreed in October 1997 not to impose sanctions in return for greater European cooperation against Iran.

Nazi past. France was forced to reexamine the collaboration of its World War II (1939–1945) Vichy regime with Nazi Germany when Maurice Papon, a senior Vichy official who served as budget minister from 1978 to 1981, was tried in October 1997 for crimes against humanity. Accused of sending more than 1,500 Jews to Nazi death camps, Papon claimed he was being unjustly persecuted. Prosecutors protested when a judge allowed Papon, 87, to be released during the trial because of ill health, a move that ensured he would not go to prison if convicted.

French Roman Catholic bishops apologized to the Jewish community in September, saying the church had agreed through its silence to the wartime deportation of more than 76,000 French Jews.

Pollution scare. The government banned half of all automobiles from the streets of Paris on October 1 to lower the extreme levels of air pollution in the capital. It was the first use of a restrictive antipollution law passed earlier in 1997.   □ Tom Buerkle

See also **Europe** (Facts in brief table); **Immigration** Special Report: **The Latest Wave.; People in the News.**

Gabon. See Africa.

Gardening continued to evolve from a money-saving backyard hobby to a multibillion-dollar segment of the leisure industry in 1997. Theme park promoters, in particular, discovered that brightly colored flowers were a big draw. The Walt Disney Company, based in Burbank, California, spent heavily on horticulture at all its theme parks in 1997 and made plans to exhibit at indoor garden shows in spring 1998. Katy Moss Warner, director of horticulture for Walt Disney World in Orlando, Florida, won the Massachusetts Horticultural Society's George Robert White medal of honor in October 1997. The prestigious award had been bestowed earlier in the century upon Frederick Law Olmsted, the "father" of landscape architecture, and Gertrude Jekyll, the "mother" of the English-style perennial border.

Garden shows. Traditional garden shows came to resemble professional trade shows in 1997 as commercial interests replaced volunteer participation. The 12-year-old San Francisco Garden Show began to be produced by Garden Expositions, Incorporated, a company affiliated with Seattle's successful 10-year-old Northwest Flower and Garden Show. The San Francisco show had previously been produced by a volunteer group. The show also moved from historic and quaint Fort Mason to the Cow Palace, a cavernous exhibition hall.

The Massachusetts Horticultural Society, based in Boston, began expanding its education and

Sunlight streams through the glass dome of the Palm Gallery in the refurbished Enid A. Haupt Conservatory at the New York Botanical Garden. The conservatory, originally opened in 1902, reopened in May 1997 after a four-year, $25-million renovation.

information programs to a new 36-acre (15-hectare) horticultural garden and educational center at the Elm Bank Reservation in the Boston suburb of Wellesley. The society built two greenhouses and offered a number of programs at the new site in 1997. The society's headquarters and some educational programs were to remain in Boston.

Gardening trends. In 1997, backyard container planting became popular, especially in the western United States, where residents grappled with water restrictions and shrinking lot sizes. Although Mexican and Italian pottery have traditionally dominated the garden container market, imports with refined designs from Thailand and other Pacific Rim countries brought welcome diversity in 1997.

Many gardeners in 1997 grew their culinary herbs and tomatoes in self-watering plastic containers. Window boxes, a staple of the 1940's, began to make a comeback. In addition, space-saving arbors and trellises decked with vines, especially roses, became more common.

Although perennial borders remained popular in 1997, the classic English border began to yield to mixed plantings of dwarf shrubs, tender bulbs, and exotic or high-performance annuals. More gardeners developed such specializations as building lily pools, using herbs, and attracting birds.

Birdfeeders and birdhouses were the top-selling accessories in many garden shops in 1997. Nature writers Lillian and Donald Stokes, famous for their "Stokes Nature Guides" series of books, launched a weekly television series in 1997 that included segments on how to use landscaping to attract birds.

Vegetables. The eternal quest to grow the first ripe tomato in the neighborhood made a top seller of new tomato seeds developed by the W. Atlee Burpee Company of Warminster, Pennsylvania. The "Fourth of July" tomato seed promised red fruit by Independence Day. Many vegetable gardeners in 1997 experimented with varying their plants by taste and ripening time and trying heirloom varieties.

Medicinal herbs were more widely offered by nurseries and seed companies in 1997 than in previous years. The most popular medicinal herb was purple coneflower, an American wildflower yielding an extract that, according to German tests, boosts the immune system. Other popular herbs were goldenseal, used to treat sinus problems, and osha root, used for sore throats and coughs. Customized blends of herbal teas grew in popularity as allergy fighters.

Fighting pests. Some new strategies to fight horticultural pests were introduced in 1997. Biologists released leaf-eating and root-eating beetles from Europe in more than 500 locations in the United States and Canada to attack the rapidly-spreading weed purple loosestrife. Since being imported from Europe in the 1800's, purple loosestrife has become one of the most troublesome weeds invading wetlands. Bernd Blossey, an ecologist at

Cornell University in Ithaca, New York, who studied the beetles, said that he hoped the insects would be able to tame the loosestrife plague within a decade.

Mark McClure, an *entomologist* (insect expert) with the Connecticut Agricultural Experimental Station in Windsor, released 15,000 Japanese ladybugs in eight Connecticut and Virginia forests in 1997 to prey upon woolly adelgids, Asian insects destroying eastern hemlock trees. McClure said that he was pleased with the preliminary results of the release.

Deaths. The horticulture world in 1997 mourned the death of J. C. Raulston, founder of the North Carolina State Arboretum in Raleigh, who was killed in an automobile accident in late December 1996 at the age of 56. Raulston had collected and studied 7,000 woody plants from 6 continents, donating many to gardens and nurseries. After his death, the arboretum he founded was renamed in his honor.

Thalassa Cruso, often called the "Julia Child of horticulture" because of her pioneering 1966–1969 public-television program "Making Things Grow," died in 1997 at the age of 88. Cruso wrote several best-selling books and was often seen giving gardening lessons to a hapless Johnny Carson on "The Tonight Show." □ Carol Stocker

Gas and gasoline. See Energy supply.
Genetic engineering. See Biology; Medicine.

Geology. Researchers from Massachusetts Institute of Technology in Cambridge, Massachusetts, Australian National University in Canberra, Australia, and the U.S. Geological Survey in Denver, Colorado, published evidence in April 1997 that advanced the understanding of *plate tectonics.* Plate tectonics is a theory that states that the Earth's surface is divided into huge slabs called lithospheric plates, the movements of which create earthquakes, volcanoes, and mountains. (Lithospheric refers to the solid portions of the Earth.) According to the research, when two moving plates meet, one of the plates is pushed deep into the *lower mantle* (a layer of hot rock extending from approximately 810 to 1,800 miles [1,300 to 2,900 kilometers] below the Earth's surface). While geologists had previously theorized that the meeting of two plates causes one to sink, many geologists had not believed that plates sink as deep as the lower mantle.

The researchers based their conclusion on an analysis of the lengths of time it took earthquake waves to travel through the Earth. Because the speed of the waves was dependent on the type of material they passed through, the researchers were able to create a three-dimensional image of the Earth's interior that revealed how deep into the mantle lithospheric plates had sunk. Geologists said that the study increased the understanding of the geological evolution of the Earth.

Tibetan plateau. In August, researchers from the

University of California at Los Angeles and other institutions reported that they had discovered evidence that the Tibetan plateau, a large, raised area in Asia that has an average elevation of 14,800 feet (4,500 meters), was much older than previously thought. The researchers said that a portion of the plateau had formed approximately 100 million years ago. The new date contradicted the long-held belief that the rise of the plateau was caused by the collision of the Indian and Asian continental plates approximately 50 million years ago. The new date also cast doubt on a common assumption that the cooling of the global climate over the past 50 million years was caused by the rise of the plateau.

The researchers used geological dating methods to study an 82 mile (132 kilometer) section of the Earth's crust across southern Tibet. They speculated that the rise of the plateau may have been caused by the collision of two lithospheric plates known as the Lhasa and Qiangtang blocks.

Orbit and climate. In July, scientists published a study proposing that *ice ages* (recurring periods in which glaciers advance southward from northern latitudes) can be explained by changes in the Earth's *inclination* (plane of the Earth's orbit around the sun with respect to the plane of the rest of the solar system). According to the researchers, from the University of California at Berkeley and the International Institute for Applied Systems Analysis in Laxenburg, Austria, ice ages may begin when the Earth's plane of orbit dips into a cloud of cosmic dust every 100,000 years, blocking a certain amount of sunlight. This theory contradicted theories that explained the cause of ice ages as changes in the Earth's *eccentricity* (shape of the orbit around the sun).

The researchers based their study on a chemical analysis of microscopic fossils deposited on the sea floor during the past 600,000 years. Chemical properties of the fossils vary depending on the amount of glacial ice that was present in the sea when the fossils were deposited. The analysis indicated that glaciers advance and retreat every 100,000 years—the period of time that it takes for Earth's inclination to go through one complete cycle. Some experts, however, doubted that changes in inclination would result in major changes in climate.

Subsurface life. Researchers from Gothenburg University in Sweden and the University of Bergen in Norway reported in September 1997 that they had found fossils of microorganisms inside granite bedrock 1.8 billion years old and 680 feet (207 meters) underground. Although no living microorganisms were found by the researchers, the fossils suggested that previous research that claimed to find living microorganisms at the site, on Sweden's Baltic coast, was valid. Scientists stated that the existence of life deep underground on Earth indicates that life may exist beneath the surface of other planets as well.

□ Henry T. Mullins

Georgia. Relations between Georgia and the United States were complicated in 1997 when a Georgian diplomat caused a three-car accident in Washington, D.C., by driving while intoxicated. A 16-year-old girl was killed in the crash. The United States threatened to suspend $30 million in foreign aid to Georgia unless it waived the official's diplomatic immunity protecing him from prosecution. Georgian President Eduard Shevardnadze agreed to the request, and in October, the diplomat, Gueorgui Makharadze, pleaded guilty to involuntary manslaughter and aggravated assault. He was sentenced to 7 to 21 years in prison in December.

Talks in Moscow in 1997 yielded progress in the conflict between Georgia and its secessionist region of Abkhazia. On August 15, Georgia and Abkhazia signed a formal commitment to finding a peaceful resolution of the conflict, without embracing the comprehensive solution proposed by Russian President Boris Yeltsin. Despite its ambiguity, nationalists on both sides attacked the declaration as an act of surrender. In November, representatives from several nations and the United Nations agreed to set up an international council to settle the conflict.

Security Minister Shota Kviraya resigned in July. An investigation led to accusations that Kviraya executed six people during Georgia's civil war in 1993 and also was a Russian spy. □ Steven L. Solnick

Georgia (state of). See **State government.**

Germany experienced during 1997 some of its worst economic difficulties since the country's near-miraculous recovery after World War II (1939–1945). Unemployment in 1997 surged to a postwar record as industry invested heavily abroad to escape Germany's tax rates and labor costs, which ranked among the highest of any industrialized country. The rise in joblessness made it difficult for the government of Chancellor Helmut Kohl to reduce its budget deficit to meet the requirements for join-ing the single European currency, expected to be launched in 1999. Political tensions mounted well ahead of the federal elections due to be held in September 1998, as the opposition Social Democratic Party blocked government attempts to stimulate the economy and reduce business costs through tax cuts.

The German unemployment rate passed 12 percent early in 1997 with a sharp slowdown in construction activity and the expiration of job-creation schemes in the former East Germany. Unemployment worsened despite an acceleration of economic growth, which the European Commission, the executive arm of the European Union (EU)—a group of 15 Western European nations—forecast would rise to 2.5 percent in 1997, from 1.4 percent in 1996. Most of the growth reflected higher exports.

Budget embarrassment. The rise in unemployment created a crisis for the government, reducing

Building cranes dominate the skyline of Berlin, as viewed from the top of the famous Brandenburg Gate, which once separated the downtown areas of East and West Berlin. Construction continued at an unprecedented rate in Berlin in anticipation of the city again becoming the German capital by 2000.

income tax revenues and increasing spending on unemployment benefits. The combined effect threatened to push the budget deficit above 3 percent of gross domestic product (GDP), the limit for countries wishing to join the single currency. GDP is the value of all goods and services produced by a country in a year. To resolve the crisis, Finance Minister Theo Waigel in May 1997 proposed revaluing the nation's gold reserves, which had been valued far below the market price. The government would use the profits from the revaluation to reduce the debt and deficit.

The proposal, however, hurt the country's reputation for sound fiscal management. Before the crisis, Germany had insisted on a strict interpretation of the economic criteria for the single currency and criticized countries that used creative accounting techniques to reduce their deficits. Many EU countries claimed that Germany was resorting to such creative methods with the gold revaluation scheme, and the German central bank that manages the reserves also opposed the plan. Weigel abandoned the plan in June. The German government raised taxes on gasoline and other fuels, sold its remaining shares in the German airline Lufthansa and part of the Deutsche Telekom phone company, and set tighter restraints on public spending in an effort to stay within the 3 percent budget deficit limit.

Political gridlock. Germany's economic problems led to a confrontation between the Christian Democratic-led government and the opposition Social Democratic Party, as both sides prepared for the parliamentary elections scheduled for September 1998. Helmut Kohl, who announced on April 3, 1997, that he would run for an unprecedented fifth term as chancellor, proposed a tax-cut package for businesses and individuals that was designed to stimulate the economy and restore the country's international competitiveness.

The Social Democrats claimed that the measures favored the rich and were reluctant to support reforms that might improve the government's popularity. In September, the Social Democrats, who control the upper house of parliament, blocked the tax reforms. The government managed in October to pass legislation to cut the country's income tax surcharge, an unpopular levy ranging from 7.5 percent to 5.5 percent used to finance the rebuilding of eastern Germany.

Local elections in Hamburg on September 21 gave some encouragement to Kohl, who called the vote a rejection of the Social Democratic Party's blocking tactics on tax reform. The Social Democrats remained the favored party. However, their share of the vote fell to 36.2 percent, 4 percent less than they had won in the previous election in 1993 and the party's worst showing in Hamburg since World War

II (1939–1945). Henning Voscherau, the city's Social Democratic mayor, resigned after the election. Voscherau had campaigned as being tough on crime and suggested delaying the start of the single currency, positions also advocated by Gerhard Schroeder, a politician seeking to run as the Social Democratic candidate for chancellor in 1998. The Christian Democrats increased their share of the vote to 30.7 percent from 25 percent, but that remained below the party's historic level of support.

Cold War crimes. German courts convicted two high-ranking officials in the former East Germany of human-rights crimes, raising questions about the government's right to prosecute citizens of its former Cold War rival. Markus Wolf, the former head of the East German foreign intelligence agency, was convicted on three counts of kidnapping by a Düsseldorf court on May 27, 1997, and received a two-year suspended sentence. Wolf was accused of imprisoning opponents of the former Communist regime in the 1950's and 1960's. Wolf had been convicted of treason in 1993 and sentenced to six years in prison, but Germany's Supreme Court threw that verdict out in 1995, ruling that East Germans could not be convicted of espionage in East Germany, because espionage was not against the law in that country.

In August 1997, East Germany's last Communist leader, Egon Krenz, was convicted of having ordered the deaths of people who attempted to flee East Germany over the Berlin Wall. He was sentenced to six and a half years in prison. Krenz appealed the verdict, saying that East Germany's Communist leaders merely followed orders from Moscow.

Mercedes flop. In 1997, automaker Mercedes-Benz suffered one of Germany's worst new-product launches. The company introduced its first compact car, known as the baby Benz, in September as part of a long-range plan to extend its line-up beyond the luxury-car class. But Mercedes was forced to recall the car in November after a Swedish automotive magazine reported that it tipped over when making sudden, sharp turns. The company estimated that modifications to the vehicle would cost about $170 million. In December, Mercedes delayed the launch of its Smart minicar (smaller than a subcompact) until October 1998 to correct a similar problem. The delay was expected to cost the company an additional $170 million. The incidents also damaged Mercedes's reputation for excellence.

Floods. Heavy rain caused severe flooding of the Oder River in eastern Germany in late July and early August 1997. Although the floods forced the evacuation of hundreds of people and caused about $270 million in damages, they also helped build feelings of solidarity between Germany's eastern and western regions, as soldiers and civilians from the west assisted people in the flooded areas. □ Tom Buerkle

See also **Europe** (Facts in brief table).

Ghana. See Africa.

Golf. For golf fans, the sport's crowning moment in 1997 came in April, when Eldrick (Tiger) Woods, the 21-year-old sensation playing in only his 15th professional competition, won the Masters Tournament with a performance that transcended the game. Woods's four-round total was an 18-under-par 270, the lowest score in the history of the event. It gave Woods a 12-stroke margin of victory over Tom Kite, the largest margin ever posted in a major U.S. tournament.

With the overwhelming conquest of the Masters, played at the Augusta National Golf Course in Augusta, Georgia, Woods became the youngest winner in Masters history. The victory also caused some observers to speculate that Woods was capable of winning the United States Open, the British Open, and the Professional Golfer's Association (PGA) Championship to complete golf's modern "Grand Slam." Even though he won none of these tournaments, he finished the 1997 golf season as the leading money winner, taking home $2,066,833.

The U.S. Open was held from June 12 to June 15 at the Congressional Country Club in Bethesda, Maryland, where Ernie Els shot a four-under-par score of 276 to top the field for the second straight year. The victory marked the second time that Els, a 27-year-old South African, left Colin Montgomerie of Scotland in second place, this time by one stroke. Tom Lehman took the lead into the final round, as he had done in two previous U.S. Opens, only to finish third.

The British Open, played July 17 to July 20 at Royal Troon Golf Club in Scotland, was won by Justin Leonard, a 25-year-old Texan who fired a 12-under-par tournament total of 272. Leonard took the lead after he sank a 35-foot (11-meter) birdie putt on the 17th hole of his last round. Darren Clarke and Jesper Parnevik tied for second place with a score of 275.

PGA Tour. One of 1997's most poignant moments occurred in August, when Davis Love III won the 79th PGA Championship at Winged Foot Golf Club in Mamaroneck, New York. Love had played in 312 PGA Tour events, including 39 majors, before he achieved his long-sought victory. He shot three rounds at 66 and another at 71 to finish five strokes in front of Justin Leonard.

The Vardon Trophy, awarded to the player with the lowest scoring average in PGA events during the year, was won by Nick Price, who shot an average of 68.98 during 1997. Tiger Woods was named PGA Player of the Year.

Seniors. Hale Irwin dominated the PGA Senior Tour in 1997. He won seven events, including the PGA Seniors Championship for the second straight year, and ranked first among his rivals in scoring, birdies, total driving, and hitting greens in regulation. He also ranked first among seniors in 1997 earnings—$2,343,364. Ranking second among seniors in earnings was Gil Morgan, with $2,160,562.

Women. The 1997 Ladies Professional Golf Association (LPGA) Tour offered a total of $30 million at 43 events, a new high in each category. Major LPGA titles went to four different golfers. Betsy King won the Nabisco Dinah Shore event in March by two strokes over Kris Tschetter. Chris Johnson beat Leta Lindley on the second hole of a sudden-death play-off to take the McDonald's LPGA title in May. In July, the U.S. Women's Open went to Alison Nicholas of England, who edged out Nancy Lopez by a stroke. Colleen Walker won the du Maurier Classic in August. Annika Sorenstam of Sweden, who won six events in the tour and a record $1,236,789 in 1997, was named LPGA Player of the Year.

Team. The golf season's biggest upset came in September at the 32nd Ryder Cup, held at the Valderrama Gold Club in Sotogrande, Spain (the first time the tournament was held outside the United States or Great Britain). Against an American team widely considered more talented, a European team captained by Seve Ballesteros of Spain held off a late rally to win by a score of 14.5 to 13.5.

Ben Hogan, whose 63 major golf victories included nine major championships, died on July 25 at the age of 84. Hogan is best remembered for winning the 1950 U.S. Open only 16 months after being in a near-fatal auto accident.　　　□ Ron Reid

Gore, Al. See People in the news.
Great Britain. See United Kingdom.

Greece made significant progress toward economic stability in 1997. The government of Prime Minister Costas Simitis sought to break the country's cycle of excessive public spending, high inflation, and devaluation by reducing the budget deficit and defending the value of the currency, the drachma.

Under budget measures adopted in early 1997, the government introduced a property tax and other levies, stopped indexing income tax rates for inflation, pledged to replace only one in five retiring civil servants, and lowered public subsidies for state-owned companies. The "hard-drachma" policy cut inflation and the budget deficit to levels unseen since the early 1970's. Inflation fell to 4.7 percent in late 1997, and the European Commission, the executive arm of the European Union (EU)—a group of 15 Western European nations—forecast that the deficit in 1997 would fall to 4.2 percent of *gross domestic product* (GDP—the value of all goods and services produced in a country in a given year). Both rates had stood at more than 10 percent in 1994.

In November 1997, the government introduced a 1998 budget designed to prepare Greece to join the single European currency in 2001, two years after most EU countries planned to launch the currency. The budget included new tax increases, plans to privatize state-owned companies, and limited pay increases for civil servants to below the rate of inflation. It aimed to cut inflation to 2.5 percent and to

reduce the deficit from 4.2 percent in 1997 to 2.4 percent of GDP in 1998, below the 3-percent ceiling for countries adopting the single currency.

Olympic victory. The country's reform efforts won a seal of approval when the International Olympic Committee voted on Sept. 5, 1997, to award the 2004 Summer Olympic Games to Athens, which defeated rival bids from Rome, Cape Town, Stockholm, and Buenos Aires. The victory restored civic pride hurt when Greece lost its bid for the centennial games of 1996 to Atlanta, Georgia.

Relations with Turkey, Greece's long-time rival, remained volatile during 1997. Foreign Minister Theodoros Pangalos endorsed Turkey's goal of membership in the EU in March. But tension flared later in the year over Cyprus, when the divided island's Greek Cypriot government decided to buy Russian antiaircraft missiles. Turkey had stationed troops in northern Cyprus since 1974 and considered the missile purchase a provocation. Relations deteriorated further in December 1997 when Turkey, which had been rejected for EU membership, refused an offer to participate in a conference with EU countries and potential members from Eastern Europe. At Greece's urging, the EU had stipulated that Turkey could join the conference only if it improved its human-rights record and submitted its territorial disputes with Greece to international arbitration.　　□ Tom Buerkle

See also **Europe** (Facts in brief table); **Turkey.**

Guatemala. Guatemalans enjoyed a year of peace in 1997 following the signing of peace accords on Dec. 29, 1996, between the government and rebel leaders. The treaty, brokered by the United Nations (UN), ended 36 years of civil war. On Jan. 22, 1997, the Inter-American Development Bank and other international-aid donors pledged $1.9 billion to help rebuild devastated areas of Guatemala.

On January 20, the UN authorized a 155-member military force to monitor compliance with key provisions of the accords. On March 3, the UN began overseeing the disarmament of some 3,600 former guerrilla combatants and reintroducing them, their families, and sympathizers into Guatemalan society. The UN forces also oversaw the reduction by one-third of Guatemala's 46,000-member armed forces.

During 1997, a law providing blanket amnesty for all those who committed crimes during the civil strife came under fire from human-rights organizations. The Guatemalan Congress had passed the law in 1996 just before the signing of the peace accords.

In May 1997, the U.S. Central Intelligence Agency declassified 1,400 pages of files that revealed the agency's role in the 1954 *coup* (takeover) that ousted democratically elected President Jacobo Arbenz Guzmán. Authorities have cited the coup as a primary cause of the civil war.　　□ Nathan A. Haverstock

See also **Latin America** (Facts in brief table).
Guinea. See Africa.

Guyana. Janet Rosenberg Jagan was elected to a five-year term as president of Guyana on Dec. 15, 1997. Jagan—the widow of former President Cheddi Jagan, who died on March 6—was the first woman to become president of Guyana.

Cheddi Jagan, whose parents immigrated to Guyana (then British Guiana) from India, and Janet Jagan, who was born in Chicago, founded the People's Progressive Party in 1950 and were influential in gaining the colony's independence from Great Britain in 1966. Cheddi Jagan had been sworn in as president in 1992.

After Cheddi Jagan's death in March 1997, Prime Minister Samuel Hinds was sworn in as the interim president, and Janet Jagan was appointed prime minister and first vice president. In the presidential campaign, opponents made an issue out of the fact that Jagan had not been born in Guyana. Her supporters, however, cited her years of dedication to Guyana and the fact that she had renounced her U.S. citizenship.

A Canadian company, Exploration Bre-X, announced in early 1997 that it had acquired Guyanese gold and diamond properties and agreed to invest at least $250,000 in exploration and development. The Guyanese government earned a 5-percent royalty on all mining production in 1997.

☐ Nathan A. Haverstock

See also **Latin America** (Facts in brief table).

Haiti. Political turmoil paralyzed the Haitian government for much of 1997. Prime Minister Rosny Smarth resigned on June 9 under pressure from political rivals who supported former President Jean-Bertrand Aristide. Smarth had charged that Aristide's followers had rigged elections held on April 6.

On August 26, Parliament rejected President René Préval's nominee for prime minister, Eric Pierre. Préval then nominated economist Hervé Denis, but by the end of 1997, the Haitian parliament had not approved the nomination.

Because of the conflict, Préval, was unable to move ahead with plans to privatize nine state enterprises—a condition set by the international donors that provide 60 percent of the Haitian government's budget. Parliament was also unable to agree on how to allocate at least $100 million in foreign aid.

United Nations peacekeeping forces, which had arrived in March 1995, departed in December 1997. A 300-member multinational police force remained to assist the Haitian National Police. About 500 U.S. military personnel also remained, primarily to assist with improvements in roads and bridges.

On September 8, an overloaded ferryboat sank in shallow waters off Haiti's western coast, killing at least 245 passengers.   ☐ Nathan A. Haverstock

See also **Latin America** (Facts in brief table).

Harness racing. See Horse racing.

Hawaii. See State government.

Health-care issues. On June 26, 1997, the United States Supreme Court ruled unanimously that, while terminally ill patients do not have a constitutional right to commit suicide with the assistance of their physicians, states were free to create laws allowing or banning the practice. The court decision upheld New York State and Washington State laws prohibiting physician-assisted suicide. The decision also let stand an Oregon law, approved by voters in 1994, allowing physician-assisted suicide. The Oregon statute was the only such law in the nation in 1997, but it had not been implemented because of legal challenges in lower courts.

In November, Oregon voters reaffirmed their support for the assisted-suicide law by defeating a ballot initiative that would have repealed it. However, the controversy over the Oregon law continued as the U.S. Drug Enforcement Administration warned Oregon physicians that they risked losing their medical licenses if they prescribed drugs to help patients end their lives.

Children's health insurance. In August, U.S. President Bill Clinton signed into law a program designed to help states expand health insurance for children. The U.S. Congress approved $50 billion to fund the program between 1998 and 2007. States were to provide additional funds. Congress estimated that as many as 2.5 million uninsured children in the United States would gain health insurance coverage under the program.

Critics of the program charged that it was too expensive and that it would lure middle-class people out of privately funded insurance. Uninsured children from families with incomes as high as twice the federally defined poverty level were to be eligible for the program.

Health-care bill of rights. In November 1997, a 34-member commission of experts appointed by President Clinton proposed a plan setting detailed federal standards for all health insurance programs and health insurance companies. The plan, called the "Consumer Bill of Rights," was designed to address such common complaints of patients as being denied insurance coverage for certain medical procedures and being unable to obtain sufficient information about health-care providers. The commission included members from business and labor organizations and from the health-care and insurance industries.

The commission proposed that patients be allowed to appeal denials of health care procedures or insurance coverage to an independent arbiter. The commission also stated that patients have a right to obtain a wide range of information to evaluate the quality of services provided by physicians, hospitals, and health plans.

President Clinton called on Congress to enact legislation based on the proposals. Insurance companies claimed that the proposals would drive up premiums and force people to drop coverage.

Hobbies

Trouble for Columbia/HCA. In July, the top two executives of Columbia/HCA Healthcare Corporation of Nashville, Tennessee, the largest for-profit hospital firm in the United States, resigned in the midst of a federal investigation into the company's billing and other business practices. The federal investigation, which began in March with raids into Columbia facilities in seven states, uncovered evidence of possible fraudulent billing of the *Medicare* and *Medicaid* programs (federal programs that pay for health care for elderly and poor Americans). In July, a federal grand jury indicted three Columbia officials accused of overcharging expenses at a Florida hospital in order to increase the hospital's compensation from federal health-care programs.

By late 1997, a total of 11 of Columbia's top 14 officials had resigned. In November, Columbia announced that it planned to either sell or *spin off* (redistribute the stocks of) approximately one-third of its more than 340 hospitals. The federal investigation of Columbia continued into 1998.

Surgeon General nominee. In September 1997, President Bill Clinton nominated David Satcher, director of the Centers for Disease Control and Prevention in Atlanta, Georgia, as Surgeon General of the United States. The post had been vacant since January 1995. □ Emily Friedman

See also **Medicine**.

Hobbies. See Toys and games.

Hockey.
After a frustrating, 42-year drought, the Detroit Red Wings finally recaptured the Stanley Cup to become the 1996-1997 champions of the National Hockey League (NHL). Although five other teams had won more games than Detroit during the regular season, the Wings's combination of speed, power, and stifling defense resulted in a succession of dominating performances in the play-offs.

Season. In contrast to the previous season, when Detroit set an NHL record by winning 62 of 82 games during the regular season, the Red Wings managed just 38 victories in 1996-1997. They finished 10 points behind the Dallas Stars in the Central Division of the NHL's Western Conference. The defending champion Colorado Avalanche compiled the league's highest total for victories (49) and points (107) and won the Pacific Division title. Competition in the Eastern Conference was considerably closer. The New Jersey Devils edged the Philadelphia Flyers by just one point to take the Atlantic Division title, and the Buffalo Sabres finished 8 points ahead of the Pittsburgh Penguins to win the Northeast Division crown.

Play-offs. Philadelphia also made up for several disappointing seasons by reaching the Stanley Cup final series for the first time since 1974-1975. To get there, the Flyers defeated Pittsburgh, Buffalo, and the New York Rangers, each by a margin of 4 games to 1. Detroit traveled a harder road, beating the St. Louis Blues (4 games to 2), Anaheim Mighty Ducks (4

National Hockey League standings

Western Conference

Central Division

	W.	L.	T.	Pts.
Dallas Stars*	48	26	8	104
Detroit Red Wings*	38	26	18	94
Phoenix Coyotes*	38	37	7	83
St. Louis Blues*	36	35	11	83
Chicago Blackhawks*	34	35	13	81
Toronto Maple Leafs	30	44	8	68

Pacific Division

	W.	L.	T.	Pts.
Colorado Avalanche*	49	24	9	107
Anaheim Mighty Ducks*	36	33	13	85
Edmonton Oilers*	36	37	9	81
Vancouver Canucks	35	40	7	77
Calgary Flames	32	41	9	73
Los Angeles Kings	28	43	11	67
San Jose Sharks	27	47	8	62

Eastern Conference

Northeast Division

	W.	L.	T.	Pts.
Buffalo Sabres*	40	30	12	92
Pittsburgh Penguins*	38	36	8	84
Ottawa Senators*	31	36	15	77
Montreal Canadiens*	31	36	15	77
Hartford Whalers	32	39	11	75
Boston Bruins	26	47	9	61

Atlantic Division

	W.	L.	T.	Pts.
New Jersey Devils*	45	23	14	104
Philadelphia Flyers*	45	24	13	103
Florida Panthers*	35	28	19	89
New York Rangers*	38	34	10	86
Washington Capitals	33	40	9	75
Tampa Bay Lightning	32	40	10	74
New York Islanders	29	41	12	70

*Made play-offs

Stanley Cup champions—
Detroit Red Wings (defeated Philadelphia Flyers, 4 games to 0)

Leading scorers	Games	Goals	Assists	Pts.
Mario Lemieux, Pittsburgh	76	50	72	122
Teemu Selanne, Anaheim	78	51	58	109
Paul Kariya, Anaheim	69	44	55	99
John LeClair, Philadelphia	82	50	47	97
Wayne Gretzky, N.Y. Rangers	82	25	72	97

Leading goalies (25 or more games)	Games	Goals against	Avg.
Martin Brodeur, New Jersey	67	120	1.88
Andy Moog, Dallas	48	98	2.15
Jeff Hackett, Chicago	41	89	2.16
Dominik Hasek, Buffalo	67	153	2.27
John Vanbiesbrouck, Florida	57	128	2.29

Awards

Adams Trophy (coach of the year)—Ted Nolan, Buffalo
Calder Trophy (best rookie)—Bryan Berard, N.Y. Islanders
Hart Trophy (most valuable player)—Dominik Hasek, Buffalo
Jennings Trophy (team with fewest goals against)—Martin Brodeur and Mike Dunham, New Jersey
Lady Byng Trophy (sportsmanship)—Paul Kariya, Anaheim
Lester B. Pearson Award (best player as voted by NHL players)—Dominik Hasek, Buffalo
Masterton Trophy (perseverance, dedication to hockey)—Tony Granato, San Jose
Norris Trophy (best defenseman)—Brian Leetch, N.Y. Rangers
Ross Trophy (leading scorer)—Mario Lemieux, Pittsburgh
Selke Trophy (best defensive forward)—Michael Peca, Buffalo
Smythe Trophy (most valuable player in Stanley Cup)—Mike Vernon, Detroit
Vezina Trophy (best goalkeeper)—Dominik Hasek, Buffalo

Red Wings coach Scotty Bowman raises the Stanley Cup in triumph after guiding Detroit to the 1997 NHL title—the team's first since 1955.

to 0, with three of the games decided in overtime), and Colorado, the team that had ousted the Red Wings the season before (4 to 2).

The final series was an unexpected mismatch that resulted in the 19th series sweep in NHL his-tory. The series was an embarrassment for the Flyers' star defenseman and team captain Eric Lindross, who scored only one goal, and for coach Terry Murray, who was fired six days after the final game.

Detroit's victory celebration proved short-lived, however. Three days after the team's victory parade before 1 million fans in Detroit, defenseman Vladimir Konstantinov was severely injured in a limousine crash that also injured his teammate, Slava Fetisov, and the team masseur, Sergei Mnatsakanov.

"Super Mario" retires. Mario Lemieux, star center for the Pittsburgh Penguins and one of hockey's all-time greats, retired in May 1997. During his stellar 12-year career, Lemieux, 31, led the NHL in scoring six times despite undergoing two back surgeries and a battle with Hodgkin's disease, a type of cancer. In November, Lemieux was inducted into the Hockey Hall of Fame, skipping the mandatory three-year waiting period after retirement.

International. Canada won hockey's world championship, held in May 1997 in Helsinki, Finland. In the five games preceding the medal round, Canada outscored its rivals 21-6. For the championship, Canada beat Sweden in a best-of-three final. □ Ron Reid

Honduras. Carlos Roberto Flores, a member of the Liberal Party and president of the Honduran National Assembly, was elected to a four-year term as president of Honduras on Nov. 30, 1997. Flores defeated the National Party candidate Nora de Melgar, the first woman to head a major party ticket in Honduras. Flores replaced President Carlos Roberto Reina, also of the Liberal Party.

On August 11, some 700 prisoners escaped after riots broke out at prisons in Santa Barbara and Trujillo in northern Honduras. Most of the escaped inmates either surrendered or were recaptured. On August 14, two inmates were killed in rioting at a prison in Santa Rosa de Copán. The riots brought attention to the living conditions within many Honduran prisons and the plight of inmates often held without being formally charged with crimes.

In January, the Pan American Health Organization (PAHO), a United Nation's affiliate, announced that some 300,000 Hondurans were among the more than 16 million people in Latin America who suffered from Chagas' disease, an infectious disorder that can lead to chronic heart failure. The disease, caused by a parasitic microorganism, is transmitted by the bite of certain insects that are commonly found in houses with dirt floors. PAHO predicted that 65,000 Hondurans would die from the disease by 1999. □ Nathan A. Haverstock

See also **Latin America** (Facts in brief table).

Hong Kong 1997:
Capitalism Comes to China

The British colony of Hong Kong, a community
that flourished on unfettered capitalism, returned
on June 30, 1997, to the sovereignty of China, the
world's largest and most powerful Communist state.

By Graham Thomas

Fireworks light up the sky over Hong Kong at midnight on June 30, 1997, to celebrate the handover of the British colony to the People's Republic of China. Chinese President Jiang Zemin, Prince Charles, and British Prime Minister Tony Blair, *inset,* attend the ceremony marking the transfer of power.

On June 30, 1997, millions of people around the world watched, via television, the pomp and spectacle of the ceremony in which the United Kingdom returned Hong Kong to the People's Republic of China. At the stroke of midnight, the control of one of the world's most important commercial centers shifted from a democratic, capitalist country to a Communist state with no tradition of constitutional law. Many viewers recalled another television broadcast in 1989, during which they watched Chinese troops attack students in Beijing's Tiananmen Square who were demonstrating against official corruption and demanding democracy in China. With these two televised images in mind, business people, politicians, economists, and others wondered what effect the Chinese communist government would have on the lifestyles, business practices, and freedoms of the nearly 6 million citizens of Hong Kong. But they also wondered what effect the Hong Kong citizens would have on the lives of their more than 1 billion fellow Chinese citizens.

British rule of Hong Kong

The conditions of the handover of Hong Kong from British to Chinese rule were established by the Sino-British Joint Declaration of 1984. This agreement called for a Chinese policy of "one country, two systems"—socialism in China and capitalism in Hong Kong. The success of that policy for another 50 years—the length of time stipulated in the 1984 agreement—was expected to influence not only the Chinese and Hong Kong economies but also international relations within in Asia and around the world.

The total land area of Hong Kong that was returned to Chinese sovereignty in 1997 had come under British control in three stages. In 1842, Hong Kong Island was ceded *in perpetuity* (forever) to Britain by the Treaty of Nanjing at the end of the First Opium War. The British had fought the war in retaliation against Chinese attempts to end the illegal opium trade that British merchants conducted with smugglers and corrupt Chinese officials. The British also opposed restrictions on legal trade that the Chinese government had imposed at the end of the 1700's. The Treaty of Nanjing gave Britain the best natural harbor in southern China and an ideal base for trade with the mainland, free of the official restrictions of the Chinese government. The defeat also heralded more than a century of Chinese humiliation, during which an increasingly weak China additionally lost territory to Russia, Japan, and the maritime powers of Europe.

The second stage of the formation of modern Hong Kong occurred in 1861 at the end of the Second Opium War, which Britain fought in alliance with France. The British gained the Kowloon Peninsula, which is a part of the mainland opposite Hong Kong Island, and the tiny Stonecutters Island, also "in perpetuity." In 1898, Britain took a 99-year lease on the much larger New Territories, an area of the mainland that is adjacent to Kowloon, as well as more than 235 small islands. The New Territories made up over 90 percent of the land area of the British colony. Long before 1997, when the lease on the New Territories was due to expire, all three parts of Hong Kong had grown into one economic and social unit. Negotiations between the United Kingdom and China over the handover of Hong Kong did not distinguish the New Territories from Hong Kong Island and the Kowloon Peninsula, which according to international treaties (that the Chinese did not recognize) were forever British.

A different kind of colony

While in name a colony, Hong Kong was a place to which few British people migrated. Hong Kong from the outset was a center for free trade, where merchants from around the world were at liberty to conduct business under the rule of British law, but with little government restriction. British merchants and bankers took full advantage of Hong Kong's economic freedoms to develop business and trade with China and the rest of East Asia.

To the surprise of the British, the Chinese also flocked to Hong Kong to escape conflict on the mainland and to benefit from the

The author

Graham Thomas is Head of the Briefing Office of the School of Oriental and African Studies at the University of London and teaches modern Chinese history.

Hong Kong since 1839

1839–1842   **First Opium War:** Britain fights China over a Chinese ban on opium trade and takes possession of Hong Kong Island.

1856–1860   **Second Opium War:** The British defeat the Chinese and take possession of the Kowloon Peninsula and Stonecutters Island.

1898   **New Territories:** Britain signs a 99-year lease for the New Territories, an area of the mainland, and more than 235 islands.

1941–1945   **Japanese occupation:** The Japanese occupy Hong Kong during World War II.

1949   **Communist revolution:** The Communists establish the People's Republic of China. Hundreds of thousands of Chinese immigrate to Hong Kong.

1959–1962   **Great Leap Forward:** Economic reforms in China cause widespread famine, and thousands of Chinese people flee to Hong Kong.

1984   **Sino-British Joint Declaration:** China and Great Britain agree to the terms of the 1997 handover of Hong Kong to China.

1989   **Tiananmen Square demonstrations:** The Chinese military kills hundreds of prodemocracy protesters, raising concerns about the rights of the people of Hong Kong after the 1997 handover.

1997   **Change of sovereignty:** At midnight on June 30, British control of the colony ends, and Hong Kong becomes a special administrative region of China.

The flag of the Hong Kong Special Administrative Region, *left bottom,* replaces the British colonial flag.

colony's political stability and economic freedom. The number of Chinese residents in Hong Kong rose from approximately 30,000 in 1851 to almost 860,000 in 1931, when the British population numbered less than 20,000. By 1939, another 750,000 Chinese had arrived as refugees from the war that Japan had been waging against China for two years. The flow of immigrants reversed when the Japanese occupied Hong Kong in December 1941 and held it until the end of World War II (1939–1945). During 1948 and 1949, hundreds of thousands of Chinese flooded back into the colony to escape the chaos of the civil war between Chiang Kai-shek's Nationalist Party and the Chinese Communists. By 1950, the population of Hong Kong had mushroomed to an estimated 2.2 million people. In 1997, the majority of the nearly 6 million people were of Chinese ancestry.

After the Communist government took control of China in 1949, Hong Kong remained under British control, but the Chinese government did not recognize British sovereignty over the territory. Consequently, China had no official diplomatic relations with Hong Kong. The Chinese government did, however, assign diplomats as "editors" to the Hong Kong offices of the Xinhua News Agency, the news service of the People's Republic of China. Also after 1949, China established companies in Hong Kong to represent Chinese state-owned trading corporations.

Rise to economic power

Hong Kong's rise to an economic center of global importance began between 1948 and 1950 with the influx of businessmen from Shanghai, then a much more important commercial center than Hong Kong. The new arrivals were refugees from the Communist government. The immigrants' entrepreneurial skills and manufacturing know-how enabled Hong Kong to industrialize rapidly. Their efforts launched what was to become one of the most competitive economies in Asia. At first, Hong Kong produced textiles, clothing, and plastic flowers. Later, companies began producing more technologically advanced goods—consumer electronic products, watches and clocks, and computer components. The growth of industry proved to be critical for Hong Kong's post-World War II economic boom.

The next crucial development in Hong Kong's rise to economic leadership came when Communist leader Deng Xiaoping rose to power in China. In

1979, Deng introduced an "open-door policy" designed to accelerate China's economic development by opening its economy to the world. The reform policy established "special economic zones," cities in which special regulations and incentives were designed to attract foreign capital.

During those changes in China's economic policy, Hong Kong became a link between China and foreign investors and corporations. That new role helped Hong Kong to develop into a major manufacturing, trading, and financial center. By 1997, Hong Kong was the world's busiest container port and a leading financial center, ranking third after New York and London. In 1996, Hong Kong's per capita gross domestic product (GDP) was valued at $24,282 —higher than the GDP of Canada, Australia, or the United Kingdom. (GDP is the total monetary value of goods and services produced, minus the net payments on foreign investments.)

Effect of Chinese economic reforms

Beijing's economic reforms benefited the Chinese economy as well as Hong Kong's, particularly in the neighboring Chinese province of Guangdong, where Hong Kong manufacturers took advantage of cheaper land values and lower labor costs. By the early 1980's, Hong Kong companies employed 3 million Chinese citizens in its factories in Guangdong. By the mid-1990's, they employed 4 million Chinese workers. The Special Economic Zone of Shenzhen, a city directly across the border from Hong Kong, grew from a city of 20,000 in 1978 to a modern, industrial metropolis of approximately 2 million people by the early 1990's.

Hong Kong was China's biggest foreign direct investor from the beginning of the "open-door policy." By 1993, the total worth of Hong Kong-financed investment projects in China exceeded $76 trillion. Hong Kong investments accounted for 60 to 80 percent of foreign direct investment in China. And while Hong Kong-financed projects accounted for less than 5 percent of China's total output of goods and services, these companies produced two-thirds of China's exports.

As Hong Kong's manufacturing activities shifted across the border into China, Hong Kong developed into an important interna-

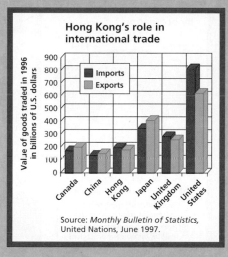

Hong Kong's role in international trade

Source: *Monthly Bulletin of Statistics,* United Nations, June 1997.

A world trade giant

Hong Kong, the busiest container port in the world, is a major player in international trade and exceeds China in its annual volume of imports and exports. Ships in 1997 fill Victoria Harbor, *below,* the hub of trade that lies between Hong Kong Island and the Kowloon Peninsula.

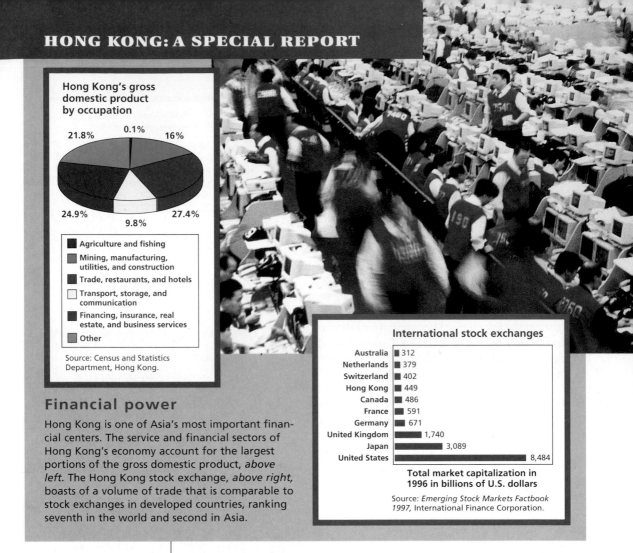

Hong Kong's gross domestic product by occupation

- 0.1%
- 16%
- 21.8%
- 27.4%
- 9.8%
- 24.9%

Legend:
- Agriculture and fishing
- Mining, manufacturing, utilities, and construction
- Trade, restaurants, and hotels
- Transport, storage, and communication
- Financing, insurance, real estate, and business services
- Other

Source: Census and Statistics Department, Hong Kong.

Financial power

Hong Kong is one of Asia's most important financial centers. The service and financial sectors of Hong Kong's economy account for the largest portions of the gross domestic product, *above left.* The Hong Kong stock exchange, *above right,* boasts of a volume of trade that is comparable to stock exchanges in developed countries, ranking seventh in the world and second in Asia.

International stock exchanges

Country	Value
Australia	312
Netherlands	379
Switzerland	402
Hong Kong	449
Canada	486
France	591
Germany	671
United Kingdom	1,740
Japan	3,089
United States	8,484

Total market capitalization in 1996 in billions of U.S. dollars

Source: *Emerging Stock Markets Factbook 1997,* International Finance Corporation.

tional business center. By the mid-1990's, the service sector accounted for approximately 75 percent of Hong Kong's GDP and employed about 70 percent of the work force. The colony became not only an international conduit to Chinese businesses, but also a center of learning for officials of Chinese enterprises involved in international trade and investment. By 1997, Hong Kong was China's most important trade and investment partner, its most important provider of business services, and a key contributor to its modernization effort.

Hong Kong had also become the linchpin of "greater China." The close economic ties of trade, technology transfers, and investment had made Hong Kong a crucial link between a rapidly developing southern China and Taiwan, the home of the Chinese Nationalist government. Despite the fact that China, Hong Kong, and Taiwan were politically distinct, the economies of all three had become more economically integrated since China's reform policies were introduced. By 1997, China, Hong Kong, and Taiwan—if considered as a single economic entity—had the world's third largest *gross national product* (total value of goods and services produced) and the largest foreign exchange reserves and trade turnover. They were also the third largest exporter to the United States after Canada and Japan.

In addition to gaining such a huge economic asset, Chinese leaders saw the transfer of power as a means to demonstrate to the people of Taiwan that they would be granted the same freedoms as Hong Kong if Taiwan returned to Chinese sovereignty. In 1997, the Hong Kong Special Administrative Region, the official title after the handover, continued to function as a *laissez faire economy* (an economy with minimal government regulations). After the handover, China and Hong Kong remained separate economic entities and continued to operate as if they were foreign trade and investment partners.

Speculation about Hong Kong's future

During 1997, however, many people debated whether the "one country, two systems" policy would work and whether Hong Kong would continue to be an economic asset. Hong Kong's elite business and professional community, foreign business people, prodemocracy leaders in Hong Kong, and the international media all speculated about the future of Hong Kong. If Communist China were to continue the "one country, two systems" policy for 50 years as planned, China could enhance Hong Kong's status as a metropolitan economy with its crucial role in the development of greater China. Hong Kong's economic dynamism would likely reinforce its preeminence in southern China and its position in the global economy. If, however, China failed to maintain the laissez faire system, China could

Crowded high-rise apartment buildings provide housing for the majority of Hong Kong's 6.5 million residents. The increasing demand for housing in Hong Kong has resulted in some of the highest real estate prices in the world. The new chief executive of Hong Kong, Tung Chee-hwa, announced in his inaugural address on July 1, 1997, that the regional government would take "resolute action" to provide new housing and to lower property costs.

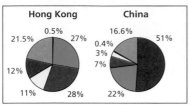

Hong Kong's and China's work forces compared by occupation

Hong Kong

0.5%
21.5%
27%
12%
11%
28%

Size of active work force in 1995: **2,970,500.**

China

16.6%
0.4%
3%
7%
51%
22%

Size of active work force in 1995: **644,330,000.**

- ■ Agriculture, fishing, and forestry
- ■ Mining, manufacturing, utilities, and construction
- ■ Trade, restaurants, and hotels
- ☐ Transport, storage, and communication
- ■ Financing, insurance, real estate, and business services
- ▨ Other

Sources: State Statistical Bureau, People's Republic of China; Census and Statistics Department, Hong Kong.

Earning a living

The percentage of people employed in service-related jobs and in agriculture varies greatly between Hong Kong's work force and China's. Agricultural employees in China, *below left,* represent more than half of China's work force. Business people and service-related employees in Hong Kong, *below right,* make up the vast majority of its relatively small work force.

damage the territory's role as a leading international business center. As a consequence, Hong Kong could decline to a regional trading center for Guangdong, overshadowed (as it was before World War II) by Shanghai, which began to regain its economic preeminence in China in the 1990's.

The international media and prodemocracy leaders, in particular, raised concerns about China's restrictions on free speech and open political disagreement. Many argued that the freedoms provided under the rule of law during British colonialism were necessary to fuel the economy's dynamism. Repressing those rights, some leaders maintained, could trigger a flight of capital from Hong Kong and an exodus of thousands of the highly educated and skilled people crucial to the functioning of Hong Kong as a business center. The Chinese leadership could also damage Hong Kong's attractiveness to international business by favoring business people and companies with strong personal and political connections to powerful factions in China.

The large-scale corruption pervasive in China could be equally damaging to Hong Kong. In 1996, an independent ranking of Asia's business environments listed Hong Kong as one of Asia's least corrupt environments after Singapore and Japan. The colony's ability to keep corruption relatively low had been due to its Independent Commission Against Corruption (ICAC) and the public support that the commission enjoyed. Economic analysts considered

the ICAC's autonomy and its public support after the handover crucial to preventing corruption in the business community.

Further speculation suggested that if China were to tolerate a genuinely autonomous Hong Kong, both the economic and political gains for China could be enormous. China would continue to benefit from the contribution that Hong Kong had already made to its modernization and to its increasing integration into the world economy. Additionally, over time the process of economic modernization in China could create a middle class of business and professional people large and confident enough to demand a share of political power in a democratic political framework. If the modernization of China were to lead to such changes, Hong Kong could serve as a model of a successfully functioning political unit run by Chinese on Chinese soil and characterized by a degree of democracy and the rule of law. This influence, however, would run counter to the "one country, two systems" formula, since the policy is based on the assumption that neither system should be allowed to undermine the other. Such significant political changes also presuppose a willingness on the part of the Chinese Communist Party to give up its monopoly on power and to introduce a multiparty political system. At the time of the handover, there was no evidence that such a situation would be likely to develop in the near future.

Possible effects on international commerce

Respecting the autonomy of Hong Kong could also positively affect China's relations with Southeast Asian countries. Such behavior toward Hong Kong would most likely reassure Vietnam, the Philippines, Indonesia, Malaysia, and Thailand—countries acutely conscious of China's growing economic and political weight in the region. Furthermore, Asian nations might be more willing to respect China's desire to bring Taiwan under Chinese sovereignty if the Chinese government were to honor the agreements of the Hong Kong handover. If China were to exert more control over Hong Kong, however, Southeast Asian countries' apprehensions regarding China would be intensified. Also, the Chinese communities in other Asian countries might reconsider the closeness of their ties with their ancestral homeland. If China were isolated, from within or without, the stability and increasing economic integration of the whole Southeast Asia region would be impaired.

China's relations with the United States and Japan would also be likely to improve if Hong Kong remained autonomous. The integration of business in the entire Asia-Pacific region could be accelerated and China's general international standing enhanced. However, if China were to infringe on Hong Kong's autonomy, the U.S. government in particular would likely be disturbed by potential damage to the territory in which American businesses have much invested. The United States would also be concerned about the effects of such a

Ranking the quality of life	
Canada	1
United States	4
Japan	7
United Kingdom	15
Hong Kong	22
Uzbekistan	100
China	108
El Salvador	112

Source: Human Development Index in the United Nations *Human Development Report 1997*.

Quality of life in Hong Kong versus China

The United Nations ranks nations and dependent territories on a scale called the human development index. The index is based on life expectancy, literacy and level of education, and standard of living. In 1997, Hong Kong ranked with the world's developed nations. China's rank was comparable to those of small, developing countries.

Political changes in China's Hong Kong

- **Protests and demonstrations:** On July 18, 1997, the Hong Kong government gave regional police the power to regulate public protests and ban demonstrations threatening "national security."

- **Legislature:** On July 1, 1997, a 60-member, Beijing-appointed Provisional Legislative Council replaced Hong Kong's democratically elected Legislative Council. Future members would be partly chosen in direct elections and partly by an electoral college and members of the business and professional community.

- **Justice system:** On July 1, 1997, a new Court of Final Appeal replaced the highest appeal court of the United Kingdom. Legal experts expected complications as new laws were passed after the handover.

Thousands of Hong Kong demonstrators participate in a candlelight vigil on June 4, 1996, to commemorate the deaths of prodemocracy protesters in Beijing's Tiananmen Square in 1989. After the 1997 handover, prodemocracy leaders questioned whether the Chinese government would permit future commemorative gatherings.

policy on Taiwan and might respond by changing the official U.S. policy toward both China and Hong Kong. In 1992, the U.S. Congress passed the United States-Hong Kong Policy Act requiring the U.S. government to deal with Hong Kong "as a separate territory in economic and trade matters." If the Chinese were to disregard the "one country, two systems" policy, U.S. leaders might seek to reverse the 1992 measure and treat Hong Kong as simply another province of China.

In 1997, Hong Kong's role in international commerce seemed secure by almost any measure. The number of foreign corporations with regional headquarters in Hong Kong had grown from 581 to 793 between 1990 and 1995. Hong Kong had the world's seventh largest and Asia's second largest stock market and the world's fifth largest foreign exchange market. Hong Kong had also become a center for project finance, fund management, and stock market analysis for the whole Asian region. It was home to Asia's largest community of professional specialists crucial to business—from lawyers and accountants to construction engineers, architects, and realtors. At the time of the handover, however, Hong

Chinese President Jiang Zemin, while delivering a speech in Beijing on July 1, 1997, called upon Taiwan to follow Hong Kong's lead and to embrace the "complete reunification" of China.

Kong's prosperity was dependent on continuing economic growth in China, since it was China's vast market that attracted Western business. Also, Hong Kong's ability to maintain its cost competitiveness against rival centers in China and the rest of Asia would affect the prosperity of Hong Kong in the years after the handover.

The test for China

The return of Hong Kong to Chinese sovereignty occurred while China was undergoing fundamental transformations. It was changing from a rural society with an inward-looking perspective to an urban society with a more international outlook. The economy had begun to move from self-reliance to international interdependence. Also, the foundations of the rule of law were being laid, at least in relation to the practice of international business. But such changes had a long way to go before they could have been considered irreversible.

In 1997, China was developing into a nation with an economy comparable to those of the United States, Western Europe, Japan, and Hong Kong. The policies and actions of the Chinese leadership toward Hong Kong would likely test their willingness and ability to move China away from a system in which economic success depended to a great extent on personal connections, political favoritism, and corrupt practices. If Hong Kong, on the other hand, were forced to fit the pattern of an only partially reformed, semimodern, one-party state, Hong Kong could become more like China. At the end of a ceremony marking one of history's most unusual and controversial transfers of power, the world waited to see how China's dealings with Hong Kong for the next 50 years would influence the economic and political environment of Asia and the wider world. ■ ■ ■

Horse racing captivated public attention in June 1997, when a potential Triple Crown winner emerged for the first time in 19 years. Nevertheless, race track attendance continued to slide in 1997, because of competition from the growing casino and riverboat gambling industry. In September, the chairman of Arlington International Race Course near Chicago said economics had forced the cancellation of racing at the track in 1998. In late 1997, the racing world mourned the passing of jockey Eddie Arcaro, two-time winner of the Triple Crown, who died on November 14, at age 81.

Four-year-old Skip Away became a favorite for horse-of-the-year honors with a record-smashing victory in the Breeder's Cup Classic, which raised his lifetime earnings to $6,876,000. Another candidate, Favorite Trick, possibly the best 2-year-old since Secretariat, won the Breeder's Cup Juvenile to finish unbeaten in his first season of racing. However, 1997 was a sad year for Cigar, the 1995 and 1996 horse of the year. In May 1997, Cigar's owners filed a $25-million infertility insurance claim after 34 attempts to breed him failed.

Three-year-olds. Silver Charm, a bargain-priced horse with a modest pedigree, focused public attention on horse racing in May, when he won the Kentucky Derby and the Preakness Stakes, the first two legs of the Triple Crown. Silver Charm won the Kentucky Derby by a head over Captain Bodgit and two weeks later won the Preakness, again by a head. Free House was second and Captain Bodgit third, in what was the closest Preakness finish in 65 years. At the Belmont Stakes on June 7, however, Silver Charm's bid to become the 12th horse to win the Triple Crown fell short by less than a length, when Touch Gold pulled ahead in the final 70 yards. The last Triple Crown winner was Affirmed in 1978. The near 20-year stretch without a Triple Crown winner was exceeded in length only by the 25-year drought between Citation in 1948 and Secretariat in 1973.

Harness. On Aug. 9, 1997, at Meadowlands Race Track in East Rutherford, New Jersey, the $1-million Hambletonian was won by Malabar Man, the favorite, who came into the race with 19 wins in 21 starts. Malvern Burroughs, the real estate developer who had helped build the Meadowlands track, became the second amateur driver to win the Hambletonian.

International. Jerry Bailey, who led all jockeys with more than $17 million in earnings for 1997, won the $4 million Dubai World Cup on April 3 in the United Arab Emirates. Bailey's mount was Singspiel, a 5-year-old, Irish-bred horse.

On April 5, the prestigious Grand National Steeplechase in Liverpool, England, was postponed by a bomb threat. Police were forced to evacuate the Aintree Race Course just 30 minutes before the race. On April 7, Lord Gyllene, a 14-to-1 shot ridden by Tony Dobbin, won the race by 25 lengths, amid the tightest security ever staged at a sporting event in Great Britain. □ Ron Reid

Hospital. See Health care issues.
Housing. See Building and construction.

Major horse races of 1997

Thoroughbred racing

Race	Winner	Value to winner
Arlington Million	Marlin	$600,000
Belmont Stakes	Touch Gold	$432,600
Breeders' Cup Classic	Skip Away	$2,288,000
Breeders' Cup Distaff	Ajina	$520,000
Breeders' Cup Juvenile	Favorite Trick	$520,000
Breeders' Cup Juvenile Fillies	Countess Diana	$535,600
Breeders' Cup Mile	Spinning World	$572,000
Breeders' Cup Sprint	Elmhurst	$613,600
Breeders' Cup Turf	Chief Bearhart	$1,040,000
Canadian International	Chief Bearhart	$600,000
Derby Stakes (United Kingdom)	Benny the Dip	$1,008,532
Dubai Cup (United Arab Emirates)	Singspiel	$2,400,000
Hollywood Gold Cup Handicap	Gentlemen	$600,000
Irish Derby (Ireland)	Desert King	$666,233
Japan Cup (Japan)	Pilsudski	$1,141,932
Jim Beam Stakes	Concerto	$360,000
Jockey Club Gold Cup	Skip Away	$600,000
Kentucky Derby	Silver Charm	$700,000
King George VI and Queen Elizabeth Diamond Stakes (United Kingdom)	Swain	$499,141
Matriarch Stakes	Ryafan	$420,000
Oaklawn Handicap	Atticus	$450,000
Pacific Classic Stakes	Gentlemen	$600,000
Pimlico Special Handicap	Gentlemen	$360,000
Preakness Stakes	Silver Charm	$488,150
Prix de l'Arc de Triomphe (France)	Peintre Celebre	$769,200
Santa Anita Derby	Free House	$460,000
Travers Stakes	Deputy Commander	$450,000

Harness racing

Race	Winner	Value to winner
Cane Pace	Western Dreamer	$159,070
Hambletonian	Malabar Man	$500,000
Little Brown Jug	Western Dreamer	$207,586
Meadowlands Pace	Western Dreamer	$120,000
Messenger Stakes	Western Dreamer	$165,650
Woodrow Wilson	Real Artist	$382,875

Sources: *The Blood Horse Magazine* and U.S. Trotting Association

Silver Charm (right) edges out Captain Bodgit to win the 123rd Kentucky Derby on May 3, 1997. Two weeks later, on May 17, he won the Preakness Stakes, again by a head. However, Silver Charm failed to win the Triple Crown.

Hungary. The opposition Christian Democratic Party broke up in July 1997 after being expelled from the European Union of Christian Democrats because of links to the extreme right-wing party of Hungarian nationalist Istvan Csurka. Although Hungary's coalition government of Socialists and Free Democrats headed by Premier Gyula Horn remained stable in 1997, midyear opinion polls revealed that public support for both parties had slipped.

NATO membership. In July, Hungary, Poland, and the Czech Republic became the first formerly Communist nations of Europe approved for admission to the North Atlantic Treaty Organization (NATO). While leaders of the far-left Workers' Party opposed NATO membership, all 312 deputies present in the parliament on July 15 voted unanimously in favor of joining NATO. In August, the government allocated $78 million—2 percent of the federal budget—to finance preparations for NATO membership and to prepare Hungary's bid to join the European Union (EU), an organization of 15 Western European countries. In June, Hungary was one of the nations chosen to begin admission talks with the EU in 1998.

In a binding referendum held on Nov.16, 1997, Hungarians voted overwhelmingly to join NATO. Opposition members in parliament had attempted to block the referendum because it included questions regarding whether citizens should be allowed to enlarge land holdings and whether foreigners should be allowed to own land in Hungary.

The economy continued to grow in 1997, with economists projecting a 2 to 3 percent increase in gross domestic product. Inflation stood at 17.8 percent in June, down from 24 percent in 1996. Real wages in 1997 grew by 3 to 4 percent in the private sphere and 2 percent in the public sphere. As part of a continuing privatization effort, officials planned to begin the sale of state-owned banks and several important state-owned companies. Foreign investment, already the highest in the region, reached $1.12 billion in the first five months of 1997.

Foreign affairs. Hungary's relations with neighboring Slovakia continued to be complicated by a dispute over the status of ethnic Hungarians in Slovakia. Hungarian leaders called on Slovakia to begin to implement the provisions of a 1996 Slovak-Hungarian treaty, which included pledges to respect ethnic minorities in each country. Hungary also urged Slovakia to adopt a law permitting the use of minority languages. In July 1997, the Hungarian parliament organized more than $1 million in flood relief donations for Slovakia, as well as for the Czech Republic and Poland.

The Russian government in July agreed to repay within four years the $650 million it owed to Hungary. In a sign of improving relations with Romania, Hungary in July reopened its consulate in the Romanian city of Cluj. □ Sharon L. Wolchik

See also **Europe** (Facts in brief table).

Ice skating. Tara Lipinski, a 14-year-old from Houston, and Elvis Stojko, an innovative, 25-year-old Canadian, were the individual gold medalists at the World Figure Skating Championships at Lausanne, Switzerland, in March 1997. Lipinski became the story of the competition with an implausible victory that made her the youngest world figure skating champion in history—younger by a month than Sonja Henie, who first won the title in 1928.

Revealing athletic ability and artistry beyond her years, Lipinski landed seven triple jumps to win the short program and put the overall title out of reach for Michelle Kwan of Torrance, California. Kwan, the reigning champion, won the long program, which accounted for two-thirds of each skater's score, with a flawless performance, but finished second in the overall standings because her scores were not high enough to top Lipinski's cumulative points in both programs. Vanessa Gusmeroli of France took the bronze medal. Lipinski had also upset Kwan a month earlier at the U.S. championships in Nashville.

Stojko took the men's title for the third time in four years with the most difficult program ever performed at a world championship. His routine included a quadruple toe-loop, triple toe-loop combination and eight triple jumps that demonstrated his exceptional jumping ability. Stojko had become the first skater to land the quad-triple jump combination in competition two weeks before at the Champions Series final in Hamilton, Ontario. Stojko won the competition, followed by Todd Eldredge, the defending world champion from Chatham, Massachusetts, and Alexei Uramov of Russia, the reigning Olympic and European champion.

Eldredge came close to retaining his title as world champion, but he fell while trying to execute a triple axel as his time ran out. Bad luck also touched Uramov, who was forced out of the competition with a severe groin injury suffered during a practice session. Somewhat surprisingly, the bronze medal went to Alexei Yagudin, Uramov's training partner.

Mandy Wotzel and Ingo Steuer of Germany captured the pairs gold medal at the world championships. Russia's Marina Eltsova and Andrei Bushkov took the silver in a reversal of the way the teams had finished at the 1997 European championships. Oksana Gritschuk and Yevgeny Platov of Russia, the European ice-dancing champions, won their fourth straight world title at Lausanne.

Speed skating. Gunda Niemann of Germany took the women's overall title for the sixth time in seven years at the world championships, held in Nagano, Japan, in February. She also won individual gold medals in the 1,500, 3,000, and 5,000 meter events. Ids Postma of the Netherlands was the men's European and world champion. □ Ron Reid

Iceland. See Europe.

Idaho. See State government.

Illinois. See State government.

In March, Tara Lipinski, at age 14, becomes the youngest world figure skating champion in history, breaking the record set by Sonja Henie who was world champion in 1927 at age 15.

Immigration. A February 1997 Immigration and Naturalization Service (INS) report revealed that the number of illegal immigrants in the United States had increased to an estimated 5 million people by October 1996. The INS report noted that approximately 41 percent of the 5 million illegal residents entered the country using tourist or worker *visas* (visitor permits), but did not return to their native country when their visas expired. The remaining 59 percent entered the country without visas.

The INS reported in April 1997 that the number of legal immigrants admitted to the United States in 1996 increased by 27 percent over 1995. According to the report, more than 915,000 people immigrated legally to the United States in 1996, compared with 720,461 people in 1995.

A new immigration law took effect April 1, 1997, making it more difficult to claim political asylum. Under the law, immigrants claiming asylum but lacking proper documents must be interviewed by an immigration official at the port of entry to determine whether the claim is valid. The new rule does not require that immigrants be told that they could claim fear of persecution if they return to their native country. The law also made it easier for the U.S. government to deport illegal immigrants. Anyone living in the United States illegally after April 1, 1997, was required to return to his or her country of origin to apply for a valid visa. If such people remained in the country illegally for six months after the law went into effect, they would be barred from returning for three years once they left the country or were deported. People who stayed without documents for one year or longer following the deadline would be barred from returning for as long as 10 years. Congress included a provision in the new law allowing illegal immigrants waiting for visa applications to be processed to remain in the country past the deadline if they paid a $1,000 fine.

INS under fire. The INS came under fire in 1997 for faults in the immigrant screening process. An independent audit of INS found that of the more than 1 million people granted citizenship between August 1995 and September 1996, approximately 180,000 were admitted before required checks for criminal records were completed. Another 71,000 people became citizens even though they had criminal records. The INS reported that 168 of 1 million applicants were ineligible.

In March 1997, the Justice Department awarded a $4.3-million contract to an independent accounting firm to study the citizenship process and recommend improvements. The study was expected to be completed in 1999. In August 1997, a federal advisory panel recommended the INS be abolished and its duties assigned to other agencies.   □ William J. Eaton

See also **Immigration** Special Report: **The latest wave; Welfare.**

Income tax. See Taxation.

Nations worldwide face tough questions as more and more people search for a better life.

Immigration: The Latest Wave

By Barry R. Chiswick

Debates over the pros and cons of immigration raged during 1997 in legislatures from the German Bundestag in Bonn to the California statehouse in Sacramento. The debates were fueled by two worldwide trends: More and more residents of the world's less-developed nations were clamoring to immigrate to the more-developed nations; many residents of the more-developed nations were responding to this clamor with fear of the continuing influx of foreigners. Political leaders, in turn, responded to voter concerns with campaign rhetoric and new laws designed either to stem the flow of immigrants or tighten control over existing foreign-born residents.

In Germany, the government ruled in 1997 that German-born children under the age 16 must carry resident *visas* (permits) if their parents were legal immigrants from Turkey, Morocco, Tunisia, or the former Yugoslavia, the countries of origin of most minority communities in Germany. In the United States, Congress passed and in August 1996 President Bill Clinton signed a bill denying food stamps to legal immigrants and allowing states to turn off financial aid and Medicare to most legal immigrants. In Ireland, better known as a source of migrants than a refuge for immigrants, a wave of illegal immigrants from Romania, Republic of Congo (the former Zaire), and Somalia led to the passage of the 1996 Refugee Act, Ireland's first significant immigration legislation since 1936.

Yet immigration is nothing new. It is one aspect of migration (the movement of people from one place to another). While immigration refers to the process of people moving from one country to another for a permanent or semipermanent stay, emigration refers to leaving a country for a permanent or semipermanent stay elsewhere.

Migration has been a characteristic of human existence since prehistoric times, resulting in the spread of people to all corners of the globe. But trends in the migration of people have not been uniform over time. Historically, immigration occurred in waves. Immigrants tended to flock to an area or country during periods of economic prosperity in that area or country. The pattern was reversed during economic recession or war.

The major immigration streams since the mid-1800's have been from the lower income countries of Europe and Asia to higher income nations, particularly Australia, Canada, and the United States. Immigration to these countries increased in the late 1800's and the early 1900's, slowed during the years from World War I (1914-1918) through World War II (1939-1945), and escalated again in the decades after 1945.

With the rapid growth of income in Western Europe and Japan after World War II, emigration declined and immigration increased. Since the 1960's, there were more immigrants to Western Europe each year than emigrants leaving the region. The overall gain in migrant population is called net immigration. People from the Caribbean, Africa, and the Middle East arrived in Europe in record numbers in the 1970's and 1980's. Following the collapse of Communism in Eastern Europe in the early 1990's, another wave of immigration within Europe washed east to west.

Japan, during a period of great prosperity in the 1980's, also became a country of net immigration, though on a much smaller scale than in Western Europe. While Japan admitted record numbers of low-skilled, temporary workers from Southeast Asia, south Asia, and parts of the Middle East, the workers were not encouraged to regard immigration as permanent. In contrast, Japan welcomed emigrants of Japanese ancestry from Peru and other Latin American countries.

Israel became a net immigration country upon its creation in 1948 by welcoming all people of the Jewish faith or of Jewish background. Israel's latest wave of immigration, in the 1990's, included refugees from the former Soviet Union and from war-torn Ethiopia.

Motives for immigration

If classified by motive, immigrants can be categorized as refugees, economic migrants, or *tied movers* (spouses, children, and dependents who travel with economic migrants). Refugees emigrate, most often involuntarily, in search of safety or freedom. In 1994, for example, more than 2 million Hutu refugees, fearing for their lives, emigrated from Rwanda to other countries, particularly Zaire (now Republic of

Congo). In 1996, revolutionary forces in Zaire forced 1 million of the same refugees to migrate again, back to Rwanda.

Economic migrants are people who move for job opportunities. Most adult immigrants to the United States in the 1990's were economic migrants. Asian, Mexican, and Latin Americans made up this wave of economic immigrants just as European immigrants had in the 1890's.

Immigration to the United States

In 1996, immigration into the United States reached its highest level since the pre-World War I era, when immigration was virtually unrestricted. According to statistics from the U.S. Immigration and Naturalization Service (INS), more than 915,000 immigrants were admitted to the United States in fiscal 1996 (Oct. 1, 1995–Sept. 30, 1996). An additional 275,000 people either overstayed their visas or entered the country illegally during the same 12-month period. The INS estimated that another 5 million undocumented residents already lived in the United States in 1996.

The foreign-born population of the United States in 1997, according to INS statistics, reached 24.6 million people, meaning that nearly 10 percent of the total U.S. population was foreign-born. By comparison, the percentage of the U.S. population that was foreign born in 1880, during unregulated mass immigration, stood at 15 percent. In 1970, it was 5 percent and in 1980, 8 percent.

During the greatest period of immigration to the Unites States—the 1840's to 1914—the vast majority of immigrants came from Europe and Asia. During the 1840's and 1850's, more than 1 million immigrants came from Ireland to escape famine resulting from a potato crop failure that occurred from 1845 to 1848. Between the 1840's and the 1880's, approximately 4 million Germans escaped economic recession, unemployment, and political unrest to seek a new life in America. In the mid-1800's, news of the discovery of gold in California prompted a wave of emigrants from China, and during the 1860's, another wave of immigrants, both Chinese and European, came to the United States to find work in the construction of transcontinental rail lines.

During the same peak immigration period, America experienced its first wave of *xenophobia* (fear of foreigners) as native-born citizens began to fear job competition from immigrants. The American Party—also called the "Know-Nothing Party"—demanded as early as the 1850's that the U.S. government enact laws to reduce immigration and to make it harder for foreigners to become citizens. Congress ignored their pleas for restrictions until a depression, following the panic of 1871, threw thousands of people out of work. In response, Congress passed legislation in 1875, banning convicts and prostitutes from entering the country. In 1882, Congress passed the Chinese Exclusion Act, which prohibited all Chinese from entering the country.

Regardless of such restrictions, immigration to the United States boomed between 1881 and 1914, when more than 23 million immigrants—predominantly northern Europeans in the 1880's and eastern and southern Europeans in the 1890's and early 1900's—poured into

The author

Barry R. Chiswick heads the Department of Economics at the University of Illinois at Chicago.

Countries of origin of largest numbers of **legal** immigrants to the U.S. in 1996	
Mexico	163,572
Philippines	55,876
India	44,859
Vietnam	42,067
China	41,728
Dominican Republic	39,604
Cuba	26,466
Ukraine	21,079
Russia	19,668
Jamaica	19.089

Countries of origin of largest numbers of **illegal** immigrants in 1996	
Mexico	2,700,000
El Salvador	335,000
Guatemala	165,000
Canada	120,000
Haiti	105,000
Philippines	95,000
Honduras	90,000
Bahamas	70,000
Nicaragua	70,000
Poland	70,000

States with largest numbers of **legal** immigrants in 1996	
California	201,529
New York	154,095
Texas	83,385
Florida	79,461
New Jersey	63,303
Illinois	42,517
Massachusetts	23,085
Virginia	21,375
Maryland	20,732
Washington	18,833

Source: U.S. Immigration and Naturalization Service.

States with highest numbers of **illegal** immigrants in 1996	
California	2,000,000
Texas	700,000
New York	540,000
Florida	350,000
Illinois	290,000
New Jersey	135,000
Arizona	115,000
Massachusetts	85,000
Virginia	55,000
Washington	52,000

Source: U.S. Immigration and Naturalization Service.

A woman protests U.S. immigration policy during a 1994 demonstration in Miami-Dade County, Florida, where 45 percent of the population was foreign born by 1990.

the country. The flow, however, slowed to a trickle during World War I and after 1921, when Congress set a ceiling on the number of Eastern Hemisphere people allowed to enter the country. The quota limited the annual number of immigrants from any one nation to 3 percent of the foreign-born people of that nationality already in the United States. Therefore, immigration was open to northern Europeans, who for the most part did not want to come. Immigration was severely restricted for southern and eastern Europeans and closed to Asians.

During the Great Depression of the 1930's, immigration to the United States dropped even further. While some 500,000 immigrants came to the United States between 1931 and 1940, an even larger number left the country, most returning to their countries of origin.

World War II led to an easing of the nation's immigration laws. The United States lifted its Chinese ban when China became an ally. The War Brides Act of 1945 admitted the spouses and children of U.S. military personnel who had married while abroad.

In the mid-1960's, the United States underwent a change in attitude toward race and ethnicity that resulted in the enactment of the 1964 Civil Rights and 1965 Voting Rights acts. The 1965 amendments to the Immigration and Nationality Act of 1952 reflected the change and dramatically refocused immigration patterns with the abolition of the

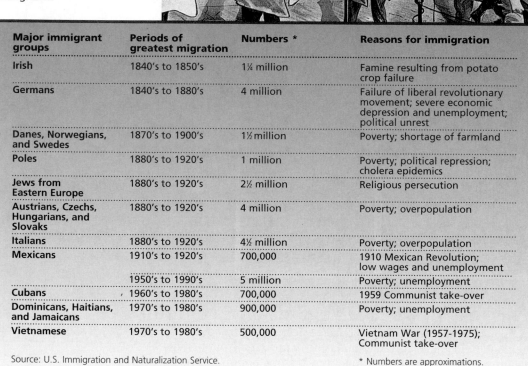

A sign of the times

An 1893 political cartoon illustrates anti-immigration attitudes among many U.S. citizens who either had been immigrants themselves or who were descendants of immigrants.

Major immigrant groups	Periods of greatest migration	Numbers *	Reasons for immigration
Irish	1840's to 1850's	1¼ million	Famine resulting from potato crop failure
Germans	1840's to 1880's	4 million	Failure of liberal revolutionary movement; severe economic depression and unemployment; political unrest
Danes, Norwegians, and Swedes	1870's to 1900's	1½ million	Poverty; shortage of farmland
Poles	1880's to 1920's	1 million	Poverty; political repression; cholera epidemics
Jews from Eastern Europe	1880's to 1920's	2½ million	Religious persecution
Austrians, Czechs, Hungarians, and Slovaks	1880's to 1920's	4 million	Poverty; overpopulation
Italians	1880's to 1920's	4½ million	Poverty; overpopulation
Mexicans	1910's to 1920's	700,000	1910 Mexican Revolution; low wages and unemployment
	1950's to 1990's	5 million	Poverty; unemployment
Cubans	1960's to 1980's	700,000	1959 Communist take-over
Dominicans, Haitians, and Jamaicans	1970's to 1980's	900,000	Poverty; unemployment
Vietnamese	1970's to 1980's	500,000	Vietnam War (1957-1975); Communist take-over

Source: U.S. Immigration and Naturalization Service.

* Numbers are approximations.

"national origins" quota. The amendments replaced quotas based on nationality with annual quotas with ceilings of 170,000 immigrants from the Eastern Hemisphere and 120,000 from the Western Hemisphere. The act established a preference system for entry visas that strongly favored relatives of U.S. citizens and permanent resident aliens, with much less emphasis on people with special skills. Wives, husbands, parents, and the minor children of U.S. citizens could enter without being counted as part of the quota.

The authors of the 1965 amendments believed that the "kinship" provisions in the amendments would produce a similar distribution of immigrants by country of origin as under the "national origins" quota system. Soon after the passage of the 1965 amendments, however, the number of Asian and Latin American immigrants increased dramatically as those from Europe shrank.

In 1978, Congress replaced the separate quotas for immigrants from the Eastern and Western hemispheres with a single annual quota of 290,000. By the 1980's, 23 percent of immigrants to the United States came from Mexico, and 25 percent came from other Latin American countries and the Caribbean; 37 percent arrived from Asia; and 2 percent from Africa. The percentage of immigrants from Europe and Canada fell to 13 percent.

More amendments in 1990 increased the number of immigrants allowed into the United States. In fiscal 1996, 18 percent of the 915,000 immigrants entering the country came from Mexico (nearly 164,000 people) and 24 percent from other parts of Latin America and the Caribbean; 5 percent were from Africa; and 33 percent were from Asia, including approximately 55,000 people from the Philippines, 45,000 from India, 42,000 from Vietnam, and 42,000 from China.

Effects of immigration on national culture

The increase in the number of immigrants and the change in their countries of origin since the 1960's dramatically affected the United States and its culture—from the demographic composition of its cities to salsa replacing ketchup as the nation's No. 1 condiment. The impact of these changes was not, however, uniformly felt across the country. In 1990, 33 percent of all foreign-born people lived in California, while only 12 percent of the entire U.S. population lived in California. Another 14 percent lived in New York. Florida and Texas each accounted for about 8 percent, and another 5 percent lived in New Jersey and Illinois. These six states—with only 39 percent of the total U.S. population—were home to nearly 73 percent of all foreign-born residents in 1990.

Immigrant populations in the same six states were further concentrated in urban areas: in the San Francisco Bay area and the southern counties of California; along the Mexican border in Texas; in Miami-Dade County, Florida; Chicago, Illinois; and the New York City metropolitan area. Of a total of 3,141 counties in the United States, only 156 counties—approximately 5 percent—had populations with 8 percent or more foreign-born residents in 1990. The population of Miami-Dade County, Florida, in contrast, was 45 percent foreign born.

Where immigrants settle

After the era of cheap farmland in America ended in the early 1900's, the places where immigrants settled has remained largely static and determined by three factors: port of entry, concentration of other foreign-born people, and job opportunities. New immigrants often settled in ports of entry, that is, they remained in the places where they entered the country. Boston, for example, became the home of America's largest concentration of Irish immigrants in the 1800's and early 1900's because it was America's nearest port to Ireland and, therefore, the cheapest passage.

According to an INS report, the majority of immigrants entering the United States in 1996 planned to settle in ports of entry. Approximately

130,000 immigrants in 1992 reported their intention of living in the Los Angeles/Long Beach area, a major Mexican, Latin American, and Asian port of entry. More than 24,000 immigrants reported plans to settle in San Diego, California, and 27,000 people planned to make their homes in Houston, Texas. Both are major ports for Mexican emigrants. More than 40,000 immigrants declared that they expected to settle in the San Francisco/San Jose metropolitan area, a primary port of entry for Asian emigrants. Attracting 128,000 immigrants in 1992, New York City remained the premier port of entry for eastern Europeans, Africans, and Middle Easterners. More than 31,000 Cubans and Latin Americans chose the port of Miami in 1992.

In the 1990's, immigrants from countries that differ in language and customs from the United States continued to settle in communities with other immigrants from their home countries. Living in an area where others speak the same language and read the same foreign language newspapers, eat the same foods, and celebrate the same holidays eases the initial adjustment.

INS statistics indicated that in fiscal 1996, more than 64,000 Mexican emigrants, interviewed before entering the United States, planned to settle in California, and more than 46,000 emigrants planned to live in Texas. California and Texas are home to the largest Mexican-American communities in the United States. More than 20,000 immigrants from the Dominican Republic reported their intention of moving to New York City, which was home to nearly 500,000 Dominicans by the mid-1990's. Chicago, a city of ethnic neighborhoods and a magnet for eastern Europeans, attracted 37,000 immigrants in fiscal 1992. Historically, Chicago also offered immigrants entry-level job opportunities—the third factor affecting settlement. Immigrants tend to go where job opportunities are best for their skills.

Arguments against immigration

Immigration policy became an intense political issue during the 1990's in most developed countries of the world, with "closed door" and "open door" advocates at the extremes. Opponents argued that an influx of foreign-born people would destroy national culture and traditions. In 1997, France's National Front political party rallied against African, Asian, and Middle Eastern immigrants by arguing that they threatened France's national identity. A similar argument was used by Japanese officials, who viewed Japan as culturally homogeneous.

Immigration opponents also argued that immigrants "took" jobs that native workers might fill, thereby hurting the employment opportunities of the native born. In the 1990's, the citizens of many prosperous countries expressed increased concern over the growing numbers of immigrants joining the work force. According to the U.S. Census Bureau, approximately 10 percent of the total work force in the United States in 1991—11.6 million people—was foreign-born. The figure included some 465,000 temporary workers. In Germany in 1995, the total number of foreign workers was 2.5 million, or 7.4 percent of the total work force, including the unemployed. In Japan in 1995, the total

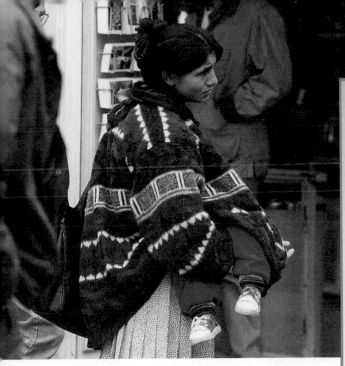

Immigrant populations in developed countries

Country*	Foreign-born population	Percentage of total population
Australia†	3.7 million	22.3
Austria	724,000	9
Belgium	910,000	9
Canada†	4.3 million	15.6
Denmark	223,000	4.2
Finland	69,000	1.3
France	3.5 million	6.3
Germany	7.1 million	8.8
Ireland	96,000	2.7
Italy	991,000	1.7
Japan	1.3 million	1.1
Luxembourg	138,000	33.4
Spain	500,000	1.2
Switzerland	1.3 million	18.9
United Kingdom	2 million	3.4
United States‡	24.6 million	10

*Data is from 1995 unless otherwise indicated.
†Data is from 1991.
‡Data is from 1997.

Sources: Organization for Economic Cooperation and Development, "Trends in International Migration Annual Report 1996"; U.S. Immigration and Naturalization Service.

number of foreign workers was 590,000, or 0.9 percent of the total work force.

In France in 1995, 1.5 million laborers—6.2 percent of the work force—were classified as foreign. French politicians in 1997 suggested that the unemployment rate of 13 percent would fall dramatically if fewer immigrants were allowed in the country.

Another concern of critics of immigration in the 1990's was the financial burden on governments forced to care for low income immigrants and their children. A 1997 report by the National Academy of Sciences and the National Research Council, Washington, D.C.-based research organizations, showed that taxpayers in states with a high percentage of immigrants—California, Florida, and Texas, for example—suffered because of income differences between immigrants and native-born residents. The taxes that many new immigrants paid fell short of covering the costs of the government services they used—including health care and public education. The report noted that the average household in California in the 1990's paid an extra $1,178 annually in taxes because of immigrants. In 1996, California Governor Pete Wilson signed an executive order ending illegal immigrants' access to certain state benefits, including public housing, prenatal care, and child-abuse programs.

Arguments for immigration

The same 1997 National Academy of Sciences/National Research Council report concluded that the overall impact of immigration on the U.S. economy was not, however, that great in relation to the national economy as a whole. The report projected that each 1990's

A Bosnian immigrant to Ireland begs, with her child in her arms, on the streets of Dublin, *above*. Thousands of such immigrants, many of them illegal, strained private and public social service resources in Ireland in 1997.

245

Arguments used
for
immigration

- Immigrants contribute to the vitality of a country's economy by improving the standard of living.

- Immigration brings professional people to more-developed nations.

- Newcomers to a country bring significant skills with them and contribute to the workplace.

- Immigrants take jobs that no one else wants.

- Immigrants, most of whom are young adults, add youth to aging populations.

- Population growth and ecological problems are global, regardless of immigration patterns.

- Immigrants can educate an adopted culture by exposing residents to the idea of bilingualism and various foreign languages.

Tens of thousands of demonstrators, *above right,* march in Paris in February 1997 in favor of human rights and the rights of immigrants.

immigrant, during his or her lifetime, provided the treasury of the United States with $80,000 in extra tax revenue, reinforcing what proponents of an open immigration policy have longed argued—that immigrants enhanced the economy of the host country. Advocates of open immigration argued that immigration can be a boon to a country's economy. Some experts favored immigration, contending that it tended to keep wages competitive and prices low. Economists and immigration scholars stated that immigrants who are highly skilled greatly benefit a national economy. In the 1990's, Chinese engineers, Russian physicists, and Indian computer programmers, for example, earned high wages in the United States, increasing the gross domestic product and the American per capita income.

Advocates for an open-door policy also pointed out that immigrants tend to be young adults. In countries with very low (below replacement) rates of fertility, young adult immigrants helped slow the gradual aging and eventual decline in the population. In fact, some countries have attempted to lure immigrants to their shores in an effort to increase and add youth to the population and to strengthen the professional work force.

In the Canadian Province of Quebec, which has a large French-speaking population, the provincial government budgeted $2 million in 1997 to recruit 4,000 workers from France. The effort was made to off-set an increase in English-speaking immigrants and a low birthrate among French-speaking Quebecers. The government offered immediate permanent residence visas to French engineers, mechanics, and cooks.

The political debate over immigration

One interesting feature of the political debate over immigration in the 1990's was how the divide between proponents and opponents did not follow the "liberal left" versus "conservative right" split that defined many political issues. Open door supporters included civil rights advocates and civil libertarians as well as business persons and labor leaders who supported free trade. The "restrictionists" included nationalists (extreme patriots), environmentalists, and business and labor leaders who supported the protection of domestic industry and workers.

Another remarkable aspect of the political debate surrounding immigration in the 1990's was the similarity of arguments from country to country and the similarity of arguments between time periods. The similarity of debate may result from the similarity of factors surrounding immigration in the 1990's and the late 1800's. While the latest wave of immigrants flowed from different directions, the force driving it remained the same: For the most part, people immigrated to better themselves economically. They settled in urban concentrations among people of similar circumstances. Large concentrates of the foreign born tended to produce fears among native-born citizens, and those fears culminated in legislation regulating immigrant flow.

Slowing the immigrant flow

In the mid-1990's, immigration did begin to slow. The Organization for Economic Cooperation and Development, a Paris-based multinational association working to promote economic and social welfare among members and to coordinate member aid to developing countries, announced in its 1996 annual report that legal immigration to many European countries began to level off and even decline in 1995 and 1996. The slowdown was attributed to new regulatory laws, rather than to a real decrease in the desire of people to leave one country for another.

Proponents of open-door immigration argue that such regulations are the products of racism or xenophobia. Some scholars of immigration, however, disagree. These scholars offer the theory that slow periods between waves—whether the result of regulation, economic downturn, or war—provide a "time out" during which cross-cultural and economic absorption can be accomplished, quietly and harmoniously.

While the immigrant waves of the past changed the United States and its culture, American culture exerted an even greater effect on the immigrant population, which in one to two generations dispersed from ethnic enclaves and came to more closely resemble the native-born population. It is likely that the latest wave of immigrants will go through a similar process, this time not only in the United States but in other prosperous nations of the world. ▪▪▪

WE DEMAND! MEXICO TAKE CARE OF YOUR OWN!

Protesters *above left,* demonstrate in Los Angeles in 1996 against immigration policies.

Arguments used against immigration

- Immigrants impose significant material burdens on their adopted country and reduce the prospects of long-term prosperity.

- Skilled professionals, such as doctors and engineers, create a "brain drain" when they leave their homeland, where they may be urgently needed.

- Immigrants take jobs from native residents.

- Immigrants cause a country's population to grow, which depletes natural resources.

- Many immigrants do not speak the native language of their adopted land, resulting in a language barrier.

- Immigrants in the 1980's and 1990's are different from those of the past and are less willing to adapt to national customs in their new country.

Tushar Gandhi pours the ashes of his great-grandfather, Mohandas K. Gandhi, into the sacred Ganges River in January 1997. The Gandhi family fought a court battle for the rediscovered ashes, misplaced since the Mahatma's assassination in 1948.

India. The 50th-anniversary celebration of India's independence from Great Britain was overshadowed in 1997 by political turmoil and scandal. In April, Inder Kumar Gujral took office as prime minister, heading India's fourth government in 11 months. Political battles that sometimes turned violent forced Gujral to resign in November and stirred Hindu-Muslim tensions in India.

Gujral was named prime minister on April 19 by India's 14-party coalition government, which had struggled for three weeks to find a successor for H. D. Deve Gowda. Gowda had been named prime minister in May 1996, after elections produced the most fractured Parliament in India's history. In the 1996 vote, 22 parties had gained seats in Parliament, and even the most successful of these parties—the Bharatiya Janata, a conservative Hindu nationalist party—had fallen short of winning a third of the seats of the 545-member lower house. Weakened by scandal, the Congress Party, which had long dominated Indian politics, had taken only 140 parliamentary seats. Following the elections, the Congress Party had supported the United Front coalition in order to keep the Bharatiya Janata out of power.

Power struggle. In March 1997, Congress Party leader Sitaram Kesri withdrew his party's support from the United Front, leaving the ruling party without a parliamentary majority. Kesri then began an unsuccessful campaign for premiership. He finally gave up his bid for the office and agreed to support a new version of the United Front Party on the condition that Gowda was not the party head. On April 14, two days after losing a vote of confidence, Gowda offered to step down as head of his United Front coalition if his withdrawal would lead to a new governing agreement with the Congress Party.

The two parties agreed to back Gujral, a two-time foreign minister, who was widely praised for improving India's troubled relations with neighboring countries. Gujral had served the Indian government in various roles since the 1970's, earning a reputation for personal integrity. He vowed to continue with economic reforms that had begun to revitalize India's sluggish economy and to pursue improved relations with Pakistan.

Tensions mounted throughout 1997 between India's warring political factions in the United Front and the Congress Party. In October, Gujral ordered United Front Party leaders to prepare for a possible general election. Coalition leaders worried that an election might oust the ruling government in favor of the Bharatiya Janata, a Hindu-backed party with a history of causing trouble between Hindus and Muslims. On November 29, Gujral resigned after the Congress Party withdrew its backing of the governing coalition. The political turmoil sent Indian financial markets into a sharp decline and brought appeals from business leaders for politicians to stop feuding and concentrate on economic problems.

Untouchable named president. K. R. Narayanan, a 76-year-old former vice president, diplomat, and cabinet minister who once served as India's ambassador to the United States, was elected on July 14 as president, a largely ceremonial post. Narayanan, an *untouchable* (a Hindi belonging to the lowest social caste in India), was the first member of the caste to be elected president. When Narayanan was a boy, untouchables were denied the right to enter Hindu temples. But by 1997, it was illegal to discriminate against untouchables, who call themselves Dalits, a Hindi word meaning "the oppressed." However, few Dalits held positions of power.

Corruption. In 1997, both the United Front and the Congress parties were weakened by corruption scandals involving party leaders. In March, former cabinet member Kalpnath Rai was sentenced to 10 years in prison for harboring the associates of an underworld figure. Rai was the first former cabinet member to be convicted of a crime.

Weeks after Gujral took office with a pledge to provide India with a "clean government," Laloo Prasad Yadav, one of the prime minister's political allies, was arrested on charges that he siphoned millions of dollars from a state-run cattle fodder fund. Yadav resigned as chief minister of Bihar, the country's poorest state, in July, naming his semiliterate wife, Rabri Devi, as successor, and vowing to continue ruling from a jail cell. Devi, who signed official documents with her thumbprint, said "I will learn governance as I did cooking and milking cows."

On September 25, P. V. Narasimha Rao, prime minster from 1991 to 1996 and the former head of the Congress Party, was charged with bribing members of Parliament to win a confidence vote in 1993. Rao was the first Indian prime minister to face criminal charges.

Kashmir conflict. India and Pakistan pledged in June 1997 to reconcile their differences over the disputed territory of Kashmir, a Himalayan region that had been at the center of a dispute between the countries since the two nations were created by partition in 1947. Each country claimed Kashmir as part of its territory. Officials of both countries said the pledge was the first time since partition that the two governments had even agreed to negotiate on Kashmir. On Oct. 7, 1997, India began to gradually withdraw its army from some towns in the Kashmir valley.

State funeral. Mother Teresa, the Roman Catholic nun who devoted her life to helping the poorest of the poor mainly in India, died at age 87 on September 5 in Calcutta. India honored her with a state funeral. However, citing security reasons, the government barred many of the country's poor from attending the funeral. □ Henry S. Bradsher

See also **Asia** (Facts in brief table); **India** Special Report: **50 Years of Independence; Pakistan; People in the news; Roman Catholic Church** Special Report: **Mother Teresa—Saint of the Gutters.**

India has made dramatic progress during 50 years of independent rule and democracy—but great problems remain.

India:
50 Years of Independence

By David Taylor

In 1997, India—one of the world's major powers and the second most populous country on Earth—celebrated 50 years as an independent country. As the world's largest democracy, India had much to be proud of in maintaining a relatively stable and free democratic system since its inception in 1947. Anniversary celebrations in India were, nevertheless, muted, as observers both inside and outside the country noted certain sobering facts.

India's population in 1997 was about 950 million. Despite a steady decline in the rate of population growth in the 1990's, India still faced the daunting problem of supporting 18 million people born each year. Although boasting a large industrial sector with a massive pool of scientifically and technically trained personnel, India in the late 1990's still contained the world's largest number of people in dire poverty. And while proud of sustaining democracy in a land of huge diversity, where the people speak more than 14 major languages and support more than 20 political parties, India had often seen its rival factions clash violently. As India reflected on its history since independence, it could celebrate a half-century of achievement, but it could also see a long agenda of improvement ahead.

The road to independence

India officially became independent on Aug. 15, 1947. Before 1947, it had been a colony of the United Kingdom (UK), the so-called "jewel in the crown" of the vast British Empire. Once a collection of separate states ruled by local princes, India—including territories that are now the nations of Pakistan and Bangladesh—gradually became part of the British Empire, beginning in the mid-1700's. The British East India Company, a powerful trading company founded in 1600, established the foundations for British settlement and expansion by setting up trading ports and developing independent armies to protect them. These armies eventually established colonial control over most of the local rulers and also eliminated competition from other European traders.

The British developed a strong bureaucratic machinery that prided itself on its ability to provide stable government that was free of corruption. By the late 1800's, British officials had responded to growing political pressure by allowing Indians to join the lower and middle ranks of the bureaucracy. After 1919, they transferred limited areas of government to the control of elected legislative councils.

A worker, *opposite top,* irons Indian flags in preparation for the nation's 50th anniversary celebrations in 1997. The contrast between the grandeur of India's famed Taj Mahal, *left,* and the polluted Jumna River running beside it points out the huge challenges still facing the world's most populous democracy.

Glossary

Cold War: the contest for world leadership that began after World War II (1939-1945) between the Communist countries headed primarily by the Soviet Union, and the countries of the West headed principally by the United States.

Confederation: an alliance among separate states or countries to form a union.

Partition: a division into parts; in Indian history, the 1947 division of British imperial India into the separate independent countries of India and Pakistan.

The author:

David Taylor is Senior Lecturer in South Asian politics at the School of Oriental and African Studies at the University of London in Great Britain.

Because the chief purpose of these concessions was to maintain British control over India, it was not surprising that an increasingly active nationalist movement began to emerge. In 1885, a group of middle-class professionals founded the Indian National Congress (also known as the Congress) as their political vehicle. Initially, the Congress sought modest reforms within the British Empire. But from the beginning of the 1900's, the more militant nationalists began to reject anything short of *purna swaraj* (complete independence).

The Gandhian vision

The key figure in the history of Indian nationalism was Mohandas Karamchand Gandhi, often known as Mahatma Gandhi or simply the *Mahatma* (great soul). Gandhi emerged in 1920 as the main exponent of a nationalism that sought to achieve its aims through nonviolent means, such as the nonpayment of taxes or the symbolic defiance of government authority through strikes or peaceful demonstrations. Gandhi's aim was an India that would not simply gain political freedom but would use its freedom as a means to find its own path of development. This development, he thought, should be essentially village-based, with only limited use of modern technology.

Freedom, Gandhi believed, would also give Indians the responsibility for dealing in their own way with questions of social equality, such as the position of the so-called "untouchables" in India's Hindu *caste* system—a rigid division of people into social groups determined by birth. In the early 1900's, the untouchables formed about 15 percent of the population, and their welfare was always one of Gandhi's prime concerns. Gandhi's India was also to be a place where national identity would be based on cultural pluralism. Religious difference would be celebrated rather than seen as cause for strife.

Gandhi's vision was rejected by the Muslim League, headed from the mid-1930's by Muhammad Ali Jinnah. Before 1947, Muslims formed about a quarter of India's population. Jinnah argued that Gandhi's vision of unity would only ensure the dominance of the Hindu majority over the Muslim minority. The League, therefore, demanded the division of India into Hindu and Muslim states.

Partition

The final negotiations that led to independence and the partition of India took place against the backdrop of World War II (1939-1945) and its aftermath. The Congress had refused to participate in the Allied war effort unless it was given a promise of immediate independence, and in 1942 it launched the Quit India movement to back its demand. In the short term, the British succeeded in controlling the movement, but by the time the war ended it was clear that the British no longer had the resources nor the will to continue to hold India by force. Elections held at the end of 1945 confirmed that the Congress and the League were the only major political parties.

The British at first tried to broker a compromise based on the idea of *confederation* (an alliance among separate states to form a union).

Their efforts failed, mainly because suspicion and fear on all sides ran high and violence began to erupt between Hindus, Muslims, and *Sikhs* (a prominent religious community in the Punjab), each group anxious for its future. The British government in March 1947 named Lord Louis Mountbatten as India's last *viceroy* (deputy sovereign), with the mission to resolve the issue as soon as possible. Mountbatten quickly came to the conclusion that partition was inevitable, including the division of the provinces of Punjab and Bengal.

The British handed over sovereignty on Aug. 15, 1947, to the two successor states, India and Pakistan, unleashing an unprecedented wave of mass migration and communal violence. Across Punjab and north India, up to a million people were killed and as many as 14 million people became refugees. Decades of nonviolent protest ended with killing on a massive scale. Gandhi himself became a casualty of independence. He was assassinated on Jan. 30, 1948, by a Hindu fanatic who blamed him for the country's partition.

The Nehru years

While Gandhi inspired most members of the generation of political leaders who took power in 1947 and laid the foundations of modern India, the man who did the most to create the modern Indian nation was its first prime minister, Jawaharlal Nehru. Despite his personal closeness to Gandhi, Nehru had his own distinct vision of the future. He viewed India in a more *secular* (nonreligious) light than Gandhi did, but he placed a similar emphasis on tolerance and inclusiveness. Nehru also believed that India was entitled to play a major role in the contemporary world. To achieve that role, it had to move rapidly down the path of industrialization. India would not become a pale copy of the West, but it would still have to endure many of the same social struggles as the West had on its road to economic and social development.

Drawing equally upon Western and Soviet models of economic development, India in the mid-1960's embarked on a program of planned industrialization. With financial and technological help from the Soviet Union and several European countries, Indian authorities set up steel mills and other basic industries. While these were placed under government control, the private sector of Indian

Major events in India's modern history

India's history goes back more than 5,000 years, but its life as an independent democratic country began in 1947.

- **1947:** Indian and British leaders agree to partition British India into independent nations, India and Pakistan. Jawaharlal Nehru becomes prime minister of India.

- **1948:** Mohandas K. Gandhi, a leader of India's independence movement who advocated nonviolent disobedience to British rule, is assassinated.

- **1950:** India adopts a new constitution, declaring the country an independent, democratic republic.

- **1964:** Prime Minister Nehru dies.

- **1966:** Indira Gandhi, Nehru's daughter, becomes prime minister.

- **1971:** India successfully assists East Pakistan in separating from West Pakistan. East Pakistan becomes the independent nation of Bangladesh.

- **1975:** Prime Minister Indira Gandhi imposes a state of emergency rather than resign after claims of illegal practices during her 1971 election campaign.

- **1977:** The state of emergency is lifted. Indira Gandhi loses her seat in parliament, and her party loses its majority.

- **1980:** Indira Gandhi again becomes prime minister of India.

- **1984:** Indira Gandhi is assassinated by two Sikh members of her security force. Her son, Rajiv Gandhi, becomes prime minister.

- **1991:** Rajiv Gandhi is assassinated. India begins a radical program of economic liberalization.

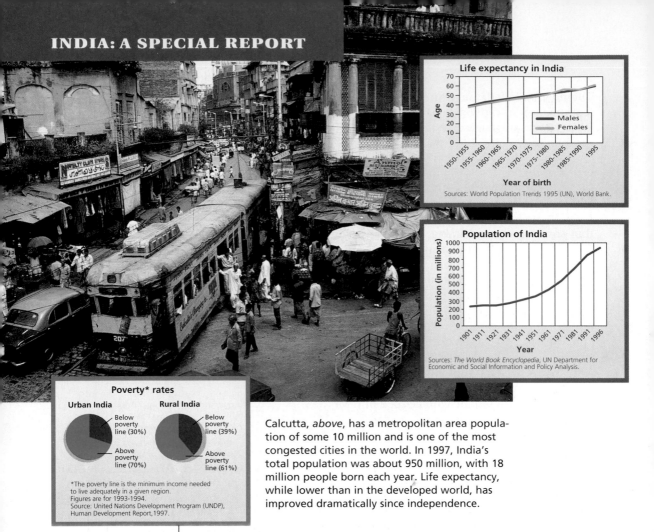

Life expectancy in India

Age / Year of birth

1950-1955, 1955-1960, 1960-1965, 1965-1970, 1970-1975, 1975-1980, 1980-1985, 1985-1990, 1995

Males
Females

Sources: World Population Trends 1995 (UN), World Bank.

Population of India

Population (in millions) / Year

1901, 1911, 1921, 1931, 1941, 1951, 1961, 1971, 1981, 1991, 1996

Sources: *The World Book Encyclopedia*, UN Department for Economic and Social Information and Policy Analysis.

Poverty* rates

Urban India

Below poverty line (30%)
Above poverty line (70%)

Rural India

Below poverty line (39%)
Above poverty line (61%)

*The poverty line is the minimum income needed to live adequately in a given region.
Figures are for 1993-1994.
Source: United Nations Development Program (UNDP), Human Development Report,1997.

Calcutta, *above*, has a metropolitan area population of some 10 million and is one of the most congested cities in the world. In 1997, India's total population was about 950 million, with 18 million people born each year. Life expectancy, while lower than in the developed world, has improved dramatically since independence.

According to most estimates, about 300 million Indians, or nearly one-third of the total population, live below the poverty line. The greater number of poor live in rural areas.

industry, many of whose members had been active supporters of the independence movement, continued to dominate consumer goods production, such as textiles. Both the private and public sectors were given extensive protection against outside competition through heavy import duties and other measures. The economy was deliberately insulated from international forces in order to give it time to develop independently.

In the 1950's and early 1960's, little investment was put into agriculture. Instead, leaders sponsored land reforms that they believed would lead to significant increases in output to meet the growing needs of the industrial sector. Land ownership rights was transferred from large landlords to small tenants, and local initiatives, such as credit unions that allowed small farmers to borrow money at low interest rates, were encouraged by the government.

India's ability to sustain a democracy and an independent economic development strategy gave it the necessary base to play a part in world affairs. India—and Nehru in particular—played a major role in the emergence, in the 1950's and 1960's, of the *nonaligned movement*, whereby countries refused to align themselves to either the

Soviet Union or the United States during the most intense years of the Cold War. However, a border conflict with China escalated into war in 1962, which India effectively lost. At the same time, poor relations with Pakistan became even more of a hindrance to India's aspirations for leadership of the non-aligned world.

The Nehru-Gandhi dynasty

After Nehru died in 1964, his successors interpreted his political vision in various ways. When his daughter, Indira Gandhi (her husband, Feroze Gandhi, was no relation to Mohandas Gandhi), campaigned to succeed him as prime minister, she emphasized the abolition of poverty through radical measures and won a famous election victory in 1971. Her response to setbacks, however, was to enhance her own power and the power of the central government. This tendency reached its peak when she imposed emergency rule from 1975 to 1977, during which the press was censored and many opposition leaders were arrested. The drive against poverty took second place to programs that emphasized social discipline, often backed up by force. In Delhi, for example, squatter settlements were cleared, and their inhabitants moved to the outskirts. Throughout India, strict population control programs were forced on unwilling people. Resentment led to Indira Gandhi's electoral defeat in 1977. However, the incompetence of the new government allowed her to return to power in 1980. Afterward, she had to contend with Sikh militants in the Punjab, who demanded an independent state. This led eventually to her assassination by Sikh security guards in October 1984.

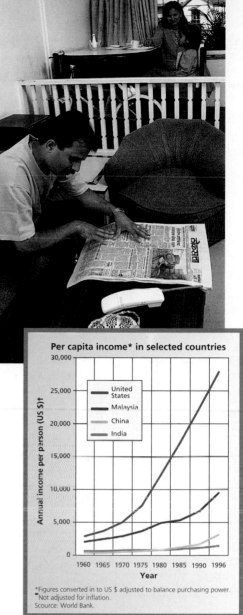

Per capita income* in selected countries

Legend: United States, Malaysia, China, India

Y-axis: Annual income per person (US $)† — 0; 5,000; 10,000; 15,000; 20,000; 25,000; 30,000
X-axis: Year — 1960 1965 1970 1975 1980 1985 1990 1996

*Figures converted in to US $ adjusted to balance purchasing power.
■Not adjusted for inflation.
Scource: World Bank.

India's rapidly growing middle class lives in comfortable accommodations, *top*, and enjoys a much higher standard of living than was possible in the 1960's or 1970's. Per capita income has risen steadily since 1947, but India's average income remains low compared with other developing nations in Asia.

Indira Gandhi was succeeded by her son, Rajiv Gandhi, the third member of the Nehru-Gandhi family to be prime minister. During his years in office, from 1984 to 1989, Gandhi maintained emphasis on a strong central government but also continued the process of economic reform and liberalization that had begun to take root in the late 1970's. During the 1991 election campaign, which he might have won, Rajiv Gandhi also was assassinated. Observers believed that the perpetrators were, most likely, Tamil militants from Sri Lanka, who were angry at India's intervention there in 1987.

The Congress did in fact win the election. The new prime minister, P. V. Narasimha Rao, took the program of economic liberalization further during his tenure in office, which lasted from 1991 to 1996.

Literacy rates in India

Source: UNESCO.

Children in India receive free education through the age of 14, but facilities remain basic. With an overall adult literacy rate of only 52 percent—65.5 for men and 37.7 for women—education remains one of India's most urgent issues for the future.

Economic reform

For many historians and economists, the reforms begun in 1991 were a crucial turning point in India's history. They were initiated more by necessity than by ideology. With government spending and subsidies skyrocketing in the 1980's and foreign debt out of control, the Indian government was forced to turn away from Nehru's vision of a planned economy and to embrace instead the free-market policies that Nehru had rejected. Under Finance Minister Manmohan Singh, most government controls were removed, and foreign companies were allowed easy entry to set up businesses and invest foreign capital in India.

The results were clear within a few years. In the early 1990's, India had managed a growth rate of only 3 to 4 percent per year. By 1997, India's economic growth rate had climbed to more than 6 percent. Foreign investment brought much-needed currency into a country that had been desperately in debt. Once restrictions on foreign investment were removed, United States companies, for example, began investing up to $1 billion a year in India.

Although India's economic growth had been uneven, by 1997 its largely agricultural economy had developed a substantial industrial sector, capable of independent technical development. Fifty years after independence, India was building its own washing machines as well as its own satellites and exporting sophisticated computer software. *Per capita* (per person) income rose slowly but steadily in most years between 1947 and 1997 and picked up pace in the 1990's.

However, by 1997 India had not yet abolished poverty, as Indira Gandhi had promised in 1971. By most estimates, some 300 million people—nearly one-third of the population—continued to live below the poverty line by the late 1990's. As many as two-thirds of children under age 5 were malnourished. Literacy—often considered the measure of a country's economic and political success—remained low, at 52 percent. In 1997, little more than half of India's adults could read and write.

India also paid a heavy price for the industrialization and urbanization of its more recent history. Water, much less abundant per person in the 1990's than it had been at independence, became more and more polluted by industrial waste and sewage, while acute air pollution became an accepted hazard in most major Indian cities. In 1996, the World Bank, a United Nations agency that provides loans for development projects, estimated that more than 40,000 Indians died prematurely each year as a result of air pollution. A 1997 report in the magazine *India Today* revealed that more than 10,000 industrial plants—many of them illegal—were generating some 2,200 tons (2,000 metric tons) of waste per day across the country.

An economy for the 2000's

After its rather bumpy transformation into a modern economic state, India led many observers to wonder how well its reforms had positioned the country to meet the next century. Despite the economic advancements of the 1990's, India by 1997 had not been able to match the explosive economic growth achieved in other Asian countries. The obvious comparison was China, which in 1947 had an average *per capita* income similar to India's. After a decade of fast growth in the late 1980's and 1990's, China had become twice as wealthy as India. By the time India celebrated its 50th birthday, the so-called "tiger economies" of the Pacific Rim were enjoying per capita incomes more than 25 times that of India.

Nevertheless, observers in 1997 still found cause for optimism in India's economy. Pointing to the greatly improved growth rate in recent years, some analysts predicted that, if trends continued, India could legitimately become one of the world's economic superpowers by the early 2000's. The software industry, one of the country's most notable successes in the 1990's, grew by more than 50 percent in 1996 alone, with a total turnover of $850 million. According to India's National Association of Software and Service Companies (Nasscom), India's revenues from software were expected to reach $5 billion by the year 2000.

Another indicator of India's development in the 1990's was the growth of a new middle class—by some estimates as large as 300 million people—with a purchasing power of immense global potential in the new century. According to the U.S. Department of Commerce, India in 1997 was one of the world's 10 largest emerging markets, with a promising future in the world economy.

Political success

It is important to note that India achieved its economic stability while still maintaining a stable and free democracy—a feat that China and many other Southeast Asian economic powers cannot claim. If India's 50-year economic record was judged as lackluster compared with Asia's "tiger" economies, its political success over 50 uninterrupted years of democratic rule was widely recognized and applauded. India's ability to sustain competitive electoral politics since 1947—apart from the two years of Indira Gandhi's emergency rule—had distinguished it from almost all other Asian countries. Although power was concentrated in the Congress Party, which ruled for the great majority of India's 50 years of independence, democratic politics had allowed many different voices to be heard and provided safety nets for the poor.

Indian citizens enjoyed such fundamental aspects of democracy as a free press and a truly independent judicial system from 1947. While many other former colonies, newly independent in the mid-1900's, lapsed into one-party rule or military dictatorship, India adopted, and sustained, a multiparty democratic system that endured. Thanks to the legacy of the independence movement and to the leadership of people like Nehru, democracy took root in India in the 1950's and became part of an everyday expectation of life. India's democratic system was far from ideal—corruption, for example, was widespread, but most ordinary Indians still recognized the value of democracy. In a 1997 poll carried out by *India Today*, 34 percent of those surveyed named corruption as the greatest contemporary evil. An overwhelming 95 percent, however, still believed that their vote was valuable. Despite its problems, Indians believed in democracy.

India's record is especially impressive when compared with its neighbors, Pakistan and Bangladesh. After 50 years, Pakistan could claim only limited political freedom, with nearly half of its years since independence spent under military rule. Bangladesh by 1997 had spent approximately 16 of its 25 years as an independent country under military control.

From a social standpoint, Bangladesh and Pakistan also lagged far behind India. While India by the late 1990's had managed only a 52 percent adult literacy rate, Bangladesh and Pakistan had even lower rates. Figures for 1995 show these countries maintaining an adult literacy rate of only 38 percent. Most commentators agreed that a crucial test for India in the next 50 years would be its ability to conquer mass illiteracy and bring a wider cross-section of its population into the political and economic arena.

Future challenges

India by 1997 had demonstrated that poor countries were capable of sustaining a vibrant democratic political system as well as a modern, fast-growing economy. However, it remained to be seen in 1997 if India's own particular democratic mechanisms might remain obstacles to continued economic reform. Despite enormous economic changes, successive governments after 1991 were still unwilling to remove subsidies, which traditionally had taken up a large part of public expenditure. These subsidies covered basic food supplies for the poor, but also paid for fertilizers and other agricultural expenses. Many economists argued that while there may have been good reasons

Although agriculture lags behind industry in India, the nation's farmers raise sufficient grain to feed nearly 1 billion Indians and produce a surplus for export.

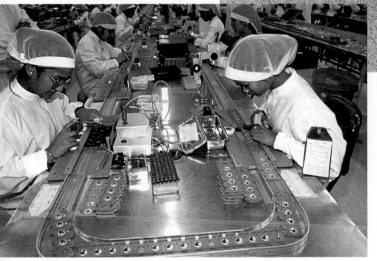

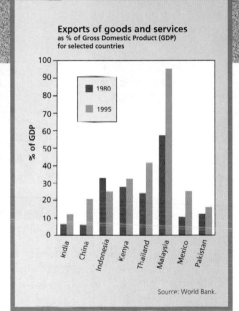

Exports of goods and services
as % of Gross Domestic Product (GDP)
for selected countries

■ 1980
■ 1995

% of GDP

India China Indonesia Kenya Thailand Malaysia Mexico Pakistan

Source: World Bank.

India's economy improved in the 1990's, with exports of goods and services improving by more than 5 percent between 1980 and 1995. But the total remains low in comparison with other developing countries.

for some of these subsidies, not all of them could be justified. Many governments in the 1990's, particularly delicately balanced coalition governments such as India's, found it difficult to decisively continue economic reform.

Another big challenge facing Indian democracy in the 1990's was the rise of Hindu nationalism, particularly as shown in the increased electoral power of the right-wing Bharatiya Janata Party (BJP). It emerged in the 1996 election as the country's single largest party, taking a third of the total seats in the national legislature. The BJP came to prominence by promoting a specifically Hindu identity for India, accepting minorities—particularly Muslims—only on BJP's own terms. The pursuit of a Hindu nationalist agenda led to extreme violence. For example, when a Muslim mosque in Ayodhya was pulled down by a mob in December 1992, it triggered widespread rioting that left more than 1,200 people dead. Nevertheless, by 1997 there was still little overall public support for an overtly Hindu religious

President K. R. Narayanan, *above*, addresses the Indian parliament in New Delhi. In July 1997, Narayanan became the first person from India's lowest social class to serve as head of state.

Indian and Pakistani soldiers, *opposite*, continued to face one another across the border dividing the two countries in 1997. Indian-Pakistani relations have remained tense since independence in 1947.

state. Commentators pointed to India's long and admirable history of religious tolerance and expressed confidence in the country's capacity to maintain its long-term stability despite any internal differences.

India's antiquated caste system was the institution that most stood in the way of its claim to full democratic freedoms for all, and in 1997 Indian politics appeared poised for a future struggle by the lower castes for political power. These castes included both the former "untouchables," now known officially as the scheduled castes or *Dalits* (the oppressed), and other lower classes, including many of the country's small farmers and agricultural laborers. These two groups constituted a majority of India's population in 1997 and would represent a formidable force if united politically. The fact that K. R. Narayanan, himself a Dalit, was elected president in July 1997 demonstrated the potential for the greatly increased influence in the coming century of India's previously excluded classes.

India and the world

By the end of the 1990's, India was still adjusting to the new world situation after the end of the Cold War. Economically, India needed to be able to attract investment and trade with the United States and other major economies. Politically, India attempted to make clear that it was unwilling to uncritically accept U.S. leadership in all fields. In terms of military strategy, India was unwilling to accept a U.S.-sponsored nuclear agreement that would deny it the chance to become a nuclear state while China was permitted to remain a nuclear power. In 1997, therefore, India was the only large country that chose not to sign the Comprehensive Test Ban Treaty. India, to maintain freedom of action, courted as wide a range of diplomatic relationships as possible, including connections with Iran, Russia, and other republics of the former Soviet Union.

India's relations with Pakistan overshadowed all other issues in 1997, with the problem of Kashmir at the center of the disagreement. India's claim to the northern state of Jammu and Kashmir has been disputed by Pakistan since partition. And the Indian government has traditionally regarded internal rebellion in the state as the work of Pakistani intelligence agencies. An uprising in the region in 1989 led to continued violence. By 1997, an estimated 20,000 people had been killed in confrontations between Muslim rebels and Indian troops over the disputed territory. Poor relations between India and Pakistan became a major factor in an arms race between the two countries, which by the 1990's encompassed weapons with a nuclear potential and sophisticated missile systems. Talks to resolve the Kashmir issue resumed in 1997, though few expected an early breakthrough. A state visit to India by Britain's Queen Elizabeth II in October 1997 was beset by controversy, largely over the issue of Kashmir. The queen's earlier comments in Pakistan about her hopes for a resolution of differences between Pakistan and India were perceived in India as British meddling in its internal affairs and proved just how sensitive and intractable the issue has remained.

The next 50 years

India's overall position as the leading power in south Asia was undeniable by 1997. If India proved able to continue the pace of economic development it set in the 1990's, it was poised during the first half of the next century to achieve the capacity to end the poverty that was still widespread in 1997. At the same time, the middle class could continue to enjoy a standard of living comparable, for example, to that already enjoyed in many countries in east Asia. However, many obstacles remained. The need for dramatic improvement in the field of education in order to conquer widespread illiteracy and the resultant social imbalance remained a top priority. Similar challenges existed in the areas of health care and housing. Tackling corruption was a top political priority, with President Narayanan calling for a nationwide movement against corruption in 1997, to mark the 50th anniversary of India's independence.

Despite the huge scale of these challenges, against a background of a vast and expanding population, Indians had good reason in 1997 to be optimistic about the prospects for their nation's medium- and long-term prosperity. Fifty years after India first took control of its own destiny, the rest of the world took careful note of this country and its great potential for the future. ■■■

Pakistan: Neighbor and rival

Pakistan, India's neighbor, became an independent nation on Aug. 14, 1947, one day before Indian independence. In response to demands for a Muslim homeland by Muslim leaders in India, the regions of East and West Pakistan were carved out of what had been British India. A country that began as a vision of a place where Muslims could live without fear of domination by Hindus (India's religious majority), Pakistan endured a turbulent first 50 years.

Beginning with the communal violence that left up to a million people dead, the relationship between India and Pakistan was one of confrontation and mutual distrust. In 1948 and again in 1965, the two countries fought over the disputed border territory of Kashmir. Civil war erupted between East and West Pakistan in 1971, as East Pakistan declared its independence and called itself Bangladesh. India successfully assisted Bangladesh's separation from West Pakistan.

Muhammad Ali Jinnah, the Muslim leader who became Pakistan's first head of government, died in 1948, only 13 months after the country was established. Political life over the following decades was unstable and often violent, with the majority of Pakistan's first 50 years spent under military rule.

The population of Pakistan included a wide variety of ethnic backgrounds, languages, and cultures—the people were united only by religion. One of the most problematic divisions came between the *mohajirs* (refugees who emigrated from India at partition) and the local population. Power struggles between the two groups over issues such as quotas for university places or government jobs led to violence. Although Pakistan in 1997 had a 69 percent higher gross domestic product per person than India, it had lower literacy rates and higher rates of infant mortality. Pakistan's spending on health care and education was among the lowest in Asia. After a difficult first half-century, Pakistan in 1997 faced many challenges in its struggle to emerge as a democratic nation.

Indian, American. The United States National Park Service in March 1997 selected a design for the Little Bighorn National Monument to memorialize the American Indians who died in the 1876 battle in which the Indians defeated the forces of Lieutenant Colonel George A. Custer. A granite obelisk erected in 1881 honors the estimated 270 soldiers and Indian scouts of the U.S. Seventh Cavalry who died in the battle. The proposed Indian memorial will honor the estimated 75 Indians who died fighting Custer's troops. Designed by Philadelphia architect John R. Collins, the proposed memorial is an earthen mound in which three bronze figures on horseback represent members of the Lakota Sioux, Cheyenne, and Arapaho tribes. Through an opening in the mound, visitors will be able to glimpse the 1881 memorial.

The Indian Land Consolidation Act of 1984, which barred American Indians from passing on to their heirs private property on reservation land, was ruled unconstitutional by the U.S. Supreme Court on Jan. 21, 1997. The 1984 law, which had made the entire tribe the recipient of property after an owner's death, had been intended to stop the division of reservation land. In an 8-to-1 ruling, the justices determined that the law violated the Fifth Amendment to the Constitution, which bars the government from taking property without compensation.

A long-contested dispute over Hopi and Navajo reservation land in northeastern Arizona ended in March 1997. The dispute began in 1882 when President Chester A. Arthur gave land in the middle of a Navajo reservation to the Hopis. When the U.S. Congress clarified the boundaries of the two reservations in 1974, about 12,000 Navajos lived on Hopi land. All but about 1,200 Navajos were relocated by the federal government. The 1997 settlement required the remaining Navajos to sign 75-year leases to remain on the property. Those who did not sign a lease had 90 days to decide whether to be relocated by the federal government or to move on their own.

Osage tribe. The 10th U.S. Circuit Court of Appeals voided in June a 1993 referendum that had given the Osage tribe of Oklahoma a democratic government. The court reinstated the Osage Allotment Act of 1906, which closed the membership rolls of the tribe in 1907, thereby recognizing the tribe as having 2,229 members and consequently 2,229 tribal or "headright" votes that could be inherited or shared among heirs. With a population of about 17,000 people in the 1990's, the tribe had deemed the old system ineffective. The referendum approved by tribal members in 1993 ratified a constitution guaranteeing universal voting rights in the tribe. A group of headright voters, however, challenged the referendum in court, and the 10th Circuit Court ruled that the tribe did not have the right to change its form of government. Advocates of the new constitution believed the ruling would have far-reaching implications about who could claim to be a member of the Osage tribe and be eligible for various benefits.

Department of Interior investigation. U.S. Attorney General Janet Reno in November extended an investigation into the role of Interior Secretary Bruce Babbitt in his department's rejection of an off-reservation casino project proposed by three Chippewa tribes in Wisconsin. Babbitt maintained that the project was rejected because the casino would not have been on or near reservation land. The Chippewa alleged that the rejection was the result of political pressure from the Clinton Administration. During the 1996 presidential campaign, other tribes with casinos in Wisconsin and neighboring states had donated at least $270,000 to President Clinton's reelection campaign and to the Democratic Party. Reno was expected to determine early in 1998 if an independent counsel should investigate the allegations.

The Intertribal Sinkyone Wilderness Park, the first Indian-owned national wilderness, was officially dedicated on Oct. 10, 1997. The 3,900-acre (1,600-hectare) park along northern California's Pacific Coast was once part of a heavily harvested redwood forest. The National Park Service and the 11 tribes that purchased the land planned to restore native plants and trees to the park and rebuild salmon jumps in the park's rivers.   □ Jay D. Lenn

Indiana. See State government.

Indonesia experienced a financial crisis in 1997 when its currency fell 32 percent, and its stock market plunged 41.6 percent. In October 1997, the International Monetary Fund (IMF), a United Nations (UN) affiliate, offered a $15-billion emergency aid package to Indonesia, and the United States committed approximately $3 billion in aid, the first direct American financial contribution to restore financial stability in Southeast Asia. The loan package included wide-ranging austerity measures for the world's fourth most populous country.

Ethnic violence. Indonesia experienced the worst ethnic violence in its history in 1997, when more than 50 people died during battles in Kalimantan, the Indonesian region of the island of Borneo. In January and February, Muslim settlers from the Indonesian island of Madura clashed with Christian Kalimantan tribesmen, known as Dayaks.

Election riots. Supporters of the ruling Golkar Party fought members of the United Development Party (PPP) in Banjarmasin on May 23, the final day of a parliamentary election campaign. Rioters set fire to a shopping center, killing more than 120 people.

On May 29, the Golkar Party claimed 74 percent of votes for parliament amid charges of fraud. The PPP won 22 percent of the vote, replacing the Democratic Party of Indonesia (PDI) as the party of protest. PDI had been led by Megawati Sukarnoputri, a daughter of Indonesia's former President

Sukarno. In 1996, the government of President Suharto had arranged for a rebel PDI faction to remove Megawati as party leader. Megawati and some of her supporters boycotted the 1997 election. The PDI's vote fell from 17 percent in the 1992 parliamentary elections to 3 percent in 1997.

East Timor. Guerrillas seeking independence killed more than 40 people in 1997 in East Timor, a former Portuguese colony that was seized by Indonesia in 1975. The UN made no progress in brokering an end to the violence, and the United States accused the Indonesian government of human rights violations in East Timor.

Jungle fires. In September 1997, smoke wafting from forest fires in the jungles of Indonesia choked much of Southeast Asia. Mixed with urban air pollution, the smoke created a smog that disrupted transportation, affected school attendance, and caused respiratory problems for millions of people. The forest fires and smog resulted in one of the worst and most widespread manmade disasters the region has known. The fires were, for the most part, intentionally set by Indonesian and Malaysian companies, which used fire as a cheap and illegal means of clearing land. Dry weather caused by *El Niño* (a powerful Pacific Ocean current that occasionally upsets weather patterns around the world) created conditions that made the fires difficult to control. □ Henry S. Bradsher

See also **Asia** (Facts in brief table); **Malaysia**.

International trade grew strongly for much of 1997, contributing to rapid economic growth and low inflation in the United States. However, the outlook for trade became a source of concern in mid-1997, after a severe crisis swept across financial markets in Asia and then struck Latin America. The turmoil raised the prospect that stricken regions would become weaker markets for imports from the United States and other trading nations, while the weakened countries would try to export more to the United States or European markets.

Granting "fast-track" trade negotiating powers to President Bill Clinton became a political battlefield during 1997. In November, Clinton withdrew his request that the U.S. Congress give him so-called "fast-track" authority after it became clear that the legislation lacked support in Congress among the president's own Democratic Party. This authority, which presidents had been granted routinely since 1974, would have given President Clinton the power to negotiate trade pacts that Congress could only vote for or against without amendments. The rebuff was seen by some as a major defeat that could curtail the president's influence in his three remaining years in office and become an obstacle to continued rapid growth in international trade.

NAFTA. In the first formal assessment of the North American Free Trade Agreement (NAFTA)—a 1994 treaty that united Mexico, Canada, and the United States into one of the world's largest free-trade zones—the Clinton Administration in July 1997 reported to Congress that the treaty had proven to be beneficial to the country. The report noted that NAFTA had created between 90,000 and 160,000 U.S. jobs and had stimulated greater exports to Canada and Mexico. American unions, however, disputed the figures and said that NAFTA had cost jobs.

Although trade relations generally flourished between the NAFTA partners, a disagreement over the movement of cargo trucks from Mexico into the United States continued in 1997. The U.S. government continued to suspend a NAFTA provision that would allow cargo trucks from Mexico and the United States to move freely across each nation's border. The regulation continued to draw objection from some U.S. unions, which feared job losses, and from American officials in such border states as California and Texas, who feared a rise in highway accidents if Mexican trucks failed to meet U.S. inspection standards. In March, however, five Republican senators from border states sent a letter to the Clinton Administration asking the president to lift the restriction "so that the border region can reap the full economic gains of free trade."

European currency. Finance ministers from the European Union (EU)—an organization of 15 Western European nations that promotes cooperation among its members—reaffirmed their intentions on September 13 to develop a single European currency by 1999. The euro, as the currency was to be called, would replace other forms of currency circulated in individual EU countries by the year 2002. Various EU nations raised interest rates or taxes in 1997 toward the goal of lowering national budget deficits and inflation. However, for much of the year, most of Europe experienced high levels of unemployment and mild overall economic growth.

China and Japan. Statistics released by the U.S. Commerce Department in November showed that the U.S. trade deficit continued to rise in 1997. A trade deficit is the shortfall between the value of a country's exports and the value of its imports.

Statistics revealed that the deficit stood at $11.1 billion in September. The major reason for the deficit was a growing trade gap between the United States and Asian nations, led by China and Japan. The trade gap in goods with China increased to $5.5 billion in September, while the monthly deficit with Japan increased to $5.1 billion. The report showed the initial effects on trade flows from currency crises that spread across Asia in 1997.

Trade in Asia was dominated by China's continued growth as a world economic power. Tensions between the United States and Japan arose as the Japanese economy stumbled in 1997 as its currency—the yen—fell against the U.S. dollar in world currency markets.

International trade

As the Japanese yen continued to weaken, the United States and other major industrial nations urged Japan to shift its focus toward stimulating domestic demand and away from dependence on exports. Instead, with its economy showing improved strength after years of mostly weak growth, Japan on April 1 increased a consumption tax on goods from 3 percent to 5 percent in an attempt to reduce the budget deficit. The unpopular tax led Japanese consumers to stockpile goods prior to March 31, resulting in sharply reduced consumer spending in the months that followed.

As China continued its emphasis on boosting exports to fuel economic growth, the Clinton Administration in May announced plans to extend China's most-favored-nation (MFN) trade status for one year. MFN is a designation under U.S. law that allows lower U.S. tariffs on imports from MFN trading partners. The Republican-led Congress approved the trade status for China, but by a narrower margin than in past years after Democratic leaders fought the extension.

However, the United States continued to oppose China's goal of joining the World Trade Organization (WTO), which administers global trade agreements and settles disputes between nations. U.S. leaders insisted that China liberalize its trade terms to meet WTO standards before being admitted.

Hong Kong. The British dependency of Hong Kong—an Asian financial and trade center that flourished on capitalism—returned at midnight on the morning of July 1 to the sovereignty of China, the world's largest Communist nation. Some analysts believed the event could have a lasting impact on trade and financial flows. China pledged not to interfere with Hong Kong's economy.

World markets in crisis. Several stock and currency markets throughout the world suffered severe declines beginning in mid-1997, in part because of a strong U.S. dollar. Currency traders, who viewed the economy of Thailand as having become too overextended to support its growth, had bid down Thailand's currency, the baht, for months. Thailand's government announced on July 2 that it would request international financial aid, which caused the value of the baht to drop even lower.

The collapse of Thailand's overvalued currency soon spread to other Asian countries as well as to Latin America. The value of currency in Malaysia, Indonesia, and the Philippines all declined, which caused some countries to raise their interest rates in an effort to protect the value of their currency. Other nations took emergency loans from the International Monetary Fund, a United Nations organization that provides short-term credit to its more than 175 member nations, to help stabilize the value of their currency.   ☐ John D. Boyd

See also **Economics; Hong Kong** Special Report: **Hong Kong 1997—Capitalism Comes to China.**

Internet. In July 1997, *The New York Times* declared that the World Wide Web had reached a "defining moment" in its development as a communications medium. For the first time in history, millions of people worldwide used the Web to gather news and information about the exploration of another planet as soon as the news became available.

Mars Pathfinder, a spacecraft sent by the United States National Aeronautics and Space Administration (NASA), landed on Mars on July 4, 1997. Hours later, the craft began transmitting photographs of the Martian landscape back to Earth. NASA immediately made these images public on several Web sites that were linked to NASA's Jet Propulsion Laboratory in Pasadena, California. In the first four days following the landing, sites featuring Pathfinder data averaged more than 80 million hits per day. A hit is a unit of measurement of the number of requests for files that visitors make to a particular site.

America Online, Incorporated (AOL), of Dulles, Virginia, rebounded from a shaky start early in 1997 to cement its position as the world's largest Internet provider. In January 1997, AOL avoided a barrage of lawsuits by signing an agreement with the attorneys general of 36 states. The agreement called for AOL to halt an aggressive expansion effort, which in 1996 had attracted more subscribers than the provider could handle. During peak usage times, many AOL subcribers found it impossible to access the service. In 1997, AOL moved quickly to upgrade its systems and add telephone access numbers in most areas.

AOL's biggest move of 1997 occurred in September, when it participated in a three-way deal to purchase competitor CompuServe Corporation of Columbus, Ohio. In the deal, WorldCom, Incorporated of Jackson, Mississippi, purchased CompuServe for $1.2 billion. AOL then acquired CompuServe's online service and its 2.3 million subscribers, plus $175 million in cash, from WorldCom. In exchange, WorldCom received AOL's ANS Communications division, which provided Internet access, mainly for large businesses. The deal made WorldCom a major provider of telecommunications networks for online services and business customers.

A mainstream medium. The Internet gained wide acceptance in 1997, particularly in the business world. Web addresses, with their familiar "www" prefix, appeared in TV ads, on billboards, and on product packaging. The number of Web sites registered was 26 million in September 1997, up from 14.7 million in 1996, according to a survey by a scientist at the Bellcore Internet Architecture Research Laboratory in San Francisco. Internet marketing firms reported that 36 million people used the Internet in 1997, up from 19 million in 1996.

The Internet emerged as a vital arena of commerce in 1997, with close to $500 million in business conducted online. In October, the Internet Advertising Bureau (IAB), an Internet marketing analysis firm, reported that consumers spent $343.9 million on the Internet in the first half of 1997—a 322-percent increase over the first half of 1996.

Growing pains. The extent to which the Internet had become a part of everyday life for many people was underscored on July 17, 1997, when a system breakdown occurred at a regional Internet computer facility in Herndon, Virginia. Two huge files in a computer containing more than a million Internet addresses became garbled during a routine program upgrade. For several hours, millions of perplexed Internet users found themselves unable to use e-mail or access World Wide Web sites.

The rise of e-mail as a common means of personal communication led to of a new phenomenon known as spamming. Lured by e-mail's ability to mass-mail cheaply to huge numbers of people, some companies bombarded e-mail users with electronic junk mail—popularly known as *spam*. Spamming rose to such an annoying level in 1997 that several Internet service providers filed lawsuits against companies engaging in the practice.

Adult content. The U.S. Supreme Court in June struck down the Communications Decency Act, a 1996 law regulating the Internet. The law had made it illegal to post "indecent" or "patently offensive" words and pictures on the Internet where children could find them. However, the law never went into effect because several groups had filed suit to block it. The court decided in 1997 that the law violated the right to open access to information.

Concern about online pornography waned in 1997 as parents, schools, and libraries purchased special programs that could block access to unsuitable sites using a set of specified keywords. Such programs ignited new controversy, however, when it was discovered that they might unintentionally prohibit access to legitimate Web sites with information on such topics as AIDS or breast cancer.

New domain names. In February 1997, the Internet Society introduced seven new domain names for use with Internet addresses. A domain name is a three-letter suffix that appears at the end of e-mail and Web addresses. Officials of the society, a standard-setting group based in Reston, Virginia, said more domains were needed because existing ones were running out of addresses. In the past, six domain names were used in the United States: *.com* for commercial businesses, *.org* for noncommercial organizations, *.net* for network services, *.mil* for military institutions, *.gov* for government agencies, and *.edu* for schools. The society added *.firm* for noncommercial businesses, such as law firms; *.store* for businesses offering goods for sale, *.info* for information services, *.web* for World Wide Web-related services, *.arts* for cultural organizations, *.rec* for recreational groups, and *.nom* for personal names. ☐ Herb Brody

See also **Computer; Telecommunications.**

Iowa. See State government.

Iran. A German court precipitated a diplomatic crisis by concluding on April 10, 1997, that Iranian leaders had approved the assassination of Iranian opposition figures living outside of Iran. The court's findings were the culmination of a trial, begun in 1993, of five people suspected of the 1992 slaying of three Iranian opposition leaders in Berlin. Four of the suspects—one Iranian and three Lebanese—were found guilty. Although the court concluded that the Berlin assassinations had been ordered by Iranian leaders, it did not specify which leaders were involved. However, testimony during the trial alleged that a "committee for special operations," which included then President of Iran Ali Akbar Hashemi Rafsanjani and spiritual leader Ayatollah Ali Khamenei, had to approve all political assassinations. Some 20 Iranian opposition figures reportedly had been killed while living in exile in Europe since Iran's Islamic government came to power in 1979.

Fourteen of the 15 countries belonging to the European Union (EU), a cooperative association of Western European nations, responded to the court's announcement by withdrawing senior diplomats from Iran. The EU also suspended discussions intended to moderate Iran's behavior. The United States, which had previously condemned Iran for supporting terrorism and attempting to acquire weapons of mass destruction, urged the EU to sever all diplomatic and commercial ties with Iran. EU leaders, however, raised doubts about the effectiveness of pursuing a hard-line policy. On April 29, 1997, the EU announced that it would restore limited diplomatic relations with Iran.

New president. On May 23, Iranian voters, in the most freely contested presidential election since the Islamic government assumed power, overwhelmingly elected moderate Muslim cleric Mohammed Khatami as president. Khatami won 69 percent of the vote, while Ali Akbar Nateq Nouri, the candidate favored by Iran's conservative religious establishment, won 25 percent. Khatami received heavy support from women, young adults, and the middle class—many of whom desired a liberalization of the strict economic and social constraints instituted by the Islamic government. Some observers hoped the election results were evidence that the fervor of Iran's Islamic revolution was finally giving way to practical concerns.

In August, the Iranian parliament approved the appointment of all 22 of Khatami's Cabinet nominees, many of whom had been resisted by the more conservative members of parliament. Ayatollah Mohajerani, who was selected to head the Ministry of Culture and Islamic Guidance, promised to ease some restrictions on cultural life. He had previously urged direct talks with the United States, commonly considered Iran's greatest enemy. Massoumeh Ebtekar, who was appointed vice president of environmental protection, became the Islamic govern-

Iranian women attend a May 1997 rally for presidential candidate Mohammed Khatami, a moderate who promised to ease restrictions on cultural life. The support of women was crucial to Khatami's May 23 victory.

ment's first female Cabinet member. Some Western critics noted, however, that conservatives still held great power in Iran, despite the new, moderate president and Cabinet members. Former President of Iran Rafsanjani, an arch conservative, remained head of the Expediency Discernment Council, which outlines long-term state policies and influences parliamentary decisions.

Foreign gas deal. In September, Iran signed a $2-billion deal with the French oil company Total SA (in partnership with a Russian and a Malaysian company) to exploit a natural gas field in the Persian Gulf. The deal led the United States to consider imposing trade sanctions against the companies under a 1996 U.S. law, which mandated sanctions against any company, including a foreign corporation, investing more than $40 million in either Iran's or Libya's energy sector. European countries responded that the United States had no authority to punish European companies for activities conducted beyond U.S. borders. The gas deal was one of many efforts made by Iran in 1997 to attract foreign investment.

Earthquakes. A series of earthquakes in early 1997 destroyed hundreds of villages in Iran. The quakes caused the deaths of more than 3,500 people, injured some 10,000 people, and left more than 50,000 others homeless. □ Christine Helms

See also **Middle East** (Facts in brief table); **People in the news.**

Iraq. On Oct. 29, 1997, Iraqi President Saddam Hussein ordered all United States personnel affiliated with United Nations (UN) inspections of Iraqi weapons programs out of the country. The UN inspectors had been attempting to verify if Iraq was complying with UN demands to destroy long-range missiles and chemical, biological, and nuclear weapons. Verification of the destruction of these weapons was the primary criterion considered by the UN for the lifting of economic sanctions imposed after Iraq's 1990 invasion of Kuwait. Observers claimed it was Hussein's frustration with the sanctions, which the UN had previously threatened to toughen—at the urging of the United States—that led Hussein to order U.S. inspectors out of Iraq. U.S. officials had implied that the sanctions should remain in effect as long as Hussein remained in power.

After Hussein ignored UN warnings to rescind his order, the UN Security Council imposed additional sanctions on Iraq on Nov. 12, 1997. The new sanctions banned foreign travel by some Iraqi officials. Hussein evicted the U.S. inspectors on November 13, and the UN withdrew all other inspectors the following day in protest. The crisis escalated in mid-November as the United States began a military build-up in the Persian Gulf and attempted to win international support for military action against Iraq.

On November 18, Russian officials announced that Iraq had accepted a plan to resolve the crisis.

The plan allowed UN inspectors to return to Iraq on November 21. Russia then proposed that the UN declare Iraq free of nuclear weapons and nearly free of long-range missiles.

Oil-for-food. On December 4, the UN Security Council voted to extend the "oil-for-food" program, originally instituted by the UN for Iraq in late 1996, for another six months. The program allowed Iraq to sell $2 billion worth of oil during a six-month period in order to buy such humanitarian supplies as food and medicine. Iraq, however, complained that the United States was blocking or delaying Iraqi purchases of humanitarian goods.

Health problems. The inability of the United States to assemble international support for military action against Iraq in November 1997 highlighted the widespread concern that many nations had for the plight of the Iraqi people. In March, the World Health Organization, a UN agency, stated that Iraq's health-care system had nearly collapsed due to delays in receiving medical supplies and to other problems related to UN sanctions. In November, the UN Children's Fund (UNICEF) stated that 960,000 Iraqi children suffered from malnutrition, a problem that was practically nonexistent in Iraq prior to the imposition of the sanctions.

Pilgrimage flights. On April 9, Iraq flouted an air embargo that was part of the 1990 UN sanctions by allowing Iraqis to fly to Saudi Arabia for the *hajj*, the annual Islamic pilgrimage to Mecca. Despite calls from the United States for a strong condemnation of the flight, the UN Security Council issued only a mild rebuke on April 16, 1997.

Turkish Kurds. In May, Iraqi officials condemned a massive assault made by Turkish forces on Turkish Kurd bases in northern Iraq. Kurds are an ethnic group inhabiting mountainous regions of southwest Asia. Turkish Kurdish rebels, who began fighting for independence from Turkey in 1984, set up bases in northern Iraq in 1994 when Iraqi Kurdish groups began fighting each other. Turkey alleged that the rebels used the bases to launch attacks on Turkish targets. In September, Iraqi officials claimed that Turkish air strikes against rebel bases in Iraq violated Iraqi sovereignty. Turkey reportedly had 20,000 troops in northern Iraq in late 1997.

Regional relations. In early October, the United States sent the aircraft carrier *Nimitz* to the Persian Gulf after Iran bombed two bases in Iraq controlled by an Iranian opposition group. U.S. officials said that the show of force was intended to prevent renewed conflict between Iran and Iraq, which fought a war from 1980 to 1988.

Iraq and Syria signed a trade accord in June 1997, following a visit in May by a delegation of Syrian businessmen to Iraq. Syrian-Iraqi relations had been severed in 1980 when Syria sided with Iran in the Iran-Iraq war. □ Christine Helms

See also **Middle East** (Facts in brief table); **Turkey.**

Ireland, with both parliamentary and presidential elections occurring in a single year, was dominated by political change in 1997. Bertie Ahern became *taoiseach* (prime minister) after the Fianna Fail Party narrowly won a general election on June 6. Outgoing Prime Minister John Bruton had called the election early, hoping that voters would reward his center-left "Rainbow Coalition"—made up of the Fine Gael, Labour, and Democratic Left parties—for Ireland's tax-cutting budget, which had passed in January. However, Ahern's center-right alliance with the Progressive Democrats won enough seats in the *Dáil* (lower house of parliament) to vanquish Bruton.

Mary McAleese, a law professor and vice-chancellor of Queen's University, Belfast, was elected president of Ireland on October 30. The election was called after Mary Robinson, who had been president since 1990, resigned on Sept. 12, 1997, to take the post of United Nations High Commissioner for Human Rights. McAleese, the candidate of Ireland's ruling coalition, was Ireland's first president to have been born in Northern Ireland.

The Irish economy continued to be strong in 1997. The European Commission forecast in October that growth would continue at the 1996 rate of 8.6 percent, though unemployment would fall only slightly to 10.8 percent. The government was also on course to meet the criteria for joining the European Union's single currency, set to be introduced in 1999.

Rising crime. The parliamentary election took place amid an unprecedented economic boom thanks to foreign investment, record growth, and government tax incentives. However, crime had become the major preoccupation of the voters. Petty crime, such as muggings and burglary, rose steadily in 1997, but there was also an increase in organized crime, especially related to drugs. Heroin abuse continued to increase sharply and spread from Dublin to other towns and cities.

The issue of illegal drugs had become a source of national concern in June 1996, when Veronica Guerin, one of Ireland's top journalists, was shot dead in her car by a suspected contract killer allegedly hired by a drug baron she was investigating. In October 1997, two men were arrested at a railway station near Amsterdam, the Netherlands, and charged with her murder. Extradition proceedings for a third man wanted in connection with the murder were begun in a London court.

Ireland's first divorce was granted by the High Court in Dublin on Jan. 17, 1997, though the legislation enacting it—the result of a 1995 referendum—only came into force on Feb. 27, 1997. A terminally ill cancer patient from Dublin had applied for a divorce so that he could marry the woman with whom he was living. The man died a few days later.

□ Ian Mather

See also **Europe** (Facts in brief table); **Northern Ireland; People in the news.**

Islam. Muslim leaders attending a meeting of the Organization of the Islamic Conference in Teheran, Iran, condemned Israel on Dec. 11, 1997, as a "terrorist state." Turkish President Süleyman Demirel, however, did not endorse the declaration and left the conference early—a move observers interpreted as a reflection of Turkey's efforts to improve cooperation with Israel. The delegates also criticized Islamic militants in Algeria, Egypt, and Pakistan, noting that the "killing of innocents is forbidden in Islam."

Fire in Mecca. On April 15, 1997, a fire swept through a camp outside Mecca, Saudi Arabia, killing more than 340 Muslim pilgrims, most of whom were from Bangladesh, India, and Pakistan, and injuring at least 1,500 other people. The fire destroyed about 70,000 tents in the encampment where devout Muslims had gathered for the *hajj*, an annual pilgrimage to Mecca.

Islamic militants in Egypt. On July 5, jailed leaders of two militant Islamic groups called for a cease-fire in their six-year conflict with the secular government of Egypt. More than 1,200 people had died since antigovernment violence began in 1992.

The proclamation coincided with a reputed weakening of Islamic radicalism in Egypt as the government continued to promote moderate forms of Islam in the media and to provide better services to poorer communities, where Islamic militants had particular success recruiting followers. Nonetheless, violent attacks on police and civilians continued. On

A fire on April 15, 1997, sweeps through a camp near Mecca, Saudi Arabia, where Muslim pilgrims were staying during the *hajj*, an annual pilgrimage. More than 340 people died in the blaze.

Nov. 17, 1997, militants murdered 58 foreign tourists and 4 Egyptians at the ancient temple of Queen Hatshepsut in Luxor.

Threat to Islamic writer. In May, scholars at Al-Azhar University in Egypt condemned Hassan Hanafi, a Cairo University professor, for carrying out a "destructive plan" against Islam. Hanafi headed the intellectual al-Turath wa al-Tajdid (Tradition and Renewal) project, which promoted philosophical creativity and endorsed reform of Islamic studies.

The Al-Azhar scholars, in their condemnation, quoted a passage from Hanafi's book *From Doctrine to Revolution:* "God does not exist except in our minds. That is, by thinking, we make God." Hanafi maintained that the passage was quoted out of context and, therefore, misinterpreted. The condemnation caused concern among more liberal Islamic and secular scholars, as a similar action led to the assassination of Egyptian writer Farag Fouda in 1992.

Islamic law in Malaysia. In June 1997, three Muslim contestants in a Malaysian beauty pageant were arrested for breaking Islamic laws requiring women to dress modestly. The incident prompted debate over jurisdictions between civil law and Islamic law, which each state interprets for its Muslim citizens. Prime Minister Mahathir bin Mohamad called for a review of Islamic laws as a step toward clarifying jurisdiction.   □ Vincent J. Cornell

See also **Egypt; Religion; Saudi Arabia.**

Israel. On Sept. 25, 1997, at least two Israeli intelligence agents allegedly attempted to assassinate Khaled Meshal, a leader of the militant Islamic group Hamas, in the Jordanian capital, Amman. The agents sprayed a nerve toxin into Meshal's ear. When Meshal's bodyguard intervened, the agents fled. The agents were later apprehended and turned over to Jordanian authorities. Observers in the Middle East believed that the attack was ordered in retaliation for a July 30 suicide bombing in which 16 Israelis were killed in Jerusalem. The bombing was attributed to Islamic extremists. Meshal survived the attempt on his life after the United States reportedly pressured Israel to provide an antidote to the toxin.

The alleged assassination attempt nearly shut down the Arab-Israeli peace process. After Jordan's King Hussein, who had been Israel's strongest supporter among Arab nations, learned of the attempted assassination, he threatened to sever ties with Israel. In response, Israeli Prime Minister Benjamin Netanyahu made a secret trip to Amman to resolve the crisis. Following the trip, Netanyahu released Sheik Ahmed Yassin, the jailed spiritual leader of Hamas, on October 1. Netanyahu also released as many as 70 other Arab prisoners, reportedly in exchange for the release of the Israeli intelligence agents captured in the assassination attempt.

Deterioration of peace process. The attempted assassination was the most serious among several incidents that threatened the Arab-Israeli peace process in 1997. The first such incident occurred in February, when Netanyahu approved the construction of 6,500 Israeli houses in East Jerusalem, the status of which remained to be resolved in Arab-Israeli negotiations. East Jerusalem was Arab territory taken during the 1967 Six-Day War that the Israeli government later annexed. The prime minister asserted that the additional settlements were needed to accommodate the growing Jewish population. Palestinians, however, charged that the Jewish settlements were meant to influence the ultimate determination of East Jerusalem's status.

The expansion of Israeli settlements triggered a number of violent incidents. On March 13, 1997, seven Israeli schoolgirls were shot and killed by a Jordanian soldier on Naharayim Island, land leased by Jordan to Israeli farmers. On March 21, in the first suicide bombing to occur since 1996, an Islamic extremist killed three people and wounded dozens of others in a Tel Aviv cafe.

Arab frustration mounted in July 1997, when the mayor of Jerusalem announced that 50 apartments would be built for Jews in an Arab neighborhood of East Jerusalem. On July 30, suicide bombings resumed with the Jerusalem bombing that killed 16 Israelis and wounded 150 others. On September 4, five Israelis were killed and more than 180 people were wounded by bombs in West Jerusalem. In addition to the bombings, bloody clashes between Palestinian youth and Israeli soldiers spread throughout the Israeli-occupied Arab territories of the West Bank and Gaza Strip during 1997.

Reaction to bombings. After the July bombing, Arafat agreed to increase efforts to suppress Hamas. Netanyahu responded to the July bombing by imposing blockades of the West Bank and Gaza Strip, preventing Palestinians from reaching their jobs in Israel. He also withheld millions of dollars of customs and tax funds that Arafat was to use as pay for Palestinian civil servants and police. The September bombing prompted Netanyahu to suspend a scheduled withdrawal of Israeli troops from a portion of the West Bank, further angering Arabs.

Albright urges restraint. On September 10, U.S. Secretary of State Madeleine Albright began a six-day visit to the Middle East in an attempt to reduce the growing tensions. She called for a suspension of provocative acts. However, on September 24, Netanyahu announced the building of a new Jewish settlement in the West Bank, and on September 25, the alleged assassination attempt was made on the life of the Hamas leader Khaled Meshal.

Yassin and Arafat. On October 22, released Hamas leader Yassin, who had received a tumultuous welcome upon his return home to Gaza, vowed to continue the "holy war" against Israel. In contrast, Arafat, who considered Yassin a political rival, had met with Netanyahu on October 8 to reaf-

An Orthodox Jew, taking part in a June 1997 demonstration in Jerusalem against archaeological excavations of Jewish gravesites, attempts to hoist a mock coffin and sign reading, "Theodore Herzl [founding father of Zionism], you too will end up in the clutches of archaeologists."

firm his commitment to peace. Netanyahu also pledged his support for peace during the meeting.

Cabinet proposal. On November 30, the Israeli Cabinet agreed to withdraw some Israeli troops from the West Bank, but Palestinians denounced the proposal for lacking details. Palestinians also accused Israel of failing to honor previous commitments to withdraw troops from the West Bank.

Observers noted that Netanyahu had made the proposal under pressure from the United States to revive the stalled peace process. Netanyahu was also under pressure from members of his political coalition who opposed any return of land to Palestinians. Earlier in 1997, Israel had withdrawn troops from 80 percent of the West Bank city of Hebron and from a small amount of other West Bank land. Palestinians, however, claimed that these withdrawals were inadequate because they did not meet Palestinian hopes that Israel would withdraw from some 80 percent of the West Bank by mid-1998.

Lebanese security zone. Twelve Israeli soldiers were killed on Sept. 5, 1997, in a commando raid against suspected pro-Iranian guerrillas in southern Lebanon. The deaths occurred in a 9-mile (14.5-kilometer) wide "security zone" maintained by Israel to deter guerrilla attacks. The incident prompted many Israelis to question the wisdom of maintaining the security zone. □ Christine Helms

See also **Middle East** (Facts in brief table).

Italy made great strides in 1997 toward reentering the economic and political mainstream of Europe. The government of Prime Minister Romano Prodi survived a challenge from his Communist allies, raising hopes that Prodi's center-left coalition might last a full five-year term and end Italy's post-World War II (after 1945) history of political instability. The government also engineered a sharp fall in the budget deficit and inflation, improving Italy's chances of joining the single European currency due to be launched in 1999.

Monetary union. The government continued to gear its policies toward meeting the economic requirements for the single currency. Prodi claimed that the euro, as the currency was to be called, offered Italy an opportunity to eliminate the high inflation and mounting government spending that had hampered its economy since the 1970's. He also insisted that Italy needed to join the monetary union to retain political influence in the European Union (EU), the organization of 15 Western European nations that is launching the euro.

The $58 billion in budget cuts and tax increases that Prodi had introduced since taking office in May 1996 bore fruit in 1997. The European Commission (the administrative arm of the EU) predicted that Italy's budget deficit, which was 6.8 percent of gross domestic product in 1996, would fall to 3.0 percent in 1997, the limit for countries joining the single currency. Inflation was expected to fall to 2.2 percent, the lowest since the 1960's. The budgetary restraint slowed the economy, however. Output was expected to grow by 1.4 percent in 1997, barely half the EU average. Unemployment stood at 12.1 percent.

Budget crisis. In September, the government proposed an additional $15-billion budget cut for 1998 to ensure that the deficit would stay below the single-currency ceiling. The Refounded Communists, a left-wing party whose support kept the government in power, promised to vote against the package, forcing Prodi to resign on Oct. 9, 1997. The Communists backtracked five days later, however, as Italians vented their outrage at the party for risking the country's chances of joining the single currency. Prodi remained in power after promising the Communists he would introduce legislation to reduce the working week to 35 hours by the year 2001.

Local elections. The government received a boost when the center-left parties of Prodi's so-called Olive Tree coalition dominated municipal elections on Nov. 16 and Nov. 30, 1997. The coalition parties won control of 57 cities with more than 15,000 residents, including some of Italy's largest cities—Genoa, Naples, Rome, and Venice. The center-right Freedom Alliance won only 25 smaller cities, while the Northern League, which wants independence for much of northern Italy, won 15.

Berlusconi convicted. The opposition suffered a further blow on December 3, when Silvio Berlusconi, the media magnate, former prime minister, and leader of the Freedom Alliance, was convicted of falsifying the price of a film company. Prosecutors in Milan said Berlusconi's company, Fininvest, purchased the film company for an artificially high price in 1989 to conceal the creation of a $6-million political slush fund. Berlusconi received a 16-month sentence but did not go to prison because of an Italian law that suspends most sentences of less than two years. He appealed the verdict. Berlusconi continued to face separate charges of bribing tax authorities and channeling money to politicians, including former Prime Minister Bettino Craxi, who remained in exile in Tunisia to escape corruption charges.

Intervention in Albania. In April 1997, the Italian government obtained a peacekeeping mandate from the United Nations and led a force of 6,500 soldiers from nine European countries into Albania after the Balkan country collapsed into near anarchy. Violence had broken out in Albania in March in response to the collapse of several fraudulent investment schemes, which wiped out an estimated $2 billion of savings in Europe's poorest country. Italy arranged for the peacekeeping force to stop a surge of immigration after 16,000 Albanians crossed the Adriatic Sea to Italy to flee the violence.

The force enabled Albania to restore order and hold elections on June 29 and July 6, in which the Socialist Party and its leader, Fatos Nano, defeated the Democratic Party of President Sali Berisha. The force withdrew from Albania in August.

Earthquakes. A series of earthquakes struck the central Italian region of Umbria beginning September 26, killing 11 people, leaving thousands homeless, and severely damaging some of the country's greatest medieval treasures. The quakes were followed by more than 400 aftershocks, forcing about 100,000 people to live in tent cities and cars in spite of the cold weather. The worst damage occurred in Assisi, where the ceiling of the basilica of Saint Francis of Assisi, built in the 1200's, collapsed, killing four people and turning some of Italy's earliest Renaissance *frescoes* (ceiling and wall paintings) to rubble.

Nobel laureate. Italian playwright and actor Dario Fo was awarded the 1997 Nobel Prize for literature by the Swedish Academy of Letters In December. Fo's dramas use medieval conventions and satire to provide social commentary.

Telephone sale. The Italian government, as part of its deficit-cutting efforts, sold its 41.8-percent stake in Telecom Italia, the national telephone company, to private investors in September and October 1997. The sale, Europe's largest single privatization to date, raised $14.9 billion. □ Tom Buerkle

See also **Albania; Art; Europe** (Facts in brief table).

Ivory Coast. See Africa.
Jamaica. See West Indies.

Japan. Ryutaro Hashimoto began a second term as prime minister in 1997. On September 5, his conservative Liberal-Democratic Party (LDP) acquired a majority of seats in the lower house, which dominates the Diet, the Japanese Parliament, by winning over defectors from other parties. LDP's power base had been weakened in the 1995 and 1996 parliamentary elections.

The realignment of Japan's political parties that began in 1992 entered a new phase in 1997 as the LDP won the support of defectors from smaller political parties. Ichiro Ozawa, a former LDP deal maker, attempted to institute political and economic reform by forming the New Frontier Party (NFP), which became the main opposition to LDP. By 1997, NFP began losing public and political support, and many officials found it difficult to work with Ozawa. On June 18, Morihiro Hosokawa, who in 1993 became the first non-LDP prime minister in Japan in almost 40 years, defected from the NFP. Another former prime minister, Tsutomu Hata, also defected from the NFP in 1997 and started his own party.

In 1997, the LDP initiated reforms that gave voters greater power in regulating government policies. It also considered proposals to reduce government bureaucracy and to deregulate the economy.

In municipal elections in Tokyo, the capital, on July 6, the LDP won 54 seats in the city's 127-seat assembly. The LDP held only 38 seats prior to the election. The Social Democrats, the LDP's main coalition partner in the national government, lost seats in the election. Observers claimed that voters had turned against the Social Democrats because the party did not offer a distinctive difference from the LDP.

The Communist Party, which in 1997 became the leading opposition party against the coalition government, doubled its strength in the Tokyo assembly—from 13 to 26 seats. The party had softened its hard-line Communist ideology and emphasized its reputation for honesty, in contrast to the corruption scandals that had plagued the LDP for decades.

Cabinet member resigns. Koko Sato, whom Hashimoto had named to his new Cabinet in September, resigned on September 22 under political pressure. Hashimoto was widely criticized for recommending Sato for a Cabinet position. Sato had been convicted in 1976 of taking bribes.

Changing role. Japan reassessed its role in east Asian military affairs in 1997 and grappled with sensitive foreign policy issues. On Sept. 24, 1997, Japan and the United States agreed on new guidelines for implementing the Japanese-American security treaty of 1960. The treaty had detailed the military measures Japan could take in defending its borders in the event of an attack by the former Soviet Union.

The new guidelines outlined 40 acts that Japan could undertake in a military emergency, such as providing search-and-rescue operations and logistical support for the U.S. military. The guidelines shifted emphasis from Japanese defense of its islands to allowing the Japanese military to work with the United States during regional military emergencies.

Japan's constitution bars its armed forces from fighting outside of the Japanese islands. The 1997 treaty, however, allowed for the possibility that Japan may enter a military conflict outside of its boundaries. On July 15, the Japanese defense ministry cautioned that Japan needed to guard against China's and North Korea's military build-up. There were also growing concerns in 1997 about Japan's role in possible conflicts between China and Taiwan.

In 1997, China threatened to attack Taiwan if it attempted to declare an independent status. Although the island of Taiwan had been governed separately from China since 1949, China still regarded Taiwan as its province. On Aug. 17, 1997, Seiroku Kajiyama, chief secretary of the Japanese Cabinet, said that the revised treaty guidelines detailed how Japan would cooperate with the U.S. military in the event of an armed conflict between China and Taiwan. China had previously asked Japan not to cooperate with the United States in protecting Taiwan's separate status.

American bases. Parliament passed a bill in April giving the government power to provide land for U.S. military bases. In 1996, residents of Okinawa had voted for a reduction in the number of U.S. bases on the island, where in 1997, 30,000 of the

47,000 U.S. troops in Japan were based. The 1997 bill extended the leases on base land. Following passage of the bill, local newspaper polls showed that only 14 to 23 percent of Okinawa residents wanted the bases to close. Many residents feared the economic consequences of closing U.S. bases.

Relations with Russia. A July agreement on a $10-billion construction project helped ease relations between Japan and Russia. The countries agreed to cooperate in the development of natural gas fields in Russia and the construction of a pipeline to Japan across Mongolia, China, and South Korea. However, Japan and Russia continued to disagree over Russia's refusal to return to Japan the islands at the southern end of the Kurile chain that the Soviet Union had seized at the end of World War II in 1945.

Economy. Japan continued in 1997 to suffer the effects of a speculative boom that rocked the nation's economy in the early 1990's, when property prices soared to nearly 20 times what they had been in 1970. By early 1997, property prices leveled off at approximately four times 1970 prices, but several banks still held loans from people who bought property at inflated prices and could not repay the notes.

From April through June 1997, economic output dropped at a monthly rate of 11.2 percent, the worst decline since 1974. Tokai Kogyo, a construction company, declared bankruptcy in July 1997, the first Japanese construction company to declare bankruptcy since 1945. Construction had been the driving force of Japan's domestic growth in the post-World War II era. In November, Yamaichi Securities, Japan's fourth-largest brokerage firm, announced that it was insolvent. It was the largest corporate failure in Japan since 1945.

Nuclear power plants in Japan were plagued with accidents in 1997, triggering public concern about building more plants because of previous accidents and cover-ups. The state-run Power Reactor and Nuclear Fuel Development Corporation (PNC) admitted falsifying reports on Japan's worst nuclear accident, which occurred on March 11 at the Tokai-mura reprocessing plant 70 miles (113 kilometers) north of Tokyo. The accident exposed at least 37 workers to low doses of radiation.

After an accident in April at a plant 220 miles (354 kilometers) west of Tokyo exposed 11 workers to radiation, PNC admitted that it had failed to report 11 earlier radiation leaks at the plant. In August, the press reported that PNC had failed to carry out a 1982 order to repair a nuclear waste storage area at Tokaimura, which may have contaminated ground water. The government pushed ahead with plans to build nuclear power plants despite reports of declining morale among plant workers and the industry's failure to attract skilled employees. Nuclear power continued to be an important alternative to Japan's heavy dependence on imported energy sources, such as oil and gas.

Child murder. The Japanese public, which takes pride in its social stability and low murder rate, was shaken in May 1997 when the severed head of an 11-year-old boy was found outside a school in Kobe. In June, police arrested a 14-year-old boy who allegedly admitted killing the younger boy. According to police, he also admitted attacking two girls in March. One of the girls died following the attack. Prime Minister Hashimoto speculated that the high pressure put on children by Japan's school system was to blame for what a Japanese newspaper called "an increase in the frequency and savagery of crimes committed by young people."

Education reform. On June 26, Japan's Education Ministry began implementing a program to reform the school system. The system in place in 1997 stressed that children learn facts. Students were rigorously tested in science and mathematics, but the system discouraged creativity and individualism. The new plan reduced the number of examinations students would be required to take so that they could concentrate on a broader range of subjects.

Transplant law. On June 17, parliament passed a law that made it possible for people to receive heart and lung transplants from patients with no brain function. Laws that tightly restricted organ donation had forced many Japanese patients to travel abroad for transplants. □ Henry S. Bradsher

See also **Asia** (Facts in brief table).

Jordan. Israeli intelligence agents on Sept. 25, 1997, attempted to assassinate Khaled Meshal, a political leader of the militant Islamic group Hamas, in the Jordanian capital of Amman. The action infuriated Jordan's King Hussein, who had been Israel's main supporter among Arab nations. Hussein responded to the attempted assassination by threatening to end Jordan's relations with Israel. After a secret trip to Amman, Israeli Prime Minister Benjamin Netanyahu released Sheik Ahmed Yassin, the popular spiritual leader of Hamas, on October 1. Israeli officials also announced that they intended to release as many as 70 other Arabs.

Embassy shootings. On September 22, Jordanian militants shot and wounded two Israeli security guards at the Israeli embassy in Jordan. Press reports, quoting Israeli intelligence sources, claimed the attack, along with the renewal in July of suicide bombings in Jerusalem, led to the Israeli assassination attempt on Khaled Meshal.

Hussein's popularity. Hussein's strong response to the attempted assassination greatly increased his popularity among Arabs, most of whom had disapproved of the king's March 16 trip to Israel to offer condolences to the families of seven Israeli schoolgirls gunned down by a Jordanian soldier. Many Israelis blamed the shooting of the girls on Arab anger incited by a letter that Hussein wrote to Netanyahu on March 9. In the letter, Hussein rebuked

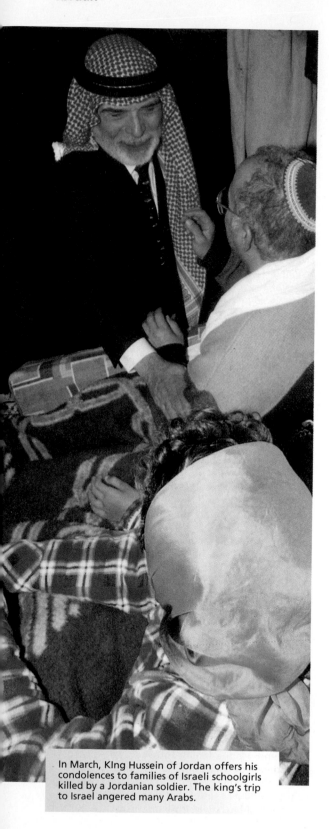

In March, KIng Hussein of Jordan offers his condolences to families of Israeli schoolgirls killed by a Jordanian soldier. The king's trip to Israel angered many Arabs.

Netanyahu for actions, such as the approval in February of a new Jewish settlement in East Jerusalem, that had seriously worsened relations between Israelis and Palestinians.

Dissent. Parliamentary elections held in November in Jordan were boycotted by nine opposition parties as a protest against what they called a steady usurpation of parliamentary power by Hussein. The opposition parties accused the government of massive fraud in the elections, in which the overwhelming majority of parliamentary seats were won by candidates loyal to Hussein.

In March, Hussein had instituted a law severely limiting freedom of the press, prompting four leaders of Jordan's professional unions to resign in protest. The unions in Jordan have a close relationship with the press. After other union leaders said they would resign, Hussein threatened to curb union political activities. Both the press and the unions had been highly critical of the Arab-Israeli peace process.

U.S. money. In June, the United States rewarded Jordanian support of the Arab-Israeli peace process by granting Jordan an additional $100 million in aid, to be used to secure stable water supplies and ease poverty. At least 21 percent of Jordan's population lives in poverty. The United States also gave Jordan $47 million in 1997, two-thirds of which could be used for military expenditures. □ Christine Helms

See also **Israel; Middle East** (Facts in brief table).

Judaism. Conservative and Reform Jews in Israel and the United States during 1997 called for *religious pluralism* (equal recognition of the major branches of Judaism) in Israel. Orthodox Jewish leaders, however, supported a bill under consideration in the Knesset, the Israeli parliament, that would establish Orthodox Judaism as the official state religion of Israel. In practice, the Orthodox rabbinate already controlled conversions to Judaism in Israel, but the proposed bill was intended to make that practice law. If the law were passed, it would officially determine who could be married in a Jewish ceremony, who could be buried with Jewish rites, and who could serve on religious councils in Israeli cities. The law could also have implications for immigration policies that grant citizenship to any person professing the Jewish faith or of Jewish heritage.

On April 1, the Knesset approved the bill 51 to 32 in the first of three required readings. In response to criticisms from Reform and Conservative leaders, the Knesset froze further action on the bill and agreed to work out a compromise. In return, the non-Orthodox leaders agreed to discontinue legal action to gain official recognition for non-Orthodox Judaism through the Israeli Supreme Court. The compromise terms included shared rabbinical leadership, that is, allowing non-Orthodox rabbis to prepare candidates for conversion, but giving the Orthodox rabbinate authority over the actual conversions. The discussions broke down, however, in October, and further action on the bill was postponed until 1998.

Impact on American Jews. The religious pluralism debate in Israel in 1997 resulted in disagreements among Orthodox, Conservative, and Reform Jews in the United States. While Conservative and Reform Jews are a small minority of religious Jews in Israel, they account for a vast majority of religiously affiliated Jews in the United States. Non-Orthodox American Jews, who have supported Israel through philanthropic organizations, saw the proposed legislation as an effort to delegitimize their faith.

In March, the Union of Orthodox Rabbis in the United States and Canada, the largest Orthodox rabbinical organization in North America, released a statement declaring that "Reform and Conservative are not Judaism at all but another religion." Reform and Conservative leaders, in turn, publicly criticized Orthodox leaders in the United States and in Israel.

Synagogue 2000, an interdenominational project, was initiated during 1997 at 16 "pilot sites"— 8 Conservative and 8 Reform synagogues in North America. Synagogue 2000 is based on the idea that synagogues must become "spiritual homes"—places of healing, prayer, study, and good deeds—rather than the ethnic centers that many Conservative and Reform Jews felt their synagogues had become in the past 100 years.

Apology from Roman Catholics. On Sept. 30, 1997, at a ceremony in Drancy, France, Roman Catholic Archbishop Olivier de Berranger apologized to French Jews for the church's silence during World War II (1939-1945). The Nazi regime had used Drancy as a relocation center for about 76,000 Jews who were sent to concentration camps in Germany. Henri Hajdenberg, head of the Representative Council of Jewish Institutions in France, responded at the ceremony by saying, "After the heavy silence of the war, the long silence of the postwar period is broken."

Switzerland and the Holocaust. In November 1997, Reva Shefer, a Jewish woman from Latvia who survived the Holocaust, received $400 from the Humanitarian Fund, which was established in February by three Swiss banks to compensate Holocaust victims or their relatives. Other businesses contributed to the fund, bringing its assets to about $200 million. The fund was in part created in response to Jewish organizations, particularly the World Jewish Congress based in New York City. The organizations had asked Switzerland, which was neutral during the war, to subject its wartime records to public scrutiny and to account for the gold and foreign currency reserves amassed from trade with Nazi Germany. Also in 1997, Swiss banks released lists of dormant bank accounts opened before or during the war that may have belonged to Jews. □ Marc Lee Raphael

See also **Religion; Switzerland.**

Kampuchea. See **Cambodia.**

Kansas. See **State government.**

Kazakstan. In 1997, foreign investors purchased major stakes in Kazakstan's lucrative natural resources and industrial sectors, which the Kazak government continued to privatize. To encourage further investment, the government passed laws offering tax exemptions for up to five years to foreign investors. Privatization was, however, generally unpopular among Kazak workers, many of whom failed to receive wages or pensions or became unemployed when new owners closed unprofitable operations. Protests were reported in several cities.

Prime Minister Akezhan Kazhegeldin, architect of Kazakstan's economic reforms, became the focus in 1997 of much criticism. Officials accused him of placing Western economic interests above those of the nation. In September, a new scandal erupted after Kazhegeldin admitted that he had worked, during the Soviet era, for the KGB, the intelligence agency of the Soviet Union. On October 10, Kazhegeldin resigned. Nurlan Balgimbayev, head of the national oil company, was named prime minister.

The transfer of Kazakstan's capital from Almaty north to the city of Akmola was completed in December 1997, when the prime minister's staff became the last office to move. A joint session of the Kazak legislature opened in the new capital on December 11. □ Steven L. Solnick

See also **Asia** (Facts in brief table).

Kentucky. See **State government.**

Kenya. An increasingly oppressive political climate and widespread corruption continued in 1997 to undermine the government of President Daniel arap Moi, Kenya's authoritarian leader. Tourism, Kenya's largest source of foreign currency, dropped in the wake of widening political violence and instability. Economic growth was also crippled by high inflation, the exodus of capital from Kenya's relatively wealthy Asian community, and a loss of confidence by foreign governments and investors.

Prodemocracy forces, encouraged by the May 16 overthrow of Mobutu Sese Seko, dictator of neighboring Zaire (renamed the Democratic Republic of Congo in 1997), opened a campaign to pressure Moi to enact constitutional reforms before elections scheduled for late in 1997. They also demanded that the government abolish laws that severely restricted opposition parties and rallies, permitted government control of the media, and allowed detention without trial. On May 31, proreform groups rallied in Nairobi, Kenya's capital. Several protesters died as police dispersed the crowd with tear gas and rubber bullets.

On July 7, opposition forces staged nationwide demonstrations, to which the government again responded violently. Nine people died, and many political activists and religious leaders, including the head of Kenya's Presbyterian Church, were severely beaten. On July 9, the government closed several universities, including Nairobi University, following a

Priests and other demonstrators flee tear gas fired by police to break up a rally in Nairobi, Kenya, in July by groups demanding democratic reforms.

series of clashes between police and students. On July 11, members of pro-reform groups in Kenya's legislature warned the government that its rigid opposition to democracy had made "violent" political change "inevitable."

Foreign governments, including the United States, loudly protested the government's behavior and threatened to cut off foreign aid. On July 17, Moi, bending to domestic and international pressure, announced a vague plan of "minimal reforms" and promised that police would not interfere with protesters. As a result, an opposition rally on July 31 proceeded peacefully. On August 13, however, gangsters employed by Moi's party attacked villages around the ocean-front city of Mombasa, Kenya's most popular tourism site. The gangsters targeted people who supported the opposition.

International pressure. Moi's failure to curb official corruption led international lending agencies to withdraw their support. On July 31, the International Monetary Fund suspended a three-year, $216-million loan package. On August 11, the World Bank withdrew $71.6 million in credits.

In late November, Moi legalized an opposition party in an effort to split support among his political rivals. Moi was re-elected president on Dec. 29, 1997.

□ Mark DeLancey

See also **Africa** (Facts in brief table); **Congo (Kinshasa).**

Korea, North. A drought in 1997 destroyed approximately 70 percent of North Korea's wheat crop and more than one-third of its rice crop, leaving much of the country's population of 24 million people malnourished or starving. The United Nations World Food Program warned that North Korea was heading toward "one of the biggest humanitarian disasters of our lifetime." The drought followed summer floods that had devastated crops in 1995 and 1996. On Aug. 21, 1997, a hurricane smashed dikes and flooded fields, further reducing harvests.

North Korea's secretive Communist government in 1997 allowed a few foreign relief workers to visit the country. Workers found hungry children abandoned by parents and starving people stripping bark from trees and digging up grass roots in search of nourishment. In June, 5 of the country's 10 food distribution centers ran out of supplies. However, supplies were reportedly available again in many of the centers by late 1997. The centers were designed to feed approximately 17 million people.

The government appealed to foreign countries for food aid, but refused to allow foreign donors to supervise its distribution. In the past, North Korea had used food aid to build its military stockpile.

Kim Chong-Il assumed the title of general secretary of the ruling Communist Party on Oct. 8, 1997. North Korea had been without a party leader since the death in 1994 of Kim's father, Kim Il Sung. The younger Kim delayed proclaiming himself leader of the party in adherence to the traditional three-year mourning period that historically was observed for Korean kings. Kim's new leadership was the first family succession in the Communist world.

Nuclear reactors. On Aug. 19, 1997, an American-led consortium began construction of two modern nuclear reactors on North Korea's east coast. The $5-billion project was financed primarily by the governments of South Korea and Japan, which agreed to pay for construction if North Korea abandoned older reactors that were suspected sites of a nuclear weapons program.

Hostile acts. North Korea continued to commit provocative acts that obstructed international peace talks convened to draft a treaty to replace the armistice that ended the Korean War (1950–1953). On July 16, 1997, 14 North Korean soldiers entered the Demilitarized Zone, a region that has separated North and South Korea since 1953, triggering the fiercest battle in the zone since 1973.

Defection. North Korea canceled one round of peace talks with the United States in August 1997, after the North Korean ambassador to Egypt, Chang Sung Gil, defected to America. Chang reportedly informed U.S. officials about North Korean sales of ballistic missiles to Middle Eastern countries.

☐ Henry S. Bradsher

See also **Asia** (Facts in brief table); **Korea, South.**

Korea, South. In December 1997, South Korea agreed to terms for the largest international economic rescue in history—a $57-billion loan package that would help the nation pay its debts. The International Monetary Fund (IMF), leader of the bailout, was joined by the World Bank, the Asian Development Bank, the United States, and several other nations in financing the loan package. South Korea, which in the 1970's through the 1990's, had grown from an impoverished nation to the world's 11th-largest economy, fell victim in 1997 to sharp devaluations of its currency and soaring debts. On December 23, the World Bank released $3 billion to South Korea. The money was originally intended to reshape the nation's banking system, but World Bank officials approved its use to help South Korea pay short-term loan obligations.

Election. On Dec. 18, 1997, Koreans, angered by the ruling party's mismanagement of the economy, elected an opposition candidate president for the first time in the country's history. Kim Dae Jung, head of the National Congress for New Politics, was elected to lead the nation, succeeding Kim Yong sam, whose five-year term in office ended amid charges of corruption and corporate collapses. Kim Dae Jung received 40.4 percent of the vote compared to 38.6 percent for his main rival, Lee Hoi Chang, the candidate of the ruling New Korea Party. In his acceptance speech, Kim Dae Jung reassured

Foreign relief workers allowed into North Korea in 1997 find abandoned, starving children, victims of a famine that began with floods in 1995.

foreign investors that he would adhere to the conditions of the International Monetary Fund bailout.

Kim Dae Jung was widely hailed as one of the most courageous campaigners for democracy in Asia. Kim Dae Jung became a prodemocracy protester in the 1950's who so angered government officials that several of the country's dictators tried to have him killed. Since 1962, Kim Dae Jung has spent five and a half years in prison (including a stay on death row), three years in exile, and six and a half years under government surveillance and frequent house arrest.

Corruption. In January, South Korean-based Hanbo Steel company filed for bankruptcy with $6.7 billion in debts. Prosecutors said the company had bribed people close to Kim Yong-sam, who influenced banks into lending money to the company. Eleven people, including Home Minister Kim Woo Suk, were arrested in connection with the scandal. Kim's son, Kim Hyun Chul, was sentenced on October 13 to three years in prison. He was fined $1.57 million for taking kickbacks worth $3.5 million.

Appeal rejected. On April 17, Chun Doo Hwan and Roh Tae Woo, two former South Korean presidents convicted in 1996 of mutiny, treason, and corruption, lost final appeals to prison sentences handed down in December 1996. However, on Dec. 20, 1997, Kim ordered their release.

□ Henry S. Bradsher

See also **Asia** (Facts in brief table).

Kuwait. On June 6, 1997, gunmen shot and seriously wounded Kuwaiti National Assembly member Abdullah al-Naibari, a leading spokesman for the opposition, as well as his wife, an act that shocked the nation of Kuwait. Five suspects, including two Iranians, were arrested within 24 hours of the shooting and were charged on June 10 with attempted murder. One of the Kuwaiti suspects had previously been criticized by *Talea,* a weekly publication backed by Naibari's political organization, for his role as a middleman in state contracts. Such middlemen earned very high commissions in multibillion-dollar state purchases of weapons following the 1991 Persian Gulf war against Iraq. In December 1996, after much public criticism of these contracts, Kuwait announced that the use of middlemen in arms deals had been stopped.

State jobs. On April 2, 1997, Kuwaiti officials reaffirmed a plan to cut the number of foreigners on the state payroll by 10 percent each year between 1996 and 2000 to ease the state's fiscal burden. Foreigners, mostly Asian or Arab, held approximately 40 percent of Kuwait's 250,000 public sector jobs in 1997. Critics of the plan claimed that it would have no fiscal benefit, because state salaries of Kuwaiti nationals were up to three times higher than those of foreigners in 1997. Critics also said they were pessimistic about another government goal—the moving of large numbers of native workers into the private sector. Foreigners held nearly 99 percent of Kuwait's 616,000 private-sector jobs in 1997. Such jobs were shunned by Kuwaitis, who typically viewed the positions as less prestigious than state jobs.

Kuwait, which devoted roughly 65 percent of its annual oil earnings to state salaries in 1996, employed more than 90 percent of the native Kuwaiti work force in 1997. Only about 4,000 Kuwaiti nationals were officially counted as unemployed. In 1997, Kuwaiti nationals numbered 720,000 people, while the foreign population in Kuwait numbered 1.2 million.

Security concerns. In August, United States companies operating in Kuwait revealed they had taken additional measures to improve security for their personnel after American officials warned of an anonymous threat against U.S. interests in Kuwait. Some 8,000 U.S. citizens, including several hundred military troops, lived in Kuwait in 1997.

Gulf relations. In 1997, Kuwaiti companies explored a number of possible joint commercial ventures with Iranian companies, including the construction of two cement plants and a steel mill. While Kuwait improved its relations with Iran, it staunchly opposed any easing of United Nations (UN) sanctions against Iraq, which had been penalized by the UN for invading Kuwait in 1990.   □ Christine Helms

See also **Middle East** (Facts in brief table).

Labor and employment. The United States economy in 1997 enjoyed another year of expansion without significant inflation. In November, the U.S. Bureau of Labor Statistics (BLS) reported that the country's unemployment rate declined to 4.6 percent, the lowest jobless rate since 1973. Such low joblessness usually triggers price inflation. But in November 1997, the BLS reported that consumer prices had increased a scant 0.2 percent in October. Consumer prices had increased 2.1 percent between October 1996 and October 1997, according to the BLS. In 1996, consumer prices rose a total of 3.3 percent. Analysts considered 1997 to be a virtual dream economic scenario—a continually expanding economy, the creation of more than 2 million jobs, low inflation, and higher salaries for employees.

Other analysts, however, wondered how long employment and wages could increase without inflation. They argued that strong global competition trumped opportunities for domestic price increases. Some workers in the United States and around the world also appeared wary of seeking big wage and benefit increases because companies had demonstrated a past willingness to pack up and move.

Automotive industry. Local plant problems that had remained unsettled following a 1996 national contract settlement with the United Automobile Workers (UAW) union came front and center in 1997. Labor difficulties hit both General Motors Corporation (GM) and Chrysler Corporation. Several local disputes with union workers at GM cost the automaker more than $490 million. A 29-day strike at a Chrysler engine plant in Detroit, which ended May 8, shut down seven assembly plants and cut vehicle shipments, costing Chrysler more than $438 million. During 1997, representatives from both GM and Chrysler settled disputes with the UAW by hiring additional employees, reducing overtime requirements, and addressing health and safety issues.

Ford Motor Company managed to settle labor contracts in 1997 without work stoppages. However, company officials announced in March plans to stop production of the Ford Thunderbird and Mercury Cougar at the end of 1997. The decision cut 1,800 jobs and closed a portion of a plant in Lorain, Ohio. Because 20 other factories nationwide built parts for both vehicles, analysts estimated that the decision would result in 700 additional layoffs. Ford also planned to stop production of the Aerostar Van, built at a plant in St. Louis, Missouri, and the Probe sports coupe, built at a factory in Flat Rock, Michigan. Employees at both factories were assigned to work on other vehicles made at the plants.

Airline industry. The Allied Pilots Association announced on January 8 that members had voted not to ratify a contract with American Airlines that had been reached in September 1996. The contract had contained stock options and pay increases of 3 percent in 1997 and 2 percent in 1999. In February 1997, President Bill Clinton used his emergency powers to block a pilots' strike and appointed a federal emergency board to oversee the contract negotiations. The pilots on May 5 approved a five-year contract, which included pay raises of more than 9 percent through the year 2001 and stock options.

At United Airlines, members of the Air Line Pilots Association and the International Association of Machinists reached a settlement in March 1997. Under the settlement, wages would increase 10 percent by 1998. The agreement included restoring wages and pension benefits the unions had given up in 1994 in return for United Airlines stock. Continental Airlines and the Independent Association of Continental Pilots union agreed in November 1997 to a tentative contract agreement for its more than 5,000 pilots that would increase Continental's payroll for pilots by 45.5 percent over a two-year period.

UPS strike. The highest profile labor-management dispute of 1997 involved the United Parcel Service (UPS) and the International Brotherhood of Teamsters. The Teamsters called a strike on August 4 for 185,000 unionized UPS employees after negotiators were unable to resolve disputes over UPS's pension fund program and the company's reliance on part-time employees.

On August 6, President Clinton announced that he would not intervene in the strike because it did not affect the national economy, public safety, or

Changes in the United States labor force		
	1996	**1997***
Civilian labor force	133,943,000	136,467,000
Total employment	126,708,000	129,715,000
Unemployment	7,236,000	6,752,000
Unemployment rate	5.4%	4.9%
Change in real weekly earnings of production and nonsupervisory workers (private nonfarm sector)†	0.2%	1.0%
Change in output per employee hour (private nonfarm sector)	1.5%	2.7%

*All 1997 data is through the third quarter of 1997 (preliminary data).

†Real weekly earnings are adjusted for inflation by using constant 1982 dollars.

Source: U.S. Bureau of Labor Statistics.

public health. However, the president approved intervention in the strike by Secretary of Labor Alexis Herman. Herman persuaded both sides to negotiate until an agreement was reached on August 18.

The new five-year contract provided wage increases for full-time and part-time workers and created thousands of new full-time jobs. Under the settlement, part-time wages would increase by $4.10 an hour over five years. Full-time wages would increase by $3.10 an hour—15 percent—over five years, resulting in an average hourly pay of $23.11. UPS also agreed to create 20,000 new full-time jobs by the year 2002. The positions would be filled largely from the company's pool of part-time workers.

Goodyear work stoppage. The United Steelworkers of America ended an 18-day strike on May 8, 1997, after ratifying a six-year contract with Goodyear Tire & Rubber Company of Akron, Ohio. More than 12,000 workers at 9 locations walked off the job on April 20. The agreement gave workers a performance bonus of between $500 and $1,500 in 1997, a 29-cent hourly wage increase in 1998, and a 35-cent hourly wage increase in 1999. Another 2,300 workers at a Goodyear's Kelly-Springfield Tire Company in Fayetteville, North Carolina, ended a 16-day strike on May 8, 1997, following a separate agreement.

General Electric Company (GE) and members of two unions representing more than 27,000 GE employees ratified a three-year contract on July 9,

The International Brotherhood of Teamsters calls a strike against United Parcel Service in August 1997, after negotiators failed to resolve pension-fund and part-time-employment disputes.

1997. Terms of the agreements included an 8.75-percent pay increase over a three-year period for members of the International Union of Electronic Workers and the United Electrical Workers.

Detroit newspaper strike. A 19-month dispute involving *The Detroit News* and *Detroit Free Press* and six unions ended in 1997 when, on February 14, the unions offered to end the strike unconditionally. Managers from the two newspapers and from Detroit Newspapers Incorporated, which runs the publications under a joint operating agreement, accepted the offer on February 19. The strikers' jobs, however, had been filled months before by nonunion workers who management refused to replace. While the National Labor Relations Board ruled that unfair labor practices by the newspapers had led to the strike and that employees who had been on strike should be rehired, a federal judge on August 14 refused to order the papers to rehire the former employees.

A 10-month steel strike over pension plans between the United Steel Workers of America and Wheeling-Pittsburgh Steel Corporation ended in August with a five-year contract. Provisions included an industry-standard defined pension plan, a $1.50-an-hour wage increase, and reimbursements of $2 million in medical costs incurred during the strike.

The strike involved 4,500 steelworkers and idled production at eight plants in Pennsylvania, Ohio, and West Virginia. The work stoppage cost the company and the union more than $150 million.

Union membership declined slightly in 1996 (the most recent year for which data are available), falling to 14.5 percent from 14.9 percent in 1995. A total of 16.3 million people belonged to unions in 1996. Approximately 6.9 million union members worked in federal, state, and local government jobs. Private industry accounted for 9.4 million union workers, with membership numbers highest in transportation and public utilities and lowest among farming, forestry, and fishing workers.

Teamster trouble. A federal election official in August 1997 overturned the 1996 election of Ron Carey as president of the powerful International Brotherhood of Teamsters, citing a controversy over campaign finance irregularities. Carey had narrowly defeated James P. Hoffa, the son of late Teamsters president Jimmy Hoffa, in the race.

Federal election official Barbara Zack Quindel had ordered that the election be rerun, but a court-appointed monitor on Nov. 17, 1997, barred Carey from running for election to the post after ruling that he had illegally funneled union money to his campaign. Carey announced plans on November 25 to take an unpaid leave of absence as president of the Teamsters Union, just hours before the three-member, federally appointed Independent Review Board accused him of diverting more than $700,000 from the Teamsters Union's treasury to finance his campaign against Hoffa.

Minimum wage increase. Millions of American workers celebrated Labor Day with a 40-cent-per-hour raise when the federal minimum wage increased from $4.75 to $5.15 on September 1. The increase was the second phase of an agreement approved by the U.S. Congress in 1996. The first phase, implemented in fall 1996, increased the minimum wage for hourly workers from $4.25 to $4.75. According to the U.S. Department of Labor, approximately 10 million minimum wage workers benefited from the increases. Of those affected by the 1997 increase, the Labor Department reported that 57 percent were women, 32 percent were youths between the ages 16 and 19, and 55 percent were part-time workers.

Despite the favorable aspects of the wage increase for hourly workers, some critics argued that the change would eventually result in a reduction in the number of hourly jobs or the numbers of available work hours.

Foreign unemployment. Many of the world's industrialized nations suffered higher unemployment than did the United States in 1997. Some countries struggled to emerge from 1990's recessions, while others worked through public and private policy problems.

Some of the factors underlying their unemployment problems mirrored those that had triggered the recession in the United States in the early 1990's. These factors included a weakened consumer demand often brought on primarily by a loss of jobs or stagnant incomes, higher interest rates, or weakened positions in the world trade market.

According to the Organization for Economic Cooperation and Development (OECD), a Paris-based multinational association working to promote economic and social welfare, member nations experienced diverse unemployment rates in 1997. In September, the average unemployment rate of all 29 OECD countries was 7.3 percent. The rate was 0.2 percent lower than in the first nine months of 1996. By August 1997, unemployment figures ranged from 2.3 percent in Korea to 19.8 percent in Spain. At the beginning of 1997, the OECD estimated that more than 30 million people were unemployed.

By mid-1997, unemployment rates had fallen in several countries, including Canada, Denmark, Finland, Iceland, Ireland, Mexico, the Netherlands, Norway, Poland, Portugal, Spain, Turkey, and the United Kingdom, compared with the same period in 1996. However, despite movement in the right direction, unemployment rates still remained in double digits in many of those nations. The unemployment rate in Ireland in August 1997 was 10.7 percent, compared with 11.8 percent in 1996. Finland reported that unemployment stood at 12.6 percent in August 1997, a drop from 15.6 percent in 1996. Spain experienced a 19.8-percent unemployment rate in August 1997, well below the 21.9 percent experienced during that period in 1996.

While double-digit unemployment rates existed in other OECD countries, in some cases the numbers reflected a slight increase. In France, for example, the unemployment rate in August 1997 was 12.6 percent, up from 12.5 percent during that same period in 1996. In Italy, the reported unemployment rate in July 1997 was 12.8 percent, compared to a 12-percent unemployment rate during the same seven months in 1996.

Although unemployment rates in some nations did not top the 10-percent mark, the OECD reported that more people in 1997 than in 1996 were looking for work. Germany, for example, reported an unemployment rate in August 1997 of 9.8 percent compared with the 8.9 percent reported in 1996. Canada reported an unemployment rate of 9 percent in September 1997, a decrease from the 10 percent reported for that period in 1996.

Some Asian countries, while able to maintain some of the lowest unemployment rates, still reported minor increases, according to the OECD. Japan reported a 3.4 percent unemployment rate in September 1997, a slight jump up from the 3.3 percent reported in September 1996. In South Korea, unemployment grew to 2.3 percent in August 1997, up from the August 1996 unemployment figure of 2 percent. ☐ Robert W. Fisher

See also **Economics; Manufacturing.**

Laos. See Asia.

Midterm elections in Mexico and Argentina, in which opposition parties unseated their long-incumbent political rivals, were among the most important political events in Latin America in 1997. In July elections in Mexico, which many observers considered a milestone in Mexico's progress toward mulitparty democracy, opposition parties won the majority of seats in the Chamber of Deputies, the lower house of the legislature, for the first time since 1929. The unseated Institutional Revolutionary Party (known in Spanish by the initials PRI) also lost key mayoral and state gubernatorial races.

Observers claimed that Mexican voters were weary of numerous accounts of political corruption and the 1997 revelations that military leaders were involved in drug trafficking. While the PRI suffered setbacks in the election, President Ernesto Zedillo Ponce de León, a member of the PRI, saw his approval rating soar to 59 percent in September, the highest rating since his inauguration in December 1994. In overseeing one of the more honest elections in Mexico's history, Zedillo was given credit for providing Mexicans with an opportunity for change.

The outcome was similar in October elections in Argentina, where an alliance of opposition parties won control of the House of Deputies. The election marked the first time in half a century that the long-dominant Peronist Party lost a midterm election when its leader was the incumbent president.

Leftists win key mayoralties. Cuauhtémoc Cárdenas Solórzano, a key figure in Mexico's 1997 elections, became the first elected mayor of Mexico's capital, Mexico City. Cárdenas, founder of the leftist Revolutionary Democratic Party, defeated his PRI opponent by a 2-to-1 margin. The post of mayor, previously filled by presidential appointment, is considered the second most important political office in Mexico. Political observers regarded Cárdenas, mayor of the Western Hemisphere's most populous urban area and son of a past president of Mexico, as a front-runner for the presidential race in 2000.

Hector Silva of El Salvador's leftist Farabundo Martí National Liberation Front (FMLN) was elected mayor of the capital, San Salvador, on March 16, 1997. The mayoralty is considered the nation's second-most-important political office. The FMLN, a party formed by Marxist rebels who traded in their guns for a chance to compete in politics in 1992 peace accords, also made significant gains in congressional elections.

Political gains for women. While not achieving equality with men in Latin American politics, women did score impressive gains during 1997. On February 9, Vice President Rosalía Arteaga Serrano de Córdova became Ecuador's first female president—albeit

for only two days—succeeding Abdala Bucarám Ortíz, whom Congress removed on grounds of incompetence and corruption. Arteaga served as the interim president until Congress elected Fabián Alarcón, the president of Congress, to the post.

In Guyana, Janet Jagan, was elected president on December 15. Jagan—the widow of former President Cheddi Jagan, who died on March 6—had served as prime minister since March 17, replacing Samuel Hinds, who served as interim president.

In February, Nora de Melgar, a former mayor of Tegucigalpa, the capital city of Honduras, became the first woman in Honduras to be selected by a major party as a presidential candidate.

Peruvian hostage crisis. In April, Peruvian commandos stormed the Japanese ambassador's residence in Peru's capital, Lima, ending a 126-day hostage crisis. On Dec. 17, 1996, members of the leftist Túpac Amaru Revolutionary Movement (MRTA) had seized the ambassador's residence and taken more than 400 people hostage. As negotiations continued into 1997, the MRTA released all but 72 hostages.

Government forces, in a meticulously planned assault on April 22, attacked the MRTA rebels through tunnels dug beneath the house. Although all 72 hostages were rescued, one was wounded by a stray bullet and later died of a heart attack en route to the hospital. Two Peruvian officers were killed, as well as all 14 of the MRTA rebels.

Neglected prisons. Media accusations against the Peruvian government for inhumane treatment of political prisoners—as well as jail riots in Colombia, Honduras, Jamaica, and Venezuela in 1997—drew public attention to the state of prisons in Latin America. A January *New York Times* editorial argued that Latin American governments could afford to improve the conditions of their prisons but chose not to. The editorial noted that in Venezuela, one of the wealthiest countries in Latin America, the prisons "are among the continent's most violent and squalid." In contrast, several countries had prisons for white-collar criminals and drug lords that were comfortable, such as the Colombian prison nicknamed" the Sheraton."

Record revenues from privatization. Latin America's revenues from privatization reached an estimated $23.7 billion in 1997—62 percent higher than in 1996—according to data compiled by the Santiago (Chile) Chamber of Commerce. Brazil took in the greatest revenues in 1997—estimated at $9 billion—from the sale of state-owned enterprises to foreign and domestic investors. Argentina followed with revenues estimated at $5.6 billion. The total number of state companies scheduled for sale to private owners in 1997 reached a record 125. Peru

In May 1997, women in San Andrés Sajcabajá, Guatemala, pray over the remains of relatives secretly buried by the military during the 36-year civil war, which ended in 1996. An estimated 400 secret grave sites exist throughout the country.

led with the sale of 22 companies, followed by Argentina with 19 and Venezuela with 18.

Gap between the rich and poor. As Latin American countries continued to pursue free-market reforms in 1997, economic growth rates averaged about 5 percent, compared with 1.5 percent in 1988. In spite of signs of progress in 1997, many of the same nations that enjoyed record economic growth were unsuccessful in reducing the gap between rich and poor citizens.

The International Monetary Fund (IMF), a United Nations agency based in Washington, D.C., made Argentina—with a 17 percent unemployment rate in 1997—a test case for lessening that gap. The IMF made a new three-year line of credit dependent on whether Argentina practiced "good governance." The terms in the loan agreement included taking steps to eliminate government corruption, open government ledgers to public inspection, remove politics from the judicial system, invest more in health and education, and create new jobs.

Trade talks. Trade ministers from 34 Western Hemisphere countries attended the Americas Business Forum at Belo Horizonte, Brazil, from May 14 through May 16. U.S. Commerce Secretary William M. Daley recommended that talks on a Free Trade Area of the Americas (FTAA), which would create the world's largest free-trade zone, should begin after the Second Summit of the Americas, a conference scheduled for Santiago, Chile, in March 1998.

Ministers at the Belo Horizonte meeting reaffirmed their support for a target FTAA start-up date in 2005, but they reached no agreement on how and when the negotiations should proceed. Representatives of the nations affiliated with South America's Southern Cone Common Market—Argentina, Bolivia, Brazil, Chile, Paraguay, and Uruguay—feared that the United States would dominate the FTAA market and hurt their healthy regional trade. They favored a gradual approach to FTAA and recommended that key issues in the trade agreements be handled one at a time rather than in a broad and immediate trade policy.

U.S. President Bill Clinton made his first trip to Latin America in May 1997. The tour was regarded by many political observers as a gesture to placate feelings that the United States had neglected its Latin American neighbors. Stopping first in Mexico City, Clinton signed an accord with President Zedillo on May 6 that called for broader cooperation in the war on drug trafficking.

Clinton attended a summit meeting on May 8 in San José, the Costa Rican capital, with leaders from Belize, Costa Rica, the Dominican Republic, El Salvador, Guatemala, Honduras, and Nicaragua. Clinton promised to soften the impact of the Illegal Immigration Reform and Immigrant Responsibility Act of 1996, which went into effect on April 1, 1997. Central American leaders were worried that provisions

of the U.S. law would lead to massive deportations of immigrants from Latin America, who had sought political refuge in the United States during various civil wars.

Clinton also signed an "open skies" accord with six Central American nations. The accord provided for free competition among airlines from all seven nations. Clinton concluded his tour by meeting with 15 Caribbean leaders at Bridgetown, Barbados, on May 10 to discuss trade agreements.

In October, President Clinton and First Lady Hillary Rodham Clinton toured Venezuela, Brazil, and Argentina, where Clinton signed agreements on energy, education, and environmental protection. Concluding his trip to Argentina, the U.S. president held a televised "town meeting," during which he answered questions from people in Buenos Aires, the capital; Los Angeles; and Miami.

U.S. lifts arms ban. The Clinton Administration announced on August 1 that it was lifting a 1978 ban on sales of advanced weapons systems, including jet fighters and tanks, to Latin American countries. In lobbying for the controversial change, U.S. arms makers estimated that the annual value of the Latin American market for sophisticated weaponry ranged from $500 million to $2 billion.

The U.S. Central Intelligence Agency (CIA) released documents on Jan. 28, 1997, revealing that in the 1980's the agency had taught techniques for mental torture and coercion to the security forces of at least five Latin American nations, which observers believe were Argentina, El Salvador, Guatemala, Honduras, and Panama. On March 2, 1997, the CIA reported that it had severed ties with about 100 foreign agents who were believed to have been involved in acts of murder, torture, terrorism, and other crimes. Approximately half of the agents were in Latin America.

U.S.-Colombian drug trafficking. In January, the U.S. Drug Enforcement Agency issued a 30-count indictment against Ludwig Fainberg, owner of a nightclub in the Miami, Florida, suburb of Hialeah, and two Cuban immigrants, Juan F. Almeida and Nelson P. Yester. In one of the strangest twists to the case, Fainberg—suspected of being a figure on the Russian organized-crime scene—and the Cubans were accused of attempting to buy a Russian-made submarine for $5.5 million, reportedly to transport cocaine from Colombia to the United States.

Growing automobile market. American, European, and Japanese automobile makers invested about $18 billion in South American production facilities in 1997. Most of the highly automated plants were built in Brazil and Argentina, which account for 80 percent of South America's auto sales. With no domestic competition and with wages one-third lower than those in the United States, car companies projected that they would boost production from 2,455,000 cars in 1997 to 3,858,000 cars by 2000.

Facts in brief on Latin America

Country	Population	Government	Monetary unit*	Foreign trade (million U.S.$) Exports†	Foreign trade (million U.S.$) Imports†
Antigua and Barbuda	67,000	Governor General James B. Carlisle; Prime Minister Lester Bird	dollar (2.70 = $1)	40	246
Argentina	35,805,000	President Carlos Saúl Menem	peso (1.00 = $1)	23,811	23,762
Bahamas	287,000	Governor General Orville Turnquest; Prime Minister Hubert Ingraham	dollar (1.00 = $1)	176	1,243
Barbados	266,000	Governor General Sir Clifford Husbands; Prime Minister Owen Arthur	dollar (2.01 = $1)	238	766
Belize	232,000	Governor General Sir Colville Young; Prime Minister Manuel Esquivel	dollar (2.00 = $1)	168	256
Bolivia	7,944,000	President Hugo Banzer Suárez	boliviano (5.31 = $1)	1,137	1,635
Brazil	169,430,000	President Fernando Henrique Cardoso	real (1.10 = $1)	47,762	56,947
Chile	14,878,000	President Eduardo Frei Ruíz-Tagle	peso (466.31= $1)	15,353	17,828
Colombia	36,694,000	President Ernesto Samper Pizano	peso (1,267.25 = $1)	10,587	13,684
Costa Rica	3,641,000	President José Maria Figueres Olsen	colón (240.05 = $1)	2,946	3,433
Cuba	11,244,000	President Fidel Castro	peso (23.00 = $1)	1,600	2,825
Dominica	71,000	President Crispin Anselm Sorhaindo; Prime Minister Edison James	dollar (2.70 = $1)	45	96
Dominican Republic	8,217,000	President Leonel Fernández Reyna	peso (14.38 = $1)	815	3,686
Ecuador	12,151,000	President Fabián Alarcón Rivera	sucre (4,219.50 = $1)	4,890	3,724
El Salvador	6,150,000	President Armando Calderón Sol	colón (8.76 = $1)	1,024	2,671
Grenada	93,000	Governor General Daniel Williams; Prime Minister Keith Mitchell	dollar (2.70 = $1)	20	107
Guatemala	11,542,000	President Alvaro Arzú Irigoyen	quetzal (6.17 = $1)	2,031	3,146
Guyana	864,000	President Janet Rosenberg Jagan	dollar (142.80 = $1)	414	485
Haiti	7,633,000	President René Préval; Prime Minister (vacant)	gourde (17.35 = $1)	90	666
Honduras	6,133,000	President Carlos Roberto Reina Idiáquez	lempira (13.22 = $1)	1,106	1,694
Jamaica	2,504,000	Governor General Sir Howard Cooke; Prime Minister P. J. Patterson	dollar (34.50 = $1)	1,380	2,756
Mexico	98,766,000	President Ernesto Zedillo Ponce de León	new peso (7.79 = $1)	47,056	45,977
Nicaragua	4,854,000	President José Arnoldo Alemán Lacayo	gold córdoba (9.74 = $1)	635	1,120
Panama	2,763,000	President Ernesto Pérez Balladares	balboa (1.00 = $1)	625	2,511
Paraguay	5,337,000	President Juan Carlos Wasmosy	guaraní (2,200.00 = $1)	919	3,144
Peru	25,124,000	President Alberto K. Fujimori	new sol (2.67 = $1)	5,897	9,472
Puerto Rico	3,522,000	Governor Pedro Rosselló	U.S. dollar	21,800	16,700
St. Kitts and Nevis	41,000	Governor General Clement Athelston Arrindell; Prime Minister Denzil Douglas	dollar (2.70 = $1)	27	118
St. Lucia	148,000	Governor General George Mallet; Prime Minister Kenny Anthony	dollar (2.70 = $1)	123	313
St. Vincent and the Grenadines	115,000	Governor General David Jack; Prime Minister James F. Mitchell	dollar (2.70 = $1)	46	132
Suriname	437,000	President Jules Wijdenbosch	guilder (401.00 = $1)	472	472
Trinidad and Tobago	1,349,000	President Arthur Napoleon Raymond Robinson; Prime Minister Basdeo Panday	dollar (6.18 = $1)	2,456	1,714
Uruguay	3,239,000	President Julio María Sanguinetti	peso (9.81 = $1)	2,397	3,323
Venezuela	23,195,000	President Rafael Caldera Rodríguez	bolívar (498.40 = $1)	18,189	11,961

*Exchange rates as of Oct. 24, 1997, or latest available data.
†Latest available data.

Amazon fish. "You come up with drastically different kinds of fish," commented John G. Lundberg, a fish specialist from the University of Arizona in Tucson, in a February 1997 report about the fish in the Amazon River, a relatively unstudied wildlife habitat in South America. Among the species that Lundberg identified were an electric fish that eats the tails of other fish and a blind catfish that can taste its surroundings with receptors on its body to help it navigate the river's murky depths. Although Lundberg had identified 240 new species, he and other researchers estimated that the Amazon and its tributaries have at least 2,000 fish species, twice the number found in the fresh waters of North America.

Archaeologists, meeting at the Dallas Museum of Natural History on February 10, agreed that radiocarbon dating methods had confirmed that humans lived in southern Chile 12,500 years ago at a place called Monte Verde. (Radiocarbon dating measures the amount of radioactive Carbon 14 in certain substances to determine their age.) Extensive excavations begun in 1977 revealed well-preserved artifacts, including tools, human fecal material, meat, and the remains of a hut. The agreement at the Dallas meeting officially supplanted the theory that a site in Clovis, New Mexico, with human remains and artifacts from 11,200 years ago, was the oldest inhabited site in the Americas. □ Nathan A. Haverstock

See also articles on the individual nations.

Latvia. Political instability continued in Latvia in 1997, as Prime Minister Andris Skele resigned twice in seven months. In January, Skele quit in protest over the controversial appointment of a finance minister. In February, President Guntis Ulmanis renominated Skele, who formed a new government. In July, Skele's government was again shaken by scandal, as four ministers were accused of violating a new anticorruption law, and Skele was investigated for misappropriating government credits. Skele's foreign policy also came under attack after Latvia failed to be invited to apply for membership in the European Union (EU), a political and economic alliance of 15 Western European countries. On July 28, Skele resigned for the second time.

This time, Skele was replaced as prime minister by Economics Minister Guntars Krasts, of the center-right Fatherland and Freedom Party. Krasts formed a coalition government in August, promising to accelerate economic reforms championed by Skele and pursue EU membership for Latvia.

Talks to settle the disputed sea border between Latvia and Lithuania continued in 1997. The conflict had stalled several international oil exploration and development ventures planned for the Baltic Sea.

□ Steven L. Solnick

See also **Europe** (Facts in brief table); **Lithuania.**

Law. See Civil rights; Courts; Supreme Court of the United States.

Lebanon. On May 11, 1997, nearly 500,000 Lebanese participated in a Mass celebrated by Pope John Paul II in the capital, Beirut, a city that was still visibly battered from the 1975-1990 civil war. The pope spent two days in Lebanon, during which he stressed the importance of reconciliation among the country's diverse religious groups that had fought each other during the civil war.

The pope also spoke of independence for Lebanon. In condemning the "presence of non-Lebanese forces" and the "menacing occupation in southern Lebanon," observers believed John Paul was referring to Syrian troops, who, in 1997, controlled much of Lebanon, and Israeli troops, who maintained a "security zone" in southern Lebanon as a buffer against guerrilla attacks. The guerrillas were part of Lebanon's pro-Iranian Hezbollah (Party of God), a militant Islamic group. The Israeli troops, in particular, were resented by many Lebanese, who believed the troops provoked guerrilla activity.

Israel. Violence pitting Israeli and pro-Israeli forces against anti-Israeli forces escalated in August in southern Lebanon. The violence threatened to undermine an April 1996 cease-fire agreement in which the combatants had pledged not to target civilians or civilian facilities. On Aug. 18, 1997, pro-Israeli Lebanese militiamen fired artillery into Sidon, the largest city in southern Lebanon. The assault killed or wounded several people and provoked an August 19 guerrilla rocket barrage on northern Israel. In response, Israel unleashed air strikes against targets in southern Lebanon, including water and power facilities, on August 20.

A September 12 clash between Israeli forces and Lebanese guerrillas near the Israeli security zone resulted in the death of the eldest son of Sayed Hassan Nasrallah, the leader of Hezbollah. Guerrillas retaliated within 24 hours by killing two Israeli soldiers with a roadside bomb.

Arrests. Lebanese radio reported on February 18 that security forces had arrested five Japanese members of the Red Army, a communist terrorist group allied with Arab nationalists. The men were arrested in Lebanon's Bekaa Valley, a haven for extremist groups. On March 6, Lebanese officials announced that the men would be indicted in Lebanon on lesser charges of forgery and illegal entry, rather than being extradited to Japan to face terrorism charges. Some Lebanese sympathized with the Red Army.

The United States announced in July that it was lifting a 10-year restriction that barred Americans from entering Lebanon. The ban had been imposed after several Westerners had been taken hostage by pro-Iranian extremists. Lebanese officials hoped the return of Americans would help counter Syrian and Iranian influence in Lebanon. □ Christine Helms

See also **Israel; Middle East** (Facts in brief table); **Syria.**

Lesotho. See Africa.

Charles Taylor, president of Liberia, attends a church service in Monrovia on July 20, 1997, the day after Liberia's first free elections in more than 25 years.

Liberia in 1997 celebrated the end of seven years of bloody civil war, the country's first free elections since 1971, and the inauguration of a new civilian government. Liberians experienced a renewed sense of optimism, though the country remained devastated by the war. At least 150,000 of Liberia's 2.8 million people had been killed, and the war left more than 2 million refugees within Liberia or abroad. Peaceful conditions, however, permitted a wider distribution of humanitarian aid and health care. While the war left the economy in a shambles, glimmerings of an economic revival appeared in 1997.

Peace process. The 1997 elections had been mandated by an August 1996 peace accord brokered by Nigeria, the leading power in the region. In 1990,

Nigeria had led a 10,000-member multinational peacekeeping force, ECOMOG, into Liberia in an attempt to establish order. The first sign that the elections scheduled for 1997 might actually take place was the surprising ease of the disarmament phase of the peace process. Under the agreement, Liberia's various military factions had agreed to surrender their arms by January 31. By the deadline, ECOMOG had collected an estimated 16,000 weapons.

Election. The Independent Elections Commission, charged with organizing and overseeing the elections, did miss the May 30 deadline. The task of registering voters, establishing electoral procedures, and setting up the voting system delayed balloting until July 19. Thirteen candidates campaigned for the six-year term as Liberia's president.

ECOMOG, as well as about 500 observers from the United Nations, the Organization of African Unity, and other groups, monitored the vote, which observers pronounced free, fair, and remarkably peaceful. More than 80 percent of Liberia's 736,000 voters participated.

Former warlord Charles Taylor, head of the National Patriotic Party (NPP), was swept into office with 75 percent of the vote. Ellen Johnson-Sirleaf, of the Unity Party, came in second with slightly more than 9 percent. The NPP won 21 of 26 seats in the Senate, the upper house of Liberia's legislature, and 49 of 64 seats in the Assembly. Taylor and his new Cabinet were sworn in on August 2.

Many foreign observers found Taylor's victory difficult to understand. Most Liberians, however, viewed him as the only candidate with the strength and leadership to restore order. He had launched the Liberian civil war in 1989 with almost no support, conquered most of the country, and managed to survive the conflict. In the process, he had accumulated wealth by selling timber and minerals from conquered areas. The wealth funded an election campaign that was far superior to those of his opponents. In addition, NPP-supported charities stepped up efforts to provide food and other relief supplies during the campaign. ☐ Mark DeLancey

See also **Africa** (Facts in brief table); **Nigeria.**

Library. Libraries won a number of major victories in 1997. In May, the Federal Communications Commission (FCC), an independent agency of the U.S. government that regulates radio, wire, and cable communication, voted unanimously to discount rates for telecommunications services to the nation's libraries and schools. The discounts, ranging from 20 percent to 90 percent, were valued at $2.3 billion annually and were scheduled to begin Jan. 1, 1998. The FCC plan also established a $4.7-billion fund to help schools and libraries purchase computer equipment and connect to the Internet.

The Communications Decency Act, a law that many librarians had opposed because of its vague wording, was ruled an unconstitutional violation of free-speech rights by the United States Supreme Court in June 1997. The court upheld a ruling by a federal district court panel that had blocked the law, signed by President Bill Clinton in 1996, from going into effect. Justice John Paul Stevens, who wrote the majority opinion for the court, stated, "It is true that we have repeatedly recognized the governmental interest in protecting children from harmful materials, but that interest does not justify an unnecessarily broad suppression of speech addressed to adults."

Following the Supreme Court decision, concerns about protecting children from pornography on the Internet focused on technological solutions such as the use of filters or blocking software. The Chicago-based American Library Association (ALA) argued that, while filters are useful for home use, they can unnecessarily block educational sites. The organization launched a parent-education campaign that included recommendations of websites for children and young adults. The ALA also helped organize the National Families Online Summit in December 1997, to focus on children's use of the new technology.

Billionaire William H. Gates, cofounder of Redmond, Washington-based Microsoft Corporation, and his wife, Melinda French Gates, announced in June 1997 the establishment of the Gates Library Foundation. Launched with the Gateses' donation of $200 million over five years and $200 million in computer equipment and software, the foundation was intended to bring computers and digital information to low-income communities throughout the United States and Canada. The funds were expected to benefit at least 8,000 libraries.

The Oprah Book Club, established by television talk-show host Oprah Winfrey, resulted in thousands of book donations for the nation's libraries in 1997. Winfrey's monthly selection of a work of fiction sent millions of viewers to bookstores and libraries. Each title Winfrey named became an instant best seller. To help libraries meet the demand, Winfrey requested that publishers of selected titles donate copies to the ALA for distribution to public and high school libraries across the country. Each publisher of a book club selection donated 10,000 copies.

The America Reads Challenge Act, introduced in the U.S. Senate in April 1997, called for a five-year, $2.7-billion investment to ensure that every American child could read well and independently by the end of the third grade. Proposed funding for the program included $260 million for the Department of Education and $200 million for the Corporation for National and Community Service. The funds were to be used for local reading programs in school, after school, and during summer vacation for children from preschool through grade three.

Renovation of the Library of Congress's Thomas Jefferson Building was completed in April 1997. Restoration and modernization of the building, one of three in Washington, D.C., that house the Library of Congress, had begun in 1980 and cost $81.5 million. The completion of the project, as well as the 100th anniversary of the 1897 building, was celebrated with an exhibit, "The Treasures of the Library of Congress." The largest permanent show in the library's history, the exhibit featured artifacts that ranged from a rough draft of the Declaration of Independence written by Thomas Jefferson to a first-edition Walt Disney comic book.

A location for a presidential library was chosen by President Bill Clinton in February 1997. Clinton announced that his library will be built on the Little Rock campus of the University of Arkansas.
☐ Peggy Barber

The Thomas Jefferson Building, one of three Library of Congress facilities in Washington, D.C., reopens in May 1997 after a 10-year renovation. The interiors, including the Great Hall, *above*, were restored to their original 1897 appearance.

Libya. The Arab League, an association of 21 Arab states (and Palestinian Arabs) dedicated to promoting closer relations among members, voted on Sept. 21, 1997, to defy a UN embargo on flights from Libya and allow planes carrying Libyan dictator Muammar Muhammad al-Qadhafi and other Libyan officials to land in their countries. The league also voted to allow Libyan aircraft to land in member countries for humanitarian and religious purposes. The flight embargo was part of UN sanctions imposed on Libya in 1992 after Qadhafi failed to aid in the investigation of the 1989 bombing (allegedly by Libyan intelligence agents) of a French plane and to turn over two Libyan agents indicted by Great Britain and the United States for the 1988 bombing of Pan Am Flight 103.

Qadhafi had violated the flight embargo at least four times since 1994. The violations included a 1996 trip to Egypt and a May 1997 trip to Niger and Nigeria. In addition, Libyan planes had been allowed to land in Saudi Arabia for the annual Islamic pilgrimage to Mecca. The vote by the Arab League highlighted the support Qadhafi had among Arab leaders in 1997. According to some experts, the vote also indicated Arab anger at the United States, the major proponent of sanctions, for failing to take a more active role in the Arab-Israeli peace process.

Arrest. The arrest of a suspected Libyan terrorist by Italian police on August 26 seemed likely to ensure that the UN sanctions against Libya would remain in place. The suspect, a former intelligence agent named Musbah Abulgasem Eter, had been sought for his alleged role in the 1986 bombing of a Berlin nightclub. On Feb. 7, 1997, a court in Berlin ruled that Libya was responsible for the bombing, which killed three people, including two U.S. soldiers, and injured 200 others. The trial of Eter and four other suspects began in Germany in November.

French trial. French intelligence officers announced on May 7 that they hoped to try six Libyans in absentia for the 1989 bombing of a French plane over Niger. Among those named was Qadhafi's brother-in-law, Abdallah Senoussi, who was once a high-ranking Libyan intelligence officer.

Other relations. In February 1997, the Organization of African Unity, an association of more than 50 African nations, held a three-day meeting in the Libyan capital of Tripoli to demonstrate solidarity with Libya. On March 10, the Vatican established full diplomatic relations with Libya in response to what it said was Libya's progress in protecting religious freedom. Despite U.S. objections, South African President Nelson Mandela visited Qadhafi in Libya twice in October and spoke out against the UN sanctions. Diplomats described Mandela's visits as a big boost for Qadhafi because of Mandela's international stature. Mandela traveled overland to avoid the UN flight embargo. □ Christine Helms

See also **Africa** (Facts in brief table); **Egypt.**

Literature, American. In 1997, publishers, booksellers, and writers debated the importance of serious fiction in the United States. The term "midlist," frequently noted in the debate, came to represent serious writers whose works usually generated modest sales. Retail booksellers chastised publishers for putting out too many midlist books and not giving the public what it supposedly wanted, while publishers complained that bookstores made no effort to sell new books. Writers felt attacked from both sides. Nonetheless, serious novels found their way to the best-seller lists and defied expectations of the midlist. Serious fiction enjoyed such popularity in 1997 that *The New Yorker* magazine humorously referred to it as the "Year of the Slow Read."

The 1997 National Book Award was given to Charles Frazier's *Cold Mountain,* an appropriate selection for an ambitious novel that seemed to lead the revival of serious fiction. *Cold Mountain,* the author's first novel, tells the story of Inman, a wounded Confederate soldier who wanders through the devastated South trying to return to the woman he loves in North Carolina. The novel is a modern version of Homer's *Odyssey,* the story of the Greek warrior Odysseus's journey home after the Trojan War. While Inman does not meet mythological monsters, he faces as many perils as the Greek hero.

Other National Book Award nominations. Don DeLillo's *Underworld* was also nominated for the National Book Award and garnered immense critical praise. The novel begins in 1951 at the famous playoff baseball game between the Brooklyn Dodgers and the New York Giants and shifts, often in reverse order, through the decades that followed. DeLillo employs a huge cast of characters—from nuns to waste technicians to former Federal Bureau of Investigation director J. Edgar Hoover—in a book that tries to distill the essence of America during the Cold War, the rivalry between Communist and non-Communist countries from 1945 to 1991. *Underworld* is a large, complex book full of ideas, analysis, and intuition about recent American history.

Three other novels were nominated for the National Book Award in fiction. Diane Johnson's *Le Divorce,* a tragicomedy about an impressionable American woman who moves to Paris to help a stepsister in a failing marriage, is a coming-of-age story that satirizes Americans' troubles with understanding the French. Ward Just's *Echo House* is the story of three generations of the Behl family in Washington, D.C. The politically powerful Behls serve as a metaphor for the city, where power, not the people who wield it, is the only thing that lasts. Cynthia Ozick's *The Puttermesser Papers*—a funny, sharp social commentary—tells the story of Ruth Puttermesser, a lawyer and New York City bureaucrat with a literary bent. After being demoted at work and dumped by her boyfriend, she goes into a trance in which she conjures a *golem,* a magically created human being of

Jewish legend. Through the golem's intervention, Puttermesser becomes mayor and embarks on grand but ultimately doomed plans.

Notable works. The publication of a novel by the reclusive Thomas Pynchon—a writer known for his dense style, vast subject matters, and literary and historical allusions—is a newsworthy literary event. His fifth novel, *Mason & Dixon,* was no exception. The book is an imaginative re-creation of colonial America, focused on the surveying expedition in the late-1700's of Charles Mason and Jeremiah Dixon, who created the line that would later divide the North and South. Pynchon displays a detailed knowledge of life in the 1700's. But his book, rather than being a historical record is a dazzling and humorous examination of reason and the universe.

Saul Bellow's novella *The Actual,* his first work of fiction since 1989, is the story of Harry Trellman, a retired man who becomes involved with a billionaire businessman while pursuing a long-lost love. Bellow once again comments on how the desire for money and love have created a dissatisfying modern life. *The Actual* satirizes the way Americans live and act, while still upholding the possibility of happiness.

Philip Roth's 1997 novel, *American Pastoral,* tells the story of a family that seems to have achieved the American Dream but finds their lives destroyed during the 1960's. Roth's characters represent three generations of the immigrant experience and depict how the potential for destruction lurks behind the obvious trappings of success.

John Updike's *Toward the End of Time* is set in the year 2020 in a lawless United States after a devastating war with China. Despite the collapse of order, Updike's hero, Ben Turnbull, lives in an isolated suburb in Massachusetts where he still manages to play golf. While Turnbull struggles through his relationships with his wife and two other women, Updike ironically points out the persistence of petty desires even as the world is coming to an end.

Kurt Vonnegut claimed that his 1997 publication, *Timequake,* was his last book. It is a combination of novel and memoir, which came about because Vonnegut decided he hated the novel he was working on. He discarded large portions of the novel and added personal stories and ideas. In the end, *Timequake* is a book about the relationship between fact and fiction and between a writer's life and work.

Short-story collections. Two important collections of short stories by authors who died before 1997 were published during the year. *The Complete Stories of Bernard Malamud,* a life's work in short fiction, documents with a comic eye the life of Jewish immigrants and their children in the United States. For all his concentration on the Jewish experience, Malamud never fails to make universal, moral points that transcend setting.

Ralph Ellison's *Flying Home and Other Stories,* a collection of 13 stories, is as notable as the 1952 novel, *Invisible Man,* which made Ellison famous. Six of the stories had not been published before Ellison's death in 1994. The critical praise for the short-story collection inspired great hope for the planned publication of Ellison's incomplete second novel.

Notable nonfiction works. Perhaps the most anticipated nonfiction book of 1997 was J. Anthony Lukas's *Big Trouble: A Murder in a Small Western Town Sets Off a Struggle for the Soul of America,* which investigates the 1905 murder of Frank Steunenberg, a former governor of Idaho. The man who admitted to planting the bomb that killed Steunenberg claimed that the act was instigated by leaders of the Western Federation of Miners. Three leaders of the mining union were allegedly kidnapped later in Colorado and put on trial in Idaho. The trial became a focus of the labor struggle and was presented by the press of the day as a choice between anarchy and order, freedom and slavery. Lukas's book re-creates the climate of America at the time and examines the ramifications of the event through the following decades.

Sam Tanenhaus's *Whittaker Chambers: A Biography* is a comprehensive effort to make sense of the man who was a key witness in 1948 before the House Un-American Activities Committee, which investigated U.S. citizens suspected of working for the government of the Soviet Union. Chambers, a self-confessed former Communist spy, testified against Alger Hiss, a former official of the U.S. Department of State, who was later convicted of perjury. Tanenhaus meticulously presents the world of Communist agents and sympathizers in the 1930's and the "red hunts" of the 1940's and 1950's.

Douglas Hofstadter's *Le Ton Beau de Marot: In Praise of the Music of Language* is a dazzling combination of science, literature, and art that is built around a short poem by French Renaissance writer Clement Marot. Hofstadter translates the poem dozens of times as he fleshes out his ideas about language and translation and personalizes his analysis with autobiographical details that memorialize his recently deceased wife. Critics hailed the book as the successor to his 1980 Pulitzer Prize-winning study of patterns in mathematics, art, and music, *Gödel, Escher, Bach: An Eternal Golden Braid.*

Peter Balakian's *Black Dog of Fate: The Legacy of Genocide in an American Family*—one of the more poetic and impassioned books of 1997—is the story of Balakian's youth in the United States in the 1950's. It is also his family's history in Armenia and the events of the attempted extermination of the Armenians by the Ottoman Empire in 1915. Balakian penetrates his family's silence on those events while interweaving three stories: his own coming of age, his family's past, and Armenian history.

☐ Robert Messenger

See also **Canadian literature; Literature, Children's; Literature, World.**

Literature, Children's. Multicultural and nonfiction informational books continued to dominate children's literature in 1997. Some of the outstanding books of 1997 included the following:

Picture Books. *Bunny Cakes; Bunny Money* by Rosemary Wells (Dial). Max gets into trouble when he tries to help make a birthday cake for Grandma and insists on buying her vampire teeth as a gift. Ages 3 to 7.

Edward and the Pirates by David McPhail (Little, Brown). Outstanding illustrations highlight a young boy's adventures in the world of books. Ages 5 to 8.

The Hunterman and the Crocodile retold by Baba Wague Diakite (Scholastic). In this West African tale, Donso the hunterman helps a crocodile family and learns the place people hold in nature. Ages 5 to 8.

One Grain of Rice: A Mathematical Folktale by Demi (Scholastic). Rani, granted a wish by the miserly raja, asks for one grain of rice doubled each day for 30 days. The raja is later sorry. Ages 5 to 8.

The Khan's Daughter by Laurence Yep, illustrated by Jean & Mou-Sien Tseng (Scholastic). A shepherd must perform three impossible tasks to wed the Khan's daughter in this Mongolian tale. Ages 5 to 8.

Cracked Corn and Snow Ice Cream by Nancy Willard, illustrated by Jane Dyer (Harcourt Brace). This almanac of country life combines photographs with events, poems, gardening tips, folk wisdom, and more for each month. All ages.

The Bone Man: A Native American Modoc Tale by Laura Simms, illustrated by Michael McCurdy (Hyperion). Nulwee is in great danger when he awakens the Bone Man. Ages 5 to 8.

Buddy by William Joyce (HarperCollins). Gertie Lintz raises a baby gorilla as if it were a child, dressing it in clothes and teaching it to eat at a table. But Gertie's life changes when Buddy matures. All ages.

Fiction. *A Picture of Freedom: The Diary of Clotee, a Slave Girl* by Patricia C. McKissack (Scholastic). Clotee learns to read while she fans young Master William during his lessons, and she keeps a diary of her daily life from 1859 to 1860. Ages 10 and up.

The Buffalo Tree by Adam Rapp (Front Street). Sura, 12, in a detention home for six months, endures bullying and injustice, but his roommate, Coly Jo, suffers even more. Ages 12 and up.

The Tulip Touch by Anne Fine (Little, Brown). In this British award-winning book, Natalie befriends angry, abused Tulip and gets drawn into Tulip's malevolent games. Ages 11 to 13.

Dancing on the Edge by Han Nolan (Harcourt Brace). Miracle, born of a dead mother, looks for love from her unreachable father, leading to a breakdown and a slow recovery. Ages 12 and up.

Hiding Mr. McMulty by Berniece Rabe (Browndeer/Harcourt Brace). When Mr. McMulty, a black man in Mississippi in the 1930's, is cheated out of his home, he takes revenge. Rass, a white boy, tries to save him from the Ku Klux Klan. Ages 10 and up.

Out of the Dust by Karen Hesse (Scholastic). In this story told in free-verse poetry, Billie Jo finds life in the Oklahoma Dust Bowl of 1934-1935 all but unbearable. Ages 12 and up.

Wringer by Jerry Spinelli (HarperCollins). Palmer dreads Pigeon Day, when 10-year-old boys wring the necks of injured birds at the town's shooting contest. Ages 8 to 12.

The Facts Speak for Themselves by Brock Cole (Front Street). Linda describes her dysfunctional family and the family's effect on her. Ages 12 and up.

The Voices of Silence by Bel Mooney (Delacorte). Thirteen-year-old Flora struggles with the deprivations of everyday life under Romania's Communist dictatorship. Ages 10 and up.

Time of Fire by Robert Westall (Scholastic). A British boy, whose parents are killed during World War II, deals with feelings of grief and revenge when faced with a downed German airman. Ages 11 to 13.

Fantasy. *Shade's Children* by Garth Nix (HarperCollins). In this Australian novel, children find refuge from the Overlords and their robotic minions with Shade, a holograph that is not as benevolent as they think. Ages 12 and up.

Ella Enchanted by Gail Carson Levin (HarperCollins). A fairy awards Ella the gift of total obedience at her christening, making Ella's life miserable. Ages 8 and up.

William Shakespeare's Macbeth retold by Bruce Coville, illustrated by Gary Kelley (Dial). Coville's version of the Shakespearean play captures the original's dark and brooding atmosphere. Ages 8 and up.

A Ring of Tricks: Trickster Animal Tales from America, the West Indies, and Africa by Virginia Hamilton, illustrated by Barry Moser (Blue Sky/Scholastic). Here are familiar (Br'er Rabbit) and unfamiliar (wren) tricksters. Ages 6 and up.

The Lion Tamer's Daughter & Other Stories by Peter Dickinson (Delacorte). Four tales explore other worlds, time shifts, and ghosts. Ages 12 and up.

The Iron Ring by Lloyd Alexander (Dutton). Tamar, king of a mythical India, forfeits his life in a game with another king, who disappears. While seeking the missing king to fulfill his promise, Tamar encounters helpers and adventures. Ages 10 and up.

The Library Card by Jerry Spinelli (Scholastic). In four unusual stories, young lives are changed by a mysterious library card and libraries. Ages 8 and up.

Poetry. *Harlem* by Walter Dean Myers, illustrated by Christopher Myers (Scholastic). The poems intertwine Harlem's colors, rhythms, sounds, sights, and history with striking illustrations. All ages.

A Child's Book of Lullabies illustrated with paintings by Mary Cassatt (DK Publishing). Lullabies are accompanied by reproductions of paintings by the noted American impressionist. Ages 3 months to 3.

Home on the Range: Cowboy Poetry selected by Paul Janeczko, illustrated by Bernie Fuchs (Dial). Twenty illustrated poems explore the lives and feelings of cowboys. Ages 8 and up.

Love Letters by Arnold Adoff, illustrated by Lisa Desimini (Blue Sky/Scholastic). Poems to people, pets, and others are amusingly presented. Ages 5 to 9.

It's Raining Laughter by Nikki Grimes, illustrated by Myles C. Pickney (Dial). Photos of African American children accompany poems about everyday life. Ages 4 to 8.

Nonfiction books. *The Best Vacation Ever; Divide and Ride; Every Buddy Counts* by Stuart J. Murphy (HarperCollins). Stories in the MathStart series teach counting, division, data collecting, and chart making. Ages 3 to 8.

A Drop of Water by Walter Wick (Scholastic). Spectacular photographs, text, and experiments explore the water. Ages 9 and up.

Passage to Freedom: The Sugihara Story by Ken Mochizuki, illustrated by Dom Lee (Lee & Low). Jewish refugees in Lithuania in 1940 flock to the Japanese consulate for visas to escape the Nazis. Defying orders, Sugihara saves thousands of lives while risking his own. Ages 7 to 11.

An Extraordinary Life by Laurence Pringle, illustrated by Bob Marstall (Orchard). Presents the story of the life of a monarch butterfly, from birth through migration to death. Ages 8 to 11.

It Came from Ohio! My Life as a Writer by R. L. Stine and Joe Arthur (Scholastic). The author of the Fear Street and Goosebumps series describes his life, family, and writing techniques. Ages 9 to 11.

Leon's Story by Leon Walter Tillage, illustrated by Susan L. Roth (Farrar, Straus & Giroux). Leon describes the cruelty and fear he experienced growing up black in a small, Southern town in the 1930's and 1940's. Ages 10 and up.

Charlotte Brontë and Jane Eyre by Stewart Ross, illustrated by Robert Van Nutt (Viking). Brontë's childhood and attempts to write fiction eventually lead to *Jane Eyre*. Ages 9 to 12.

Our Common Ground: The Water, Earth, and Air We Share by Molly Bang (Blue Sky/Scholastic). Presents an allegory that shows why the natural resources of our planet must be shared. Ages 7 to 10.

Awards. E. L. Konigsburg won the 1997 Newbery Medal for her novel *The View from Saturday*. The

Golem, the story of a giant created by a rabbi of the 1500's to protect the Jews of Prague, wins the 1997 Caldecott Medal for author and illustrator David Wisniewski.

award is given by the American Library Association (ALA) for "the most distinguished contribution to children's literature" published the previous year. The ALA's Caldecott Medal for "the most distinguished American picture book for children" was awarded to David Wisniewski for *Golem.*

Deaths. Matt Christopher, author of more than 120 sports novels for children and young adults, died Sept. 20, 1997, at the age of 80. Christopher played minor league baseball while trying to establish his career as a writer. His best-known works included *The Lucky Baseball Bat* and *The Kid Who Only Hit Homers.*

☐ Marilyn Fain Apseloff

293

The Creator of Thomas, the Tank Engine

By Cynthia A. Clampitt

T he Reverend Wilbert Awdry, creator of *Thomas, the Tank Engine*, and other railway stories for children, once told an interviewer, "I should like my epitaph to say, 'He helped people see God in the ordinary things of life, and he made children laugh.'" By the time of his death on March 21, 1997, Awdry, through the sale of more than 20 million copies of his books, had made children laugh in more than 40 countries throughout the world. Awdry's creations— Thomas the tank engine, James the red engine, the carriages Annie and Clarabelle, and all the other inhabitants of the mythical Isle of Sodor— joined the ranks of literary characters beloved by generations of children.

Wilbert Vere Awdry was born June 15, 1911, at Ampfield, near Southampton, England. His father, an Anglican clergyman, was a train enthusiast, and Awdry's earliest recollections were of walking along railway tracks with his father. When the family moved to Box, a town near Bath, they lived adjacent to one of the Great Western Railway's main lines. The young Awdry would lie in bed, listening to the trains nearby. "It needed little imagination," Awdry later said, "to hear, in the sounds they made, the engines talking to each other."

Wilbert Awdry went on to study at Oxford University, where he was ordained a priest in the Church of England in 1937. However, the young minister had no thought of becoming a writer when, in 1943, he sat by the bed of his son, telling the 3-year-old stories about trains that talked. He simply wanted to cheer up Christopher, who

Thomas, the tank engine, pulls his coaches through the countryside of the mythical Isle of Sodor. The Reverend Wilbert Awdry created Thomas in 1943, to amuse his son.

Photographic image provided courtesy of Britt Allcroft Inc.
© Britt Allcroft (Thomas) Limited 1985, 1986.

was confined to bed with the measles. The delighted child insisted on hearing the stories again and again. To keep the details straight, Awdry scrawled his tales on odd scraps of paper, illustrating them with simple sketches of engines with faces on their smoke boxes.

When Christopher was better, Awdry built him toy engines. One was like Edward, the first train Awdry had named, but another one, a wooden tank engine painted blue with the number 1 on its side, had no name. According to family legend, Christopher immediately identified it as Thomas and began demanding tales of "his" engine.

Margaret Awdry believed her husband's stories deserved a wider readership. She located an agent and then prodded her husband to send in his stories. Awdry was amazed that they were warmly received. *The Three Railway Engines,* which related the stories of the engines Edward, Gordon, and Henry, was published in 1945. Soon, the agent was calling for another book, and in 1946, *Thomas, the Tank Engine,* made his debut. In all, Awdry produced 26 titles in the Railway Series. The last, *Tramway Engines,* was published in 1972.

All of Awdry's stories—including Gordon's derailment into a sewer ditch and Thomas's descent down an abandoned mine shaft— were based on events that had occurred in railroading history. Awdry took great care to provide his fictional engines with the capabilities of real steam locomotives. The gentle tales impart more than just facts about trains. They include moral lessons applicable to life: there are consequences to mischief; it is not good to boast or be mean; being obedient and "really useful" can lead to fullfilment and happiness. Lessons of forgiveness and redemption are interwoven through many of the stories. As Awdry noted, "The important thing is that the engines are punished and forgiven, but never scrapped."

Children particularly enjoy Awdry's repetitive dialog that mimicks the rhythm of a moving train. As Edward and Henry prepare to pull a broken-down Gordon, the two engines puff, "Pull hard we'll do it. Pull hard we'll do it. Pull hard we'll do it." Another endearing aspect of the stories is the distinctly human personalities and failings of such engines as naughty, cheeky Thomas, pompous Gordon, and grumpy James.

Awdry retired from the ministry in 1965 and moved to a modest house, which he named Sodor, in the city of Stroud, west of London. His work was later honored by the Dean Forest Railway Company, which christened one of its three steam locomotives Wilbert, Awdry's first name. In 1995, the Isle of Man issued postage stamps featuring Thomas and friends, and in 1996 Queen Elizabeth II awarded Awdry the Order of the British Empire.

Wilbert Vere Awdry's death at the age of 85 did not signal the end of the line for Thomas. Awdry's son, Christopher, had already taken over as author of the series, writing his first railway tale in 1983, for his own son. ■ ■ ■

The author:

Cynthia A. Clampitt is a free-lance writer, editor, and photographer who specializes in the areas of literature, history, travel, and geography.

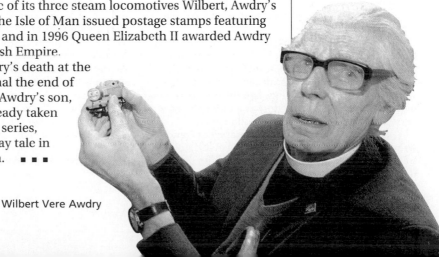

Wilbert Vere Awdry

Literature, World. The 1997 Nobel Prize for literature was awarded to Italian dramatist Dario Fo. His satirical political farces, *Accidental Death of an Anarchist* (1970) and *Can't Pay, Won't Pay* (1974), have made him one of Europe's most widely performed playwrights. The award stirred controversy among critics, some of whom argued that the controversial nature of Fo's plays rendered him an unsuitable recipient. Other critics saw the award as an indication of the Nobel jury's acceptance of the realities of contemporary European culture.

The United Kingdom and Ireland. Ulster poet Seamus Heaney's *The Spirit Level,* a collection of poetry, was named the 1997 Whitbread Book of the Year. The poems employ a range of forms—including *elegies* (poems that mourn the dead) and translations of older texts—to comment on contemporary politics and culture in Northern Ireland. The Whitbread award recognizes works published in the United Kingdom or Ireland.

Three popular writers published fictional fables that rethink traditional Christian beliefs. Jim Crace's *Quarantine* retells the story of Jesus Christ's 40 days in the wilderness. In this account, Jesus is joined by other travelers in the desert, and Satan is embodied in a merchant. Michele Roberts's *Impossible Saints* examines women who are made saints and reveals how their lives and sainthoods are influenced by men. In Bernard MacLaverty's *Grace Notes,* an Irish composer and single parent rejects her Roman Catholic faith to embark on a journey of artistic self-discovery and, in the process, releases herself from a legacy of grief by writing a musical masterpiece.

Ian McEwan's *Enduring Love* draws on the conventions of the genre of the thriller to create a menace-laden account that begins with a hot-air balloon accident and produces a probing study of human relationships. In Martin Amis's detective novel, *Night Train,* a female police officer narrates her struggle to make sense of the apparently motiveless suicide of the daughter of a high-ranking police officer.

Interest in Jane Austen continued unabated in 1997 with the publication of two biographies, both entitled *Jane Austen,* by David Nokes and by Claire Tomalin. Other notable literary biographies included Andrew Motion's *Keats* about John Keats and the first volume of Robert Foster's *Yeats* about William Butler Yeats.

Other European countries. In France, Marie Darrieussecq's first novel, *Pig Tales (La Truismes),* received critical acclaim in 1997. The book's subtitle, *A Novel of Lust & Transformation,* aptly describes the story of a prostitute who finds herself turning into a pig. Critics interpreted the story as a satirical allegory of far-right politics and moral judgments.

Olivier Todd's monumental biography of French writer *Albert Camus* became available in an English translation in 1997. Also available in English translation was Gennadi Aigi's *Selected Poems: 1954–1994,* a volume that provides a variety of work by one of the most original and controversial of Russian poets.

The Caribbean and Latin America. In 1997, Derek Walcott published *The Bounty,* his first collection of poems since winning the Nobel Prize for literature in 1992. The title poem is both an elegy for the poet's mother and an examination of his diverse personal allegiances. Like much of Walcott's poetry, the volume focuses on a traveling character whose roots remain within the poet's native St. Lucia.

Earl Lovelace's novel, *Salt,* published in 1996, was awarded the 1997 Commonwealth Writers' Prize, an award given to a writer from the countries of the British Commonwealth. Set in Trinidad, *Salt* tells the story of two men trying to give their fellow Trinidadians a better life in a country still influenced by its colonial past.

Martiniquan author Patrick Chamoiseau's *Texaco,* which won France's Prix Goncourt in 1992, was published in English in 1997. The novel blends storytelling traditions, magic, and history as it follows a family through nearly two centuries of the island's history. British-Guyanese writer Pauline Melville's *The Ventriloquist's Tale* explores European colonial attitudes toward native Guyanese through an Englishwoman who is researching British writer Evelyn Waugh's portrayal of the Guyanese.

St. Kitts-born Caryl Phillips's *The Nature of Blood* is a study of racism and ethnic hatred. The novel spans about five centuries, weaving together the stories of four characters, including the Shakespearean character Othello and a Jewish girl living during the *Holocaust* (Nazi Germany's persecution of Jews in the 1930's and 1940's).

Fred D'Aguiar, a Guyanese writer living in Great Britain, published *Feeding the Ghosts* in 1997. The novel offers a fictional account of a real-life scandal involving the slave ship *Zong* and its crew, which had thrown 132 sick or dead African slaves overboard during an Atlantic crossing in 1783. *News of a Kidnapping* by 1982 Nobel Prize winner Gabriel García Márquez is a nonfiction account of the kidnappings by cocaine baron Pablo Escobar Gaviria in Bogotá, Colombia, in 1990.

Asia. Arundhati Roy won the 1997 Booker Prize for her first novel, *The God of Small Things,* the story of young twins in India. As their family comes to terms with the death of a relative, the twins watch as the "big things"—truths about sexual and caste conflict—are revealed. (The Booker Prize recognizes writers from the Commonwealth and other former British colonies.) Indian novelist Gita Mehta's personal memoir, *Snakes and Ladders: Glimpses of Modern India,* offers reflections on politics, the arts, history, and a host of other subjects.

Australasia. Peter Carey's 1997 novel, *Jack Maggs,* provided a significant addition to the expanding genre of post-colonial novels that explore issues of cultural identity by telling a story derived from British literature of the 1700's and 1800's. Carey's novel revisits Charles Dickens's character Magwitch, from *Great Expectations,* a convict who is transported to the penal colony of Australia. Carey provides an ingenious investigation of Australian identity as Maggs returns to Great Britain, bent on revenging himself on the "motherland."

Australia's most acclaimed poets, Les Murray and Peter Porter, both published books in 1997. Murray, who won the 1997 T. S. Eliot Prize for *Subhuman Redneck Poems,* published *A Working Forest: Selected Prose,* which explores his formative influences and the religious impulse behind his poetry. Peter Porter's poetry collection, *Dragons in Their Pleasant Palaces,* moves between various Australian locations and allusions to classic European culture.

Nicholas Jose's *The Custodians* follows a diverse group of Australian friends—custodians of an unclear heritage—who confront problems of personal and national identity. Madeleine St. John, an Australian writer living in London, was a surprise 1997 Booker Prize nominee for her novel, *The Essence of the Thing.* Set in contemporary London, the rather conventional story of a broken relationship captures the comic and bittersweet possibilities of failed love.

Other notable works to appear in 1997 included *Collected Stories* by Gillian Mears, one of Australia's finest younger writers of short fiction, and novelist and literary scholar Mudrooroo's *Milli Milli Wangka,* a study of literature by Australia's Aboriginal writers. Mudrooroo's book aroused controversy when the author's claim to be an Aborigine was challenged by members of his own family.

New Zealand novelist Maurice Gee—best known for his trilogy *Plumb, Meg,* and *Sole Survivor*—reinforced his reputation for the subtlety of his studies of family life in his homeland with the 1997 publication of *Loving Ways,* which presents an ever-darkening picture of the author's usual subject matter.

Africa. The most significant publications in Africa in 1997 were nonfiction works. The 1997 Noma Award for Publishing in Africa was awarded to Albert Adu Boahen for *Mfantsipim and the Making of Ghana: A Centenary History, 1876–1976.* Boahen traces the evolution of modern Ghana and examines the role of education in gaining national independence by telling the story of one secondary school from its founding during British colonization to post-colonial freedom. South African J. M. Coetzee's *Boyhood: Scenes from Provincial Life* is a memoir of the author's youth in the Western Cape. Written as a third-person narrative rather than in the usual first-person style of memoirs, Coetzee offers a vivid account of a sensitive boy growing up troubled by his relationship with his English-speaking Afrikaner family and by the deep divisions among racial and ethnic groups.   □ John Thieme

See also **Canadian literature; Literature, American; Literature for children.**

Lithuania. In January 1997, a new coalition government led by Prime Minister Gediminas Vagnorius of the conservative Homeland Union party settled into power in Lithuania. With the swearing-in of the new government officials on Dec. 10, 1996, Homeland Union leader Vytautas Landsbergis became speaker of the parliament. During 1997, the government focused on greater integration with Europe.

Despite vigorous campaigning for membership in NATO, Lithuania's hopes for early membership were dashed in July, when NATO invited only Poland, Hungary, and the Czech Republic to join the alliance. Lithuanian leaders were particularly concerned that a new NATO treaty with Russia, signed in May, would permanently freeze Lithuania out of NATO. Landsbergis claimed that American officials assured him that Lithuania and the other Baltic states could still be considered for membership in the future.

In July, Lithuania was again disappointed when it was not invited to apply for membership in the European Union (EU), a political and economic alliance of 15 Western European countries. After the EU's decision was announced, Vagnorius said he would continue to press for Lithuania's inclusion in the EU.

In December, Lithuanian voters again went to the polls, to elect a new president, Algirdas Brazauskas V. Landsbergis.   □ Steven L. Solnick

See also **Estonia; Europe** (Facts in brief table); **Latvia.**

Los Angeles. On June 30, 1997, Richard J. Riordan began his second, and final, four-year term as mayor of Los Angeles, California's largest city. Riordan, a Republican, defeated Democratic state senator Tom Hayden on April 8 by an almost 2-to-1 margin. Riordan's victory was credited to his support among Hispanic citizens. The April election was the first in Los Angeles history in which Hispanic voters outnumbered black voters, who supported Hayden in substantial numbers.

New budgets. On May 19, the Los Angeles City Council approved a $4.1-billion budget to expand library hours and to increase funds for parks, the fire department, and neighborhood improvement. On April 23, the Los Angeles County Board of Supervisors approved a $12-billion budget that significantly cut county health department funding to help eliminate a large budget deficit.

New police chief. On March 10, the Los Angeles Police Commission announced that controversial Police Chief Willie L. Williams would not be reappointed to a second term. Williams, Los Angeles's first African American police chief, had been hired in 1992 to reform the department, following a wave of rioting triggered by alleged police brutality and racism. The commission found that Williams had failed to implement sufficient reforms.

Mayor Riordan announced on August 6 that Bernard C. Parks, a 32-year veteran officer, would become the new police chief. Parks, also an African American, was sworn into office on August 22.

New UCLA hospital. Officials at the University of California at Los Angeles (UCLA) unveiled plans on July 8 for a new state-of-the-art medical center. The medical center, designed by architect I. M. Pei, was budgeted at $1.1 billion. At more than 1.7 million square feet (158,000 square meters), it was to be the largest construction project undertaken by UCLA to date. Construction was scheduled to begin in 1998 and be completed by 2010. UCLA's current medical center was damaged in a 1994 earthquake.

New arts center. Getty Center, the largest nonprofit arts institution in the world, opened to the public on Dec. 16, 1997, with a large civic celebration attended by President Bill Clinton and other dignitaries. Architect Richard Meier's six-building, 110-acre (45-hectare) complex, which cost $1 billion and was largely financed by the estate of the late oil magnate J. Paul Getty, was widely acclaimed by both architectural critics and museum patrons.

Disney concert hall. In August, civic leaders reached an accord to begin work on the long-planned Walt Disney Concert Hall in downtown Los Angeles. The accord stipulated that as much as $14 million in Disney-family funds could be used to enable architect Frank O. Gehry to produce working drawings for the hall, on which contractors would then bid. The Disney family had previously donated approximately $100 million to the project. The Walt Disney Company of Burbank, California, announced in December that it would donate $25 million to the project. Other donations came from various corporations, foundations, and private donors, including Mayor Riordan. Groundbreaking for the hall, which is to be the centerpiece of a reinvigorated downtown, was scheduled for early 1998.

Sports stadium. Plans were announced in 1997 for a new downtown sports arena and entertainment center, to be codeveloped by Edward P. Roski, Jr., part owner of the Los Angeles Kings hockey team. Some of the $300-million cost was to come from public funds. Work on the stadium, to be used by the Kings and the Lakers basketball team, was to begin in January 1998.

Dodgers sold. Australian-born media mogul Rupert Murdoch agreed on Sept. 5, 1997, to buy the Los Angeles Dodgers baseball team for $350 million. The previous owner, Peter O'Malley, had announced his intentions to sell the Dodgers in January.

Trade. In 1997, the Los Angeles Customs District, which includes all the ports and airports in the Los Angeles metropolitan area, was, for the fourth year in a row, the nation's busiest port complex. The total value of imports and exports passing through the complex in 1997 was projected to be $180 billion. The customs district's top trading partner was Japan.

□ Margaret A. Kilgore

See also **Architecture; City.**

Magazine. The American Society of Magazine Editors (ASME), a professional group located in New York City, urged editors in June 1997 to resist pressure from advertisers trying to influence the kinds of stories and other editorial material published in magazines. Editors, not advertisers, traditionally determined editorial content of magazines.

The trade group expressed concern that the use of a policy called "early warning" could open the door to greater advertiser influence over editorial content. An early warning is an advance notice that magazine editors sometimes give to advertisers when their magazine plans to run stories that an advertiser may not want associated with its products. The warning gives advertisers a chance to withdraw ads and avoid offending potential customers.

ASME did not condemn the use of early warnings, but said that in some cases, advertisers may use their advance knowledge to pressure editors or publishers to change or drop stories, cartoons, photographs, and other editorial material they find offensive. In September, ASME and the Magazine Publishers of America issued a joint statement asking members of their groups not to "submit tables of contents, text, or photos from upcoming issues to advertisers for prior review."

Esquire's problems. In February, Will Blythe, literary editor of *Esquire* magazine, resigned in protest after Edward Kosner, the magazine's editor in chief, dropped a short story scheduled for publication. Blythe argued that the homosexual-themed story, by novelist David Leavitt, was killed because the magazine was afraid it would offend advertisers. Kosner insisted that his decision was a matter of taste. In June, Kosner resigned after failing to stop a decline in *Esquire*'s circulation and advertising sales.

Women and sports. Publishers in 1997 continued to take advantage of the sports and physical fitness boom among women. In April, Time Inc. began selling *Sports Illustrated Women/Sport*. Weider Publications Inc. in August introduced *Jump*, which focused on sports and fitness for teen-age girls. In September, Conde Nast Publications debuted *Sports for Women*.

Rodale Press announced in July its purchase of *New Woman* magazine from K-III Communications Corporation. Rodale, which publishes *Prevention* and other healthy lifestyle magazines, banned cigarette and hard-liquor ads from *New Woman*.

Gambling. The popularity of gambling casinos led to the introduction of two magazines. *Milton: The Luxury Gaming Magazine*, issued by Berle-Moll Enterprises, publishes gambling strategy and terminology and rates casinos. *Chance*, a quarterly issued by ARC Publishing, focuses on helping people improve their chances of winning at casino gambling.

□ Michael Woods

Maine. See State government.
Malawi. See Africa.

A construction worker gazes at the Kuala Lumpur skyline engulfed in the haze of smog generated by jungle fires in Indonesia that burned out of control in September 1997.

Malaysia. The severe economic problems that plagued Malaysia in 1997 halted several large development projects, including a $5-billion dam on the Island of Borneo and a $2-billion, mile-long building in Kuala Lumpur, and slowed progress on a new capital south of Kuala Lumpur. In Kuala Lumpur, the capital in 1997, a currency crisis caused shares on southeast Asia's largest stock market to drop in value in July and August. In September, the national currency, the ringgit, plunged to record lows against the U.S. dollar.

The Malaysian economy began to weaken in 1997, after more than a decade of rapid growth. The demand for workers in new industries exceeded the number of workers available. Approximately one-fifth of wage earners were foreigners who came to Malaysia to fill jobs. Wages rose faster than productivity, which pushed up costs of goods and services. As a result, foreign investment that had fueled the economic boom slackened, and many international companies moved production to countries with less expensive work forces, such as China and Indonesia. These factors, combined with heavy borrowing from abroad by Malaysian businessmen, created a foreign trade deficit.

Reaction. Prime Minister Mahathir bin Mohamad blamed the economic decline on foreign currency traders who, he claimed, were intent upon weakening the Malaysian economy. He considered protecting local investors from plunging stock prices by using state money to boost the market, but decided against this action when economists warned that it would put Malaysia at risk of isolating itself from the international investment world. On September 5, Mahathir lifted stock market restrictions.

Fighting corruption. Malaysian Deputy Prime Minister Anwar Ibrahim stepped into the role of acting prime minister for two months in 1997 while Mahathir took a vacation. Many observers said Anwar's actions—such as his attacks on corruption—increased the likelihood that he would succeed to the premiership. However, the 71-year-old Mahathir showed no signs of retiring. Anwar's anti-corruption campaign targeted the ruling United Malays National Organization. The Anti-Corruption Agency forced a state party boss and party leaders to resign and prosecuted several officials.

Serious smog. The Malaysian state of Sarawak, in northwest Borneo, declared a state of emergency in September 1997, after smoke from jungle fires in Indonesia lowered visibility to an arm's length. The smoke, combined with urban pollution, produced smog that seriously impaired the ability of residents of Malaysian cities to breathe. In September, Malaysian officials announced plans to prosecute the companies believed to have intentionally set the fires to clear jungle land. ☐ Henry S. Bradsher

See also **Asia** (Facts in brief table); **Indonesia**.

Manufacturing

Manufacturing. The manufacturing sector in the United States showed considerable strength in 1997, along with remarkably low costs for most raw materials. Some observers wondered if increasingly computer-driven companies may have produced a new era in which the economy can grow faster and make more goods with lower inflation than in past years. Yet output from the nation's factories was periodically threatened by labor unrest and problems at major freight transportation companies. Reduced sales of products also led to the reduction of the work force at some companies. Analysts expected that U.S. manufacturing could be slowed in 1998 following economic turbulence across much of Asia in 1997.

Threats to manufacturing. Manufacturers and government officials who managed economic policy became concerned in 1997 that demand for products was growing faster than the ability of factories to produce goods without having to increase prices. Part of that concern stemmed from a tight labor market, resulting in employers having to offer higher wages to bring in new workers.

The U.S. Bureau of Labor Statistics reported that the nation's November unemployment rate—the percentage of workers unable to find a job—fell to 4.6 percent, the lowest unemployment rate since October 1973. Historically, such a decline pointed toward higher consumer price inflation. Many economists argued in 1997, however, that there was no sign that inflation would increase. Lower prices for raw material and finished products resulted in a mild increase in consumer prices of just 2.1 percent between October 1996 and October 1997.

Gross domestic product. The U.S. gross domestic product (GDP)—the total value of goods and services produced in the United States—grew at a rate of 4.9 percent in the January-March quarter of 1997. Watching such fast growth, the Federal Reserve System (the Fed), the nation's central bank, cautioned that consumer demand threatened the ability of manufacturers to supply goods at low cost, a situation that could result in inflation. This factor led the Fed on March 25 to slightly retard the pace at which new money was created, which increased the interest rate banks charged to one another from 5.25 percent to 5.5 percent. The Fed explained that the rate increase was designed to prolong economic expansion by sustaining a lower inflation.

The GDP slowed to 3.3 percent in both the second quarter and third quarter of 1997.

Manufacturer's survey. A much-watched index of industrial activity showed that the U.S. factory sector enjoyed solid growth throughout 1997. The National Association of Purchasing Management (NAPM) polls more than 300 U.S. manufacturers monthly about new orders, employment, cost of materials, delivery problems, and other factors. Index values above 50 percent mean a growing economy.

Values below 50 percent indicate that the factory sector is contracting. In January the NAPM index reading was 52 percent. It never fell below that level through November 1997. The index reached 58.6 percent in July and dipped to 54.4 percent in November.

Cigarette settlement. The highly profitable cigarette manufacturing industry on June 20 agreed to a proposed arrangement with states' attorneys general in a bid to settle lawsuits in which state governments were seeking reimbursement for health-care costs for treating tobacco-related illness. A major part of the proposed settlement involved an agreement by the five major tobacco manufacturers in the United States to pay the states and the federal government $368.5 billion over a 25-year period. After 25 years, the annual fine would be reduced to $15 billion but would continue indefinitely. The tobacco settlement needed to be approved by the U.S. Congress and President Bill Clinton before going into effect. Republican leaders in Congress predicted in October that the tobacco legislation might be approved in early 1998.

Company layoffs. Signs that even a year of economic strength could include employment problems for manufacturers were apparent throughout 1997. A decrease in sales forced automaker Ford Motor Company to close a portion of a Lorain, Ohio, plant that made the Ford Thunderbird and the Mercury Cougar. The decision to close a portion of the plant and stop production of the two automobiles led to the loss of 1,800 jobs. An additional 700 jobs were expected to be lost at other factories nationwide that built parts for both vehicles.

Sagging sales led to an announcement in November by jeans manufacturer Levi Strauss & Company of San Francisco that it would close 11 plants in four states, costing nearly 6,400 jobs.

The Eastman Kodak Company of Rochester, New York, a longtime photography powerhouse, announced in November that it would reduce its work force by 10,000 jobs—one of the biggest layoff announcements by any U.S. company in 1997. Kodak blamed foreign competition and a lack of interest in high-tech photographic products.

With prices falling in the highly competitive market for personal computers, International Business Machines Corporation (IBM) revealed in November that it would begin an immediate layoff of hundreds of employees in its North American division.

Interruptions to supply lines plagued manufacturers in 1997 as shipments important to business operations were disrupted following problems at two major U.S. freight companies.

On August 4, the International Brotherhood of Teamsters, one of the most powerful U.S. unions, called a strike against United Parcel Service (UPS), the nation's largest small-package delivery system. The strike, which was the result of disputes over em-

ployment issues and pensions, forced many customers to scramble for alternative carriers, including
UPS business competitors and the U.S. Postal Service.
Many companies had to delay shipments until the
company was back in operation.

The strike ended on August 18 after union and
management representatives reached a new five-
year contract. However, UPS required several weeks
to clear a backlog of shipments stuck in its system by
the strike.

The federal Surface Transportation Board declared a transportation emergency in October after
Union Pacific Railroad, the largest U.S. rail network,
became overwhelmed by increased volumes of
freight. The board ordered Union Pacific to open a
section of track in its 36,000-mile (57,600-kilometer)
long network to a small competitor, the Texas Mexican Railway, in order to ease rail congestion. The
traffic tie-up spread over Union Pacific lines across
the United States, affecting other railroads that connected with or used the railway's tracks. The massive
congestion affected all types of manufacturing, including chemicals, paper, grain, automotive parts,
lumber, and metals.   □ John D. Boyd

See also **International Trade**.

Maryland. See **State government**.
Massachusetts. See **State government**.
Mauritania. See **Africa**.
Mauritius. See **Africa**.

Medicine. A controversy about the age at which
women should begin having mammograms to detect breast cancer at an early stage was apparently
settled in 1997. In March, the National Cancer Institute (NCI) recommended that women begin having
a regular mammogram at age 40. The NCI is an
agency of the National Institutes of Health (NIH) in
Bethesda, Maryland, which provides government
funding for biomedical research.

The NCI said that women in their 40's should
have a mammogram, a special X ray of the breast,
every one or two years. The institute advised women
at higher risk for breast cancer, such as women with
a family history of the disease, to speak with their
doctor about starting regular screening earlier than
age 40. Regular mammography for women in their
40's, according to the NCI, reduces deaths from
breast cancer by 17 percent. Patients diagnosed early have a better chance of being cured.

The NCI guideline was an about-face. In 1993, the
agency withdrew a previous recommendation that
women begin regular mammograms at age 40. At
that time, there was insufficient scientific evidence
that mammography actually reduces mortality from
cancer. Other agencies and health groups, however,
continued to recommend mammograms for women
in their 40's. The disagreement created confusion
among women and concerns that health insurers
might not pay for mammograms.

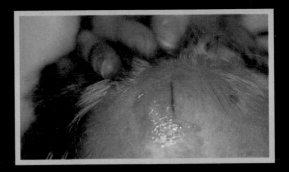

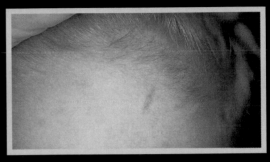

A laceration on a forehead,
top, heals, *above,* with only a
faint scar after being closed
with a medical glue. In 1997,
glues replaced stitches for closing many kinds of wounds.

In March 1997, the American Cancer Society also
stated that mammography was beneficial for wom-
en in their 40's and urged that the test be done annually. But there was still a lack of consensus on the
advisability of mammograms beginning at age 40. In
January, a panel of experts convened by the NIH said
the benefit of mammograms for women in their 40's
was not clear and that women should decide for
themselves if they wish to undergo regular testing.

Breast cancer genes. Two genes involved in
breast and ovarian cancer play a less important role
in causing cancer than previously believed, scientists
at the NCI reported in May. New research showed
that women who inherit *mutated* (abnormal) genes,
called BRCA1 and BRCA2, were less likely to develop
breast and ovarian cancer than earlier studies suggested, though their cancer risk was still significant.

Previous studies had indicated that women with
the mutations had up to an 87-percent chance of developing breast cancer and an 84-percent chance of
getting ovarian cancer by age 70. The risks for wom-
en without the defects were about 8 percent and
1.6 percent, respectively. The new study showed
that women with the mutations had a 56-percent
chance of developing breast cancer and a 16-percent
chance of developing ovarian cancer by age 70.

Parkinson disease. A gene that causes some
cases of Parkinson disease was identified in June by
scientists at the National Human Genome Research

Institute, a part of the NIH. About 500,000 Americans had Parkinson disease, a progressive nerve disorder that results from the death of nerve cells in the brain. It causes trembling of the limbs, difficulty with walking, and other symptoms.

The normal version of the gene spells out instructions for the manufacture of a protein, alpha-synuclein, which is critical for the function of nerve cells. In Parkinson disease, a mutation in the gene results in production of a faulty protein. Scientists said the discovery may help in developing new treatments for Parkinson disease.

Diet and blood pressure. A nationwide study reported in April by the National Heart, Lung, and Blood Institute (NHLBI) concluded that a low-fat diet rich in fruits and vegetables lowers blood pressure as effectively as some drugs. The NHLBI is a division of the NIH. In the study, the diet worked especially well for people with high blood pressure, or hypertension, a disease that affects about 1 of every 4 Americans. The diet also proved effective in people with only slight elevations in blood pressure who were considered at high risk for developing hypertension. High blood pressure increases the risk of heart attack, stroke, and a number of other diseases. NHBLI Director Claude Lenfant described the low-fat, high-fruit and -vegetable diet as one of only a few non-drug approaches that have been proven effective in reducing blood pressure. The others include exercise, weight control, and avoidance of salty foods.

New calcium guidelines. The National Academy of Sciences (NAS) recommended in August 1997 that everyone—not just women—should eat more calcium-rich foods. Calcium is important to prevent osteoporosis, bone loss that often causes fractures in older people. The National Academy of Sciences, advises government officials on science policies.

The report noted that all adults should consume at least 1,000 milligrams of calcium daily, an intake achieved by only 10 percent of adults in the United States. That goal can be met by consuming three to four servings of calcium-rich food a day. One serving equals one glass of milk or cup of yogurt.

People over 50, the approximate age at which many bone-thinning problems begin to occur, were advised to consume 1,200 milligrams of calcium each day. The previous recommendation for all adults over age 25 was 800 milligrams. The NAS also raised its calcium recommendation for adolescents, whose growing bones need a great deal of calcium, from 1,200 milligrams to 1,300 milligrams.

The NAS issued the new guidelines as the first step in revising its Recommended Dietary Allowances (RDA's). RDA's had originally been created in 1941 to prevent diseases caused by severe nutritional deficiencies. Such disorders are now rarely seen in the United States. The revised guidelines, called Dietary Reference Intakes, are intended to help people attain optimal health. They were to be issued in stages through the year 2000.

Controlling asthma. Asthma should be treated earlier and more aggressively in order to avoid the needless deaths that sometimes result from the disease. That advice was contained in new medical guidelines issued in February 1997 by a special panel convened by the NHLBI.

The panel found that some people with asthma were not being properly diagnosed and treated, factors that contribute to a high level of hospitalization and death from the disease. Asthma is a chronic respiratory disorder that causes wheezing, difficulty in breathing, and other symptoms. The panel emphasized the importance of early treatment of asthma with anti-inflammatory inhalant drugs. These medicines reduce inflammation in the lungs and bring symptoms under control.

Screening for diabetes. All people age 45 and older should be tested for Type II diabetes, a panel organized by the American Diabetes Association recommended in June. Type II diabetes, also called adult-onset diabetes, affects about 15 million Americans. The panel said testing would greatly improve the diagnosis of Type II diabetes and help millions of people avoid heart disease, eye damage, and other complications of diabetes. The disease usually can be controlled without insulin. Type I diabetes, also called juvenile diabetes, usually occurs in childhood or adolescence and must be treated with insulin.

Help for epilepsy sufferers. The first alternative to drugs or surgery for the treatment of epilepsy was approved by the U.S. Food and Drug Administration (FDA) in July. The FDA approved an implantable nerve stimulation device, the NeuroCybernetic Prosthesis (NCP) System, made by Cyberonics, Incorporated, of Webster, Texas.

The device, which is implanted in the chest, electronically stimulates the vagus nerve in the neck, sending signals to the brain that can stop an epileptic seizure. About 2.5 million Americans suffer from some form of epilepsy. About 200,000 people, who have a form of the disease that cannot be treated adequately with drugs, could be candidates for the NCP system. The only alternative treatment is a surgical procedure, considered risky, that destroys brain tissues involved in epileptic seizures.

Another implantable stimulator, the Activa Tremor Control System, made by the Medtronics Corporation of Minneapolis, Minnesota, was approved by the FDA in August. The device controls tremors caused by Parkinson disease or a condition called essential tremor, a nerve disorder that affects about 2 million Americans. The stimulator consists of a pulse generator implanted in the chest and connected to a wire placed in the brain. Electrical pulses to brain cells block tremors. ☐ Michael Woods

See also **AIDS; Drugs; Mental health; People in the news; Public health and safety.**

Mental health. In April 1997, scientists at Rockefeller University in New York City and four other institutions reported that men who have inherited two copies of an altered gene, one from each parent, have a greater risk of developing obsessive-compulsive disorder (OCD). People with OCD perform repetitive rituals, such as hand washing, cleaning, and checking or counting items. They also may have recurrent, unwanted thoughts, such as anxiety about being contaminated with germs or being injured.

The researchers identified a gene that instructs cells to produce the enzyme catechol-O-methyltransferase (COMT), which helps control chemicals that transmit nerve signals in the brain. An altered COMT gene can result in a biochemical imbalance. The researchers noted no increased risk among men with only one copy of the altered gene and found no association between the gene and the development of OCD among women. Also, some men with two copies of the altered gene had no OCD symptoms. The scientists concluded that the COMT gene was only one of several factors causing OCD.

Guidelines for treating Alzheimer's disease were issued for the first time in April by the American Psychiatric Association (APA), a professional society of psychiatrists based in Washington, D.C. Alzheimer's disease, the most common form of *dementia* (deterioration of the mind), is caused by the gradual destruction of brain cells.

The APA recommended giving Alzheimer's patients low doses of vitamin E, which can slow the progression of the disease in patients with moderate symptoms. Vitamin E is inexpensive, safe, and does not interact dangerously with other recommended medications, such as drugs that enhance brain activity and slow the progression of symptoms.

The guidelines also suggested that physicians write on prescription forms "Do not drive" for patients whose symptoms prevent them from doing simple tasks, such as preparing meals or doing household chores. The APA suggested that such prescriptions offered support to family caregivers who may be reluctant to restrict a patient's driving.

Schizophrenia treatment. In June, researchers led by psychiatrist Michael Green of the University of California at Los Angeles (UCLA) reported that the drug risperidone can treat aspects of schizophrenia that other medications cannot. Schizophrenia, which affects about 3 million people in the United States, causes distorted thinking, hallucinations, and delusions. It impairs a person's ability to make decisions, manage emotions, and relate to other people.

Risperidone, like other medications, reduces hallucinations and delusions. But according to the UCLA study, risperidone also improves a patient's memory, problem-solving abilities, and reasoning. Without these higher level skills, people with schizophrenia have difficulty resuming independent lives. In the study, patients on risperidone showed significant improvement in these abilities compared with patients on other medications. In a series of mental function tests, people taking risperidone scored an average of 20 percent higher than people taking other drugs.

Also in 1997, the National Alliance for the Mentally Ill (NAMI) published several articles that endorsed early detection and treatment of schizophrenia to reduce the lifelong disability that can result from the disease. NAMI is a health organization based in Arlington, Virginia, that works to improve the lives of people with severe mental illness and advocates changes in mental health care policies.

Researchers who were featured in NAMI's spring 1997 edition of the magazine *The Decade of the Brain* cited evidence that permanent mental deterioration occurs in the early stages of the disease, usually during the first five years. Prompt treatment with antipsychotic drugs, the researchers reported, may reduce the permanent damage and enable patients to live more normal lives.

Attention deficit/hyperactivity disorder. In June, Russell J. Schachar, a psychiatrist at the Hospital for Sick Children in Toronto, Canada, reported that the standard twice-daily Ritalin treatment, which has been shown to improve a child's behavior in school, may not be adequate to improve behavior at home. Ritalin is a medication widely used to treat attention deficit/hyperactivity disorder (ADHD). ADHD is characterized by a persistent inability to sit still, control impulses, and focus attention.

Schachar studied 91 children using the standard Ritalin treatment, taking the medicine at breakfast and lunch. He found that the effects of that regimen often wore off by the end of the school day. Parents, he reported, often saw only the side effects of Ritalin, such as loss of appetite or difficulty sleeping, and not the benefits. Those parents were inclined to take their children off the medication. Schachar advocated a third dose of Ritalin late in the afternoon that could improve a child's behavior at home.

Teen-agers and depression. In May, psychiatrist Gail A. Bernstein of the University of Minnesota in Minneapolis reported that teen-agers who miss many days of school because of dizziness, upset stomachs, or menstrual problems may be experiencing clinical depression or anxiety. Bernstein studied 44 adolescents who frequently missed school because of symptoms of physical illness. On average, they were absent 3 out of 4 days. She concluded that anxiety and depression, rather than physical illness, were largely responsible for the symptoms.

Bernstein said parents, physicians, and school officials should be more aware of the role of anxiety and depression in causing physical symptoms. She suggested an increased awareness could eliminate unnecessary diagnostic tests, permit more rapid treatment, and avoid chronic absences from school.

☐ Michael Woods

Mexico. Change of historic proportions dominated Mexican politics in 1997. In July midterm elections, parties in opposition to the Institutional Revolutionary Party (known in Spanish by the initials PRI) won 261 of the 500 seats in the Chamber of Deputies, the lower house of the legislature. The leftist Revolutionary Democratic Party (PRD) and the conservative National Action Party led the victory. The PRI, which had held power in Mexico since 1929, retained control of the Senate, but opposition parties also made gains in state and local elections.

Mayor of Mexico City. Cuauhtémoc Cárdenas Solórzano, 63, founder and leader of the PRD, became the first popularly elected mayor of Mexico City, the capital, by taking almost 48 percent of the vote—well ahead of his PRI rival, who took about 26 percent of the vote. The mayoralty of Mexico City, a post previously filled by presidential appointment, is considered the second-most-powerful political office in Mexico. Cárdenas, who had run unsuccessfully for the presidency in 1988 and 1994, therefore, established himself as a front-runner for the presidential elections in 2000. At his swearing in as mayor on Dec. 5, 1997, Cárdenas faced an enormous challenge, governing a capital beset by poverty, high crime rates, and severe environmental pollution.

U.S. loan repaid. On January 15, Mexico repaid the remaining $3.5 billion balance on its $12.5 billion loan from the U.S. government during Mexico's economic crisis in February 1995. Mexico also paid $1.5 billion of the $13.4 billion it borrowed from the International Monetary Fund, a United Nations agency based in Washington, D.C.

U.S. President Bill Clinton, accompanied by First Lady Hillary Rodham Clinton, traveled to Mexico City in May 1997 to begin his first state visit to Latin America. President Clinton and Mexican President Ernesto Zedillo Ponce de León signed accords on May 6 that covered a broad, if vague, range of collaborative efforts, such as border patrols, drug trafficking enforcement, and environmental protection. Clinton also met with representatives from all three major political parties, to demonstrate U.S. support of fair democratic elections.

Drug chief ousted. The Mexican defense ministry announced on February 18 that General Jesús Gutiérrez Rebollo had been dismissed as head of Mexico's National Institute to Combat Drugs. Gutiérrez, who had been appointed in December 1996, was accused of taking payoffs from drug traffickers and participating in their turf wars by cracking down on some drug traffickers while protecting others.

Barry R. McCaffrey, head of the U.S. Office of National Drug Control Policy, responded that the United States was "extremely disappointed" in the report about Gutiérrez, who was privy to U.S. policies on the war against drug trafficking. By July 1997, 34 current and former military officers had been arrested for complicity in drug trafficking.

U.S. certification. Despite evidence of high-level corruption among Mexican officials, the Clinton Administration on February 28 certified Mexico as a country that was being cooperative in the war on drugs. The certification guaranteed that the United States would continue to provide military and economic assistance to Mexico.

The Clinton Administration supported its decision by citing the Mexican government's promise to extradite more suspected drug traffickers to the United States, to enforce new money-laundering laws, and to root out government corruption. The Administration's confidence in Mexico was shaken, however, when the Mexican government, shortly after the certification was given, reported that Mexican investigators had released from custody Humberto García Abrego, brother of a convicted drug trafficker.

The U.S. Congress responded to the news by passing a resolution that threatened to "decertify" Mexico if the Clinton Administration could not provide evidence of Mexico's progress in controlling drug trafficking. The Administration conceded in a September 16 report that rampant corruption and lack of punishment for drug traffickers in Mexico had impeded the war against drugs. Nonetheless, the report cited evidence of progress and affirmed the certification of Mexico.

March on Mexico City. On Sept. 8, 1997, about 1,100 members of the leftist Zapatista National Liberation Army emerged from their hideouts in the southern state of Chiapas to make a five-day journey of 750 miles (1,200 kilometers) to Mexico City. Covering the route on foot as well as by bus, the Zapatistas hoped to bring national attention to Indian rights issues and to the rebels' campaign for social justice, which began with a bloody uprising on Jan. 1, 1994. When the Zapatistas reached Mexico City on Sept. 12, 1997, tens of thousands of people turned out for their rally at the city's central square despite rain and rush-hour traffic.

Massacre in Chiapas. On December 22, gunmen killed 45 Tzotzil Indians, including 15 children, in the mountain village of Chenalhó in Chiapas. The incident was the worst act of violence in Chiapas since the beginning of the Zapatista unrest. Survivers of the massacre claimed that the killers were Indians belonging to a government-backed paramilitary group.

Phone competition. On Jan. 1, 1997, a new law ended the monopoly on long-distance telephone service held by Teléfonos de México (Telemex), touching off international competition to capture Mexican markets. In Querétaro, a city in central Mexico, Telemex retained only 30 percent of the market. Forty-two percent of customers chose AT&T, and 27 percent chose Avantel, a joint venture of MCI and Grupo Financiero Banamex-Accival, Mexico's largest financial group. ☐ Nathan A. Haverstock

See also **Latin America** (Facts in brief table).

A tornado threatens downtown Miami on May 12, 1997, after touching down on the city's southwest side, where trees were uprooted and buildings damaged.

Miami. Miami voters on Sept. 4, 1997, rejected a referendum that would have abolished the city and merged it with unincorporated Dade County, which was the name of the county where Miami is located. The referendum had been championed by a group of business leaders who claimed that the city government was too corrupt and poor to govern effectively. In 1997, a number of city officials, including the commissioner and city manager, were imprisoned for soliciting kickbacks from vendors bidding on city contracts. In addition, Miami was near bankruptcy in 1997 due to a $64-million budget deficit uncovered by outside auditors in 1996.

New county name. On Nov. 14, 1997, residents of Dade County voted to change the county's name to Miami-Dade County. Business leaders believed the new name would make it easier to market the county in the rest of the nation and in Europe.

New mayor. Miami Mayor Joe Carollo lost to former Mayor Xavier Suarez in a November 14 runoff election. The runoff was needed because no candidate received a majority of votes in the regular election, held on November 4. The regular election was marred by allegations of voter fraud.

Executive mayor. Miami voters in 1997 also approved the creation of an "executive mayor" form of city government and an election system whereby each city commissioner would be chosen by district rather than by citywide voting. The executive mayor was to have the power to veto commission decisions and to hire and fire the city manager. Advocates for electing commissioners by district argued that such a system would increase representation of African and Haitian Americans.

Versace murder. On July 15, renowned Italian fashion designer Gianni Versace was shot to death on the steps outside his mansion in the South Beach area of Miami Beach. Police identified the assailant as Andrew Cunanan, a 27-year-old fugitive wanted for four other murders committed over a three-month period in three states. The death of Versace, the most famous of the five men allegedly killed by Cunanan, focused national attention on the Miami metropolitan area. On July 23, Cunanan took his own life in a houseboat that was docked not far from Versace's mansion.

Cargo jet crash. On August 7, a Fine Air DC-8 cargo jet crashed seconds after taking off from Miami International Airport and plunged into a business district west of the airport. The crash, which occurred in the middle of a workday, destroyed three storefronts and killed the four crewmen and a man in a car. Officials from the National Transportation Safety Board, the government agency that investigates airplane accidents, attributed the crash to improper loading of the plane's cargo.

Raising a child. A report released in August by Zero Population Growth, a population-control advocacy group based in Washington, D.C., rated Miami as one of the worst cities in the United States in which to raise a child. The report rated 219 U.S. cities on 20 factors, including population density, student-teacher ratio, and the percentages of teen pregnancies, school dropouts, and juvenile arrests. Miami ranked 202 out of 219.

Kids and guns. A study published in June by the *Miami Herald* indicated that 42 percent of 17- to 19-year-old boys in Dade and Broward counties (Broward is adjacent to Miami-Dade) had carried firearms, been with friends who had carried firearms, or had played with parents' guns. (The study results did not include the use of guns for hunting or target practice.) The study, based on telephone interviews with hundreds of randomly selected teen-agers, also indicated that more than half of the boys knew where on the street to easily obtain a gun.

Marlin mania. The Florida Marlins baseball team won the seventh and deciding game of the World Series by defeating the Cleveland Indians 3-2 in an 11-inning game that began on October 26 and concluded after midnight on October 27. The game, played at Miami's Pro Player Stadium, gave southern Florida its first professional sports championship since 1974, when the Miami Dolphins football team won the Super Bowl. The 5-year-old Marlins team was the youngest baseball franchise ever to win the World Series. ☐ Geoffrey Tomb

See also **City.**

Michigan. See **Detroit; State government.**

Middle East

Events in 1997 revealed that the political consensus that the United States had developed with its Arab and Western allies after Iraq's 1990 invasion of Kuwait had frayed. In November 1997, Arab leaders openly refused to support U.S. calls to threaten Iraq with military action. Moreover, Arabs accused the United States of not placing sufficient pressure on Israel to abide by terms of the Arab-Israeli peace process. In addition, frustration with the United States was cited as a motive behind the November massacre of foreign tourists by Egyptian Islamic militants.

Crisis with Iraq. The United States failed to find international support for military action against Iraq following Iraqi President Saddam Hussein's October order that all U.S. personnel working for United Nations (UN) weapons inspection teams leave Iraq. The UN inspectors had been trying to verify if Iraq was complying with UN demands to destroy weapons of mass destruction. Verification of the destruction of these weapons was the primary criteria considered by the UN for the lifting of economic sanctions imposed after Iraq's 1990 invasion of Kuwait.

The crisis escalated after Hussein, who accused the U.S. inspectors of spying, ignored UN warnings to rescind his order. The United States began a military build-up in the Persian Gulf in mid-November.

On November 18, Russian officials announced that Iraq had accepted a plan to resolve the crisis. On November 21, UN inspectors returned to Iraq, and Russia urged the UN to take steps leading to the lifting of the economic sanctions. The United States had previously urged the UN to toughen the sanctions. UN agencies in 1997 suggested that the sanc-

A Palestinian youth, protesting the expansion of Jewish settlements in Arab neighborhoods, hurls a fire bomb at Israeli soldiers in the West Bank city of Hebron in June 1997. The soldiers responded by firing rubber bullets into the crowd of demonstrators.

tions had played a part in the near collapse of Iraq's health-care system and in widespread malnutrition among Iraqi children.

Egyptian massacre. On November 17, Islamic militants killed 58 foreign tourists and 4 Egyptians at the ancient temple of Queen Hatshepsut in Luxor, Egypt. Islamic militants, who had declared war on the Egyptian government in 1992, targeted tourists in an attempt to weaken Egypt's economically vital tourist industry. Al-Gamaa al-Islamiya (The Islamic Group) claimed responsibility for the attack, saying that it had originally planned to take the tourists as hostages in order to secure the release of its spiritual leader, Sheik Omar Abdel Rahman, who had been convicted in the United States in 1995 of conspiring to blow up buildings in New York City.

Peace process crisis. The Arab-Israeli peace process began unraveling on Feb. 28, 1997, when Israeli Prime Minister Benjamin Netanyahu announced the construction of new Jewish settlements at Har Homa, in East Jerusalem. Prior to Netanyahu's election, the Israeli government had suspended Jewish settlements in East Jerusalem, the status of which remained to be resolved in Arab-Israeli negotiations. Palestinians hoped that East Jerusalem would become their capital. Israel had also revoked the residency permits of some 1,000 East Jerusalem Arabs since 1996. Palestinians feared the new settlements and the residency revocations would weaken the Arab position in final negotiations over the city.

After Netanyahu's announcement, the militant Islamic group Hamas unleashed its first suicide bombing in over a year, killing three people in Tel Aviv on March 21, 1997. In June, Israeli officials said they suspected Palestinian security officials were involved in the May murders of three Arab land dealers who had sold land in Arab areas to Jews. A Palestinian official had proclaimed in May that any Arab selling land to Jews should receive the death penalty. On July 30 and September 4, suicide bombings in Jerusalem killed a total of 21 people and wounded more than 300. In other violence, Arab youth and Israeli soldiers clashed repeatedly in the Israeli-occupied Arab territories of the West Bank and Gaza Strip.

In response to the September 4 suicide bombing, Netanyahu suspended a scheduled withdrawal of Israeli troops from a portion of the West Bank. Earlier in 1997, Israel had withdrawn troops from 80 percent of the West Bank city of Hebron and from a small amount of other West Bank land. Palestinians claimed that these withdrawals and other withdrawal offers made by Israel in 1997 were inadequate because they did not meet Palestinian hopes that Israel would withdraw from some 80 percent of the West Bank by mid-1998.

Albright visit. On Sept. 10, 1997, with the Arab-Israeli peace process on the brink of collapse, Madeleine Albright began her first official visit to the Middle East as U.S. Secretary of State. Albright secured a pledge from the Israelis and Palestinians to continue talking to each other, but accomplished little else during her six-day stay. On September 24, Prime Minister Netanyahu announced the building of a new Jewish settlement in the West Bank.

Jordan and Israel. The peace process nearly ended on September 25, when the Israeli intelligence agency Mossad allegedly tried to assassinate Khaled Meshal, a leader of Hamas, in the Jordanian capital of Amman. Upon learning of the assassination attempt, Jordan's King Hussein, Israel's strongest Arab supporter, threatened to end Jordan's relations with Israel. A diplomatic rift was avoided, however, when Netanyahu visited Jordan on September 28. Following the secret visit, Israel released Sheik Ahmed Yassin, the spiritual leader of Hamas, from prison, and Jordan released Mossad agents captured in the assassination attempt.

In May, Hussein had defused an earlier international crisis involving Israel when he allowed the United States to deport Mousa Mohammad Abu Marzook, the alleged political leader of Hamas, to Jordan. The crisis had begun in April, when Israel abruptly canceled an *extradition* (surrender of a prisoner from one state to another) request for Marzook. The cancellation stunned the United States, which had detained Marzook in 1995 at Israel's request. At the time, Israel had stated that it wanted to try Marzook on terrorist charges. Observers speculated that Israel canceled the extradition request either because it lacked evidence to convict Marzook or feared that a trial would incite more terrorism.

Arab-U.S. relations. The Arab world criticized the United States in 1997 for a number of actions that were seen as favoring Israel in the peace process. Arabs cited the U.S. refusal to support a March UN Security Council resolution condemning the construction of the Israeli Har Homa settlements. Most Islamic countries as well as all 15 members of the European Union, a cooperative association of Western European nations, had supported the resolution.

In June, Arab states decried the passage of an unbinding resolution by the U.S. House of Representatives that recognized Jerusalem as Israel's undivided capital. The resolution called for the U.S. embassy to be moved from Tel Aviv to Jerusalem by 1999.

In October 1997, Egyptian President Hosni Mubarak denied the validity of a U.S. intelligence report implicating Egypt in the abduction and extradition of a prominent Libyan dissident. The report charged that former Libyan Foreign Minister Mansour Kikhia, missing since 1993, had been abducted by Egyptian officials and turned over to Libya. Mubarak charged that the United States had issued the report to pressure Egypt into returning to Israel Azam Azam, an Israeli convicted of espionage by an Egyptian court in August 1997. Israeli Prime Minister Netanyahu maintained that Azam, who was sentenced to 15 years of hard labor, was innocent.

Facts in brief on Middle Eastern countries

Country	Population	Government	Monetary unit*	Foreign trade (million U.S.$)	
				Exports†	Imports†
Bahrain	604,000	Amir Isa bin Salman Al Khalifa; Prime Minister Khalifa bin Salman Al Khalifa	dinar (0.38 = $1)	4,113	3,716
Cyprus	762,000	President Glafcos Clerides (Turkish Republic of Northern Cyprus: President Rauf R. Denktash)	pound (0.52 = $1)	1,387	3,977
Egypt	66,547,000	President Hosni Mubarak; Prime Minister Kamal Ahmed al-Ganzouri	pound (3.40 = $1)	3,540	13,041
Iran	71,569,000	Leader of the Islamic Revolution Ali Hoseini-Khamenei; President Mohammad Khatami-Ardakani	rial (3,000.00 = $1)	16,000	13,000
Iraq	22,345,000	President Saddam Hussein	dinar (1,200.00 = $1)	no statistics available	
Israel	5,883,000	President Ezer Weizman; Prime Minister Benjamin Netanyahu	new shekel (3.59 = $1)	20,474	30,603
Jordan	4,480,000	King Hussein I; Prime Minister Abd-al-Salam al-Majali	dinar (0.71 = $1)	1,817	4,428
Kuwait	1,702,000	Amir Jabir al-Ahmad al-Jabir Al Sabah; Prime Minister & Crown Prince Saad al-Abdallah al-Salim Al Sabah	dinar (0.30 = $1)	14,803	7,541
Lebanon	3,173,000	President Ilyas Harawi; Prime Minister Rafiq al-Hariri	pound (1,531.50 = $1)	1,014	7,568
Oman	2,425,000	Sultan Qaboos bin Said Al Said	rial (0.39 = $1)	5,713	4,248
Qatar	582,000	Amir Hamad bin Khalifa Al Thani; Prime Minister Abdallah bin Khalifa Al Thani	riyal (3.64 = $1)	3,181	1,891
Saudi Arabia	19,801,000	King & Prime Minister Fahd bin Abd al-Aziz Al Saud	riyal (3.75 = $1)	42,614	23,338
Sudan	30,392,000	President Umar Hasan Ahmad al-Bashir	pound (1,428.60 = $1)	556	1,185
Syria	16,180,000	President Hafiz al-Assad; Prime Minister Mahmud Zubi	pound (41.85 = $1)	3,999	5,244
Turkey	65,331,000	President Süleyman Demirel; Prime Minister Mesut Yilmaz	lira (183,136.00 = $1)	23,083	42,465
United Arab Emirates	2,022,000	President Zayid bin Sultan Al Nuhayyan; Prime Minister Maktum bin Rashid al-Maktum	dirham (3.67 = $1)	25,300	21,700
Yemen	15,957,000	President Ali Abdallah Salih; Prime Minister Faraj Said bin Ghanim	rial (124.00 = $1)	934	2,087

*Exchange rates as of Oct. 24,1997, or latest available data.
†Latest available data.

The Arab League, an association of 21 Arab states and Palestinian Arabs passed a resolution in March, after Israel began constructing the Har Homa settlements, urging Arab states to slow economic, cultural, and scientific ties with Israel. In November, most Arab states refused to attend a U.S.-backed economic summit with Israel in Qatar, saying that economic cooperation with Israel should wait until progress was made in the peace process. In contrast, a December meeting of the Organization of the Islamic Conference, a group of 55 Islamic nations, was attended by most Arab states. The organization met in Iran, a country condemned by the United States for sponsoring terrorism.

The Arab League approved a resolution in September permitting airplanes carrying Libyan dictator Muammar al-Qadhafi and other Libyan leaders, as well as religious pilgrims and humanitarian goods, to land in Arab League states. The resolution defied a UN flight embargo that was among sanctions imposed on Libya in 1992 as punishment for Libya's sponsorship of terrorism. The United States had been the main proponent of the sanctions. The resolution was viewed by some experts as an expression of Arab anger at the United States for not taking a more active role in the peace process.

Export of terrorism. The U.S. State Department's 1997 report on terrorism listed Iran, Iraq,

Libya, Sudan, and Syria as among countries that sponsor terrorism. However, Iran was the only country that the State Department linked directly to specific terrorist activities in 1996, including the assassination of political opponents living abroad.

In January 1997, at least 18 letter bombs were mailed from Egypt to the United States, England, and Saudi Arabia. Most of the bombs had been addressed to the Washington, D.C., New York City, London, and Riyadh offices of the privately owned Saudi newspaper *Al Hayat.* Two London mail clerks were injured by one of the bombs. The other bombs were detected before they blew up. The origins of the bombs remained unknown. In November, a Palestinian and a Jordanian were convicted of detonating the bomb that exploded in the World Trade Center in New York City in February 1993, killing 6 people and wounding more than 1,000 others.

In early January 1997, France sentenced three members of a radical Islamic group to one to eight years each in prison for their role in killing two tourists in Morocco in 1994. In late January 1997, French authorities arrested at least 22 alleged Islamic militants to stem the growth of Islamic networks in France. The arrests coincided with a similar crackdown in Germany on Arab immigrants suspected of supporting militant groups.

Kurdish rebels. Turkey launched major ground assaults in May and September against rebel bases in northern Iraq belonging to the militant Turkish Kurdish Workers Party (PKK). Air strikes bolstered the September assault. The PKK began its war for independence from Turkey in 1984. The Kurds are an ethnic group who inhabit the mountainous region of southwest Asia. Fighting between Kurdish factions broke out in 1994. The Turkish assaults threatened to draw Syria, Iran, and Iraq, which have supported various Kurdish factions, into the fighting.

Yemen. On April 27, 1997, the party of Yemen President Ali Abdullah Saleh, the General People's Congress (GPC), won an overwhelming victory in the first general elections held since the 1994 civil war. The victory allowed Saleh to form a cabinet dominated by the GPC. In 1994, secessionist forces had failed to reestablish independence for South Yemen, which had united with North Yemen in 1990.

Dredging of the port of Aden, on the Gulf of Aden in southern Yemen, began in April 1997. The work was part of a $500-million project to turn the port into an international shipping hub capable of reviving Yemen's economy, which was still suffering from the effects of the civil war. Yemen, one of the poorest Arab countries, also developed plans in 1997 to increase its crude oil production and export liquefied natural gas.

Water scarcity. An international group of scientists and other authorities meeting in Morocco in March for the World Water Forum warned that competition over scarce water supplies could lead to armed conflict in the Middle East and Africa after the year 2000. The forum was sponsored by the UN Educational, Scientific and Cultural Organization (UNESCO). In February 1997, delegates from Arab states attending a conference in Damascus, Syria's capital, had charged that Turkish and Israeli water-use policies were heightening problems of water scarcity in the Middle East.

Human rights. The Arab Organization for Human Rights, based in Cairo, Egypt, reported in June that human rights in the Middle East had deteriorated during 1996 due to foreign intervention, tensions between Islamic extremists and secular governments, and conflicts that had killed and displaced thousands of people. The report criticized six countries, including Israel, as well as Palestinian authorities, for using torture. It also criticized the restriction of freedom in many countries and the harsh impact of UN sanctions on Libyans and Iraqis.

☐ Christine Helms

See also the various Middle Eastern country articles (Facts in brief table).

Mining. See Energy supply.

Minnesota. See State government.

Mississippi. See State government.

Missouri. See State government.

Moldova. See Europe.

Mongolia. See Asia.

Montana. See State government.

Montreal. Mayor Pierre Bourque and his Vision Montreal party lost their majority on Montreal's City Council on July 23, 1997, when Councillor Robert Gagnon became the 15th Vision member to resign from the party in 1997. As a result, Vision Montreal's caucus in the 52-member council was reduced to 25, and Bourque became the first Montreal mayor since 1954 to head a minority council. The defecting councillors accused Bourque of making major decisions without consulting them. Many councillors were especially outraged by Bourque's decision to sell to Quebec province the closed Hippodrôme de Montréal, which includes 4.6 million square feet (430,000 square meters) of land and a racetrack.

In an attempt to dissuade growing disloyalty, Bourque had fired two dissident Vision councillors from the city's executive committee on Jan. 19, 1997. But 19 days later, a Quebec Superior Court judge ordered the immediate reinstatement of the two members, ruling that Bourque had acted illegally.

Bourque's woes worsened on June 17, when Quebec Municipal Affairs Minister Rémy Trudel gave the city four months to clean up its finances. In May, Montreal's auditor had released a report alleging $17 million in improper city expenditures. The city also learned in June that it would have to find an additional $46.7 million—2.6 percent of its $1.8-billion operating budget—to pay for services previously funded by the province.

Law and order. The drug-turf war between the Quebec chapter of Hell's Angels and the Rock Machine, a rival criminal gang, claimed the lives of two prison guards in 1997. Diane Lavigne and Pierre Rondeau were ambushed in separate incidents in June and September. Rondeau's murder sparked a one-day wildcat strike by 2,000 guards across Quebec. More than 50 people have been killed since the biker feud began in 1995.

The Montreal Urban Community, an agency that administers the police department in Montreal and surrounding communities, agreed in February 1997 to pay more than $218,000 to the mother and four children of Marcellus François. The unarmed François was fatally shot in 1991 by police, who mistook him for a murder suspect.

Major projects. An $82-million restoration plan for the Lachine Canal, a contaminated dumping ground that once served as Canada's main commercial artery, was announced on April 10, 1997. The 8-mile (12.5-kilometer) canal, which was built in 1821, was closed to navigation in 1970. The governments of Quebec and Montreal and several other agencies agreed to rebuild the canal's locks and walls, replace adjoining streets and walkways, and create marinas and docks. The restored canal was expected to attract 1.2 million people and 5,000 pleasure boaters annually and serve as a catalyst for economic development in southwestern Montreal.

Claude Brochu, president of the Montreal Expos baseball team, unveiled plans on June 20, 1997, for a new $250-million stadium next to the Molson Centre hockey stadium. Although Brochu warned that the survival of the Expos depended on the proposed 35,000-seat, open-air stadium, widespread government cutbacks raised doubts about public support.

International flights began arriving at Montreal International Airport (Dorval) on September 15, as part of a restructuring by Aéroports de Montréal, the private company that operates the city's two airports. The Supreme Court of Canada in August had ended a legal battle attempting to stop the transfer of the flights from Montreal International Airport (Mirabel) to Dorval by groups representing municipalities around Mirabel. In February, an injunction from a lower court had halted renovations at Dorval.

Plant expansion. Montreal's sluggish economy in 1997 got a boost with the September announcement that Northern Telecom, Canada's largest high-technology firm, would invest $160 million to expand its suburban St. Laurent facility and another $110 million on a new complex nearby. The company also expected to hire an additional 500 workers.

Youngest grandmaster. Alexandre Lesiége, 21, of suburban Longueuil became Canada's youngest chess grandmaster in August at the Quebec Open tournament. He was also the first French-speaking Canadian to hold that title. □ Mike King

See also **Canada; Canadian provinces; Cities.**

Motion pictures. Independently produced films with relatively unknown casts outshone most Hollywood-backed motion pictures at the Academy Awards in March 1997, leading some critics to conclude that audiences prefer fresh concepts and storylines to familiar and safe plots. Moviegoers in 1997 enjoyed a few artistic and appealing films in what many critics and audiences otherwise considered a generally disappointing year. Successful new releases focused on 1970's nostalgia, the lives of historical figures and events, and adaptations of literary classics. One of 1997's biggest film events was the re-release of the most successful film trilogy of all time.

***Star Wars* returns.** George Lucas's re-release of his *Star Wars* trilogy in early 1997 made the films smash hits among a new generation of science-fiction fans. Lucas used advanced computer technology to digitally enhance special-effects images and add new scenes to *Star Wars,* first released in 1977; *The Empire Strikes Back,* released in 1980; and *Return of the Jedi,* released in 1983.

The overwhelming success of the trilogy led to renewed fan interest in plans for the first of three *Star Wars* prequels (films that deal with earlier events than those in the original). The first new installment was expected to be released in theaters in 1999.

***Titanic* watch.** James Cameron, known for directing action films such as *The Terminator* and *True Lies,* turned to the 1912 sinking of the luxury liner *Titanic,* one of the most famous maritime disasters in history, for a 1997 film. Fans awaiting the $200-million picture—the most expensive film ever made—were disappointed when work on the movie's special effects pushed the original summer release date to the end of the year.

Titanic made a big splash following its release, with audiences judging it a spectacular film with varying degrees of romance, comedy, and adventure. In addition to recreating the ship and the formation of the fatal iceberg, Cameron sought to create an air of intimacy by concentrating on a youthful love affair between characters played by Kate Winslet and Leonardo DiCaprio.

Summer film doldrums. Many of Hollywood's highly anticipated movie sequels of 1997 turned out to be either critical or box-office duds. Steven Spielberg's dinosaur-laden *The Lost World: Jurassic Park* was reviewed as a needless and uninspired sequel. Similarly, the action thriller *Speed 2: Cruise Control* never fired viewer interest. *Father's Day,* an expensive comedy starring Robin Williams and Billy Crystal, was considered one of the summer's biggest failures. Both *Speed 2* and *Father's Day* ended their theater runs taking in less than one-third of production costs. In the United States, audiences found *Batman & Robin* mindless and overblown, but audience reaction to the film was more favorable overseas.

The summer's most successful film, *Men in Black,* skillfully combined science-fiction special effects

Ralph Fiennes and Kristin Scott Thomas star in *The English Patient,* which won nine Academy Awards, including best picture, in 1997.

F O C U S

O N

Academy Award-winning films in 1997 swept movie audiences from the frozen landscape of Minnesota into the mind of a mentally ill pianist and onto a North African desert during World War II.

Motion pictures 1997

Frances McDormand, *left,* portrays a rural Minnesota sheriff in *Fargo,* a role that earned her the Academy Award for best actress.

John Gielgud plays a music professor and Noah Taylor plays a young David Helfgott, a mentally disturbed pianist, *above,* in *Shine.* The role won Geoffrey Rush, who played Helfgott as an adult, the 1997 Academy Award for best actor.

with sardonic wit. Julia Roberts's performance in the comedy *My Best Friend's Wedding* earned her some of the most favorable reviews of her career. Rupert Everett enjoyed a major success in the same film as Roberts's gay confidant. Another big screen success that tackled the subject of homosexuality was *In & Out,* starring Kevin Kline and Tom Selleck. Although the film came under some fire because of its story-line, *In & Out* became one of the first major Hollywood studio films with top male stars in a romantic scenario. *Hollow Reed* and *Kiss Me, Guido* also treated gay characters with compassion.

One of the summer's biggest surprise success stories came from England. Peter Cattaneo's *The Full Monty* told the story of unemployed steel workers who become male strippers. The film, a low-budget comedy-drama, proved successful with a variety of audiences, playing to packed houses in *multiplexes* (multiroomed theaters with up to 18 screens) as well as in small art theaters. To build interest in *The Full Monty*, which had no major stars, its producers used an aggressive marketing campaign in major American cities, where ads asking "What is *The Full Monty?*" were placed in newspapers and retail stores. When the film was released in August in a limited number of theaters in New York, Los Angeles, and San Francisco, theaters reported record-breaking attendance figures, eventually triggering additional

releases in Boston, Chicago, Philadelphia, San Diego, and Seattle.

Robert Zemeckis's modestly successful *Contact,* a film starring Jodie Foster as an astronomer who detects an extraterrestrial radio signal, made headlines in July after the Clinton Administration charged that the movie improperly manipulated President Bill Clinton's statements and image. The film incorporated real 1996 footage of the president speaking about the discovery of a rock from Mars that may display signs of ancient life.

Although many summer films were scorned by critics, the season was profitable at the box office. By the end of the Labor Day weekend, summer box office receipts totaled $2.2 billion. However, the summer of 1997 had more releases and higher admission prices, which for many brought the record-breaking figure into perspective.

Return to the 1970's. High expectations from films and filmmakers marked the final months of 1997. Director Ang Lee's *The Ice Storm,* a depiction of alienation and seduction in the Connecticut suburbs of the 1970's, received rave reviews from several critics. The film starred Kevin Kline and Sigourney Weaver. *Boogie Nights,* another financially and critically successful film set in the 1970's, took a look at the early years of the adult film industry. Mark Wahlberg's performance was regarded as one of the finest of 1997. Veteran actor Burt Reynolds also won his best reviews in years as a producer with delusions of artistry. The positive responses to *Boogie Nights* and *The Ice Storm* caused observers to wonder if the Hollywood establishment was better at exploring the past than the present.

Critical hits. Veteran actor Peter Fonda, father of actress Bridget Fonda, brother of Jane Fonda, and son of the late Henry Fonda, received the best reviews of his career for playing an withdrawn, saddened old man in the film *Ulee's Gold.*

Deconstructing Harry, a comedy directed by Woody Allen and starring Allen, Billy Crystal, Elisabeth Shue, and Robin Williams, was released in December to Allen's eager and loyal audience. *Deconstructing Harry* was Allen's most complex film, in both plot and character development, since *Crimes and Misdemeanors* in 1989.

Oliver Stone gave viewers the sensual and violent *U-Turn,* starring Sean Penn. While *U-Turn* was unable to capture audience attention, Curtis Hanson's multilayered adaptation of James Ellroy's dark crime novel, *L.A. Confidential,* drew rave reviews and large box office attendance. The film, starring Kevin Spacey and Kim Basinger, presented a cynical look at the Los Angeles police department and the fame and corruption in Hollywood during the 1950's. Basinger bolstered her career with high praise for a performance that transcended the stereotype of a gold-hearted prostitute.

Another bright release in 1997 was *Shall We*

Academy Award winners in 1997

The following winners of the 1996 Academy Awards were announced in March 1997:

Best Picture, *The English Patient*
Best Actor, Geoffrey Rush, *Shine*
Best Actress, Frances McDormand, *Fargo*
Best Supporting Actor, Cuba Gooding Jr., *Jerry Maguire*
Best Supporting Actress, Juliette Binoche, *The English Patient*
Best Director, Anthony Minghella, *The English Patient*
Best Original Screenplay, Ethan Coen and Joel Coen, *Fargo*
Best Screenplay Adaptation, Billy Bob Thornton, *Sling Blade*
Best Cinematography, John Seale, *The English Patient*
Best Film Editing, Walter Murch, *The English Patient*
Best Original Dramatic Score, Gabriel Yared, *The English Patient*
Best Original Music or Comedy Score, Rachel Portman, *Emma*
Best Original Song, Andrew Lloyd Webber and Tim Rice, "You Must Love Me" from *Evita*
Best Foreign-Language Film, *Kolya* (Czech Republic)
Best Art Direction, Stuart Craig, *The English Patient*
Best Costume Design, Ann Roth, *The English Patient*
Best Sound, Walter Murch, Mark Berger, David Parker, Chris Newman, *The English Patient*
Best Sound Effects Editing, Bruce Stambler, *The Ghost and the Darkness*
Best Makeup, Rick Baker, David Leroy Anderson, *The Nutty Professor*
Best Visual Effects, *Independence Day*
Best Animated Short Film, *Quest*
Best Live-Action Short Film, *Dear Diary*
Best Feature Documentary, *When We Were Kings*
Best Short Subject Documentary, *Breathing Lessons: The Life and Work of Mark O'Brien*

Motion pictures

Dance? The Japanese film portrays the life of a rigid businessman who learns to relax while taking ballroom dancing lessons. The film's sense of happiness and liberation spoke to worldwide audiences and became one of the most popular Japanese films ever released in the United States.

Lighter fare late in 1997 included the release of the special effects-laden *Starship Troopers* and *Anastasia,* which was the first animated feature to come out of the new Fox Animation Studios.

Historical views. The Dalai Lama, the Tibetan Buddhist leader, was the subject of two 1997 films. *Seven Years in Tibet,* a picturesque film with a relatively weak plot, was released in October. The film featured Brad Pitt as an Austrian mountain climber and former Nazi who befriends the young Dalai Lama. In December, Martin Scorsese's *Kundun* was released. The Dalai Lama was actively involved in Scorsese's film, spending several days meeting with the film's screenwriter. The Dalai Lama also reportedly sketched from memory the floor plan of the palace from which he escaped in 1959.

The British film *Mrs. Brown,* starring Dame Judi Dench as Great Britain's Queen Victoria, scored highly with viewers in 1997. Attention was also focused on the historical *Amistad,* which told the story of an 1839 slave mutiny and subsequent trial. *Amistad* was the second film released by DreamWorks SKG, a new studio formed by entertainment heavyweights Steven Spielberg, Jeffrey Katzenberg, and David Geffen. In September 1997, the studio released its first film, *The Peacemaker,* a disappointing spy drama starring George Clooney and Nicole Kidman.

New classics. The movie industry continued its interest in literary classics as two versions of Henry James novels received mostly positive reviews. *The Wings of the Dove* was considered an outstanding adaptation of James's novel, while *Washington Square* opened to mixed reviews. *Washington Square* director Agnieszka Holland and producers Roger Birnbaum and Julie Bergman Sender cast Jennifer Jason Leigh in the role that won an Oscar for Olivia de Havilland in *The Heiress* in 1949. Although Leigh's performance as the shy, repressed heroine did not match de Havilland's, the new film ranked as a more rounded, faithful version of the James novel.

The success of historical dramas also spurred filmmakers to present Charles Dickens's novel *Great Expectations* in a contemporary setting. The tale was moved to a New York City artists' colony and featured Ethan Hawke and Gwyneth Paltrow as characters similar to Dickens's Pip and Estella.

Adrian Lyne's long-expected adaptation of Vladimir Nabokov's novel *Lolita* opened to mixed reviews in France, Germany, Great Britain, Italy, and Spain in September 1997, but failed to find an American distributor willing to handle the controversial film. *Lolita,* which starred Jeremy Irons and 15-year-old unknown actress Dominique Swain, followed Nabokov's controversial novel about a middle-aged man's passion for a teen-age girl. Some film publications reported that Hollywood executives were more fearful of the quality of Lyne's version of *Lolita* and its poor box-office potential than of its controversial subject matter.

Horror films continued to thrill audiences in 1997. The unexpected success of *Scream,* which had opened late in 1996 but was still playing in theaters during the summer of 1997, led to a spate of horror films. The fact that horror movies are traditionally shot quickly and cheaply made them appealing to studio executives. None of the new films, however, including *Mimic* and *I Know What You Did Last Summer,* matched *Scream's* roaring success. *Scream,* however, was not shown in Japan, which banned the film because of unrelated serial killings in that country. American moviegoers lined up for the release of the sequel, *Scream 2,* in December.

Foreign success. The German film industry in early 1997 enjoyed its strongest showing at the box office since the 1950's. Thirteen German films released during the first three months of 1997 accounted for 37 percent of that quarter's box office receipts in Germany. Such German films as *Rossini* and *Knockin' on Heaven's Door* topped the profits of such Hollywood movie heavyweights as *Ransom* and *Jerry Maguire* in Germany.   □ Philip Wuntch

See also **People in the news.**

Netherlands held the presidency of the European Union (EU), a group of 15 Western European nations, during a difficult six-month period in the first half of 1997. The government's main task was to lead the negotiations on a new EU treaty that was supposed to prepare the Union to accept as many as a dozen new members from Eastern and Southern Europe. But most EU countries were preoccupied with cutting their budget deficits to qualify for the single currency that the group planned to launch in 1999. Many countries also opposed some of the main treaty proposals, such as restricting the ability of individual countries to veto EU policies.

Treaty of Amsterdam. The negotiations were concluded at a June summit meeting of EU leaders in Amsterdam chaired by Dutch Prime Minister Wim Kok. The treaty gave the EU new powers in areas such as environmental policy, employment, and human rights, but it imposed only modest limits on the ability of national governments to veto EU policies. A decision on curbing the growth of members in the European Parliament and the European Commission, the EU executive agency, was deferred until after 2000. The summit meeting also produced an agreement on a Pact for Stability and Growth that was intended to ensure the strength of the euro, as the single currency was to be named. The pact set permanent limits on national budget deficits and steep fines for any country that violated those limits.

More than 16,000 skaters participate in the Netherland's Eleven Cities Skating Marathon, held in January 1997 for the first time in 11 years. The race takes place only when ice freezes 6 inches (15 centimeters) thick along the entire course—125 miles (200 kilometers) of canals linking 11 medieval Dutch cities.

Economy. The Netherlands outperformed most of its EU partners in 1997 as growth remained strong and unemployment continued to drop. The economy benefited from policies adopted in the 1980's that increased employment by limiting wage increases and encouraged people to take part-time jobs. The European Commission forecast that the country's gross domestic product (GDP) would grow by 3.1 percent in 1997, above the 2.6 percent EU average. Unemployment was forecast to fall to 5.5 percent in 1997, the EU's third-lowest rate. Economic growth produced higher tax revenues that were expected to lower the budget deficit to 2.1 percent of GDP, well below the 3 percent limit set for countries wishing to join the single currency.

EU bank chief. In July, Wim Duisenberg, the president of the Dutch central bank, was appointed president of the European Monetary Institute, the EU body charged with preparing for the single currency. The Netherlands and most EU governments wanted Duisenberg to continue as president after the institute is converted to the European Central Bank, which was to be established in 1999 to manage the single currency. However, the French government in November 1997 nominated Jean-Claude Trichet, president of the Bank of France, for the post. The European Central Bank presidency was to be filled in 1998. □ Tom Buerkle

See also **Europe** (Facts in brief table).

New York City. Rudolph W. Giuliani was re-elected to a second four-year term as mayor of New York City on Nov. 4, 1997. Giuliani campaigned on themes of reduced crime, a strong local economy, and record tourism to defeat the Democratic candidate, Manhattan Borough President Ruth Messinger. Giuliani was the first Republican mayor since Fiorello La Guardia in 1937 to win back-to-back terms.

Giuliani's victory came despite serious allegations of police brutality when four police officers were accused of torturing Haitian immigrant Abner Louima on Aug. 9, 1997, in a holding cell of the 70th precinct stationhouse in Brooklyn. Critics charged that the administration's tough crackdown on crime had given too much latitude to police officers, and thousands of immigrants and supporters held an antipolice rally in front of City Hall.

On August 18, the mayor reacted by announcing the appointment of a citizen task force to investigate ways to improve relations between the police department and minority communities. However, Giuliani continued to support the police department's own civilian complaint review board, which Giuliani had opposed in his 1993 race for mayor.

The city council also considered plans for an independent body of citizens to monitor complaints against police officers. At a council hearing on Sept. 23, 1997, former detective Frank Serpico testified that New York needed the proposed board to "cre-

Confetti rains down on crowds in New York City's newly revitalized Times Square theater district to celebrate the "Broadway on Broadway" launch in September of the 1997 theater season.

ate an atmosphere where the crooked cop fears the honest cop, and not the other way around." Serpico's charges of corruption against the department in 1971 resulted in a major investigation and made him the subject of a popular film starring Al Pacino.

Tourism increased to an all-time high in New York in 1997, in part because of a decrease in the rate of serious crime—a category that includes all violent crime and theft. Serious crime in New York City declined 39 percent between 1993 and 1997. The city's Convention and Visitors Bureau estimated that 32 million people visited New York City for business and leisure in 1997, up 2 percent from 1996 and more than 10 percent since 1994. Visitors were estimated to have spent about $14 billion in 1997.

As the numbers of tourists increased, new attractions opened to meet demand. New York City's 42nd Street and Times Square, a historic theater district that became an area of adult entertainment in the 1970's, made a comeback in 1997 as a family entertainment center. The landmark New Amsterdam Theater, purchased and restored by the Walt Disney Company as a home for its musicals, reopened in May. In November, the theater was the scene of the premiere of *The Lion King*. Based on the animated film and budgeted at $15 million, *The Lion King* was the most expensive show in Broadway history.

The New York City school system, the nation's largest, added 15,000 new pupils to bring enrollment to a record 1.1 million for the 1997–1998 school year. However, there were no overcrowding problems for the first time in several years, thanks to the use of classroom trailers and an $8.6-billion school budget, one-fourth of the city's operating budget. School authorities continued to await legislative approval for year-round schools, proposed in 1996 as a long term answer to increasing enrollment. The growing enrollment reflected an increase in the number of children from middle-class households returning to New York City public schools.

On Sept. 25, 1997, a group of Greenwich Village parents won a victory with national implications for other urban school districts. In a bid to keep class sizes down at PS 41, the parents collected enough money to pay the salary and benefits of a fourth grade teacher who was being reassigned to another school. Schools Chancellor Rudolph F. Crew initially rejected the offer, saying it was unfair to children in poor districts whose parents lacked the means to subsidize additional teachers. But after a public outcry and the threat of a court suit, Crew, while rejecting the parents' offer, authorized the use of public funds to pay for the additional teacher.

The new Arthur Ashe Stadium was the site of the U.S. Open tennis championship, which began Aug. 25, 1997. The nearly 23,000-seat arena was dedicated to the memory of the African American tennis star, who died of AIDS in 1993.   □ Owen Moritz

See also **City.**

New Zealand. New Zealand's coalition government, consisting of the National Party and the New Zealand First Party, faced a number of political problems in 1997. The coalition had been formed in December 1996 under new rules that required political parties to be represented in the government in proportion to the share of votes they received in elections. The most serious political problem of 1997 occurred in November, when Prime Minister Jim Bolger was forced to resign after Jenny Shipley, his transport minister, took over leadership of the National Party from him. Deputy Prime Minister and Treasurer Winston Peters, leader of the New Zealand First Party, considered leaving the coalition after Bolger's ouster, believing that Shipley was too conservative. Peters stayed on, however, after receiving written assurances from Shipley that she would not change the direction of the government.

Other political problems. In May, a parliamentary committee found Peters guilty of having assaulted a National Party legislator in Parliament in March. The committee formally rebuked Peters but did not find him in contempt of Parliament.

In August, New Zealand First Party member Neil Kirton was dismissed as associate health minister after reportedly disobeying party orders not to give interviews to the press. Kirton had opposed government efforts to privatize the health care industry. In September, National Party member Christine Fletcher resigned from her local government, women's affairs, and cultural affairs portfolios, claiming that she was not being consulted over policy.

Tax inquiry. A commission of inquiry concluded in August that, contrary to charges by Peters, there was no evidence of fraud in tax deals made between New Zealand companies and the government of the Cook Islands, semiautonomous bodies northeast of New Zealand. Peters had charged that the deals allowed companies to evade taxes and that government agencies had inadequately investigated the deals. In November, Peters asked New Zealand's High Court to rule that the commission's conclusions were incorrect.

Economy. An economic slowdown in 1997 caused unemployment in New Zealand to rise to 6.7 percent by mid-1997, from 6.1 percent in mid-1996. Inflation remained low at under 2 percent. In late 1997, the Reserve Bank, New Zealand's central bank, predicted that annual economic growth from March 1997 to March 1998 would be 2.4 percent.

Rabbit virus. In August 1997, farmers illegally introduced a rabbit-killing virus to areas of New Zealand's South Island where rabbit populations had become a serious nuisance. The government had hesitated to release the virus due to ecological concerns. In September, however, the government announced that it would arrange controlled spread of the virus on the North Island.   □ Gavin Ellis

See also **Pacific Islands** (Facts in brief table).

The following people and events made headlines in 1997:

Roswell case closed. In June 1997, the United States Air Force released a 231-page report dealing with the mysterious "Roswell Incident" of 1947, which allegedly involved a spacecraft from another planet that crash-landed in the desert near Roswell, New Mexico. Believers in the Roswell crash charged that government and military officials conspired to cover up the incident to prevent widespread panic. Over the years, several people claimed to have seen evidence of space ships and aliens in the area of Roswell.

The 1997 report was the Air Force's latest and most detailed attempt to explain what it said actually inspired the accounts of aliens and extraterrestrial artifacts. It concluded that "incomplete and inaccurate intermingling" of actual events that took place over many years resulted in a "sensational story" that did not hold true when compared to official records.

The report revealed that highly secret military projects were conducted at the Roswell Army Air Field in the 1940's and 1950's. Many involved the development of intelligence equipment and high-altitude escape systems. According to the Air Force, these projects explained both the unusual events and the veil of secrecy that surrounded them.

When a local ranch foreman told a newspaper about finding pieces of unusual, metallic wreckage in July 1947, the Army responded that the wreckage came from a crashed weather balloon. The 1997 report stated that the balloon actually was carrying highly classified sensors developed to detect nuclear detonations by the Soviet Union.

An eyewitness's description of a bulbous-headed alien with slitlike eyes, the report said, may have arisen after an accident in 1959 involving a secret high-altitude parachute test. Official records noted that a test parachutist suffered a serious injury that caused swelling of his head and face, making his eyelids swell almost shut. He was brought to the Roswell base under tight security.

The U.S. Navy's Blue Angels fly over the frigate U.S.S. *Constitution* on July 21, 1997, in celebration of the 200th birthday of "Old Ironsides." The refurbished *Constitution,* normally on display in the Charlestown Navy Yard in Boston, sailed under her own power for the first time in 116 years.

Another famous account—a mass autopsy of several small, dark aliens—may have been inspired, according to the Air Force report, by a June 1956 military plane crash. Army records showed that 11 badly burned bodies were pulled from the wreckage and taken to the Roswell air base to be identified.

Despite these and other Air Force explanations, believers in the Roswell aliens discounted the report. The New Mexico Department of Tourism estimated that more than 40,000 people attended a week-long celebration in July 1997 of the 50th anniversary of the Roswell Incident.

Bush takes a dive. Former U.S. President George Bush captured nationwide media attention in 1997, but in an unusual way—he jumped out of an airplane. Bush had jumped from a plane once before, as a pilot in World War II (1939-1945), when he had been forced to abandon his crippled aircraft over the Pacific Ocean. Bush had been struck by the plane as he jumped, and his parachute had ripped. After that ordeal, Bush said, he had promised himself that he would jump again one day. At the age of 72, he fulfilled that goal when he completed a 12,500-foot (3,800-meter) jump over the Arizona desert in March 1997. Unlike most novice skydivers, Bush was provided with some special help. He jumped with eight members of the U.S. Army's Golden Knights exhibition skydiving team. For most of the jump, Bush was attached to two Army skydivers, and six more were on hand on the way down, in case something went wrong.

Burger blitz. Two American fast-food titans, McDonald's Corporation of Oak Brook, Illinois, and Burger King Corporation of Miami, Florida, squared off in 1997 in an increasingly heated competition for the American fast-food dollar. Long the nation's dominant hamburger chain, McDonald's watched its share of the fast-food market slip in 1997 due to vigorous competition from other burger makers, as well as from a growing number of other fast-food operations that featured chicken, tacos, and pizza.

Burger King fired the first salvo in September, when it launched the Big King, a large double cheeseburger that intentionally bore a striking resemblance to McDonald's flagship burger, the Big Mac. Burger King ads promoted the fact that the Big King had more beef than the Big Mac. Burger King reported that Big Kings were selling at a rate of 3 million per day. This rate slowed after the promotion ended.

McDonald's responded to the Burger King assault by rolling out its version of Burger King's signature hamburger, the Whopper. At the end of 1997, neither company had decided whether their new burgers would permanently join their menus.

L-I-T-I-G-A-T-I-O-N. Attorneys for Barney, the beloved purple dinosaur character whose public television show became a favorite of millions of young viewers, filed a copyright and trademark infringement suit in a Texas federal court in November 1997. The defendant was another character played by a person in an animal suit—the free-lance sports mascot known as the San Diego Chicken.

Ted Gianulis—the man in the Chicken suit—appeared for many years at major sporting events across the United States, entertaining crowds with humorous skits during breaks. One of the Chicken's routines featured a Barneylike purple dinosaur, which the Chicken attacked and beat to the roaring approval of the crowd. Texas-based Lyons Partnership, owner of the rights to the Barney costume, said Gianulis first had been notified in 1994 that using the Barneylike costume in his act constituted infringement of Lyons's trademarks and copyrights.

Gianulis (in full Chicken costume) and his attorney appeared on a network TV news program to respond to the charges. "I think the law is well established that parody of the kind performed by [the

Employees and members of the environmentalist group Greenpeace dangle precariously for 48 hours from a bridge near Seattle, Washington, during an August 1997 protest of overfishing in the Bering Sea. After the protest, three of the participants learned they were being laid off along with 300 other employees due to declining revenues.

In 1997, the Ford Motor Company announced that it was halting production of the Thunderbird, first introduced in 1954. Sales of the legendary sports car had slumped to a mere 80,000 in 1996.

Chicken] is protected," the lawyer said. "It doesn't constitute copyright infringement." When asked if he thought his antics would upset young children, the Chicken replied "Well, I personally have not encountered that kind of reaction . . . I've seen children cry on the lap of Santa Claus. I know I myself—when I was younger—I was traumatized by the Easter Bunny, but I turned out to be fairly and somewhat normal since then."

Going with the wind. Millionaire Chicago businessman and adventurer Steve Fossett in 1997 made his third attempt to become the first individual to circle the globe in a balloon. Fossett's voyage, which began on Jan. 13, 1997, covered 9,672 miles (15,566 kilometers) in 6 days, 2 hours, and 54 minutes. Fossett's planned route was to take him over Europe, but wind shifts forced him to fly over northern Africa. On January 17, Libyan authorities denied Fossett permission to enter Libyan airspace, forcing him to change course again.

The unexpected detours caused Fossett to use up his propane fuel, which heats the air that keeps a balloon aloft, faster than anticipated, forcing him to end his flight on January 20, near Sultanpur, India. Although he failed to complete the journey, Fossett set endurance and distance records for a solo balloon flight.

In December 1997, Fossett and his support team were gearing up for another attempt. This time, they faced competition from at least four other teams bidding to complete a balloon flight around the world. One competitor, British millionaire Richard Branson, was forced to delay his flight after his balloon broke free of its moorings and flew away just hours before his planned take-off from Morocco on December 9. A sudden gust of wind apparently snatched the balloon while Branson's team was filling it with helium. Moroccan military officials offered to shoot down the balloon, but it eventually came down on its own in the Algerian desert.

Tune in, turn on, and blast off. Timothy Leary, the former Harvard psychologist and 1960's cultural icon who once advocated mind expansion through psychoactive drugs, took one last trip in 1997. Leary, who died on May 31, 1996, had requested that his remains be launched into space. In April 1997, a lipstick-sized capsule carrying 0.25 ounce (7 grams) of Leary's ashes was attached to the side of a corporate-owned rocket launching a Spanish satellite into orbit. The ashes of 23 other people, including space physicist Gerard O'Neill and Gene Roddenberry, creator of the television series "Star Trek," were also attached to the rocket. The capsules were expected to remain in orbit for up to 10 years before falling back toward Earth and burning up in the atmosphere.

Ted Turner, the billionaire cable television tycoon, pledged in September 1997 to donate $1 billion to the United Nations (UN). Turner made the surprise announcement at a UN dinner in New York City. The enormous gift, the largest in philanthropic history, was to be paid in installments of $100 million a year over a period of 10 years. Turner stipulated that the money be used only to fund UN aid programs and not for UN administrative costs.

To oversee the allocation of the funds, Turner established the United Nations Foundation. In November, he named Timothy E. Wirth, a former U.S. Senator from Colorado and Undersecretary of State for Global Affairs, as president.

In the past, the brash, outspoken Turner had publicly chastised other wealthy individuals for not donating some of their fortunes to charitable causes. "If you want to lead," Turner said of his donation, "you got to blow the horn and get out in front of the parade."

Turner received a 10-percent stake in the broadcasting corporation Time Warner Incorporated when the media conglomerate purchased his successful cable TV empire in 1995. The billion-dollar pledge, some observers estimated, amounted to one-third of his net worth.

Car breaks the sound barrier. On Oct. 15, 1997, Thrust SSC (for "supersonic car"), a jet-propelled automobile from Great Britain, set a new land-speed record and officially became the first automobile to break the sound barrier. The car, driven by Royal Air Force pilot Andy Green, completed two supersonic runs down a 14-mile (22.5-kilometer) course on Nevada's Black Rock Desert.

In order for the land-speed record to be declared official by the United States Auto Club (USAC), two runs had to be made within one hour of each other. USAC used the average of Thrust SSC's two runs to calculate an official speed of 763.035 miles (1,227.886 kilometers) per hour. The speed of sound, which varies according to altitude and weather conditions, was calculated that day at 748.11 miles (1,203.966 kilometers) per hour. Richard Noble, who served as the leader of the Thrust SSC project, had set a land-speed record in 1983 of 633.47 miles (1,019.47 kilometers) per hour.

Suicide cult. One of the largest mass suicides in U.S. history occurred in March 1997, when 39 members of Heaven's Gate, a California doomsday cult, were found dead in a house they had oc-

Thrust SSC, a jet-powered automobile from Great Britain, sets a new land-speed record in October and becomes the first car to exceed the speed of sound.

cupied in Rancho Santa Fe, California. Investigators revealed that the suicides were planned to coincide with the closest approach to Earth of the Hale-Bopp comet. Heaven's Gate members practiced a blend of Christianity and belief in extraterrestrial beings. They spread their philosophy over the Internet. A posting on the group's home page indicated that they believed that the comet signaled the arrival of a spaceship sent to carry its members to heaven. The dead cult members were found wearing identical black outfits, their faces covered by purple shrouds. They had each packed a suitcase and carried a $5 bill and several quarters in their pockets. Authorities said the suicides were carried out by drug overdose.

A Hollywood ending. In December 1997, a federal bankruptcy judge approved the sale of the famous Hollywood Memorial Park Cemetery, apparently laying to rest speculation that it would be shut down. The owner of a Hollywood mortuary company agreed to purchase the 98-year-old park—the final resting place of Cecil B. DeMille, Rudolph Valentino, Charlie Chaplin, and hundreds of other Hollywood stars—for $375,000, plus the substantial costs of repairs and maintenance at the neglected site.

The property, which had fallen into disrepair in recent years and suffered significant damage in the 1994 earthquake that struck Los Angeles, was in need of approximately $1 million in repairs. Its owner declared bankruptcy April 1, 1997, amid allegations of fiscal improprieties.

The sale price was far below the $3 million that the Santa Monica Boulevard property was estimated to be worth. The purchase was contingent on the buyer's review of the cemetery grounds and its financial status. It was due to be finalized in mid-January 1998. *The New York Times* reported that the happy ending "could have been directed by Frank Capra (who is not buried at Hollywood Memorial)."

The international pastime. Figures released in October 1997 by baseball's National and American leagues showed that the percentage of Latino players in the major leagues had nearly doubled in the

Paul McCartney displays his insignia after being knighted by Britain's Queen Elizabeth II in March 1997. McCartney, a member of the rock group the Beatles, was honored for his contributions to music.

1990's. In 1997, nearly 25 percent of Major League Baseball players and 30 percent of minor leaguers were Latinos. A record eight native Puerto Rican players participated in Major League Baseball's All-Star Game in Cleveland on July 8. Cleveland Indians catcher Sandy Alomar, Jr., hit the two-run homer that won the game for the American League. He became the first Puerto Rican to be named the Most Valuable Player of the All-Star Game.

Perhaps the biggest impact of the rising proportion of Hispanic players in Major League Baseball was seen in the 1997 World Series victory of the Florida Marlins, based in Miami—a city with a large and diverse Hispanic population. The championship quest seemed to fuse the many ethnic communities in the team's hometown. Marlins shortstop Edgar Renteria, a native of Colombia, drove in the run that clinched the final game. Rookie pitcher Livan Hernandez, a 22-year-old Cuban defector, was named

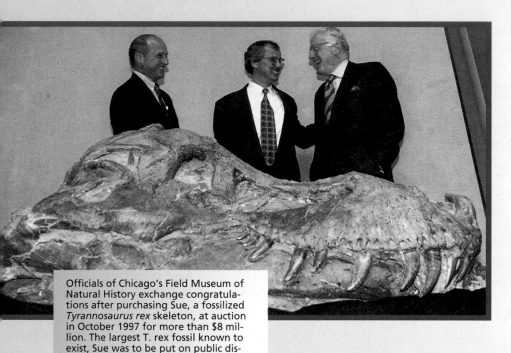

Officials of Chicago's Field Museum of Natural History exchange congratulations after purchasing Sue, a fossilized *Tyrannosaurus rex* skeleton, at auction in October 1997 for more than $8 million. The largest T. rex fossil known to exist, Sue was to be put on public display around the year 2000.

the Most Valuable Player of the series. The Marlins's roster included another Cuban, Alex Fernandez; three Dominicans, Moises Alou, Felix Heredia, and Antonio Alfonseca; a Puerto Rican, Bobby Bonilla; and a Jamaican, Devon White. "No matter how well, or poorly, the Marlins do in subsequent years," the *Miami Herald* declared, "for now they're the glue that bonds a disparate community."

Underground Sue. The largest and most complete *Tyrannosaurus rex* fossil ever unearthed was

sold in October 1997 at an auction at Sotheby's in New York City. It sold for just over $8 million, the highest price ever paid for a dinosaur fossil.

The 65-million-year-old skeleton was named after Susan Hendrickson, a private fossil hunter who discovered the skeleton in 1990 near Faith, South Dakota. The fossil was found on the property of Maurice Williams, a Native American of the Cheyenne River Sioux tribe, whose land was being held in trust by the federal government. Peter Larson, head of the Black Hills Institute of Geological Research, Incorporated, in South Dakota, excavated the tyrannosaur after purchasing it from Williams for $5,000. However, the United States government, Williams's trustee, claimed that Larson had not received government permission to remove the bones. In 1992, FBI agents —supported by National Guard troops—raided Larson's institute and seized the dinosaur.

Larson and his colleagues were charged with 148 felonies and 5 misdemeanors related to taking fossils from federal land. A federal judge later threw out most of the charges, and Larson was found not guilty of stealing fossils from government land. The courts finally awarded ownership of Sue to Williams. As his trustee, the government decided to sell the skeleton at auction, with the proceeds going to Williams.

Members of the scientific community feared that a collector might outbid public institutions for Sue, possibly making the fossil unavailable for scientific study. Officials of Chicago's Field Museum of Natural History, however, assembled a partnership of corporate and private donors to raise the money to purchase Sue. After the sale, museum officials announced that three life-size replicas, built from casts of the bones, will be given to McDonald's Corporation, the museum's largest partner. McDonald's planned to put one replica on display at Walt Disney World. The other two will go on tour worldwide. After a two-year project to restore and preserve the fossil, the real Sue is to be assembled and placed on permanent display at the Field Museum.   □ Peter Uremovic

Newspaper. In an unusual move, the executive editor of *The San Jose* (California) *Mercury News* stated in a May 11, 1997, editorial that a well-publicized, three-part series of articles in August 1996 on the rise of crack cocaine in urban America was flawed. The editorial stated that suggestions in the 1996 articles that the sale of crack cocaine in Los Angeles in the 1980's was initiated by Nicaraguan drug suppliers, who used the profits to support antigovernment rebels known as *contras,* and that the U.S. Central Intelligence Agency was linked to the operation, were not supported by fact. The editorial admitted that the series "through imprecise language and graphics . . . created impressions that were open to misinterpretation. . . ." The articles failed to make clear that dollar-amounts were estimates and that the issue of how the crack epidemic in the United States grew was oversimplified.

Major sale. Knight-Ridder Incorporated announced on April 4, 1997, that it would pay the Walt Disney Company $1.65 billion for *The Kansas City* (Mo.) *Star, The Fort Worth* (Texas) *Star-Telegram,* and two smaller newspapers, *The Belleville News-Democrat* in Illinois and *The Times Leader* in Wilkes-Barre, Pennsylvania. The four newspapers had a total revenue in 1996 of $500 million.

Detroit strike ends. A 19-month strike at *The Detroit News* and *Detroit Free Press*, the city's two major daily newspapers, ended in February 1997. On February 14, six labor unions representing about 2,500 striking employees unconditionally offered to return to work. On February 19, managers from the two newspapers and from Detroit Newspapers Inc., the agency that runs the papers under a joint operating agreement, accepted the offer.

During the strike, the newspapers, which have combined printing and business operations, had hired approximately 1,300 replacement workers and had continued to publish without interruption. Although the National Labor Relations Board concluded that the strike was caused by unfair labor practices by the newspapers, a federal judge on August 14 refused the board's request that the newspapers rehire more than 1,000 former strikers.

British newspaper reform. Britain's Press Complaints Commission on September 25 recommended changes to the newspaper industry's code of conduct. The recommended changes included a request that editors no longer purchase pictures by *paparazzi* (aggressive free-lance photographers) that were obtained either illegally or unethically.

The proposed changes to the British newspapers' code of conduct came in the wake of criticism that members of the press were partially responsible for the August 31 death of Diana, Princess of Wales, her companion Emad (Dodi) Fayed, and their driver, Henri Paul, in a high-speed Paris car crash.

□ Mark Fitzgerald

See also **Diana, Princess of Wales,** Special Report.

Nicaragua. Arnoldo Alemán Lacayo, 51, was sworn in for a five-year term as Nicaragua's president on Jan. 10, 1997. Alemán called for national unity, a matter that political observers considered urgent, after the Liberal Alliance, a coalition of conservative parties that backed his election, won only 42 of the 92 seats in the national legislature.

In February, Alemán announced austerity measures for the government, including the elimination of thousands of government jobs. The president claimed that Nicaragua must fight "an entrenched bureaucracy, many years of corruption, and the idea that the state should be the great generator of employment." To demonstrate his personal commitment to change, Alemán stripped senior administrative officials of perks, such as cellular phones and new automobiles. With press cameras flashing, he took scissors to credit cards previously furnished to members of Nicaragua's presidential Cabinet.

In February, Nicaraguan police seized a large cache of armaments—rifles, grenades, submachine guns, rocket launchers, plastic explosives, and land mines—at a ranch belonging to a retired military officer of the former leftist Sandinista government. Nicaraguan authorities suspected that the weapons had belonged to a former leftist guerrilla movement in neighboring El Salvador. □ Nathan A. Haverstock

See also **Latin America** (Facts in brief table).

Niger. See Africa.

Nigeria. The military government of General Sani Abacha continued its relentless persecution of political opponents in 1997, while at the same time exercising leadership in efforts to promote democracy in neighboring countries. Although human rights groups had no difficulty documenting the regime's abuse of human rights, the international community refused to take serious action against Nigeria, such as banning imports of Nigerian petroleum, the country's largest source of income. Moreover, Nigeria won international praise in 1997 for its successful supervision of free elections in Liberia and its efforts to restore civilian government in Sierra Leone.

Elections. Abacha's government trumpeted elections for 774 local councils, held on March 15, as a first step in a transition to civilian government. The elections, the first multiparty vote since the regime seized power in 1993, attracted a heavy turnout. The five participating parties, however, were all supportive of the government. Independent opposition parties remained outlawed. The National Democratic Coalition (NADECO), the country's leading prodemocracy party, was shut out of the election. NADECO condemned the elections and criticized the participating parties as government puppets.

Transition plan. Although Abacha continued to promise to restore elected government in 1998, a government-orchestrated campaign to persuade Abacha to run for the presidency as a civilian candidate suggested that the return to civilian rule might not be a return to democracy. Government opponents denounced the plan as a sham, pointing out that Nigeria already had a civilian president—Moshood Abiola—whose 1993 election had been annulled by the military. Abiola, arrested on charges of treason in 1993, remained imprisoned in 1997.

More treason charges. On March 12, the government charged 12 political dissidents with treason for their alleged involvement in a series of nationwide bombings in 1996 and 1997. Among the accused was exiled author Wole Soyinka, winner of the 1986 Nobel Prize for literature. Eight of those charged were still living in Nigeria and were jailed. Like other political prisoners in Nigeria, they faced torture, foul prison conditions, and a corrupt legal system. Human rights groups condemned the charges and insisted that the government lacked any evidence connecting the accused to the bombings.

Rights abuses. The World Council of Churches, a worldwide organization of some 300 Protestant, Anglican, Old Catholic, and Orthodox churches based in Geneva, Switzerland, accused the Nigerian government in January 1997 of repressing the country's oil-rich Ogoniland region. The report detailed incidents of rape, torture, and looting by government soldiers. □ Mark DeLancey

See also **Africa** (Facts in brief table); **Liberia; Sierra Leone.**

Nobel Prizes

Nobel Prizes in literature, peace, the sciences, and economics were awarded in October 1997 by the Norwegian Storting (parliament) in Oslo and by the Royal Swedish Academy of Sciences, the Karolinska Institute, and the Swedish Academy of Literature in Stockholm. Each prize was worth $1 million.

The 1997 Nobel Prize for literature went to Italian playwright and actor Dario Fo, who according to the Swedish Academy, "emulates the jesters of the Middle Ages in scourging authority and upholding the dignity of the downtrodden." Fo's dramas incorporate such medieval conventions as the comic comments of court jesters to examine social and political themes.

Fo's most famous play, *Comic Mystery* (1969), is built around a single character who satirizes landowners, the government, and the Roman Catholic Church. Fo's play *Accidental Death of an Anarchist* (1970) was based on the true story of a bombing suspect who fell to his death from a fourth-story window while being interrogated by Milanese authorities. *The Devil with Boobs* (1997) is a Renaissance courtroom drama centered on a woman possessed by the devil and the judge who determines her fate.

The 1997 Nobel Prize for peace was awarded to the International Campaign to Ban Landmines (ICBL) and its American coordinator, Jody Williams. The prize money was split equally between Williams and the organization. Since its founding in 1991,

ICBL members have worked to ban and clear antipersonnel land mines. According to the organization's estimates, the more than 100 million such mines deployed throughout the world maimed or killed 26,000 people in 1997, 80 percent of whom were civilians. The ICBL grew under Williams's direction from a coalition of a few antiland mine groups to a worldwide organization of more than 1,000 such groups.

The Nobel Committee cited Williams and the ICBL for starting a process that "in the space of a few years changed a ban on antipersonnel mines from a vision to a feasible reality." An international treaty mandating such a ban was adopted by 89 countries in September 1997.

The 1997 Nobel Prize for physiology or medicine was awarded to American physician and medical researcher Stanley B. Prusiner of the University of California in San Francisco, for his discovery of prions. Prions are infectious agents linked with brain-wasting disorders such as mad-cow disease and Creutzfeldt-Jakob Disease (CJD). After one of his patients died of CJD in 1972, Prusiner set out to find the cause of the disease. Ten years later, he identified prions, after isolating them in diseased hamster brains.

Prions are apparently a new form of infectious agent, a kind of rogue protein. Prion proteins exist normally in a harmless form. However, according to Prusiner's still-unproven theory, they can be changed into a disease-causing form by coming into contact with a prion from outside the body or by genetic mutation (change). Toxic prions destroy nerve cells. If true, this may lead to a new understanding of Alzheimer's disease, which may be caused by changes in ordinary proteins.

The 1997 Nobel Prize for economics went to American Robert C. Merton of Harvard University in Cambridge, Massachusetts, and Canadian-born Myron S. Scholes of Stanford University in Palo Alto, California, for devising a formula to determine the value of derivatives. Derivatives are lucrative, but risky, investments based on predicting the future value of such assets as stocks, bonds, or interest rates. Investors can purchase the option to buy or sell shares of an asset at a particular price at a particular time in the future. Merton and Scholes's formula became the standard for options valuation, contributing to the development of the options market, which in 1997 handled $70 trillion in transactions.

The 1997 Nobel Prize for chemistry was awarded to three researchers for their contribution to the understanding of the chemical properties of adenosine triphosphate (ATP), the compound that stores the energy that fuels living cells. Half the prize went to Danish chemist Jens C. Skou of Aarhus University in Denmark. In the late 1950's, Skou discovered an enzyme that helps regulate the amounts of potassium and sodium in a cell. The other half of the prize was split between American

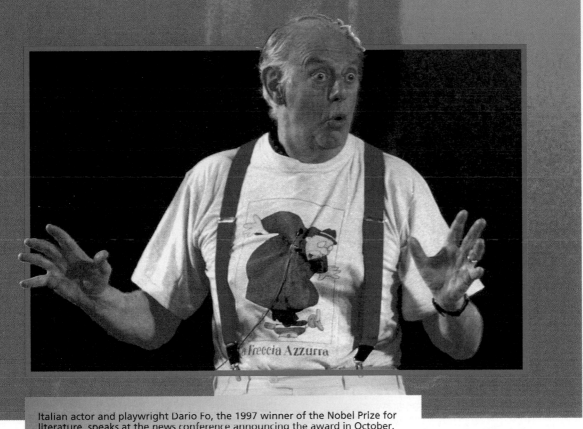

Italian actor and playwright Dario Fo, the 1997 winner of the Nobel Prize for literature, speaks at the news conference announcing the award in October.

chemist Paul D. Boyer of the University of California at Los Angeles and British chemist John E. Walker of the Medical Research Council Laboratory of Molecular Biology in Cambridge, England. Their work explained how enzymes, such as the one Skou discovered, make ATP.

The 1997 Nobel Prize for physics went to Steven Chu of Stanford University, Claude Cohen-Tannoudji of the Collège de France and École Normale Supérieure in Paris, and William D. Phillips of the U.S. National Institute of Standards and Technology, in Gaithersburg, Maryland, for the development—worked out independently—of "methods to cool and trap atoms with laser light."

Cooling is vital to the study of atoms because low temperatures slow the speed at which atoms travel, making them easier to examine. Chu developed a method of rendering atoms nearly motionless by corraling them with laser beams. Philips and Cohen-Tannoudji achieved even greater cooling: Phillips used magnetic fields; Cohen-Tannoudji developed a method of converting atoms to a state in which they will not absorb light. These methods made it possible to construct an improved atomic clock accurate to within one second over a 3-billion-year span. Earlier atomic clocks were accurate to within a second in 32 million years. □ Lisa Klobuchar

North Carolina. See **State government.**
North Dakota. See **State government.**

Northern Ireland. The Irish Republican Army (IRA), an unofficial military force that seeks to unite Northern Ireland with the independent Republic of Ireland, launched a campaign of bombings and bomb threats in Great Britain in the weeks before the British general election on May 1, 1997. Two IRA bombs placed in Wilmslow, near Manchester, on March 26, and two more bombs discovered next to the M6 motorway in central England on April 3 resulted in widespread chaos on the British rail system as well as vast traffic jams. The Grand National Steeplechase, one of Britain's biggest sporting events, was postponed on April 5 for two days because of an IRA bomb threat at the racecourse. London traffic ground to a halt April 21 after bomb threats closed five railway stations and four airports.

Elections. The IRA ceased operations in Northern Ireland before Britain's May election to avoid harming the chances of Sinn Féin, the political wing of the IRA. The tactic worked, and Sinn Féin gained nearly 16 percent of the vote. Sinn Féin President Gerry Adams and the party's chief negotiator, Martin McGuinness, won seats in the British House of Commons. However, they refused to swear a loyalty oath to the queen and were not allowed to take their places.

Peace negotiations. After nearly three decades of strife, Northern Ireland's feuding political parties began full-scale peace negotiations in Belfast on October 7. The talks were hailed as the most significant development in Northern Ireland since 1921, when the partition of Ireland left the province of Northern Ireland united with Great Britain. The real impetus for the talks came from Britain's new prime minister, Tony Blair, who had declared his determination to achieve a new constitutional settlement in Northern Ireland. Blair met with Sinn Féin President Adams at 10 Downing Street, the prime minister's residence, on Dec. 11, 1997, the first such meeting in 76 years.

The Ulster Unionist Party, the largest party in Northern Ireland and the one that represents most Protestants and seeks to maintain the union with Great Britain, took part in the October talks. However, the more extreme Democratic Unionist Party and the tiny United Kingdom Unionist Party refused to join. An IRA cease-fire on July 20 allowed the British government to invite Sinn Féin to take part in the talks, reversing an earlier ban. Another obstacle that had held up the start of the talks was cleared on September 9, when Sinn Féin agreed to principles of nonviolence and democracy laid down by the Mitchell Commission—a team led by former U.S. Senator George Mitchell—in 1996. The British government set a deadline of May 1998 to reach a settlement that was to be put to the vote in separate referendums in Northern Ireland and Ireland.   □ Ian Mather

Northwest Territories. See Canadian Territories.

Norway. A centrist-party coalition took control of Norway's government in 1997 for the first time in 25 years, after voters spurned the long-ruling Labor Party in an election for members of the Storting (parliament) on September 15. The coalition, made up of the Christian People's Party, the Center Party, and the Liberal Party, promised to use the country's oil-driven economic boom to increase spending for education, health care, and care of the elderly. The coalition won 42 seats in the 165-seat Storting and formed a minority government on October 17 led by Christian People's Party leader Kjell Magne Bondevik as prime minister. The Labor Party—the country's largest—won 65 seats, a decline of two from the previous election in 1993. However, Thorbjoern Jagland, who had succeeded veteran politician Gro Harlem Brundtland as prime minister in 1996, resigned, as he had promised to do if Labor did not match or surpass its 1993 electoral score.

Land mine ban. Diplomats from 89 countries endorsed a treaty to ban the manufacture and use of land mines at an international conference in Oslo on Sept. 18, 1997. Although the United States refused to sign the treaty, President Boris Yeltsin said Russia would sign.   □ Tom Buerkle

See also **Europe** (Facts in brief table).

Nova Scotia. See Canadian provinces.
Nuclear energy. See Energy supply.
Nutrition. See Food.

Ocean. New evidence that a huge meteorite crashed into the Caribbean Sea on the north side of Mexico's Yucatán Peninsula about 65 million years ago was reported in February 1997 by an international team of marine geologists. The researchers, who had been studying sea-floor sediments off the coast of South Carolina, found evidence of the impact 1,000 miles (1,600 kilometers) from the crater.

The investigators examined cores of sediment and found that they contained layers of debris that appeared to be from a blanket of material ejected into the atmosphere when the meteorite struck the Earth. The material had settled onto the sea and sunk to the bottom. Many scientists believe the impact led to the extinction of many of Earth's species, including the dinosaurs.

Roman ships. Oceanographer Robert Ballard, the man who located the sunken remains of the *Titanic* in 1985, reported another important find in July 1997. Ballard announced that he and his research team had discovered five ancient Roman shipwrecks in the Mediterranean Sea at depths of nearly 2,500 feet (760 meters). Previously, no major ancient shipwreck had been discovered at a depth of more than 200 feet (60 meters).

The oldest ship, among a cluster of five dating from about 100 B.C. to A.D. 400, was 100 feet (35 meters) long and carried ceramic *amphorae* (large two-handled jugs) used to transport wine, oil, fish sauce, and fruit preserves. A second ship, from the first century A.D., carried precut Roman columns and giant cut blocks of either granite or marble—a cargo that Ballard called "prefab Roman buildings." Ballard and his colleagues also discovered the wrecks of three more-modern ships in the same area.

A record El Niño? What promised to be the most intense El Niño of the century was underway in late 1997. El Niño is a periodic warming of the waters of the eastern tropical Pacific Ocean that occurs every three to seven years and disrupts weather patterns around the globe. The name—Spanish for *the* (Christ) *child*—was coined by South American fishermen, who noticed that an El Niño usually peaks around Christmastime. To people in the fishing industry, an El Niño means a disappearance of the fish off their coasts. To others in the world, it means drastic changes in precipitation patterns—good for some, disastrous for others.

The El Niño phenomenon has been intensely studied by scientists involved in an international effort called the World Climate Research Program (WCRP). By 1997, the investigators had made great strides in predicting El Niños and understanding how interactions between the ocean and the atmosphere affect the global weather patterns. With the aid of computer *models* (simulations), climate researchers predicted the 1997 El Niño several months before the surface waters of the Pacific began to grow warmer. In contrast, scientists were not even aware of the El Niño of 1982-1983, previously the strongest El Niño of the 1900's, until it was in full swing.

Nations participating in WCRP operate some 70 moored buoys, extending across the tropical Pacific equipped with both surface and subsurface temperature sensors. The sensors provide data that enable computer models to make long-range forecasts about the occurrence and effects of El Niños.

The dynamic ocean. After seven years of collecting data, a major component of the WCRP, the World Ocean Circulation Experiment (WOCE), was revealing in 1997 that the ocean is far different from the classic textbook sea. WOCE found that the ocean has surprising variability. Preliminary data analyses showed that ocean waters were warming in just the way that climate models had predicted as a consequence of the rising levels of so-called greenhouse gases in the atmosphere.

Cousteau dies. Jacques-Yves Cousteau, the underwater explorer who revealed the wonders of the sea to millions of people around the world, died on June 25 at the age of 87. The wiry, bespectacled Cousteau was a household name for two generations through his highly popular undersea TV series and filmed documentaries, many of them involving his famous boat, the *Calypso*. Cousteau was a co-inventor of the aqualung, the breathing device that for the first time freed divers from the need to be connected to a surface air source.   □ Arthur G. Alexiou

Olympic Games. In September 1997, the International Olympic Committee (IOC) selected Athens to host the 2004 Summer Games. Stockholm, Rome, Buenos Aires, and Cape Town, South Africa, had also bid to host the Games. A group of citizens in Rome began a campaign in February 1997 opposing their city's bid. In Stockholm a predawn bombing in August damaged the historic stadium where the 1912 Olympic Games had been held.

Mal Hemmerling, chief executive of the Organizing Committee of the 2000 Summer Olympics in Sydney, Australia, resigned in March 1997 after a difficult tenure. In July, Thomas Welch, the chief organizer of the 2002 Winter Olympics in Salt Lake City, Utah, resigned after he was charged with domestic violence.

With one year to go before the scheduled start of the 1998 Winter Olympics in Nagano, Japan, critics in 1997 pointed to several potential problems with facilities planned for the games. Among the problems identified were the limited seating capacity of the hockey arena (8,000 seats) and the ice-skating arena (7,300 seats), a short (5,500-foot [1,680-meter]) downhill skiing course, and potentially dangerous wind conditions at the ski-jumping venue.   □ Ron Reid

Oman. See Middle East.
Ontario. See Canadian provinces.
Opera. See Classical music.
Oregon. See State government.

Pacific Islands. Political change dominated events in the Pacific Islands in 1997. New leaders took office in several nations, Fiji adopted a new constitution, and Australia and New Zealand became more active in regional politics.

Papua New Guinea. Bill Skate, the governor of Papua New Guinea's capital Port Moresby, replaced Sir Julius Chan as prime minister following national elections held in June 1997. The main campaign issue was the so-called "Sandline Affair," a scandal triggered by a secret agreement that Chan had made with Sandline International, a British firm of mercenary soldiers. According to the agreement, Papua New Guinea was to pay the mercenaries $36 million to supervise military operations against rebels seeking to gain independence for Bougainville Island, one of Papua New Guinea's larger islands. The rebellion began in 1988. The secret agreement was revealed to the press by the head of Papua New Guinea's army, Brigadier General Jerry Singirok. He complained that the money spent for the mercenaries should instead be used for his troops, who lacked many basic supplies.

After Chan survived a no-confidence vote in Parliament on March 25, 1997, more than 1,000 soldiers and civilians surrounded the Parliament building demanding Chan's resignation. Approximately 100 members of Parliament were confined in the building by the protesters. Chan, however, escaped. On March 26, Chan stepped down, but shortly before the June elections, he resumed the premiership.

After the elections, Skate joined forces with several of Chan's associates to form a coalition government. Skate proved more receptive than Chan to diplomatic efforts by Australia and New Zealand to seek a peaceful solution to the conflict over Bougainville Island.

El Niño. In September, Papua New Guinea began to feel the effects of drought, which proved to be the nation's worst in 50 years. Meteorologists believed the lack of rain was caused by *El Niño*, a periodic warming of tropical Pacific Ocean currents that disrupts normal weather patterns. The government of Papua New Guinea declared a state of emergency due to food shortages and, aided by Australia and New Zealand, mounted a massive relief effort to avert famine and disease.

Solomon Islands. In August, Bartholomew Ulufa'alu was chosen as prime minister of the Solomon Islands by the Parliament. His coalition government replaced that of Solomon Mamaloni, who had been implicated in a financial scandal involving Malaysian corporations. Observers expected that Ulufa'alu's government would make progress in settling various problems with Papua New Guinea, including an ongoing border dispute. Ulufa'alu graduated from the University of Papua New Guinea, and members of his cabinet also had ties of education or church affiliation with Papua New Guinea citizens.

A member of the Moge tribe of Papua New Guinea's western mountainous region waits to vote in national elections in June 1997. A record 2.6 million people registered to vote in the South Pacific country of 4.3 million people.

Facts in brief on Pacific Island countries

Country	Population	Government	Monetary unit*	Foreign trade (million U.S.$)	
				Exports†	Imports†
Australia	18,758,000	Governor General William Deane; Prime Minister John Howard	dollar (1.41 = $1)	60,536	65,428
Fiji	820,000	President Ratu Sir Kamisese Mara; Prime Minister Sitiveni Rabuka	dollar (1.46 = $1)	653	947
Kiribati	84,000	President Teburoro Tito	Australian dollar	7	34
Marshall Islands	59,000	President Imata Kabua	U.S. dollar	21	70
Micronesia, Federated States of	135,000	President Jacob Nena	U.S. dollar	29	141
Nauru	12,000	President Kinza Clodumar	Australian dollar	25	21
New Zealand	3,683,000	Governor General Sir Michael Hardie-Boys; Prime Minister James B. Bolger**	dollar (1.60 = $1)	14,442	14,725
Palau	18,000	President Kuniwo Nakamura	U.S. dollar	1	25
Papua New Guinea	4,596,000	Governor General Wiwa Korowi; Prime Minister William Skate	kina (1.47 = $1)	2,650	1,452
Samoa	180,000	Head of State Malietoa Tanumafili II; Prime Minister Tofilau Eti Alesana	tala (2.65 = $1)	10	100
Solomon Islands	416,000	Governor General Sir Moses Pitakaka; Prime Minister Solomon Mamaloni; Bartholomew Ulufa'alu††	dollar (3.74 = $1)	142	142
Tonga	104,000	King Taufa'ahau Tupou IV; Prime Minister Baron Vaea	pa'anga (1.30 = $1)	15	77
Tuvalu	10,000	Governor General Tulaga, Manuella; Prime Minister Bikenibeu Paeniu	Australian dollar	1	4
Vanuatu	182,000	President Jean Marie Leye; Prime Minister Serge Vohor	vatu (118.80 = $1)	30	97

*Exchange rates as of Oct. 24, 1997, or latest available data. **Bolger was replaced as prime minister by Jennifer Shipley on December 6.
†Latest available data. ††Ulufa'alu replaced Mamaloni as prime minister on August 27.

Fiji. In July, the Fijian Parliament approved a new constitution to increase the political influence of the country's various non-Fijian ethnic groups, which include people of Chinese, European, Micronesian, and Polynesian ancestry. Twenty-five seats in the lower house were to be reserved for "ethnic" candidates, and Fijian nominees for president were required to select vice presidential nominees from other ethnic groups.

Nauru. In February, Nauru's Parliament selected former finance minister Kinza Clodumar as the country's fifth president in five months. The appointment followed special elections held to end political instability. A series of parliamentary no-confidence votes brought down the previous leaders, who were accused of mismanaging the trust fund generated from past phosphate mining. In 1997, revenues from phosphate mining were exhausted, making the country's high per capita income dependent on careful management of investments.

Samoa. In July, Western Samoa dropped "Western" from its name to become the "Independent State of Samoa." The name change angered some residents of American Samoa, a U.S. territory, who felt that the new name implied that American Samoans were somehow "less Samoan" than residents of Samoa. □ Eugene Ogan

See also **Australia; New Zealand.**

Painting. See Art.

Pakistan. In 1997, Prime Minister Nawaz Sharif prevailed in a prolonged constitutional conflict that involved President Farooq Leghari and Chief Justice Sajjad Ali Shah, both of whom had moved to oust Sharif. On December 2, Leghari resigned, and Shah was demoted by the other members of the Pakistani Supreme Court. The resolution of the crisis after several months of political feuding brought a sense of relief to Pakistanis, who feared that Sharif's removal could have led to a return to military rule.

The Pakistan Muslim League and its allies won 181 out of 217 seats in the lower house of parliament in the Feb. 3, 1997, elections. Sharif became prime minister on February 17. He had served as prime minister from 1990 until 1993, when he was dismissed by President Ghulam Ishaq Khan on charges of corruption.

The Muslim League's landslide victory in the 1997 elections left the Pakistan People's Party with only 19 seats in parliament. In 1993, the Pakistan People's Party had won control of parliament, and party leader Benazir Bhutto had become prime minister. In November 1996, Leghari had dismissed Bhutto and her government on charges of corruption.

Shifting power. Observers viewed Sharif's 1997 conduct of the government as a return to full parliamentary democracy, which had been curtailed in 1985. On April 1, 1997, Sharif won unanimous approval from parliament for a constitutional amendment removing the president's power to oust elected governments, which had happened four times since 1988. On Dec. 2, 1997, a three-member panel of the supreme court, convened by Shah, stayed the amendment, which opened the door for Leghari to remove Sharif. Based on the panel's action, Leghari informed the army that he intended to dismiss Sharif. However, the army refused to back the ouster. A majority of supreme court justices met later in the day on December 2 to declare the stay order illegal and to remove Shah as chief justice.

Americans killed. Four Americans and their Pakistani driver were killed on November 12 in Karachi, Pakistan, when gunmen leaped on their car and fired at them at point-blank range. Police linked the attack to the November 11 conviction of Mir Amal Kansi, a Pakistani, in the killing of two U. S. Central Intelligence Agency (CIA) employees. In 1993, Kansi had shot and killed two CIA employees and wounded three other men outside CIA headquarters in Langley, Virginia.

Militants in Kansi's native province, Baluchistan, vowed to seek revenge after Kansi was seized by American and Pakistani agents in Pakistan in June 1997 and flown to the United States without an extradition hearing. Following the November attack, the U.S. State Department issued an advisory warning to Americans in Pakistan of possible risks involving retaliatory violence.   □ Henry S. Bradsher

See also **Asia** (Facts in brief table).

Paleontology. Paleontologists Mikhail Fedonkin, of the Russian Academy of Sciences in Moscow, and Benjamin Waggoner, of the University of California at Berkeley, published a study in August 1997 that described *Kimberella,* an extinct animal previously thought to have been a jellyfish, as a mollusk or mollusk ancestor. Mollusks are a large group of animals that includes snails, slugs, clams, and octopuses. The study, based on the discovery of 35 well-preserved fossils of the animal in northern Russia, indicated that *Kimberella* may have been similar to the ancestor of most bilaterally symmetrical animals, such as mollusks and mammals, which have bodies with similar left and right sides. In contrast, radially symmetrical animals, such as jellyfish and starfish, have body parts arranged circularly around a central point.

Kimberella had been known since the 1950's from four poorly preserved 550-million-year-old fossils from Australia. The new fossils revealed that *Kimberella* was a small, sluglike animal that had a "pleated skirt" of tissue along its margins. *Kimberella* appeared just before the *Cambrian explosion,* a major diversification of animal life that occurred, according to most paleontologists, from approximately 540 million years ago to 510 million years ago.

Cause of Cambrian explosion. In July 1997, geophysicist Joseph Kirschvink of the California Institute of Technology in Pasadena published a study

Supporters of former Prime Minister Benazir Bhutto rally on Jan. 29, 1997, in Larkana after the Supreme Court upheld the dismissal of her government.

claiming that the Earth's *litho-sphere* (the outer rocky layers of the planet) tilted 90 degrees relative to the Earth's axis of rotation approximately 550 million years ago. According to Kirschvink, the tilting, which moved land that was located at the poles to the equator, caused major changes in seawater circulation and climate patterns. Kirschvink speculated that these changes could have caused much of the Cambrian explosion by forcing species to adapt rapidly in order to survive.

Kirschvink analyzed the orientation of magnetic fields in iron-bearing grains within certain ancient rocks. When these rocks formed, they "locked in" an orientation towards the Earth's magnetic poles. By plotting changes in the apparent position of the poles as determined from the rocks, researchers demonstrated that North America moved rapidly from near the equator to near the South Pole, possibly due to tilting of the entire lithosphere.

Oldest sponges. In April 1997, a team of paleontologists led by Martin Brasier of Oxford University in England reported that it had discovered evidence pushing back the date of the earliest sponges. The team found spicules, tiny glassy spikes that make up the skeletons of sponges, in rocks 544 million years old, immediately before the Cambrian explosion, in southwestern Mongolia.

Sponges are among the Earth's most primitive animals. Although they are made up of many cells, the cells are not organized into tissues. Sponges function more as cooperative associations of individual cells than as multicelled organisms. Despite the simplicity of sponges, the oldest fossil evidence for them had previously come from rocks tens of millions of years younger than fossils of more complex animals. The discovery supported the contention that the record of earliest fossil animals remains incomplete.

Dinosaur bonanza in China. A group of researchers led by paleontologist John Ostrom of Yale University in New Haven, Connecticut, announced the discovery of a major new site of dinosaur fossils in China's Liaoning Province in April. The site yielded hundreds of extremely well-preserved fossils dating from approximately 120 to 140 million years ago.

A *Sinosauropteryx*, one of hundreds of dinosaur fossils discovered in China's Liaoning Province in 1997, is the first dinosaur fossil to be discovered with preserved internal organs.

The most remarkable fossil from the site was of a new dinosaur, dubbed *Sinosauropteryx prima*. The fossil appeared to show a series of feathery impressions along the back and tail of the dinosaur. Paleontologists debated throughout 1997 whether these impressions represented feathers, featherlike scales, supporting tissue from beneath the skin, or tissue that was distorted from decay. Although the impressions seemed to lack the branching pattern of true feathers, some paleontologists speculated that they could represent a type of early, primitive feather.

Paleontologists said that if the impressions proved to be of feathers, they would provide confirmation of the generally accepted theory that birds evolved from dinosaurs. Scientists hoped to find other fossils at the Chinese site to settle the debate.

More evidence for dinosaur-bird link. In May, paleontologists Fernando Novas, of the Argentine Museum of Natural Sciences in Buenos Aires, and Pablo Puerta, of the Patagonian Paleontological Museum in Trelew, announced the discovery of the remains of a small, birdlike dinosaur in southern Argentina. The dinosaur, *Unenlagia comahuensis,* had a shoulder joint that faced outward, enabling the animal to fold its front limbs in a manner similar to the way birds fold their wings. The dinosaur also had certain birdlike features of the pelvis and hind limbs. *Unenlagia* belonged to a group of dinosaurs called maniraptorans, from which birds are thought to have evolved. However, *Unenlagia* itself lived too recently—90 million years ago—to have been an ancestor of birds, which are thought to have evolved at least 150 million years ago.

In October 1997, a group of paleontologists led by Mark Norell of the American Museum of Natural History in New York City reported that they had found remains of a *Velociraptor,* a maniraptoran dinosaur made famous in the film *Jurassic Park,* with a *furcula* (wishbone). This bone, in birds, acts as a spring to lift wings in flight.

Despite the new fossil finds of 1997, some scientists continued to doubt that birds evolved from dinosaurs. According to most of these scientists, dinosaurs and birds each evolved separately from more primitive reptile ancestors. □ Carlton E. Brett

Panama. President Ernesto Pérez Balladares drew public criticism in 1997 for exhibiting political favoritism. In September, *La Prensa,* Panama's leading newspaper, lampooned the president for appointing 4 relatives to the 11-member board of directors that was scheduled to take over the management of the Panama Canal from the United States in 1999. Pérez Balladares also allegedly allowed his cousin's television broadcasting company, in which the president owned shares, to gain a near monopoly on the broadcasting market in 1997.

In August, the government ordered the expulsion of Peruvian journalist Gustavo Gorriti, an editor at *La Prensa.* Gorriti had written several controversial articles, including one in 1996 that accused the president of receiving campaign money from Colombia's Cali drug cartel. The expulsion, criticized internationally as an attempt to silence the press, remained under review by Panama's Supreme Court in 1997.

On April 28, Panama granted asylum to Abdala Bucarám Ortíz, the former Ecuadoran president who was removed from office in February for incompetence and corruption. Bucarám joined other exiled leaders in Panama, including Jorge Serrano Elías, a former Guatemalan president, and Raoul Cédras, a former Haitian dictator. □ Nathan A. Haverstock

See also **Latin America** (Facts in brief table).

Papua New Guinea. See **Asia; Pacific Islands.**

People in the news in 1997 included those listed below, who were all Americans unless otherwise indicated.

Ahern, Bertie (1951–), was elected *taoiseach* (prime minister) of Ireland on June 26, 1997, by a minority coalition in the *Dail Eireann* (lower house of Parliament). The youngest taoiseach in Ireland's history, Ahern won his post two weeks after his conservative Fianna Fail party, which has close ties to the Roman Catholic Church, bested the ruling Fine Gael party in national parliamentary elections.

Ahern, a member of the moderate wing of Fianna Fail, has long been sympathetic to efforts to unite Northern Ireland, part of the United Kingdom, with the Republic of Ireland. He stated that his first priority as taoiseach would be to work toward resolving the conflict between Catholics and Protestants in Northern Ireland. He also promised to cut taxes and prepare Ireland for membership in the Economic and Monetary Union, a 1992 pact establishing a common currency and central bank among members of the European Union, scheduled to begin in 1999.

Bartholomew Patrick Ahern was born on Sept. 12, 1951, in Dublin. Ahern earned a degree in accounting from the University of Dublin. He first won a seat in the Dail in 1977. From 1986 until 1987, he served as lord mayor of Dublin. In 1987, he was appointed labor minister and in 1991 became finance minister. Ahern was elected leader of Fianna Fail in 1994.

See also **Ireland.**

Albright, Madeleine Korbel (1937–), was sworn in as the first female secretary of state on Jan. 23, 1997. From 1993 until her appointment to the State Department, Albright had served as United States ambassador to the United Nations (UN). In that position, she was regarded as an effective and tough representative, who helped revitalize the UN after decades of decline during the Cold War, the intense rivalry between the United States and its allies and the former Soviet Union and its allies from the mid-1940's to the early 1990's.

Albright served as chief legislative assistant to Senator Edmund S. Muskie of Maine from 1976 to 1978. She worked on President Jimmy Carter's staff and the staff of the National Security Council from 1978 to 1981. From 1982 to 1993, Albright taught international affairs at Georgetown University in Washington, D.C., where she was repeatedly voted best teacher.

The daughter of a diplomat, Albright was born on May 15, 1937, in Prague in the former Czechoslovakia. Albright's family fled to London in 1938 when Nazi Germany invaded Czechoslovakia. The family returned to their native country after the war, but fled to the United States in 1948 when the Communists took over the government. Albright, who speaks five

Madeleine Albright, U.S. secretary of state (left)
and Jiang Zemin, president of China

languages, received a bachelor's degree from Wellesley College in Wellesley, Massachusetts, in 1959 and a
master's degree in 1968 and a doctoral degree in
1976 from Columbia University in New York City.

See also **Cabinet, U.S.**

Annan, Kofi A. (1938–), a career official at the
United Nations (UN), took office as that organization's secretary-general on Jan. 1, 1997. He had been
elected to the post by the UN General Assembly on
Dec. 17, 1996. A native of what is now Ghana, Annan
became the first UN secretary-general from an
African country south of the Sahara.

Annan succeeded Secretary-General Boutros
Boutros-Ghali of Egypt, whose reelection to a second
five-year term had been vetoed by the United States.
The United States had charged Boutros-Ghali with
failing to institute sufficient reforms to reinvigorate
the organization and had blamed him for the failure
of the UN peacekeeping effort in Somalia. The United States argued that Annan's popularity and highly
regarded diplomatic skills would provide the leadership necessary to bring about UN budget cuts and
other reforms.

Kofi Atta Annan was born on April 8, 1938, in Ku-
masi in the southwest African country of Ghana, then
a British colony called the Gold Coast. He received a
bachelor's degree in economics at Macalester College
in St. Paul, Minnesota, in 1961 and a master's degree
in management from the Massachusetts Institute of
Technology in Cambridge in 1972. In 1959, he joined
the World Health Organization, a UN agency. From
1974 to 1976, he served as head of Ghana's tourism
development agency. In 1976, he rejoined the UN,

where he served in a variety of posts until 1993, when
he was appointed undersecretary-general for peacekeeping operations. He supervised the withdrawal of
UN troops from Somalia and in 1995 oversaw the
transfer of the UN peacekeeping mission in Bosnia to
forces of the North Atlantic Treaty Organization.

See also **United Nations.**

Blair, Tony (1953–), became prime minister of
Great Britain on May 2, 1997, after his Labour Party
won a 179-seat majority in the House of Commons in
national parliamentary elections on May 1. Blair replaced Prime Minister John Major of the Conservative
Party, which had controlled Parliament since 1979. At
age 43, Blair became the youngest man to serve as
prime minister since 1812.

Blair is considered a moderate who has sought to
move his party away from its traditional support of
nationalized industries and social welfare by emphasizing free enterprise. Blair also has attempted to reduce union influence in the Labour Party and has promoted a law-and-order social policy that he characterizes as "tough on crime and tough on the causes
of crime."

Anthony Charles Lynton Blair was born on May 6,
1953, in Edinburgh, Scotland. He earned his under-
graduate degree from Oxford University in 1975,
then worked as an attorney specializing in employment law.

Blair first was elected to the House of Commons
in 1983 and served in various party positions. In 1994,
he was overwhelmingly elected leader of the Labour
Party, the youngest man to hold that position. His
new party platform called for controlling inflation,

333

reducing the budget deficit, improving worker training, and establishing more rigorous academic standards for students.

See also **United Kingdom**.

Cohen, William S. (1940–), was sworn in as U.S. secretary of defense on Jan. 24, 1997. A Republican member of the U.S. Senate for 18 years, Cohen had been an occasional critic of Democratic President Bill Clinton's defense policies. Nevertheless, Clinton made Cohen his first Republican Cabinet appointee and praised his nonpartisan legislative work. Clinton also noted Cohen's role in developing the 1991 Strategic Arms Reduction Treaty, an agreement between the United States and the former Soviet Union to reduce stockpiles of nuclear weapons.

Cohen was born on Aug. 28, 1940, in Bangor, Maine. He earned a bachelor's degree in Latin from Bowdoin College in Brunswick, Maine, in 1962 and a law degree from Boston University Law School in 1965. While working as a lawyer, he served on the city council of Bangor from 1969 to 1972 and was that city's mayor from 1971 to 1972.

In 1972, Cohen won a seat in the U.S. House of Representatives, where he served until his election to the Senate in 1978. He devoted his three terms in the Senate to defense, military, and national security issues. He served on the Senate Armed Services and Governmental Affairs committees from 1979 to 1997 and on the Select Committee on Intelligence from 1983 to 1991 and from 1995 to 1997. In addition to authoring numerous pieces of defense-related legislation, he played a pivotal role in efforts to eliminate waste in the government's acquisition of goods and services.

See also **Cabinet, U.S.**

Cuomo, Andrew M. (1957–), an advocate for the homeless, was sworn in as U.S. secretary of the Department of Housing and Urban Development (HUD) on Jan. 29, 1997. Cuomo spearheaded President Bill Clinton's successful efforts to prevent the U.S. Congress from cutting a HUD program that provided low-income housing in 1997 for more than 4 million Americans through rent vouchers and subsidies to landlords.

Cuomo, the oldest son of former New York Governor Mario Cuomo, was born on Dec. 6, 1957, in New York City. He earned a bachelor's degree from Fordham University in New York City in 1979 and a law degree from Albany Law School in Albany, New York, in 1982. In 1982, he also ran his father's first victorious gubernatorial election campaign. He subsequently joined the New York City district attorney's office.

In 1986, Cuomo founded Housing Enterprise for the Less Privileged (HELP), a private organization that provides transitional housing for the homeless. He served as chairman of the New York City Commission on the Homeless from 1991 until 1993, when he was appointed HUD's assistant secretary for community planning and development. In that post, he was the principal

Linda Finch, pilot

author of a widely praised report that urged the government to expand its definition of the homeless to include people who temporarily lack shelter because of a divorce, illness, or job loss. Cuomo also helped win a $300-million increase in the HUD budget in 1994.

See also **Cabinet, U.S.**

Daley, William M. (1948–), was sworn in as U.S. secretary of commerce on Jan. 30, 1997. His agenda as commerce secretary included doubling the number of small exporters, modernizing the U.S. Weather Service, and maintaining America's lead as an innovator of advanced technologies.

William Michael Daley was born on Aug. 8, 1948, in Chicago. He is a son of Richard J. Daley, mayor of Chicago from 1955 until his death in 1976. William Daley earned a bachelor's degree in 1970 from Loyola University and a law degree in 1975 from John Marshall Law School, both in Chicago. He worked for a private law firm from 1975 to 1977, when he became a member of the Advisory Council on Economic Development in the Administration of President Jimmy Carter.

From 1990 to 1993, he served as president and chief operating officer of the Amalgamated Bank of Chicago. He then became a partner in a private law firm. He also has served as an adviser to his brother, Chicago Mayor Richard M. Daley.

A longtime supporter and adviser to President Bill

Clinton, Daley served as Clinton's Illinois campaign chairman in the 1992 presidential campaign. In 1993, Daley successfully spearheaded Clinton's efforts to win congressional approval of the North American Free Trade Agreement (NAFTA), which called for the elimination of trade barriers between the United States, Mexico, and Canada.

See also **Cabinet, U.S.**

Finch, Linda (1951–), pilot, businesswoman, and restorer of vintage airplanes, in May 1997 completed a historic around-the-world flight that retraced as closely as possible the route U.S. aviator Amelia Earhart was attempting when she disappeared over the Pacific Ocean in 1937. American flyer Ann Pellegreno in 1967 became the first to complete Earhart's intended flight along the equator. Finch, however, was the first to make the trip in the same type of plane that Earhart flew—a twin-engine, 1935 Lockheed Electra 10E. Finch's Electra is one of only two in existence. Finch restored the plane, modified it to hold extra fuel, and equipped it with modern navigational equipment.

Finch began her flight at Oakland (California) International Airport, also Earhart's take-off point, on March 17, 1997—60 years to the day Earhart began her ill-fated flight. She touched down at Oakland 72 days later, on May 28. Finch's 26,000-mile (42,000-kilometer) journey took her to 18 countries.

Finch was born on March 13, 1951, and grew up in San Antonio, Texas. She dropped out of high school at age 16, married, and had a daughter. Divorced in 1970, Finch studied accounting at Southwest Texas State University in San Marcos and worked as a bookkeeper. In the 1970's, she returned to San Antonio, working at a company that owned nursing homes. In 1979, she started her own nursing home business. She earned her pilot's license at age 29.

See also **Aviation.**

Gore, Albert, Jr. (1948–) Accusations in 1997 of illegal fund-raising threatened Vice President Albert Gore's reputation for integrity and his position as the leading contender for the Democratic nomination for U.S. president in the 2000 campaign. In March 1997, Gore was accused of breaking a 1983 law that bans political fund-raising on federal property by calling potential contributors to the Democratic National Committee from his White House office. Gore argued that there was "no controlling legal authority" that barred him from making such calls. But he said he would end the practice because of the "concern and comment" it aroused.

Gore's contention that his activity failed to violate the law was challenged by a Re-

publican-led Senate panel probing campaign finance abuses. Gore's case was also weakened by conflicting reports. In March 1997, he said he made calls from his vice-presidential office phone on only "a few occasions." In August, however, the Clinton Administration said Gore had made 46 calls. In documents made public in late August, the total was raised to 80. In September, Gore was criticized for appearing at an April 1996 Democratic fund-raising event at a Buddhist temple in Los Angeles. Donations received at that event were later returned because of doubts about their legality.

On Feb. 12, 1997, a commission headed by Gore announced a series of proposals to improve aviation safety and security, including faster development of satellite-based air traffic control.

See also **Democratic Party.**

Gujral, Inder Kumar (1919–), was named prime minister of India on April 19, 1997, by that country's multiparty ruling coalition, known as the United Front. He replaced coalition leader H. D. Deve Gowda, who resigned after a no-confidence vote. Gujral promised to continue the coalition's program of economic liberalization, including encouraging foreign investment and reducing trade barriers. Gujral was unsuccessful in his efforts to end political chaos in India and resigned his premiership on November 28 after three weeks of turmoil in Parliament forced the speak-

Bertie Ahern, prime minister of Ireland

er of Parliament to adjourn the session indefinitely.

Gujral said that his main priority would be to improve India's relations with neighboring Pakistan. Gujral met with Pakistan's Prime Minister Nawaz Sharif several times during 1997. In September and October, however, Indian and Pakistani forces clashed along the border of Kashmir state, claimed by both countries.

Inder Kumar Gujral was born on Dec. 4, 1919, in Jhelum, in what is now Pakistan, into a well-to-do Hindu family. In 1930, Gujral was jailed for his participation in efforts to win India's freedom from Great Britain. He emigrated to India in 1947 after anti-Hindu riots broke out in Karachi, Pakistan, where he worked in his family's timber business. He entered politics in 1959 as a member of the New Delhi Municipal Council, where he served until being elected to Parliament in 1964. From 1967 to 1997, he held various cabinet positions, including foreign minister.

See also **India**.

David Ho, AIDS researcher

Herman, Alexis (1947–), was sworn in as U.S. secretary of labor on May 1, 1997. The first African American to head the Labor Department, Herman has devoted much of her career to expanding employment opportunities for women, minorities, and the hard-to-employ.

Herman was born on July 16, 1947, in Mobile, Alabama. She received a bachelor's degree from Xavier University in New Orleans in 1969, after which she conducted worker training with a social services agency. From 1977 to 1981, she served as director of the Women's Bureau at the Labor Department, where she developed programs to assist low-income and young female workers.

In 1981, Herman founded A. M. Herman & Associates, a marketing and management company. She served as deputy chair and chief of staff of the Democratic National Committee from 1988 to 1991, when she was named chief executive officer of the 1992 Democratic National Convention Committee. In 1992, she was appointed deputy director of newly elected Bill Clinton's Presidential Transition Office. From 1993 until her appointment as Labor secretary, Herman served as an assistant to the president and director of the White House Public Liaison Office.

See also **Cabinet, U.S.**

Ho, David (1952–), a molecular biologist, won acclaim in 1997 for discovering a drug treatment that slows the progress of AIDS (acquired immunodeficiency syndrome) in its early stages in some patients. Research teams led by Ho also made surprising discoveries about the life cycle of the human immunodeficiency virus (HIV), which causes AIDS.

Ho was born in Taiwan on Nov. 3, 1952. In 1964, he and his mother and brother moved to Los Angeles, where his father had immigrated nine years earlier. Interested in science at an early age, Ho graduated from the California Institute of Technology in Pasadena in 1974 and received a medical degree from Harvard University in Cambridge, Massachusetts, in 1978. In the early 1980's, while on the staff of Cedars-Sinai Medical Center in Los Angeles, he became one of the first physicians to treat patients with AIDS, then an unknown disease.

In 1982, Ho took a research post at Massachusetts General Hospital in Boston. There, he discovered that HIV grows in immune cells called macrophages. In 1986, he returned to Cedars-Sinai and joined the faculty at the University of California, Los Angeles.

Alexis Herman,
U.S. secretary of labor

In 1990, Ho was named head of the newly formed Aaron Diamond AIDS Research Center in New York City. In 1995, Ho and fellow researchers devised an AIDS treatment that involved flooding a HIV-infected person's system with a "cocktail" of antiviral drugs that attack the virus at different stages in its reproductive cycle. If used within weeks of infection, the drugs can reduce HIV in the bloodstream to almost undetectable levels for at least 12 months in some patients. The treatment, which may result in severe side effects, cannot cure AIDS.

See also **Medicine.**

Jiang Zemin (1926–), president of China, became that country's supreme authority after the death of China's paramount leader, Deng Xiaoping, in February 1997. Jiang ousted many of his political rivals from positions of power in October at the Communist Party Congress. Jiang, hand-picked by Deng as his successor in 1989, assumed increasing authority as the aging Deng gradually withdrew from public life. Deng, however, continued to exercise authority from behind the scenes until shortly before his death.

While continuing Deng's capitalistic reforms, Jiang also promoted state-run industries. He demonstrated his commitment to maintaining the dominance of China's Communist Party by cracking down on the prodemocracy movement and closing dissenting newspapers.

Jiang was born on Aug. 17, 1926, in Yangzhou City in eastern China. He joined the Communist Party in 1946 and in 1947 earned a degree in electrical engineering from Jiaotong University in Shanghai. Jiang entered politics in the late 1970's. In 1989, he was appointed chairman of the Central Military Commission, which controls China's military forces, and became general secretary of the Communist Party that same year. Jiang was named president of China in 1993.

In October 1997, Jiang met with President Bill Clinton in Washington, D.C. The two leaders agreed on trade pacts between China and the United States, but they clashed over American concerns about political and religious rights in China.

See also **China.**

Jobs, Steven P.
(1955–), a computer executive and founder of Apple Computer Inc. of Cupertino, California, rejoined Apple in December 1996, 11 years af-

ter having been ousted by that company's board. Jobs agreed to step in as acting chief executive—his former post—to replace Gilbert F. Amelio. In August 1997, Jobs announced that Apple would form an alliance with arch-competitor, the Microsoft Corp. of Redmond, Washington, whose Windows operating system dominates the personal computer market.

Steven Paul Jobs was born on Feb. 24, 1955, and grew up in Los Altos, California. In 1972, Jobs enrolled at Reed College in Portland, Oregon, but dropped out after 18 months. After traveling in India, he went to work for computer game maker Atari.

In 1976, Jobs founded Apple Computer with Steve Wozniak. The two built the Apple II, the world's first successful personal computer. In 1984, they unveiled the Macintosh computer, which revolutionized computer operating systems. The Apple board of directors fired Jobs in 1985 after early sales of the new computer fell far short of expectations.

Jobs went on to found another computer company, NeXT, Inc., intending to make a computer for college students. When that venture failed, he turned NeXT into a software company. In 1986, Jobs bought Pixar, the computer graphics division of a film studio owned by director George Lucas, and created Pixar Animation Studios, a computer animation company. Pixar created the animation for the hit motion picture *Toy Story* (1995), the first completely computer-animated movie. Jobs sold NeXT to Apple in 1996.

See also **Computer.**

Jospin, Lionel R. (1937–), became prime minister of France on June 3, 1997, after his Socialist Party, along with the allied Communist and Green par-

Lionel Jospin, prime minister of France

Mohammed Khatami, president of Iran (left)
and Nawaz Sharif, prime minister of Pakistan

Kabila, Laurent (1939–),
declared himself head of state
of the newly renamed Democratic Republic of the Congo
(formerly Zaire) on May 17,
1997, after a seven-month military campaign to oust long-
time dictator Mobutu Sese
Seko. A former Marxist, Kabila
had fought for more than 30
years against Mobutu, who had
reportedly looted $4 billion
from Zaire during his 32-year
reign, destroying the economy
and leaving Zairians in poverty.

Western nations, which had
long supported Mobutu, expressed cautious approval of
Kabila's government. Later in
1997, however, Kabila's refusal
to cooperate with a UN investigation of human rights abuses
by his forces during the campaign threatened his international support.

Laurent Désiré Kabila was
born in 1939 in Jadotville (now
Likasa) in the Congo, then a
Belgian colony. He studied in
France and Tanzania. After
Congo won its independence in
1960, Kabila served as a youth
leader of a party allied with
that of the country's first prime minister, Patrice Lumumba. Months after taking office, Lumumba was
ousted by Mobutu. In 1964, Kabila led an unsuccessful
revolt against Mobutu.

In 1967, Kabila founded the Marxist People's Revolutionary Party, which controlled an eastern region of
Zaire. In the 1980's, Kabila moved to Tanzania and
worked in the gold trade. In 1996, he organized another revolt against Mobutu by ethnic Tutsis in eastern Zaire that grew into the nationwide revolt that
toppled Mobutu.

See also **Africa; Africa** Special Report: **The Hutu
and Tutsi: A Conflict Beyond Borders.**

Khatami, Mohammed (1943–), was elected
president of Iran on May 23, 1997, in that country's
first free presidential election since its Islamic revolution in 1979. Khatami won about 69 percent of the
vote, despite opposition from Iran's hard-line clerics
and politicians. He replaced Ali Akbar Hashemi Rafsanjani, who had served as president for the legal limit of two four-year terms.

Khatami, generally recognized as a moderate,
pledged to improve Iran's economy by limiting the
power of its state-run monopolies and permitting increased economic ties with Western nations. He also

ties, won a majority in parliamentary elections held
two days earlier. Jospin replaced Prime Minister Alain
Juppé, whose conservative coalition had lost public
support because its unpopular austerity measures
had failed to solve France's economic problems.

Jospin advocated a "humane" approach to economic policy. He pledged to create 700,000 jobs to
lower France's 12.8-percent unemployment rate and
to shorten the work week by four hours without raising taxes or cutting wages.

Lionel Robert Jospin was born in Meudon, a suburb
of Paris, on July 12, 1937. He graduated from the
School of National Administration, an elite training
ground for government officials, in 1965. He joined
the foreign ministry in 1965 and served until 1970.

Jospin joined the Socialist Party in 1971 and was
elected to the National Assembly in 1977. In 1981,
then-President François Mitterrand named Jospin first
secretary of the Socialist Party. He served in that post
until 1988, when he became minister of education.
Several of his decisions displeased Mitterrand, however, and Jospin was replaced in a cabinet reorganization
in 1992. Jospin also lost his seat in Parliament in 1992.
In 1995, he ran unsuccessfully for president. Despite his
loss, he became leader of the Socialist Party in 1996.

See also **France.**

promised to reduce government press censorship and increase personal liberties that had been curtailed by the Islamic regime. Because the post of president in Iran is largely ceremonial, his power to effect real change remained limited.

Khatami was born in Ardakan, Iran, and studied theology before earning degrees in philosophy and education. He rose to the rank of *hojatolislam*, a mid-level position in Islam.

During the 1960's and 1970's, Khatami opposed the government of Iran's secular leader, Shah Mohammed Reza Pahlavi. In 1982, he was named minister of culture and Islamic guidance in the fundamentalist regime of Ayatollah Ruhollah Khomeini. But Khatami's tolerant position regarding freedom of the media led to his dismissal in 1992. That same year, he became director of Iran's national library.

See also **Iran**.

McDormand, Frances (1957–) won an Academy Award for best actress on March 24, 1997, for her performance in the black comedy *Fargo* . She played Marge Gunderson, a pregnant police chief in rural Minnesota who investigates a murder spree. Her performance in *Fargo* also won her a number of other nominations and awards, including best actress from the Broadcast Film Critics Association.

The daughter of a minister, McDormand was born on June 23, 1957, in rural Illinois. She began acting in high school and earned a degree in theater in 1979 from Bethany College in Bethany, West Virginia, and a master's degree in 1982 from the Yale Drama School in New Haven, Connecticut.

In 1984, McDormand landed a role in *Blood Simple,* the first film of the moviemaking brothers Joel and Ethan Coen. She won her first Oscar nomination for her role as the wife of a Ku Klux Klan member involved in the murder of civil rights workers in *Mississippi Burning* (1988). Her other films include *Raising Arizona* (1987), *Short Cuts* (1993), *Palookaville* (1995), *Lone Star* (1996), *Primal Fear* (1996), *Paradise Road* (1997), and *Talk of Angels* (1997).

Her stage credits include *Painting Churches* in 1984, *Moon for the Misbegotten* in 1992, and *The Sisters Rosensweig* in 1993. McDormand was nominated for an Antoinette Perry (Tony) award for her role as Stella in a 1988 production of *A Streetcar Named Desire*.

See also **Motion pictures.**

Rush, Geoffrey (1950–), an Australian actor, on March 24, 1997, won an Academy Award for best actor for his performance in the motion picture *Shine* (1996). *Shine* tells the true story of David Helfgott, a concert pianist who developed a mental illness in adolescence and spent 13 years in institutions before returning to performing. Rush's portrayal of Helfgott's rapid-fire, stream-of-consciousness prattle and musical gifts charmed both audiences and critics. Rush also won a Golden Globe award for the role and was named best actor of 1996 by the Los Angeles Film Critics and the New York Film Critics Circle.

Rush was born in Toowoomba, Australia. He attended the University of Queensland and in 1970 joined a professional theater group. In 1975, he went to Paris to study mime and movement.

During the 1980's and 1990's, Rush built a successful stage career in Australia, winning acting awards for his performance in a 1989 production of *The Diary of a Madman* and award nominations for his work in *Oleanna* in 1993 and *Hamlet* in 1994. He also directed a number of plays. His film work included roles in *Starstruck* (1982), *Dad and Dave—On Our Selection* (1995), and *Children of the Revolution* (1996).

See also **Motion pictures.**

Sharif, Mohammad Nawaz (1949–), began a second term as prime minister of Pakistan on Feb. 17, 1997. In national parliamentary elections held two weeks earlier, Sharif's Pakistan Muslim League scored an overwhelming victory over the Pakistan People's Party of former Prime Minister Benazir Bhutto, capturing 136 of 217 seats. Bhutto, who had defeated Sharif in elections in October 1993, had been dismissed from office in November 1996 by Pakistan's President Farooq Leghari on charges of corruption. Sharif, who first became prime minister in 1990, had been forced from office in July 1993 after being similarly accused.

Geoffrey Rush, Academy Award winner for best actor

In elections held on March 12, 1997, the Pakistan Muslim League also won control of Pakistan's upper house. This majority enabled Sharif on April 1 to push through parliament a constitutional amendment that stripped the office of president of its power to dissolve parliament, fire the prime minister, appoint a transitional government, and call elections.

In March, Sharif announced a plan to cut import tariffs and reduce taxes. In August, he signed a law giving police the power to arrest without a warrant and to shoot suspected terrorists. Sharif also met with India's Prime Minister Inder Gujral several times in 1997 in an effort to end border clashes between the two countries.

Mian Mohammad Nawaz Sharif was born on Dec. 25, 1949. He was educated at Government College and earned a law degree from Punjab University, both in Lahore, Pakistan. He served as finance minister in Punjab province from 1981 to 1985 and as chief minister of the Punjab province from 1985 to 1990.

See also **Pakistan.**

Slater, Rodney (1955–), was sworn in as U.S. secretary of transportation on Feb. 14, 1997. Slater was widely considered an able transportation administrator, and his appointment was applauded by transportation industry executives as well as by members of both parties in Congress.

Slater announced that one of his main priorities as transportation secretary would be to improve transportation safety. He also stressed the importance of making public transportation widely available so that former welfare recipients could get to work. In addition, he submitted a plan to Congress to increase spending on new highways and mass transit systems.

Slater was born in Tutwyler, Mississippi, on Feb. 23, 1955, and he grew up in Marianna, Arkansas. He received a bachelor's degree from Eastern Michigan University in Ypsilanti in 1977 and a law degree from the University of Arkansas in Fayetteville in 1980.

From 1980 to 1982, Slater was the assistant attorney general for the state of Arkansas, and from 1983 until 1987, he served as assistant to then-Governor of Arkansas Bill Clinton. In 1987, Slater was appointed to the Arkansas State Highway and Transportation Commission, becoming chairman in 1992. In 1993, he became the head of the Federal Highway Administration. He also helped develop the National Highway System (NHS) Designation Act of 1995, which provided $5 billion to the states for highway and transportation projects and created the NHS, a 160,000-mile (260,000-kilometer) network of roads considered vital to the nation's economy and defense.

See also **Cabinet, U.S.**

Wilmut, Ian (1944–), a British embryologist, announced on Feb. 22, 1997, that he had become the first person to successfully *clone* (produce an exact genetic copy of) an adult mammal. Wilmut produced a sheep, named Dolly, from an udder cell taken from an adult ewe. Previously, only cells from *embryos* (developing animals) had yielded clones. In early 1966, Wilmut and fellow researchers at the Roslin Institute near Edinburgh, Scotland, had produced two sheep clones using cells from embryos.

To produce Dolly, Wilmut's team fused the ewe's udder cell with a different ewe's egg cell (whose genetic material had been removed). The resulting cell, which was implanted into the womb of a third ewe, developed into a lamb whose genetic makeup was identical to that of the first ewe.

The announcement of Dolly's birth created world-

Tiger Woods, Masters golf tournament champion

wide controversy, because the experiment raised the possibility of human cloning. Many political and religious leaders called for strict limits on cloning. Wilmut himself said that he supported a ban on human cloning. His research involved producing animals for commercial and medical use.

Wilmut was born on July 7, 1944, in Hampton Lucey, England. He earned his doctorate degree in 1973 at Cambridge University. In 1993, he became the first scientist to reproduce a calf from a frozen embryo. In 1974, he joined the Animal Breeding Research Station, renamed the Roslin Institute.

See also **Biology; Biology** Special Report: **Is It Wrong to Clone People?**

Woods, Tiger (1975–), became the youngest Masters golf tournament champion in history by winning that prestigious competition on April 13, 1997, at age 21. Woods recorded a record 12-stroke margin of victory, and his four-day total of 270 strokes—18 under par—also set a Masters record. Woods, whose racial heritage includes Thai, Chinese, African American, Caucasian, and Native American ancestors, also became the first person of color to win the Masters.

Eldrick Woods was born on Dec. 30, 1975, in Long Beach, California, the only child of Earl Woods, a retired U.S. Army lieutenant colonel, and his wife, Kultida. Earl Woods, a veteran of the Vietnam War (1957-1975), nicknamed his son "Tiger" after a South Vietnamese combat buddy. Woods began training his son to be a champion golfer when Tiger Woods was only 11 months old. By age 3, Woods had played nine holes in fewer than 50 strokes and gained national attention as a child prodigy. In 1993, he won his third straight Junior Amateur title. With his victory in the 1994 U.S. Amateur Championship, Woods became the only player to win both competitions. He won an unprecedented third straight Amateur title in 1996.

At age 16, Woods became the youngest player to participate in a Professional Golfers' Tour event. Woods entered Stanford University in Palo Alto, California, in 1994 on a full golf scholarship but dropped out in August 1996 to play professional golf. Woods won three professional tournaments in 1996 and became the only rookie ever to finish in the top five in five consecutive tournaments.

See also **Golf.**

Yilmaz, Mesut (1947–), became prime minister of Turkey for the third time on June 30, 1997. He had served briefly in that post in 1991 and in 1996. Yilmaz led the center-right Motherland Party, the largest of three *secular parties* (parties not associated with a religion) that formed a coalition government after the June 1997 resignation of Prime Minister Necmettin Erbakan, leader of the Muslim Welfare Party. Erbakan's 1996 election was a departure

Mesut Yilmaz, prime minister of Turkey

from Turkey's 74-year history of secular rule.

Yilmaz, a pro-Western politician who supported a free-market economy, accused Erbakan of appointing Islamic militants to key government positions and failing to implement necessary economic reforms. Yilmaz's victory pleased Western nations, who expressed satisfaction with Turkey's return to its secular tradition.

Yilmaz was born on Nov. 6, 1947, in Istanbul, Turkey. He received a degree in political science from Ankara University in 1971. After earning a master's degree in economics and social science from Cologne University in Germany, he worked for several industrial firms. In 1983, Yilmaz became deputy chairman of the Motherland Party at its founding and was elected to parliament. He served as minister of culture and tourism from 1986 to 1987, when he was appointed foreign minister.   □ Lisa Klobuchar

See also **Turkey.**

Peru. On April 22, 1997, Peruvian commandos stormed the Japanese ambassador's residence in Lima, the capital, ending a 126-day hostage crisis. On Dec. 17, 1996, members of the leftist Tupác Amaru Revolutionary Movement (MRTA) had taken more than 490 people hostage at a party at the ambassador's residence. The MRTA had threatened to kill hostages if the Peruvian government did not release imprisoned MRTA members. The rebels did not kill their prisoners and released all but 72 hostages before the April 1997 rescue. In the meticulously planned attack, the remaining hostages were freed, but Peruvian Supreme Court Justice Carlos Giusti Acuña, who was hit by a stray bullet, later died of a heart attack. Two Peruvian commandos as well as all 14 members of the MRTA were killed in the raid.

Peruvian President Alberto K. Fujimori won praise in the wake of the hostage crisis for not bending to terrorist demands. Later in 1997, however, Fujimori saw his popularity plummet amid charges that he had assumed near-dictatorial rule in his effort to eliminate terrorism and that he had given too much authority to military and intelligence leaders. In particular, Ivan Vladimiro Montesinos, the head of national intelligence, and General Nicolás Hermoza Rios, chairman of the joint chiefs of staff, were accused of compromising civil liberties in Peru.

Judges dismissed. On May 29, Peru's congress, dominated by Fujimori's Change 90 party, dismissed three judges from the seven-member Constitutional Court. The judges had ruled in 1996 that legislation allowing Fujimori to run for a third consecutive term was unconstitutional. They were dismissed in 1997 for exceeding their authority by allegedly representing the opinion of the entire court in their decision when in fact three other judges had abstained from voting on the issue. Protesting the dismissals, the chief justice resigned on May 30, 1997.

Citizenship revoked. On July 13, the government revoked the Peruvian citizenship of Israeli-born Baruch Ivcher Bronstein, majority shareholder of the television station Frecuencia Latina TV. Earlier on the same day, the station had reported that Peru's intelligence services had wiretapped telephone conversations of prominent citizens. Since Peruvian law forbids foreigners from owning majority shares in media companies, the revocation forced Ivcher to give up control.

On July 14, thousands of Peruvians took to the streets of Lima to protest the action against Ivcher, and on July 17, Defense Minister General Tomás Castillo Meza and Justice Minister Carlos Hermoza resigned in protest. When progovernment minority shareholders took control of the station on September 19, many of the station's journalists resigned in protest. ☐ Nathan A. Haverstock

See also **Latin America** (Facts in brief table).

Petroleum and gas. See **Energy supply.**

Peruvian soldiers rescue hostages on April 22 from the Japanese ambassador's residence in Lima, where 72 men had been held by Tupác Amaru guerrillas for 126 days—the longest terrorist siege in Latin American history.

Philadelphia. President Bill Clinton and former presidents George Bush, Jimmy Carter, and Gerald Ford were among the dignitaries who gathered in Philadelphia on April 27, 1997, to kick off the Presidents' Summit for America's Future—a three-day event focusing on the importance of volunteerism and community service. Following a morning rally at Marcus Foster Stadium, the dignitaries joined more than 5,000 volunteers in cleaning up 8.5 miles (13.5 kilometers) of Germantown Avenue, a street lined, in some areas, with graffiti-covered buildings and strewn with litter and drug paraphernalia.

Other participants in the event included retired U.S. Army General Colin Powell, who chaired the summit, Vice President Al Gore, Philadelphia Mayor Edward Rendell, First Lady Hillary Rodham Clinton, and a number of governors, mayors, and members of the U.S. Congress. Celebrities included members of the Philadelphia Eagles football team, television personality Oprah Winfrey, actor John Travolta, and singers Tony Bennett and LL Cool J.

Racial tension. An African American woman's accusations, made in February, that six white men assaulted her son and nephew triggered increased racial tension in Philadelphia's Grays Ferry neighborhood in 1997. On April 14, in response to a number of violent race-related incidents, Louis Farrakhan, leader of the Nation of Islam religious movement, held an antiracism rally at a church in the neighborhood of South Philadelphia. The rally, attended by 3,000 people, was praised by political and community leaders but failed to end the racial incidents, which continued throughout the year.

Farrakhan was persuaded to hold the rally by Mayor Rendell, who hoped it would draw participants away from a planned march of thousands of blacks through Grays Ferry. Rendell feared that the march would incite violence. About 500 participants ultimately walked in the April 14 march, which proceeded peacefully.

Rendell was criticized by Jewish leaders for inviting Farrakhan, whose remarks have often been interpreted as anti-Semitic. At the rally, Farrakhan said that Rendell, who is Jewish, showed "courage and strength" in inviting him to Philadelphia. Farrakhan referred to himself as a "Jew and a Muslim and a Christian" and implored Americans of all faiths to work together to repair "the internal rot in America."

Million Woman March. On October 25, hundreds of thousands of African American women gathered on Philadelphia's Benjamin Franklin Parkway in what was called a demonstration of unity against shared family and community problems. Winnie Madikizela-Mandela, ex-wife of South African President Nelson Mandela, was the key speaker at the event, which was called the Million Woman March. The event was modeled after the 1995 Million Man March, organized by Louis Farrakhan.

School strike. On Sept. 11, 1997, Roman Catholic high school lay teachers approved a three-year contract with the Archdiocese of Philadelphia, ending an eight-day strike. The strike closed 22 schools and affected 23,000 students in five counties, including many students in Philadelphia. The contract called for small salary increases for the archdiocese's teachers. It also required teachers to attend Mass and other religious events during the school year.

Sports icon dies. Baseball Hall of Fame centerfielder Richie Ashburn, who achieved a career batting average of .308 and was the most popular member of the Philadelphia Phillies baseball team throughout the 1950's, died of a heart attack on Sept. 9, 1997. He was 70 years old. After retiring in 1962, Ashburn became a radio and television announcer for the team.

Classical radio. Fifty years of classical music on Philadelphia's only classical radio station, WFLN FM, ended on Sept. 5, 1997, to a storm of protests. Officials at Greater Media, Incorporated of Philadelphia, which purchased the station in April 1997, said they could generate greater revenue by playing popular music. Greater Media's acquisition of the station marked the fifth time in 13 months that the station had been sold. On September 15, WRTI, a jazz station owned by Temple University, began to play classical music during the daytime.   □ Howard S. Shapiro

See also **City.**

Philippines. Political maneuvering in the Philippines intensified in 1997 as politicians prepared for the 1998 presidential elections. President Fidel V. Ramos was widely criticized for supporting an effort to change a constitutional one-term limit on the presidency and members of Congress. Throughout 1997, Ramos denied that he wanted to serve an additional six-year term, but he failed to voice opposition to changing term limits until public pressure forced him to do so in September.

Many political analysts considered Ramos's presidency to be one of the most successful in Philippine history. Ramos, a West Point-educated former general, restored military discipline, stabilized democratic institutions, and introduced financial reforms that brought economic growth to the Philippines. In 1986, Ramos had led troops in support of Corazon Aquino, who championed the "people's revolt" that overthrew President Ferdinand Marcos. Marcos had been president since 1965. Ramos was Aquino's primary military supporter, deflecting attempted *coups* (overthrows) that threatened her presidency and the future of democratic rule.

Political maneuvers. In March 1997, Ramos's backers collected more than half the signatures needed for a referendum on term limits. The Supreme Court, however, ruled that a referendum was insufficient to amend the constitution. In response, Ramos's supporters in the lower house of

Philippines

Congress—one-third of whom were barred from seeking reelection—attempted to enact legislation to change the constitution. Jaime Cardinal Sin, archbishop of Manila, the capital, led a popular opposition campaign against the measure. Sin, who had helped end Marcos's dictatorship of the largely Roman Catholic nation, said that a second term for Ramos would return the nation to "political dynasties, warlordism, corruption, sham democracy, and debilitating poverty."

Former President Aquino publicly denounced the proposed amendment. Ramos denied rumors that he might declare martial law to avoid elections, as Marcos did in 1972. Ramos and many businessmen were expected to support Defense Minister Renato de Villa for president in the May 1998 presidential election.

Business fears. The movement to extend term limits was supported by business and financial leaders, who feared that Vice President Joseph Estrada would win the May 1998 presidential election. Estrada, a former movie star, was an extremely popular figure, despite the fact that he lacked government or business experience. The business community expressed concern that Estrada would be unable to carry on Ramos's economic reforms.

Economic slowdown. Political turmoil damaged business confidence in the Philippines, slowing the economic boom of the 1990's. Growth in the gross national product declined. Late in 1997, turmoil in Asian currency markets caused the Philippines national currency, the peso, to lose value and investment to slow. The troubled Philippine government also delayed reforms needed to end widespread tax evasion.

Civil war continued in the southern islands of the Philippines. The Moro Islamic Liberation Front (MILF), which had rejected a peace treaty offer made by the government in 1996, waged guerrilla warfare throughout 1997, mainly in parts of the islands of Mindanao and Basilan where Muslims outnumbered Christians. A faction of rebels formed MILF after breaking from the Moro National Liberation Front, which had signed a treaty with the government in 1996 to end 25 years of civil war. The MILF continued to fight for an Islamic state.

In February 1997, a Roman Catholic bishop was shot and killed outside his cathedral on the island of Jolo, which lies just off Mindanao. The murder dashed the government's hopes for peace talks. The government, which blamed the MILF for bombings, raids, and kidnappings, attacked MILF jungle camps with artillery and air strikes. The fighting forced tens of thousands of people to flee their villages.

Monsoon rains in mid-August flooded large regions of the Philippines. Twelve people died from flooding on August 18 when 9.6 inches (24.4 centimeters) of rain fell on Manila. □ Henry S. Bradsher

See also **Asia** (Facts in brief table).

Physics. In the spring of 1997, a team of Italian and Dutch astrophysicists studying mysterious bursts of gamma rays from outer space got their first clues to where the radiation is coming from. Gamma rays are similar to X rays but have higher energies. Both are forms of electromagnetic energy, as is ordinary light. The new observations suggested that gamma-ray bursts originated in titanic explosions that happened long ago in far-distant parts of the universe.

Gamma-ray bursts, which typically last a few seconds, were first observed in 1967 by U.S. spy satellites. None of these bursts came from the location of a known celestial object, and there were never two bursts from the same place in the sky. More sensitive modern satellites have revealed that these bursts are fairly common—several are observed each week.

The key to the 1997 observations was a new satellite called BeppoSAX, a joint venture by space scientists from Italy and the Netherlands. The name BeppoSAX combines the nickname of the Italian space science pioneer Giuseppe Occhialini and the initials of the Italian society for X-ray astronomy.

On February 28, BeppoSAX detected a gamma-ray burst, and scientists were able to reprogram an X-ray telescope on the satellite to look for the location of the burst. They found a faint glow of X rays in the direction of the burst's origin. Two days later, the glow was still there, but it had faded to about 5 percent of its earlier strength. A similar observation was made after another burst on May 8.

In addition to making their own observations of the bursts, the BeppoSAX team alerted astronomers throughout the world. Several observatories trained their telescopes on the points in the sky from which the bursts came and observed faint starlike objects. The biggest of the instruments, the giant 33-foot (10-meter) Keck Telescope in Hawaii, managed to analyze the light spectrum of the object producing the May 8 burst just four hours after the gamma rays were detected. This observation revealed that the object was at least 7 billion light-years from Earth, and thus the explosion had occurred more than 7 billion years ago in another galaxy. (A light-year is the distance light travels in one year—about 5.9 trillion miles [9.5 trillion kilometers]).

Astronomers using the Very Large Array radio telescope near Socorro, New Mexico, also zeroed in on the object four hours after the May 8 burst but saw nothing. However, follow-up observations on May 13 and 15 detected a radio signal that was actually growing in strength.

To be observable at such an enormous distance, the gamma-ray burst had to have come from an event that emitted, for a few seconds, millions of times more energy than an entire galaxy. Not even a *supernova* (exploding star) releases that much energy, so scientists are not sure how the enormous burst was generated. The collision of two extremely dense objects called neutron stars offers one explanation.

Excited atom. In March 1997, scientists at the National Physical Laboratory in Teddington, England, reported the discovery of an unusually long-lasting "excited" state of an atom. This discovery could provide the basis for a better atomic clock.

An excited atom is one that has been raised to a state higher in energy than its normal condition, known as the ground state. Every excited state has a natural frequency of vibration, the frequency of the radiation the atom emits when it sheds its excess energy and returns to the ground state. The longer the excited state lasts, the more accurately this frequency can be determined. Most excited atoms return to the ground state in a few hundred millionths of a second. The state created by the British scientists has an estimated lifetime of 10 years.

The British researchers trapped a single ion of ytterbium—an ytterbium atom with one electron removed—with electromagnetic forces in a vacuum. A beam from a sapphire laser was carefully tuned to provide the exact amount of energy to raise the atom into an excited state. The experimenters inferred the lifetime of the state from the rate at which the laser light was absorbed by the atom.

An atomic clock based on the frequency of this state should be accurate to one part in a trillion trillion—about a billion times more precise than the current standard, based on atoms of cesium.

☐ Robert H. March

Poetry.

In 1997, a relatively unexciting year in American verse, several prize-winning poets published new collections, but no single book garnered outstanding reviews. The most valuable overview of the year was the annual volume of *The Best American Poetry*, guest-edited by poet James Tate. The anthology offered readers a sense of American poetry at its most contemporary.

Voices from the past. Two of the most outstanding books of poetry in 1997 were not new works, but a translation of poetry by the ancient Roman poet Horace and a collection of poems by Amy Clampitt, who died in 1994. David Ferry's *The Odes of Horace* brilliantly conveys the autumnal wisdom of the great Latin poet: *Carpe diem* (seize the day). *The Collected Poems of Amy Clampitt* gathers everything by the much-admired, much-missed Clampitt, who wrote a surprising amount of poetry, considering that her first book, *The Kingfisher*, didn't appear until 1983, when she was 63. On any page of her collected works, the reader finds striking lines, as in this image of a hurricane: "Wheeling, the careening / winds arrive with lariats / and tambourines of rain."

Collections from award-winning poets. In *The Errancy*, Jorie Graham takes up the theme of desire in its many forms, but her treatment is highly philosophical and somewhat overwrought. She knows how to make words sing or cast images: "the cicadas again like kindling that won't take." But

then she moves into realms of speculation that can try the reader's patience. The evocation of the chirpy insects continues: "The struck match of some utopia we no longer remember / the terms of— / the rules."

The first half of Frank Bidart's impressive and powerful *Desire* is devoted to short lyrics, but the long visionary poem in the second half, "The Second Hour of the Night," is a major effort that contrasts the death of the writer's mother with scenes from the life of the French composer of the 1800's Hector Berlioz. The poem then explores the nature of desire with allusions to the Roman poet Ovid, remembered for his sophisticated love poems. The effect of this rolling thunder of a poem is that of a gorgeous litany: "On such a night, at such an hour. . . ."

C. K. Williams is best known for his long prosy lines, so much so that his poems really should be printed in books that are wider than they are tall. Still, he has a powerful autobiographical voice. In *The Vigil*, Williams's best poems are stories that are as moving for their content as for the choice of language. In "Secrets," for example, he relates the sad life of a friend who slides into petty crime and ends up shot dead in an alley. "Well, Sid, what now? Shall I sing for you, celebrate you with some truth? Here's truth: / add up what you didn't know, friend, and I don't, and you might have one conscious person."

Present by Alfred Corn reflects the writer's significance as a poet, essayist, anthologist, and teacher on the East Coast literary scene. The collection contains poems about the homeless; a sequence that juxtaposes scenes from the lives of Johann Sebastian Bach, the German baroque composer of the 1700's, and Franz Kafka, the Czech writer of tortured lives in the early 1900's; a meditation on life in Israel; and a piece about discovering in a library book the art of Francisco Goya, the Spanish artist born in 1746. Corn can be philosophical or witty. The poem "Wonderbread" opens "Loaf after loaf, in several sizes, / and never does it not look fresh / . . . Amazing that bread should be so weightless."

Other notable books. Some less well-known poets produced appealing collections in 1997. In *The Actual World*, Erica Funkhouser tells amiable stories about her life: "Mine was not a religious family, so when my father / arrived home on Christmas Eve with the three Hungarians, / none of us was thinking of kings." William Bronk continues to write his brief, edifying observations about life in *The Cage of Age*: "All the real worlds of one or another sort / we escape into can as well abandon us there."

Other collections of poetry in 1997 that deserve recognition include Rika Lesser's *Growing Back: Poems 1972–1992*, Baron Wormser's *When*, Dabney Stuart's *Long Gone*, Cynthia Macdonald's *I Can't Remember*, Mary Oliver's *West Wind*, and *Thomas Lux: New and Selected Poems*. ☐ Michael Dirda

See also **Canadian literature; Literature, American; Literature, World; Pulitzer Prizes.**

Poland

Poland. In March 1997, the Polish government's decision to shut down the historic shipyard in the port of Gdańsk and lay off the more than 3,000 workers sparked protests and rioting. The Gdańsk shipyard was the birthplace of the Solidarity labor union, which led the popular revolt against Communism in the 1980's. On March 13, 1997, approximately 2,000 protesters blockaded all motor and rail traffic into and out of Gdańsk for two hours. The protests failed to avert the shutdown. However, in August, one of the facility's warehouses was reopened as a nightclub.

Flooding. Widespread flooding struck 250 Polish towns and cities in July and August, killing more than 50 people and causing an estimated $2.8 billion in damage. The Polish government sought to borrow $300 million from the World Bank for reconstruction. The European Union (EU), a political and economic alliance of 15 Western European countries, granted Poland $70 million in flood-relief aid.

Government. On May 25, Polish citizens approved Poland's first new constitution since the end of Communist rule. In July, President Aleksander Kwasniewski signed into law a measure abolishing the death penalty. In August, a law went into effect that required top government officials to reveal whether they had collaborated with Poland's secret police during the Communist era.

In parliamentary elections held on September 21, the resurgent Solidarity movement regained control of the government from the Democratic Left Alliance. The center-right Freedom Union party, headed by former Solidarity leaders, agreed to form a coalition government with Solidarity. On October 31, the new government was installed, with Jerzy Buzek as Poland's new prime minister.

Poland's previous coalition government, led by the Democratic Left Alliance, had been weakened in August by disagreements over agricultural policies. The Peasant Party, junior partner of the coalition, had proposed a vote of no-confidence in Prime Minister Wlodzimierz Cimoszewicz over the issue of advance payment to farmers for grain purchases. The government survived the no-confidence vote on August 27 only because it struck a compromise deal with the Peasant Party, which then agreed not to support its own motion.

Economy. Poland's economy continued to grow in 1997. Economists expected the nation's gross domestic product to grow by 6 percent during the year. Direct foreign investment, led by the United States and Germany, totaled more than $16 billion in the previous five years. The nation's unemployment rate dropped to 12 percent in April—the lowest rate in five years—and to 11.6 percent in June.

NATO membership. In July 1997, Poland, the Czech Republic, and Hungary were accepted for membership in the North Atlantic Treaty Organiza-

Workers at Poland's Gdańsk shipyards warm themselves in March 1997 at a roadblock set up to protest the closing of the yards where the Solidarity movement began in 1980.

tion (NATO), a military alliance of 16 Western European and North American nations. In February, current NATO members Denmark and Germany had formally agreed to establish a joint defense force with Poland, indicating their optimism that Poland's NATO membership would succeed despite Russian opposition. Polish leaders had worried that the Russian government's resistance to the expansion of NATO would prevent them from joining the alliance. In May, however, NATO and Russia signed an agreement on NATO expansion that cleared the way for NATO to accept new members.

EU membership. In June, the European Union (EU), a political and economic organization of 15 Western European countries, placed Poland and five other nations on a short list of candidates to be invited to preliminary talks on possible membership. The talks were scheduled to begin in early 1998.

President Kwasniewski and Ukrainian President Leonid Kuchma signed a joint declaration of reconciliation in May 1997. The treaty was aimed at ending the centuries of enmity that existed between Poland and Ukraine, most recently in the aftermath of World War II (1939–1945). Each country viewed the other as a potential trade partner. In addition, Poland regarded a strong Ukraine as a buffer between it and Russia. □ Sharon L. Wolchik

See also **Europe** (Facts in brief table).

Pollution. See Environmental pollution.

Popular music. Female artists and teen-age fans redirected the course of popular music in 1997, a year that experienced both a gender and generational takeover. Such female artists as Fiona Apple and Jewel, both of whom were in their 20's, and teen-age country singer LeAnn Rimes, continued to develop as favorite performers of younger listeners, who seemed to be more interested in singers closer to their own age than in older and more established performers.

Lilith Fair. The strongest indication that women dominated the music industry in 1997 was the successful Lilith Fair tour, a music festival that celebrated female artists. The all-female tour was the idea of Canadian singer-songwriter Sarah McLachlan, who recruited a rotating lineup of performers including Fiona Apple, Tracy Chapman, Paula Cole, Sheryl Crow, Jewel, and Joan Osborne, to appear at various stops on the summer tour, which started in July.

Until the Lilith Fair tour, promoters had regarded female artists as in competition with each other. The common practice in the music industry had been to mix female with male acts on a concert bill, rather than featuring two female performers. Lilith Fair, however, proved to be the most successful festival package of 1997, drawing male and female fans.

"Girl power." Among the most successful yet controversial sensations of 1997 were the Spice Girls, a British quintet whose debut album, *Spice*, sold more than 14 million copies following its release in February 1997. The group released their second album, *Spiceworld*, late in 1997. Detractors claimed that the popularity of the singers, most of whom were in their 20's, owed more to marketing than music and that the girls, who had nicknames such as Baby Spice and Posh Spice, had been cast for their roles based more on looks than on talent. Critics compared the group to the 1960's band the Monkees, who also offered fans more in appearance than musical talent. Although the Spice Girls were not taken seriously by most older listeners, younger listeners, especially young girls, rallied to the group's prowoman "girl power" slogan.

Hanson, a band consisting of three teen-age brothers from Tulsa, Oklahoma, became one of the biggest young breakthrough acts of 1997. Featuring 16-year-old Isaac Hanson on guitar, 13-year-old Taylor Hanson on keyboards, and 11-year-old Zachary Hanson on drums, the band found success with their single, "MMMBop." Hanson reminded listeners and critics of such earlier hitmaking teams of young brothers as the Jackson 5 and the Osmonds. The success of Hanson reinforced the search for younger new artists with appeal for a teen-age fan base.

"Candle in the Wind 1997." The death of Diana, Princess of Wales, on August 31 in a car accident in Paris inspired singer Elton John and lyricist Bernie Taupin to rewrite their 1973 song, "Candle in the Wind," in her memory. The song originally had been recorded in tribute to Marilyn Monroe. John performed the new version of the song, titled "Candle in the Wind 1997," at Diana's funeral. A studio version of the song was released in Great Britain on September 13 and in the United States on September 23. By the end of 1997, the single had sold more than 35 million copies worldwide and raised more than $32 million for the Diana, Princess of Wales, Memorial Fund, a charitable organization established following Diana's death.

Stadium tours. As fresh sounds and emerging acts filled radio airwaves, stadiums were filled with the fans of more established artists, such as U2, the Rolling Stones, and a reunited Fleetwood Mac.

In April, U2 kicked off its PopMart tour, one of the most expensive and elaborate productions ever to go on the road. Special effects for the concerts included a 40-foot (12-meter) tall mechanical lemon and a huge backdrop of video screens.

Rock icons the Rolling Stones returned to action in September with a tour to promote their *Bridges to Babylon* album. There was the usual speculation that the 1997 tour might be the band's last, though members of the Rolling Stones insisted that they had no intention of retiring from the road.

Members of Fleetwood Mac, which first gained a strong following with the release of *Rumours* in 1977, put aside their differences in 1997 and reunited for a live album titled *The Dance* and a successful

Grammy Award winners in 1997

Record of the Year, "Change the World," Eric Clapton

Album of the Year, "Falling Into You," Celine Dion

Song of the Year, "Change the World," Gordon Kennedy, Wayne Kirkpatrick, and Tommy Simms

New Artist, LeAnn Rimes

Pop Vocal Performance, Female, "Un-break My Heart" Toni Braxton

Pop Vocal Performance, Male, "Change the World," Eric Clapton

Pop Performance by a Duo or Group with Vocal, "Free As A Bird," The Beatles

Traditional Pop Vocal Performance, "When I Fall in Love," Natalie Cole and Nat King Cole

Pop Instrumental Performance, "The Sinister Minister," Bela Fleck & the Flecktones

Rock Vocal Performance, Female, "If It Makes You Happy," Sheryl Crow

Rock Vocal Performance, Male, "Where It's At," Beck

Rock Performance by a Duo or Group with Vocal, "So Much To Say," Dave Matthews Band

Hard Rock Performance, "Bullet With Butterfly Wings," Smashing Pumpkins

Metal Performance, "Tire Me," Rage Against the Machine

Rock Instrumental Performance, "SRV Shuffle," Jimmie Vaughan, Eric Clapton, Bonnie Raitt, Robert Cray, B. B. King, Buddy Guy, Dr. John, and Art Neville

Rock Song, "Give Me One Reason," Tracy Chapman

Alternative Music Performance, "Odelay," Beck

Rhythm-and-Blues Vocal Performance, Female, "You're Makin' Me High," Toni Braxton

Rhythm-and-Blues Vocal Performance, Male, "Your Secret Love," Luther Vandross

Rhythm-and-Blues Performance by a Duo or Group with Vocal, "Killing Me Softly With His Song," Fugees

Rhythm-and-Blues Song, "Exhale (Shoop Shoop)," Babyface

Rap Solo Performance, "Hey Lover," LL Cool J

Rap Performance by a Duo or Group, "The Crossroads," Bone Thugs-N-Harmony

New-Age Album, "The Memory of Trees," Enya

Contemporary Jazz Performance, "High Life," Wayne Shorter

Jazz Vocal Performance, "New Moon Daughter," Cassandra Wilson

Jazz Instrumental Solo, "Cabin Fever," Michael Brecker

Jazz Instrumental Performance, Individual or Group, "Tales From the Hudson," Michael Brecker

Large Jazz Ensemble Performance, "Live At Manchester Craftsmen's Guild," Count Basie Orchestra (with The New York Voices)

Latin Jazz Performance, "Portraits of Cuba," Paquito D'Rivera

Country Album, "The Road To Ensenada," Lyle Lovett

Country Vocal Performance, Female, "Blue," LeAnn Rimes

Country Vocal Performance, Male, "Worlds Apart," Vince Gill

Country Performance by a Duo or Group with Vocal, "My Maria," Brooks & Dunn

Country Vocal Collaboration, "High Lonesome Sound," Vince Gill featuring Alison Krauss and Union Station

Country Instrumental Performance, "Jam Man," Chet Atkins

Bluegrass Album, "True Life Blues: The Songs of Bill Monroe," Various Artists

Country Song, "Blue," Bill Mack

Rock Gospel Album, "Jesus Freak," dc Talk

Classical Album, "Corigliano: Of Rage and Remembrance (Sym. No. 1, Etc.)," Leonard Slatkin, conductor

Music Video, Long Form, "The Beatles Anthology," The Beatles

Music Video, Short Form, "Free As A Bird," The Beatles

concert tour that began in September. Although the band had featured countless lineups since it was formed by drummer Mick Fleetwood and bassist John McVie in 1967, the 1997 tour reunited the group's most commercially successful incarnation—Fleetwood, McVie, Lindsey Buckingham, Stevie Nicks, and Christine McVie. The tour sparked hopes among fans of a more permanent reunion.

Father and son. Folk-rock artist Bob Dylan, whom many critics have called the best and most influential songwriter in the history of rock music, released *Time Out of Mind* in the autumn of 1997. Critics viewed the album, a collection of songs that deal with issues of mortality, as a return to Dylan's most inspired form.

The album marked a comeback of sorts for Dylan, who had battled a potentially fatal heart ailment in May 1997. Dylan had been forced to cancel a June European tour after he was hospitalized with a fungal infection called pericarditis, which caused the membrane surrounding his heart to swell.

On September 27, Dylan performed before Pope John Paul II and a crowd of more than 250,000 people at the World Eucharistic Congress in Bologna, Italy.

Bob Dylan's son, Jakob Dylan, singer and song-writer for Jakob's band, the Wallflowers, emerged as one of the more popular and promising new artists of 1997. The band's album, *Bringing Down the Horse*, was frequently and favorably compared with the music of a younger Bob Dylan.

"Gangsta" rap. In March, music fans mourned the death of Christopher Wallace, better known as Biggie Smalls or the Notorious B.I.G. Wallace was murdered in a drive-by shooting in Los Angeles a few weeks before the release of his second album, prophetically titled *Life After Death*. The murder had not been solved by the end of 1997.

Wallace's death disrupted what was considered by many music experts to be a comeback year for big-ticket live performances by rap music artists. Tours by several artists, including Snoop Doggy Dogg and Wallace's collaborator and producer, Sean "Puffy" Combs, were put on hold or canceled.

In September, the rap group Wu-Tang Clan abruptly ended a national tour as the opening act for the rock group Rage Against the Machine. Members of Wu-Tang Clan were investigated in 1997 for allegedly inciting a riot in August at a concert in Indianapolis, Indiana. Band members were also investigated in August for allegedly beating a record company promoter following a concert at a suburban Chicago arena.

Jazz musician and composer Wynton Marsalis received the 1997 Pulitzer Prize for music for *Blood on the Fields,* a three-hour oratorio on slavery. Marsalis, who wrote the piece in 1994 for New York's Lincoln Center for the Performing Arts, became the first jazz composer to receive a Pulitzer Prize.

Country music. Garth Brooks on Aug. 7, 1997, became the first country artist to stage a free concert in New York City's Central Park. The event drew more than 250,000 fans from across the country, according to New York City police estimates. The concert was broadcast live on cable television and on radio stations nationwide.

Brooks had intended the concert to serve as the promotional launch for his new album, *Sevens,* but delayed the album's release following a corporate upheaval at his record label, EMI. Brooks had been displeased with the way the company had planned to market the album. *Sevens* was finally released on November 25 and sold more than 1 million copies within the first few weeks.

A second highly anticipated release in 1997 was *Come On Over* by the Canadian singer Shania Twain, "Love Gets Me Every Time," a single from the album, entered the country music charts in September at number 20—the highest debut onto the charts by a female country artist and the second highest by any country artist.

Despite the continued appeal of such performers as Brooks and Twain, country music lost much of its popular momentum in 1997. Some music experts maintained that fans had begun to view mainstream country artists as having lost touch with the music's Nashville roots in favor of a wider variety of musical influences. □ Don McLeese

Population. The United Nations Population Fund (UNFPA) in May 1997 estimated the world's population at 5.85 billion people. That figure reflected a slight decrease in the world's annual population growth rate, from 1.57 percent in 1994 to 1.48 percent in 1995. The UNFPA also reported that the population of the world grew by 81 million people a year in the mid-1990's, down from 87 million in the mid- and late-1980's. Nevertheless, the UNFPA cited funding for family planning and women's reproductive health programs as its top priority in 1997. The UNFPA predicted that the world's population would reach 9.4 billion by the year 2050.

The State of the World Population Report, issued by the UNFPA in May 1997, charged that industrialized nations were not keeping their commitment to financially support family planning and reproductive health care programs in developing nations. At the International Conference on Population and Development in Cairo, Egypt, in 1994, the world community had estimated that by the year 2000 it would annually need $17 billion to adequately fund population programs. Developing countries agreed to provide 67 percent of the funds, while industrialized nations agreed to provide 33 percent. Data for 1995 (the most recent available) showed that developing countries spent $10.7 billion on the programs, while industrialized countries contributed $2.5 billion of the $5.7 billion they had pledged.

The UNFPA report noted that if the shortfall in financial aid to developing countries continues, it could result in 120 million unwanted pregnancies from 1995 to 2000. The UN agency predicted that an estimated 49 million of those pregnancies would end in abortions, 5 million would result in the deaths of infants and young children, and more than 65,000 would result in maternal deaths.

The UNFPA report attributed the shortfall in funds to budget cuts for overseas development assistance by industrialized nations. The UNFPA decried the "massive violation" of human rights of women because of the continued "widespread discrimination and violence against women."

The lack of financial aid also hampered efforts to stop the spread of sexually transmitted diseases, according to the UN agency. The UNFPA estimated that worldwide more than 300 million new cases of sexually transmitted diseases develop each year, and that teen-agers account for more than half of the new cases. The annual rate of HIV infection, the virus that causes AIDS, was estimated at more than 3 million cases. About 1.5 million people worldwide annually die from AIDS-related causes. In presenting the report, Nafis Sadik, executive director of the UNFPA, noted that "for millions of women, sexual and reproductive rights are quite literally the key to survival." □ J. Tuyet Nguyen

See also **AIDS; Census; City.**

Portugal. The Portuguese economy grew strongly in 1997, boosting hopes of qualifying for the single European currency to be launched in 1999. The government of Prime Minister Antonio Guterres claimed that joining the single currency was necessary to keep attracting foreign investment to the country and to ensure that Portugal retained an influence among leading European nations.

Portugal, like its neighbor, Spain, benefited in 1997 from the significant creation of new jobs, higher investment by industry, and a sharp decline in interest rates. The European Commission, the administrative arm of the European Union (EU—a group of 15 Western European nations), forecast that unemployment in Portugal would fall to 6.8 percent in 1997, down from 7.3 percent in 1996 and well below the average rate of more than 10 percent for EU countries. Economic growth was expected to rise to 3.5 percent, nearly one percentage point above the EU average.

Strong growth and government efforts to reduce tax evasion helped to swell tax revenues and shrink the budget deficit. The European Commission forecast that the deficit would decline to 2.7 percent of gross domestic product, well within the 3.0 percent requirement for joining the single European currency and down from 3.2 percent in 1996. The deficit also shrank because of a decline in interest rates, a trend that reflected confidence in the economy.

Portugal

Nazi gold. In 1997, Portugal became involved in the controversy over gold dealings with Nazi Germany during World War II (1939-1945). According to declassified American government documents disclosed in July and December 1997, the Portuguese government bought tons of gold during the war from Nazi Germany. The transactions were conducted through the Swiss National Bank and involved gold held on deposit for Portugal by the U.S. Federal Reserve Board and the Bank of Canada. The Bank of Canada appointed an historian to investigate its wartime dealings with Portugal.

Macao. Following in the footsteps of the United Kingdom, which transferred control of its former colony of Hong Kong to China in July, Portugal in 1997 prepared to hand control of Macao, a small colony west of Hong Kong, to China on Dec. 20, 1999. President Jorge Sampaio traveled to Beijing in February and received assurances from President Jiang Zemin that China would respect the human rights of Macao's 450,000 people.

Floods. A severe storm with heavy rains and winds of more than 60 miles (97 kilometers) per hour lashed Portugal in early November 1997. Ten people were killed, and towns were flooded along the Guadiana River, which marks part of the Portuguese-Spanish border. □ Tom Buerkle

See also **Europe** (Facts in brief table); **Switzerland.**

Prison. Federal and state prisons in the United States held 1,182,169 inmates as of Dec. 31, 1996—more than double the number of inmates in 1985—according to a 1997 report by the U.S. Department of Justice's Bureau of Justice Statistics (BJS). The BJS also reported that jails, which hold people who are awaiting trial or serving sentences of one year or less, held another 518,000 inmates on June 30, 1996.

Imprisonment rates in 1997 were vastly higher in the United States than in other Western countries. Incarceration rates in the 1990's in jails and prisons ranged from 60 per 100,000 people in Sweden and the Netherlands to 120 per 100,000 people in Canada. The comparable U.S. figure at mid-year 1997 exceeded 650 inmates per 100,000 people.

The high prison population in the United States in the 1990's was due in part to an increase in the number of prosecutions for drug and weapon offenses and an increase in the amount of time prisoners actually served before being released. Federal and state "three-strike" laws, which mandate a life sentence after a third conviction for some serious crimes, also increased prison populations.

Women in prison. The number of female prisoners in the United States grew 9.1 percent from December 1995 to December 1996—a much faster rate than the 4.3-percent increase of male prisoners. As the number of women in state and federal prisons increased, totaling 74,730 as of Dec. 31, 1996, the

The *Resolution,* a prison ship, sails into harbor at Portland, England, on March 13, 1997. The British Prison Service purchased the ship, capable of housing about 500 prisoners, from New York City's Department of Corrections.

problems facing women prisoners also increased.

In March 1997, the U.S. Department of Justice (DOJ) filed a lawsuit against the state of Arizona, charging that guards in state prisons had subjected female prisoners to sexual assaults and violations of their privacy. In a separate lawsuit against the state of Michigan, the DOJ charged that women were subjected to similar offenses and were denied adequate medical and mental health care.

In July 1997, the state of California settled a lawsuit that claimed the state provided inadequate medical treatment for the 5,400 female inmates at facilities in Chowchilla and Frontera. As part of the settlement, the prisons' health care services were to be monitored for eight months.

AIDS in prison. The number of federal and state prisoners who were infected with the human immunodeficiency virus (HIV) fell slightly from 2.4 percent of prisoners in 1994 to 2.3 percent in 1995, according to a 1997 report of the BJS. HIV is the virus that causes AIDS.

Although 30 states reported that 1 percent or fewer of prisoners were HIV-positive in 1995, the rates were much higher in New York, with 13.9 percent, and Connecticut, with 5.1 percent. Overall, the number of AIDS cases in prisons was six times higher than the national average. ☐ Michael Tonry

See also **Crime.**

Prizes. See Nobel Prizes; Pulitzer Prizes.

Protestantism. On Oct. 4, 1997, an estimated 500,000 men gathered in Washington, D.C., for Stand in the Gap, an event sponsored by Promise Keepers, an evangelical Christian men's organization. Promise Keepers promoted the rally as a "day of heartfelt confession and prayer" that would encourage men to be faithful to their families and churches, to seek racial reconciliation, and to provide spiritual and moral leadership.

News coverage of the event highlighted criticism of Promise Keepers. Opponents of the organization maintained that it threatened women's rights and that it was a political arm of the conservative religious right rather than a spiritual movement.

Church unity. In 1997, the Evangelical Lutheran Church in America (ELCA), the United Church of Christ (UCC), the Presbyterian Church (U.S.A.), and the Reformed Church in America agreed to recognize each other's sacrament of communion and to exchange their clergy under certain circumstances. The ELCA finalized the Formula of Agreement in August at its biennial Churchwide Assembly.

The ELCA delegates at the assembly narrowly rejected a similar measure with the Episcopal Church, the Concordat of Agreement, which the Episcopalians approved in July. ELCA delegates voiced concerns about the Episcopal Church's hierarchy and the lifetime ordination of bishops. Comparable ELCA leaders remain bishops only during terms of office.

Controversial Bible publication. In May, the International Bible Society and Zondervan Publishing canceled publication of a revision of the New International Version (NIV) of the Bible, a popular translation among evangelical Christians. The revision of the NIV Bible was to have included gender-inclusive words—such as substituting "people" for "mankind" —while retaining the masculine pronouns referring to God. The publication was canceled, however, after *World* magazine, Focus on the Family, and other evangelical organizations criticized the Bible translators for being under the sway of a secular "feminist agenda" and "political correctness."

IRS controversy. In July, the joint Congressional Committee on Taxation opened an investigation of the Internal Revenue Service (IRS) to determine if the IRS targeted conservative religious-interest groups for audits. During the 1990's, the IRS had denied or revoked the tax-exempt status of several groups for allegedly endorsing politicians—a role denied to tax-exempt organizations. The religious groups maintained, however, that the audits were politically motivated harassments that limited freedom of religion guaranteed by the First Amendment. The focus of the controversy was the accusation by watchdog groups that the Christian Coalition, a conservative organization that is devoted to preserving what it considers traditional American values, used its publications and political training sessions to influence elections.

New leadership. In May 1997, James Kenneth Echols of Philadelphia was elected president of the Lutheran School of Theology at Chicago, an ELCA seminary. Echols became the first African American to lead a Lutheran seminary in North America.

In July, Bishop Frank Griswold III of Chicago was elected to a nine-year term as the presiding bishop of the Episcopal Church. Griswold succeeded retiring Bishop Edmond Browning, who served for 12 years.

Homosexuality. In June 1997, the Southern Baptist Convention, the largest Protestant body in the United States, voted 4 to 1 to boycott the Walt Disney Company. The church criticized Disney for providing benefits to same-sex partners of employees, allowing "gay days" at Disney parks, and producing "gay-friendly" entertainment.

Also in June, a Presbyterian Church (U.S.A.) policy that required "fidelity in marriage" and "chastity in singleness" for ordained clergy went into effect. Although the policy did not mention homosexuality, opponents claimed it was intended to ban practicing homosexuals from the pulpit. At the annual General Assembly in June, a more moderate measure was introduced that required clergy to demonstrate "fidelity and integrity in marriage or singleness." If a majority of the church's 172 presbyteries approved the measure before the 1998 assembly, it would become an official policy. ☐ Martin E. Marty

Psychology. See Mental health.

Public health and safety.

Children exposed to high electromagnetic fields (EMF's) at home are no more likely to develop leukemia than children in homes with lower levels of EMF's, according to a major study reported in July 1997. The eight-year, $5-million study was the largest ever conducted on the controversial issue, which had worried parents and been debated by health experts since the 1970's. The study was sponsored by the National Cancer Institute, an agency of the National Institutes of Health in Bethesda, Maryland.

© OHMAN—OREGONIAN

Previous investigations had suggested that EMF's in the vicinity of high-voltage power lines increase the risk of cancer, including acute lymphoblastic leukemia (ALL). ALL is the most common childhood cancer, striking about 1,600 children annually.

In the study, researchers compared 638 children suffering from ALL with 620 healthy children. Technicians measured EMF's in the children's houses and in the room where each child's mother slept during pregnancy. They also recorded the distance of each house from high-voltage power lines. The investigators found no link between exposure to high EMF's and ALL.

Tainted beef. Concerns about the safety of ground beef arose in August after Hudson Foods, Incorporated, of Rogers, Arkansas, recalled 20,000 pounds (9,080 kilograms) of frozen hamburger patties produced at its Columbus, Nebraska, processing plant. The beef, contaminated by a strain of *Escherichia coli* bacteria, was implicated in at least 16 cases of food poisoning in Colorado. Under the urging of the United States Department of Agriculture (USDA), Hudson later recalled a total of 25 million pounds (11 million kilograms) of meat. The Columbus plant was closed and later sold to the Iowa Beef Processors company. The rest of the Hudson company was purchased by another Arkansas company, Tyson Foods, Incorporated, of Springdale, Arkansas, the country's largest poultry producer.

Regulating tobacco. A federal judge in Greensboro, North Carolina, ruled in April that the U.S. Food and Drug Administration (FDA) has the authority to regulate tobacco as a drug. The judge ruled that cigarettes are drug-delivery devices, much like hypodermic syringes, and that the tobacco and nicotine in cigarettes fit the legal definition of drugs.

The decision came after tobacco companies asked the court to strike down FDA regulations, issued in August 1996, restricting children's access to tobacco.

Those rules included requiring stores to verify that customers who buy tobacco are at least 18 years old.

The many dangers of smoking. Smoking kills at least 6,200 children each year through disease and fire, researchers at the University of Wisconsin in Madison reported in July 1997. Their study indicated that 2,800 deaths result annually from low birth weight in babies born to women who smoke during pregnancy. Low-birth-weight babies are frail and vulnerable to disease. According to the study, another 2,000 deaths each year result from sudden infant death syndrome attributed to secondhand smoke. A thousand deaths are due to respiratory diseases, 250 are caused by fires, and 14 result from asthma triggered by secondhand smoke.

In May, scientists at Harvard University in Cambridge, Massachusetts, reported that regular exposure to secondhand smoke almost doubles the risk of heart disease. Their 10-year study of more than 32,000 nurses found that exposure to secondhand smoke is more dangerous than previously believed.

Distracting cell phones. Talking on a cellular telephone while operating a vehicle distracts drivers and increases the risk of an accident, researchers at the University of Toronto, Canada, reported in February. The scientists studied 699 drivers with cell phones who were involved in highway accidents, comparing the number of accidents that occurred during phone calls with the number that happened when the individuals were not using their phones. They found that the accident rate was more than four times higher during phone conversations—approximately the same accident risk as driving while intoxicated.

Airbags. A major safety controversy in 1997 centered on the use of airbags. Although airbags had saved some 2,600 lives in the United States between 1990 and 1997, they were blamed for the deaths of approximately 85 adults and children between 1991 and 1997. Most victims were killed by the force of the airbag inflation. In response to the concern, federal safety regulators on Nov. 18, 1997, announced that some consumers, beginning in January 1998, would be able to purchase on-off switches to temporarily deactivate airbags. Motorists eligible for the switches would include people with medical conditions that place them at high risk from an airbag deployment and people who could not avoid placing rear-facing infant car seats in the front passenger seat. Consumers had to obtain permission from the National Highway Traffic Safety Administration to have switches installed in a vehicle.

Nontraditional computer keyboards, designed for more comfortable use, provide no major benefit in protecting people from fatigue or from wrist and arm pain, according to a National Institute for Occupational Safety and Health (NIOSH) study reported in January. NIOSH researchers studied 50 female clerical workers who used either a conventional keyboard or one of three alternative-design keyboards. The nontraditional units had a split configuration, with keys for the left and right hands on separate units. Users reported little fatigue and discomfort with either type of design. The investigators concluded that keyboard design is not a major cause of the discomfort reported by some computer users.

□ Michael Woods

See also **Courts.**

Puerto Rico. In February 1997, the United States-Puerto Rico Political Status Act was introduced in the U.S. Congress. The bill, supported by pro-statehood Puerto Rican Governor Pedro J. Rosselló, called for a referendum to be held by Dec. 31, 1998, that would offer Puerto Ricans an opportunity to remain a U.S. commonwealth, become a U.S. state, or claim national independence.

The political status of Puerto Rico has been debated since the United States gained the territory at the end of the Spanish-American War in 1898. Since 1952, Puerto Rico has been a U.S. commonwealth, a political status that makes Puerto Ricans U.S. citizens but does not allow them to vote for president or entitle them to full representation in Congress.

On April 14, 1997, Rosselló announced that the Puerto Rican government would sell the publicly owned Puerto Rico Telephone Company to private investors. The company, under public management, was reportedly unable to compete with private businesses. On October 1, about 100,000 Puerto Ricans gathered in San Juan to protest the sale.

A record eight native Puerto Rican baseball players participated in the 1997 All-Star Game in Cleveland on July 8. Sandy Alomar, Jr., the first Puerto Rican to be named the All-Star Game's most valuable player, hit the two-run homer that won the game for the American League. □ Nathan A. Haverstock

See also **Latin America** (Facts in brief table).

Pulitzer Prizes in journalism, letters, and music were awarded on April 7, 1997, by Columbia University in New York City on the recommendation of the Pulitzer Prize Board.

Journalism. *The Times Picayune* of New Orleans, Louisiana, won the public service award for a series of articles analyzing the decline in the world's fish supply. The *Picayune* also won a Pulitzer for Walt Handelsman's editorial cartoons. *The Seattle* (Washington) *Times* won the investigative reporting prize for disclosure of corruption in the federal housing program for Native Americans by Eric Nalder, Deborah Nelson, and Alex Tizon. The same paper won the beat reporting prize for Byron Acohido's unearthing of rudder control problems on the Boeing 737 as part of an investigation of the aerospace industry.

Newsday, of Long Island, New York, won the spot news reporting prize for coverage of the crash of TWA Flight 800. The prize for explanatory journalism was awarded to reporter Michael Vitez and photographers April Saul and Ron Cortes of *The Philadelphia* (Pennsylvania) *Inquirer* for a series about how terminally ill patients attempt to die with dignity. The national reporting award went to *The Wall Street Journal* for its coverage of the impact of AIDS research on the science, business, and medical industries. John F. Burns of *The New York Times* won the international reporting award for his coverage of Afghanistan's Taliban regime.

The Baltimore Sun took the feature writing prize for Lisa Pollack's profile of a baseball umpire, two of whose sons were born with a rare genetic disorder. Eileen McNamara of *The Boston Globe* won the commentary award for her columns on Massachusetts and its people. The prize for criticism went to *The Washington Post's* music critic, Tim Page. The board awarded the editorial writing prize to Michael Gartner of *The Daily Tribune* of Ames, Iowa, for commentaries on local issues.

In the spot photography category, Annie Wells of *The Press Democrat* of Santa Rosa, California, won the award for her photograph of a teen-ager being rescued from floodwaters. Alexander Zelianichenko of the Associated Press won the feature photography award for his photograph of Boris Yeltsin, the president of Russia, dancing at a rock concert.

Letters and music. Steven Millhauser won the fiction award for *Martin Dressler: The Tale of an American Dreamer.* The history prize went to Jack N. Rakove for *Original Meanings: Politics and Ideas in the Making of the Constitution.* Frank McCourt won the biography prize for his memoir *Angela's Ashes.* Lisel Mueller's *Alive Together* won the poetry award. *Ashes to Ashes* netted the general nonfiction prize for Richard Kluger. Wynton Marsalis won the music prize for *Blood on the Fields,* the first jazz composition to win the music award. No prize for drama was awarded in 1997. □ Lisa Klobuchar

Quebec. See **Canadian provinces.**

Radio. The consolidation of radio stations into larger corporate entities continued to be the main business trend in United States commercial radio in 1997. Radio stations, which often post annual profits of 40 percent or more because of low operating costs, are extremely lucrative media properties.

The radio industry, which traditionally was dominated by small "mom-and-pop" operations, was transformed by the Telecommunications Reform Act of 1996, which removed most restrictions on radio ownership. As a result, big radio companies were permitted to buy up to eight stations in a single market. In 1996, more than 2,100 of the 10,300 commercial radio stations in the United States had changed hands in deals worth a record $15.5 billion. By 1997, seven companies owned almost 20 percent of all commercial stations nationwide.

On February 18, the merger of three networks—Evergreen Media Corporation, Chancellor Broadcasting Corporation, and Viacom Incorporated—formed the Chancellor Media Corporation, the largest independent U.S. radio broadcaster. The new company, controlled by the Dallas-based investment firm of Hicks, Muse, Tate & Furst, Inc., comprised 93 stations with revenues of $700 million.

On August 25, Hicks, Muse became the largest U.S. radio conglomerate with its purchase of SFX Broadcasting Inc. SFX's 71 stations were merged with the 273 stations of Capstar Broadcasting Corporation, another Hicks, Muse subsidiary. Less than one month later, on September 19, Westinghouse Electric Corporation became the highest grossing U.S. radio broadcaster with its purchase of American Radio Systems Incorporated for $2.6 billion in cash and debt. The new 175-station chain collected $1.5 billion in revenues in 1997, compared to an estimated $1.45 billion for the Hicks, Muse conglomerate.

All-talk radio. The number of all-talk radio stations continued to climb in 1997, to more than 1,000 from approximately 200 in 1987. While many shows with politically conservative hosts offered tempestuous discussions of politics, race, and the economy, an increasing number of programs addressed personal issues. Among these were "Here's to Your Health," hosted by Deborah Ray, and "The Dr. Laura Schlessinger Show." Ray and Schlessinger were typical of the growing number of women program jockeys. Others included Nanci Donnellan, the aggressive host of "The Fabulous Sports Babe," Dr. Joy Browne, and exercise and nutrition guru Susan Powter.

Stern goes north. On Sept. 2, 1997, Howard Stern, the leading U.S. purveyor of "shock radio," took his act to Montreal and Toronto in Canada. Stern, who has incurred almost $2 million in fines from the U.S. Federal Communications Commission, immediately upset some listeners with insulting comments about French-Canadians. In March 1997, Stern's autobiography, *Private Parts*, was released as a movie and became a top-grossing attraction.

Trouble at Pacifica. In February 1997, WRTI-FM at Temple University in Philadelphia was accused by local critics of censoring radio content when, at the last minute, WRTI-FM cancelled a series of commentaries made by a death-row inmate convicted of killing a police officer. The commentaries were to have aired on "Democracy Now!" a news program produced by Pacifica Radio, a West Coast programmer. WRTI-FM, Pacifica's only subscriber in Pennsylvania, also canceled its contract with the programmer, as did 11 other affiliates that carried Pacifica's news and public affairs programs. WRTI said it had replaced "Democracy Now!" with a jazz show, because a musical program would more effectively highlight the Temple University role in the community. The other stations argued that a convicted killer should not be given such a wide public forum.

In April, the Corporation for Public Broadcasting (CPB), after auditing Pacifica, accused the Pacifica Foundation, which governs the network, of violating federal open meeting laws and interfering with the operation of the advisory boards of local stations. The audit had been requested by opponents of Pacifica's decisions to cancel several of its less popular programs. The CPB gave Pacifica six months to open its meetings to the public or risk losing its $1-million grant. □ Brian Bouldrey

See also **Telecommunications; Television.**

Quebec. See **Canadian provinces; Montreal.**

Religion. Rioters in Rengasdenglok, Indonesia, attacked two Buddhist temples and four Christian churches on Jan. 30, 1997. The incident reflected an ongoing religious conflict in Indonesia, where about 90 percent of the more than 200 million people are Muslim. Most of the remaining 10 percent of Indonesians are Buddhist, Christian, or Hindu. About 200 houses of worship—mostly Christian churches—have been destroyed since 1995.

The rioting in January 1997, during Ramadan, the Islamic month of fasting, allegedly began when non-Muslims complained to authorities about Muslim youths who were awakening their neighbors to make sure that they ate before dawn in accordance with the traditions of the fast. Days before the riot, President Suharto had called for unity among all religious people in Indonesia.

Tung Chee-hwa, the chief executive of Hong Kong, addressed delegates on July 9 at an assembly in Hong Kong of the Lutheran World Federation, a world-wide communion of Lutheran churches with headquarters in Geneva, Switzerland. Tung promised the delegates that the Hong Kong government would protect the religious freedoms of its citizens. People of all faiths had expressed concerns about religious rights after June 30, 1997, when Hong Kong returned to the sovereignty of China, where the Christian church was growing rapidly and religious groups are closely regulated by the government.

Religious groups with 150,000 or more members in the United States*

African Methodist Episcopal Church	3,500,000
African Methodist Episcopal Zion Church	1,230,842
American Baptist Association	250,000
American Baptist Churches in the U.S.A.	1,517,400
Antiochian Orthodox Christian Archdiocese of North America	300,000
Armenian Apostolic Church of America	180,000
Armenian Church of America, Diocese of the	414,000
Assemblies of God	2,387,982
Bahá'í Faith	300,000
Baptist Bible Fellowship International	1,500,000
Baptist Missionary Association of America	231,191
Buddhism	780,000
Christian and Missionary Alliance	307,366
Christian Church (Disciples of Christ)	929,725
Christian Churches and Churches of Christ	1,070,616
Christian Methodist Episcopal Church	1,000,000
Christian Reformed Church in North America	206,789
Church of God (Anderson, Ind.)	224,061
Church of God (Cleveland, Tenn.)	753,230
Church of God in Christ	5,499,875
Church of God in Christ, International	250,000
Church of Jesus Christ of Latter-day Saints	4,711,500
Church of the Nazarene	601,900
Churches of Christ	1,655,000
Conservative Baptist Association of America	200,000
Coptic Orthodox Church	180,000
Episcopal Church	2,536,550
Evangelical Free Church of America	242,619
Evangelical Lutheran Church in America	5,190,489
Full Gospel Fellowship of Churches and Ministers International	195,000
Greek Orthodox Archdiocese of North and South America	1,950,000
Hinduism	910,000
International Church of the Foursquare Gospel	227,307
International Council of Community Churches	250,000
International Pentecostal Holiness Church	157,163
Islam	5,100,000
Jehovah's Witnesses	966,243
Judaism, Conservative	2,242,000
Judaism, Orthodox	472,000
Judaism, Reform	2,301,000
Lutheran Church—Missouri Synod	2,594,555
National Association of Free Will Baptists	213,716
National Baptist Convention of America, Inc.	3,500,000
National Baptist Convention, U.S.A., Inc.	8,200,000
National Missionary Baptist Convention of America	2,500,000
National Primitive Baptist Convention, Inc.	500,000
Orthodox Church in America	2,000,000
Pentecostal Assemblies of the World	1,000,000
Presbyterian Church in America	267,764
Presbyterian Church (U.S.A.)	3,669,489
Progressive National Baptist Convention, Inc.	2,500,000
Reformed Church in America	306,312
Reorganized Church of Jesus Christ of Latter Day Saints	177,779
Roman Catholic Church	60,280,454
Salvation Army	453,150
Seventh-Day Adventist Church	790,731
Sikhism	190,000
Southern Baptist Convention	15,663,296
Unitarian Universalist Association	204,046
United Church of Christ	1,472,213
United Methodist Church	8,538,662
United Pentecostal Church International	550,000
Wisconsin Evangelical Lutheran Synod	412,478

*A majority of the figures are for the year 1995.

Sources: Representatives of individual organizations; *Yearbook of American and Canadian Churches 1997.*

Decline in religious interest. The German magazine *Der Spiegel* reported in January that in 1996 for the first time atheists and agnostics outnumbered religious believers among the more than 82 million people in Germany. In the survey, 50 percent of former West Germans said they are religious, while only 20 percent of former East Germans identified themselves as such.

In the United States, attendance at a church or synagogue in a given week dropped to 38 percent of the American population in 1996 from 43 percent in 1995, according to a Gallup Poll released in April 1997. The 1996 figure was the lowest since 1940, when Gallup reported that 37 percent of Americans attended services. Attendance reached its highest level—49 percent—in 1955 and 1958.

Awards. At a May 6, 1997, ceremony in London, Pandurang Shastri Athavales, a 71-year-old Hindu activist, was presented the 1997 Templeton Prize for Progress in Religion, a $1.21-million award given to an individual who has advanced people's understanding of God or spirituality. Athavales was recognized for the volunteer movement he founded in 1954 to assist poor people. The movement is based on a Hindu text that promotes self-respect and love for God and all people.

Larry L. Rasmussen, a social-ethics professor at Union Theological Seminary in New York City, received the 1997 Grawemeyer Award in Religion at a ceremony in April 1997. The $150,000 award is presented annually by the Louisville Presbyterian Theological Seminary and the University of Louisville in Kentucky. Rasmussen was cited for his 1996 book, *Earth Community, Earth Ethics,* a study of environmental problems, including a history of religious concern or disregard for the earth.

Religion and state. The U.S. Supreme Court overturned the Religious Freedom Restoration Act of 1993 by a vote of 6 to 3 in June 1997. The law had specified that the government must show a "compelling interest" before it could limit the religious practices of individuals. The law had been passed in response to a 1990 Supreme Court decision that upheld the state of Oregon's right to withhold government assistance to two Native Americans who used peyote, an illegal drug, in a religious ceremony.

Justice Anthony M. Kennedy noted in the majority opinion that the Religious Freedom Restoration Act interpreted the degree of religious protection guaranteed by the U.S. Constitution—a power that belongs to the judiciary, not the legislature. Justice Sandra Day O'Connor, writing the dissenting opinion, noted that the law reflected the "legitimate concerns" of Congress that the 1990 ruling had "restricted religious liberty." □ Leon Howell

See also **Eastern Orthodox Churches; Islam; Judaism; Protestantism; Roman Catholic Church; Roman Catholic Church** Special Report: **Mother Theresa—Saint of the Gutters; Supreme Court.**

Republican Party

Republican Party. The Republican Party in 1997 scored major victories in off-year elections and escaped much of the harsh criticism for fund-raising practices that was directed at the Democratic Party. However, Republicans in 1997 did face some questions about campaign finance irregularities. GOP (for Grand Old Party) leaders also came under attack following claims of unethical conduct.

Gingrich reprimanded. Republican Speaker of the U.S. House of Representatives Newt Gingrich (R., Georgia) on January 21 was formally reprimanded and fined $300,000 for bringing discredit upon the House of Representatives. The sanction was the first imposed on a speaker in the 208-year history of the House. In the historic decision, the House voted 395 to 28 to reprimand Gingrich for improperly using tax-exempt donations for political purposes and then submitting false information to the House Ethics Committee. A House subcommittee report concluded that Gingrich failed to seek adequate legal advice regarding the use of tax-deductible donations to help finance a college course he taught and that Gingrich supplied inaccurate statements to the ethics panel. Gingrich admitted responsibility as part of a plea bargain with the ethics panel in late 1996.

Two Democrats and 26 Republicans voted against the penalty, while 196 Republicans and 198 Democrats voted in favor. Twelve House members did not vote. Gingrich was absent during the vote.

On April 17, 1997, Gingrich announced that he would borrow $300,000 from retired Republican Senator Bob Dole (R., Kansas) to pay the fine. Under terms of the loan, Gingrich would not have to repay the $300,000 until the year 2005, two years after the date Gingrich announced he would leave Congress.

Failed coup. In July 1997, Gingrich fought off an attempted *coup* (overthrow) by junior GOP House members who tried to oust him from the speakership. Some members argued that Gingrich was not conservative enough and had damaged the GOP through questionable actions. Reports differed on who was involved in the internal rebellion, but on July 17, Representative Bill Paxon (R., New York), who some viewed as Gingrich's potential successor, resigned as head of the House GOP leadership team. Paxon denied involvement with the coup.

Campaign finances. At U.S. Senate Governmental Affairs Committee hearings on campaign finance irregularities in July, former Republican National Committee (RNC) Chairman Haley Barbour denied using the National Policy Forum, a conservative

organization he founded, to funnel as much as $2.2 million from a Hong Kong-based company to the RNC. Democrats on the Senate committee had alleged that Barbour asked Hong Kong businessman Ambrous Tung Young, head of Young Brothers Development Corp., for funds that were sent to the RNC.

GOP presidential hopefuls gathered in Indianapolis in August for the Midwest Republican Leadership Conference. The meeting took place more than two years before the first presidential primary in 1999. Speakers included former Vice President Dan Quayle, 1996 vice presidential nominee Jack Kemp, former Tennessee Governor Lamar Alexander, publisher Steve Forbes, and radio host Alan Keyes. Speaker of the House Gingrich, Texas Governor George W. Bush, and Senator Fred Thompson (R., Tennessee) also attended the conference. No clear front-runner for the GOP nomination in the year 2000 emerged at the meeting, which was attended by more than 1,200 Republicans.

Elections. The GOP, better supplied with cash than the Democratic Party, helped finance candidates to victory in New Jersey and Virginia in the Nov. 4, 1997, election.

In Virginia, former State Attorney General James S. Gilmore III led a Republican sweep of the state's top three offices by winning the race for governor. Gilmore defeated Lieutenant Governor Don Beyer, a Democrat, to succeed Governor George Allen, a Republican. John Hager was elected lieutenant governor, while state Senator Mark Earley won the race for attorney general.

In New Jersey, Governor Christine Todd Whitman, a Republican, was narrowly reelected to a second term by defeating Democrat Jim McGreevey, a state senator. Analysts said that Whitman, who was once

regarded as a rising star within the party, was hurt by her moderate position on such issues as abortion.

Republicans scored major victories in several mayoral races in 1997, including the nation's two largest cities. New York City Mayor Rudolph Giuliani crushed his Democratic opponent, Ruth Messinger, on November 4 to win a second term, and Richard J. Riordan won a second term as mayor of Los Angeles by defeating Democratic state Senator Tom Hayden on April 8.

Staten Island and Brooklyn voters gave Republican Vito Fossella an easy victory over Democratic state assemblyman Eric Vitaliano in a race for an open congressional seat in New York City. Fossella replaced Representative Susan Molinari (R., New York), who resigned on August 1 to become a television anchorperson.

Governors. Arizona Governor Fife Symington, a Republican, resigned on September 5, after a jury convicted him on September 3 of seven felony counts of defrauding lenders while working as a commercial real estate developer before being elected governor. On June 11, an Alabama state parole board pardoned former GOP Governor Guy Hunt, declaring him innocent of ethics violations. In 1993, Hunt was convicted of diverting $200,000 from his 1987 campaign fund.   □ William J. Eaton

See also **Democratic Party; Elections.**

Rhode Island. See **State government.**

Roman Catholic Church. Mother Theresa, a Roman Catholic nun who devoted her life to comforting the dying and aiding the poor, died on Sept. 5, 1997, in Calcutta, India, at the age of 87. Mother Theresa had founded a religious order of nuns, the Congregation of the Missionaries of Charity, in 1950 and served as its leader until March 1997, when she was succeeded by Sister Nirmala. Mother Theresa was honored worldwide for her compassion for and service to the neediest and most neglected people.

Apology to French Jews. On September 30, Archbishop Olivier de Berranger of the Roman Catholic Church in France apologized to French Jews for the church's silence during World War II (1939-1945). The archbishop issued the apology at a ceremony in Drancy, a French city from which about 76,000 Jews were sent to Nazi death camps in Germany. In his address, de Berranger claimed that among Roman Catholics, "silence was the rule" during the German occupation of France.

Excommunication of theologian. In January 1997, the Vatican excommunicated Sri Lankan Tissa Balasuriya, a Roman Catholic priest and well-known theologian, on the grounds of *heresy* (holding beliefs contrary to church teachings). The Vatican had imposed sanctions against Balasuriya in 1996 when he refused to recant statements he made on doctrinal matters. In his publications, Balasuriya had challenged the church's teachings on veneration of Mary, ordination of women, the uniqueness of Jesus Christ as the redeemer, and *original sin* (belief that sin is a natural condition inherited from Adam).

In spite of Balasuriya's appeal to the pope, the Vatican severed his tie to the church—the harshest action taken against any Roman Catholic theologian during the papacy of Pope John Paul II. In response to the ruling, some Roman Catholics called for reforms in the church's due process procedures.

Chicago's new Archbishop. On April 8, 1997, the Vatican appointed Archbishop Francis E. George of Portland, Oregon, to head the Roman Catholic Archdiocese of Chicago, the second largest archdiocese in the United States. George, 60, succeeded Joseph Cardinal Bernardin, who died on Nov. 14, 1996. George was known among Roman Catholics as a conservative on matters of theology and church doctrine, but a moderate on social issues. He was formally installed as archbishop on May 6, 1997.

Sexual abuse case. A jury on July 14 awarded 11 plaintiffs $118 million in a sexual abuse case brought against former parish priest Rudolph Kos and the Roman Catholic Diocese of Dallas. Kos was found liable before the trial, because he did not respond to the suits. The jurors found the diocese guilty of gross negligence, fraud, and reckless disregard for the safety of others. Kos was accused of sexually molesting minors over a period of 12 years. Diocesan officials were accused of failing to heed warnings of Kos's conduct and of concealing evidence after complaints were filed.

John Paul II visits Paris. In a visit to Paris in mid-August, Pope John Paul II drew large crowds as he continued his world travels, despite the infirmities of advancing age. The pope, 77, visited Paris to participate in World Youth Day festivities, a gathering of approximately 500,000 youth from 160 nations. The activities of the six-day event included the half-million young people, hand-in-hand, forming a ring around the city. On the final day of the papal visit, the pope celebrated the mass with estimates of about 1 million people in attendance. In his address, he stated that the faithful youth would "receive the enlightenment needed to build the civilization of love, to help our brothers and sisters to see the world transfigured by eternal wisdom and love."

Teachings about Mary. Joaquin Navarro-Valls, a Vatican spokesperson, announced on August 18 that the church would not consider new proclamations about the doctrine of Mary. The announcement was a response to requests to the pope by some conservative Roman Catholics to proclaim Mary *coredemptrix* (coredeemer), *mediatrix* (mediator), and advocate. Such changes in church doctrine would be a significant turn from tradition by attributing roles to Mary that the church teaches as belonging only to Jesus Christ.   □ Thomas C. Fox

See also **Religion; Roman Catholic Church** Special Report: **Mother Theresa—Saint of the Gutters.**

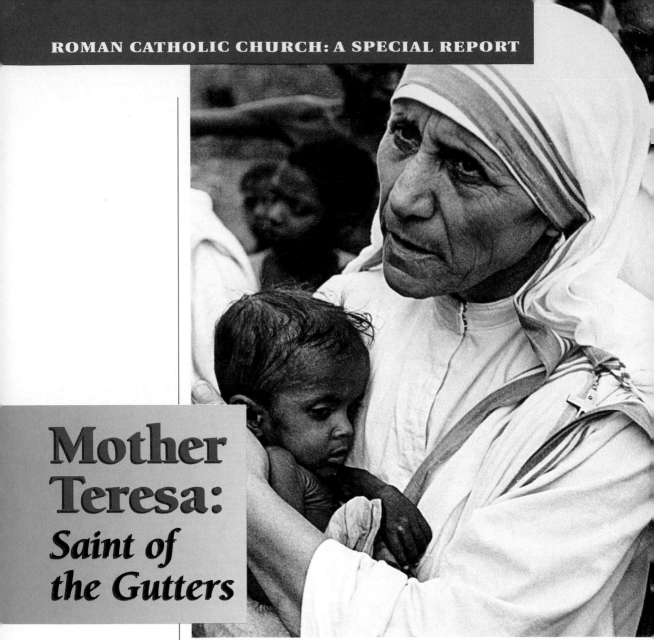

Mother Teresa:
Saint of the Gutters

The author

Jennifer Parello is a Managing Editor with World Book Annuals.

Mother Teresa, a Roman Catholic nun who devoted her life to helping the poorest of the poor, once said that she did not fear death because "I see it all the time." From the 1950's until her death at age 87 on Sept. 5, 1997, Mother Teresa served the diseased, the destitute, and the dying, mainly in the slums of Calcutta, India. Through her efforts, seriously ill people received medical care, hungry children were fed, and those people who might otherwise have died frightened and alone spent the final hours of life cradled in the tiny nun's arms.

Mother Teresa's work and her extraordinary success at fund-raising for that work brought her to a level of media attention usually reserved for heads of state and film stars. Her deeply lined face framed by a blue-bordered sari came to symbolize the plight of the poor and the desperate. Yet, despite her fame, Mother Teresa spent much of her life out of the reach of the spotlight, ministering to society's outcasts in some of the darkest corners on Earth.

Mother Teresa was honored by people of all religious affiliations and economic backgrounds for the compassionate and effective way she provided care and comfort to the desperately poor and sick. Her admirers—from Diana, Princess of Wales, to former Haitian dictator Jean-Claude (Baby Doc) Duvalier—called her "a living saint." She referred to herself as a mere instrument in God's hands. "I am like a little pencil in [God's] hands," she said. "He does the thinking. He does the writing. The pencil has only to be allowed to be used."

During a lifetime devoted to charity, she founded a Christian order, health clinics, orphanages, centers for the malnourished, rehabilitation centers, homes for alcoholics and drug addicts, treatment centers for AIDS patients, shelters for the homeless and battered women, and hospices for the dying in countries across the world. However, Mother Teresa, the woman who Indians called a "saint of the gutters" also had her critics. She was criticized for her practice of accepting donations from anyone who offered to help the needy and for her condemnation of both abortion and contraception. Few people, however, questioned her dedication or sincerity.

A call to the slums

Mother Teresa was born Agnes Gonxha Bojaxhiu, the daughter of an Albanian building contractor, on Aug. 26, 1910, in what is now Macedonia. Childhood friends, who called her "Nana Loke" (mother of my spirit), were not surprised when at age 12 Agnes announced her intention of becoming a nun. At age 18, Agnes joined the Sisters of Loreto, a religious order in Ireland, where she became known as Sister Teresa. She chose the name Teresa in honor of the French saint Therese of Lisieux, renowned for her goodness, piety, and courage in the face of illness and death.

After two months in Ireland, Teresa was sent to India, where she spent 17 years as a teacher and then principal of a Calcutta high school for privileged girls. In 1946, during a train ride to a religious retreat, Teresa received "a call within a call." She later related that God had ordered her to leave the school and move into the slums of Calcutta. "I was to give up all," she later wrote in her 1995 book *A Simple Path*, "and follow Jesus into the slums."

The call came at a time of revolutionary change in India. British colonial rule of the country ended in 1947, creating an independent

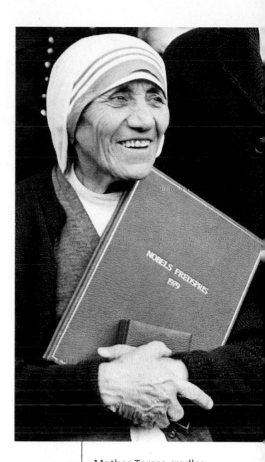

Mother Teresa cradles the Nobel Prize for Peace following the 1979 awards ceremony in Stockholm, Sweden. She received the prize for combating poverty and distress, which "also constitute a threat to peace."

India and Pakistan and spurring religious warfare between Hindus and Muslims. One million refugees flooded into India and onto the already crowded streets of Calcutta from the newly created state of Pakistan, triggering widespread disease and poverty.

Sister Teresa became Mother Teresa in 1950, after receiving permission from Pope Pius XII to move into the slums of Calcutta and establish her own religious order. A dozen nuns joined the newly formed Congregation of the Missionaries of Charity. During the next 47 years, her order grew to include 5,000 nuns and brothers operating more than 2,500 orphanages, clinics, and hospices in more than 120 countries, including the United States.

Mother Teresa insisted that nuns who joined the order pledge to serve the poor and needy in addition to taking vows of chastity, obedience, and poverty. The nuns of the order wore a white sari with blue trim, a habit designed by Mother Teresa.

One of the first projects the order undertook was the establishment of an open-air school for slum children whose parents were too poor to send them to school. In 1952, Mother Teresa became interested in the care and comfort of the dying after she found a woman lying in a Calcutta street who had been nearly devoured by rats. "We tried to get someone to take her to a hospital," said Sister Agnes, a long-time associate of Mother Teresa, "but before we could, she died. Mother said there should be a place where people can die with dignity and know that they are wanted."

Building shelters for the dying became Mother Teresa's signature endeavor. The first shelter, located in a shabby, one-story former hostel in Calcutta, was named Nirmal Hriday, or Home for the Dying. Mother Teresa persuaded Calcutta's municipal authorities to help finance the project—her first major success as a fund-raiser.

International acclaim

A motion-picture documentary released in 1969 on the work of Mother Teresa and the Missionaries of Charity brought Mother Teresa international attention as well as millions of dollars in donations. The donations allowed her to set up homes for abandoned children, leper colonies, soup kitchens, and a number of other charitable institutions. Mother Teresa regarded celebrity as the price for expanding her missionary programs.

In 1979, Mother Teresa received the Nobel Peace Prize because "poverty and distress also constitute a threat to peace." At her request, the banquet following the ceremony was canceled, and the $7,000 budgeted for the luncheon was given to the poor. She used the $190,000 that accompanied the prize—as well as all other donations and monetary awards that came to her—to fund projects for the needy. When Pope Paul VI gave Mother Teresa the limousine he had used during a visit to India, she sold it to finance a new leper colony.

Mother Teresa claimed never to worry about funding the many activities of her order. "Money is really no problem," she once explained. "We depend on divine providence. The Lord sends [money]. We do his work; he provides the means." When her order opened a center in New York City, the New York archdiocese offered to establish an endowment to finance the center. "I didn't want to hurt [Terence Cardinal Cooke, the cardinal who made the offer]," Mother Teresa said, "but I didn't know how to explain to him that our services are purely for the love of God and that we cannot accept maintenance. I expressed it the only way I could: 'Your Eminence, I don't think God is going to become bankrupt in New York City.'"

However, the funds did not come from prayer alone. Mother Teresa sought and accepted donations from many sources, a practice that occasionally drew harsh criticism. "Hell's Angel," a 1994 British television documentary that examined the life of Mother Teresa, claimed she accepted donations from unsavory individuals, which allowed infamous people to buy international respectability. Mother Teresa replied that she had no right to refuse donations given for the sick and poor.

Neither criticism nor age slowed the nun's pace. In 1982, when she was 72, Mother Teresa visited war-torn Beirut, Lebanon, walking across the front lines of battle to rescue dozens of children. A Red Cross official who observed Mother Teresa in action commented, "What stunned everyone was her energy. We didn't expect a saint to be so efficient."

In early 1990, Mother Teresa, who was suffering from heart disease, resigned as head of her order. At the election for a new head, members of the order could not decide on a successor and, so, reelected Mother Teresa to the post. In March 1997, Mother Teresa finally relinquished control as her health continued to decline.

After Mother Teresa died of heart failure in September, world leaders praised her for her work that transcended boundaries of religion and nationality. India, her adopted homeland, honored her with a state funeral. In Washington, D.C., the U.S. House of Representatives, which had awarded Mother Teresa the Congressional Gold Medal earlier in 1997, observed a moment of silence in her honor. At the Vatican in Rome, Pope John Paul II considered lifting her to sainthood by waiving the lengthy canonization process.

"By blood and origin I am Albanian," she once said. "My citizenship is Indian. I am a Catholic nun. As to my calling, I belong to the world. As to my heart, I belong entirely to the heart of Jesus." ∎ ∎ ∎

Nuns of the Missionaries of Charity, the order Mother Teresa founded, hold a vigil after her death on Sept. 5, 1997.

Romania

Romania. Non-Communists took control of Romania's government in 1997 for the first time since the dictatorship of Nicolae Ceaușescu fell in 1989. The new government quickly began to enact the promised broad slate of economic and social reforms that had swept it into power in November 1996.

Reforms. In February 1997, Prime Minister Victor Ciorbea launched a radical program of economic reform, drafted with the aid of the International Monetary Fund (IMF) and World Bank, two international economic organizations with ties to the United Nations. Romania reduced state subsidies to businesses, tightened monetary policy, doubled prices for energy, and deregulated food prices. A massive campaign was scheduled to privatize some 3,600 state companies by the end of 1997, and several large, inefficient factories were closed. Direct foreign investment increased dramatically to $190 million in January and February. In April, Romania secured $960 million in loans from the IMF and the World Bank.

In July 1997, the government passed a law granting ethnic Hungarians in Romania the right to use the Hungarian language in dealings with local government officials and in education at all levels. The Hungarian Democratic Union, representing ethnic Hungarians—a substantial minority in Romania, was a junior partner in the ruling center-right coalition. Ethnic Hungarian ministers were given the portfolios of minority affairs and tourism in the new cabinet.

Economy. The new government's economic policies led to a 25-percent decline in personal income in 1997, while prices for many goods doubled by mid-year. However, unemployment, which reached 8.7 percent in early 1997, dropped to 6.9 percent in September. Inflation, which reached 30.8 percent in March, declined to 3.3 percent in September. The volatility led to sporadic strikes and protests. However, the president and prime minister continued to enjoy firm public support. The government increased social assistance payments to buffer the transition.

Foreign affairs. General Ioan Talpes, head of Romania's foreign intelligence service, resigned in July, after a Swiss diplomat was arrested in Switzerland for spying for Romania. The incident revealed a Romanian intelligence operation that was trying to trace funds allegedly embezzled by Romania's former Communist regime and hidden in Swiss banks.

Relations between Romania and Hungary improved in 1997. Hungarian President Arpad Goncz visited Romania in May, the first time that a Romanian leader entertained a Hungarian head of state. In October, the two nations agreed to create four new border crossings and improve road and rail links between their countries.

In 1997, Romania failed to be included in the first wave of NATO expansion. However, several NATO members, including France, Italy, and Greece, supported Romania's bid. □ Sharon L. Wolchik

See also **Europe** (Facts in brief table); **Hungary.**

Russia. President of Russia Boris Yeltsin began 1997 with a case of double pneumonia. However, by spring Yeltsin's health had dramatically improved, and he actively reasserted control over the Russian political scene. A reorganized and reinvigorated government attempted in 1997 to breathe new life into political and economic reforms that in 1996 had appeared to have run out of steam.

Yeltsin required 12 days of hospitalization in January 1997, just weeks after he had returned to work following heart bypass surgery in November 1996. The president's return to the hospital prompted opposition leaders like Gennadiy Zyuganov, who lost to Yeltsin in the 1996 presidential election, to call for the president's resignation on grounds of ill health.

By March 1997, however, Yeltsin returned to work and wasted little time in announcing his dissatisfaction with the current workings of the Russian government. In a speech to parliament on March 6, Yeltsin announced that he would be shaking up his Cabinet and launching a new program to establish "order based on law." Within two weeks, Yeltsin appointed two new deputy prime ministers—Anatoliy Chubais and Boris Nemtsov—to restart stalled economic and political reforms.

Chubais and Nemtsov had both risen to prominence after the collapse of the Soviet Union in 1991. Observers in Moscow, the capital, noted that while Chubais and Nemtsov served under Prime Minister Viktor Chernomyrdin, both appointees had Yeltsin's full support and confidence and could, therefore, act with great autonomy.

Chubais, who was also appointed finance minister, had until 1995 managed the Russian program to privatize the country's vast network of state-owned industrial enterprises. Chubais, as privatization chief, had permitted a small network of bankers and industrialists to amass great fortunes, even as many industrial workers were forced to go without pay. He became a favorite target of Communist and nationalist politicians, who blamed many of Russia's ills on a mismanaged "giveaway" of the nation's wealth through hasty privatization. In the wake of the Communist Party's victories in the December 1995 parliamentary elections, Chubais had been forced from the government.

However, Chubais's connections with bankers and financiers had proved instrumental in enabling him to salvage Yeltsin's faltering 1996 presidential campaign. By successfully managing Yeltsin's reelection bid, Chubais had ensured his own political comeback. Western investors and businessmen, who appreciated his commitment to liberal market principles and tight fiscal controls, hailed Chubais's March 1997 return to the government.

Boris Nemtsov rose to prominence as the governor of the Nizhniy Novgorod region. Despite the region's history as a center of defense industries, Nemtsov had managed to transform it into a showplace of economic reforms. By appointing Nemtsov to a top cabinet position, Yeltsin brought into the government a reformer with practical experience beyond Moscow's usual corridors of power. Nemtsov had notable success as a politician, such as handily winning reelection as governor in 1995, and there was speculation that Yeltsin might be grooming Nemtsov as a successor.

The challenges facing Nemtsov and Chubais in 1997 were so complex that Nemtsov likened the appointment to that of a suicide mission with little chance of survival. Nemtsov focused primarily on reforming the heavily subsidized housing and energy sectors. Chubais launched a plan aimed at improving Russia's dismal performance in collecting taxes and reforming the freewheeling banking system. By the end of 1997, they had won a series of political battles connected to the budget. But more fundamental reforms, including a new tax code, remained elusive.

In November 1997, Chubais became the center of a political scandal when it was revealed that he and three other government officials had each received a $90,000 advance for contributing to a book on Russia's privatization effort. The money had come from a publishing company with ties to a top bank that had purchased substantial amounts of former state property in privatization auctions, which were under Chubais's authority. Yeltsin moved quickly to resolve the controversy, relieving Chubais and Nemtsov as finance minister and energy minister, respectively. Both men, however, retained their far more powerful positions as deputy prime ministers.

Political opposition to Yeltsin's revitalized government was weak and disorganized. The Communist Party, led by Gennadiy Zyuganov, was incensed by the appointment of the new reformers to the cabinet, but could not agree on an effective strategy of protest. In October, the Communists attempted to organize a vote of no confidence against the government over the proposed 1998 budget. However, they abandoned the effort when Yeltsin threatened to dissolve the parliament. Under the Russian constitution, the president was not required to change the government after a vote of no confidence in parliament, but could force new parliamentary elections instead. Zyuganov feared that the Communists would lose valuable seats in the *Duma* (the lower house of Russia's parliament) in such elections.

While the Duma wielded little power over the president, Yeltsin faced greater challenges from some regional officials, including Yevgeniy Nazdratenko, the governor of Primorye, Russia's far eastern maritime province. Widespread corruption was strangling Primorye's economy, and mismanagement of the energy sector had led to cutoffs of heating supplies during the winter of 1996-1997. Yeltsin's attempts to remove Nazdratenko from office were unsuccessful, mainly because Nazdratenko was a popular governor. Other governors also feared that Naz-

dratenko's removal by Yeltsin would establish a precedent that could later be used against them. Although Yeltsin stripped Nazdratenko of some powers in June, the showdown was a reminder of the federal government's uncertain reach.

Yeltsin faced a constant reminder of the limits of federal power even within Moscow. On several occasions in 1997, Moscow's mayor, Yuri Luzhkov, openly defied federal decrees and regulations, essentially exempting Moscow from elements of reform in areas of housing and taxation. These measures gained Luzhkov the solid support of most Moscow residents, and many observers felt he was preparing himself for a future presidential bid. In September 1997, Luzhkov presided over the celebration of Moscow's 850th anniversary. The lavish festivities and the massive building projects undertaken by Luzhkov's government since 1992 demonstrated the independent power of Moscow's mayor.

Economic oligarchy. Russian political and economic life continued to be dominated by a small group of bankers and businessmen who controlled vast financial, industrial, and media empires across Russia. In 1995, a group of these bankers had agreed to make large loans to the federal government in return for control over the government's shares in Russia's largest companies. Beginning in 1996 and continuing in 1997, the bankers were able to purchase these shares at below-market prices, enabling them to gain control over some of the world's largest conglomerates. A few of these financiers capitalized on their wealth to secure prominent positions in the Yeltsin administration.

During 1997, however, the united front of these tycoons began to crumble. In July, the sale of the national telecommunications monopoly, Svyazinvest, prompted charges of favoritism and collusion between government officials and the winning bidders. A fight erupted and was aired in the newspapers and on television, as rival industrialists traded slanders through the media outlets they owned.

In November, Boris Berezovsky, one of Russia's wealthiest businessmen and a part owner of Russia's largest national television network, was fired from his post on Russia's Security Council. Observers suggested that Nemtsov and Chubais were taking advantage of the disunity among Russia's new tycoons to consolidate control over the government.

Economy. The Russian economy showed signs of growth during 1997 for the first time since the Soviet Union collapsed in 1991. The ruble remained essentially stable, with only moderate inflation. In August 1997, the government announced that it would redenominate the Russian currency on Jan. 1, 1998, by removing three zeroes from all ruble notes. The move indicated the government's faith that the devastating inflationary period, which began in 1992, was ending. The sharp rise of Russia's stock market, which began shortly before Boris Yeltsin's reelection

Workers complete the reconstruction of Moscow's Christ the Savior Cathedral in August 1997, in time for its scheduled rededication during the city's 850th anniversary in September. Soviet dictator Josef Stalin had pulled down the original cathedral in 1931.

in mid-1996, ended in November 1997, when stock prices fell by as much as 40 percent.

Relations with NATO. When officials of the North Atlantic Treaty Organization (NATO), a military alliance of 16 Western European and North American nations, made it clear in 1997 that they intended to invite former allies of the Soviet Union to join the Western alliance, Yeltsin vigorously opposed NATO's eastward push. He warned that the inclusion of former Soviet republics such as the Baltic republics of Latvia, Lithuania, and Estonia in NATO would be totally unacceptable to Russia. However, on May 27, Yeltsin went to Paris to sign the "Founding Act on Mutual Relations" with NATO. The agreement established a permanent joint council to discuss European security arrangements. Yeltsin indicated that he had accepted the inevitability of NATO expansion and declared that the agreement would "promote stability throughout Europe." American officials were quick to claim that the document did not give Russia any sort of veto over NATO actions.

International relations. Yeltsin signed important agreements in May with the two largest republics on Russia's western border, Belarus and Ukraine. On May 23, he signed a charter of political and economic union with Belarus. However, the Belarusian treaty stopped far short of the political integration and monetary union that both sides had earlier anticipated.

A week later, Yeltsin made a long-awaited visit to Kiev to sign a treaty of friendship with the president of Ukraine. The pact became possible only after the two countries agreed on a plan to jointly control the Black Sea Fleet. Russia and Ukraine had argued over which country owned the fleet ever since the Soviet Union broke up in 1991.

With his health restored, Yeltsin made a series of international diplomatic trips in 1997. In March, he met with United States President Bill Clinton in Helsinki, Finland, and in June he attended a summit of industrialized nations in Denver, Colorado. In November, Yeltsin visited China to sign a border demarcation treaty and to discuss expanding economic ties between the two large countries.

Religion. Russia drew widespread international criticism in September 1997, when Yeltsin signed a new law on the status of religions in Russia. The law, which was sought by the Russian Orthodox Church, was particularly aimed against missionary activity by dissident Orthodox congregations, Roman Catholics, evangelical Christians, and other groups. It gave higher status to religions that had been officially recognized in Russia for at least 15 years than to religions or sects either not recognized under Soviet rule or introduced since 1991. Critics feared the law could be used to strip legal status from certain religious groups.   □ Steven L. Solnick

See also **Belarus; Eastern Orthodox Churches; Europe** (Facts in brief table); **Ukraine.**

Rwanda. An upsurge in violence between the Tutsi and Hutu in 1997 inflicted severe hardships on Rwandans and blocked any hope of economic recovery. In early 1997, hundreds of people died in clashes between forces of the Tutsi-dominated government and Hutu guerrillas in northwestern Rwanda. The clashes occurred in the wake of the return of more than 1 million Hutu refugees from Zaire (renamed Democratic Republic of Congo) and Tanzania in late 1996. In December 1997, Hutu guerrillas attacked a Tutsi camp in northwestern Rwanda and killed at least 272 people.

UN Trials. Both the government of Rwanda and the United Nations (UN) in 1997 began trying more than 120,000 imprisoned Hutu for involvement in the 1994 *genocide* (extermination of a racial or cultural group) of Tutsi. By December 1997, Rwandan courts had heard only about 200 cases. Approximately 80 of the accused were sentenced to death. Sixty men received sentences of life in prison. The judicial process was hampered by a severe shortage of defense lawyers and the intimidation and murder of witnesses by Hutu militants. Critics charged the UN court with corruption, inefficiency, and lacking the cooperation of neighboring governments, which were slow to hand over suspects.   □ Mark DeLancey

See also **Africa** (Facts in brief table); **Africa** Special Report: **The Hutu and Tutsi; Congo (Kinshasa)**

Sailing. See Boating.

San Francisco. In 1997, San Francisco continued to experience an economic and population boom, thanks to an increase in jobs in growing businesses, such as multimedia products, film, and tourism. Many affluent younger adults, working in the computer industry in the region south of the city known as the Silicon Valley, continued to move into San Francisco to take advantage of the city's cultural and entertainment resources.

While such growth benefited the city, residents of San Francisco, famous for its Victorian single-family houses, became acutely aware in 1997 of the lack of affordable housing for middle- and low-income residents. With an unprecedented rental vacancy rate of only 1 percent and a growing average income per person, the cost of housing in San Francisco rose 20 percent between the summers of 1996 and 1997. The number of houses for sale in the same period dropped to a record low, creating sharp price increases in an already inflated market.

Bicycle battles. Critical Mass, a bicycling program intended to remind motorists of alternative forms of transportation and to promote safety for bicyclists, drew attention to the challenges of the city's population density. Since the program's beginning in 1992, it had been more a monthly event than an organization, with bicyclists riding along major commuter routes. In 1997, however, Critical Mass frequently slowed and sometimes snarled traffic dur-

Morning rush-hour traffic into San Francisco on Sept. 8, 1997, backs up across the Bay Bridge to Oakland, California, because of a strike by Bay Area Rapid Transit workers. The six-day strike created the worst traffic delays in the city's history.

ing peak commuting hours. Mayor Willie L. Brown, Jr., threatened to impound bicycles and arrest riders who did not comply with police-escort routes, after a particularly unruly ride in June. The mayor's criticism only fanned the flames. On July 25, an estimated 5,000 to 10,000 bicyclists protested the mayor's edict by disregarding the designated route. The result was traffic gridlock and violence that led to more than 250 arrests. After the July incident, Critical Mass events resumed the peaceful and orderly pattern of earlier rides.

Transit strike. In September, a six-day strike by Bay Area Rapid Transit (BART) workers shut down the city's main commuter rail service. Alternative forms of transportation—ferries, buses, and carpools—were overwhelmed, and traffic jams were labeled the "worst in Bay Area history." Because of chronic problems with several public transportation organizations, many commuters felt the strike—which ended favorably according to union leaders—was inconvenient and irresponsible.

The Golden Gate National Recreation Area, a group of parks throughout the San Francisco area, was the focus of heated debates in 1997. In January, 2 miles (3.2 kilometers) of Ocean Beach, part of the recreation area on the city's Pacific Coast, was closed to off-leash dogs in order to protect the roosting areas of the Western snowy plover, an endangered bird. Dog sympathizers protested that the ban was issued without any public hearings on the matter.

An ongoing debate also continued in 1997 over another part of the national park, the Presidio, a closed military base near the Golden Gate Bridge. Special-interest groups rallied in support of various proposals for the area—from housing for the homeless to reclaimed wetlands.

49ers stadium. In June, voters narrowly approved funding of a new $525-million stadium for the city's professional football team, the 49ers. Proponents of the new state-of-the-art arena promised the creation of jobs and economic improvements in the depressed area where the facility was to be built. The campaign for the stadium came with a hefty price as well—about $22 per San Francisco voter. After the victory, accusations arose about questionable voting procedures, including opening some polling places a week early, double-voting, and using the names of deceased persons to vote. By late 1997, the voting process for the stadium was under investigation by federal, state, and local authorities.

Herbert Caen, a journalist for the *San Francisco Chronicle,* died at the age of 80 on February 1. Caen, who had written a column about life in the city since 1938, was best known for his "three-dot" style—a brief coverage of topics, usually gossip or entertainment, separated by three periods.   □ Brian Bouldrey

See also **City.**

Saskatchewan. See **Canadian provinces.**

Saudi Arabia. Increasing unemployment and a growing population fueled concerns in 1997 about Saudi Arabia's future stability. The unemployment rate for Saudi nationals was unofficially estimated at 20 percent in 1997. Population pressures caused the government to place a greater emphasis in 1997 on a five-year plan designed to create 659,000 new jobs for Saudis by the year 2000—mainly by replacing foreigners in private-sector jobs with Saudi nationals. Foreigners held nearly 93 percent of private-sector jobs in 1997. Critics said the five-year plan was inadequate because it was not designed to create enough jobs for the 1.6 million young Saudis expected to be entering the work force by 2000.

Bombing investigation. In January 1997, U.S. government officials criticized the Saudis for failing to cooperate fully in the investigation of the June 25, 1996, terrorist bombing of a U.S. airbase in Dhahran, Saudi Arabia. The bombing killed 19 U.S. military personnel and wounded more than 380 other people. United States investigators believed that the Saudis had evidence that the bombing was the work of Saudi extremists who had been aided by Iran's government and trained by Lebanon's pro-Iranian Hezbollah (Party of God). Some experts claimed that the Saudis were reluctant to cooperate because they did not want to antagonize Iran.

In March 1997, Canada arrested a Saudi named Hani Abdel Rahim al-Sayegh as a suspected lookout in the bombing. Canadian officials said that Sayegh belonged to Saudi Hezbollah, a small dissident group associated with Iran. Sayegh, who agreed to help in the bombing probe in exchange for pleading guilty to lesser charges and not being returned to Saudi Arabia, was deported to the United States in June. However, after arriving in the United States, he refused to cooperate. In September, the United States dropped charges against him and began the process to deport him, possibly to Saudi Arabia.

Diplomatic crisis. The 1997 murder convictions of two female British nurses by a Saudi court led to a diplomatic crisis between Saudi Arabia and Great Britain. The women were convicted of the 1996 killing in Dhahran of an Australian nurse. One nurse was sentenced to eight years in prison and 500 lashes. The other faced a verdict of death by beheading. British officials strongly protested the sentences. In October 1997, the slain nurse's family said that they would accept financial compensation in order to spare the convicted women such punishments.

Tragedy. On April 15, more than 340 people were killed and about 1,500 injured when a fire swept through a tent city erected near Mecca to house Muslims, mostly from Bangladesh, India, and Pakistan, attending the annual *hajj* or Islamic pilgrimage. A gas cooking stove was the source of the fire, which spread quickly due to strong winds. □ Christine Helms

See also **Islam; Middle East** (Facts in brief table).
School. See Education.
Senegal. See Africa.

Sierra Leone. Sierra Leone was buoyed early in 1997 by its steady progress toward political stability and improved economic conditions. Democratic elections in 1996 had replaced a military regime with a civilian government, and a cease-fire had ended a five-year civil war. By the end of 1997, however, Sierra Leone had reverted to a state of civil strife and economic chaos.

Return of war. The peace agreement between the government, headed by President Ahmed Tejan Kabbah, and the rebel Revolutionary United Front (RUF), led by Foday Sankoh, began to unravel in February. The government reported intercepting a message from Sankoh in which he ordered his troops to attack national forces. On March 15, high-ranking officers in the RUF announced that Sankoh had been deposed. Later that month, fighting broke out between the RUF's rival factions.

On May 25, a group of junior military officers led by Major Johnny Paul Koromah seized control of the government. Kabbah fled to neighboring Guinea. In a surprising move, Koromah immediately offered to share power with the RUF, and on May 27, RUF troops entered Freetown, Sierra Leone's capital. Following the *coup* (overthrow), Koromah announced the formation of a governing Armed Forces Revolutionary Council that included Sankoh.

Nigerian intervention. In response to the upheaval, Nigeria stepped up its presence in Sierra Leone. Nigeria had commanded a peacekeeping force from the Economic Community of West African States (ECOWAS) in Sierra Leone since 1994. On May 27, 1997, Nigeria moved another 900 soldiers into Freetown. Fighting between ECOWAS troops and RUF forces and Koromah's backers broke out on June 2 after Nigerian warships in Freetown's harbor bombarded the rebels' headquarters and ECOWAS forces attacked the airport.

On June 3, the Organization of African Unity authorized the Nigerian-led peacekeeping force to use "appropriate" action to reinstate Sierra Leone's civilian government. ECOWAS also imposed a trade embargo that included food. Talks to end the embargo faltered in late July after Koromah reneged on his June promise to restore democratic government as soon as possible. He said the regime would not hold elections before 2001. After bombing attacks by Nigeria in October, Koromah agreed to restore Kabbah to power in April 1998.

By December 1997, Sierra Leone had reverted to stalemate. In rural areas, RUF soldiers and bandits terrorized residents, who also suffered from food shortages. Hundreds of thousands of Sierra Leoneans—who had fled to Guinea, Gambia, and Liberia during the civil war and had returned when Kabbah was elected—fled again. □ Mark DeLancey

See also **Africa** (Facts in brief table); **Nigeria.**
Singapore. See Asia.
Skating. See Hockey; Ice skating; Sports.

Italy's Deborah Compagnoni turns in one of two gold medal-winning performances at the World Alpine Ski Championships in Italy in February.

Skiing. The World Cup professional season ended on a historic note at Vail, Colorado, in March 1997, when Luc Alphand became the first Frenchman to win the men's overall World Cup championship since Jean-Claude Killy in 1968. With his victory, Alphand also became the first downhill specialist to win the overall title since Austria's Karl Schranz in 1970.

World Cup. Alphand's success was all the more impressive because he competed in only two alpine skiing disciplines—downhill (in which he was a three-time world champion) and the super-giant slalom (super-G). However, in June 1997, Alphand retired from skiing, announcing that he would not compete in the 1998 Winter Olympics in Nagano, Japan. Sweden's Pernilla Wiberg captured her first women's World Cup overall title with 1,960 points—a World Cup record. Her nearest rival, Germany's Katja Seizinger, won silver medals in the giant slalom and super-G. Thomas Sykora of Austria won the men's World Cup overall slalom title in decisive fashion, winning 5 of the season's 10 slalom events.

Alpine champions. The World Alpine Ski Championships were held Feb. 3 through Feb. 15, 1997, in Sestiere, Italy. Deborah Compagnoni of Italy led the women with gold medals in both the slalom and giant slalom. Hilary Lindh of Juneau, Alaska, gave the United States its second consecutive downhill world title. In March, Lindh also announced her retirement.

Italy's Isolde Kostner won the gold in the super-G, and Renate Goetschi of Austria won the gold in the combined event.

Also at Sestiere, Bruno Kernen of Switzerland won the gold medal in the downhill, and Sebastien Amiez won the silver. Italy's Alberto Tomba pleased thousands of his local fans with a brilliant second run that earned him the downhill bronze. Tomba battled illness and a broken wrist in the 1996-1997 season. Switzerland's Michael Von Gruenigen won the giant slalom, and Tom Stiansen of Norway took the slalom competition. Atle Skaardal of Norway won the super-G title, and another Norwegian, Kjetil-Andre Aamodt, won the gold medal in the combined race.

Other champions. Norway's Bjorn Daehlie and Elena Valbe of Russia dominated cross-country skiing in 1997. Daehlie ran his career victory total to 36 and took the men's World Cup title for the fifth time. Valbe won five gold medals at the Nordic world championships in Trondheim, Norway, earning her fifth World Cup crown.

Freestyle skier Kirstie Marshall brought Australia its first championship in winter sports by winning the World Cup aerials title. Canada's Jean-Luc Brassard took the World Cup title in men's moguls for the third time. Primoz Peterka, an 18-year-old from Slovenia, won both the World Cup ski-jumping and ski-flying championships.   □ Ron Reid

Slovakia. In May 1997, a national referendum on whether Slovakia should join the North Atlantic Treaty Organization (NATO), a military alliance of 16 Western European and North American nations, was declared invalid due to faulty procedures, the latest episode in a political battle between Prime Minister Vladimir Mečiar and opposition forces. An election commission declared the referendum invalid because it was supposed to have included a question on permitting direct presidential elections.

Political strife. In March 1997, Slovak President Michal Kovač declared that a May referendum on NATO membership would include a question on making the presidency a directly elected office. Slovakia's constitution specified that the president was elected by the parliament. Kovač's term was due to expire in February 1998, but no party or coalition in the Slovak parliament held enough seats to elect a president. Most Slovak leaders believed that the situation would result in a deadlock that could last from February to September 1998, when the next national elections were scheduled. The opposition feared that, without a president in office for six months, Mečiar would expand his power as prime minister.

In April 1997, Mečiar's cabinet appealed to Slovakia's Constitutional Court on the legality of using a referendum to change how a president is elected. On May 22, the court ruled that the question could be included in the referendum but stated that a constitutional amendment would be needed to permit direct presidential elections. The presidential election question was removed from the ballot. As a result, only 10 percent of registered voters turned out for the referendum, which made the vote invalid. In June 1997, five opposition parties overcame years of internal conflict to form a strong coalition. This coalition was potentially a serious challenge to Mečiar's ruling coalition in the 1998 national elections.

Slovakia's economy continued to grow in 1997, but the federal deficit and foreign debt rose significantly. Gross domestic product grew by an estimated 4.6 percent in 1997. Inflation, which stood at 5.8 percent in January, increased to 6.5 percent in August. Unemployment was 12.45 percent in July. Foreign investment totaled $1.05 billion in late March.

NATO and the EU. Slovakia was not invited to join NATO in July 1997. Officials of NATO and the European Union (EU), an alliance of European countries, had criticized the government's manipulation of the referendum. They also criticized the government's apparent disregard for the constitution, treatment of the Hungarian minority, and lack of respect for the rights of the opposition. However, the government refused in July to enact changes that the EU had suggested as conditions for including Slovakia as a future EU member. As a result, Slovakia was also excluded from EU expansion talks scheduled for 1998. □ Sharon L. Wolchik

See also **Europe** (Facts in brief table).

Soccer in 1997 was highlighted by South Africa's joyous advance to its first World Cup final and the fourth-straight women's world championship won by the United States. For the second year in a row, D.C. United took the Major League Soccer (MLS) championship in the United States, and Borussia Dortmund of Germany won the European Cup, the continent's most prestigious club tournament.

While the MLS tried with varying success to establish itself as a major professional sports league, critics abroad complained that with three European Cup competitions—consisting of a record 181 teams—the game's standards and quality had been diminished. Many of the year's most thrilling matches came in qualifying competition for the World Cup final, scheduled to be played in France in 1998.

Major League Soccer. Shortly after the MLS opened its regular 1997 season, which ran from March 22 through September 28, the league announced it would expand from 10 to 12 teams in 1998, with the addition of franchises in Miami and Chicago. The MLS, through the first 40 games of 1997, drew an average attendance of 15,800 per game—6,200 less than in its 1996 inaugural season.

On July 9, 1997, the MLS All-Star game drew nearly 25,000 fans to Giants Stadium, home of the troubled New York/New Jersey Metro Stars. Because soccer is best played on a grass field, every Metro Stars game required the installation of 6,124 trays of natural sod over the stadium's artificial turf-covered playing surface. The time required for resurfacing the playing field became the focus of a dispute between the team and the New Jersey Sports and Exposition Authority, which operated the stadium. The dispute turned into a black eye for the team and the MLS when the Metro Stars were forced to play their final four home games on the artificial turf.

The MLS championship game, played at Washington, D.C.'s RFK Stadium on October 26, drew a sellout crowd. More than 57,000 fans watched D.C. United defeat the Colorado Rapids by a score of 2-1.

U.S. Women's Cup. In June, the U.S. women's team took the U.S. Women's Cup championship with a 2-0 victory over Italy in the finals before a crowd of 11,200 people at RFK Stadium. The win extended the U.S. streak to 30 international games without a loss.

World Cup qualifying. South Africa earned its first trip to the World Cup finals with a 1-0 victory over Congo (Brazzaville) in Johannesburg, South Africa, on August 16. A frenzied crowd of 90,000 fans saw striker Phil Masinga score the game's only goal in the 14th minute of play.

Borussia Dortmund captured the European Cup in a 3-1 victory over an Italian team, Juventus of Turin. Schalke, another team from Germany's Ruhr Valley, beat Italy's Internationale Milan in the UEFA Cup final. Schalke won, 4-1, in a penalty shoot-out to claim its first European Cup trophy in 93 years.

□ Ron Reid

Social Security. The Advisory Council on Social Security recommended in January 1997 that the government invest a portion of social security tax funds in the stock market for the system to remain solvent through the year 2072. Investing in stocks involves a higher level of risk, but usually results in a higher return. Traditionally, social security tax funds are invested in safe, low-return government bonds.

Under various alternatives proposed to the U.S. Congress by the 13-member panel, between $1.2 trillion and $4.2 trillion would be shifted from U.S. Treasury securities to stocks by the year 2015. The panel was split over what level of financial risk was suitable. They were also divided over whether individuals or the government should have more control over social security investment decisions. However, panel members agreed that state and local workers should no longer be exempt from the social security payroll tax. The panel also agreed that U.S. income taxes should be increased on social security benefits that exceed a recipient's total lifetime contribution.

Internet access. The Social Security Administration announced plans in September 1997 to resume offering social security information on the Internet. Internet service was first offered in March but shut down in April over concern that information, such as a person's earnings history, could be obtained and misused. The new Internet site included safeguards to enhance personal privacy.   □ William J. Eaton

Somalia continued to be divided in 1997, as it had been since the outbreak of a civil war in 1991. While Somalia remained relatively peaceful in 1997, its warring factions made little progress in resolving their differences. In northern Somalia, President Mohammed Ibrahim Egal won reelection in February. In the south, militias or the elders of various clans controlled the countryside, while the Somali Salvation Alliance (SSA) and the Somali National Alliance (SNA) ruled Mogadishu, the capital. Clashes between these forces disrupted the city, and the airport and harbor remained closed.

Negotiations to establish a central authority for the south, which had begun in November 1996 in Ethiopia, continued into January 1997. On January 3, the leaders of 26 factions agreed to form a National Salvation Council to develop a transitional charter for a new government. The SNA refused to participate. However, the leaders of the SNA and the SSA agreed during talks held in Egypt in May to end their violence and restart peace talks.

Floods devastated southern Somalia in October and November, killing at least 2,000 people and leaving hundreds of thousands homeless. The raging water also destroyed the newly harvested sorghum crop, intensifying food shortages caused by drought earlier in the year.   □ Mark DeLancey

See also **Africa** (Facts in brief table).

South Africa. President Nelson Mandela, in his fourth state-of-the-nation address, on Feb. 7, 1997, identified three major problems facing South Africa. The first was a lack of financial resources that prevented the government from undertaking essential projects. The second was corruption in the civil service. The third was a weak economy unable to create the new jobs needed to reduce an unemployment rate stuck at about 40 percent. Mandela also called attention to the country's epidemic crime problem, which included what is likely the world's highest incidence of rape.

Healing wounds. Reconciling citizens of all races after years of *apartheid* (racial separation) also remained a daunting problem. In 1997, the Truth and Reconciliation Commission, headed by retired Anglican Archbishop Desmond Tutu, began to hear cases in public. The government-appointed commission had been created in 1995 to receive testimony about abuses under the country's former system of racial separation and to grant amnesty to those who confessed their crimes voluntarily. Because fewer than 200 of the more than 6,000 cases before the Truth and Reconciliation Commission had been heard, its mandate was extended beyond the original December 1997 deadline.

Among the major cases heard by the commission in 1997 were the 1977 torture and murder of anti-apartheid activist Steven Biko; the 1993 murder of Chris Hani, the leader of South Africa's Communist Party; and allegations that Winnie Madikizela-Mandela arranged killings of political foes during the late 1980's, when her then-husband Nelson Mandela was incarcerated on charges of conspiring to overthrow the government.

An official inquiry had concluded that the massive head injuries Biko suffered during a police interrogation were the result of an accident. In January 1997, however, a defense lawyer reported that five former police officers had admitted killing Biko. The five, against whom authorities had gathered mounting evidence, reportedly filed amnesty applications with the commission in order to avoid criminal prosecution.

In August, Janusz Walus and Clive Derby-Lewis, both former policemen, testified that they had shot Hani in order to throw South Africa into political chaos so the far right-wing could take control of the government. Although both men were serving life sentences for Hani's murder, they could be released if the Truth and Sentencing Commission concludes that they have told all they know about the murder and that they acted for political reasons.

In November, Madikizela-Mandela faced the Truth and Sentencing Committee, which delved into allegations that she had played a role in the murders of political foes. She was accused of persuading members of the Mandela United Football Club to help her discredit and assassinate political enemies.

De Klerk testifies. Former President Frederik Willem de Klerk also appeared before the commission. On May 14, de Klerk conceded that the government, controlled for 42 years by the National Party (NP), had spied on and unjustly imprisoned opponents of apartheid. But de Klerk denied that high government officials had ever approved assassination and murder. Commission members reported being "devastated" by de Klerk's refusal to take personal or political responsibility for violence against antiapartheid activists. On May 16, the NP said it would no longer cooperate with the commission, because the commission was biased against it.

Race and politics. In 1997, each major political party was supported almost exclusively by a particular race. In response to the NP's withdrawal from Mandela's national unity government in 1996, the African National Congress (ANC) attempted to expand its ruling coalition by negotiating with other parties. On Aug. 26, 1997, de Klerk announced his resignation as head of the NP to underscore, he said, the party's break with its racist past. He was succeeded by Marthinus van Schalkwyk. Thabo Mbeki became ANC party president after Mandela relinquished the post in December.   □ Mark DeLancey

See also **Africa** (Facts in brief table).

South America. See Latin America.
South Carolina. See State government.
South Dakota. See State government.

Space exploration in 1997 was marked by both triumphs and tribulations. Spacecraft photographed Jupiter, its moons, and an asteroid, explored Mars, and set off for Saturn. U.S. space shuttles flew eight missions. However, Russia's Mir space station experienced a spate of problems, triggering concern in the United States because a U.S. astronaut was aboard.

The first space shuttle mission of 1997 was flown by Atlantis, which carried astronaut and physician Jerry M. Linenger to Mir on January 12. Linenger replaced retired U.S. Air Force Colonel John E. Blaha, who returned with the shuttle to the Kennedy Space Center (KSC) in Florida on January 22.

The Russian space station, whose core module was launched in 1986, suffered a number of system failures in 1997. On February 23, an oxygen-producing canister caught fire. Although no one was hurt, the station filled with smoke, forcing the American, four Russians, and one German on board to don oxygen masks and wear filtration masks for two days, even while they slept. By late March, Mir was deemed safe enough for Linenger and station commander Vasili Tsibliyev to undertake a spacewalk. Linenger was the first U.S. astronaut to conduct a spacewalk in a Russian space suit.

Service call. The shuttle Discovery flew from KSC on February 11 to update science instruments on the Hubble Space Telescope. The crew alternated in five

Frederik Willem de Klerk, South Africa's last president under apartheid, announces his resignation as head of the National Party on August 26.

days of spacewalks to install the new equipment, which astronomers hoped would provide the farthest view into the universe—and thus the furthest look back in time. Discovery landed on February 21.

Spacelab. The shuttle Columbia was launched April 4 for a Spacelab mission. The flight was to have lasted 16 days, during which experiments, including up to 200 involving small fires to study combustion, were scheduled. However, one of the shuttle's three electricity-producing fuel cells malfunctioned, forcing Columbia to return to Earth after just four days in space. Columbia flew again on July 1—with the same crew and payloads—performing the experiments as planned and landing at KSC on July 17.

Collision in space. On May 15, the shuttle Atlantis flew C. Michael Foale, a British-born NASA astronaut, to Mir to replace Linenger. Atlantis returned to Earth May 24. On June 25, a Progress cargo spacecraft—a supply ship that had used an automated system to home in on Mir many times—struck Mir, damaging a set of solar arrays and puncturing Spektr, one of Mir's modules. Flight controllers had instructed cosmonaut Vasili Tsibliyev to test a manual device similar to a computer "joy stick" to control the Progress. However, the Progress approached too quickly. As a result of the collision, air inside Mir started to escape. The crew considered abandoning the station and returning to Earth in the Soyuz capsule docked to Mir. However, they managed to seal off Spektr.

In late August, two Russian cosmonauts who had replaced Tsibliyev and his partner on Mir on August 7 restored some of the power the station had lost in the accident. However, the cosmonauts, inspecting the module inside and out, could not find the leak. In addition, Mir's main computer failed five times between July and the end of September. NASA reconsidered keeping a U.S. astronaut aboard Mir but eventually determined that the station was safe. Foale was retrieved by the space shuttle Atlantis, which was launched on September 25 carrying Foale's replacement, astronaut David Wolf. Atlantis returned to KSC October 6.

The spacecraft NEAR (Near Earth Asteroid Rendezvous) photographed and measured Mathilde, an asteroid in a belt between Mars and Jupiter, as it passed the dark rock on June 27, 1997, at 22,000 miles (35,400 kilometers) per hour. NEAR, launched in 1996, flew one of a number of planetary missions whose purpose was to show that NASA can learn much even with small, inexpensive spacecraft. NEAR was to reach its target, the asteroid Eros, in 1999.

Mars Pathfinder, a small spacecraft weighing just 1,250 pounds (567 kilograms), landed on Mars on July 4, 1997, tethered to a parachute and protected by inflatable airbags. The base station was designed to photograph and analyze the surface and atmosphere of Mars for at least a month, and the Sojourner rover—about the size of a child's wagon—

was expected to last at least 10 days. Both pieces of hardware worked far longer, sending scientists on Earth detailed pictures of a diverse group of rocks in a plain where scientists believe water had once flowed on Mars. Pathfinder stopped transmitting data to Earth on September 27.

Goals of the August flight of the shuttle Discovery included atmospheric science experiments and the testing of a new Japanese robotic arm. The shuttle's crew also launched an ozone-mapping satellite and retrieved it—filled with data—before returning to KSC on August 19.

Mars Global Surveyor, launched in 1996, began to orbit Mars on Sept. 11, 1997. The spacecraft used a technique called *aerobraking* (using atmospheric friction to reduce speed) to lower the Surveyor's orbit, but because one solar array appeared to be broken, controllers had to proceed more slowly than planned. Surveyor was thus expected to begin its mapping mission in 1999, a year behind schedule. Surveyor did make a major discovery during its first week in Martian orbit—a magnetic field on Mars approximately $1/800$th as strong as Earth's.

Cassini/Huygens, a U.S.-European combination spacecraft, was launched on Oct. 15, 1997, from Cape Canaveral Air Force Station in Florida on a 2.2 billion-mile (3.5-billion-kilometer) voyage to Saturn. The $3-billion mission was the most complex and expensive planetary launch yet undertaken. The Cassini spacecraft, weighing more than 6 tons (5.4 metric tons), included an orbiter and a probe—Huygens—that was to land on Titan, Saturn's largest moon. The spacecraft was to twice loop close to Venus, pass Earth once, and then fly out to Jupiter to use gravity to sling itself faster toward Saturn, where it was due to arrive in July 2004.

A new Ariane 5 launch vehicle, largely developed by the French space agency, carried test satellites into orbit nearly a year and a half after the first Ariane 5 exploded on its maiden flight. The 740-ton (670-metric-ton) rocket lifted off from French Guiana on Oct. 30, 1997. Ariane 5's mission was declared a success, even though the test satellites were placed into orbit 5,600 miles (9,000 kilometers) lower than intended.

The final shuttle mission of 1997 was a 16-day flight by Columbia. Launched November 19, the mission included microgravity experiments and the first spacewalk by a Japanese astronaut. Takao Doi, an aerospace engineer from Tokyo, and his American partner, Winston Scott, captured a slowly spinning, malfunctioning satellite in their gloved hands. Columbia returned to Earth on December 5.

Work on the international space station fell behind schedule when Russia was late in providing critical components. NASA was forced to build expensive backup hardware and delay the launch of the first components to 1998. □ James R. Asker

See also **Astronomy.**

The U.S. space shuttle Atlantis, *below,* docks in May with the Russian space station, Mir, to deliver supplies and a new crew member, U.S. astronaut C. Michael Foale. Throughout 1997, Mir, *above,* experienced a series of mishaps that called into question the future of the aging space station.

Spain. The 30-year struggle between Spain and Basque separatists intensified in 1997. The separatists seek independence for the Basque region of northern Spain. The conservative government of Spain's Prime Minister José María Aznar, which took power in 1996, favors a strong central government over regional autonomy.

Supreme Court Judge Rafael Martínez Emperador was assassinated outside his house in Madrid, the capital, on Feb. 10, 1997. The government blamed the guerrilla group Basque Homeland and Freedom (abbreviated in Basque by the initials ETA) for the attack. The murder occurred while the Supreme Court investigated leaders of ETA's political wing, Herri Batasuna, about the party's use of an ETA videotape in their campaign during the 1996 parliamentary election. On Dec. 1, 1997, all 23 of the party's leaders were convicted of collaborating with ETA guerrillas for using the videotape and were sentenced to seven years in prison.

Outrage at slaying. Tensions escalated when the ETA kidnapped and killed Miguel Angel Blanco, a government official in the Basque town of Ermua, in July. The ETA had demanded that Basque prisoners be jailed in their native region, instead of in prisons throughout Spain. The government had refused the demand. After the assassination, several million people marched in cities around Spain to protest Basque violence, which had claimed approximately 800 lives since 1968. The ETA in November 1997 suspended all armed action on behalf of Basque inmates. In December, the Spanish government moved 15 of about 500 Basque inmates to prisons closer to the Basque region as a good-will gesture.

González cleared. The Supreme Court on September 30 ordered Spain's former interior minister, Jose Barrionuevo, and 11 other former officials to stand trial on charges of involvement with antiterrorist death squads. The squads allegedly had killed 27 people in a "dirty war" against Basque separatists in the 1980's. The court decided not to charge the former prime minister, Felipe González Márquez. Allegations of González's involvement in the death squads had contributed to the Socialists' defeat in the 1996 parliamentary election.

The economy performed strongly in 1997, raising Spain's hopes of joining the single European currency, scheduled to be launched in 1999. The European Commission, the administrative arm of the European Union—a group of 15 Western European countries—forecast that Spain's economic output would grow by 3.3 percent in 1997 from 2.3 percent in 1996. The unemployment rate was expected to decline to 21 percent in 1997 from 22.1 percent in 1996. The budget deficit was forecast to decline to 2.9 percent of gross domestic product in 1997, and inflation was expected to fall to 2.1 percent, the lowest level since the late 1960's.   □ Tom Buerkle

See also **Europe** (Facts in brief table).

Sports. The 1997 sports year was highlighted by athletes achieving remarkable successes at early ages. A 14-year-old, 4-foot, 8-inch (140-centimeter) skater, Tara Lipinski of Houston, won both the 1997 U.S. and World figure skating championships. Eldrick "Tiger" Woods, 21, the California golf wonder, overwhelmed the famed Augusta National course in April to win the 1997 Masters championship by 12 strokes. His four-round total of 270—18 under par—was the lowest score in the 61-year history of the Masters tournament. Woods, playing in his first Masters, became the youngest player in tournament history to win a major golf championship.

Tennis star Martina Hingis of Switzerland won the 1997 Australian Open, Wimbledon, and U.S. Open championships at age 16. German cyclist Jan Ullrich won the Tour de France at age 23. In track and field, Maurice Greene, 23, and Marion Jones, 21, of the United States each won the gold medal for the men's and women's 100-meter sprints, respectively, at the World championships in August. Greene and Jones also won their respective sprint titles at the U.S. championships in June.

Corporate take-over. Another piece of baseball history was made in September 1997, when Los Angeles Dodgers owner Peter O'Malley agreed to sell the team to a corporation headed by Australian-born billionaire Rupert Murdoch, the tabloid publisher and owner of the Fox Television Network. Murdoch's group announced it would purchase a majority interest in the Dodgers—major league baseball's last family-owned franchise—from the O'Malley family, which had owned the Dodgers since 1950, for $350 million. The deal was contingent upon the approval of other major league owners, but that was thought to be a formality.

Record chase. Another major baseball story of 1997 included a season-long chase for the single-season home run record in major league baseball. Mark McGwire, traded from the Oakland A's to the St. Louis Cardinals in July 1997, and Ken Griffey, Jr., of the Seattle Mariners, both came close to breaking major league baseball's single-season home run record—61—set by Roger Maris of the New York Yankees in 1961. McGwire hit 34 homers with Oakland and 24 more with St. Louis to finish the season with a total of 58. Griffey ended the season with 56 home runs, despite being moved up in the batting order during the final week of the regular season to gain more chances at bat. The run for the record probably enlivened the season more than did interleague play, which major league baseball tried in 1997 for the first time in history.

The stadium issue. Sports headlines in 1997 often told of professional sports franchise owners asking for—and frequently receiving—new stadiums built at taxpayer expense. Several owners of professional sports teams pressured communities for new facilities built at taxpayer expense, under the veiled threat of moving their teams to new cities. Even such long-established clubs as the New York Yankees, Boston Red Sox, Philadelphia Phillies, and Pittsburgh Pirates lobbied hard for new facilities by suggesting the possibility of moving.

In the National Football League (NFL), the Washington Redskins played their first game in Jack Kent Cooke Stadium, a new facility outside Landover, Maryland, on Sept. 14, 1997. The stadium, completed in less than 18 months, opened five months after the death of Redskins owner Jack Kent Cooke, who had worked 10 years to complete the stadium that bears his name. Also in 1997, construction or renovation projects of NFL stadiums began or were approved in Baltimore; Cincinnati, Ohio; Nashville, Tennessee; San Diego; San Francisco; Seattle; and Tampa, Florida.

Transgressions. Stories of sports figures or teams running afoul of rules or the law made news in even greater numbers than usual in 1997. The most shocking occurred when former heavyweight boxing champion Mike Tyson was banned from boxing in the U.S. for at least one year for biting off part of Evander Holyfield's ear during a heavyweight title bout in Las Vegas on June 28, 1997. Tyson also was fined $3 million.

Officials of soccer's world governing body, FIFA, investigated reports in 1997 that Iraq's national soccer team had been jailed and beaten after being eliminated from World Cup qualification by Kazakstan. A London newspaper reported in July that the Iraqi players, upon their return to Iraq, were taken to a military base, where they were beaten and shorn of their hair and mustaches. FIFA officials announced in November that they had found no evidence to support the accusations.

The Russian sports world suffered two apparent contract killings in 1997. Valentin Sych, president of the Russian Ice Hockey Federation, was shot and killed outside his house in April. In June, Larisa Nechayeva, director of one of the nation's most popular soccer teams, was shot outside her country house east of Moscow. Both killings were attributed to Russian organized crime figures, who may have been trying to extort money from sports organizations.

Dallas Cowboys owner Jerry Jones, trying to polish his team's image, installed video surveillance cameras in the players training camp dormitory and declared a popular off-campus drinking establishment off limits. Controversy continued to haunt the team, however. In August, authorities at Dallas-Fort Worth Airport confiscated a loaded handgun from the bag of Cowboys head coach Barry Switzer.

In December 1997, the National Basketball Association (NBA) suspended Golden State Warriors guard Latrell Sprewell for attacking and threatening Warriors head coach P. J. Carlesimo. Sprewell, whose $32-million contract was terminated by the Warriors, was banned from the NBA for one year—the longest suspension in the league's 51-year history.

Mary Slaney, the top U.S. female middle-distance runner, was banned from competition by both the world and U.S. track and field governing bodies, for allegedly testing positive for elevated levels of the hormone testosterone during qualifying trials for the 1996 U.S. Olympic team. (Testosterone, the hormone responsible for secondary sex characteristics in males, is an illegal performance-enhancing drug.) The ban excluded Slaney from competition in the 1997 U.S. championships, which was also the qualifying meet for the world championships in Athens in August. Slaney appealed the ban, and USA Track and Field, the sport's U.S. governing body, exonerated her in September 1997.

Awards and milestones. The 50th anniversary of Jackie Robinson's breaking the "color line" in major league baseball was commemorated in 1997 in ball parks from coast to coast. In 1947, Robinson joined the Brooklyn Dodgers, becoming the first black player in the major leagues. Until 1947, only white baseball players were allowed to play in the major leagues. Blacks formed and played in all-black baseball leagues known as the Negro Leagues.

In January 1997, runner Michael Johnson, winner of two gold medals at the 1996 Olympic Summer Games in Atlanta, became the first athlete in history to receive the prestigious Jesse Owens International Trophy Award for the second year in a row. In March 1997, he received the Sullivan Award as the best amateur athlete of 1996. The native Texan was the 37th track and field athlete to win the award, which is voted on by U.S. media and sports figures. Finalists for the award included golfer Tiger Woods; basketball standout Teresa Edwards; track stars Gail Devers and Dan O'Brien; softball player Dot Richardson; swimmer Amy Van Dyken; and college football star Danny Wuerffel.

Carl Lewis, the winner of nine Olympic gold medals and arguably the greatest track and field athlete of all time, retired at age 36. Mario Lemieux, the six-time National Hockey League (NHL) scoring champion, retired at age 32, after 12 seasons and more than 700 games with the Pittsburgh Penguins. Lemieux returned to the NHL for his final two seasons after being diagnosed and treated for Hodgkin's Disease.

Jim Kelly, 37, the Buffalo Bills quarterback who played in four Super Bowls, and Mike McCormack, 67, whose 46-year career in the National Football League included stints as a player, head coach, and president of the Carolina Panthers, both retired from the NFL in 1997. Brazil's Emerson Fittipaldi, 50, the former Formula One racing champion, retired after injuring his spine in a private-plane crash in September 1997. Fittipaldi, who had broken his neck in a 1996 race, said he considered his latest brush with death an "order" to give up dangerous sports.

Competitors in the 1997 Tour de France race through the scenic French countryside on July 16.
On July 27, Jan Ullrich became the first German cyclist ever to win the 21-stage Tour de France.

NCAA. In 1997, the National Collegiate Athletic Association (NCAA), the chief governing body of collegiate sports, stripped the University of California, the University of Connecticut, and the University of Massachusetts of their victories in the 1996 men's basketball tournament. California was hit hardest, drawing 3 years' probation, forfeiting its 28 season victories, and losing $54,000 from its share of the tournament winnings. The penalties resulted because Todd Bozeman, the team's former head coach, had made illegal payments totaling $30,000 over three years to a player's family. Massachusetts and Connecticut were also punished for making illegal gifts to student athletes. Massachusetts was forced to return $151,617, its share of the tournament purse. Connecticut returned $90,970. Kansas State University drew two years' probation and forfeited 11 games for making illegal payments to players and recruits in its women's program.

Among the winners in 1997 were—

Cycling. In July 1997, Jan Ullrich, 23, became the first German cyclist to win the Tour de France. Ullrich finished the 2,454-mile (3,950-kilometer) race 9 minutes and 9 seconds ahead of Richard Virenque of France, the runner-up. In a race marked by several crashes and injuries, Ullrich took the lead in the 10th stage with a remarkable climb of the Arcalis peak in Andorra. The effort won him the overall leader's yellow jersey, which he retained through the race. All nine cyclists competing for the U.S. Postal Service team, a first-time entrant, finished the race.

Diving. In the U.S. championships for men, Troy Dumais of Ventura, California, took the 1-meter springboard title; P. J. Bogart of Mesa, Arizona, won the 3-meter championship; and David Pilcher of Fort Lauderdale, Florida, was first among the platform divers. In women's competition, Carissa Zenorini of Demarest, New Jersey, took the 1-meter title; Doris Glenn Easterly of Midlothian, Virginia, won off the 3-meter board; and Lizzy Flynt of Auburn, Alabama, captured the platform championship. Tyce Routson of Coral Gables, Florida, won both the 3-meter and platform titles in the NCAA men's championships. His teammate, Rio Ramirez, took the 1-meter competition. Vera Ilyina of Texas won the 1- and 3-meter titles in the women's NCAA championships and her teammate, Laura Wilkinson, won the platform title.

Gymnastics. The Romanian women and Chinese men captured, for the third time in succession, their respective team titles in the World Gymnastic Championships at Lausanne, Switzerland, in early September. China mastered a variety of difficult routines that added up to a 4.5-point margin of victory over Belarus, the silver medalist in the men's meet. The U.S. men finished fifth. The Romanian women performed superbly in the vault and floor exercise to finish ahead of Russia and China. The U.S. women's team, with Dominique Moceanu as the only returning member of the 1996 Olympic team, finished sixth. Ivan Ivanko of Belarus, who had missed the 1996 Atlanta Olympic Games because of a torn Achilles' tendon, came back to win his second world all-around title. Svetlana Chorkina of Russia won the women's all-around for the first time, with a near-perfect routine on the uneven parallel bars.

Marathon. The Boston Marathon was won by a Kenyan for the seventh straight year. Lameck Agusta took the lead with not quite 2 miles (3.2 kilometers) to go and stayed there the rest of the way. No fewer than eight of his countrymen, including runner-up Joseph Kamau, finished in the top 14. Fatima Roba of Ethiopia took the women's race to end the three-year winning streak of Germany's Uta Pippig. In the New York City Marathon in November, two Kenyans led the men—John Kagwe was first (2 hours 8 minutes 12 seconds), followed by Joseph Chebet (2:09:27). The first female finisher was Franziska Rochat-Moser of Switzerland (2:28:43).

Rowing. In the World Rowing Championships in Chambery, France, the United States won the men's eight, the premier event of the competition. Germany led the competition with five gold medals. The U.S. won four. The eight oarsmen representing the Nottingham Rowing Association pulled off a huge upset in the Henley Royal Regatta in July. Outweighed an average of 38 pounds (17 kilograms) per man by the University of Washington's intercollegiate champions, the British rowers beat the Huskies by one foot. In the 143rd Boat Race, Cambridge beat Oxford by two lengths in 17 minutes, 38 seconds. It was the fifth straight victory for Cambridge, and one of the closest races ever contested.

Other champions

Biathlon. World champions: men's 20-kilometer, Ricco Gross, Germany; women's 15-kilometer, Magdalena Forsberg, Sweden.

Canoeing. World Cup whitewater champions: men's canoe, Patrice Estanguet, France; men's kayak, Scott Shipley, United States; women's kayak, Irena Pavelkova, Czechoslovakia.

Cricket. Sahara Cup championship, India.

Equestrian. World cup champions: jumping, Hugo Simon, Austria; dressage, Anky Van Grunszen, the Netherlands.

Fencing. World champions: men's foil, Sergei Golubiitsky, Ukraine; women's foil, Giovanna Trillini, Italy.

Lacrosse. U.S. college champions: men, Princeton University; women, University of Maryland.

Modern pentathlon. World champions: men, Russia; women, Italy.

Motorcycle racing. World 500-cc champion: Michael Doohan, Australia.

Rugby. Tri Nations champion: New Zealand.

Sled dog racing. Martin Buser won the 25th Iditarod Trail Sled Dog Race from Anchorage to Nome, for the third time. His team covered the 1,150-mile (1,851-kilometer) Alaskan race in 9 days, 8 hours, 30 minutes, and 45 seconds.

Soap Box Derby. Masters champion: Wade Wallace, Elkhart County, Indiana.

Triathlon. World champions: men, Chris McCormack, Australia; women, Emma Carney, Australia.

Volleyball. World League men's champion: Italy.

Weightlifting. European super heavyweight champion: Tibor Stark, Hungary.   □ Ron Reid

Iditarod: Celebrating the Dog Days of Winter

In March 1997, mushers and their teams of dogs competed in Alaska's 25th annual Iditarod Trail Sled Dog Race, an event often heralded as the "last great race on earth."

By Bill Sherwonit

O n a cold, sunny afternoon in March 1997, Joe Redington, Sr., driving a nine-dog team into Nome, Alaska, completed his run of the 25th annual Iditarod Trail Sled Dog Race. He finished 36th in the race standings, nearly four days behind three-time champion Martin Buser. Nonetheless, hundreds of people cheered the arrival of the 80-year-old founder of the race and a veteran of 19 Iditarods. In 1973, amid almost universal skepticism, Redington organized the first sled dog race to cover more than 1,000 miles (1,600 kilometers). In the years since, the Iditarod became Alaska's premier sporting event and the world's most famous sled dog race.

Redington had not competed in the race since 1992, so his return was a highlight of the 25th annual event. But his journey also had a downside. Like four other entrants in the 1997 Iditarod, Redington had a dog die. As with many Iditarod dog deaths, race veterinarians could not determine what killed the 4-year-old male named Nip, but they emphasized it had been well rested and well cared for. Since the first run in 1973, the Iditarod has drawn criticism for such deaths. In spite of that continued controversy, however, the 1997 race attracted thousands of fans to an event that pits mushers and dogs against the challenges of an Alaskan winter. For Alaskans, the occasion was a celebration of a history closely linked to the legacy of dog sledding.

The history of the Iditarod Trail

Centuries ago segments of the trail used by the Iditarod racers were developed by Native Alaskans. Russian fur traders also used portions of the route during the early 1800's. The Iditarod Trail's heyday, however, was during Alaska's gold rush era, from the late 1880's through the mid-1920's. Primarily a winter pathway, the original trail was a network connecting mining camps (including one named Iditarod, now a ghost town), trading posts, and other settlements. Although many people used the trail, one group earned special acclaim—mail carriers. Until airplanes replaced dog teams in the 1920's and 1930's, mail-carrying mushers were the "kings of the trail." Sled dog racers, who competed in events such as the All-Alaska Sweepstakes in Nome, also built heroic reputations in the early 1900's.

The greatest race of that era, however, was not a sporting event. In 1925, 20 drivers and more than 100 dogs participated in a 700-mile (1,130-kilometer) relay run that became known as the Great Race of Mercy to Nome. Their mission was to deliver diphtheria medication to Nome, where an outbreak threatened to reach epidemic proportions. Traveling through blinding snow storms and temperatures running to -60 °F (-51 °C), mushers and dogs delivered the serum in time to divert disaster. Among the serum run's many highly publicized participants, Leonhard Seppala became a celebrated hero after driving his team for more than 90 miles (145 kilometers)—the longest stretch of the relay—through a treacherous storm along the coast.

In spite of the long history of dog sledding, mushing went into decline throughout much of Alaska as snowmobiles began to replace sled dogs in the 1960's. Joe Redington, Sr., a devoted musher, was

A musher races his team through Ruby, Alaska, *above*, one of the towns along the route of the 1925 relay that delivered diphtheria serum to Nome to stem an epidemic. The route of the Iditarod Trail Sled Dog Race, *right*, begins in Anchorage and ends in Nome on the Bering Sea coast. In even-numbered years, racers follow the northern route; in odd-numbered years, they take the southern route.

380

upset by this decline but could find no remedy—until he met Dorothy Page in 1966.

Page, a self-described history buff, had been chosen to organize an event celebrating the 100th anniversary of the 1867 United States purchase of Alaska from Russia. She proposed a race along the Iditarod Trail to pay tribute to Alaska's pioneer mushers. Redington loved the idea. The two planned a race for February 1967. Despite predictions of failure, the race proved to be a great success with 58 mushers competing for $25,000 in prize money. The race, run in two 25-mile (40-kilometer) heats, was officially called the Iditarod Trail Seppala Memorial Race, named for musher Leonhard Seppala. Over the years, the Iditarod race's origins were closely linked with the 1925 serum run because of Seppala's heroic role in that event. In reality, "Seppala was picked to represent all mushers," Page explained. The event was patterned after sweepstakes races rather than the serum run.

Enthusiasm for an Iditarod race waned after the initial event, but Redington kept the dream alive. In 1973, he staged the first Iditarod Trail Sled Dog Race from Anchorage to Nome with 34 drivers competing for $51,000 in prize money. Redington billed the Iditarod as a 1,049-mile (1,688-kilometer) race—still the official distance. There was no question that the route was at least 1,000 miles long, and "49" was intended to symbolize Alaska, the 49th state. In reality, the trail is more than 1,100 miles (1,770 kilometers) long.

By the time of the 25th annual event, the Iditarod had earned international acclaim as the "last great race on earth," attracting entrants from 14 countries. The Iditarod's success also sparked a mushing revival in rural Alaska. Race highlights have included victories between 1974 and 1976 by Native Alaskan mushers Carl Huntington, Emmitt Peters, and Jerry Riley; Libby Riddles' gamble across the sea ice in 1985, resulting in the first Iditarod victory by a woman; Rick Swenson's record five championships; the "Susan Butcher era" in which Butcher won four races in five years (1986–1990); and the 1995 win by Doug Swingley of Simms, Montana—the only Iditarod victory by a non-Alaskan. Another highlight has been the increasing speed at which the course is completed. It took the 1973 winner, Dick Wilmarth, 20 days to reach Nome, but the 1997 last-place finisher, Ken Chase, made it to Nome in less than 16 days. The record—9 days, 2 hours, and 42 minutes—was set by Doug Swingley in 1995.

The author

Bill Sherwonit is a free-lance writer in Anchorage, Alaska. His publications include *Iditarod: The Great Race to Nome*.

Mandatory racing gear:

- ax
- cold-weather sleeping bag
- snowshoes
- eight "booties" for each dog
- cooking pot
- veterinarian notebook
- at least two pounds of food per dog (restocked at each checkpoint)
- at least one day's ration of food for musher

Other necessities:

- stove
- fuel
- extra clothing and boots
- headlamp and batteries
- first-aid kit
- repair equipment

The musher's sportswear:

- insulated boots
- two pairs of socks
- long underwear
- fleece pants, shirt, and sweater
- insulated bib overalls
- parka with a fur muff
- ski mask
- fur hat
- insulated glove liners
- fur-lined mittens

An extraordinary team sport

The 1997 Iditarod began on the first Saturday in March in downtown Anchorage with a ceremonial start, staged before thousands of fans. Mushers drove their teams several miles through snow-covered streets and trails, carrying passengers who had bid for the chance to ride on a sled. Afterward, teams were trucked to Wasilla, where the race officially began on Sunday.

From start to finish, the 1997 teams passed through 23 checkpoints. Along the way, mushers and dogs crossed the Alaska Range and two smaller mountain ranges and followed the Yukon and Kuskokwim rivers. In the final stages, teams traveled along the often stormy Bering Sea coast. Beginning in the 1970's, the race's middle section took two paths, to give more villages a chance to serve as checkpoints. In even-numbered years, teams follow the northern route; in odd-numbered years, they travel the southern route.

The journey to Nome has presented every imaginable winter challenge. Iditarod racers have endured temperatures as low as -50 °F (-46 °C), waist-deep snow, hurricane-force winds, blizzards, moose attacks, dog fights, exhaustion, and hallucinations. The dogs, however, have remained the stars of this marathon. They have been bred, raised, trained, and conditioned to run long distances in harsh conditions. Mushers have bred Siberians and other huskies with hounds, setters, German shepherds, and even wolves. Their goal was to produce fast, tough-footed dogs of proper size and shape, with great endurance, a willingness to please, and a strong desire to run.

No matter how talented, a team cannot perform to its potential unless all members remain healthy. Therefore, care of the dogs has been a top priority in the 25 years of the race. In 1997, as in past years, veterinarians examined all Iditarod teams during a prerace checkup, and vets were stationed at all of the checkpoints. A comprehensive set of rules governed the treatment of dogs. Mushers had to begin with at least 12 and no more than 16 dogs and were required to have at least 5 dogs in the harness at all times. No dogs could be added once the race was started. Mushers could leave tired, sick, or injured dogs at designated drop-off sites, where the Iditarod staff cared for them. Also, racers were required to make two 8-hour layovers and one 24-hour layover. Race officials established penalties, including expulsion, for participants who broke any of the rules.

During the 1997 race, as is customary in most sledding competitions, mushers allowed the dogs to rest about the same amount of time as they ran. During the rest periods, dogs were tended to first. Mushers made certain the dogs were fed and bedded down, feet were checked, and sick or injured dogs were treated. Because Iditarod dogs burn up to 10,000 calories per day, most racers fed them high-energy foods and supplemented commercial dog food with eggs, vegetable oils, and such meats as lamb, chicken, beef, fish, liver, seal, or beaver. Mushers slept as little as one to two hours a day, or sometimes less, but the dogs got plenty of rest. To make up for the loss of sleep, some racers took short naps on the sled while the team was running.

To ensure the safety of the dogs and mushers, the race officials over the years also established a list of mandatory gear: an ax, a cold-weather sleeping bag, snowshoes, a cooking pot, a veterinarian note-book, and eight "booties" for each dog to protect feet on icy trails. Race officials also required mushers to depart checkpoints with suffi-cient food for themselves and each dog.

Controversies surrounding the Iditarod

Over the years, few entrants in the Iditarod have been full-time pro-fessional mushers. For most Iditarod mushers, sled dog racing has been a part-time business or hobby, albeit an expensive one. Race-related costs in 1997 ranged from $10,000 to more than $30,000, including a $1,750 entry fee plus dog food, equipment, kennel main-tenance, dog-care expenses, and transportation to the trail. In 1997, all of the rac-ers who finished below 20th place received $1,049 from a purse of nearly $400,000. While the top 20 finishers received larger prizes, only the 4 top finishers received more than $30,000—enough money to cover the maxi-mum expenses.

The cost of running the Iditarod increased steadily over the years, and by the 1990's, many rural Alaskans could no longer afford to enter. This trend was reflect-ed in the race's declining numbers of Native Alaskan mushers. Because most Native Alaskans live in remote rural areas—far from media outlets, corporate sponsors, and high-paying jobs—they have found it difficult to raise the money to build competitive Iditarod teams. In the early years of the race, many top Iditarod mushers were rural Inuit and Athabaskan Indians, but no Native Alaskan has won the race since 1976. In 1997, only a handful of the 53 entrants were Native Alaskans. Their decreased participation was widely regarded as a significant loss to the event.

Since its inception, the biggest controversy surrounding the Iditarod was the death of dogs. In the race's first year, an estimated

A race veterinarian gives a dog a checkup along the route of the 1997 Iditarod. The dogs wear fleece booties to protect their feet while run-ning along hard and icy trails.

16 to 30 dogs died along the trail. This triggered protests, especially among animal rights groups, which have asserted that the mushers force the dogs to perform beyond their physical limits. Throughout the controversy, mushers, race organizers, and veterinarians have maintained that dogs are endurance athletes that live to run and that they receive the best training, food, and medical care possible. Over the years, the number of deaths dropped dramatically because of improved dog-care practices and strict rules to protect the dogs. Race veterinarians have admitted, however, that even with the best care available, unforeseeable accidents and deaths still occur.

In the 1990's, several animal rights groups attacked the Iditarod as inhumane, and the Humane Society of the United States (HSUS) vigorously campaigned to end the race. Pressure from the HSUS prompted the Iditarod's largest corporate sponsors to withdraw support. In the early 1990's, the HSUS had even held a seat on the Iditarod Trail Committee and had strongly influenced race rules pertaining to dog care and dog deaths. Iditarod officials severed that link, however, when the HSUS condemned the race in 1994.

The costs of the animal rights attack on the Iditarod were high. The race lost hundreds of thousands of dollars in sponsorship money and got what one musher called a "national black eye." Yet even as it was being attacked, mushers and officials continued to develop better

Musher Vern Halter with his team of 16 dogs sets off to cross the Alaska Range during the 1997 25th annual run of the Iditarod Trail Sled Dog Race.

dog-care practices. To keep the race afloat, Alaskan businesses and individuals began to sponsor teams and help underwrite costs.

A celebration of Alaska's heritage

Regardless of the controversy, the Iditarod became more and more popular in Alaska and retained its international appeal, helping to boost winter tourism in Alaska. Iditarod supporters have maintained that the race's true importance, however, cannot be measured in dollars. In the 1990's, Alaska was in many ways a land divided, split into factions by emotionally explosive issues: subsistence rights, resource development, federal management of parklands, Native sovereignty, fisheries allocations, and wildlife management. The Iditarod enthusiasts claim that as the race takes center stage each March, those divisions dissolve. Residents throughout the state become united by their passion for a sporting event that transcends athletic competition.

As in the past, the 25th annual running of the Iditarod not only pitted competitors against each other but also against the wilderness and Alaska's often brutal winter weather. It was a contest in which women and men competed as equals and one that renewed the primal bond between humans and dogs. Perhaps most important, many Alaskans saw the Iditarod Trail Sled Dog Race as a true celebration of Alaska's frontier past and spirit of adventure. ■ ■ ■

Sri Lanka. The two main political parties of Sri Lanka's Sinhalese Buddhist majority agreed in 1997 upon a united approach in negotiating an end to a 14-year civil war with the guerrilla army of Tamil Hindus. The governing Sri Lanka Freedom Party (SLFP), headed by President Chandrika Kumaratunga, pledged in April to join forces with the United National Party (UNP), the government opposition party, in mounting a negotiation campaign. Great Britain, the colonial ruler of Sri Lanka (then called Ceylon) until 1948, facilitated the accord.

The Tamils, a minority group, sought an independent state in northern and northeastern Sri Lanka. Between 35,000 and 50,000 people died since the Liberation Tigers of Tamil Eelam (LTTE) began the civil war in 1983. On Nov. 8, 1997, the LTTE rejected a compromise with the government on its demand for an independent state.

Fighting. The LTTE engaged in heavy fighting and terrorist attacks throughout 1997. The fiercest battles occurred in the northern jungles of Sri Lanka, where the Sri Lankan army attempted to clear rebel forces from a 43-mile (69-kilometer) stretch of road leading to the Jaffna peninsula. The army had captured the town of Jaffna from the LTTE in 1995, but LTTE blocked the road to the town, forcing the army to enter the town by boat or air.

The army launched an offensive to open the road into Jaffna at 5:20 a.m. on May 13, 1997—a time chosen by astrologers. The LTTE counterattacked, using artillery it had captured from the army. More than 3,000 people were killed in ensuing battles that continued throughout 1997. On October 6, rebels stormed a military base in northern Sri Lanka that housed government troops engaged in capturing the road. At least 180 people were killed and 260 wounded in the battle.

The LTTE launched attacks in eastern Sri Lanka in 1997. On March 6, rebels killed 89 government soldiers in a raid on an army camp near Batticaloa. On May 11, LTTE forces stormed a police station near Trincomalee, killing 19 people. Navy gunboats intercepted an LTTE supply boat off the coast of Trincomalee in June and killed about 40 rebels.

On October 15, LTTE guerrillas detonated a truckload of high explosives in the center of Colombo, the capital. Eighteen people were killed, and seven buildings were wrecked in the blast. The explosion came a week after the U.S. State Department formally labeled the LTTE a terrorist group, thus blocking its legal fund-raising in the United States.

Elections were held on March 21 in seven of Sri Lanka's nine provinces lying outside war zones. The SLFP gained control of 194 of the 238 local councils. The UNP won control of 43 councils.

Boating disaster. A boat carrying Tamil refugees fleeing Sri Lanka overturned on February 20, killing more than 165 people. □ Henry S. Bradsher

See also **Asia** (Facts in brief table).

State government. State governments enjoyed a relatively quiet legislative year in 1997. Most states benefited from a strong economy, and many ended their fiscal years with a surplus of funds.

Fiscal surpluses. Many states ended fiscal 1997 on June 30 with their highest average financial balances since fiscal 1980, the National Conference of State Legislatures reported in August 1997. Among the states ending the year in the black were California, with a $1.4-billion surplus; Minnesota, with a $2.3-billion surplus; and Wisconsin, which had a $588-million surplus. An exception to the economic boom was Hawaii, which suffered a recession in 1997 due to a decrease in tourism. The report revealed that overall state spending grew by nearly 5 percent nationwide. The largest average increases went to education, corrections, and Medicaid.

Approximately half of the state legislatures reduced taxes in 1997. Iowa reduced its income tax rate by 10 percent, while Maryland approved plans to reduce income taxes by 10 percent by 2002. In Michigan, legislators provided income tax relief with new and expanded tax credits and deductions, while lawmakers in both Missouri and North Carolina lowered the state sales tax on food. New York legislators enacted $5 billion in tax cuts, to be phased in through the year 2002. In August 1997, Texas voters approved a $1-billion property tax cut that raised the homestead exemption from $5,000 to $15,000. Minnesota lawmakers approved giving homeowners and renters a 20-percent property tax rebate totaling about $500 million. Maine enacted personal income, sales, and property tax relief measures.

Cigarette taxes increased in several states, including Alaska, Maine, New Hampshire, and Utah. States increasing motor vehicle taxes in 1997 included Utah and Vermont.

Tobacco settlement. The nation's four largest tobacco companies and 40 state attorneys general on June 20, 1997, agreed to a settlement to end lawsuits brought by the states over health-care costs resulting from smoking. The proposed settlement called for the tobacco companies to pay states and the federal government $368.5 billion over a 25-year period. The companies would then pay $15 billion annually for an indefinite period.

The proposed settlement permits future individual claims to recover health-care costs related to smoking, but bans any other class-action lawsuits or suits for punitive damages. The tobacco settlement needed to be approved by President Bill Clinton and the U.S. Congress before it could go into effect. In October, Republican leaders said Congress would not vote on the proposed settlement until 1998.

On July 3, 1997, the tobacco industry reached a $3.6-billion settlement with Mississippi. Mississippi was the first state to sue the tobacco companies in order to recover state funds spent on Medicaid and other health programs related to smoking illnesses.

Selected statistics on state governments

State	Resident population*	Governor†	Legislature† House (D)	(R)	Senate (D)	(R)	State tax revenue‡	Tax revenue per capita‡	Public school expenditure per pupil§
Alabama	4,273,084	Fob James, Jr. (R)	70	35	22	13	$ 5,258,000,000	$1,230	$ 4,740
Alaska	607,007	Tony Knowles (D)	15	25	6	14	1,519,000,000	2,500	10,390
Arizona	4,428,068	Jane Dee Hull (R)	22	38	12	18	6,409,000,000	1,450	4,390
Arkansas	2,509,793	Mike Huckabee (R)	#85	14	28	7	3,709,000,000	1,480	4,500
California	31,878,234	Pete Wilson (R)	#42	37	**23	16	57,747,000,000	1,800	5,330
Colorado	3,822,676	Roy Romer (D)	24	41	15	20	4,820,000,000	1,260	5,550
Connecticut	3,274,238	John G. Rowland (R)	96	55	19	17	7,830,000,000	2,390	8,860
Delaware	724,842	Tom Carper (D)	13	28	13	8	1,688,000,000	2,330	7,690
Florida	14,399,985	Lawton Chiles (D)	55	65	17	23	19,699,000,000	1,370	6,050
Georgia	7,353,225	Zell Miller (D)	#100	79	34	22	10,292,000,000	1,400	6,030
Hawaii	1,183,723	Ben Cayetano (D)	39	12	23	2	3,069,000,000	2,590	6,210
Idaho	1,189,251	Phil Batt (R)	11	59	5	30	1,857,000,000	1,560	4,740
Illinois	11,846,544	Jim Edgar (R)	60	58	28	31	17,277,000,000	1,460	6,050
Indiana	5,840,528	Frank L. O'Bannon (D)	50	50	19	31	8,437,000,000	1,440	6,430
Iowa	2,851,792	Terry E. Branstad (R)	46	54	22	28	4,441,000,000	1,560	6,060
Kansas	2,572,150	Bill Graves (R)	48	77	13	27	3,979,000,000	1,550	6,170
Kentucky	3,883,723	Paul E. Patton (D)	64	36	20	18	6,489,000,000	1,670	6,230
Louisiana	4,350,579	Murphy J. (Mike) Foster (R)	77	28	25	14	4,906,000,000	1,130	4,880
Maine	1,243,316	Angus King (I)	**81	69	**19	15	1,897,000,000	1,530	6,710
Maryland	5,071,604	Parris N. Glendening (D)	††98	41	32	15	8,167,000,000	1,610	7,050
Massachusetts	6,092,352	Paul Cellucci (R)	**130	29	33	7	12,453,000,000	2,050	7,630
Michigan	9,594,350	John Engler (R)	58	52	#16	21	19,129,000,000	1,990	7,320
Minnesota	4,657,758	Arne H. Carlson (R)	70	64	**42	24	10,056,000,000	2,160	6,400
Mississippi	2,716,115	Kirk Fordice (R)	‡‡84	36	35	18	3,863,000,000	1,420	4,580
Missouri	5,358,692	Mel Carnahan (D)	**86	76	19	15	7,300,000,000	1,360	5,370
Montana	879,372	Marc Racicot (R)	35	65	16	34	1,256,000,000	1,430	5,970
Nebraska	1,652,093	E. Benjamin Nelson (D)	unicameral (49 nonpartisan)				2,369,000,000	1,430	5,650
Nevada	1,603,163	Bob Miller (D)	25	17	9	12	2,889,000,000	1,800	5,520
New Hampshire	1,162,481	Jeanne Shaheen (D)	§§145	249	9	15	837,000,000	720	6,560
New Jersey	7,987,933	Christine Todd Whitman (R)	31	49	16	24	14,385,000,000	1,800	10,130
New Mexico	1,713,407	Gary E. Johnson (R)	42	28	25	17	3,061,000,000	1,790	5,900
New York	18,184,774	George E. Pataki (R)	97	53	26	35	34,150,000,000	1,880	9,700
North Carolina	7,322,870	James B. Hunt, Jr. (D)	59	61	30	20	11,882,000,000	1,620	5,250
North Dakota	643,539	Edward T. Shafer (R)	I†26	70	††18	29	985,000,000	1,530	4,840
Ohio	11,172,782	George V. Voinovich (R)	39	60	12	21	15,649,000,000	1,400	5,910
Oklahoma	3,300,902	Frank Keating (R)	65	36	33	15	4,618,000,000	1,400	4,530
Oregon	3,203,735	John Kitzhaber (D)	29	31	10	20	4,416,000,000	1,380	6,590
Pennsylvania	12,056,112	Tom J. Ridge (R)	#99	103	20	30	18,725,000,000	1,550	7,570
Rhode Island	990,225	Lincoln C. Almond (R)	84	16	41	9	1,549,000,000	1,560	7,880
South Carolina	3,673,287	David Beasley (R)	##52	70	25	21	5,113,000,000	1,380	5,350
South Dakota	732,405	William J. Janklow (R)	22	48	13	22	730,000,000	1,000	4,960
Tennessee	5,319,654	Don Sundquist (R)	61	38	18	15	6,185,000,000	1,160	5,270
Texas	19,128,261	George W. Bush (R)	82	68	14	17	21,259,000,000	1,110	5,940
Utah	2,000,494	Michael O. Leavitt (R)	20	55	9	20	2,914,000,000	1,460	4,090
Vermont	588,654	Howard Dean (D)	***89	57	17	13	841,000,000	1,430	7,560
Virginia	6,675,451	James S. Gilmore III (R)	**51	48	20	20	8,900,000,000	1,330	6,370
Washington	5,532,939	Gary Locke (D)	41	57	23	26	10,586,000,000	1,910	6,220
West Virginia	1,825,754	Cecil H. Underwood (R)	74	26	**25	9	2,771,000,000	1,520	7,040
Wisconsin	5,159,795	Tommy G. Thompson (R)	#47	51	17	16	9,617,000,000	1,860	7,370
Wyoming	481,400	Jim Geringer (R)	17	43	9	21	626,000,000	1,300	6,290

*July 1, 1996, estimates. Source: U.S. Bureau of the Census.
†As of November 1997. Source: state government officials.
‡1996 figures. Source: U.S. Bureau of the Census.
§1996-1997 figures for elementary and secondary students in average
  daily attendance. Source: National Education Association.
#One vacancy.

**One independent.
††Two vacancies.
‡‡Two independents.
§§Two independents; four vacancies.
##One independent; one vacancy.
***Three progressive; one independent.

On August 25, the tobacco industry settled a lawsuit brought by Florida by agreeing to pay the state $11.3 billion.

Education. Court rulings pushed state legislatures to end funding disparities in public education attributed to different levels of property wealth. The Vermont legislature in September adopted a statewide property tax to replace local property taxes for school support. In May, New Jersey's Supreme Court declared that the state's school finance system was unconstitutional and ordered the state to spend as much on schools in 28 low-income districts as it spent in 120 wealthier districts.

Legislators in Illinois adjourned in June without passing a proposed plan to shift the burden of paying for schools from local property owners to a statewide income tax. The Ohio Supreme Court in March ruled the current school finance system unconstitutional and gave the state until 1998 to design a new system. Nebraska also provided more state aid for schools to compensate for a lid on local property taxes passed in 1996.

More states approved legislation in 1997 for charter public schools. Charter schools are typically created and run by parents, teachers, community groups, or other groups outside of a school district's authority. The schools receive public funding but operate free of many state and local regulations. Mississippi, Ohio, and Pennsylvania were among the states approving the creation of charter schools. In fall of 1997, some 780 charter schools operated in at least 23 states. Texas amended its law to allow 100 new charter schools to open through 1999, up from the 20 allowed under the former state law. However, attempts to pass charter school laws in states such as Alabama, Indiana, Missouri, Nevada, Tennessee, Virginia, and Washington were unsuccessful in 1997.

In July, the Ohio legislature gave control of the Cleveland school district to the mayor of that city after two years of state control. The Ohio legislature also approved funding for a tuition voucher program for Cleveland schools through 1999. Under the system, 3,000 children chosen through a lottery would receive vouchers worth as much as $2,500.

State lawmakers in Connecticut in August 1997 passed legislation to take over the troubled Hartford school district.

Several states in 1997 agreed to put more funding into early-childhood learning initiatives. North Carolina budgeted $23 million in fiscal 1998 to expand its early-childhood education program, called Smart Start, statewide. Connecticut appropriated $50 million to expand preschool education to reach 55,000 children. New Hampshire increased funding from $500 to $750 per child to expand public kindergartens. State lawmakers also agreed to cover 75 percent of construction costs in school districts that either needed to improve kindergarten facilities or did not have kindergarten facilities in 1997.

Welfare reform. Leaders from al 50 states met the July 1 federal deadline to file welfare-reform plans mandated by welfare-reform legislation passed by the U.S. Congress in 1996. State plans were required to outline how the state would provide financial assistance to needy families with children. States also faced an Oct. 1, 1997, federal deadline to have 75 percent of two-parent families participating in work or work-related activities. However, several states were unable to meet the federal deadline. Some state officials described the more stringent work goal as being too "unrealistic."

Governors. Republicans defeated Democratic challengers in the only two gubernatorial races held on Nov. 4, 1997. New Jersey Governor Christine Todd Whitman narrowly defeated Democratic challenger Jim McGreevey, a state senator, to win a second term in office. In Virginia, former attorney general James S. Gilmore III, a Republican, defeated Lieuten-ant Governor Don Beyer, a Democrat, in a race to succeed Republican Governor George Allen.

A jury on September 3 found Republican Governor Fife Symington of Arizona guilty of seven felony counts of defrauding lenders while he was a commercial real estate developer. The jury acquitted Symington on three related charges. U.S. District Judge Roger Strand declared a mistrial on 11 remaining counts after the jury was unable to reach a verdict. Symington, who was elected governor in 1991, resigned from office on Sept. 5, 1997. Secretary of State Jane Dee Hull, a fellow Republican, succeeded him.

Massachusetts Governor William Weld, a Republican, resigned from office in July 1997 in order to pursue congressional confirmation as U.S. ambassador to Mexico. Weld was later denied a congressional hearing for the post. On July 29, Massachusetts Lieutenant Governor Paul Cellucci became acting governor.

In Rhode Island, Republican Governor Lincoln Almond appointed Republican Bernard Jackvony lieutenant governor in January 1997. Jackvony replaced Bob Weygand, a Democrat, who won election to the U.S. Congress in November 1996.

Marriage laws. A bill approved by the Louisiana legislature in June 1997 set up an alternative marriage contract, called a "covenant marriage." The new Louisiana law required couples who chose a covenant marriage to undergo premarital counseling and sign an affidavit that they understand the seriousness of marriage. The only grounds for a divorce in a covenant marriage became adultery, physical or sexual abuse, abandonment, or conviction of a felony.

In Hawaii, a law that legally recognized the rights of same-sex couples in the areas of insurance, property, pension, and hospital visitation took effect in July.
□ Elaine Stuart

See also **Courts; Education; Elections; Welfare.**

Stocks and bonds. Lower interest rates, improved business productivity, and robust corporate profits made 1997 the third straight banner year in U.S. stocks and bonds, despite a speed bump in October. Currency devaluations and tumbling stock markets in several Asian nations added a note of caution to the upbeat year. But a 7.2-percent Dow Jones Industrial Average (the Dow) in decline on October 27 failed to shake investor confidence. Agreement between the U.S. Congress and President Bill Clinton to eliminate the annual federal deficit helped strengthen investor sentiment.

The Dow Jones Industrial Average—a composite of the stock prices of 30 major companies traded on the New York Stock Exchange—experienced four rallies and three slumps in 1997. A January advance, when many investors choose their investments for the year, was followed by a March sell-off. Investors feared that popular technology stocks had become overpriced, prompting a retreat in stock prices. The Dow industrials fell to 6392 on April 11, below the 6448 close at the end of 1996. The swoon of March and April 1997 initiated a rally through early August. The Dow industrials peaked at 8259 on August 6. Stocks began slipping shortly thereafter but recovered somewhat in September.

By October 26, a crash was underway in Hong Kong, the former British colony that on July 1 had come under the rule of the People's Republic of China. Global investors feared that Hong Kong would sever the 14-year link between the Hong Kong dollar and the U.S. dollar, following currency devaluations during the summer in Thailand, Malaysia, and Indonesia. The Hang Seng Index of 33 major companies traded on the Hong Kong Stock Exchange sank 46 percent between August 7 and October 28, including a 6-percent drop on Monday, October 27.

In New York, the Dow industrials plunged 554 points on October 27, the Dow's biggest point drop in history. For the first time since the crash of 1987, the New York Stock Exchange halted trading, once after the Dow lost 350 points from Friday's close and again after the Dow fell 550 points. Stocks rebounded Tuesday, Oct. 28, 1997, as a record-high 1.2 billion shares were traded on the New York Stock Exchange. The Dow industrials jumped a record 337 points. By November 19, the Dow had fully recovered from the October 27 plunge.

By mid-December, the Dow stood at 7920, up 23 percent for the year, compared to a 26-percent advance for all of 1996. Broader market indexes also recovered from the October slump. The Standard & Poor's 500 index of 500 company stocks was up 30 percent. The NASDAQ composite index of all stocks traded on the electronic NASDAQ Stock Market operated by the National Association of Securities Dealers was up 19 percent. The Russell 2000 index of small-company stocks tracked by the Frank Russell Company was up 16 percent.

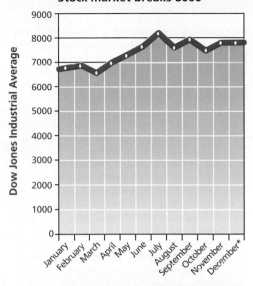

Stock market breaks 8000

Dow Jones Industrial Average

Closing monthly averages for 1997

*December figure is as of the 12th.

The Dow Jones Industrial Average broke 8000 for the first time in July but plunged a record 554 points on October 27. The trading of 1.2 billion shares on October 28 presaged the recovery of the market by November 19.

The Asian financial crises and currency devaluations in export-driven economies meant lower import prices for U.S. consumers. That trend, plus increased worker productivity in U.S. businesses, kept U.S. inflation low and interest rates falling. After peaking at 7.17 percent in April, the yield on 30-year Treasury bonds fell to 5.98 percent in mid-December. Lower bond yields mean lower interest rates for home mortgages and other long-term debt. Lower interest rates pull investors away from fixed-income debt securities and into stocks. Lower rates also boost corporate profits, making stocks more attractive. Yields on three-month Treasury bills gyrated during 1997 but stood at about 5.2 percent in early December, near the 5.17 percent at the end of 1996.

Winners and losers. Computer technology stock results were lackluster in 1997. International Business Machines Corporation (IBM) was up 30 percent for the year by mid-December, to $99 a share. Intel Corporation of Santa Clara, California, the giant semiconductor manufacturer, was up only 8 percent, to $71, compared with a 131 percent gain in 1996. Dell Computer Corporation of Round Rock, Texas, tripled in value, to $85 a share, as demand for personal computers stayed strong, but modem-producer 3 Com Corporation of Santa Clara lost half its value amid a glut of computer modems.

AT&T Corporation of New York City rebounded to a 39-percent gain for 1997 through mid-December, to $57, compared with a 31-percent loss in 1996. Prospects for global consolidation among telecommunications companies helped spark interest in AT&T and other phone giants. MCI Communications rose 33 percent to $44 amid competing bids by other phone companies to acquire MCI.

Employer pressure on managed-care providers to lower costs and consumer dissatisfaction with health maintenance organization (HMO) services made 1997 a bad year for HMO operators. The stock of Oxford Health Plans, Incorporated, of Norwalk, Connecticut, sank nearly 73 percent by mid-December, to $16. Another loser was Eastman Kodak Company of Rochester, New York. Despite restructuring efforts and attempts to compete with lower-priced Japanese camera film, Kodak stock sank to about $53 in mid-December, from $94.75 in mid-February.

International stock markets. Asian stock markets turned in the worst performances of 1997 on the world's exchanges. The Nikkei 225 index of major Japanese companies listed on the Tokyo Stock Exchange stood at 15909 in mid-December, off 18 percent for 1997. The year's strongest stock market was in Mexico, where the IPC Bolsa index of 35 leading companies advanced 46 percent to 4960. The Financial Times-Stock Exchange index of 100 stocks traded on the London Stock Exchange rose 24 percent to 5122. The main German stock index, the DAX index, was up 43 percent to 4029. ☐ Bill Barnhart

Sudan. Allied rebel forces launched a major military offensive on Jan. 12, 1997, against Sudanese government forces, raising fears that Sudan's 14-year-old civil war might fragment the country. The rebels hoped that their capture of several military garrisons would spark a popular uprising against Sudanese President Umar Hasan Ahmad al-Bashir, but by April the offensive had lost steam. On April 21, Bashir and a number of rebel groups signed a peace agreement.

The agreement brought little hope of real peace, however, because John Garang, leader of the strongest rebel group, the Sudan People's Liberation Army (SPLA), refused to sign the accord. The SPLA, consisting mainly of Christian and *animist* (believing that souls are present in all parts of nature) forces from southern Sudan, had fought to win autonomy from the mainly Muslim north since 1983. In 1989, after Bashir led a group of military officers to power, he instituted a harsh Islamic government. In 1991, northern opposition groups allied themselves with the SPLA and other southern rebel groups.

Civilian toll. War in Sudan continued to take its toll on civilians in 1997. In June, about 75,000 students graduating from secondary school were ordered to report to military training camps. Public servants in 1997 were required to give 10 percent of their salaries to defray the war's cost—estimated to be $1 million per day. In addition, tens of thousands of civilians were displaced from their houses and became refugees.

Regional relations. Fears of a wider, regional conflict grew during 1997 as the government accused Ethiopia, Uganda, and Eritrea of aiding the rebels. On January 13, the government claimed that Ethiopia supported the January 12 rebel offensive with artillery fire. Also in January, the government said that Uganda was allowing rebel troops to mass along the Sudanese border. In June, a Sudanese official said that Communists recently arrested for plotting subversive acts against the government had been supported by Eritrea.

United States. In November, the United States tightened sanctions against Sudan, citing Sudanese support of terrorism and abuse of human rights. While not breaking all diplomatic ties with Sudan, the United States in 1996 had withdrawn its diplomatic corps from the country, fearing for the safety of individuals.

Despite U.S. recommendations that outside nations not get involved in the affairs of the region, the United States announced in 1997 that it was increasing its military aid to Ethiopia, Eritrea, and Uganda to help those countries fight Sudanese-sponsored rebels. Some observers claimed that the aid would be used to support the rebels fighting Sudan's government. ☐ Christine Helms

See also **Middle East** (Facts in brief table).

Supreme Court of the United States.

In 1997, the Supreme Court of the United States issued important rulings on assisted suicide, gun control, free speech on the Internet, and the president's veto power.

Brennan dies. Justice William J. Brennan, Jr., who retired in 1990, having written more than 1,200 opinions for the Supreme Court, died on July 24, 1997. He was 91. Appointed by President Dwight D. Eisenhower in 1956, Brennan was considered a civil rights champion, a staunch opponent of the death penalty, and the author of some of the Supreme Court's most significant decisions in the areas of free speech, affirmative action, and individual liberties.

Brennan was born in Newark, New Jersey, and served on the New Jersey Superior Court from 1949 to 1952 and the New Jersey Supreme Court from 1952 to 1956. Among the decisions Brennan wrote was *Baker v. Carr* in 1962, which gave federal courts the power to ensure the fairness of voting districts. It established the principle of "one person, one vote." In 1964, Brennan wrote *New York Times v. Sullivan,* which protected the news media from libel suits by public officials unless the reporters intentionally or recklessly published falsehoods. In 1989, Brennan wrote *Texas v. Johnson,* which decided that burning the U.S. flag as an expression of political discontent is protected by the First Amendment guarantee of free speech.

Assisted suicide. In one of the most closely watched cases of the term, the court on June 26 unanimously upheld bans imposed by the states of New York and Washington on physician-assisted suicides. Both restrictions had been struck down by federal appeals courts that found terminally ill patients had a constitutional right to die.

In reversing the appeals courts' decisions, the Supreme Court ruled that there is no general constitutional right to physician-assisted suicide. However, the court noted that it might find in a future case that there is constitutional protection for a dying patient to control the manner of his or her death. The decision did not bar individual states from legalizing the process.

During the fall 1997 session, the court rejected an appeal to block Oregon's Death with Dignity Act, which had been approved by Oregon voters in 1994. The court's action, announced Oct. 13, 1997, made Oregon the first state to have legalized doctor-assisted suicide available for terminally ill patients.

Gun control. On June 27, the court struck down, in a 5-to-4 vote, the part of the 1993 Brady gun-control law that delegated responsibility for checking the background of people buying handguns. The majority opinion noted that the federal government cannot force local law enforcement officials to conduct background checks to determine whether a felony record, mental illness, or other problems in a buyer's personal history should prevent the sale of a gun. The ruling did not change the provision of the Brady law that requires a five-day waiting period before completing a gun purchase.

The decision's impact was expected to be short-lived. On Nov. 30, 1998, the law will require gun dealers to immediately check names of buyers against a computerized list of offenders prepared by the Federal Bureau of Investigation. Twenty-three states were covered by the Brady law in 1997. Twenty-seven states had enacted gun purchase screening measures that were more stringent than those laid down by the Brady law.

Congressional power. In a major ruling on the balance of powers between Congress and the courts, the justices on June 25, 1997, found the 1993 Reli-

Former Supreme Court Justice Harry A. Blackmun (center) is escorted from the July 29 funeral of former Justice William J. Brennan, Jr., by current members of the Supreme Court.

gious Freedom Restoration Act unconstitutional. The act provided that no level of government could enforce laws that would "substantially burden" religion without demonstrating a "compelling need."

The religious freedom act had been challenged by officials in Boerne, Texas, during a zoning dispute with a Roman Catholic congregation that wanted to renovate its historic building. In a 6-to-3 vote, the Supreme Court ruled that Congress had gone beyond its right to enforce the Fourteenth Amendment's provision for equal protection.

Buffer zones. On Feb. 19, 1997, the court upheld key parts of a federal judge's order designed to reduce confrontations outside abortion clinics in upstate New York. The justices voted 6 to 3 that antiabortion demonstrators can be kept 15 feet (4½ meters) away from clinic entrances, forming a buffer zone. However, the court ruled 8 to 1 that individual protesters cannot be barred from getting within 15 feet of anyone entering or leaving a clinic.

On a third issue, the court voted 6 to 3 that two protesters at a time could enter the 15-foot buffer zone to talk with women entering the clinics, but the protesters would have to leave if the women asked them to do so.

Church-state relations. The justices lowered the wall separating church and state in a June 23 ruling that allowed public school teachers on parochial school property to provide remedial education and guidance counseling to children struggling academically. Voting 5 to 4, the justices reversed a 1985 ban on the practice.

The decision affected children eligible for help through a federal program that channels money for remedial classes through local public schools. Because of a 1985 high court ruling, religious school students had to go off-campus for the special courses to avoid violating the First Amendment ban on the establishment of a state religion.

Presidential immunity. On May 27, 1997, the court unanimously ruled that Paula Jones could pursue a sexual harassment suit against President Bill Clinton while he was in office. The justices noted that the U.S. Constitution does not protect sitting presidents from lawsuits stemming from acts unrelated to their official duties.

Jones claimed that in 1991, when Clinton was governor of Arkansas and she was a state employee, Clinton met her in a Little Rock, Arkansas, hotel room and requested sexual favors. In 1994, Jones filed suit against Clinton, seeking a public apology and $700,000 in damages. Clinton denied the event occurred. In August 1997, U.S. District Judge Susan Webber Wright in Arkansas set a May 1998 date for the start of jury selection.

Free speech. In a 7-to-2 decision, the justices on June 26, 1997, struck down the 1996 Communications Decency Act, which made it illegal to post "indecent" or "patently offensive" words and pictures on the Internet where children could find them. Penalties for breaking the law included up to two years in prison and a $250,000 fine. The ruling was the court's first judgment involving the Internet.

The majority opinion stated that the law violated the Constitution's First Amendment because it limited communication among adults. The justices noted that the government cannot limit adults to seeing "only what is fit for children." The justices also wrote that the Internet is not as "invasive" as radio or television and that users seldom encounter content "by accident."

Following the court's decision, opponents of the Communications Decency Act said that Congress should encourage, rather than thwart, growth of the Internet. Supporters of the law argued that the court's action would harm parents' efforts to protect their children.

Line-item veto. The court on June 26, 1997, ruled that members of Congress do not have a legal right to challenge the constitutionality of the law giving the president power to cancel individual items of federal spending without vetoing the entire measure. In a 7-to-2 ruling, the court wrote that five members of Congress who challenged the president's "line-item veto" power in court had no legal right to do so because they had not suffered any personal injury from its use.

The court's ruling overturned a decision by Judge Thomas P. Jackson in U.S. District Court in Washington, D.C. Jackson said that a line-item veto violated the law-making procedure established by the Constitution and shifted too much power over spending and taxes from Congress to the president.

President Clinton used the line-item veto for the first time on August 11, when he vetoed two narrow tax breaks and a provision designed to help New York State gain more federal Medicaid money.

□ Geoffrey A. Campbell and Linda P. Campbell

See also **Civil rights; Courts; Internet; Religion; U.S. President.**

Surgery. See Medicine.

Suriname. See Latin America.

Swaziland. See Africa.

Sweden maintained an uneasy relationship with its partners in the European Union (EU), an organization of 15 Western European countries, in 1997. The Social Democrat-led government announced in June that Sweden would not join the single European currency scheduled to begin in 1999, even though the government continued to pursue budgetary policies that would qualify Sweden for participation. Prime Minister Goran Persson said that the Swedish people remained skeptical about closer cooperation with the EU, while the government feared that the euro, as the new currency was to be called, would be weak. Sweden was one of the EU's newest members, having joined in 1995. The country had briefly fixed its currency, the crown, to EU monies in the early 1990's but was forced to devalue the crown in the face of massive speculation in 1992.

Economy. The government in 1997 continued the tight spending policies adopted in 1996 and stayed on track in its goal to achieve a balanced budget in 1998. The European Commission (EC), the executive arm of the EU, forecast in October 1997 that Sweden's budget deficit would decline to 1.9 percent of gross domestic product (GDP) in 1997, down from 3.7 percent in 1996. Sweden's economy, along with the economies of other European countries, accelerated in 1997. The EC forecast in October that Sweden's GDP would rise by 2.1 percent in 1997 from 1.1 percent in 1996.

Unemployment edged above 10 percent in 1997. Prime Minister Persson resisted political pressure for tax cuts, and his Social Democratic Party promised in September to make permanent Sweden's temporary 5-percent income tax surcharge on high incomes if the Social Democrats won the next parliamentary election. The opposition conservatives promised to lower taxes, suggesting that taxes would be the main issue of the September 1998 election.

Nuclear power. The government in February 1997 announced its intention to shut down all of Sweden's nuclear power plants, though it did not set a deadline for doing so. In June, the government won parliament's approval for the first closures to be carried out at Barsebaeck in southwest Sweden. The site's first reactor was scheduled to be closed in July 1998, and its second, in 2001. Sweden's 12 nuclear reactors supply about half of the country's electricity.

Forced sterilizations. A Swedish newspaper triggered nationwide debate when it revealed in August 1997 that Sweden had sterilized as many as 60,000 citizens from 1935 to 1976 under a policy of *eugenics* (the suppression of genetic traits deemed to be inferior). Under the policy, sterilizations were carried out on a range of people: the mentally retarded; Gypsies; people of mixed race; and unmarried mothers. ☐ Tom Buerkle

See also **Europe** (Facts in brief table).

Swimming. In August 1997, Russia's Aleksandr Popov, returning to competition after being stabbed in a 1996 street altercation in Moscow, made the comeback of the year at the European Championships in Seville, Spain. He extended his winning streak in the 50 and 100 meters that began at the 1992 Olympics. The defending Olympic and European champion in the 100-meter freestyle, Popov won that race in 49.09 seconds, the year's fastest time. He achieved a second seasonal best when he won the 50-meter race in 22.30 seconds. He also won gold medals in the 4x100-meter individual freestyle and the 4x100-meter relay, leading a Russian team to victory in a European record time of 3:16.85.

De Bruin controversy continues. Ireland's Michelle de Bruin also received considerable attention in 1997, but for different reasons. De Bruin, the winner of three gold medals at the 1996 Olympics (under her maiden name, Michelle Smith), hoped to win five gold medals at the 1997 European Championships in Seville. However, she won only the women's 400-meter individual medley and the 200-meter freestyle, taking the silver in the 400-meter freestyle and the 200-meter butterfly races.

The crowds in Seville responded to de Bruin's performances, even her victories, with only tepid applause. After the meet, de Bruin announced that she was filing libel suits against four newspapers in Ireland and Great Britain. She claimed that her reputation had been damaged by speculation that her surprising 1996 Olympic performance was drug enhanced. The newspapers in question noted that the phenomenal improvement de Bruin showed in Atlanta came at age 26—relatively late in a swimmer's career—and that her husband, Erik de Bruin, was a former Dutch shot-put and discus thrower who had received a four-year suspension for using performance-enhancing drugs.

Record breakers. In nine days in February 1997, Russia's Denis Pankratov set four short-course (25-meter) pool world records in three different European meets. He set records in the men's 50-, 100-, and 200-meter butterfly. His fourth record came when he broke the 100-meter mark for the second time in a week.

Jenny Thompson of the United States also set a world record in 1997 and boosted her remarkable tally of national titles to 17, the most by any active swimmer. In April, at the World Short-Course Championships in Gothenburg, Sweden, Thompson set a world record for the women's 100-meter butterfly of 57.79 seconds. In August, she won five gold medals at the Pan Pacific Championships in Fukuoka, Japan, and was named outstanding female performer of the meet. Claudia Poll of Costa Rica set two world short-course records at Gothenburg—4:00.03 in the women's 400-meter freestyle and 1:54.17 in the 200-meter freestyle. ☐ Ron Reid

Switzerland continued to struggle in 1997 with allegations that the country and its banks had profited from World War II (1939–1945) dealings with Nazi Germany. The controversy began in 1996, when the British government opened wartime archives that indicated that Swiss banks had held at war's end as much as $4 billion in gold looted by the Nazis. Relations with the United States soured in 1996, when the U.S. Congress and President Bill Clinton put pressure on Switzerland to examine its records.

Swiss banks, industry, and the country's central bank established a fund of almost $200 million in February to compensate Holocaust victims and their heirs. The Holocaust was the systematic killing during World War II of 6 million Jews and other people considered undesirable by Germany's Nazi government.

In July, a number of Swiss banks released a list of 1,756 dormant accounts, worth $40 million, that had been opened by foreigners before 1945. Some of the accounts presumably belonged to people who were later victims of the Nazis. Another list, of 14,445 dormant accounts containing $8.2 million, was released in October. Jewish groups believed the real number of accounts to be higher, and a commission headed by Paul Volcker, former chairman of the U.S. Federal Reserve Board, continued its own investigation. At a December meeting in London, the United States and Britain pledged money for an international fund to compensate Holocaust victims. In March 1997, the Swiss government tried to restore its reputation by proposing to revalue the nation's gold reserves and use some of the resulting profits for a $4.7-billion Solidarity Fund, to generate annual income to aid victims of poverty, abuse, and natural disasters.

Banks merge. Switzerland's largest bank, Union Bank, agreed on December 8 to merge with the third-largest, Swiss Bank Corporation. The deal, expected to be completed in 1998, would create the world's second-largest bank in terms of assets and the largest fund manager, controlling $920 billion in investments. Swiss executives expected the merger to make the banks more competitive in the global banking market. The merger would eliminate about 13,000 jobs, including 7,000 in Switzerland, the country's largest layoff in history. In August 1997, Credit Suisse, Switzerland's second-largest bank, agreed to pay $9 billion for Winterthur Insurance. Both mergers attempted to cut costs, because the slow Swiss economy had lowered corporate profits.

Economy. The Organization for Economic Cooperation and Development, a group of 25 Western European, North American, and Pacific nations, forecast that Switzerland's 1997 economic growth would remain below 1 percent for the seventh straight year and that unemployment would rise to 5.4 percent in 1997 from 4.7 percent in 1996.   □ Tom Buerkle

See also **Europe** (Facts in brief table); **Judaism.**

Syria. On Sept. 12, 1997, U.S. Secretary of State Madeleine Albright met with Syrian President Hafiz al-Assad in an attempt to revive the failing Arab-Israeli peace process. Only minor progress was reported from the meeting, but Assad agreed to additional talks between Syrian and U.S. officials.

Although Syrian agreement was essential for a comprehensive Arab-Israeli peace, Israel had suspended peace talks with Syria in March 1996 after suffering a number of terrorist attacks. Assad had since refused to restart negotiations because Israeli Prime Minister Benjamin Netanyahu objected to returning the Golan Heights, territory captured from Syria by Israel in the 1967 Arab-Israeli Six-Day War. Negotiations with the Israeli government that preceded Netanyahu's government had led Assad to hope for the return of the Golan Heights.

Instead of returning the Golan Heights, Netanyahu reportedly proposed that Israel would withdraw its troops from southern Lebanon if Syria stopped attacks by Lebanese guerrillas against northern Israel. Syria, however, claimed that it had no control over the guerrillas. On Sept. 5, 1997, after a serious clash between guerrillas and Israeli commandos that left 12 commandos dead, Netanyahu insisted that Israeli troops would remain in southern Lebanon.

Syrian-Iraqi relations. As prospects for a comprehensive Arab-Israeli peace worsened in 1997, Syria attempted to improve its relations with Iraq. In mid-May, a delegation of six Syrian businessmen visited Iraq to discuss trade issues. The meeting was followed in mid-June by the visit of a 37-member Iraqi trade delegation to Syria. Syrian merchants hoped to sell food, soap, and pharmaceuticals to Iraq as a result of the permission, granted by the United Nations in late 1996, for Iraq to trade oil in exchange for humanitarian goods. On June 2, 1997, the border between Syria and Iraq was opened at three points for the first time in 17 years.

Syrian-Iraqi relations had been severed in 1980 when Syria supported Iran in the 1980-1988 Iran-Iraq war. Relations between Syria and Iraq worsened when Syria joined the U.S.-led multilateral force that ousted Iraqi forces from Kuwait in 1991.

Terrorism. The U.S. State Department's annual report on terrorism, released on April 30, 1997, continued to list Syria as a nation that sponsors terrorism. Some U.S. and Saudi officials claimed that Syria had failed to cooperate in 1997 with U.S. investigations of two terrorist bombings that killed American citizens in Saudi Arabia in 1995 and 1996. These officials claimed that Syria refused to apprehend a Saudi suspect who was linked to both incidents. Following a U.S. query about another Saudi suspect linked to the 1996 incident, Syrian officials responded that he had committed suicide.   □ Christine Helms

See also **Iraq; Israel; Lebanon; Middle East** (Facts in brief table).

Taiwan. The Taiwan National Assembly approved constitutional changes on July 18, 1997, that brought the island closer to formal independence from China. The island of Taiwan had separated from China in 1949, but China still regarded Taiwan as its province. The amendment expanded presidential power and virtually eliminated the provincial government. China warned that the amendment would not lessen China's claim to Taiwan and threatened that the act may lead to war.

The constitution used by Taiwan had been written in 1946 when the Kuomintang (KMT) Party ruled mainland China. When the Communist Party took control of China in 1949, the KMT, including leader Chiang Kai-shek, fled to Taiwan and set up a central government, but also retained the provincial government, which in 1997 employed hundreds of thousands of people and provided much of the same services as the central government.

President Li Teng-hui campaigned for the elimination of the provincial government. The ruling KMT and its opposition, the Democratic Progressive Party, both backed the measure, approving the amendment in a 261 to 8 vote. The KMT said that the amendment was intended to increase government efficiency and not to change Taiwan's national identity. The Democratic Progressive Party, which favors complete independence from China, hailed the move as "opening a chapter for a new Taiwanese history."

A Chinese ship arrives in Taiwan's Kaohsiung port on April 19, the first Chinese ship to dock in Taiwan in more than 40 years. In 1997, Taiwan eased a ban on Chinese shipping.

Chinese officials protested the amendment, stating that the move was another step toward abandoning reunification. Branding Taiwan as a "rebel province," Chinese leaders had repeatedly threatened to use force against Taiwan if it moved toward formal independence. A public opinion poll conducted in July showed that 43 percent of the Taiwan population favored independence and 34 percent supported reunification with the mainland.

Trade relations between Taiwan and China improved in 1997, when Taiwan eased a ban on shipping from China. In April, the first legal commercial shipping link across the Taiwan strait was opened. Extensive trade also went through Hong Kong.

Boycott. Many world leaders stayed away from a September conference in Panama to discuss the future of the Panama Canal. China, attempting to block Taiwan from retaining diplomatic relations with other countries, called for a boycott because of Taiwan's participation in the event.

Resignation. Taiwan's government survived a no-confidence vote in May 1997 that was brought by legislators over a series of unsolved murders and rising crime. The KMT defeated a move by opposition parties to force the resignation of Prime Minister Lien Chan's cabinet. However, on August 21, Lien resigned and was replaced by Vincent Siew, a former economics minister. □ Henry S. Bradsher

See also **Asia** (Facts in brief table); **China**.

Tajikistan. The five-year civil war in Tajikistan ended on June 27, 1997, with the signing of a peace accord in Moscow. The document was signed by both Tajik President Emomali Rahmonov and Said Abdullah Nuri, leader of the United Tajik Opposition (UTO). The wars erupted in 1992 after rebel forces backed by Russia toppled a popularly elected Islamic government in Tajikistan. United Nations troops had maintained an intermittent cease-fire since 1995.

Under the agreement, the UTO was to receive 30 percent of the posts in the Tajik government. In addition, the political parties comprising the UTO were legalized, and the UTO army was to merge with the Tajik army. While delays in exchanging prisoners of war and repatriating refugees threatened to derail the agreement, a compromise was reached shortly before the peace accord was signed.

Extremists on both sides, however, opposed the peace plan, and political violence in Tajikistan continued. In August 1997, Tajikistan's Islamic spiritual leader, Amonullo Negmatzoda, and his son were kidnapped in separate incidents; a series of bombings in September and October damaged several government buildings in the capital, Dushanbe; and an October 16 attack on the presidential guard barracks by some 80 gunmen left 14 soldiers and 3 attackers dead. □ Steven L. Solnick

See also **Asia** (Facts in brief table).

Tanzania. See Africa.

395

Taxation. President Bill Clinton and the U.S. Congress announced in July 1997 the largest federal tax cut since 1981. The cut, a legislative compromise, benefited families with children, investors, and college students and provided total tax cuts worth more than $90 billion through the year 2002. The agreement was reached after negotiations between the Clinton Administration and Republican congressional leaders on tax cuts and spending reductions designed to achieve a balanced budget by 2002.

Major provisions of the agreement included a $400-per-child tax credit—set to begin in 1998 and to be raised to $500 in 1999—for children 16 or younger. The credit would be phased out for couples earning more than $110,000 a year. A maximum tax credit of $1,500 for the first two years of college tuition was approved, with credits for additional years of college set at $1,000.

The agreement also lowered the individual tax rate for *capital gains* (profit on the sale of assets) from a maximum of 28 percent to 20 percent, retroactive to May 7, 1997. Assets held for five years would have a top capital-gain rate of 18 percent after the year 2001. The exemption for estate taxes was raised from $600,000 to $1 million, to be phased in over the next 10 years. The law also increased taxes on cigarettes by 10 cents a pack in the year 2000 and by another 5 cents a pack in the year 2002.

President Bill Clinton signed separate budget and tax bills on Aug. 5, 1997, at a bipartisan White House ceremony. Critics, claiming that the changes complicated an already complex tax code, said that the tax cuts would lead to increased revenue losses after the year 2002.

On Aug. 11, 1997, President Clinton used the line-item veto for the first time to block three specific provisions from budget and tax bills. The president struck down two narrow tax breaks and a provision designed to help the state of New York gain more federal Medicaid money.

IRS criticisms. The Internal Revenue Service (IRS) came under harsh criticism in both houses of Congress in 1997. In November, the House of Representatives voted 426 to 4 in favor of a bill that would overhaul the IRS. If approved by the Senate, the legislation would create an 11-member independent board to supervise the IRS; it would give taxpayers 28 new rights and shift the burden of proof from taxpayers to the IRS on disputes that go to court; and it would implement changes to improve customer service.

The bill followed a series of taxpayer complaints and claims of IRS mismanagement. Senate Finance Committee hearings held in September 1997 focused on the abuse and harassment of some taxpayers. During the hearings, acting IRS Commissioner Michael P. Dolan apologized for the department's conduct and promised new programs to improve the handling of taxpayer complaints.   ☐ William J. Eaton

Telecommunications. The competition for local telephone and television cable service in the United States promised by the 1996 Telecommunications Reform Act failed to materialize in 1997. While the act permitted telephone and cable operators to enter one another's businesses, most communities were still being served by only one cable operator at the end of 1997, and telephone competition was limited to the long-distance arena. All but a few cable operators decided to avoid the telephone business, and regional telephone companies decided to stick to their core business. Industry observers noted that the threat of competition from such long-distance giants as AT&T Corp., Sprint Corp., and MCI Incorporated scared off most regional telephone companies, which could not invest the money necessary to launch broad-scale cable operations while protecting themselves against competition for local phone service.

Telephone competition. The Telecommunications Act also allowed regional telephone companies to offer long-distance service outside their local areas after they opened their own markets to competition. On June 26, the Federal Communications Commission (FCC) rejected a plan by SBC Communications Inc., a regional Bell, to offer national long-distance services in Oklahoma. The FCC said SBC subscribers had no other options for regional long-distance service. The rejection marked the first time the FCC had blocked an attempt by a regional telephone company to enter the long-distance market.

An FCC attempt to boost competition between regional and national long-distance carriers was struck down by a federal appeals court on July 18. The FCC rules had provided guidelines for regulating prices among competing long-distance carriers in a particular market. According to the guidelines, regional long-distance companies would have been required to levy uniform charges for access to local phone networks on all companies operating in the market. The court ruled, however, that under the Telecommunications Act, only the states had the power to regulate prices.

The decision was expected to slow the competition for long-distance service. Industry observers predicted long-distance carriers would be reluctant to launch new operations that would be governed by multiple sets of regulations.

World telecommunications pact. More than 65 countries, including the United States, members of the European Union, an organization of 15 Western European nations, and Japan, agreed to open their domestic telephone markets to international competition in an accord announced on February 15. The pact covered more than 90 percent of the $600-billion international telecommunications industry.

The FCC estimated that the agreement, scheduled to take effect on Jan. 1, 1998, would cut the cost of an international telephone call by 80 percent over a period of several years. However, the pact did not completely deregulate global communications. Some participating countries retained the right to prevent foreign companies from gaining controlling ownership of their major telephone companies.

Judicial decisions. The Supreme Court of the United States on March 31, 1997, dealt the cable industry a major defeat by upholding a 1992 federal law that required cable television systems to carry local broadcast channels. The court rejected the cable industry's arguments that the so-called "must carry" law violated its right of free speech. The justices contended that the government had a legitimate interest in ensuring that all households had access to a wide range of local programming.

On June 26, 1997, the high court struck down the Communications Decency Act. The act, a provision of the 1996 Telecommunications Reform Act, had imposed stiff penalties on anyone who distributed "indecent or patently offensive material" online. The law was partly intended to protect children from sexually explicit articles, photographs, and other material carried on the Internet, the global communications network. The majority opinion supported the argument of free speech advocates that the right of adults to freedom of expression overrode any interest, however compelling, in protecting children from pornography.　　　□ Tim Jones

See also **Internet; Radio; Television.**

Television. The television industry's voluntary rating system for programming went into effect on Jan. 1, 1997. The system mandated that a small icon, displaying an "age rating," appear for 15 seconds at the start of each program in the upper-left corner of the screen. Shows were rated TV-G (general audience), TV-PG (parental guidance), TV-14 (inappropriate for children under 14), or TV-MA (for mature audiences only). Ratings for children's programming carried the ratings of TV-Y (for all children) or TV-Y7 (may be unsuitable for children under 7).

Shortly after the debut of the system, some parent and teacher groups criticized the ratings as vague and inconsistent. In July, the television industry agreed to an additional set of ratings, which were implemented on October 1. The expanded system contained four more specific labels: D (explicit dialogue), L (coarse language), S (sexual situations), and V (violence). Although most of the major broadcasting and cable networks agreed to use the rating system, the National Broadcasting Company (NBC) declined to participate, using instead its own advisory warnings.

Special events programming attracted record television audiences in 1997. More than 65 million people watched Steven Spielberg's 1993 film "Schindler's List," broadcast by NBC on Feb. 23, 1997, without commercial interruption. The total number of television viewers of the three-hour

Academy Award-winning film on a single night was more than twice the film's total audience during its theatrical run.

More than 50 million viewers in the United States watched the London funeral of Diana, Princess of Wales, during the early morning hours of September 6. In Great Britain, more than 31.5 million people watched the funeral, which was shown on most broadcast and cable channels. The funeral culminated a week of almost around-the-clock television coverage that began almost immediately following the princess's death August 31 in Paris in an automobile accident.

Lawsuit settled. A federal jury in Greensboro, North Carolina, on January 22 awarded the Food Lion supermarket chain $5.5 million in punitive damages in its lawsuit against the American Broadcasting Company (ABC). The lawsuit stemmed from a 1992 story on "Prime Time Live," an ABC news show, that reported that the grocery chain had deliberately sold spoiled meat and produce.

To research and film the story, two ABC producers had obtained jobs in the meat department of Food Lion stores in North Carolina and South Carolina and had taped practices with hidden cameras. Food Lion sued ABC for fraud, accusing the two producers of trespassing and of submitting false resumes. On Aug. 29, 1997, a federal judge reduced the damages in the case to $315,000.

Cable television. The U.S. Supreme Court on March 31 upheld a 1992 federal law requiring cable TV systems to carry the signals of local broadcast channels. The "must carry" law had been challenged by cable companies, which claimed that the requirements were an unconstitutional challenge to their freedom of speech.

Broadcast television received another boost on April 3, 1997, when the Federal Communications Commission (FCC) approved a plan to introduce high-definition television programming (HDTV) in the United States. HDTV provides clearer, sharper pictures on wider screens. In a separate decision on April 3, the FCC also voted to lend all 1,600 U.S. television stations a second channel for HDTV programming. Each station would operate both traditional and HDTV channels until the year 2006, when HDTV was scheduled to completely replace conventional TV signals.

Daring subjects. Television programs tackled a few daring subjects in 1997, to the chagrin of some major advertisers. In a special hour-long episode of "Ellen" on April 30, the ABC situation comedy's title character, played by Ellen DeGeneres, revealed that she was gay. Although TV shows had featured gay characters for several years, "Ellen" became the first program to have a gay character in the leading role.

The highly publicized episode captured a large viewing audience. However, ratings gradually declined as the season continued. In the wake of much publicity preceding the episode, some television critics reported that the only surprise was in the line-up of advertisers. Bowing to pressure from conservative organizations, most regular advertisers—including major fast-food, beverage, and car companies—chose not to purchase airtime during the episode.

Another *sitcom* (situation comedy), CBS's "Murphy Brown," proved controversial when it returned for its 10th season in October. The title character, played by Candace Bergen, discovered that she had breast cancer and underwent treatment. While some critics applauded the series for tackling a real-life situation, other critics and organizations blasted the character's use of marijuana in order to relieve the side effects of chemotherapy.

Few runaway hits emerged during the 1997 fall line-up. An exception, "Ally McBeal" on the Fox Network, depicted the life of a young lawyer, played by Calista Flockhart, and combined drama with workplace comedy and wild fantasy. The other new sitcom hits of the 1997 fall season were "Dharma and Greg" on ABC and "The Gregory Hines Show" on CBS.

Old favorites. Several favorite stars returned to TV in new fall shows. Bob Newhart, a veteran of "The Bob Newhart Show" and "Newhart," teamed with Judd Hirsch, star of "Taxi," in a CBS sitcom. The duo played "George & Leo," two disparate fathers-in-law. On the NBC show "Veronica's Closet," Kirstie Alley, formerly of "Cheers," starred as a former model who owns a lingerie catalog company. Not all the returning veterans were actors. "Public Eye with Bryant Gumbel" on CBS brought back the former "Today" show host in a television newsmagazine format.

Religion on TV. Religion was a common theme on a number of fall season shows that were inspired by the CBS series "Touched by an Angel." The dramatic series, which depicts two angels in human form bringing hope to troubled people, had grown steadily more popular and influential since its debut in the 1994 season. Similar offerings in 1997 included "Nothing Sacred," in which a young priest, played by stage actor Kevin Anderson, deals with his

In May, NBC agreed to pay Michael Richards (left), Julia Louis-Dreyfus (second from left), and Jason Alexander (right) a reported $600,000 per episode of the hit comedy "Seinfeld." Jerry Seinfeld, (second from right) was reported to earn $1 million for each half-hour show.

Top-rated U.S. television series

The following were among the most-watched television series for the 1996-1997 regular season, which ran from Sept. 16, 1996, to May 21, 1997.

1. "E.R." (NBC)
2. "Seinfeld" (NBC)
3. "Suddenly Susan" (NBC)
4. (tie) "Friends (NBC)
   "The Naked Truth" (NBC)
6. "Fired Up" (NBC)
7. "NFL Monday Night Football" (ABC)
8. "The Single Guy" (NBC)
9. "Home Improvement" (ABC)
10. "Touched by an Angel" (CBS)
11. "60 Minutes" (CBS)
12. "20/20" (ABC)
13. "N.Y.P.D. Blue" (ABC)
14. "CBS Sunday Night Movie" (CBS)
15. "Prime Time Live" (ABC)
16. "Frasier" (NBC)
17. "Spin City" (ABC)
18. (tie) "NBC Sunday Night Movie" (NBC)
    "The Drew Carey Show" (ABC)
20. (tie) "The X-Files" (FOX)
    "Dateline NBC (Tuesday)" (NBC)
22. (tie) "Soul Man" (ABC)
    "Cosby" (CBS)
24. (tie) "Walker, Texas Ranger" (CBS)
    "Mad About You" (NBC)
    "NBC Monday Night Movie" (NBC)
    "Caroline in the City" (NBC)

Source: 1998 A&E Entertainment Almanac.

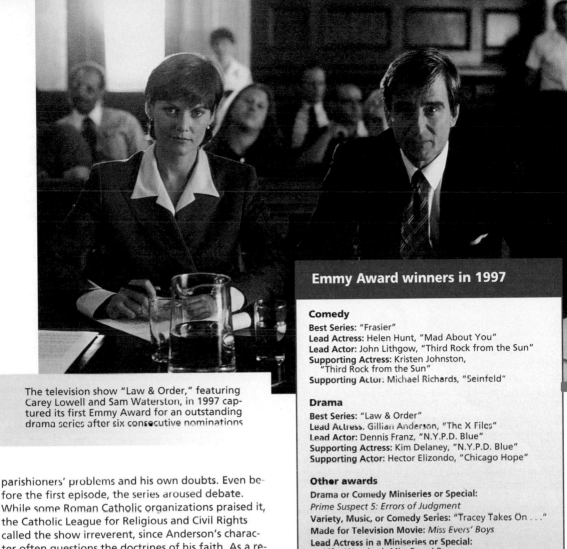

The television show "Law & Order," featuring Carey Lowell and Sam Waterston, in 1997 captured its first Emmy Award for an outstanding drama series after six consecutive nominations.

parishioners' problems and his own doubts. Even before the first episode, the series aroused debate. While some Roman Catholic organizations praised it, the Catholic League for Religious and Civil Rights called the show irreverent, since Anderson's character often questions the doctrines of his faith. As a result, several of the show's sponsors withdrew their advertising.

Less controversial new shows included two other ABC programs. "Soul Man" starred comedian Dan Aykroyd as a motorcycle-riding minister and widower. "Teen Angel" focused on a deceased adolescent who acts as his best friend's guardian angel. The United Paramount Network (UPN) launched "Good News," featuring an African American pastor.

New dramas. Veteran producer Steven Bochco was back in 1997 with another police drama, CBS's "Brooklyn South." "Brooklyn South" was the first show in several years to concentrate on uniformed officers, rather than plain-clothes detectives.

Lawyers were also well-represented in the fall 1997 television lineup. David Caruso, one of the original stars of "N.Y.P.D. Blue," played crusading district attorney "Michael Hayes" on CBS. Defense attorneys struggled in "The Practice," a 1997 spring replacement show that ABC carried into the fall.

Live broadcast. The season premiere of the NBC drama "E.R.," the highest-rated show of the 1996–1997 season, provided the network with healthy rat-ings on Sept. 25, 1997, when it broadcast the episode live. The season opener drew 42.7 million viewers, television's largest audience ever for the season premiere of a drama series.

Federal regulations requiring broadcast stations to carry three hours of educational children's programming each week took effect September 1. Few stations offered much innovation, however. Most stations either repeated old children's programs or added brief educational messages to slapstick comedies and sports shows. One of the few exceptions was ABC's "Science Court," a cartoon that combined humor with scientific theory.   ☐ Troy Segal

See also **Telecommunications.**

Tennessee. See State government.

399

On July 5, 1997, Switzerland's Martina Hingis, at age 16, becomes the youngest player to win a Wimbledon singles final in 110 years.

age of 15. The grand-slam victory earned Hingis more than $522,000 in prize money.

Hingis proved to be less successful five months later, when her streak of 37 victories was spoiled on June 7 by Iva Majoli of Croatia in the women's final of the 1997 French Open tennis tournament in Paris. Hingis was still recovering from arthroscopic knee surgery when she lost to Majoli, 6-4, 6-2. The victory made Majoli the first Croatian player to win a grand-slam title.

On July 5, Hingis became the youngest player in more than a century to win a Wimbledon singles title. She defeated third-seeded Jana Novotna of the Czech Republic, 2-6, 6-3, 6-3, in the British tournament. Hingis put on a superb tennis demonstration highlighted by well-placed, two-handed backhand shots. It was her 44th victory of 1997.

Hingis recorded her third grand-slam and 10th tournament title in 1997 on September 7 at the U.S. Open, which was held for the first time at the newly constructed Arthur Ashe Stadium in New York City. In the women's singles final, Hingis defeated Venus Williams of Florida, 6-0, 6-4. Williams, an unseeded 17-year-old, was the first African American woman to reach the U.S. Open final since Althea Gibson won the tournament in 1957. Williams hurt her chances for victory with a combined 38 errors in both sets. Hingis won $650,000, and her record improved to 63-2.

Tennis. Martina Hingis, a teen-ager from Switzerland, and Pete Sampras, a 25-year-old veteran from the United States, were the world's outstanding tennis players in 1997. Hingis, who turned 17 on September 30, won three grand-slam titles and more than $3 million in 1997. Sampras won two of the four grand-slam tennis titles—the Australian Open and Wimbledon—and earned $6 million.

Women. Hingis captured the first grand-slam title of her career on January 25, when she defeated Mary Pierce of the United States in the Australian Open singles final at Melbourne. Hingis needed only one hour to complete her 6-2, 6-2 victory. At the age of 16 years, 3 months, she became the youngest winner of a grand-slam tournament since Charlotte "Lottie" Dodd won at Wimbledon in 1887, at the

Men. Sampras, ranked as the best men's player throughout 1997, got off to an impressive start with a decisive victory on January 26 over Carlos Moya of Spain for the men's title at the Australian Open in Melbourne. Sampras defeated Moya in straight sets, 6-2, 6-3, 6-3. Moya, who defeated Boris Becker and Michael Chang in earlier tournament rounds, never found his rhythm against Sampras in the finals. Sampras's point tally against Moya included 12 *aces* (points won by a single stroke—usually a serve that an opponent is unable to return).

The season's most celebrated grand-slam victory occurred on June 8, at the French Open, when Brazil's Gustavo Kuerten upset Sergi Bruguera of Spain to win the men's title. Kuerten, 20, came into the tournament ranked 66th in the world. He finished as the first Brazilian to win a men's grand-slam title. The French Open men's final was only the 49th match of Kuerten's professional career.

Sampras staged a comeback on July 6 at Wimbledon to take the men's singles championship for the fourth time in his career, boosting his grand-slam titles to 10. Sampras easily defeated Cedric Pioline of France, 6-4, 6-2, 6-4, in a match that took only 94 minutes to play. Sports observers noted that Sampras had shown especially impressive quickness in reaching the net against Pioline, who was the first Frenchman to reach a Wimbledon final since 1946.

In an unexpected final matchup, Patrick Rafter of Australia, seeded 13th, captured the men's title at the U.S. Open on Sept. 7, 1997, by defeating an unseeded opponent, Greg Rusedski of Great Britain, 6-3, 6-2, 4-6, 7-5. The U.S. Open was only the second tournament championship of Rafter's professional career. Rafter was the first Australian to win the U.S. Open men's championship since John Newcombe in 1973.

Davis Cup. Sampras and Michael Chang were selected for the singles spots in the Davis Cup semifinals versus Australia and led the United States to a 4-1 victory in September 1997 in Washington, D.C. The United States, however, was defeated 5-1 by Sweden in the Davis Cup final, which was held in Goteborg, Sweden, in November. ☐ Ron Reid

Terrorism. Violent campaigns by extremist groups plagued nations worldwide in 1997. *Religious nationalists*—people intent upon making their religion the dominant political force in their nation or region—carried out much of the bloodshed. Governments were accused of responding to violent attacks with terrorist acts as well.

Algeria and Egypt. In Algeria, where more than 80,000 people died in religious struggles between 1992 and 1997, Islamic militants carried out civilian massacres in 1997. On August 29, approximately 300 people were killed in an attack on the village of Reis. The Algerian government was accused by human-rights groups of responding to such attacks by forming vigilante squads to massacre civilians suspected of siding with Muslim extremists.

In Egypt, where the government believed it had suppressed most religious extremists, members of the outlawed Islamic Group attacked and killed 58 foreign tourists and 4 Egyptians at an ancient temple in Luxor on November 17. The attack was the deadliest yet in a nearly six-year campaign to replace Egypt's secular government with an Islamic state.

Israel. In 1997, members of the militant Islamic group Hamas claimed responsibility for two suicide bombing incidents: On March 21, a suicide bombing killed three Israelis in Tel Aviv; and on July 30, two other suicide bombers killed 16 people and injured approximately 150 others in a Jerusalem market. Ob-

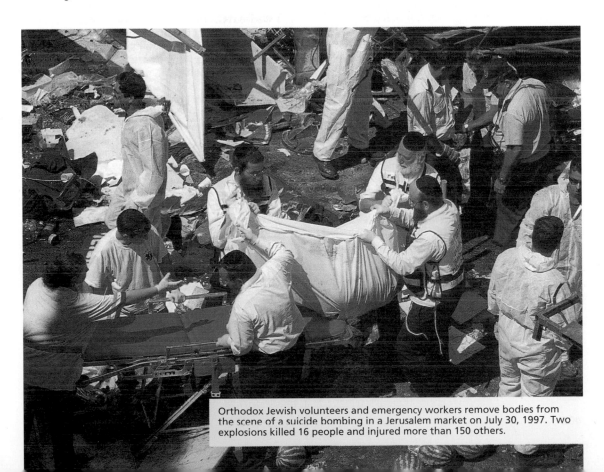

Orthodox Jewish volunteers and emergency workers remove bodies from the scene of a suicide bombing in a Jerusalem market on July 30, 1997. Two explosions killed 16 people and injured more than 150 others.

servers believed that the bombings, the first in Israel for more than a year, had been set in retaliation for the building of Jewish housing settlements in East Jerusalem, an area claimed by both Israelis and Palestinians. Israeli intelligence agents on September 25 allegedly attempted to assassinate Hamas leader Khaled Meshal in Amman, the capital of Jordan. The attempt misfired, straining Israeli relations with Jordan and embarrassing the government of Israeli Prime Minister Benjamin Netanyahu.

South Asia. Terrorist violence continued in 1997 in strife-torn Pakistan, where more than 300 people were killed as a result of rivalries among various Islamic sects and armed groups, many of which had been formed to fight in Afghanistan during the former Soviet Union's occupation in the 1980's. On Nov. 12, 1997, unidentified Pakistanis shot and killed four visiting American businessmen and their Pakistani driver in Karachi. The attack was believed to be in retaliation for the November 11 conviction in Fairfax, Virginia, of Mir Aimal Kasi, a Pakistani. Kasi was convicted of shooting five people in 1993, two of whom died, outside U.S. Central Intelligence Agency headquarters in Langley, Virginia.

Ethnic Bodo separatists, seeking an independent state in northeastern India, claimed responsibility in January 1997 for a 1996 train bombing in the state of Assam that had killed 38 people. The attack was one of a series of bombings that continued into 1997. In New Delhi, India's capital, at least 19 bombings claimed seven lives in 1997. A Sikh group seeking independence in the state of Punjab claimed responsibility for some of the attacks. Groups representing clashing Hindu and Muslim interests continued to battle in 1997 in Kashmir, the disputed border territory between Pakistan and India. In Sri Lanka, the armed struggle intensified between the government, representing the Sinhalese Buddhist majority, and the Liberation Tigers of Tamil Eelam, representing ethnic minority Tamils. Since the beginning of a major military offensive in May, more than 3,000 rebels and soldiers had been killed.

Latin America. On April 22, 1997, Peruvian commandos launched a surprise attack to rescue hostages held by members of the leftist Tupác Amaru Revolutionary Movement (MRTA) in Lima, Peru's capital. In December 1996, the MRTA had taken hundreds of hostages at a party at the residence of the Japanese ambassador. The rebels, who demanded that imprisoned MRTA rebels be set free, later released all but 72 hostages. In the April attack, soldiers killed all 14 MRTA guerrillas and rescued the hostages, one of whom died shortly afterward.

In Colombia, feuding drug lords and leftist guerrillas fought a small-scale civil war during 1997. Warring factions assassinated scores of police officers, officials, and candidates running for office. Health Minister María Teresa Forero estimated that violence caused 1 of every 3 deaths in Colombia in 1997.

United States. New York City police officers arrested two Palestinian men on July 31 and charged them with conspiring to bomb the city's subway system. On November 12, Ramzi Ahmed Yousef and Eyad Ismoil were convicted for their roles in the 1993 bombing of New York City's World Trade Center.

On June 13, a federal jury in Denver recommended the death sentence for Timothy J. McVeigh, who was convicted on 11 counts of murder and conspiracy in connection with the 1995 bombing of the Alfred P. Murrah Federal Building in Oklahoma City, Oklahoma. On Dec. 23, 1997, a federal jury found a codefendant, Terry L. Nichols, guilty of conspiring to bomb the building and of involuntary manslaughter.

On April 27, members of the militia group, Republic of Texas, kidnapped two people, initiating a seven-day standoff with state and local police near Fort Davis, Texas. The militia maintained that Texas had been illegally annexed by the United States in 1845 and was, therefore, an independent country. Six members of the group surrendered on May 3, 1997, and two others escaped, one of whom was killed in a gun battle with police. In November, Richard McLaren and Robert Otto, two of the leaders, were convicted of plotting the kidnapping.

☐ Richard E. Rubenstein

See also **Algeria; Colombia; Egypt; India; Israel; Peru; Sri Lanka; United States, Government of the.**

Texas. See **Dallas; State government.**

Thailand. The Thai economy crashed in 1997, abruptly halting a decade of rapid growth and triggering a financial crisis throughout Southeast Asia. Thailand devalued its currency, the baht, in July, causing it to tumble more than 30 percent against the U.S. dollar. The financial crisis resulted in the collapse of the Thai government in November.

From the late 1980's through the mid-1990's, Thailand's economy grew at an average of 8 percent a year. The economy began to slow in 1996, when growth fell to 6.7 percent from 8.5 percent in 1995. The economy was expected to grow less than 2 percent in 1997, and unemployment soared. Exports were down sharply, and Thailand faced a budget deficit for the first time in decades. From 1994 to 1997, the Thai stock market fell 65 percent. Growth was funded primarily by foreign investment. The debt created by these investments became increasingly harder to pay as demand for exports slowed.

Foreign investment also financed the real estate boom in Bangkok, the capital. The boom turned into a bust in the mid-1990's, when occupancy rates fell for luxury housing and office space, burdening banks with $17 billion in unpaid property debt. The government compounded the financial crisis by spending 8 percent more than it received in revenues.

After long denying the severity of its problems, the Thai government devalued its currency in an attempt to shore up the country's faltering economy.

The move, which economists hoped would attract investors to Thai exports and stocks, caused foreign investors to lose confidence in the country and made it harder for the government to repay loans and borrow from abroad.

IMF bailout. On Aug. 11, 1997, the International Monetary Fund (IMF), a United Nations agency, and a group of Asian nations led by Japan agreed to a $16-billion rescue of Thailand's economy. IMF terms required that the Thai government raise taxes, cut spending, and keep inflation below 9 percent.

New constitution. On Sept. 27, 1997, the Thai Parliament approved a new constitution, the 16th charter since Thailand became a constitutional monarchy in 1932. The constitution was drafted to change Thailand's electoral system, under which the buying of votes had been widespread and had drained the country's treasury.

Government collapse. Demonstrators in October 1997 called for the resignation of Prime Minister Chavalit Yongchaiyudh, who had been widely criticized for his handling of the economic crisis. Chavalit resigned from office on November 3. Thailand's new 48-member Cabinet, led by Prime Minister Chuan Likphai, was sworn in by King Bhumibol Adulyadej on November 15. Chuan said he did not expect Thailand to fully recover from its financial crisis until the year 2000.   □ Henry S. Bradsher

See also **Asia** (Facts in brief table).

Theater. The flurry of productions in New York in the spring of 1997 were remarkable more for their quantity than for artistic innovation. While the burst of excitement in the musical genre generated by 1996's *Rent* and *Bring in 'Da Noise, Bring in 'Da Funk* was not duplicated in 1997, the Antoinette Perry (Tony) Award judges did have a healthy quantity of musicals to choose from at awards time in June.

Tony Awards. *Titanic,* an operatic but less an dramatic pageant about the sinking of the famous ocean liner, swept the awards over more conventional productions—*The Life, Steel Pier, Dream, Play On!, Jekyll and Hyde,* and *Candide*—indicating that Tony voters were interested in honoring artistic aspiration over commercialism.

Alfred Uhry's *The Last Night of Ballyhoo,* about a Jewish family in Atlanta, Georgia, in the 1930's—which had received mixed reviews—won in the best-play category over two highly acclaimed British plays, *Stanley* and *Skylight,* and over the 1995 Pulitzer Prize winner *The Young Man from Atlanta* by Horton Foote. A British production of Henrik Ibsen's *A Doll's House,* which played on Broadway, was awarded best play revival of 1997. It featured an astonishingly vibrant leading performance by Janet McTeer, who won the Tony for best actress.

Critics widely agreed that the most exciting production of early 1997 was *Chicago,* a concert-style revival of Bob Fosse's dark, sexy musical. Winning six

Tony awards, *Chicago* continued to play on Broadway through 1997, and a national tour and London production opened before year's end. *Noise/Funk* and *Rent,* meanwhile, proved that their appeal extended beyond New York. As their Broadway productions continued to play to capacity audiences, national tours for both shows were launched in 1997.

Other New York productions. The off-Broadway hit of 1997 was *Gross Indecency: The Three Trials of Oscar Wilde,* about Wilde's infamous prosecution for indecent behavior. (In 1895, Wilde was accused of having homosexual relations and was later sentenced to two years in prison.) Director and writer Moisés Kaufman funded the initial production himself, which moved to an open run at a larger off-Broadway house following outstanding reviews. Another off-Broadway hit was Paula Vogel's *How I Learned to Drive,* a troubling but moving look at incest, which seemed destined for a long run in New York and multiple regional restagings.

In the fall, a burst of vital new musicals opened on Broadway: *Ragtime,* an epic-scale musical about the United States in the early 1900's, based on the 1975 novel by E. L. Doctorow; *The Lion King,* a stage version of the Disney movie; *Triumph of Love,* a musicalization of a 1732 French comedy by Pierre Marivaux; and *The Scarlet Pimpernel,* a musical version of the swashbuckling classic set during the French Revolution (1789–1799).

New writers. A young generation of Anglo- and Anglo-Irish writers brought a disturbingly violent burst of energy to British stages in 1997. The Royal Court Theatre maintained its commitment to the most outspoken young writers with its premiere of a play by 30-year-old Mark Ravenhill that equated human interaction to commercial transactions and featured a title so profane that most publications would not print it. At the Royal National Theatre, 31-year-old Patrick Marber's *Closer* was a bracingly—some critics said depressingly—honest look at romantic relationships. Both Ravenhill and Marber were courted by American producers.

The hot young playwright of 1997 was 26-year-old Martin McDonagh, a Londoner of Irish descent. Although McDonagh claimed to have no interest and background in the theater, his plays displayed a kinship with the Irish plays of John Middleton Synge and the high-octane violence in the films of Quentin Tarantino. First premiered at the Druid Theatre in Galway, Ireland, McDonagh's plays, including *The Cripple of Inishmaan* and *The Beauty Queen of Leenane,* enjoyed success on the West End of London and on international tours in 1997. New York productions of both were planned for early 1998.

The Globe. The long-awaited royal opening of Shakespeare's Globe Theatre on the South Bank of the River Thames in London in June 1997 was nothing if not dramatic—Queen Elizabeth II arrived by barge to give the official blessing to the theater. The

Scenic designer Stewart Laing's re-creation of the *Titanic,* the ill-fated ocean liner, sails onto Broadway in 1997 in the Tony Award-winning musical *Titanic.*

new Globe, a replica of the original structure, presents Shakespearean and other Elizabethan plays.

London theater news. Richard Eyre's nine-year term as artistic director of the Royal National Theatre ended in September. Under Eyre's direction, the three-theater complex on the South Bank experienced popular and critical success that was unprecedented since the National's 1963 founding by Laurence Olivier. The productions that opened prior to Eyre's departure typified his embrace of new plays from emerging and established writers and the bold revitalization of the classics. Productions included new works by David Hare and Tom Stoppard; new productions of Bertolt Brecht, Peter Weiss, and Shakespeare; and a joyous revival of the classic musical *Guys and Dolls,* directed by Eyre himself.

The National replaced Eyre with Trevor Nunn, former artistic director of the Royal Shakespeare Company. His selection was seen by many as a conservative choice, but Nunn's reign at the National started strong, with new works by Michael Frayn and Caryl Churchill; revivals of Henrik Ibsen, George Bernard Shaw, and Arnold Wesker; and *Peter Pan,* featuring Sir Ian McKellan as Captain Hook.

Composer and producer Andrew Lloyd Webber's production company Really Useful Group (RUG) suffered a round of setbacks in 1997. Lloyd Webber's latest megamusical, *Whistle Down the Wind,* closed after a troubled tryout in Washington, D.C., without

Tony Awards winners in 1997

Best Play, *The Last Night of Ballyhoo,* Alfred Uhry
Best Musical, *Titanic*
Best Play Revival, *A Doll's House*
Best Musical Revival, *Chicago*
Leading Actor in a Play, Christopher Plummer, *Barrymore*
Leading Actress in a Play, Janet McTeer, *A Doll's House*
Leading Actor in a Musical, James Naughton, *Chicago*
Leading Actress in a Musical, Bebe Neuwirth, *Chicago*
Featured Actor in a Play, Owen Teale, *A Doll's House*
Featured Actress in a Play, Lynne Thigpen, *An American Daughter*
Featured Actor in a Musical, Chuck Cooper, *The Life*
Featured Actress in a Musical, Lillias White, *The Life*
Direction of a Play, Anthony Page, *A Doll's House*
Direction of a Musical, Walter Bobbie, *Chicago*
Book of a Musical, Peter Stone, *Titanic*
Original Musical Score, Maury Yeston, *Titanic*
Orchestration, Jonathan Tunick, *Titanic*
Scenic Design, Stewart Laing, *Titanic*
Costume Design, Judith Dolan, *Candide*
Lighting Design, Ken Billington, *Chicago*
Choreography, Ann Reinking, *Chicago*
Regional Theater, Berkeley Repertory Theater, California
Lifetime Achievement, Bernard B. Jacobs

making a planned move to Broadway, though RUG insisted it would resuscitate the show. Also, the New York and London productions of RUG's *Sunset Boulevard* closed by mid-year at a considerable loss despite lengthy runs and healthy audiences.

Ireland. The approaching 100th anniversary of Oscar Wilde's death (1900) sparked an interest in the Anglo-Irish wit's life and work. In addition to New York's *Gross Indecency,* Dublin's Abbey Theatre premiered Tom Kilroy's *The Secret Fall of Constance Wilde* about Wilde's troubled relationship with his wife. London's Almeida Theatre drew much publicity in 1997 with the announcement that famed Northern Irishman Liam Neeson was being cast as Wilde in the 1998 production of David Hare's *The Judas Kiss.*

It was also a banner year for Irish playwright Frank McGuinness, translator and adapter of the award-winning *A Doll's House* and a lauded production of Brecht's *Caucasian Chalk Circle* at the Royal National Theatre. McGuinness's *Mutabilitie,* a story about a 1598 Irish uprising against the English, made its world premiere at the National in autumn 1997. Another Irish playwright, Sebastian Barry, enjoyed stellar reviews in London, Dublin, and New York for his play *The Steward of Christendom,* as did actor Donal McCann for his portrayal of the play's aging Dublin policeman whose inner struggle was a metaphor for modern Ireland. ☐ Karen Fricker

Togo. See Africa.

Toronto experienced a year of upheaval in 1997. A bill merging the six municipalities of Metropolitan Toronto into one city—popularly known as Megacity—passed the Ontario provincial legislature in April, despite formidable opposition from citizens and politicians. On November 10, voters in Metro Toronto elected a new city council and a new mayor for their consolidated city, scheduled to come into existence on Jan. 1, 1998.

The struggle to unity. The unification of Metro Toronto was a major element in a massive restructuring of government financing and services in Ontario undertaken in 1997 by Premier Mike Harris and his Progressive Conservative Party government. Harris insisted that the consolidation of the six municipalities—Toronto, York, East York, North York, Etobicoke, and Scarborough—would slash government spending and streamline the delivery of public services. Many residents of Metro Toronto, however, adamantly opposed the plan, arguing that the merger would destroy their distinctive neighborhoods and lead to a reduction in services.

Opponents attacked the merger on several fronts. On February 15, an estimated 4,000 people marched in protest in downtown Toronto. On March 3, the six city councils that would be eliminated by the merger held a nonbinding referendum on the Megacity legislation. An overwhelming 75.6 percent of voters rejected the consolidation.

In the provincial legislature, members of the opposition New Democratic Party (NDP) introduced more than 11,000 amendments to the Megacity bill. Legislators from the NDP and the Liberal Party also staged a 10-day, 24-hour-a-day filibuster in April.

The new Toronto. In the end, Ontario Premier Harris prevailed, and on April 21, the legislature unified Toronto. The new city, to be known as Toronto, would have a population of 2.3 million, greater than the population of six of Canada's 10 provinces. Under the law, the city was to be governed by a mayor—elected citywide—and by a 56-member city council elected from 28 newly established wards. The law also created six community councils, representing the formerly independent municipalities, that were given responsibility for local and neighborhood issues. Each of these councils also was to elect a representative to the new city's executive committee.

Court challenge. Six days after the passage of the Megacity law, three coalitions, including a group of four Metro Toronto cities, launched civil lawsuits against it. The challengers contended that Ontario's government failed to consult the citizens of Metro Toronto—as required by Canada's constitution—before it imposed unification on the six municipalities. In July, the judge in the case ruled against a key element of the challenges.

Mayoral election. The suits against Megacity also figured into the November 10 election for the first city council and mayor of the unified Toronto. Mayoral challenger Mel Lastman, campaigning on a platform of fiscal conservation, criticized incumbent Mayor Barbara Hall for wasting $300,000 on the challenge. Although Lastman, the 10-term mayor of North York, had opposed the unification plan, he had refused to join the lawsuits.

Despite several missteps, Lastman, who had an enviable reputation for delivering municipal services in North York, maintained a lead throughout the campaign. In the vote, Hall took only old Toronto. Lastman swept all five other areas of Metro Toronto.

Lastman faced serious challenges, including a growing number of homeless people, as the new mayor of Metro Toronto. He had made promises to freeze city spending and hold the line on taxes while finding additional money for municipal services. As part of its restructuring plan, the provincial government passed on to Toronto and other Ontario cities full financial responsibility for subsidized housing, public health, and other services previously funded by the province. Most worrisome to Torontoans was their increased responsibility for welfare. Previously, Metro Toronto had contributed 20 percent of the cost of welfare for people who were employable. The federal and provincial governments had funded assistance for single mothers, the elderly, and the disabled. Under the new arrangements, Toronto would be responsible for 20 percent of the cost of these payments as well. ☐ David Lewis Stein

Tamagotchi, Japanese for "cute, little egg," requires its owner to feed, exercise, and clean up after it by pressing buttons when the pet beeps demands. The handheld "cyberpet" was one of the most popular toys of 1997.

Toys and games. Retail toy sales in the United States in 1997 rose by approximately 3 percent over 1996 sales. The gain was considered average in the toy industry, which keeps its prices low to appeal to consumers who generally purchase toys with discretionary income. Several companies debuted online toy shopping on the World Wide Web in 1997. The virtual toy stores followed the lead of more and more retailers that offered consumers the option of purchasing products from their home computers.

Snoozer's no loser. It was back to Sesame Street in 1997, as Sing & Snore Ernie, a resident of the fictional neighborhood, followed in the sold-out footsteps of his Sesame Street neighbor, Tickle Me Elmo, the holiday hit of 1996. Made by Tyco Preschool of Mount Laurel, New Jersey, Sing & Snore Ernie yawned, said "I'm so sleepy," sang "Twinkle, Twinkle, Little Star," and snored. As the snoring sounds began, Ernie's tummy rose and fell in imitation of a sleeper's breathing pattern.

Virtual blockbusters. Virtual pets—also known as cyberpets and introduced in the United States in the spring of 1997, were instant hits not only with children ages 8 and up, but with many adults as well. The egg-sized, interactive, handheld electronic toys featured a digital "pet"—a puppy, kitten, chicken, or space creature—that "hatched" on a liquid-crystal display screen. The toy beeped when the pet needed to be fed, exercised, cleaned up after, or giv-

en medicine when ill. If the virtual pet owner failed to respond by pressing the appropriate buttons, the neglected pet died.

Tamagotchi, made by Bandai America Incorporated of Cypress, California, was the first virtual pet to debut in the United States. Playmates Toys Incorporated of Costa Mesa, California, also introduced its version, Nano Pals, in 1997, and Tiger Electronics Incorporated of Vernon Hills, Illinois, unveiled Giga Pets.

Loaded for bear. Winnie the Pooh—despite his 71 years—enjoyed a resurgence of popularity in 1997. Stuffed toys, board games, lunch boxes, clothing, and other children's accessories featured the image of the honey-loving bear. One of the best-selling Pooh items was the Hug 'n Wiggle Pooh electronic stuffed toy. Manufactured by Mattel Incorporated of El Segundo, California, Pooh wiggled his nose, giggled, and talked when hugged.

Return of the Star Wars Empire. The year 1997 marked the 20th anniversary of the space epic *Star Wars*, one of the most successful movie franchises in cinematic history. The movie trilogy, which also included *The Empire Strikes Back* and *Return of the Jedi*, was rereleased in theaters and on videocassette in 1997, with added scenes and an enhanced soundtrack. Hasbro Incorporated of Pawtucket, Rhode Island, reissued action figures of many of the movies' characters, some in special collectors' series. Shipments of the most popular characters sold out quickly, forcing some retailers to limit the number of items per customer.

Mars mania. The National Aeronautics and Space Administration's (NASA) launch of spacecraft to Mars triggered a demand for Mattel Inc.'s Hot Wheels Mars Rover Action Pack in 1997. The pack featured detailed replicas of the Mars Pathfinder lander and the Sojourner rover. A small portion of the proceeds from sales of the toy went to NASA.

Barney and Barbie do Windows. Windows, the graphic user interface from Microsoft Incorporated of Redmond, Washington, gave life to two new toys introduced in 1997. Microsoft unveiled ActiMates Barney, a 16-inch (41-centimeter) plush version of preschoolers' favorite purple dinosaur. The toy contained a microchip that allowed it to play 12 games, sing 17 songs, and instruct or encourage a child. The manufacturer offered additional accessories that enabled Barney to interact with videotapes, CD-ROM software, or to live broadcasts of the Barney television show.

Mattel Inc.'s Talk With Me Barbie also plugged into a PC. The doll came with a CD-ROM, which prompted the child to enter personal information, such as name, birthday, friends' names, and favorite activities. The child then selected a topic, and Barbie, mouth in motion, responded with appropriate conversation.
□ Diane P. Cardinale

See also **Computers.**

Canada's Donovan Bailey, *right*, and American Michael Johnson compete in a "One-to-One Challenge" race in June. Johnson, who pulled a leg muscle, did not finish.

World outdoor track and field records established in 1997

Men

Event	Holder	Country	Where set	Date	Record
000 meters	Wilson Kipketer	Denmark	Cologne, Germany	Aug. 24	1:41.11
2 miles	Daniel Komen	Kenya	Brussels, Belgium	July 19	7:58.61
3,000-meter steeplechase	Bernard Barmasai	Kenya	Cologne, Germany	Aug. 24	7:55.72
5,000 meters	Daniel Komen	Kenya	Brussels, Belgium	Aug. 22	12:39.74
10,000 meters	Paul Tergat	Kenya	Brussels, Belgium	Aug. 22	26:27.85

Women

Event	Holder	Country	Where set	Date	Record
5,000 meters*	Jiang Bo	China	Shanghai, China	Oct. 23	14:28.09
Pole vault	Emma George	Australia	Melbourne, Australia	Feb. 20	14 ft., 11 in. (4.55 m)
Hammer throw	Olga Kuzenkova	Russia	Munich, Germany	June 22	239 ft., 10 in. (73.1 m)

m = meters
*Awaiting IAAF ratification
Source: International Amateur Athletic Foundation (IAAF)

Track and field.

Track and field. Poorly marketed in the United States and embroiled in politics abroad, track and field continued to suffer in 1997 from the erosion of its audience, drug problems among its athletes, and diminished media attention.

In July, Craig Masback, a Washington attorney, television analyst, and former world-class miler, was elected the new executive director of USA Track and Field, the sport's national governing body. Masback replaced Ollan Cassell, who had headed the organization for 31 years before being voted out of office in December 1996. Masback took over a financially troubled organization in dire need of sponsors. He said he hoped to resolve this major problem by returning the sport to a more significant place in the American consciousness. He vowed to enlist the cooperation of elite U.S. athletes, a group that often had been at odds with Cassell.

Carl Lewis, the nine-time Olympic gold medalist considered by many to be the greatest track-and-field athlete of all time, retired in September 1997 at age 36. Lewis made five U.S. Olympic teams during his career, including the team that boycotted the Moscow Games in 1980. He set 11 world records in 17 years of competition and went undefeated in the long jump—the event in which he won four Olympic gold medals—for a record 65 consecutive meets.

Match race. Donovan Bailey of Canada, the 100-meter world record holder, beat Michael Johnson of the United States, the world 200-meter champion, in a controversial 150-meter race run on June 1, 1997, on a makeshift two-lane track in the Toronto Sky-Dome. Bailey won easily, in 14.99 seconds, as Johnson pulled his left quadriceps and did not finish. At a post-race press conference, Bailey, who won $1 million for his victory in addition to the $500,000 appearance fee given to both sprinters, called Johnson a "coward" and made other disparaging comments about his American rival. The injury idled Johnson for almost four weeks and caused him to miss the U.S. championships at Indianapolis, Indiana, two weeks later.

World championships. The World Track and Field Championships were held in Athens in August. The meet was plagued by poor attendance and by the questionable conduct of Primo Nebiolo, the president of the International Amateur Athletic Foundation (IAAF), track and field's world governing body. Nebiolo was an ardent supporter of the city of Rome's bid to host the 2004 Olympic Summer Games. During the meet, Nebiolo belittled Athens, which also was vying for the games, and the meet's organizing committee. Greek fans, who booed Nebiolo during the closing ceremonies, had the last laugh when the International Olympic Committee awarded the 2004 Games to Athens.

The world championships, for the first time in track and field history, awarded prize money and invited the participation of "wild-card" athletes, who were not required to qualify through competition. The wild-card system permitted Michael Johnson and other defending champions who missed their qualifying meets due to injury to participate. The gold, silver, and bronze medalists received $60,000, $30,000, and $20,000 respectively. The 1997 world championships produced no new world records, for which $100,000 was to be awarded.

New stars. On Aug. 4, 1997, Maurice Greene of Kansas City won the men's 100-meter final in 9.86 seconds, and Marion Jones of Los Angeles won the women's 100 in 10.83. Greene was too strong for Bailey, who finished second. On August 5, Johnson claimed his third world 400-meter title. He moved from third to first place over the final 60 meters to win in 44.12 seconds. Jones later teamed with Chryste Gaines, Inger Miller, and Gail Devers to win the 4x100-meter relay in 41.47 seconds, the second best time in history.

Grand Prix. On Aug. 13, 1997, Wilson Kipketer, a Kenyan middle-distance runner competing for Denmark, broke Sebastian Coe's 1981 world record in the 800 meters (1:41.73) with a time of 1:41.24 at a Grand Prix meet in Zurich, Switzerland. In Cologne, Germany, on August 24, he lowered the mark again to 1:41.11. Kipketer and German shotputter Astrid Kumbernuss won $200,000 each as overall champions of the Grand Prix series. □ Ron Reid

See also **Olympic games; Sports.**

Transportation. On March 12, 1997, President Bill Clinton proposed spending $175 billion over the next six years to repair the nation's crumbling bridges and highways. The proposed bill, the National Economic Crossroads Transportation Efficiency Act (NEXTEA), was to replace the Intermodal Surface Transportation Efficiency Act (ISTEA) of 1991, which expired Sept. 30, 1997. The new act would increase spending for transportation by 11 percent over the expenditure approved in 1991, including a 10 percent increase in highway spending and a 3 percent decrease in mass transit spending.

The new act would allow states to collect tolls on interstate highways—if the funds were used for road upkeep—and would improve roads in national parks and national forests and on Indian reservations. The act would also increase spending for programs to improve truck safety, to prevent drunk driving, and to help people move from welfare to work.

Members of the House of Representatives had not agreed on funding for the bill when Congress adjourned in autumn. While some representatives wanted to increase transportation funds, others refused to violate the balanced-budget legislation that President Clinton had signed into law on August 5. As a compromise, House and Senate negotiators agreed in November to give each state at least half of the funding that it had received in 1997, allowing Congress until March 31, 1998, to work out a new

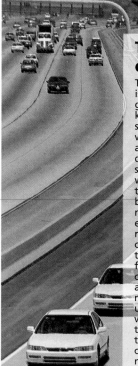

The future of driving?
The first automated highway is tested in California in August 1997. A 7.6-mile (12.2-kilometer) stretch of Interstate 15 north of San Diego was embedded with magnets and radar-reflective tapes to demonstrate two competing systems. General Motors cars were equipped with sensors that "read" the patterns of buried magnets, while cars made by Honda used a camera and computer to follow reflective tapes. Steering, acceleration, and braking all took place without input from a driver. The experiment, conducted by a consortium of auto manufacturers, government transit departments, and university research centers, was mandated by the 1991 Intermodal Surface Transportation Efficiency Act. Passengers commented that, after the novelty wore off, "driving" a car without handling any of the controls "gets really dull."

six-year plan. Such an extension was expected to cost $15 billion, an amount that would not violate the balanced-budget accord.

Railroad consolidation. The bidding war between Norfolk Southern Corp. of Norfolk, Virginia, and CSX Transportation Corp. of Jacksonville, Florida, for Philadelphia-based Conrail, Inc., ended in April 1997. The bidders agreed to partition Conrail between themselves. In a $10.2-billion deal that raised the price of Conrail stock to $115 a share, Norfolk Southern would acquire 58 percent of Conrail and CSX would take 42 percent.

Conrail, a government-owned corporation, was formed in 1976 from Penn Central and other bankrupt eastern railroads. The U.S. Surface Transportation Board, a Washington, D.C.-based government agency that regulates railroad mergers, was expected to rule on the merger in June 1998.

Railroad privatization. The government of Great Britain completed the privatization of the former state-owned British railroad system in March 1997. Track and signalling systems were transferred to an infrastructure company, Railtrack, which subsequently issued shares on the London stock exchange. Passenger train operation was awarded to 25 regional companies under franchises lasting between 7 and 15 years.

The British privatization model was considered by other countries as well. The Portuguese government in April proposed to split the existing state-owned railroad into infrastructure and operating companies and to invite bids from private companies for the operation of some lines. An advisory group to the U.S. House Transportation and Infrastructure Committee suggested in June that a similar restructuring might help Amtrak, the government-owned rail passenger company, recover from its financial troubles. Amtrak lost more than $700 million a year during the 1990's and narrowly avoided bankruptcy in 1997 when Congress approved an extension of its line of credit in November.

A high-speed rail service between Paris and Brussels, called Thalys, inaugurated on December 10, cut travel time between the two capitals from 1 hour 55 minutes to 1 hour 25 minutes. The Thalys

Firefighters attempt to cool down the TPAO, Turkey's largest oil tanker, which caught fire on February 13, following an explosion while docked in Istanbul for repairs. More than 20 people were injured in the blaze.

service, which runs on specially built high-speed track, is part of a system being developed by the European Union, a group of 15 Western European nations, to provide links across national borders and make rail travel competitive with air travel.

The Channel Tunnel linking France and Great Britain reopened for full passenger service in May 1997 and for full freight service in June. Service had been reduced after a freight truck fire aboard a shuttle train damaged the tunnel in November 1996. Though use of the tunnel fell only slightly in 1997, Eurotunnel, the owner and operator of the project, was forced to seek shareholder approval to restructure its debt in July 1997 to avoid bankruptcy.

The world's largest cruise ship, the Grand Princess, featuring a virtual reality center, five pools, and a nine-hole putting course, was launched at Monfalcone, Italy, in May 1997. The 109,000-ton vessel, which can carry 3,300 passengers, became the flagship of Britain's Peninsular and Oriental (P&O) Princess Cruises.

The container shipping industry experienced major company consolidations in 1997. Britain's Peninsular and Oriental Steam Navigation Company and Holland's Koninklijke Nedlloyd Group announced in late 1996 the formation of a joint venture to operate 112 container ships. In April 1997, Neptune Orient Line of Singapore purchased Oakland, California-based APL (formerly named American President Line), forming a new 113-container-ship company. Both mergers provided competition to market leaders Maersk and Evergreen of Taiwan and Sealand, a subsidiary of CSX Corp., of the United States.

GE Capital Services, a unit of General Electric, announced a joint venture with Bermuda-based Sea Containers, Ltd., in September 1997. The new company—GE SEACo Ltd.—began operations with a fleet of 1.2 million 20-foot (6-meter) marine containers, making it one of the largest shipping-container lessors in the world. □ Ian Savage

Trinidad and Tobago. See **Latin America** (Facts in brief table).

Tunisia. See **Middle East.**

Turkey. Turkish Prime Minister Necmettin Erbakan resigned on June 18, 1997, ending the first Islamic-oriented government in Turkey's 74-year history. Since Erbakan came to power as leader of a coalition government in June 1996, Turkey had become increasingly polarized between Islamic and *secular* (nonreligious) forces. Although Turkey is predominantly Muslim, it has traditionally honored the separation of church and state. Observers said that Erbakan's resignation possibly averted a *coup* (overthrow) by the military, which had accused Erbakan of fomenting the growth of Islamic extremism. The military had seized power three times since 1960 to preserve the tradition of a secular government.

On Feb. 4, 1997, the military sent tanks through Sincan, a town near the capital Ankara, after an Islamic rally there called for an Iranian-style Islamic government and voiced opposition to the Arab-Israeli peace process. On February 28, the military demanded that Erbakan adopt 18 reforms, including a curb on the influence of Islamic schools, a crackdown on Islamic groups thought to be accumulating weapons, and the enforcement of a law banning Islamic clothing. Erbakan agreed to the demands but later reneged on his promises.

Erbakan was forced to resign after a scandal caused several lawmakers to defect from the True Path Party, which made up the governing coalition with Erbakan's Welfare Party. The defections caused the coalition to lose its parliamentary majority. The scandal grew from January reports that some Turkish government officials had allegedly used criminals to kill political opponents in exchange for protecting drug smuggling and other illegal activities.

Following Erbakan's resignation, Turkish President Süleyman Demirel asked Mesut Yilmaz, leader of the secular center-right Motherland Party, to form a new government. Yilmaz became prime minister on June 30, after he formed a coalition with two smaller center-right parties. Yilmaz rejected a role for the Welfare Party in his coalition.

Curbing Islam. In May, the military reportedly purged more than 50 officers thought to have had pro-Muslim beliefs. In June, the military announced that it would stop purchasing supplies from some 100 companies with Islamic ties. In August, the parliament passed a bill mandating that children spend eight years in public secular school (instead of the previously required five years) before being eligible to enroll in Islamic religious academies. In November, Turkey's chief prosecutor recommended that the Welfare Party be banned from politics for its plotting to impose Islamic law in Turkey.

Kurds. On May 14, at least 10,000 Turkish troops launched an offensive into northern Iraq against guerrilla bases of the militant Turkish Kurdish Workers Party (PKK). Kurds are an ethnic group inhabiting the highlands region along the borders of Turkey, Iraq, Iran, and Syria. The PKK, which began fighting for independence from Turkey in 1984, set up bases in northern Iraq in 1994 when Iraqi Kurdish groups began fighting each other.

Rebels downed two Turkish helicopters with Russian-made antiaircraft missiles in May and June of 1997. The helicopter hits marked the first time that the rebels had used the hand-held missiles.

Turkey announced in early June that its forces would remain in Iraq indefinitely despite condemnation by Arab states. In September, Turkey launched another ground assault, as well as air strikes. Turkey reportedly kept 20,000 troops in northern Iraq after the assaults. Between 1984 and late 1997, the PKK war for independence had led to the deaths of at least 24,000 people and the displacement of more than 550,000 people

Europe. Turkish hopes were dashed when the European Union (EU), a cooperative association of 15 Western European countries, announced in December that it would exclude Turkey from a group of states invited to start EU membership talks. Although some European officials cited Turkey's human-rights record as a reason for the exclusion, Turkish officials claimed that the EU was biased against Islam. □ Christine Helms

See also **Iraq; Middle East** (Facts in brief table); **People in the news.**

Turkmenistan. See **Asia.**

Uganda. See **Africa.**

Ukraine. On May 31, 1997, President Leonid Kuchma of Ukraine and President Boris Yeltsin of Russia signed a treaty of friendship between their two countries. Negotiations over the treaty had clouded Russian-Ukrainian relations for the last five years, mostly over the division of the former Soviet Black Sea Fleet. Both Ukraine and Russia had been republics of the Soviet Union. In May 1997, the two sides agreed on a plan to divide the fleet on terms allowing Russia to continue basing ships and personnel at Sevastopol, a Black Sea port held by Ukraine.

New prime minister. In June, Kuchma removed Prime Minister Pavlo Lazarenko from office. The official reason was poor health, but Lazarenko had been plagued by accusations of corruption. In July, a new government was formed, and Valery Pustovoitenko, a close ally of Kuchma, was named prime minister. Kuchma hoped that the new government could reinvigorate Ukraine's economic reform program. However, economic reform had fewer supporters in the parliament than in the Cabinet. On Nov. 4, 1997, the parliament voted to suspend Ukraine's privatization program, demanding that Kuchma appoint a new privatization chief. The episode gave Ukrainian voters a preview of issues likely to dominate the national elections scheduled for 1998.

Economy. While Ukraine's rate of inflation dropped to its lowest point since the collapse of the Soviet Union in 1991, the economy continued to shrink during 1997. Ukraine's gross domestic product was expected to decline in 1997 by approximately 5 percent. Many observers felt that Ukraine's economic restructuring had stalled as a result of half-hearted reforms and official corruption.

Foreign policy. In August, Kuchma announced a change in foreign policy direction. He indicated that Ukraine would no longer be bound by the collective security agreement signed in 1992 by seven former Soviet republics—including Ukraine and Russia. Kuchma announced that Ukraine, instead, would be "a state outside a state" and pursue relations with other nations on an individual basis. This shift reflected Kuchma's desire to play a bigger role in the European community. It also calmed Russian fears that Ukraine wished to join the North Atlantic Treaty Organization (NATO), an alliance of 16 European and North American nations.

In November 1997, the G-7, an organization of seven major industrialized nations, pledged $300 million to help Ukraine close the Chernobyl nuclear facility by the year 2000. Parts of the Chernobyl complex were destroyed in a catastrophic accident in 1986. European officials had long favored shutting down the remaining Chernobyl reactors, which they considered unsafe. However, Ukrainian officials complained that they had not received the financial help that other countries had promised to help them build replacement reactors. ☐ Steven L. Solnick

Unemployment. See Labor and employment.

United Kingdom. The Conservative Party, after 18 years in power in the United Kingdom (U.K.), was defeated by the Labour Party in elections held on May 1, 1997. The Labour Party, led by Tony Blair, won with an overwhelming majority of 179 seats in Parliament. Blair, at age 43, became the youngest prime minister in more than a century.

Reforms. Labour moved swiftly to establish itself as a reform government. On May 14, the party published plans to push 26 bills through Parliament before September 1998. The program focused on Labour's five key campaign promises: to cut primary school class sizes; shorten hospital waiting lists; crack down on young offenders; move 250,000 young people off welfare and into work; and lay the foundation for lasting prosperity.

On June 11, 1997, Members of Parliament (MP's) voted to ban handguns in Great Britain, fulfilling a pledge Labour had made after a gunman massacred 16 young children and their teacher at a school in Dunblane, Scotland, in 1996. The government backed off from a promise to ban fox hunting in the face of fierce resistance from the fox hunting community and many farmers, who argued that hunting controlled foxes. Blair also gave a new impetus to the peace process in Northern Ireland, which led to all-party talks in October 1997, the first all-party talks in the province.

Bomb threats. The Irish Republican Army (IRA), an unofficial military force fighting for a united Ireland, carried out a campaign of disruption in England in April, just before the election. IRA threats that bombs had been planted at railway stations and on motorways seriously disrupted road and rail traffic. Another bomb threat, on April 5, led to the postponement of the Grand National Steeplechase. April 21 bomb threats closed five railway stations and four airports in London. Relations between the British government and the IRA improved in December, when Blair met with Sinn Féin President Gerry Adams. It was the first meeting between an IRA leader and a British prime minister at 10 Downing Street, the prime minister's residence. in 76 years.

New Tory leader. John Major, who had been prime minister for six-and-a-half years, resigned as Conservative leader following the party's defeat in May, its worst defeat since 1832. On June 19, 1997, Conservative MP's chose William Hague, age 36, as the new leader. Hague, who held a Cabinet position under the Conservatives as the Welsh secretary, was identified with the party's right wing

Assemblies for Scotland and Wales. The people of Scotland voted, in a September 12 referendum, in favor of establishing the first Scottish parliament in nearly 300 years by a 4 to 3 margin. The voters also gave the parliament powers to impose some taxes in Scotland. The new 129-seat parliament will control education, health, the environment, agriculture, and the arts in Scotland. The Conserva-

Tony Blair, newly elected prime minister of the United Kingdom, and his wife, Cherie, arrive at 10 Downing Street, their official London residence, on May 2.

tives opposed a Scottish parliament, arguing that it was the first step to the breakup of the United Kingdom. By a very narrow margin of 50.3 percent, Welsh voters on September 18 also set up an assembly, though it was to have no legislative or tax-raising powers.

Death of the Princess of Wales. The British were stunned by the death in the early hours of August 31 of Diana, Princess of Wales, in a car crash in Paris. Diana had left the Paris Ritz Hotel accompanied by Emad (Dodi) Fayed, son of Egyptian tycoon Mohamed Al Fayed, and had been pursued by photographers on motorcycles. The accident, which occurred in a traffic tunnel, killed Diana, Fayed, and the driver and injured Diana's bodyguard. In the week that followed, as many as 100,000 people a day visited Kensington Palace, which had been Diana's London residence, to lay flowers and sign books of condolences. Many commentators blamed the media and, in particular, paparazzi photographers and the publications that bought their pictures, for hounding the princess to death. More than 1 million people lined the route of the funeral procession on September 6, and more than 1 billion people worldwide watched the funeral broadcast live on television from Westminster Abbey.

Privacy laws. The British government came under pressure to introduce privacy laws following the death of Diana, because of accusations that British

newspapers had harassed her to death. There was particular concern about protecting her sons, Prince William, 15, and Prince Harry, 12. On September 25, the Press Complaints Commission, which regulates the conduct of newspapers, introduced new guidelines. Photographs obtained by "persistent pursuit" were banned, and areas where public figures could expect privacy were extended to include restaurants, churches, and some secluded beaches.

Economic policy. On May 6, Chancellor of the Exchequer (treasury head) Gordon Brown announced that the Bank of England would control interest rates, which had previously been set by the government. Under the new system, a monetary policy committee was established by the bank to set interest rates to meet inflation targets laid down by the government. Brown said that the previous system had aroused suspicions that governments manipulated interest rates for political advantage. In 1997, the Bank of England increased interest rates five times between May and December, until rates reached 7.25 percent, their highest level since 1992.

Brown introduced in his first budget on July 2, 1997, a welfare-to-work program for young people, to be paid for by taxing windfall profits of formerly state-owned utilities, which Labour argued the Conservatives sold too cheaply to private interests. Brown also announced more money for schools and hospitals from extra taxes on pension funds.

European Union relations. Labour promised a fresh start in the U.K.'s relations with the European Union (EU)—an organization of 15 Western European nations—which had bitterly divided the previous Conservative government. In a reversal of Conservative policy, Blair on October 2 ended the U.K.'s opposition to the Social Chapter of the Maastricht Treaty covering workers' rights, which gave British workers the same rights as their EU counterparts. The Conservatives had argued that the extra costs required by the Chapter, particularly a minimum wage, would dissuade foreign companies from establishing facilities in Britain.

Hong Kong. The U.K. returned the former British dependency of Hong Kong to the People's Republic of China in a ceremony culminating at midnight on the morning of July 1. The colony, made up of the island of Hong Kong, the Kowloon Peninsula on the mainland of China, and the New Territories (an area of mainland China adjacent to Kowloon plus more than 235 islands), had come under British control in stages between 1842 and 1898. In 1984, the Chinese and the British had agreed that the U.K. would return the colony to China and that China would allow Hong Kong to maintain its economic system of capitalism for another 50 years. The rest of China was to continue its socialist economic policy. International economists were hopeful that, after the handover, Hong Kong would maintain its position as a leader in international commerce, particularly since China's economic policy in the 1990's had begun to develop similarities to Western economies.

Queen Elizabeth's visit to Pakistan and India in October 1997 to mark the 50th anniversary of both countries' independence from British rule was marred by embarrassing incidents. During a speech to Pakistan's National Assembly on October 8, the Queen suggested that Pakistan and India should settle their differences over the state of Kashmir, which was divided between them in 1947. I. K. Gujral, then prime minister of India, responded by blaming the U.K. for the problems in Kashmir. Prince Philip, the queen's husband, caused outrage at a wreath-laying ceremony at a memorial to Indians killed when British troops opened fire on unarmed demonstrators in Amritsar in 1919. Philip said he doubted if the number of people killed was actually 2,000, as indicated on a plaque.

Sheep cloned. Scientists at the Roslin Institute near Edinburgh, Scotland, announced on Feb. 22, 1997, that they had successfully *cloned* (made an exact genetic duplicate of) a sheep. The resulting animal, called Dolly, was produced by taking cells from an adult *ewe* (female sheep). The cells were then deprived of nutrients for five days to "starve" them into an inactive state. The scientists extracted the nucleus from another ewe's unfertilized egg and used an electric charge to fuse the two types of cells. The resulting fused cell contained the nucleus from only one ewe. The nucleus contains DNA (deoxyribonucleic acid)—the molecule that genes are made of. The new cell, which began to grow and divide, was then implanted into a third ewe, which gave birth to Dolly. The news of the cloning sparked an international debate over its implications.

Nurses sentenced. British nurses Deborah Parry and Lucille McLaughlan, who were charged in Saudi Arabia in 1996 with murdering Australian nurse Yvonne Gilford, were sentenced in 1997. All three nurses had lived and worked at the King Fahd Military Medical Complex in Dhahran. In September, Parry was found guilty of murder, punishable by death by beheading, and McLaughlan was found guilty of being an accessory and sentenced to receive 500 lashes and eight years in prison. The sentences, which U.K. Foreign Secretary Robin Cook called "wholly unacceptable," severely strained relations between Britain and Saudi Arabia. Under Saudi law, which is based on Islam, the relatives of a murder victim have the right to have the death sentence waived in return for "blood money." Yvonne Gilford's brother accepted a $1.2-million settlement, which observers believed was offered by British companies doing business in Saudi Arabia.   □ Ian Mather

See also **Biology** Special Report: **Is It Wrong to Clone People; Diana** Special Report; **Europe** (Facts in brief table); **Hong Kong** Special Report: **Capitalism Comes to China; Northern Ireland.**

United Nations. Kofi Annan of Ghana began his term as the new secretary-general of the United Nations (UN) on Jan. 1, 1997. The 58-year-old Annan replaced Boutros Boutros-Ghali of Egypt, who did not win reelection for a second 5-year term. Annan had begun working for the UN in 1959. He had been serving as undersecretary-general for peacekeeping operations when the UN General Assembly approved his nomination by the Security Council for the secretary-general position.

Annan made reform of the 52-year-old organization his top priority. By March 1997, he had ordered the elimination of 1,000 staff positions in the Secretariat, the administrative arm of the UN. Annan also reduced the budget by $123 million for the 1998-1999 period to about $2.4 billion. In July 1997, Annan began the second phase of his reform package. The secretary-general ordered deep cuts in administrative costs to channel more resources to development projects. He consolidated some two dozen UN agencies into four departments: economic and social affairs, humanitarian affairs, peace and security, and development. Annan also formed a cabinet of senior managers and appointed a deputy UN secretary-general to help run the organization.

The Security Council, the highest political body of the UN, elected five new members for two-year terms in October 1997. Bahrain, Brazil, Gabon, Gambia, and Slovenia replaced Chile, Egypt, Guinea-Bissau, Korea, and Poland as nonpermanent members for the 1998-1999 term. The newly elected countries joined the permanent members of the council—the United States, Russia, China, France, and Great Britain—and the five other nonpermanent members who were elected for the 1997-1998 term—Costa Rica, Japan, Kenya, Portugal, and Sweden.

The General Assembly opened its 52nd annual session on Sept. 16, 1997. Representatives of 182 of 185 UN members elected Hennady Udovenko of Ukraine as president of the Assembly. In addition to debating UN reforms, the Assembly discussed the organization's mounting debt. By September 1997, scores of countries owed the UN more than $2.3 billion in peacekeeping and administrative expenses. President Bill Clinton, in a speech to the Assembly on September 22, said that the United States was prepared to begin paying its debt—which the UN estimated to be $1.4 billion, while the U.S. claimed it to be about $1 billion—but only if the UN continued to lower administrative costs and cut the U.S. share of costs from 25 percent to 20 percent.

UN High Commissioner for Human Rights Jose Ayala Lasso resigned his post on March 15 to become foreign minister of Ecuador. Secretary-General Annan appointed Mary Robinson, president of Ireland, to fill the post. Robinson resigned the Irish presidency on September 12 to accept the UN position.

The Middle East. Israel's decision to build a new settlement for about 32,000 Jews at Har Homa in East Jerusalem, which is predominantly Palestinian, created conflict in the Security Council in early 1997. On two separate occasions in March, the Security Council tried to pass resolutions declaring the Jewish settlement "illegal and a major obstacle to peace" and calling on Israel to stop the construction. However, in both instances U.S. Ambassador Bill Richardson vetoed the resolution. The Palestine Liberation Organization (PLO) then took the issue before the General Assembly. The 185-nation Assembly approved the resolution. However, the resolution was nonbinding, and Israel continued the construction.

In June and in December, the Security Council voted to extend a 1996 program that allowed Iraq to sell $2 billion in oil every six months to raise money to buy humanitarian goods for Iraqi civilians. The program, known popularly as "oil-for-food," was designed to alleviate civilian suffering after the UN imposed economic sanctions on Iraq in August 1990 for invading Kuwait. Part of the oil money was also used to compensate victims of the Iraqi invasion and to eliminate Iraq's weapons of mass destruction. On Oct. 29, 1997, Iraq expelled American arms inspectors—who were part of a UN monitoring team required by Gulf War sanctions—from the country. The Security Council imposed additional sanctions on Iraq on November 12, including restrictions on travel for Iraqi officials who interfered with the

team's work. After a series of negotiations carried out by Russia, Iraq allowed UN inspectors to reenter Iraq on November 21.

Environment. The UN General Assembly convened a session called Earth Summit+5 in June 1997, to assess the implementation of Agenda 21, a program developed at the 1992 Earth Summit in Rio de Janeiro, Brazil. Agenda 21 was meant to stop the deterioration of the earth's environment. A report presented at Earth Summit+5 indicated that little progress had been made during the five years.

Representatives of nearly 180 countries at Earth Summit+5 failed to agree on goals to solve such problems as global warming, the cutting and burning of forests, and the shortage of fresh water. The governments pledged that by 2002 they would show concrete and measurable progress in attaining sustainable development. President Bill Clinton on June 26, 1997, acknowledged that the United States, with only 4 percent of the world population, produced 20 percent of the world's greenhouse gases. Clinton promised $1 billion to help developing countries reduce greenhouse gas emissions.

Gift for UN. On Sept. 18, 1997, American media mogul Ted Turner announced that he would donate $1 billion to the UN for humanitarian relief programs. The gift was to be presented in increments of $100 million a year for 10 years.   □ J. Tuyet Nguyen

See also **People in the news.**

United States, Government of the.

The United States government launched a five-year balanced-budget plan on Aug. 5, 1997, when President Bill Clinton signed separate budget and tax bills designed to eliminate the national deficit by the year 2002. The legislation also offered tax cuts for the middle class, including a child-care tax credit and tax breaks for college tuition and homeowners. Analysts said the legislation benefited investors, college students, and families with children. The legislation ended months of negotiations between the president and the Republican-led U.S. Congress over spending and tax cuts.

Shrinking deficit. On Oct. 27, 1997, President Clinton announced that the deficit for fiscal 1997, which ended September 30, was $22.6 billion—the lowest annual deficit since 1974. The shortfall was less than some analysts had predicted and was far below the deficits of the early 1990's, such as the $290-billion deficit of 1992. Some analysts credited the continuing economic boom of 1997 with the lower figure.

Veto power. For the first time in U.S. history, President Clinton on August 11 used a line-item veto to block specific provisions from budget and tax bills while signing the rest of the bill into law. The president struck down two tax breaks and a provision designed to help the state of New York gain additional federal Medicaid money.

President Clinton was widely criticized in October for vetoing 38 items worth $287 million from the military construction bill and rejecting 13 additional research and development projects in the defense bill. On November 14, the president vetoed a bill that would have restored the 38 items cut from the military construction bill.

Fund-raising investigation. President Clinton remained under fire throughout 1997 for alleged illegal fund-raising activities during his 1996 reelection campaign. Republicans in Congress repeatedly called for the appointment of an independent counsel to investigate allegations of fund-raising abuses. Attorney General Janet Reno repeatedly put off taking such a step, saying that she had not uncovered sufficient evidence of criminal activity. On Dec. 2, 1997, Reno announced that she would not name an independent counsel to look into allegations that either President Clinton or Vice President Al Gore violated federal law by making phone calls from their executive offices to solicit contributions to the Democratic National Committee. Reno reported that a thorough investigation indicated that no laws had been broken.

However, Reno also announced on December 2 that the Justice Department would continue its investigation into alleged fund-raising abuses.

Inauguration. President Clinton was sworn in for a second term on Jan. 20, 1997. Clinton's tone was subdued as he called for racial harmony and an end to "petty bickering and extreme partisanship." In his State of the Union message to Congress on February 4, the president proposed no major new legislation, but promised to make education his top priority during his final term in office.

Terrorist convictions. A federal jury in Denver, Colorado, on June 2, 1997, convicted Timothy J. McVeigh on 11 counts of murder and conspiracy in connection with the bombing of the Alfred P. Murrah Federal Building in Oklahoma City, Oklahoma. The terrorist attack on April 19, 1995, had killed 168 people. The jury recommended on June 13, 1997, that McVeigh, a veteran of the Persian Gulf War (1991), be executed for his role in the attack.

A federal jury on Dec. 23, 1997, found Terry L. Nichols, a second defendant charged in the 1995 Oklahoma City attack, guilty of conspiring to bomb the federal building. The jury also found Nichols guilty of involuntary manslaughter in the deaths of eight federal law enforcement officials. The jury acquitted Nichols of charges of carrying out the attack.

A federal jury in New York City on Nov. 12, 1997, convicted Ramzi Ahmed Yousef of the 1993 bombing of the World Trade Center in New York City. The jury found a codefendant, Eyad Ismoil, guilty of driving a van filled with explosives into the basement garage of the World Trade Center. Both men faced being sentenced to life in prison.

Federal spending
United States budget for fiscal 1997*

	Billions of dollars
National defense	270.1
International affairs	15.4
General science, space, technology	18.5
Energy	1.6
Natural resources and environment	21.0
Agriculture	10.7
Commerce and housing credit	– 14.0
Transportation	39.7
Community and regional development	11.7
Education, training, employment, and social services	51.5
Health	123.4
Social security	365.3
Medicare	190.0
Income security	230.4
Veterans' benefits and services	39.3
Administration of Justice	20.2
General government	12.8
Interest	244.1
Undistributed offsetting receipts	–50.0
Total budget outlays	**1,601.7**

*Oct. 1, 1996, to Sept. 30, 1997.
Source: U.S. Department of the Treasury.

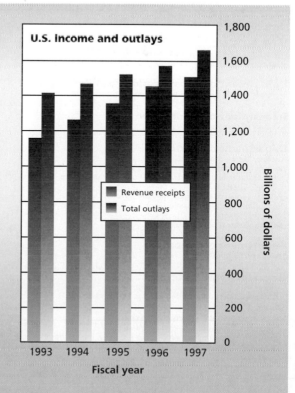

U.S. income and outlays

Legend: Revenue receipts, Total outlays

Fiscal year: 1993 1994 1995 1996 1997

Billions of dollars

Source: U.S. Department of the Treasury.

Selected agencies and bureaus of the U.S. government*

Executive Office of the President
President, Bill Clinton
Vice President, Albert Gore, Jr.
White House Chief of Staff, Erskine B. Bowles
Presidential Press Secretary, Michael McCurry
Assistant to the President for Domestic Policy, Bruce N. Reed
Assistant to the President for National Security Affairs, Samuel R. Berger
Assistant to the President for Science and Technology, John H. Gibbons
Council of Economic Advisers—Janet L. Yellen, Chairperson
Office of Management and Budget—Franklin D. Raines, Director
Office of National Drug Control Policy—Barry R. McCaffrey, Director
U.S. Trade Representative, Charlene Barshefsky

Department of Agriculture
Secretary of Agriculture, Daniel R. Glickman

Department of Commerce
Secretary of Commerce, William M. Daley
Bureau of Economic Analysis—J. Steven Landefeld, Director
Bureau of the Census—Martha F. Riche, Director

Department of Defense
Secretary of Defense, William S. Cohen
Secretary of the Air Force, F. Whitten Peters (acting)
Secretary of the Army, Togo D. West, Jr.
Secretary of the Navy, John H. Dalton
Joint Chiefs of Staff—
General Henry H. Shelton, Chairman
General Michael E. Ryan, Chief of Staff, Air Force
General Dennis J. Reimer, Chief of Staff, Army
Admiral Jay L. Johnson, Chief of Naval Operations
General Charles C. Krulak, Commandant, Marine Corps

Department of Education
Secretary of Education, Richard W. Riley

Department of Energy
Secretary of Energy, Federico F. Peña

Department of Health and Human Services
Secretary of Health and Human Services, Donna E. Shalala
Office of Public Health Service—John M. Eisenberg, Assistant Secretary (acting)
Centers for Disease Control and Prevention—David Satcher, Director
Food and Drug Administration—vacant
National Institutes of Health—Harold Varmus, Director
Surgeon General of the United States, J. Jarrett Clinton (acting)

Department of Housing and Urban Development
Secretary of Housing and Urban Development, Andrew M. Cuomo

Department of the Interior
Secretary of the Interior, Bruce Babbitt

Department of Justice
Attorney General, Janet Reno
Bureau of Prisons—Kathleen M. Hawk, Director
Drug Enforcement Administration—Thomas A. Constantine, Administrator
Federal Bureau of Investigation—Louis J. Freeh, Director
Immigration and Naturalization Service—Doris M. Meissner, Commissioner
Solicitor General, Seth P. Waxman

Department of Labor
Secretary of Labor, Alexis M. Herman

Department of State
Secretary of State, Madeleine K. Albright
U.S. Ambassador to the United Nations, Bill RIchardson

Department of Transportation
Secretary of Transportation, Rodney E. Slater
Federal Aviation Administration—Jane F. Garvey, Administrator
U.S. Coast Guard—Admiral Robert E. Kramek, Commandant

*As of Dec. 31, 1997.

Department of the Treasury
Secretary of the Treasury, Robert E. Rubin
Internal Revenue Service—Charles D. Rossotti, Commissioner
Treasurer of the United States, Mary Ellen Withrow
U.S. Secret Service—Lewis C. Merletti, Director
Office of Thrift Supervision—Ellen S. Seidman

Department of Veterans Affairs
Secretary of Veterans Affairs, Hershel W. Gober (acting)

Supreme Court of the United States
Chief Justice of the United States, William H. Rehnquist
Associate Justices—
John Paul Stevens
Sandra Day O'Connor
Antonin Scalia
Anthony M. Kennedy
David H. Souter
Clarence Thomas
Ruth Bader Ginsburg
Stephen G. Breyer

Congressional officials
President of the Senate pro tempore, Strom Thurmond
Senate Majority Leader, Trent Lott
Senate Minority Leader, Thomas A. Daschle
Speaker of the House, Newt Gingrich
House Majority Leader, Dick Armey
House Minority Leader, Richard A. Gephardt
Congressional Budget Office—June E. O'Neill, Director
General Accounting Office—James F. Hinchman, Comptroller General of the United States (acting)
Library of Congress—James H. Billington, Librarian of Congress

Independent agencies
Central Intelligence Agency—George J. Tenet, Director
Commission on Civil Rights—Mary Frances Berry, Chairperson
Commission of Fine Arts—J. Carter Brown, Chairman
Consumer Product Safety Commission—Ann Winkelman Brown, Chairman
Corporation for National Service—Harris Wofford, Chief Executive Officer
Environmental Protection Agency—Carol M. Browner, Administrator
Equal Employment Opportunity Commission—Gilbert F. Casellas, Chairman
Federal Communications Commission—William E. Kennard, Chairman
Federal Deposit Insurance Corporation—Andrew C. Hove, Chairman (acting)
Federal Election Commission—John Warren McGarry, Chairman
Federal Emergency Management Agency—James Lee Witt, Director
Federal Reserve System Board of Governors—Alan Greenspan, Chairman
Federal Trade Commission—Robert Pitofsky, Chairman
General Services Administration—David J. Barram, Administrator
International Development Cooperation Agency—J. Brian Atwood, Director (acting)
National Aeronautics and Space Administration—Daniel S. Goldin, Administrator
National Endowment for the Arts—vacant
National Endowment for the Humanities—Bruce A. Lehman, Chairman (acting)
National Labor Relations Board—William B. Gould IV, Chairman
National Railroad Passenger Corporation (Amtrak)—Thomas M. Downs, Chairman
National Science Foundation—Neal F. Lane, Director
National Transportation Safety Board—James E. Hall, Chairman
Nuclear Regulatory Commission—Shirley A. Jackson, Chair
Peace Corps—Mark D. Gearan, Director
Securities and Exchange Commission—Arthur Levitt, Jr., Chairman
Selective Service System—Gil Coronado, Director
Small Business Administration—Aida Alvarez, Administrator
Smithsonian Institution—I. Michael Heyman, Secretary
Social Security Administration—Kenneth S. Apfel, Commissioner
U.S. Arms Control and Disarmament Agency—John D. Holum, Director
U.S. Information Agency—Joseph D. Duffey, Director
U.S. Postal Service—Marvin T. Runyon, Postmaster General

Espionage crimes. A former Federal Bureau of Investigation (FBI) agent pleaded guilty in February 1997 to conspiracy to commit espionage and attempted espionage after selling classified information to the former Soviet Union and to Russia for $224,000 between 1987 and 1992. In June 1997, Earl Edwin Pitts was sentenced to 27 years in prison.

Former Central Intelligence Agency officer Harold James Nicholson pleaded guilty in March 1997 to selling top-secret information to Russia. Nicholson, who accepted $300,000 from Russia between 1994 and 1996, was sentenced to 23 years in prison in June 1997.

In an espionage case dating back to the 1960's, Robert Lipka pleaded guilty in May 1997 to conspiracy to commit espionage. Lipka sold secrets to the former Soviet Union for $27,000 while working as an Army clerk at the National Security Agency. In September, Lipka was sentenced to 18 years in prison, the maximum sentence allowed under his plea agreement.

Robert C. Kim, a former civilian intelligence analyst for the U.S. Navy, pleaded guilty in May to conspiracy to commit espionage after giving secret documents to South Korea. In July, Kim was sentenced to nine years in prison.

Allegations of sexual misconduct in the military made headlines in 1997. In May, 1st Lieutenant Kelly Flinn, the first female B-52 bomber pilot, was discharged from the U.S. Air Force following allegations that she lied to a superior officer about a relationship she had with a married civilian. Flinn, a pilot at Minot Air Force Base, North Dakota, accepted a general discharge in exchange for avoiding a court-martial. In February, Flinn was accused of adultery, fraternization, making false statements, conduct unbecoming an officer, and disobeying orders to end a relationship with a Minot soccer coach married to a woman enlisted in the Air Force.

In the wake of a national debate over the Flinn case, Air Force General Joseph W. Ralston withdrew his name from consideration as chairman of the Joint Chiefs of Staff in June. He admitted to an extramarital relationship in the 1980's when he was separated from his wife. Army General Henry Hugh Shelton, commander of U.S. Special Operations Command, was sworn in as chairman of the Joint Chiefs of Staff in October 1997, succeeding retired Army General John Shalikashvili.

Foreign policy. The U.S. State Department issued its annual human rights report in January. The report concluded that the president's policy of "constructive engagement" had failed to alter China's attitude toward human rights. According to the report, "widespread and well-documented human rights abuses," including the repression of dissent and the abuse of prisoners, had continued in China in 1996. The State Department report also criticized Burma, Colombia, Cuba, Indonesia, Iran, Iraq, Israel,

Libya, Nigeria, North Korea, and Syria for human rights inadequacies.

A U.S. government report released in May concluded that the Swiss government had aided Nazi Germany's war effort during World War II (1939–1945). The report stated that Switzerland had held gold that the Nazis stole from Jewish prisoners and from the banks of conquered nations. In addition, the report concluded that Switzerland had provided Germany with credit to help finance the war. Switzerland was officially neutral during World War II.

On July 16, 1997, President Clinton suspended for the third time in two years a provision of a controversial 1996 law designed to strengthen an economic embargo of Cuba. The president suspended for a six-month period Title III of the Helms-Burton Act, which was designed to allow U.S. citizens whose property was seized after the Cuban revolution in 1959 to sue foreign companies currently using that property. Republican congressional leaders criticized the president for not enforcing the law. However, Canadian and European leaders applauded the move.

The Clinton Administration announced in February 1997 that Mexico had been certified as a nation cooperating with U.S. antidrug officials in the war against drugs. The certification came less than two weeks after the arrest of General Jesús Gutiérrez Rebollo, Mexico's top antidrug official, who was suspected of having links to a powerful drug cartel. The United States also decertified Colombia for the second consecutive year. Certification was denied to Afghanistan, Burma, Iran, Nigeria, and Syria.

The United States refused, during a meeting in Oslo, Norway, to sign a treaty, adopted by 89 countries on September 18, to ban the use, production, transfer, and stockpiling of land mines. President Clinton said he would not compromise the safety of U.S. soldiers by signing the treaty.

Economics. The Federal Reserve Board's Federal Open Market Committee voted on March 25 to raise a key short-term interest rate by one-quarter of a percentage point. The federal funds rate—the interest rate banks charge on overnight loans made to one another—increased from 5.25 percent to 5.5 percent. The increase was the first since 1995 and the first rate change since 1996.

The U.S. Treasury Department issued its first inflation-indexed securities on Jan. 29, 1997. The Treasury Department sold about $7 billion worth of the 10-year notes, called Treasury Inflation Protection Securities (TIPS). The securities, which carry an interest rate of 3.449 percent plus any increase in the inflation rate before maturity, were designed as a kind of "insurance policy" against inflation.

Airline crash reports. The National Transportation Safety Board (NTSB) in August 1997 released its final report on the 1996 crash of ValuJet Flight 592 in the Florida Everglades, which killed all 110 people aboard. The report blamed ValuJet Airlines and the

United States, Government of the

Federal Aviation Administration, concluding that oxygen generators carried as cargo accidentally ignited, starting a fire that downed the airliner. The NTSB also criticized the FAA for not implementing an earlier recommendation that smoke alarms and sprinklers be installed in aircraft.

In November 1997, the Federal Bureau of Investigation sent letters to the families of passengers who had died in the explosion of Trans World Airlines (TWA) Flight 800, explaining that "absolutely no evidence" had been found to support the idea that a criminal act had caused the crash and that the agency was closing its investigation. The 1996 explosion of the Paris-bound jet off the coast of Long Island, New York, killed all 230 people aboard the air-liner. The National Transportation and Safey Board, however, continued on with its investigation of the TWA airline crash.

Crime lab criticized. The U.S. Department of Justice issued a report on April 15 that harshly criticized the FBI crime laboratory. The report concluded that work performed by some scientists at the laboratory was "deficient," that some testimony presented at trials by FBI lab officials was "flawed" and "inaccurate," and that several high-profile cases may have been affected by tainted evidence.

◻ William J. Eaton

See also **Armed forces; Aviation; Congress of the United States; Farm and farming; Iraq; Terrorism; Welfare; U.S. President.**

United States, President of the. President Bill Clinton (1946–) took the oath of office on Jan. 20, 1997, to begin his second term. He was the first Democratic president since Franklin D. Roosevelt in 1936 to be elected to a second term in office. During his 22-minute inaugural address to a crowd of more than 200,000 people, President Clinton supported limiting the role of government, saying that the government should provide people with the chance to build better lives.

Campaign funds. Republicans attacked the president throughout 1997 for his alleged involvement in fund-raising excesses during the 1996 presidential election campaign. On Dec. 2, 1997, Attorney General Janet Reno announced that she would not appoint an independent investigator to look into allegations that the president and Vice President Al Gore broke a law by making telephone calls from their executive offices to solicit donations to the Democratic Party. The Justice Department in 1997 continued an investigation into other alleged political fund-raising abuses.

President Clinton also came under fire for allegedly inviting political contributors to stay overnight in the White House and for hosting fund-raising coffees in the Executive Mansion. The president denied any wrongdoing in raising funds for his reelection campaign and for the Democratic Party.

In October, the U.S. Senate Governmental Affairs Committee ended its probe into campaign financing without uncovering hard evidence of abuses. The House of Representatives Government Reform and Oversight Committee was still investigating election fund-raising improprieties when House and Senate adjourned in November.

"Fast-track" setback. On November 10, President Clinton withdrew his request that Congress grant him so-called "fast-track" trade negotiating powers after it became apparent that the legislation lacked the support of Democrats in Congress. The trade legislation would have enabled the president to negotiate trade deals that Congress could not amend before bringing them to a vote.

The proposal was a routine trade-negotiating authority that all presidents have had since 1974. Some analysts concluded that many House Democrats were punishing President Clinton for negotiating too much with Republicans in order to garner their support for such legislation as a 1997 balanced budget agreement and tax cut.

Civil trial. The Supreme Court ruled unanimously on May 27, 1997, that Paula Jones, a former Arkansas state employee, could pursue a sexual harassment case against Clinton, despite his request to delay a civil trial until after he left office. Jones claimed that in 1991, when Clinton was governor of Arkansas, he had requested sexual favors from her. In August 1997, a judge set a May 1998 date for the start of Jones's civil case.   □ William J. Eaton

See also **Democratic Party.**

Uruguay. See Latin America.

Utah. See State government.

Uzbekistan. Despite the assurances of President Islam Karimov that Uzbekistan would work to expand political and religious freedoms, international observers in 1997 noted little real progress on human rights. In January 1997, the U.S. State Department gave Uzbekistan a poor rating in its annual global human-rights report, despite limited areas of progress. In June, the Organization for Security and Cooperation in Europe (OSCE), of which Uzbekistan is a participating state, reported an "erosion of religious liberty" in Uzbekistan. In April, Karimov urged the Uzbek parliament to show "more courage" in reporting human rights violations.

In February, Karimov became chairman of a new International Fund for Saving the Aral Sea. By 1997, the Aral Sea had shrunk to less than half its size in the 1960's. Poor water management policies and contamination from toxic chemicals used in fertilizers and pesticides created a host of medical problems for residents of neighboring regions. In Karakalpakistan, the Uzbek region's most severely affected, birth defect rates skyrocketed and agricultural production collapsed. Central Asian leaders agreed in 1997 to devote a share of their national incomes to the Aral Sea fund. In August, the World Bank approved a $75-million loan to fund construction of new water treatment and distribution systems for affected regions.   □ Steven L. Solnick

Vanuatu. See Pacific Islands.

President Bill Clinton, standing before the west front of the Capitol in Washington, D.C., delivers his second inaugural address on Jan. 20, 1997.

419

Venezuela. The Venezuelan government was able to sell $4 billion in 30-year bonds on the international market in September 1997. Investment analysts saw the sale as a sign of renewed confidence in the strength of Venezuela's economy.

Venezuela's penal system was sharply criticized in in a March report by Human Rights Watch/Americas, an organization based in New York City. The 1997 report estimated that 3 inmates were killed and more than 20 wounded weekly in 1996 in attacks in Venezuelan jails by both inmates and guards.

President Rafael Caldera Rodríguez, symbolically showing his intent to change prison conditions, threw a switch on March 16, 1997, that reduced to rubble El Retén de Catia, one of the most notorious prisons in South America. Violence in Venezuela's prisons continued, nevertheless. In August, members of a prison gang murdered 29 inmates belonging to a rival gang at a maximum-security prison.

Venezuelan banker Orlando Castro Llanes was sentenced on April 10 to three years in prison by the New York State Supreme Court. Castro was convicted on charges of defrauding Venezuelan investors through his Banco Progreso Internacional de Puerto Rico. □ Nathan A. Haverstock

See also **Latin America** (Facts in brief table).

Vermont. See State government.

Vice President of the United States. See People in the news.

Vietnam voters elected to office a younger generation of Communist leaders in 1997. In June, Vietnam's top three leaders—Prime Minister Vo Van Kiet, President Le Duc Anh, and Communist Party General Secretary Do Muoi, all in their 70's or 80's—announced that they were stepping down to make way for new leadership. All 450 seats of the National Assembly were up for election in July. Only a fifth of the departing Assembly members sought reelection.

Although more than 80 percent of the candidates represented the Communist Party, voters could choose among candidates who were nominated by state-backed organizations or ran as independents with party permission. The candidates were younger and better educated than candidates in previous elections. Eighty-two percent of the 660 candidates held college degrees, compared with 56 percent of the outgoing Assembly. There were also more women among the candidates than in past elections. Sixty-six non-Communists, including a former South Vietnamese army officer, won seats in the Assembly.

New leaders. The Communist Party's central committee met secretly September 15 and September 16 in the capital, Hanoi, to choose successors for Anh and Kiet. On September 24, the Assembly elected Tran Duc Luong president. Luong, a 60-year-old mining engineer, was a deputy prime minister who had been elected in 1996 to the politburo, the Communist Party's power center. In selecting Luong, the

Assembly had broken a pattern of electing a senior military officer president. The change reflected the weakened influence of the military in the 1990's, as the government had emphasized economic reform over military power.

The Assembly elected Phan Van Khai, 63, prime minister on Sept. 25, 1997. Khai was a native of South Vietnam and a deputy prime minster since 1991. Officials regarded Khai, an economic planner, as a leader in economic reform. In late 1997, the Communist Party considered candidates to succeed Muoi, who announced he would retire in 1998.

Economic troubles. Vietnam, which had experienced an average annual growth rate of 8.5 percent since 1990, suffered an economic downturn in 1997. In August, the World Bank, a United Nations agency, urged the Vietnamese government to boost domestic savings and make efforts to regain the confidence of foreign investors. In April, Vietnam agreed to repay the United States $145 million in debts incurred by South Vietnam before North Vietnam conquered the region in 1975 and unified the country.

A typhoon pummeled Vietnam's southern coast on November 3, killing hundreds of people, sinking hundreds of fishing boats, and flattening thousands of houses. □ Henry S. Bradsher

See also **Asia** (Facts in brief table).

Washington (state of). See State government.

Washington, D.C., in 1997 remained at or near the top in almost every negative category of urban statistics—infant mortality, drug addiction, high-school dropout rates, AIDS cases, rape, and armed robbery. Although the city's overall crime rate in 1997 was 18 percent lower than the 1996 figures, Washington trailed far behind other major U.S. cities in reducing crime.

The crisis debate. A 1996 publication, *The Orphaned Capital: Adopting the Right Revenues for the District of Columbia* by Carol O'Cleireacain, a former finance commissioner in New York City, fired debate in 1997 over federal responsibilities to the capital. O'Cleireacain asserted that most of the city's troubles were caused by a lack of access to financial aid. She noted that most U.S. cities received around 30 percent of their general revenues from the states, while the federal government's annual payment to Washington, D.C., contributed only 19 percent of the city's revenues. Since 1995, Washington had been run by a control board appointed by the U.S. Congress. While the board had seriously cut into the city's budget deficit, services had also been cut to a minimum. O'Cleireacain maintained that even if the control board could restore order to the city's finances, questions about the city's future remained. Eleanor Holmes Norton, the city's nonvoting member of Congress, continued in 1997 to push for a flat 15-percent income tax to lure residents to the city.

Federal action. On January 14, President Clinton entered the debate by proposing a plan that would form the basis for a bailout package included in the federal budget bill, signed on August 5. The bill allotted $1 billion in federal aid to the city for five years and stipulated that the federal government would assume responsibility for the city's pensions, prisons, roads, courts, and Medicaid payments. It also included tax relief for new residents, business investment, and job creation. The budget bill provided a huge boost to the city, which had already shown signs of economic growth. Job creation was up in the first six months of 1997. The city's credit rating was upgraded. And tax revenues were $50 million over projections.

However, the plan shifted control of most city agencies from the mayor to the control board. Mayor Marion S. Barry, Jr., who had sparred frequently with the board, called the bill a "rape of democracy." Federal officials feared the bill could propel Barry, who was widely blamed for the city's woes, to a fifth term in 1998 elections.

Sports and culture. The Jack Kent Cooke Stadium, the new home of the Washington Redskins and the largest open-air football stadium in the United States, opened to great fanfare on Sept. 14, 1997, in the nearby suburb of Raljon, Maryland. On December 2, the MCI Center opened in downtown Washington as the new venue for the basketball and hockey teams.

The Washington Opera's acquisition of an old department store for conversion into an opera house by 2001 offered another sign of revitalization. The driving force behind the purchase was celebrated tenor Placido Domingo, who became the artistic director of the opera in 1996. The Newseum, an admission-free interactive museum devoted to American journalism, opened in April 1997 in nearby Arlington, Virginia.

Memorials. The Franklin Delano Roosevelt Memorial opened on the Tidal Basin in Washington's West Potomac Park in May. The memorial sparked controversy among disability-rights activists because it did not depict Roosevelt, who was disabled by poliomyelitis, in a wheelchair. Plans for a national memorial honoring the veterans of World War II

Washington's National Airport new passenger terminal opens to the public in July. The high arches of steel and glass were likened by some critics to the classic train stations of the 1800's.

(1939–1945) also evoked public discord. The proposed site—between the Lincoln Memorial and the Washington Monument on the National Mall—pleased few people, and many of those who approved of the site disapproved of the design. The rancorous debate threw into question whether the $100-million memorial would ever be built.

National Airport. A $1-billion renovation of Washington's much-maligned, but much-utilized, National Airport was finished in July 1997. The steel and glass arches of the terminal offered superb views of the city, and new connections to the public transit system and parking made the airport more convenient.   □ Robert Messenger

See also **Washington, D.C.** Special Report: **A Look at the FDR Memorial.**

O n May 2, 1997, President Bill Clinton dedicated the Franklin Delano Roosevelt Memorial on the Tidal Basin in Washington, D.C.'s West Potomac Park. The memorial, decades in the planning, is only the fourth major presidential memorial in Washington. The others include the Washington Monument and the Lincoln and Jefferson memorials. The Roosevelt Memorial was built to honor a man, known to many Americans as FDR, who has been assessed by many historians as the greatest president of the 20th century.

Roosevelt, elected to four consecutive terms, served as president from 1933 until his death in 1945. He became president during the Great Depression, the most devastating economic crisis in the country's history. Through his self-confidence and ability as a communicator, FDR helped to restore hope to the nation. He also sponsored legislation—collectively known as the New Deal—consisting of a series of reform programs that gave the federal government authority to regulate the nation's economy and assist its financially strapped citizens. Despite the fact that the New Deal failed to end the depression, many historians credit Roosevelt's programs with enabling democracy and free enterprise to survive in the United States.

In 1941, the United States entered World War II (1939-1945) after Japanese planes attacked Pearl Harbor Naval Base in Hawaii. In FDR's role as commander in chief of the U.S. armed forces, he guided the United States to victory against the most powerful military adversaries the nation had ever faced—Nazi Germany and imperial Japan. The United States emerged from the war as the leading economic and military power in the world.

The Roosevelt Memorial

The Roosevelt Memorial, designed by landscape architect Lawrence Halprin, is a 7.5-acre (3.0-hectare) landscape of four exterior "rooms" formed by granite walls that provide a backdrop for sculptures amid waterfalls. The sculptures were created by Neil Estern, George Segal, Robert Graham, Leonard Baskin, and Tom Hardy. Quotations from FDR were cut into the walls by master stonecarver John Benson.

The opening of the memorial was greeted with criticism from disability-rights activists objecting to the fact that nowhere in the memorial was FDR portrayed seated in a wheelchair. (Stricken with poliomyelitis, FDR was unable to walk, except for short distances with crutches or canes.) Many historians, however, claim that depicting FDR in a wheelchair is inappropriate. While Roosevelt did not hide the fact that he was crippled, he also did not make a public display of his disability.

A Look at the FDR Memorial

The largest of six waterfalls in the
Franklin Delano Roosevelt Memorial
represents the exuberance and excitement felt by the American people at the
victorious conclusion of World War II.

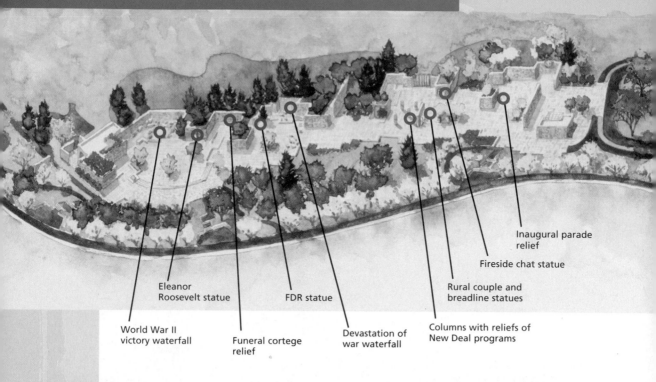

Inaugural parade relief

Fireside chat statue

Rural couple and breadline statues

Eleanor Roosevelt statue

FDR statue

World War II victory waterfall

Funeral cortege relief

Devastation of war waterfall

Columns with reliefs of New Deal programs

I SEE ONE-THIRD OF A NATION ILL-HOUSED, ILL-CLAD, ILL-NOURISHED

THE TEST OF OUR PROGRESS IS NOT WHETHER WE ADD MORE TO THE ABUNDANCE OF THOSE WHO HAVE MUCH, IT IS WHETHER WE PROVIDE ENOUGH FOR THOSE WHO HAVE TOO LITTLE.

Sculptures by George Segal depict Americans during the hard times of the 1930's. A rural couple, *above left,* represents the despair faced by farmers. A breadline, *above right,* represents hunger. A man listening to one of FDR's "fireside chats," *right,* represents the hope FDR inspired in many.

A visitor old enough to remember Roosevelt's wife, Eleanor, touches a sculpture, by Neil Estern, *left,* that honors Mrs. Roosevelt's highly active role as first lady and her later work as a delegate to the United Nations. Another sculpture by Estern, *below,* depicts FDR with his beloved dog Fala during the war years of 1941 to 1945.

THEY (WHO) SEEK TO ESTABLISH SYSTEMS OF GOVERNMENT BASED ON THE REGIMENTATION OF ALL HUMAN BEINGS BY A HANDFUL OF INDIVIDUAL RULERS... CALL THIS A NEW ORDER. ...T NEW AND IT IS NOT ORDER.

FOCUS ON

Weather 1997

A resident of South Fargo, North Dakota, *right,* stands behind a dike protecting her house from the raging Red River in April 1997. A mild winter and exceptionally deep snowpack on the northern Plains resulted in record-breaking floods in western Minnesota, the eastern Dakotas, and southern Manitoba.

Workers blockade a roadway, *right,* near Seattle, Washington, washed out by flooding caused by heavy rains and rapid snowmelt in the Pacific Northwest in early January.

Pedestrians cross snow-covered Commonwealth Avenue in Boston, Massachusetts, on April 1, 1997. A late-season storm dumped 25 inches (64 centimeters) of snow on Boston, the city's third-largest snowstorm in history.

Significant Weather Events of 1997

- January 1–4. As much as 40 inches (102 centimeters) of rain and rapid snowmelt in California and the Pacific Northwest cause widespread flooding.

- March 1. Tornadic thunderstorms from Arkansas to Tennessee kill 26 people, 16 of whom perish when a tornado packing 200-mile- (320-kilometer-) per-hour winds tears through Arkadelphia, Arkansas.

- March 31–April 1. A storm drops a record 33 inches (84 centimeters) of snow on Worcester, Massachusetts, and covers Boston with its third-largest snowfall in history—25 inches (64 centimeters).

- May 27. Thunderstorms rip through four Texas counties, from Waco to Austin. One tornado destroys an entire subdivision in Jarrell, killing 27 people.

- July. Recurrent storms deluge central Europe, triggering the worst flooding in 200 years. More than 1 million people in Germany, Poland, Hungary, Romania, Slovakia, and the Czech Republic are affected.

- September 16–26. Hurricane Nora lands on Mexico's Baja Peninsula with 110-mile- (177-kilometer-) per-hour winds and then, in a rare move, strikes California and Arizona, leaving flooding in its wake.

- September 18–October 2. A drought in Indonesia attributed to El Niño—a warming of equatorial eastern Pacific Ocean waters that affects weather patterns worldwide—is blamed for the area's worst ecological disaster. Forest and peat fires blazing out of control because of a delay in seasonal rains blanket Southeast Asia in smog.

- October 6–10. Hurricane Pauline skirts Mexico's Pacific Coast, striking hardest at Acapulco, where 150 people are killed in flash floods and landslides.

- October 24–25. A blizzard sweeps across Colorado, Nebraska, and Iowa, blanketing areas of eastern Colorado with as much as 23 inches (58 centimeters) of snow, closing roads and knocking out electrical power for as many as 100,000 residents.

Raging waters and mudslides triggered by Hurricane Pauline sweep part of a house through an Acapulco neighborhood on October 9. The hurricane, which was associated with El Niño—a warming of equatorial eastern Pacific Ocean waters that affects weather patterns worldwide—left 150 people dead.

A tornado slams into a subdivision at Jarrell, Texas, on May 27, 1997, killing 27 people. The tornado was one of a number of twisters that cut across Texas from Waco to Austin.

Weather

Weather. The winter of 1997 was among the wettest of the century in the Western and North-central United States, but drier than normal in much of the Southwest. In the Northeast, an unusually warm winter ended with a major snowstorm and was followed by abnormal chill in April and May. A Texas tornado in late spring rated a 5—the highest value on the Fujita tornado damage scale. El Niño—a periodic warming of tropical eastern Pacific waters that affects weather patterns worldwide—may have contributed to abnormal wetness in much of the West during the middle and late autumn.

Winter floods. The first week of January 1997 brought excessive precipitation to much of California and the Pacific Northwest. Some areas of northern California received as much as 40 inches (102 centimeters) of rain. The rain, combined with rapid melting of the deep mountain snowpack, caused widespread flooding, especially in the foothills of the Sierra Nevada Mountains and the northern Central Valley. In California alone, total damage to property exceeded $1.6 billion, causing more than 40 counties to be designated federal disaster areas.

Heavy rain and snowmelt also brought Lake Tahoe, in Nevada, to its highest level since 1917. Many casinos in Reno, Nevada, were extensively damaged. In western Idaho, as many as 10,000 people were isolated by floodwaters. Overall, 36 people died from the January rains and subsequent flooding.

Heavy snow repeatedly blanketed the northern Plains and upper Midwest in January 1997. On January 3 and 4, a powerful storm dropped over 2 feet (60 centimeters) of snow on portions of the Dakotas and Minnesota. Blizzard conditions continued in the storm's wake as 50-mile- (80-kilometer-) per-hour winds created 10-foot (3-meter) drifts. A surge of Arctic air crossing the Great Lakes produced a narrow band of intense snow in upstate New York on January 11 and 12. East of Lake Ontario, residents of Montague, New York, received 95 inches (241 centimeters) of snow in a 36-hour period. In mid-January, a severe ice storm moved across Texas, causing 300,000 people to lose electrical power.

Spring roared in like a lion in 1997 across the lower Mississippi and Ohio valleys. Tornadic thunderstorms erupted on March 1 from Arkansas to Tennessee, killing 26 people—the deadliest tornado outbreak since 1994. In the town of Arkadelphia, Arkansas, 16 people perished as a tornado packing winds near 200 miles (320 kilometers) per hour tore through the town. Farther north, the same weather system brought heavy rain and extensive flooding to the Ohio River Valley. A 24-hour state rainfall record was broken at Louisville, Kentucky, on March 7, 1997, when 10.48 inches (26.61 centimeters) fell. Meanwhile, 8 feet (2.4 meters) of water inundated Falmouth, Kentucky, leaving the town in muddy ruins. Total flood damage along the Ohio River and its tributaries in March was pegged at $1 billion.

A late-season storm dropped heavy snow from eastern Pennsylvania to New England on March 31 and April 1. Traffic was immobilized for over 12 hours on I-80 in the Pennsylvania Poconos as strong winds produced 3- to 4-foot (1- to 1.2-meter) drifts. In Massachusetts, the storm forced a state of emergency when the high winds and snow disrupted electric power to more than 250,000 customers. Worcester registered a record snowfall of 33 inches (84 centimeters), while Boston received 25 inches (64 centimeters), its third heaviest snowfall in history. A 72-mile- (116-kilometer-) per-hour wind gust was clocked at the Blue Hill Observatory south of Boston.

Flooding in the Plains and Manitoba began to develop in late March, when very mild weather quickly melted the region's exceptionally deep snowpack. In early April, additional cold and snow recharged the snowpack, setting the stage for the highest river crests on record at numerous sites in western Minnesota and the eastern Dakotas. The Red River at Grand Forks crested 26 feet (8 meters) above flood stage on April 21, leaving more than 90 percent of the city under water. Flood damage and cleanup costs in Grand Forks alone were estimated at $1 to $2 billion. Meteorologists noted that a flood of such magnitude is only expected to occur once in 500 years. By the end of April, river levels had fallen at most locations, but remained critically high along the northern reaches of the James and Red rivers. On April 22, the floodwaters reached southern Manitoba, resulting in the province's worst flood in over 100 years.

Unusual cold in the east and unseasonable warmth in the west persisted through much of April and May. During the second week of April, a complex storm spread moderate to heavy snow from the Colorado Rockies to the central Great Lakes. Over 14 inches (36 centimeters) of snow fell in southern Iowa and northern Missouri. Spring snows helped push seasonal snowfall tallies to record levels of 117 inches (297 centimeters) at Fargo and 102 inches (259 centimeters) at Bismarck, North Dakota. On May 13, Omaha, Nebraska, and Gilbert, Arkansas, experienced their latest spring freeze on record. By the end of May, Lansing, Michigan; Pittsburgh, Pennsylvania; and Bristol, Tennessee, established new records for below average May temperatures. In contrast, the month ended with a temperature of 95 °F (35 °C) in Salt Lake City, Utah, the highest ever recorded there in the month of May.

The severe weather season began slowly over the southern Plains. Only one tornado was detected in Oklahoma during March and April, a record low for twisters. However, on May 27, an explosive line of thunderstorms spawned violent tornados, which ripped through parts of four central Texas counties from Waco to Austin. One powerful tornado destroyed an entire subdivision in Jarrell, Texas, where 27 people died and dozens more were injured.

The Atlantic tropical storm season began when weak Tropical Storm Ana formed in the central Atlantic on July 1. It was the first of four tropical storms and hurricanes in July, tieing a record for most named storms for that month. The only storm to hit land was Hurricane Danny, which passed the mouth of the Mississippi on July 18 before stalling near Dauphin Island, Alabama, on July 19. While more than 12 inches (30 centimeters) of rain fell on Mobile, Alabama, nearly 30 inches (76 centimeters) of rain was estimated to have fallen over parts of southern Alabama. The remnants of Danny drifted northeastward and regained tropical storm strength near the Virginia coast on July 20. Moisture from the same storm broke New York City's 24-hour July rainfall record when 3.75 inches (9.5 centimeters) fell.

Thunderstorms over the mountains were unusually frequent in the West during July and August. After a thunderstorm dropped 8 inches (20 centimeters) of rain in five hours near Fort Collins, Colorado, on July 29, a wall of water up to 20 feet (6 meters) high swept through two trailer parks near Colorado State University, claiming five lives.

A powerful blizzard in Colorado, Nebraska, and Iowa was the first major snowstorm of the 1997-1998 season. The storm left over 2 feet (61 centimeters) of snow in parts of eastern Colorado and Nebraska on October 24 and 25.

Recurrent storms deluged central Europe with torrential rain in July. The worst flooding in 200 years disrupted the lives of more than 1 million people in parts of Germany, Poland, Hungary, Slovakia, the Czech Republic, and Romania. The cost of the disaster was estimated at over $2 billion.

El Niño, a warming of equatorial eastern Pacific Ocean waters that can alter global weather patterns was blamed for a variety of meteorological conditions in North America and Asia. Drought conditions contributed to widespread fires in Indonesia, causing dangerous pollution levels over parts of the tropical western Pacific and Southeast Asia in the late summer and fall. Powerful hurricanes struck the West Coast of North America in the fall. Hurricane Nora hit Mexico's Baja Peninsula on September 24, bringing heavy rains and 155-mile- (250-kilometer-) per-hour winds. Nora then hit California—a rare occurrence—before moving on to Arizona. Yuma received 3.6 inches (9 centimeters) of rain—the average annual rainfall—in a single day. Hurricane Pauline, which developed off the west coast of Mexico, was even more destructive. Pauline struck Acapulco on October 9, causing flash floods that killed 150 people.

Typhoon Linda—the worst storm to hit Southeast Asia in nearly 100 years—struck the southern coast of Vietnam on November 3. As many as 2,000 people are believed to have died at sea.

☐ Fred Gadomski and Todd Miner

See also **Disasters.**

Weightlifting. See **Sports.**

Welfare. President Bill Clinton, in his Feb. 6, 1997, State of the Union address, announced that 2 million people had moved off of welfare rolls since 1993. The president set a new goal of reducing the number of people on welfare by another 2 million by the year 2000. During the address, President Clinton repeated a call to private companies to hire welfare recipients. In January 1997, the president asked the U.S. Congress to provide a tax credit to firms that hire welfare recipients. Under the proposal, a company would receive a tax credit equal to half of the first $10,000 annual salary paid to anyone hired from welfare rolls. The credit would apply only to those people who had been receiving welfare for at least 18 months.

In April, the president announced that the U.S. government would hire 10,000 welfare recipients over the next four years as its contribution toward moving people off welfare. Most of the new federal jobs would be entry level positions, paying approximately $12,500 a year. Approximately 4,000 jobs would involve assisting the government to prepare for the 2000 census.

Benefits restored. As part of a balanced budget bill passed by Congress in June 1997, legislators restored some benefits for elderly and disabled legal immigrants that had been eliminated when the welfare system was revised in 1996. Congress restored Supplemental Security Income program payments, averaging $410 a month, to legal immigrants who had been living in the United States when welfare legislation was signed in August 1996. However, other restrictions mandated by the revised welfare law went into effect in April 1997. For example, legal immigrants who were not U.S. citizens were denied access to food stamps. In addition, adults who were single, childless, able to work but unemployed, were declared ineligible for food stamps.

Welfare numbers fall. The U.S. Department of Health and Human Services announced in February that the number of people receiving Aid to Families with Dependent Children (AFDC), a federal welfare program abolished in 1996, fell 18 percent nationwide between 1994 and 1996. Recipients totaled 11,864,000 in October 1996, down from a record high of 14,398,286 set in March 1994. Declines occurred in all states except Hawaii. The decrease was attributed to a strong economy, low unemployment, and efforts to place welfare recipients in jobs.

Ambitious goals. Many states reported difficulty in meeting an Oct. 1, 1997, federal deadline requiring that a majority of welfare recipients be placed in private sector jobs. Under the deadline, 75 percent of all two-parent families receiving welfare were required to perform some type of work as a condition of receiving welfare benefits. Some state officials said that job applicants often lacked skills or experience to satisfy employers' needs.

☐ William J. Eaton

The Soufriere Hills Volcano on the Caribbean island of Montserrat erupts on Aug. 8, 1997. A series of eruptions during the summer left much of the island uninhabitable and forced at least 8,000 people to evacuate.

West Indies. The world looked on helplessly in the summer of 1997 as a series of eruptions from the Soufriere Hills Volcano on Montserrat destroyed much of the British colony in the Caribbean. On June 25, the volcano, which had been active since July 1995, spewed a river of ash, rock, and gas, killing at least 19 people and forcing the evacuation of thousands. In late July and August, the volcano erupted again for several weeks.

The British government, which was criticized for delaying relief efforts, announced in August an assistance program that included relocation expenses, British work permits, income support, and housing benefits. By October, about 3,000 of the island's 11,000 citizens remained on the island.

The North American Free Trade Agreement (NAFTA)—which had provided duty-free access between Canadian, Mexican, and U.S. markets since 1993—produced a disastrous impact on small Caribbean nations, according to a 1997 study by the World Bank, an agency of the United Nations based in Washington, D.C. The report predicted that increased competition from Mexico could cut Caribbean exports to the United States, worth about $12.5 billion annually, by more than one-third.

Summit with Clinton. U.S. President Bill Clinton, at a meeting with 15 Caribbean leaders in Bridgetown, Barbados, on May 10, made no commitment to requests for trade agreements similar to NAFTA. Clinton also refused to end U.S. efforts to convince the World Trade Organization, which negotiates international trade regulations, to end quotas on banana exports to Europe. U.S. banana companies claimed that the quotas gave an unfair preference to Caribbean banana producers.

Elections. On March 14, voters in the Bahamas reelected Prime Minister Hubert A. Ingraham to a second five-year term. His Free National Movement party won 34 seats in the 40-seat parliament. On May 23, the St. Lucia Labor Party won 16 of 17 seats in parliament. Kenny Anthony became prime minister. The election ousted the United Workers' Party, which had controlled the government since 1982.

St. Kitts and Nevis. On Feb. 24, 1997, voters in Nevis gave the pro-independence party, Concerned Citizens Movement, only three of five seats in the island's parliament. The party needed four seats to call for a vote to make Nevis independent from St. Christopher (commonly called St. Kitts), the much larger partner of the two-island federation.

Michael Norman Manley, a fomer prime minister of Jamaica and an outspoken advocate for third-world countries, died on March 6 at age 72.

See also **Latin America** (Facts in brief table).

□ Nathan A. Haverstock

West Virginia. See State government.
Wisconsin. See State government.
Wyoming. See State government.
Yemen. See Middle East.

Yugoslavia. Widespread popular protests against Serbian President Slobodan Milošević continued in early 1997. The protests had begun in November 1996. In February 1997, Milošević gave in to demands to allow opposition representatives who had won local elections held in November 1996 to take office. The opposition Zajedno (Unity) coalition, which had led the demonstrations, collapsed in June, amid interparty rivalry. In July, opposition groups ended their boycott of parliament.

Political scene. In July 1997, Milošević was elected president of Yugoslavia. He was barred by law from seeking a third term as president of Serbia—the office from which he had dominated Yugoslav politics for 10 years. (Yugoslavia in 1997 consisted of the republics of Serbia and Montenegro.) While the federal presidency was a ceremonial office, Milošević hoped to change Yugoslavia's constitution to give the office all executive authority. This plan was delayed when Milošević's Socialist party lost its parliamentary majority in elections in September.

In September, Zoran Lilić, a Milošević protege, won 36 percent of the vote in Serbia's presidential elections, far below the 50 percent needed to become president. Low voter turnout invalidated the second and third rounds of elections in October and December. After a third round of voting in late December, another Milošević ally, Milan Milutinović, was proclaimed the winner, with 59 percent of the vote, despite widespread evidence of election fraud.

Opposition groups organized two days of protests after the city council of Belgrade, the capital, ousted Mayor Zoran Djindjić and the directors of an independent television station on September 30. Police used force against protesters in several cities.

In Montenegro, Milo Djukanović defeated a Milošević ally, Momir Bulatović, in presidential elections in October. Many Montenegrins blamed Serbia for international sanctions imposed on Yugoslavia and sought greater economic autonomy.

Kosovo. In 1997, protests flared up in Kosovo, a formerly autonomous region of Serbia whose population of about 2 million is more than 90 percent ethnic Albanian. Some 20,000 students in the region demonstrated on October 1 to demand Albanian language instruction at Priština University. Ibrahim Rugova, president of Kosovo's shadow government—Serbia had dissolved Kosovo's government in 1990—called for a suspension of the protests after Serbian police attacked and beat the protesters with clubs, injuring 150 people. The European Union (EU), an organization of 16 European countries, denounced Serbia's use of force against the protesters.

In 1997, a group known as the Kosovo Liberation Army stepped up its attacks on Serbian security forces in Kosovo. In December, two Serb policemen were killed when a police convoy was ambushed by gunmen armed with automatic weapons and grenade launchers. Some observers believed the attacks could escalate into a well-armed guerrilla movement in Kosovo.

Economy. Living standards in Yugoslavia continued to decline, the result of EU sanctions and the Yugoslavian government's unwillingness to adopt economic reforms. According to government reports, 30 percent of the population in 1997 was unemployed. Economists estimated the true figure was much higher. Among people with jobs, the average monthly salary was $100. In May, pensioners protested over nonpayment of benefits and poor living standards. Many had not received benefits since February. In June, ethnic Serb refugees from the now-independent states of former Yugoslavia called on Yugoslavia to provide them with social assistance.

International relations. The EU eased restrictions on trade with Yugoslavia in April, after Milošević allowed opposition parties greater access to the media. By September 1997, however, the Yugoslav telecommunications ministry had reportedly closed down 55 independent television and radio stations. In December, Yugoslavia's foreign minister walked out on an international conference on Bosnia in Bonn, Germany, after conference members called on the Yugoslav government to negotiate with Albanians in Kosovo. □ Sharon L. Wolchik

See also **Europe** (Facts in brief table).
Yukon Territory. See Canadian territories.

Zoos. The San Diego Wild Animal Park opened "Heart of Africa," a 30-acre (12-hectare) representation of the diverse habitats of central and southern Africa in May 1997. A winding trail offered visitors areas of forest, savanna, and wetland. Among the 11 mammal species to be seen were cheetahs, Kikuyu colobus monkeys, Allen's swamp monkeys, white rhinoceroses, wildebeest, warthogs, duikers (small antelopes), and okapis (relatives of giraffes). Bird species included white and shoebill storks, white-breasted cormorants, sacred ibises, southern ground hornbills, flamingos, and crowned cranes.

Monkeys and water birds inhabited small islands in the middle of a lagoon fed by streams and waterfalls. Visitors participated in field research activities with scientists at a research station on another island in the lagoon.

Oklahoma rain forest. In June, Oklahoma's Tulsa Zoo opened its "Tropical American Rain Forest," a building with 13,000 square feet (1,209 square meters) of exhibit space containing more than 3,100 plants representing 250 species and about 500 animals representing 100 species. The exhibit simulated the rain forests of Central and South America. Animals included jaguars, black howler monkeys, golden-headed lion tamarins, poison-dart frogs, iguanas, and an anaconda. Hummingbirds and other birds flew freely among visitors. In parts of the exhibit, visitors were able to peer through cutaway windows to see various animals, including piranhas and leaf-cutter ants.

Besides wildlife, the exhibit contained several replicas of artifacts from ancient Middle American civilizations, including a colossal head similar to those carved 3,000 years ago by the Olmec people of what is now Mexico.

Oklahoma cats. Considerable roaring heralded the opening, in May 1997, of "Cat Forest/Lion Overlook" at the Oklahoma City Zoo. This exhibit contained 2.5 acres (1 hectare) of feline habitats from around the world and featured 10 different species of cats. The "Cat Forest" part of the exhibit re-created an Indonesian bamboo forest with Sumatran tigers, a Himalayan Alpine forest with snow leopards, a Mexican dry forest with jaguars, and other habitats with ocelots from Latin America, servals and caracals from Africa, and Pallas's cats from Asia. A path led to "Lion Overlook," which re-created an African savanna—home to a pride of lions.

Arizona rain forest. In January, the Phoenix Zoo opened "The Forest of Uco," a representation of the tropical forests of the Andes Mountains in Colombia. The word "uco," which means "bear" in an Andean dialect, refers to the featured animals of the exhibit—spectacled bears. From an overlook, visitors watched bears beside a pond filled by a waterfall. Other animals included boa constrictors, freshwater tropical fish, howler monkeys, helmeted curassows (crested forest birds), and scarlet macaws.

Chicago's Pacific coast. The Brookfield Zoo, near Chicago, opened "The Living Coast" in May. Focusing on the western coast of South America, the exhibit simulated habitats where the world's driest desert (the Atacama Desert) meets one of the world's most fertile ocean areas.

Near the exhibit building's entrance, a 6-feet by 10-feet (2-meter by 3-meter) window revealed numerous moon jellies (jellyfish about the size of dinner plates) drifting with the current. Lighting effects made the moon jellies appear to glow. Other animals seen in the "open ocean" area of the exhibit included green sea turtles and various fish, including bonnethead sharks and cownose rays. In the "where land meets sea" part of the exhibit, a 50,000-gallon (189,250-liter) tank displayed Humboldt penguins and fish, including moray eels and small sharks, swimming through tall strands of artificial kelp, a type of long, greenish-brown seaweed. A variety of invertebrates, including crabs, starfish, sea urchins, and sea anemones, lived by the shore's edge. In the "rocky shores" part of the exhibit, Inca terns, gray gulls, and brown pelicans flew overhead or perched on rocks, while penguins paddled offshore. Other animals on the shore included chinchillas, leaf-eared mice, and boa constrictors. Vampire bats could be seen roosting in a cave.

New mammal and reptile house. In May, Chicago's Lincoln Park Zoo opened the Regenstein Small Mammal-Reptile House, a building housing more than 200 species of mammals, reptiles, birds, amphibians, and invertebrates. The building was divided into two segments—the "gallery" and the "ecosystem." The mammal walk within the "gallery" displayed such rarities as naked mole rats from Ethiopia, fennec foxes from the Sahara, and golden-headed lion tamarins from Brazil. The "gallery's" reptile walk displayed 15 species, including Virgin Island boas (among the world's rarest snakes) and Aruba Island rattlesnakes.

Visitors passed through a replica of a giant African baobab tree (a cavelike home to two fruit bat species) to reach the "ecosystem," where nine mixed-species exhibits depicted rain forest, savanna, desert, swamp, and dry forest habitats in Africa, Asia, South America, and Australia. Visitors could observe Asian small-clawed otters, African dwarf crocodiles, and koalas from Australia.

Kentucky islands. In April, the Louisville Zoo in Kentucky opened "Islands Pavilion," the second phase of the zoo's island theme inaugurated by "Island Village" in 1996. The "pavilion" exhibit presented animals from islands and coastal regions around the world. Among the exhibit's animals were Rodriguez fruit bats from an Indian Ocean island, rockhopper and Humboldt penguins from South America, Cuban crocodiles, and Komodo dragons (giant lizards from Indonesia). An aviary contained more than 100 tropical birds.   □ Eugene J. Walter, Jr.

1997

Dictionary Supplement

A list of new words added to the 1998 edition of *The World Book Dictionary* because they have been used enough to become a permanent part of our ever-changing language.

definition

word

(werd), *n., v. –n.* ...und or a group of ...s that has meaning ...an independent ... speech; vocable: ...ak words when ... *A free form which* ... *phrase is a word.* ..., *then, is a free form which does not consist entirely of . . . lesser free forms; in brief, a word is a minimum free form* (Leonard Bloomfield).

spell | ing

dic|tion|ar|y (dik´shə ner´ē), *n., pl.* –ar|ies.
1. a book that explains the words of a language, or some special kind of words. It is usually arranged alphabetically. One can use a dictionary to find out the meaning, pronunciation, or spelling of a word.

1. a way of pronouncing:
pro|nun|ci|a|tion *a foreign pronunciation.*

sup|ple|ment
(sup´lə mənt), *n.* 1. So...ng added to complete a thing, or to make it larger or bett...

A a

access code, a code for gaining entry to a computerized system, especially a computer network: *Current voice-mail systems are vulnerable because their access codes are relatively easy to crack* (John D. Keller).

animal activist, a person who will resort to militant action in order to protect animals from abuse and exploitation: *Overnight the rules were rewritten. Now a traipse of fur makes animal activists furious* (James Wolcott).

Apec or **APEC** (ā'pek), *n.* Asian Pacific Economic Conference or Asia-Pacific Economic Cooperation (a group of eighteen Asian and Pacific nations, including the United States, that aims to foster free trade between member states): *The Jakarta declaration two weeks ago by President Bill Clinton and the other 17 Apec members is a "giant step in the march of capitalism," according to the Washington Post* (John Gittings).

assignment worker, a part-time or temporary employee: *Employment agencies call them . . . assignment workers. Some labor economists, by contrast, call them disposable and throwaway workers. Whatever they are called, their [numbers] are climbing* (Peter T. Kilborn).

Atlantic Rim, the nations bordering the Atlantic Ocean, especially the North Atlantic: *Boston's prominence on "the Atlantic Rim" . . . when Europe is scheduled to unite economically* (Boston Globe).

B b

back-to-the-future (bak'tə ᴛнə fyü'chər), *adj.* of or having to do with something that may become a future trend but which suggests past experience or practice: *And as at least four more new major league stadiums are due to open in coming years, this back-to-the-future style might become as much a part of baseball as eight-figure, multiyear player contracts* (New York Times).

bereavement counseling, psychological counseling offered to surviving family members who have lost a relative: *The therapy offered . . . inevitably leads to bereavement counseling, a fairly well-explained branch of psychology . . . working with survivors in the family and a unique set of problems* (Lou Ann Walker).

bleaching disease (blē'ching), a disease in corals, possibly brought on by rising water temperatures, which causes coral to release the algae on which they live and to lose their color: *Last year the most severe outbreak on record of another coral disease, bleaching disease, struck corals from Colombia and Venezuela as far north as the Florida coast . . . the outbreaks have left scientists worried that some unknown, long-term factor is affecting the world's reefs* (New York Times).

boomerang child, a young person living with his or her parents after having left home for a period of time to work or to study: *Ugly new phrases ("latchkey child," "throwaway child," and later "boomerang child") joined the sad new lexicon of youth* (Atlantic).

brand equity, the reputation and value of a product based on its advertisers and consumers: *Chris Moseley, . . . said cable channels were trying to build "brand equity." "Everybody is trying to solidify what a channel means to the consumer," she said* (New York Times).

box-cutter (boks'kut'ər), *n.* a small sharp hooked blade wrapped around the knuckles with a strap and used to open or take apart boxes, especially corrugated boxes: *The stabbing left many students calling for better security . . . to protect them against the box-cutters and knives that some students smuggle in* (New York Times).

C c

Cambrian explosion, the time during the Cambrian in which multicellular life developed: *The crucial time, beginning some 550 million years ago . . . called the Cambrian explosion* (Natural History).

captive breeding, the breeding of wild animals in captivity, often in an attempt to save them from extinction: *The Peregrine Fund's captive-breeding program ensured the availability of birds for falconers* (Atlantic).

cover sheet, a form with spaces for names, fax and phone numbers, and a short note sent with material being faxed: *It will prepare a fax for you . . . , create a cover sheet . . . and . . . keep dialing Bob's fax machine until it gets through* (New York Magazine).

cultural literacy, knowledge of the history, literature, music, art, science, and other aspects of a particular culture: *How, for instance, would Amy and her peers perform on Prof. E.D. Hirsch's recently published test of the 5,000 indicators of "cultural literacy?" . . . of "what every American needs to know" but often doesn't* (Manchester Guardian Weekly).

D d

dream team, a specially skilled group of people, usually experts in a given field: *A "dream team" of 12 cardiologists assembled by the Celtics' physician, Arnold Scheller, made a diagnosis of cardiomyopathy, an abnormal stretching or thickening of the heart* (Time).

E e

Ebonics (ē bon'iks, e-), *n.* a form of black English: *Oakland [California]*

schools and ebonics—the name scholars have given to the black slang of the ghetto—are suddenly front-page news (Jesse Jackson). [< *eb*(ony) + (ph)*onics*]

exit strategy, a plan for ending some undertaking, such as a military operation: *Seeking an exit strategy before sailing into harm's way is smart, but it must be related to the mission's goal* (Time).

F f

fringe market, a stock market in a developing or underdeveloped country: *Exotic equity markets, called fringe markets or emerging markets in the securities trade, are continuing their surge . . . leading performers include such surprises as Colombia, India, Indonesia and Nigeria* (Time).

G g

gene sequence, the sequence of nucleotides in the segment of DNA composing a specific gene: *Watson's vision collided with the Bush Administration's decision to seek patents on gene sequences that the project was beginning to turn up* (New Yorker).

ghost net, a fishing net broken free and left adrift: *Every year an additional 500 miles of drift nets—so-called ghost nets—are left floating in the ocean, where for centuries they will continue to ensnare fish, mammals and birds* (Rolling Stone).

golden hour, the period of time when treatment is most effective after a serious injury: *Doctors refer to "the golden hour" after a trauma, before irreversible shock sets in, when life-saving treatment is most likely to succeed* (Time).

Greenmarket (grēn'mär kit), *n.* a small, innercity market where farmers sell their produce retail: *The more that Greenmarkets become fixtures in city neighborhoods, the more they resemble the proverbial backyard fence where neighbors exchange recipes and gossip* (New York Times).

growth hormone releasing factor, a protein normally found in very small amounts in the hypothalamus serving to stimulate the pituitary gland to release growth hormone: *Growth hormone releasing factor also may be able to stimulate release of growth hormone to reverse thinning bones in aging and to treat tissue-wasting conditions* (Science News).

Gulf War syndrome or **Gulf syndrome**, an illness of veterans of the Gulf War, whose symptoms include chronic fatigue, aches, diarrhea, rashes, hair loss, memory loss, cancer, and birth defects in offspring. Theories as to the cause of this syndrome include a reaction to a combination of drugs with antinerve gas pills administered to U.S. soldiers and inhalation of chemicals. *The drugs dispensed during the Gulf war* [will] *be investigated at a veteran's committee public hearing on Gulf syndrome. The Congressional hearing will also examine the plight of ill children fathered by Gulf veterans* (Manchester Guardian Weekly).

H h

ho|tel|ing or **ho|tel|ling** (hō tel′ing), *n.* the practice of sharing desk space in an office by several employees at different times or of working from a virtual desk in a business computer network: *A similar switch to telecommuting and hoteling by the Chicago staff . . . enabled the firm to reduce the number of individual offices by nearly 100* (Time).

hot zone, an area of infestation by virulent disease-causing microorganisms: *The monkey house had to be treated as a "hot zone"—Army lingo for a place contaminated with a lethal and incurable virus* (Technology Review).

I i

in|fo|bahn or **In|fo|bahn** (in′fō bän), *n.* the Internet, as it is also known outside the United States: *But the door is now ajar for non-English users on the infobahn* (British Financial Times). [< German *Infobahn*]

in|tra|net (in′trə net), *n.* a private, internal computer network of a company, institution, or other organization.

K k

Kui|per belt (kī′pər), a ring of small celestial bodies orbiting through the outer solar system, beyond the farthest planets, Neptune and Pluto. It is believed that the Kuiper belt is a source of comets: *The number of new solar system bodies found so far is sufficient to establish beyond doubt the existence of the Kuiper belt* (Scientific American). [< Gerald Peter *Kuiper,* 1905-1973, American astronomer, who first proposed the existence of this region in the solar system]

L l

Le Shuttle, the trains and train service running between England and France through the English Channel tunnel: *The tunnel's operator, Eurotunnel, is offering a four-band fare struc-*ture for its *Le Shuttle passenger services* (Manchester Guardian Weekly).

line in the sand, a point beyond which nothing will be yielded; limit: *President Clinton's latest line in the sand in the budget battle is education spending* (Investor's Business Daily).

M m

man|da|tory min|i|mum, a minimum sentence that must be imposed for a particular crime: *As* [Senator] *Orrin Hatch concedes, "Mandatory minimums are a political response to violent crime"* (Atlantic).

men|tor|ing (men′tə ring), *n.* the giving of advice and assistance: *Without effective modeling, mentoring, and support, student teachers face . . . probable early exit from the teaching profession* (English Journal).

mi|cro|man|ag|ing (mī krō man′ə jing), *n.* control and direction of the smallest details of business; overattention to particulars: *Given to micromanaging, the publicity-shy ex-lawyer even chooses the pictures for the covers of flight schedules* (Wall Street Journal).

min|i|com|pact (min′ē kom′pakt), *n.* a passenger car smaller than a subcompact car: *The "Youthful" group will appeal to entry-level buyers on a budget, with products such as the Aspire minicompact and the Escort subcompact* (Investor's Business Daily).

N n

nat|u|ral burn, allowing a forest fire to burn until it is put out by rain or other precipitation: *The fires . . . sparked a political fire storm over the "natural burn" policy of the United States National Park Service* (World Book Year Book).

O o

off-lead (ôf lēd′), *adj.* of or having to do with the second most important front-page story in a newspaper: *Mort Zuckerman's purchase of the News made the off-lead story on the front page of* The New York Times (Vanity Fair).

or|bit|al de|bris, anything lost in space that orbits the earth, including equipment or parts, as of a spacecraft, artificial satellite, or the like: *Johnson, a leading authority on orbital debris, has found no confirmed case of injury or significant property damage from space junk* (USA Today).

out|sourc|er (out′sôr sər, -sōr-), *n.* a business or individual that supplies contract services or employees to a company that outsources: *Many of the small outsourcers have focused prima-*rily on the banking industry, and others have concentrated on health care, utilities, and telecommunications (Business Week).

S s

search engine, a computer program that enables the user to find specific information in a database or on the Internet: *Cheap or free software "search engines" make it simple to track down sites where you can find a topic of interest* (U.S. News & World Report).

soc|cer mom, a middle class, usually suburban, woman who devotes a significant portion of time to her family's needs and activities: *Hillary is the soccer mom . . . who went grocery shopping and to baseball games and firmly hitched her wagon to her husband's star* (Time).

SUV (no periods), sports-utility vehicle: *Kid-carrying, grocery-hauling SUV's, are still hot* (Daniel McGinn).

U u

up|size (up′sīz′), *adj., v.,* **-sized, -sizing.** —*adj.* larger; expanded: *For its part, G.M. plans to introduce two new upsize models later this year* (John Tagliabue).
—*v.i., v.t.* to increase in size or scope; expand: *Whether you're upsizing or downsizing, nobody knows how to ensure systems reliability . . . better than IBM* (Time). **up′siz′ing,** *n.*

V v

V chip, a computer chip placed in television sets that allows viewers to screen out programs with a high rating for violent or sexual content: *The current V-chip technology . . . when installed in TV sets . . . can receive encoded information about each show* (Richard Zoglin). [< V(iolence) + chip]

vid|e|o|cam (vid′ē ō kam′), *n.* = video camera: *La Budde smuggled a videocam aboard a Panamanian tuna boat and shot striking first-time footage of how dolphins were still being slaughtered by the netters* (Tom Harton). [video + cam(era)]

W w

World Wide Web, the portion of the Internet capable of handling multimedia computer programs, including images and sound: *Businesses are taking their cues from the Internet's multimedia segment, the World Wide Web, when setting up companywide computer systems* (U.S. News & World Report).

Pronunciation Key: hat, āge, câre, fär; let, ēqual, tėrm; it, īce; hot, ōpen, ôrder; oil, out; cup, pùt, rüle; child; long; thin; ᴛʜen; zh, measure; ə represents **a** in about, **e** in taken, **i** in pencil, **o** in lemon, **u** in circus.

AFRICA ▪ AIDS ▪ ALBANIA ▪ ALGERIA ▪ ANTHROPOLOGY RCH

AUSTRALIA ▪ AUSTRIA ▪ AVIATION ▪ B

▪ BOXING ▪ BRAZIL ▪ BUILDING AND CO BULGARIA

CITY ▪ CLASSICAL MUSIC ▪ COAL ▪ COLOMBIA

DISASTERS ▪ GS TERN OF CH

▪ EDUCATIO S

NIA ▪ ETHIOPI

▪ FRANCE ▪ RGIA

HAITI ▪ HOCKEY ▪ HONG KONG SE

1997 World Book Supplement

▪ KENYA A NORTH ▪ KOREA SOUT

▪ LATIN AME

LITERATURE ▪ LITE

MENTAL HEALT

▪ NEWSMA ERS

PRIZES ▪ NORTHE

PACIFIC ISLANDS ▪ PAKISTAN ▪ PERU ▪ PETROL

PINES ▪ PHYSICS ▪ POLAND ▪ POPULAR MUSIC

▪ PORTUGAL ▪ PROTESTANTISM ▪ PSYCHOLOGY ▪ ROMAN CATHOLIC CHURCH

▪ SIERRA LEONE ▪ SKIING ▪ SLOVAKIA ▪ SOMALIA ▪ SOUTH AFRICA ▪ SPAC

MIMING ▪ SWITZERLAND ▪ SYRIA ▪ TAIWAN ▪ TELECOMMUNICATIONS ▪ TEL

▪ UKRAINE ▪ UNITED KINGDOM ▪ UNITED NATIONS ▪ UNITED STATES ▪

© Lawrence Migdale

WORLD BOOK photo by Steven Spicer (Jones Metropolitan High School of Business and Commerce, a Chicago Public High School)

During adolescence, relationships with *peers* (people of one's own age) take on great importance. Teen-agers spend much time with their peers in such activities as eating together or chatting after school. The students shown above right attend a high school with a strict dress code.

Adolescent

Adolescent refers to a person who is experiencing the period of development between childhood and adulthood. This period is often called *adolescence.* Many experts in human development believe adolescence begins at about the age of 10. They recognize adolescence as a period of growth with many distinctive features. These features involve changes in the individual's body, thinking abilities, psychological concerns, and place in society.

Human beings, like all mammals, go through a series of physical and biological changes, called *puberty,* that prepares them for sexual reproduction. As a biological phenomenon, therefore, adolescence has always existed as a period in human development. However, adolescence as a separate psychological and social stage is a concept that was developed in industrialized nations during the mid-1800's.

The "invention" of adolescence

Before the 1800's, adults did not make important distinctions among children of different ages. However, new patterns of work and family life came with industrialization in the 1800's. Individuals from age 12 to 16 were greatly affected by these changes. As work shifted away from farming and became less tied to the family, young people needed a new kind of preparation for adulthood. Children in working-class families often took jobs in mines, factories, and mills. Others were apprenticed to craftworkers to learn a trade. Adolescents in middle-class families were expected to attend school, where they were grouped with others of the same age.

Laurence Steinberg, the contributor of this article, is Professor of Psychology at Temple University and co-author of You and Your Adolescent: A Parent's Guide for Ages 10 to 20.

At school, they could be better educated for a rapidly changing workplace.

By the early 1900's, adolescence in some societies and some social and economic classes had become a lengthy period of preparation for adulthood. During this time, young people remained grouped with people their own age, often referred to as their *peers,* and were economically dependent on adults. This role is still what is expected of adolescents in most societies today.

How society regards adolescence has a tremendous impact on the psychological and social development of individuals. Before the 1800's, the lives of adolescents did not revolve around socializing with their friends. There was no such thing as a "teen culture." Young people seldom felt compelled to take a certain action, adopt certain values, or otherwise conform to be accepted by the group. Today, social pressure from people their own age, known as *peer pressure,* is a major influence on many adolescents.

Before adolescence became defined as a distinct developmental stage, most young people did not struggle to develop a clear sense of self or to sort out what they would become in the future. Most young people had few real choices open to them. Today, psychological experts use the term *identity crisis* to refer to the psychological distress many adolescents feel as they seek a sense of purpose and an acceptable role in the world. Peer pressure, popular culture, and identity crises may seem to make up the core of adolescence, but they are actually consequences of how adolescence is defined today.

Physical development

Puberty is the most obvious sign that an individual has entered adolescence. Technically, puberty refers to the period during which the individual becomes capable of sexual reproduction. More broadly, however, puberty is used as a collective term for all the physical changes that occur in a growing girl or boy as the individual passes from childhood to adulthood.

The physical changes of adolescence are triggered by *hormones* (chemical substances in the body) that act on specific organs and tissues. In boys, a major change is increased production of the hormone *testosterone,* while girls experience increased production of the hormones called *estrogens.* In both sexes, a rise in growth hormone produces a growth spurt. During this spurt, which lasts two or more years, an individual commonly grows 2 to 4 inches (5 to 10 centimeters) taller per year.

Sexual development. Many of the most dramatic changes of puberty involve sexual development. Internally, adolescents become capable of sexual reproduction. Externally, as secondary sexual characteristics appear, girls and boys begin to look more like mature women and men. The term *secondary sexual characteristics* refers to a variety of physical traits, such as body shape, voice, and facial hair.

Not everyone goes through puberty at the same time or rate. In Western industrialized societies today, the adolescent growth spurt occurs, on average, between the ages of 12 and 14 in boys, and 10 and 12 in girls. But some young people start puberty when they are 8 or 9, and others not until they are in their mid-teens. Generally, girls begin puberty about two years earlier than boys. The duration of puberty also varies greatly, from $1\frac{1}{2}$ to 6 years in girls and from 2 to 5 years in boys.

Adolescent "awkwardness." Because different parts of the body grow at different rates during puberty, many adolescents temporarily look and feel awkward. For many years, psychologists believed that puberty was stressful for young people. According to one theory, changes in hormones made young adolescents moody, irritable, and depressed. We now know that most emotional disturbances in adolescence result from changes in the teen-ager's roles and relationships. Adolescents can minimize difficulties associated with adjusting to puberty by knowing what changes to expect and having healthy attitudes toward them.

National Archives/Photo Researchers

An adolescent of the past worked long hours in a factory, *above.* Before the 1800's, adolescence was not regarded as a separate psychological and social stage of development.

The timing of puberty may affect an adolescent's social and emotional development in important ways. Because early maturing boys and girls appear older physically, people often treat them as if they were more mature psychologically than they are. Early maturers will more likely engage in risky behavior during early adolescence, such as experimentation with drugs, sex, or delinquency. Many psychologists believe these risky actions result from the influence of older teen-agers, who befriend early maturers more often than they befriend younger-looking adolescents.

Because of the emphasis many boys place on athletics, early-maturing boys may have temporary advantages over their peers. As a result, during the first years of adolescence, early-maturing boys tend to be more popular, have higher self-esteem, and have more self-confidence than average- or late-maturing boys.

Average height and weight for adolescents

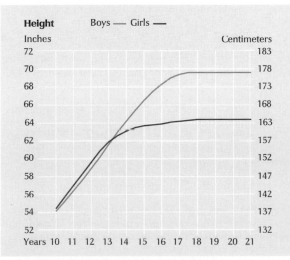

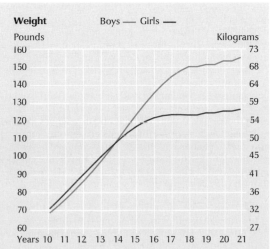

Source: National Center for Health Statistics, U.S. Public Health Service.

In contrast, the effects of early maturation on girls are more mixed. Early-maturing girls tend to be more popular with their peers. But they are also more likely to feel awkward and self-conscious, perhaps because they are uncomfortable with the attention, both welcome and unwelcome, their new appearance draws.

Over time, puberty has begun at younger and younger ages. Part of the trend is due to improvements in nutrition and health care. The trend appears to be leveling off, however.

Intellectual development

Compared with children, adolescents begin to think in ways more like adults. Their thinking becomes more advanced, more efficient, and generally more effective. These improvements appear in five chief ways.

(1) An adolescent's thinking is less bound to concrete events than that of a child. Children's thinking focuses on things and events that they can observe directly in the present. Adolescents can better compare what they observe with what they can imagine.

(2) During adolescence, individuals become better able to think about abstract things. Adolescents have an increased interest in relationships, politics, religion, and morality. These topics involve such abstract concepts as loyalty, faith, and fairness.

(3) Adolescents think more often about the process of thinking itself. As a result, they can develop better ways to remember things and to monitor their own thinking.

(4) Adolescents have the ability to think about things in several ways at the same time. Adolescents can give much more complicated answers than children to such questions as "What caused the American Civil War?" Adolescents have more sophisticated, complicated relationships with others because they can better understand other people's feelings. They also understand that social situations can have different interpretations, depending on one's point of view.

(5) Children tend to see things in absolute terms. Adolescents often see things as relative. They are more likely to question statements and less likely to accept "facts" as unquestionably true. This change can be frustrating to parents, who may feel that their adolescent children question everything just for the sake of argument. However, such questioning is normal and helps teen-agers develop individuality and personal convictions.

One by-product of these changing aspects of intellectual development is the tendency for adolescents to become self-conscious and self-absorbed. This tendency is sometimes called *adolescent egocentrism.* Intense self-consciousness sometimes leads teen-agers mistakenly to believe that others are constantly watching and evaluating them. A related problem is an adolescent's incorrect belief that his or her problems are unique. For example, a teen-ager who has just broken up with a girlfriend or boyfriend may say that nobody else could possibly understand what he or she is feeling, even though such breaking up is a common experience.

Psychological development

Identity and self-esteem. As individuals mature, they come to see themselves in more sophisticated, complicated ways. Adolescents can provide complex, abstract psychological descriptions of themselves. As a result, they become more interested in understanding their own personalities and why they behave the way they do. Teen-agers' feelings about themselves may fluctuate, especially during early adolescence. However, self-esteem increases over the course of middle and late adolescence, as individuals gain more confidence.

Some adolescents go through periods when they genuinely wonder what their "real" personality is. Adolescents who have gone through a prolonged identity crisis may feel a stronger sense of identity as a result of taking the time to examine who they are and where they are headed.

Independence and responsibility. During adolescence, individuals gradually move from the dependency of childhood to the independence of adulthood. Older adolescents generally do not rush to their parents whenever they are upset, worried, or need assistance. They solve many problems on their own. In addition, most adolescents have a great deal of emotional energy wrapped up in relationships outside the family. They may feel just as attached to their friends as to their parents. By late adolescence, children see their parents, and interact with them, as people—not just as a mother and father. Unlike younger children, adolescents do not typically see their parents as all-knowing or all-powerful.

Being independent also means being able to make one's own decisions and behave responsibly. In general, decision-making abilities improve over the course of the adolescent years, with gains in being able to handle responsibility continuing into the late years of high school.

During childhood, boys and girls are dependent upon and relate closely to their parents rather than their peers. During early adolescence, conformity to parents begins to decline, while peer pressure and conformity to peers increase. Peer pressure is particularly strong during junior high school and the early years of high school.

Adolescents yield more often to peer pressure when it involves day-to-day social matters, such as styles of dress, tastes in music, and choices among leisure activities. But teen-agers are mainly influenced by their parents and teachers when it comes to long-range questions concerning educational or occupational plans, or decisions involving values, religious beliefs, or ethics.

Becoming independent involves learning how to cope with peer pressure. During middle adolescence, individuals begin to act the way they think is right, rather than trying to impress their friends or please their parents.

Social development

Relationships with peers change in four important ways during the teen-age years: (1) There is a sharp increase in the amount of time adolescents spend with their peers compared to the time they spend with adults or their families. (2) Peer groups function much more often without adult supervision than they do during childhood. (3) In most societies, there is much more contact with peers of the opposite sex. (4) Adolescents tend to move in much larger peer groups than they did in childhood. Crowds tend to dominate the social world of the school.

The increased importance of peers during early adolescence coincides with changes in an individual's need for intimacy. As adolescents begin to share secrets with their friends, a new sense of loyalty and commitment grows between them. An adolescent's discovery that he or she thinks and feels the same way as someone else becomes an important basis of friendship and helps in the development of a sense of identity.

Dating and sex. In industrialized societies, most young people begin dating sometime during early to mid-adolescence. Dating can mean a variety of activities, from gatherings that bring males and females together, to group dates, in which a group of boys and girls go out jointly. There can be casual dating in couples or serious involvement with a boyfriend or girlfriend.

Most adolescents' first experience with sex does not involve another person. Many boys and girls report having sexual fantasies about someone they know or wish they knew. It is also fairly common for adolescents to *masturbate* (handle or rub their sex organs).

By the time many adolescents have reached high school, they have had some experience with intimate sexual contact, such as kissing, caressing, or sexual intercourse. During the 1970's and 1980's, more adolescents became sexually active than in the past and they became sexually active at an earlier age. Surveys in the late 1990's, however, indicated that the trend toward becoming sexually active at an early age might be leveling off. Many individuals and religious groups consider sexual activity outside of marriage to be morally wrong. They also urge adolescents to avoid sexual activity for health reasons.

Family relationships change most about the time of puberty. Conflict can increase between parents and adolescents, and closeness between them diminishes somewhat. Changing adolescent views on family rules and regulations may contribute to increased disagreement between young people and their parents.

Although young people may distance themselves from their parents as they enter adolescence, this period is not normally a time of family stress. Most conflicts take the form of minor arguments over day-to-day issues. In many families, the decline in closeness between parents and children in early adolescence results from the adolescent's increased desire for privacy. In addition, teen-agers and parents may express affection for each other less often. Generally, this distancing is temporary, and family relationships become closer and less conflict-ridden during middle and late adolescence.

Certain constants remain in family life. Among the most important is an adolescent's need for parents who are both nurturing and demanding. This combination of warmth and strictness is associated with healthy psychological development. Children raised by loving parents who maintain clear and constant personal and social standards are more likely to have good feelings about themselves than children brought up by harsh or lax parents. Adolescents raised with both warmth and firmness are more likely to excel in school, to have close and satisfying relationships with others, and to avoid trouble with drugs and delinquency.

Special problems and challenges

Adjusting to school life. A young person's move from elementary school to middle school or junior high

© Bob Higbee, Berg & Associates

Dating normally begins during adolescence. Learning to enjoy a new kind of closeness with another person is among the normal developmental tasks of this period of life, as well as learning to think of oneself as a sexual being and to deal with sexual feelings.

school can be difficult. In elementary school, the child had a single homeroom teacher who knew him or her personally. In middle school or junior high, the child usually has a different teacher for each subject. In elementary school, children are rewarded for trying hard. In middle or junior high school, grades are based more on performance than on effort. In elementary school, children work under close supervision all day. In middle school or junior high, young people must learn to work more independently.

For such reasons, many students are temporarily disoriented during the transition between schools. Their self-esteem falters, and their grades may drop off slightly. Their interest in school activities declines. They may feel anonymous, isolated, and vulnerable. Parents can help by talking to the child before school begins about the differences he or she will experience.

Alcohol and drug abuse. Many adolescents in industrialized countries experiment with alcohol, tobacco, and marijuana. Adolescents may experiment with such substances because of a desire to fit in with their friends. Many adolescents see smoking, drinking, and using drugs as a key to popularity. Other reasons adolescents experiment with drugs and alcohol include boredom, and a desire to feel grown-up—that is, they see drugs as a way to prove they are adults and no longer under adult control.

Young people who abuse drugs and alcohol are more likely to experience problems at school, to suffer from psychological distress and depression, to have unsafe sex, and to become involved in dangerous activities. Alcohol and drugs often contribute to automobile

Conflicts between adolescents and their parents can arise because adolescents are more likely than children to question what they are told and more likely to disagree with family rules.

© Billy E. Barnes, Photo Edit

accidents, the leading cause of death among American teen-agers. Adolescent substance abusers also expose themselves to long-term health risks that result from drug addiction or dependency.

Pregnancy. Some young women become pregnant before the end of adolescence. Adults can help adolescents prevent unwanted pregnancies. For example, parents and teachers can provide sex education to instruct young people in how to deal with their sexual feelings before they become sexually active. Adults also can make adolescents feel more comfortable about discussing sexual matters so that young people will examine their own behavior seriously and thoughtfully.

Establishing a sexual identity. Normal developmental tasks of adolescence include learning to think of oneself as a sexual being, to deal with sexual feelings, and to enjoy a new kind of closeness with another person. Part of this involves developing a sexual identity. Sexual identity includes *sexual orientation*—that is, whether a person is sexually attracted to the opposite sex or the same sex. People who are primarily attracted to members of their own sex are called *homosexual*, *gay*, or, if they are women, *lesbian*. People who are attracted to the opposite sex are called *heterosexual* or *straight*. No one factor determines sexual orientation.

At some time, almost all young adolescents worry that they might be homosexual. At the age when children enter puberty, they still spend most of their time with members of the same sex. As a result, many adolescents begin to experience sexual feelings before they have much contact with the opposite sex. This does not mean that all of these young adolescents have homosexual desires. Their sexual development is just ahead of their social development.

Unfavorable attitudes toward homosexuality may cause significant psychological distress for adolescents who experience gay and lesbian feelings, especially if they encounter hostility from those around them. The psychological tasks of adolescence, such as developing a sense of identity, present great challenges for all teenagers. These challenges may be intensified for those adolescents attracted to members of the same sex. They may have to resolve these issues without the social support available to their heterosexual peers.

Eating disorders. Some adolescents, especially females, become so concerned about weight control that they take drastic and dangerous measures to remain thin. Some overeat and then force themselves to vomit to avoid gaining weight. This pattern is associated with an eating disorder called *bulimia.* Young women with a disorder called *anorexia nervosa* actually starve themselves to keep their weight down. Adolescents with eating disorders have an extremely disturbed body image. They see themselves as overweight when they are actually underweight. Bulimia and anorexia nervosa are rare before the age of 10. It was once believed that eating disorders were more common in North America and Western Europe than in other parts of the world, and were more common among the prosperous and well educated. However, research in the late 1990's found these disorders to be common among all social and economic levels, and in many countries throughout the world.

Although the incidence of anorexia and bulimia is small, many adolescents, especially females, remain unhappy with their body shape or weight. Many girls whose weight is normal by medical and health standards believe they are overweight. A majority of adolescent girls report that they would like to be thinner. Most believe that being thinner would make them happier, more successful, and more popular.

Delinquency. Violations of the law are far more common among adolescents and young adults than in any other age group. Violent crimes and crimes against property peak during high school.

Violent crime is a serious concern to youths as well as to adults. Adolescents are the age group most likely to become victims of such crimes as theft, robbery, rape, and assault. However, adolescents may also commit such violent crimes. Delinquents who repeatedly commit serious crimes typically come from disrupted or badly functioning families, and they frequently abuse alcohol or drugs. Hostile, neglectful, or unfit parents may mistreat children and fail to instill in them proper standards of behavior or the psychological foundations of self-control.

Risk taking. Many adolescent health problems result from behaviors that can be prevented. These behaviors include substance abuse, reckless driving, unprotected sex, and violence. One particular concern is sexually transmitted diseases, such as AIDS, among teen-agers. Some people mistakenly consider AIDS a homosexual disease, but the virus can be transmitted from male to female or female to male. The virus is also transmitted through needles and syringes that are used in taking drugs. It may even be spread by tattooing or body piercing if the instruments were previously used on an infected person.

Suicide. The suicide rate among teen-agers has risen dramatically since the mid-1900's. Four factors in particular place an adolescent at risk for a suicide attempt: (1) suffering from low self-esteem or an emotional problem, such as depression; (2) being under stress, especially in school or because of a romantic relationship; (3) experiencing family disruption or family conflict; and (4) having a history of suicide in the family or a friend who has committed suicide.

Any threat of suicide demands immediate professional attention. Anyone who suspects an adolescent is considering suicide should immediately call a suicide hot line or the emergency room of a local hospital.

Planning for the future

Career planning is part of the identity development process during adolescence. Occupational plans develop in stages. Prior to adolescence, children express career interests that are often little more than fantasies and have little bearing on the plans they eventually make. In adolescence, individuals begin to develop self-concepts and ideas about work that will guide them in their educational and occupational decisions. Although adolescents may not settle on a particular career at this point, they do begin to narrow their choices according to their interests, values, and abilities.

One problem all young people face in making career plans is obtaining accurate information about the labor market and the best ways of pursuing positions in various fields. One goal of career education is to help adolescents make more informed choices about their careers and to free them from misinformation that inhibits their choices. For a discussion of how to choose and plan a career, see the **Careers** article.

Education is essential today for anyone who wants a well-paying job with a promising future. Young people need at least a high school education to compete in the job market. Those who want to go into a craft or trade usually need a two-year course of college study.

Most of the better jobs go to individuals with at least some college education. However, getting a job is not the only reason for going to college. College plays a critical role in a young person's psychological development. College not only provides occupational advantages but also affects where individuals will live, who they will marry, who their lifelong friends will be, and, most important, who they become.   Laurence Steinberg

Related articles in *World Book* include:

Acne	Guidance	Rite of passage
Anorexia nervosa	High school	Sex education
Boys Town	Homosexuality	Sexuality
Bulimia	Junior high school	Sexually transmitted disease
Child	Juvenile delinquency	Student government
Developmental psychology	Marriage	Universities and colleges
Drug abuse	Middle school	Vandalism
Family	Minor	
Gang	Personality	
Growth		

Outline

I. **The "invention" of adolescence**
II. **Physical development**
    A. Sexual development
    B. Adolescent "awkwardness"
    C. The timing of puberty
III. **Intellectual development**
IV. **Psychological development**
    A. Identity and self-esteem
    B. Independence and responsibility
V. **Social development**
    A. Relationships with peers
    B. Dating and sex
    C. Family relationships
VI. **Special problems and challenges**
    A. Adjusting to school life   E. Eating disorders
    B. Alcohol and drug abuse   F. Delinquency
    C. Pregnancy   G. Risk taking
    D. Establishing a sexual   H. Suicide
       identity
VII. **Planning for the future**
    A. Career planning
    B. Education

Questions

What is *peer pressure?*
How does puberty affect an adolescent's social and emotional development?
What challenges does an adolescent face in moving into a middle or junior high school?
Why is education important for an adolescent?
What actions should individuals take if they suspect an adolescent is considering suicide?
How do an adolescent's thinking patterns differ from those of a child?
When did the term *adolescent* first emerge?
How do family relationships change for an adolescent?
What are the chief reasons why some adolescents experiment with alcohol, drugs, and tobacco?
What are the two most important adolescent eating disorders?

Additional resources

Atwater, Eastwood. *Adolescence*. 4th ed. Prentice Hall, 1996.
Broude, Gwen J. *Growing Up: A Cross-Cultural Encyclopedia*. ABC-Clio, 1995.
Chadwick, Bruce A., and Heaton, T. B., eds. *Statistical Handbook on Adolescents in America*. Oryx, 1996.
Fenwick, Elizabeth, and Smith, Tony. *Adolescence: The Survival Guide for Parents and Teenagers*. Dorling Kindersley, 1994.
Graff, Harvey J. *Conflicting Paths: Growing Up in America*. Harvard Univ. Pr., 1995.
Kutner, Lawrence. *Making Sense of Your Teenager*. Morrow, 1997.
Lerner, Richard M., and others, eds. *Encyclopedia of Adolescence*. 2 vols. Garland, 1991.
Meyer, Linda. *Teenspeak! A Bewildered Parent's Guide to Teenagers*. Peterson's, 1994.
Noel, Carol. *Get It? Got It? Good! Serious Business*, 1996. A guide for teen-agers.
Palladino, Grace. *Teenagers: An American History*. Basic Bks., 1996.

Marice Cohn Band, © *The Miami Herald*

Cuba is a mountainous island in the West Indies. The beautiful Sierra Maestra range, *above,* on the southeast coast has played an important role in Cuba's history. It has served as a refuge for various rebel groups, including the one that brought Fidel Castro to power in the late 1950's.

Cuba

Cuba, *KYOO buh,* is an island nation that is the only Communist state in the Americas. It lies about 90 miles (145 kilometers) south of Key West, Florida. Havana is Cuba's capital and largest city.

Cuba is the largest island and one of the most beautiful islands in the West Indies. Towering mountains and rolling hills cover about a third of the island. The rest of Cuba consists mainly of gentle slopes and broad grasslands. Cuba has a magnificent coastline marked with deep bays, sandy beaches, and colorful coral reefs.

Cuba's geographic location has greatly influenced its history. The island lies at the intersection of major sea routes between the Atlantic Ocean, the Caribbean Sea, and the Gulf of Mexico. The famous explorer Christopher Columbus landed in Cuba in 1492, and the island later became an important strategic outpost of Spain's empire in the New World.

During the late 1700's and early 1800's, sugar cane became Cuba's single most important crop. Sugar cane was grown on large plantations that depended heavily on human labor. The desire for cheap labor for the plantations led to the importation of thousands of African slaves to Cuba.

During the 1800's, many Cubans began to call for independence from Spain. In 1898, the United States helped defeat Spain, which then gave up all claims to

Cuba. A U.S. military government ruled Cuba from 1899 until 1902, when the island became a republic. But the United States maintained close ties with Cuba and often intervened in the island's internal affairs. During most of the period from the 1930's to the 1950's, Cuba was controlled by a dictator, Fulgencio Batista y Zaldívar.

In 1959, Fidel Castro led a revolution that overthrew Batista. The rebels later set up a Communist government, with Castro as its head. Relations between Cuba and the United States became tense soon after the revolution. The Castro government developed close ties with the Soviet Union, then the main rival of the United States in a struggle for international power. In 1961, the United States ended diplomatic relations with Cuba.

Facts in brief

Capital: Havana.
Official language: Spanish.
Official name: República de Cuba (Republic of Cuba).
Area: 42,804 sq. mi. (110, 861 km²). *Greatest distances*—northwest-southeast, 708 mi. (1,139 km); north-south, 135 mi. (217 km). *Coastline*—2,100 mi. (3,380 km).
Elevation: *Highest*—Pico Turquino, 6,542 ft. (1,994 m). *Lowest*—sea level.
Population: *Estimated 1998 population*—11,244,000; density, 263 persons per sq. mi. (101 per km²); distribution, 74 percent urban, 26 percent rural. *1981 census*—9,723,605. *Estimated 2003 population*—11,539,000.
Chief products: *Agriculture*—coffee, fruits, sugar cane, tobacco, vegetables. *Manufacturing*—cement, cigars, fertilizers, food processing, leather goods, paper and wood products, refined petroleum, refined sugar, textiles. *Mining*—chromium, cobalt, copper, iron, manganese, nickel.
National anthem: "La Bayamesa" ("The Bayamo Song").
Money: *Basic unit*—peso. One hundred centavos equal one peso. See **Peso.**

Louis A. Pérez, Jr., the contributor of this article, is J. Carlyle Sitterson Professor of History at the University of North Carolina at Chapel Hill. He has written extensively on Cuba.

Today, the government of Cuba is highly centralized, and Castro has strong control. The government provides many benefits for the people, including free medical care and free education. But political and economic freedom is severely limited.

Government

According to the Cuban Constitution, which was adopted in 1976, Cuba is a socialist state. It is governed by a single political party—the Partido Comunista de Cuba (Communist Party of Cuba), also known as the PCC. The Constitution established the Communist Party as the leading authority in the government and society. The Central Committee of the PCC is responsible for making the highest levels of policy, and it exercises control over all formal government institutions.

Until the 1990's, membership in the PCC was highly restricted. For example, people who attended religious services were barred from membership. In the 1990's, however, the party began to expand its membership and started allowing churchgoers to join. The PCC also sought to attract greater numbers of young people, women, and Cubans of African descent.

National government. The National Assembly of People's Power is Cuba's chief legislative body. The people elect the 589 deputies of the Assembly to five-year terms. All candidates must have the approval of the Communist Party to appear on the ballot. Citizens who are at least 16 years of age may vote.

The National Assembly holds two regular sessions a year. Between sessions, the Assembly is represented by the Council of State. The council consists of 31 members elected by the National Assembly from among its deputies. The president of the council is the most powerful official in the Cuban government and serves as both the head of state and head of government.

The president, with the approval of the Assembly, appoints the members of a Council of Ministers. This council enforces laws, directs government agencies, and conducts Cuba's foreign policy.

Provincial and local government. Cuba has 14 provinces, which are divided into about 170 municipalities for purposes of local government. Each province and municipality has an assembly. The people elect the members of each municipal assembly. The municipal assemblies of a province elect the members of the provincial assembly. Cuba's largest offshore island, the Isle of Youth, does not belong to any province and is ruled directly by the central government.

Municipal assemblies supervise and control local economic enterprises, including retail operations and factories that produce goods for the local market. Municipal assemblies also exercise authority over schools, health services, motion-picture theaters and sports facilities, and all transportation within municipal boundaries.

Courts. The People's Supreme Court is Cuba's highest court. It consists of a president, a vice president, and the members of the court's five divisions. These divisions, called *chambers,* are civil and administrative, criminal, labor, military, and state security. Each chamber consists of a president, at least two other professional judges, and a number of *lay judges.* Lay judges are citizens who hold their regular jobs while serving on the Supreme Court.

© Bill Lyons, Gamma/Liaison

The old Capitol in Havana served as the meeting place of the Cuban legislature from 1929 to 1959. Today the Cuban legislature meets in the Palace of Conventions, and the old Capitol houses the Ministry of Science and a natural history museum.

Cuba's flag was officially adopted in 1902, shortly after Cuba became a republic. The star stands for independence.

Coat of arms. The key means Cuba is the key to the Gulf of Mexico. The stripes are taken from the nation's flag.

WORLD BOOK map

Cuba is an island country between the Caribbean Sea and the Atlantic Ocean, about 90 miles (145 kilometers) south of Florida.

Justices of the Supreme Court are elected by the National Assembly. The president and vice president of the court are nominated by the president of the Council of State and approved by the National Assembly.

Cuba also has a number of lower courts. They include 14 provincial courts and about 170 municipal courts, which operate throughout the island.

Armed forces. Cuba has one of the largest armed forces in Latin America. Approximately 105,000 men and women serve on active duty in the Cuban army, navy, and air force. An additional 135,000 men and women serve in an army reserve. All Cuban men must serve two years of active duty after they reach the age of 16.

People

Ancestry and language. Most Cubans are descendants of people who came to the island from Spain and Africa, but specific information about the ancestry of individual Cubans is often unreliable. According to many authorities, however, about 40 percent of the people are white and of Spanish ancestry, and approximately 10 percent are black. About 50 percent of the people are *mulattoes*—that is, people of mixed white and black ancestry. Cuba also has a small percentage of people of Chinese descent. Spanish is Cuba's official language.

Way of life. The majority of Cuban people live in urban areas. Havana is Cuba's capital, largest city, and commercial and cultural center. Many people in the cities are employed by government agencies or small factories. Some people operate their own small private businesses. Cuba's cities have a severe housing shortage. Many people live in crowded high-rise apartment

© José Acosta, Gamma/Liaison

Small apartment buildings provide some housing for Cuba's urban dwellers. Many other city people live in high-rise apartments. In many cases, two or more families share an apartment.

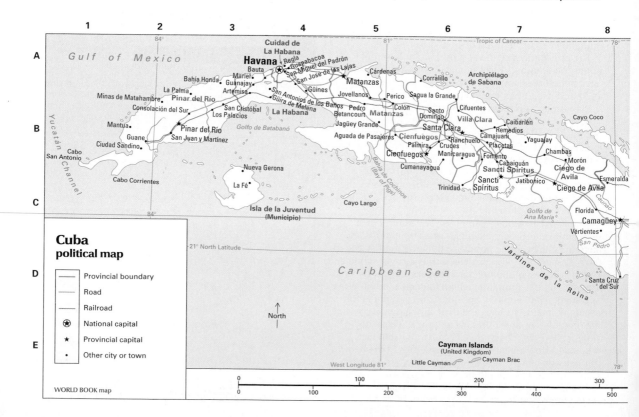

Cuba
political map

——	Provincial boundary
——	Road
----	Railroad
⊛	National capital
★	Provincial capital
•	Other city or town

North

WORLD BOOK map

buildings. In many cases, two or more families share an apartment. Many buildings are in need of repair. Energy shortages at times result in blackouts, the closing of factories, and a reduction in transportation services.

Most of the people in rural areas work on farms. Many rural people live in *bohíos*. Bohíos are thatch-roofed dwellings with dirt floors.

Before the 1959 revolution, many rural communities lacked health facilities, schools, adequate transportation and communication, and housing. Since 1959, however, the government has built hospitals, clinics, and schools in the countryside. It has also expanded transportation and communication facilities and increased housing construction. Nevertheless, many rural areas of Cuba continue to have housing shortages and to lack certain necessities.

Food and drink. Many Cuban foods are spicy. Rice is the most common Cuban food. It is often served with various kinds of beans, or it is mixed with tomatoes, onions, and green peppers in a dish called *arroz con pollo*. Another popular dish is *picadillo*, which consists of ground beef, pork, or veal mixed with onions, garlic, tomatoes, and other ingredients. Corn meal is used in tamales and many other dishes. Coffee and rum are popular beverages.

Many types of food are scarce in Cuba. As a result, the government has organized a rationing system for the distribution of food. This system is designed to provide all households with minimum quantities of rice, beans, meat, chicken, eggs, sugar, milk, and coffee.

Recreation. Cubans are enthusiastic sports fans. Baseball arrived in Cuba from the United States in the

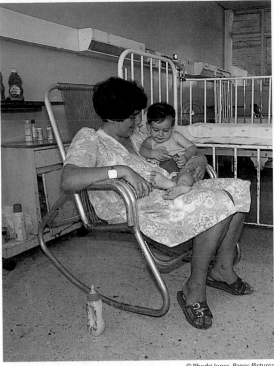

© Rhodri Jones, Panos Pictures

Health care in Cuba improved under the Castro government. The government built many hospitals, clinics, and dental care facilities. The hospital shown above is in Havana.

Provinces

Camagüey	727,700	.C	8
Ciego de Avila	355,500	.C	7
Cienfuegos	356,700	.B	5
Ciudad de La Habana	..2,068,600	.A	4
Granma	777,300	.D	9
Guantánamo	...487,900	.E	11
Holguín	927,700	.D	10
Isla de la Juventud*	70,900	.C	3
La Habana	633,400	.A	4
Las Tunas	481,500	.D	9
Matanzas	599,500	.B	5
Pinar del Río	. 681,500	.B	2
Sancti Spíritus	422,300	.C	7
Santiago de Cuba	974,100	.E	10
Villa Clara	788,800	.B	6

Cities and towns

Aguada de Pasajeros	12,171	.B	5
Artemisa	34,024	.B	3
Banes	31,282	.D	11
Baracoa	35,558	.D	12
Bauta	17,734	.A	3
Bayamo†	128,167	.D	9
Cabaiguán	25,348	.B	7
Caibarién	32,094	.B	7
Camagüey†	286,404	.C	8
Camajuaní	17,537	.B	6
Campechuela	...14,151	.E	9
Cárdenas	59,501	.A	5
Ciego de Avila†	80,500	.C	7
Cienfuegos†	...125,000	.B	6
Colón	35,098	.B	5
Consolación del Sur	16,995	.B	2
Contra-maestre	22,204	.D	10
Cruces	18,123	.B	6
Cueto	13,552	.D	10
Florida	39,700	.C	8
Fomento	14,925	.B	7
Gibara	14,511	.C	10
Guanajay	21,042	.A	3
Guantánamo†	..203,371	.E	11

Güines	41,552	.A	4
Güira de Melena	21,145	.B	3
Havana (La Habana)	2,119,059	.A	3
Holguín†	232,770	.D	10
Jagüey Grande	15,540	.B	5
Jatibonico	14,863	.C	7
Jiguaní	15,042	.D	10
Jovellanos	20,899	.B	5
La Maya	13,939	.E	10
Las Tunas†	120,897	.D	9
Los Palacios	13,928	.B	3
Manzanillo	87,471	.D	9
Matanzas†	115,466	.A	5
Mayarí	21,139	.D	11
Moa	26,850	.D	11
Morón	40,396	.B	8
Niquero	15,544	.E	8
Nueva Gerona	30,898	.C	3
Nuevitas	35,103	.C	9
Palma Soriano	55,927	.E	10
Palmira	9,856	.B	6
Pedro Betancourt	9,033	.B	5
Pinar del Río†	.124,100	.B	2
Placetas	37,535	.B	7
Puerto Padre	...23,239	.C	9
Ranchuelo	14,644	.B	6
Remedios	16,176	.B	6
Sagua de Tánamo	15,327	.D	11
Sagua la Grande	42,741	.B	6
San Antonio de los Baños	..27,550	.A	4
San José de las Lajas	...27,279	.A	4
San Luis	23,638	.E	10
Sancti Spíritus†	75,600	.C	7
Santa Clara†	...197,189	.B	6
Santiago de Cuba†	418,721	.E	10
Santo Domingo	12,945	.B	6
Trinidad	32,809	.C	6
Vertientes	22,440	.C	8

*Municipality responsible to central government.
†Provincial capital.
Sources: Official estimates for 1990 and earlier years for provinces and large cities; 1981 census for smaller cities and towns.

late 1800's and quickly became the island's national pastime. Other popular sports include basketball, boxing, swimming, track and field, and volleyball. Soccer also has a national following.

Religion. About 40 percent of the Cuban people are Roman Catholics. Several Protestant groups have widespread membership in Cuba, including Anglicans, Methodists, Baptists, and Presbyterians. A small Jewish community is concentrated mostly in Havana.

Some Cubans believe in Santería, a religion that combines certain traditional African religious beliefs and some Roman Catholic ceremonies. Followers of Santería believe that the Catholic saints correspond to African spirits called *orishas*.

Education. Cuba has one of the most extensive networks of schools in Latin America, from preschool facilities to graduate and professional programs. All Cubans from the ages of 6 to 14 are required to attend school. Education is free. Centers of higher education include the University of Havana, the Central University of Las Villas in Santa Clara, and the University of Oriente in Santiago de Cuba. Nearly all adult Cubans can read and write. For the country's literacy rate, see **Literacy** (table).

The arts. Cuba has a distinguished tradition in the arts. The Cuban government strongly supports the arts and sponsors free ballets, plays, and other cultural events for Cubans. The work of the government-sponsored Institute of Cinema Art and Industry has made Cuba a center of the Latin American film industry.

Cuban paintings are known primarily for their strong colors and portrayals of dramatic actions. Armando Menocal, who began painting in the late 1800's, became

famous for his murals and depictions of historical events. Well-known Cuban painters of the 1900's include Amelia Peláez and Wifredo Lam. Peláez pioneered the introduction of modern art in Cuba. Lam combined both African and Cuban elements in his works.

José Martí was the most famous Cuban writer of the 1800's. Martí, who helped lead Cuba's fight for independence from Spain, wrote eloquently on political subjects. He also was a poet. The most prominent Cuban novelists of the early and middle 1900's included Carlos Loveira, Alejo Carpentier, and José Lezama Lima. Loveira wrote about social and political injustice. Carpentier produced works in the style of *magic realism*. Magic realism blends dreams and magic with everyday reality. Lezama published poetry and literary reviews. Guillermo Cabrera Infante became one of Cuba's outstanding novelists and short-story writers of the late 1900's. His innovative works of fiction are filled with puns and other kinds of wordplay.

Cuban popular music has gained worldwide renown. This highly rhythmic music combines African and European, especially Spanish, traditions. Much Cuban music features guitars and such percussion instruments as castanets, maracas, and a variety of drums, including bongo drums. Cuban music has given rise to a number of dances, including the *cha-cha-cha, conga, mambo, rumba, son*, and *Cuban bolero*.

The land

Cuba lies about 90 miles (145 kilometers) south of Key West, Florida. It consists of a main island (Cuba) surrounded by more than 1,600 smaller islands. The Cuban mainland extends about 710 miles (1,150 kilometers) from northwest to southeast. The mainland and its surrounding islands cover 42,804 square miles (110,861 square kilometers). At its widest point, the island measures 135 miles (217 kilometers). At its narrowest point, it reaches only about 20 miles (32 kilometers).

Cuba consists mainly of three mountainous regions separated by gentle slopes, rolling plains, and wide, fertile farmlands. The three mountainous regions rise in the west, in south-central Cuba, and in the southeast.

The westernmost mountainous region of Cuba consists of two mountain ranges—the Sierra de los Órganos and the Sierra del Rosario. The south-central mountainous region is known as the Sierra de Escambray. It includes the Sierra de Trinidad and the Sierra de Sancti Spíritus ranges. The southeastern mountainous zone has several ranges. Among them is the Sierra Maestra range, which rises abruptly from the southeastern coast. The highest point in Cuba, the Pico Turquino, stands 6,542 feet (1,994 meters) high in the Sierra Maestra.

Cuba has more than 200 rivers and streams. Most of them are short, narrow, and shallow. Few inland waterways on the island can be navigated for any great distances. The longest river, the Cauto, flows about 150 miles (240 kilometers) through southeastern Cuba. It is navigable for only about 40 miles (65 kilometers).

The coastline of Cuba measures approximately 2,100 miles (3,380 kilometers) long. It is marked with deep bays and sandy beaches. Much of the southern shoreline of Cuba in the west consists of a band of low marshland that is broken up into hundreds of *coral keys* and *mangrove swamps*. Coral keys are low islands that

© Mel Rosenthal, The Image Works

Baseball is highly popular in Cuba and is played in parks and stadiums and on playgrounds throughout the island. The game arrived in Cuba from the United States in the late 1800's.

Cuba physical map

Numerous coral reefs and small islands form bays along the Cuban coast. Cuba also has many small rivers. Pico Turquino, the country's highest mountain, rises in the Sierra Maestra range.

Geographical Terms

Archipiélago..........................islands
Bahía...bay
Cabo..cape
Golfo..gulf
Pico......................................mountain
Río..river
Sierra.....................mountain range

★   National capital
•   Other city or town
+   Elevation above sea level
＝   Swamp

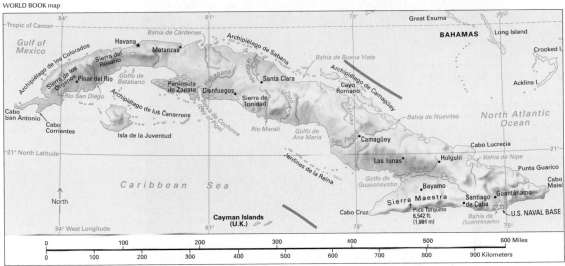

WORLD BOOK map

form when coral growths build up above the water. Mangrove swamps are created when the spreading roots of mangrove trees catch and hold soil. West of Cienfuegos lies the Zapata Peninsula, a vast swampland.

Cuba has over 200 natural harbors along its shoreline. The larger harbors have narrow entrances, which protect the inner area against winds and waves. Important northern harbors include Antilla, Cabañas, Cardenas, Gibara, Havana, Honda, Manatí, Mariel, Matanzas, Nuevitas, and Puerto Padre. The chief southern harbors include Cienfuegos, Guantánamo, and Santiago de Cuba.

Climate

Cuba lies within the northern tropics and has a semitropical climate. Cool ocean breezes during the summer and warm breezes in the winter give the island a mild climate throughout the year. Average daily temperatures in Cuba range from about 70 °F (21 °C) in winter to about 80 °F (27 °C) in summer. The interior has a greater temperature range than the coastal regions. Temperatures on the island rarely fall below 40 °F (4 °C) or rise above 100 °F (38 °C). Frosts sometimes occur in the mountains.

Cuba has a dry season and a rainy season. The dry season lasts from November through April, and the rainy season runs from May through October. Cuba has an average annual rainfall of more than 50 inches (125 centimeters). Thunderstorms occur almost daily in the rainy season.

Hurricanes frequently strike the island. Hurricane season lasts from June to November. The strong winds from hurricanes occasionally destroy buildings and crops and create high waves that flood the coastal lowlands. Earthquakes also occasionally hit Cuba. They occur most frequently and most severely along the southeastern coast.

Economy

Cuba has a *gross domestic product* (GDP) of about $15 billion. A country's GDP is the total value of all goods and services the country produces in a year. Cubans have a *per capita* (per person) income of about $1,300.

From 1961 to the early 1990's, government planning dominated the key economic decisions of the country. During that time, the Cuban economy declined. The country relied heavily on aid from, and trade with, the Soviet Union and the nations of the Communist bloc of Eastern Europe.

© Marc Pokempner

Workers harvest sugar cane on a government-operated farm. Sugar cane has long been Cuba's most important crop by far, and Cuba ranks as one of the world's leading producers of sugar.

World-famous Cuban cigars rank among the island's leading exports. The best cigars are made from tobacco grown in the Vuelta Abajo region in northwestern Cuba. Skilled workers, *left,* roll the cigars by hand, the traditional method of making high-quality cigars.

© Alex Quesada, Matrix

Communism collapsed in Eastern Europe during the late 1980's, and the Soviet Union broke apart in 1991. These political changes resulted in a loss of economic aid for Cuba. To combat the severe economic crisis brought on by this loss of aid, the Cuban government somewhat loosened its control over the economy. Foreign investment, which had previously been discouraged by the government, began to return to the island, principally in tourism. In 1993, some private enterprise was gradually permitted. Many Cubans began to open small businesses, including restaurants and clothing stores.

Manufacturing centers on sugar production. Cuba has more than 100 sugar mills throughout the country. The manufacture of cigars is also important. Cuba is famous for fine hand-rolled cigars made from high-quality tobacco. Most cigar factories are in Havana. Other important industrial activities in Cuba include oil refining and the production of fertilizer, food products, cement products, textiles, paper and wood products, and leather goods.

Agriculture. Sugar cane has long been Cuba's most important crop by far, and Cuba is one of the world's leading producers of sugar. Sugar cane is grown throughout the island. Tobacco and coffee are also important crops.

Through the years, the government has promoted attempts to grow other crops as a way for the country to supply more of its own food. As part of these efforts, the government has tried to increase the production of bananas, citrus fruits, corn, rice, potatoes, and tomatoes.

The government has also attempted to increase the production of livestock farming, particularly the raising of beef and dairy cattle, hogs, and chickens.

During the 1960's, nearly all farmland came under state control. Most farms were run as *state farms,* owned and operated by the government. Some farms were reorganized and operated as *farm cooperatives,* which were owned jointly by the government and groups of farmers. Some small farms remained under the control of individual owners. In all cases, farmers were required to sell their products to the state at prices set by the government. In 1994, however, the government authorized farmers to sell their surplus production on the open market after certain quotas had been met. Soon, small farmers' markets sprang up across the island and sold directly to the public a variety of products, including fruits, vegetables, and other foods.

Mining. Cuba's mines produce chromium, cobalt, copper, iron ore, manganese, and nickel. Most of the country's nickel mines are on the eastern end of the island. Cuba also produces small quantities of petroleum, mostly for its own use.

Fishing industry. State-owned Cuban fishing fleets range over the Caribbean Sea and parts of the North Atlantic Ocean. The chief fish caught include tuna and such shellfish as lobsters and shrimp. Caibarién, Cienfuegos, and Havana are among the important fishing ports.

Service industries are those industries that produce services rather than manufactured goods or agricultural products. They include banking, education, and health care. One of the fastest-growing service industries in

Cuba's gross domestic product

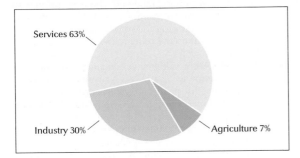

Services 63%

Industry 30%

Agriculture 7%

The gross domestic product (GDP) is the total value of goods and services produced within a country in a year. The GDP measures a nation's total economic performance and can be used to compare the economic output and growth of different countries. Cuba's GDP was $14,700,000,000 in 1995.

Production and workers by economic activities

Economic activities	Percent of GDP produced	Employed workers	
		Number of persons	Percent of total
Community, social, & personal services*	34	1,413,000	30
Manufacturing, mining, & utilities	21	1,036,000	22
Wholesale & retail trade	19	518,000	11
Transportation & communication	10	330,000	7
Construction	9	471,000	10
Agriculture	7	942,000	20
Total	100	4,710,000	100

*Includes government and financial services.
Figures are for 1995.
Source: *World Book* estimates based on data from the U.S. Central Intelligence Agency.

Cuba is tourism. Largely as a result of foreign investment, new hotels and motels have been constructed, and old ones have been restored. Tourists are arriving in growing numbers, mainly from Canada, Europe, and Latin America.

International trade. From about 1900 to 1960, Cuba's principal trading partner was the United States. During the 1950's, about 65 percent of Cuban exports and about 75 percent of all imports were related to Cuban-U.S. trade. Beginning in the early 1960's, Cuban trade shifted largely to the Soviet Union and the Communist countries of Eastern Europe. By the mid-1980's, about 85 percent of all Cuban trade was with the Communist bloc. The collapse of Communism left Cuba in search of new trading partners. After 1991, Cuba's chief trading partners became Canada, China, Italy, Japan, Mexico, Russia, Spain, Ukraine, and Venezuela.

Through the years, sugar has remained Cuba's principal export product. Other exports include citrus fruits, coffee, fish and shellfish, medical products, nickel, rum, and tobacco products. Among Cuba's chief imports are chemical products, food, machinery, and petroleum.

Transportation and communication. More than 18,000 miles (29,000 kilometers) of roads crisscross the island. The Central Highway extends between Pinar del Río and Santiago de Cuba. However, gasoline rationing, problems in obtaining spare parts, and a scarcity of new vehicles make automobile transportation difficult. In the cities, many people travel by bicycle. Railroads cross the island, but more people ride buses—when the buses have enough fuel to operate—than trains. José Martí International Airport is the country's largest airport.

More than 15 newspapers are published on the island. The principal newspaper is *Granma,* published by the Cuban Communist Party. The government controls all newspapers, magazines, and television and radio broadcasts. Advances in telecommunications, however, including satellite broadcasts, have enabled Cubans to receive TV and radio broadcasts from the United States. In addition, Radio Martí, which is operated by the United States government, provides daily news broadcasts to the island.

History

Early years. The famous explorer Christopher Columbus landed in Cuba in 1492. At the time of Columbus's arrival, three groups of Indians inhabited the island: the Guanahatabey, the Ciboney, and the Taíno. Estimates of the size of the Indian population at the time of European arrival vary widely—from as few as 16,000 to as many as 600,000.

Spanish soldiers and priests arrived in Cuba in 1511. The Indians resisted the Spanish effort to take over the island but were soon defeated. The Spaniards then forced the Indians to work in agriculture and mining. Many Indians died from diseases and harsh treatment. By the mid-1500's, only a few thousand Indians remained. As the Indian population declined, the Spaniards began to import African slaves. The first African slaves arrived in Cuba in the 1520's.

The island became strategically important to the Spanish colonial system in the New World. Control of Cuba offered Spain command of sea routes to Mexico, the Gulf Coast, western Florida, and Central America, as well as the chief sea lanes of the Caribbean. In 1564, Spain officially introduced its *fleet system.* Under this system, its merchant vessels, carrying treasure from the New World, sailed together in groups called *convoys,* which were protected by warships. Havana became the gathering place for the treasure ships before they set sail in convoys for Spain. Havana soon emerged as the political, administrative, economic, and cultural hub of the country.

In 1762, the British seized Havana during the Seven Years' War, known in the United States as the French and Indian War. During their occupation, the British introduced reforms and established new trade ties between Cuba and the British colonies of North America.

The British returned control of Havana to Spain in 1763. In the years after the restoration of Spanish rule, Spain eased trade restrictions, abolished all duties on Cuban imports, and opened Cuban ports to unlimited free trade in slaves. These actions helped the Cuban economy flourish.

In the late 1700's, a rebellion of black slaves in the French colony of Saint Domingue (now Haiti) destroyed the production of sugar and coffee on that island. About the same time, the world price of these products soared. In response to this situation, Cuban producers soon launched coffee production in eastern Cuba and expanded sugar cane cultivation throughout the island, beginning in the west.

Through the years, sugar emerged as the most important Cuban export. Expanding sugar production led to the desire for more cheap labor. As a result, tens of thousands of African slaves were brought onto the island. Many owners treated their slaves brutally. In 1812, a group of slaves, headed by José Antonio Aponte, planned a revolt. The Spaniards discovered the plot and hanged Aponte and his followers.

Struggle against Spain. By the mid-1820's, nearly all of Spain's colonies in Latin America had won their independence. During the 1800's, various Cuban groups sought to end Spanish rule of their country as well.

During the mid-1800's, some Cubans and Americans supported a movement to *annex* (join) Cuba to the United States. The annexation movement received much support from Cuban and American slaveholders. These people feared that ongoing unrest among the slaves on the island would lead Spain to end slavery in Cuba. Other groups in Cuba and the United States favored American control of the island for economic and military reasons. The United States made several offers to buy Cuba, but Spain rejected them.

Cuba's struggle against Spanish rule led to the outbreak of the Ten Years' War in 1868. Carlos Manuel de Céspedes, a landowner, headed a revolutionary group largely made up of poor whites, mulattoes, free blacks, and slaves. The group demanded independence from Spain, the establishment of a republic, and the emanci-

pation of the slaves. Spain rejected the group's demands, and bitter fighting followed. The war ended with the signing of the Pact of Zanjón in 1878. This treaty provided for political reforms and for the liberation of slaves who had joined the rebel army. Slavery was abolished in Cuba in 1886.

By the early 1890's, Cubans were again preparing to fight for independence. Largely as a result of the efforts of the writer José Martí, the separatists organized the Cuban Revolutionary Party. In 1895, they launched a new war for the independence of the island.

President William McKinley of the United States claimed that the fighting on the island threatened American interests. He told the Spanish government to either change its policy toward Cuba or give up the island completely. In February 1898, the U.S. battleship *Maine,* which had been sent to Havana to protect Americans in Cuba, exploded mysteriously. The United States blamed Spain for the explosion and, in April, declared war on Spain. This war became known in the United States as the Spanish-American War. In Cuba, the war that was fought from 1895 to 1898 is called the Spanish-Cuban-American War.

The U.S. intervention delivered the final blow to the Spanish army in Cuba. The Spanish army in Cuba surrendered in July 1898, and an armistice in August ended the fighting. Under the Treaty of Paris, which was signed on December 10, Spain gave up all rights to the island. The United States then set up a military government in Cuba. Consequently, the Cubans did not achieve the independence they had hoped to gain. Instead, Cuba

National Archives

The U.S. battleship *Maine* arrived in Havana in 1898 to protect Americans during Cuba's fight for freedom from Spain. The ship exploded mysteriously, triggering the Spanish-American War.

was occupied by another foreign country—the United States.

The Platt Amendment. In 1901, Cuba adopted a constitution. The United States insisted that the Constitution include a set of provisions called the Platt Amendment. The amendment limited Cuban independence by permitting the United States to intervene in Cuban affairs. It also limited the Cuban government's power to make treaties with other governments. The amendment required Cuba to allow the United States to buy or lease land for naval bases on the island. Under a treaty with Cuba in 1903, the United States received a permanent lease on Guantánamo Bay and began to build a large naval base there.

The government of Cuba from 1902 to 1934, except for the years 1906 to 1909, is sometimes called the Platt Amendment Republic or the Plattist Republic. The period of the Plattist Republic was marked by political instability, public corruption, and popular protest. During this period, the United States gained increasing control over the economic affairs of Cuba. The United States began to dominate Cuban trade.

In 1901, the Cuban people elected Tomás Estrada Pal-

Important dates in Cuba

1492 Christopher Columbus landed in Cuba.

1520's The first African slaves arrived in Cuba.

1762 The British seized Havana. They returned it to Spanish control in 1763.

1868-1878 Cuban revolutionaries fought Spanish rule in the Ten Years' War. Under the Pact of Zanjón, which ended the war, Spain promised reforms.

1886 Slavery was abolished in Cuba.

1895 A revolution, led by José Martí, broke out in Cuba against Spanish rule.

1898 The United States, supporting the Cuban rebels, defeated Spain in the Spanish-American War. Spain gave up all claims to Cuba.

1899-1902 A U.S. military government controlled Cuba.

1901 Cuba adopted a constitution that included a set of provisions called the Platt Amendment. The amendment allowed the United States to intervene in Cuban affairs.

1902 Tomás Estrada Palma became the first president of the Republic of Cuba.

1906-1909 United States forces again occupied Cuba.

1933 A revolutionary group led by Fulgencio Batista y Zaldívar took control of the government.

1934 The United States and Cuba signed a treaty that canceled the Platt Amendment.

1959 Fidel Castro's forces overthrew Batista's government, and Castro became ruler of the country.

1961 Cuban exiles sponsored by the U.S. Central Intelligence Agency (CIA) invaded Cuba at the Bay of Pigs and were quickly defeated by Castro's army.

1962 The Soviet Union agreed to U.S. demands that it remove its missiles from Cuba and dismantle the remaining missile bases on the island.

1976 Cuba adopted a new constitution that established the Communist Party as the leading authority in the government and society.

1991 The Soviet Union, which had been an important source of economic aid to Cuba, was dissolved. Cuba's economy suffered greatly as a result.

1993 Cuba instituted economic reforms that allowed some workers to start private businesses.

ma as the first president of the Republic of Cuba. American troops left the country. In 1906, violent protests broke out in Cuba over the disputed outcome of a presidential election. United States troops then returned to Cuba. A government headed by Charles E. Magoon of the United States ruled Cuba from 1906 to 1909. The United States returned control of the country to the Cubans in 1909. American forces left the country, but the United States retained naval bases on the island.

A black uprising broke out in Cuba in 1912. The protesters objected to the lack of political opportunity for blacks in Cuba. In 1917, a revolt protesting electoral fraud broke out. During both uprisings, the United States sent military forces into the country.

The Cuban people elected Gerardo Machado president in 1924. During his campaign, Machado had attacked the Platt Amendment and had promised reforms. But after becoming president, he ruled as a dictator. In August 1933, a general strike and an army revolt forced Machado out of office. A month later, an army sergeant named Fulgencio Batista y Zaldívar and a group of university students and professors led a military revolt that overthrew the new government. They named a five-man government, headed by a former university professor named Ramón Grau San Martín, to rule Cuba.

The Grau government wanted to reduce U.S. influence in Cuba and make far-reaching changes. The government passed a number of measures, including laws that established an eight-hour workday and required all Cuban businesses to employ Cubans for at least half of their total work force. The United States and many

Fulgencio Batista, famous for his fiery speechmaking, ruled Cuba as dictator from 1934 to 1940, as an elected president from 1940 to 1944, and again as dictator from 1952 to 1959.

Cubans refused to recognize the Grau government.

The Batista era. Batista forced Grau to resign from office in 1934. Until 1940, Batista ruled Cuba as dictator through presidents who served in name only. The United States recognized and supported Batista's government. In 1934, the United States and Cuba signed a treaty that canceled the Platt Amendment, except for the Guantánamo Bay lease. United States investments in Cuba continued to expand during the 1940's and 1950's. For example, American interests eventually controlled more than 90 percent of Cuba's telephone and electrical services and about 40 percent of its sugar production. The United States also continued to be Cuba's most important trading partner.

In 1940, Cubans adopted a new constitution and elected Batista president. The Constitution prevented Batista from seeking reelection in 1944, and Grau became president again. Carlos Prío Socarrás won the 1948 election.

In 1952, Batista overthrew Prío's government and became dictator again. Batista stressed the development of light industry and encouraged foreign companies to build businesses in Cuba. He also improved public works. But many Cubans remained unemployed and in poverty, and political conflict expanded across the island. Strikes and demonstrations became common.

The Castro revolution. On July 26, 1953, Fidel Castro, a young lawyer, tried to start a revolution against Batista by attacking the Moncada army barracks in Santiago de Cuba. Castro was captured and imprisoned. Many of his followers were either imprisoned or murdered. Castro was released from prison in 1955 and went to Mexico. In 1956, he organized the 26th of July Movement, which was named after the date of his first revolt. Castro's forces landed in Oriente Province in December 1956. Most of the rebels were imprisoned or killed. However, Castro and about a dozen of his followers escaped to the Sierra Maestra.

In 1957, Castro's forces began to wage a guerrilla war against the Cuban government. The same year, university students stormed the presidential palace in an attempt to assassinate Batista. Attempts by the government to crush the revolution increased the people's support of the rebels. Continued poor economic conditions also led to growing support for the rebels, particularly among workers, peasants, students, and the mid-

dle class. By mid-1958, Batista's government had lost the support and confidence of both the United States and the Cubans.

On Jan. 1, 1959, Batista fled the country. Castro's forces then took control of the government. Later, Castro became prime minister of Cuba. The revolutionary leaders did away with the political and military structure of Batista's government. Many former political officials and military officers were tried and executed. A large number of middle- and upper-class Cubans went into exile in Florida.

The new Cuban government immediately set out to change Cuban relations with the United States. In particular, it sought to reduce U.S. influence on Cuban national affairs. In 1960, for example, the Cuban government seized U.S.-owned businesses, including sugar estates. As a result, relations between Cuba and the United States quickly became strained.

As relations with the United States declined, Cuba developed stronger ties with the Soviet Union and became a Communist country. In early 1960, Castro's government signed a broad economic pact with the Soviet Union.

In June 1960, the Castro government took over American and British oil refineries in Cuba after the refineries refused to process crude oil imported from the Soviet Union. The United States then stopped buying sugar from Cuba. Over the next few months, the Castro government took over all the remaining American businesses in Cuba and accepted Soviet military assistance. In October, the United States placed an economic embargo on Cuba, which banned all U.S. exports except medicines and some food products. In January 1961, the United States ended diplomatic relations with Cuba.

The Bay of Pigs invasion. In April 1961, Cuban exiles sponsored by the United States Central Intelligence Agency (CIA) invaded Cuba at the Bay of Pigs on the south coast. Castro's forces crushed the invasion and captured most of the exiles. Castro later released many of the exiles to the United States in exchange for nonmilitary supplies.

The Cuban missile crisis. Cuban leaders feared another direct U.S. invasion. The Soviet Union offered military aid to Cuba, and Cuba agreed to let the Soviet Union send missiles and materials to build launch sites. In October 1962, the United States learned that Cuba had nuclear missiles in place that could be launched toward American cities. President John F. Kennedy ordered a naval blockade to halt the further shipment of arms. He demanded that the Soviet Union remove all missiles from the island and dismantle the remaining missile bases. For several days, the world stood on the brink of nuclear war. Finally, the Soviet Union removed the weapons under protest from Castro. The Soviet action came after Kennedy privately agreed not to invade Cuba. Kennedy also agreed to remove U.S. nuclear missiles from Turkey, which the Soviets considered to be a threat.

Social programs. The Castro government built many new schools and improved old ones, and school enrollments and literacy rates increased dramatically. The government also improved medical and dental care facilities across the country and built new ones. The number of doctors and other health professionals increased.

UPI/Corbis-Bettmann

Fidel Castro, a young revolutionary, became the head of the Cuban government in 1959 after he and his supporters waged a guerrilla war and overthrew the dictatorship of Fulgencio Batista.

Health conditions improved, and life expectancy increased. Social reforms also led to more opportunities for minorities. Women began attending universities in greater numbers. Larger numbers of women joined the labor force. Blacks also received increased educational, employment, and political opportunities.

On the other hand, many opponents of the government were jailed, and Cuba came under sharp criticism from international human rights groups. In addition, the Cuban people were denied many political and economic freedoms. The Cuban economy declined under Castro, and the people suffered from shortages of food and housing.

Foreign relations. From the 1960's to the 1980's, Castro tried to spread revolution throughout Latin America, mainly by supplying military aid to guerrilla groups in a number of Latin American countries. Cuba also sent troops and civilian military advisers to aid certain groups in Angola and several other African countries. The Soviet Union provided most of the military supplies for Cuba's African operations.

Relations between Cuba and the United States remained strained, despite occasional signs of improvement. The United States kept its embargo, first imposed in 1960, firmly in place. During the 1990's, the United States passed legislation, including the Helms-Burton Act of 1996, to broaden trade sanctions against Cuba.

Another serious issue between Cuba and the United States involved the immigration of Cubans to the United States. After the revolution, hundreds of thousands of Cubans left the country because of their opposition to Castro or because of dissatisfaction with their social and economic conditions. Most of these people settled in the United States, which had a policy of providing political asylum to all Cubans who reached its shores. Other Cuban exiles settled in such Spanish-speaking countries as Mexico and Spain.

An especially large immigration wave took place between April and September of 1980, when more than 125,000 Cubans moved to the United States. This event became known as the Mariel boat lift because the refugees left from the Cuban port of Mariel. After another large immigration in 1994, Cuba and the United States reached an immigration agreement. The United States said it would admit at least 20,000 new immigrants from Cuba annually. In return, Cuba pledged to do more to prevent illegal departures.

Recent developments. In the late 1980's, the Soviet Union and other European Communist countries began programs to give their people more political and economic freedom. Castro criticized these reform efforts. Non-Communist governments replaced Communist governments in most of the Eastern European countries during the late 1980's. In December 1991, the Soviet Union was dissolved, its Communist government was replaced, and Cuba lost its most important source of aid. Cuba's economy suffered severely as a result.

Cuba soon took a number of steps aimed at easing its economic crisis. For example, it undertook limited reforms that loosened state control over parts of the country's economy. It also sought to improve relations with other countries, particularly Canada and European and Latin American nations, in an attempt to stimulate foreign investment in Cuba.   Louis A. Pérez, Jr.

Related articles in *World Book* include:

Cities

Guantánamo	Havana	Santiago de Cuba

History

Batista y Zaldívar, Fulgencio	Guevara, Ché
Castro, Fidel	Kennedy, John F. (Cuba)
Columbus, Christopher	Martí, José Julián
Cuban missile crisis	Reed, Walter
Finlay, Carlos Juan	Spanish-American War
García Iñiguez, Calixto	Wood, Leonard
Guerrilla warfare (History)	

Other related articles

Organization of American States
West Indies

Outline

I. **Government**
   A. National government
   B. Provincial and local government
   C. Courts
   D. Armed forces
II. **People**
   A. Ancestry and language
   B. Way of life
   C. Food and drink
   D. Recreation
   E. Religion
   F. Education
   G. The arts
III. **The land**
IV. **Climate**
V. **Economy**
   A. Manufacturing
   B. Agriculture
   C. Mining
   D. Fishing industry
   E. Service industries
   F. International trade
   G. Transportation and communication
VI. **History**

Questions

Why did Cuba suffer a severe economic crisis in the early 1990's? What are some of the steps the government took to ease the crisis?

What is Cuba's most important crop?

What was the Platt Amendment?

What are some Cuban dances?

What was the 26th of July Movement?

Why does Cuba have a mild climate the year around?

In what ways was Cuba important to Spain's empire in the New World?

What official is the most powerful person in the Cuban government?

What was the Cuban missile crisis?

What is Cuba's national pastime?

How have the Cuban people benefited from the Castro government? In what ways have the people of Cuba been limited by the government?

Additional resources

Crouch, Clifford W. *Cuba.* Chelsea Hse., 1991. Younger readers.
Pérez, Louis A., Jr. *Cuba.* 2nd ed. Oxford, 1995.
Rice, Earle, Jr. *The Cuban Revolution.* Lucent Bks., 1995.
Smith, Wayne S. *Portrait of Cuba.* Turner Pub. Inc., 1991.
Suchlicki, Jaime. *Cuba.* 4th ed. Brassey's, 1997. *Historical Dictionary of Cuba.* Scarecrow, 1988.

House is a building that provides shelter, comfort, and protection for its inhabitants. Houses range in size from small cottages to huge mansions. Many rise two or more floors, and others spread in long, low lines across the ground. Houses vary greatly in appearance, depending on when and where they were built and what building materials were used.

Building materials

Houses are often classified according to the chief type of building material used. For example, we speak of *frame* (wood) houses; brick houses; and stone houses. A combination of materials may also be used. For example, a thin layer of brick or stone called *veneer* may be applied over wood. *Prefabricated* houses are built with factory-made sections assembled at the building site. *Manufactured* houses are built completely in factories and moved to the homesite. The kind of materials used in the construction of a house depends mainly on the size of the house, its location, its design, and the climate.

Wood has long been a popular building material because it is usually more plentiful and cheaper than other materials. Houses are often made of fir, pine, hemlock, redwood, and spruce. Redwood and cedar often are used for the *siding* (outer covering), if the siding is not going to be painted. Other woods, including oak, cypress, maple, walnut, and birch, are used for such interior features as stairways, cabinets, floors, and doors.

Brick is one of the oldest and most common building materials. Brick wears well and, like wood, is usually easy to obtain. Builders often use brick when building codes require a more fire-resistant material than wood—for example, in the construction of row houses. Bricks are available in a number of colors and finishes.

Concrete block and stone make strong, attractive houses that are relatively cheap to maintain. Concrete blocks are made by pouring a mixture of cement, sand, water, and other materials into a mold. Builders also make houses of stone that has been taken from quarries and split into usable sizes. Because stone is an expensive building material, it is usually applied as a veneer over an inner wall of brick or concrete block.

Other materials. Builders often cover a house's exterior with aluminum or vinyl siding. These types of siding provide insulation, prevent rotting, and save much repainting and repairing. Window frames may be made of aluminum or vinyl, or wood clad with aluminum or vinyl for protection against the weather. Manufacturers coat nails for use in home construction with zinc, copper, nickel, or aluminum to make them rustproof.

Building a house

A person building a house must first select a *lot* (piece of land). The next step is to consult an architect or builder. This expert will check local zoning laws and electrical, building, and plumbing codes. Knowledge of these codes protects the homeowner in both the present and the future. For example, the building code in an area may specify how deep the foundation must be, based on soil conditions and the depth to which the ground freezes.

The architect then designs the house according to the owner's ideas and budget. The architect must also consider the size and shape of the lot and the location of the house on the lot. The architect prepares construction drawings, which provide information on the size of the house and details of how it is to be built. These drawings are the basis of the contract between the builder and the homeowner. The architect also prepares *specifications,* a written description of the house materials. The drawings and specifications are used to determine the cost of the house and to obtain a *building permit* from the community.

The following sections describe the steps involved in building a typical frame house.

The foundation supports the house. First construction workers begin e*xcavating* (digging) holes or trenches for the *footings,* the lowest part of the foundation. The footings support each wall load. They are made by pouring concrete into wood or steel forms that workers place below the *frostline,* the depth to which the ground freezes. This is done so that the footings will not freeze and shift. Builders generally use concrete or concrete block for the house's foundation. The foundation walls rest on the footings. These walls rise from 8 inches to 3 feet (20 to 90 centimeters) above the ground.

An area within the foundation below the first story is called a *basement.* Basements add to the cost of building a house, but they provide extra room. Many basements have separate rooms for the home's heating unit and laundry equipment, and for storage. Some basements also have a recreation room.

Most of the houses built today do not have basements. In many low or damp regions, houses are raised above the ground on concrete *piers* (supports). Sometimes a *slab* foundation is laid directly on the ground, especially if the earth beneath the house is hard. The ground must first be *graded* (leveled). Workers then spread a *filler,* usually stone, and cover it with a thin plastic sheet called a *moisture barrier.* The workers pour concrete over the moisture barrier, forming a slab about 4 inches (10 centimeters) thick. The barrier prevents moisture from coming through the slab.

Some house-building terms

Attic is the space directly below the roof and above the ceiling.
Ceiling joists are beams that rest on the top plate of the studs and support the ceiling.
Conduit is a tube that protects electrical wires.
Dry wall is an interior wall finish made in panels of dry material, usually gypsum. It is covered with paper on both sides.
Duct is a metal pipe for distributing air from the heating and cooling equipment to the rooms of a house.
Eaves are the part of the roof that hangs over the outside wall.
Girder is a heavy piece of timber or steel used for support.
Header is a beam perpendicular to the joists. It is nailed to the joists to make a frame for a chimney, stairway, window, door, or other opening.
Joists are beams that support floors and ceilings. They are supported at the ends by walls, girders, or larger beams.
Lath is a strip of wood, sheet of metal mesh, or panel of plasterboard attached to the inside of the frame. Laths provide support for plaster and tile walls.
Rafter is a sloping piece of lumber that extends from the *ridge* (top edge) of the roof to the eaves. It supports the roof covering.
Sash is the framework that holds glass in a window or door.
Sheathing refers to boards or other materials that cover the wall or roof before the finished siding or roofing is added.
Siding is the outer covering of a frame house. It may be made of wood, metal, or various composition materials.
Stud is a vertical part of the frame.

Some styles of houses

The Georgian house originated in England during the 1700's. It is built on a simple square or rectangular plan. The house has two or more stories and a prominent central entrance.

A Greek revival house displays some characteristics of ancient Greek architecture, such as a row of columns at the front and a *pediment,* a triangular area above the columns.

The Queen Anne style emerged in the late 1800's in England. The house's exterior has irregular shapes and textures, a steep roof, narrow siding, and a large, projecting main entrance.

The shingle style in the United States grew out of the Queen Anne style. It was popular in the late 1800's for houses of wealthy families and was distinguished by shingled walls.

A Tudor house is based on English architecture that was popular during the 1500's. This picturesque style features gables, a large chimney, numerous windows, and elaborate paneling.

The prairie style emerged in the United States during the early 1900's. A prairie house has a low, horizontal profile, with eaves that project beyond the roof and long rows of windows.

The International Style became popular starting in the mid-1900's. The house features geometric shapes, white walls, and a flat roof. The exterior has little or no ornamentation.

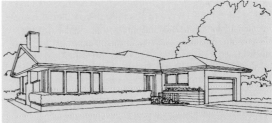

WORLD BOOK illustrations by Mark Nelson

The ranch house became popular in the United States in the mid-1900's. All the rooms are arranged on ground level. The house has several windows, including a large picture window.

The frame is the skeleton around which the rest of the house is built. After the footings and foundation have been formed, workers bolt wooden beams called *sills* to the foundation. The sills support the outside walls. *Floor joists,* beams that support the floor, are attached to the sills about 16 inches (40 centimeters) apart. In many cases, the joists run from one sill to the sill on the opposite side of the house. In other cases, the joists run to an intermediate support beam or an interior support wall called a *bearing wall.* Floorboards or plywood nailed on top of the joists make the bottom layer of the floor. The structure is then solid enough to hold the *wall frames.*

Wall frames include vertical pieces of lumber called *studs* and horizontal pieces called *plates.* Carpenters assemble and nail together each wall frame separately before attaching it to the sill. Then they lift each frame into place and brace it temporarily. When all the outside walls have been raised, they are nailed together and braced permanently.

The *sheathing* (the inner layer of the outside walls) may be wood, fiberboard, or plywood nailed to the studs. Usually, builders cover the sheathing with waterproof paper called *building paper* or with a thin plastic sheet called *house wrap.* Then they add the siding. Siding may be aluminum, brick, stone, or wood.

The roof seals the top of the house. Some roofs are flat, but most are slanted to shed rain and snow. Slanted roofs are often formed by pieces of lumber called *rafters.* Carpenters nail the bottom ends of the rafters to the plates at the top of the outside walls. The rafters slant from the plates and meet at the *ridgeboard,* a board placed at the *ridge* (top edge) of the roof, or at a similarly placed *ridge beam.* Rafters support the roof's weight.

After carpenters nail sheathing to the tops of the rafters, they add heavy building paper or roofing felt to it. Then they add the final layer of asphalt, wood, or slate shingles. They usually cover flat roofs with asphalt or with a *membrane roof* of rubber sheet roofing. *Flashing* (strips of sheet metal) placed around the chimney and other roof openings prevents water leakage.

Interior construction includes (1) floors, (2) walls, (3) windows, and (4) doors.

Floors have a lower layer and upper layer. The lower layer, called the *subfloor,* usually consists of sheets of plywood that are $\frac{3}{4}$ inch (1.9 centimeters) thick. Some subfloors may consist of boards nailed at an angle across the floor joists.

The upper layer is known as the *finished* floor. Finished floor coverings include wood; carpeting; linoleum; rubber; cork; and vinyl, ceramic, and stone tile. Wood flooring is often made from *tongue-and-groove boards.* One side of each board has a projecting piece called a *tongue,* and the other side has a matching slot called a *groove.* The tongue of one board fits snugly into the groove of another board. Carpenters drive nails through the groove side so that the nailheads do not show on the finished floor. Most finished floors are made of hardwoods, such as maple or oak, that have been finely sanded. The wood may then receive an application of wax, shellac, varnish, or plastic, or it may be covered with a carpet.

Walls. Rooms are made by building inside walls after the outside walls have been attached to the foundation. Inside walls, also called partitions, are really small-sized frames like the outside walls. They have studs and must

be supported by plates, joists, and girders.

If plaster is to be applied, the interior walls must first be covered with *lath*—horizontal strips of wood, metal mesh, or plasterboard. Gypsum wallboard is commonly used instead of plaster on partitions. Wood or plywood boards may also be used.

Windows. Most parts of a window come from a lumber mill or are manufactured by window companies. Windows that open have two parts, the *frame* and the *sash.* The sash, which holds the glass, swings or slides open. The frame fits into the opening left in the structure's frame and is nailed into place. Window frames and sashes may be made of wood, metal, or vinyl.

Doors. Both doors and doorframes may usually be bought ready-made. Carpenters attach the doors high enough to swing over rugs or carpets. A *threshold* fills in the space under an outside door and provides protection against the weather.

Electrical wiring provides lighting and furnishes outlets for lamps, washing machines, and other appliances. In some houses, electric power also provides heat. Before construction starts, the builder determines the location and type of wiring. Wires vary in size, depending on the equipment in the house and how far the current must travel. Standard wiring in the United States is designed for 110-volt current. But builders often specify heavy-duty, 220-volt wiring if large electrical appliances or an air conditioning system are installed.

Electricians install wiring after carpenters have built the frame. Wiring is done in a series of circuits. Each set of wires has several outlets. Electricians often place the wiring for a furnace on a separate circuit. This keeps the furnace running in case another circuit breaks down.

Wires become hot and can cause fires if they are overloaded, so electricians may install a protective switch called a *circuit breaker* for each electrical circuit. If the circuit becomes overloaded, the circuit breaker automatically cuts off the current. Instead of circuit breakers, many older houses have protective devices called *fuses,* which contain a wire that melts easily. If too much current passes through a circuit, the wire in the fuse melts, or "blows." A *fuse box* holds all the fuses.

Plumbing. During construction, plumbers install the pipes that will supply gas and water, and carry away waste. They install bathroom fixtures and sinks just before other workers add the finishing touches to the house. Plumbers also install *traps* to keep out sewer gas. The trap used for bathroom washbasins, for example, is a P-shaped pipe directly below the drain. Water settles in the lower part of the pipe and prevents sewer gas from backing up and leaking into the room. To function properly, traps must have outside ventilation. The *vent* or *vent stack,* the small pipe that projects from the roof of a house, is a ventilating pipe for sewer gas.

A cast-iron waste-disposal pipe runs from inside the house to the outside, where it connects to the city sewerage system. In areas without a city sewerage system, a *septic tank* near the house holds sewage until it dissolves. Water from the sewage flows through pipes into the ground. The sludge remaining in the tank must be removed at intervals.

Insulation reduces the amount of heat or cold that passes through walls, floors, and ceilings. When the air around the house is warmer or colder than the air inside, heat passes from the warm air to the cold air. This means that in winter, the heat will pass to the outside, and the house will become cold. In summer, the heat outside passes into the house. Insulation fills the air spaces in walls, floors, and ceilings and creates *dead-air space.* This helps prevent heat from passing through. Insulation can save fuel costs in heating a house.

Insulation is made from many materials, including cellulose, rock wool, a glassy lava called *perlite,* gypsum, certain plastics, and fiberglass. Insulation comes as blankets, boards, paper, and sheathing. It is also available in a loose, crumblike form. The type of insulation used depends on the climate and on whether it insulates floors, ceilings, or walls.

Heating and air conditioning. Most houses have *central heating* systems. One furnace or boiler supplies heat for the entire house. Such houses are heated by warm air, steam, or hot water. In hot-air heating, a fan connected to the furnace blows warm air through *ducts* (pipes) into the rooms. In steam or hot-water heating, the steam or hot water produced in a boiler passes through radiators that stand throughout the house. In *radiant* heating, hot-water pipes run under the floors or in the ceilings or walls.

Air-conditioning units may be used to cool houses. An air conditioner takes warm air from the house, cools it, removes moisture, and recirculates cool air. An air conditioner with a heat pump may warm cold air, add moisture, and recirculate warm air.

Interior design. In a new house, the builder usually paints the rooms and finishes the floors as part of the contract with the homeowner. The owner generally selects, buys, and arranges the furnishings. But sometimes the owner hires a professional designer to do this job.

Landscaping is the last step in building a house. Most builders try to keep the natural outline of the land and to preserve the trees. After the house is finished, the builder may plant seed or lay rolls of grass turf for a lawn around the house. The builder may also plant trees and shrubs. The homeowner may have a firm of *landscape contractors* provide landscaping. The homeowner also may hire a *landscape architect* to design a garden or landscape.   Stuart E. Cohen

Some parts of a house

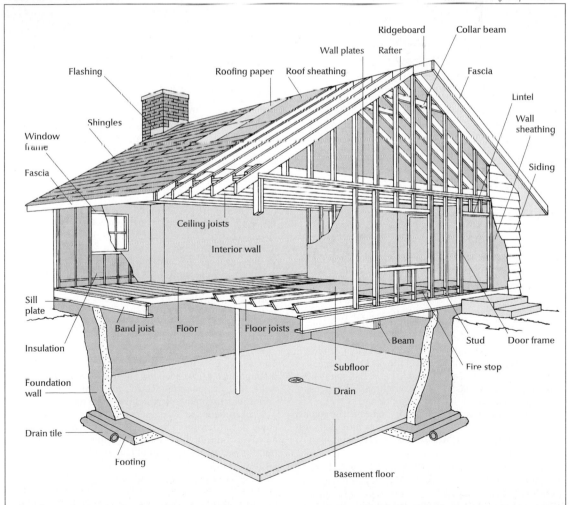

WORLD BOOK photo by David R. Frazier

India is one of the largest and most densely populated countries in the world. The country has many crowded cities, such as Bangalore, *above.* However, most of India's people live in rural areas.

India

India is a country in southern Asia that ranks as the second largest country in the world in population. Only China, its neighbor to the north, has more people. India is also one of the most densely populated countries in the world and one of the largest in area. Its capital is New Delhi. Bombay, also known as Mumbai, is its largest city.

Much of India forms a peninsula that extends southward into the Indian Ocean. India is bordered on the west by the Arabian Sea and Pakistan; on the north by China, Nepal, and Bhutan; and on the east by Burma, Bangladesh, and the Bay of Bengal. India, Bangladesh, Bhutan, Nepal, and Pakistan are sometimes said to make up a region called the Indian subcontinent.

India is a land of great variety and contrast. The mighty snow-capped Himalaya, the world's tallest mountain system, rises along its northern border. A vast, scorching

The contributors of this article are Vinay Lal, Assistant Professor of History at the University of California at Los Angeles, and Anil Lal, Instructor in English at Truman College in Chicago.

desert lies in the west, but parts of eastern India receive some of the highest rainfall in the world. The country also has broad plains, winding rivers, lush rain forests, and tropical lowlands.

The people of India belong to a variety of ethnic groups and speak hundreds of dialects and languages. Hindi is the national language and is widely spoken in north and central India.

The people of India practice a number of religions. A large majority are Hindus, but India has one of the largest populations of Muslims in the world as well.

Indians vary widely in terms of education and wealth. The nation has a growing number of scientists and engineers, but a large part of the population cannot read and write. India is one of the world's major manufacturing countries, but many of its people live in extreme poverty.

Most Indians are farmers, and they depend on seasonal rains to grow their crops. These farmers live in villages throughout the land. On the other hand, a growing number of Indians work in offices and factories in the country's cities. The urban centers of Bombay, Calcutta, and Delhi are among the largest in the world.

India has been home to several major empires and civilizations through the ages. The first of these civilizations, the Indus Valley civilization, was established about 4,500 years ago. Through the centuries, travelers to India described it as a land rich in gold, spices, textiles, and other valuables, and India became fabled for its wealth. Eventually, it attracted European traders, and in the late 1700's, India came under British rule. In 1947, after a long struggle for freedom, India became independent.

Government

India is a republic made up of 25 states and 7 union territories. Its Constitution went into effect on Jan. 26, 1950. The Constitution guarantees equal rights to all citizens, and it prohibits discrimination on the basis of race, sex, *caste* (social class), religion, or place of birth. The Constitution also includes guidelines called *directive principles of state policy*. These principles call for the government to promote the welfare of the people. For example, they urge the government to establish a minimum wage, provide education and jobs for people from disadvantaged backgrounds, and improve public health.

Central government. India has a parliamentary system of government. The president of India is the head of state, and the prime minister is the head of the government. Parliament is the chief lawmaking body of India. It consists of the president and two houses—the Lok Sabha (House of the People) and the Rajya Sabha (Council of States).

The president of India is elected to a five-year term by an electoral college consisting of the elected members of Parliament and the state and territorial legislatures.

WORLD BOOK photo by David R. Frazier

The art treasures of India rank among the greatest in the world. The Taj Mahal at Agra, *below,* is India's most famous building. The beautiful white marble tomb was built in the Islamic style about 1650. Colorful statues of Hindu divinities, *left,* decorate a temple at Bangalore. Most Indians are Hindus.

WORLD BOOK photo by David R. Frazier

India in brief

Capital: New Delhi.
Principal official language: Hindi. *Other languages with official status:* English ("associate national language"), Sanskrit, and 16 regional languages.
Official name: Bharat Ganarajya (Republic of India).
National anthem: "Jana-gana-mana" ("Thou Art the Ruler of the Minds of All People"). *National song:* "Vande Mataram" ("I Bow to Thee, Mother").
Largest cities: (1991 census)

Bombay (9,925,891)   Madras (3,841,396)
Delhi (7,206,704)   Bangalore (3,302,296)
Calcutta (4,399,819)

सत्यमेव जयते

India's flag was adopted in 1947. It has horizontal stripes of orange-yellow, white, and green. The wheel is an ancient symbol called the *Dharma Chakra* (Wheel of Law).

India's national emblem is copied from a pillar built by Ashoka, an ancient Indian emperor. The words in Sanskrit beneath the pillar mean "Truth alone triumphs."

Land and climate

Land: India lies in southern Asia, north of the Indian Ocean. It borders Pakistan, China, Nepal, Bhutan, Burma, and Bangladesh. Most of northern India is a low-lying plain that includes the valleys of the Ganges and Brahmaputra rivers. The Himalaya rises in the far northern parts of the country. The large triangular peninsula that forms southern India is a plateau bordered on the east and west by mountains that drop down to coastal plains.

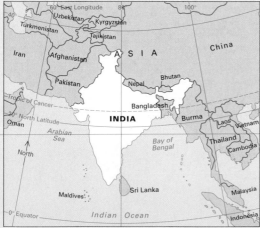

WORLD BOOK map

Area: 1,269,346 sq. mi. (3,287,590 km²). *Greatest distances*—north-south, about 2,000 mi. (3,200 km); east-west, about 1,700 mi. (2,740 km). *Coastline*—4,252 mi. (6,843 km), including 815 mi. (1,312 km) of coastline of island territories.
Elevation: *Highest*—Kanchenjunga, 28,208 ft. (8,598 m) above sea level. *Lowest*—sea level along the coast.

Climate: Northern and central India have mild, cool temperatures from October to February. In the northwest and north-central regions, temperatures occasionally drop below freezing. Southern India lacks a true cool season, but the period from October to February is not as hot as the rest of the year. The entire country, except the mountains, is hot from March to June. From June to September, rains brought by seasonal winds called *monsoons* bring relief from extreme dry heat. The northeast and west coast receive heavy rainfall.

Government

Form of government: Federal republic.
Head of state: President.
Head of government: Prime minister.
Legislature: Parliament of two houses—Lok Sabha (545 members) and Rajya Sabha (a maximum of 250 members). The Lok Sabha is more powerful than the Rajya Sabha.
Executive: President and prime minister. The prime minister selects the members of the Council of Ministers, who are then appointed by the president.
Judiciary: Highest court is the Supreme Court.
Political subdivisions: 25 states and 7 territories.

People

Population: *Estimated 1998 population*—986,026,000. *1991 census*—846,302,688. *Estimated 2003 population*—1,069,021,000.
Population density: 777 persons per sq. mi. (300 per km²)
Distribution: 73 percent rural, 27 percent urban.
Major ethnic groups: 72 percent Indo-Aryan, 25 percent Dravidian.
Major religions: 82 percent Hindu, 12 percent Muslim, 2 percent Christian, 2 percent Sikh.

Population trend

Millions

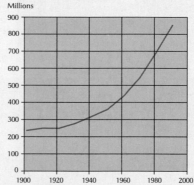

Year	Population
1901	238,396,000
1911	252,093,000
1921	251,321,000
1931	278,977,000
1941	318,661,000
1951	361,088,000
1961	439,235,000
1971	548,160,000
1981	696,833,000
1991	846,303,000

Economy

Chief products: *Agriculture*—bananas, beans, chickpeas, coconuts, cotton, jute, mangoes, onions, oranges, peanuts, pepper, potatoes, rice, sesame seeds, sorghum, sugar cane, tea, wheat. *Manufacturing and processing*—bicycles, brassware and silverware, cement, chemicals, clothing and textiles, fertilizer, food products, iron and steel, jute bags and rope, leather goods, machinery, medicines, motor vehicles, paper, petroleum products, rugs, sewing machines, sugar, wood products. *Mining*—coal, iron ore, limestone, petroleum.
Money: *Basic unit*—rupee. One hundred paise equal one rupee.
International trade: *Major exports*—chemicals, cotton textiles and clothing, cut diamonds and jewelry, engineering goods, handicrafts, iron ore, leather goods, tea. *Major imports*—chemicals, fertilizer, industrial machinery, pearls and gemstones, petroleum products. *Major trading partners*—Germany, Japan, Saudi Arabia, United Kingdom, United States.

New Delhi is the capital of India. Both houses of the Indian Parliament meet in the circular Parliament House, which appears in the foreground. The British built the structure in the early 1900's, during their rule of India. Government office buildings stand behind Parliament House.

WORLD BOOK photo by David R. Frazier

Bills approved by Parliament must receive the president's signature before they can become law.

The prime minister, who is appointed by the president, is the most powerful person in the Indian government. The prime minister is usually the leader of the party that has the largest number of seats in Parliament. The prime minister heads the Council of Ministers. Members of the council are appointed by the president on the prime minister's recommendation. They assist in running the day-to-day operations of the government. A prime minister who loses the support of a majority in the Lok Sabha can be dismissed by the president. The president can then dissolve the Lok Sabha and call a new election.

The most important of the two houses of the Indian Parliament is the Lok Sabha. States and territories with larger populations send more representatives to the Lok Sabha than do those with smaller populations. Voters elect 543 of the 545 members of the Lok Sabha. The president names the other 2. Members serve a five-year term unless the president calls for elections earlier.

The Rajya Sabha has a maximum of 250 members, who serve six-year terms. The state and territorial legislatures elect all but 12 of the members. The president may nominate up to 12 remaining members, who are well-known academic or cultural figures.

State governments. Most Indian states have one legislative body, but some have two. Most members are elected by the people. Each state has a governor and a chief minister. The governor is appointed by the president of India. The chief minister is appointed by the governor and is typically the leader of the party with the most seats in the legislature.

The states traditionally have had little power in relation to the central government. For example, Parliament has the right to establish or abolish states and to change state boundaries and names. In addition, Parliament taxes the largest sources of revenue, such as business and personal income. The states have extremely limited and poorer sources of income, including real estate taxes and licensing fees. As a result, most states rely largely on assistance from the central government for their income.

Courts. The Supreme Court is India's highest court. Its justices are appointed by the president. The Supreme Court hears cases that involve disputes between states or between a state and the central government. It also acts as the final court of appeal in certain criminal and civil cases. In addition, the Supreme Court serves as the final interpreter of the Constitution and can declare legislation passed by Parliament to be unconstitutional.

India has 18 high courts, which serve the individual states and territories. The high courts hear original cases as well as appeals from lower courts.

Politics. India has many political parties. The Congress Party, or one of the branches that developed from it, dominated Indian politics for nearly all the years from 1947 to the 1980's. Since then, the party's strength has declined. Other national parties in India include the Bharatiya Janata Party (BJP-Indian People's Party), the Janata Dal (People's Party), and the Communist Party (Marxist).

Regional parties play an important role in Indian politics. In some parts of the country, political parties representing certain language, religious, or ethnic groups have successfully formed governments. All Indians who are at least 18 years old can vote.

Armed forces. India has an army, navy, and air force. More than a million people serve in the armed forces. Military service is voluntary.

People

Ancestry. India's people belong to a variety of ethnic groups. The two largest groups are the Dravidians and the Indo-Aryans. Most Dravidians live in the south. Most Indo-Aryans live in the north.

The Dravidians are descended from some of the earliest inhabitants of India. About 2500 B.C., these early people are believed to have established an advanced civilization that spread through the Indus Valley in what are now Pakistan and western India. The Indo-Aryans trace their ancestry to a central Asian people called the Aryans. Around 1500 B.C., the Aryans invaded India. They gradually conquered the Dravidians and drove some of them south.

From about the A.D. 400's to the late 1400's, central Asian peoples settled in northern India. Many of their descendants live in the area now occupied by the states of Jammu and Kashmir, Uttar Pradesh, and Bihar. Some groups who live in the far north and northeast are closely related to peoples of East and Southeast Asia.

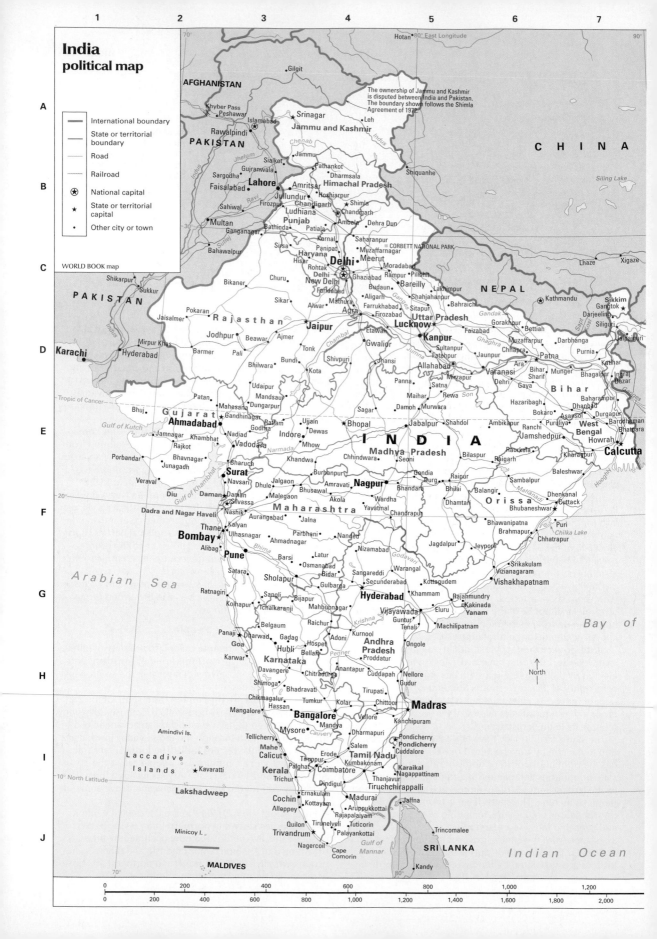

India
political map

▬▬▬	International boundary
───	State or territorial boundary
───	Road
-----	Railroad
⊛	National capital
★	State or territorial capital
•	Other city or town

WORLD BOOK map

The ownership of Jammu and Kashmir is disputed between India and Pakistan. The boundary shown follows the Shimla Agreement of 1972.

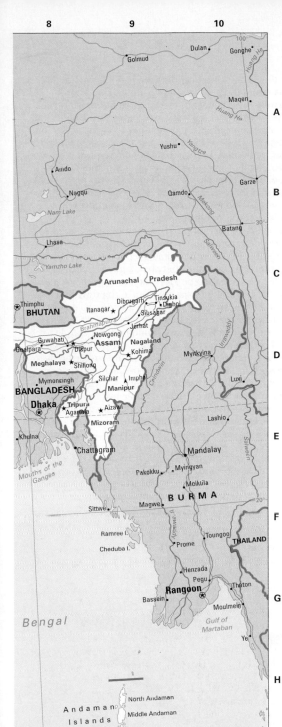

India map index

States

Map key	Name	Population	Area In sq. mi.	In km²	Capital
A 4	Andhra Pradesh	66,508,008	106,204	275,068	Hyderabad
C 9	Arunachal Pradesh	864,558	32,333	83,743	Itanagar
D 9	Assam	22,414,322	30,285	78,438	Dispur
D 6	Bihar	86,374,465	67,134	173,877	Patna
H 3	Goa	1,169,793	1,430	3,702	Panaji
E 2	Gujarat	41,309,582	75,685	196,024	Gandhinagar
C 4	Haryana	16,463,648	17,070	44,212	Chandigarh
B 4	Himachal Pradesh	5,170,877	21,495	55,673	Shimla
A 4	Jammu and Kashmir	7,718,700	85,806	222,236	Srinagar
H 3	Karnataka	44,977,201	74,051	191,791	Bangalore
I 3	Kerala	29,098,518	15,005	38,863	Trivandrum
E 4	Madhya Pradesh	66,181,170	171,215	443,446	Bhopal
F 3	Maharashtra	78,937,187	118,800	307,690	Bombay
D 9	Manipur	1,837,149	8,621	22,327	Imphal
D 8	Meghalaya	1,774,778	8,660	22,429	Shillong
E 9	Mizoram	689,756	8,139	21,081	Aizawl
D 9	Nagaland	1,209,546	6,401	16,579	Kohima
F 6	Orissa	31,659,736	60,119	155,707	Bhubaneshwar
B 3	Punjab	20,281,969	19,445	50,362	Chandigarh
D 3	Rajasthan	44,005,990	132,139	342,239	Jaipur
C 7	Sikkim	406,457	2,740	7,096	Gangtok
I 4	Tamil Nadu	55,858,946	50,216	130,058	Madras
E 8	Tripura	2,757,205	4,049	10,486	Agartala
D 5	Uttar Pradesh	139,112,278	113,673	294,411	Lucknow
E 7	West Bengal	68,077,965	34,267	88,752	Calcutta

Territories

Map key	Name	Population	Area In sq. mi.	In km²	Capital
	Andaman and Nicobar Islands	280,661	3,185	8,249	Port Blair
H 9	Andaman Islands				
J 9	Nicobar Islands				
B 4	Chandigarh	642,015	44	114	Chandigarh
F 2	Dadra and Nagar Haveli	101,586	491	190	Silvassa
C 4	Delhi	9,420,644	573	1,483	Delhi
	Daman and Diu	101,586	43	112	Daman
F 3	Daman District				
F 2	Diu District				
	Lakshadweep	51,707	12	32	Kavaratti
I 2	Amindivi Islands				
J 2	Minicoy Island				
I 2	Laccadive Islands				
	Pondicherry	807,785	190	492	Pondicherry
I 4	Karaikal District				
I 3	Mahe District				
I 4	Pondicherry District				
G 5	Yanam District				

Cities and towns

Name	Population	Key
Agartala	157,636	E 8
Agra	955,694	D 4
Ahmadabad	2,954,526 †3,297,655	E 2
Ahmadnagar	221,710	F 3
Aizawl	154,343	E 9
Ajmer	401,930	D 3
Akola	327,946	F 4
Aligarh	479,978	C 4
Allahabad	858,213	D 5
Alleppey	†264,287	J 3
Alwar	211,162	C 4
Amravati	433,746	F 4
Amritsar	709,456	B 3
Asansol	763,854	E 7
Aurangabad	592,052	F 3
Bally*	181,978	E 7
Bangalore	3,302,296 †4,086,548	H 4
Bardhaman	244,789	E 7
Bareilly	607,652	C 5
Belgaum	401,619	G 3
Bellary	245,758	H 4
Bhagalpur	261,855	D 7
Bhatpara	315,976	E 7
Bhavnagar	403,521	E 2
Bhilai	395,360	F 5
Bhiwandi*	391,670	F 2
Bhopal	1,063,662	E 4
Bhubaneshwar	411,542	F 6
Bihar Sharif	200,976	D 6
Bijapur	193,038	G 3
Bikaner	415,355	C 3
Bilaspur	233,570	E 5
Bokaro	415,686	E 6
Bombay	9,925,891 †12,571,720	F 2
Brahmapur	210,585	F 6
Burhanpur	172,809	E 4
Calcutta	4,399,819 †10,916,272	E 7
Calicut	800,913	I 3
Chandigarh	574,646	B 4
Chennai, see Madras		
Cochin	1,139,543	I 3
Coimbatore	1,135,549	I 4
Cuttack	439,273	F 6
Darbhanga	218,274	D 6
Darjeeling	†57,603	D 7
Davangere	287,114	H 3
Dehra Dun	367,411	B 4
Delhi	7,206,704 †8,375,188	C 4
Dhanbad	†817,549	E 7
Dhule	277,957	F 3
Dindigul	182293	I 4
Dispur	†1,725	D 8
Durgapur	415,986	E 7
Eluru	212,918	G 5
Erode	357,427	I 4
Faridabad	613,828	C 4
Farrukhabad	207,783	C 5
Firozabad	270,534	D 4
Gandhinagar	104,392	E 3
Gangtok	25,024	C 7
Gauhati	577,591	D 8
Gaya	293,971	D 6
Ghaziabad	519,508	C 4
Gorakhpur	489,850	D 6
Gulbarga	309,962	G 4
Guntur	471,020	G 5
Gwalior	720,068	D 4
Howrah	950,453	E 7
Hubli	647,640	H 3
Hyderabad	3,145,939 †4,280,261	G 4
Imphal	200,615	D 9
Indore	1,104,065	E 3
Itanagar	†14,116	C 9
Jabalpur	887,188	E 5
Jaipur	1,514,425	D 4
Jalgaon	241,603	F 3
Jamnagar	365,464	E 2
Jamshedpur	834,535	E 7
Jhansi	368,580	D 4
Jodhpur	648,621	D 3
Jullundur	519,530	B 3
Kakinada	327,407	G 5
Kalyan	1,014,557	F 3
Kanchipuram	169,813	I 4
Kannur*	463,951	I 3
Kanpur	1,879,420 †2,111,284	D 5
Kavaratti	†6,601	I 2
Kharagpur	279,736	F 7
Kohima	†34,340	D 9
Kolhapur	417,286	G 3
Kota	166,178	D 3
Kottayam	166,178	I 3
Kumbakonam	150,502	I 4
Kurnool	274,795	G 4
Lucknow	1,642,134	D 5
Ludhiana	1,012,062	B 4
Machilipatam	159,007	G 5
Madras	3,841,396 †5,361,468	H 5
Madurai	1,093,702	I 4
Malegaon	342,431	F 3
Mangalore	†425,785	H 3
Mathura	233,235	C 4
Meerut	846,954	C 4
Moradabad	432,434	C 4
Mumbai, see Bombay		
Muzaffarnagar	247,729	C 4
Muzaffarpur	240,450	D 6
Mysore	652,246	I 3
Nadiad	170,018	E 3
Nagercoil	189,482	J 4
Nagpur	1,661,409	F 4
Nanded	308,853	F 4
Nashik	722,139	F 3
Nellore	316,445	H 5
New Delhi	301,297	C 4
Nizamabad	240,924	F 4
Panaji	443,165	G 3
Panihati*	275,000	E 7
Patiala	268,521	B 4
Patna	1,098,572	D 6
Pondicherry	401,337	I 4
Port Blair	74,955	I 9
Pune	2,485,014	G 3
Quilon	362,402	J 3
Raipur	461,851	I 5
Rajahmundry	403,781	G 5
Rajkot	651,007	E 2
Rampur	242,752	C 4
Ranchi	614,454	E 6
Ratlam	195,752	E 3
Raurkela	398,697	F 6
Rohtak	215,844	C 4
Sagar	256,878	E 4
Saharanpur	373,904	C 4
Salem	573,685	I 4
Sangli	363,728	G 3
Shahjahanpur	260,260	C 5
Shillong	222,273	D 8
Shimla	109,860	B 4
Shimoga	192,647	H 3
Sholapur	620,499	G 3
Siliguri	226,677	D 7
Silvassa	†6,914	F 3
South Dum Dum*	232,811	E 7
Srinagar	595,000	A 3
Surat	1,517,076	F 3
Thane	803,389	F 2
Thanjavur	200,216	I 4
Tiruchchirappalli	711,120	I 4
Tirunelveli	365,932	J 4
Tiruppur	305,546	I 4
Trivandrum	825,682	J 3
Tuticorin	284,193	J 4
Udaipur	307,682	D 3
Ujjain	367,154	E 3
Ulhasnagar	369,000	F 3
Vadodara	1,115,265	E 3
Varanasi	1,026,467	D 6
Vellore	304,713	I 4
Vijayawada	845,305	G 5
Vishakhapatnam	1,051,918	G 6
Warangal	466,877	G 4

*Does not appear on map; key shows general location.
†Population of metropolitan area, including suburbs.
‡1981 census.
Source: 1991 census, except where indicated by ‡.

A number of smaller groups of peoples live in remote forests and hills throughout India. Often referred to as tribes or tribal groups, these peoples include the Bhils, Gonds, Khasis, Mizos, Mundas, Oraons, and Santals.

Languages. People in India speak over 1,000 languages and dialects—more than in any other part of the world. Most Indian languages belong to two main language groups: Indo-Aryan, which is a branch of the Indo-European family of languages, and Dravidian.

Modern Indo-Aryan languages are based on an ancient language called Sanskrit. About three-fourths of the Indian population, mainly in north and central India, speak one or more of the main Indo-Aryan languages. These languages include Assamese, Bengali, Gujarati, Hindi, Kashmiri, Marathi, Oriya, Punjabi, and Sindhi.

The four principal languages of southern India—Kannada, Malayalam, Tamil, and Telugu—belong to the Dravidian family of languages. About a fifth of the population speaks these languages.

In the Himalayan region of the northeast and along the border with Burma, many people speak Kuki, Manipuri, Naga, and other Sino-Tibetan languages. Some groups in the northeast and certain central areas use Mundari and Santali, which belong to the Mon-Khmer, or Austro-Asiatic, family of languages.

India's national language is Hindi, one of the Indo-Aryan languages. More than two-fifths of the people speak one or more of the dialects of this language, and at least some Hindi is understood by as many as two-thirds of the population. The study of Hindi is required in elementary and secondary schools in India.

English has an official status as an associate national language. It is the common language among educated people across India, and much of the nation's official business is conducted in English. In cities especially, many parents try to send their children to English-language elementary and secondary schools. English is widely used at colleges and universities.

Through the years, the Indian government has at times sought to introduce Hindi in non-Hindi speaking areas. Immediately after independence, the Indian government argued that national unity would be best promoted by encouraging the spread of Hindi, the most widely spoken Indian language. But non-Hindi speakers feared that they would face discrimination in their search for jobs. They also wanted recognition for their own languages. They urged that Indian states be reorganized according to language groups. After much pressure on the Indian government, the first of such states, Andhra (now Andhra Pradesh), was established for Telugu speakers in 1953.

Today, the boundaries of India's states are based largely on language. But each state still includes people from multiple language and dialect groups. Several states have large numbers of Hindi speakers. Each state also has its own official language. For example, Bengal's official language is Bengali and Tamil Nadu's is Tamil.

Way of life

India is such a large and varied country that there is no one way of life practiced by all—or even most—Indians. Food and clothing vary throughout the country. People follow a number of religious beliefs and practices. Social structure differs from place to place. Neverthe-

less, there are some features of Indian life that are common among most people throughout the country.

Family life. Family ties are important to most Indians. The number of *nuclear families*—that is, households that consist of only parents and their children—is increasing, especially in cities. However, many families continue to live as traditional *extended families*. In a typical Indian extended family, three generations live together in one household. Upon marriage, a woman leaves her parents' home and shares a household with her husband and his relatives, including his brothers and their wives, his unmarried sisters, and his parents.

Parents usually arrange marriages, though a couple may reject an arrangement made by the parents. Marriages for love do occur, but many people think of marriage more as an alliance between families than as a relationship between two people. The bride's family typically pays a dowry to the husband's family. The dowry may be money, goods, or both. Today, the paying of a dowry is illegal, but the practice continues nonetheless.

Indians generally expect a young married couple to have a child within a few years after marriage. In India, as in most other rural societies, sons are preferred over daughters. In rural areas, sons are expected to work on the land and take care of their parents.

Village life. Most of India's people live in villages. Most villagers are farmers who work in nearby fields. A typical Indian village is a collection of mud-and-straw dwellings. These homes are generally small, consisting of one or two rooms with mud floors. Wealthier families live in brick or concrete houses.

Population density and language groups

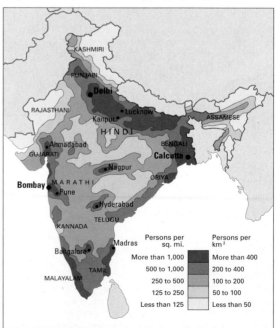

WORLD BOOK map

India ranks second in population—after China—among the world's countries. This map shows where the people of India live and the location of the largest cities, as well as where the major languages are spoken.

Village life in India has changed little through the years. Most Indians live in such rural communities. They raise livestock and grow crops in nearby fields. This village is located on the plains of the Deccan Plateau near the city of Aurangabad.

WORLD BOOK photo by David R. Frazier

Bombay, also known as Mumbai, is the largest city in India. Modern high-rise apartment and office buildings stand in parts of the city, but most of Bombay's people live in crowded slums.

WORLD BOOK photo by David R. Frazier

Most villagers own few possessions. These belongings typically include brass pots for cooking and clay pots for carrying water and storing grain. Village people cook foods on a *chula,* a clay oven that burns coal. People sit and sleep on cots of woven string, which are dragged outside on warm days. Many people also sleep outside. If the village is without electric power, kerosene lanterns are used for light. A local well or nearby pond or river provides water for most villages. Some larger villages have running water.

A council of elected elders, called a *panchayat,* governs most villages. The panchayat has the power to hear complaints and administer punishments.

City life. Varanasi (also called Banaras or Benares), Patna (formerly called Pataliputra), and some other Indian cities were commercial, political, and religious centers in ancient times. They attracted pilgrims, traders, and people seeking their political fortunes. After arriving in India in the 1600's, the British developed the fishing villages of Bombay, Calcutta, and Madras (also known as Chennai) into major ports. These cities are now among the largest in India.

Older Indian cities have a densely populated center. Many of these cities once had walls surrounding them for protection against enemies. After the city expanded outside its walls, the section inside became known as the *walled city.* Buildings occupy most of the space in city centers, which bustle with activity. People, animals, automobiles, and smaller vehicles, such as rickshaws, hand-pulled carts, and bicycles, compete for space on the narrow, twisting streets. Various traders sell their wares in shops with fronts open to the street. Entire families live in, above, and behind the shops.

During the British rule of India, the Britons who lived in Indian cities made their homes in areas called *cantonments.* The cantonments had pleasant bungalows and wide, treelined streets, and lay far from the crowded sections where the Indians lived. Today, politicians, military officers, wealthy business people, and other leaders live in the cantonments. These areas now include modern buildings and shopping districts.

Most Indian cities have a growing middle class, which includes government employees, office workers, and shopkeepers. A large number of urban dwellers work at manual labor or in factory jobs. Many vendors, such as vegetable and fruit sellers, cobblers, and plumbers, peddle their goods and services on the street.

The population of Indian cities has increased tremendously since independence. Millions of people have moved from rural to urban areas in search of jobs. This rapid population growth has strained city resources. For example, the supply of water and electric power has not kept up with the needs of the increasing population. Despite efforts to build low-cost and improved housing, many people—including some members of the middle class—still lack adequate homes. As a result, they must live in slums or on the streets. In the slums, as many as 10 people may be crammed into a one-room shack, and toilet facilities may be shared by the entire slum.

Social structure. Indians, especially Hindus, have traditionally been organized into social groups called *castes.* A person's caste determines his or her social status within the community and influences what occupations a person might hold.

Ancient Hindu texts described four main groups called *varnas.* The Brahmans (priests and scholars) were the highest group, followed by Kshatriyas (rulers and warriors), Vaishyas (merchants and professionals), and Shudras (artisans, laborers, and servants). Over time, each varna came to include smaller castes called *jatis.* Altogether, the caste system has thousands of categories.

Complicated rules govern contact and behavior between the castes. For example, marriages between people of widely different castes are rare, and the upper castes do not eat with the Shudras. In principle, when members of a caste eat cooked food, it should be prepared only by someone of the same caste or a higher caste. For example, Brahmans would eat only food cooked by other Brahmans. Many members of the upper castes do not eat meat, fish, or eggs.

Today, caste barriers are weaker than they have been in the past, especially in cities. There the various castes mix with one another every day. They work side by side in factories and offices, ride in buses and trains together, and mingle on the streets. In the cities, too, rules against castes dining with one another have greatly relaxed.

A large group of people—approximately 15 percent of the population—is considered to be outside the caste system. Known as *untouchables, harijans* (children of God), *dalits* (downtrodden), or the *scheduled castes,* this group has an even lower status than the Shudras. Untouchables have traditionally held the most undesirable jobs, such as the cleaning of toilets and the disposal of garbage. Some upper-caste people believe that they will be polluted by the touch of members of this group.

Under the Indian Constitution, the untouchables are supposed to have equal rights. Discrimination in jobs and education against the untouchables is forbidden by law. The government has also set aside for them and other disadvantaged groups a significant percentage of government jobs, scholarships, and legislative seats. Nevertheless, the untouchables remain an oppressed group, especially in villages. There, for example, they are often denied entry to Hindu temples and forbidden to draw water from certain village wells. They also may be excluded from participation in village political life.

Religion plays a vital role in the lives of most Indians. India has no official religion, and people of various faiths

WORLD BOOK photo by David R. Frazier

A street market in Bangalore offers fruits and vegetables to shoppers. Many Indians in the cities work as food vendors or craftworkers, selling their goods and services on the street.

practice their religion freely. More than 80 percent of the people are Hindus. About 12 percent are Muslims. Smaller percentages of Indians practice other religions. They include Buddhists, Christians, Jains, and Sikhs.

Hinduism. The religious beliefs and practices of Hindus vary enormously. Hindus have many sacred texts, including the Vedas, the Upanishads, and the Puranas. These writings serve as a guide to moral conduct.

Hindus believe in *reincarnation*—that is, that the body alone dies, and the soul, which does not die, is reborn in another body. This process can be repeated for thousands of years. Liberated beings are those whose souls, having achieved spiritual perfection, enter a higher state of existence. Hinduism also teaches such virtues as *ahimsa* (nonviolence), *yoga* (a spiritual discipline that involves fitness of body and mind), and the unimportance of material goods. Hindus consider cows to be sacred and therefore do not believe in eating beef.

Hindus believe there is a single spiritual force—God, also called Brahman—that takes many forms. These forms make up the many gods and goddesses of Hindu belief. People worship whichever form—that is, whichever god or goddess—pleases them the most. Most Hindus worship Shiva or Vishnu. Vishnu's two most popular *incarnations* (human forms) are Krishna and Rama. Popularity of the individual gods and goddesses varies from place to place. In Bengal, for example, worship of the goddess Kali is common, but in Maharashtra, people worship Ganesh, an elephant-headed god.

There are a number of Hindu religious festivals. They include Holi, which marks the arrival of spring, and a festival popularly called Diwali, which is celebrated in the fall. During Holi, people sprinkle colored water and powders on one another. Fireworks light up the night during Diwali, which honors several Hindu deities.

Islam. India has one of the largest Muslim populations in the world. Most Indian Muslims live in the north, but there are also major Islamic centers, such as Hyderabad, in the south. Many Muslims live in urban areas.

Islam came to India in the 700's, but most Muslims in India are descendants of Hindus who converted to the new faith. There have been outbreaks of violence between Muslims and Hindus through the years. But they have also lived together peacefully. Over time, they have developed a common culture in some areas.

Buddhism was founded in India about 500 B.C. by Siddhartha Gautama. It flourished in ancient India. It later spread to other countries but declined in India. Today, Buddhists are mainly converts from the lower castes.

Christianity existed in several small communities when Europeans came to India about 1500. But it spread mainly after the Europeans arrived. Indian Christians live largely in the southern states of Kerala and Tamil Nadu, and in the tribal regions of northeast India.

Jainism was founded in India in the 500's B.C. by a religious reformer named Mahavira. Jains believe all life is sacred, and most are strict vegetarians. They have been especially successful in business and the professions.

Taurus

Muslims, followers of Islam, make up India's largest religious minority. The people pictured here are praying at one of the country's many beautiful *mosques* (Islamic houses of worship).

Sikhism is a religion founded in India by Nanak, a *guru* (religious teacher) who lived in the late 1400's and early 1500's. Sikhs pride themselves on their bravery and do not believe in caste. As a mark of equality, many Sikh men use the same last name, Singh, which means *lion.* Most Sikhs are farmers and traders. They also make up a large part of the Indian army.

Other religions. India also has the largest population of Zoroastrians in the world. Usually called Parsis in India, the Zoroastrians fled Persia (now Iran) over 1,000 years ago when it was being converted to Islam. They have become business leaders. India has had a Jewish community since about the A.D. 100's, though many Indian Jews moved to Israel during the 1950's and 1960's. Many Indians also practice folk religions.

Clothing worn by Indians varies greatly by region. Members of the various religious or ethnic groups also may dress differently. But most Indians wear light, loose clothing because of the hot climate.

Most Indian women wear a *sari.* This garment consists of a straight piece of cloth about 5 yards (6 meters) long that is draped around the body as a long dress. Its loose end is flung over a shoulder or used to cover the head. A sari is usually worn with a blouse. Unmarried women and young girls, especially in northern India, commonly wear long flowing trousers called a *shalwar* and a long blouse known as a *kameez.* Tribal women wear long skirts. Many Christian women in the south wear Western-style skirts and blouses. Some young women in cities, especially wealthier women, wear jeans.

Many men wear a *dhoti.* This simple garment, which is usually white, is wrapped between the legs to form a kind of loose trousers. It can also be wrapped around

WORLD BOOK photo by David R. Frazier

A Hindu religious festival called Holi celebrates the arrival of the spring season. Celebrants sprinkle colored water and powder on one another and parade through the streets.

the lower half of the body like a skirt and is then knotted at the waist. A shirt is worn over the upper half of the body. Poor laborers and farmers may wear only a *loincloth,* which is a piece of cloth wrapped around the hips and between the thighs. On formal occasions, some men wear a long, tight coat over loose trousers called a *pajama* that are wide at the top and sharply taper toward the bottom. In the cities, Western-style shirts and trousers, and increasingly, jeans, are popular.

Food and drink. Rice, wheat, and other grains rank among the chief foods of India. *Pulses,* which are the seeds of such pod vegetables as beans, chickpeas, and lentils, are also widely consumed.

Indian cooking is extremely varied, and foods eaten in one part of the country may be completely unknown elsewhere. For example, a typical north Indian meal consists of *chapattis, dal,* and a vegetable dish. Chapattis are thin, flat breads. Dal is a porridge made with specially prepared lentils. A typical meal in West Bengal would probably also include fish, and rice would substitute for the chapattis. In the south, a typical meal would consist of rice, *sambar* (a lentil preparation that resembles dal), and vegetables. Yogurt, pickles, and such fresh fruits as apples, bananas, guavas, and mangoes are part of most meals throughout the country.

Most Indian meals are cooked in *ghee* (liquid butter) or vegetable oil. A number of spices, such as coriander, cumin, garlic, ginger, mustard seeds, red pepper, and turmeric, flavor most dishes. Chicken and mutton are expensive and are eaten mainly on special occasions. Hindus do not believe in eating beef, and Muslims do not believe in eating pork. Many Indians are vegetarians.

The most popular beverage in India is tea, though many southern Indians prefer coffee. Western soft drinks are widely available, but fairly expensive.

Food production in India increased enormously in the late 1900's, and today the country exports wheat and rice. Even so, the nutritional needs of at least a third of the population are not being met, in part because many people cannot afford sufficient food. Many women, in particular, have trouble getting adequate nourishment. Especially in traditional homes, the men and children are

WORLD BOOK photo by David R. Frazier

A family dinner in India may consist of a variety of dishes, depending on the region. Rice is India's chief food. In the north, meals usually include thin, flat breads called *chapattis.*

served by the women and older girls, who eat what is left at the end of the meal.

Health care. Life expectancy rates for both women and men are much lower in India than in the United States and Europe. Infant death rates are much higher. See **Life expectancy** (table).

Dismal living conditions account for many diseases. Standards of sanitation, hygiene, and nutrition are poor, especially in villages and urban slums. High levels of pollution in the cities have led to a sharp increase in illnesses of the lungs.

On the other hand, India has made great strides in controlling cholera, malaria, and other infectious diseases. Government clinics across the country provide cheap medical care to government employees and their families. Other public clinics and hospitals attend to the needy. In addition, the government runs family-planning clinics to help control the growing population. In urban

WORLD BOOK photo by David R. Frazier

Public education in India provides free schooling for children from age 6 through 14. This class is studying in a New Delhi public school. Despite the availability of education, many Indian children must leave school early for economic reasons. As a result, illiteracy remains a problem in the country.

areas, thousands of doctors have set up private practices, often at their own homes.

Recreation. The most admired and widely played sport throughout India is cricket. Field hockey and soccer are also popular. Indians enjoy playing cards and chess. Kite flying is also a common recreational activity. Many people spend their evenings watching television or going to motion-picture theaters. In large cities, people also attend concerts and plays.

Education. The Indian Constitution provides for free education for children from age 6 through 14. Nearly all Indian children receive some schooling, but only about half of those 10 years of age or older continue their education. There are several reasons why children drop out of school. Some children leave school because their parents put them to work on the family farm. Other children have to get jobs to help support their families or are needed at home to look after smaller children.

Because Indians receive little formal education, illiteracy is a major problem in India. Since about 1950, the government has spent much money on training teachers, publishing schoolbooks, and building schools. As a result, literacy rates have improved, and school attendance has increased substantially. However, about half of India's adult population still cannot read and write. For the country's literacy rate, see **Literacy** (table).

Indian universities are run by the central or state governments. India has over 8,000 universities and colleges. The University of Delhi alone has about 200,000 students.

The arts

The arts of India have a long history. They had reached high levels thousands of years ago. Indian arts also include a wide variety of forms and styles.

Architecture and sculpture. Sculpture flourished during the Indus Valley civilization, which was established about 2500 B.C. Buddhism was the next great influence on Indian architecture and sculpture. Several ruins of Buddhist monasteries and dome-shaped *stupas* (monuments) have survived from ancient times.

Caves were cut into a cliff of solid rock at Ajanta in western India between the 100's B.C. and the A.D. 600's. They feature spectacular examples of *frescoes* (wallpaintings on plaster) and sculpture. Artists worked at the nearby caves at Ellora until about A.D. 1000. The greatest monument at Ellora, dating from the late 700's, honors the Hindu god Shiva. It was carved out of the cliff like a great piece of sculpture. Magnificent sculptures of Hindu gods and goddesses were also carved in the caves at Elephanta, near Bombay, mainly from the 600's to 900's.

Hindu temples are noted both for their architecture and for their exquisite sculptures. The temples have rows of sculptured columns, richly carved exteriors, and open porches. Temples in northern India have tall towers with curving sides that taper at the top. South Indian temples have gateway towers shaped like trapezoidal pyramids and made of steplike layers of stone. Each step has carvings that tell a story.

Muslims conquered parts of northern India during the 1200's and introduced their style of architecture. Muslim architecture in India reached its peak in the 1500's and 1600's. The outstanding Islamic building in India is the Taj Mahal (about 1650) in Agra. The Emperor Shah Jahan ordered the Taj Mahal built as a tomb for his favorite wife. The building features magnificent Islamic-style decoration, in which geometrical patterns and floral designs are inlaid in marble with semiprecious stones. Islamic art and architecture use such patterns and designs because Islam forbids the depiction of God or the human form.

The British and other Europeans added many buildings in Western styles to India after their arrival. During the 1700's, the British constructed churches and other buildings in the neoclassical style. Neoclassical architecture reflected a renewed interest in Europe in the architecture of ancient Greece and Rome. In the 1800's, the British designed many public buildings in India in the Gothic Revival style, with tall spires and pointed arches. Some British buildings include curved domes and other features of Islamic architecture.

Modern Indian architecture borrows from many styles. For example, the internationally recognized works of Charles Correa and Balkrishna Doshi mix traditional Indian forms with contemporary designs.

Painting. The frescoes in the caves at Ajanta are the most important early examples of Indian paintings. Wall-paintings that show scenes from Buddhist stories are commonly found in Buddhist temples and monasteries.

Miniature paintings on small pieces of paper developed into a distinct art form in India from 1500 to 1800. These paintings portrayed rulers, members of the nobility, scenes of hunting, or stories from Hindu legends.

In the 1800's, Indian painting was mainly an imitation of Western styles. Many artists of the 1900's, including

The Art Institute of Chicago, gift of Mr. and Mrs. Robert Andrew Brown
Sculpture ranks among India's greatest artistic achievements. An unknown sculptor carved this stone statue of the Hindu god Vishnu between the A.D. 900's and 1200's.

WORLD BOOK photo by David R. Frazier

Temples carved from rock at Ellora in western India rank among India's most important historical monuments. The temples represent the Buddhist, Hindu, and Jain religions.

© R. G. Everts, Photo Researchers

The tower of a temple in Madras rises in steplike stone blocks. The numerous sculptures that decorate each step tell stories about Hindu gods and goddesses.

Maqbool F. Husain and Amrita Sher-Gil, show both Indian and Western influences. Husain's paintings resemble those of the European *expressionists*, who attempted to give form to powerful emotions. Sher-Gil studied art in France but painted mostly Indian subjects. Nandlal Bose's works are based mainly on Indian folk forms.

Literature. All of India's major languages have written literatures, many of which are at least 1,000 years old. The earliest Indian written works—the Vedas—are about 3,000 years old. Composed in an early form of Sanskrit, these Hindu scriptures are poetical compositions that discuss God, the universe, and the nature of life.

India's two great epics, the *Mahabharata* and *Ramayana*, were also composed in Sanskrit. Parts of the *Mahabharata*, which includes the *Bhagavad-Gita,* are probably more than 2,500 years old. The *Ramayana* was likely begun about the same time. These poems have inspired Indian literature through the centuries. Today, they are generally read not in Sanskrit but in other Indian languages and English.

Many of the world's fables and folk tales come from India. The oldest collection of fables in India, the *Panchatantra,* may date from as early as the 200's B.C.

From about A.D. 500 to 1600, a social and religious movement called *bhakti* swept across India. Bhakti influenced the development of regional languages because it emphasized people's everyday speech. Many bhakti poets, including Jnaneshwar, Kabir, Mirabai, Surdas, and Tulsidas, are still among the most widely read authors in India. Their hymns are also set to music.

Later Indian literature continued to be written in all the major Indian languages and English. For example, Bankim Chandra Chatterji, sometimes called the father of the Indian novel, wrote in Bengali. His historical novels about Indian heroes helped spread Indian nationalism in the 1800's. Bengali-language writers of the early 1900's include Rabindranath Tagore, whose spiritual poetry won the Nobel Prize for literature in 1913, and Saratchandra Chatterji (also spelled Saratcandra Chattopadhyaya), whose novels emphasize social issues. Among the best-known Indian-born writers of the late 1900's are two who write in English—R. K. Narayan, whose novels depict Indian village life; and Salman Rushdie, whose writings combine fantasy, satire, and Hindu and Islamic lore.

Music and dance. The beginnings of Indian classical music date to ancient times. Styles, forms, and principles of composition developed over the centuries. Indian music sounds different from Western music partly because it uses different scales and musical instruments. The notes of the Indian scale are arranged in various patterns called *ragas*. Each raga has a special meaning and may be associated with a particular mood, emotion, season, or time of day. Indian instruments include the sitar, sarod, and vina, which are plucked stringed instruments; the tambura, which produces a *drone* (continuous tone); and the tabla and mridangam, which are drums.

Music for motion pictures, called *film music,* is extremely popular in India. Film music combines Indian classical, folk, and religious music with certain features of Western music. Film music, for example, is typically played by a large orchestra that includes both Indian and Western instruments.

There are several major styles of classical Indian dance. They include the Bharata Natyam of southern India and the Kathak of northern India. Both of these styles, like all classical Indian dances, draw upon the Hindu epics and other poems and stories about the lives of the Hindu deities. They use highly stylized hand, foot, and arm gestures, and movements of the eyes and other facial features to indicate moods and tell stories.

Folk dancing is also popular and varies from region to region. For example, a favorite folk dance in the Punjab is the lively bhangra, in which male dancers jump high in the air. Like other folk dances, the bhangra has a freer form than classical dances.

Motion pictures. India's motion-picture industry produces hundreds of films annually. Centered in Bombay, the industry is sometimes called by the nickname "Bollywood." Indian movies are made in many languages, often for regional audiences. The most popular motion pictures are those made in Hindi, which are shown throughout the country. Hindi films also attract audiences in the Middle East, North and East Africa, the Caribbean, and in Indian communities overseas.

Indian popular films include love stories, crime thrillers, and social dramas. Like American musicals of the 1930's, all Indian popular films feature song-and-dance sequences.

The Indian motion-picture industry is also known for its art films. These motion pictures are more realistic than popular films. They explore such serious social themes as the problems of life in the city, the oppressiveness of the caste system, the difficulty of human relations, and the nature of guilt.

WORLD BOOK photo by David R. Frazier

Motion pictures are popular throughout India. The Indian film industry produces hundreds of movies every year. Most are filmed in Hindi, but some are made in regional languages.

Several Indian directors have won international recognition for their work. Satyajit Ray won particular praise for his Apu Trilogy, a series of three motion pictures describing the growth of a boy to manhood in modern India. Other directors noted for making realistic films about Indian life include Shyam Benegal, Ritwik Ghatak, Adoor Gopalakrishnan, and Mrinal Sen. Ismail Merchant, an Indian film producer, won international acclaim for his film adaptations of literary works.

The land

India covers 1,269,346 square miles (3,287,590 square kilometers) in South Asia. Tall mountains separate most of northern India from the rest of Asia. The southern half of the country is a triangular peninsula that juts into the Indian Ocean. The Arabian Sea laps India's shores to the west, and the Bay of Bengal lies to the east.

India has three main land regions. They are (1) the Himalaya, (2) the Northern Plains, and (3) the Deccan, also called the Southern Plateau.

The Himalaya, the highest mountain system in the world, extends for about 1,500 miles (2,400 kilometers) from northernmost India to the northeastern part of the country. The three almost parallel ranges of the Himalaya in India are nearly 200 miles (320 kilometers) wide at some places. The tallest mountain in India, Kanchenjunga, stands 28,208 feet (8,598 meters) high on the border of Nepal and India in the Himalaya. Dozens of other peaks in the system are more than 20,000 feet (6,100 meters) high. Snow covers the tall peaks throughout the year. The foothills of the Himalaya have many kinds of wildlife, including tigers, deer, and rhinoceroses, and many wildflowers.

The Northern Plains lie between the Himalaya and the southern peninsula. They stretch across northern India for about 1,500 miles (2,400 kilometers) and are from 150 to 200 miles (240 to 320 kilometers) wide. The flat plains include the valleys carved by the Brahmaputra, Indus, and Ganges rivers and their branches. This region is

The Art Institute of Chicago

Indian painting is primarily religious art. This colorful miniature painting from about 1650 shows the Hindu god Krishna sitting with a young prince below and four milkmaids standing above.

the great heartland of India and forms the largest *alluvial plain* in the world. An alluvial plain is land formed of soil left by rivers. The soil in the Northern Plains is fertile, and farmers have tilled the land for centuries. The majority of Indians live in this region.

The Ganges, also known as the Ganga, is the greatest river in India. It originates high in the Himalaya and flows into the Bay of Bengal. Many important towns and cities, including Allahabad and Varanasi, lie along its banks. The Ganges is sacred to Hindus, and many Hindus bathe in the river to cleanse and purify themselves.

WORLD BOOK photo by David R. Frazier

Fertile cropland stretches across the Deccan Plateau in southern India. This plateau also has forests and mineral deposits. The Vindhya and other mountains separate it from the rest of India.

The Thar Desert (also called the Great Indian Desert or the Indian Desert) lies in the western part of the Northern Plains. It covers much of the state of Rajasthan and parts of Gujarat. Few people live in this area.

The Deccan Plateau forms most of the southern peninsula. It is separated from the Northern Plains by a mass of mountain and hill ranges, most prominently the Satpura, Vindhya, and Aravalli. On the eastern edge of the Deccan, a rugged mountain range called the Eastern Ghats rises to an average height of 2,000 feet (610 meters) before slanting down gradually to a wide plain. The Western Ghats form the western boundary of the Deccan. This range reaches a height of about 8,000 feet (2,440 meters) before falling sharply to a narrow coastal plain. The southernmost point of the plateau is formed by the Nilgiri Hills, where the Eastern and Western Ghats meet.

Major rivers of the Deccan Plateau include the Cauvery (also spelled Kaveri), Godavari, Krishna, and Mahandi. Most of the Deccan is farmland. Parts of the Eastern and Western Ghats are heavily forested and are home to elephants, monkeys, and other wildlife.

Climate

Most of India has three main seasons. They are (1) the cool season, (2) the hot season, and (3) the rainy season.

The cool season lasts from October to February. During the cool season, the foothills of the Himalaya receive much snow, though the highest peaks are snow-covered the year around. During the cool season, the temperature in the Himalaya region drops well below the freezing point of 32 °F (0 °C). The northwestern and north-central parts of the Northern Plains have a wide range of

© Gurmeet Thukral, Black Star

The majestic Himalaya is the world's highest mountain system. It consists of several mountain ranges that rise in steps from the plains of northern India along India's borders with China and Nepal. *Himalaya* means *House of Snow* or *Snowy Range* in Sanskrit, an ancient language of India.

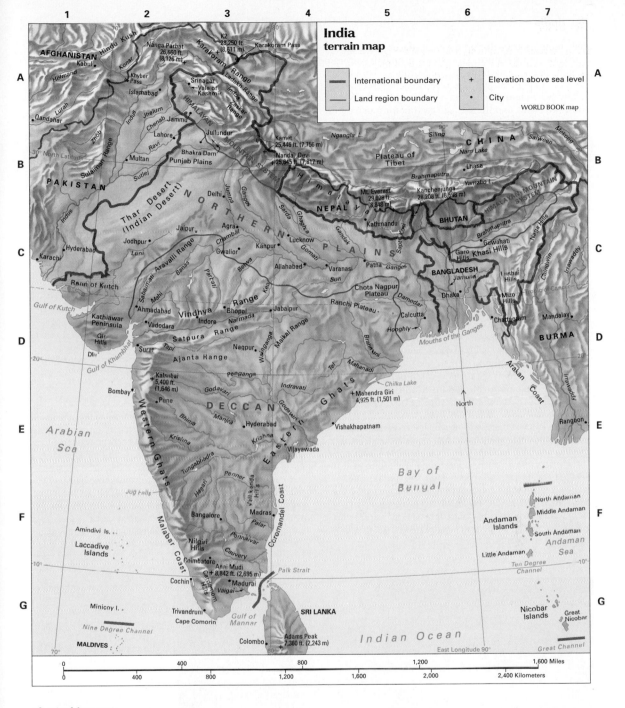

India terrain map. WORLD BOOK map.

Physical features

daily temperatures during the cool season. Days are warm, but temperatures sometimes drop below freezing at night. In the eastern part of the Northern Plains and in the Deccan, the temperature never reaches freezing.

The hot season lasts from March to June, though the Northern Plains and the Deccan are hot for much of the year. In the hot season, temperatures in the plains routinely go up to 115 °F (45 °C). Temperatures often rise to 123 °F (49 °C) in the desert region. Temperatures on the coastal plain average 85 to 90 °F (29 to 32 °C). In the Deccan, daytime temperatures in the hot months generally average from 90 to 100 °F (32 to 38 °C).

The rainy season can last from June to September. However, India usually receives rain from five to seven weeks during this period. During the rainy season, seasonal winds called *monsoons* blow across the Indian Ocean and pick up moisture on the way. The monsoons, which strike from the southeast or the southwest, bring heavy downpours. Although there is some rain at other times of the year, most of India receives its rain through the monsoons.

There is much Indian lore about the monsoons, which provide relief after months of scorching heat. The monsoons also are of great importance to India's agricultural production and the health of the economy. If the monsoons bring enough rain to the country, crops will grow. Sometimes the rains fail to arrive on time, and crops are poor as a result. Some monsoons drop too much rain and cause rivers to overflow, crops to be ruined, villages to be washed away, and many lives to be lost.

Rain falls most heavily in northeastern India. Some hills and mountain slopes in this region receive an average of about 450 inches (1,140 centimeters) of rain a year. The world's heaviest recorded rainfall for a one-year period fell at Cherrapunji. This village had almost 1,042 inches (2,647 centimeters) of rain from August 1860 to July 1861. The Thar Desert in the northwestern part of the country receives less than 10 inches (25 centimeters) of rain a year. Some sections of the desert get less than 4 inches (10 centimeters) of rain annually.

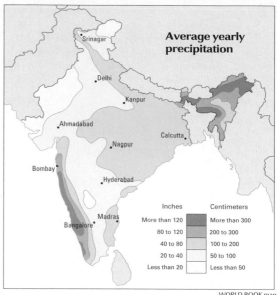

Average yearly precipitation

Inches	Centimeters
More than 120	More than 300
80 to 120	200 to 300
40 to 80	100 to 200
20 to 40	50 to 100
Less than 20	Less than 50

WORLD BOOK map

Rainfall in India varies greatly during the year. The heaviest rainfall occurs in summer, when winds called *monsoons* blow from the southwest, bringing moisture from the Indian Ocean.

Economy

India has one of the largest economies in the world in terms of its *gross domestic product* (GDP). Gross domestic product is the value of all goods and services produced in a country in a year. However, India has such a large population that the country has an extremely low per capita GDP. This figure is determined by dividing a nation's GDP by its population. As a result of its low per capita GDP, India is considered a developing country and one of the poorest countries in the world.

Until 1991, the Indian government firmly controlled the economy. It owned all major industries. It also

The rainy season in India extends from June to September. During those months, seasonal winds called *monsoons* blow across the Indian Ocean, picking up moisture that brings heavy downpours. Monsoons frequently cause flooding. A monsoon created problems for traffic in the northern city of Varanasi (also called Banares or Benares), *left*.

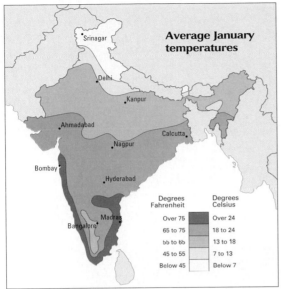

Average January temperatures

Degrees Fahrenheit	Degrees Celsius
Over 75	Over 24
65 to 75	18 to 24
55 to 65	13 to 18
45 to 55	7 to 13
Below 45	Below 7

WORLD BOOK map

In January—during the cool season—cool, dry monsoons from the northeast bring mild temperatures to northern India. Most of southern India has high temperatures all year.

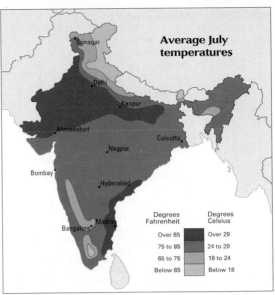

Average July temperatures

Degrees Fahrenheit	Degrees Celsius
Over 85	Over 29
75 to 85	24 to 29
65 to 75	18 to 24
Below 65	Below 18

WORLD BOOK map

Temperatures in July, a rainy season month, are not as high as during the hot season, which lasts from March to June. Much of the Himalayan region remains cool all year.

placed heavy *duties* (taxes) on the import of goods from other countries and allowed foreign companies to invest and trade only under strict supervision. Since 1991, however, India has moved closer to a free enterprise system. The government has encouraged foreign investment and corporate ownership, ended many government monopolies, and greatly reduced duties on goods imported from other countries.

Agriculture provides the main source of income for a majority of the population. Farms cover about half the country's land. About three-fourths of the farmland is used to grow India's major grains and *pulses* (seeds, beans, and lentils). The major grains include rice, wheat, corn, sorghum, and millet. Rice leads all crops in land area. Only China produces more rice than India.

India is the world's leading producer of such crops as cauliflower, a fiber called jute, mangoes, millet, pulses, sesame seeds, and tea. It is a major grower of bananas, cabbages, coconuts, coffee, cotton, onions, oranges, peanuts, potatoes, rapeseeds, rubber, sugar cane, and tobacco. Cardamom, ginger, pepper, turmeric, and other spices are also important products.

In the past, India imported much of its food. Today, however, it is essentially *self-sufficient* in food production—that is, it produces enough food to meet its needs. The increase in agricultural production came about partly because of the Green Revolution, the introduction of high-yielding seeds in the 1960's. Improved farming techniques, greater mechanization, and irrigation have also increased agricultural production. In addition, farmers are paid high prices for their crops to encourage them to grow more, and many rural development programs make credit and machinery easily available.

Large farms, such as those in the Punjab, which is called India's "breadbasket," grow food for sale. However, most Indian farmers are subsistence farmers, who grow crops mainly to feed their families, not for com-

mercial purposes. About two-thirds of India's farmers own the land on which they work.

Most Indian farms are small. Half the farms are less than $2\frac{1}{2}$ acres (1 hectare) in area, and only a few are larger than 25 acres (10 hectares). Indian farms are so small in part because of inheritance customs. After a farmer dies, his farm is divided among his sons. After these sons die, the land is further divided among their sons. With each generation, the size of the farm decreases, and it may become too small to provide a living.

India has more cattle than any other country. The animals serve a variety of purposes. In most of rural India, farmers still use oxen to plow the land. Dairy farming is important. Milk from water buffaloes is also sold commercially. The hides of dead cattle and water buffaloes are used to produce leather and leather goods. There is almost no beef farming in India, because Hindus are not supposed to eat beef.

Manufacturing. India is one of the world's top producers of iron and steel. Huge iron and steel mills operate in Bhilai, Bokaro, Durgapur, and Raurkela. Indian factories use the iron and steel to manufacture such products as aircraft, automobiles, bicycles, electrical appliances, military equipment, railway cars, sewing machines, and tractors. Factories also produce cement, drugs, dyes, fertilizer, food products, industrial chemicals, paper, pesticides, petroleum products, and wood products. One of the largest employers in India is the textile industry. Cotton mills are in western India, near Bombay and Ahmadabad.

Millions of Indians work at home or in small plants. Some of these workers produce cotton textiles on hand looms. Others manufacture matches, incense sticks, and a variety of handicrafts, including brassware, embroidered textiles, jewelry, leather goods, and woodcarvings. Although craft goods are made throughout the country, individual regions tend to specialize in certain

India's gross domestic product

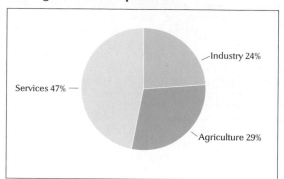

India's gross domestic product (GDP) was $304,002,000,000 in 1995. The GDP is the total value of goods and services produced within a country in a year. *Services* include community, government, and personal services; finance, insurance, real estate, and business services; trade, restaurants, and hotels; transportation, storage, and communication; and utilities. *Agriculture* includes agriculture, forestry, and fishing. *Industry* includes construction, manufacturing, and mining.

Production and workers by economic activities

Economic activities	Percent of GDP produced	Employed workers Number of persons	Percent of total
Agriculture, forestry, & fishing	29	191,300,000	59
Manufacturing	16	28,700,000	9
Community, government, & personal services	15	59,100,000	18
Trade, restaurants, & hotels	15	21,300,000	7
Transportation, storage, & communication	8	8,000,000	2
Construction	6	5,500,000	2
Finance, insurance, real estate, & business services	6	2,600,000	1
Utilities	3	2,800,000	1
Mining	2	1,800,000	1
Total	100	321,100,000	100

Figures are for 1995.
Source: *World Book* estimates based on data from Central Statistical Organization, New Dehli.

ones. For example, Kashmir is famous for carpets, South India for brass, and Rajasthan for puppets.

Mining. India has valuable deposits of a variety of natural resources. The country is one of the world's leading producers of iron ore. Iron ore deposits lie mainly in Bihar, Madhya Pradesh, and Orissa. India also has large deposits of coal and petroleum. Coal accounts for about 40 percent of the yearly value of all minerals mined in India, and petroleum accounts for about 35 percent. Enormous coal deposits lie in Bihar, Orissa, Madhya Pradesh, and the western end of West Bengal. There are some inland deposits of petroleum, mainly in Assam and Gujarat, but most drilling is off the shore of Bombay.

India exports much manganese ore, which is used in steelmaking. India has large deposits of bauxite, chromite, gypsum, limestone, magnesite, mica, natural gas, and titanium. There are smaller deposits of copper, lead, sulfur, and zinc. India also has supplies of two radioactive metals, thorium and uranium.

© Bernard Pierre Wolff, Photo Researchers

Workers plant rice seedlings in a flooded paddy in the southern state of Andhra Pradesh. India is a leading world producer of rice. Farmland covers about half the country's area.

India has deposits of a number of precious metals and stones, including diamonds, emeralds, gold, and silver. Cut diamonds are one of India's biggest exports.

Forestry and fishing. Forests cover only about 10 percent of India. India's forestland has shrunk rapidly since the mid-1900's, because each year more trees are cut down than are planted. Conservation movements are now working to restore Indian forests. In most cases, the previous forests, which had a variety of trees, are being replaced by fast-growing eucalyptus or pine trees. Villagers cut down trees for use as fuel. Deodar cedar, rosewood, sal, and teak trees are cut for timber.

Fishing is a way of life for millions of people who live on India's coasts, and it is one of the chief industries in such coastal states as Andhra Pradesh, Kerala, Orissa, Tamil Nadu, and West Bengal. The main varieties of fish caught from the seas around India include mackerel, perch, prawn, and sardines. Carp and catfish are the most important freshwater fish.

Service industries are economic activities that provide services, rather than produce goods. A growing urban population and increasing commercial and communication links between India and the rest of the world have led to a dramatic expansion of the country's service industries. Government is the largest service industry. Other important service industries include business, computer programming, education, finance, health care, insurance, public administration, real estate, social work, tourism, transportation, and utilities.

India's major stock exchange is in Bombay, which is the nation's business, finance, and trading capital. Calcutta ranks as the world leader in the wholesale trade of jute. Bangalore is the center of the country's computer industry.

Energy supply. India has rich deposits of coal, and petroleum production is increasing. Nevertheless, India still imports large amounts of petroleum because it uses more than it produces. Plants that burn petroleum or coal generate about 80 percent of India's electric power. Most of the rest comes from hydroelectric plants.

International trade. The value of India's imports is greater than the value of its exports. The main import is petroleum, which comes from the Middle East. Other imports include chemicals, fertilizer, industrial machinery, and pearls and gemstones. Among India's exports are chemicals, cotton textiles and clothing, cut diamonds and jewelry, engineering goods, handicrafts, iron ore, leather goods, and tea. India's main trading partner is the United States. Its other trading partners include Germany, Japan, Saudi Arabia, and the United Kingdom.

Transportation. India's railway system, which is owned and operated by the government, is one of the largest in the world. It has more than 7,000 stations and more than 38,000 miles (62,000 kilometers) of track. It is also the single largest employer in the country. Railroads transport most goods in India and serve as the main carrier of passengers. About 4 billion passengers travel by train in India annually. The government keeps the price of train travel low enough for most people to afford it.

India is well connected by roads, but the roads generally are not well maintained. Each of the states has a long-distance bus system. There are many private bus companies as well, which operate mainly in the tourist regions or between large cities.

Although few Indians own an automobile, car and motorcycle ownership is growing rapidly. Many people ride bicycles. In urban areas, buses are a popular form of transportation. In rural areas, many people travel on buggies or carts drawn by horses or oxen. The Brahmaputra, Ganges, and other major rivers carry boat traffic.

The government owns and operates two major airlines. Air India provides international service to many countries throughout the world. Indian Airlines flies within India and to nearby countries. Several private airlines also operate within India. Bombay, Calcutta, Delhi, Madras, and Trivandrum (also spelled Thiruvananthapuram) have major airports.

Communication. Telephone and telegraph services reach throughout India. However, few families have telephones. In towns and cities, especially, public telephones are widely available.

The radio remains the main source of news for most Indians. However, almost every village with electric power has at least one television set, and an entire village may gather around it for a film or special program. The number of connections to cable and satellite sys-

Economy of India

Agriculture is a major economic activity throughout much of India. This map shows the nation's leading agricultural areas and major farm products. It also indicates the country's chief forestlands, fisheries, manufacturing centers, and mineral deposits.

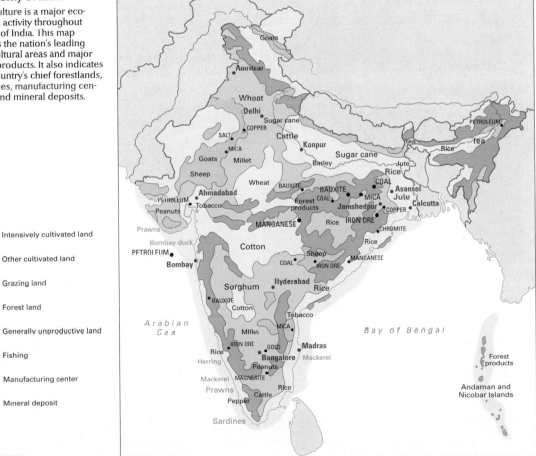

Intensively cultivated land

Other cultivated land

Grazing land

Forest land

Generally unproductive land

Fishing

● Manufacturing center

● Mineral deposit

WORLD BOOK map

Traditional crafts play an important part in Indian manufacturing. This woman uses a carved wood block to paint a design on fabric. Millions of people work at home or in small plants.

© Emil Muench, Photri

WORLD BOOK photo by David R. Frazier

Modern technology is growing rapidly in India's cities. The communications laboratory shown above is located in Bangalore, the center of the country's computer industry.

tems is growing rapidly, making more channels and a wider variety of television programs available to many viewers.

India has a lively newspaper culture. Newspapers are privately owned, and they freely criticize the government. India has about 3,500 daily newspapers, which are published in a variety of languages. The major English-language newspapers include the *Times of India, Indian Express, Statesman,* and *The Hindu.* These papers are published nationally and are highly influential.

History

Earliest times. People have lived in what is now India for at least 200,000 years. About 4,500 years ago, a civilization began to flourish in the Indus Valley in what are now western India and Pakistan. Archaeological excavations in the early 1920's uncovered extensive ruins of two cities named Harappa and Mohenjo-Daro.

The people of Harappa, Mohenjo-Daro, and other Indus Valley cities had a system of writing. However, scholars have not yet succeeded in deciphering this script. The Indus Valley people also had systems of counting, measuring, and weighing. About 1700 B.C., the Indus Valley civilization gradually broke up. Scholars believe that changing river patterns, including a series of floods, may have caused the end of the culture.

The Aryans. About 1500 B.C., groups of warlike people left their homes in central Asia, possibly near the Caucasus Mountains, and came to India. These people called themselves *arya* (kinsmen or nobles). They are now known as the Aryans.

When the Aryans arrived in India, they found people with an advanced civilization living there. These people, called the Dravidians, lived in towns and grew crops. The Aryans gradually conquered the Dravidians and drove some of them southward. Eventually, the Aryans extended their rule over all of India except the south.

The Aryans tended sheep, goats, cows, and horses. They measured their wealth in herds of cattle. Over time, the Aryans settled into villages. Each village or group of villages was led by a headman and council.

Over many centuries, the caste system became established. The Brahmans—the priests—were the highest caste and the Shudras, who may have been Dravidians, were the lowest. The Brahmans perfected Sanskrit, the language of the Aryans; conducted elaborate rituals and sacrifices; and passed sacred knowledge from one generation to another. Beginning about 1400 B.C., the earliest known Hindu scriptures—the Vedas—were composed. The most important Hindu sacred writings, called the Upanishads, appeared between 800 and 600 B.C.

In the 500's and 400's B.C., two religions were founded in India. The great religious and social reformer Siddhartha Gautama, who became known as Buddha (Enlightened One), founded Buddhism. Another reformer, Mahavira, founded Jainism. Both religions rejected the authority of the Vedas and the Brahmans, and both spread rapidly throughout India.

Persian and Greek invasions. About 518 B.C., Persians gained control of the Gandhara region in the northwest, now in Pakistan. Alexander the Great of Macedonia led his Greek army into India in 326 B.C., but he went only as far as the Beas River in the northwest. He wanted to push eastward to the Ganges River, but his troops, tired and worn out by disease, refused to go farther. Alexander left India and named some of his generals as *satraps* (governors) of the conquered provinces. In a few years, Indian forces drove most of the satraps out.

The Mauryan Empire was established by Chandragupta Maurya about 324 B.C. By the end of Chandragupta Maurya's rule in about 298 B.C., the empire extended over nearly all of northern India and into what are now Afghanistan and parts of central Asia.

Chandragupta Maurya's grandson Ashoka became

one of India's most famous emperors. He ruled from about 272 to 232 B.C. In 261 B.C., Ashoka conquered the kingdom of Kalinga (now Orissa). The bloodshed caused by his war of conquest left Ashoka stricken with sorrow and regret. He converted from Hinduism to Buddhism and gave up war.

Ashoka spent the rest of his life trying to spread a message, based on Buddhist teachings, that emphasized nonviolence and the importance of duty. He sent members of his family as Buddhist missionaries to other parts of India and to what is now Sri Lanka. Ashoka had laws and moral teachings carved on great pillars that were installed throughout his kingdom. India's state emblem, a group of lions, is taken from one of these pillars.

The Mauryan Empire began to break up after the death of Ashoka in 232 B.C. The empire ended about 185 B.C. For about the next 500 years, groups of central Asian peoples, including the Scythians and the Kushans, moved into northern India. The Kushans established a dynasty in northern India around A.D. 50.

The golden age. Indian emperors of the Gupta dynasty reunited northern India about 320. Gupta territory eventually extended to what is now Afghanistan in the northwest and to the Vindhya mountains in the south. The Gupta Empire, which lasted until about 500, is often referred to as India's "golden age." Indian art, literature, mathematics, philosophy, and science achieved great heights under the Guptas, especially during the reign of Chandragupta II, who ruled from about 375 to about 415. India's most famous dramatist and poet, Kalidasa, wrote works of great charm and beauty in this period. The finest frescoes at Ajanta were also painted at this time, and many Hindu temples were built. A system of medicine called Ayurveda also developed about this time.

Southern India. From about 50 B.C. to about the A.D. 1000's, several dynasties competed for control of southern India and established a great civilization there. These dynasties included the Andhras, also called the Satavahanas; the Cholas; and the Pallavas. Southern India forged trading links with Southeast Asia that lasted for centuries. Indian traders and other voyagers spread Indian culture throughout Southeast Asia.

Period of invasions. From about 455 to the early 1500's, armies from what are now Afghanistan, central Asia, and Iran invaded India. First, the Huns invaded from central Asia. Muslim armies came from Arabia in the early 700's. Mahmud of Ghazni, a warrior from Afghanistan, began a series of 17 raids into India about 1000. During these attacks, Mahmud destroyed Hindu temples and looted Indian cities.

In 1206, the Muslim general Qutb ub-din Aybak proclaimed himself *sultan* (ruler) of northern India and established the Delhi Sultanate. In 1398, the armies of the central Asian leader Timur, also known as Tamerlane, swept over India. Timur sacked Delhi before returning to his capital at Samarqand (Samarkand) in what is now Uzbekistan. After Timur's attack, the Delhi Sultanate began to break apart.

The Mughal Empire. In 1526, a central Asian leader named Babur defeated Ibrahim Lodi, the last sultan of Delhi, at the Battle of Panipat. Babur, a descendant of both Timur and the Mongol conqueror Genghis Khan, then established the Mughal Empire in India. Babur ruled until 1530 and conquered much of northern India.

Babur's grandson Akbar became the greatest Mughal emperor. He ruled from 1556 to 1605. He expanded his empire as far west as what is now Afghanistan and as far south as the Godavari River. Akbar was a tolerant ruler. A Muslim, he won over the Hindus of India by making many of their leaders government administrators and military commanders, and by giving them honors. The Mughal Empire under Akbar was among the most powerful in the world at that time.

Akbar's grandson Shah Jahan, who ruled from 1628 to

Important dates in India

c. 2500 B.C.	The Indus Valley civilization began to flourish.
c. 1500 B.C.	The Aryans invaded India.
c. 1400 B.C.	The earliest known texts of the Hindu faith—the Vedas—were beginning to be composed.
326 B.C.	Alexander the Great reached what is now India.
A.D. 320-c. 500	The Gupta dynasty unified northern India.
1498	Vasco da Gama of Portugal reached India.
1526	The Mughal Empire was established by Babur, a Muslim ruler from central Asia, who conquered India.
1757	The British East India Company's agent Robert Clive won the Battle of Plassey. The company soon gained control of Bengal.
1774	Warren Hastings, the first British governor general of India, took office.
1857-1859	The British put down the Indian Rebellion, an uprising against their rule by Indians in northern and central India.
1858	The British government took over the direct rule of India from the East India Company.
1885	The Indian National Congress was formed.
1906	The All-India Muslim League was organized.
1919	Demonstrations against British rule became widespread. In an incident known as the Amritsar Massacre, British troops in Amritsar opened fire on an unarmed crowd of Indians.
1920	Mohandas K. Gandhi became the leader of the Indian National Congress and started a program of nonviolent disobedience against the British.
1935	The British government created a new constitution that gave Indians more political power.
1940	The Muslim League demanded that a separate Muslim country, Pakistan, be carved out of India.
1947	India became independent on August 15, the day after Pakistan was created. Jawaharlal Nehru became India's first prime minister.
1947-1949	India and Pakistan fought over Kashmir.
1948	Mohandas Gandhi was assassinated.
1950	India's Constitution took effect.
1965	India and Pakistan fought a second war over Kashmir.
1966	Indira Gandhi, Nehru's daughter, became India's first woman prime minister.
1971	India assisted East Pakistan in a war against West Pakistan. The West was defeated, and East Pakistan became the independent nation of Bangladesh.
1984	Indira Gandhi was assassinated. Her older son, Rajiv, then became prime minister.
1991	Rajiv Gandhi was assassinated.
1996	The Congress Party, which had ruled India for all but four years since the nation won independence in 1947, was voted out of office, and India entered a period of coalition governments.

WORLD BOOK maps

The Mauryan Empire, which lasted from about 324 B.C. to 185 B.C., united almost all India for the first time. The empire's capital was Pataliputra (now Patna).

The Gupta Empire extended across northern India from about A.D. 320 to about 500. At this time, India became a center of art, learning, and medicine.

The Mughal Empire was established by central Asian Muslims in 1526. By about 1600, the Mughals ruled most of India. The empire lasted until the 1700's.

1658, built a new capital in Delhi. He was also responsible for the construction of the Taj Mahal at Agra and many other great buildings.

Aurangzeb, one of Shah Jahan's sons, became head of the Mughal Empire in 1658. Aurangzeb was a strict Muslim and a harsh ruler. He reimposed a tax on Hindus that had been abolished by Akbar. Hindus hold him responsible for destroying many Hindu temples and trying to forcibly convert Hindus to Islam. His policies caused many revolts. Under the Hindu leader Shivaji Bhonsle, the Marathas of western India launched attacks against Aurangzeb's empire. Many local leaders in the south also rebelled. Partly as a result of Aurangzeb's rule and his costly wars, the Mughal Empire began to fall apart.

© Paolo Koch, Photo Researchers

Ruins at Mohenjo-Daro in the Indus Valley include a citadel from the 2000's B.C. and a dome-shaped Buddhist monument called a *stupa* from the A.D. 100's. Mohenjo-Daro was a center of the Indus Valley civilization, India's first advanced civilization.

The coming of the Europeans. The first European explorer to reach India was Vasco da Gama of Portugal. He arrived in Calicut in 1498. At the time, Portugal was challenging Turkish Muslims and traders from Italian city-states for control over the European trade with Asian countries in silk, spices, and other highly valued goods. The Portuguese gained control over Goa and some other areas on the western coast of India.

In 1600, Queen Elizabeth I of England granted a charter for the formation of a company to open trade with India and East Asia. This company, called the East India Company, received permission from the Mughal Emperor Jahangir, Akbar's son, to trade in India. The company soon set up trading posts and forts at Bombay, Calcutta, and Madras. During the 1600's, the English became the leading European power in India. Meanwhile, the French established a trading post at Pondicherry.

The rise of the East India Company. By the mid-1700's, little remained of the Mughal Empire, and there was no effective central power. In these circumstances, the Europeans in India prospered. The East India Company expanded its trade and increased its political power. It also began collecting taxes in some regions. When Indian rulers refused to agree to the company's terms, the company used force against them.

At the Battle of Plassey in 1757, the forces of Robert Clive, an agent of the East India Company, defeated the army of the *nawab* (Mughal governor) of Bengal. Most historians regard this British victory as the starting point of the British Empire in India, though at that time, most of the country still remained under the rule of Indian princes. Over the next 100 years, however, British political influence and territorial control expanded. In 1774, Warren Hastings was appointed the company's first governor general of India.

The Indian Rebellion. Through the years, resentment against British rule grew, especially in the north. Land taxes imposed by the British caused many difficulties for farmers. Large numbers of people went hungry. British land reforms took away land from many Indian people. In addition, many Indians resented what they believed to be a growing British interference in Indian customs and religion. In 1857, the Indian people rebelled.

The rebellion, sometimes called the Sepoy Rebellion or Sepoy Mutiny, began at an army base in Meerut, near

Manuscript painting (late 1500's-early 1600's); Musée Guimet, Paris (Giraudon/Art Resource)

Babur, *seated at the far left,* was a Muslim ruler from central Asia who founded the Mughal Empire in 1526. Babur conquered much of northern India before his death in 1530.

Delhi. There, Indian soldiers called *sepoys* revolted after British officers instructed them to bite open rifle cartridges believed to have been greased with cow and hog fat. Both Hindus and Muslims objected to the order. The religious beliefs of the Hindu sepoys forbade them to eat beef, and the Muslim sepoys could not eat pork.

The Indian Rebellion quickly spread from Meerut to the rest of northern and central India. However, the rebels were poorly organized, had few weapons, and lacked good leadership. By 1859, they had been defeated. Although the rebellion had failed, the British had faced a serious threat to their rule.

British India. In 1858, the British government decided to govern India directly. The direct British rule of India is often called the British Raj. *Raj* means *rule* or *administration.* Parliament took control of the East India Company's Indian possessions, which became known as British India. In most other parts of India, called the *princely,* or *native, states,* the British governed indirectly, through local rulers. A few small areas of coastal land remained French or Portuguese colonies until the mid-1900's.

The British monarch appointed an official called a *viceroy* to govern British India. An executive council of five members—all British and all appointed by the monarch—helped the viceroy. The viceroy appointed

from 6 to 12 additional members, who met together with the executive council to form a legislative council. A few Indians could serve on the legislative council.

British India was divided into several provinces. An appointed governor or lieutenant governor headed each province. The provinces also had their own executive council and legislative council.

Britain placed a representative, called a *resident,* in each princely state. The resident advised the local prince about political and economic matters. The local prince had no power to make laws relating to foreign affairs, defense, relations with other princely states, and certain other matters. In internal affairs, however, the local prince generally had complete authority.

In 1876, Queen Victoria of Britain was given the title Empress of India by the British Parliament. Although the British did not engage in further expansion of their territory within India, they were involved in several wars in which they used Indian troops. Indian troops serving under British officers fought the Second Afghan War (1878-1881). This war helped establish India's boundary with Afghanistan. British India defeated the Burmese in the Third Burmese War (1885). Burma then became a province of India. It remained part of India until 1937.

In the second half of the 1800's, the British built railroad, telephone, and telegraph systems in India. They also established universities. Although the British enlarged the Indian irrigation system, agricultural production improved only slightly. Poverty levels remained high. The British spent little money on elementary education and did little to promote industrialization.

Rise of Indian nationalism. Indians did not generally feel content about British rule in India. Indians lacked equal job opportunities. They were not allowed to advance to high positions in government service or to become officers in the army. In 1885, a number of Indian lawyers and professionals formed the Indian National Congress. Members of the organization belonged to various religions and came from all parts of India. Congress members debated political and economic reforms, the future of India, and ways for Indians to achieve equal status with the British.

Some Muslims believed the Indian National Congress was a Hindu organization aiming for Hindu rule. In 1906, several Muslim leaders, encouraged by the British, formed the All-India Muslim League. Members of the organization sought to give the Muslims a voice in political affairs. However, most Muslims continued to support the Indian National Congress.

In 1905, the British divided the state of Bengal into separate Hindu and Muslim sections. Indians protested this action with a boycott of British goods and a series of bombings and shootings. In an effort to stop the violence, the British introduced the Morley-Minto Reforms of 1909. These reforms enlarged the viceroy's executive council to include an Indian. They also allowed Indians to elect representatives to the provincial legislative councils. In 1911, the British reunited Bengal.

When World War I broke out in 1914, Britain declared that India was also at war with Germany. Indian troops fought in many parts of the world. In return for Indian support, the British promised more reforms and agreed to let Indians have a greater role in political affairs. Nevertheless, protests against the British continued.

In March 1919, the British passed the Rowlatt Acts to try to control protests in India. The acts attempted to restrict the political liberties and rights of Indians, including the right to trial by jury. But demonstrations against the government increased in response to the acts.

On April 13, 1919, thousands of Indians assembled in an enclosed area in Amritsar. Troops entered the meeting place and blocked the entrance. The British commander then ordered the soldiers to open fire on the unarmed crowd. The shots killed about 400 people and wounded about 1,200. This event, called the Amritsar Massacre, proved to be a turning point. From then on, Indians demanded complete independence from British rule. The British promised more reforms, but at the same time, they tried to crush the independence movement.

The Montagu-Chelmsford Reforms were passed in late 1919 and went into full effect in 1921. The reforms increased the powers of the provincial legislative councils, where Indians were most active. The central legislative council was replaced by a legislature with most of its members elected. However, the viceroy and the governors still had the right to veto any bill. The Indians did not believe the reforms gave them enough power.

By 1920, Mohandas K. Gandhi had become a leader in the Indian independence movement and in the Indian National Congress, which had become the most important Indian political organization. Gandhi persuaded the Congress to adopt his program of *nonviolent disobedience,* also known as *nonviolent noncooperation.* Gandhi's program asked Indians to boycott British goods, to refuse to pay taxes, and to stop using British schools, courts, and government services. As a result, some Indians gave up well-paying jobs that required them to cooperate with the British. Gandhi changed the Indian National Congress from a small party of educated men to a mass party with millions of followers.

New Constitution. In 1930, Gandhi led hundreds of followers on a 240-mile (386-kilometer) march to the sea, where they made salt from seawater. This action was a protest against the Salt Acts, which made it a crime to possess salt not bought from the government. The salt march and other acts of civil disobedience in the early 1930's led the British to give the Indian people more political power. In 1931, Gandhi and the viceroy, Lord Irwin, signed an agreement. Gandhi agreed to give up his campaign of civil disobedience. The British agreed to release thousands of political prisoners.

The Government of India Act of 1935 created a new constitution. This Constitution gave provincial legislatures control over lawmaking in the provinces. It also increased the representation of Indians in all branches of government. However, the viceroy and the governors still kept their veto power over all bills, and the government controlled finances. As a result, many important changes that Indians wanted were never approved by the government.

Meanwhile, the Muslim League had become more politically active. In 1934, Muhammad Ali Jinnah, who had been an important Congress leader, was chosen to head the Muslim League. Under Jinnah's leadership, the league won a number of seats in the provincial legislatures, and membership increased rapidly. However, the provincial elections of 1937 showed that most Muslims still supported the Indian National Congress.

Jinnah increased his political activity and declared that the Congress could not speak for Muslims. In 1940, he demanded that a new country be carved out of India for Muslims. The name *Pakistan*, which means *land of the pure* in the Urdu language, came to be used for this proposed nation. According to Jinnah, India was to be for Hindus, and Pakistan for Muslims.

World War II (1939-1945). Britain declared war on Germany on Sept. 3, 1939. As it had done before, in World War I, Britain again said that India was also at war with Germany. Indian leaders were angered because they had not been consulted. They continued to demand independence. Britain promised independence for India after the war. But members of the Indian National Congress demanded immediate self-government instead, and they refused to support the war effort.

Nevertheless, India was already helping Britain. Indian troops fought in Africa and the Middle East. Indian factories produced supplies for the British and Allied armies. The British exported coffee, tea, rice, and wheat from India to Allied nations. The export of these products contributed in part to the Bengal famine of 1943, in which about 3 million Indians died.

In December 1941, Japan entered the war on Germany's side. Within a few months, Japanese troops had captured Burma. The Japanese invaded eastern India in

The British East India Company controlled much of India by the early 1800's. Areas not held directly were allied states, except for the Maratha Confederacy.

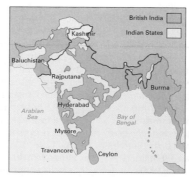

British India was set up in 1858. Britain took over East India Company lands and indirect control of the remaining states. It gradually expanded India's boundaries.

WORLD BOOK maps

Independent India was founded on Aug. 15, 1947, the day after the northeast and northwest became Pakistan. Burma and Ceylon won independence in 1948.

© Black Star

Mohandas K. Gandhi led the people of India to independence. He was assassinated in 1948, the year after achieving his goal.

March 1944. Many thousands of Indian troops decided to aid the Japanese in the hope of driving the British out of India. These soldiers, most of whom had been captured by the Japanese when they seized Burma, called themselves the Indian National Army. But British and Indian troops soon drove them back.

During the war, Britain continued to hold talks with the Indian National Congress. In a final effort to free India of the British, Gandhi launched another civil disobedience campaign, called the Quit India Movement, in August 1942. In response, the British jailed all Congress leaders for the rest of the war. The Muslim League, on the other hand, cooperated with the British during the war, with the understanding that their demands for a separate nation would receive serious consideration.

Independence and partition. At the conclusion of the war in 1945, Congress leaders were released and negotiations for independence were resumed. The British declared early in 1946 that they would grant India independence if Indian political leaders could agree among themselves on a form of government. Britain sent a special Cabinet mission to India, but the Congress and Muslim League could not settle their differences.

To show its strength and to warn the British not to make a separate agreement with the Congress, the Muslim League declared Aug. 16, 1946, as Direct Action Day. On that day, Muslims held nationwide demonstrations calling for the establishment of Pakistan. Bloody rioting broke out between Muslims and Hindus in Calcutta. Similar violence later occurred elsewhere in India.

In 1947, Indian and British leaders agreed to *partition* (divide) the country into India and Pakistan. They saw no other way of bringing to an end the violence between Hindus and Muslims.

India became an independent nation on Aug. 15, 1947. Pakistan had become an independent nation the day before. Partition was accompanied by more violence and bloodshed. More than 10 million people became refugees, as Hindus and Sikhs in Pakistan fled to India, and Muslims in India fled to Pakistan. About half a million people were killed in Hindu-Muslim riots.

Gandhi also fell victim to violence. On Jan. 30, 1948, while on his way to a prayer meeting in New Delhi, he was assassinated. A Hindu fanatic who hated Gandhi for his tolerance toward Muslims and disagreed with Gandhi's policy of nonviolence shot him to death.

Although British India had become partitioned, an agreement also had to be reached with the princely states. Most local rulers agreed to merge their states into India. In return, the Indian government offered them annual payments. A few princely states joined Pakistan.

One state that initially merged into neither India nor Pakistan was Kashmir. Its ruler was Hindu, but the majority of its people were Muslims. Pakistani Muslims launched an invasion to take Kashmir by force, and Pakistan laid claim to the state. Kashmir's ruler responded by seeking India's protection and by making Kashmir part of India. The war between India and Pakistan lasted until 1949, when the United Nations (UN) arranged a cease-fire and set up a truce line. See **Kashmir.**

In India, Jawaharlal Nehru, a close associate of Gandhi, became the first prime minister after independence. A constituent assembly drew up a new constitution. The assembly approved the Constitution in November 1949. The Constitution went into effect on Jan. 26, 1950. January 26 is now celebrated each year in India as a national holiday, Republic Day.

India in the 1950's and early 1960's. India's first general election was held in 1951 and 1952. The Congress Party, under Nehru's leadership, won a huge majority of the seats in India's Parliament. Nehru sought to develop the country and raise the standard of living. Under Nehru, the central government ran the economy and controlled industry.

In 1951, India began its first *five-year plan,* a program designed to improve the country's standard of living. This plan resulted in some notable achievements. Agricultural and industrial production grew rapidly, and school enrollment rose sharply. A rationing system enabled people to buy essential food items at low prices. New laws made it possible for more poor farmers to own the land they worked on. Women gained the right to divorce and to inherit property. Malaria was brought under control.

Nehru also sought to achieve the political unity of India. France gave up the last of its Indian territories in 1954, but Portugal refused to do so. It still had three small colonies in India—Damão (now Daman), Diu, and Goa. In 1961, Indian troops invaded these areas and defeated the Portuguese forces there. Goa became a state in 1987. Daman and Diu remained a territory.

Regional, language, and ethnic differences among Indians created difficulties for national unity. In 1953, after much pressure on the Indian government, the state of Andhra (now Andhra Pradesh) was created for Telugu speakers. In 1955, the States Reorganization Commission recommended the creation of other states based on language. At that time, the state boundaries were those that the British had drawn up. In 1956, most of India's major language groups were given their own states. Additional states based on language were created later.

In foreign affairs, Nehru adopted a position of nonalignment. During the Cold War, a period of intense rivalry between the United States and the Soviet Union, most nations were allied with one side or the other. Nehru, however, refused to support either side. He chose to use the UN to resolve international conflicts and strongly supported UN peacekeeping operations.

© Brian Brake, Magnum

Jawaharlal Nehru, *on horseback*, worked for independence with Mohandas Gandhi and became India's first prime minister.

Border disputes between India and China erupted into armed violence in October 1962, when Chinese forces swept into northeastern India. In November, the Chinese pulled back, and a cease-fire took effect. Nehru, who had been surprised by the Chinese invasion, decided that military spending should increase. As a result, more of the budget went to the armed forces and less to education, health, and social reform.

India under Indira Gandhi. Nehru died in office in 1964. He was succeeded by Lal Bahadur Shastri, a member of his cabinet. In early 1965, fighting broke out along the Pakistan-India border, but Shastri and President Muhammad Ayub Khan of Pakistan quickly agreed to a cease-fire under UN supervision. There were many violations of the cease-fire, and later that year, Pakistan and India fought over Kashmir. Once again, a UN-sponsored cease-fire took effect.

In 1966, Shastri and Ayub Khan signed a peace treaty. Shastri died shortly after signing. A brief leadership struggle within the Congress Party followed Shastri's death. Nehru's daughter, Indira Gandhi, eventually became the prime minister in 1966.

In 1971, civil war broke out in Pakistan, and millions of East Pakistani refugees fled into India. India assisted East Pakistan in the fight against West Pakistan. West Pakistan was defeated , and East Pakistan became the independent nation of Bangladesh.

Gandhi had taken office during widespread unrest because of severe food shortages, unemployment, and other problems. The economic situation remained poor in the early 1970's, and there were many demonstrations urging her removal. In June 1975, a high court found Gandhi guilty of using illegal practices in her 1971 election campaign. Rather than resign, Gandhi had the president declare a state of emergency. She claimed that external enemies and internal forces of disorder were trying to break India apart. She had her opponents jailed and imposed strict censorship. In November 1975, the Supreme Court of India overturned her conviction.

In 1977, Gandhi declared the state of emergency over. Political prisoners were released, and preparations were made for elections that year. For the first time, the Congress Party lost, and the newly formed Janata Party came into office. But the Janata Party, which was a coalition of

several parties, could not hold itself together. By 1980, elections had to be held. Gandhi's party, Congress-I (the *I* stood for *Indira*), won back power, and Gandhi once again became prime minister.

In the early 1980's, a militant Sikh movement grew in the Punjab. The leaders of this movement claimed that the Sikhs suffered from widespread discrimination. They wanted a separate state only for Sikhs. Some Sikhs carried out acts of terrorism and violence against people who opposed the movement. Sikh militants occupied the Golden Temple in Amritsar, the most sacred Sikh shrine. In 1984, government troops attacked the temple. The leaders of the militants died in the fighting. Many Sikhs were angry that their shrine had been attacked, and two Sikh members of Gandhi's security force assassinated her on Oct. 31, 1984. The assassination touched off riots in which several thousand Sikhs were killed. Gandhi's elder son, Rajiv, succeeded her as head of the Congress-I Party and as prime minister.

Religious and ethnic unrest. In the late 1980's, Muslim groups in Kashmir began to hold demonstrations against Indian rule. Many received the support of the Pakistani government. In 1989, the demonstrations turned violent. Since then, thousands of people have died as a result of clashes between Indian military forces and the Muslim groups.

In 1989 and 1990, violence between Hindus and Muslims erupted over the status of a *mosque* (Muslim place of worship) in the town of Ayodhya in the state of Uttar Pradesh. Some Hindus claimed that a Muslim ruler of the 1500's had built the mosque at the site after destroying a Hindu temple there. They also claimed that the Hindu god Rama was born where the mosque had been built. They demanded that the mosque be removed and a temple be built to honor Rama. In 1992, Hindu extremists destroyed the mosque. This action led to violence between Hindus and Muslims in many areas of India.

A number of ethnic separatist groups emerged in the 1980's and 1990's. They included the United Liberation Forces of Assam, which called for independence for Assam, and the Bodo movement, which favored autonomy for the region inhabited by the Bodo people. In 1993 and 1994, violence broke out, mainly in Manipur, between Nagas wanting independence and Kukis, who also live in

Wide World

Indira Gandhi was the first woman prime minister of India. She held that position from 1966 to 1977 and from 1980 to 1984.

the region. The clashes left hundreds of people dead and many villages destroyed.

Recent developments. During Rajiv Gandhi's term, the government—and the prime minister himself—came under suspicion of corruption. In 1989, the Congress Party lost its majority in Parliament, and Gandhi resigned. The National Front, a coalition of parties, then formed the government. The coalition proved unable to hold together, and new elections were called. While campaigning in May 1991, Gandhi was assassinated.

The 1991 elections returned the Congress Party to power, and P. V. Narasimha Rao became prime minister. Rao began a far-reaching policy of reform to liberalize the Indian economy by reducing government control over it. He ended many government monopolies and introduced competition in key industries. Investment by foreign corporations in India increased dramatically.

In elections in 1996, the Congress Party suffered a major defeat. At the time, many members of Rao's cabinet had resigned due to charges of corruption and bribery. Rao himself was later charged with bribery and fraud. A Hindu nationalist party called the Bharatiya Janata Party won the largest number of seats but not a majority. The Bharatiya Janata Party failed to gain enough allies to form a government, and a coalition of 14 parties called the United Front governed India. The political situation remained unstable, however.   Vinay Lal and Anil Lal

Related articles in *World Book* include:

Political and military leaders

Akbar	Gandhi, Indira	Kanishka
Asoka	Gandhi, Mohandas	Nehru
Aurangzeb	Karamchand	Pandit, Vijaya L.
Babar	Gandhi, Rajiv	Ranjit Singh
Besant, Annie W.	Harsha	Rao, P. V. Nara-
Chandragupta	Hastings, Warren	simha
Maurya	Jinnah, Muhammad	Shah Jahan
Clive, Robert	Ali	

Animal and plant life

Adjutant	Cashmere goat	Rhinoceros
Banyan tree	Elephant	Tiger
Cardamom	Gaur	Water buffalo

Cities

Agra	Bangalore	Delhi	Madras
Ahmadabad	Bombay	Hyderabad	New Delhi
Allahabad	Calcutta	Kanpur	Varanasi
Amritsar	Darjeeling	Lucknow	

States and regions

Kashmir	Punjab	Sikkim

History

Alexander the Great	Delhi Sultanate	Kushan Empire
Aryans	East India Company	Mauryan Empire
Black Hole of	Gupta dynasty	Mogul Empire
Calcutta	Indus Valley	Mongol Empire
Colombo Plan	civilization	Sepoy Rebellion

Physical features

Arabian Sea	Ganges River	Thar Desert
Bay of Bengal	Himalaya	
Brahmaputra River	Indian Ocean	

Religion

Asceticism	Caste	Juggernaut
Brahman	Hinduism	Muslims
Buddha	Islam	Reincarnation
Buddhism	Jainism	Shiva

Sikhism	Vedas	Vishnu
Upanishads		

The arts

Architecture (Indian architecture)	Mahabharata	Sanskrit literature
	Music (Asian music)	Sculpture (India)
Bhagavad-Gita	Painting (Asian painting)	Sitar
Dancing (picture)	Ramayana	Tagore, Sir Rabindranath
Drama (Asian drama)	Rushdie, Salman	
Furniture (India)		Taj Mahal

Other related articles

Asia	Jute	Suttee
Bangladesh	Nepal	Thug
Bhutan	Pakistan	World, History of
Clothing (pictures)	Rajah	the (pictures)
Dravidians	Rupee	Yoga
Hindi	Sanskrit language	
Indigo	Surgery (History)	

Outline

I. Government
   A. Central government   D. Politics
   B. State governments   E. Armed forces
   C. Courts

II. People
   A. Ancestry   B. Languages

III. Way of life
   A. Family life   F. Clothing
   B. Village life   G. Food and drink
   C. City life   H. Health care
   D. Social structure   I. Recreation
   E. Religion   J. Education

IV. The arts
   A. Architecture   C. Literature
      and sculpture   D. Music and dance
   B. Painting   E. Motion pictures

V. The land
   A. The Himalaya   C. The Deccan Plateau
   B. The Northern Plains

VI. Climate
   A. The cool season   C. The rainy season
   B. The hot season

VII. Economy
   A. Agriculture   F. Energy supply
   B. Manufacturing   G. International trade
   C. Mining   H. Transportation
   D. Forestry and fishing   I. Communication
   E. Service industries

VIII. History

Questions

Who is the most powerful person in the Indian government?
What is the caste system?
What major religions were founded in India?
What are *monsoons*? Why are they important?
Why does Indian music sound different from Western music?
What are some of the methods Mohandas K. Gandhi used in his campaign for Indian independence?
How does climate affect the way people in India live?
What are the earliest Indian written works? What language were they written in?
What was the Indian, or Sepoy, Rebellion? Why was it important?
What factors have had a negative effect on Indian unity?

Reading and Study Guide

See *India* in the Research Guide/Index, Volume 22, for a *Reading and Study Guide.*

Additional resources

Kalman, Bobbie. *India: The Culture.* Crabtree Pub. Co., 1990. *India: The Land.* 1990. *India: The People.* 1990. Younger readers.
Mansingh, Surjit. *Historical Dictionary of India.* Scarecrow, 1996.
McNair, Sylvia. *India.* Childrens Pr., 1990. Younger readers.
Muthiah, S., ed. *An Atlas of India.* Oxford, 1990.
Nehru, Jawaharlal. *The Discovery of India.* Oxford, 1990.

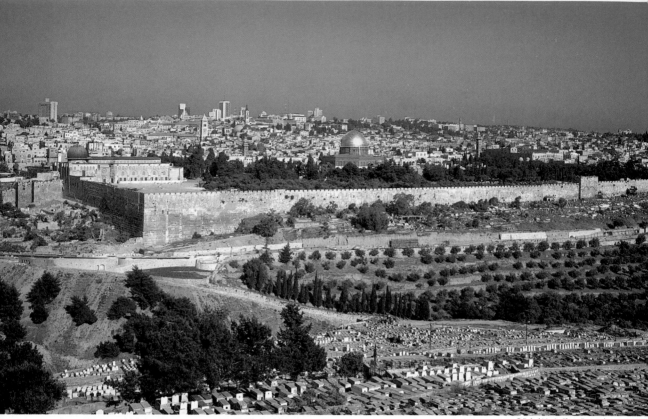

© Rafael Macia, Photo Researchers

Jerusalem is the capital of Israel and the country's largest city. This view shows Jerusalem from the east as seen from the Mount of Olives. A Muslim cemetery appears in the foreground. The golden Dome of the Rock, a Muslim shrine, rises above the walls of the Old City, Jerusalem's oldest district.

Jerusalem

Jerusalem is the capital and largest city of Israel and one of the world's holiest cities. It is also one of the oldest continuously inhabited cities in the world. For centuries, Jerusalem has been a spiritual center to Jews, Christians, and Muslims. Jews consider Jerusalem a holy city because it was their religious and political center during Biblical times. Christians consider Jerusalem holy because many events in the life of Jesus Christ took place there. Muslims also revere the city and believe that the Prophet Muhammad rose to heaven from there.

Nearly three-fourths of Jerusalem's population are Jews. The remainder includes Muslims and a small number of Christians, including Roman Catholics, Eastern Catholics, Protestants, and members of Eastern Orthodox Churches.

Jerusalem is a city of three Sabbaths—Friday (Muslim), Saturday (Jewish), and Sunday (Christian). Businesses in Jerusalem may be closed on any of these three days. The Jewish Sabbath, however, is by far the most widely observed. After it begins on Friday night, much of Jerusalem closes down and most public transportation stops.

Jerusalem lies about 40 miles (64 kilometers) east of the Mediterranean Sea. The city is surrounded on the north, east, and south by the West Bank, a disputed territory inhabited by both Palestinians and Israelis. In 1949, at the end of the first Arab-Israeli War, Jerusalem was divided between Israel and Jordan. Israel controlled the western part of the city. Jordan controlled the eastern section, including the Old City, a walled section of Jerusalem dating from Biblical times. Israel took control of the entire city in 1967. Jerusalem today is claimed by both the Palestinians and the Israelis as their capital.

Facts in brief

Population: 567,100.
Area: 41 sq. mi. (107 km²).
Altitude: About 2,500 ft. (760 m) above sea level.
Climate: *Average temperature*—January, 55 °F (13 °C); July, 85 °F (31 °C). *Average annual precipitation* (rainfall, melted snow, and other forms of moisture)—22 in. (56 cm).
Government: *Chief executive*—mayor; elected by the people to a four-year term. *Legislature*—Municipal Council of 31 members; elected by the people to a five-year term.

Bernard Reich, the contributor of this article, is Professor of Political Science and International Affairs at George Washington University.

© George Chan, Photo Researchers

The Western Wall in the Old City is the holiest site in Judaism. The wall was part of the Second Temple built by Herod and destroyed by the Romans in A.D. 70. Jews from throughout the world come to pray at the wall and insert messages and prayers in its crevices.

WORLD BOOK maps

Jerusalem

Park or forest

City boundary
Major highway
Other road or street
Railroad
▪ Point of interest

Location of Jerusalem

Mediterranean Sea — Syria — Golan Heights — Israel — West Bank — JERUSALEM — Gaza Strip — Jordan — Suez Canal — Egypt

Area of Jerusalem

Bet Horon — Atarot Jerusalem Airport — Qiryat Anavim — WEST BANK — Shoafat — AREA OF MAIN MAP — JERUSALEM — ISRAEL — Abu Dis — Gilo — Bethlehem

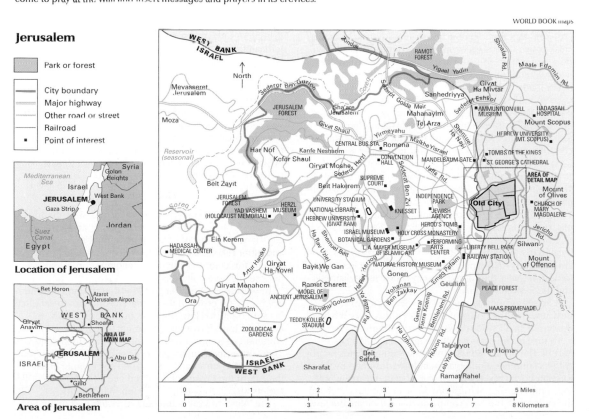

The city

Jerusalem lies on hilly, rocky land in the Judean Hills. The city is divided into three sections: (1) the Old City; (2) West Jerusalem, also called the New City; and (3) East Jerusalem.

The Old City, which occupies much of the area of Biblical Jerusalem, is the historical heart of the city. It covers a rectangular area of about $\frac{1}{3}$ square mile (1 square kilometer) in the eastern part of Jerusalem.

The Old City is enclosed by stone walls about 40 feet (12 meters) high and $2\frac{1}{2}$ miles (4 kilometers) long. Although Jerusalem has always been a walled city, its present walls were built during the 1500's. Some sections of its foundation are much older. A number of gates open into the walls, including the Jaffa Gate, Zion Gate, Dung Gate, Lion's Gate (also known as St. Stephen's Gate), Damascus Gate, New Gate, and Herod's Gate (also known as Flower Gate). Until the late 1800's, these gates were closed at night to protect inhabitants.

The skyline of the Old City is dominated by a Muslim shrine called the Dome of the Rock. The shrine stands on a raised area called the Temple Mount, the site of the first and second Jewish Temples in ancient times.

The Old City is divided into four neighborhoods—the Armenian, Christian, Jewish, and Muslim quarters. The Armenian quarter is occupied primarily by members of the Armenian Church, an Eastern Orthodox Church. The largest religions in the Christian quarter are the Roman Catholic Church and Greek Orthodox Church. Most inhabitants of the Jewish and Muslim quarters are followers of Judaism and Islam, respectively.

The narrow cobblestone lanes that wind through the Old City have remained largely unchanged for hundreds of years. Houses, many with inner courtyards, stand crowded together. The busiest streets are the *suqs* (markets), which have small, windowless shops that sell food, pottery, jewelry, and souvenirs. Most of the streets are too narrow for automobiles. Donkeys and pushcarts transport heavy loads.

From 1948 to 1967, the Old City was under Jordanian control. The area had a poor sanitation system and inadequate supplies of electric power and water. After Israel took control in 1967, it expanded public services into the Old City, including modern electric and water systems, garbage collection, and social welfare programs.

West Jerusalem is the most modern part of the city. The main downtown area of Jerusalem centers on a triangle formed by King George Street, Jaffa Road, and Ben-Yehuda Street in West Jerusalem. Fashionable shops, hotels, restaurants, and tall office buildings line these streets.

Several modern public buildings in West Jerusalem are located in a neighborhood called Givat Ram. Among them are buildings on the new campus of Hebrew University of Jerusalem. Near the campus are the Knesset (parliament) and the Supreme Court.

A neighborhood known as Mea Shearim, north of downtown, is the home of many Orthodox Jews. It has dozens of small synagogues and study houses.

To the southwest is a picturesque area called Ein Kerem. The huge Hadassah Medical Center stands nearby, with its famous stained glass windows designed by the Russian-born artist Marc Chagall. Also in the area is Yad Vashem, a memorial museum dedicated to the victims of the Holocaust, the Nazi campaign to exterminate the Jews.

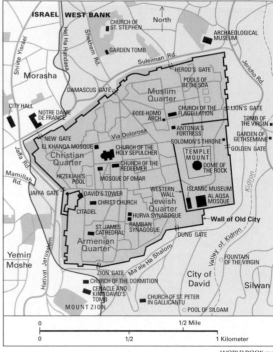

WORLD BOOK map

The Old City, in eastern Jerusalem, contains many sites sacred to Christianity, Islam, and Judaism. The city is divided into the Armenian, Christian, Jewish, and Muslim quarters.

East Jerusalem, north of the Old City, is where most of Jerusalem's Arabs live. Some neighborhoods in East Jerusalem are run-down, with old, neglected housing. Other East Jerusalem areas are more modern. Israel built several modern Jewish neighborhoods, including Ramat Eshkol and Gilo, after taking control of East Jerusalem in 1967. There are also modern buildings on the original campus of Hebrew University on Mount Scopus, which was rebuilt and expanded in the 1970's.

East Jerusalem has many Arab restaurants and shops. On Friday evenings and Saturdays, when restaurants in West Jerusalem are closed, many people go to East Jerusalem for meals.

Holy places

Jerusalem has a central place in the worship, doctrine, and daily practice of Judaism, Christianity, and Islam. The city's large number of synagogues, churches, mosques, and other religious institutions reflects the significance of the city for all three faiths. Each religious community supervises its own holy sites.

Jewish sites. According to Jewish tradition, Jerusalem is where God ordered the patriarch Abraham to sacrifice his son, Isaac, to Him. The Jews built their Temple, the center of Jewish worship in ancient times, at the site of Abraham's sacrifice on the Temple Mount in the Old City. Two successive buildings, the First Temple and the Second Temple, stood at the site. The First Temple housed the Ark of the Covenant, a sacred chest holding the tablets inscribed with the Ten Commandments.

The Western Wall is the only surviving part of the Sec-

The Church of the Holy Sepulcher is in the Christian Quarter of the Old City. The church stands on Calvary, the site where, according to Christian tradition, Jesus Christ was crucified. Much of the present church dates back to the 1100's.

© Lawrence Migdale, Photo Researchers

ond Temple and Judaism's most sacred shrine. It is a stone retaining wall that reinforced the western side of the Temple Mount in ancient times. The wall is sometimes called the *Wailing Wall* because of the sorrowful prayers said there to mourn the destroyed Temple.

Other sites in the city sacred to the Jews include King David's tomb on Mount Zion in West Jerusalem, and the Jewish Cemetery and the Tombs of the Prophets on the Mount of Olives, a hill just east of the Old City. Many sites associated with Biblical figures are sacred to Christians, too.

Christian sites. Many monasteries, convents, shrines, and religious seminaries in Jerusalem mark events in the life of Jesus Christ and in the formation of the Christian Church. Jesus taught in Jerusalem and performed numerous miracles there. The Last Supper supposedly took place in a room known as the Cenacle (also called *Coenaculum)* on Mount Zion. The Church of the Holy Sepulcher in the Old City occupies the site said to be the place of Jesus's Crucifixion (called Calvary or Golgotha), as well as His burial and Resurrection. Several Christian sects share custody of the church, which was originally built by Constantine the Great, then rebuilt and dedicated by the Crusaders in A.D. 1149. The building stands at the end of the Via Dolorosa (Way of Sorrows), believed to be the path over which Jesus carried His cross to Calvary. Jesus was last seen by His followers on the Mount of Olives before He ascended to heaven. All of these sites attract many religious pilgrims each year.

Islamic sites. Jerusalem is Islam's third holiest city, after Mecca and Medina in Saudi Arabia. According to tradition, the Prophet Muhammad originally selected Jerusalem as the *qibla,* the direction the faithful should face during prayer. However, the prophet redirected his followers to face Mecca instead of Jerusalem when pray-

ing, to symbolize the independence of Islam. This change helped ease the tension that had existed between Muslims and Jews. Muhammad is said to have ascended to heaven from a stone now enclosed by a golden-domed shrine called the Dome of the Rock. The Dome of the Rock and an ancient mosque called Al Aqsa Mosque rank among the holiest sites in Islam. They form the central features of the Temple Mount, which Muslims call the Haram ash-Sharif (Noble Sanctuary).

The people of Jerusalem

Nearly three-fourths of Jerusalem's people are Jews. Palestinian Arabs make up nearly all the remaining one-fourth of the population. Generally, Jews live in West Jerusalem and Arabs in East Jerusalem. Growing numbers of Jews also live in new neighborhoods in East Jerusalem. The central business district, in West Jerusalem, is almost entirely Jewish, and the markets of the Old City are mostly Arab. The most common languages are Hebrew, Arabic, and English.

The population of Jerusalem has grown substantially since Israel became independent in 1948. The city continues to add to its population through both natural growth and immigration. Only about half of Jerusalem's people are native-born Israelis. Many others are Jews who have immigrated to Israel from countries around the world. Large numbers have come from Poland, Russia, and other Eastern European countries; from other Middle Eastern countries; and from northern Africa, including Ethiopia. As a result, Jerusalem's Jewish citizens represent a mixture of cultures and nationalities.

Jerusalem's Jewish citizens also differ in the extent to which they follow the laws and practices of Judaism. Some people, called *secular Jews,* have a strong sense of Jewish identity but observe few religious traditions. A group of

The Cardo in the Jewish Quarter of the Old City is a street dating back to Roman and Byzantine times. The original Cardo was a wide avenue of columns and roofed arcades. At one time the Cardo ran the entire length of the city. It is now the main entry to the Jewish Quarter from the Christian and Muslim sections of the Old City.

Israel Ministry of Tourism

Israel Ministry of Tourism

Ben-Yehuda Street is a popular commercial area in downtown Jerusalem. The portion of the street shown above is a mall closed to automobile traffic. Residents of Jerusalem and tourists visit the street for its shopping and to relax at the area's many cafes and restaurants.

An Arab market in the Old City attracts shoppers seeking traditional arts and crafts. This street is known as the Via Dolorosa (Way of Sorrows). According to Christian tradition, Jesus Christ carried His cross down this street on the way to His Crucifixion.

extremely traditional Orthodox Jews called *haredim* (pronounced *hah ray DEEM)* make up about a third of Jerusalem's Jews and are the fastest-growing group in the city. Many haredim follow ways of life that developed among Jewish communities in Poland, Russia, and other Eastern European countries hundreds of years ago. These haredim speak a Germanic language called Yiddish instead of Hebrew and dress in the style of Eastern Europe in the 1800's. Most of the men wear long black coats, black or fur-brimmed hats, and beards or dangling side curls. The women typically wear long coats and dresses, black stockings, and headscarves or wigs to follow religious laws that call for modesty.

Confrontations have occasionally developed between Jews of different religious convictions over observances of Jewish law. Many extremely religious Jews believe that only a life of prayer and religious study is proper for the holy city. For example, they have protested the opening of nonkosher restaurants. They have also demanded that streets be closed to traffic for the duration of the Jewish Sabbath, from sundown Friday to sundown Saturday. Some haredim do not even recognize the state of Israel. They believe that only the Messiah, whom God will send, can establish the Jewish state.

Architecture

Jerusalem's architecture is a mixture of old and new. The Old City contains architectural examples from each major period in the city's history. Many ancient historical sites and places of worship stand near modern shopping centers and industrial zones. Architecture from the late 1800's and early 1900's displays European influences. Usefulness rather than style characterizes many new apartment buildings constructed by the government as housing for immigrants. Many buildings, old and new, have matching exteriors because all construction is required to be faced with a cream-colored limestone called *Jerusalem stone,* produced by nearby quarries.

Culture

Jerusalem can be described as a vast open-air museum because of the many archaeological sites throughout the area. The city also has many indoor museums, some dealing with the city's Biblical history. Notable museums include the Rockefeller Museum and the Bible Lands Museum, both famous for their archaeological treasures; the L. A. Mayer Museum of Islamic Art, which displays Islamic textiles, pottery, and other arts and crafts; and the Israel Museum, which has collections of fine art and archaeology. The Israel Museum includes a white-domed building with black walls, called the Shrine of the Book, where several of the ancient manuscripts called the Dead Sea Scrolls are exhibited.

Jerusalem is a major educational center. Students from throughout the world attend seminaries there to become rabbis, ministers, priests, or Islamic religious leaders.

Israel Ministry of Tourism

Mea Shearim is a center of Orthodox Jewish life in Jerusalem. The neighborhood lies near downtown Jerusalem. In addition to apartments, Mea Shearim includes many religious schools called *yeshivas* as well as stores that sell religious books and religious articles.

Jerusalem's Islamic seminaries are supported by Muslim foundations called *waqfs* (pronounced *wuhkfs)*, which receive income from endowed land and other property throughout the Islamic world. The foundations also support Islamic law schools, prayer rooms, colleges, orphanages, homes for the poor, public fountains, baths, mosques, and tombs. Jerusalem also has many schools called *yeshivas* for study of the Talmud, a collection of Jewish religious and civil laws. Hebrew University of Jerusalem offers courses in many areas of scholarship but is especially famous for science and Jewish studies.

The Jerusalem Symphony Orchestra plays regular concerts at Henry Crown Symphony Hall. Music lovers can also enjoy concerts by chamber music ensembles and choirs, and performances by several dance companies. Night life flourishes at many of the city's restaurants and cafes, and at motion-picture theaters. Local and international festivals provide a wide variety of cultural events that range from opera and theater to classical music and rock music.

Economy

Tourism is Jerusalem's main economic activity. The city has hundreds of hotels, restaurants, travel agents, taxis, and guides to serve tourists.

Construction has become a major source of employment as the city continues to grow. Jerusalem is also the headquarters of many technology companies and government-related activities.

Jerusalem has almost no heavy industry but does have

© Esaias Baitel, Gamma/Liaison

Housing developments have been constructed on the outskirts of Jerusalem to accommodate the large population increase in the city since the 1967 war. The distinctively designed development called Ramat Polin, *above,* in northwestern Jerusalem houses many Orthodox Jewish families. A shortage of housing ranks among Jerusalem's major social problems.

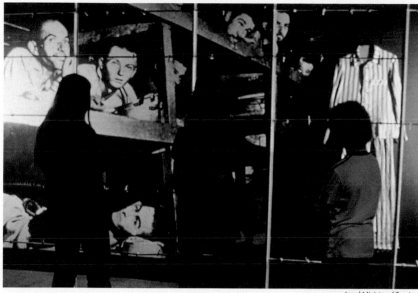

Israel Ministry of Tourism

Yad Vashem is a memorial in western Jerusalem to the Jews who were killed during the Holocaust, the mass murder of European Jews by the Nazis. The memorial includes an archive, a shrine, a monument, the Avenue of the Righteous Gentiles, and a Museum of Holocaust Art. The scene at the left comes from the permanent exhibition at Yad Vashem called "Warning and Witness," which illustrates the horrors of the Nazi period.

some modern factories. Most factories are in West Jerusalem. They produce chemicals, clothing, leather goods, machinery, and plastics. There are also printing, diamond-polishing, and food-processing industries. Older handicraft industries include embroidery, pottery and glassware, silverwork, and wood carvings.

Government

After Israel took control of East Jerusalem and the Old City in 1967, the Knesset established Jerusalem as a single city under Israel's administration. The citizens of Jerusalem elect a 31-member Municipal Council for five-year terms. The citizens elect the city's mayor for a four-year term.

History

Ancient times. Jerusalem's origin dates back about 4,000 years. About 1,000 B.C., King David captured the city from a people called the Jebusites and made it the capital of the Israelites. David's son, King Solomon, built a magnificent place of worship, the First Temple, in his capital city. Solomon also built a great palace complex consisting of many buildings. After Solomon died in about 928 B.C., his kingdom split into a northern kingdom called Israel and a southern kingdom called Judah. Jerusalem remained the capital of Judah.

In 587 or 586 B.C., the Babylonians conquered Judah, destroyed Solomon's Temple, and took many Jews to Babylonia as captives. In 538 B.C., Cyrus the Great, king of Persia, allowed the Jews to return to Jerusalem after he conquered the Babylonians. The returning Jews then rebuilt their center of worship, the Second Temple.

By about 400 B.C., priests and scribes of the Temple had established laws governing Jerusalem. They helped the city recover as a religious center. Alexander the Great of Macedonia conquered King Darius III of Persia in 331 B.C. and took control of Judah in 332 B.C. Alexander and the kings who succeeded him granted administrative power to the priests and allowed the Jews to follow their own religion. But in 168 or 167 B.C., King Antiochus IV

tried to stop the practice of Judaism. He angered the Jews by dedicating the Temple to the Greek god Zeus. The Jews, led by the warrior Judah Maccabee, overthrew Antiochus. About 165 B.C., the Jews recaptured the Temple and rededicated it to God. Judah Maccabee's family, the priestly Hasmoneans, established an independent state that lasted about 80 years.

Roman rule. In 63 B.C., the Roman general Pompey the Great captured Jerusalem and made it part of the Roman Empire. In 54 B.C., the Roman general Marcus Licinius Crassus stole the Temple's funds. The Romans named Herod the Great king of the Jews, and he took control of Jerusalem in 37 B.C. Herod began a huge building program and made major architectural changes in the city. He also restored the Temple.

Beginning in A.D. 6, Judea (the Roman name for Judah) had no king. Jerusalem was ruled by a Roman *procurator* (administrator). Roman rule was generally peaceful, but riots were sometimes set off by leaders who claimed to be sent by God to preserve Judaism. The Romans arrested most of these leaders, who were called *Zealots,* and crucified them. Jesus of Nazareth arrived in Jerusalem in about A.D. 28 and declared the coming of the Kingdom of God. His followers believed He was the Messiah. But Jewish leaders said He had *blasphemed* (insulted God). They forced the Romans to accuse Him of treason and brought Him before the procurator, Pontius Pilate, who sentenced Him to be crucified.

Roman rule became harsh, and the Jews, led by the Zealots, began a major revolt in A.D. 66. They seized Jerusalem and held it until the Roman emperor Titus retook it in A.D. 70. The Romans destroyed the Temple and much of the city's fortifications. Only part of the Western Wall of the Temple Mount remained. Many Jews died during the siege. Survivors were either executed or enslaved and exiled.

Jerusalem remained largely uninhabited until about 130, when the Roman emperor Hadrian announced plans to build a Roman city on the site. He renamed the city Aelia Capitolina and built temples to Roman gods, including one to the god Jupiter on the Temple Mount. The Jews, led by a warrior named Bar Kokhba, rebelled again in 132 and recaptured the city. Hadrian drove out the rebels three years later and tried to end all Jewish hope of regaining Jerusalem by prohibiting Jews from visiting or living there. But the city's importance as a spiritual center continued.

By the early 300's, the ban against Jews visiting the city was no longer strictly enforced. After Constantine the Great became the sole emperor in 324, he made Christianity the official religion of the Roman Empire. He replaced Jerusalem's Roman structures with Christian monuments and built several churches there, including the Church of the Holy Sepulcher. He also restored Jerusalem as the city's name.

In 395, the Roman Empire split into the West Roman Empire and the East Roman Empire, also called the Byzantine Empire. Jerusalem became part of the Byzantine Empire.

Muslim rule. In the early 600's, control of Jerusalem changed three times. First, Persian troops captured the city and held it from 614 to 629. Byzantine forces regained control but lost Jerusalem again in 638, this time to Muslim Arabs. The Caliph Abd al-Malik constructed the Dome of the Rock, which was completed in 691.

During the 900's and 1000's, a number of Muslim groups fought for control of Jerusalem. In 1099, the Crusaders, who were European Christians, captured Jerusalem from the Muslims in the First Crusade. The Crusaders killed both Muslims and Jews and established a Crusader state called the Kingdom of Jerusalem. Jerusalem served as capital of the kingdom until 1187, when the Muslim leader Saladin reconquered the city. Saladin repaired the city walls, and Muslims and Jews returned to the city in large numbers. Except for a brief period in the 1200's, Jerusalem remained under Muslim control for more than 700 years. The city was controlled by the Mamelukes, Muslims from Egypt, from 1250 to 1516. Then the Ottoman Empire, a Muslim empire centered in what is now Turkey, took the city.

Under the Ottoman Empire, Jerusalem began to grow. At first, most of the city's population were Muslims, and even Christians greatly outnumbered Jews. However, increasing numbers of Jews immigrated to the city. By about 1870, Jews had become the majority group.

By the mid-1800's, construction had spread outside of the walls of the Old City. New communities in West Jerusalem included Yemin Moshe, constructed in 1860 with the financial assistance of Sir Moses Montefiore, a Jewish philanthropist from England. Orthodox Jews built several neighborhoods north and west of the Old City, particularly Mea Shearim, established in the mid-1870's. Many haredim still live there. Christian and Muslim groups also built new communities outside the walls.

British rule. In December 1917, during World War I, British troops under General Edmund Allenby captured Jerusalem and ended Ottoman control over the city. A month earlier, the British government had issued the Balfour Declaration, an official document supporting a national homeland for Jews in Palestine. The League of Nations, a forerunner of the United Nations, made Palestine a *mandated territory*—that is, an area administered by Britain, under the League's supervision, in preparation for self government. The British administration of Palestine

centered in Jerusalem. As a result, many new houses and government buildings were erected.

Jewish immigration to Jerusalem increased during the 1920's and 1930's. Two factors stimulated immigration. One was the increasing strength of the Zionist movement, which advocated a Jewish homeland in Palestine. The other was the rise of the Nazi regime in Germany, which had anti-Jewish policies. Many new Jewish neighborhoods, such as Rehavia and Beit Hakerem, were established, primarily in West Jerusalem.

Anti-Zionist feelings developed among the Arabs in Palestine who wanted to create an independent Arab state. By the 1930's, severe anti-Jewish riots had broken out in Jerusalem. In 1947, the British turned over the question of Palestine's future to the United Nations (UN). The UN voted to end the British mandate and divide Palestine between the Arabs and the Jews. Jerusalem would be an international city under UN control.

Arabs quickly responded to the UN resolution by attacking the Jews. In May 1948, British control ended and Israel declared its independence. Arab armies invaded the new state. Jerusalem's Old City came under heavy shelling, and many civilians were killed. By the end of 1948, Israeli soldiers held West Jerusalem, and Jordanian troops controlled East Jerusalem and the Old City. The loss of the Western Wall and other Jewish shrines bitterly disappointed the Israelis. Armistices between Israel and neighboring Arab countries ended the war in 1949.

In an agreement that Jordan (then called Transjordan) and Israel signed in 1948, the two countries established a border called "no man's land." This strip of land formed the frontier between Israeli and Jordanian territory. The border ran along the west wall of the Old City and extended north and south of the wall. Israel established its seat of government in West Jerusalem. However, many countries refused to recognize Jerusalem as Israel's capital because of the UN plan to make it an international city. These countries instead established their embassies in Tel Aviv, Israel's chief commercial, financial, and industrial center.

Israeli control. War again broke out between the Arabs and Israelis in June 1967. After a brief conflict that Israelis call the Six-Day War and others call the June War, Israel captured the Old City and East Jerusalem. Huge crowds of joyful Jews entered the Old City for the first time in 19 years to pray at the Western Wall. Israel extended the boundaries of Jerusalem to make East Jerusalem, the Old City, and nearby villages part of the city. The people of East Jerusalem were granted the same rights and responsibilities that all other Israeli residents had, and were given the opportunity to apply for Israeli citizenship.

In 1980, the Knesset passed a law restating Israel's position that Jerusalem is the capital of Israel. The law also guaranteed protection for the holy places of all religions and continued free access to them.

The future of Jerusalem remains one of the most complex and delicate issues in the Arab-Israeli conflict. The Palestine Liberation Organization, the political body that represents the Palestinian people, would like to establish an independent Palestinian state with Jerusalem as its capital. The Israeli government remains committed to keeping Jerusalem as both the Israeli capital and an undivided city.   Bernard Reich

Index

How to use the index

This index covers the contents of the 1996, 1997, and 1998 editions of *The World Book Year Book.*

Each index entry gives the edition year and the page number or numbers—for example, **Crace, Jim, 98:** 296. This means that information on this topic may be found on page 296 of the 1998 *Year Book.*

When there are many references to a topic, they are grouped alphabetically by clue words under the main topic. For example, the clue words under **Crime** group the references to that topic under numerous subtopics.

When a topic such as **CROATIA** appears in all capital letters, this means that there is a *Year Book* Update article entitled Croatia in at least one of the three volumes covered by this index. References to the topic in other articles may also appear after the topic name.

An index entry followed by *WBE* refers to a new or revised *World Book Encyclopedia* article in the supplement section, as in **CUBA:** *WBE*, **98:** 444. This means that a *World Book Encyclopedia* article on Cuba begins on page 444 of the 1998 *Year Book.*

The "see" and "see also" cross references—for example, the one at the end of the **Currency** heading—refer the reader to other entries in the index.

When only the first letter of a topic, such as **Cyclones** is capitalized, this means that there is no article entitled Cyclones but that information on this topic may be found in the edition and on the pages listed.

The indication (il.) means that the reference on this page is to an illustration only, as in the **Dade County, Florida,** picture on page 241 of the 1998 edition.

Index

A

Abacha, Sani, 98: 38, 323-324, **97:** 40, 51, 295, **96:** 40, 310
ABC. See **American Broadcasting Cos.**
Abdel Rahman, Omar, 98: 308, **97:** 404, **96:** 185, 303, 448
Abdullah, 97: 354
Abe, Takeshi, 97: 250
Aberdeen Proving Ground, 98: 150
Abiola, Kudirat, 97: 296
Abiola, Moshood, 98: 38, 324, **97:** 51, 295-296, **96:** 40, 310
Abkhazia, 98: 217, **97:** 228
Aborigines, 98: 91-92, **97:** 74, 75, **96:** 66-67
Abortion: Germany, **96:** 232; Ireland, **96:** 246-247; "Jane Roe," **96:** 305; laws and court cases, **98:** 391-392, **97:** 139, 233; pill, **97:** 233; population studies, **98:** 349; Roman Catholic Church, **96:** 357, 358; violence, **97:** 157, **96:** 431
Abu Nidal, 96: 432 (il.)
Abu Qurgas, Egypt, 98: 195
Abu Sayyaf (group), **96:** 331
Abu Zeid, Nasr, 97: 246-247
Aburto Martínez, Mario, 96: 285
Academy Awards, 98: 313, **97:** 286, **96:** 300
Accidents. See **Disasters; Safety**
Acquired immunodeficiency syndrome. See **AIDS**
Activa Tremor Control System, 98: 302
Actual, The (Bellow), **98:** 291
Actual World, The (Funkhouser), **98:** 345
Adair, Virginia Hamilton, 97: 319
Adam Opel AG (company), **96:** 231
Adams, Bud, 96: 239
ADAMS, GERRY, 96: 38; Northern Ireland affairs, **98:** 325, 326, **96:** 311, 313, 319-321
Adams, John, 96: 144, 145
***Adarand Constructors, Inc., v. Peña*, 96:** 87, 131, 143
Addiction. See **Drug abuse; Smoking**
Adela (boat), **98:** 116
Aden. See **Yemen**
Adenosine triphosphate, 98: 325
Adkins, Derrick, 96: 439
Adkisson, Perry L., 98: 54
ADM Milling, 96: 298
Adolescence, 96: 208; *WBE,* **98:** 438. See also **Teenagers**
Advanced boiling water reactor, 97: 199
Advertising, 98: 265, 298
Aegean Sea, 97: 232, 390
Aerospace industry. See **Aviation; Space exploration**
A-Faran (group), **96:** 241
AFDC. See **Aid to Families with Dependent Children**
Affirmative action, 98: 150, 195, **97:** 135-137, 185, 187, **96:** 87, 130-143, 209-210, 401, 403
AFGHANISTAN, 98: 38, **97:** 38, **96:** 38; Pakistan, **97:** 38, **96:** 38; tables, **98:** 84, **97:** 70, **96:** 62
AFL-CIO. See **American Federation of Labor and Congress of Industrial Organizations**
AFRICA, 98: 38-53, **97:** 38-54, **96:** 39-45; AIDS, **98:** 43, **97:** 41, **96:** 45; conservation, **98:** 164, **96:** 171; early humans, **98:** 58-59, **96:** 49; Eastern Orthodox prelate, **96:** 205; literature, **98:** 297, **97:** 267; water project, **98:** 122; zoos in U.S., **98:** 432
"Africa" (exhibit), **96:** 468
African Americans: affirmative action, **98:** 195, **96:** 131, 134-143; baseball, **98:** 375; census, **97:** 116, **96:** 120; church arsons, **98:** 150, **97:** 137, 332; early religions, **97:** 60; education, **98:** 194, 195, **97:** 184; health, **97:** 55, 277, **96:** 204, 341; Judaism, **96:** 254; law enforcement, **97:** 371-372, **96:** 338; marches, **98:** 343, **96:** 130, 247, 354, 453; mortgages, **98:** 100; religion, **96:** 247; Republican Party, **96:** 356-357; Simpson trial, **96:** 130, 273; Texaco lawsuit, **97:** 135; voting rights, **97:** 370. See also **Civil rights; Race relations**
African National Congress, 98: 371, **97:** 358, **96:** 380
Agassi, Andre, 97: 379, **96:** 423
Agates, 96: 120
Agee, William, 96: 87
Agenda 21 (program), **98:** 414
AGRICULTURE, 98: 54-55, **97:** 207-218, **96:** 220-222; cloning, **98:** 112; government policy, **98:** 163, **97:** 148, **96:** 221-222; Russia, **97:** 350; water supply, **97:** 410. See also **Food** and individual country articles
Agriculture, U.S. Department of, 98: 54, 163, 352, **97:** 207-209, **96:** 104, 220, 222, 224
Agriculture Improvement and Reform Act, 98: 54, **97:** 207
Agusta (company), **96:** 80
AHERN, BERTIE, 98: 332
Ahmed, Shahabuddin, 97: 82
Aho, Esko, 96: 224
Aid to Families with Dependent Children, 98: 429, **97:** 414, **96:** 399
Aida (opera), **98:** 152 (il.)
Aideed, Hussein, 97: 358
Aideed, Mohamed Farah, 97: 40, 358, **96:** 380
AIDS, 98: 55, **97:** 55, **96:** 45-46; emerging diseases, **96:** 345-349; Ho, David, **98:** 336; Japan, **97:** 250; Memorial Quilt, **97:** 409 (il.); prisons, **98:** 351, **96:** 338; world population, **98:** 349. See also **Africa**
Ainley, Neil, 96: 147
Air Force, U.S. See **Armed forces**
Air France, 97: 80
Air Line Pilots Association, 97: 257
Air pollution. See **Environmental pollution**
Air traffic control, 96: 70-71
Airbags, 98: 94, 352-353, **97:** 77, **96:** 363
Airbus Industrie, 98: 206, **97:** 80
Airline Pilots' Association, 98: 279
Airlines. See **Aviation**
Aitken, Jonathan, 96: 443
Akaev, Askar, 97: 255
Akmola, Kazakstan, 98: 275
Alabama, 98: 357, 388, **97:** 365, 367, 371; tables, **98:** 387, **97:** 366, **96:** 400
Alarcón, Fabián, 98: 193, 282
Alaska, 98: 200, 378-385, 386, **97:** 365, **96:** 175, 182, 454; tables, **98:** 387, **97:** 366, **96:** 400
Al-Azhar mosque, 97: 246
Al-Azhar University, 98: 268-269
ALBANIA, 98: 57, **97:** 55-56, **96:** 46; financial crisis, **98:** 206; Italy, **98:** 271-272; tables, **98:** 204, **97:** 204, **96:** 218
Albanians, in Yugoslavia, 98: 431, **96:** 466
Al-Bashir, Umar Hasan Ahmad, 97: 51, **96:** 402
Albert II, 97: 90
Alberta, 98: 136, **97:** 112, **96:** 116
ALBRIGHT, MADELEINE KORBEL, 98: 332-333; appointment, **98:** 124, **97:** 100; Croatia, **98:** 206; Middle East affairs, **98:** 269, 308, 394
Alcan Aluminum Ltd., 98: 137
Alcohol, Tobacco, and Firearms, Bureau of, 96: 186, 254, 425, 426
Alcohol consumption, 98: 189, **97:** 180
Aleman, Harry, 98: 144
Alemán Chiari, Alfredo, 97: 315
Alemán Lacayo, José Arnoldo, 98: 323, **97:** 295
Alesana, Tofilau Eti, 97: 312
Alexander, Jason, 98: 398 (il.)
ALEXANDER, LAMAR, 96: 46; election, **97:** 189-191
Alexei II, 98: 190, **97:** 181, **96:** 205
Alfalfa, 98: 209
Alfred P. Murrah Federal Building (Oklahoma City), **98:** 62, 164, 415, **97:** 405, **96:** 186, 425-426, 448
Algae, 96: 322
Al-Gamaa al-Islamiya (group). See **Islamic Group**
ALGERIA, 98: 57-58, **97:** 56-57, **96:** 46-47; Islamic movements, **96:** 187; tables, **98:** 40, **97:** 42, **96:** 42. See also **Terrorism**
Al Hayat (newspaper), **98:** 310
Alho, Arja, 98: 208
Ali, Muhammad, 97: 300
Alias Grace (Atwood), **97:** 110, 267
Aliens. See **Extraterrestrials; Immigration**
Alitalia (airline), **98:** 95, **97:** 80
Aliyev, Heydar A., 98: 97, **97:** 82, **96:** 72
Al Khalifa family, 98: 97, **97:** 82
All Eyez on Me (recording), **97:** 322
Allen, George F., 96: 210
Allen, Gracie, 97: 169-172
Allen, Woody, 98: 313
Alley, Kirstie, 98: 398
Alliance of Democratic Forces for the Liberation of Congo-Zaire, 98: 49-51, 155-156
Allied Pilots Association, 98: 96, 279
"Ally McBeal" (TV program), **98:** 398
Almeida, Juan F., 98: 284
Almond, Lincoln, 98: 388
Almsick, Franziska van, 96: 405 (il.), 406
Alomar, Sandy, Jr., 98: 322, 353
Alphand, Luc, 98: 368
Alpirez, Julio Roberto, 97: 232, **96:** 264
Al Saud family, 97: 282, 354
Altamirano Duque, Tomás, 97: 315
Al-Tayyib, Salih, 97: 267
Alternative Public Schools, 96: 209
Al Thani, Hamad bin Khalifa, 96: 297
Al Thani, Khalifa bin Hamad, 97: 283, **96:** 297
Alvin Ailey American Dance Theater, 98: 171
Alzheimer's disease, 98: 190, 303, 325, **97:** 276, 329, **96:** 278
Amalgamated Clothing and Textile Workers Union, 96: 258
Amazon region, 97: 260
Amazon River, 98: 286
Amelio, Gilbert F., 98: 154
America Online, 98: 264, **97:** 387
America Reads Challenge Act, 98: 288
America³ (boat), **96:** 81
American Airlines, 98: 95-96, 279, **97:** 80, **96:** 71, 259
American Ballet Theatre, 98: 170, **97:** 161, **96:** 191-192
American Basketball League, 98: 104
American Broadcasting Cos., 98: 397-399, **97:** 377-379, **96:** 84, 420, 421
American Cancer Society, 98: 301
American Civil Liberties Union, 97: 316
American Federation of Labor and Congress of Industrial Organizations, 96: 86, 259
American Federation of Teachers, 98: 195
American Frozen Food Institute, 97: 221
American Indian. See **Indian, American**
American League. See **Baseball**
American Library Association. See **Library; Literature, Children's**
American Pastoral (Roth), **98:** 291
American Psychological Association, 96: 280
American Radio Systems Inc., 98: 354
American Society of Magazine Editors, 98: 298
American Telephone & Telegraph Co. See **AT&T Corp.**
Americans with Disabilities Act, 97: 175
Americas Business Forum, 98: 284
America's Cup. See **Boating**
Ameritech Corp., 97: 264, **96:** 258
Amir, Yigal, 97: 248, **96:** 247, 297
Amis, Martin, 98: 296
Amistad (film), **98:** 314
Amman, Jordan, 98: 269, **97:** 251
Ammons, A. R., 97: 320
Amnesty International, 96: 131
Amory, Vance, 97: 415
Amplicor HIV-1 Monitor, 97: 55
Amputation, 96: 340
Amsterdam, Treaty of, 98: 179, 202, 314
Amtrak, 98: 409, **96:** 187, 440, 448
Anabolic steroids, 97: 362, **96:** 384
Anand, Viswanathan, 96: 121
Anarchists, 96: 429
Anasazi Indians, 98: 61
Anatolepsis (animal), **97:** 314
Ancram, Michael, 96: 311, 320
Andean Community, 97: 258
Anderson, George (Sparky), 96: 77
Anderson, Kevin, 98: 398-399
Andersonville (TV series), **97:** 379
Ando, Tadao, 96: 52
Andorra, tables, **98:** 204, **97:** 204, **96:** 218
Andrade, Pedro Antonio, 98: 196
Andreotti, Giulio, 97: 249, **96:** 251
Andrew, Prince, 97: 393-395
Andrews, Julie, 97: 383
Angara, Edgardo, 96: 331
Angela's Ashes: A Memoir (McCourt), **97:** 267
Anglicans. See **England, Church of**
Angola, 98: 42, 43, 45, 49-50, 155, **97:** 41, 53, **96:** 44; tables, **98:** 40, **97:** 42, **96:** 42
Animal rights, 98: 383-385, **96:** 443
Animals. See **Biology; Cloning; Fossils; Paleontology**
Animated film, 98: 313, **97:** 285, **96:** 299
ANNAN, KOFI A., 98: 333; UN affairs, **98:** 413, **97:** 402
Antarctica, 97: 199-200, **96:** 214
Anthony, Earl, 97: 94
Anthony, Kenny, 98: 431
ANTHROPOLOGY, 98: 58-59, **97:** 57-58, **96:** 47-49
Antibiotics, 96: 349
Antigua and Barbuda, tables, **98:** 285, **97:** 261, **96:** 262
Antimatter, 98: 87
Antineoplaston (drug), **97:** 237
Anti-Semitism, 96: 130, 254
Antiterrorism and Effective Death Penalty Act, 97: 370-371
Ants on the Melon (Adair), **97:** 319
Anvil Range Mining Corp., 98: 140
Anwar Ibrahim, 97: 274, **96:** 275
Apache Indians, 97: 241
Apartheid. See **South Africa**
Apes, 98: 164
Apostasy (Islam), **98:** 269, **97:** 246-247, 254
Apple Computer, Inc., 98: 154, 337, **96:** 164
Apple trees, 98: 110
Aqua-Leisure Industries, 97: 334
Aquariums. See **Zoos**
Aquino, Corazon, 98: 343, 344
Arab League, 98: 290, 309, **97:** 186, 280
Arabs. See **Islam; Middle East; Palestinians**
Arafat, Yasir, 98: 269-271, **97:** 247, 248, 280, 283, **96:** 250, 294-296
Aral Sea, 98: 419
Arbenz Guzmán, Jacobo, 98: 220
Arbour, Louise, 97: 403
Arcaro, Eddie, 98: 234
Archaea (organisms), **97:** 91, 298
ARCHAEOLOGY, 98: 59-61, **97:** 58-60, **96:** 49-52; Amazon region, **97:** 260; Chile, **98:** 286; Honduras, **96:** 264; Israel, **98:** 270 (il.)
Archean Eon, 96: 231
Archer, Dennis W., 98: 196, **96:** 200
Archer Daniels Midland Co., 96: 222
Archery, 97: 364, **96:** 385
ARCHITECTURE, 98: 61-62, **97:** 60-61, **96:** 52-53. See also **Building and construction**
Arctic, 96: 322, 467
ARGENTINA, 98: 64-65, **97:** 62, **96:** 54; anti-Jewish terrorism, **96:** 297; Clinton visit, **98:** 284; elections, **98:** 282; Latin American affairs, **97:** 258, **96:** 261-263, 263; Pan American Games, **96:** 328; privatization, **98:** 282; tables, **98:** 285, **97:** 261, **96:** 262
Argonauts, Toronto, 98: 212, **97:** 223
Ariane 5 (rocket), **98:** 372
Aristide, Jean-Bertrand, 98: 221, **96:** 235

Index

Index

Index

Index

512

Index

Index

Acknowledgments

The publishers acknowledge the following sources for illustrations. Credits read from top to bottom, left to right, on their respective pages. An asterisk (*) denotes illustrations and photographs that are the exclusive property of *The Year Book*. All maps, charts, and diagrams were prepared by *The Year Book* staff unless otherwise noted.

6 Reuters/Archive Photos; AP/Wide World
7 © Dilip Banerjee, *India Today*; AP/Wide World
8 Agence France-Presse; AP/Wide World; Camera Press/Archive Photos
9 AP/Wide World; Reuters/Archive Photos; AP/Wide World
10-13 Reuters/Archive Photos
14-16 AP/Wide World
18 © Scott Takushi, Sygma
20 AP/Wide World
22 Agence France-Presse
24-25 Jet Propulsion Laboratory/NASA
27-31 AP/Wide World
32 Reuters/Archive Photos
35 © Kaku Kurita, Gamma/Liaison
36 AP/Wide World
39 Agence France-Presse
44 © Noel Quidu, Gamma/Liaison; Agence France-Presse
47 Reuters/Archive Photos
50 © Peterson, Gamma/Liaison
52 © Radhika Chalasani, Sipa Press
56-58 AP/Wide World
60 Agence France-Presse
62 Monona Terrace
63-64 AP/Wide World
67 AP/Wide World; Reuters/Archive Photos
68 Reuters/Archive Photos
71 U.S. Department of Defense
72 © New China Pictures from Gamma/Liaison
73 Reuters/Archive Photos
74-77 U.S. Department of Defense
81 AP/Wide World; Reuters/Archive Photos
83 Seth Mydans, NYT Pictures
88 Jet Propulsion Laboratory/NASA; Marijn Franx (University of Groningen, the Netherlands), Garth Illingworth (University of California, Santa Cruz), and NASA
89 AP/Wide World; NASA
90 Brad Whitmore (STScI), and NASA; Don F. Figer (UCLA), and NASA
94 General Motors Corporation; Porsche Cars North America; Mercedes Benz of North America
96 Reuters/Archive Photos
98 Agence France-Presse
102-113 AP/Wide World
114 © Brad Markel, Gamma/Liaison
117 Agence France-Presse
119 AP/Wide World
121 Sky City Auckland Ltd.
123 Reuters/Archive Photos
125 AP/Wide World
127 Reuters/Archive Photos
132-138 AP/Wide World
142 Reuters/Archive Photos
143 Agence France-Presse
145 Reuters/Archive Photos
152 © Franco Fainella, Ente Lirico Arena di Verona
154-156 Reuters/Archive Photos
161 Stephen Crowley, NYT Pictures
163 Reuters/Archive Photos
165 AP/Wide World
167 Reuters/Archive Photos
168 Canapress
171 © Drew Donovan
172 Archive Photos; Columbia University

173 RKO Pictures/Archive Photos; Archive Photos
174 AP/Wide World; UPI/Corbis-Bettmann
175 UPI/Corbis-Bettmann; Reuters/Archive Photos; AP/Wide World
176 Fred Patterson Collection/Archive Photos; Archive Photos
177 AP/Wide World; AP/Wide World; Archive Photos; Chicago Symphony Orchestra
178 AP/Wide World
180 Reuters/Archive Photos; AP/Wide World
182-183 © Tim Graham, Sygma
184 © Jonathan Buckmaster, Rex USA
185-186 AP/Wide World
191 James Hill, NYT Pictures
195-203 AP/Wide World
207 AP/Wide World; Steven Spicer*
210 Reuters/Archive Photos
213 AP/Wide World
215 © Allen Rokach, The New York Botanical Garden
218 AP/Wide World
223 Reuters/Archive Photos
224 Agence France-Presse
227 © M. Setboun, Sygma
228 Reuters/Archive Photos
229 © Wolfgang Kaehler
230 © Michele Burgess, The Stock Market; © Alvin Chung, Sygma
232-235 AP/Wide World
237 Reuters/Archive Photos
238 © Hardy A. Saffold, Sipa Press
241 © Essdras Suarez, Gamma/Liaison
242 Granger Collection
245 © Eamonn Farrell, Photocall
246 © Albert Facelly/Thierry Chesnot from Sipa Press
247 Reuters/Archive Photos
248 AP/Wide World
250 © Dilip Banerjee, *India Today*; AP/Wide World
254 © Steve McCurry, National Geographic Society
255 © Pablo Bartholomew, Gamma/Liaison
256 Archive Photos
259 © Nickelsberg, Gamma/Liaison; Reuters/Archive Photos
260 © Pablo Bartholomew, Gamma/Liaison
261 AP/Wide World
266 Agence France-Presse
268-270 AP/Wide World
274-276 Reuters/Archive Photos
277 © Kilcullen/Trocaire from Sygma
280 Agence France-Presse
283 Reuters/Archive Photos
287 AP/Wide World
289 Michael Dersin, Library of Congress
293 Cover from *Golem* by David Wisniewski, © 1996 by David Wisniewski. Reprinted by permission of Clarion Books/Houghton Mifflin Company. All rights reserved.
295-299 AP/Wide World
301 Closure Medical Corporation
305 Arthur Harvey, © *The Miami Herald*
306 Reuters/Archive Photos
312 Michael Tackett/Polygram Film

International from Shooting Star; Phil Bray, Shooting Star; Fine Line Pictures from Shooting Star
315 AP/Wide World
316 Chris Maynard, NYT Pictures
318 AP/Wide World
319 Archive Photos; AP/Wide World
320 AP/Wide World; Reuters/Archive Photos
322 AP/Wide World
325 Reuters/Archive Photos
328 AP/Wide World
330 Agence France-Presse
331 © David Bubier, Academy of Natural Sciences of Philadelphia
333-335 Reuters/Archive Photos
336 AP/Wide World; © Greg Girard, Contact Press Images
337 Reuters/Archive Photos
338 Agence France-Presse
339 © Deidre Davidson, SAGA/Archive Photos
340-341 Reuters/Archive Photos
342 AP/Wide World
346 Agence France-Presse
350 AP/Wide World
352 © Tribune Media Services, Inc. All rights reserved. Reprinted with permission.
356 Ann Telnaes. Reprinted with special permission of North American Syndicate.
358 Camera Press/Archive Photos
359 Reuters/Archive Photos
361 Agence France-Presse
364 © R. Poderni, Sygma
366 AP/Wide World
368 Agence France-Presse
371 AP/Wide World
373 NASA; AP/Wide World
376 AP/Wide World
378 © Tom Soucek, Alaska Stock
380-381 The Anchorage Museum of History & Art
383-385 © Jeff Schultz, Alaska Stock
391 Amy Thompson, NYT Pictures
395 Reuters/Archive Photos
398 AP/Wide World
399 © 1996 Universal Television
400 Agence France-Presse
401 AP/Wide World
404 © Joan Marcus
406 Bandai America
407 Reuters/Archive Photos
408 AP/Wide World
409 Reuters/Archive Photos
412 AP/Wide World
418 Angel Franco, NYT Pictures
421-422 AP/Wide World
423 © Carol M. Highsmith, Parks & History Association
424 © Phil Thys, Parks & History Association; © Carol M. Highsmith, Parks & History Association; National Park Service
425 Agence France-Presse; © Richard Ellis, Sygma
426 AP/Wide World; AP/Wide World; Reuters/Archive Photos
427 © Ted S. Warren/*Austin American-Statesman* from Gamma/Liaison; AP/Wide World
430 © Savino, Sipa Press
436 Israel Ministry of Tourism

January

1 New Year's Day.

1-2 Major college football bowl games played by top teams.

6 Epiphany celebrated by many Christians to commemorate the visit of the Magi.

19 Birthday of Robert E. Lee celebrated as a legal holiday in most Southern States.

Martin Luther King, Jr., Day.

22 25th anniversary of Roe vs. Wade, the U.S. Supreme Court decision legalizing abortion.

24 150th anniversary of the beginning of the California Gold Rush in Coloma.

25 Super Bowl XXXII played in San Diego.

27 25th anniversary of the end of the American participation in the Vietnam War (1957-1975).

28 Chinese New Year.

Ramadan, Islamic month of fasting, ends.

31 The 40th anniversary of U.S. space exploration. The United States launched its first successful satellite, Explorer 1, on this date in 1958.

S	M	T	W	TH	F	S
				1	2	3
4	5	6	7	8	9	10
11	12	13	14	15	16	17
18	19	20	21	22	23	24
25	26	27	28	29	30	31

February

S	M	T	W	TH	F	S
1	2	3	4	5	6	7
8	9	10	11	12	13	14
15	16	17	18	19	20	21
22	23	24	25	26	27	28

1 African American History Month, or Black History Month, begins.

2 Ground-Hog Day celebrated. According to legend, if a ground hog emerges and sees its shadow, six weeks of winter weather will follow.

4 Halfway point of winter.

7 Opening ceremonies for the 1998 Winter Olympic Games in Nagano, Japan.

8 90th anniversary of the Boy Scouts of America.

12 Abraham Lincoln's birthday.

14 Valentine's Day.

16 President's Day, honoring Lincoln, Washington, and other past U.S. Presidents.

19 525th anniversary of the birth of Nicholas Copernicus, the Polish astronomer who discovered that the sun is the center of the solar system instead of Earth.

120th anniversary of Thomas Edison's patent on the phonograph.

22 Closing ceremonies of the 1998 Winter Olympic Games in Nagano, Japan.

George Washington's birthday.

25 Ash Wednesday marks the beginning of Lent.

S	M	T	W	TH	F	S
1	2	3	4	5	6	7
8	9	10	11	12	13	14
15	16	17	18	19	20	21
22	23	24	25	26	27	28
29	30	31				

March

1 National Women's History Month begins, to celebrate the achievements of women.

National Nutrition Month begins.

2 Lent begins for Eastern Orthodox Christians.

3 National Anthem Day commemorates the anniversary of the bill designating "The Star-Spangled Banner" as the national anthem.

7 The Iditarod sled dog race from Anchorage to Nome, Alaska, begins.

85th anniversary of the game Monopoly.

8 The 85th anniversary of the U.S. federal income tax.

Girl Scout Week begins.

12 Jewish festival of Purim celebrates Queen Esther's intervention to save the Jews of ancient Persia in the 500's B.C.

15 National Agriculture Week begins.

National Poison Prevention Week begins.

17 St. Patrick's Day.

19 80th anniversary of the Standard Time Act in the United States, which created standard time zones and daylight-saving time.

20 Spring begins.

21 Naw-Ruz, or New Year's Day for those of the Baha'i faith.

22 Camp Fire Boys and Girls Sunday.

29 Daylight-saving time begins in the United Kingdom and Europe.

145th birth anniversary of painter Vincent Van Gogh.

S	M	T	W	TH	F	S
			1	2	3	4
5	6	7	8	9	10	11
12	13	14	15	16	17	18
19	20	21	22	23	24	25
26	27	28	29	30		

April

1 April Fools' Day.

Alcohol Awareness Month begins, to raise awareness of underage drinking.

4 30th anniversary of the death of Martin Luther King, Jr.

180th anniversary of the adoption by the U.S. Congress of a national flag with 13 stripes and 1 star for each state.

5 Daylight-saving time begins in the United States.

Palm Sunday celebrated by many Christians to mark the triumphal entry of Jesus into Jerusalem, when palm branches were spread before him.

10 Passover, or Pesah, begins at sundown to celebrate the deliverance of the ancient Israelites from Egypt.

Good Friday observed to mark the crucifixion of Christ.

11 **30th anniversary of the Civil Rights Act of 1968.**

12 **Easter,** celebrated by many Christians, to mark the resurrection of Christ.

15 **The *Titanic* sank in 1912.**

19 **Eastern Orthodox Easter.**

National Infants' Immunization Week begins to increase parents' awareness of the need to immunize their children on time.

21 **100th anniversary of the beginning of the Spanish-American War.**

28 **National Day of Mourning** in Canada for workers killed on the job.

30 **50th anniversary of the founding of the modern nation of Israel.**

60th anniversary of the first public television broadcast.

S	M	T	W	TH	F	S
					1	2
3	4	5	6	7	8	9
10	11	12	13	14	15	16
17	18	19	20	21	22	23
24	25	26	27	28	29	30
31						

May

1 **May Day.**

Law Day celebrated in the United States.

Mental Health Month begins, to heighten public awareness of mental health.

2 **Kentucky Derby** is run.

3 **Be Kind to Animals Week** begins.

National Family Week begins.

5 **Cinco de Mayo,** commemorating an 1862 battle in which Mexican forces defeated invading French troops.

National Teacher Day.

6 **Spring is half over.**

7 **National day of prayer** in the United States decreed by presidential proclamation.

10 **Mother's Day.**

National Nursing Home Week begins.

National Police Week begins.

11 **140th anniversary of Minnesota statehood.**

15 **80th anniversary of regular airmail in the United States.**

18 **Queen Victoria Day in Canada** celebrates the birth of Queen Victoria.

19 **National Volunteer Week** begins.

22 **Immigrants' Day in Canada,** recognizing the contributions by immigrants to Canada.

25 **Memorial Day** celebrated in the United States.

29 **150th anniversary of Wisconsin statehood.**

30 **130th anniversary of the first Memorial Day.**

31 **Pentecost observed** by many Christians.

S	M	T	W	TH	F	S
	1	2	3	4	5	6
7	8	9	10	11	12	13
14	15	16	17	18	19	20
21	22	23	24	25	26	27
28	29	30				

June

1 **Hurricane season begins** in the Atlantic Ocean, the Caribbean Sea, and the Gulf of Mexico.

National Safety Month begins.

5 **30th anniversary of the assassination of Robert F. Kennedy.**

World Environment Day, sponsored by the United Nations.

8 **National Flag Week** begins.

National Little League Baseball Week begins.

12 **100th anniversary of Philippine Independence.**

Russian Independence Day.

13 **100th anniversary of the formation of the Yukon Territory.**

14 **Flag Day** celebrated in the United States, to commemorate the 1777 adoption of the Stars and Stripes.

21 **Father's Day.**

Summer begins.

23 **130th anniversary of the patent on the first U.S. typewriter.**

24 **John the Baptist Day** celebrated by many Christians.

50th anniversary of the Berlin airlift to supply the Communist-blockaded city.

S	M	T	W	TH	F	S
			1	2	3	4
5	6	7	8	9	10	11
12	13	14	15	16	17	18
19	20	21	22	23	24	25
26	27	28	29	30	31	

July

1 **Canada Day** celebrated, to commemorate confederation of Upper and Lower Canada with certain Maritime provinces to form the Dominion of Canada in 1867.

2 **210th anniversary of the ratification of the U.S. Constitution.**

3 **Earth reaches aphelion**—the point in its orbit when it is farthest from the sun—at 8 p.m. (E.S.T.)

4 **Independence Day** celebrated in the United States.

6 **70th anniversary of the first all-talking movie,** *Lights of New York*.

7 **100th anniversary of the annexation of Hawaii** by the United States.

August

S	M	T	W	TH	F	S
						1
2	3	4	5	6	7	8
9	10	11	12	13	14	15
16	17	18	19	20	21	22
23	24	25	26	27	28	29
30	31					

1 **Children's Vision and Learning Month** begins.

National Day in Switzerland commemorates the formation of the Swiss Confederation in 1291.

2 **Jewish observance of Tisha B'av,** commemorating the destruction of the first and second temples in Jersusalem in 586 B.C. and 70 A.D.

4 **Coast Guard Day** celebrates the founding of the U.S. Coast Guard in 1790.

7 **Summer is half over.**

Lunar eclipse visible in eastern North America, Central America, South America, Europe, and Africa.

8 **61st annual Soap Box Derby** in Akron, Ohio.

United Nations International Day of the World's Indigenous People.

10 **50th anniversary of the television show "Candid Camera."**

16 **50th death anniversary of baseball legend Babe Ruth.**

17 **National Aviation Week begins.**

21 **Solar eclipse** visible in the Indian Ocean, India, southern China, Indonesia, the Philippines, southern Japan, and Australia.

140th anniversary of the beginning of the Lincoln-Douglas presidential debates.

26 **Women's Equality Day.**

27 **90th birth anniversary of Lyndon B. Johnson,** 36th President of the United States.

28 **35th anniversary of Martin Luther King, Jr.'s,** "I have a dream" speech in Washington, D.C.

10 **25th anniversary of the independence of the Bahamas.**

11 **World Population Day,** sponsored by the United Nations to focus attention on the problems of overpopulation.

12 **Jewish holiday Fast of Tammuz.**

14 **Independence Day** in France.

19 **150th anniversary of the first women's rights convention** in the United States, held in Seneca Falls, New York.

20 **Space Week** begins commemorating the first human landing on the moon on July 20, 1969.

24 **100th birth anniversary of Amelia Earhart,** famed aviator.

27 **45th anniversary of the armistice that ended the Korean War** (1951-1953).

October

1 Breast Cancer Awareness Month begins.

United States 1998 fiscal year begins.

4 Fire Prevention Week begins.

Jewish Feast of Tabernacles (Sukkot) begins.

5 The U.S. Supreme Court begins its 1998-1999 term.

Child Health Day.

9 Leif Ericson Day.

10 25th anniversary of the resignation of Spiro Agnew as Vice President of the United States.

12 Columbus Day celebrated in many cities in the United States.

Thanksgiving in Canada.

S	M	T	W	TH	F	S
		1	2	3	4	5
6	7	8	9	10	11	12
13	14	15	16	17	18	19
20	21	22	23	24	25	26
27	28	29	30			

September

1 National Cholesterol Awareness Month begins.

National Sickle Cell Month begins, to focus public support on efforts to find a cure for sickle cell anemia.

6 Lunar eclipse visible in most of North America, Australia, South America, and New Zealand.

7 Labor Day in the United States and Canada.

8 55th anniversary of Italy's surrender to the Allies during World War II (1939-1945).

12 Federal Lands Cleanup Day.

13 National Grandparents' Day.

15 National Hispanic Heritage Month begins.

Independence Day in Nicaragua, Guatemala, El Salvador, Honduras, and Costa Rica.

17 Citizenship Day.

20 Rosh Ha-Shanah begins at sundown.

22 National Centenarians Day, honoring people who have lived to 100.

23 Autumn begins.

22 485th anniversary of Balboa's sighting of the Pacific Ocean.

29 Yom Kippur begins at sundown.

S	M	T	W	TH	F	S
				1	2	3
4	5	6	7	8	9	10
11	12	13	14	15	16	17
18	19	20	21	22	23	24
25	26	27	28	29	30	31

16 **130th anniversary of the first department store** in the United States (in Salt Lake City).

17 **Sweetest Day.**

18 **National Health Education Week** begins.

24 **United Nations Day.**

25 **Daylight-saving time ends** and standard time resumes.

Reformation Day observed by many Protestant churches.

30 **60th anniversary of Orson Welles's** "War of the Worlds" radio broadcast.

31 **Halloween.**

National UNICEF Day.

1 **All Saints' Day.**

National Alzheimer's Disease Month begins to increase awareness of Alzheimer's disease.

Day of the Dead begins in Mexico.

3 **General election day** in the United States.

5 **Guy Fawkes Day** in the United Kingdom.

6 **Halfway point of autumn.**

11 **Veterans Day** celebrated in the United States.

Remembrance Day celebrated in Canada.

80th anniversary of the armistice that ended World War I (1914-1918).

15 **American Education Week** begins, to call attention to the importance of public education in the United States.

National Geography Awareness Week begins.

18 **70th birth anniversary** of Mickey Mouse, who first appeared in the animated cartoon "Steamboat Willie."

115th anniversary of the adoption of standard time zones in the United States.

19 **135th anniversary** of Abraham Lincoln's Gettysburg Address.

20 **National holiday in Mexico** to celebrate the beginning of the Mexican Revolution, which led to establishment of democracy.

United Nations Universal Children's Day.

21 **215th anniversary of human flight.** Frenchmen Jean Francois Pilatre de Rozier and Marquis Francois Laurent d'Arlandes ascended in a balloon over Paris.

22 **35th anniversary of the death** of John F. Kennedy.

National Bible Week begins.

26 **Thanksgiving Day** in the United States.

November

S	M	T	W	TH	F	S
1	2	3	4	5	6	7
8	9	10	11	12	13	14
15	16	17	18	19	20	21
22	23	24	25	26	27	28
29	30					

S	M	T	W	TH	F	S
		1	2	3	4	5
6	7	8	9	10	11	12
13	14	15	16	17	18	19
20	21	22	23	24	25	26
27	28	29	30	31		

December

1 **United Nations' World AIDS Day** celebrated, to focus attention on the prevention of AIDS.

2 **175th anniversary** of the Monroe Doctrine.

3 **180th anniversary** of Illinois statehood.

5 **65th anniversary of 21st amendment**, ending prohibition.

6 **Saint Nicholas Day,** celebrated in Europe.

7 **Pearl Harbor Day** commemorates the 1941 bombing of the U.S. fleet in Hawaii by the Japanese.

10 **100th anniversary of the Treaty of Paris** between Spain and the United States ending the Spanish-American War.

14 **Hanukkah,** the eight-day Jewish Feast of Lights, begins.

16 **225th anniversary** of the Boston Tea Party.

17 **95th anniversary** of the Wright Brothers' flight at Kitty Hawk.

20 **195th anniversary** of the completion of the Louisiana Purchase.

21 **Winter begins.**

24 **Christmas Eve.**

25 **Christmas Day.**

26 **Kwanzaa begins,** an African American holiday based on African harvest festivals. Continues through Jan. 1, 1999.

Boxing Day in Canada and the United Kingdom.

30 **35th anniversary of "Let's Make a Deal"** television show.

31 **New Year's Eve.**